By the same author

Supertips to Make Life Easy
Supertips 2
Pasta for Pleasure

THE COMPLETE
HOME REFERENCE BOOK

ENQUIRE

within

UPON EVERYTHING

MOYRA BREMNER

CENTURY

London   Sydney   Auckland   Johannesburg

To H.R.H. With Love

Text copyright ©Moyra Bremner 1988
Illustrations copyright ©Century Hutchinson 1988
All rights reserved

First published in 1988 by Century Hutchinson Ltd,
Brookmount House, 62-65 Chandos Place, Covent Garden,
London WC2N 4NW

Century Hutchinson Australia Pty Ltd, 89-91 Albion Street,
Surry Hills, Sydney, New South Wales 2010, Australia

Century Hutchinson New Zealand Ltd, PO Box 40-086,
Glenfield, Auckland 10, New Zealand

Century Hutchinson South Africa Pty Ltd, PO Box 337,
Bergvlei, 2012 South Africa

British Library Cataloguing in Publication Data
Bremner, Moyra
   Enquire within upon everything: the
   complete home reference book.
   1. Household management - Practical information
   I. Title
   640

ISBN 0 7126 1932 1

Designed by Julian Holland
Illustrated by Paul Saunders, Martin Smillie and Taurus Graphics

Typeset in Paladium by TND Serif, Ipswich
Printed and bound in Great Britain by
Butler and Tanner Ltd, Frome

Contents

INTRODUCTION

This is a book with a curious and fascinating history. The first *Enquire Within*, published in 1856, was a runaway bestseller and, between 1856 and 1976, ran to 126 editions - claiming to be 'the most famous book of domestic reference in the world'.

Its author - an anonymous man who wrote of 'my wife's little suppers' - had created a quirky, highly individual and delightful hotch-potch. It covered everything a Victorian family needed to know: from the making of 'mouth glue' (presumably the kind you licked) to 'hints for wives' - on tolerance towards their husbands.

Unfortunately, 120 years of revising and updating left it full of good details but like a suit which has been altered too often and isn't quite sure what fashion it represents. So I was asked to write a totally new edition, which would solve the daily problems of the 1980s and 1990s as effectively as the first edition solved those of the 1850s.

We don't need to make our own 'mouth glue' but most domestic chores loom as large as they ever did. We may have washing machines but self-removing stains and trouble-free pets and children are not yet on sale. This meant the book had to cover almost all the domestic topics covered by the old one: and this it does in totally modern terms.

However, life today is infinitely more complex than it was for the Victorians. We can no longer sit back, as our ancestors could, certain that the world we have to confront today is much as it was yesterday and that we know how to deal with it. In the time it has taken to write this book there have been major changes in consumer law, social security, and the educational system. And the financial world has been both shaken and stirred to produce a cocktail unlike anything that has ever existed before.

To keep abreast of such changes we need to be better informed than we have ever been. For example, to a Victorian we would seem positively swaddled in consumer protection, but the law only protects us *if* we know and use it.

Our grandmothers had a simple choice over where to put their earnings or their savings: the bank, the teapot, or a sock under the bed. Today we face choices our parents would not have dreamt of; and people are falling over themselves to lend you money. But choices cut both ways and every year ordinary people lose their homes because they don't know enough to make the right decision. Similar opportunities and pitfalls can be found in almost any area of modern living.

So I decided that, for the 1980s and 1990s, *Enquire Within Upon Everything* would need to take on every aspect of modern living, guiding readers through the maze, explaining what to do and where to go for help with the problems that beset private life. The result is a survival guide for life today.

Where organizations are given, you will find not just their addresses but a briefing on what they offer. For those who want to read more on any topic I have also recommended books which expand the facts I have given. Often they are the latest books, but I believe that a first-rate book from a library is worth two second-rate ones from a bookshop, so not all the recommended books are in print.

To find the very latest facts in every field, I have sifted through not only a substantial range of books but also drawn on almost three-quarters of a ton of letters and leaflets which arrived in reply to over 2,000 letters I sent out asking for information. But this is not a book written simply from theory. Having brought up three children, alone, for over 21 years, I have had first-hand experience of almost every area I cover. And where my personal life left gaps I have found my professional experience has stepped in. In fact, part of the pleasure and excitement of writing this book has been the satisfaction of seeing the varied threads of my life all adding to some aspect of it.

However, despite its name, it makes no claim to say everything about everything: that would take a library. Instead it is a first source which will give the basics and provide pointers to where to find out anything else you want to know.

It is organized into sections and alphabeticized sub-sections. For example, the section on law is sub-divided into consumer law, criminal law and so on.

Within each sub-division the headings are usually in alphabetical order. But a natural order sometimes overrules that. In First Aid, for example, it was safest to start with the emergency procedures which must be done first, and work through the correct stages in saving life. Basic tasks like making a curtain or cooking a chicken also have their own overriding order which has been followed in preference to the alphabet. I suspect that these deviations will seem as natural to you as they do to me, and make the book even easier to use. For those who like to go straight to the page, with no browsing on the way, there is also a detailed index. I hope you will turn to it even when you seem to have found what you need. Often topics overlap and useful information could appear in more than one place.

Not being sexist, yet equally reluctant to distort the English language, hims appear randomly in some paragraphs and hers in others and I hope readers will assume that what is written applies equally to both sexes - unless logic dictates otherwise.

The author of the 1856 *Enquire Within* ended his introduction with the words: 'Our Interviews [paragraphs] will be varied, genial, and entirely original in their arrangement. The pleasure of your company is earnestly solicited.'

I hope you will find my paragraphs just as 'varied and genial'. Having little time for useful books which aren't interesting, I have woven into its pages curious facts, quotations from far and wide, and extracts from the first *Enquire Within*, so you can pick it up from time to time for nothing more serious than a contented browse. In this, most of all, the pleasure of your company is indeed most earnestly solicited.

ACKNOWLEDGEMENTS

The anonymous author of the Victorian edition of *Enquire Within* said he compiled his book with the help of his friends and quaintly directèd his readers to find 'a schoolmaster at [paragraph] 1925', 'a surgeon at 2186' and so on. I have continued his tradition and my first thanks must go to my friends. It is no exaggeration to say that this book could not have been written without them. They have given this book inside information which I could have found in no other way. Their generosity in giving me their time and sharing their knowledge is something for which I am more grateful than I can express.

To make this book totally up to date it has been necessary to draw most of my information from people rather than from books. So I have also been helped by an army of experts, officials, and press officers in almost every major organization in Britain, to them I also owe a great debt. Their kindness in answering endless queries, reading my text and correcting my errors, has been extraordinary, and many went well beyond the call of duty to assist me. I would like to name them all, but that would be a book in itself, so I can only name a selection of those to whom I owe a particular debt or whose organizations do not appear in the book. I hope that all those who do not appear below will feel no less warmly thanked. I will long remember with gratitude the many individuals who gave me so much help and encouragement.

My particular thanks go to the following (in random order):
Bruce and Amanda Weatherill
Dr Graham White
Imperial Chemical Industries
The Health and Safety Executive
Metropolitan Police
David Butcher
Nella Opperman
Ian Wood
Deborah Carnworth
Corinne Julius
Anne Beeching
Jennifer Bonner
Alison Bonner
Pat Buckingham
The London Fire Brigade
Black & Decker
Barbara Davies
Paint Research Association
Slumberdown
Harrods
Relyon Beds
Lever Bros
Michael Simmons and Emma Lodge-Patch of Malkin
Cullis and Sumption
The Worshipful Company of Goldsmiths
Caroline Hunt
Kim Bertram
Melvin Brown
Doyin Lawumi
Paul Newman
Automobile Association
Brian Davis
British Agrochemical Association
Christopher Peel
Laura Ponsonby
John Brennan
Banking Information Service
British Insurance Association
National Westminster Bank
Barclays Bank

Lloyds Bank
Midland Bank
Nicholas Carew Hunt
The Stock Exchange
Rosemary Burr
Phillida Dally
National Consumer Council
British Farm Produce Council
Dornay Foods
Sea Fish Industry Authority
Shellfish Association of Great Britain
H.J. Grimes
Rex Thomas
Sharp Electronics
J. Sainsbury
Whitworth's Foods
Cherry Valley Ducks
Meat and Livestock Commission
Jenny Salmon of The Food Dimension
Diane Roberts of the Public Health Laboratories
Tony Hein
David Cossart
Wine of Australia
Italian Trade Centre
Bulgarian Vintners Co
German Wine Information Service
Food and Wine from France
The Sherry Institute of Spain
Wines from Spain
Portuguese Government Trade Office
Wine Institute of California
Tim Stanley-Clarke
William Warre
Stanley Holland
American Airlines
Penny and Roger Holland
Graham Marr
Smith Brothers
Digital Equipment Corporation

Zena Edmunds
Dunlicraft
Paton & Baldwin
H. Milward & Sons
Coats
Peter Jones
Donald Wadsworth
Bradley Viner
J.R. Bainbridge
Chrissie Nicholls
British Equine Veterinary Association
The Zoological Society
The Natural History Museum
Coral Bazaar Aquariums
Dr J. Brett
Dr Emond
David Simpson
Dr Stephen Inman
Dr Ione Inman
Dr Victoria Murday
Dr Richard Cotterell
Kate Start (Chief Paediatric Dietician, Guy's Hospital)
Professor J.R. Mitchell
Dr Ilya Kovar
Dr Bronwyn Hughes
Dr Sheena Sutherland
Dr C. Robinson
Dr Lynda Howard
Dr Tony Martin
Dr David Barlow
Dr Clarke of the London School for Hygiene and Tropical Medicine
Dr E.L. Rhodes
Rand Rocket
J. Cork of St John Ambulance
Mr Peter Diggory
Lorraine Hewitt of the Standing Conference on Drug Abuse
Marks & Spencer
Clarks Shoes
Dr Jon Darius

Cassandra Darius
J.C. Wells (Reader in Phonetics,
   London University)
Collins Publications
Oxford University Press
BBC Pronunciation Department
Rowena Gedye
Adam Leyland
Sophie Bennett
Andy Smith

Donatella Rovera
Simon and Esther Herrtage
Monique Sandoz
Smythson of Bond Street
Lars Gorton
Liz Filippini
Ian Hope Morley
Fiona Hunter
Pat Verity
Deborah Cullen

Dr A. Martin
The Science Museum
The Royal College of Physicians
Suzanne Tarlin
Felise Tucker
The Electricity Council
English Abrasives
GKN

My thanks also go to my editors Gail Rebuck, Sarah Wallace and Valerie Buckingham, without whose support and patience this book could not have been completed, and to Julian Holland and my illustrators who have so excellently converted my words into a book. I particularly want to thank Sarah Riddell who edited my words with a sensitive and restrained pencil, and showed such great understanding of what I was trying to achieve.

Finally, there are no words for the debt I owe to my children, Siobhan, Fergus and Rory, who endured with infinite tolerance and understanding my preoccupation, the massive invasion of paper, and the domestic chaos which writing a book of this diversity has inevitably caused; and who also helped me in my research and lent me their knowledge in their own special fields.

Key

This key explains the symbols used after organizations throughout this book. But most are constantly developing and may now be offering services or facilities which were not on offer when I contacted them. Also I noted the points they emphasized. So if an organization told me they specialized in giving advice in the telephone I put 'Tel Ad' - but that doesn't mean that all the organizations without 'Tel Ad' *don't* give advice on the phone. So please take my summaries as a broad indication of what is being offered, rather than as a hard and fast guide which allows no change or deviation.

M£L	membership fee low - under £10 pa
M£M	membership fee moderate - £10-20 pa
M£H	membership fee high - over £20 pa
M£var	membership fee variable
M£Vol	at your discretion

Children, OAPs and other special categories are often much less, and most charities provide free basic help and information to non-members.

A	activities are organized
Ad	advice is given on the subject in question
B	book list or books on mail order
C	career advice is available
CC	credit card orders accepted
Cl	runs clinics
Comp	competitions/shows organized
CS	for children with the complaint
Disc	membership provides certain discounts
E	sells equipment
Ed	educational facilities or information
EI	information on equipment
Ex	exhibitions run or visited
F	sells or hires films on the topic
F&F	for the family and friends of sufferers
Fest	members take part in festivals

G	there are local groups or clubs which can be contacted and/or joined, these may be branches of the main body or loosely affiliated
GP or Dr	referral from a doctor needed
H	holidays are offered
HC	holiday or residential courses run
HD	the handicapped are catered for
Inf	information provided
Ins	insurance cover via the organization
Int Comp	international competitions arranged
Jun	junior section for children to join
L	they have leaflets on the topic
Lec	lectures are given on relevant topics
Leg	offers relevant legal advice
Lib	members may use a special library
M	magazine or newsheet sent to members
O	older people (i.e. elderly) catered for
RC	registered charity
Res	respite care - of sick/old/handicapped to give relative a rest
Rg	regional centres
S	for sufferers from this condition
sae	send a stamped, self-addressed envelope with any query
T	travel opportunities for members
Tel:	telephone number as follows
Tel Ad	telephone advice
Th	therapy offered
TR	hires or sells tape recordings on the topic
V	sells or hires videos on the topic
vg	very good, shows I am most impressed
Vis	visits to relevant places of interest

Social Behaviour

Social Behaviour • Entertaining • Hospitality •
Events • Manners and Dress • Overseas Manners •
Writing and Speaking

SOCIAL BEHAVIOUR

Social behaviour is decided by conventions of manners and etiquette which are such minefields of prejudice and misconception that I am tempted to open by saying 'Abandon hope all ye who enter here'. For a start, you cannot discuss either without class raising its unfashionable head. But unfashionable I shall have to be.

Etiquette is the conventional code of behaviour within a particular group or class - embellished, of course, with regional or national variations. It is a behavioural uniform by which people tell the world the social group to which they belong - or aspire to belong. The British make a habit of asserting that England is the most class-conscious country in the world. In fact, class consciousness exists everywhere (even behind the Iron Curtain), and most of the foibles and snobberies which we think of as distinctly English are found in every sophisticated country in Europe.

Good manners, on the other hand, are barrier breakers, based on consideration for others. They involve adapting to make others feel comfortable. So good manners tell you a lot about someone's character, while etiquette tells you a lot about someone's class.

I would prefer to write only about good manners. But etiquette has to be covered because there are still situations in which not knowing what to wear or do, in a group other than your own, can be a disadvantage. So this chapter concentrates on the established form. It isn't *the* correct way to behave; it is *a* correct way to behave. Some of it may sound both bossy and snobbish. But it is impossible to write about rules of any kind without laying down the law and, for example, nobody needs to know how to dress to go and stay in ordinary houses: it only becomes a problem if those you are visiting live rather more grandly than you do.

However, bossiness and encouragement of snobbery are not my intention. So far as I am concerned the best social behaviour is what comes naturally to people who are gentle and genuinely considerate, and social niceties are unimportant in comparison. But not everyone would agree with me, and the trivial points of etiquette can still be hidden traps for people in both their career and their social life. It therefore seems essential to include them. However, nobody should imagine for a moment

that I am suggesting people should alter their ways to those I outline. If any of my readers choose to do things differently that is their right. I don't always follow all these rules either. Those who want to know about general points not covered here should read Debrett's *Etiquette and Modern Manners*, or turn to Debrett's *Correct Form* for the details on how to address, either in speech or writing, every kind of dignitary.

Accidents and Breakages

If someone breaks or damages something belonging to someone else, the first step should be to try to put it right, or help the owner or hostess to put it right. If food or drink has been spilt, mop it up - but if you are inexperienced at such jobs ask her how she would like it handled. If an item needs to be cleaned or replaced offer to pay for it (unless it is so expensive that this would be ridiculous). Whatever happens, there should never be any attempt to conceal the accident. Concealing it is a form of lie.

The person whose property has been damaged should always try not to embarrass their guest further by making much of it. Whether or not the offer to pay for the cleaning or repairs is accepted is a matter of their relative situations.

General Courtesies

The first edition of *Enquire Within* enjoined its readers to: 'Be polite. Politeness is the poetry of conduct - and like poetry it has many qualities. Let not your politeness be too florid, but of that gentle kind which indicates a refined nature.'

At that time the gestures of courtesy tended to be a one-way traffic; from men to women, young to old. Now things are far more flexible. Those with the best manners extend their consideration in all directions. So a woman will open a door for a heavily laden man, or give her seat up for a younger woman who is pregnant or carrying a child, just as much as for someone elderly. But she in turn should have a seat given to her or the door opened by any child or man, unless they are more heavily laden than she is.

The bonus of teaching such manners to children is that it sets a pattern for thoughtfulness within the family too.

ENTERTAINING

Buffet Meals

With a buffet meal almost anything goes. Buffets usually start with the main course (which is generally cold), move on to pudding and may include cheese and fruit. If you care for your guests at all try to have food which can comfortably be eaten with just a fork. This applies not only to the type of food but to how it is prepared. Lettuce torn into sizeable pieces is nothing but a nuisance, but chop it finely as they do in Arab salads and it is perfect for fork meals. .

The organization of any buffet can be adapted to fit the household, but here are some points to bear in mind.

- There are always laggards. If you can arrange things so you don't have to clear the main course in order to serve the pudding and cheese you do both them and yourself a favour.
- The placing of the table should make it easy for people to queue to get at the food and encourage them to leave the room afterwards.
- If you have people helping on one side of the table it is fastest to have one serving the meat or fish and another the salads, rather than both serving everything. This keeps people moving along.
- Put the plates at the entry but the forks at the far end to move people away.
- If someone is around to usher them to where they can sit down, they won't stand by the food and stop others getting at it.
- If you have the drink well away from the food it makes people circulate.
- Avoid all foods which stain badly - beetroot, purple fruits and curry are among the worst.
- Remember some guests feel compelled to open bottles - even if plenty are already open. So only bring them out as the others run low, or you'll be left with a mass of half-empties.
- Expect drink to be spilt - so choose colourless drinks if you can.
- Have white paper napkins. Someone is bound to mop up spilt drink with their napkin, and the dye from coloured ones will ruin your carpet.

★ Small French polished tables which would be marked by glasses can be covered with cling film. Carefully stretched it is invisible in low light.

It is, incidentally, perfectly good form for guests at a buffet meal to return for second helpings once everyone else has been served. They don't have to wait to be asked.

Cocktail Parties and Drinks Parties

A formal 'At Home' invitation can be issued for any type of drinks party and they normally start at 6.00 or 6.30 pm. Usually, they only last two hours and the leaving time is often given on the invitation. Drinks parties can also start closer to 9 pm and be designed to go on all evening - often with dancing. For these no end time is given.

The drink can range from champagne, through spirits to cheap wine cup, according to the occasion. Cocktails are rarely served. The food is scanty - nuts, crisps and dips predominate, and canapés are served by those who use caterers. For late evening drinks parties buffet food or a substantial selection of cheese is often offered. In this case, the invitation should make it clear by saying 'Buffet Supper' or 'Wine and Cheese'.

The host and/or hostess should keep moving people round and introducing them. This doesn't mean breaking up groups or couples who are clearly having a great time together, but it does mean having an eagle eye for the simulated interest of someone who has been stuck for too long. Take someone who is at a loose end to join some others, introduce them and then extract a guest you want to move. Having taken that person on to the next group you can extract someone else from there - and so on.

However, guests don't have to be dependent on the host or hostess; anyone can introduce themselves to anyone else, and it makes the party go a lot better if they do. It is everyone's responsibility to see that no stranger is left standing by themselves.

If you have been stuck with a group for too long, you can either melt out of a large group without comment, or openly excuse yourself saying there is someone you have to go and talk to (even if there isn't), then vanish from sight. If you are stuck with one person take him or her to meet someone else and then excuse yourself. If you know nobody, manoeuvre him or her into a crowd - via getting a drink or food - then excuse yourself and head for the loo.

Formal Lunches and Dinners

Advance Planning

The secret of enjoying one's own entertaining is to do as much as possible well ahead. It always seems to be the so-called 'little jobs' which take the time. So it helps to have a running 'battle plan' permanently on file giving a count-down on what needs to be done on each of the days that lead up to the event.

Ideally, the battle plan enables you to do all the little jobs at least 24 hours ahead, and your choice of foods lets you have no more than one course which needs to be cooked on the day. That way you should still be ready by a whisker even if - as tends to happen - the cat is sick, the phone never stops ringing and a child throws the tantrum of its life.

Planning is very much easier if you keep a note of any previous entertaining. It is useful to jot down who came, what you gave them to eat, how much was made of each dish and how much was left, any foods they said they disliked or obviously avoided, any foods they obviously loved, and whether they drank coffee, or something else. This means you don't keep bringing the same groups of people together, give pâté to the same couple three times running, or foist fish on someone who clearly loathes it.

All this may sound like a system for those with leisure. Far from it. It's those who have the most work who find systems most useful.

HOSPITALITY

Arriving

Lunch invitations are usually for between 12.30 and 1 pm, and dinner/supper invitations for half an hour before the time when you plan to serve dinner. As dinner tends to start between 8 pm and 9 pm, people are usually invited for 7.30 pm, 8 pm or 8.30 pm. In picking the time, thoughtful hosts and hostesses take account of how late the guests may have to work and how far they have to come.

In Britain guests are expected to arrive 15 to 20 minutes late for dinner, but be rather more punctual for lunch. Some countries have very different rules of punctuality (see page 24).

Presents from Guests

It used to be unusual for guests to arrive with presents for their host. They are still not essential, but more and more people take flowers, after-dinner chocolates or a bottle of wine. It all depends on who is at the receiving end. Those on a relatively small budget may particularly welcome wine to eke out what they have bought for the meal - and friends can offer to bring a bottle, when they are invited. Others may prefer chocolates or flowers. It is tactful for the hostess to show her appreciation by using the present at the meal. The exception to this is a fine bottle of wine which will not be at its best after a journey; ask the guest whether he or she thinks it can be drunk immediately or whether it should be allowed to rest until another day. If it is mainly for their own delectation the guests will opt for drinking it immediately (however ill-advised this is). But if they have brought it for your pleasure they will tell you to keep it.

Canapés

Those who enjoy making fiddly canapés to munch with the drinks will probably find their guests fall on them with shouts of glee, but they aren't essential. Small bowls of nuts or crisps are fine, and some people offer nothing at all. Alternatively, those who hate washing up can dispense with a first course by having some interesting and substantial dips which guests eat with their drinks. This is an unconventional ploy, but I find it works. And if anyone is particularly late, or you have worked all day and are late cooking the meal, it salves your guests' impatience.

Drinks

Drinks are usually served in the sitting room before both lunches and dinners; if the weather is hot few places are better than a garden. Pimms and Kir are the garden drinks par excellence, but inside or out anything goes, provided it suits the occasion, from beer before an impromptu barbecue to champagne before a black-tie dinner. Nowadays wine is often served. But a guest should never ask for wine as an aperitif unless it has been offered - the host (or hostess) may have no wine which is suitable, or too little to go round at dinner if it is drunk before. Offering a guest a choice of specific drinks guards against this, as well as making it easier for the guest. The usual selection is gin, whisky and sherry or vermouth plus, perhaps, campari. There should also be at least one enjoyable, not too sweet, non-alcoholic drink clearly on offer: drivers don't necessarily have a passion for tap water.

Laying the Table

There used to be a lot of debate over whether mats or a cloth should be used when laying a table. Now you can use either, provided the cloth is a plain colour. If the table has a lovely surface it may be a shame to cover it, but a tablecloth conceals a multitude of sins and allows you to cover the surface with a protective undercloth. There are two kinds: bulgomme and heat-resistant felt. Both are sold by the yard in good furnishing fabric departments. You can also use a layer or two of blanket, if the cloth will conceal it. The padding gives a hospitable softness to the table as well as protecting it.

Knives and All That

The rules for table laying are the same for both lunch and dinner. The places are set so that the guests are evenly spaced round the table. Knives and spoons go to the right of each place and forks to the left, arranged in the order in which they will be used - with those which will be used first on the outside. Apart from the small knife for buttering bread, everything is laid in pairs. So the large knife should be there, with its blade facing the mat, even if the food only needs to be eaten with a fork, and the small fork should be there even if the pudding does not need a fork. Whether it is or is not correct to put the pudding spoon and fork head to tail above at the top of the mat is a matter of dispute, but it is never wrong to put them at the side.

An ample number of serving spoons should be on the table, unless they are to be put in each dish as it comes to the table. There should also be a knife (or knives) for the butter, plus suitable spoons for mustard, bread sauce, whipped cream and so on.

The normal order of courses is:

First course	soup, pâté or some other light starter
Second course	fish - this is often omitted or eaten instead of a first course

Main course	meat, or a major fish, usually with hot vegetables
Fourth course	green salad - very optional but increasingly popular, though the French deplore a vinegar dressing when wine is drunk
Fifth course	pudding
Sixth course	cheese
Seventh course	fresh fruit
Eighth course	coffee sometimes accompanied by chocolates and/or liqueurs.

At home people rarely have more than three or four courses, plus coffee, even when giving a formal dinner; and at lunch three courses are ample. This means you can start either with the main course and have both pudding and cheese, or have a first course and forget the cheese.

Whatever the meal, the fourth, fifth and sixth courses are very flexible. Fresh fruit is often eaten with cheese and, at an informal meal, this combination may take the place of pudding. Equally, at a formal meal, at which a dessert wine will be served, it may be better to have cheese before pudding - as the French do.

Glasses

The glasses go above the spoons and knives. At most meals only one wine will be served, but provide two glasses and have water on the table as well. If you have more than one wine there should be a fresh glass for each. There are no rules for how these should be arranged, provided it looks good, but there are rules on the size of glass.

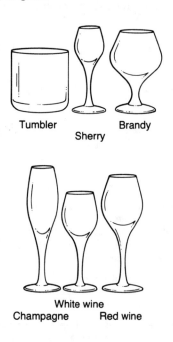

Tumbler   Brandy
Sherry

White wine
Champagne   Red wine

To wine lovers tulip-shaped glasses are best. This is because the in-curving rim holds the scent of the wine, which is a large part of its pleasure.

★ Storing glasses is tricky as they easily pick up the smell of a cupboard - especially if stored upside down on a wood shelf. So, if the glasses aren't used daily, keep smells out by standing them upright with a piece of cling film covering each one.

Napkins and Plates

The classic system is to have a dinner service with matching plates for every course. But matching isn't essential; one of the prettiest dinner services I know consists entirely of unmatched antique plates, of similar styles, picked up in junk shops. Failing such originality, anyone buying a dinner service might consider plain white, which shows off food extremely well. For large numbers you can also add any other white china you like and, by candlelight, only your most critical guests will notice the mismatch.

A small plate, for bread, goes to the left of the forks (even if you don't intend to serve bread) and the table napkin goes on it. If you enjoy napkin origami, do it; but there is really no need and very elaborate napkins call for food which lives up to them. Double damask dinner napkins (as in the tongue-twister) are ideal for formal meals, but any fabric napkin can be used, and nowadays large soft paper napkins, in a colour which suits the table setting, are perfectly good for many occasions.

Making Serving Easier

Have all the plates which will be used cold - and even the hot ones if you have a warmer - already in the dining room before the meal. Medium-sized plates are used for first courses, such as pâté, and for puddings. They can also be put under small containers, such as cocotte dishes, small soup bowls or glasses of sorbet. So, when buying a dinner service, it is worth getting twice as many of these as of the meat plates.

At an informal meal, you can let guests eat a salad course from their meat plate. But it does depend on the food. The juices of some meat are delicious with lettuce; but fish juices can be vile, so it is useful to have a separate salad plate. This can be a crescent shaped plate, but is more often a middle-sized plate or a small bowl. Equally, cheese should really have a separate plate - but by this stage hostesses are often running out, so people often use their bread plates.

Pepper, Salt and All That

There are all kinds of extras which people may need with their food - pepper, salt, butter, sauces, mustards and so on. Ideally, everyone passes these to everyone else. In reality, nobody passes anything. So put as many on the table as you can muster. The butter can stay on until after the cheese, but every pepper, salt and sauce container should be removed after the main course - or the salad, if you are having one.

Decorating the Table

Except for occasions like Christmas, tables don't really need much decorating - the food and the guest provide the colour. The main point is not to let any central flowers create a hedge between the two sides of the table; nothing dampens cross-table conversation quite like shouting through foliage.

Lighting the Table

Bright light is a great conversation-stopper and can reduce a party of friends to stilted small talk. But put even strangers in the cosy softness of candlelight and the shy unwind and the confident become garrulous - which is just what makes an evening go. But the light shouldn't be so dim that you are left fumbling for your fish bones.

If you dislike candles use low lamps or dimmed lights which don't point directly at the table. And if you want the conversation to keep flowing when everyone returns to the sitting room its lighting must be equally dimmed.

Seating People at Table

Hostesses usually decide who will sit where. At a large or formal gathering there can be a name card at each place. At smaller gatherings she can tell each person where to sit. But even for quite small groups it can be useful to draw a plan: a good arrangement is not as easy as it seems.

There are three standard rules for seating. First, men and women should alternate. Second, husbands and wives (or couples of less classic mould) should not be next to each other. Third, the most important man should sit on the hostess's right, and the most important woman (often the important man's wife) should sit on the host's right. This last is often abandoned (as is the charming tradition of giving a new bride priority among the women). But it is a rule worth observing if there is any guest sufficiently old, or eminent, to be offended by having less than the best place.

It's also worth pairing people who will get on well together, and placing anyone shy and silent near a good talker who will keep that part of the table going. (The malicious use the vengeance system, and place the most boring person next to whoever they like least.)

Strictly speaking, each man should pull back the chair of the woman on his right and push it in as she sits down. It's charming when men do.

If it's a large group, someone is bound to wish they were next to someone who is just out of reach. So I like to ask all the men to move round two male places after each course - taking their glass and napkin with them. This is not conventional and doesn't suit a *very* formal meal but people do seem to enjoy having two new people to talk to at each course - and the 'Mad Hatter's Tea Party' air it gives tends to help things go.

Serving Food

If there are staff the food should be served to the most important woman first, then to the other women in order of importance (for formality) or simply according to where they are sitting. Then this pattern repeated with the men. For the main course, the plate of meat or fish should be put in front of each person and the vegetables then offered separately, so everyone can help themselves to what they want. If two people are serving it is quickest to have two sets of vegetables and let them each offer them down one side of the table. All plates and dishes are served from the left of each guest - to avoid a raised glass and a proffered plate colliding.

If you yourself are serving, adopt the order of precedence staff would use, but simply pass the plates down the table. Or, if there is plenty of room to move round the table, it may be easier to have one member of family serve and the other take the plates to each person. The vegetables and other extras should be on the table and it is up to the guests to offer these to the person on their right and hold the dish while they take what they need.

Serving Wine

Wine is served from the right of the diner, and a wine glass should never be more than half full: to fill it further is to leave no room for the bouquet. If (as usually happens) there is only one wine, and it will go with the first course, it is served from the start of the meal. But if the flavours will clash it can be held back until the main course.

At a very formal meal the staff serve each guest and stay in the room to refill glasses as necessary. More often, the wine is served, and then put on the table so guests may top up their glasses as they wish. The host should make sure that they do and pour more if necessary. At informal meals the host may ask guests to help themselves from the start - in which case the men should pour the wine for the woman on their left.

Empty bottles should be taken from the table, and if there is more than one wine, each wine is removed before the next is served. If port is served, it arrives with the cheese. Tradition has it that the host pours port only for the person on his right, he then helps himself and passes the port to his left, and it then continues to progress clockwise.

Clearing the Table

One of the worst developments in modern restaurants is that waiters often take people's plates away as soon as they finish - even though others at the table are still eating. This should *never* happen - nor should hosts permit it. It makes those who are slow feel guilty that they are holding other people up. No plate should ever be removed until the last person has finished - and even then, not until a few minutes after.

To Stack or Not to Stack

In the early 1950s there was a *Punch* cartoon of a wife at a dining table turning to her husband and saying 'Do we stack or are we gentry?' An allusion to the fact that, lacking staff, only those who clung very determinedly to their pre-war standards continued to carry the plates off one at a time after family meals. However, it *is* correct and there is an argument for doing so when entertaining.

Serving Coffee

Some people serve coffee at the dinner table, so the flow of conversation is uninterrupted. Others go to the sitting room. In this case, the hostess often removes the women from the table slightly earlier to allow time for loos and retouching make-up. But the days are long gone when men could tell stories over the port, while the women talked about babies over coffee.

As fewer people are drinking coffee, more smart hostesses are offering a choice of coffee, an after-dinner tea or herbal tisane. This is still unusual, but perhaps worth considering. It doesn't matter whether the hostess asks each guest if they want sugar or cream and puts it in, or lets them do it themselves, but there should be a coffee spoon on every saucer, whether or not people take sugar.

Leaving

Urban (if not urbane) lunch parties usually end at about 3.00 pm - though business lunches are usually shorter. In the country at weekends lunch may flow into a walk and then tea (in which case the hosts should indicate that this will be the form). Dinner parties usually end between 11 pm and 12 pm, although they can last into the small hours if the hosts look as if they want everyone to stay and the guests are keen to do so.

If guests have a special reason for needing to leave early (for example, to catch an early plane next morning) it is tactful if they tell the hosts about this when they accept the invitation - then there won't be doubts about whether they enjoyed themselves. Normally, guests say good-bye (without formalities) to other dinner guests, but when leaving early it may be best to leave inconspicuously. Then they won't spoil the party by starting a general exodus.

Guests should take their cue for leaving from what they know about the host and hostess. If someone is an early riser it's thoughtful to leave early. If they like nothing better than to talk into the small hours, early leaving (unless you have to) is spoiling their fun.

Hosts should accept that not going to bed at the usual time is a price they pay for the pleasure of having guests, and if guests outstay their welcome there is no *good* way to get them to go. However you wrap it up, making someone leave before they choose to is saying you have tired of their company or that you care more about your comfort than their pleasure - and neither is very hospitable.

On leaving, guests should thank the hosts, and the hosts should accompany them to the door and wait as they go to the street. If a woman is leaving alone at night the host should walk with her to her car, or see that she has other transport.

Tea

Tea, as I remember it from childhood, with meltingly wonderful home-made cakes, is, sadly, a vanishing tradition. But, laden as it is with forbidden fruits - fats, sugar and bread - it is an occasional delight which is worth maintaining.

Except for children's parties, invitations to tea are seldom written. Unless the tea is mainly for the benefit of young children, it is eaten in the sitting room, not at a table. Each person has a cup and saucer, with a teaspoon, and a small plate with a small knife. Neither doilies nor cake forks should be used - if a cake is too messy to eat with the fingers the pundits say it should not be served.

The hostess pours the tea for each person and, if you are bothered about such things, the tea goes in first. The up-market tea is China, drunk with a thin slice of lemon and no milk, but Indian is more popular. Lump sugar can be added to either. The usual food is sandwiches, cake(s) and possibly biscuits. The hostess should at first offer the food to guests, but this is one meal at which people may help themselves, within reason, as the meal progresses.

The official method of drinking tea is to hold the saucer just above the knees and lift the cup to the mouth - head ducking and little finger crooking are out. When eating, the cup and saucer are put down on a side table (there should be one close to each chair) and the plate is held like the saucer or put on the lap. Small cakes are eaten as they are. Large slices of cake may be eaten in sections which you cut off, and small napkins aren't essential unless the cakes are sticky.

Teenage Parties

At an informal party there is, in my view, only one rule: don't go out and leave teenagers alone in your home. I know this is contentious, and it would be a shame to hover about and spoil their fun, or embarrass them to bits by trying to join in. But it is one thing to keep out of their hair, and another to give them totally free rein. When drink is poured into inexperienced and undisciplined heads there is always a risk that some of their friends will try to take things too far. If that happens they need an adult within call. Today there is also the risk of violent gate-crashers to be considered.

Weekends and More

It is said that in-laws should live far enough away to have to put their hats on, but not so far that they have to stay the night. But friends are a different matter - provided everyone sticks to the ground rules.

The respective roles of the host and his or her house guest are summed up in the anonymous quote: 'The perfect host makes his guests feel at home; the perfect guest never behaves as if he *is* at home.' But achieving this ideal state of affairs demands a lot from both sides - especially from the host and hostess, for it is up to them to express welcome and attentiveness, while subtly conveying enough house rules to let guests fit in smoothly. This latter is essential, as much for the guests as for themselves: it is impossible to feel at home when you don't know what to expect next.

Issuing Invitations

Most invitations to stay are issued on the phone or informally in a letter. If you are inviting guests for a particular date you should say when you expect them to arrive. The best way is to indicate the time of the first meal for which they are expected, for example, 'Do come for dinner on Friday night. We usually eat at about 8 o'clock, so we'll expect you sometime after 6.' This gives them decent leeway for hold-ups on a long journey, but makes it clear that arriving at 8 would be too late. It is also wise to indicate a departure time. Again, meals are a good reference point. You can easily say, 'We do hope you'll stay for Sunday lunch', whereas you can't say, 'We do hope you'll go after Sunday lunch' - which is what it means.

The Length of the Stay

How long friends should stay is really a matter of how far away they live and how well you know them. A rough guide is one night for every 1 to 1½ hours of travel to reach you. So if you live 3 hours' drive away you can't decently invite them for less than 2 nights.

The same rule applies when inviting yourself to stay with someone who has issued an open invitation. But a week is about the maximum - even if you fly round the world - unless you are genuinely pressed to stay longer. Be specific about the time you'd like to arrive and depart and, unless an invitation includes pets and/or children, they should not be taken.

If guests are arriving by train the host(ess) usually tries to meet them at the station. Those who invite themselves shouldn't expect this consideration, but a good host (or hostess) will give it.

Briefing Guests on Clothes

Guests should be casually briefed on whether they need to bring special clothes. So tell them if you have a swimming pool, or tennis court, or if you are going to a point-to-point on Saturday, or usually change for dinner, or even if you want them to help with DIY. If a host (or hostess) forgets to do this a guest can always ask.

House Rules

Once guests arrive they need to be kept briefed on the form for the house - the times of meals, whether they can have a bath whenever they want, plus the quirks of difficult taps and lavatories. They also need to know the rules on getting up. Some people insist that their guests are on parade for breakfast at set hours, but if you are happy to let them get up at any time, say so - making it clear whether or not food will still be available for latecomers. It is not unreasonable to say, 'Breakfast is sometime between 8 and 9, but if you want to skip breakfast and sleep late you can just make yourself a cup of tea whenever you get up.' This absolves you from the duty to fry eggs all morning and lets guests get a rest - and a sleeping guest is never any bother. But some people can sleep like the dead, so tell them if they need to be up by midday - and offer to wake them.

Conversely, guests who wake early and hungry should conceal this and not sit around waiting to be fed, like a family dog. Unless there is clear evidence to the contrary, they should also assume everyone is fragile and needs quiet at breakfast time.

Privacy

Unless two people are married or you are *certain* they sleep together, give them separate rooms - preferably close enough for them to creep across surreptitiously. All guests need hangers, and towels; Americans may expect a face flannel too, and flowers in the room make up for a multitude of shortcomings.

Once guests are in their room hosts should regard it as private. To knock and walk in, even with cups of early morning tea is to invite embarrassment. Instead, knock and say you are leaving the tea outside the door.

Bedtime and Waking

It is up to the guests to go to bed first (just as it is up to them to leave a party). Not all guests know this, so there can be a stalemate as each side sits waiting for the other to make the first move. Once a reasonable hour has been reached the hosts can cure this by offering a nightcap or hot drink 'before bed'.

Before saying good-night hosts should check that guests have enough blankets on their beds, and brief them *fully* on any alarm system. It is all too easy to tell them not to go downstairs but to forget to tell them not to go upstairs, or not to let the dogs out.

As people often wake early and thirsty in a strange house it is also a good idea to show guests where they can make themselves tea or coffee early in the morning. If an alarm system prevents this they can at least be given a thermos of boiling water, and what they need to make instant coffee, or even a jug of orange juice to cheer the early hours. To lie awake unable even to make a drink is miserable.

If guests are able to go down to the kitchen hosts needn't take the odd clink as a signal to leap up and start breakfast. This will only make the guests feel guilty. Equally, guests should avoid clattering about 'helpfully' preparing breakfast - it will only make the hosts feel they should have risen earlier. The only thing worse than a guest who does nothing is one who does too much.

Gifts on Arrival

It's conventional to arrive bearing gifts when going to stay with people. This can be anything you choose, but food and drink are the most usual. Or, you can take flowers, or send them afterwards. The size of the present should suit the length of your stay.

Food and Drink

Anyone who has any serious food allergy should warn the hostess - no one wants to make guests ill. A hostess should also try to ask about food likes and dislikes, if only to spare herself the depressing sight of guests picking at her food.

Some households tell guests to help themselves to any food or drink they feel like. Guests should use this privilege with great moderation. If that invitation isn't issued they should always ask before taking anything, and keep their asking to a minimum.

Helping

The main role of any guest is to be good company - but that isn't quite all.

Unless there are staff, good guests should look to see what needs to be done and either do it unobtrusively or offer to do it: vague offers of help are simply annoying. However, there are limits to how much work a guest should do. Nobody wants a guest to turn into a demon cleaner in the middle of a sociable visit, and a quick way to have the hostess smiling through gritted teeth is to clean things far more thoroughly than she does. The matter of contributing to the food budget also needs tact. Money, in any form, should *never* be handed to the hostess (unless perhaps to split a specific bill when you are shopping together), but contributions in kind are always welcome and may be expected if someone is staying several days.

On leaving ask the hostess if she would like the beds stripped. But *only* do it if she says yes. Underblankets are not always designed for guests' eyes.

The Host's Children and Animals

Unlikely as it may seem to devout child and animal lovers, some perfectly civilized people regard both as they regard adults - they like some and dislike others. Liking the parents or owners does not guarantee any affection for their offspring and pets. So little darlings, of both kinds, should be prevented from molesting the guests. By the same token, guests must do all they can to treat them well and deflect them tactfully.

Staff

If there are staff one of them may well unpack a guest's suitcase - so consider before you pack anything embarrassing. On leaving, guests should tip any members of staff who have helped them - including the daily woman who has cleaned their room during the stay. It is always wisest to ask your host or hostess how much you should give.

EVENTS

Christenings

Parents who want their child christened should ring the clergyman, priest or appropriate official of their church, and make an appointment to discuss the arrangements. Some Church of England clergymen prefer to make christenings part of the morning service, but it is normally possible to have it as a separate service - especially if you offer to bring the child for a blessing with the whole congregation at another time.

The exact forms of service vary with each branch of the Church, but they are all easy to follow and need no advance preparation. One difference, however, is that in the Church of England the godmother usually holds the child before baptism; in the Roman Catholic Church the mother holds it.

Announcing the Christening

Christenings can be announced in the court and social pages of *The Times* and the *Daily Telegraph* and should be submitted to the social editor in writing. Just give the parents' names, the name of the clergyman, what the child was christened, the date and place and who the godparents were.

Choosing Godparents

The parents usually select two godfathers and two godmothers. They are normally expected to be baptized, confirmed and practising Christians - though this is usually taken for granted without questions being asked. The idea is to give the child an even better extended family, and more loving (and Christian) guidance than nature provided.

It is an honour to be asked to be a godparent, but it carries long-term responsibilities and it is unfair to the child if you accept when you really don't feel inclined to carry these out. If you want to refuse a good excuse is needed. One possibility is to say you have so many godchildren already that you don't feel it would be fair to take on another - much as you'd like to. The important thing is to give no hint to parents that you don't like their child - which may well be the truth.

Godparents are expected to give the child presents and so are the immediate family. The presents should be something lasting - jewellery or small items of silver are traditional. Godparents can make life easier for themselves if they choose something to which they can add at every birthday. Then the problem of what to give is solved for years ahead. Others who are invited to the service have no obligation to give anything, but they may feel more comfortable giving at least a token - unless they visited the mother in hospital and gave her something for the baby then.

The Occasion

Dress is very much like a wedding so far as women are concerned, but men wear dark suits. The baby traditionally wears a white christening robe - but any good white garment is suitable.

Everyone who attends the christening usually goes back to the parents' house for a small party. It could be a lunch, tea or evening drinks - depending on the time of the christening - but, whatever the hour, it is traditional to have a special cake (rather like a wedding cake) and perhaps champagne. A godfather usually proposes a toast to the baby.

Funerals

The formalities which used to surround death dwindled almost to nothing during the two World Wars, but there are certain conventions which remain. There are also legal requirements and these can be found in the section under Law.

Announcing a Death

When someone dies relatives and close friends should be notified immediately. This can be done in person, by telephone or by letter. An announcement can also be put in the papers, and *The Times,* the *Daily Telegraph,* the *Scotsman* and the *Guardian* all have deaths columns. Some regional papers, like the *Yorkshire Post*, and some local papers, do too. The announcement should briefly give the name of the deceased, the date and place of death, and the date, time, and location of the funeral. If flowers are not welcome it should say so. For example:

> **PETRIE** - On 5 April at Great Ormond Street Children's Hospital, Anne-Marie, darling daughter of John and Isobel Petrie. Funeral the Brompton Oratory 4 pm, 10 April. No flowers please, donations to the Leukaemia Research Fund if desired.

Dress
People no longer go into mourning by wearing black, but a man should wear a dark suit and white shirt, and a woman a dark dress, suit or coat. A hat isn't essential, but it is preferable, especially for women, and showy jewellery shouldn't be worn. The only exception is if a widow wants to wear clothing or jewellery which her husband loved to see her in. If his favourite colour was red, then red she can wear.

There is no longer any need to wear black in the weeks which follow, although if people feel they want to make this visual expression of their sense of loss it would be cruel to try to jolly them out of it. A time for mourning is needed if the bereaved are to recover fully in the long run, and to hurry people into some phoney 'normality' is to paper over cracks which are best left to heal in their own time.

Letter Writing
It is still customary to write a letter of sympathy to friends and relatives, when they are bereaved. These should be written swiftly, as the whole purpose is to give support to the bereaved during the difficult and lonely days immediately after the death, but those who are less close to the family may prefer to write in the second week.

It can be hard to know what to write, but this shouldn't put you off writing. You only have to say how very sorry you are to hear of the death. Offer your sympathy and let them know that they are being thought of, and are not alone in their grief. The simplest and most genuine words are the best.

Letters of condolence should always be answered, unless the writer says there is no need for a reply - and clearly means it. All that is needed is one sentence saying how much their kind and understanding letter was appreciated, another saying something about the deceased - for example, that mercifully they died very peacefully - and perhaps a final sentence saying that you are sure they understand that you are not able to write more, but that you hope to be in touch before too long. If there are a lot of replies to write the whole family can share the task, making it clear that they are writing on behalf of the chief mourner. Nowadays ordinary writing paper and envelopes, not mourning paper, are used.

The Flowers
Flowers from either family or friends are sent to the funeral director, so they can be put with the coffin on its journey. Those who wish to send flowers should ask the family where to send them.

Undertakers/ Funeral Directors
Undertakers are called undertakers because they undertake all the arrangements for a funeral, though they now like to be called funeral directors. Most operate a 24-hour service and will collect a body as soon as the death has been certified by a doctor. From then on the relatives need only tell the funeral director what they wish to have arranged and he does everything for them.

Funerals are expensive and made more so by the fact that only complete packages are available. You can expect to spend over £400, and the price will rise with extra options, such as an elaborate coffin or a headstone. But prices also vary considerably from one company to another for exactly the same 'package'. The costs come out of the dead person's estate (see under Law). So if someone would have resented his or her saving being spent on inflated funeral costs you should ring round and ask for comparative prices. But this must be done *before* the body is collected. Once any company has collected the body there is, effectively, no changing. (See also under Law). The most basic package usually includes:
- the collection of the body from the home or hospital
- keeping the body in a chapel of rest
- all arrangements - phoning the crematorium, church, minister etc., a simple coffin
- taking the body to the cemetery or crematorium
- the staff required for this
- It may also include one car for the family on the day, and more can be provided at extra cost.

If the family wants to view the body it will normally be embalmed - possibly at extra cost. But some funeral directors embalm *every* body they handle - unless you ask them not to.

The costs don't end there. In cities, obtaining a plot and having the grave dug costs several hundred pounds, and in some places the bill is close to a thousand pounds (but see under Law). Although the undertaker makes the arrangements for the crematorium, the fees involved are *not* included in his charges. There will be fees for the extra medical certificates needed for a cremation, and there will also be a fee for the use of the crematorium and possibly for an officiating minister.

Most good funeral directors belong to the **National Association of Funeral Directors** (57 Doughty Street, London WC1 2NE Tel: 01 242 9388) and its members operate a code of practice agreed with the Office of Fair Trading. They will deal with complaints, if any.

The Funeral
The date and time of the funeral may depend on what the officiating priest can manage, but the family should tell the undertaker their preferences. Occasionally,

people put requests regarding the service in their will, and in religions and denominations that allow variations the family usually discuss their special requirements with the priest and, choose the hymns.

The chief mourners are usually collected from the deceased's house, and the funeral cars take them both to and from the service. Other mourners should arrive about 15 to 20 minutes before and there should be a verger or family friend there to see the correct pews are filled and that enough space is left for the family at the front.

If the body is being buried the coffin will be carried out to the grave after the service and the family will lead the mourners out to the graveside for the final moments.

Cremations

Cremation is becoming more popular and crematoriums permit services of all religions and also non-religious services - such as those of the humanists. If the body is to be cremated, there are two possibilities. The service can be held in the non-denominational chapel at the crematorium, with the dead person's local priest or someone on the crematorium roster officiating. Alternatively, the service can be at the deceased's usual place of worship and the coffin taken to the crematorium afterwards. In this case, it is usually only accompanied by the family. The crematorium will need to know what should be done with the ashes.

What Happens After the Funeral

After the funeral, the relatives and close friends usually return to the house of whoever has died for some kind of food and drink. Often this is prepared by friends or relatives and brought along in advance, to spare whoever is in mourning the work involved. If food and drink is available anyone who would be welcome to return for it should be told in advance - there is no need for a proper invitation - and anyone who turns up unexpectedly at the funeral and would be welcome can be invited too.

Weddings

Engagement rings were once part of an intricate system of ring signals. In the first (1856) edition of *Enquire Within* I found these signals described in a section called 'Love's Telegraph', which explained:

> If a gentleman wants a wife, he wears a ring on the first finger of the left hand; if he is engaged he wears it on the second finger; if he is married on the third; and on the fourth if he never intends to be married. When a lady is not engaged she wears a hoop or diamond on her first finger; if engaged, on her second; if married, on her third; and on the fourth if she intends to die a maid.

This subtle signalling didn't stop at a ring, for the writer continues:

> When a gentleman presents a fan, flower, or trinket, to a lady with the left hand, this, on his part, is an overture of regard; should she receive it with the left hand, it is considered as an acceptance of his esteem; but if with the right hand, it is a refusal of the offer. Thus by a few simple tokens, explained by this rule, the passion of love is expressed: and, through the medium of the telegraph, the most diffident man may, without difficulty, communicate his sentiments of regard to a lady, and, in case his offer should be refused, avoid experiencing the mortification of a refusal.

It seems rather a pity that we have retained the engagement ring, and discarded all the other useful signals. It might save a lot of heartbreak if those who had no intention of marrying announced it on their hands.

Even without these aids some 400,000 people get married in Britain each year. Although Church of England weddings predominate, there are numerous other forms and even the C of E conventions vary with the region. Much as I would like to include traditions of Scots Presbyterians, Bah'ais or Buddhists, I am limited for space and can only cover the classic Church of England conventions. The civil requirements are covered opposite.

Church of England Weddings

For most Church of England marriages the civil preliminary is the calling of the banns, but there are other options (see below).

The Banns

A Church of England wedding can only take place if the banns have been called on three Sundays. For this, the bride and groom each visit their own parish priest, ask for banns to be called and pay a statutory fee. Some clergy like seven days' notice before the first banns are called. If the couple is marrying at a church which isn't in either of the parishes the banns must normally be called there too. The banns involve asking the congregation if they know any reason why these two people should not be married, and the clergyman will usually talk to the couple and check this.

Common Licence

For a common licence to get married one of the couple must have lived in the parish for 15 days before applying. Together they then apply for the licence to whoever represents the bishop in that area. If it is granted the couple can get married the next day.

Special Licence

It is a legal requirement to get married in either your own parish or that of your fiancé. If you want to get married anywhere else you need a special licence from the Archbishop of Canterbury which allows a wedding to take place anywhere - for example, in a hospital. You get an application from the **Registrar of the Faculties,** 1 The Sanctuary, Westminster, London SW1P 3JT Tel: 01 222 5381.

Church Weddings Not in the Church of England

All weddings not conducted by the Church of England must be preceded by the preliminaries needed to obtain either a certificate or a licence for a registry office wedding (see below). That doesn't necessarily mean that there has to be a registry office wedding as well as a religious service. Once the Superintendent Registrar has issued an authorization for the wedding to take place the marriage can often be conducted in the place of worship.

Some priests and ministers are registered as 'authorized persons' and allowed to register a marriage; others are not. This is not a matter of some denominations or religions being registered, but of some individuals being registered. So the fact that one Catholic priest registers marriages doesn't mean the next one necessarily can. If whoever conducts the service is not authorized, a registrar of marriages may be able to come to the place of marriage and register the wedding. Only when this is not possible is it necessary to have a registry office ceremony as well as a religious ceremony.

Civil Weddings

For a marriage to be valid it must be registered - any religious service is, from the legal point of view, just icing on the cake. Registration can either take place in a Registry Office or in a building which is authorized by the state - such as most of the Christian churches.

If a marriage is purely in a registry office there are two options - a certificate or a licence. To obtain either the bride or groom must live in the area of the registry office being used. For a **certificate** each takes their birth certificate and a fee to the registry office in the area where they live (those who have been married before must also take a decree absolute or a death certificate). If they live in two different areas one registry office just accepts notification that the person intends to marry, and a booking is made at the other. This must all be done not more than 3 months and not less than 21 days before the day they wish to marry. The couple book a definite time and day - book early for Saturdays. It is also worth asking how many guests may come and whether a photographer will be allowed in; some registry offices are very small.

For a **licence** the documents and fees for both the bride and groom are taken to the registry office where they intend to marry. This must be done at least one clear working day before the wedding, and both of them must have been living in the area of the registry office for at least 15 days.

On the day they must bring a further fee (it is considerably more for a licence than for a certificate) and two witnesses. They exchange vows, in a ceremony lasting about 10 minutes, and sign the register. A ring isn't a legal requirement, though most couples use one. If there is a reception afterwards it is often paid for by couple, especially if it is a second marriage. Invitations can be issued in exactly the same way as for a church wedding and the reception can follow the same formula if they wish.

Scottish Civil Weddings

In Scotland the procedure is very similar. It's a myth that you can just run away to Gretna Green and get married. Only in an emergency can you have a sheriff's licence which allows the wedding almost immediately. Normally, even to apply for a civil wedding in Scotland one of you must have lived there for the past 15 days. You then have to sign application forms in the presence of two local householders and the forms must be displayed for seven days before the Certificate of take place during the next three months.

> There is a special form of licence which allows someone to be married anywhere - for example, in hospital - if he or she is too ill to be married in any of the usual places.

Second Marriages

Second marriages present no legal problems. So any couple free to marry can have a registry office marriage without question. The same is true of religious ceremonies if both their previous partners are dead. But problems arise if one or other of them is divorced - even if he or she was the 'innocent' party. Some branches of the Christian Church do permit second marriages in certain circumstances but not all. Those who care deeply about this, and have been barred from a service in their own church, can contact the main offices of other denominations (see Organizations) and ask if a marriage service would be possible.

Where a second church marriage is possible the bride can still wear white, but there are usually no bridesmaids; she may be given away by a male relative if she wishes or she can dispense with this. Unless she is a young girl and her family want to give her a second reception she normally pays the wedding expenses which fell to her parents the first time round.

Planning a Wedding

A wedding is the largest, and most expensive, festivity that most families ever arrange, and to make it a success takes a great deal of planning. It needs to be regarded as a military operation, for which every move is planned as far ahead as the length of the engagement allows.

At one time weddings followed set rules. Today most weddings keep fairly close to them, but there is far more variation than there used to be. What follows is the classic format, but couples can have anything they want. It is, after all, their big day and if the bride wants to wear puce and turn the reception into a disco she has a perfect right to do so.

Who Decides What

Most of the work of planning a wedding falls to the bride and her mother. Both should remember that for weddings everything is priced individually: the reception food doesn't include the cake, the church music doesn't include the bells, the bride's bouquet doesn't include a buttonhole for her father etc. So bills can escalate alarmingly. The decision making divides like this:

Wedding invitation printing	Bride's family
Wedding service printing	Bride's family
Whether there will be carpet and an awning to the church	Bride's family
Where the wedding presents will be displayed (if at all)	Bride's family
Wedding service details	Bride and groom
Wedding present list	Bride and groom
Bridesmaids'/pages' outfits	Bride
Bridesmaids' and bride's flowers	Bride
Reception details	Bride's family
Flowers for the church	Bride - but if others are being married there the same day it is wise to agree one lot of flowers for all the weddings - and much cheaper.
Guest list	Whoever is paying for the reception decides how many will be invited. Then each family lists about half that number with names and addresses. The groom's list is then given to the bride's family, and they send the invitations.

Who Pays for What

Weddings now cost so much that the old rules about who pays for what are often ignored. The main expense is the reception, and the bride, the groom and even the groom's family may well contribute to it. However, the conventional division of costs makes a good starting point for discussion.

Bride's father
Press announcements of the engagement and wedding
Printing wedding invitations
Flowers in the church
Flowers for the reception
Wedding dress and trousseau
Music in church
Carpet and awning at church (if used)
All costs related to the reception
The photographer
Cars apart from those for the groom and best man
Printing the service sheet

Groom
Engagement ring
Fees for licence or banns
Bride's and bridesmaids' flowers
Buttonholes for himself and best man
Cars for himself and best man
Wedding ring
A present for the bride
Church expenses other than music or flowers
   (e.g. bells, banns)
A present for each bridesmaid
A present for best man and possibly for each usher
The honeymoon

The bride chooses the bridesmaids' and pages' outfits, but they or their parents usually pay for them. So it's considerate to consult them and try to choose dresses they will like and be able to wear on other occasions.

Some magazine articles imply that you not only need to have printed invitations but also printed table napkins, book matches and so on. If this is all the rage in your area you may want to go along with it, but it is most certainly not the standard form and is one expense which can be avoided.

There is so much to consider that it is well worth reading all the details in the chapter on weddings in Debrett's book *Etiquette and Modern Manners*, which includes Roman Catholic, Quaker and Jewish weddings. There is also **Debrett's Information Service** (73 Britannia Road, London SW6 Tel: 01 731 4221). **Brides Magazine** (Vogue House, Hanover Square, London W1R 0AD Tel: 01 499 9080) has an information service on all aspects of weddings, which answers all queries personally. Send an sae for their list of shops all over Britain which hire wedding dresses. Other magazines for brides have useful information if you can't find something you need. Some are not reliable in their information on etiquette - but not everyone wants to observe it anyway. The **National Association of Toastmasters**, Albany House, Albany Crescent, Claygates, Esher, Surrey RT10 0PF Tel: 01 0372 68022 will put people in touch with toastmasters in their area.

Preparations

How far in advance you need to book anything depends on the time of year. In peak wedding periods everything gets booked up months in advance, while in the low season you can get away with less forethought. It looks as if the saying that 'in spring a young man's fancy lightly turns to thoughts of love' is very true: most engagements are 3 to 6 months long and the peak

Planning a Wedding

As Early as Possible

☐ Make a guest list.

☐ Find out the dates on which both the church and a good venue for the reception are available *before* deciding the date of the wedding.

☐ Book the church.

☐ Book wherever you will hold the reception (or a marquee).

☐ Book the caterers, a cake maker and staff, if the reception will be in a private house.

☐ Book music for the reception if you want it (most weddings don't have it, but if you want a string quartet in the garden or a disco for dancing don't delay).

☐ Book a photographer or a video company - the best get *very* booked up.

☐ Book cars for the bride, bridesmaids and her family and for the groom and best man.

☐ Book a toastmaster (see page 15) - if one is being used.

☐ Book the honeymoon, and plan clothing.

☐ Ask the best man, bridesmaids etc. as soon as possible.

☐ Find, or order, a wedding dress, and headdress and bridesmaids'/pages' clothes.

☐ Decide on the service and the hymns you want.

☐ Order the wedding invitations (printing usually takes 2 to 4 weeks).

Well in Advance

☐ Arrange a wedding list at a suitable shop.

☐ Talk to florists, get comparative prices and ideas, and book your choice.

☐ All men involved must book morning dress if they need to hire it (allow 6 weeks).

☐ Confirm with the minister the dates of the banns and the details of the wedding.

☐ Order the service sheets for the wedding.

☐ Agree the food and drink with the caterers.

☐ Buy a wedding ring.

☐ Get suitable luggage for going away - if you don't have it.

☐ Buy shoes for the wedding and wear them round the house so they are comfortable on the day.

☐ Get a passport or check your passport (you can't have it put into your married name until you have a marriage certificate to show them). Apply for visas, if needed.

☐ Have any immunizations needed for the honeymoon (if they last long enough). Some make you feel rough so *don't* leave it to the last minute.

☐ Get family planning advice.

☐ Send out invitations 6 to 9 weeks before.

☐ Check off each acceptance or refusal.

☐ Start a wedding present list and note who gives you what *as you open it*. Then if you get behind on letters you still know whom to thank.

The Last Month

☐ Check that guests who have failed to reply have received their invitations.

☐ Arrange accommodation for guests travelling long distances, if needed.

☐ Book a hair appointment for the day.

☐ Make final arrangements for the flowers for: the reception, the church, the bride, the bridesmaids and buttonholes for the bride's father, the groom and ushers.

☐ If you are having a sit-down meal make a seating plan.

☐ Give the final numbers to the caterers 2 weeks before the wedding.

☐ Book a hotel for the first night if you will need it.

☐ Arrange the incidental music with the organist.

☐ Prepare a newspaper announcement of the wedding and submit it.

☐ Make arrangements for any stag (or doe) nights - preferably *not* the night before.

☐ Bride buys presents for pages; groom for the bridesmaids.

☐ Bride and groom buy presents for each other.

☐ Bride's parents buy a present for the groom.

☐ Groom's parents buy a present for the bride.

The Last Week

☐ Rehearse the wedding ceremony.

☐ Confirm or double check any arrangements not yet totally certain.

months for weddings are always July, August and September, with April, May and June being runners up. Whereas January to March has only a fraction of the nuptials.

Invitations

As the bride's father usually pays for the reception, the wedding invitations are normally worded to show that the bride's parents are the hosts. This can be the case even if they are divorced - provided they themselves are happy with this. But if, for example, the father is dead and the mother and an uncle are giving the reception, or the bride and groom are giving their own reception, the wording will reflect this.

People are normally invited to both the service and the reception, but for a registry office wedding the invitation can be simply to the reception. When inviting guests of another faith, who may feel unable to attend the service, one solution is to enclose a note saying that they will be most welcome at the reception if they are not able to be at the service, and say when the reception is expected to start.

The name of each guest is hand-written at the top left-hand side of their invitation, and if children are welcome at the wedding their names should be with those of the parents. If they aren't, the parents should assume they won't be welcome. As many guests may be coming to an unknown place it can also be useful to enclose a map or diagram showing how to find the church and/or reception.

Presents

Everyone who accepts the invitation is expected to send a present in advance, and relations and very close friends usually give presents whether or not they accept. The couple often put a list of what they would like in a department store - or in several. The list(s) should be reasonably long and include items to suit every pocket. They can be quite specific, and even give the design of dinner service wanted. This allows guests who can't get to the shop to do the whole business by phone and still know they are giving something which will be enjoyed.

The presents are sent to the bride's home before the wedding - or elsewhere if the couple prefer - with a card bearing good wishes and the full name of the sender. At one time it was traditional for the presents to be displayed at the reception, but the practice is almost dead.

The Best Man and Bridesmaids

The groom picks one of his closest friends as best man who then has a key role in the proceedings. He normally knows all the plans and his duties usually include the following:

- discussing the timing of events in the reception with the toastmaster if one is being used
- organizing the ushers
- arranging for the church fees to be paid before the wedding
- making sure the groom's clothes and luggage for going away are in place on the day

- arranging the groom's stag night
- getting the groom to the church (accompanying him in a car or driving him) and taking him in through a side entrance
- standing beside him before the ceremony on his right in the front right-hand pew
- handing the wedding ring to the minister
- accompanying the chief bridesmaid into the vestry when the register is signed and down the aisle at the end
- being the timekeeper who gets the bride and groom into place at each stage of events at the reception
- being master of ceremonies and introducing the speakers if there is no toastmaster
- proposing the speech to the bridesmaids
- making sure the bride and groom leave on time.

There are no rules about how many bridesmaids a bride can have, and both they and pages are entirely optional, but it may be useful to have one good friend to help with getting in and out of the wedding dress.

Giving the Bride Away

The bride is normally escorted to the church by her father and he stands beside her and gives her away. If there is no father she can be escorted by another male relative and he can give her away, or her mother can step forward for the giving away.

Heritage Placements Ltd, 4 Wellington House, Greenberry Street, London NW8 7AB Tel: 01 586 3665 has on its books castles, country houses and islands, all over Britain, and will find a suitable location among its clients for a social occasion of any kind, at no charge to you. Plus companies for all the trimmings - from food to music.

Despite its name **London Convention Bureau,** 26 Grosvenor Gardens, London SW1W 0DU Tel: 01 730 3450 is not just a convention organization. Its numerous members cover locations, within a 25-mile radius of London, which you can hire for every type of entertaining. The places range from discos to castles. Plus companies which provide all the extra services. The service is free to the enquirer. Their publication *Convention and Exhibition Venues in London* is also free.

Historic Houses, Castles and Gardens, British Leisure Publications lists such places county by county and says what type of function each will accommodate.

Dress

A formal wedding invitation indicates that guests are expected to dress formally too. This means women wear smart day clothes. Anyone in white or cream should relieve it with black or a strong colour so as not to steal the bride's thunder. Men traditionally wear morning dress (see page 23) for a church wedding, but a dark suit is sometimes substituted and is worn at most registry office weddings and receptions.

The Wedding Ceremony

- The best man makes sure the groom gets ready and gets to the church on time, and he has charge of the wedding ring.
- Ushers arrive at a wedding 40 minutes before it is due to start; it is their job to hand out service sheets and show people to their seats.

- The organist plays and the bells peal for 30 minutes before it starts.
- The groom and best man should be seated 20 minutes before the start.
- Guests arrive *at least* 15 minutes before the service starts. The bride's relations and friends sit on the left of the aisle (as you look at the altar), the groom's relations and friends on the right.
- The bride's mother should be the last person to take her seat, 5 minutes before the bride arrives. This acts as a signal that the bride is on her way.
- The bridesmaids and pages arrive 5 minutes before the bride and get in position near the main door.
- The priest and choir then wait, ready to process up the aisle before the bride.
- The bride arrives and once she has adjusted her veil, and possibly posed for photographs, processes up the aisle on her father's (or a substitute's) right arm.
- After the wedding the bride and groom leave first.

Confetti

Confetti is almost universally hated by church wardens and hoteliers. In theory, it can be thrown either as the couple leave the church or as they leave on honeymoon.But permission should be asked of the church or hotel beforehand. It is best avoided in the rain as some confetti is not colour-fast and can ruin a light dress.

The Reception

The loveliest wedding receptions are often those in a private house with a beautiful garden. And the home of a relative or friend may be borrowed to provide one. But, given the risk of a deluge, it must have enough flat lawn to take a marquee. As most people don't have the space the reception is usually in a hotel or a suitable club, but you can also hire stately homes, or anything from an island to a swimming pool for a wedding reception.

Food and Drink

Champagne is the stuff of which weddings are made. Non-vintage is usual and there is often a back-up of white wine for those who don't like fizzy drinks. It is also essential to serve non-alcoholic drinks. If the reception runs into tea-time, tea is usually served towards the end of the reception.

Though some people do have a sit-down 'wedding breakfast', the classic format is still for everyone to stay standing and be offered light buffet food. In choosing it, the appetites of guests who have driven a long way without eating should be borne in mind.

It should be delicious, festive, easy to eat with the fingers when smartly dressed. So ban anything with deep-fried crumbs which could leave a greasy trail down dresses. Ideally, some of the food is laid out on tables and some circulated on trays, so even guests who get stuck with deaf Aunt Amy will get a morsel.

Avoid the paddling pools on stems which caterers may offer as champagne glasses. The tall glasses called flutes are far less likely to spill.

Arriving at the Reception

The receiving line which traditionally greets guests as they arrive at the reception is: the bride's mother and father, groom's mother and father, bride and groom - in that order - and the guests shake hands with each as they enter. This can lead to a very tedious delay, and even queueing in the rain.

Before the last war the bride's mother, as hostess, was the only person to greet guests, so the receiving line is not sacrosanct, and some stylish weddings have abandoned the formal line-up; instead its members circulate more freely during the reception, which is much more enjoyable for the guests.

Speeches

Speeches are traditional but it's a rare bride whose menfolk are all entertaining speakers. The speechmakers should make it easy for themselves - and everyone else - by remembering the dictum that 'brevity is the soul of wit', unless, of course, *other people* rate them as wits.

Normally, the best man urges the bride and groom into position at a pre-arranged time (about an hour after the reception starts, or later if there has been a long line-up). The toastmaster, or best man, then asks for silence, and the bride's father (or an old family friend chosen by him) makes a speech proposing the health and happiness of the bride.

Next the bridegroom makes a speech in which he thanks the bride's parents for letting him marry their daughter and for the reception, and thanks the guests for their presents. Finally, he proposes a toast to the bridesmaids.

The best man replies on behalf of the bridesmaids and may read out a *few* telegrams and greetings cards provided they really are entertaining and if most of the guests know the people concerned.

Cutting the Cake

The cake is cut after the speeches. The bride and groom jointly use a knife (or service sword) to cut one slice while guests stay silent. The other slices are then cut by the caterers, and the cake is passed round to all the guests.

Leaving the Reception

The bride and groom always leave first, driving off in their going-away clothes. The timing is up to them, but the other guests are expected to follow very soon afterwards.

If it is raining the ushers should be armed with umbrellas to hold over the bride and groom and over guests as they leave.

At one time it wasn't only those in the forces whose path was lined with symbols of their profession - though a guard of honour might not like to be called that. In country districts wood shavings would be strewn for a carpenter, cloth for a tailor and so on. It would be amusing to see this revived with computer chips and dummy share certificates strewing the path.

What Happens Next

What happens next is beyond the scope of this chapter but the Victorian edition of *Enquire Within* gave clear guidelines for how to live happily ever after:

> *HOW TO TREAT A WIFE. - First, get a wife; secondly be patient. You may have great trials and perplexities in your business with the world, but do not carry to your home a clouded or contracted brow. Your wife may have many trials, which, though of less magnitude, may have been hard to bear. A kind, conciliating word, a tender look, will do wonders in chasing from her brow all the clouds of gloom... oh! bear with her; she has trials and sorrows to which you are a stranger, but which your tenderness can deprive of all their anguish. Notice kindly her little attentions and efforts to promote your comfort. Do not treat her with indifference, if you would not sear and palsy her heart, which, watered by your kindness, would, to the latest day of your existence, throb with sincere and constant affection. Sometimes [!] yield your wishes to hers. Do you find it hard to yield sometimes? Think you it is not difficult for her to give up always? If you never yield to her wishes there is a danger that she will think you are selfish, and care only for yourself, and with such feelings she cannot love you as she might.*

While the 'Advice to Wives' reads as follows:

> *...She must study never to draw largely on the small stock of patience in a man's nature, nor to increase his obstinacy by trying to drive him; never, never if possible, to have scenes.... If irritation should occur a woman must expect to hear from most men a strength and vehemence of language far more than the occasion requires. Mild, as well as stern men, are prone to exaggeration of language; let not a woman be tempted to say anything sarcastic or violent in retaliation. The bitterest repentance must needs follow if she do. Men frequently forget what they have said, but seldom forget what is uttered by their wives. They are grateful, too, for forbearance in such cases; for whilst asserting most loudly that they are right, they are often conscious that they are wrong. Give a little time, as the greatest boon you can bestow, to the irritated feelings of your husband.*

Needless to say, the author of *that* edition of *Enquire Within* was a man.

Wedding Anniversaries

The only anniversaries which are usually celebrated with presents and parties are the silver, ruby, golden and diamond wedding anniversaries. By tradition, silver presents are given for a silver wedding, gold for a gold and so on, but this can be expensive. Happily, the tokens associated with other anniversaries have charm without great cost.

1st Paper	pottery	16th China
2nd Cotton	9th Pottery or	25th Silver
3rd Leather	willow	30th Pearl
4th Fruit or	10th Tin or	35th Coral
flowers	aluminium	40th Ruby
5th Wood	11th Steel	45th Sapphire
6th Iron	12th Silk or linen	50th Gold
7th Wool or	13th Lace	55th Emerald
copper	14th Ivory	60th Diamond
8th Bronze or	15th Crystal	

MANNERS AND DRESS

General Table Manners

In France, at one time, socially selective mothers would vet prospective sons or daughters-in-law by serving raw peaches at dinner. Anyone who failed to eat one with due elegance - and a knife and fork - was unlikely to gain acceptance. Such deliberate testing has surely died out, but good table manners still make an impression - and the more so as they become rarer.

The details vary from country to country, but the underlying aim is usually to avoid eating in a way which is an eyesore and look after other people's needs as well as your own. This leads to certain dos and don'ts. You may think them too obvious to mention. For, in this era of fast food, it's easy to forget the niceties of behaviour and it may be useful for parents to have a check list to wave at children who insist that *nobody in the world* really expects the manners their parents are trying to instil.

Do's for Good Guests

Be guided by the behaviour of your host and hostess. Do as they do, not as you do at home - unless their manners are so dreadful that you can't go quite that far.

It is far better manners to drink beer from a can, when the host is serving it that way, than to discomfort everyone by finding a glass. As with any manners the touchstone is consideration for others. So the rules are these - and, of course, they aren't limited to social occasions.

- Look to see who needs something passed to them, and pass it. If it is on a dish, hold it while they help themselves.
- Look to see how many helpings will be needed from a dish before helping yourself, and adjust your portion accordingly - though without looking as if you are *counting* the peas, however few there are.
- Avoid the temptation to take all the best bits, or most luscious cakes.
- Avoid taking more than you need, want or will eat.
- If you discover you have been given food you hate there is a dilemma. At one time you had to eat everything on your plate, however much you loathed it. Few people keep to this now. But, if a hostess' feelings matter to you, leave only a *very* little.
- If *offered* a food you dislike ask for a smaller than average portion, giving some plausible excuse - for example, the previous courses were so delicious you

hardly have room for more. *In extremis* you can even claim an allergy to it.

- If you have to get rid of a bone, or other debris raise your fork or spoon to your mouth and *discreetly* eject the offending morsel. Then slip it neatly on to the side of your plate - tucking it under other leftovers if it is something which might embarrass the hostess. When eating fruit with your fingers, a stone can be ejected into the hole formed by the thumb and forefinger of a lightly clenched fist, then placed on the plate.
- Spare any slow eater the embarrassment of eating alone by dawdling a little yourself, so you finish only just before them.
- Make sure that nobody is left out of the conversation for any length of time.

Don'ts for Good Guests
- Don't reach across other people to get what you need - ask if they can pass it.
- Never start eating until the last person at the table has been served (unless the hostess tells you to). With central heating food only gets cold if the numbers are immense and, unless there are people waiting at table, it is essential that guests pass things to others instead of eating. Starting immediately also leaves the poor host and hostess, who are served last, eating alone when others have long finished.
- Don't put your own knives, forks or spoons into serving dishes.
- It's 'not done' to handle food which others are going to eat - so don't check the peaches for ripeness or pick up hard cheese to cut it.
- There is a story that a woman was once so used to feeding children that at a formal dinner she automatically turned to the man next to her and cut all his food into tiny pieces - while he looked on aghast. Perfectly possible. It's amazing how many women play 'mother' at other people's dinner tables and 'helpfully' serve other people with food. *Don't* - unless they ask you to. They are adults able to choose how many potatoes they have, not children who need it decided for them.
- Don't eat so fast that you finish before everyone else. Someone who wolfs their food neither talks nor listens - which makes them a poor guest.
- Don't make noises or chew food with your mouth open - half-chewed food looks awful. The worst example I have seen of this was someone who put whole baby crabs into his mouth and extruded the shells on to his plate, in a continuous stream as he munched.
- Don't even attempt to smoke between courses. The smell of smoke in a room can ruin many people's enjoyment of food. In France, in a famous Normandy restaurant called 'La Mère Corbeau', those who lit cigarettes while waiting for their meal to arrive would instantly be presented with coffee and the bill. If they protested the patron would explain that since they had no palate left there was no point in cooking for them.

- Never start clearing before the hostess does so - she may want to offer second helpings and you can ruin her plans. This includes buffet meals.
- Don't automatically stack plates to help the hostess clear away. Look to see what she does. If she takes the plates off individually do the same.
- Don't insist on getting up to help a hostess unless she looks as if she wants (as opposed to needs) the help. Getting up breaks the conversation, so it may be far more helpful to keep the conversation flowing and allow her to take her time in the kitchen.
- Don't reach for more drink, unless you have been told to help yourself, and *never* put the bottle on the floor beside you.
- Don't insist on helping to wash up. Offer, if it's appropriate, but listen to the reply. If the 'no' sounds as if the host or hostess is sure leave it there. Guests charging round the kitchen when the cook is dying just to sit and talk are trying, not helpful.
- Don't push your chair back from the table during the meal or rock on its two back legs - it may break.

The Details of Table Manners
The general table manners I've given above apply almost everywhere. But the details of table manners are like pronunciation: there is a 'correct' form - equivalent to standard English. If anyone is being vetted for a job, or even a marriage, they are the ones which those who care about such things will be looking for. But people can eat tidily, and give no offence to anyone, without following them.

Which Knife and Fork to Use
A correctly laid table should make the choice of cutlery easy. The rule is: start at the outside and work in. If the order looks wrong remember that the largest fork and knife will be for the meat, and the smallest spoon and fork for the pudding - you may then be able to decide when to use the rest. There may or may not be fish knives and forks - they were considered rather 'lower class' for many years and fish was eaten with normal forks and knives. But recently fish knives have begun to become fashionable again. The rules for wielding them are:
- take food up to your mouth; don't duck your mouth down to it
- manoeuvre the cutlery while keeping your elbows close to your sides, so as not to nudge your neighbour
- when not actively in use, rest any cutlery on your plate with the handles apart, in an upside-down V.

(The handles shouldn't ever rest on the table). If you are holding cutlery, keep it low, with the tips lower than the handles

- you show you have finished by placing the cutlery side by side close together, with the prongs of the fork pointing up and the blade of the knife facing towards it.

Finger-Bowls

These are placed above the forks when food is eaten with the fingers. You dip the tips of your fingers in the water, brushing them across the lemon if there is some, and discreetly dry them on your napkin. If a finger bowl arrives on your fruit plate you put it in position yourself, usually with the lace mat it is sitting on.

Forks

When a fork is used without a knife, a right-handed person holds it in the right hand with the prongs pointing up, and food may be cut by turning it on its side and pressing down with its inner edge. It is used like this for fork suppers and for food which needs no knife - pasta, and rice dishes like risotto or pilaff. In Britain, when a knife is added, the knife and fork form a marriage: once you have picked up both they have to work together. You cut one mouthful at a time and use the knife to press the food on to the fork, which is held with its tines pointing *down*. But the difficulty of balancing peas on that side of a fork means that forks are turned over more and more. This is now almost acceptable, provided it is done elegantly and the food pushed on to the inner edge. But many people still regard it as 'kitchen manners' to be used only within the family - if then.

Knives

The correct way to hold a knife is to grasp it so the top of the handle lies *inside* the palm of the hand, and the

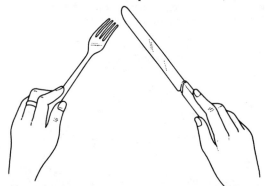

forefinger lies along the top of the knife, without resting on the blade. It shouldn't be held so it rests between the thumb and first finger, like a pen.

Napkins

You unfold a napkin to make a long strip and place it across the knees (never tucked into your front). Apart from wiping drips from your chin (which shouldn't be necessary), it stays there until you dump it unfolded on the table at the end of the meal. It is only folded if you are a house guest and napkin rings have been provided.

Spoons

Spoons are one of the big catches: a soup spoon, unlike a knife, should be held rather like a pen, but the wrist turned so the spoon faces across the body and is parallel to the table. The soup is then quietly sipped from the *side* of the spoon as you tilt it towards the mouth. You don't blow on it, nor do you put the spoon in your mouth. Then, as the soup gets low in the bowl, tilt it away from you, and if you cannot lift a spoonful to your mouth without dripping, lightly brush the drips from the back of the spoon against the farther edge of the bowl, before lifting it to your mouth.

A pudding or cereal spoon is used in rather the same way. But if a pudding is served on a plate, a small fork must *always* be used to help the food on to the spoon. You only omit the fork for mousses and creams in small containers, and for these a teaspoon may be used instead of a pudding spoon.

Problem Foods

A Victorian book of etiquette warned its readers to 'avoid embarking on an orange, as it requires long experience, a colossal courage, any amount of cool self-possession and great skill to attack and dispose of one without harm to yourself or your neighbours.' A warning anyone who has been squirted in the eye would endorse. But happily, with most foods, it is just a matter of knowing what to do, and today few people mind if the style is unconventional provided the spectacle isn't unpleasant. If in doubt the golden rule is: watch everyone else and do as they do. But for those who like to know in advance the conventions are these.

Artichokes (Leaf)

If you are offered sauce, put some on the side of your plate - unless the centre of the artichoke has been removed to take it. Pull off the leaves with a finger and thumb, one at a time, starting at the outside. Dip the fat base of the leaf into the sauce and place it between your teeth. Then pull the leaf out as you bite hard enough to squeeze out the flesh from the base without biting through the skin. Stack the bitten leaves neatly on the side of your plate or they will fall off on to the table. Near the centre the leaves become papery and not worth eating. Under them is the choke, a tight cluster of fibrous seeds rather like those of a dandelion. Pull, or cut, these off in neat lumps to reveal the delicious fleshy base which you eat with a small knife and fork.

Asparagus
This is a real test of dexterity if the asparagus is thin and floppy. Pick up the spears, one at a time by the base, with your fingers. Dip the tip in the sauce on your plate and bite it off; dip it in sauce again and bite some more. If the skin is tough, you may press the flesh out from inside it with your teeth instead of biting right through. You only eat the part which is tender; the rest is stacked neatly at the edge of the plate. The art is neither to expose your teeth while biting nor to drip the sauce on your chin.

Bread and Rolls
With rolls or French bread you break off one bite-sized piece at a time, butter it and eat it, and slices of bread for breakfast or tea, or with cheese, pâté or smoked salmon, should be cut into quarters, not just halves.

Butter should be taken from its container with a butter knife (not your knife) and marmalade or jam with or a jam spoon - and put on the side of your plate. Only then do you apply them to the bread, a little at a time - not spread right across the slice, except perhaps at breakfast.

Though some sauces beg to have bread dipped in them, almost the only time you can correctly use your bread to mop up the juices from food is when eating snails.

Cheese or Pâté
Serve yourself from a wedge of cheese so that you take the rind as well as the middle - don't cut the point off and leave the less moist bit for everyone else. Put the wedge on your plate and eat it by cutting off a small piece, placing it on your buttered biscuit, or on a small piece of bread (see Bread, above) and eating the two together. Do the same with pâté.

Stilton buffs insist that Stilton should be cut from the round in thin wedge-shaped portions, but those who have a whole round still tend to scoop it out in large crumbs.

Crab
Crab is usually served already dressed (see under Food) and is easily eaten from the shell. But if it is served whole you scoop the flesh out of the red, upper part of the body. Then crack the legs with nutcrackers the flesh can be taken from them with a special implement made for the purpose which has two little hooks on the end. The white under-section of the body also contains a good deal of meat which can be hooked out with the same implement. It is always messy food and finger bowls are needed.

Fish
It is best to lift fish from its skin and bones a little at a time, as you eat it, rather than fillet it. Otherwise your plate immediately becomes littered with unsightly bones.

Fruit
If a table is laid with a fruit knife and fork you don't touch the fruit with your hands at all (except to help yourself). Instead you use them to cut the fruit into quarters, and peel it (if appropriate). Then cut off small slices and eat them on the fork. If there is only a fruit knife cut the fruit in quarters, peel it if you wish (holding it close to the plate) cut off a small section at a time and eat it in your fingers. Small fruit, such as cherries or plums, are simply eaten in the fingers.

Lobsters
Lobsters are no problem, as the flesh is usually served in a halved shell, to be eaten with a knife a fork. Claws are treated like crab claws (see above).

Mussels
The British usually pick up a mussel in their fingers and remove the contents with a small fork. The empty shells are either put in a separate dish or neatly stacked round the edge of the plate. Many mussel recipes have liquid which can be spooned up and drunk like soup.

Oysters
As Jonathan Swift wrote, 'He was a bold man that first ate an oyster.' But if you are feeling bold lift the raw oyster from its half shell with a fork, while you hold the shell down. Having eaten it, you then drink the juice from the shell.

Pasta
Pasta is never cut up. To eat long pasta, such as spaghetti, stick your fork into the *edge* of the pasta, so only two or three strands are caught within the prongs, then twist the fork so the pasta is wound into a neat bundle with a minimum of trailing ends. The trick is to get it to your mouth before it undoes.

Prawns
Prawns have to be shelled with the fingers. Hold the body while you pull off the head. Pull the under edges of the shell so they open out and release the body. Remove this main shell and then pull off the tail. Place the prawn on the plate and eat it with a knife and fork, or fork alone, according to what accompanies it.

Snails
Snails are held with a pair of tongs designed for the purpose and the flesh lifted out with small, sharp fork. Dip each in the sauce before eating it.

Restaurant Manners

If you are going to entertain someone give them as much consideration as possible. Ring and reserve a table. If it's winter and you really want to please your guest, ask for a table well out of the draught; in hot weather ask for one by a window or in the garden. Having made your reservation keep to it, ring the restaurant and cancel the booking.

Arriving
A host should always arrive before his or her guests - unless he or she accompanies them - and use the time

to make sure the table is correct, to arrange the method of paying (if there might be problems) and make tentative decisions about the wine.

If a woman arrives at a restaurant with a man she should enter before him but then allow him to draw abreast, or even ahead, so that he can ask for a table or confirm his booking. He should then stand aside to let her walk ahead of him to the table. If a waiter does not pull out a chair for her the man should do this. Continental manners, however, dictate that the man enters the restaurant first.

Choosing Food and Ordering

The food-conscious choose the main course first, and then pick other courses to balance the meal. All ordering should be done through the host, and the host should ask his or her guest what they want before the waiter arrives. So another advantage of choosing the main course first is that you can tell your host what this will be and wait to see if you are asked to choose a first course too. Which gets you over the dilemma of not knowing what is expected of you.

The first two courses are usually ordered together, but the choice of pudding or cheese is left until after the main course is finished. Coffee or liqueurs are then ordered later - if you are having them. Offering coffee is basic, offering liqueurs is a luxury extra. Although ordering tea after lunch or dinner used to be bad, it is gradually becoming more acceptable - provided it is a smart tea such as a tisane.

If you order anything which can be served in more than one way - for example steak well done, medium or rare - a good waiter will ask how you want it cooked. If he forgets, tell your host how you would like it *before* the waiter leaves.

All that is fine if you can understand the menu. If you can't don't let it bother you. When a menu is in a foreign language nobody should be afraid to ask what the names of the dishes mean. Some names may be well-known dishes, but an inexperienced diner can avoid showing ignorance by asking the waiter to explain how they cook dish X or Y 'here' - thus implying familiarity with the normal way of making it. But avoid wording it like this if the dish says *à la maison* or *dans notre façon* - which indicate a recipe created by the restaurant. If you ask a waiter if the steak is good or the melon ripe 'today', a good waiter will tell you the truth. But beware of asking his advice over what dish to have. Many managers instruct waiters to suggest any dishes which are selling poorly on that particular day.

Whatever you choose, avoid the most expensive dish unless you are paying or your host urges you to have it. Any host who is planning to splash out should let guests know if by picking out some of the more expensive dishes and suggesting they might like them. In restaurants where the guest is given a menu with no prices it's best to ask hosts who don't have bottomless pockets, which dishes they recommend.

Ordering Drink

The choice of drinks is up to the host, who should bear in mind the food the guests have chosen (see under Drink). When the wine is brought the waiter will pour some for the person who ordered and wait while it is tasted. In fact, your nose should tell you if wine is all right or not, and if it isn't say so. But don't make the common mistake of saying wine is 'corked' because bits of cork float on the top.

A considerate host should also ask if guests want water with their meal. Failing that a guest can ask if some can be ordered. Heavy advertising means that in many restaurants 'water' means Perrier unless you ask for something else, but Badoit, which is less gassy, goes better with many foods. Or ask for tap water and let water snobs be damned.

Attention During a Meal

It is up to the host to see that his or her guests have what they ordered. If someone ordered a rare steak the host should ask if it is how the guest likes it, and *look* to see if it *is* rare - the guest may be embarrassed to admit it isn't. If anything isn't right the host should calmly ask for the problem to be corrected. There's no need to make a song and dance about complaining, but neither is there any need to eat anything which is not right. When the food returns check it again: some restaurants just rearrange the plate and send it back.

If a host needs to call a waiter during a meal raising the head and looking questioningly should work. If it doesn't, a small indication with the hand should attract attention. Only when these fail is it permissible to call 'waiter'.

To call a waiter over if you are a guest is to imply that the host isn't looking after your needs. So, if you are a guest and need something during the meal, the correct form is to ask the host if you may have whatever is needed (say a glass of water) and let him call a waiter. But if this is impractical wait until a waiter passes very near and then quietly make your need known to him.

Whenever a waiter serves food or drink it is usual to say thank you, speaking quietly enough not to interrupt the conversation. If you are being spoken to at the time, just glance at the waiter and nod or smile slightly to indicate your thanks silently. The same holds true when being served by staff in a private house.

Going Dutch

How a bill is divided between friends can be a very sore point. Traditionally, if people agree to 'go Dutch' everyone splits the bill. Fine, provided they all eat and drink much the same amount. But if anyone wants to eat or drink conspicuously more than the rest that person should be sure to chip in with more than his or her basic share, so the others don't have to pay for somebody else's indulgence.

Obtaining and Paying the Bill

A small writing movement in the air is an international signal for a waiter to bring the bill. But sometimes, even asking for the bill brings no results and you are left marooned and unable to leave. If need be, the swiftest course is for the whole party to get up, as if to leave, and walk towards the manager. It galvanizes even the slowest waiter.

Tipping

If service is included in the bill there is no need to leave a tip in Britain unless you feel the waiter has been exceptional. But small change is left if you pay in cash. When service is not included a 12 per cent tip is average, and 10 per cent is enough for below average service, but give 15 per cent (or more) if it was especially good. The tip can be included in a cheque or credit card payment or given as cash. The same tips apply in bars where drinks are brought to the table. If you need a copy of a bill ask for it as you pay.

What to Wear When

Dress is a tribal matter. I say tribal because the purpose of tribal dress is to celebrate certain rituals or to show which group of people you identify with, and want others to know that you belong to. Whether by the studded jacket of a Hell's Angel, or a businessman's dark suit, we are all, whether we realize it or not, walking around in uniform, with our garments proclaiming our tribe to everyone we meet. We all conform, even if we conform by a particular style of rebellion - as do the punk rockers.

Nobody needs this book to tell them how to dress as they please. The only time when reading about dress is any use is when you need to take part in a tribal ritual (such as Ascot) which is new to you or to camouflage yourself as belonging to some other 'tribe'. So, while there's no need for anyone to conform to the following rules, they can be useful.

Formal Dress for Men

The 1856 edition of *Enquire Within* instructed men to:

> *Dress well but not superfluously.*
> *Be neither like a sloven, nor like a stuffed model.*
> *Keep away all uncleanly appearance from the person. Let the nails, and teeth, and, in fact, the whole system receive SALUTARY rather than STUDIED care. But let these things receive attention in the toilette - not elsewhere.*
> *Avoid displaying excess of jewellery. Nothing looks more effeminate upon a man.*

Very little has changed in over two hundred years. Jewellery, apart from a signet ring, is still frowned on and the essence of a man being well dressed is still immaculate cleanliness and understatement. Not even the smallest spot is permissible. But, true to not looking like a 'stuffed model', nothing must look too new or too carefully arranged. An appearance which suggests a total lack of effort is the keynote. An attitude which Dorothy Sayers caught perfectly when, in one of the Lord Peter Wimsey books, Lord Peter turns to his valet and says, 'How do I look?' The valet replies, 'Perfect. That is to say, slightly flawed - the sign of a true gentleman.'

For business and formal occasions the essential garments for this look are a dark suit in a good wool cloth, without a conspicuous pattern in the fabric, worn with a white, pastel-coloured or discreetly striped shirt, plain dark socks and a good quality tie which does not draw attention to itself. There are also a host of details which make the difference between looking 'right' or just missing the look. For example:

- the lowest button on a waistcoat should be left undone
- the top and bottom buttons of a single-breasted jacket are undone
- a wallet goes in the inside jacket pocket not in the trousers
- the outside breast pocket of a jacket is left empty
- the socks never show when standing
- with a black, grey or navy suit the shoes are always black - never grey - and the ornamentation should be minimal, unless they are brogues.

Some of the rules for correct formal dress spill over into informal and evening occasions and among the points which conventional bosses and mothers-in-law might especially frown on, at any time, are:

- ready-tied ties (though ready-tied bow ties are creeping in)
- ties with very large knots
- ties of organizations to which the wearer does not belong
- very dark shirts with suits
- frilly or embroidered shirts - even in the evening
- dinner jackets decorated with braid
- white socks, except for sport
- suits, trousers or jackets in strong colours or very conspicuous checks (Prince of Wales check apart)
- shirt collars smoothed out over the jacket collar, when tieless
- socks which allow the skin of the ankle to show when seated.

Of course, it is all a matter of personal preference and there are always exceptions. For example, Prince Charles breaks the rule about breast pockets. But that, it seems, is no criterion. For when I pointed out this fact, to a very elegant Old Etonian, he remarked, 'But, my dear, the royals never *did* have any style'. So those who find themselves breaching the sartorial code can comfort themselves that they are, at least, in good company.

Dress for Women

Since women are always more individualistic in their dress than men, there are fewer rules and a woman can usually get away with whatever she can carry off. Mercifully, thanks to the Princess of Wales, the old rule that it was suspect to be glamorous is beginning to disappear. But there is also an international 'Sloane Ranger' uniform to be found among established families whether in London, Paris or seemingly egalitarian Amsterdam. It neither follows fashion nor totally ignores it and, as in the male equivalent, minute details are important. As it changes fractionally from year to year it is almost impossible to pin down except to say that good quality is essential.

How far anyone follows fashion, or seeks to conform

to a social group, is simply a matter of taste, but on occasions, such as interviews when making an impression counts, it is hard to go wrong with the following:
- natural fibres (or blends which look natural)
- well-cut shirts in plain colours
- well-cut suits or skirts
- understated make-up
- accessories which match each other - but not too emphatically

particularly if you avoid wearing:
- white shoes with dark stockings
- exotically patterned fabrics - except Liberty prints
- ankle chains
- imitation anything
- clothes so tight they have a VPL (visible panty line)
- clothing that is rampantly sexy
- very decorated shoes.

As with men, everything must be immaculately clean and perfectly pressed - someone can look well-dressed with only one good garment in their wardrobe, if it is always pressed before wearing, or look a mess with a wardrobe full of model clothes, if they are uncared for.

When in doubt, it is considered correct to be underdressed rather than overdressed. Neither too smart, too fashionable nor too conspicuous. The classic rule for jewellery, for example, is to put on as much as looks exactly right, and then remove one piece. This ultra-discretion is not simply a British foible; I have observed it in other European drawing rooms as well. But my personal sympathies are with the splendidly outrageous older wife of a young academic who once told me, 'Darling, I always put on what looks exactly right - and then *add* some.' She looked marvellous and knew it. Such flamboyance is no good at all as social camouflage - which is what a lot of dressing is about - but it has an indiscreet charm.

Dressing for a Country House Weekend

For anyone not brought up in an English country house, dressing for the country is one of the hardest tasks. Country-house dwellers seem blissfully unaware of the huge range of clothes which their seemingly casual lifestyle demands. The list varies with the people and the season, but might include:
- wellingtons - for walks in the wet
- jeans - clean but with a decidedly lived-in look
- inconspicuous shirt(s) and jumper(s) to go with the jeans
- something suitable for going to church (if they do)
- cords for a man, plus V-neck pullover, shirt and possibly a casual cravat for neater wear - such as informal drinks with neighbours
- smart trousers or skirt, shirt and jumper for a woman
- a black-tie outfit or a dress formal enough to pass muster if they decide to dress up for dinner - still not uncommon in large country houses (but anyone who doesn't own one can always ask if there will be changing for dinner, and only acquire one if it's needed)

- a dark suit or dress which is suitable for an ordinary dinner party
- tennis clothes in summer, if there's a tennis court
- if there may be shooting it's essential to have really warm waterproof clothes which are dark enough not to scare the birds. The ideal for a woman is a Puffa (a waistcoat mated with an eiderdown) and/or the dark-green waterproof jacket called a Barbour (pronounced barber). A new Barbour is almost a contradiction in terms, so anyone who doesn't want to look like a new boy in school should try to wear it in while gardening or pushing through woods
- possibly clothes for a point-to-point or racing.

If that list seems daunting and expensive don't worry. Wearing the right clothes may make you feel more 'in' but, unless you are being summed up for a job or marriage, or wear bright clothes to a shoot, nobody will care a hoot what you wear. Only those who are socially fragile themselves are critical of other people's lapses in clothing conformity. In some country houses jeans, a jumper and wellingtons are all you need in a week.

To Dress or Not to Dress

For most invitations people blithely insist that dress is casual. And casual is whatever the speaker chooses to make it from cocktail dress to track suit.

However, saying dress is casual or informal is at least better than saying it is 'optional'. That means so little that one friend of mine, with a quirky sense of humour, punished his hosts for such an invitation by taking it literally, and arrived stark naked - upon which, they turned the tables by making him stay that way all evening.

Given the immense variation in what people mean, hosts owe it to their guests to give them some guidance over what to wear. This doesn't mean you have to push them around. It's perfectly easy to say, 'It's just an informal evening, so I'll probably wear jeans but do dress up if you feel like it', or vice versa. When hosts don't do this it is perfectly reasonable to ask how casual it is going to be. If you can't do that the correct form is to underdress rather than overdress. But this can be taken too far: as a friend of mine wisely remarked, 'How you dress reflects your opinion of what your hostess is inviting you to.'

White Tie

Men

The full evening dress implied by 'white tie' is seldom worn, except for very formal occasions. Men are expected to conform to a formula of black trousers with braid at the sides, black tail coat, waistcoat, stiff-fronted white shirt with stiff detachable wing collar, and white piqué (Marcella) bow tie and waistcoat. Gold or mother-of-pearl studs and cufflinks fasten the shirt and black silk socks are worn with plain shoes in either black patent leather or fine calf. Dandies can even add a black cloak, black silk top hat, white kid gloves and a black, silver-topped cane - and go looking for Scarlett O'Hara if they wish.

Women

A white tie invitation opens the door to the grandest ballgown you can muster and, unless long dresses are totally out of fashion, most women wear long rather than short. If you have gems prepare to show them now. Long gloves, of the sort which open at the wrist and roll up, used to be essential for white-tie evenings. They aren't absolutely essential for balls - though they have recently had a considerable come-back - but they are needed for royal and diplomatic occasions on which evening dress is worn. Bracelets go over them and rings go under, and they are kept on for shaking hands and dancing but removed for eating. If they have buttons at the wrist they are not removed entirely but the hands are slipped out and the hand part rolled neatly inward so it tucks under the wrist section. They can be any colour which suits the dress.

Morning Dress

Men

Morning dress is the daytime equivalent of white tie. It is used for weddings, Royal Ascot, state openings of parliament and other elegant occasions. It consists of black or dark-grey trousers, with a fine stripe, a dove-grey waistcoat and a black or dark-grey morning (tail) coat. For very formal occasions, such as Ascot and the smartest weddings, there must also be a grey top hat - correctly called a 'white hat' - but for ordinary weddings fewer and fewer men bother with them. Either way, classic black calf shoes are worn, plus a white shirt usually with a stiff collar, and a light-grey silk tie or cravat. This is one of the few occasions on which a man may be dandified and wear a tie pin. Creamy yellow chamois gloves are also correct, though very little used. (See following page for hiring.)

Women

The female counterpart is a really smart dress in summer - often in silk - or an elegant suit, or coat. If you are buying something for a morning dress occasion a suit is the best buy, as it can be adapted to any weather, whereas a dress just looks chilly on a bad day. Strictly speaking, morning dress means a hat should be worn, and they are one of the features of Ascot, but at weddings the young increasingly flout this convention.

Black Tie

Men

The words 'Black Tie' are an invitation for both sexes to dress up. For a man it's easy. The set formula is a dinner jacket with matching trousers (on braces not a belt) which usually have a single strip of black braid down the outer seam. This is worn with a white evening shirt and a formal black bow tie, of a kind designed to go with the shirt and jacket. The shirt usually has a piqué or finely pleated front, and sleeves with double cuffs and cufflinks. A single-breasted suit may have a matching waistcoat but is more often worn without one and with a cummerbund in black or dark-red silk. Double-breasted suits don't need a waistcoat or a

cummerbund (but they are less often in fashion). In hot climates the black jacket is replaced by a white one. The footwear used to be patent leather shoes, but these are only worn now by those who have clearly had them for years. To wear new patent is just not done, and fairly plain black calf shoes are the usual footwear, plus black socks (ideally in silk). In winter the whole lot can be topped by a black overcoat, and a long white silk scarf.

If a man doesn't want to wear the classic outfit he can simply wear a dark suit (a pity, as almost every man looks more handsome in evening dress). Alternatively, he can wear a more original version of black tie by sporting a dark velvet jacket with evening trousers instead of a matching jacket.

Conventional bow ties come in two kinds: single-ended and double-ended. The single-ended is worn with wing collars, the double-ended with turn-down collars. They are tied like this:

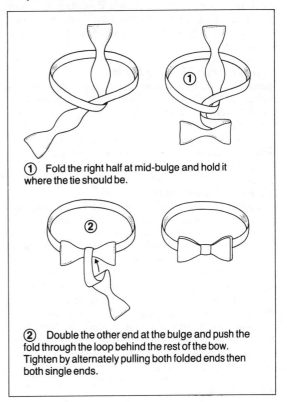

① Fold the right half at mid-bulge and hold it where the tie should be.

② Double the other end at the bulge and push the fold through the loop behind the rest of the bow. Tighten by alternately pulling both folded ends then both single ends.

Women

For women it is less easy. At one time when full evening dress of white tie and tails was the form a long dress was needed, and a black tie invitation indicated that a short evening dress would almost certainly do. Now white tie is very little used and black tie spans both occasions - even when a long dress would be preferable for a woman. One guide to what to wear is the type of people who will be there. Another rough guide is the place where the event is being held. If it is somewhere grand then there is a good chance that you are being offered an excuse to wear a long evening dress, though a short one will probably be fine. It's worth thinking about coverage as well as mere length. A seductive dress which would be perfect for a film première may be not be the thing for a black-tie dinner at the rotary club or an Oxford college.

Scottish Formal Dress

If you are wearing a kilt there is no sharp distinction between black tie, white tie and morning dress. There are two styles of jacket which can be used for either: a black barathea (Prince Charlie) with silver buttons, or a black velvet (Montrose). The Prince Charlie is usually worn with an evening shirt and black bow tie, the Montrose with a softer shirt and a lace jabot. In both cases, a man wears either cream knee socks or dark socks to pick out a dark tone in the tartan. The shoes are either heavy leather shoes called gillie brogues, or black patent with cross-over straps. Whatever the occasion, a man does not wear a dress tartan. Dress tartans are said to be one of Queen Victoria's inventions and are strictly reserved for women to wear on evening occasions.

Clothes for Early Evening Parties

Standard clothing is a dark suit, a plainish shirt and darkish tie for a man, with black shoes. Women wear cocktail dresses, evening suits, or evening trousers and tops. Adjust the clothing to your hosts — in some circles anything goes and no man would dream of wearing a jacket; in others he wouldn't be allowed through the door without one.

Point-to-points and Races

At point-to-points the chief aim is to keep warm and dry so the clothes are the same as for shooting (see page 22). The races are a different matter. They vary considerably in smartness but - Ascot aside - men tend to wear dark suits and women elegant tweeds. Trilbys are often sported by men and elegant hats with a country air by women, which - when they are in fashion - may well be a female trilby. This is an occasion on which the classic Englishwoman's shoes, with heels which are not particularly high or narrow, come into their own for walking on grass. Ascot is an occasion for morning dress and women dressed up to the tens - be warned.

Hiring Clothes

C. & W. May Ltd, 9-11 Garrick Street, London WC2E 9AR Tel: 01 836 5993/4 hires out fantasy fancy dress and period costumes and will make one to order.

Moss Bros, (21-26 Bedford Street, London WC2 9EQ Tel: 01 240 4567) and **Young's Formal Wear for Men,** (1-2 Berners Street, London W1P 3AF Tel:01 580 7179) both have branches in major provincial towns.

One Night Stand, 44 Pimlico Road, London SW1 Tel: 01 730 8708; and in NW1 hires out evening dresses from cocktail frocks to ball dresses.

Simpsons Dress Hire, 9-11 Garrick Street, London WC2E 9AR Tel: 01 836 2381 hires out evening dresses from cocktail frocks to ball gowns and has branches in several major towns.

OVERSEAS MANNERS

Foreign manners can be perplexing and the nuances often elude the visitor. Here are just a few of the pitfalls.

Arriving

It's easy to assume that everyone does it the British way, arriving 10 to 15 minutes late to allow for a host or hostess who isn't quite on time. This isn't the case. The French expect their guests within 15 minutes of the invited time, in southern Italy they expect them to be on time - knowing they will be late - while Scandinavians, northern Italians and some Germans expect guests to be perfectly punctual. The Dutch take it even further: in Holland the time you are invited for is the *latest* you can arrive and in courtesy you should be 10 to 15 minutes early. Which would make for disaster if the Dutch invite the Portuguese. In Portugal you should be *at least* half an hour late and an hour late is quite normal.

Encounters between the Japanese and the Dutch may be no easier. The Dutch never arrive empty-handed and it is considered very rude for the person receiving the present to fail to open it immediately and express appreciation. The Japanese also take presents but in Japan the present must *never* be opened while the giver is there. The idea is that it cannot possibly be good enough, so the giver will be embarrassed that it isn't better.

Swedes may arrive bearing flowers or chocolates, but don't expect the French or Italians to do this. In both these countries it is thought more considerate to send flowers the next day, though the ultra-thoughtful guest may send them on the morning before.

In most of Europe shaking hands on first meeting is essential. But in Thailand and Japan they prefer not to shake hands, and use a traditional half bow as greeting. In the Middle East people go to the other extreme and often shake hands *every* time they meet, not just on the first occasion of the day. This may not apply to greetings between the sexes; some Arab women may touch no man except their husband.

Kisses on greeting have an etiquette all of their own. For example, few people know that in France hand-kissing is strictly for the ungloved hand of a married woman. Or that cheek-kissing between close friends is limited to two kisses in France and Italy and three in Belgium, while the Scandinavians hardly kiss (in that sense) at all - though this is changing in the younger generation. However, in Japan social kissing is totally taboo and considered most upsetting behaviour.

At Table

In all Muslim countries the left hand must never be used to touch food. Muslims aren't the only people to have hand conventions. In Italy, home of the Borgias, it is essential to keep your hands in sight throughout the meal. They should rest lightly on the edge of the table, never on your lap. In France you may put your hands where you like, but to put salt or pepper on food without tasting it (and even then) is to insult your host, and anyone who drinks anything but water with salad is thought to show a total lack of palate. Another sidelight on French meals is that, since crests are put on the underside of the handles, spoons and forks are usually laid with the bowl or prongs towards the tablecloth.

There are few rules on second helpings, but in France they will be offered first to the most senior woman and she should always accept, even if she only toys with the food, or other guest may feel compelled to follow her lead and refuse too.

At social functions in Sweden it is traditional to 'skäla'. This involves a man raising his glass to one of the women and saying 'Skäla Anna' (or whatever her name is). Then both drink from their own glasses while keeping eye contact. To drop the eyes is considered rude. The skäla must also be returned soon after, and nobody may skäla the hostess unless there are fewer than six guests.

Functions do not always end when you might expect. In both the Arab world and among the Chinese in Hong Kong guests are expected to leave almost as soon as the coffee has been drunk. To linger and talk is not polite.

Naming Names
Most of northern Europe has caught the British and American habit of using first names almost immediately, even in business situations. Not so the French. The young may switch quickly to first-name terms and use *tu*, but the older generations still stick to *vous*, and *Monsieur, Madame* or *Mademoiselle* and the surname until they are invited to use the first name and *tu*. Foreigners should do the same, for *tu* used in the wrong place can be a sign not of friendship but of contempt. In talking, they also refer to their friends and acquaintances as *Monsieur* or *Madame* plus the surname, and in Portugal it is correct to apply this same formality, using Don or Donna when speaking to, or about, anyone older than oneself, which lends a certain period charm to conversation in both countries.

Body Language
Quite apart from the hazards of uncovering too much flesh in regions where flesh is considered indecent, the ways in which the body is used can also be considered insulting. For example, to cross your legs in the company of Arabs in such a way that the sole of the shoe even slightly faces towards someone is to say, 'You are lower than the sole of my shoe.' In Thailand not only is the sole of the foot considered so low that it is insulting even to stand so that your toes point towards somebody, but also the top of the head is the highest point and must be respected. So ruffling a child's hair affectionately is a serious breach of respect for the child and its family.

Praising
I once made the mistake of telling a Japanese that he had a very beautiful wife, only to be astonished at his assertions that she was a 'very ugly and horrible wife'. It is not polite for a Japanese to admit to having a lovely wife because a wife is considered part of the husband and he is therefore bound to be modest. In Arab countries it is even worse. If you admire an object the owner may feel obliged to give it to you. This can, in some circumstances, extend to women - even today.

At the Cinema
The French and Italians will all make their way to an inside seat facing the screen. But in Germany or Sweden it is considered insulting to pass another person with your behind pointing towards them.

Language
Words don't always mean quite what they seem to mean in translation - which is perhaps one reason why British prime ministers tend to avoid speaking in foreign languages. Americans are not always so cautious. After a visit to a foreign country one American president made a farewell speech in which he expressed his great pleasure at having had the opportunity to 'get to know' so many of the people of that country. His speech caused quite a stir: his speechwriter had unfortunately used the verb which in that language meant to 'know' in the purely carnal sense.

There is also the pitfall of the double meaning. President Kennedy made a famous speech in Germany at the climax of which he proclaimed *'Ich bin ein Berliner'*. Everyone roared their approval but what he had said could be translated not only as 'I am a Berliner' but also as 'I am a doughnut' (a *Berliner* being a type of doughnut).

Anyone setting forth for the Middle East should read *Manners and Correct Form in the Middle East* by Sir Donald Hawley KCMG, MBE, Debrett.

WRITING AND SPEAKING
Rules of English
As recently as 1965, that highly respected work, *Fowler's Modern English Usage*, could say, 'Received Pronunciation is the pronunciation considered correct for an educated Englishman.' Today that statement is unacceptable: 'education' is no longer thought to be limited to those with a particular background and accent. That doesn't alter the fact that it is necessary to define a standard pronunciation which can be given in dictionaries, taught to foreigners, and so on.

Today's Received Pronunciation (RP), or Standard English, is almost literally 'the Queen's English' - for it is very close to her style of speech. This means it is fundamentally the pronunciation which comes naturally to those who were born into the landed gentry and the professions, and educated at public schools, though they are by no means the only people to speak the 'Queen's English'.

Its official position doesn't mean that Received Pronunciation is 'right' in any absolute sense. But, since it has been chosen as the benchmark, it does mean that words should be pronounced that way unless the speaker has a regional or national accent which overrides it. But Received Pronunciation isn't fixed for ever. Language is a living thing and the accepted patterns of speech gradually change, rather as hairstyles do. Today's Received Pronunciation is not the same as it was in our mother's day, still less our grandmother's time. Even if your dictionary is only 20 years old it may not be right to settle an argument by referring to it.

The Maverick H
One of the classic changes in pronunciation concerns the letter 'h', which has always been a vexed letter. When the first edition of *Enquire Within* came out in 1856 the author wrote, 'Few things point so directly to a want of CULTIVATION as the misuse of the letter "h" by persons in conversation.' He told his readers, 'H should always be sounded except in the following words':

A heir, honest, honour, hour, hostler

B herb, hospital, humble, humour and words made from them.

He could have added hotel, and history from which the 'h' was also dropped in correct speech at that time, as was the g in huntin', shootin' and fishin'.

The interesting thing is the way these words have changed. In correct British speech, the g is now sounded on all 'ing' words; the 'h' is still not sounded on the words in list A, but *is* sounded in list B, and in hotel and history. In other parts of the English-speaking world the changes have not been the same: for example, Americans still pronounce herb as 'erb, just as the Victorians did.

None of this would matter were it not for the confusion which it creates over whether to use 'a' or 'an' before such words. The rule, of course, is that 'a' is used before words starting with a consonant, while 'an' is used before vowels. But words beginning with 'h' are sometimes one and sometimes the other. Despite what you may see in conservative publications, the top authorities on pronunciation say it is now correct both to say *and* write 'a' before words like humble, hospital, and hotel in which the 'h' is sounded.

The 'h' also causes trouble in words beginning with 'wh'. The Victorians used to pronounce the 'h' before the 'w', saying h-wite, and h-wen. But correct speech has changed: as the 'h' isn't *written* before the 'w', in Standard English the 'h' is simply left out altogether.

BBC Pronouncing Dictionary, Oxford University Press

Simple Speech
Many of the greatest writers in the English language have commented on the power and excellence of plain words. Yet, on television, you can often hear nervous spokesmen using long words which clearly aren't those they would use at the breakfast table. They obviously feel their ordinary speech isn't good enough, or impressive enough. They are quite wrong: most of Shakespeare's greatest speeches, and those of any great orator, are written in words anyone could say at break-fast. Saying utilize, for example, when you mean 'use' diminishes rather than enhances the strength of a phrase.

Nor is it only in the choice of general vocabulary that simplicity is best. Understatement rules at every level. So a car is called a car, even if it's a Rolls-Royce, and a mink is just a coat. And if you spent the weekend at Great Grandure Castle with Lord Havealot you either don't mention it at all or you say you were at Great Grandure visiting Jim Havealot.

Singulars and Plurals
It can sometimes be difficult to tell a singular from a plural - which makes it hard to use a verb correctly after it. The United States is a good example - it ends in an s, and refers to a collection of states, so it could well be a plural: it isn't, it is a united country. So you would say 'The United States *is* going to declare war...'. The same holds true of group nouns - like the government or the committee - which usually take the singular, so 'the committee is in session.' The exception comes when the members of the group are clearly acting as individuals. So you would say 'The committee are in the garden having drinks' - to use 'is' would suggest they had one drink between the lot of them. The rule for getting this right is mentally to replace the noun with 'it' or 'they', and let whichever sounds right dictate the rest of the sentence.

Split Infinitives
Splitting infinitives is a fault schoolteachers love to point out. The perfect example came in the opening words of the television series *Star Trek* - 'To boldly go where no man has gone before.' The word 'boldly' splits the 'to' away from 'go' - which is the infinitive form of the verb. (Infinitives are all the basic verbs as you'd see them listed in a grammar book - to run, to sit, and so on.) So the sentence should have been, 'Boldly to go where no man has gone before.'

However, sometimes it is better to deliberately split an infinitive, and have the emphasis right rather than stick to the rule and sound flat. That sentence is an example. Putting 'deliberately' before the 'to' gives it far less emphasis yet it is the key word in that sentence, so there is an argument for having it right where it is.

Subject or Object
People sometimes agonize over whether they should say I or me in sentences like 'Harry and I went to Ascot.' There is a very simple rule: use the form which would let you drop the other person from the sentence and still allow it to sound correct. You can shorten 'Harry and I went to Ascot' to 'I went to Ascot', but you couldn't say 'Me went to Ascot', so I is correct there. But though 'Pass it to Harry and I' may sound reasonable, it is shown to be wrong the moment you drop Harry. 'Pass it to me' works; 'Pass it to I' doesn't.

The Written Word

Capital Letters

There has been a trend towards the effusive capital. That is, capitals used just because the writer feels the word is important, as in 'my Boss'. This seventeenth-century practice is not really correct today, but the correct use of capitals isn't as obvious as it may seem. In some instances there are rules on the use of capitals; in others it is a matter of taste, but the current guidelines are these.

- Although capital letters start each new sentence, and so follow full stops, they don't always come after exclamation marks.
- Capital letters are always used for the initials of people or organizations, e.g. J. B. Priestley.
- Capitals start each major word of the name of a person, place, official position, organization or creative work, e.g. Mrs Hippy, Loch Ness, Lever Bros, *Gone With The Wind.*
- Capitals are used for full titles, so you write 'the Duke of York'. You may write either 'the Duke' or 'the duke' - though the first has the edge.
- Some words have two meanings - in one case it is used as the shortened name of an organization, in the other as a basic noun. Only the shortened name takes a capital letter. So you would write, 'I am going into the church' but, 'The Church still forbids the ordination of women.'
- The capital is always dropped if the word doesn't mean one particular person, organization, etc. So you would write, 'I would like to be a managing director', but 'Ian Kairn, Managing Director of Kairn Industries'.
- When it comes to place names associated with objects you write 'french windows' and 'Cheddar cheese'. This is not consistent.
- On the points of the compass and the seasons of the year it is up to you.

Punctuation

I write about punctuation with some trepidation, since to do so is to throw every stop and comma in this book open to criticism - and in a book this long there are bound to be misplacements.

Though it's easy to get it wrong when in a hurry, punctuating is much easier than people think. After all, most punctuation is just designed to indicate the position and length of the pauses you would leave if you were talking. So, the first rule is to read the words with as much expression as possible (gabbling won't work) and listen to where the natural pauses come. When you know where they *feel* right you can then decide how big each pause needs to be, and choose the punctuation mark accordingly.

The remaining punctuation marks are a kind of shorthand to tell people the things they would know automatically if the words on the page were a live scene which they could watch. For example, speech marks tell you someone is speaking, and an exclamation mark tells you someone is speaking with force. To put those in you only have to decide what is happening.

The only tricky punctuation marks are colons and semi-colons. Even the greatest experts are not entirely agreed about the finer points of their use, but you can write perfectly clear English without ever using them - as most newspapers show.

The following list is in order of the length of the pause - except where two marks have much the same length, but are used in different situations.

Punctuation for Pauses

comma

Commas are used for the shortest pause and are the Swiss army knife of the writer's tools - they can be used for almost everything. In modern writing, of the less literary kind, they are even used instead of the slightly longer pause correctly indicated by a semi-colon. But the correct uses of commas are as follows.

1 To separate items in a list (e.g. The thieves stole rubies, emeralds, and diamonds). People sometimes argue over whether there is a comma before the 'and' in such a list. If you read the list you will hear it is there in speech. However, some authorities feel that in lists the 'and' provides the pause and no comma is needed before it.
2 Before and after a word or phrase which is added to the main sentence but is not essential (e.g. The Prime Minister, unfortunately, lost his voice...). In this situation it must be possible to remove the words inside the commas without altering the sense. If you can't you have put the commas in the wrong places.
3 Between two adjectives describing the same noun (e.g. A long, dark night).
4 To divide direct speech from the words introducing or explaining it (e.g. 'I'm going out,' she said).
5 To separate the main part of a sentence (which makes sense by itself) from a less important section - which doesn't - (e.g. She didn't eat her potatoes, because she was slimming).
6 After 'Dear John', or whoever, when starting a letter and after the final phrase - 'Yours faithfully,' etc.

dash

This gives almost the same length of pause as a comma but is used in slightly different situations.

1 Like the commas in (2) above, dashes mark off words inserted in the middle of a sentence. But you put them before and after words which interrupt the flow of the sentence (e.g. She was immensely beautiful - though I know you, Susan, disagree - and her charm was extraordinary.) They can also be used to draw attention to the words within them.
2 A dash can also be used to divide two contradictory sections of a sentence (e.g. I will meet you at the station - unless you prefer to come by car).
3 In direct speech, a dash is used to indicate that someone has been interrupted in mid-sentence (e.g. 'I was only -'
'Don't give me any excuses.').

semi-colon

This is a longer pause than a comma and suggests a slightly heavier style of speech or writing. It is used between two statements which are too closely linked to be separate sentences but need a decided pause between them. Often the two have very similar structure and counterbalance one another, as if on scales, with the semi-colon as the fulcrum. The classic example is: 'To err is human; to forgive divine.'

colon

A colon is a slightly longer pause than a semi-colon but very similar.

1   Like the semi-colon, it divides two sections of a sentence, but the colon is mainly used if what follows it extends and elaborates the idea set up in the first half, as in examples of cause and effect. Nancy Mitford used it perfectly when she wrote, 'An aristocracy in a republic is like a chicken whose head has been cut off: it may run about in a lively way, but in fact it is dead.'
2   It introduces a list of any kind (e.g. There was a cast of three: James Mason, Anna Neagle and Cary Grant).
3   It is used after these words: to sum up, for example, namely, the following.

full stop

This is the longest pause of all.

1   It ends all sentences that don't end in an exclamation mark or a question mark. But if there is a sentence within another sentence, as can happen with a quotation (see 2 above), you only use the full stop at the end of the main sentence.
2   Full stops follow some abbreviations.
3   Initials of people have full stops, e.g. F.E. Smith, whereas organizations which are pronounced as a name do not, e.g. NATO.

Tradition has it that full stops can never be used before an 'and' or a 'but'. Popular journalism has thrown that rule away. Inelegant as it may seem, this only reflects how people speak - 'ands' often do follow long pauses, and semi-colons and colons are not always appropriate.

Punctuation for Explanation

apostrophe

1   This shows that at least one letter has been missed out, and replaces the vanished letters (e.g. do not becomes don't; he will becomes he'll).
2   It is also used to show that something belongs to someone (or to a group of people) and it comes after the main word and before the final *s* which is used to make the possessive (e.g. the dog's dinner, women's rights). It is a touch trickier when a word already ends in s:
     a after singular words ending in *s* the possessive is still *'s* (e.g. Queen Bess's soldiers, Charles's children). The only exceptions to this are words pronounced *iz* at the end (e.g. Moses' son), classical names (e.g. Herodotus' books) and long words like Nicholas

which can take the apostrophe or *'s*.
     b after plurals ending in *s* or *es* the apostrophe is added *without* an extra *s* (e.g. a girls' school).

brackets

1   They are used to insert a little comment directed at the reader: e.g. James (more often known as Tubby) sat down heavily.
2   They contain an explanation, reference note or translation.
3   Square brackets contain additional information which was not put in by the original writer. So they are often used in translations and edited diaries (e.g. 'My darling Pebbles [Jane Seymour], how I have missed you...').

exclamation mark

An exclamation mark is only needed when the words before it are an exclamation (e.g. Damn! Good Heavens! Ow!) and occasionally in novels to show that someone is saying something seemingly mild with more than usual emphasis (e.g. 'What a horrid day this is!' is quite different from 'What a horrid day this is').

In all other situations if a sentence is well worded it doesn't need an exclamation mark; the words say it all. It is the punctuation equivalent of a nudge and a wink - and just as unnecessary if the joke or remark made the point. The sole exception is perhaps a letter between close friends.

hyphen

Hyphens are used when you need to split a word in writing it, because it won't fit on to the line. In this case split the word where the syllables break naturally. It can also link two words and replace a word like 'to' (e.g. The London to Brighton express could be written as the London-Brighton express). It is also used to link nouns, more neatly than words could manage (e.g. 'the Anglo-French agreement' is much neater than 'the agreement between the English and the French').

question mark

Obviously, this shows that someone is asking a question. It is always used, even when the words clearly indicate a question without it.

inverted commas, quotation and speech marks

There are two kinds - single ' and double " - and either can be used in the following situations.

1   At each end of words which are spoken, e.g. 'I love you,' he said and the punctuation relating to the spoken words goes *inside* the marks. Only the words showing who is speaking stay outside.
2   Inverted commas go round quotations of all kinds when the words are *exactly* what was said or written, or where any omissions are indicated by ... but don't go round compressed extracts, or inexact quotes.
3   Inverted commas go at each end of any quoted titles but not round the name of any book of the Bible. (Italics are usually used for titles of books, films and plays.)

Although there are no fixed rules about when to use double inverted commas, and when single, the most usual convention is to use single ones as much as possible. This means speech is in single marks, and if someone uses a quotation in the course of speaking the quotation is in double marks to distinguish it from the rest.

The Oxford Guide to English Usage, Oxford University Press

Job Interviews

An interview is a situation in which every aspect of someone's social behaviour is being looked at, and looked at critically. Those who are experienced at being interviewed have probably developed a technique for handling it. So what follows is mainly intended for those new to the game.

The time leading up to the interview should be used for careful preparation. This starts with taking all the focus *off* yourself. Instead of thinking about how you feel about the interview, put yourself in the shoes of the interviewer. Bear in mind the sort of job it is and the type of person who will be interviewing you (if you know) and what they will want to know. Interviewing people is tough, and often boring, work. Think how you'd like a good interviewee to be and then work out how to be like that.

Almost any interview boils down to three issues:

Why do you want this job?
Why do you want to work for this company?
Why are *you* right for the job?

Why Do You Want this Job?

Decide why you *do* want that particular job. The fact that you haven't got another and need work is not enough. You have to seem as if their particular job is the very one you want. If you don't know enough about the job to sound convincing *find out.* Then work out some good reasons *why* it really appeals to you. If you want the job enough to apply there must be things you genuinely like about it. Don't down-play them.

Why Do You Want to Work for this Company?

Showing an interest in a company is one of the most vital aspects of an interview - and one of the most neglected. Yet even those applying for senior jobs in management sometimes fail to take this basic step. So find out all you can about this particular company and think of some good reasons why you would like to work for it. Good reasons mean reasons which will seem good to *them.* You may be applying because they have a great pension scheme, but *they* may be more impressed if you say you are excited by their latest business activities.

To find out about a public company just ring its head office and ask for the latest report and accounts to be sent to you. If it's a small firm all you may be able to find out is what they do in general. In that case, just work out the questions you need to ask.

Why Should They Employ You?

There are several aspects to this and you need to think about each of them.

What qualifications do they want?
If there was an advertisement this will tell you. Decide the best way of talking about your qualifications. They should already have the bald facts in writing, but was some aspect of your training angled in the perfect direction? If so, prepare to tell them about it.

What previous experience would they like someone to have?
Decide which aspect of your previous work or school provides the best springboard for the job you are applying for. Then decide how best to bring this out. You should be able to sound as if you enjoyed your other work and took an interest in it.

What sort of personality are they likely to want for the job?
The ideal salesman has a very different personality from the ideal bank manager. Work out how you can bring out the aspects of yourself which most suit the job.

What are your hobbies and interests?
If you have a hobby prepare to answer questions about why you took it up and why you enjoy it. Watch yourself. If you are applying for a job which means you have to be with people, don't say you like birdwatching because you prefer to be alone. If you have no real hobbies or interests *find at least one.* Then learn enough about it to answer a question on it. For most jobs it doesn't matter whether you say it is disco dancing or backgammon, but admitting to spending every evening in front of the television is like admitting you have brain death - even if you only watch serious documentaries.

Other Questions to Prepare For

There are obviously no rules about which questions will be asked, but the following are some others which are most likely to crop up. So plan your answers.
- In your last job/in school what were you best at?
- Have you ever lost your job? And why was that?
- If you get the job how long do you plan to stay?
- Tell me about yourself.
- If we can't take you for this job but can offer you one at a lower salary will you take it?
- What are your ambitions/ goals in life (or in your career)?

Whatever you do don't try to write down the answers you will give and learn them up, as it will leave you totally tongue-tied if the question isn't worded as you expect or you forget your lines.

What Do You Need to Know?

When you have found the best answers to all those questions you will have a very good idea of how to show you are right for the job. Having seen it from their point of view, you can now see it from your own.

What do you want to know about the job?

You may only have time to ask one question, and you are very unlikely to have time for more than three. So work out what you want to know and be ready to put your questions in the order of importance to you; then think what impression your questions will make on that particular company. The best questions are the ones which suggest you are really interested in the job - not the perks.

How Will They Expect Someone in that Job to Dress?

Packaging counts. If you have to wear a city suit to work, you need to turn up in a city suit - if that means borrowing or hiring it, do so. Equally, if it's a job where casual clothes are the rule wear something appropriate. The role of your clothes is to make others feel you are one of them, that you will fit in. Make it easy for them to think that (see page 21).

On the Day

The rules on the day are very simple.
- Before going for the interview read the copy you kept of your letter or application form and memorize what you said on it.
- Make sure you look right for the job.
- Take with you everything you have been asked to take.
- Be early - not hours early, but have time to spare so you can go in five minutes ahead of time without rushing.
- Take something to do while you wait; they may run behind time and if you sit doing nothing the nerves may mount.
- When you enter the interview be guided by the interviewer as to whether you shake hands or not. If you do so make it firm (but not gripping) and decisive, and look at the person you are greeting.
- Follow the plan you have worked out above but listen carefully for any cues the interviewer gives. The way a question is worded will often suggest the answer which is wanted.
- Look at the interviewer.
- Don't smoke unless the interviewer invites you to.
- Never criticize a previous employer.

After the Interview

Some people suggest that you should write a pleasant businesslike letter to the interviewer the next day - you should have made a note of his or her name and initials. In it you should:
- thank them for the interview
- say how much you appreciated the chance to learn more about the job
- say how interesting you found it
- tell them briefly anything *vital* you omitted from the interview - if really necessary
- let them know that you do want the job and are looking forward to hearing from them.

This does have the advantage of allowing you to say something vital which you forgot in the interview, but to some people it could seem pushy. So the situation needs to be judged carefully.

Making Conversation

I have to confess that I simply cannot tell anyone how to make small talk. It is not one of my skills and, like origami napkin folding, I have always left it to those who do it better. As with origami, it is quite extraordinary the lengths to which some take it. Some people have talk that is both so small and so incessant that listening to it is like being choked to death with talcum powder. Mercifully, now that women are allowed to have brains, small talk is getting bigger.

Opening Gambits

There are books which give you all kinds of advice on how to start conversations with people. But there is only one rule: it doesn't matter what you say so long as you take an interest in *them*. As the 1856 edition of *Enquire Within* put it:

> The true art of being agreeable is to appear well pleased with all the company, and rather to seem well entertained with them than to bring entertainment upon them.

Avoid talking about yourself; praising your own works; and proclaiming your own deeds. If they are good, they will proclaim themselves; if bad, the less you say of them the better.

Ask them a question about themselves which is likely to produce an interesting answer. Listen very attentively to the answer, pick up a point from it, and ask another question - the more flattering, the better. Given an attentive ear almost anyone will find something interesting to say, in time. It's a technique with which you can't go wrong: the unimportant and shy are flattered that, for once, someone is listening to them; the important and self-opinionated are getting what they regard as their due. Even the shyest person can adopt the tactic with ease, as it involves deflecting attention away from oneself.

Topics of Conversation

The basic rule is never to talk about anything which will upset anyone else who is present. Nor should you say anything which is likely to stop the conversation dead with surprise. So what you say at a Hampstead drinks party is rather different from what you say at a tea with a country vicar. Religion and politics are no longer banned - but they do have to be carefully handled if they are not to touch anyone on a sensitive spot. Sex is rather the same. General comments are now acceptable at many tables, but the personal or anatomical usually brings conversation to a halt.

The permissible level of debate is a matter of taste and nationality. The British tend to be more afraid of debate than other Europeans, but restrained arguments are tolerated, provided they are intellectual, not personal. The old *Enquire Within* put it rather well:

> Avoid Disputation, for the mere sake of argument.

The man who disputes obstinately and in a bigoted spirit, is like the man who would stop the fountain from which he should drink. Earnest discussion is commendable; but factious argument never yet produced a good result.

Once anyone starts to get heated the host or hostess should deflect the conversation towards something less controversial. Whatever the topic, anyone who has not spoken for a long while should be brought into the conversation by a direct question and not left out in the cold.

Making Introductions

Introductions are an essential oil in the wheels of social encounters. Whenever anyone finds themselves with two acquaintances who don't know each other, he or she is duty-bound to introduce them. It makes no difference whether the meeting was engineered or a chance encounter in the street.

If the two people are more or less equal in age, sex and standing you can introduce either to either. If you need to bring them together across a room, and there is any inequality, you always take the less important person to meet the more important one - therefore, given equal status, you take a man to meet a women, not vice versa, and you introduce them on the same basis.

When making the introduction the counsel of perfection is to work a few words into the introduction which allow them to start a conversation easily. So look for something which they have in common. For example, to introduce a medical student to a doctor, the format would be 'John' (assuming you are on first name terms) 'I'd like you to meet Dr Scapula. Dr Scapula (or his first name if you normally use it), John Sternum is studying medicine at Barts - that's your old hospital, isn't it?' (assuming it is).

The issue of how to introduce someone with a title is a vexed one. If the title owner is likely to be offended at it not being used then it must be used. But it may put both sides at a disadvantage, so since good manners should never make anyone feel uncomfortable, the title can often be omitted. There are no rules; you can only judge each situation as it comes.

If people don't appear to be linked, but are - such as wives who keep their maiden name, and lovers - it is useful to introduce them both at the same time and throw in some phrase which clearly tells the rest of the room that they are a couple. It doesn't matter whether it's that they have enchanting children or have just got back from a holiday in Casablanca; it saves the rest of the room wondering.

Children tend to get left out of such courtesies. They shouldn't be. A child deserves an introduction just as much, and they tend to behave better if they are treated with a touch of formality.

When introducing a person or a couple to a large group of people the usual method, unless one of the people is particularly important, is to start off by giving the names of the newcomer(s) and then to name all the others going round the group. It is convenient to go round the circle in the order that people are standing, but some still introduce all the women before the men. Whether you use Christian names or surnames or whether people shake hands on introduction will depend on the formality of the occasion and the age of the guests.

On the Telephone

According to Debrett, the correct way to answer a private telephone is simply with the word 'Hello'; 'Hello, this is 234 6789' or 'Hello, Susan Selby [or whoever] speaking' should be reserved for work. I disagree. Good manners are about making things easier for other people. Only if you give your number or name do callers know if they have got through to the right number. It also gives them a chance to realize who has answered - so they don't launch into a long conversation only to find they are talking to the daughter, not the mother.

Stopping people talking is a common problem. The classic British solution is to express your pleasure at having talked to them but say you mustn't keep them. If they ignore this go for a range of excuses - you'd love to go on talking but...you can smell something burning in the kitchen, or your husband/wife/boss/mother/child is calling you about something urgent.

Answering Machines

Many owners make it almost impossible for their callers to leave a message by failing to say whether their particular machine will only take a brief message or gives unlimited time. When recording the message to callers:

- tell them your number
- ask them to leave a message
- *tell them how long the message can be* (some machines have unlimited time, others only 30 seconds)
- ask them to wait for the tone before speaking.

It is then basic politeness for the caller to leave a message, and not let the poor machine owner return to the tantalizing series of burrs and clicks which show someone rang and left no message.

Ringing Up

Telephones are extraordinary: dial someone and you walk right into their life - interrupt them in mid-sentence, get them out of the bath, or wreak havoc with their love-making. Thoughtful telephoners start by trying to avoid times which won't suit other people. Next, let them know who you are: it's amazing how many people ring and say 'Hi, it's me' or 'Hello, it's Susan', forgetting that there are an awful lot of mes and Susans around. And whether telephoning an office or a home, it's considerate to ask if it is a good moment to talk, or would they rather you rang later (even, or perhaps especially, if you are a relative) - it is surely presumptuous to suppose anyone, however close, is free to talk to you at any minute you choose. If you are busy when the phone goes perfectly within your rights to say so and ask if you can call them back later - but some people are reluctant to do this. If it's a business call keep it very much to the point - so decide exactly what you want to say before you ring.

Paying for Calls
Whether one should or should not pay for calls made on a friend's telephone is a tricky matter. Some people are insulted at being offered money; others are upset if calls aren't paid for. So, avoid phoning long distance or overseas and be brief. But if you have to make a long or expensive call you can see that a proud friend isn't out of pocket by putting money to cover it beside the telephone. Then, as you leave you can mention that you put it there. Alternatively, scribble a note and put it with the money, saying you've done so because it was a rather long call.

Public Speaking
Being a first-rate public speaker is an ability which, like that of being a racing driver, is inborn as much as learnt. However, almost everyone can get from A to B as a speech maker, just as they can as a driver. It is a matter of knowing what to do.

Introducing a Speaker
Someone who introduces a speaker simply has to be the oil which eases the speaker into place. You don't have to be clever or witty, just pleasant and competent and keep it short.
1   Say how pleased you are to be able to welcome the speaker. And if you are an official of the organization to which the speech is being made, say you are delighted to be able to welcome the speaker on behalf of that organization. (You can also add that it is a personal pleasure, if there is some reason why that is true.)
2   Introduce the speaker by name and give an indication of their position. Make sure you include any qualifications relevant to the subject to be spoken on.
3   If the speaker has spoken to your organization before say something to indicate that he or she is particularly welcome because everyone enjoyed his or her last speech so much.
4   Give an indication of the subject the speaker has come to speak on. *Only* do this if you have had a chance to find out beforehand what the speaker's subject *is*. He or she may have changed the speech in the train, and it is embarrassing if you announce that the subject is flower arrangement and the speaker launches into the mating habits of the mongoose or vice versa.
5   Finish with 'Ladies and gentlemen' (or whatever is appropriate), and the person's name, then start the applause, and sit down when it ends.

Thanking the Speaker
This should be *very* brief - people's patience wears a bit thin after a speech. Just say a few very warm words of praise about what you have just heard. Sound really appreciative, however awful the speech was. For someone who is bad at speaking to have made a speech at all was probably an immense effort which deserves thanks. Try to pick out a particularly memorable point which the speaker made and remark on it. Then say where everyone should go from there. It may be that the speaker was speaking on behalf of a charity - in which case you will be expected to urge people to make donations. On the other hand, if the talk was just for everyone's pleasure and the next move is a cup of tea or a drink announce it, or nobody will know when they can get up.

If the applause at the end of the speech failed to materialize, or was less than enthusiastic, you can smooth this over by saying something like, 'But before we all go to tea I'm sure we'd all like to give [the speaker's name] a *big* round of applause.' Then lead the applause loudly, egging the others on with your example.

Making a Speech
Most people who have to give a speech are worried sick about what they are going to say. That is totally unnecessary. Talking is rarely a problem. What does matter is getting together *thoughts* which will make a talk worth listening to. The bad speaker is someone who says what everyone has heard before, in words which are all too familiar.

The other route to a bad speech is (in most cases) to write it out. Actors, professional broadcasters and a few politicians apart, very few people can read a speech so that it sounds alive and immediate. Usually the written word becomes a barrier between the speaker and the audience. Only by picking your words as you go along can you be certain to speak *to* people not *at* them, and so hold their attention.

Nobody can teach anyone how to be witty or charming, but the following method should allow anyone to create a speech which is well organized and has a chance of being effective, and perhaps original. Yet it relies entirely on notes which will fit on a series of postcards, and is extremely easy to use.

Preparing a Speech
In the early stages of preparation the essential thing is not to try too hard. Relax and let your mind wander over the topic you have to speak on. Each time you think of something connected with it write it down in just *one* or *two* words each. It should be a disordered jumble of ideas, let them be as crazy and far-fetched as you like. Give your imagination free rein, don't sit there being critical. Ideas are shy things: your brain only has to sense you criticizing one of its suggestions and, like a criticized person, it will stop being original and interesting and start coming up with the safe and the boring.

When you run out of ideas, go through what you have written down and pick out the three key areas, or topics, which your jumbled notes suggest to you. They may be there as words already, or you may see several patterns in what you have written down and think of a heading for each. (If your words are really dreary have another go from the beginning.)

Make these the three main headings for your talk (you could pick out five for a very long speech). Put each one at the top of a separate sheet of paper.

Under each heading write down any relevant ideas and points you would like to make on that particular aspect of the subject. Don't worry about structure; write things down just as they come into your head.

Look at what you have written down in the light of the type of speech you are wanting to make. Cross out the things you don't want to say on this particular occasion. Leave in those that you do want to say. For example, suppose you are making a wedding speech. You have chosen three headings: The Past, The Present and The Future. You find that under 'The Future' your random jottings include 'One marriage in three ends in divorce', so you cross it out. But if you were making a speech in a debating society and the motion was 'Marriage has no future in our society', you would certainly keep that statistic in.

Having sorted out which ideas you will use, decide the order in which your three headings should go, and mark them A, B and C. Remember that your speech should build to some sort of climax, not shoot its bolt in the early minutes and go downhill from there.

Once you know the order of the main headings you can start to arrange the order of the ideas within them. They need to lead easily from one to another within a section, and they also need to be planned so the last idea in each section takes you easily into the next heading. Once that is done you have the backbone of what you will say. The invariable structure of all but the frothiest speech is this:

1   Your introduction gets the audience interested and outlines what you will talk about.
2   The body of your speech is made by building point on point or witty remark upon witty remark, according to the nature of the subject.
3   You summarize what you've just said and round the speech off smoothly.

You now need to decide on an attention-catching opening, and find an entertaining way to summarize all the main points of the speech. Then flesh out the bones of section 2 with clever comparisons, examples, statistics, jokes or anything else that will give interest to what you have to say. This is the bit you have to work at and polish until you are sure that every idea can be made really interesting. But don't try to be precise about the words you will use. Keep noting your ideas in one or two words beside the point they relate to.

When that is done take five postcards. Write the notes for the introduction on one, and the headings and summary on the other four. Under each heading list the one or two word reminders of the points to be made - in the order you have decided - plus a memory jogger for anything you need to flesh each out. Your speech is now ready.

★ The technique of jotting down random ideas and then organizing them under headings is one worth practising. Once you get the hang of it there is no faster way of preparing an examination answer and making sure it reads well.

Debating

Each debating society tends to have small variations on the rules of debating, but the basics are very simple. First, a motion is formulated as a statement; for example, the motion on one radio debate in which I took part was 'Women aren't funny'. There then have to be four speakers:

- one to propose the motion
- one to second (agree with) the motion
- one to oppose the motion
- one to second the opposition motion

There must also be a chairman, and a 'house', which is a participating audience. In some debates there are six speakers, each side having an extra seconder.

Each of the speakers prepares a speech, the length being set beforehand so they all speak for the same time - 10 to 15 minutes is average. At the start of the debate the chairman announces the motion and calls on the first speaker to propose the motion. The proposer then puts forward an argument in favour of the motion, producing as many persuasive points as possible, and trying to win the audience over to agreeing.

Next the chairman calls on the other side to oppose the motion. This should be an equally persuasive argument against it.

After that the seconders alternate in the same way, putting forward new arguments and ideas for their side. They are allowed to refer to what the other side has said and point out how their arguments refute it.

When all four have spoken the debate is normally 'thrown open to the floor'. At this stage anyone can catch the chairman's eye - usually by raising a hand - and the chairman can call on that person to speak from the floor. He or she will then put points on either side but always addressing the chairman, not the speakers, so the opening words must be 'Mr Chairman' or 'Madam Chairman'.

Nobody should interrupt anyone else or speak unless the chairman has called on them to do so. But there are two exceptions. Anyone on the floor can leap to their feet and say, 'On a point of fact/information, Mr Chairman ....' and go on to correct a factual inaccuracy by any speaker or by anyone else on the floor. They can also leap up and say, 'On a point of order, Mr Chairman...' and point out how someone has broken the rules of debate.

Good chairmen will not allow speakers from the floor to go on for more than three minutes and will cut them off sooner if they are boring. They allow a set amount of time for the debate on the floor, after which they first call on the opposer to sum up his or her argument and then on the proposer to do the same. After that the motion is put to the vote. Only those on the floor vote, not the chairman or speakers.

Running a Meeting

The chairman's job is to make sure that everyone gets a fair chance to put his or her point of view, that the meeting proceeds at a decent pace and that decisions get taken. To do this he or she must start by making it clear that the meeting will be held with a certain degree of formality. This doesn't have to mean the elaborate pseudo-parliamentary protocol which is still used by the highly traditional. It just means being businesslike. However, a degree of protocol does bring it home to people that chatting is out of order. So the most basic procedure is given below.

The Agenda

It is usually helpful to have an agenda listing the topics which will be discussed and voted on. It can be drawn up by the chairman on the basis of topics which other members of the committee ask him or her to include.

The agenda should have attached to it the minutes of the last meeting. These are brief but accurate notes on every decision which was taken and on who agreed to do what. So at every meeting someone must take these down, even if there is no official secretary. If this doesn't happen there will be decisions but no action.

The agenda and the minutes of the last meeting should be circulated, in advance, to everyone who will be coming to the meeting and they should read them before they come.

At the Meeting

The chairman should sit at the head of the table or in a dominant position. He or she should check that everyone is present and allow only a brief grace for late arrivals. From that point on every comment should be addressed to the chair. So 'Mr Chairman' or 'Madam Chairman' will precede each person's opening words.

The chairman should then outline the purpose of the meeting, and perhaps check that everyone has an agenda, with the minutes. He or she will then ask the secretary to read any apologies for absence. The minutes of the last meeting are then gone through, point by point.

If a decision for someone to take action was minuted, the chairman should ask that person what was done and what the outcome was.

He or she should make his or her reply short and to the point. If people ramble in reply the chairman should bring them gently to the nub of the matter. If this part of the proceeding is allowed to drag there will be no time to discuss any fresh issues or make new decisions.

If any action decided on in the last meeting is completed it is said to be 'adopted'. If it needs further action it is re-minuted so it will be brought up again at the next meeting. This proceeds until all the minutes have been dealt with.

Next the points on the agenda are considered one by one. Each point is discussed in detail and the chairman can call on whoever put an item on the agenda to speak first. It is the chairman's job to keep things moving forward and decide when any point has been discussed for long enough. He or she then sums up the general mood of the meeting and steers people firmly towards a decision. For example, 'Are we all agreed that there should be a cake stall at the Bring and Buy?' If everyone agrees, there is no problem. If they don't, the chairman asks for a vote. The decision is taken on a majority vote, through a show of hands, and the chairman votes last,

making the final decision if an equal number are for and against.

★ Things go more smoothly if decisions are kept simple. Decide to have a cake stall; *then* decide who will run it. Once any point has been voted on the topic is closed. If anyone tries to take the discussion back to it the chairman should intervene at once, or the meeting will get nowhere.

When all the points on the agenda have been dealt with, the last item is usually 'any other business'. This is a chance for people to raise issues which failed to get on the agenda and need to be dealt with. The chairman then closes the meeting - having, of course, arranged the date of the next one, if this is appropriate.

Business Letters

The best letter is the one which expresses what you have to say simply and clearly. Just write as you would speak. It is far better to say, 'If you need more information please let me know', than to use the cliché, 'If you need more information do not hesitate to contact me.' Hesitation about business matters went out years ago.

However, there are a couple of special rules. Business letters should have the address of the person to whom the letter is being sent written at the top left-hand corner. If your letter is a reply your first sentence must also give the date and reference number (if there is one) of the letter you are replying to. The simple form is:

Dear ....
In reply to your letter of (date), reference number (quote the reference numbers or letters on their letter).

Then say what you want to say. Time is money - sometimes it's their money, but if you are consulting professionals it is *your* money. They need only the key points (don't be embarrassed by bare paper). If you need to give more than a few facts, it can often be useful to split the information. Suppose you have an appointment with a lawyer, write confirming the appointment and say what you are consulting him about (problems with a neighbour, a divorce or whatever) and what help you hope to get from him. Then say the background facts are enclosed, and on the separate sheet give all the main facts he might need to know to advise you. Giving him a chance to read a clear outline can save you a lot of time and money when you actually see him.

Spend time deciding which facts really *are* relevant and important. He doesn't need to know that it was your birthday when the neighbour's tree fell, breaking your fence, but he will need to know who is legally responsible for the fence.

Keep a copy of every business letter you send or receive, and only destroy them when they could be of no possible use. The same holds good for all documents and evidence - guarantees, receipts and so on - never post them without keeping a copy, or better still, keep the original and send the copy. If there is any chance that someone may say you did not write, pay a bill or return goods at an appointed time, ask the post office for a free certificate giving proof of posting.

Complaining

The golden rule for complaints is to praise first. If you have usually had satisfactory service from the company start by saying so. Then explain what was wrong. Ask them for whatever redress you feel is appropriate (see Consumer Rights) and either tell them what evidence you are enclosing or ask them to arrange to see the problem (you could not after all post a faulty sofa). If you are sending items by post remember to get proof of posting

Most big businesses have Customer Relations Departments which deal with complaints. But if in doubt write to the Managing Director - complaints, like water, filter down very easily, but if you send them to somebody too low down the ladder they never rise to the level of someone who can deal with them.

Job Applications

When applying for a job bear in mind that you are advertising yourself. A good advertisement gives the key facts, briefly and cleverly, and says no more than is needed to get the reader interested. The aim is to get them to take a look at the product - and this time the product is you. So don't be tempted to go on and on: instead give the full details in a curriculum vitae (CV, see below). If the job needs you to apply by phone, make a note of what you will say before you phone. If the application must be in writing, plan the letter carefully.

Start by saying which job you are applying for and how you knew it was available. Briefly say why you are especially qualified for the job and sound as if you are genuinely interested in work of its type. Finally, tell them about any enclosures and politely show that you expect a reply. For example:

Dear ....,

I am writing to apply for the job of senior crocodile keeper, which was advertised in The Animals' Friend *of Saturday 25 September.*

For the past three years I have been assistant reptile keeper in Animal Haven, a large private zoo in California, and have had special responsibility for crocodiles and alligators.

Crocodiles have always been my special interest, and I have studied and applied the latest developments in their care and handling. Last year, for example, I attended an advanced course on the subject at Las Bestas State Zoo where, as I am sure you know, they have pioneered captive breeding of the more difficult crocodile species.

A curriculum vitae, giving full details of my qualifications and experience is enclosed, and I will be glad to supply references from my two previous employers if you need them.

I believe that I have both the qualifications and the experience which are needed for the post you advertised, and I am greatly attracted by this opportunity to work in a operation which is so dedicated to conservation and research.

I very much look forward to meeting you and learning more about what sounds like a most interesting job.

Yours faithfully,

Needless to say, a job application must never go on to a second page, should be totally free from errors of spelling, punctuation and grammar, and be typed, or written in good hand-writing. The managing director of one dynamic company told me he always rejects, without further reading, an application - for a post at *any* level - if he finds even one small error in it. In his view, 'If someone can't be bothered to check that everything is absolutely correct, when *their* future and income are at stake, what chance is there that they will take trouble over details which matter to the company?'

Curriculum Vitae (CV)

A CV lists all the background details a prospective employer might need to know. But it must be carefully selected and compressed into no more than two sides of A4 paper. The key facts are:

- schools/colleges/universities attended
- all exams passed, plus the standard achieved if it was good
- all special awards
- special achievements - head boy/girl, captain of cricket and so on
- any further training you received
- every job or position held - unless you are so senior that only recent experience is relevant
- key hobbies and interests in private life.

Select hobbies to suggest abilities which could be useful in the job - working in a team, being creative and so on.

The dates go, in exact sequence, down the left-hand side. Some people write CVs starting with their most recent job and working *back* to their birth; others start at their birth and work through. Start with whichever end of your life is most impressive - if you sound dull at the start of the CV the prospective employer may not bother to read to the end.

The CV is your one chance to reveal yourself, and you should be very careful about what you reveal accidentally. There is a difference between the person who writes:

1981-85   Export Manager for YT Industries PLC. The need to pull out of South Africa made this a difficult time for the company. However, by working on our existing markets in the Far East I was able to minimize the impact of this and maintain profits.

and the one who writes:

1981-85   As Export Manager for YT Industries PLC I faced the challenge of restructuring the company's export strategy. By moving strongly into new markets it was possible substantially to increase the company's profits from exports, despite the fact that key markets had to be dropped by the board for political reasons.

It isn't just a matter of giving the facts but of giving the facts in a way which sounds appealing. So work out what the prospective employer is looking for - using the advertisement as guidelines, and then write a CV which combines the two. Some employers frown on CVs prepared by agencies, as they simply don't reveal enough about the real person to show whether they are worth interviewing.

As employers are usually suspicious of those who take time off to do nothing, and seem to fear it may be a recurrent disease, there should be no unaccounted-for years. But be careful, if you are someone who feels the need to account for idle years, never to claim to have done something which you haven't done at all. Anything in a CV is open to questions at the interview and you can't be sure that the interviewer won't have been to the place you claim to have visited or done what you claim to have done.

Invitations

Sending Invitations

The etiquette of invitations is a legacy from the days when, instead of directly inviting people to your house, you let them know that you regarded them as worthy of your acquaintance and would be 'at home' on a certain day if they called. This curious wording is still the classic style of invitation to send out for almost all occasions except weddings or children's parties. A typical invitation would read:

If the event is to take place at a country house, but the hosts find it more convenient to receive replies at their London address, they would put 'at Grandthorpe Manor, Little Airs, Buckinghamshire' under the date, and the RSVP address would remain at the bottom left-hand corner. Strictly speaking, the words 'At Home' can only be used when a *woman* is sending out the invitations. So a wife issues the invitations in her name only. Stiff white card, 4 x 6¾ in (10 x 17 cm), is traditional. The name and address, and the words 'At Home' should be printed. But the time and date can be either printed or hand-written, and the names of the guests are then hand-written at the top left-hand corner.

One of the hazards of the basic wording is that the poor benighted guests are left wondering just what sort

of a party they are being invited to. So drinks or dinner (or whatever) is usually written or printed above the time. If there is a special reason for the party this should also be given. So if parents are giving a party for one of their children they will put 'For John' or 'For Miss Susan Bold' - according to how formal they wish to be (the latter is more correct) - under the date.

If a man is giving a party or a couple wish to use their joint names on an invitation, the words 'At Home' are replaced by 'request(s) the pleasure of your company'. These words can also be used if the party is not being held at the hostess's home.

Other Parties

Invitations to casual parties and parties for the young can take any form you like, from bought cards to felt-pen writing on balloons, and be varied according to the age of those concerned. For children's parties put the time the party ends. After entertaining a hoard of children that will be the time you really care about.

Accepting Invitations

The convention for answering invitations is to repeat the wording of the invitation. A reply to the invitation by Mrs Bold (page 000) should read:

> *Dr and Mrs Pillue thank Mrs John Bold for her kind invitation for Saturday 25th May, from 6 - 8 pm, and have much pleasure in accepting.*
> **or**
> *- very much regret that they are not able to accept as they will be abroad/have a prior engagement/or whatever.*

It looks minimal but it says all that needs to be said and, well placed, on the smallest size of writing paper it is perfectly adequate. Nothing further is added and it is not signed.

A solo guest bringing a partner should include his or her name in the reply - it may be someone the hostess already knows, or the ex-husband or ex-wife of one of her other guests, and she needs to be forewarned.

Inviting People to Dinner

There are no rules for how far ahead anyone should be invited to dinner - or any other social event. People who lead dynamic social lives are best invited a month beforehand, while most people are perfectly content with two to three weeks' notice.

As dates may need to be juggled, the initial invitation, to anything but a very formal dinner party, is usually by phone. If the arrangements are at all vague, it is then wise to drop the guests a short note confirming the date and time. For a more formal occasion, Debrett suggests sending an At Home card with the RSVP crossed out and 'To Remind' written above. I personally prefer 'To Confirm' which smacks less of the suggestion that the recipient is absent-minded.

Those who follow in the footsteps of Pussy Gladstone, as she was known (Lord Gladstone's wife), and invite people and then forget they have done so, can even send one to themselves.

Inviting Single Guests

The days when guests had to arrive and go into dinner, two by two, like animals entering the ark, are long gone. But some hostesses still feel awkward on behalf of a single person. There is no need to. In general, only the very newly bereaved or divorced find it embarrassing to be solo. And, though a great excess of either sex can be difficult, it is insulting to someone of either sex to suppose that he or she is not worth inviting without a partner, or that a partner *has* to be produced.

Guests may, however, have an 'opposite number' they would like to bring with them. It's tactful to make it clear, by a telephone call or a note with the invitation, that they are invited solo, but that if *they* particularly want to bring someone, they are welcome to do so. That way, a guest who lacks a suitable partner won't feel that he or she has to scrape around to find someone to bring. Putting 'and guest' on an invitation, though kindly meant, can make solo friends feel that if they can't bring a guest they won't be welcome, which can be hurtful.

Stationery

Paper and Envelopes

Today there is nothing to stop you having purple writing paper ornamented with puce kisses, if you want to. But, as with clothes, there are certain conventions, which apply if someone wants to make a particular type of impression. Colours are more flamboyant than they used to be - but the more striking the choice, the harder it may be to carry off. Those who want to impress would-be employers or parents-in-law should bear in mind that a gentleman's (or woman's) writing paper should be rather like a classic suit: good quality and understated, with discreet details. That means good quality unlined paper in white or pale-blue in any size, with matching envelopes. The address can be printed at the top in a neat, unshowy typeface, either in the centre or at the right-hand corner. Failing that, it is hand-written at the top right. Printed addresses usually include the telephone number (not preceded by the word 'tel:' on private stationery); hand-written ones do not.

Notes and Cards

It is conventional to use plain postcards with your address printed or handwritten along the top edge. Christmas cards always used to have the sender's address printed inside at the bottom-right hand corner, but nowadays many people avoid this expense, except for business. However, only the address should be printed, not the name, and each card must be hand-signed.

Business Cards

Today's business cards sprang from the days before telephones when, to make contact without intruding, people would visit the house and leave a card to show they had called. Flurries of excitement were created when the local big-wigs condescended to leave their card on a newcomer. Today cards are mainly used for business, but in some parts of the world failing to exchange business cards is like failing to return a greeting.

Engraving v Printing

The best cards, business cards and other stationery are engraved and the letters feel raised, whereas ordinary printing feels flat. Engraving is undoubtedly more elegant, but today few people recognize engraving and although, in some people's eyes, the niceties of engraving versus printing, and of good quality card versus light card, are a matter of status, there is now a printing process which mimics engraving.

Social Letters

Writing or Typing

Typing used to be reserved for business letters, and type-written social letters were considered cold and unfriendly, at best. In America this view has long since died out. As hand-writing has deteriorated and typewriters and computers have entered more homes, type-written social letters have become acceptable here too. But a hand-written letter, in good hand-writing, still makes a better impression especially in ink not biro - and a type-written one should still contain a sentence excusing the type-writing. Business letters can be hand-written or typed - but the latter looks rather more efficient and makes it easier to keep a duplicate copy.

How to Start Letters

The etiquette of how you start and end letters, and address an envelope to those with ranks or titles is so complex that I cannot cover it here. But Debrett's *Etiquette and Modern Manners* gives every nuance.

For ordinary situations:

- 'Dear Sir,' or 'Dear Madam,' is the correct business opening if you know the sex but not the name.
- 'Dear Sir/Madam,' is now used, if you don't know the name or sex.
- If you know the name 'Dear' followed by Mr or Mrs (or Dr) and the surname is the correct business opening.
- 'Dear' followed by the first name is increasingly used between those on first-name terms either in business or socially.
- Nowadays 'Dear' plus first name and surname seems to be creeping in, when people are not on first name terms but Mr or Mrs might seem too deferential.
- For letters to those close to you any variation goes - My Dear, Dearest, Darling, as you will.
- On postcards use no opening at all, but go straight into the message.

How to End Letters

There is a simple hierarchy of friendliness for the endings to letters. Starting with the coolest, this is:

Yours faithfully,	For formal business letters, especially to someone you have not met, or when starting with Dear Sir - or Madam.

Yours sincerely,	For business letters to those you know (e.g. your bank manager) or for social letters when you wish to show a fair amount of distance and respect.
Yours truly,	Slightly dated, but useful for acquaintances.
Yours,	A neutral ending, neither very formal nor affectionate, useful when you don't want to define the closeness - for example, when writing to a friend's husband or wife.
With very best wishes Yours,	Like this 'Yours' can remain non-intimate but you express more warmth. And the wishes can be extended to a particular person.
Yours affectionately,	Affectionate but slightly distant - say to a relative who is not close enough for 'With love', or to someone for whom you feel real affection but not intimacy.
Yours ever,	A slightly dated ending between friends.
With love, All my love, Much love,	At one time these endings were little used. Today they are used, not only between relatives and lovers, but between friends of the opposite sex (who won't misunderstand), and between women friends.

Thank-yous

Nowadays thank-yous are often overlooked entirely, but it is correct to thank people after any major hospitality - lunch, dinner, going to stay or a party. You don't, however, send thank-yous after cocktails, weddings, funerals or royal garden parties.

If a letter can't be written then a quick, enthusiastic telephone call will do - unless it was a long visit or a formal occasion. And many hostesses actually prefer a phone call, which allows them to mull over the evening's events, to a letter, which allows no chance to gossip.

When writing the rules are the same whether you have been entertained or received a present:

1   Thank them for the dinner/party/present and say how much you enjoyed/like it, etcetera.
2   Pick out one or two reasons why you enjoyed/like it so much. If the evening was boring, or the present ghastly, be creative; thank-yous are about making other people feel good, not a game of truth. But keep within the bounds of reason; if the food was a disaster, praise the flowers or the choice of guests. If the object is terrible, there are plenty of complimentary adjectives you can use without lying about *liking* it. Then say how very kind they were to invite you/give it to you.
3   End with some good wishes, such as that you hope to see them again soon.

If you have large writing paper this may leave a lot of blank space but there is no need to pad thank-you letters with chat.

Styles for Envelopes

It is not just what you call someone on an envelope that matters but how you place the writing on the paper. The name and address should start about half-way down and not threaten to embrace the stamp. They are *only* preceded by 'To' on a parcel address, when there could be confusion between to whom it's addressed to and to whom it's from.

A woman with no special title can be Miss, Mrs or Ms. But Miss and Ms are followed by her first name or initials, then surname, whereas Mrs is followed by the husband's first name or initials. On widowhood, and often on divorce, the husband's initials or name are replaced by her own. Dr is always followed by the woman's first name or initials as the qualification belongs to her not her husband.

The use of Master for young boys is outdated and the first name and surname will do until late adolescence. For a man, the first name or initials (one initial will do) and surname are used. If you don't know his initial, and can't discover it, there is no convention on what to do. Nancy Mitford used to resort to the Greek letter θ (theta) instead of an initial; I myself simply put A.

The classic form of address is to put Esq after the man's name, so it will read A. E. Jones Esq. Mr is used when both the husband and wife are being written to, as in Mr and Mrs Gettogether, or when writing to a surgeon, in which case Mr is - confusingly - the correct title. But, under American influence, more and more people are writing Mr for any man, and I fear that Esq will eventually pass into history. It is not, however, there yet and there is still a certain prestige in using it. If a husband and wife are doctors you put Dr John and Dr Joan Cutabout, or whatever. But, strictly, if a letter is intended for both husband and wife it should be written and addressed solely to the wife.

Food

Additives and Labelling • Dairy Products • Eggs •
Fish and Shellfish • Food Hygiene • Frozen Food and Freezing •
Fruit and Nuts • Game and Poultry • Grains •
Herbs, Spices and Flavourings • Meat •
Methods and Problems • Pulses • Quantities and Temperatures •
Special Cooking Methods • Storage Times • Vegetables

ADDITIVES AND LABELLING

Food Additives

There have always been additives, and we are lucky to have been spared some of those experienced by our ancestors. A hundred years ago milk was watered, tea and flour adulterated and wine, beer, cheese and oil debased. Sugar was as much as 50 per cent sand, causing the popular jingle:

> Little bags of sugar
> Little grains of sand
> Make the artful grocer
> The richest in the land.

Sand was one of the more harmless additives of the time - others were outright poisons, like red lead and verdigris. No wonder it wasn't considered respectable to be 'in trade'.

Reformers fought, and won, a battle for stricter controls. Yet today our food contains more additives than it has ever done. Some do stop food going bad, and a tiny minority improve its flavour. But most simply make food look more appealing than it really is, or are just a modern version of the grocer's old trick of increasing profits by making a small quantity of food go farther.

There is also a new phenomenon. A hundred years ago even the most adulterated food had *some* real food in it. This is no longer true of all food. Today more and more 'food' is totally a laboratory creation: 'fruit' drinks which haven't even had the fruit in question waved over them, snacks which haven't a genuine food element in them, instant desserts, spreads which look like butter and milk substitutes unrelated to milk. The list is endless.

Never in the history of the world have human beings consumed such vast numbers of chemicals which do not occur naturally in food. Moreover the positive safety of many of them is just not proven. All that has been established is a lack of evidence of them being unsafe. But if manufacturers have a right to make these phoney products, we have an equal right to avoid them. And the failure of such products to sell will make them vanish from the shops far more swiftly than any government legislation.

Defining

Some additives are old friends like salt, sugar and vitamins. But the term also covers the whole caboosh of artificial colourings, flavourings, flavour enhancers, emulsifiers, thickeners, sweeteners, bleaches, anti-oxidants, anti-foaming agents (yes, in food not detergent), humectants, propellants, solvents and preservatives. Some 6,000 different chemicals all told, and almost *a quarter of a million tonnes* of them are added to British food each year. That means each of us consumes 8 to 10 pounds of additives per year - whether we want to or not.

There is so much protective legislation around nowadays that we tend to assume that if something is permitted it must be safe. This is not true where additives are concerned. The 'E' before the code numbers of most additives may not stand for Evil - in fact, it shows that the additive is permitted in the EEC - but many permitted additives are known to produce ill effects in *some* people.

To give you some idea of how widespread the use of certain additives is: tartrazine (E102) - which may cause asthma, hayfever and hyperactivity - is used in 2,995 different products including:

17 types of sausages	59 canned vegetables
21 toppings and sauces	64 preserves
24 milky desserts	86 ice cream products
26 frozen desserts	104 dessert mixes
32 coatings	109 toffees and caramels
48 types of chocolate	188 soft drinks
49 confectionery fillings	201 gums, jellies and
49 soups	pastilles
50 jellies	301 boiled sweets

> Those figures came, not from some pressure group trying to make much of the over use of additives, but from a report by the Ministry of Food and Agriculture in 1987.

Interactions

It is not simply a matter of any given additive being bad for us. There is also the question of interaction. As additives are seldom used singly, we are being exposed to unpredictable chemical cocktails. With over 6,000 additives being added in different combinations to a huge variety of foods it would be mathematically impossible for the food industry or any government organization to test *even a useful fraction* of the possible interactions to see if any dangerous by-products were produced. It is entirely possible that the additives now in our food do most people no harm at all. However, since the potential for interactions makes it almost impossible to prove either way, it is not unreasonable to limit our intake.

Government Restrictions

The law says that the use in food of substances which are of no nutritional value must be restricted. The Ministry of Agriculture, Fisheries and Food and the Ministry of Health are jointly responsible for vetting additives. However, their decisions are curious. For example, they have decided that the British food industry 'needs' food dyes which the rest of the EEC does very well without, and they allow the use of flavourings which have never been tested for safety at all.

Hazards from Additives

People vary enormously in their sensitivity to certain additives, so that something which will be safe for 9 people out of 10 can produce an acute reaction in the tenth. Whether it is foolish to ban something which seems to do most people no harm, or whether 1 in 10 people should not be put at risk by using a chemical which has no food value is a matter of debate.

Each consumer should be able to decide whether to take this risk or not. Current labelling means that most food additives have to be listed on most labels - but not all. The exceptions are additives used in manufacturing processes - for example, to stop food sticking to a mould - and those used in alcoholic drinks, vinegar, butter, milk, cream, cheese, chocolate and some confectionery. And that's an awful lot of food.

The Good Es

There is no need to be alarmed if you see the following Es on food labels. They are either harmless or positively good for you.

Number	Name
E101	Vitamin B2/riboflavin
101a	riboflavin/5'-phosphate
E140	chlorophyll
E141	chlorophyllins
E160a,c, e,f }	extracts of plant colourings

E170	calcium carbonate
E172	iron oxides & hydroxides
E260	acetic acid
E261	potassium acetate
E262	sodium hydrogen, acetate, sodium diacetate
E300	vitamin C & l-ascorbic acid
E301	sodium l-ascorbate
E302	calcium l-ascorbate
E304	6-0-palmintoyl-l-ascorbic acid
E306	vitamin E (natural tocopherols)
E307	alpha-tocopherol vitamin E (synthetic)
E308	gamma-tocopherol vitamin E (synthetic)
E309	delta-tocopherol vitamin E (synthetic)
E322	lecithin
E330	citric acid
E331	sodium citrates
E331a-c	other citrates
E332 } E333 }	potassium and calcium salts of citric acid
E334	tartaric acids
E335 } E336 } E337 }	various salts of tartaric acid
E339a-c	derivatives of phosphoric acid
E340a-c	as E339
350/1/2	derivatives of malic acid
353	metatartaric acid
355	adipic acid
375	nicotinic acid/niacin
E400	alginic acid
E401	sodium alginate
E406	agar
E410	carob gum
E415	corn sugar gum
E440a-b	pectin
518	magnesium sulphate
526	calcium hydroxide
540	calcium hydrogen phosphate
552	calcium silicate
553a	magnesium silicate
570	stearic acid
576	sodium gluconate
903	carnauba wax
920	l-cysteine hydrochloride
---	glycine
---	nitrogen

The Bad Es

Some people would say that any E that isn't a good E is a bad E. But some additives are only bad in high doses or to a small minority who are sensitive to them - like the young - while others may possibly affect many of us. These latter I term the bad Es, though maybe I should call them the very bad Es. The following are those to which quite large numbers of people are sensitive and which may carry a risk for the rest of us. Possible reactions include: hay fever, blurred vision, breathing problems, skin rashes, swollen blood vessels, vomiting, gastric trouble, hyperactivity, asthma, swelling, damage to an unborn child, possible cancer risk, sensitivity to light and blood pressure changes. Yet many of these additives are widely found in basic manufacturers foods, especially in those such as sweets, cakes and fast foods - which we are likely to give to children. And some are banned in other countries.

Number	Name
E102	Tartrazine
E104	quinoline
107	yellow G2
E110	sunset yellow FCF
E120	cochineal red
E122	carmoisine
E123	amaranth
E124	ponceau 4R
E127	erythrosine
128	red 2G
E131	patent blue V
E132	indigo carmine
E133	brilliant blue FCF
E150	caramel
E151	black PN
E153	carbon black
154	brown FK
155	brown HT
E210	benzoic acid
E211/2/ 3/4/5/6/ 7/8/9	various benzoates
E220	sulphur dioxide
E221/2/ 3/4/6/7	various sulphites
E230/1/2	various phenols
E236/7/8	formic acid variants
E239	benzene derivatives
E249 E250/1/2	various nitrites & nitrates
E310/11/12	various gallates
E320	butylated hydroxyamisole (BHA)
E321	butylated hydroxytoluene (BHT)
E407	carrageenan, seaweed extract
420/1	sorbitol/mannitol
430/1	various stearates
432/3/ 4/5/6	sorbitol derivatives
E450a-c	various phosphates
E466	carboxymethyl/cellulose sodium salt/CMC
493	sorbitol derivative Span 20
513	sulphuric acid
535	sodium ferrocyanide
536	potassium ferrocyanide
553(b)	talc
621	monosodium glutamate (MSG)
627	guanosine 5'-disodium phosphate
631	inosine 5'-disodium phosphate
635	sodium 5'-ribonucleotide
907	micro-crystalline wax
924	potassium bromate
925/6	chlorine & chlorine dioxide
---	aspartame
---	dichloromethane
---	dioctyl sodium sulphosuccinate
---	hydrogenated glucose syrup
---	isomalt
---	nitrous oxide
---	extract of quilaia
---	saccharin
---	xylitol

Hyperactivity, often coupled with asthma and/or eczema, is one of the main problems which occur when children react badly to additives. The Hyperactive Children's Support Group (see In Sickness) suggests that the parents of hyperactive children should avoid giving them synthetic colours (E100 - 180 are colours) and flavours, glutamates, nitrates, nitrites, BHA, BHT and benzoic acid. In addition to the list above, anyone with asthma or eczema may find it useful to contact the organizations in In Sickness for information on the additives which most aggravate those conditions.

Paradoxically, medicines do not have to declare the colourings used in them and some children's medicines use colourings which are among the bad Es. It may be worth querying the colouring agent with your pharmacist.

Additive Free Food
Many products are additive free, but most fresh foods have been sprayed with chemicals or grown on land fertilized by man-made fertilizers. If you want to know that food reaches you without the addition of any man-made chemicals at all you will have to buy organic produce. This is being sold more and more widely and even reaches the shelves of supermarkets like Safeway. However, organic is a fairly woolly term. So if you want to be sure of what you are getting, the food should meet some set standard such as that set by the Soil Association. Before produce can carry the Association's symbol, the land it was grown on must have been free from chemical fertilizers for 2 years or more, and chemical sprays must not have been used for 2 years. They must also pass inspections and spot-checks.

Protection Against Additives
It would be nice if we could totally avoid all potentially harmful additives. The truth is we can't. Even if we cut them out of our own shopping - which is well nigh impossible - we are bound to encounter them if we ever eat out. Happily, studies in animals have shown that a diet rich in vitamins and fibre helps to minimize the ill effects.

Understanding Food Labels
The usefulness of any label depends on whether you can decode the curious, if not misleading, language which is defined by law.

What's in a Name
Flavour: The word 'flavour' is code for a total lack of the natural ingredient which would provide that flavour. So the word flavour in 'Blackcurrant Flavour Dessert' shows it is a complete fake and hasn't even looked at a blackcurrant. The manufacturer does not have to say 'imitation flavour', or 'synthetic flavour'. Flavourings are not regulated as colourings are - even though some, such as caramel made by modern processes, may possibly be health hazards (see page 40).

Flavoured: The 'ed' at the end of flavoured in 'Blackcurrant Flavoured Dessert' tells you blackcurrants were involved in its making - but just how many is the manufacturer's secret. He doesn't have to say.

Blackcurrant dessert: Tells you real blackcurrants played a reasonable part in the process.

Natural flavourings: This may also be written as 'free from all artificial flavourings', which sounds good, but the food industry is allowed to define as 'natural' man-made flavourings whose chemistry mimics natural ones - though they are no more natural than a china monkey. But full details of flavourings do not have to be given.

Added vitamins: Most products which have added vitamins are made with ingredients which had their natural vitamins removed - or are made of such unnatural ingredients that they never had any in the first place. What's more, manufacturers don't always add as many vitamins and minerals as the food would contain naturally. So those which proclaim 'added vitamins' may not be the best for you.

Health food drink: It is perfectly legal to call a product a 'health food' or a 'health drink' without any real evidence that it is especially good for you.

Contents

The contents must be listed in order, starting with the ingredient which the food contains most of. But this can be misleading. If food contains three different types of sugar, for example, they will each be listed separately. So, even if the three put together would make sugar as the largest ingredient, this may not be clear from the label.

Watch out for water. More and more meat products are being doctored with chemicals which make them mop up water - bad from your point of view but money for old water for the manufacturer. Water only has to be listed in the ingredients if it is more than 5% of the total weight. Polyphosphates are the chemicals used.

Since July 1986 all pre-packed foods have had to list any food additives by serial number (E code if they have one) or their full name, and also have a descriptive term - such as 'stabilizer'.

Freshness

Many foods which keep fresh for less than 18 months must carry a datemark. There are two terms in use and if food bought within their given date has gone off you can expect a refund from the shop. This applies even if it was sold at a reduced price just before the sell-by date. If the shop refuses, contact your local Trading Standards Officer (listed in the telephone book under your local council), or write to the manufacturer giving all the facts and enclosing a sample - if this is possible.

The **Ministry of Agriculture** (see Organizations) has leaflets on additives and on food labelling.

The **National Eczema Society** (see In Sickness) mentions the makers of additive free food in its magazine.

The Vegetarian Society's Handbook lists suppliers of organic food.

Maurice Hanssen, *E for Additives*, Thorsons

Additives - Your Complete Survival Guide, Felicity Lawrence ed., Century

DAIRY PRODUCTS

Cheese

We don't have much choice about the age at which we eat our cheese, and according to Cooper's *Thesaurus* of 1565 we should be thankful, for he informed his readers that:

> *new, sweet, and fresh Cheese, nourisheth plentifully; middle-aged Cheese nourisheth strongly, but old and dry Cheese hurteth dangerously: for it stayeth siege* [constipation?], *stoppeth the Liver, engendereth choler, melancholy, and the stone, lieth long in the stomack undigested, procureth thirst, maketh a stinking breath, and a scurvy skin...*

Look at the surface of cheese before buying; the cut face should be moist and fresh. If a cheese looks dry or sweaty avoid it. Check Brie and Camembert carefully - especially in cold weather. If they have a white chalky slab in the centre, and runny layers top and bottom they are not worth buying. This is the sign that they have been over-chilled in transit; after that the cheese will never ripen evenly. If, however, there is a thin white line though the middle and a firm but creamy layer above and below you can expect it to ripen well at room temperature. But don't expect all soft cheeses to run. The more fatty they are, the less likely they are to run. So Brie labelled 62 per cent *matier gras* will keep its shape, while one in the 40 per cent range will ooze.

A letter to *The Times* once claimed that the writer had kept a piece of cheddar under a glass for 41 years, and found it to be still good 'but rather hard'. Curious but not to be recommended. The ideal place is a larder which keeps below 10°C (50°F). Failing that a refrigerator at 5°-10C (40°-50°F). It needs to be closely wrapped to prevent it losing moisture or taking up the smell of other food.

The **English Cheese Bureau**, P.O.Box 194A, Thames Ditton, Surrey KT7 0EE - has a list of farms which make cheese and welcome visitors. Visit cheese makers in the morning; the work is often finished by lunch.

Andronet, *Guide du Fromage*, Aidan Ellis

P. Rance, *The Great British Cheese Book*, Papermac

Cream and Milk

Anyone who has been lucky enough to taste milk straight from the cow is all too aware of the processing our pintas are subjected to. It may all be commendably healthy, but what exactly are we getting for our money? The table below shows you.

First, to explain how milk and cream are treated. The typical processes are these (though there are others):

- For **pasteurization** they are heated to 63°-71.7°C (145°-161°F) for not less than 15 seconds. This kills all the major bacteria.

- For **sterilization** they are homogenized, sealed and heated to 108°-130°C (226°-266°F) for at least 10 to 45 minutes; this destroys bacteria more thoroughly than pasteurization.

- Under **Ultra Heat Treatment** (UHT) they are taken to 132.2°-140°C (270°-284°F) for not less than 1 to 2 seconds. This is slightly more sterilized.

Those processes are to kill off bacteria. **Homogenization** is different - the liquid is forced through an extremely small hole to create uniform fat globules and make them distribute themselves evenly throughout the liquid.

Facts about Cream

	Calories per ¼ pt	Calcium mg per ¼ pt	Percentage fat	Treatment	Flavour
Clotted cream	693	54	55	Scalded to above pasteurization	
Double cream	657	73	48	Pasteurized	
Whipping/whipped cream	546	90	35	Pasteurized	
Sterilized cream	355	126	23	Homogenized and heat treated	Distinct smoky taste very
Sterilized half-cream	241	145	12	and may have additives.	unlike fresh cream.
Cream/single cream	288	133	18	Homogenized to stabilize	
Half-cream	241	145	12	Homogenized	

Whipping Cream

Cream can be whipped if its fat content is between 30 to 42 per cent, but whips best above 38 per cent. This means you can whip double cream, whipping cream and also equal amounts of single and double cream mixed together. Cream must be fridge cold when you whip it. If it is warm it rapidly goes grainy.

Whipping cream doubles its volume when whipped, but double cream is denser and only increases by 1½ times. To give it greater bulk, stir 1 to 1½ tablespoons of milk into 125 ml (¼ pt) of double cream before beating. If you add ½ teaspoon of lemon juice per 125 ml (¼ pt) cream it will whip faster.

Extra thick double and spooning cream are now sold, which have been thickened by homogenization, but heavily homogenized cream won't whip.

Facts about Milk

Top style	Calories per pt	Calcium mg per pt	Fat per pt	Character	Result
Gold	445	702	4.8	Rich tasting milk from Jersey and Guernsey cows. Pasteurized: see Silver top.	Food values scarcely changed
Silver	380	702	3.8	Pasteurized by heating to 71.7°C then rapid cooling.	Food value almost unchanged.
Red	380	702	3.8	Homogenized to break down fat globules, and pasteurized.	Food value scarcely changed but 'smoky' taste.
Metal style blue	380	702	3.8	Sterilized at 115° to 130°C.	Distinctly cooked taste. Slight vitamin reduction.
Red stripe	263-280	729	1.5-1.8	Semi-skimmed, pasteurized.	Slightly less vitamins A & D but calcium and other vitamins unchanged.
Blue check	195	761	0.1	Pasteurized, skimmed milk, not for young children or babies.	No vitamins A or D, but other vitamins and calcium retained.
UHT carton	380	702	3.8	Homogenized and heated to 132.2°C+.	Food value hardly changed, but slightly altered taste.
Calcia	227	783	2.35	Pasteurized.	Calcium enriched.
Vital	197	978	0.47	Pasteurized.	

Milk and cream contain vitamins A, D, B1, B12, B2, protein and fat. In addition to calcium, milk contains most other minerals, including about a third of our daily requirement of zinc.

Curd Cheese

To make curd cheese: Heat 1 pt of milk to 38°C (120°F). Remove from the heat and add the juice of 1 lemon *or* 1 tsp of rennet (as for junket). Leave for 15 minutes (if lemon) or 20 minutes (if rennet). Transfer the curds to a colander lined with a large square of muslin. Tie the corners of the muslin together diagonally and hang it to drip for 1 hour. Turn out, season to taste and eat.

Yoghurt

Yoghurt can be made with no more equipment than a thermos flask, but if you prefer it set, use a yoghurt maker.

1 Heat 1 pt of milk to 43°C (110°F) or bring it to the boil and cool it to that temperature. (At this temperature your finger should be able to stay in it comfortably for at least 10 seconds.)

2 Stir in 1 level tablespoon of any plain yoghurt.

3 Pour into a pre-warmed vacuum flask, close and leave for 7 hours.

4 Turn it into a basin and cool by standing the basin in cold water and stirring the yoghurt.

5 Refrigerate for 4 hours to let it thicken slightly more.

At stage (2) you can make the yoghurt richer and thicker by adding 50g (1¾ oz) of dried skimmed milk powder or whole milk powder. You can make yoghurt with any type of milk, including UHT, and even with diluted evaporated milk or with evaporated milk instead of part of the milk.

Be warned: Any of the following can make yoghurt go wrong.

- adding extra yoghurt to start it
- disturbing it before the time is up
- leaving it in the warm for longer than recommended.

But yoghurt is temperamental; it can sometimes fail for no obvious reason. Don't let that put you off. Use scrupulous hygiene in making it. Sterilize the flask with Milton, the solution for sterilizing babies' bottles.

National Dairy Council, 5 John Prince's Street, London W1M 0AP Tel: 01 499 7822 - has leaflets.

EGGS

The size of egg you use in a recipe really only matters in mixtures like cakes and soufflés where the right balance of ingredients is important. The British Egg Information Service tells me that when a recipe says 'take one egg' it means a size 3 egg.

Brown v White

I'm sorry to have to tell you, but the idea that brown eggs are better for you is pure fantasy. The only difference between them is the type of chicken which lays them or the type of food they have been given - the difference in diet makes no difference to the food values.

Large	◯	SIZE 1	**70 g or more**	**Grade A eggs are perfect.**
	◯	SIZE 2	**65–69 g**	
Standard	◯	SIZE 3	**60–64 g**	**Grade B eggs may have to be cleaned or have a crack, or oversized air cell.**
	◯	SIZE 4	**55–59 g**	
Medium	◯	SIZE 5	**50–54 g**	**Grade C eggs cannot be sold to the public, only as broken eggs to the trade.**
	◯	SIZE 6	**45–49 g**	
Small	◯	SIZE 7	**under 45 g**	

Eggs Other than Chickens'

Ducks are messy creatures and the shell on a duck egg forms late. So there is a risk of duck eggs being contaminated with salmonella bacteria. For safety, duck eggs should be well cooked. So should those of any other bird whose laying conditions may be uncertain - gulls' eggs, for example, need 15 minutes despite their diminutive size.

Testing for Freshness

If you have put eggs into the egg compartments and aren't sure which are the freshest there is a simple test. Put an egg in a jug with about 10 cm (4 in) of water and watch how it behaves. If it lies on the bottom it is fresh. If one end tilts up it is beginning to age. If it floats to the top it is either bad or only fit for omelettes in which its slackness will not be noticed.

If you crack an egg its freshness is easily judged. A very fresh egg has a ring of *firm bulgy* white around the yolk. The older the egg is, the wider and thinner the white spreads, and the slacker the casing of the yolk. Old slack eggs are almost impossible to whip - even when they are perfectly good to eat - and will spread everywhere if you try to poach them. Very fresh and very old eggs peel badly when boiled.

Baked Eggs

The most foolproof method of cooking eggs looks the most sophisticated: it's baking. Just put the egg in a buttered cocotte dish and bake on a high shelf in a preheated oven for 15 minutes at gas no 5 or (190°C) 375°F.

Beating (or Whipping) Eggs

Beating eggs correctly is the secret of so many delicious dishes that it is well worth mastering. And it isn't difficult. Start with a reasonably fresh egg; slack watery ones can be almost impossible to beat. If possible have the egg at room temperature: the proteins which stabilize the foam work best when not chilled.

Egg whites won't beat properly if there is any grease present. To an egg white, a drop of yolk is grease and can reduce the volume of the foam by two-thirds. Egg white also objects to traces of fat on the bowl, and beats less well in plastic bowls (or with plastic beaters), since plastic is oil-based.

If a white is chilled adding just under a tablespoon of warm (not hot) water is useful in increasing the volume. You can also increase the volume by standing the bowl over gently simmering water as you beat - as Italians do for making zabaglione (but don't overdo the heat). Traditionally, chefs have always used a copper bowl for this job and science has just proved they were right: copper helps egg whites to foam.

The great thing is to know when to stop. Egg white is like a rubber band: you can pull it so far, but go that bit further and it snaps. And when an egg white snaps it won't hold air. If a recipe says 'beat the whites until very stiff' it usually means until the bowl can be turned upside down without the froth falling out. 'Stiff peaks' means the point of a peak sticks straight up; 'soft peaks' means that the tops just turn over.

Once the eggs begin to stiffen keep stopping to test the stiffness of the peaks at regular intervals - lest you overbeat. Once they are perfect use them immediately: eggs go flat again quite quickly after beating and, once flattened, it is much harder to get them to stand well again.

★ If you are short, put the bowl in the sink, to make it lower.

Boiling Eggs
Curiously, the secret of good boiled eggs is not to boil them. Boiling makes the albumen in egg go rubbery, so they should be simmered. A medium-sized, fresh shop egg, straight from the fridge, put into boiling water for 4½ minutes will have a white which is just set and a runny yolk. In 6 to 6½ minutes it will reach the stage the French call *oeufs mollets*, when the white is firm enough for you to peel the egg, but the yolk is still runny in the middle. Large or very new eggs will need longer.

For hard-boiled eggs at their best put them into boiling water, simmer for 5 minutes, remove from the heat, and leave them in the water to cool. But if speed is needed simmer them for 10 minutes.

★ Pierce the round end of each egg with a drawing pin before boiling it, so that the air can escape, as it heats and expands, without breaking the egg.
★ To shell hard-boiled eggs easily hold them under a cold tap, and let the water run under the shell.
★ Hard boiled eggs cut most easily with a wet knife.
★ Only a hard-boiled egg can spin in an even circle, others have a lolloping motion.
★ It is easier to grate a hard-boiled egg for sandwiches than to chop it.

Omelettes
For a good omelette eggs should be lightly beaten with pepper and salt and a dessertspoonful of water for each egg. Over-beating makes them rubbery. It is also best to cook omelettes in ½ tbsp oil and ½ tbsp of butter - so you get the taste of butter but it won't burn easily.

Poaching Eggs
The rules for poaching eggs successfully are very easy.
● Have a fresh egg broken into a cup.
● Have a dash of vinegar in the boiling water (it helps the egg solidify).
● Stir the water into a whirlpool and slide the egg into the centre.
● Turn the heat down and simmer *very* gently.
● Drain briefly on kitchen roll.

Scrambled Eggs
There are five secrets to good scrambled eggs: use only a dessertspoonful of milk per egg; beat only lightly; use lots of butter; stir all the time; and stop cooking the egg before it is how you like it - it always goes on cooking as you serve it.

Separating Yolks from Whites
Tap the centre of the egg firmly on the edge of a pan. Cup it between eight finger-tips and - with the bowl underneath - gently insert both thumb nails into the crack and pull *slightly*. As the white trickles into the bowl through the crack, tilt the egg on end and pull off the top. The yolk can now be juggled between the two halves while letting the white trickle out. For safety crack your eggs into an empty bowl and transfer each one to whatever you will cook them in. Then an accident won't ruin them all.

★ If you can't manage that crack it on to a plate, cover the yolk with a glass, allowing a tiny gap, and tip the plate up.
★ Separated whites or yolks will keep several days in a refrigerator. Simply cover them closely, or drop a little water on unbroken yolks to stop them drying up.

The British Egg Information Service Ltd, Bury House, 126-8 Cromwell Road, London SW7 4ET Tel: 01 370 7411

FISH AND SHELLFISH

There is something special about picking at the succulent white flesh of a fresh crab in a summer garden. But since the early 1970s the trend has been away from fresh shellfish and towards frozen. So much so that, sadly, the humble winkle is now the only shellfish to escape the freezer.

Most taste very much better fresh. So, the chart on page 46 shows when you ought to be able to obtain fresh ones, though price and availability are greatly influenced by the weather - something you can buy in May one year may not arrive until August in another.

Usually, the best months to buy fish are when summer turns to autumn, around September/October, when they are fat and plentiful from the summer warmth. But the price per pound may be lowest earlier on, when the numbers are ample but the proportion of flesh to bone on any fish is less good. Many fish are unobtainable from March to May.

Buying Wet Fish
Fish is not a food to buy passively, by just asking for it. More than any other fresh food, it needs to be carefully looked at and checked. Most fish are not bred as meat is, so they are far more variable. You must pick

and choose to get the best - and the freshest.

With fish freshness is everything. Get close to them and sniff - fresh fish smell of nothing but crisp saltiness (and fresh water fish are odourless). Look at the eyes, and get the fishmonger to turn the fish over and open its gills. The eyes should be bright and domed, the skin should have a smooth sheen to it, and inside the gills should be a rich pinky-red. After a couple of days out of the water the eyes begin to go dull and hollow, the inside of the gills goes browner and the skin also loses its sheen and becomes slimy. As one of the best fish buyers in Billingsgate fish market summed it up, 'You buy by the eye. There's fish what looks dead and there's fish what looks alive.'

★ If you find yourself looking for white fish which will make a basic dish like fish pie, take a look at hake; it's an undervalued fish with a good flavour and big bones, it can be used in a lot of dishes which call for the more expensive cod.

Buying Shellfish

Molluscs (mussels, clams and so on) must be alive - which means they are either waving their little valves at you, as they do in the markets of Italy (where even the sea life waves its arms about), or they should be keeping the stiff upper lip which distinguishes the British mollusc and be tightly shut - if you tap them, they should clamp themselves too tight to open.

Shellfish, such as crab, should be odourless, and a crab will often have frothy, brownish-white bits still clinging to the shell from the cooking - though some fishmongers brush these off, because the public dislikes them. A freshly cooked lobster should have a certain spring to its tail, so uncurl it. If it has lost its elasticity it is over a day old.

When buying a crab or lobster always pick it up and feel the weight for the size. Good ones feel heavy for their size, light ones may have starved too long as they waited to be sold, or may have just shed their shells and acquired larger ones. On crabs, look at the width of the tail (which is tucked under the shell); females have broader tails, and are less good value as the claws are also smaller.

Cleaning Fish

Fish are much easier and more pleasant to gut than animals, and even a slightly squeamish cook should be able to manage it. But first have a very sharp knife. Insert the point of the knife in the hole at the base of the belly near the tail. Then cut it open, like slitting an envelope - and with as much care not to slit the contents. Tip the insides out, and use a spoon to scrape away any that remain, including any blood that clings inside, as it will spoil the fish if left in. Rinse the fish well inside and out and remove the head, unless it is needed. Then slide your knife point along the lie of the bones holding the fins in place, cut the flesh away to either side. Tug the fins off firmly, pulling towards the head, and their 'root' bones should come away too.

Seasons for Fish and Shellfish

r - rare and likely to be expensive
* - available
** - a plentiful time when prices may drop
W - wild salmon are in the shops

Shellfish and Molluscs	J	F	M	A	M	J	J	A	S	O	N	D
Clams	*	*	*	*					*	*	*	*
Cockles	*	*	*	*	**	**	*	*	*	*	*	*
Crab (whole)				*	**	**	**	*	*			
Crawfish						r	r	r	r	r	r	
Crayfish							*	*	*	*	*	*
Dublin Bay prawns	*	*	*	*	*	*	*	*	**	**	**	*
Lobster	*	*	*	*	*	**	**	**	*	*	*	*
Mussels	**	*	*				r	r	r	*	**	**	**
Oysters (native)	**	*	*	*					**	**	**	**
Oysters (Pacific)	*	*	*	*	*	*	*	*	*	*	*	*
Prawns	*	*	*	*	*	**	**	**	**	*	*	*
Scallops	r	r	*	**	**	*	*	*	*	*	r	r
Shrimp	*	*	*	*	*	**	**	**	*	*	*	*
Whelks	*	*	*	*	*	*	*	*	*	**	**	**
Winkles	*	*	*	*	*				*	*	*	*
Octopus	*	*	*	*	*	*	*	*	*	*	*	*
Squid (calamari)						*	*	*	*	*	**	

White Fish - flat	J	F	M	A	M	J	J	A	S	O	N	D
Brill	*	*				*	*	*	*	*	*	*
Dab	*	*	*	*	*				*	*	*	*
Flounder			*	*	*		*	*	*	*	*	
Halibut	*	*	*				*	*	*	*	*	
Megrim	*	*	*				*	*	*	*	*	*
Monkfish (anglerfish)	*	*	*	*	*			*	*	*	*	*
Plaice	*	*				*	*	*	*	*	*	
Skate	*	*				*	*	*	*	*	*	
Sole - Dover	*	*				*	*	*	*	*	*	
Sole - lemon	*	*	*			*	*	*	*	*	*	
Turbot	*	*			*	*	*	*	*	*	*	
Witch	*	*				*	*	*	*	*	*	

White Fish - round	J	F	M	A	M	J	J	A	S	O	N	D
Bass	*	*	*					*	*	*	*	*
Cod	*	*				*	*	*	*	*	*	
Coley	*	*					*	*	*	*	*	
Conger eel			*	*	*	*	*	*	*	*		
Haddock	*	*				*	*	*	*	*	*	
Hake	*	*	*				*	*	*	*	*	*
Huss	*	*	*	*	*			*	*	*	*	*
John Dory	*	*	*	*	*			*	*	*	*	
Ling	*	*	*	*	*	*			*	*	*	
Mullet - grey	*	*							*	*	*	
Mullet - red					*	*	*	*	*			
Pollack					*	*	*	*	*			
Sea Bream	*	*				*	*	*	*			
Whiting	*	*					*	*	*	*	*	

Oily Fish	J	F	M	A	M	J	J	A	S	O	N	D
Herring						*	*	*	*	*	*	*
Mackerel	*	*	*			*	*	*	*	*	*	*
Salmon	*	*	*	*	*W	*W	**W	**W	**W	*	*	*
Sprat	*	*	*							*	*	*

Cooking Fish

Poached or steamed fish used to be invalid food - and fish got a bad name as a result - but poaching is the basic method of cooking fish and the preliminary to a lot of excellent dishes. A typical poaching liquid (court bouillon) would be 2 l (4 pt) of water with 12 peppercorns, ¼ pt of wine or cider vinegar, 2 onions and 2 carrots. Boil this court bouillon up for an hour and strain it.

You don't need a fish kettle to poach fish. Simply take a large piece of muslin - or any perfectly clean white cotton fabric. (If it is old linen, boil it several times, throwing the water away each time, to get rid of any left-over soap.) Place the fish on your fabric and tie the ends together above the head and the tail. (To stop the fish buckling in the middle as you lift it out, place a couple of long metal skewers or long bamboo chopsticks between the fish and the cloth, if you have them.)

Bring the liquid just to simmering point, then lower the fish into the pan. It is important that the water never boils. High temperatures can spoil the texture of fish and boiling may break up the flesh. When the fish is cooked you just lift the knots with a fork and (wearing thick rubber gloves) take hold of as much of the edges of the fabric as you can, so the fish is supported along its whole length as you lift it out, on its little sling.

Time it from the moment the water returns to simmering point - at which it should barely tremble. Fish is cooked when the flesh turns white (in the case of white fish), opaque and firm.

Fillets	6-12 mins depending on thickness
Steaks	10-20 mins depending on thickness
Whole small fish	4-6 mins a pound
Large whole fish	3½ - 5 mins a pound

Fish can also be cooked in the poaching liquid in the oven at gas no 4 or 180°C (350°F). The times are much the same.

> When cooking large fish you can't simply multiply the number of minutes per pound by the weight of the fish, and say 5 minutes per pound means a 10-pound fish takes 50 minutes. The shape of a fish and the nature of its flesh mean that *the larger the fish, the less time it needs per pound.* A 10-pound fish takes 30 minutes not 50 minutes.

Baking Fish in Foil

Baking in foil is one of the best ways of cooking fish, as all its delicate flavour is parcelled up. It also means that your pans don't limit the size of fish you can cook. Simply oil the foil to stop it sticking to the skin, place the fish on it - with any delicious flavourings and seasonings you wish - and make a tightly closed parcel of it. How long it will take to cook depends on the thickness of the fish as well as the total weight. But on average you need about 8 minutes per 500 g (1 lb) at gas no 4 or 180°C (350°F), plus 5 to 10 minutes. But bear in mind the rule on cooking large fish given above.

For serving cold it is often best to let it cool in its wrapping.

Grilling Fish

The smell of fish tends to cling to a grill; a sheet of foil over the grid - with the edges turned up to stop the juices running off - prevents that. For grilling, fish should be de-scaled (below) and dried well, and thick skin should be slashed in places. Flat fish need 2 to 6 minutes a side; round fish and steaks take 4 to 7 minutes a side. But steaks tend to become dry and are much better baked in foil.

De-scaling a Fish

Fish can have the scales removed if they are large and would feel unpleasant in the mouth in a particular dish in which the skin is eaten. Just hold the fish firmly by the tail (dipping your fingers in salt will give you a better grip) and run the back of a knife firmly up the fish *from tail to head* until the scales come off. Then rinse well and dry.

Keeping Fish and Shellfish

Spanking fresh, fish is firm and delicious; as time passes the flavour fades and the flesh gradually becomes soggy and woolly. So, though fish will usually keep for 2 days in a refrigerator without going bad, it may be little pleasure to eat at the end of that time. The only exceptions are plaice, skate and lemon sole which develop a better flavour by their third day out of the sea - but remember they may have had 3 days out before you buy them. All fish keep best on an open plate in the refrigerator.

If you have to keep white fish a day longer than you should, sprinkle salt all over it, but rinse this off before cooking. If fish is a touch older than it should be, but still safe to eat, it can be redeemed by firmly rinsing any slime off the skin under a cold tap and then wiping with equal parts vinegar and water - then cook it at once. But this should only be done if fish is *just beginning* to age - and never with any shellfish.

Shellfish are even more fragile than other fish. Mussels, clams and similar molluscs should be eaten the day you buy them. Prawns, lobsters and other crustaceans should be eaten in 1 to 2 days. But you can never tell how fresh they are when you buy them. So if they even begin to smell other than sweet and fresh throw them away.

It is no coincidence that the fish which are smoked are the oily ones which generally keep least well when fresh. Even when smoked they should be eaten within 3 days, and though they will freeze, they need to be eaten quickly as they rapidly go rancid. Rancid smoked salmon is vile beyond belief and a dreadful waste.

Skinning and Filleting Fish

Skinning and Filleting Whole Flat Fish

Sole is sometimes half skinned, removing only the dark side. So start there. For Dover sole cut a crosswise slit in the skin near the tail. Wiggle your fingers inside to loosen the skin from the flesh as much as possible. Then hold it with a cloth or dip both thumbs and forefingers in salt. Hold the tail firmly with one hand and rip the skin from tail to head with the other. Do the same on the other side. For plaice and lemon sole you reverse this and start at the head end and peel the skin off diagonally downwards, but you need to both cut and pull or flesh may come off with the skin.

Flat fish make four fillets. Lie the fish flat and cut through the flesh down the length of the spine. Hold it flat and cut the flesh carefully off the bones, working from the slit out to the edge, until one fillet is free. Repeat for the other three fillets. If you need to skin fillets, proceed as for skinning round fish - below.

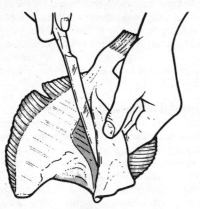

Skinning and Filleting Round Fish
With round fish the jobs are done in reverse order, and you get two fillets per fish. Slice through the skin down the back from head to tail. Starting at the head end slide the blade close to the bones and cut the flesh carefully from them, working down to the tail. Free the fillet from the head and the tail. Repeat on the other side.

There are two schools of thought on skinning fillets; one says you lay the fish skin-side down, the other advocates skin-side up. Try it both ways and see which feels right for you. Either way the tail is towards you. I favour skin-side down, so place the skin-side on a board. With a very sharp knife cut the flesh from the skin at the tail end. Then hold the skin firmly between salted fingers and angle the blade of the knife into the gap between skin and flesh and half cut, half push the flesh from the skin, being very careful not to cut through thin skins like haddock.

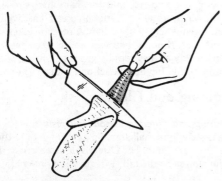

Filleting Herrings
Slice through the flesh near the tail and head, at each side. Run your thumb firmly all along the spine, to loosen it from the flesh, with as many bones as possible.

Skinning eel
Raw eel is the very devil to skin. If you can possibly get it done for you, do so. If you have to do it, cut the skin right round the neck, and make a slit down the whole length. Hang it on a butcher's hook (if you have one) or get someone to hold the head *very* firmly; hold the edge of the skin with a cloth and yank the skin sharply off with all your might.

Fish with Special Needs

Crabs and Lobsters
Most crabs and lobsters are sold ready boiled, but if you acquire a live one it should be alive until the moment of cooking. It will live out of water for about 24 hours if it is kept moist. Cover it completely in a damp cloth or - better still - place it on damp sawdust and sprinkle damp sawdust all over without pressing it down. Putting ice with these creatures damps down their nervous system and makes them sluggish and easier to handle. But once a crab grabs you it will not let go unless you sever its limb. A medium-sized crab serves 2-3, a lobster 2.

Cooking Crabs and Lobsters
There is no easy answer to which cooking method is least cruel. None of these creatures has a brain as we have. A crab has two nervous centres and a lobster has thirteen. So far there is no conclusive research to show how much they feel hurt, or whether one method is more or less hurtful than another: even the RSPCA doesn't know. The Universities Federation for Animal Welfare has looked into the matter, and recommends stabbing both a crab's nervous centres - as illustrated - just before cooking. However, they concede that not everyone can bring themselves to do that and there is no way of getting at the thirteen nerve centres of a lobster. In this case they say that plunging the lobster into boiling liquid, and holding it under, seems to be the least cruel.

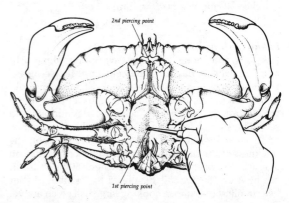

2nd piercing point

1st piercing point

To stab a crab lie it flat on its back, and thrust a strong skewer straight down into the hole which lies near the centre of the body. Stab it in and out, at slightly different angles, until the legs relax and stop moving. Next, pierce the other nerve centre by inserting the skewer below the mouth parts, as illustrated.

For once, kindness chimes with gastronomy, for chefs say that plunging the creatures into court bouillon also produces the best flavour. So plunge it in, turn down the heat, and cook it gently for 10-15 minutes per 450g (1lb). You may need to reduce the number of minutes per pound as you do in fish. One expert recommends 8 minutes a pound after the first pound.

Once cooked, both crabs and lobsters should be removed from the liquid and put in a cool place to chill, but they should not be icy cold on serving, as this kills their flavour.

Preparing a Cooked Crab

To open a crab, anyone who is not a judo black belt should put on an oven mit. Stand the crab on its flatter edge and give a swift karate chop, with the mittened hand, on the upper edge. This breaks the upper part from the lower. You can then lift the front and open it up like a book. Clinging round the body there are grey fern-like structures called 'dead men's fingers' which should all be discarded - but they are nothing to be frightened of, despite the name. Also remove the tiny grey bag of the stomach, just behind the mouth. All the rest can be eaten. Serve it with good brown bread, mayonnaise, lemon wedges and a crisp salad. Few meals are nicer than one spent slowly picking the succulent flesh from a good crab, and savouring it morsel by morsel, as you can never do when it is dressed.

The small legs of a crab are best broken with nutcrackers; the claws need to be put in a plastic bag and hit gently with a hammer. Without the bag the pieces tend to ricochet about the room.

If you want to dress a crab, simply scoop the brown part out of the upper part of the shell and mash it with seasoning. Then pick every morsel of white from the body and legs - there is a great deal in the body if you cut it open. Rinse and dry the shell, and break off any surplus rim. Then combine both types of meat elegantly in the half shell and garnish it.

Preparing a Cooked Lobster

Split the lobster down its length, for serving, and remove the bag in the head and the intestine - which is a thin charcoal-grey line running the length of the tail. The greenish substance near the top is the liver and perfectly edible. Once cleaned, lobster can be served plain or briefly reheated with a sauce, but brevity is important or it becomes rubbery.

Crawfish (langouste) and Crayfish (écrevisse)

The situation on crayfish and crawfish is confusing. In Britain a crayfish is a fresh-water lobster, complete with claws. A crawfish is a clawless lobster which lives in the sea. However, in some other parts of the world they call the fresh-water ones 'crawfish', and the salt-water ones 'rock lobster'.

Crayfish are unusual among crustaceans in needing to be thoroughly washed and gutted before cooking. To gut them you twist the central section of the tail and pull, and the long tube of intestine should come away. It runs down the middle of the underside of the tail, and needs to be cut out if it doesn't come away as it can make the fish bitter. Crayfish take 10 to 15 minutes per pound to cook in court bouillon as for lobster (see above).

Crawfish is cooked exactly like lobster, except that the shell is opened up on the underside, so the meat can be removed, sliced and put back in the trough created by the back.

Eel

Smoked eel is served skinned and filleted like smoked trout.

Haddock

The best smoked haddock is pale creamy Finnan haddock, which should be plump and moist. There are also delicious little Arbroath smokies which are younger haddock heavily smoked to an almost brown tone. The worst haddock is the bright-yellow-dyed variety, and watch out for fish which looks like haddock but isn't: 'smoked fillets' may be cod or haddock, and 'golden cutlets' may be whiting.

Smoked haddock can be over-salty. To cure this either bake it in water with a tablespoon of vinegar per pint (for inferior haddock), or (for good haddock) cook it in milk.

Herrings by Other Names

Bloaters are herrings which have been left whole, cured and smoked, with their guts in to give them a gamey flavour. Remove the guts before grilling. Like smoked mackerel, they keep badly.

Kippers are herrings which have been gutted, salted and cold smoked. The best kippers are undyed and the flesh is a soft creamy colour from natural smoking. These taste infinitely superior to the rest, which have been dyed a very nasty shade of yellow. Look for a plump oiliness to the flesh and a good smoky smell. If they are very salty poach them in milk, though they are usually grilled and only take 4 to 5 minutes to cook.

The most labour-saving and least smelly way to cook kippers is the traditional method of jugging. Cut off the heads and tuck them, on end, into a tall jug. Pour in boiling water right to the top and leave them for 6 to 7 minutes. Remove them and pat them dry before serving.

Buckling are herrings which have been hot smoked and, to my mind, are far more delicate and delicious than any other smoked herring. They are eaten cold, with sour cream and dill pickles, either whole or skinned and filleted - which is very easy to do. They also make a very good pâté.

Sprats These are smoked baby relatives of herrings.

Mussels, Clams and Cockles

In Portugal you can see men standing by the hour up to their knees in the sea patiently pumping a flat-bottomed cockle net rhythmically to and fro in the sand to acquire these elusive molluscs. In Britain, though cockle gathering used to be much practised on certain parts of the coast, such diligence in search of food is a lost art, and the cry of 'cockles and mussels alive, alive 'o' has long since ceased to echo in London's streets. Fortunately, mussels and clams have not yet vanished from the scene. They must be absolutely fresh when you buy them. Then you can clean them and plump them up, if you wish, by putting them in water for a day *or* a night (not longer) with 2 cupfuls of porridge oats to each gallon of water.

To prepare them for cooking you rinse them well, swirling them around in several changes of water until no sand comes out. Then beard them. This is just a matter of scrubbing them clean, and pulling off any straggly bits visible on the outside of the shell. You may have to scrape the shell with a tough little knife to clean them, if washing and pulling aren't enough. As you do this check them over. It is only safe to cook and eat them if they are alive until you cook them. So discard any which:

● have cracked or chipped shells
● are open and fail to close in a minute or two after being tapped with the knife
● are closed and will let you easily open them with your fingers
● are unusually heavy - they may be full of sand, which will ruin your meal.

Cook them within the hour, or you will have to check for dead ones all over again. You need only heat them with a cup of white wine, shaking the pan with the lid on over fierce heat for about 5 minutes, until they open. But you can cook them with chopped onion and parsley, and add cream to the sauce if you wish.

> All shellfish of this type are filter feeders, which means that if they are in water contaminated by sewage or chemicals the contaminants will stay in their bodies. It is therefore unwise to gather mussels yourself unless it is in an area where there is no possible risk of contamination.

Oysters

Don't worry about there being an R in the month before you eat an oyster. The prohibition wasn't because it was bad for *you*, but because it was bad for the oysters. There are two types of oyster. The native ones spawn in British waters and may not be taken during the summer months when they are spawning. The smaller Pacific oysters are farmed in British waters but, though they will grow here, they wisely deem our chilly waters too spartan for their offspring and refuse to breed. So they have no closed season and can be bought all year.

Prawns and Shrimps

In Britain shrimps are often called prawns. To explain the difference: Dublin Bay prawns (also known as Scampi or Norwegian lobster) have a fairly tough shell and a pair of claws, like miniature lobster claws. Shrimps are thinner shelled, have no claws and come in three sizes. There are the tiny brown shrimps, which are so delicious with brown bread and butter, the slightly larger pink shrimp and the fleshy deep water shrimp, which is most often called a prawn.

If you are tempted to go prawning take a big fabric bag in which you can keep the prawns with plenty of seaweed: they will die in plastic from lack of air. Prawns have to be kept moist or they die. A dead or dying prawn is no joking matter because chemical changes take place in a slowly dying prawn which make it poisonous.

Cook your prawns as soon as you get them home. But first throw away any that don't look lively, or are beginning to look cloudy and pale pink - these are dead or dying. Live prawns are almost translucent. Have ready a pan of well-salted rapidly boiling water, with a lid, and prepare to put the lid on. Throw in the prawns and cover instantly - or they may jump out. Let the water return to the boil. When it has boiled for about 30 seconds and all the prawns have risen to the top, and are pink, remove the pan from the fire, drain the prawns and let them cool. Sprinkle them with salt to improve their looks and taste. This brief cooking should produce the best prawns you have ever eaten.

The timing above is for prawns which are about 8 to 10 cm (3 to 4 in) long and about the size of a finger or thumb. Shrimps are cooked in the same way, but will be ready even sooner.

Recipes often fail to specify whether they mean raw or cooked prawns or shrimps. The difference is important; their flesh goes rubbery and tasteless with overcooking. If any recipe suggests cooking prawns, as opposed to warming them through, you can assume they are meant to be raw. So you may need to adapt the recipe and just throw in cooked ones to warm near the end. It won't taste as good as using raw ones, but it is better than eating rubber.

Salmon

If you intend to cut a salmon into steaks, first arm yourself with a very sharp knife and a good knife sharpener. Nothing blunts a knife like fish skin and it is essential to keep the blade perfectly sharp or you will be pressing at the flesh and making it pulpy.

Nothing short of a guillotine will cut through the bones in a salmon's back, so the thickness of your slices is set by the length of the backbones. If necessary, feel with a sterilized hat pin to gauge the length of the bones. They are almost the same length from head to tail so, once you have the measure of them, it's no trouble at all.

Slicing a side of smoked salmon is a much slower job than it might seem. Give yourself plenty of time; it is not a job to leave until just before guests arrive. First, feel over the surface and meticulously remove every fine bone with tweezers. For elegance if the salmon has a seam of dark meat down the centre it is removed with a V-shaped cut before you start slicing. It is perfectly good to eat - though stronger and oilier in flavour than the rest of the flesh. Then take a thin-bladed, *very* sharp knife and start slicing towards the tail, cutting along the surface and making each slice as thin as paper. But don't worry if you can't match a master chef: it will taste no worse.

Scallops

A scallop is one shellfish which doesn't have to be alive until you cook it. Even so they are freshest and best if they are opened as you buy them and haven't sat around ready opened. If you buy them closed, slip a knife blade through any cranny between the two shells and run it round the edge. Only then try to prise the shell open. Slice the flesh carefully from the shell. Keep the nice circular eye of flesh, and the half crescent of orange and beige coral and discard all the thin slithery bits. Rinse the shell and the scallop briefly under a tap and it is ready to cook. If you wish you can also use the point of a knife to slit open the dark vein of intestine that runs through the coral and rinse it clean.

In a pan they need only the briefest of cooking (3 to 5 minutes at low to moderate heat) and the simplest of presentation to bring out their delicate flavour. Scallops are cooked the moment the flesh becomes white and firm, and they should be served immediately. Overcooking or waiting spoils their flavour and texture. Bake them gently in a fairly low oven on their curved shells (fishmongers will give these to you if you ask) with a rub of butter, milk (or cream), seasoning and a scrap of parsley and garlic. No fuss, no washing up, and perfection.

Skate

The wings are the only edible part of skate, and their skin is covered in an almost gluey substance which must be scrubbed off with plenty of cold water. Skate is then poached in court boullion (page 47) and skinned before serving.

Squid

To prepare a squid, cut open the body sac and remove the transparent 'bone' and any slithery bits - leaving only the flesh. Also peel off any loose skin from the outside. It is then usually cut in rings or slices. It can be battered and deep fried as they do in Spain and Greece, or cooked in white wine and tomatoes as a sauce for pasta.

Trout

Trout needs no attention - just grilling or frying - and can be wrapped in cleaned leek leaves to keep it moist during cooking.

Smoked Trout

Smoked trout is often served lamentably dry and fishmongers sometimes suggest this is in the nature of smoked trout. It isn't. It should be beautifully plump and moist. Serve it as it is, or filleted, with brown bread and a good horseradish sauce.

British Trout Association, PO Box 189, London SW6 5LN Tel: 01 385 1158
J Muus and Preben Dahlstrom, *Collins Guide to Seafishes of Britain and North Western Europe,* Collins
Collins Guide to Freshwater Fishes of Britain and Europe by the same authors

FOOD HYGIENE

From some television advertisements you'd think germs behaved like some demon army, scurrying everywhere and leaping at us and our families from all directions, hell-bent on spreading death and disease. They don't. Germs are lazy things and usually let us do their dirty work for them.

Of course, they can be carried on droplets in the air - a sneeze sprays them for a truly astonishing distance. But most germs don't walk if they can ride, so they let us kindly carry them to where they'd like to be. And most of us all too often do so.

The Bacteria in Food Poisoning

Whatever may be said to the contrary, most diarrhoea is caused by bacteria. Of course a little bit of dirt never did anyone any harm; but the important word is - *little*: a small contamination with bacteria doesn't stay small. In the right conditions food poisoning bacteria divide to produce double their number every 20 to 30 minutes. So 1 cell becomes 2 million in 7 hours, and 7,000 million in 12 hours - and some can multiply much faster. One cell would do you no harm - but a few million can. Thousands of people in Britain go down with food poisoning every year. Most get over it, but it can kill - especially the young and the old.

Food poisoning is like burglary - it needs opportunity and it needs time. The bacteria are there, in small numbers, in the environment most of the time - up our noses, in excreta, in our pets, and particularly in the raw meat we buy. To cause poisoning they need both food to multiply on and enough time, at the right temperature, to do so. Bacteria multiply well on: meat, poultry, fish, shellfish, milk products, eggs, rice, anything made with any of these.

Not Giving Bacteria an Opportunity

The rules for preventing bacteria getting on to the food are very simple:

1 Hands should be washed before handling food if you have been:
- using the lavatory
- touching sites of infection, like spots, cuts etc
- using a handkerchief (or nose picking)
- touching pets
- handling other raw meat or fish
- doing dirty cleaning jobs which get bacteria on to the hands.

2 Don't let raw meat or fish:
- drip on to other food in the refrigerator
- touch other food in the refrigerator

- touch kitchen equipment (knives, boards etc) later used for cooked foods, without washing them in between.

3 Prevent flies, cockroaches or other pests and even pets contaminating food - by keeping it covered.

Not Giving Bacteria Time

However clean we are, some food will always come into our homes with food poisoning bacteria on it. Salmonella, in particular, are in many animal foodstuffs, and production line gutting means that they are often transferred out of the guts on to the flesh of poultry and meat. So it can be safer to avoid buying ham and other cooked meats, from a butcher - unless the shop is set up so the cooked meat is well away from the raw meat, and has different staff and different equipment.

As bacteria on food need both time to breed and the right temperature to breed at, the biggest single preventer of food poisoning is the refrigerator (see temperature chart opposite). To give bacteria the least chance:

- cool food as rapidly as possible (but don't put it in the refrigerator while hot or it will warm up the other food)
- put cooked food in the refrigerator as soon as it is cool: don't wait for it to get cold
- when cooked food isn't being actively used refrigerate it *all* the time; don't let it sit in the warm ready for the next person to take some
- if food is being kept warm do so at temperatures above those at which bacteria will multiply
- don't keep warming food up and cooling it down: if you make a big stew, heat what you need for each meal and keep the rest fridge cold or, better still, frozen
- if possible thaw frozen meat and poultry in the refrigerator or microwave, not by leaving them for hours in a warm kitchen
- remember neither refrigeration nor freezing kill bacteria; cold may just stop them multiplying, but each time the food is brought into the warm they start to multiply once more.

Be extra careful with poultry and with rolled joints, especially large ones. Rolling the outside to the middle carries bacteria from the outer part of the meat into the centre where they are unlikely to get enough heat to kill them, and where conditions are perfect for one major food poisoning organism (clostridium perfringens, see table opposite) to grow. Both poultry and rolled joints must be fully thawed before cooking: unthawed areas may not get hot enough in cooking to kill food poisoning bacteria. And some bacteria only die at exceedingly high temperatures. Cooking is no substitute for hygiene.

How To Tell If Food Is Unsafe

It would be helpful if one could tell at a glance whether food was safe to eat. You can't always do so. The appearance of food is no sure guide to whether it is safe. Food can carry enough food poisoning bacteria to make you seriously ill while looking and smelling fresh and lovely. And raw meat can be smelly, and even taste unpleasant when cooked, without containing organisms which will do you harm. Though food can, of course, be both off and poisonous. Knowing you treated it correctly is the best guide.

★ It is a myth that highly spiced food, such as curry, can't carry food poisoning. Some spices are anti-bacterial, but food poisoning bacteria have been found living in tins of curry powder.

Some food poisoning bacteria can have a bacterial version of an afterlife. So when the main part of a bacterium dies it leaves the essence of itself behind in a minute spore which has extraordinary powers of survival, withstanding quite extreme levels of heat, cold and dehydration. Then, when conditions are more congenial, the bacterium is reincarnated from its spore. So you can kill the active part of every single bacterium in a piece of food only to have it become dangerous all over again when the bacteria are reborn from the spores, and multiply. Luckily, not all bacteria make spores, and even spores can be killed by certain temperatures.

★ Raw pet food often carries food poisoning bacteria: it should be well cooked before storing in your refrigerator or freezer.

The Temperatures Bacteria Like

Food poisoning bacteria vary in the temperatures they prefer, and in the temperatures needed to kill them (see chart opposite).

On the whole, food poisoning organisms stay on the surface of solid meat, but they will penetrate cracks, such as the slight gap between two sections of muscle. So, for safety, the *centre* of the food must reach the required temperature and stay at it for at least 20 minutes. However, for the *food* to reach that temperature the oven must be far hotter.

Types of Food Poisoning

In Britain 70 per cent of those known to have had food poisoning can blame salmonella: not too surprising since there are over 2,000 types of salmonella. Next comes clostridium perfringens, then staphylococcus aureus and bacillus cereus. All the others are rare here.

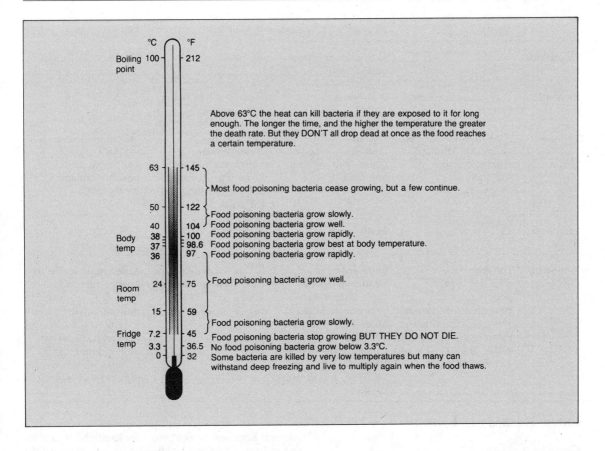

Above 63°C the heat can kill bacteria if they are exposed to it for long enough. The longer the time, and the higher the temperature the greater the death rate. But they DON'T all drop dead at once as the food reaches a certain temperature.

Most food poisoning bacteria cease growing, but a few continue.

Food poisoning bacteria grow slowly.
Food poisoning bacteria grow well.
Food poisoning bacteria grow rapidly.
Food poisoning bacteria grow best at body temperature.
Food poisoning bacteria grow rapidly.

Food poisoning bacteria grow well.

Food poisoning bacteria grow slowly.
Food poisoning bacteria stop growing BUT THEY DO NOT DIE.
No food poisoning bacteria grow below 3.3°C.
Some bacteria are killed by very low temperatures but many can withstand deep freezing and live to multiply again when the food thaws.

	Bacillus cereus	**Clostridium perfringens**	**Salmonella**	**Staphylococcus aureus**
Source	Widely found in nature, especially on rice and other cereals. Not always killed in cooking. The bacteria multiply in rice kept for reheating. The most likely cause of food poisoning after a Chinese take-away.	Human and animal excreta, raw meat, fish, poultry, insects, dehydrated food. Typically causes illness when food has been cooked and left to cool too long in a warm room, then eaten cold or inadequately reheated.	In animals' guts - are transferred to the flesh when excreta spilled in slaughter. Poultry most likely carriers. Raw pet food and pets may be carriers, but tinned pet food should be safe. Also in human excreta and water or raw foods, polluted with sewage.	Mainly the skin and the nose, of carriers, also in boils, styes, spots, cuts and burns. It can be carried deep in the pores, so does not wash off easily. Most likely to contaminate cold meat, poultry and custards. Also comes in untreated milk from cows and goats.
Special characteristics	Multiply in moist conditions, with or without air, creating poisons in food. Prefer temperatures of 28°-35°C (82°-95°F) (more usual in a hot commercial kitchen than a home). Produces spores which can survive cooking.	Very hardy - spores can survive dehydration and boiling. Grow without air. Ideal temperatures 43°-47°C (109°-117°F), but up to 50°C (122°F), so multiply during long slow cooling and can release poison in the gut.	Can grow with or without air, and cause an infection.	Multiplies with or without air, forming a poison in the food as it does so.

	Bacillus cereus	Clostridium perfringens	Salmonella	Staphylococcus aureus
Occurrence		Common in Britain and in many countries	Common worldwide.	Common in Britain and in many countries
Incubation	1-16 hours according to type.	8-22 hours	Usually 12-24 hours, 6-36 possible	2-6 hours
Symptoms	Violent vomiting and diarrhoea, stomach cramp, collapse; or just pain and diarrhoea.	Stomach pains, massive diarrhoea, nausea but seldom vomiting or fever.	Fever headache, aching limbs, diarrhoea and some vomiting. It can kill babies, the old, and the weak.	Severe vomiting, stomach cramps, diarrhoea, and possibly collapse, but rarely fatal.
Length of Illness	12-24 hours	24-48 hours	1-7 days	6-24 hours
Removing the Danger	Difficult: two different types of poison can be produced; one causes vomiting, the other diarrhoea. Former still active after 1½ hrs at 121°C (250°F).	Some forms are rapidly killed by cooking; but spores may not be killed by hours of boiling. To kill them needs temperatures of *over* 100°C (212°F) - only achieved in a pressure cooker.	Killed by cooking the food to a temperature above 55°C (131°F) for 20 minutes.	Killed quite easily by temperatures above 55°C (131°F). But the poison they create is only destroyed by temperatures *above* boiling point for 30 minutes — which requires a pressure cooker.

Other Hazards in Food

Ciguatera

Ciguatera causes weakness and loss of sensation and can lead to paralysis and death. It is generally caused by eating large fish in the Pacific and Caribbean, and one theory is that a small creature which produces a poisonous substance in the environment is eaten by small fish. And this is concentrated up the food chain, as lots of small fish containing it are eaten by middle-sized fish, and lots of middle-sized fish are then eaten by the big fish.

Diseases Carried by Food

Typhoid, paratyphoid, cholera and related infections can pass from person to person, so they are not strictly speaking food poisoning, but they also pass from human and animal (especially rodent) excreta into water. From there they can contaminate shellfish, food washed in contaminated water, ice made with it, and also cows (and their milk) if streams are contaminated. In less developed countries there is a danger that any food, or ice, may carry these infections.

Milk (and milk products) from cows and goats, which has not been sterilized or pasteurized, can contain the organisms which cause brucellosis (undulant fever). This is a serious disease which can make someone ill for months and even years. It has almost been stamped out in Britain, but overseas it is always wisest to boil untreated milk. Herds which are 'tuberculin tested' can still carry brucellosis and, even in Britain, there are several hundred cases a year. (Incidentally, it gets its name from a doctor called Bruce who first identified it.)

Moulds

There are at least 150 moulds which can produce substances which are harmful to men or to animals (mycotoxins). The best known of these is the one which grows on peanuts and peanut butter. In animals the poison this mould produces causes liver damage and cancer, but nobody is sure what it does to man. Most peanut butter doesn't go mouldy but, if any does, throw it *all* away. The same applies to sauces, such as saté sauce, in which peanuts are an ingredient.

The full range of moulds which can be harmful is still not known and it will be some while before we have any clear picture of which moulds are harmful to man and which aren't. Excellent as organically grown food may be in other ways, it is worth remembering that, as it has not been treated with fungicide, it needs more careful storage if moulds are not to be a problem.

The standard advice is that if jam becomes mouldy you can remove the mould, plus half an inch of jam under it, and eat the rest. But any jam which is liable to go mouldy is best kept in a refrigerator and eaten before mould appears.

Mould is so much part of the nature of cheese that it is reasonable to assume that if some cheese like cheddar goes mouldy it is safe to cut off the mould and eat the rest. But only time, and more research, will tell whether this is correct.

Shellfish

Mussels, and similar shellfish, can be poisoned when they consume large quantities of plankton, popularly known as the Red Tide, which contain a poison. These plankton occur mainly off the east coast of America and Canada, but they are also found off parts of Scotland and Yorkshire. Eating such mussels causes weakness and vomiting and can be fatal.

★ Certain combinations of food can give some people symptoms very similar to food poisoning. Combining spirits and shellfish is a common one.

Travellers' Food Poisoning

Reading the preceding pages should alert travellers to the major hazards. The risk depends entirely on the country, but it is easy to get mild food poisoning, when travelling, simply because each bacterium has numerous slightly different versions. So though you may be immune to your local variety of a bacterium, like escherichia coli, a new version can trigger diarrhoea. On top of that, less developed countries may combine unhygienic practices with unpurified water and inadequate refrigeration to create quite serious hazards. However, in most places which seem unhygienic the worst can be avoided with simple precautions.

- Stick to *freshly* cooked food - not cold food or dishes which may have been rewarmed.
- Keep to bottled drinks, even for teeth cleaning (preferably bottled in a hygienic country), or use water sterilizing tablets such as Boots' Sterotabs.
- Take no ice.
- Peel all fruit.
- Don't eat shellfish.
- Be wary of milk and milk products; they may be unpasteurized and carry TB or undulant fever.
- Avoid salads, unless you are sure the hygiene is good and the water they are washed in is clean.
- Avoid undercooked meat and fish.

Obviously, clean restaurants are better than dirty ones. But in countries where food hygiene isn't really understood, and cleanliness may not extend to the kitchen, it can sometimes be safer to eat from a stall, where you can see the raw food being cooked in front of you, than in a large hotel where the food may pass through more (potentially contaminated) hands and sit around for longer in the warm.

Betty C. Hobbs and Diane Roberts, *Food Poisoning and Food Hygiene*, Edward Arnold - a standard work on the topic yet remarkably readable.

FROZEN FOOD AND FREEZING

Defrosting

Freezers need to be defrosted when the layer of ice inside is about 1 cm (½ in) thick. You can scrape most of it off with a plastic spatula with the freezer filled and running. But every few months turn it off, remove the food and thaw the freezer. You can speed up the job by standing bowls of hot water in it - though *not* on any working parts. In the meantime, keep the food in a refrigerator, or in the big insulated sacks from freezer food shops, and cover them well with newspaper and other insulation to keep out warm air. Run the freezer for about half an hour before replacing the food. Whatever the method, choose a cool day.

Freezing Fresh Food

Containers and Wrappings for Freezing

There are three types of food spoilage which can be prevented or slowed down by the right packing:
- loss of moisture
- oxidation from the effects of oxygen in the air (see page 56).
- the picking up of odours (and flavours) from other food.

So the best packing is a strong one which holds in moisture and keeps out air, and the air must be pressed out of containers.

The more closely containers can be packed together in a freezer, the better. So my favourites are the brick-shaped cartons used for fruit juice and milk. Put a freezer bag inside, pour in food such as soups or stews, tie up the bag, and freeze. The carton excludes more air than a bag alone.

Foil contains smell well and is specially recommended for fish and cheese, but the standard kitchen type is thinner than is ideal, and very easily pierced. For long storage you need heavy duty foil of around 0·03 mm, but you'll have a job finding it. It's far easier to wrap food in foil and put it inside a plastic bag for extra protection. Any acid in food eats into aluminium - which means it's probably getting into the food itself, so put a plastic film under.

★ Glass containers are risky, unless the glass is designed for freezers.
★ Lined tins such as coffee tins with air-tight plastic lids are good - if you doubt the lining, put a plastic bag inside. Nothing which could rust should be near food.
★ Baking tins can be frozen with pastry in them - but some tins may rust, so line them.
★ Freezer bags closed with a clothes peg are easiest for stiff hands to undo.

Labelling Frozen Food

The cheapest label is a piece of masking tape on which you write with a marker pen. The vital information is the type of food, the date and the quantity (e.g. 2 pork loin chops 5.6.88). Once frozen, it can be hard to see what's what, even in a clear plastic bag.

Packing Food for Freezing

I learnt the hard way that it was far better to divide food into portions for one or two - which allows one to thaw as many as one needs. Any items which may need to be removed individually should have two pieces of greaseproof paper between each one. Then you can slide a knife between the two layers of paper to separate them and speed thawing.

Food expands as it freezes, so allow headroom in containers or they will crack or push off their lids. This doesn't apply to bags - so press as much air as possible out of them. Air is the great damager of frozen food, so pack food to make the air spaces between loose food as small as possible.

Freezing Techniques
Freezing techniques are designed to help the food keep its shape and minimize the ill effects of freezing. Which you use depends on the type of food but food for freezing should be in prime condition.

1 Berries keep their shape best if rinsed clean, spread on a baking sheet and frozen, then packed in containers. Plums can be rinsed, stoned, packed and frozen.

2 Fruit which would go brown if sliced and frozen (e.g. apples, pears, sliced peaches) can be blanched (see page 93) for 1 to 2 minutes in water or steam, chilled and packed.

★ Some people suggest freezing raw fruit in loose sugar or in a sugar syrup. As sugar draws the juices out of fruit this is just what you *don't* want. If fruit won't freeze well by methods 1 or 2 cook it before freezing instead.

3 I am told that fruit which needs blanching will also keep well after dipping in solutions of ascorbic acid (vitamin C) or lemon juice. I have never bothered with this - but if you want to try it dip the fruit in a solution of 1,000 mg per 250 ml (½ pt) water, pack and freeze immediately. Alternatively, use the juice of a lemon in 500 ml (½ pt water).

4 Vegetables need to be prepared and blanched in water or steam (see page 93), or cooked in some other way. Blanching stops the action of enzymes which, even at very low temperatures, slowly make them taste 'off'. For easy access to loose vegetables treat them like berries above. If you are only going to keep a vegetable for a week or two you can use method 1. But don't risk this with cabbages, sprouts or broccoli or they will stink.

5 Meat simply needs to be bagged, or wrapped, chilled and frozen. It keeps best if excess fat is trimmed off.

6 Fish can be treated like meat but is best in cling film and then foil. If a fish is *very* special it may be worth using an ice glaze. For this you freeze it unwrapped then dip it in iced water, so the water freezes on it in a thin coat and freeze again. Repeat this 2 to 3 times until the ice coat is 3 mm (⅛ in) thick. Wrap it carefully in foil without cracking the glaze.

Putting Food to Freeze
Slow freezing and unstable freezer temperatures both badly affect the look and texture of frozen food: large ice crystals form inside the food and break down its texture. So ideally food should be frozen at -21° to -23°C (-5° to -10°F). The other rules for freezing food from fresh are as follows.

- Only one tenth of a freezer's space should be used for freezing food from fresh in any day.
- Set the freezer to 'fast freeze' an hour or two ahead. If you only have a thermostat a good temperature is between -21° and -23°C (-5° and -10°F). Keep it on fast freeze for about 18 hours if you have put several items in to freeze.
- Chill the food in the refrigerator before putting it in the freezer.
- Freeze food in the coldest part of the freezer: a fast freeze compartment, the bottom parts close or to walls.
- Don't put food you are freezing next to already frozen food, or it will increase spoilage.

Ill Effects of Freezing
Freezer burn: This leaves food looking much paler and means that water has left the surface of the food, making it tough and dry, and probably rancid. It is most likely to happen if there is a hole in the container and high protein foods such as meat, poultry and shell fish, are the most vulnerable.

Reduced setting: If frozen fruit is used in jam making it will set less well than fresh fruit because freezing affects the pectin. So extra pectin must be added.

Oxidation: interaction with air can turn fats rancid - oily fish and pork are especially vulnerable - in other food it allows discoloration and loss of fat soluble vitamins.

Keeping Times
On the storage of food which you buy frozen there is only one thing to say - *follow the manufacturer's instructions.*

If food is stored at the standard freezer temperature of -18°C (0°F) it will be safe to eat however long you keep it, *but* it will only be *enjoyable* for a relatively limited time. This is because chemical alterations slowly occur which affect food's colour, texture and flavour. On top of that, the action of freezing affects the structure of food, and fluctuations in freezer temperature every time you open the door aggravate this. So the longer food is kept, the less delectable it becomes.

Different experts give different storage lives for food. The truth is that storage life is never certain. It couldn't be, because it depends on so many unpredictable factors, like how often you open your freezer and whether it's in a warm or a cold place. The following are maximum storage times within which, on average, food should be reasonably pleasant to eat. Try to eat it before the lower figure - if there are two - by the upper one it may only be much less of a pleasure. The times are for raw food in a domestic freezer at about -18°C.

Keeping Times for Frozen Food

Food	Months	Comments
Bacon joints and rashers not vacuum packed	1	
Bacon rashers vacuum packed	6	
Bacon joint vacuum packed	3	
Beef	12	
Bread	3-6	The richer doughs keep least.
Cakes	3-9	The less fat, the longer the keeping time. Fast freeze decorated cakes unwrapped, and wrap when the icing is hard.
Casseroles	3-4	Cooked and containing meat or poultry.
Cheese (hard)	6-9	Tends to go crumbly, best grated.
Chicken	9-12	Fatty birds keep the shorter time. Giblets only keep 3 months.
Cooked sliced meat	2-3 weeks	It becomes very dry on long keeping and must be well packed.
Cream (whipped)	2-6	Separates unless whipped. Some say it only freezes well at over 40% butter fat (i.e. double cream), but whipping cream, which is slightly less fatty, often freezes even better. Either keeps best with a little sugar in.
Duck	3	
Eggs (whole beaten) (yolks beaten) (whites)	6 6 12	Add a good pinch of *either* salt or sugar per whole egg. Add salt or sugar, as for whole eggs. Whites need nothing added.
Fish shellfish white fish oily fish	 1-3 6 3	Try to eat it well before this.
Fruit in sugar or syrup cooked plain juice sorbet	 9-12 9-12 9 4-6 1-2	Usually holds its flavour well, but the texture of soft fruit with thin skins spoils easily. Berries (e.g. currants) with firm skins freeze best and may keep even longer.
Game	4-6+	
Goose	4-6	
Hare	6-8	Salt the blood lightly and store separately for jugged hare.
Ice cream	1-2	The foam structure begins to break down after that.
Lamb	9-10	
Mince	2-3	
Offal	2	

Food	Months	Comments
Pancakes	4-6	Home-made layered with greaseproof.
Pastry	6	Flaky pastry even improves with freezing. Choux pastry should be cooked first.
Pâté	1	
Pies	3-4	Cooked pies containing meat or fruit.
Pork	9	
Potato (chips)	4-6	Store in a box to prevent breakage.
(crisps)	3	
Sandwiches	1	
Sausages	3	Sage tend to keep their flavour longest.
Spices in food	3-4	After that some alter their flavour.
Turkey	9	As chicken.
Veal	9	
Vegetables	6-12	If blanched.
Venison	6-8	
Yeast pastry	3-6	If cooked.
Yeast - fresh	3	Freeze well wrapped and pre-cut into 25g (1 oz) pieces.

★ Freeze egg whites in an ice cube tray for easy access.

★ If you add 2 teaspoonfuls of gelatine to each 500 ml (1 pt) of cooled fruit mixture, when making sorbets, the sorbet will hold its iciness for longer when you serve it.

Nutrition and Frozen Food

Vitamin C starts being lost from the moment vegetables are picked. But it is lost fastest under warm conditions (in 5 days peas lose a third of it). So fresh vegetables, which have spent time in the shop, often have less vitamin C than those which have been picked and frozen. But vitamin C continues to be lost while they are frozen. However, the lower the temperature and the shorter the time they are kept, the less will be lost.

Organizing Frozen Food

It is all too easy to keep using the food nearest you in the freezer (often the newest) only to find, months later, that the food at the back is past eating. There are two good ways to keep track of things. One is an exercise book divided into sections (say - starters, meat, fish, vegetables, fruit and puddings, other), and cross off as you use food. Another method is always to write two labels - one for the food and one for the door or lid of the freezer (work down or across the door to indicate newness). You then remove a label from the door as you remove the food (masking tape removes easily, other labels may not). This looks perfectly awful, but even my disorganized offspring manage to remove labels, whereas my book was totally ignored after the first week.

Power Failure and Doors Ajar

Don't think all your food has spoiled if there's a power cut. *Keep the freezer door shut;* then none of the cold is lost. If the power cut is in cold weather the temperature in a freezer will hardly change in several hours, and the food will be fine for a while.

1 If the food is icy in the centre and only thawed at the edge you can refreeze it, but when you thaw it next time remember its life will be shorter.
2 If it is fully thawed but cold you can refreeze bread, raw pastry, fruit and cakes. Raw meat and fish can be cooked immediately and refrozen. Other food will be as it would be after a similar time in a larder.
3 If the food is warm it will have been thawed a good while and it is safest to destroy all precooked dishes, meat, fish and vegetables. But fruit may be edible and can possibly be refrozen after cooking. Bread and cakes may also be refrozen if they look and smell all right - unless they have cream in.

★ Most freezer centres can tell you how to take out insurance against accidents which ruin frozen food.

★ As a precaution, keep a bag of ice cubes in the top of your freezer. Then if there is a cut you can look at the ice cubes afterwards. The amount they have melted will show you how much your food must have thawed, and help you decide what must be done. This is also useful if your family tends to leave the door ajar.

Refreezing Thawed Food

People say you can't refreeze thawed food. You can. Manufacturers put 'never freeze once thawed' on packets for two reasons. First, thawing and refreezing causes more damage to the texture of food than freezing once and they don't want their product looking tacky. Second, every time food thaws it reaches temperatures at which harmful bacteria can multiply *if they are in the food* (they may not be). So the more thaws it undergoes, the greater the risk.

Safety depends on what happens to food when it's *out* of the freezer. If you observe the rules of hygiene (page 51) and make pâté, freeze it immediately, thaw it, put it in sandwiches and freeze them immediately, you will have safe sandwiches to eat the day you thaw them. *But* if you let the pâté sit about going bad, or infect it with bacteria causing food poisoning and then leave it in the warm don't expect the freezing to make it fresh and kill the bugs for you. It won't. The double thawing will mean two periods in the warm when the bacteria can breed. So if your family gets the trots once you buy a freezer don't blame the freezer, improve your hygiene.

Thawing

The worst effects of thawing are from 'drip' - the loss of liquid from the food because cells have been damaged by freezing, which makes meat seem tough and soft fruits soggy. So, ideally, food should be cooked as soon as it is thawed. The rule is the faster it was frozen, the faster it should thaw.

Will it Freeze Well?

Don't be misled into thinking you can only freeze special freezer recipes. Most food freezes well. The main exceptions are given below.

Aspic loses its texture.
Apples cannot be frozen whole and raw.
Bananas go black - but are still fine for banana bread.
Bread dough is hard to freeze well in a domestic freezer.
Celery: inedible raw after freezing but all right for cooking.
Cream cheese: the fat separates from the water.
Cloves tend to become stronger with freezing - go easy on them.
Cornflour tends to separate, leaving the liquid thin again.
Custard and custard-style puddings tend to separate (cooked quiche).
Eggs: boiled, poached and fried eggs lose their texture. But fine in a cake or mousse. Raw eggs freeze separately.
Garlic: some people say this makes food taste 'off' after freezing.
Gelatine takes on a nasty texture, but it isn't noticeable in mousses and other mixtures into which air is beaten.

Icing: boiled sugar types become sticky.
Jelly develops a poor texture.
Mayonnaise separates.
Melon can't be frozen whole, and even in pieces it's on the soggy side.
Meringue weeps.
Milk: the fat separates from the water unless homogenized but you can still cook with it. (Don't freeze in a glass bottle.)
Pears vary in their reaction to freezing, test your variety.
Potatoes: boiled ones may go watery; with other foods cut very small.
Salad vegetables: lettuce, cucumber, radishes, endive, chicory all go inedibly soggy.
Tomatoes go soggy but are great for sauces.
Vanilla: if synthetic, becomes overpowering. Pod vanilla is fine.
Yoghurt separates on thawing unless highly sweetened. Even sweet ones need beating afterwards.

Using Frozen Food Compartments

Frozen food compartments are not the same as freezers. Only those which bear the symbol ★ ★★★ can freeze food from fresh. The others should only be used for keeping pre-frozen food because they are not as powerful as a freezer. How long any such compartment will keep frozen food depends on its star rating.

★ -6°C (21°F) keeps frozen food 1 week
★★ -12°C (10°F) keeps frozen food 1 month
★★★ -18°C (0°F) keeps frozen food 3 months (if the food will keep that long

Most freezers are also designed to run at -18°C (0°F). If you are wondering why freezers can keep food for far longer than frozen food compartments, even though the temperature is the same, it's because the small size of the compartments means that putting unfrozen food into them raises the temperature far more than it would in a big freezer. The constant opening of a fridge door also causes variations in temperature which spoil frozen food.

FRUIT AND NUTS

Fruit and Nut Seasons

Nowadays you can buy most fruit at almost any time. As each one goes out of season in one country it comes into season in another, and we import it. But those which are grown in Britain do have peak times when they are considerably cheaper, and even some imported fruit is more plentiful at one time than another.

Apples

A far wider range of apples can be found through farm shops and Pick Your Own places than you can buy in shops. When picking apples cup them underneath, lift and twist slightly. If they are ready for picking they should come free. Place them gently in a basket; if they are banged and bruised there will be no keeping them.

As each apple has distinct characteristics, noticing how each type of apple behaves, and choosing the right one for the job, rather than always using some all-purpose cooking apple, makes it very much easier to get good results. The beloved British Bramley, for example, is perfect for baked apples or apple snow, but its tendency to break up makes it a poor apple for tarts or blackberry and apple. Yet the French Golden Delicious, so dreary as eaters, really are delicious cooked in tarts, and keep their shape perfectly.

When eating apples it is worth exploring their affinity with cheese. Not for nothing are the apple growing areas of Britain close to some of the best cheese making ones. For almost every British cheese there is an apple which suits it to perfection - Cox's with Cheddar, and Red Worcesters with Double Gloucester are only two of the lovely combinations.

Apricots
There is a luscious and exotic air to ripe apricots. They not only make beautiful puddings and pastries but their pervasive sweet-sour flavour goes excellently with duck, pork or lamb. Choose those which are firm and glowing and deepest in colour to eat raw. If you cook them the flavour is greatly improved by using vanilla sugar or even a little pure vanilla essence in the cooking water. But keep the water to a minimum or the final dish will be too watery. They poach beautifully in a low oven, but tend to go brown if microwaved too slowly.

I was first persuaded to buy the dull-looking little brown dried Hunza apricots by a man running a fruit stall on a station platform in south Wales. They are a real find, with a beautiful flavour that more than makes up for their lack of looks. But pick them over before soaking, discarding those with holes as they may be inhabited. Soak and cook them without adding sugar or they will be too sweet. Ordinary dried apricots are perfect if simply soaked for 2 to 3 days with no cooking.

Bananas
Bananas should never be put in a refrigerator as the cold blackens them. However, if they do become black for any reason they are still perfectly good to eat. But if you find them unappealing you can peel and freeze them as they are, for use in milk shakes or banana bread - which is one of the best of tea breads.

West Indian recipes often call for plantain. This is a variety of banana that does not become sweet even when ripe, but sweet bananas can be cooked like plantain when they are green.

Blackberries
Blackberries are rich in names, being called brambles, brumbleberries, brumble-kites and even 'lawyers'. They are at their best early in the season when the tip blackberry in each spray ripens, those that come later are fine for jam but never have the full rich flavour of the master berry. This is perhaps why old wives spun

the tale that it is unlucky to eat them after Michaelmas - 29 September - 'when the devil tramples on them'. Try soaking fat sweet ones in whisky for a night and eating them with cream. They freeze excellently.

Blueberries
Blueberries or blayberries offer more in ornament than they do in flavour, as they seem to make only a faint impression on the palate. They are probably at their best in open tarts, as the French cook them in the Auvergne, but if you only have a few they can be used as delicate juicy morsels in pancakes or scattered in a fruit salad.

Carambola (Star Fruit)
The five-ridged sides of the pale green-yellow carambola give it its common name of star fruit. But, confusingly, there are two members of the family - both called star fruit - one more sour than the other. The one which is increasingly seen in British supermarkets is the sweeter one, correctly called carambola. Though refreshing in a very hot climate, and pretty when sliced into stars, it tastes to me like a very disappointing apple. It can be eaten raw or poached in syrup like any other fruit.

Cherries
Cherries have so brief a season that they need to be used to the full. When buying always ask to taste - looks can be deceptive. But if they are sour, and you have a yen for cherries, make a pie with them.

Cherries go mouldy fast, especially after rinsing. Store them in the refrigerator and rinse them only when you need them. If you want stoneless cherries for a tart scald a hairpin and poke the U of it into the stem end and hook the stone out; or use an olive stoner to push them out.

Coconuts
Coconuts don't belong here but they are closer to fruit than to other nuts and need to be bought just as carefully. Shake a coconut before you buy it. It should have liquid inside and three dry eyes. To open it use a hammer and strong skewer to make holes in two eyes, and pour out the milk - surely one of the most perfect drinks in nature. Then crack the nut open with a hammer. The flesh will freeze but, being fatty, it is not a good candidate for long storage.

Crab Apples
If you have acquired a garden with a crab apple tree, and are wondering whether you can make crab apple jelly, the answer is: you can. Kew Botanical Gardens tells me that all types of crab apple are safe to eat - but some are very much better than others.

Cranberries
The secret of a good cranberry sauce is to use just a few spoonfuls of liquid and only add the sugar after the berries have cooked to tenderness. Adding it sooner toughens their skins. When adding the sugar do so little by little, tasting as you go - curiously there comes a

point when more sugar increases rather than reduces their bitterness.

Currants
Currants are an exception to the usual rules for keeping soft fruit. They store best rinsed, stripped from their stalks and sprinkled with castor sugar. Like this, they keep for several days in a refrigerator and the sugar draws out enough juice to bathe them, without bleeding the firmness from them. Once the juice surrounds them they are perfect eaten just as they are - with thick cream. To strip them quickly pull the stalk between the prongs of a fork.

Dates
Unless you like a little extra protein with your fruit it is wisest to cut open fresh dates before eating as they can be inhabited. If you chill them in the freezer, and bring them to the table very cold, it stops their sweetness being cloying.

★ Dried dates cut most easily if you dip the knife in hot water between slices. So, indeed, does all candied and crystallized fruit.

Durian
Durians look like monstrous horse chestnuts and have a smell so overwhelming that, in the East, where they grow, it fills whole streets and causes the fruit to be banned from most hotels. You are unlikely to come across one in Britain but may be tempted to taste one abroad. Be careful: one of the oddities of this smelliest of all fruit is that it interacts with alcohol. To drink alcohol and eat durians in quick succession - or together - can make you seriously ill. To eat one you split it open and scoop out the pulpy white flesh which lurks in pockets. Whether you will find it heaven or hell is a matter of taste, but indifference is impossible.

Figs
There is a world of difference between the soft sensuously ripe figs one can buy in hot countries and most of their tight-lipped sisters sold in Britain. But look for ones which are well rounded and give when gently pressed. Rinse them well and place them in the sun or a warm room, for they are not at their best chilled. Eat them just as they are, all but the stalk, or slice and serve them with cream delicately flavoured with Pernod - a strangely good combination.

Guavas
Fresh guavas seem related to their tinned selves only in scent. They need to be bought carefully for the guava is unusual among fruit in giving off a strong odour long before it is ripe. And an unripe guava is a rocky and disappointing affair. Only buy ones which 'give' slightly as you press them. Either pare off the skin and slice them, or cut them in half and scoop out the flesh. You can also halve them, scoop out the seeds (eating them some other way) and fill the hollow with other fruit and perhaps whipped cream.

Gooseberries
Gooseberries only store for a day or two, even in the refrigerator. To prepare them simply rinse them and use a sharp knife to snick off the parts which stick out at either end.

Whether gooseberries should be eaten raw or cooked depends more on ripeness than on type. Those which are plump and soft when pressed can be eaten raw. Those which are hard can be stewed with sugar for puddings or used in savoury sauces. But they are at their best cooked with elderflower.

If a recipe calls for puréed gooseberries do not liquidize them, the pips will create nasty wood chips; either mash them for a rough purée or rub them (tediously) through a sieve.

Grapefruit
One shouldn't have to do battle to extract the segments from a half of grapefruit at table. To avoid this run a sharp knife round the grapefruit just inside the outer skin of the segments. Then slip the knife down between the skin and the flesh to each side of every division and quickly cut them apart. Each half segment can then be eaten whole and skinless.

Grapes
There is no easy way to peel grapes; just pick ripe ones, but the seed can be hooked out with the scalded bend of a hairpin or kirby-grip.

Kiwi (Cape Gooseberry)
One of the endearing things about the kiwi, apart from its prettiness when sliced, is that even when fully ripe it keeps for weeks in a refrigerator. If you find good ones at the right price, buy them for when you may need them. Store unripe fruit at room temperature until it ripens and has a little give when pressed. You can eat the skin, but the texture detracts from the fruit and it is easy to pull off those which are very ripe. It is a shame we don't have as charming a name for them as the French do, for in France they call them *souris vegetals* - vegetable mice. Use them raw in fruit salads, simply with one other fruit or as a garnish.

Lemons and Limes
The less air that circulates round a lemon, once cut, the better it keeps. To keep it longest, sit the cut side on a plate and put a glass over it. If you are using a lemon for juice it is useful to remove the zest, with a grater, zester or potato peeler, and freeze it for use later in cakes, apple pies, with stewed prunes, or for garnishing - according to how you removed it.

★ To get the most juice from these fruit warm them - in hot water, or a microwave.
★ Keep the squeezed halves of lemons in the refrigerator and stick your fingertips in them to remove smells from the skin.

Mangoes
When ripe, mangoes are golden or rosy, just soft to touch, and with a delicate perfume. If ripe keep them in a refrigerator, but unripe mangoes, will ripen

wrapped in paper in a warm kitchen, though they sometimes develop brown spots before they are fully ripe - and must be eaten at once for they will only spoil.

If a mango is really fresh and ripe you can slice round the middle, twist the two halves in opposite directions so that they separate from the stone. In Britain they seldom do. So the easiest way to serve this luscious fruit is to stand it on end and slice through the fruit at either side of the stone, to remove two shallow cups of flesh. Then cut across these in each direction, without going through the skin. They can now be pushed up, under the centre to open out the little cubes for eating with a spoon and fork. If you want to eat them less elegantly do it in the bath, for the juice runs everywhere.

Medlars
Medlars can't be bought, but you may come across a medlar tree. If you do, the curious feature of medlars is that they need to be picked and kept some weeks until they are bletted (soft). You then eat the brown mush with cream and sugar. I am told it is wonderful, but have never had the good fortune to find a medlar in fruit.

Melons
People say you should feel the end of a melon to see if it is ripe. This only works if everyone else hasn't been feeling it too - even the hardest melon softens if enough thumbs press it. So smell is a better guide. A distinct sweetness should waft from both the round and the rugger ball types - though it is weaker from the latter. In most round varieties there should also be a ring of cracking round the base of the stalk. These signs don't hold true for water melons, which remain odourless and rocky, so choosing them is pure guesswork. Having cut into a melon keep it very closely covered or it will lend its flavour unpleasantly to other foods near it.

Mulberries
Mulberries are lovely fruit. For picking them wear clothes which can stay stained - for it seems impossible to pick them from the beautiful spreading mulberry tree without others falling on you, and the stains may well be permanent. Serve the mulberries heaped on their own leaves (which are so loved by silk worms) with sugar and cream, or use them in summer pudding.

Oranges
Oranges need no explanation, but people are sometimes puzzled about preparing them for salad. You do it like this. Slice the top from the orange with a sharp knife, cutting both pith and skin from the top segments. Then cut round in a spiral, removing both pith and skin, to leave a juicy outside. After that you can either slice it thinly into rounds or create skinless segments. For segments you run your knife down between a dividing skin and the flesh, repeat on the other side of the segment and free it. Continue round the orange until all the segments are freed. Prepared ahead of time and sprinkled with sugar they create their own juice. Grapefruit can be cut in the same way.

Lychees
To my mind, lychees are one of the most delicious of all fruit. Simply peel off the thin leathery skin with your fingers and eat the white flesh, discarding the stone. They need no addition, no elaboration.

Papaya (Paw-paw)
The papaya must surely be one of the ugliest trees in existence, with its solitary, almost leafless, stem and clusters of pendulous ripening fruit looking like so many green bottoms, but the fruit is delicious. In Britain they are seldom sold fully ripe, so keep them in a warm place until they turn golden and yield slightly when pressed. But if any soft patches appear the whole fruit must be eaten at once or it will quickly spoil. If the fruit is still unripe you can peel, dice and cook it briefly in a sugar and water syrup. Ripe papayas are best sliced open, like an avocado, and their glistening black seeds removed, before the flesh is eaten as it is, with lemon or lime juice sprinkled over. Papaya is a natural meat tenderizer.

Passion Fruit
Passion fruit look like shrivelled plums with particularly leathery skins. Cut them open and you find a cluster of seeds coated in delicate bitter-sweet pulp. Eat this as it is or fold it into cream for a delicate and unusual fool.

Peaches and Nectarines
A ripe peach or nectarine is firm, but not hard under pressure. However, even ripe peaches can be unexpectedly tasteless if they have travelled badly. If you find you buy such fruit they can be salvaged if you peel and steep them in white wine and sugar. To peel peaches or nectarines drop them in a jug of boiling hot water for a minute or two and then into cold water. The skin then slips off easily.

To slice peaches simply make a series of cuts right through to the stone and the segments will fall off, if the peach is ripe.

Pears
Homer wrote of pears being one of the gifts of the gods and were it not for their habit of ripening rapidly, from perfect to soft and woolly, they would indeed be an ideal fruit. Keep bought pears in a refrigerator, bringing them into the warm a few at a time as you want them. Eat them with the softer cheeses, like Stilton and Brie, which are discordant with apples. Only the early varieties of pears ripen well on the tree. Pick the others as soon as they begin to soften round the stem and keep them, well spaced, in a cool place until ripe. They do not freeze well.

Pineapple
To check whether a pineapple is ripe try tugging out one of the leaves in its tuft. From a ripe pineapple they will come out easily.

The least wasteful way to remove the eyes is that practised by the thrifty Chinese on the street stalls of Penang. They carve diagonal Vs round the fruit, neatly removing the diagonally placed eyes. Then slice off the other skin more thinly. But it takes a sharp knife to do this. I find the flesh then tastes better cut thinly, as they do in parts of Africa, rather than in the doorstep slices we are used to.

Like paw-paw, pineapple contains an enzyme which breaks down protein. Unfortunately, this isn't as useful as it sounds because instead of just making it tender it makes the meat lose its texture. This enzyme also destroys gelatine. So, if you want to use pineapple in a dish with gelatine, you must boil the pineapple first to kill the enzyme or it will prevent the gelatine from setting.

Plums, Greengages and Damsons
When cooking plums first slit them open, down their length, and check inside. They are more prone to caterpillars than most fruit and this is better discovered before cooking. Slitting also enables you - if you feel diligent - to remove and crack open the stones to add the kernels to the cooking fruit. Tedious though this operation is it lends a certain excellence to the final flavour, especially of damson cheese, though it is a job only a true gourmet undertakes.

Most plums freeze well, but remove the stones first or they may give an overwhelming flavour of almond during long storage, and cook them from frozen to prevent the fruit going brown.

It is hard to think of the sweet and delicately flavoured greengage as a plum, but plum it is. Which means it is just as easy to grow, making a small compact tree almost any garden could accommodate. It is a shame few gardens have one: few things are more delightful than freshly picked ripe greengages for breakfast on a fine morning. And, although you can stew greengages or make jam from them, they are so excellent fresh that such efforts are only worthwhile if there's a glut.

Pomegranates
Eaten by themselves pomegranates can be disappointing, but the shiny garnet seeds of pomegranate are one of the prettiest and easiest garnishes. And inexpensive too, for if you simply pick a hole in the leathery skin, fish the seeds out as you need them, and cover the fruit with cling film a good pomegranate keeps for several weeks in a refrigerator.

Quinces
Quinces are one of the great fruit surprises, rocky and tasteless when raw but giving a beautiful flavour when cooked. First wash off the down which covers them. Then prepare them as directed in the recipe.

Quinces are so rare it is worth practising a little parsimony. If you have to peel and core them, keep the peel and core and boil them up. You can use the quince-flavoured liquid they yield for stewing apples. If you make quince jelly the quince has such strength of flavour that you can use equal amounts of apples and quinces (or even slightly more apples) and still have a jelly tasting purely of quince. This also improves the set. The purée which remains can make beautiful apple and

quince snow, or fool, if you sieve it to remove the pips. Deep freeze it, if you can, to give the autumnal delights of quince at intervals through the winter.

★ Leave quinces about the house. The scent is delicious and, pear-like though they look, they have none of the pear's weakness of heart and will not go woolly.

Rambutan
In Malaysia rambutan stalls are vivid with the rose-pink and golden bunches. Fresh from the trees, their horse chestnut prickles erect, they look very different from the sad brown offerings which reach our supermarkets. But the taste, so close to that of lychees but somehow lacking their almost perfumed delicacy, is not so altered. They should simply be peeled and eaten.

Rhubarb
I am told that in forcing houses rhubarb can grow 5 cm (2 in) a day, and you can hear it growing. Poached in syrup thickened with potato flour, this uninviting stalk can be remarkably good, and rhubarb upside-down cake, made with the youngest forced rhubarb, is an interesting alternative to apple - if you add enough extra sugar.

Boiled up, the leaves and off-cuts produce an acid water that will clean aluminium and brass - which is why rhubarb should never be cooked in an aluminium pan (see page 64).

Sloes
Traditionally, sloes were gathered after the first frost which softened them. Sloe gin was then made by simply washing the sloes, pricking them well, packing them in jars and pouring gin over to cover them. Like that they produce a very dry sloe-flavoured spirit, but about 350 g (12 oz) sugar is usually added, with the sloes, for 1 l (2 pt) gin. But oversweetness is a common fault in sloe gin so, unless you have a sweet tooth, it may be wise to reduce the amount you put in at first and add more later if you wish. Damson gin can be made the same way, and with both sloes and damsons you can by-pass nature by putting them in the freezer for a day or two to soften.

> WARNING: People have been seriously ill through mistaking poisonous berries for sloes. Only go sloe picking if you know your sloes.

Strawberries, Raspberries, Loganberries
Soft fruit needs careful buying - look at the bottoms of the punnets as well as the tops. Staining speaks of crushed and useless fruit.

Soft fruit, like strawberries and raspberries, lasts best if it is left unwashed with stalks on, and spread out in a very cool place (preferably the refrigerator) so the air can get all round each berry, or use a dry colander instead. Once sugar is put on these fruits it draws the juice out of them and they gradually become flabby. Loganberries are an exception in being at their best when lightly stewed.

Tamarillos (Tree Tomatoes)

Looking like plum tomatoes, this South American fruit has a strong sweet-sour flavour which is an acquired taste. Cut tamarillos in half and scoop out the soft parts to eat raw, or cook them to a purée.

Cooking Fruit

Fruit is very easy to cook but a few small points make a difference.

- It should be cut with stainless steel (ordinary steel can taint it), which is why some very old books refer to cutting it with a silver knife.
- Apples, pears and peaches must immediately be dropped into water containing lemon juice to stop them turning brown with the air.
- If you are preparing soft fruits and want a rich syrup you can draw out the juices by sprinkling the fruit with caster sugar. This dissolves better than granulated and so it suits fruit which will be briefly cooked or not cooked at all.
- For stewing, most fruit needs rather less water than would cover it and it should be cooked very gently. Often the best way is to poach the fruit in a low oven rather than on the top of a stove as there is less risk of rushing it to ruin.
- Fruit should not be cooked in aluminium. The acid in it dissolves some of the aluminium and you will be eating metal which you are better off without.

Preserving Fruit and Vegetables

Freezers have almost done away with the need to put fruit and vegetables by for the winter in bottles and jars. But even if a modern housewife has no need to bottle fruit, home-made pickles are infinitely superior to most one can buy. Making them is a soothing occupation for an autumn Sunday, and spiced pears or - better still - peaches can give a lift to a slice of cold ham or poultry which nothing else can quite achieve. And, tucking produce into boxes hardly compares to the pleasure of contemplating a row of gleaming jars, their contents softly glowing through the glass.

Bottling

Bottled fruit does not go bad for two reasons:

- all bacteria in the bottles, fruit and the water round them, have been destroyed by heat
- air has been shut out so no new bacteria can enter.

In addition, the acid in the fruit helps them to keep. Vegetables lack that acid and are more likely to go off - which can be dangerous. For that reason, the only exception is really a fruit - the tomato.

For bottling anything which needs to be sterilized you must have jars with rubber rings which will seal the air out, and it is best to have fresh rings every year. The steps are these:

1 Check the jars for chips on the rim.
2 Wash the jars well, rinse and leave wet.
3 Put the rubber seals to soak in warm water.
4 If you want to use syrup, sweeten water to your taste - there is no set amount - heating it gently until the sugar is dissolved. Boil for 2 minutes, skim off any froth, and leave to cool.
5 Choose unblemished fruit which is just ripe.
6 Prepare the fruit as you would for stewing.
7 Put a heap of fruit on your scales and note the weight.
8 Pack the fruit carefully into the jars, without bruising it.
9 Note the weight of fruit you put into each jar.
10 Leave the top 1 cm (½ in) empty.
11 Fill to just over the fruit with syrup or water - noting how much liquid went into a jar.
12 Let the bubbles come out, helping them by tapping the base of the jar on a folded cloth.
13 Dip the rubber rings in boiling water, and place them on the jars.
14 Put the lids on. Those which screw on *must* be released a quarter turn before heating *or the bottles may burst.*
15 Sterilize by one of the methods below.

★ When bottling soft fruit which packs closely together it is best to add the syrup in stages, as you pack the jar, or there may be air bubbles which can't escape.

Hot Water Bath Sterilizing 1

There are numerous ways of sterilizing but this method is one of the most reliable. However, you do need a pan deep enough for the water to come right over the bottles, and a thermometer which will register 86°C (212°F).

Place something in the base of the pan to stop the jars resting on it. (Crumpled wire netting will do.) Put the jars in the pan. Cover them with cold water and take 1 hour to bring it up to 55°C (130°F). Then heat to the temperature given in the chart opposite and hold the water at that temperature for the recommended time. ★ ★ Lift the jars out on to a room temperature surface - if you put them on to a chilly surface they may crack. Tighten screw caps immediately. Leave undisturbed for a day and check the seal after 48 hours by removing the screw cap or clip and lifting the jar *slightly* by the sealed lid. If any are not sealed check the rim and underside of the ring for the reason, re-sterilize.

★ If you have no thermometer bring the pan to simmering over 1½ hours. Keep at simmering point for 6 to 15 minutes for soft fruit, 20 minutes for firm fruit, and 30 minutes for tomatoes.
★ When storing screw-top jars unscrew them, dry inside the screw threads, wipe a touch of oil round, then replace without making them too tight. Then they won't rust solid over the winter.

Quick Hot Water Bath Sterilizing 2

Pack fruit into *warm* jars, pour hot liquid over the fruit, put the jars in hot water and heat to simmering (87°C, 190°F) in 25 to 30 minutes and hold at simmering point for the time the fruit needs (see above). Then remove and treat as for 1. The fruit won't look so good by this method but it will taste fine.

Oven Method

There are several oven methods. A simple one is to fill the jars as above but only to within 2.5 cm (1 in) of the top. Leave any screw covers off. Stand them in the centre of the oven on a baking sheet which is covered with a piece of cardboard, leaving a 5 cm (2 in) space between the bottles. Set the oven to gas no 2, 150°C (300°F) and cook for the time given below. Remove and treat as for the water method above from ★ ★.

Bottling Cooking Times

	Water 1	Water 2	Oven		
Apple slices					
Gooseberries	165°F for	2 min	1-4 lb	30-40	min
Rhubarb	10 min		5-10 lb	45-60	min
Soft fruit					
Stone fruit	180°F for	10 min	1-4 lb	40-50	min
Citrus fruits	15 min		5-10 lb	55-70	min
Pineapple	180°F for	20 min	1-4 lb	50-60	min
	15 min		5-10 lb	65-80	min
Pears	190°F for	40 min	1-4 lb	60-70	min
	30 min		5-10 lb	75-90	min
Tomatoes	190°F for	50 min	1-4 lb	70-80	min
	40 min		5-10 lb	85-100	min

1 The weights given for each oven time are for the total weight of fruit in the oven, regardless of the size of the jars.
2 More than 11 oz of fruit in a jar, or less than 5 fl oz of liquid, demand slightly longer at the final temperature.

★ Bottled pears tend to go brown, and tomatoes may be more usefully bottled once skinned and chopped. Sterilize them as for whole tomatoes.
★ Having used up fruit from a bottle with clips, don't put the clips back on the bottle or they may lose their spring.

Candying

Any spare orange, lemon or grapefruit peel can be converted into candied peel, including those from mandarin oranges. I find my candied peel does not look quite as smart and dry as the bought sort, nor does it keep so long, but the flavour is very good.

Wash the outside of the skins well and cut out any dye stamps. Put it in a pan with cold water to cover, bring to the boil and drain. Do this at least once more. Cover with fresh water and simmer until really tender (the sugar you add later will tend to toughen them). Drain well.

For 6 average oranges put 350 g (12 oz) of granulated sugar in a pan, with 175 ml (6 fl oz) of water, and 1½ tablespoons of golden syrup. Heat gently until the sugar

dissolves, then add the peel and simmer until it is clear and the syrup almost absorbed. Drain on a wire rack. Then set the peel to dry on greaseproof paper in a warm place, like an airing cupboard. Cut it in pieces with sharp scissors some way through the drying process. Once dry, shake it in a bag with castor sugar before storing in a tightly closed jar.

Crystallizing

Crystallizing is almost a lost art but in *Elinor Fettiplace's Receipt Book* - a book of recipes dating from 1604 edited and put in context by Hilary Spurling - I found this:

to drie Apricocks, Peaches, Pippins or Pearplums

Take your apricocks or pearplums, & let them boile one walmes in as much clarified sugar as will cover them, so them lie infused in an earthen pan three dayes, then take out your fruits, & let boile your syrupe againe, when you have thus used them three times then put half a pound of drie sugar into your syrupe, & so let it boile till it come to a verie thick syrup, wherein let your fruits boile leysurelie 3 or 4 walmes, then take them foorth of the syrup, then plant them on a lettice of rods or wyer, & so put them into yor stewe, & every second day turne them & when they bee through dry you may box them & keep them all the yeare; before you set them to drying you must wash them in a little warm water, when they are half drie you must dust a little sugar upon them throw a fine Lawne.

Hilary Spurling says the method is to put the fruit in the pan with sugar to cover them and dissolve it *very* slowly, only bringing it to the boil when fully dissolved, then remove the pan from the heat. The fruit can then sit in its pan for the 3 days. The instruction to 'take out your fruits' meant to put both them and their syrup in a pan which would allow boiling. So you can ignore that - unless you did put them in an earthenware bowl. They are then brought to the boil and allowed to cool on 3 consecutive days. A missing instruction is that the fruit should then be taken out of the syrup before the final sugar is added. In boiling it down, be careful not to take it to caramel. Stop if it hints at turning colour and put back the fruit. Hilary Spurling says the '3 or 4 walmes' is to bring it to the boil three or four times and explains that a stewe was a drying stove - use a plate warmer or airing cupboard instead. It is a recipe I have yet to try, but it has the touches which suggest it would work well.

Drying

Drying is a more hit-and-miss business than any other process. I suggest you try with a single apple, and find where in your house is dry enough, and then try with more. The late varieties tend to dry best.

Peel and core an apple and slice it in rings. Blanch the rings in a colander over boiling water, with a lid on, for 5 minutes. Thread on a clean (undyed) string or a bamboo pole in a dry place, spacing the rings so air gets between them. Or you can try them in the oven on a rack. You need a temperature of about 50°C (120°F) to start with, but this can be raised to 65°C (140°F) after an hour or so. Pears can be dried in the same way.

Frosting Fruit
This is a wonderfully easy way to produce a table decoration. Wash the fruit and dry it well. Beat up 1 egg white with 2 tablespoons of water and brush the mixture all over the fruit. Roll the fruit over a plate of castor sugar, and set it on a rack to dry.

Glazing Fruit
This is the way to produce those grapes coated in a crunchy sugar coating which are served among petit fours. Heat 500 g (1 lb) of sugar very gently with 125 ml (¼ pt) of water in a large pan. When the sugar has totally dissolved boil rapidly *without stirring* until a little dropped into cold water makes a crisp droplet. Let it cool slightly then dip your fruit (grapes, cherries) and put them to cool on waxed paper. To make toffee apples you just cook the sugar until golden brown.

Pickling and Spicing
- If you want a vegetable pickle to stay crisp - as for pickled onions or cabbage - let the vinegar get cold before you pour it over.
- If a recipe calls for spiced vinegar you can make it by allowing 2 to 3 oz of pickling spice (Boots often sells it when supermarkets don't) to each litre (2 pt) vinegar. Heat the vinegar with the spice in until almost bubbling. Turn it off *before* it bubbles and leave it to stand for 2 hours before straining.

Making Jams and Jellies
If you haven't got preserving sugar you can make perfectly good jam with granulated, but using preserving sugar gives a greater clarity. You can make jam with any fruit, and even with some vegetables: marrow jam flavoured with lemon, pineapple or ginger is delicious - and cheap.

Jar Preparation
Wash the jars scrupulously clean before starting to make the jam. Drain but don't dry them. Then, without touching the inside, put them in a cold oven and turn it on to about gas no 2 or 150°C (300°F). Do this just as you start to cook the jam and leave them in for the time it takes to cook. Remove, holding them by the outside and fill while still fairly hot.

★ An old trick for reducing the amount of froth produced as the fruit boils is to wipe the preserving pan round with a butter paper before putting in the fruit. And buttering the base makes the jam less likely to stick.
★ Your jam will have a brighter colour if the sugar is heated in the oven before it is added to the fruit.

Jelly Bag
A jelly bag is a bag of thick cloth which is traditionally used for straining jellies of any kind. But several layers of muslin or a piece of well-boiled sheeting (to get the

residue of detergent out), tied to the legs of an upturned chair, work just as well as pricey bags.

Graining/crystallization
To avoid crystals let the sugar melt *totally* on a low heat before attempting to boil it, and once it is at around 118°-121°C (245°-250°F) stir to the bare minimum needed to stop it catching on the bottom. Adding a little liquid glucose or cream of tartar mixed with a touch of water also helps to prevent it from forming crystals.

Setting
To set well jams and jellies need to be made from fruit with a fairly high acid content and enough pectin, as acidity helps pectin to gel. Fruits vary with the season but some, such as strawberries, never have much pectin while others, like blackberries and blackcurrants, set beautifully. If you doubt the setting ability of your fruit you can test it once you have stewed it, by putting a teaspoonful of the juice from the stewed fruit in a glass and adding 3 teaspoons of methylated spirits. When you stir gently it should clot. If it doesn't you may need to add pectin.

For poor setters, buy a pectin additive such as Certo or use Tate and Lyle's special preserving sugar called 'Sugar with Pectin' - but, be warned, if you increase the pectin for fruits which gel well anyway you will get a very solid jam which will shrink in the jar. Alternatively, put the sugar over the fruit overnight to draw out the juices; you can then cook most fruit with no added water. This produces a full-flavoured preserve with so little liquid to gel that you don't need a firm jelly-like result.

For a good set, jam must boil hard, and it will rise up the pan - only half fill the pan. If you are interrupted when jam is half boiled, turn it off or it may burn when you are not watching. Afterwards bring it back to the boil slowly and just continue boiling - it should be none the worse. But only cook for just long enough to get a good set - over-boiling will break down the set and darken the jam.

The setting point of jam can be found by putting a spoonful on a plate in the refrigerator. At setting point it will wrinkle slightly as you draw a finger through it, when cold, and the drop on your finger will not drip off.

Potting up
Let the jam stand until it forms a slight skin, then stir, before potting up. Cover at once with waxed paper circles, but leave until cold before covering with cellophane. Moisten the cellophane on the outside before covering the pot.

Jane Grigson's Fruit Book, Penguin
Leslie Johns and Violet Stevenson, *Complete Book of Fruit,* Angus and Robertson

Storing Fruit - Long Term

Ripe fruit gives off a gas which speeds the ripening of other fruit near it. So if you wish to ripen some unripe fruit put it in a paper bag with a piece of ripe fruit and close the bag. To keep fruit do the reverse, removing any that become ripe, so they don't hurry on the rest.

One needs to know one's fruit: most apples store well, but not all, and, though some pears store well, many do not.

For storing, hard fruit must have its stalk on and be perfect. If it isn't, it will spoil quickly. Pears must be picked before they are ripe, but apples can be allowed to ripen on the tree. If you have a choice of which fruit to store, small apples have smaller cells and this makes them store better.

Both pears and apples should be stored, spaced out in a cool airy place, away from strong smells. If there is a chance of them getting dusty, wrap them in newspaper. Check them regularly to remove any that are ripening or going bad. With pears this is more a matter of smell than look, as they ripen from the inside out.

GAME AND POULTRY

Game Seasons

The times of year at which each type of game may be killed in Britain are strictly controlled.

S = shooting forbidden on Sundays throughout Great Britain

X = shooting forbidden on Christmas Day throughout Great Britain

SS = shooting forbidden on Sunday in Scotland and some other UK areas

XS = shooting forbidden on Christmas Day in Scotland and some other UK areas

Blackgame	S X	20 Aug - 10 Dec
Capercaillie	SS XS	1 Oct - 31 Jan
Duck - Wild	SS XS	1 Sept - 20 Feb (below spring high tide mark) 1 Sept - 31 Jan (elsewhere)
Geese - Wild	SS XS	as duck
Grouse	S X	12 Aug - 10 Dec
Guinea Fowl		Late spring to early summer
Hares	S X	11 Dec (Scotland 1 July) - 31 March - on moorlands, elsewhere no closed season
Partridge	S X	1 Sept - 1 Feb
Pheasant	S X	1 Oct - 1 Feb
Plovers - Golden		1 Sept - 31 Jan
Ptarmigan	S X	12 Aug - 10 Dec (Scotland only)
Rabbits		No closed season
Snipe	SS XS	12 Aug - 31 Jan
Woodcock	SS XS	1 Oct - 31 Jan (England and Wales) 1 Sept - 31 Jan (Scotland)

Deer		England and Wales	Scotland
Red	Male	1 May - 31 July	21 Oct - 30 June
	Female	1 March - 31 Oct	16 Feb - 20 Oct
Fallow	Male	1 May - 31 July	1 May - 31 July
	Female	1 March - 31 Oct	16 Feb - 20 Oct
Roe	Male	1 Nov - 31 March	21 Oct - 31 March
	Female	1 March - 31 Oct	1 April - 20 Oct

The dates were kindly provided by The Game Conservancy, Fordingbridge, Hants SP6 1EF Tel: 0425 52381

Hanging Game

In some of the houses I remember from my childhood there were chilly larders with thick walls and flagstone floors, through whose zinc-meshed air vents the sun never shone. In some, tall pine cupboards mesh-panelled against flies, covered whole walls. Few homes today are so well equipped for hanging game and, if you find yourself with birds to hang, careful thought should be given to where to hang them. They need a very cool place with plenty of air and - and here's the catch - absolutely no flies. Contrary to what many people think, feathers are not a protection against flies. Few culinary experiences are nastier than starting to pluck a bird and discovering it heaving with maggots. So great care has to be taken in the early part of the season.

Hanging birds and beasts for the right length of time makes an enormous difference to the flavour. It isn't just a matter of giving a bird the 'gameyness' one associates with pheasant. The hanging time is needed so that enzymes in the flesh can work on it, softening it and enriching the taste. Tradition has it that, among game birds, swimmers (e.g wild duck) are hung by their feet and flyers are hung by their necks. Don't ask me what difference it makes - but that is how it is usually done.

Unless you are an old hand who can tell by the feel of the air how a bird is doing you should check them daily, as the hanging times vary greatly with the weather. Thundery weather can turn a bird rapidly, even if the temperature isn't high, and birds hung in warm muggy weather need much shorter hanging than they would if it was cool and crisp and game tastes best when it matures slowly at a very low temperature.

★ The standard way of freshening up game which has become a bit too whiffy - but is still safe to eat - is to wipe it with equal parts of vinegar and water.

Feathered Game

Grouse
Check if a bird is young with the bursa test (see opposite). Old birds may be shedding a toe nail or have a line across the nail where one has been shed.

Freshly shot grouse are sometimes eaten at once - to launch the shooting season; after that they are generally hung for 2 to 10 days, according to the weather. When ready they smell slightly 'high' but not unpleasantly so.

Partridge
If you have a choice, go for partridge with yellow or greyish legs. These are the native grey partridge and considered superior in flavour to the red-legged kind which are comparative newcomers - only having been introduced under Charles II.

Use the bursa test opposite to check the age and look at the legs: the legs of yellow-legged partridge are only yellow in their youth. Also look at the long feathers in the wing: in a young bird they open in a V at the ends; in an older bird they end tidily.

Early in the season partridge need only be hung for 3 to 5 days; later on old birds can be hung for as long as 7 to 10 days. This is another bird which some people like very gamey. A friend of mine has an aged aunt who even insists they aren't fit to eat until the heads fall off. However, for most people's palates they should not have more than a hint of a gamey smell.

Pheasant
Hang pheasants in feather by the neck for 3 to 10 days - and preferably singly, not in pairs, so the air can reach all sides. Country lore has it that a pheasant should be hung until the tail feathers drop out. But, for most people's taste, 7 days is the average hanging time. Use the bursa test opposite to check the age and cook it within 2 days of plucking.

As Dorothy Hartley rightly says: 'There is as much difference between pheasant well hung and cooked as game and the same bird cooked fresh, as there is between two different breeds of bird. One is game; the other practically brown chicken.'

Pigeon
Pigeons are best from May to October and should be plucked, drawn and eaten soon after killing. They are tasty but tend to be dry. So, except when very young, they are much better as a pot roast than as a roast. As there is little meat on the legs it is thrifty to serve only the breast and keep the carcass for making soup - for pigeon soup is excellent.

Quail
Quail can be hung for 3 to 4 days. Beloved by Italians, these birds were hugely popular in Victorian England but have become something of a curiosity today, though they make very good eating.

Snipe
Snipe are only hung for 3 to 4 days and then plucked, and possibly gutted - though they can be cooked ungutted, like woodcock.

Wild Duck
The ducks which are most likely to arrive in a kitchen are teal, mallard and widgeon. You should be able to tell them by weight, if nothing else. Teal are the smallest, weighing only 300 to 370 g (11 to 13 oz), widgeon weigh 700 to 900 g (1½ to 2 lb), while mallard weigh 1 to 1.3 kg (2½ to 2¾ lb). One of the curiosities of teal is that, by a quite remarkable piece of casuistry, they are classified as fish by the French Catholic Church, and may be eaten as such during Lent.

Young ducks have soft webbing which you can tear easily. Whatever the age, they only need to hang for 1 to 3 days, and when the weather is warm it may be best to gut them first. In cleaning them, make sure you remove the oil gland near their vent - with which they keep their feathers waterproof; leaving it in makes the flesh taste of turpentine.

Wild duck also have a bad reputation for tasting fishy. If you suspect this may be the case, Julia Drysdale says you should put an onion and a potato in the body cavity and place the bird in 0.5 cm (¼ in) boiling water and bake at gas no 4 or 180°C (350°F) for 10 minutes basting frequently. Then drain, throw away the onion and potato and cook as normal. These ducks are not fatty like most farm ducks and they need to be cooked like other game birds to keep them moist when cooking.

Wild Goose
On a young goose the markings are softer and less distinct than on an older bird and until November the tips of young tail feathers are separated into a V quite different from the normal closed feathers of older birds. Whatever their age, they need to hang for up to 3 weeks. They can only be roasted when young and the method for ordinary geese on page 73 should be followed - but

wild geese are less fatty and need to be totally enclosed in foil before cooking to keep them moist.

Woodcock
Woodcock are diminutive birds eaten in a distinctly curious manner, which some rave about, but which is hard to stomach. They are plucked, but not gutted; and cooked and eaten, head, entrails and all. They are hung by the feet for 3 to 14 days (some like them almost decomposed) and are said to be ready when a droplet of blood forms on the beak. Traditionally they are roasted sitting on a slice of toast which catches their juices, with bacon covering them.

The Bursa Test
According to the Game Conservancy, this is a good test for judging the age of the major game birds once they are dead. When young they have a short cul-de-sac passage, called the bursa, between their vent (anus) and tail. As the birds age the bursa shortens and may vanish. So you can check the age of a bird by how far you can push the end of a matchstick into the bursa. The distances for young birds are these: grouse 1 cm (½ in); partridge 1 cm (½ in); pheasant 2.5 cm (1 in).

Plucking Game and Poultry
Any bird is most easily plucked when just killed and still warm, but if a bird has to be hung this is impossible. In that case you can dip it for 30 seconds (not more) into boiling water. But only dip it in water if you are going to cook it as soon as it is plucked, or the warmth may make it go bad. To pluck it, just grab small feathers in handfuls, and large ones individually, and tug in the direction in which they lie. Go gently if game is very high or you will remove lumps of flesh. It is tedious, tough on the hands and takes far longer than you might expect, but it is very easy. Singe any remaining fluff with a candle.

Once plucked, game should usually be cooked the same day, but birds vary in their keeping time in a refrigerator, according to how high they already are. But they freeze well.

Drawing Game and Poultry
The only tricky part about drawing a bird is that you have to be very careful not to break the gall bladder. The yellow bile is very bitter and will spoil the bird, so go gently.
1 Slit the skin on the underside of the neck.
2 Cut the neck off very close to the body but leave the neck skin to leave a flap hanging from the body.
3 Remove the crop and the windpipe from the neck end.
4 Insert two fingers and gently loosen the contents of the body cavity.
5 Cut a slit crosswise between the tail stump and the vent (anus).
6 Insert two fingers through the hole and loosen the body contents.
7 Hold the bird firmly at the head end while drawing out the gizzard and intestines the other end.

8 Then carefully remove the heart and liver with the gall bladder attached.
9 Cut the gall bladder from the liver without breaking it, and split and clean the gizzard, stripping off all yellow parts.
10 Wash or wipe out the bird and set aside the giblets - heart, liver, neck (without head) and cleaned gizzard.

Cooking Game Birds
The best way to cook any game bird depends entirely on its age; old birds always need long slow cooking with lots of fat and moisture or they are tough and dry. If you have some old game and don't know how to cook it any good recipe for *coq au vin* will make a passable dish.

In autumn young birds are those which hatched the previous spring. But birds age fast, and one of the best game cooks I know reckons that past Christmas even these are getting on the old side. So she roasts young birds until Christmas, and casseroles all birds after that. Below are simply the key times and temperatures for roasting - from which you can probably deduce casserole times if you wish to be inventive.

The basic method for roasting all game is to put butter inside and out, season it and cover it with strips of fatty bacon or with thin slices of pork fat (if you don't like the bacon flavour). It also helps to moisten game birds by putting a peeled apple or sliced orange in the body cavity. Despite all this, they should then be basted *very* frequently during cooking. A more labour-saving method is to prepare them as above and just tuck the birds - singly or in groups - into roasting bags or in well-closed foil parcels. Then they baste themselves. An old version of this was to wrap game birds in vine leaves. Whatever the method, heat the oven first and lie the birds on their breasts - turning them to the other side at half time. Then the best meat is also the juiciest. Turn them right side up when nearly done and open the bag or foil if you wish to brown.

Game	Time to Cook the Bird	Oven Settings to Roast Gas/Electric	Servings per Bird
Blackgame	casserole		3
Capercaillie	casserole		1-2
Grouse	25-40 mins	5, 190°C (375°F)	1-2
Partridge	20 mins	7, 220°C (425°F)	1-2
or	20-25 mins	5, 190°C (375°F)	
Pheasant	45-60 mins	5, 190°C (375°F)	3-4
Pigeon	20-30 mins	6, 200°C (400°F)	1
Ptarmigan	casserole		1
Quail	15 mins	5, 190°C (375°F)	1
Snipe	10 mins	7, 220°C (425°F)	1

Game	Time to Cook the Bird	Oven Settings to Roast Gas/Electric	Servings per Bird
Wild Duck:			
Mallard	30-35 mins	6-7, 200°-220°C (400°-425°F)	2-3
Teal	15-20 mins	6-7, 200°-220°C (400°-425°F)	1-2
Widgeon	20-25 mins	6-7, 200°-220°C (400°-425°F)	1-2
Woodcock	10-15 mins	7, 220°C (425°F) bloody	1
	20-30 mins	5, 190°C (375°F) medium	

Carving Game Birds

Game birds, large enough to be carved, are carved like chicken (page 72), except that the smaller breasts can be served whole, and they may be the only part of the bird worth eating. In this case, it is prudent to keep the rest of the carcass for soup.

★ An excellent and classic addition to game soup is dry sherry in which a few chillies have steeped. A cleaned-out Worcester Sauce bottle is the best container as the dropper top lets you administer it in moderate amounts.

Furred Game

Hare

Hares are at their best from September to February and at that time a young hare has small sharp white teeth, while in an older one the teeth are large and yellow. Some people paunch the hare the instant it is killed, as the guts come away most easily then. Others gut it after hanging. It is hung, head down, in fur, for 5 to 10 days (5 often being long enough), with a bowl containing a teaspoon of vinegar under to catch the blood - the vinegar keeps the blood from congealing. A good Jack (male) hare will serve 6 to 8 people.

Skinning and Gutting Hare and Rabbit

Tie the back legs together and hang the hare up with a bowl underneath. Cut round the legs, and slit the skin down their length, then pull it off down the body, like removing a dress. Cut the feet off at the first leg joint, and remove the head. Slit the animal down the stomach (without letting the knife pierce the contents) and carefully remove the insides, letting the bowl catch the blood. After gutting, remove the thin blueish membrane which coats the body and wipe it with a cloth damped in vinegar and water - but don't wash it. (In theory, washing is supposed to take the flavour away, but I know those who do wash hares with no ill effect.) Rabbits are skinned in the same way but you need not catch the blood. Cut away any pulpy areas where a bad shot has bruised the flesh.

Roasting

Only a young hare is suitable for roasting and even then it should first be marinaded in red wine, seasoning and herbs for 24 hours. It may also be more interesting only to roast the saddle, and casserole the legs or use them in some other dish.

If you need to divide a hare up treat it much like a chicken (page 72).

Roast a saddle for 35 minutes at gas no 6 or 200°C (400°F) covered with bacon fat and baste it often. Roast a whole hare in the same way for 45 to 50 minutes.

Rabbit

Rabbits are best from October to February. They should be gutted as soon as they are killed, and are best when hung for only 24 hours in a cool place then skinned like a hare (above). A young animal will have sharp teeth and claws, and ears which are easily torn. A whole rabbit serves 4 to 6 people; a saddle serves 2.

Trussing and Jointing

Pull all four legs towards the middle and tie them with white cotton string. Traditionally, a skewer is pushed through the head and into the back so the head is upright - but few people would welcome this sight today, and the head is best removed. Joint it like a chicken (see page 72).

Cooking

Rabbit tends to be dry and it is usually better in a casserole than roasted. If you wish to roast it, a thrifty and practical old way to remedy its dryness is to thread fatty left-over bacon rinds through the back to both moisten it and improve the flavour. * Otherwise, truss, spread with butter, season and cover with bacon slices before roasting. Best of all, marinade it overnight in red wine with a touch of oil, onion, garlic and bay leaf. Then proceed as from *, basting with marinade. Test if it is cooked, as for chicken (page 72); it should not be pink. An average rabbit takes 1 hour at gas no 6 or 200°C (400°F).

Venison

It is said that venison gave us the phrase to 'eat humble pie' for the 'umbles' of venison are (or were) pieces of offal such as sweetbreads, and 'stones', liver and so on. These are said to have been given to the people who sat at the bottom of the table, while those at the head of the table ate the flesh. It benefits from marinading for 24 hours in red wine with some onion, carrot, juniper berries, bouquet garni and just a hint of *wine* vinegar.

He did give us the meanest dinner of beef shoulders and umbles of venison.

Samuel Pepys

Venison needs to be skinned, gutted and hung for a fair while or it will be tough - say, 7 to 10 days after shooting. In preparing the meat, check for any flesh which is pulpy and bruised and cut it out. The cuts are very similar to those on beef and the best part is the haunch, which can be roasted, as can the shoulder. If the meat is likely to be tender, steaks can be cut from the leg and chops from the neck, while the other cuts make excellent casseroles.

Venison lacks fat, so it really needs to be larded with pork fat. But if you lack a larding needle just stick a slim-bladed knife well into the flesh and then push a strip of fat down the hole with the point, at intervals all over the meat.

In addition to larding it needs to be well covered with fatty bacon. Then roast at gas no 5 or 190°C (375°F) for 15 minutes per lb (450 g), or for 20 minutes per lb if under 4 lb (1.8 kg). Baste it constantly.

Venison should be rather underdone when you take it from the oven. As it tends to hold the heat and continue cooking for some while longer it can easily become overdone and leathery. It needs a rich gravy and a sweet-sour fruity flavour, such as red currant jelly, to go with it.

Julia Drysdale, *Classic Game Cookery*, Papermac

Poultry

Chicken and Turkey

One used to test the youth of a fresh chicken by feeling whether the tip of its breast bone was bendy like the end of one's nose. Now you'd be hard put to it to find an old bird if you wanted one. On a fresh chicken look for eyes which are clear not sunken, and flesh that is fresh. Most birds have white skin, but maize-fed birds are sunflower yellow, and the new *poulets noirs* have curious black legs. But be very dubious if anyone says they are offering you a capon. A capon was a cock which was neutered with a hormone pellet. This practice is now illegal and there must be few farmers who take the trouble to castrate their cocks - which is the ancient way to make a capon.

Check any frozen bird over, looking for pale dry-looking patches (freezer burn, showing it may be rancid) or signs of bruising. Then check the label. If it says polyphosphates anywhere they have been added to make the flesh soak up water, and who wants to buy water at the price of meat?

- Poussins and double poussins are very young birds (under 1 kg, 2 lb) which usually have very little flavour.
- Broilers are fairly young birds (weighing about 1.35 kg, 3 lb).
- Roasting chickens are at their best when 1.8 to 2.25 kg (4 to 5 lb) and have more flavour than the younger birds.
- Boiling fowl are older larger birds weighing upwards of 2.7 kg (6 lb), but with lots of flavour.

A free-range chicken which has had a good diet, is undoubtedly the best chicken. The next best are chill-fresh chickens which have been kept under free-range conditions, and there are more and more of these on the market.

Keeping

It is best to cook fresh or thawed poultry within 24 hours of buying, even if it is kept in a refrigerator. But if it has travelled around in a warm car, or the weather is thundery, it could go off before that. Under the wings is usually the first place to go - so check for any change of colour or smell. If it is close wrapped in plastic open it slightly to let the bird breathe. Removing the giblets from the inside and inserting a peeled onion also makes it keep better. Do NOT let uncooked poultry touch or drip onto other food - see page 51.

Thawing

Because of the risks of food poisoning and because they go bad easily it is best to thaw frozen birds in the refrigerator. This takes a very long time with a large bird, so if you do thaw a bird in a room cook it immediately after; don't let it hang around.

Thawing Times

Weight	Room temperature 16°C (65°F)	Refrigerator 5°C (40°F)
2 lb (900 g)	8 hrs	28 hrs
3 lb (1.35 kg)	9 hrs	32 hrs
4 lb (1.80 kg)	10 hrs	38 hrs
5 lb (2.25 kg)	12 hrs	44 hrs
6 lb (2.70 kg)	14 hrs	50 hrs
7 lb (3.15 kg)	16 hrs	56 hrs
9 lb (4.23 kg)	19 hrs	65 hrs
12 lb (5.40 kg)	22 hrs	70 hrs
15 lb (6.75 kg)	24 hrs	75 hrs
18 lb (8.10 kg)	27 hrs	80 hrs
22 lb (9.90 kg)	36 hrs	96 hrs

I am indebted to the British Chicken Information Service for the thawing times for the lighter birds and to the Turkey Information Service for other times.

Take any giblets (neck, liver and gizzard in a bag) out of the body as soon as you can. Poultry *must* be fully thawed before it is cooked.

Roasting Preparation

Remove giblets if they are inside the bird. Pre-heat the oven. Rinse the bird inside and out under a tap. Dry the skin well with kitchen paper (*do not use a tea towel or other kitchen cloth* - unless you want food poisoning).

★ Spread the outside well with butter and put a lump inside (unless you are stuffing it). Dust with pepper and salt, inside and out. Half a lemon inside is also good.

Stuffing

The food safety pundits now say it is best not to stuff a bird in its body cavity, but only under the flap of skin at the neck. This is because of the risk of an inexperienced cook failing to allow for the extra time which a stuffing needs and serving undercooked stuffing which has been contaminated with salmonella from the chicken. If you do stuff a bird remember you *can't* assume the stuffing is cooked just because the meat on the thickest part of the thigh is done.

Roasting Cooking Chicken and Turkey

Chicken and turkey go dry very easily, so roast them

in a roasting bag, or totally wrapped in foil, with the ends of the foil rolled to close it well. Place the bird on its breast - switching to the other side at half time. Near the end, right it and remove the paper so the breast will brown. If you have neither foil nor a bag, cover it with discarded butter papers and baste it every 15 to 20 minutes.

Roast chickens and *very small* turkeys for 20 minutes per lb (450 g) at gas no 5 or 190°C (375°F), plus perhaps 20 minutes extra, depending on the size of the bird and whether the oven is up to temperature. Roast a turkey of 8 lb or more for 18 minutes per lb (450 g) at gas no 3 or 160°C (325°F). The not-so-great British tradition of Christmas turkey spoiling - having dried it all day at gas no 5 110°C (225°F) - should long since have been abandoned.

> Weigh any bird when oven ready - and count the stuffing as part of its weight when calculating the cooking time. *Never go by the timing alone; always test that a bird is cooked.* To test for this push a skewer deep into the high. If clear juice runs out when you remove it the bird is cooked. If it is at all pink it isn't. Never eat undercooked poultry. See also Stuffing, page 71.

★ While the bird cooks, the giblets (totally cleaned of any yellow bits) would be boiling up to make the liquid for the gravy. Cook them with a carrot and an unpeeled onion - the onion skin makes the liquid brown so you don't need browning.

Boiling a Chicken
Put a large pan of water to boil. Prepare as for roasting (above) to ★ Place in boiling water just to cover, with a washed carrot, 3 sprigs of parsley, a whole onion and a bay leaf (and possibly lemon zest or garlic). When it returns to boiling reduce the heat so the water hardly bubbles. An average modern bird takes 1¼ to 1½ hours; a tough old hen will take longer. Test as for roast chicken. If you are not serving the bird at once let it cool in the liquor. The liquid can be used for sauces and soups, and the fat you skim from its surface when cold is excellent for frying.

Trussing a Chicken
Professional methods of trussing need a trussing needle - and who has one? Tie the ends of the drumsticks together with a figure of eight in white cotton string and use string or small skewers to fix each wing to the body. You remove the string before the bird goes to the table, so use any method that *works*; elegance is icing on the cake.

Jointing a Chicken
Pull the 'knee' above the drumstick away from the body. Cut through the skin linking limb to breast. Pull the knee towards the table until the 'hip' joint shows. Cut *between* the two bones. Cut an arc through the breast, close to the rib bones, and down towards where the

wing must, logically, join the body, pull the meat away and sever the joint as above. Use kitchen scissors to cut through the lower ribs, to remove the breast. The breast can be split in half along the bone, if you wish, and the thigh separated from the drumstick. There is a lot of good meat on the lower ribs and base of the carcass which are left behind and these can be cooked as for boiled chicken to make soup.

Carving a Chicken or Duck
Poultry should be served so that each person has some white (breast) meat and some brown (leg, thigh and wing) meat. So, unless you are pre-carving the whole bird, alternate your cuts. Remove the leg and thigh as for jointing (above). The drumstick may be separated from the thigh afterwards by cutting through the joint. Then pull the wing away from the body in the same way and slice through the joint attaching it to the body. Now, slice the breast downwards in fairly thin slices, parallel to the breast bone, sliding the blade down the ribs in slices thin enough to be elegant but not so thin they fall apart.

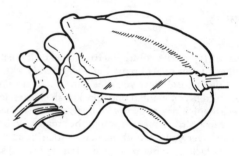

Carving a Turkey
The limbs of most turkeys are too big, and often too sinewy, to serve whole. So you simply slice meat off the drumstick and thigh, and off the breast, to give portions of both types of meat. The drumstick meat is the driest, so slice the meat on the thigh first. Keep the slices fairly thin and cut through the skin joining thigh to breast to give a larger breast area to carve.

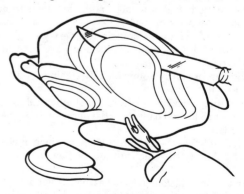

Duck
Contrary to popular belief, most ducks are now Pekin duck hybrids - not Aylesbury ducks - and they are really

ducklings of about 49 days old, as mature ducks can be very tough.

If choosing a duck in feather check the bill and feet; young ducks have a pliable bill and feet with soft webbing which is easily torn. A freshly killed duck, in feather, should hang for 24 to 36 hours.

Ducks have big heavy bones and a shallow breast, so a 4-lb duck will only give 2 good servings, though you could stretch it round 4 in the family, with plenty of vegetables. For the rest:

2 - 2¼ kg (4½ - 5 lb) serves 3-4
2½ - 2¾ kg (5½ - 6 lb) serves 4-5
3 kg + (6½ lb +) serves 5-6

Trussing and Jointing
Truss a duck like a chicken. If you need to joint a duck the breast is so small that it is best to cut it down through the breast bone and then simply split each half into two through the breast.

Roasting a Duck
There are all kinds of stories about how to get crisp duck; one friend of mine singes her ducks with a blow lamp to help the fat on its way and another goes over it with a hair dryer. Ingenious though such methods are, the secret of cooking duck with crisp skin outside and succulent flesh inside is simply as follows - but it works best with gas:

- Preheat the oven to gas no 7 or 220°C (425°F) while you prepare a duck as for chicken (page 71) to ★ making sure the skin is really dry.
- Prick the skin *well* with a fork all over, so its fat can run out, but don't pierce the meat. To get deliciously crisp skin sprinkle it well with salt (preferably Maldon Sea Salt), adding pepper to flavour. Preheat the oven.
- Place it on a grid over the roasting tin - to keep it right out of its fat. Put it into the middle of the oven, uncovered at gas no 7 or 220°C (425°F) for 15 minutes, then cook at gas no 4 or 180°C (350°F). Allow a total of 20 to 25 minutes per lb (450 g). *Do not* baste it while cooking, but prick it from time to time as it cooks to help the fat run out. Keep the fat which runs out; it is excellent for frying potatoes. *Check that the bird is cooked a little ahead of time. Serve when ready, as timings are always slightly variable* (see Carving, opposite).

Goose
A goose is a lovely bird and rightly lorded over the Christmas table until it was ousted by the fleshier charms of the turkey. Charles Dickens must have thought the same, for only an enthusiast could write, as he did in *A Christmas Carol:*

There was never such a goose. Bob said he didn't believe there was such a goose ever cooked. Its tenderness and flavour, size and cheapness, were the themes of universal admiration ...everyone had had enough, and the youngest Cratchits in particular were steeped in sage and onion to the eyebrows!

Geese are bigger than ducks and slightly less fatty, but the same cooking methods apply, with or without the traditional sage and onion stuffing, but allow 13 to 15 minutes per pound (450 g). Like ducks, geese have heavy bones and a 12-lb goose only serves 8 to 10 people. If a goose has very little fat - as a wild goose may - baste it regularly during cooking and even cook it breast down or cover the breast loosely with foil. Carve like a turkey.

Before boiling up the giblets set aside the liver, to make liver pâté, and afterwards be sure to keep the fat from the goose. Like duck fat, it is excellent for frying.

Guinea Fowl
Guinea fowl taste half way between a chicken and a pheasant, but cook them as pheasant - page 69.

British Chicken Information Service, Bury House, 126-128 Cromwell Road, London SW7 4ET Tel: 01 373 7757
British Turkey Federation Ltd, High Holborn House, 52-54 High Holborn, London WC1V 6SX Tel: 01 242 4683
Duck Information Service, Thames View House, 6 St Peters Road, Twickenham, Middx TW1 1QX Tel: 01 892 2720

GRAINS

Flours
Probably no food has such an ancient history of snobbery as flour. Even in ancient Greece the nobility had white bread, while the plebeians ate brown. This was still going strong in Chaucer's time: the prioress ate white bread while the poor widow had to make do with brown and it remained a poor relation until the 1970s. But, there may have been more than snobbery in it.

Brown v White
Wheat grains aren't uniform. There is a small germ (the embryo of a new plant) which is rich in fat, protein and certain B vitamins. Then there is a big fibrous area (the bulk of flour) surrounded by a thin layer of protein, and a tough coating (the bran). These different areas react to grinding in different ways. When wheat is milled for white flour the coarser particles - the bran and wheatgerm - may be left behind and only the finer whiter areas made into flour.

The oils in wheatgerm mean that flour containing it will go rancid quite quickly. But once the germ has been extracted, flour will keep very much better. So the big white-brown divide was probably between the rich who ate white (and therefore unrancid) bread, and the poor who had to stomach a bit of rancidity near the end of the season. Of course, the millers have had a vested interest in pushing white flour, which would give them two spin-off products - bran and wheatgerm - to sell separately.

Wholemeal flour is the whole grain in flour. This gives it three times the fibre of white flour, but in most modern grinding, the speed of the rollers generates enough heat to kill some of the enzymes and vitamins. To have all the enzymes and vitamins you normally have to buy stoneground flour, though some millers -

such as Jordans - produce the same effect by setting metal rollers to slow grind.

> Nowadays the enzymes which caused wholemeal flour to turn rancid more quickly can be made inactive. So most wholemeal flour now has a good shelf life.

Nutrition

Nutritionally you *can't* simply say - brown bread and brown flour = good; white bread and white flour = bad. Some brown bread and flour isn't really brown at all. It is white flour tinted brown by adding caramel - one of the more dubious additives. And, by law, calcium carbonate (chalk to you and me) *must* be added to all bread and flour except wholemeal, self-raising and wheat-malt.

So, if you want to avoid such additives you have to buy **100 per cent** wholemeal or **100 per cent** wheatmeal - as there would be little point in adding caramel to 100 per cent wholemeal bread and flour. However, that doesn't mean it is always additive-free. Preservatives are permitted, and used.

We should perhaps be grateful at the relative purity of our bread: in the mid-eighteenth century a tract was published entitled *'Poison detected, or Frightful Truths...a treatise on bread and the abuses practised in making that food'* and a hundred years later the first edition of *Enquire Within* said:

> *Bread and flour are adulterated with flour of inferior grain, Indian corn flour, potato flour, pea and bean flour, bone dust [!] &c. None of these are positively injurious. But they are also adulterated with plaster of Paris, chalk, alum, &c, and these are highly prejudicial to health, especially when taken continuously.*

Strong and Weak Flour

So far as performance is concerned, the big divide is between the grains which behave like chewing gum and the grains which behave like bubble gum. Certain kinds, notably Canadian wheat, contain a substance called gluten in a form which is very elastic. When it is stretched and puffed up by yeast, it holds the air bubbles, as bubble-gum does, and produces the lightest bread. Other forms of wheat and other grains either have no gluten at all or have a form which behaves like chewing gum - stretching perfectly, but not being able to hold a bubble for the life of it.

For reasons best known to history, wheat flour made from the bubble-gum type is called strong, and the chewing-gum kind is called weak. Obviously strong flour is ideal wherever you want air to be held, while weak flour is ideal for flat crisp textures like biscuits.

Arrowroot

Arrowroot is very fine flour which, for some curious reason, you buy at chemists not at grocers. Yet no less a gourmet than Escoffier admired its cooking qualities and wrote: 'It is ... infinitely probable that before long starch, fecula or arrowroot obtained in a state of absolute purity will replace flour in the roux.' It is invaluable for thickening sauces or glazing tarts, as it thickens quickly and gives no floury taste. Like cornflour, it needs to be mixed with a little water and then added to the other ingredients and cooked, while stirring, as the liquid thickens rapidly.

Barley

This is a low gluten flour which has a pleasantly earthy taste, but makes a rather grey dry bread when used alone. It is best as a small proportion of the flour in yeast bread, as a minor ingredient in soda bread or as rolled whole barley in wholemeal bread or muesli.

Buckwheat

This gluten-free flour is one of the biggest things Russia and America have in common: being as popular in American pancakes as in Russian blinis. But its lack of gluten means it is not a flour for bread making.

Cornflour (Cornstarch, Maizena)

This is a very fine flour made from maize, which must be mixed with water before being added to other ingredients. It thickens rapidly, to a slightly cloudy, jelly-like consistency. It must not be overcooked or, by some disconcerting alchemy, it becomes thin again - a trick it repeats if frozen.

Durum Flour

Durum wheat is a very hard Italian wheat, with plenty of gluten, which gives firmness to dried pasta. Good pasta should say *semolino* (or *semola*) *di grano duro* or just *grano duro* on the packet, to show it uses this wheat. The term *semolino* (semolina) shows that the wheat was coarsely ground, but *any* wheat can be coarsely ground to make semolina.

> Durum flour takes longer to digest than other flour, so pasta releases its energy slowly - which is why it is often eaten the night before a sporting event.

Maize Flour (Cornmeal, Masa Harina)

Maize flour is a rich yellow flour, and usually has a much coarser feel than most other flours. It is unique among the grains in being rich in vitamin A and it is used all over the world - in American spoonbreads or cornmeal muffins, in Mexican tortillas, in the heavy porridge-like mixtures which are staple in much of Africa and in a more sophisticated form in Italian polenta. What it lacks in lightness it makes up for in taste and nutrition and it deserves to be more used.

Oatmeal

Dr Johnson's *Dictionary* defines oats as, 'A grain, which in England is generally given to horses, but in Scotland supports the people.' The Scots get it right. Oats have the highest fat, protein and calcium content of all the cereals, and the most thiamin. Oatcakes and porridge are decidedly good for you, and oatmeal can be stirred into stews at the start of the cooking time to slowly thicken them.

Plain Flour

This is what is meant when a recipe says 'flour'. It is a fine flour milled at a low extraction rate, but with the vitamins thiamin and niacin added, plus iron and calcium. Being an all-purpose flour, it is normally a blend of strong and weak grains.

Potato Flour (Fécule de pommes de terre)

Potato flour behaves very like cornflour and is treated in the same way. It is excellent for thickening soups, and in Denmark they use it to thicken the juice of stewed fruit to give it a delectable gelatinous consistency which is most successful with rhubarb.

Rice Flour

This is a very fine flour which can be used to thicken sauces or to dust over bread to remove surplus moisture. It is not the same as ground rice, which is far coarser. Elizabeth David, in her bread maker's bible *English Bread and Yeast Cookery* (see page 76), says it is particularly good for drying the surface of rich and sticky bread doughs.

Rye

This is the cereal on which the fungus ergot can grow, and rye bread got a bad reputation because of the ergot poisoning it caused. But this is not a problem with commercial rye flour today. Rye has quite a high gluten content, but it's a gluten of inferior elasticity. It is rich in fibre and vitamin B and though it makes a heavy dense bread the flavour is deliciously nutty.

Self-raising Flour

This is plain flour with raising agents (mono-calcium phosphate and bicarbonate of soda) added to make it rise. It is excellent in scones and certain cakes. You can also get self-raising flour made from grains chosen specially for making cakes.

★ A proportion of self-raising flour in shortcrust pastry makes it lighter and more crumbly.

Strong Flour

This wheat flour is explained on page 74. It is essential for yeast cooking and is also good in other situations where air is held, such as puff pastry, and choux pastry.

Wholemeal or Wholewheat

As the main use is for bread, this flour normally has a high proportion of strong Canadian wheat in it. But the very properties which make this flour excellent for bread make it dreadful for pastry, cakes and biscuits. To be 'short' and crumbly is quite against its nature, whatever recipe you use.

Other Flours

This is by no means the full range of flour; there is also sweet potato flour, chestnut flour, water chestnut flour, banana flour, chickpea flour, cassava flour, almond flour, green bean flour and several others. But these are used mainly in the Far East and are not easily found in most parts of Britain.

Bread Making

Give me for a beautiful sight, a neat and smart woman, heating her oven and setting her bread! And if the bustle does make the sign of labour glisten on her brow, where is the man that would not kiss that off, rather than lick the plaster cheek of a duchess.
William Cobbett in *Cottage Economy*

Bread making is not the great hurdle most people suppose, though I reckon one batch always has to go to the devil before one gets the hang of it - my first effort broke a steel knife. Once you master it, the pleasure of this gentle art is enormous.

Yeast

Recipes may be written for fresh or dried yeast - 28 g (1 oz) dried yeast equals 56 g (2 oz) fresh yeast.

Mix yeast with water at 37°-42°C (98°-108°F) - it needs that temperature to get it going. If you lack a thermometer the water should feel neither hot nor cold to your finger. Mix water slowly into fresh yeast. For dried yeast reverse that - always add dried yeast to water *not* vice versa and stir *fast* as you do so, or it will clump. Dried yeast needs to work until frothy on top before being added to flour, but fresh yeast can be added immediately it dissolves - unless the recipe says otherwise. A pinch (*not* more) of sugar helps dried yeast to work, but too much checks it and fresh yeast does best without it. Salt holds yeast back, and vitamin C makes it work faster. So salty dough takes longer to prove, and if you want to hurry dough along dissolve 25 mg of vitamin C for every ounce (28 g) of yeast. But with dough, the more haste the less taste. (1 oz (28 g) will raise 3½ lb (1½ kg) flour.

Don't believe that the slightest draught will kill yeast. It prefers an even temperature and multiplies fastest in gentle warmth but, once it is mixed with the dough and has started to rise, you can leave it overnight in the refrigerator, and bake fresh rolls in the morning - if you are up to it at that time.

Kneading and Proving

To **knead** you press dough firmly away from you with your knuckles, then fold in back into a lump, and repeat this again and again until the dough is supple and springs slowly back if you press a dent in it. Rub your hands over with a butter paper before you start and it won't stick to them.

Leaving dough to **prove** means standing it in gentle warmth, but *not* in direct heat, until it has doubled in size. The ideal temperature is 18°-21°C (65°-70°F); if you feel comfortably warm in your shirt sleeves so will the dough. Keep it well covered during proving or the top will dry into a crust. Cling film over the bowl is ideal as you can have the pleasure of watching it rising

Knocking back is pushing or punching risen dough so that it returns to about the size before rising - surely the most disappointing moment in baking.

★ To tell if a loaf is cooked through knock on its base: if it sounds hollow it's done. If it has cooked in a tin remove it while hot (or it will go soggy) and place it on its side across the top of the tin to cool. If you want a soft crust, wrap it in a clean tea towel first.

Elizabeth David, *English Bread and Yeast Cookery*, Allen Lane

Pasta

Somehow, since the Sunday supplements discovered pasta-making machines, the idea has grown up that fresh pasta is the 'best' and the 'correct' pasta to use and that dried pasta is a second-rate substitute. This is totally untrue. The Italian pasta cooking tradition is that dried pasta is correct for some dishes and fresh pasta for others. So, usually, the best pasta is the shape which is right for a particular sauce, and this really does make far more difference than you might imagine.

A good pasta should have a distinctive flavour and there is a great deal of difference between the best dried pasta and the worst. Among the brands most highly regarded in Italy are Agnesi, Barilla, Ponte and Spigadoro, and my personal favourite is de Cecco.

The names of the shapes can be confusing. If you see two different names on what seem like identical pastas worry not. The Italians have never liked conformity and each region, and manufacturer, may have a different name for exactly the same shape and although the right shape does make a difference to the finished dish, it need only be approximately right.

Some brands of lasagne claim to need no precooking. Use them if you wish, but please don't call the dish you make lasagne. It is no more lasagne than a pancake is an omelette. It is some other dish with certain ingredients in common.

When buying fresh pasta ask about the proportion of eggs to flour and whether fresh eggs or dried ones are used. A good recipe should be similar to the one below.

* If you are making cannelloni buy big sheets of lasagne, cook them, cut each in half and roll the flat sheets round the filling. This is far easier than shoving stuffing down a tube with a teaspoon.

Cooking Pasta

The second great misunderstanding is the belief that pasta should be a soggy mess which sticks to the wall when thrown at it. To an Italian this is sacrilege.

Cooking pasta perfectly is very easy. Have a very large saucepan - for this you need at least 1 l (2 pt) of water *per helping of pasta* - and add 1 to 2 teaspoons of salt. Have the water boiling rapidly, drop in the pasta (but not lasagne, see below) and stir once to separate it. Let it cook at a rolling boil, giving a quick stir very occasionally. Putting 1 teaspoon of oil in the water

before you add the pasta (fresh or dried) helps to keep it separate.

Lasagne has a great tendency to stick together. Slide it into the water one sheet at a time and don't cook too many at once. When it is cooked it is best to lift it out on a large perforated spoon and lay it flat immediately on clean tea-towels. If you have to tip it into a colander run cold water over it instantly so it is cool enough for you to pick up and separate at once.

A very fine fresh pasta may be cooked in 1 minute; an average spaghetti usually takes about 7 minutes; a big rustic pasta may take over 15 minutes. The only way to know when it is done is to take a piece out and bite into it. Dried pasta should be just *slightly* firm in the centre but not crunchy. This is what the Italians call *al dente*, literally 'to the tooth'. Fresh pasta will have lost the taste of uncooked flour and have a cooked look right through. Then drain it *immediately* and combine it with the sauce before it has time to stick together.

Reheating Pasta

Pasta doesn't reheat (or freeze) well. But if you have pasta left over with no sauce on you can microwave it or put it in a pan, pour boiling water over and leave it for just long enough to absorb the heat without over-cooking. If it already has a sauce it can be *briefly* heated in a sauce, but some sauces - especially those with cream in - will turn oily and unpleasant.

Making Fresh Pasta

Making fresh pasta is one of the easiest and most soothing forms of cooking. All kinds of combinations of flour are used for different regional pastas, but what you need for most pasta is just plain flour. The proportions are 1 large egg for each 100 g (3½ oz) of flour and a pinch of salt. Work them into the flour with a fork or your fingertips (or whizz the whole lot in a blender as for pastry). Occasionally you may need to add a drop of water to get the right consistency. It should be soft and pliable but neither moist nor crumbly. Knead for 15 minutes, then put it under an upturned bowl to rest for 30 minutes.

For hand rolling you just roll as for pastry, turning the pasta constantly. For a machine start with the rollers at their widest spacing and keep re-rolling and folding the strip of pasta and passing it through again until it is perfectly thin and easy to handle (it may break up in the first few passes, but just repeat the process until it becomes more elastic).

Once the pasta is thin enough it can be cut to shape by hand or put through cutting blades on the machine. The essential point is not to have it too wet or it will stick to itself as you cut it.

If you ever feel daunted by cooking or eating pasta bear in mind the slogan on an advertisement in Italy for a brand of pasta from Naples, which boasts that it had the first pasta factory. It was addressed to other Italians and read:

Think twice before laughing at the way foreigners eat pasta. Every Neapolitan may smile at the way you eat it.

More information
Moyra Bremner and Liz Filippini, *Pasta for Pleasure*, Fontana - gives regional pasta dishes from the whole of Italy.

Rice
Rice is the staple food in some of the world's most primitive kitchens, yet it has somehow become surrounded with mystery and labelled 'difficult to cook'. In fact, it's as easy to cook as a frozen pea, and almost as instant and there are all sorts of delightful variations to be tried, from the beautiful saffron rice of the Spanish paella to rice delicately cooked in coconut milk, which Malaysians eat for breakfast with a quite remarkable combination of chillies, 'whitebait' and peanuts.

Amounts
One cup of rice bulks up to 3 cups when cooked - or to 4 cups if it's easy-cook rice. Allow about 25 to 50 g (1 to 2 oz) per person, depending on how it is being used. It only has 31 calories an ounce.

Preparation
Round rice for puddings isn't washed, but the big question with long grain rice is to wash or not to wash. The answer depends on the type, brand and method of cooking. A lot of the free starch is removed in washing, so it is less likely to stick together or stick to the bottom of the pan. However, some of the vitamins in the rice go down the plug-hole too.

With most Basmati you have to get the bits of straw and stones out. But 'easy-cook' or American long grain cooks very well without washing if you use the draining method.

To wash it, swirl the rice around in a large pan of water, picking out any impurities as you do so. Use several changes of water until it looks clear. Then let the rice soak for about 15 minutes if you can (brown rice is greatly improved by soaking and is better with twice as long). Drain it well.

Cooking Long Grain Rice
The cooking time depends both on its variety and on the method of cooking. Rice is cooked when the centre is no longer hard, but it should be slightly firm and retain its shape. Don't let the publicity blurb about 'fluffy rice' mislead you. Rice *isn't* fluffy: it's light and separate.

No one method is 'right': using lots of water is quickest and virtually foolproof, but the absorption method gives you a better flavour. I shall start with the easy one.

★ If you plan to fry rice later let it be a little undercooked.

Surplus Water Method
For this method you only need to wash the rice if it has debris. You take at least 500 ml (1 pt) of water for every 50 g (2 oz) rice (5 mugs water to 1 mug rice). Bring the water to the boil, add about ⅓ teaspoon of salt per pint, throw in the rice, give it one stir to separate it and let it boil almost unstirred for about 15-20 minutes - but start testing at 12 minutes (see above). Drain the water, and serve.

If you can't serve it at once, leave it in the colander. If it clumps or goes cold just pour some very hot water through it, separating it as you do so. Drain and serve.

Absorption Method
For this method most brands of rice must be washed (see above). To cook it, you need 1½-2 cups of water for every cup of rice - 2-2½ cups of water for easy cook long grain rice.

The usual method is to bring the water to the boil with a little salt, add the rice and a tablespoon of oil, stir, put the lid on tightly and simmer gently - without removing the lid - until the rice is cooked. For ordinary long grain this will be about 15 minutes. In theory, this produces perfect rice. In practice, there is a fine line between just cooked and just burnt. In some countries they make a virtue of necessity and regard the bits which are stuck together and browned on to the pan as great delicacies. Inventive, but not accurate.

- If it boils dry before it is cooked add *boiling* water, lightly fork it apart and continue cooking.
- If it is cooked before the water is absorbed you just drain it.
- If it is cooked and too damp but not drainable this can be cured with a *short* time uncovered in a warm oven - or a *brief* microwave. Watch it and fork it over if necessary or the top grains will be too dry.

A method needing less clairvoyance is to use the same amount of rice, boiling water and oil, cover closely and put it in the oven at gas no 4 or 180°C (350°F). It takes longer like this (how long depends on the rice, but a rice which cooks in 15 minutes on top of the stove could take 20 or more in the oven), however it is more likely to be perfect.

The advantage of the absorption method is that you can give the rice more flavour by using stock instead of water, or by frying onions, garlic and spices in oil, then adding the boiling water and rice - which is the ideal way to cook Basmati rice to go with Indian dishes.

Types of Rice
There are some 2,500 different kinds of rice. We are lucky if we can find half a dozen of them, but using the right type of rice for a recipe makes a difference.

The big divide is between **long grain** rice and **round** rice. Long grain rice is hard, stays separate more easily and suits savoury dishes. Round rice is mainly European and includes the round pudding rice and the Italian Arborio rice which is essential for risotto.

Brown rice has lost none of its vitamins and minerals, and tastes rather nuttier and more interesting. It normally needs very gentle cooking for about 40 minutes, but some brands take much less.

Wild rice is a brown rice which was found growing wild near the Great Lakes in North America. It is very long and thin, full flavoured and a good deal more chewy than other rice. Allow quite a bit more per person, as it does not bulk up very much.

White rice has been processed to remove the outer layers and with them much of the goodness. Just how much is lost is shown by the fact that in Asian countries beri-beri, which is caused by a lack of one of the B vitamins, only became a major problem after efficient rice milling was introduced. As we get plenty of vitamin B from other sources nobody should suppose white rice is bad for them. It isn't. But, if you feel strongly about the loss of vitamins, buy brown or go for easy-cook rice which has retained more of its vitamins (see below).

Long Grain Cookability
Long grain rice divides into three types - pre-cooked, easy-cook, and rice which makes no claims at all.

Pre-cooked rice has been cooked and dried; all it needs is enough cooking to put the water back into it. This makes it the rice equivalent of instant coffee - with much the same pros and cons.

Easy-cook rice is also sold as 'par-boiled', 'pre-fluffed', 'non-stick' or 'boil in the bag'. Usually the rice has been steamed and partly cooked under pressure before being milled. This allows the goodness, which is normally isolated in the outer layer, to seep into the body of the grain. So less is lost in milling. Surprisingly, most easy-cook rice takes longer to cook than ordinary rice.

Untreated rice ranges from the cheapest and most basic rices to Basmati rice, from India and Pakistan, which has a fine flavour and a premium price.

★ Italians store truffles in rice, so the scent of the truffle permeates the grains. That way they have two truffle meals: the truffle and the truffle-flavoured rice.

HERBS, SPICES AND FLAVOURINGS

There is no easier way to make simple food delicious than by using fresh herbs. As M.F.K. Fisher wrote (in *How to Cook a Wolf*): 'The possibilities of their flavours, blended or alone, are limitless: the basils, the marjorams, thyme, the sages, mint, anise...what delights they conjure if you want them to!'

The same is true of spices, and their use is not limited to the exotic. Ground cumin sprinkled into home-made hamburgers, juniper berries tucked into pork chops or chillies added to basic pasta sauces (as they do in Southern Italy) bring verve to food which might otherwise be dull.

Buried deep in culinary history there is also the almost forgotten art of using herbs so that they not only delight the palate but also benefit the body. And scientists are discovering that their benefits are not old wives' tales.

It used to be thought that meat was more digestible if it was accompanied by tracklements - sauces and relishes based on the types of plants which grew where the animal had grazed. A charming idea, and certainly many herbs are markedly digestive and often included in food which is liable to cause wind. Others such as thyme, marjoram and chillies are preservatives, containing substances which kill bacteria, and food which contains them keeps better - as does food which contains alcohol.

Fresh v Dried
Though there are exceptions, like bay and rosemary, most dried herbs are not just ghosts of their fresh selves but desiccated and unpalatable corpses. Dried herbs can be used in a bouquet garni and other cooking, but as a garnish they do only harm. If you can't find fresh herbs for a garnish, they are best left out.

Obtaining Herbs and Spices
More and more shops sell fresh herbs but nicer still is to grow your own. If you have a garden you can tuck them into any border and many deserve a place on looks alone: few small shrubs are more attractive than variegated sage, and golden marjoram is the perfect ground cover, dense but not invasive. You can even grow many of them on city window sills.

When buying dried herbs and spices avoid the dusty packets of ill-frequented stores and buy them from ethnic shops where they sell quickly, for they lose flavour with age. Especially good are the small re-sealable tins of the Rajah brand, which is widely and cheaply sold in Indian shops.

Storing Herbs and Spices
For winter, fresh herbs can be easily frozen: spread out on a tray before packing in plastic bags. They will be too soft for garnishing, but impart a wonderfully fresh flavour.

Chopped basil can also be kept in olive oil, but it must be below the surface as any which meets the air will go mouldy. To keep mint for mint sauce the easiest way is to chop it finely and then push it well down in a small container of golden syrup. Then you can simply take a little out and heat it with vinegar to taste and your sauce is made.

Those herbs which dry well should be stored in dark glass jars in a cool place, for the flavour lies in their volatile oils, which are harmed by light. Spices are equally vulnerable to heat and light.

Popular Herbs and Spices
In naming the following herbs and spices I have given the English name first, followed by the botanical name and the French name where appropriate. Finally, as ethnic food shops are the best source of many herbs and spices, I have given some names in Hindi.

Allspice *(Pimenata officinalis; poivron de Jamaïque; kabab chini)*
This dried berry is a distinct spice quite different from 'mixed spice', which is a mixture of spices. Looking like an outsized peppercorn, it tastes like a combination of cloves and cinnamon. Use a clean pepper mill to grind it lightly over meat before grilling, or add it to traditional fruitcakes and buns.

Angelica *(Archangelia officinalis; angélique)*
The soft, almost scented flavour of candied angelica is lovely in cakes and subtly delicious in cream cheese desserts. It's a ridiculous price, so it is well worth growing your own if you fancy the job of candying it. It makes a handsome addition to any garden, and seeds

freely when happy.

Balm *(Melissa officinalis; mélisse)*
Balm is an easy-going perennial with a lemony flavour. Three hundred years ago it was described as *'a sovereign remedy for the brain...chasing away melancholy'*. A few sprigs infused in boiling water make a soothing, and calming tea. Some leaves placed in the bottom of a sponge cake tin give a hint of lemon to the cake.

Basil *(Ocimum basilicum; basilic; tulsi)*
To the Romans this was the herb of fertility, and in the Middle Ages they said it would only flourish if tended by a beautiful woman. Be that as may be, this herb seems to capture the essence of summer. Dry basil is a pale shadow of the original, so this is one for a warm window ledge, where it happily doubles as a fly deterrent, and lasts well into the autumn. Its great partner is the tomato, whether in sauces or salads.

Bay Leaves *(Laurus nobilis; laurier; tej patta)*
Bay leaves are equally good fresh or dried, and their main use is in *bouquet garni*. A branch from a tree will dry in any warm room.

Borage *(Borago officinalis)*
A curious herb this, with tiny brilliant blue flowers and leaves so hairy that they feel rough in the mouth. With the aroma of cucumber, it is a traditional ingredient in Pimms, and can also be used to flavour soups and sandwiches.

Bouquet Garni ('or faggot of herbs')
This is a sprig of thyme and several sprigs of parsley plus a bay leaf, tied together with white cotton (so you can remove them easily later) and used to flavour stews, casseroles and certain sauces. In some parts of France garlic is added, and in others orange peel.

Camomile *(Anthemis nobilis)*
Camomile makes a fragrant and soothing tea which has long been used as a tranquillizer and a treatment for insomnia, especially in children. Close-planted in the garden it makes a dense carpet of glaucous foliage topped with attractive daisy-like flowers. It is the flower heads which are used to make the tea. Camomile tea is also available in packets.

Capers *(Capparis spinosa; câpre)*
Capers are the pickled buds of the caper plant which grows in the southern Mediterranean. They are particularly good at cutting the richness of other ingredients and are essential in steak tartar, and *salade Niçoise,* and add a very special pungency to a number of sauces.

Caraway *(Carum carvi; carvi)*
These sickle-shaped seeds, with their aniseedy flavour, were the feature of Edwardian 'seedy cake'. That treat seems long lost but they are still popular in Central Europe for flavouring sauerkraut, dill pickles and certain cheeses, but use them sparingly for aniseed is a pervasive flavour.

Cardamom *(Elettaria cardamomum; illaichi)*
These aromatic little black seeds in their papery, three-sided cases are used mainly in Eastern dishes, but they were also very popular in ancient Rome. Their soft, almost scented flavour enhances rice, lentils and many other dishes. Cook them in or out of their lightly crushed seed cases, which should be a smoky green or a natural straw colour (or occasionally black), not bleached an unnatural off-white. The seeds can be crushed or ground in a pestle, but they need to be used that day as the flavour quickly fades.

Chewed and swallowed, the seeds are an antidote to the smell of garlic on the breath, and they are said to cure nausea.

Cayenne Pepper
Cayenne is a fiery red pepper, used mainly as a garnish, made from a blend of ground capsicums. It can, for example, be sprinkled on a prawn cocktail to give it a little zip.

Celery Seeds
You can harvest these tiny seeds just by letting a celery plant run to seed. They can be used to give a hint of celery to casseroles when celery sticks are not to hand, and on top of cheese before it is toasted or in cheese straws.

Chervil *(Anthriscus cerefolium; cerfeuil)*
Old recipes often suggest garnishing with 'chopped parsley or chervil', so it must have been a common herb at one time. It seems a curious alternative to parsley as its aniseed flavour is very different. But, its feathery leaves and frothy white flowers make it a charming decoration to cold food.

Chillies *(Capsicum annuum; hari mirch - green, lal mirch - red)*
Chillies are one of the very ancient flavourings, cultivated in Mexico for 9,000 years. There they eat 126 different varieties, and the market stalls are stacked high with their shining shapes in scarlet, orange, green and deepest rust, each for a different purpose. Even those on sale here vary greatly in their flavour and fierceness, so it is always worth - cautiously - tasting each chilli before adding it to food. Red are not necessarily fiercer than green, but as a rule the smaller, the hotter. Bland flesh may conceal powerful little seeds, so the seeds are often discarded. But, whatever the variety, try to get them fresh or dried; most pickled chillies in jars have an unpleasant, metallic taste. South American jalapeño chillies are an exception. Fat, fleshy and green, they look as innocent as pimentos, but their fire is daunting and there are some excellent tinned brands.

Wear rubber gloves when handling chillies, lest you accidentally rub your eye with a fiery finger.

Chives *(Allium schoenoprasum; ciboulette, civette* or *cives)*
This tiny member of the onion family, with its long cylindrical leaves, is an easily grown pot herb. Both the leaves and flowers give a delicate onion flavour to salads or vegetables which they garnish.

Cinnamon *(Cinnamomum zeylanicum* or *loureirii; canelle; dalchini* and *cassia)*
Cinnamon was one of the most popular spices of the Middle Ages. Strictly speaking, it is the bark of the Sri Lankan cinnamon tree, but cassia bark from India is so similar that it too is sold as cinnamon. Powdered cinnamon makes a delicious addition to apple dishes and certain cakes, and can add a certain warmth to meat dishes. But the little sticks of rolled up bark are best

in recipes, such as mulled wine, which have liquid to draw the flavour from them.

Cloves (Eugenia aromatica; clous de girofle; lavang)
In the West Indies you can see little bushes smothered with the rosy-pink clove buds, like icing rosettes, waiting to be picked and dried. It seems strange that such delicate blooms should have such a pungent aroma, but whether in bread sauce, mulled wine or apple pie, cloves are to be used sparingly and extracted before the dish is eaten, or they will overwhelm it. Which is why in savoury dishes like bread sauce they are stuck into an onion which can be easily lifted out.

They are also one of the oldest dental pain killers. Many dentists still put a dab of clove oil on a cavity they have drilled deeply, to desensitize the nerve, and clove oil placed on an aching tooth is often more effective than aspirin. Failing that chew cloves with the teeth which hurt, until you can get to a dentist.

Coriander (Coriandrum sativum; coriandre; dhania patta or kotmil, dhania - coriander seeds)
Coriander leaves, sometimes called Chinese parsley, are a herb, while the dried seeds are one of the oldest known spices, used by the Egyptians as long ago as 5000 BC. The flavour of the leaves and seeds is so different that one cannot be substituted for the other.

The fresh fan-shaped leaves of fresh coriander are one of the most pungent and versatile herbs. Try a touch in a green salad, or add a few to a fresh tomato sauce just before serving. Buy it in bunches from Greek and Indian shops and keep it in the refrigerator in a plastic bag, or standing in an inch of water. You can grow it from seed if you have a sunny border.

The seeds have a warm, totally different flavour, with a slight hint of orange, which goes particularly well with lamb and is a vital part of many curries. They can be dry-roasted over gentle heat in a heavy pan, to bring out the flavour and ground in a coffee grinder. But once ground, they lose their flavour quite quickly. So if you buy ready-ground seeds get small amounts, keep them tightly closed and fry them lightly to bring out the flavour before mixing with other ingredients.

Cumin (Cuminum cyminium; graines de cumin; jeera or zeera)
Cumin is one of the key spices in the combination which the British think of as curry. The little crescent-shaped seeds are best when newly roasted for 2 to 3 minutes in a heavy pan over a moderate flame until the spicy aroma rises, then crushed in a pestle and mortar. Powdered cumin quickly loses its flavour and must be kept in an airtight container. Like many of the 'curry' spices, it needs to be lightly fried until its spicy aroma tickles your nostrils. It's a flavour to give spice, but not hotness, to a whole range of food, from meat balls to plain yoghurt.

Curry Leaves (curry patta or meetha neem)
Curry leaves look like small bay leaves and give a distinctive curry flavour which is delicious in many Eastern dishes, especially lentils. They dry badly, losing their lovely aroma, but freeze well.

Curry Powder/Curry Paste
These are mixtures of ground spices largely created for the convenience of the British. They are *not* the basis of what Indians think of as curry, but rather the spice equivalent of chips with everything. True Indian curries are made by selecting varying proportions of the individual spices needed for that particular dish. All the same, the blend of flavours is useful in certain British dishes.

To develop its full flavour curry powder needs to be fried for a few minutes in oil or fat. So, when flavouring cold foods, such as mayonnaise, it is very much better to use curry paste.

Dill (Anethum graveolens; anet(h))
This pretty feathery annual is much more than an ingredient in dill pickles - good though these are. Most of all it has a special affinity with potatoes. New potatoes or even a plain potato salad can be lifted out of the ordinary by a good sprinkling of freshly chopped dill or, better still, dill and sour cream. It also goes beautifully with fish, either as a garnish or as an ingredient in marinades and sauces. But its flavour fades dreadfully with drying.

Elderflowers (Sambucus)
Elderflower syrup tastes rather like muscatel grapes and combines exquisitely with gooseberries in fool, and with some other summer fruits. If you can find elderflowers which have definitely *not* been sprayed with pesticides or herbicides pick whole heads. (They keep for 24 hours in a closed plastic bag.) Simmer the flower heads, petal side down, in a light sugar and water syrup. When the liquid tastes deliciously of the flowers strain it and add it to your fruit.

Fennel (Foeniculum vulgare; fenouil)
Fennel is not one plant but a small family. You pass the flat yellow heads and feathery leaves of wild fennel in waysides all over the Mediterranean. There is also a delicate mountain fennel, whose tender shoots flavour Italian sauces, plus various types of the bulbous vegetable variety.

Fennel is also used against flatulence (which is why Italians eat wedges of the bulbous vegetable variety after meals). Equally, fennel water, made by steeping the seeds in boiling water (then cooling it), is an excellent remedy for wind in babies. Indians also dry roast them for a few minutes in a heavy pan over moderate heat and offer them in little bowls to be chewed at the end of meals as a mouth cleanser and digestive combined.

Fenugreek (Trigonella foenum-graecum; methi ke dane or methre)
Fenugreek is best known as a sprouting seed, but if you have seeds which are past their fertility period their distinctive, slightly bitter 'curry' flavour makes a pleasant addition to aubergine dishes, if they are used sparingly.

'Fines Herbes'
This French term is correctly used to describe a mixture of fresh chopped parsley, chervil, chives and tarragon used to flavour omelettes and grilled fish. But parsley, thyme, marjoram and chives, are an equally good combination for an omelette and these herbs are easier to acquire. Only in stuffing can dried herbs be substituted for fresh *fines herbes*.

Garam Masala

Indian recipes quite often call for this ingredient. It is a mixture of spices, and there is no one recipe for the combination.

Garlic (Allium sativum; ail)

Garlic may be almost as health-giving as the old wives' tales claimed it to be. It may not keep away the devil, but it does seem to be strongly anti-bacterial and to contain a natural antidote to the substances in saturated fats which can silt up the bloodstream. So granny's claim that it purified the blood may have had a lot in it.

Ginger (Zingiber officinale; gingembre; adrak or soanth)

There is a world of difference between the flavour of fresh ginger root and that of the dried powder. A whole rhizome keeps several weeks in the refrigerator, or you can peel, slice and deep freeze it. Since the sixth century BC the Chinese have prized it as a medicine as well as a flavouring, and the ginger tea which the Chinese drink after rich meals is an excellent digestive. They have long used ginger to prevent or relieve nausea, and in the West Indies it is used to treat morning sickness. It certainly works on some types of nausea: in recent scientific tests in America ginger proved to be as effective as any of the motion sickness tablets, but, without the sleepiness which some of them induce. The easiest way to take it is as crystalized ginger or ginger in heavy syrup.

Horseradish (Armoracia rusticana; raifort)

The twisted, dock-like leaves of horseradish can be found growing wild all over Britain. But in the garden it is monstrously invasive and hard to get rid of once established. Plant it in a sunken bucket and wear rubber gloves to peel and grate the fiery root. It can then be used to garnish steak or to make horseradish sauce by mixing 25 g (1 oz) of grated horseradish with 600 ml (1 pt) of whipped seasoned cream, and perhaps a hint of wine vinegar.

Juniper Berries (Juniperus communis; genièvre)

The colour of grapes and size of a blackcurrant, the pungent berries of the juniper tree are used mainly in marinades for game, and in the making of gin. They are also a good flavouring for pork.

Lemon Grass (Cymbopogon citratus; sereh)

Looking like a coarse grass with a slightly bulbous base, this is the ingredient which gives many Thai dishes a delicate and delicious flavour, which is like lemon but not lemon. If you can't buy it fresh, 2 to 3 tablespoons of dried lemon grass are the equivalent of one stalk, but it is best to soak it in a little liquid for an hour or so before use. If you buy the powder form use it very sparingly as it is highly concentrated. An Indonesian friend tells me it makes an unusual house plant, from which you can pick stems as you need them.

Lemon Zest and Juice

Lemon zest is the yellow part of lemon peel, without the bitter white pulp underneath. Use a lemon zester, or a fine potato peeler, or a grater, to remove it. It's also useful to take the zest from lemons before squeezing them and keep it to hand in a tiny box in the freezer.

It usually makes a big difference if you use freshly squeezed juice: bottled juice has the sourness without the fullness of flavour. But it is perfectly good to use in acidulating water.

Lovage (Ligusticum scoticum)

This attractive perennial was once thought to be an aphrodisiac, hence its name. It's a minor herb which can be used in salads, but its flavour is particularly good with eggs.

Mace (Macis)

You find this neglected spice ground or in delicate dried tendrils around the shell of a whole nutmeg. Just as tarragon enhances the flavour of chicken, so mace has the ability to make beef more beefy, and improves beef casseroles.

Marjoram (Marjorana hortensis; marjolaine)

There is a good deal of confusion between marjoram and oregano and some people use the words interchangeably. But, in fact, they are two distinct plants with similar flavours. *Origanum vulgare* is the wild origanum which features in Greek cooking and grows in many parts of the Mediterranean. Either plant is useful in casseroles and in salads.

Mint (Mentha; menthe)

Nobody needs to be told about mint cooked with new potatoes or with peas, but it is also very good in a whole range of cold soups, in varied Middle Eastern meat dishes, and chopped into yoghurt for eating with curry. A wide range of mints can be grown by anyone who has the space for this pushy herb. Mint tea is both refreshing and very digestive, and a sprig or two of ordinary mint in a pot of china tea makes an excellent cold tea for hot weather.

Mustard (Rai or Sarson; moutarde)

Surprisingly, since it takes moisture to bring out the pungency in mustard seeds, it gets its name from the must (fermented grape juice) with which the seeds were originally moistened.

In Indian cooking both brown and black mustard seeds are used, the black being the stronger. The Indians treat both types of seeds in two completely different ways. Either they quickly cook the little seeds in oil to flavour the oil with a subtle sweetness quite different from the usual heat of mustard; or they crush them with a little liquid in a pestle or a coffee grinder to bring out the hotness. Buy mustard seeds in small quantities, as they go bitter if stored too long.

Nasturtium (Tropaeolum)

I cannot agree with those who say pickled nasturtium seeds are a good substitute for capers: the flavour is completely different. However, the flowers, seeds and leaves of nasturtiums all add an attractive peppery taste to salads. And nothing can convert a simple green salad into a party dish as swiftly as a scattering of these beautiful scarlet and orange blooms - but add them after the dressing.

Nutmeg (Myristica fragrans; noix de muscade)

Nutmeg is the nut-sized seed of a tropical evergreen tree. It is usually linked with cakes and puddings, but its delicate aroma has far wider uses. It is excellent with potatoes and with spinach, and makes a great difference to white sauce for lasagne and cannelloni. As it swiftly loses its flavour once ground, try to buy it whole, preferably in the hard seed case, keep it in a tightly closed jar, and grate it on a very fine grater when needed.

Orange Flower Water
Part flavour, part perfume, this is distilled from orange blossom petals and lends a delightful nuance to all kinds of summer fruits, and also to yoghurt.

Oregano See Marjoram.

Paprika
A mild, almost sweet, red powder made from ground capsicum, which is used in Central European cooking.

Parsley (Carum; persil commun or persil frisé)
Parsley is becoming increasingly expensive. To make the most of it keep the stalks and freeze them for use when casseroles require a *bouquet garni;* they have just as much flavour as the leaves. And, if you have a freezer, freeze bags of finely chopped parsley when it's cheapest. It lacks the crispness of fresh parsley but has all the colour and flavour - which dried parsley does not.

Persillade is a mixture of finely chopped parsley and garlic used in French cooking.

Pepper (Piper nigrum; poivre)
Far and away the world's most popular spice, pepper is the fruit of a tropical vine which is treated in different ways according to whether white, green or black pepper is required. Whole pepper keeps its flavour well in a closed container but once ground it fades quite quickly. Keeping a few whole peppercorns with it counteracts this slightly, but freshly ground pepper is so good that it is well worth investing in a pepper grinder.

Poppy Seeds (Papaver somniferum; graines de pavot)
Poppy seeds have a delicate, almost insipid taste, but are the basis of some excellent Central European cakes. In the north east of Italy, which was once part of the Austro-Hungarian Empire, they eat them with sugar and unsalted butter on home-made fettuccine - rather delicious. Keep them tightly closed in the dark lest they go rancid.

Rocket (Arugula; roquette)
Perhaps this is really a vegetable not a herb. But, being a lovely addition to salads, rather than a total vegetable it seems to fit here. In season, you can get it in any Italian market, but here it is only sold in the most superior shops. In fact there is nothing superior about it: you can grow it in any sunny patch.

Rosemary (Rosmarinus officinalis; romarin)
Rosemary dries well but, with its grey-green leaves and soft-blue flowers, it's a lovely shrub to have in a garden, though not completely hardy in the north. It is always associated with roast lamb, but I like it almost better with pork. It is best removed before serving as its spiky leaves feel unpleasant in the mouth.

Rosewater
This is a popular flavouring in the Middle East. It is distilled from rose petals, and there are some delicious desserts which can be made with it. Buy it from a chemist but be sure to ask for *culinary* rosewater, and keep it refrigerated.

Saffron (Crocus sativus; safran)
Saffron is the world's most expensive spice for it takes 13,000 of the yellow stigmas of the saffron crocus to make an ounce of saffron and every one of them has to be hand-picked. But half a dozen threads is all a dish needs. Dry roast them first by shaking them over heat in a tiny pan until they darken to reddish brown, and crush them slightly in a pestle. Then steep them for several hours in a few tablespoons of milk, or of the warm liquid from the dish you are cooking, until the colour runs, before adding this to your dish. Being very expensive, saffron substitutes and adulterated saffron are common, so it is safer to buy the threads, sometimes called 'leaf saffron', than powdered saffron.

Sage (Salvia officinalis; sauge)
Dried sage has a musty, almost unpleasant, taste but fry a few fresh leaves in the pan with liver to give it a subtle overtone, or tuck them under roasting pork - don't use too much or it can overwhelm the dish. Being powerfully digestive and antiseptic, it lends its benefits to any rich meat - pork, goose, turkey or offal. And if food tends to 'repeat', eating a sage leaf sandwich will often cure the problem.

Savory (Satureia montana and S. hortensis; sariette)
Both the summer and winter varieties of savory are useful in cooking. Both are easily grown and have a special affinity with broad beans - for which they are also companion plants to ward off greenfly.

Sesame Seeds (Til or gingelly)
These tiny seeds are best known for their presence on top of hamburger buns, where they give their deliciously nutty flavour to the bland dough. But they are rich in calcium and lend themselves to use in both sweet and savoury dishes, and are at their best lightly fried or toasted. But, beware, they turn colour very fast and burn easily. They also tend to jump as they heat, so you may need an anti-splash cover. The flavour of sesame oil is also an excellent addition to many foods and the perfect oil for carrot salad.

Shallots (Allium ascalonicum; échalote)
Smaller, and perhaps more subtle, than their relatives the onions, shallots (scallions) emulsify more easily and are therefore the basis of a number of French onion sauces. Being smaller than onions, they are also useful whenever a small quantity of onion is needed..

Sorrel (Rumex acetosa; oseille)
The acid, highly piquant leaves of both wild and garden sorrel appear in omelettes, salads and soups in various regions of France, but its culinary high-point is an excellent sorrel sauce used to accompany fish, such as shad, in the Loire area. Hardy and very easy to grow, it is well worth experimenting with if acid tastes appeal to you, and tradition has it that it helps rid the body of poisons like alcohol.

Soy Sauce
Soya beans produce a whole range of dark-brown sauces which are used in the Far East, and each region has its own style. They range from the sweet types, favoured in Indonesia, to the dry, salty, Japanese varieties, and anyone interested in Far Eastern cooking will enjoy experimenting with them.

Tamarind (Tamarindus indica)
Tamarind is the bean-like seed pod of the tamarind tree. It has a most distinctive acid taste which is used in certain Indian and Far Eastern dishes. The paste is sold

in packets and keeps well in the refrigerator, though one uses such small quantities that it is more practical to store it in the freezer. When you need tamarind pulp just break a piece off, soak it in a little water for a few hours and sieve the resulting pulp, adding more warm water until you have got the most from your lump. Keep it away from aluminium, copper and brass. The acid in tamarind can dissolve the surface of all these metals into your food.

Tarragon (Artemesia dracunculus; estragon)
Tarragon is the classic French herb for using with chicken, and it has a remarkable ability to enhance its flavour. This ability is doubly welcome when dealing with tasteless battery birds. Put a sprig or two, with a lump of butter, inside the chicken and baste it with the juices during cooking to get the fullest flavour. Or cook a sprig with any consommé or aspic destined for a chicken dish.

Thyme (Thymus; thym, faringoule - wild Provençal thyme)
Thyme is a key ingredient in *bouquet garni*, and good in omelettes, and lemon thyme is lovely in veal stuffing. But dried thyme has an unpleasant, musty taste unless it is cooked for a long time, so it is not for garnishing or for briefly cooked food.

It also has a long history as a medicine. Its essential oil, thymol, is antiseptic and has been shown to fight salmonella and staphylococcus bacteria, and extracts of thyme are still used in certain gargles and mouthwashes.

Turmeric (Circuma longa; haldi)
We may think of this powder, made from a ground dried root, as an Eastern spice, but it's also the distinctive yellow spice in piccalilly. It has a soft, almost scented flavour, but it is a spice to use cautiously as too much can give a bitter undertone. It also becomes bitter if kept too long, so it is best bought from Indian shops which have a rapid turnover. Some recipes requiring saffron suggest using turmeric instead. The colour may be the same, but this is a recipe for disaster: the flavour is utterly different.

Vanilla (Vanilla plonifolia; gousses de vanille)
There is a world of difference between the flavour you get from a vanilla pod, which is the seed pod of a climbing orchid, and from vanilla essence. Put 2 or 3 vanilla pods in a large jar of caster sugar. It will give a delicious flavour when sprinkled over peaches, or used in cakes or stewing apricots. This way pods last for years. Where recipes require you to cook milk or cream with a vanilla pod you can rinse the pod in water afterwards and re-use it. Vanilla is the second most expensive flavouring, so such thrift is not just penny-pinching. When buying vanilla essence, check that it is pure vanilla essence not mere vanilla flavouring.

MEAT

As the price of meat has risen, butchers have had to resort to new devices to tempt their customers and boost profits. When we buy packet 'convenience foods' we

usually know we are paying highly for them. In butchers we may be less aware that every bit of creating, trimming and boning is costing us money. For example, one meat industry journal told butchers that, although a whole turkey would sell for £19.20 (giving a profit of £5 to £6), the same bird could be sold in portions for a total of £30 (giving a profit of £15 to £16). The butcher's profit is our loss - and it isn't hard to portion a turkey.

Nor is it just a matter of cutting meat up. Butchers' journals advertise mixes to add to meat when making sausages, faggots, fillings for crown of lamb and so on. 'We help you add value' proclaims the advertisement of one major manufacturer - a phrase which means the very opposite of what it says. For 'added value' is marketing jargon for inexpensively altering a product (or basic ingredients) in a way which makes it more attractive to the consumer, and allows the producer to charge far more than cost of the raw materials. So the consumer gets *less* value.

With poor value may come more additives: most mixes contain them. By law any additives butchers use should be declared close to the place where the food is displayed - but have *you* ever seen a list of additives by a tray of sausages or faggots?

Despite that, a good butcher often offers better value for money, in terms of both flavour and goodness, than you can get in pre-packed food - and you can buy precisely the quantity and cut that you want.

Buying Meat
Meat is muscle and its tenderness varies according to how much work the particular muscle has done. The less work, the more tender it will be. So veal is far more tender than beef, and lamb more tender than mutton. On beef the fillet, which lies under the rib bones and does virtually nothing, is the prized cut, while the neck, which held up a heavy head, is only fit for the stew pot.

All meat should look fresh and firm, not flabby, dry or discoloured, and should smell perfectly sweet and fresh. But it doesn't have to be bright red. Meat changes colour slightly in contact with air and perfectly fresh meat can go a deeper red. Dryness or a sweaty surface - not its colour - spell age.

Bulk Buying
In deciding whether you will save money by buying part of a carcass for freezing remember to re-calculate the quoted price to allow for wastage in bones, connective tissue and excess fat. The exact wastage will depend on the breed of animal and its weight, but of the following cuts the usable weight is typically:

beef hindquarter	67 per cent	side of pork	92 per cent
beef forequarter	70 per cent	side of lamb	92 per cent

This means that if you buy a 135 lb forequarter at £1 a pound, you will in reality pay £1.43 per pound for the cuts which are usable. Quite a difference.

It can be simplest to ask the butcher for a price based on the usable weight you will get from a carcass (even though you pay for the lot). Unless you say you don't want it the butcher should give you everything - bone, waste fat and all. If you want to use bones for stock ask the butcher to saw the shin bones into short cookable lengths. And don't forget about *marrow bone* (the soft centre of the bone) on toast - with plenty of pepper and a hint of sea salt. It's such a delicacy that Queen Victoria is said to have eaten it every day. The marrow bone ends are traditionally spread with a flour and water paste (to stop the centre running out) before being wrapped in muslin and boiled in water for about 2 hours.

To render spare fat into dripping simmer it for 2 to 3 hours in a pan of water. Let it cool in the water. When solid, lift it out, melt it down and pour it into containers for storage.

Fat v Lean

Given a choice between two steaks, one marbled with fine lines of fat and the other an unbroken lean, most shoppers buy the lean one. They are not getting the best buy. Fat in meat melts and runs between the fibres of the meat separating, softening and making it far more tender, as well as adding flavour. So often the most tender beef has a tiny marbling of fat through it, and although spare rib pork chops look less elegant than loin chops they can make far better eating. Meat which lacks this needs a good layer of fat over the outside and should be basted constantly in roasting. The growing demand for meat with little or no fat will only produce meat with less and less taste and tenderness.

Frozen Meat

To cook evenly, frozen joints should be totally thawed before cooking, especially if it is a rolled joint. It is also best thawed in the refrigerator. Chops and steaks can be cooked from frozen if you wish.

	Fridge thawed	Room thawed
Joint 3lb +	4-7 hrs per lb	2-3 hrs per lb
(1.5 kg+)	(500 g)	(500 g)
Joint under 3 lb	3-4 hrs per lb	1-2 hrs per lb
(-1.5 kg)	(500 g)	(500 g)

Raw Meat Storage

When you get meat home remove it from any plastic bag, handle it as little as possible - and only with freshly washed hands - and put it in the coldest part of the refrigerator. It is less likely to go dry if you cover it, but it won't keep better.

● Joints of beef, veal, lamb and mutton should keep 3 to 5 days.
● Joints of pork should keep 2 to 4 days.
● Mince, of any kind, keeps only 1 day.

★ To keep the surface of meat sweet if you can't cook it immediately coat the outside thickly with finely ground pepper. The pepper can be washed off before cooking. But don't try to keep meat longer than the recommended time.

Cooking Meat

Braising and Pot Roasting

The best way to deal with tougher joints of meat is to braise them. This is a delicious combination of roasting and stewing. The meat is browned all over in a little dripping or oil, then rests on a bed of diced vegetables, such as onions and carrots, in a pan with a tightly fitting lid, with just enough liquid (usually stock or wine) to stop it burning. It is then cooked gently on a burner or in the oven. Pot roasting is essentially the same but you add no liquid.

At gas no 4 or 180°C (350°F) allow the following number of minutes per pound, plus one extra pound 'for the pot': lamb 25 minutes, pork 30 minutes, beef 30 to 40 minutes.

These times assume the meat is tough and needs to be tenderized in the steam, so it will be served well done. If tender meat is cooked like this the time can be shortened.

Grilling and Frying

The exact timing will depend on the thickness of the meat and the fierceness of the heat, and the distance from the grill - (when grilling), so the following is only a rough guide. The pan or grill needs to be very hot before you start.

A 1 in (2.5 cm) thick, rare steak needs 2½-3 minutes per side, a ¾ in (2 cm) thick well-done pork chop needs 4½-5½ minutes.

Roasting

The logic of meat cooking is obvious if you look at two extremes. To dry meat - to make African biltong, for example - you expose it to a very low temperature for a very long time. But if you want steak to be well done on the outside but very juicy and underdone in the centre you do the reverse, giving it fierce heat for a very short time.

With most roast meat you want something between those two. So moderate heat makes sense. At the same time you have to consider the size of the joint or bird. Heat takes time to get to the centre, and if large joints are cooked in too hot an oven the outside is overdone before the inside is ready.

Pre-heat the oven. Dust the joint with pepper. Whether you add salt or not is debatable. Salt draws out the blood, but if you add it just before cooking and start with the heat high, I doubt if it has time to do so - and it does improve the flavour of the outer slices.

Pork and lamb are improved if you make small holes deep into the meat, with a skewer or the point of a knife, and insert tiny pieces from a peeled clove of garlic. Both are also good with a sprig of rosemary under them in the roasting pan - either as well as the garlic or instead.

Pork with rind on needs to have this slashed at 1 cm (½ in) intervals with a very sharp blade in two directions - to form diamonds. To get crisp crackling brush pork skin with olive oil and stand it on a grid over the baking tin, so the crackling doesn't get moist in the meat juices. *Do not baste* - moisture and fat each make crackling leathery.

Traditionally, meat is roasted uncovered, with a little dripping in the container if it lacks fat, and basted regularly while cooking. But for meat, such as veal, which is inclined to go dry a roasting bag can save a lot of basting. The dripping doesn't have to be the same as the meat. Beef dripping, which many butchers sell, will baste all meat if you have no matching dripping. Failing that, use butter or put slices of fatty bacon over the top, if the flavour will suit the meat.

★ If you put two unskinned onions, with just their roots cut off, to cook in the roasting pan with the joint they give off dark brown juices which brown the gravy naturally.

Roasting Beef or Veal

Sear at gas no 7, 220°C (425°F) for 20 minutes. Then cook for 15 minutes per lb (550 g) at gas no 5, 190°C (375°F); 20 minutes for pink or 25 minutes for well done. However, joints under 3 lb (1½ kg) need about 5 minutes less per lb. Those over 10 lb (5 kg) need about 3 minutes less per lb.

Add 4 to 5 minutes a pound for lamb and 5 to 7 minutes for pork. Using a roasting bag extends the time. However, bones can affect the cooking time; so can the shape of the joint and whether you are cooking at peak time. So timing alone won't work - you must check the meat (see below). Pork must be well done (unlikely though it is with modern meat inspection, pork can carry tapeworms).

Roasting with Microwaves

Microwaves are not ideal for roasting meat. As microwaves can only penetrate a limited depth, you will get uneven cooking if the shape isn't uniform. However, the speed of cooking is appealing, and shoulders of lamb - being shallow and naturally tender - cook very well. Choose rounds of meat not more than 12 cm (5 in) across and turn all meat over at half time. Since meat is easily spoiled by the wrong timing I strongly recommend you to go by the handbook for your particular microwave, which will be right for its wattage. But the following is a rough guide.

First cover all projections and very thin areas with smooth foil - without it touching the sides of the oven. The approximate times per lb (550 g) using a 600-700 watt oven are these:

On Medium	On High
10½-12½ mins	5½-6½ min rare
13-15 mins	7-8 min pink
15-17 mins	8-9 min well done

Cover the meat completely with foil, shiny side in, and stand for 15 minutes.

Testing that Meat is Cooked

You can test any meat by thrusting the skewer into the deepest part. On pork look for clear juice, with no blood in it. With other meat look for the degree of bloodiness - you may like it very bloody, or you may want to have it so well done no red blood oozes out at all.

Gravy

Gravy making is fast becoming a lost art, yet it is very easy. Tip all the fat and juices from the roasting pan into a jug (preferably a pyrex one). The fat will rise to the top. Spoon 2 to 3 tablespoons of fat into the roasting pan, let it warm on a burner and vigorously stir in enough flour to make a thick creamy mixture. Cook, stirring constantly, until it turns golden brown. *Immediately* pour in a cup of liquid, stirring fast with a loop whisk (or a wooden spoon). The best liquid is stock; failing that use a Knorr or Sainsbury's bouillon cube (the quality makes a lot of difference). Keep adding liquid little by little. If you have to use a spoon add the liquid very slowly, mixing well to avoid lumps. If you have a loop whisk you can be quite slap happy. Don't get it too thin before adding the meat juices. These should now have sunk to the bottom of the jug, so gently pour the fat into a bowl and add the juices and a little of the fat to the gravy. Darken with gravy browning if the gravy is too pale.

Keep the dripping for roasting potatoes or Yorkshire pudding, or basting other meat. Once it sets you may find some meat juices underneath which are delicious as they are, or can be frozen to add to the next gravy or sauce.

Carving

Meat carves best if you leave it for 15 minutes to settle, after removing it from the oven. This conveniently gives you time to make the gravy. Cover it with foil to keep it warm, and allow for the fact that it may continue cooking slightly as it sits. Meat for eating cold will be best if none is cut until it *is* cold: cutting into it when hot lets it bleed and makes it less moist.

The first (1856) *Enquire Within* had these words of wisdom:

> Carving knives should be put in edge before the dinner commences, for nothing irritates a good carver, or perplexes a bad one, more than a knife which refuses to perform its office; and there is nothing more annoying to the company than to see the carving knife dancing to and fro over the steel, while the dinner is getting cold and their appetites are being exhausted by delay.

Carving Beef

Beef is carved *across* its grain, and rounds of beef should be cut in the thinnest possible slices. This isn't meanness - though the joint does serve more; it is because it tastes better. The round should be stood on end and cut across the top with a *very* sharp thin-bladed knife. If you cut it on its side, like a loaf of bread, it is harder to cut it thinly and you tend to press the juices out of it. For safety, use a fork with a knife guard.

Carve sirloin on the bone down towards the bones and then release the slices by running the knife round close to the bone. You can't cut quite as thinly as on a round of beef, but the slices shouldn't be hunky - despite the lumps served at many carveries. The undercut or fillet (the smaller of the two eyes of meat beside the bone) is an exception: it is carved into slightly thicker slices along its grain.

Carving Lamb

Lamb is the easiest meat to carve as is served in fairly

thick slices. The bone is off centre in the **leg,** so prod with a fork to find which side is fleshiest. Place the meat so the fleshy part is farthest from you, and tilt the joint, with the fork, so this section is slightly away from the plate. Make several slices across the leg, into the middle of this area, cutting right down to the bone. The slices should be about ¼ inch thick and slightly slimmer at the bottom. Every few slices turn the knife sideways at the bottom of a cut so it severs them from the bone.

The bones in a **shoulder** form a Z, and one arm of the Z is the shoulder blade, which has a raised section down its centre. You need to know where these bones lie before you can start cutting. So poke with your fork. Try to cut the largest slices the bones allow, angling them across the grain of the meat wherever possible.

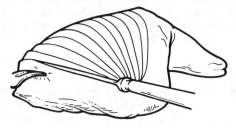

A **crown of lamb, rack of lamb,** and **best end of neck** are cut between the long bones to divide them into cutlets. The bones slope diagonally, so feel carefully for the spaces. A saddle of lamb is cut in long - fairly thin - slices, along the spine. So, carve with the grain of the meat, not across it.

Carving Pork
A leg of pork is carved like a leg of lamb but slightly thinner, and a loin is carved like a sirloin. But a hand of pork is a curious cut which is hard to carve elegantly; prod well with a fork, decide where the bones lie and cut into the fleshiest parts first, cutting across the grain. When joints are boned and rolled carve like a loaf of bread - but thinner. Pork is carved less thickly than lamb but not as thinly as beef.

Types of Meat

Beef

Beef is good meate for an Englyssheman so be the beest yonge... Olde beef and cowe flesshe doth ingender melancholye humoures [yet] if it be moderately powdeyd and the grose blode by salte be exhawtyd it doth make an Englysshman strong.
Anonymous, 14th century

Although the good cuts of beef are always more expensive than stewing cuts, the prices vary according to the demand. In many areas the better cuts - mainly hindquarter meat - are most expensive in summer when families are barbecueing steaks in the garden and roasting joints for cold cuts, and tourists are eating steak *ad nauseam.* To balance this the price of unwanted forequarter meat goes down in summer and this is the

CUTS OF BEEF		
Leg or shin Hough/Skink £	The lower part of a back leg tends to be called leg, while the same part of the foreleg is shin. It can include the shin bone for flavour and marrow bone when stewing.	Stewing, potted beef
Silverside ££	A hard-worked leg muscle which is made into salt beef and tied in long rolls. Needs much basting if roasted.	For boiled beef/pot roasting/ stewing
Toprump/ Thick flank/ Fleshy end ££	Coarser textured than topside. With more fat, but tender.	Pot roast braise
Topside ££	The top part of the leg where it joins the buttock. Tender, fine textured, full flavoured. Excellent for rare roast beef.	Roast
Rump steak/ Pin bone/ Pope's eye/ Hip bone £££	Fine grained tender meat with a layer of fat.	Grill/fry
Sirloin £££	Very tender fine grained meat with a very good flavour. Best cooked on the bone. But often boned and rolled, or sliced as steak. The home of entrecôte and T-bone steaks. A prime cut. Buy the thick end if you want the undercut (fillet) included.	Roast joint/ grill/fry steak
Fillet ££££	A long tender muscle running along the back *under* the bones. From it come medallions, tournedos and chateaubriand steaks.	Grill/fry
Baron ££££	This is the sirloin, on the bone, at both sides of the back – very expensive but good eating.	Roast
Hind quarter flank £	This is usually minced.	Any mince dish
Wing rib ££	Boned and rolled. Good meat from near the sirloin.	Roast/pot roast
Fore rib ££	Lying near the sirloin and almost as good but without the undercut. Best on the bone but can be boned and rolled.	Roast/pot roast
Middle rib Top rib £	Boned and rolled.	Braise/stew
Chuck £	Lean but tough, and often used for butcher's steak and kidney pie mix. A good cut for a long slow casserole.	Stew/braise
Clod Boasum Sloat/Lyre Gullet/Vein £	A very rough tough cut, mingling meat and fat. Often minced. Distinguished only in its names.	Stew
Sticking Neck £	Very tough meat which needs very long slow cooking.	Stew
Brisket ££	Boned and rolled, a joint with a horseshoe of lean and a core and rim of fat – much roasted in mass catering. Good but watch for gristle in the centre. Often salted.	Pot roast
Flat rib £	Mingled fat and lean.	Stew
Skirt ££	There are two kinds of skirt: goose skirt and feather skirt. One comes from the diaphragm, the other from near the belly. Both are thin and very lean, but only tender when rare. Excellent for steak tartare and Chinese beef dishes.	Steak tartare or stir fry

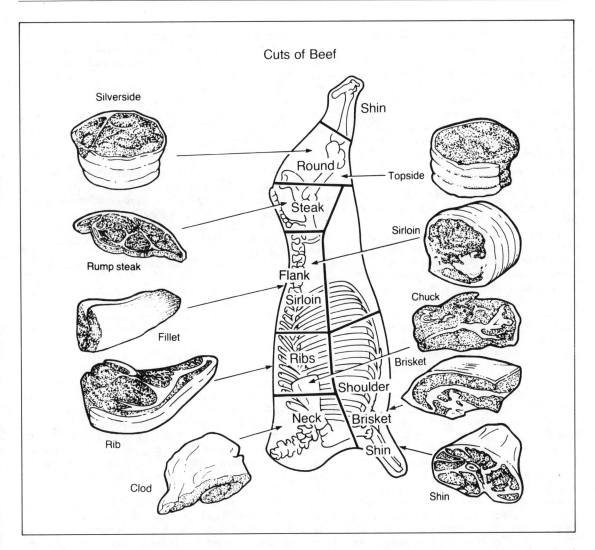

Cuts of Beef

Silverside

Shin

Round

Topside

Steak

Sirloin

Rump steak

Flank

Sirloin

Chuck

Fillet

Ribs

Brisket

Shoulder

Rib

Neck

Brisket

Clod

Shin

Shin

cheap time to buy it for freezing. The reverse is true in winter when the demand for casseroles and stew pushes up the price of the cheaper forequarter cuts, and demand for the expensive ones eases. So autumn and winter is the time when the prices of the better cuts of beef are most likely to fall.

For the best flavour and tenderness beef must be hung properly so the natural enzymes can work on it, and even with modern methods it needs two weeks. Not all butchers allow this. Quite apart from problems of space, it loses water in hanging - and that means lower weight and smaller profits. Talk to your butcher about how long his meat is hung. The more customers ask for properly hung meat, the more likely we are to get it.

Beef fat should be creamy in colour. If beef is very cheap check the fat. Very yellow fat is probably from cows not bullocks. It will taste much the same but usually be older, harder-worked and tougher. Though despised in the south of England cow meat has always been used more in the north and, if money is short, it can be a good buy for a long slow casserole. If your butcher doesn't have it look in areas where ethnic food is sold.

Cuts of Beef

The trouble with defining beef cuts is that the carcass can be divided in various ways according to the cuts which are needed. For example, a sirloin can be sold on the bone as a big carvery joint, be cut into T-bone steaks, or be boned and rolled into a traditional round of beef. This last leaves the meat from under its main bone free to be sold as fillet steak. So two cuts may well come from the same piece of meat butchered in different ways. To complicate matters still further, most cuts have different names in different parts of Britain.

Anyone who has become used to eating only the roasting and grilling cuts of beef, and is only acquainted with canteen stews of faded rubbery meat floating in tasteless gravy should have some pleasant surprises if they try some of the cheaper cuts in good recipes. With slow cookers they are very little trouble.

Ham and Gammon

Beef may have been the food of old England, but for most people it was the accommodating pig that provided the most meals. It would eat scraps, live in any yard and - best of all - its flesh lent itself to salting. To 'bring home the bacon' was to do well enough to feed your family. Their bacon would have been rather different from ours, and at one time each area had its own 'cure' using dry salt, brine, saltpetre, sugar, treacle and juniper berries in varying amounts before hanging the hams in wide farmhouse chimneys or special smokehouses.

Names and Their Meaning

Most bacon is **'Wiltshire cured'**. Whole sides of pig are injected with a solution of pickling salts, then left to soak in salt water for 2 to 4 days before being hung up to mature for a week. At the end of the week it can be sold. This is 'green', 'pale' or 'plain' bacon and has pale rind and deep pink flesh. If it is to be sold as smoked bacon it is then hung over smouldering wood sawdust. The flavour will depend on the type of sawdust. Oak gives one of the best flavours, and is part of the secret of York ham. Legend has it that the original hams were smoked in the sawdust from York Minster. Sadly, bacon is not normally sold by its cure or its type of wood smoke. A pity, for there is a world of difference between the mass produced wet cured bacon often sold, and the best dry cured bacon.

Among other ways of treating bacon one of the most distinctive is the **Ayrshire** method used in Scotland. For this the side is skinned, boned and rolled before being brined.

Sweetcure, mild cure or tender cure bacon has not been laid down for salting. Instead a curing solution, which includes sugar as well as salt and spices, has simply been injected into the flesh over 2 to 3 days.

Gammon is a leg of pig, cured as for smoked bacon. When cooked and cold it is called ham. Other parts of the pig cured in the same way can also be sold as joints, but they are called joints of bacon, not gammon. There are also hams, such as Bradenham ham and York ham, which have been specially cured, smoked and cooked to give them a distinctive flavour.

TYPES OF BACON

Prime back	sold as rashers or boneless chops	£££
Prime collar	a good braising joint	£££
Prime forehock	not as elegant as gammon, but it tastes the same; can be divided into slipper (top) and butt (bottom)	££
Slipper	another slipper can come from inside the back leg	££
Prime streaky	as bacon rashers, or as a casserole joint	£
Middlecut or throughcut	rashers or joint to stuff and braise	££
Corner of gammon	a thrifty boiling or braising joint	££
Middle gammon	the best joint or steaks	££££
Gammon hock/knuckle	a cheap, but bony gammon joint	£
Long back	frying rashers	£££

Water in Cured Meat

Some bacon has been reported as having as much as 16 per cent added water and not all the water has to be declared on the packet. If moisture comes out of your bacon when you fry it, or it spits a lot, it has more water in it than it needs for the curing process. If you see a white froth, polyphosphates have been used to make the bacon hold that water. There is only one solution: stop buying it. There are few things as powerful as a purse which doesn't open for bad goods.

> A monastery at Dunmow used to give a flitch (side) of bacon to any couple who could swear that they had not quarrelled for a year and a day and that neither of them had wished they were not married. In the 500 years from 1244 to 1772 only eight couples won it.

★ Gammon steaks can be too salty for pleasure. Soak them for a few hours in cold water to cure this.
★ Before cooking bacon or gammon rashers either cut off the rind or snip it at points with scissors, so it won't make the rasher curl up in the heat.

Cooking Gammon for Ham

Gammon varies in its saltiness; if you find some you like, and cook it perfectly, note its details so you can buy the same next time, or it will remain hit and miss. Ask if it is salty when you buy it. If it is, soak it overnight in cold water - most gammon needs this even if it's not especially salty, but you can always check - if the shopkeeper *really* knows. If it is likely, to be *very* salty bring it to the boil in plain water, throw this away and continue as below.

Drain and place in cold water with 12 peppercorns, a sliced carrot and a bay leaf. Ideally, you should also add a handful of clean hay to sweeten the meat. A romantic idea but, hay being hard to come by in cities, a tablespoonful or so of dark brown sugar (for a large ham) does the job just as well. Bring to the boil and then simmer it gently until the skin will peel off easily when you lift a corner - about 15 to 25 minutes per pound (500 g) from when it boils. The larger the gammon, the less time it takes per pound. For eating cold and plain remove the skin and leave it to cool in its juice, but it is more interesting if you glaze and bake it.

For baked ham you can boil it as above, but stop cooking 30 minutes before the end, and then bake it for about 30 minutes at gas no 6, or 200°C (400°F). It will also bake very well next day provided it cools in its liquor.

To prepare a boiled ham for baking remove the skin and slash the fat in two directions to make diamonds. It is traditional to stick it with cloves and coat it with moist brown sugar and a hint of mustard. I find it is even more delicious coated with dark marmalade, but honey is another possibility, and ginger addicts may like to try ginger marmalade. To keep it moist put 2 to 3 soup ladles of cider, or its cooking liquid, in the dish.

★ Any coating for baked ham stays on best if you sprinkle the fat lightly with flour before coating it.

Braised and Casseroled Bacon

Bacon can also be braised. In this case cider is a good liquid to use. Cook it at gas no 4 or 180°C (350°F) for 20 minutes to the pound (500g), but be sure it is well soaked, to remove the surplus salt.

Off-cuts and off ends of bacon which are going cheaply should not be despised. There are good casseroles to be made from them. Simmered with plenty of onions, garlic and lentils, and served with a tasty mustard, they can be most cheering on a cold day. Soak them (see above) to remove the excess salt, before use.

★ Don't throw away ham water. If it is not too sweet it is the best possible liquid for cooking lentils, beans or dried peas, especially as the basis for soups.

Lamb

Never you mind about the piece of needlework, the tambouring and the maps of the world made by her needle. Get to see her at work on a mutton chop...
William Cobbett, Advice to a Young Man Getting Married

Lamb prices go up and down with the season, usually being cheapest in August and September, when spring lambs are put on the market, and most expensive in April and May. But this varies with the region and the type of lamb being sold. We know far less about lamb now than we used to. At one time even thieves chose carefully.

*The mountain sheep are sweeter,
But the valley sheep are fatter,
We therefore deemed it meeter,
To carry off the latter.*

Thomas Love Peacock

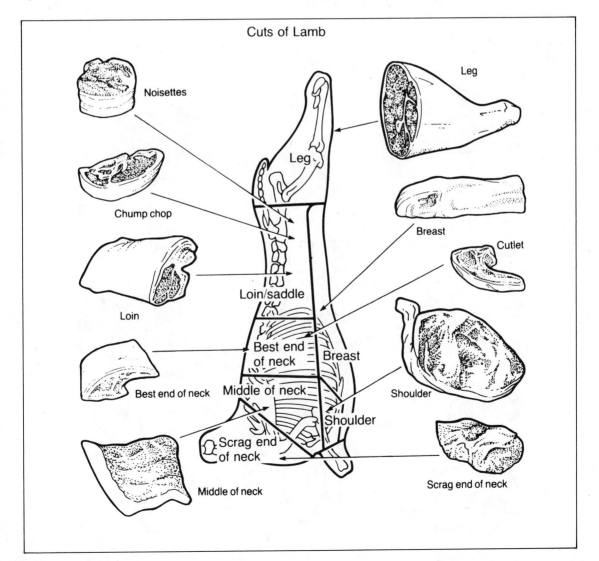

Cuts of Lamb

Noisettes

Leg

Leg

Chump chop

Breast

Cutlet

Loin

Loin/saddle

Best end of neck

Breast

Best end of neck

Middle of neck

Shoulder

Shoulder

Scrag end of neck

Middle of neck

Scrag end of neck

To realize how recently such knowledge has been lost one only has to read *Food in England* by Dorothy Hartley, which - though published in 1954 - implored readers to cook different breeds of sheep differently, and bemoaned the recent loss of lambs' tails for making lambs' tail pies.

Today when cross breeds dominate the industry, we are deemed skilled if we can tell British from New Zealand. And mutton is almost impossible to find. Though I am very much with the author of the 1858 edition of *Enquire Within* who wrote:

> *If you wish mutton tendere it must be hung as long as it will keep; then a good eight-tooth [i.e. 4-year-old] mutton is as good eating as venison.*

Lamb should have white fat and be fine grained and a firm pinkish brown, but it darkens in colour as the season progresses. It should have been hung for about 3 to 4 days, but hanging is not as critical with lamb as with beef or mutton. Being young all lamb is tender enough to roast or grill, but the nature of some cuts may dictate other treatment.

Pork

> *Look at Pork. There's a subject! If you want a subject, look at Pork!*
> Charles Dickens, *Great Expectations*

The gusto of Dickens's tone makes me almost want to rush out and buy some. Whether that would be a good idea would depend on the weather. Pork goes bad faster than other meat, especially when it's thundery. This applies especially to brawn which, in muggy weather, can go very nasty very fast.

Pork is, therefore, a very seasonal meat little eaten in June, July and August. So that is when prices drop and you can get good value for a freezer. Its peak prices are November, December and January. The meat should be pale pink and smooth, and the fat firm and white. Whatever the weather play safe: cook it within 24 hours of buying and eat it in 2 days.

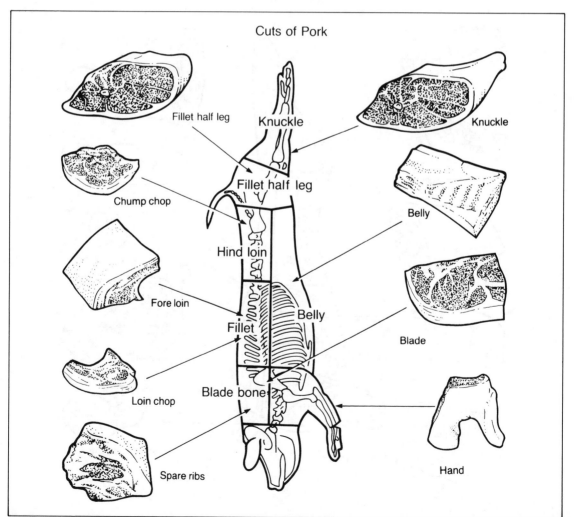

Cuts of Pork

Fillet half leg · Knuckle · Knuckle · Chump chop · Fillet half leg · Belly · Hind loin · Fore loin · Belly · Fillet · Blade · Loin chop · Blade bone · Spare ribs · Hand

Veal

Veal is beef killed when very young - usually only 13 to 20 weeks, but the age varies from country to country. For Bobby veal the animal is only a week old. At one time air was blown into the meat, but this no longer happens. The meat should be pale pink and is almost fatless, and all cuts are so tender that only the shape determines the way it is cooked. Lacking fat it dries out easily, so it is best to cook it in a roasting bag. It can be almost too delicate a flavour unless enhanced with herbs or other flavourings, such as mushrooms.

Cuts of Veal

Being small, veal animals are cut up more like a sheep than like an ox, and goats are butchered in much the same way.

Offal

Offal is the term used for all the bits and pieces of the animal. They include some of the most delectable parts, but offal is being eaten less and less and it is increasingly hard to find certain items. Even when offal was popular, we ate far fewer parts of a beast than many other countries. When writing *Pasta for Pleasure* on Italian regional pasta cooking, I had great difficulty in persuading my co-author in Italy that there was no point in including a sauce made from small pieces of intestine in a book for the British.

Nor do Italians leave it there. The most surprising piece of window dressing I ever saw was in a butcher's shop in the backstreets of Naples: hanging plumb in the centre - with evident pride - were the genitalia of an enormous bull. And Elizabeth David recounts how when she told a French cook that it would not be possible in England to use a recipe needing a pig's bladder the astonished retort was, 'What do you mean? Why can you not get a pig's bladder in England? You have pigs, do you not?'

One person's lines between what is normal or unpleasant seem illogical to someone else, but those who eat none of the offal given below are missing some of the most nutritious parts of the animal - and some of the easiest to cook. Some offal is more fragile than others, but it is always best to eat it the day you buy it.

Brains

You can buy calves', lambs' and ox brains. Calves' have the best flavour. They should look glossy and a greyish-pink and have no smell. You need about 500 g (1 lb) for 4 people. They *must* be cooked and eaten the day you buy them. Pull the membranes off the outside and soak them for a couple of hours in cold water. Then blanch them by plunging them into boiling salted water with a dash of vinegar, and turning down the heat the instant they are in, so they *just* simmer for 15 minutes. Drain and cook as the recipe suggests.

Feet and Trotters

Both calves' feet and pigs' trotters are cleaned and scalded for sale. They have no real meat on them but they are useful for boiling with other ingredients to make a broth which will set to a firm gel.

Wash them well and remove any hairs. Soak in cold salted water for at least an hour, changing the water several times. Bring them to the boil in a saucepan of cold water, drain and wash again (often the butcher will have got them to this stage). Cook by simmering in liquid with other meat (to lend gel to the cold juice) or simply with an onion, carrot, stick of celery, peppercorns and a little lemon peel, salting lightly - the broth will be concentrated later and too much salt will ruin it. It may be 2 hours before the meat is tender. Once cooked, it may, for example, be served cold with a vinaigrette or deep fried.

Head

A much despised joint nowadays, but those on slim budgets could consider it. A pig's head can make an excellent dish of pork brawn. The lower jaw is sometimes sold separately as pork jowl. Being a mixture of fat and lean, it can be substituted for belly of pork in some recipes. Both calves' and pigs' heads can be treated just like feet above.

Pigs' cheeks are sometimes boiled, coated in breadcrumbs and sold as Bath chaps. They are hard to find, and rather fatty, but cheap and tasty.

Heart

Heart is a delicious meat. Lambs' or calves' hearts are the best, as ox heart tends to be tough. Recipes often make a palaver of preparing and cooking them. There is no need. Simply rinse them out under a cold tap, season, place in a small dish with a lid and bake, just like that, at gas no 5 or 190°C (375°F) for about 40 minutes. By that time they will be cooked but pink. Don't over-cook them or they become tough. They can be eaten just as they are, cutting off the rubbery and fatty top part: very plain but very tasty. Hearts are also good stuffed or as part of the meat in kebabs.

Ox heart needs to be diced and given long slow cooking. Any good recipe for a rich beef stew can be used, and the same timing. Trim out all rubbery ends of blood vessels, as you chop it.

Kidney

Lambs' kidneys can be bought nude or neatly encased in firm white fat. The fat is useful: if they are grilled with it on, it keeps the outside perfectly moist. Veal and ox kidney comes with a section of fat, and a few blood vessels on the inside, and these need to be removed.

Kidneys have three stages of tenderness: if you cook them until they *just* lose their pinkness they are deliciously tender with a good texture; cook them a little more and they become rubbery, and if you then cook them a long while they become tender again. In the last stage of tenderness, the texture is more grainy and the flesh less succulent. This is the stage to which they are usually cooked, but it seems a pity. If you try the short-cook method, cut the kidney really thinly; then the outside won't turn rubbery before the inside is cooked.

★ Soaking ox or veal kidney in salt water or milk for a few hours improves the flavour.

Liver

Calves', lambs' and pigs' livers are priced in that order, and that is also the order of their quality. Liver has the same three stages of tenderness as kidney. It either needs to be cooked very fast or have long slow cooking in a casserole - a good use of pigs' liver as the other ingredients can mask its rather coarse flavour.

Liver is often breadcrumbed, but it is unnecessary work. Persuade your butcher to cut lambs' (or calves') liver almost paper thin (only easy if the liver is chilled to firmness and he will cut it *much* thicker unless you insist). Season it. No more than wipe the bottom of a thick pan with oil, get it hot, put in the liver and when it has hardly had time to kiss the pan turn it over. If you have it thin enough it should be cooked through in no more time. (If it is thin enough it needs under 30 seconds a side.) Serve it *immediately* with lemon juice sprinkled over it and a scattering of parsley. Nothing could be quicker or easier, and it could revise your view on this highly nutritious meat.

★ To soften the flavour of pigs' liver soak it in salted water, in the refrigerator, for an hour or two.

Ox Tail

An ox tail has small nuggets of meat, cased in deep yellow fat, surrounding the tail bone. The meat has a distinctive flavour, but any oxtail dish needs to be cooked a day ahead. Then you can chill it and remove the fat once it hardens as it is excessively fatty.

Sweetbreads

These are the thymus and pancreas glands of a calf, ox or lamb. They look unappealing but their delicate flavour is very special. They must be blanched before cooking. First put them in a bowl of cold water under a trickling tap, so the water is changed constantly. Leave for 2 to 3 hours. Cover the sweetbreads with cold water, salt lightly, bring them very slowly to the boil and simmer for 6 minutes. Drain and wash them in cold water. Pull away any rubbery bits of casing which will come off. Pat dry on kitchen paper. Cook them as you wish, but lambs' sweetbreads simply need to be fried in butter until golden and served with lemon juice, and larger sweetbreads can be sliced and fried - they are particularly good when egg-and-breadcrumbed.

Tongue

Ox and lambs' tongues are sold both fresh and salted, and ox tongue is occasionally smoked. Salted or smoked tongues have the best flavour.
- Soak lambs' tongues for 1 to 2 hours if unsalted, 2 to 4 hours if salted.
- Soak ox tongues for 3 hours if unsalted, 8 to 12 hours if salted or smoked.

Having drained the tongue, place it in cold water, bring it to the boil and then simmer for half an hour. Drain it again before putting it in cold water and adding 6 peppercorns and a bayleaf (salt too if the meat is not salted or smoked). Bring to the boil, turn down and simmer until a blunt knife easily pierces the tongue tip (lamb 1 to 1½ hours, ox 3 to 4 hours). It is easiest to remove the skin while it is still quite hot, simply pulling it off with your fingers. Find any small bones and pull them out. Tongue can then be carved across in slices and eaten hot with a piquant sauce to cut its richness. Or it can be pressed and eaten cold. For pressed tongue you simply curl it round in a circular container, pour in some good jellied stock (its own may be too salty, put a plate on top and press with at least 3½ kg (7 lb).

Tripe

This is the stomach lining of an ox. The first stomach is known as blanket, the second as honeycomb, the third as thick seam. Their textures are different but they all taste the same. They are opened, cleaned and scalded before sale. The length of the scalding affects the cooking time, so ask the butcher to advise you. Allow 4 to 6 oz per person. Some recipes call for 'cooked' tripe, simmer them in salted milk and water for about 1 to 1½ hours (unless your butcher has suggested otherwise).

The Meat and Livestock Commission, 5 St John's Square, London EC1M 4DE Tel: 01 251 2021

METHODS AND PROBLEMS

Cooking Methods and Terms

Acidulate(d)
To acidulate is to add acid, as when you add lemon juice or vinegar to water into which you will put fruit or vegetables. The acid stops the oxygen turning the cut surfaces brown. Ideally, use lemon for fruit and vinegar for vegetables.

Agitate
To agitate a pan you shake it gently to and fro. The idea is to prevent fragile food from sticking, without stirring or turning.

Arroser
This either means to sprinkle with liquid or to baste.

Aspic
This is clarified stock or cooking juices from meat or fish, which will set into a firm jelly when cold. Well-cooked meat with a high proportion of gristle (e.g shin) sets easily; fish stock may need a little gelatine added. Adding white wine to either improves the flavour. If you are only using a small quantity there are passable packet versions, such as Knorr.

Coating food in aspic is tricky as it tends to slide off. To prevent this chill the food and stand the aspic in a bowl over ice until nearly setting. When applied to the chilled food it should set beautifully. To coat a mould with aspic chill it, and tip the cold aspic around in it.

Au Gratin/Gratin
When food is *au gratin* it is coated with a sauce, sprinkled with breadcrumbs - and/or cheese, and browned under a hot grill or in the oven.

Bain-marie
This is the technique to use when you want to cook something very gently with no direct heat reaching it - as you do when thickening sauces with egg. A *bain-marie* is any container half full of water, in which you sit the pan or dish containing the food that is being cooked.

You can also use this method to keep sauces hot without spoiling them. For a *bain-marie* in the oven the water is simply round the sides of the inner container. But on top of the stove the water must always be underneath.

Baking Blind
Baking blind means you line a tart tin with pastry and cook it before you fill it. It's best to refrigerate the pastry-lined tin for 30 minutes or so before baking, if you can. Then tuck greaseproof paper into it, pressing the paper into the sides, and three-quarters fill it with dried beans to keep it from rising. Remove the beans and paper 5 minutes before the end of the cooking time and, if the filling may make the pastry soggy, brush the inside with beaten egg to seal it, before finishing the baking.

Bard
This is to tie slices of fatty bacon over the breast of game or poultry to stop it drying out in cooking. It is usually removed near the end to let the breasts brown.

Baste
Basting is spooning over the food some of the fat or liquid in which it is cooking. This prevents it becoming dry, and regular basting makes a great difference to joints, chicken and roast potatoes.

Batter
Batter is the basis of many dishes - pancakes, Yorkshire pudding, toad in the hole, drop scones, fish and chips, and fritters. Pat food dry before battering it or the batter may slide off it.

The most basic batter is: 1-2 eggs, 100 g (4 oz) sifted flour, about ¼ l (½ pt) milk, and a tablespoonful of melted butter. The flour is flavoured with a little sugar or seasoning (according to its destination), the eggs stirred in and milk then stirred in *very* gradually until it is a thick cream which coats a spoon. Finally, the cool butter is mixed in and the mixture beaten with a whisk, more liquid being added if necessary. It must then rest for ½ hour to 4 hours so the starch can swell and the mixture lighten.

The liquid can be water and milk, beer, lemonade or even wine - beer and lemonade giving a lighter mixture. Some batters also use a little yeast, and others have a beaten egg folded in at the last minute to give lightness. You can use oil instead of butter - for greater crispness.

Blanch/Blanchir
If you are blanching large quantities by the first method you really need a basket to hold the food so you can lift it quickly out and still have the boiling water for the next batch.

a The most usual form is to throw the prepared food very briefly into boiling water, then drain it and plunge it into cold water. This is the method when preparing vegetables for freezing. The vital point is to have a lot of water - at least 4 l (7 pt) - to 500 g (1 lb) vegetables. Then the coldness of the vegetables doesn't lower the water temperature too much, and it rapidly returns to the boil. Have the burner on high and time the blanching from the moment the water returns to the boil. For freezing this should be for 2-4 minutes.

Lift the food out and run it immediately under a cold tap. Instantly place in a big bowl of iced water to chill. When cold drain immediately and put to dry on kitchen paper over newspaper.

b Put food into cold water, bringing it just to the boil before draining. This draws out excess salt or blood from foods such as bacon or brains.

Steam blanching can be used to blanch foods before freezing when they are fragile. Simply place the food in a *thin* layer in a steamer or metal colander over rapidly boiling water and put a lid on. Time the blanching from the moment you put the lid on and allow half as much time again as for blanching in water. After blanching treat as for method **a**.

To blanch nuts put them in a bowl of boiling hot water until the skins are loose enough to pull off. Remove a few at a time.

Blend
Originally, this simply meant to mix ingredients together. Sometimes it now means to mix in an electric blender. But do beware of over-using the blender. The slippery softness of a slice of peach or the resilient starchy stickiness of a chunk of parsnip are far more delectable than a totally smooth peach or parsnip purée could ever be.

Boil
Boiling is the fiercest way to cook in water, and to be at boiling point (212°F 100°C) water must bubble and give off steam. A rolling boil is when it bubbles very fast. Some food is put into cold water and brought to boil (often to draw out the flavour); other food is put into the water when boiling. Assume the latter if the recipe gives no clue.

Bouillon
Bouillon is unclarified stock or broth from meat, fish or vegetables. If you have none, Knorr cubes can be substituted in some recipes - but only when the bouillon is not a central feature of the dish.

Browning
Browning food usually involves cooking it over a fairly brisk heat in a little fat, turning until it is brown all over.

Whether you need a pale golden brown or a richer tone depends on the flavour you want; the darker the colour, the stronger the flavour; but too dark and the flavour is spoilt. You can also set food under a grill to brown or even in a hot oven.

Cake Making

Weighing Sticky Ingredients
The easy way to weigh sticky ingredients like treacle is to put the container on the scales, note what the total weight is and then remove spoonfuls, into your mixing bowl, until the scales have gone *down* by the amount you need.

Butter
If a cooking book tells you to butter a cake tin rub a used butter paper round it, for you only need a thin film. Better still, for most cakes, is to run a lard paper round, as lard is far less likely to burn.

Creaming
This is beating something - usually butter - until it is like thick lightly whipped cream. The aim is both to soften it and to incorporate air which will lighten the cake. It's easy with a mixer, but if you have to do it by hand, warm the bowl and put it in the sink (so it isn't too high) and grate the fat into it first. However, as I pointed out in my book *Supertips 2* no less a cook than Eliza Acton wrote: 'For all large and rich cakes the directions are to beat the butter to a cream: but we find that they are quite as light when it is cut small and gently melted with just so much heat as will dissolve it.... It must on no account be *hot* when added to the other ingredients.' I totally agree. But you *do* need to cream when making cakes where there is no raising agent and a spongy texture is needed.

Once you have added the flour mix well but don't beat - beating at this stage makes a cake heavy.

Lining Tins
Time spent lining a cake tin with greaseproof paper is well spent - it's a shame for a good cake to be broken in being levered from the tin. But if a cake will be even

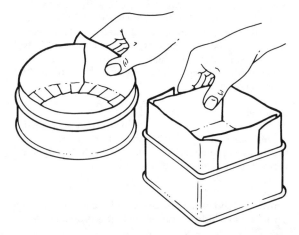

partly microwaved have no paper sticking up outside or it may catch fire.

Meringues are a special case. They must be put on vegetable parchment if they are not to stick. If you have none, oil greaseproof paper *very* well.

★ If you want the mixture to come easily off the spoon or spatula, and not leave a a cook's treat sticking to it at the end, rub vegetable oil on the spoon first. (This works best on plastic.)
★ If you want a flat top spread the mixture so it dips in the middle.

Timing
Books seldom say whether the timing given for a cake is for a conventional tin or an aluminium one. Aluminium tins cook cakes a good deal faster. So when using one check the cake periodically to see if it's ready.

Peeking
Peeking in the later stages won't ruin the cake provided you avoid great whooshes of cold air entering. So open the door slowly, look quickly and close it *very* gently.

Testing that a Cake is Done
To test if a cake is cooked push a clean skewer deep into the centre. If it comes out clean (bar a cooked crumb or so) it is done. If there is even a hint of gunge on it the cake needs more time.

After Baking
For most cakes run a knife round inside the tin to loosen it as soon as it leaves the oven. Place a wire rack over the cake and turn the two upside down, so the cake comes out on to the rack. Then leave it on the rack to cool before filling or icing. However, Swiss rolls roll best while still warm, so turn them on to a sheet of greaseproof and fill with jam when not hot and roll immediately. If you want to fill one with cream just roll it up, rolling the paper in too, while hot. Then unroll it carefully and fill with cream when cool enough.

Fragile Cakes
Once baked leave a fragile cake - with a small proportion of flour - to cool and firm before removing it from the tin. A roulade should be rolled when cool but not solidly cold. A light roulade will almost certainly crack - don't worry, the bursting look of it is part of the appeal.

Caramel/Caramelize
Caramel is sugar which has been cooked in a heavy pan over a gentle heat, with or without a hint of water, until it is a good brown. Browning starts at about 154°C (310°F) and darkens as the temperature rises. The strength of flavour increases as it darkens, and becomes unpleasant when too dark. Poured on to an oiled tin the caramel sets to a brittle toffee which can be broken into fine splinters which are delicious decoration on cakes and puddings - but keep them dry and airtight.

Chocolate
Don't be surprised if chocolate doesn't always melt in

quite the way you'd expect. Even the makers couldn't give me any foolproof rules for success, as it is altered by how it has been stored on its way to you. Use plain, never milk chocolate; put it on a plate over hot *not* boiling water; don't stir it until completely melted and then use it at once. Or microwave on low until melting and glossy.

Chopping

Chopping may not seem worth mentioning; everyone knows how to chop. But if you haven't come across it, the swiftest way to chop an onion is to stand it on its root, cut a series of slices *almost* to the bottom in one direction, turn it and cut another set of slices across them. Then you turn it on its side and slice it, and it is chopped. You can space your slices so as to chop it coarsely or into minute pieces, and the chopping is perfectly even. Almost all other vegetables can be done on the same principle.

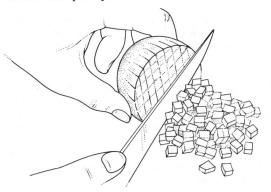

To chop parsley place it on a board, hold the tip of a sharp knife still (watching for your fingers) and lever the blade quickly up and down over the parsley with the other hand. Repeat, cutting the other way.

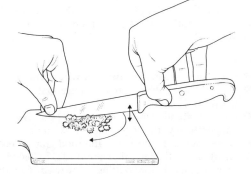

Clarifying Butter

This is butter which has been heated until foaming, then skimmed or strained through a coffee filter, to remove the milk particles which make it look cloudy and burn easily.

Clarifying Fat

Clarifying fat is just getting rid of the impurities by heating it and simmering it a while with about half as much water. Then pour it into a tall container to cool and when the fat sets lift it out (and scrape the underside if necessary) leaving the debris in the water. This is the method for cleaning dripping - if you need to.

Clarifying Stock or Broth

Broth is clarified by heating it with egg whites (first whipped until frothy but not stiff), with their shells added and preferably a small amount of minced beef and a little wine. Whip the mixture as it heats to boiling. Once it rises to the top of the pan remove it from the heat. Once it subsides, put it over low heat for 10 to 60 minutes without disturbing the crust which will form. It then needs to be strained slowly through a muslin or other fine cloth. Let the egg crust lie in the cloth so it acts as a second filter, and strain the broth through it several times if necessary.

For 1½ l (3 pt) broth you need about 2 egg whites, and 350 g (¾ lb) minced beef. The beef helps both the flavour and the clarification, but it can be left out if the broth already has a good flavour, in which case cook the broth for a shorter time.

Clotted Cream

Clotted cream is just thick cream which has been skimmed from the top of milk after it has been heated to boiling point and then left to stand in a wide pan. Anyone can make it - you don't have to leave it to the Cornish - but you can't make it with skimmed or homogenized milk. The richer the milk, the better.

Coulis

Strictly, this is the concentrated liquid, normally from meat or fish, obtained by long slow cooking.

Croquettes

Croquettes are cork-shaped mixtures of minced or puréed food, dipped in beaten egg, then in breadcrumbs, and deep fried.

Court Bouillon

A *court bouillon* is the liquid in which fish is cooked, and usually contains vinegar, onion, carrot and seasoning.

Croûtons

Croûtons are tiny cubes of bread, deep-fried until golden. They are mainly used to garnish soups, and add style and texture.

Dariole

A small, sometimes decorative, mould used for setting rice salads, jellies or creams.

Deglaze/Déglacer

With this technique you first cook some food in a pan - say meat browned in butter - and (usually) remove it. Then pour in some liquid, such as a little wine, and heat it while you scrape up the tasty morsels and juices which have browned on to the bottom of the pan. This makes the basis for a sauce.

Devil

Food which is devilled has been coated or marinaded in a mixture of fiery ingredients - mustard, Worcestershire sauce, chillies or any combination of hot spices which take your fancy. After that it is usually grilled or fried.

Dropping Consistency

A mixture that will drop easily from a spoon which is lightly shaken, but neither trickles off nor hangs on.

Duxelle

This is a purée of very finely chopped mushrooms, cooked in a nut of butter, with a little chopped shallot, until they are cooked but not too moist. The mixture can then be used for stuffing meat, or as a basis for sauces, and it freezes well until you need it. A great way to use up stalks - for, if you really love food, life's *not* too short to stuff a mushroom.

Flame/Flamber

This is to pour spirits - often brandy - on to a dish, let it warm, then set light to it. This burns off most of the alcohol as well as looking spectacular. But, spirits won't burn when cold: so, for example, Christmas pudding must be on a warm dish and the brandy warmed first.

Fold

Folding is a method of mixing two different ingredients or mixtures together without vigorous stirring. It must be very gentle, so as not to remove the air which has just been beaten into one of them. It is most easily done with a flexible plastic spatula, but a spoon will do. Slide

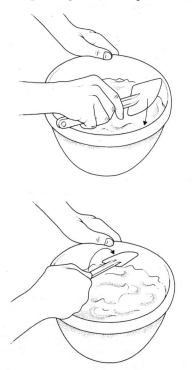

the spatula down to the bottom of the bowl. Now make a C-shaped movement - starting at the bottom. Go across the bottom, then up, turning your wrist over at the top as you lift. This takes the mixture from the bottom and deposits it on top. Turn the bowl a fraction and repeat. Keep going until the mixture is *just* combined.

Fool

A fool is a fruit purée into which has been folded about half its own volume of thickly whipped cream. Mash the fruit rather than liquidize it, so an occasional fruity nugget will land on the taste buds. Puréed it is too bland and uniform, and to purée gooseberries or raspberries is sheer disaster as the seeds become wood chips. Provided it is not over-sweetened, the acidity of the fruit makes it a beautiful (and easy) ending to a meal.

Frying
General Rules

Frying is cooking in fat on top of a stove, and the type, quantity and heat of the fat makes a big difference to the end result. Two rules hold good for all frying:

- The hotter the fat, the less it is absorbed into the food so the less greasy the food is.
- The hotter the fat, the faster the food cooks.

Each fat has a different temperature above which it cannot be heated without burning and giving an unpleasant flavour. In unclarified butter, for example, this happens at only 121°C (250°F), whereas lard reaches 205°C (400°F) before burning. The best fats for deep frying are those which reach high temperatures without burning.

Shallow Frying

For shallow frying use only just enough fat to stop the food sticking to the pan, then the food won't be greasy.

Stir Fry

This is shallow frying, often in a wok, over brisk heat while constantly turning the food over to prevent browning.

Deep Frying

- Use a heavy pan containing a wire frying basket.
- Have the food at room temperature so it won't cool the fat too much.
- Use a fat/oil which can reach the necessary temperature without burning or catching fire.
- Have enough fat to cover the food completely.
- Gently bring the fat/oil to about 182°C (360°F) - or slightly above before putting in the food. To test the temperature drop in a cube of bread. The oil should fizz hard and the bread bounce back to the surface and brown in about a minute.
- Adjust the temperature to the needs of the food. Raw food, which needs longer cooking, should fry at about the temperature given above. For cooked food, which only needs to brown on the outside and heat through, the temperature can be enough to brown

the bread (as above) in under a minute - nearer 204°C (400°F).

- You don't need to use a thermometer, but if you want to use one make sure it can handle the temperature and preheat it in hot water, then dry it before putting it in the fat - or it could be dangerous.
- Don't let *any* water or other liquid get in the fat or it will spit dangerously. So dry the food before adding it.
- Don't add too much food at once or the temperature will drop and the food cook badly.
- Breadcrumbed food fries best after a spell in the refrigerator, as the crumbs cling better.
- The frying basket should not be used for battered food as the batter will cling to it.
- If the fat seethes up DO NOT move the pan. Just lift the basket to remove the food.
- Drain the cooked food on kitchen roll over thick newspaper.
- Once cool, the fat should be strained through muslin to remove particles.
- If deep fat takes on the taste of food which has been cooked in it - such as fish - this can be removed by frying some raw potato in it.
- The smoking point - which comes before burning - is around 191°C (375°F) for animal fats and 232°C (450°F) for vegetable fats.

WARNING At very high temperatures fat or oil will catch fire by itself. It must not be allowed to overheat and needs *constant* attention. NEVER move a pan of hot fat. *If fat catches fire DO NOT put water on it or move it. Cover it as closely as possible with a lid or thick cloth.*

Fumet
A *fumet* is the concentrated liquid in which fish (or occasionally meat) has been cooked, or which has run from it during cooking.

Glaze
Glazing is coating food with a shiny finish. Like a tie on a man, it makes it look much smarter. On fruit tarts this is done with melted jam (especially apricot), on cold meat with jellied meat juices, on pastry with beaten whole egg, yolk or white, according to what is to hand. Bread and buns can have all kinds of glazes and the glaze can alter the crust: melted butter (soft crust), milk or water (crisp crust), sugar and water (or milk) syrup (soft sticky crust), egg and/or cream for a dark crust.

Grill
Grilling is cooking food rapidly under strong heat, without fat or liquid - though it can first be brushed with butter or oil, if you wish. Slow grilling will dry the food out, so preheat the grill. Americans call this broiling, as we used to in other centuries.

Icing
For smooth icing always sieve icing sugar before use.

Butter Icing
Adding one egg yolk makes it far more luscious - though softer. Add the yolk before the sugar. (Basic butter icing is just creamed butter into which is beaten twice its weight in icing sugar, then flavouring added - 75 g (3 oz) butter to 150 g (6 oz) sugar are the standard weights for an average cake.)

Fondant/Fondant Icing
This is just sugar and water boiled to 114° to 116°C (238° to 240°F), beaten with a wooden spoon until it becomes white, then kneaded on a board. It can be used to make sweets or thinned a little with sugar syrup - sugar cooked to a thin syrup with a touch of water - for icing a cake. Either way, it can be flavoured, for example with lemon juice.

Glacé Icing
This is simply sifted icing sugar worked with a little water and flavouring to the right thickness. I always like the look of it running down the sides of a cake, it has a certain generosity about it. But if you dislike trickles wrap a band of greaseproof paper tightly round the cake, so it stands slightly above the top, before you ice it. Then peel it off after the icing is set.

Royal Icing
To prevent royal icing being so rock-like that granny will break her dentures add a teaspoonful of glycerine (from a chemist but perfectly safe to eat) for each 450 g (1 lb) of icing sugar. To stop it being sickly sweet add the same amount of lemon juice.

To fill an icing bag easily, drop the end in a clean jam jar, and fold the top out over the edge of the jar.

Infuse
Infusing is letting a flavouring stand in hot liquid, or be gently heated with it, until the liquid takes on the flavour.

Julienne Strips
Cutting vegetables into *julienne* strips means cutting them to the size and shape of a matchstick - not as slow as it sounds if you cut thin slices one way, stack them, and cut equally thin slices across the other.

The quick way to make *julienne* strips of orange or lemon zest is to use a lemon zester - a cheap and invaluable tool.

Jus/Jus de viande
The natural juices which run from meat in its cooking and set into a delicious jelly when cold.

Knock up
You knock up flaky pastry by making tiny cuts horizontally along its raw edge with a sharp knife, so that the layers separate more easily in cooking.

To Lard

To lard meat you use a special larding needle to thread thin strips of fat through it, to give it flavour and moisture when cooking. This is done when meat lacks its own fat.

Leavening or Raising

Any ingredient which will make others rise in cooking is leavening - yeast, baking powder, bicarbonate of soda, egg and so on.

Bicarbonate of soda and baking powder both foam when mixed with any acid, so using sour milk, lemon juice or even a touch of vinegar in any recipe which contains them produces a lighter result.

Baking powder tends to leave a dry after-taste in the mouth and, although it is often recommended in scones, I find a much better result is obtained by just mixing self-raising flour with sour milk and sugar. And bicarbonate and sour milk can be used in most cakes which use both baking powder and a liquid.

Macédoine

This is a mixture of vegetables, diced small, or occasionally a mixed fruit salad, perhaps of dried fruit.

Macerate

To soak food in a liquid, usually alcohol of some kind.

Marinade

To marinate meat or fish is to leave it for a number of hours in a combination of liquid and seasonings, to improve the flavour and/or tenderize it. The marinade is often wine of some sort.

Most recipes for marinades only use a small quantity of liquid, which may not cover the meat, so it needs to be turned over at half time. The easy way is to put the whole lot in a plastic bag. Then, to turn the food, you just turn the bag over.

Medallions

Small rounds of meat or vegetables.

Oiling a Mould

This is simply brushing a tasteless oil over the inside of a container, with a pastry brush, so that it will later be easy to turn food out. Get into all the nooks and crannies of shaped moulds, that is where food may stick. Then leave the mould upside down, on paper, to drain.

Papillote

A *papillote* is a paper casing folded round food so that the flavour is contained during cooking. Use greaseproof paper or foil.

Parboil

To part-boil or half cook by boiling.

Paupiette

A paupiette is a very thin slice of meat, or fish, which is then covered with a stuffing, rolled into a log, and tied for cooking.

Poach

This is to cook food in an open pan of liquid which is at slightly below simmering point i.e. 77° to 82°C (170° to 180°F). Most poaching is done on a burner, but it can be done in the oven, and confusingly the *bain-marie* technique (see page 93) of cooking may be called poaching. For poached eggs see page 45.

Purée

Puréed food has been sieved, mashed or liquidized. Whether you remove all the lumps or leave a rougher texture depends on what you want to do with it.

Reduce

Contrary to what you might suppose, reducing liquid doesn't mean chucking half down the sink. Instead you boil it rapidly so it evaporates and the flavour is concentrated. This will intensify the saltiness, so go gently before reducing.

Rest or Relax

This is the process of leaving batters, for pancakes or Yorkshire pudding, to stand for half an hour or so while the starch grains swell before cooking, so you get lighter results. It is also to put pastry in a cool place for an hour or two to let the gluten in the flour contract after the mixing and handling, so it is less likely to shrink in baking.

Rub

Rubbing in fat is a matter of literally rubbing the fat and flour lightly between the tips of your fingers to a crumb-like mixture. Lightness of touch is essential or the mixture will become hot and heavy. For good results freeze the fat, and grate it into refrigerated flour on a coarse grater. This keeps the mixture cool and makes rubbing in very easy.

Sauce Making

Béchamel/White Sauce

A *béchamel* is white sauce, made of flour, butter and milk, in which the milk is first flavoured by heating it with carrot, celery and an onion stuck with a clove. Start it with a *roux* (see below). The secret is to add the liquid gradually while stirring hard with a loop whisk - in that way you won't get lumps.

Beurre Manié/Kneaded Butter

This is equal weights of flour and butter worked together into a paste. Small balls of it can be dropped into casseroles to thicken the liquid, but there must be sufficient cooking time afterwards to remove the taste of raw flour. It can be kept ready for use in the refrigerator. But, though it's considered fearfully expert, I am no great fan. Lacking the prior cooking of a *roux*, the flour takes an interminable time to lose its uncooked taste. Being impatient, I prefer to make a quick *roux* and stir that in (see below).

Alternatively, thickening with a little cornflour, potato flour (*fécule*) or arrowroot, mixed with a spoonful or two of water gives a more translucent look to the liquid, which can be even better - though classically incorrect for some sauces, and not right for some dishes, such as soups. The advantage of potato flour or arrowroot is that these root flours never give the raw taste of uncooked cereal flours. Whatever you use, stir well as you add it to the hot liquid - using a loop whisk to avoid lumps - and simmer gently until thick. These flours thicken quickly, so you can add a little until the sauce is perfect.

Cream-thickened Sauces

To use cream there must only be a small quantity of other liquid, such as a little juice and fat from frying the meat and a little wine, which has been used to deglaze the pan. Into this you stir double cream, which should really be at room temperature (the acid in the wine is then less likely to curdle it). Cook it gently, stirring continuously, and it will slowly thicken. It's beautifully easy so long as the pan is wide. If you bottle a lot of cream up in a narrow pan you can wait till kingdom come before it thickens. And single cream won't thicken at all.

Egg-thickened Sauces

Sauce béarnaise is the classic among egg-thickened sauces, and egg thickening is, admittedly, tricky if it is not to end up scrambled. The essential ingredient is patience. Any sauce thickened with egg yolks must be cooked in a bain-marie (page 93), and the water underneath must not boil. This means that the sauce thickens very slowly, and you need to stir it all the time. When thick it will be tepid, not hot. That is how it should be.

French Dressing

Whatever bastardized mixtures restaurants produce under this name, the correct and invariable ingredients are salt, pepper, olive oil and either wine vinegar or lemon juice. Sugar, mustard, garlic and other herbs can all be added - if you wish - but they are not fundamental. The proportions are about 1 part vinegar to 3 to 4 parts oil, and the ingredients are stirred together or put in a screw-top jar and shaken. It must be re-stirred just before pouring, as it separates rapidly.

It will only be as good as your ingredients - there is a world of difference between the result you get with sea salt, freshly ground black pepper, full-flavoured olive oil and good vinegar, and the sad affair concocted with table salt, packet pepper, malt vinegar and a tasteless cooking oil.

Roux

To make a roux you melt butter, stir in flour and cook it gently stirring constantly until white and frothy. This is the basis for sauces, such as white sauce, for thick soups and for the basic mixture in soufflés.

Brown Roux

For a brown roux dripping often replaces butter, and the fat and flour are cooked together until they are light brown before any liquid is added. This gives a brown sauce, and is a way to make brown gravy without using gravy browning. Finish as for Béchamel.

Vinaigrette Sauce

This is really French dressing (see above) with finely chopped onion and other flavourings, such as gherkins, parsley or capers, added to it to suit the food it dresses. In haute cuisine the different combinations of ingredients each form a sauce with its own special name.

Sauter/Sautéing

Sauter is French for to jump, so the food is jumped in the pan. This means it is cooked quite rapidly in a little hot butter or other fat while you shake or turn it so it cooks evenly.

Scald

Scald has two meanings: to heat milk to the point where it begins to bubble and rise, and to pour boiling water over something.

Season

This is to add salt and pepper to a dish until it tastes right. Cooked food should be tasted to check how much to add, but most raw meat should not be eaten, so seasoning it is guesswork.

Shelling Nuts

Don't believe those who say you should boil chestnuts before shelling them - it's a quick route to broken nails and a frayed temper. Instead cut a slit across the bump from side to side and pop them in a hottish oven until the slit just widens into a smile. Remove a few at a time and, while still very hot, hold them with a cloth and press the corners of the slit together. If the nuts are firm and fresh the shell should crack off most of the nuts easily and the rest can be dislodged with a knife end. Once shelled, you can boil them for stuffing or cakes.

★ Microwaving is even better than a normal oven. A few at a time, they need about 40 seconds on 700 watts.
★ Brazil nuts are far easier to shell when well chilled after several hours in the freezer.

Simmer

Liquid cooked on top of a stove is simmering when it shudders gently with only the occasional bubble at 85°-93°C (185°-200°F). If it bubbles all over it is boiling.

Skinning/Peeling

If you drop thin-skinned fruit such as ripe tomatoes and peaches into a bowl of boiling hot water for a minute or so, then run them under cold water the skins come off easily. You can also freeze whole tomatoes for sauces and, when you need them, run them under a hot tap, when rock solid, and the skin will peel off easily.

Aubergines and Pimentos

To skin aubergines and pimentos you need to grill them all over, until black, and then pull off the skin, rinsing the charred fragments from pimentos under a cold tap.

Nuts

Almonds, walnuts, pecans and pistachio nuts can be skinned after blanching (page 93), but add a pinch of bicarbonate of soda to make pistachios greener. Hazelnuts need to be grilled lightly; the skins will then shake off in a paper bag.

Fish - see page 47

Rabbit or Hare - see page 70.

Tongue and Gammon - see page 92.

Slake

To mix cornflour, arrowroot or similar substances to a thin paste with a little cold liquid. Use just enough liquid to give the thickness of thick pouring cream.

Steam

There are two ways of cooking food in steam:

1 Place it in a steamer (or any other heatproof container with holes which allows the steam through) over boiling water until cooked - a metal colander will stand in for a proper steamer. This suits vegetables, fish and so on.

2 Put the food in a heatproof basin, cover it well, place it in boiling water to within 4 cm (1½ in) of the rim and boil with the lid on the pan. The method for steamed puddings.

If long cooking is involved, by either method, top up with boiling water from time to time - adding cold water would alter the cooking time and maybe crack the basin. When covering puddings which will rise, make a pleat in the centre of the paper or foil to allow for expansion. If fragile food will need to be turned out of its mould after steaming, leave it to stand for a few minutes after removing it from the steamer.

Stewing

Stewing is really simmering at its gentlest: the liquid should hardly tremble. It is ideal for food, such as fruit, which would break up with rapid cooking. Normally, this is done on top of the stove, but on gas it can be hard to get the heat low enough. In this case, use a heat-reducing mat under the pan, or put the food in a covered dish in a low oven instead.

Sweat

This is the process of cooking vegetables very slowly, in butter or oil, to draw out moisture and soften them.

Sweet Making

The **crack** stage in boiling sugar is when it will form a brittle strand, when dropped into cold water, which cracks. This happens at around 154°C (310°F).

Hard ball is the stage when boiled sugar mixtures form a hard ball when dropped in cold water. This happens at about 121°-124°C (250°-255°F).

Soft ball is the stage in boiling at which sugar, or mixtures used in sweet making, can be made into a soft ball with the fingers, after being dropped into a bowl of cold water - about 115°C (240°F).

When boiled rapidly sugar mixtures reach a point when they will pull into a fine **thread**. Short threads are about 1 cm (½ in) long, and long threads 5 cm (2 in) - give or take a bit.

Tenderize

Tenderizing is making meat more tender, and there are two methods. You can beat it into submission with a meat hammer or use pineapple (page 63).

Problems with Food

Bean Sprouts Going Soggy

Unlikely though it sounds, bean sprouts need to be stored under water. Put them in a large jar of water, keep it covered, and change the water every 2 days. But once they have gone soggy they are past rescue.

Biscuits Misshapen

If a recipe tells you to cut out biscuits and put them on a baking tray it is almost impossible to make them perfectly round. Instead, roll the biscuit mixture out on the *back* of the baking sheet, cut the biscuits out and peel away the surplus mixture from around them. Bake them where they are.

Bread

If you want a thawed, or less than fresh, loaf to taste like new just pass it *rapidly* under a cold tap - top and bottom - and place it in an oven at gas no 2 to 3 or 150° to 165°C (300° to 325°F) for about 20 minutes. You can use the same method for rolls and croissants, but they will be ready in as little as 3 to 5 minutes To refresh bread in slices microwave 10-20 seconds.

Bread not Rising

The yeast could be dead. When baking, check this by mixing the yeast with a little warm water and a hint of sugar and leaving it in a warm place. If it doesn't froth (called spongeing) in 15 minutes the yeast is dead and there is no point in mixing it with the flour. If the yeast has sponged, the bread will rise - in its own time - unless you have done something very odd.

Burnt Stews or Vegetables

Tip the food out into a clean pan *without* scraping the burnt bits in with it. Check whether it tastes of burning. With vegetables, cut the burnt side off and taste the remainder. Serve whatever tastes normal. If a casserole still tastes of burning you may be able to mask the taste by adding some fried cumin powder or other spice - but do choose flavours which go with the dish or it will only taste worse.

Burnt Roast Meat

Put a clean damp cloth on the burnt part for a minute or two. You should then be able to scrape it off.

Butter Desalting

If you need unsalted butter, and have none, cut butter

into small pieces, pour boiling water over it and put the mixture to chill. The salt will be washed away in the water and the butter will solidify free from salt.

Butter Clarifying

The virtue of clarified butter is that it can be taken to quite a high temperature without burning, whereas ordinary butter burns easily. If you need clarified butter in a hurry your nearest Indian shop probably sells it as ghee (make sure it is butter not vegetable ghee) or, for most recipes, equal parts butter and vegetable oil is a very good substitute.

Cakes

Burnt or Dry

Cut off the burnt outside. Sprinkle on some suitable alcohol - sherry, brandy (or even fruit juice if you're teetotal) - to reduce the dryness. If it is very dry pierce skewer holes to help the moisture down. Ice completely, or ice in thin layers as for unrisen cake.

Cherries Sinking to the Bottom

Whole glacé cherries look wonderful when a cake is cut, but they do have a tendency to drop to the bottom of the cake. Tossing them in flour before you add them to the mixture, or washing the syrup off them, helps to stop this.

Dry

If an un-iced sponge type cake has been around a little too long and become rather dry you can revive it for family consumption by steaming it briefly in a colander over boiling water - but don't let water actually touch it. Microwaving for 10-20 seconds does the same.

Rising Poorly

There are several possible causes:
- you opened the oven door in the early stages
- you may have over-beaten the cake after adding the flour
- the cake tin was the wrong size
- you didn't sift the flour
- it was a bad recipe anyway.

You may be able to salvage it by slicing it into several layers linked by a good icing.

Stuck in the Tin

When a cake is stuck, run a sharp knife right around the edge of the tin to loosen the sides and then stand the hot tin on a folded wet cloth for a few minutes. It may then come out quite easily. If that fails you just have to prise it out and glue the broken bits together with icing.

Next time line the tin with greaseproof paper and it won't happen. To do that draw round the base of the tin on the paper and cut it out. Cut a strip slightly higher than the sides, fold up the bottom 1·5 cm (½ in) and then unfold and slash it. Put the strip in first with the fold at the bottom, and the circle on top.

When Short of Eggs

If you are an egg short and the cake recipe uses a raising agent or self-raising flour you can substitute a tablespoon of vinegar for one of the eggs with no harm.

Icing Sliding Off

Icing is less likely to slide off if you either stick it on with a thin layer of jam (under marzipan and royal icing, or if you sprinkle a *minute* mount of flour on the cake first - use cornflour, potato flour (*fécule*) or arrowroot, so it won't taste floury.

Cheese Fondue Curdling

If a cheese fondue suddenly curdles, you can rescue it by mixing 2 or so teaspoonfuls of potato flour with a very little white wine (or water) and stirring this into it with a loop whisk, over the heat, until the mixture comes together.

Chocolate Going Grainy on Melting

Chocolate is naturally unpredictable (see page 95), but you may also have over-stirred it. You can smoothe it by stirring in a hint of boiling water - if you want it to stay liquid - or a little butter if you want it to set later.

Choux Pastry Heavy

Choux pastry goes heavy if you don't pierce it straight after cooking to let the steam out.

Coffee Tasting Bitter

Coffee is far less likely to go bitter if you wait a few moments after the water has boiled and pour it on when off the boil.

Coffee Grounds Floating in the Jug

If you are making coffee by the simple expedient of pouring boiling water on to coffee grounds in a jug, the easy way to get the grounds to sink is to drop a spoonful of cold water into the jug. But only do this after the coffee has brewed for a few minutes.

Cream Going Grainy on Beating

This can't be rescued. To prevent it next time, have the cream refrigerator-cold and don't beat for so long.

Cream Sauce not Thickening

Pour the sauce into a *very* wide pan and continue heating - if the cream is double it will thicken. Or add a *little* cornflour or arrowroot mixed with a touch of milk and stir hard.

Custard Baking with Bubbles in

Custard will almost always go bubbly if you cook it too fast. Very slow cooking is needed. It also helps to prevent bubbles if you bring the milk to the boil, let it cool, then mix in the eggs and bake it standing in a tin of water - use gas no 1 or 140°C (275°F) Use 2 eggs to ½ l (1 pint).

Custard Curdling

If real egg custard - made in a double boiler - starts to curdle you can rescue it if you act fast. Either tip it into a bowl and beat hard with a whisk, or whizz it in a food processor, or put it in a clean jar or bottle and shake like mad. Speed is vital; if it goes too far nothing can be done.

Fat on the Surface of Food

The best way to remove fat is to chill the food and lift the fat off when it hardens. But when in a hurry mop it off with kitchen roll.

Fat Spitting

Fat spits when it reacts with water. If shallow frying, sprinkle in a little flour to absorb the moisture. If deep frying turn off the heat and cover - spitting can start a fire. Food should be dry before going into deep fat.

Fruit and Vegetables

Going Brown when Cut

A lot of white-fleshed fruit and vegetables go brown when cut because enzymes and other substances in them react with the air. To prevent it have a bowl of water with a squeeze of lemon juice in and drop them in as you slice them. The acid slows down the action of the enzyme. You can then drain and dry them for cooking. But the brown doesn't do you any harm.

Fizzy Fruit Salad

When fruit salad goes fizzy it is spontaneously fermenting and trying to make itself into alcohol. It feels oddly prickly on the tongue but is perfectly edible.

Hollandaise Separating

To make Hollandaise successfully all the ingredients should be at room temperature when you start, the sauce should be in the top of a double saucepan, and even the water underneath should only be *just* simmering. It should thicken *very* slowly. If it suddenly thickens it may be about to curdle. Remove it from the heat and stir in a teaspoon of cold water to cool it down.

If it separates *slightly* remove it from the heat, put a fresh yolk into a pan over slightly lower heat and very gradually work in the curdled sauce. But if it forms grains, it is past rescue.

Jelly or Aspic Stuck

Run the very tip of a knife all round the upper edge of the mould. Run the plate on to which you are turning it out under a tap and shake off the surplus water, but leave it damp. Have a basin of hot water and dip the mould in the hot water almost up to the rim, for just a *moment.* Put the plate *over* the mould and hold the two together as you turn the mould over. The layer of water should allow you to slide the jelly or aspic on the plate if it doesn't land in the centre.

Lettuce Limp

Lettuce can be crisped up by simply leaving it in cold water, but it crisps fastest if you put a peeled potato or two in the water with it. Curiously, a lump of coal is another aid.

Mayonnaise Separating

Remove the mayonnaise from the blender or bowl. Put in a fresh yolk and *very gradually* mix the curdled mayonnaise into it, as if starting again. It probably happened because you added the oil too fast; next time go more slowly. It is also easier to make mayonnaise if you have two egg yolks, not one, and if there is some mustard in the mixture. Mustard is a natural emulsifier and makes food hang together.

Marmalade Cloudy

Marmalade is much clearer if you add a dessertspoonful of glycerine for every 4 kg (8 lb) of jam half way through cooking.

Meringues Stuck to the Tin

Once stuck, there is no way to remove them without breaking - though heating the tin over a gas flame or candle and removing them instantly may sometimes help. Next time put them on vegetable parchment and they shouldn't stick at all. Failing that, oil greaseproof paper *very* well first.

Mince Rubbery

Mince tends to go rubbery if you add salt before it is cooked. Very long slow cooking may soften it - if you have made enough to warrant it. This doesn't apply to hamburgers and other dishes in which mince is cooked as a block of meat.

Pasta Stuck Together

Treat like rice. But if flat pieces are stuck they may be inseparable - it depends whether they stuck at the start of cooking or only later. Next time use *much* more water - pasta should be cooked in a very big pan not crammed together in a small one.

Pastry too Heavy

The main causes of heavy pastry are over-mixing, over-handling, hot hands, too much water and adding too much flour during rolling. But, there are some people who can't make pastry however closely they stick to the rules - I'm one. You may be too.

Pastry Shrinking

Pastry stretches in the making and needs at least 10 minutes in the refrigerator to 'relax' before use. Cover it with cling film while it does so or it will dry out. Some people stretch pastry more than others. If you do, then roll out the pastry and line your tin with it and cut off the surplus, leaving a large extra rim, and only trim it to size after it has shrunk in the cool.

Potatoes Going Brown or Black

Peeled raw potatoes rapidly go brown because air reacts with certain chemicals in them. So drop them in a bowl of water as you peel them. If you are leaving them for any time put lemon juice or vinegar in the water - but leaving potatoes in water reduces their vitamins.

Potatoes go black or grey when cooked if they have a lot of iron in. To stop (or reduce) this reaction just add vinegar or lemon juice to the cooking water.

Salad Soggy

Any dressing put on lettuce will rapidly turn it soggy. Once this happens there is no redeeming it. The French trick for avoiding the problem is to put the dressing in the bottom of the salad bowl, then cross the salad servers over it and rest the salad on top. The salad is then tossed in the dressing just before serving.

Salty Stew

If a soup or casserole tastes too salty put a large peeled potato in it, cut in chunks, and cook it for about 10 minutes. Remove it and taste. There is a limit to how much salt it can absorb but it should cure mild over-salting.

Sauce - Béarnaise Curdling

If a béarnaise sauce separates, but isn't too far gone, it can be saved by adding a teaspoonful of lukewarm water for every 2 egg yolks and by beating furiously until it comes together. If it has become much too hot it will be past saving.

Sauce Having Lumps

Beat hard with a loop whisk or an egg beater - best of all, liquidize in a blender. The lumps probably happened because you added the liquid too fast, if you are adding liquid to a roux you need to go slowly at first. If you are adding cornflour and water (or any similar thickener) to thicken liquid, it too has to be added slowly while beating hard to prevent lumps. The lumps may be because it cooled and formed a skin.

Sauce Having a Skin

The lumps created by skin on sauces and custards can be removed by beating very hard with a loop whisk or whizzing them in a food processor. To stop skin forming next time spoon a thin layer of whatever liquid you are using in the sauce on to the surface before you let it stand. Alternatively, if it suits the sauce - let tiny pieces of butter melt on the surface. You can also keep sauces hot and skin-free by simply putting them in a thermos - useful when entertaining.

Soufflés not Rising

There is no rescue. It probably happened because the eggs were over- or under-beaten or folded in with a heavy hand, or because you looked to see how it was doing and let in cold air. Next time beat the whites until you can create a peak which just flops its tip over. Fold in and rub the inside of the soufflé dish with butter, so the mixture won't stick before it has risen, and only look when there are five minutes to go.

Tarts Stuck

If a jammy filling trickles over and sticks tarts to the tin, hold the tin over a flame to melt the stickiness and flip them out while still hot.

Tinned Meat Stuck in the Tin

Easy - open the other end and push it out. You can also open the wrong side of some sardine cans if the key breaks.

Toast Burnt

Remove the crusts. Slice through between the two toasted layers (to create two thinner slices) and toast the cut side of whichever half isn't burnt. The result is a slice of melba toast.

Yorkshire Pudding Heavy

The secret of light Yorkshire pudding is to leave the mixture to stand for an hour, and to have the fat in the baking tin *very* hot when you pour it in.

PULSES

Those who share my love of unusual information may enjoy knowing that the legume family, with its host of peas and beans, is the third largest flowering plant family, after orchids and daisies. In fact, they were considered so important in ancient Rome that they had the singular honour of giving their names to four of Rome's most distinguished families - Cicero getting his family name from the chick pea (then known as *cicer arietinum*). Italians often get it right where food is concerned.

The legume family is endlessly adaptable, cropping up in delicious dishes the world over: in hearty minestrones in northern Italy, smooth chick pea pastes in Greece and Arabia, cassoulets in France, refried red beans in Mexico and spicy dals in India. Yet in Britain we exalt only the pea - and the frozen pea at that - and let the other lovely possibilities pass us by. This is a pity because, besides tasting good, this family is rich in protein and in most B vitamins, and low in fat.

I am indebted to Harold McGee for the following figures.

	PERCENTAGE			
	Water	Protein	Carbohydrate	Fat
Mung bean	11	24	60	1
Soya bean	10	37	34	18
Lentil	11	25	60	1
Chick peas	11	21	61	5
Pea	12	24	60	1
Beef	60	18	-	22
Pork	42	12	-	45
Lamb	56	16	-	28

Since the type of protein is important it doesn't automatically follow that pulses are better for you than meat but the poor children who once sang the skipping rhyme:

> Pease porridge hot
> Pease porridge cold
> Pease porridge in the pot
> Nine days old

weren't eating so badly after all, and pulses could cut any family budget.

Dried Peas, Beans and Lentils

Cleaning
Twigs and stones often appear in packets of beans and lentils. So put them in plenty of water in a big metal pan and swirl them round with your hand; twiggy bits will float to the surface and stones clink against the metal. Change the water until it stops looking dusty, picking out the stones on draining. But don't expect the water from washing split lentils to come clear; they always release a milky starch.

Soaking
Leave the beans or lentils to soak overnight in plenty of cold water. The little red lentils are an exception. Unless they are very old and tough, they can be cooked after soaking for as little as half an hour.

If you are short of time put the beans in cold water, bring them to the boil for a couple of minutes and let them soak in it for at least an hour. How well they respond to this shock treatment will depend on their age.

Cooking Dried Peas and Beans
Beans and lentils are accommodating peasant food, and wonderfully easy to cook. Pulses cook in their own time, and it's no good trying to be precise and modern with them. The timing varies with their age. The older they are, the longer they take to cook. So prepare them a day ahead. I have known very fresh mung beans become perfectly tender in just over 15 minutes, but old or large beans can take almost 2 hours, and very ancient chick peas can be boiled for an entire day without softening at all. Whatever their vagaries on first cooking, once cooked they reheat excellently and freeze well.

Dried Peas, Beans and Lentils - in Rough Order of Size

Name	Description	Cooking Time (approx)
Butter beans/ Lima beans	flattish, white and as large as two thumb nails	45+ mins
Black beans	similar to red kidney beans but bigger and black-skinned	35+ mins
Borlotti beans	pinkish cream with a marbling of wine, shaped like kidney beans	50+ mins
Pinto beans	very similar to borlotti but wider in proportion to their length than most	1+ hrs
Red kidney beans	a distinctive wine-red oblong bean	50+ mins

Name	Description	Cooking Time (approx)
Cannellini beans	white twins to the red kidney bean	55+ mins
Dried peas	round and an unmistakably smoky green	40+ mins
Flageolet beans	a soft smoky green but long and narrow	50+ mins
Chick peas/ 'garbanzos'	quite unlike other pulses, with a distinct growing point even when dry	1+ hrs
Black-eyed beans	small and creamy white with a distinct black eye at one side	30+ mins
Haricot beans	creamy white, very chubby and only a little longer than their width	1+ hrs
Soya beans	very like haricot beans but yellower and rounder	3+ hrs
Field beans	almost round and a pinkish brown	25+ mins
Ful medames beans	almost identical to field beans but browner	50+ mins
Split peas	round and yellow, like half a ball	25+ mins
Chana dal	almost the same as split peas but a little smaller: they are interchangeable if need be, but the flavours are not identical	20+ mins
Adzuki beans	very small beans, with almost square corners, like little pillows the colour of milky chocolate	25+ mins
Mung beans	distinctive tiny olive green beans	15+ mins
Moong dal	skinned and split mung beans used in Indian recipes	15+ mins
Brown/Continental lentils	little discs a dull greeny brown	25+ mins
Red split lentils	shiny and skinless little half discs in melon yellow, called Masoor dal in Indian recipes	15+ mins

★ If you have to cook any of this family in a hurry putting a pinch of bicarbonate of soda in the water greatly reduces the cooking time - but you do lose some vitamins. McGee suggests ⅛ of a teaspoon of bicarb per cup of beans - but there is no need to be very exact.

★ Acid toughens the skins of beans by preventing the cell structure from being broken down by heat. This makes the beans remain hard no matter how long you cook them. The degree to which this happens varies with the acidity of the liquid, but if you want to mix them with an acid sauce - such as the tomato in chilli con carne - cook them in water first, and drain and add them to the tomato base when tender.

Beans and Wind
Scientists have identified, and given a cumbersome name to, the substance which they think is responsible for bean's legendary ability to cause wind. *Why* it causes wind is still mysterious. However, they do confirm that, as cooks have always known, some beans are more windy than others.

To reduce the wind-making tendencies of dried beans, put them in fresh cold water and bring it to the boil. Let it boil hard for 15 minutes, then throw away the water and start again from cold. Let the beans simmer in this second water until cooked. The less water they are cooked in the less food value is lost and the faster they cook. But, as they absorb water, they are more likely to dry out and burn while your back is turned - especially lentils.

> WARNING Red kidney and lima (butter) beans can contain substances which are poisonous. Red kidney beans are neutralized by boiling the beans *hard* for at least 10 minutes *with the lid off the pan*. After this treatment they are perfectly safe, and the rest of the cooking can be fast or slow. People have been ill after eating red beans which have been cooked slowly - even though the beans were completely cooked. Lima beans possess a different type of poison. Expert opinion seems divided as to whether it is driven off by cooking, but the American and European varieties, sold to Britain, have been bred to restrict the substance to a level so low it is no longer a hazard. However, there have been cases of poisoning in the tropics where other varieties are grown and neither bean should be sprouted.

To know when any of this family are cooked simply taste them. For some recipes, you must cook them until almost mushy; for others - such as baked beans - you need them firm and whole. Suit the cooking to the dish, but don't expect soya beans to go soft and floury like other beans; they have an almost waxy texture which never changes.

Sprouting Beans
The best beans for sprouting are mung beans. Freshly sprouted they taste 100 per cent tastier and crunchier than those bought from a shop. You need no special equipment but whatever you use must be *perfectly* clean. Having sprouted seeds successfully once, either scald the container or clean it with Milton, as bacteria can build up which rot the sprouts.

They grow to 6 times their volume, so only start with a tablespoon or two: when crowded they won't grow. Cover the beans with cold water and leave them overnight. Next morning, drain, rinse and put them in a large container. Stretch some very clean cotton across the top of the container and put in a warm dark place - such as an airing cupboard. Then, every few hours, pour water in through the cloth, and drain it without disturbing the beans. They mustn't dry out. Eat them when nicely sprouted.

I find beans are temperamental, sometimes sprouting perfectly and sometimes being a complete flop. It may well depend on the age of the beans. Buying them from seedsmen is more reliable, but also more expensive. However, seedsmen such as Thompson and Morgan do offer other seeds such as alfalfa and fenugreek, which give variety to salads.

★ A good container for sprouting beans is a large plastic sweet jar - free from sweet shops. If you pierce a few small holes in the bottom, with a hot skewer, water will wash through the beans without them being tipped up and disturbed.

QUANTITIES AND TEMPERATURES

Amounts of Food per Person
Judging exactly how much food to cook is a tricky business. Some people have far larger appetites than others, there is also the question of how many courses the meal has and what else you are serving at any course. The following quantities are, therefore, just starting points from which to decide what works for your own family and friends. But if you are cooking for a large number you can't simply multiply one portion by the number of people.

Prue Leith shows it exactly when she gives these amounts. Biscuits 3 each for 10 people; 2 each for 30 people; 1 each for over 30 people.

> Small roasting joints tend to shrink dramatically and serve fewer than their weight suggests. Also meat which is well done shrinks far more than meat that is underdone. Unskilled carvers, with blunt knives, who hack off chunks of meat instead of nice slices make a joint go nowhere. A large loaf usually has 18 slices if thinly cut. 8 oz softened butter will spread about 60 slices of bread.

Comparative Oven Temperatures

> The container the food is in makes a difference. For example, thick iron and earthenware casseroles heat slowly, so the food takes longer to cook than it would in some other containers. This means oven temperatures are really only guidelines for working out how to get the best results in your particular situation, and deviation from them is not the heresy it may seem.

Variations Within an Oven

Gas ovens vary considerably in their behaviour even if they are the same size. At any temperature setting a gas oven normally has different heat zones within it. Recipes assume food is in the middle.

● The top of the oven will be higher than the setting.
● The middle of the oven will be at the temperature the oven is set for.
● The bottom of the oven will be cooler than the setting.

The difference in temperature is considerable. This means that by placing each dish on the shelf where it will get the temperature it needs, you can cook an entire meal in the oven at once, thus saving a great deal of time and fuel. The disadvantage is that if you want to cook a large quantity of small cakes, you can't fill the whole oven with them and expect them all to cook in the same time and come out equally well.

Some cooking books say which shelf any dish should be put on. Shelves are always counted from the top, so shelf 1 is the highest. The following table shows the variations in an average gas oven.

Temperature Variation in Electric Ovens

In electric ovens with fans - the middle and upper end of the electric market - there is no difference in temperature between the top and the bottom of the oven. In a standard, non-fan-assisted oven, with side panels, the top is usually a few degrees hotter than the bottom, but it's not usually enough to make much difference to how food cooks. So you can't cook a wide range of foods at a single oven setting the way you can with gas, but if you are cooking a lot of small cakes you can be sure they will all cook correctly whatever shelf they are on.

This table shows the difference between the oven setting and the actual temperature on each shelf.

Setting	E	1	2	3	4	5	6	7	8	9
Shelf 1	1½	2	3	4½	5½	6½	8	9	9	9+
Shelf 2	1	1½	2½	4	5	6	7	8	9+	9+
Shelf 3	E	1	2	3	4	5	6	7	8	9
Shelf 4	E	E/1	1	2	3	4	5	5½	6	7
Shelf 5	−E	E	E	E/1	1½	2	2½	3½	4½	5
Floor	−E	−Ė	E	E	E/1	1	1½	2½	3	4

E stands for Gas ¼–½.

Weighing and Measuring

People are sometimes worried by rough quantities such as a 'nut of butter'. They wonder exactly how big a pinch or a handful should be. But if a good recipe uses these terms it does so because precision really doesn't matter. A 'nut' means a lump about the size of a walnut, a 'pinch' is the amount you can pinch up between thumb and forefinger and if your 'handful' is bigger than the next person's the food will still taste good. Few recipes require total accuracy.

Comparative Oven Temperatures					
Description	Gas	Fahrenheit	Centigrade	Solid Fuel	Convection
very cool	¼	150°-225°	70°-110°	very slow	cooks at the same
very cool	½	225°-250°	110°-120°	slow	centigrade temperature
cool	1	275°	140°		as a normal electric
cool	2	300°	150°	warm	oven but it may take
moderate	3	325°	160°-170°	moderate	a touch longer
moderate	4	350°	180°		
fairly hot	5	375°	190°	fairly hot	
fairly hot	6	400°	200°	hot	
hot	7	425°	220°		
very hot	8	450°	230°	very hot	
very hot	9	475°-550°	240°-290°		

Measuring without Scales

Those who don't have scales can improvise. But the weights will only be *very* approximate; a great deal depends on how level your 'level' is and how large your spoon. So don't use this form of measuring where precision is needed.

	Level tablespoons per 25 g, 1 oz	Weight per ½ pt measuring jug
Breadcrumbs - fresh	5	75 g (3 oz)
- dried	3	175 g (6 oz)
Cheese - grated fairly dry	4	110 g (4 oz)
Cornflour	3	175 g (6 oz)
Custard powder	3	175 g (6 oz)
Currants	3	110 g (4 oz)
Butter, margarine, lard	2	225 g (8 oz)
Flour - unsieved	3	175 g (6 oz)
Oats - rolled	4	110 g (4 oz)
Sugar - caster, Demerara, brown, granulated	2	225 g (8 oz)
- icing	2½	175 g (6 oz)
Sultanas, raisins	2	200 g (7 oz)
Syrup or treacle	1	400 g (14 oz)

Those who lack a measuring jug could substitute a mug. Most mugs take slightly over ½ pt.

For other quantities use a fraction of the packet.

Metric and Imperial Weights	
10 g	½ oz
25 g	1 oz
50 g	2 oz
75 g	3 oz
110 g	4 oz
150 g	5 oz
175 g	6 oz
200 g	7 oz
225 g	8 oz
250 g	9 oz
275 g	10 oz
300 g	11 oz
350 g	12 oz
375 g	13 oz
400 g	14 oz
425 g	15 oz
450 g	1 lb
700 g	1 lb 8 oz

Liquid Measures		
2 fl oz	55 ml	
5 fl oz	150 ml	(¼ pt)
10 fl oz	275 ml	(½ pt)
15 fl oz	425 ml	(¾ pt)
20 fl oz	570 ml	(1 pt)
35 fl oz	1 litre	(1¾ pt)

Converting American Measurements

Perhaps because of their wagon-train past, Americans like measuring with spoons and cups rather than scales. This can be disconcerting if you bring home an American cook book. What is more there aren't any standard conversion tables, because it all depends what you are measuring. An ounce of feathers may weigh the same as an ounce of lead, but a cup of rice crispies does not weigh the same as a cup of butter. The following table is not exact, but a working guideline, as no two cooks seem to agree remotely on the conversions. An American cup is similar to a British cup but not quite identical. It probably doesn't make much odds; you can just go ahead and use a teacup - filling it to the brim.

	US cups	gr	oz
Flour	1	140	5
Caster or granulated sugar	1	225	8
Moist brown or Demerara sugar	1	170	6
Butter	1	225	8
Raisins or sultanas	1	200	7
Currants	1	140	5
Treacle or syrup	1	340	12
Rice - uncooked	1	200	7

Another difference between British and American measuring is that if a British recipe says 1 tablespoon it means one *rounded* tablespoon. If an American recipe says 1 tablespoon it means one *level* tablespoon.
- American fluid ounces are the same size as ours.
- American pints only = 16 fl oz; British pints = 20 fl oz.
- 3 teaspoons to an American tablespoon.
- 4 teaspoons to a British tablespoon.
- American spoonfuls are flat, British are rounded.
- 1 US pack of dry yeast = 7 g (¼ oz).
- 1 US packet of fresh yeast = 20 g (⅔ oz).
- 1 US packet of gelatine = 5 g (¼ oz).

Gelatine Measuring

All sachets of gelatine sold in Britain are the same weight. But if you have gelatine in other forms the equivalent measures are these:

6 leaves of gelatine, each 15 x 10 cm (6 in x 4) = 2/5 oz powdered gelatine = 1 sachet = 3 slightly rounded teaspoons

Each of those amounts will set one pint of liquid and, according to the manufacturers, it doesn't matter whether it is thin liquid like fruit juice, or a thicker one like a mousse mixture.

SPECIAL COOKING METHODS

Microwave Cooking

I used to scorn microwave ovens. It was sheer prejudice: having tested them for a magazine article I'm totally converted. They reduce cooking to a fraction of the time. They also make it possible to thaw rapidly small items straight from the deep freeze. So the contents of a freezer suddenly become accessible without forethought. On top of that, they save fuel and washing up, allow you to cook vegetables without losing goodness into the water and enable dieters and those cutting down on fat to use fatless cooking.

Explaining Microwaves

Microwaves are much easier to use successfully when you know what is going on. This is very simple. Instead of heat flowing all round the food, as it does in other cooking, microwaves behave more like a beam of light. Like light, they travel in a straight line - hence the need for a turntable which presents every side of the food to their beam. They are beamed into the cooker in such a way that they hit the metal-lined walls and are bounced back at the food on the turntable, as light might bounce off a mirror. Even this doesn't give a very wide scatter, so some microwaves have rotating metal paddles, off which the beam will bounce in several different directions - like the light off a mirror ball in a discotheque.

Also like light, they can pass through some substances (e.g. glass), penetrate others slightly (e.g. food) and are reflected off others (e.g. metal). Microwaves aren't hot but they *are* energetic. So when they penetrate food they vibrate its molecules *billions* of times a second. It is the friction of the molecules rubbing against each other, as they vibrate, that creates the heat which does the cooking. It's like a dense crowd of people in which one shove gets everyone moving.

Transferring their energy to the food uses microwaves up, just as a light bulb uses up electricity. So they are not stored in the food - any more than light is stored in a room after you turn off the switch. In fact, they are high-frequency waves closer to radio waves than to the hazards of X-rays (see Facts and Figures).

Key Facts when Using Microwaves

Always position the oven so there is 5 to 8 cm (2 to 3 in) of ventilation space at the top or side - depending on the model.

You don't have to use any special recipe to cook with microwaves but you do need to shorten the times greatly, and arrange the food slightly differently. The best course is to find a similar microwave recipe, allow for any difference in quantities, then set the timer for slightly less. If the food isn't done by the end you can always give it a few more minutes. Whatever you do, *experiment*. You won't go far wrong if you keep to the following rules.

1 **Microwaves can only go 2·5 to 5 cm (1 to 2 in) into food.** Thicker food only cooks because the heat created by the microwaves is conducted to the centre - as it would be in normal cooking - which considerably increases the cooking time. So:
   a cook food in a layer no more than 2·5 cm (1 in) thick - e.g. peas should not be heaped up
   b turn items like baked potatoes over at half time
   c stir foods such as sauces at intervals during cooking, so what was in the middle gets to the edge

   d with larger amounts of food move sides to middle at half time - if possible
   e for large single items don't just multiply up the time needed for a small item, allow a good deal more and turn them several times
   f use round containers where possible as food cooks more evenly
   g try to space items so that all sides can be reached by the microwaves, e.g. place cup cakes in a ring use ring moulds which allow the microwaves to get at food from the middle as well as the sides - or stand a glass in the middle of the dish and put the food around it.

2 **Microwaves cannot pass through metal; they bounce off it, and small quantities of metal can cause sparks which could damage the oven.** This means:
   a you *can't* cook food in metal cake tins or pans as the waves just won't reach it (or will reach the top but not the sides - disaster to a cake)
   b you *can't* cook food in containers made of metal but enamelled on the outside - e.g. Le Creuset casseroles
   c you *can't* use containers with metal parts anywhere - rims, handles, or even as part of a pattern (patterns cause arcing - i.e. sparks)
   d you *can't* close oven bags with metal ties as these can cause sparks.
   e you *can* use foil to protect small areas, like the ends of drumsticks which, being thin, would otherwise cook much faster than the rest. Use smooth foil, in small pieces, dull side out - and it must be 2·5 cm (1 in) away from the sides of the oven as the food goes round.
   f if the oven has a metal trivet for use when convection cooking it shouldn't be used when just microwaving, but it *can* be used when cooking with microwaves and convection at the same time.

WARNING Metal used incorrectly in an oven may cause sparks which can damage the cooker. If you see sparks, turn the oven off *at once* and remove whatever metal is causing them.

3 **These can be used for cooking because microwaves pass through them:**
   a **glass** - provided it can stand the heat of the food (remember liquids may reach boiling point) but *not* leaded glass, cut glass or other high quality glass as it may be damaged
   b **china** - if it can stand the heat and has no gilding on it (see 2c)
   c **pottery** - but heavy earthenware slows down the cooking
   d **plastic** - provided it can stand heat - yoghurt pots etcetera won't but some heavier containers will, so will roasting bags and cling film.

e   **paper** - but only for very brief cooking or heating or it may catch fire, and not if wax or plastic-coated.

Test the vessel by putting a cup of water in it and microwaving for 1 to 2 minutes. If the container gets hot and the water doesn't, don't use it.

4   **Microwaves heat different types of good at different speeds:**
   a   The fattier a food, the faster it cooks so:
   - cheese, cream, rich fish and shellfish overcook easily
   - cream sauces tend to separate on reheating in a microwave
   - the fatty yolk of an egg cooks before the white.
   b   Sugar cooks very fast so:
   - sugary toppings may be done before the food they top
   - the inside of jam tarts turns to caramel before the pastry is done (nasty)
   - larger tarts will be dangerously hot inside when straight from the oven
   c   Food which is moist cooks more slowly than dry food.
   d   Open textured food, such as bread, cooks faster than dense food like meat.

Don'ts for Microwaves
- Don't cook an egg in its shell - it may explode from the steam.
- Don't heat alcohol, oil or melted fat which is not mixed into the food they could overheat and catch fire.
- Don't try to cook bread, pizzas, batters, roast potatoes, small tarts, meringues or soufflés.
- Don't expect food to brown - it usually won't.
- Don't expect it to make reheated food crisp - a microwaved slice of bread is moist and delicious, a microwaved croissant is as depressing as a soft watch.
- Don't try to use a normal thermometer in a microwave.
- Don't add salt to meat, fish or vegetables until they are cooked as it can make them dry if added earlier.
- Don't try to cook a cake in a tin more than 20 cm (8 in) across: the middle may remain soggy - unless it's a ring mould.
- Don't use as much fat as usual. Less fat is absorbed in microwave cooking. (Great for slimmers.)

Do's for Microwaves
- Cover foods which may spit with kitchen roll.
- Cut the amount of liquid you use, by a third or a half as it won't evaporate away. Vegetables will cook in a tablespoonful or so.
- Cut food into even-sized pieces.
- Keep in the moisture by covering food with cling film - but allow a space for steam to escape.
- If heating whole foods with skins (e.g. tomatoes or apples) pierce the skins with a fork to let steam escape.

- Place pastry or bread on kitchen paper when reheating so the bottom won't become soggy.
- Use roasting bags for poultry and joints of meat, as it prevents spattering. But close them with string, and pierce them to allow the steam out.
- Remember that things cook faster at the edges so place portions of meat or fish with the thickest part to the outer edge.
- Reheat at the level to suit the food.
- Cook pastry cases blind; then fill them.
- Put a dish of water in the microwave when heating tiny quantities to stop it arcing (sparking).
- Stand cakes on a cooking rack at least 3 cm (1¼ in) off the oven base to ensure the underside is fully cooked.
- Remember that the food goes on cooking for a little after the oven switches off.

Safety with a Microwave
Microwaves may only be sold in Britain if they meet a set standard. All the authorities agree that microwaves made to that standard are safe - there is no risk of radiation or anything else. But before buying a cooker check that it does carry an approval label, and follow the safety rules when using it.
- Never operate one which has a fault in its door.
- Never try to repair a microwave yourself.
- Keep a dish of water in the bottom when not in use, in case it is accidentally switched on.
- Keep the seal round the door perfectly clean and in good condition.
- Don't worry about opening the door during a cycle - the microwaves will automatically switch off.

Timing Food in a Microwave
Most foods can be cooked very quickly on high. But eggs, cheese, shellfish and fish, and meats which are tough, need longer cooking, and a medium or low setting is best.

The more you put in the oven, the longer the food will take to cook. This isn't simply a matter of a big cake taking longer than a small one (it would in any oven), but of four small *individual* items - say four chicken drumsticks, nicely spaced - taking longer than one cooked on its own. This means that you can never predict exact times for anything cooked by a microwave unless you follow a recipe and use exactly those quantities. But everything cooks so fast that if you have to put anything back to cook for longer it seldom takes more than a minute or two. Generally speaking, if you double the quantity you must add a third to a half to the cooking time. If you reduce the quantities by half reduce the cooking time by rather more than half.

When the microwaves are turned off cooking doesn't stop immediately. The molecules in the food keep on bouncing. This is why recipes often allow a standing period after the oven is turned off. During this, cover the food with foil to keep in the heat.

Wattages
The wattage of a microwave is whatever it gives out

at its highest setting. At lower settings the wattage is lower. Unfortunately, microwaves haven't been standardized but the vast majority are 650 to 700 watts and most microwave recipes are written for them. If you need to adjust timings for less than 650 watts the rules are these:

Time at 650 watts	Equivalent time at 500 watts
10 seconds	13 seconds
15 seconds	20 seconds
30 seconds	40 seconds
45 seconds	1 minute

For larger amounts, needing longer cooking, you can work the timing out by the following rule. For each minute of cooking time at 650 -

add 10 to 15 seconds for a 600 watt oven
add 15 to 20 seconds for a 500 watt oven
add 20 to 25 seconds for a 400 watt oven.

Hints and Tips
★ Citrus fruits yield more juice if microwaved on full power for a few seconds.
★ To melt gelatine stir it into the water and give it 2 minutes on defrost.
★ To soften butter for cake making 'defrost' for 30 to 40 seconds.
★ When baking cakes use a soufflé dish instead of a cake tin - but line it so you can remove the cake easily.
★ Although food doesn't brown, you can make it look less ghostly by brushing it with paprika, or soya sauce or (if the flavour works) brown sugar and Worcestershire sauce before you cook it. Better still finish it under a grill.
★ If you have to cook food in a square container shield the corners with foil to stop them overcooking.

Microwave Association, Lansdowne House, Lansdowne Road, London W11 3LP Tel: 01 229 8225/6/7
The Microwave Cooking School, Apple Tree Cottage, 2b South Hill Park, London NW3 2SB Tel: 01 794 8567 - runs day-long courses.
Claire Ferguson, *Gourmet Vegetarian Microwave Cookery,* Grubb Street Publishers
Good Housekeeping (Ebury Press) do an excellent range of microwave cooking books.

Pressure Cooking
The principle of a pressure cooker is that when water reaches boiling point in an ordinary pan it lets off steam and that stops the water getting any hotter. A pressure cooker holds the steam in and allows the water to reach a much higher temperature - making the food cook faster.

It is most useful for foods which take a long time to cook - dried beans, bottling fruit, Christmas puddings and certain casseroles.

The precise instructions for each cooker *must* be followed but these points apply to all brands.
● Pressure cookers should only be used with the recommended amount of liquid in. There will usually be a set minimum and maximum.
● It is dangerous to try to remove the lid before the pressure has dropped. Check the indicator and do not open it until it shows it is safe.

● Foods should not be cooked in pressure cookers which might rise up and block the vents.
● In working out the pressure cooking time for a normal recipe you can calculate that it will take about one-third of the time of ordinary cooking.

★ When steaming puddings add lemon juice or vinegar to the water to reduce the discoloration of the pan.
★ After use wash and dry it well and leave with the lid upside down so air can get in. If you leave it closed it may smell musty when you next open it.

Haybox Cooking
Haybox cooking is an ancient way of cooking by simply holding the heat in a pot after taking it from the fire. Take a strong wooden box like a tea chest and line it with about 25 layers of newspaper. Cover this with brown paper and fix it in place. Put a thick layer of unchopped hay in the bottom of the box and place on it the casserole you will want to use. Check there will be space round it for a thick lining of hay. Make a bag which will exactly fit the top of the box, and fill it with hay to make a cushion and sew up the opening. Cook the food in the pan, on a normal stove and, when it is at the stage where you would normally simmer it bring it to the boil. Then, *without* opening the lid, put it in the hay box and pack hay tightly round it. Cover it with a sheet of newspaper - to keep the hay off the lid - and cover it with the hay cushion and more newspaper to keep in as much heat as possible. Put a lid on the box and leave it.

How long the food needs to stay in the box is a matter of your convenience, unless it is likely to spoil with overcooking. Some foods will be ready to eat; others will need to be finished on top of the stove.

It is a useful way of cooking some foods which would otherwise consume a lot of time and fuel, such as vegetable soups (allow 3 hours) or stewed fruit (allow 2 to 3 hours), but it is not advisable for meat or fish as the temperature could drop to a point which would allow food poisoning bacteria to multiply.

Vacuum Flask Cooking
A wide-necked vacuum flask can be used to cook any kind of dried fruit. Simply put the fruit in, pour on boiling water and close. By next day the fruit should be cooked or almost so - saving both fuel and trouble.

★ Put cling film round cork tops to vacuum flasks or they take up the smell of the food.
★ When vacuums are empty, lumps of sugar inside stop them smelling stale.

STORAGE TIMES
No matter how tightly sealed anything seems, it probably isn't totally impervious to air - unless it's a tin or a sealed glass jar. Even plastic fizzy drink bottles aren't airtight - only they do the reverse and allow a minute amount of gas to escape *out* through the plastic itself. So everything will spoil with time.

There are two issues here - how long the food lasts

at its best and how quickly it goes bad. The times given below are for using the food at its best, unless otherwise stated. After that food may become unpleasant and lose food value but, in many cases, it will do you no harm.

General Store Cupboard Foods
If food is sold well packed in sealed bags or packets leave it like that. Don't transfer any foods to a home container until you are ready to use them, as it will shorten their shelf life. Once opened, all dried foods are easily contaminated by mice and attacked by biscuit beetles, so then they are best kept in jars. Failing more decorative containers, most sweet shops throw away large plastic sweet jars which will hold bulky dry goods like cereals. But check the plastic hasn't cracked, as they can be brittle.

The counsel of perfection (and thrift) is to date all goods, with a marker pen, as you put them in a store cupboard and put them at the back of the shelf, moving older food to the front. The following times are for a cool, dry kitchen cupboard, unless otherwise stated.

Food	Time	Comments
Biscuits - cream-filled	3 mths unopened 1 wk opened	Store in a tightly closed jar or metal box, once opened.
Biscuits - plain or crispbread	5 mths unopened 10 days opened	Store in a tightly closed jar or metal box once opened. Will stay crisp longer if sugar lumps are put with them.
Bouillon cubes	9 mths	
Coffee - ground - beans	18 mths in a sealed pack 1 wk opened 9 mths in a sealed pack 1 wk opened	For longer keeping once opened roll up the top, close tightly with a bulldog clip and freeze.
Coffee - instant	12-18 mths unopened 4 wks opened	Avoid leaving lid off, as the flavour 'dies'.
Dried beans and lentils	9 mths	Will last for years but become harder to cook.
Dried fruit or crystallized fruit (except prunes)	9 mths unopened 6 mths opened	May become drier, with sugar crystals on the outside, but still usable unless mouldy. Soak very dry ones in water to restore juiciness.
Fizzy drinks	9-12 mths unopened 1 day reclosed	These times are for those in plastic bottles.
Flour - plain	13 mths	Most flour usable longer. Flour will sweat if closed in a plastic bag. Use a container which keeps mice and biscuit beetles out, yet lets air in.
Flour - self-raising	10 mths	As plain flour
Flour - wholemeal (rye, wheat, barley, buckwheat)	3-6 mths	Some stoneground or cool-ground flour keeps the shorter time.
Jam and honey	Indefinitely unopened but best within 18 mths. Use as soon as possible once opened.	Pure fruit jams need cool and are best in the fridge.
Muesli and rolled grains	5-6 mths	May have additives which allow longer keeping.

Food	Time	Comments
Nuts - shelled	4+ mths	Nuts can go rancid. Best in the freezer.
Oats - rolled, porridge, or oatmeal	9-12 mths	This assumes the oats have been heat-treated, as most modern oats have been, to stop the enzymes turning them rancid.
Oil	3-12 mths	Oils go rancid with heat and light, best stored in a cool dark place. Use walnut in 3 mths, olive will keep a year.
Pasta (dry), rice, custard powder	9 mths	Pasta and rice usable longer but may need more cooking.
Pastes and spreads	3-6 mths unopened. Once opened refrigerate and use rapidly.	Go bad more easily than many foods. Don't store longer, eat rapidly once opened.
Peanut butter	1 yr unopened	See page 54.
Prunes	2-12 mths	Modern prunes don't keep well. For long storage freeze them. Cook in tea with lemon zest.
Sugar	18 mths at best	To stop moist brown sugar going solid, put a piece of bread with it and keep well closed.
Tea	18 mths unopened. Use within weeks once opened.	Best kept airtight as it takes up the taste of other foods.
Yeast - dried	6 mths	Keep tin well closed.

Fresh Food

The keeping time of fresh food is far more variable than the times for dried foods. For meat, fish and poultry, see index.

Bacon - slices or joints vacuum packed	15 days in fridge	They may not have a packing date but you may be able to judge how fast they are moving in the shop.
Bacon - slices or joints not vacuum packed	10 days in fridge	Bacon also freezes well. Cut whole packs crosswise, when frozen, to make chopped bacon - but have a sharp knife.
Butter	8 wks (from packing) in fridge	Butter has no packing date, but a good shop shouldn't keep it long so it should keep several weeks.
Cake	3 days - 1 yr + In cake tin in a kitchen cupboad	Each type has its own time limit: fatless sponges become dull in a day or two, while rich fruit cakes are excellent after a year. Keep longer with a slice of bread or a chunk of apple.
Cheese - goat	1-2 days at their best in a cool place	Wrap in foil and put in vegetable drawer of refrigerator.
Cheese - hard or hardish blue	3 wks in vacuum pack; 1-3 wks opened in cool place or a fridge vegetable drawer	Keep in foil, in a tin, in a cool place. Put at room temperature for 1 hr before eating - but cheese will spoil if repeatedly warmed and cooled. For cooking, grate and freeze.

Food	Time	Comments
Cheese - soft curd style	4-7 days ideally chilled at 1-5°C	Grows mould very easily. Ricotta is extra fragile.
Cheese - soft ripened (e.g. Brie)	2-3 days in a cool place	Wrap in foil and put in a cool place. Will ripen in cool but not in fridge. If it must go in a refrigerator, use the vegetable drawer. Put at room temperature for 1 hour before serving to restore softness.
Cheese - mozzarella	about 6 days in a fridge	For eating raw, keep in water. For cooking it can be frozen.
Eggs - natural	Several wks below 10°C (50°F)	Eggs are coated with a natural preservative, only broken down by water - so do not wash before storage. Store pointed end down.
Eggs - lard-coated	2-4 wks if room temperature, 4-6 mths in a cold place	To keep eggs longer rub lard all over the shell to hold moisture and carbon dioxide in the shell.
Ham and similar cold meats	Sliced - 2 days in fridge	Home-cooked ham joints keep longer.
Macaroons	A wk in cupboard	Put a slice of bread in the tin to keep their soft centre.
Mayonnaise - fresh	Several days in fridge	To stop home-made going oily: when you finish making it, beat in 2 tbsps hot water for every 3 egg yolks.
Milk	Varies with the weather; 2-3 days average in fridge	Must be tightly closed or it will pick up smells from other food and taste odd. A metal top pressed open with a thumb is replaceable.
Olives	9 mths in fridge	Cover unstuffed olives in olive oil in a clean jar. Any keep 6 mths in a freezer and can be sliced from frozen for a garnish.
Pasta - freshly made	24 hrs in fridge	If it is really freshly made - and not fresh chilled - it can go mouldy very quickly.
Pâté	3 days in fridge	If pâté has been out of the fridge much eat that day.
Yeast - fresh	2 wks in fridge	In a screw-top jam jar, or wrapped in plastic film.

★ When camping, or if the fridge fails, stand the bottle in an inch of water and put a cloth over the bottle with its bottom edge in the water. The evaporating water will cool the bottle. You can also use this on a doorstep if you have a friendly milkman and are out when he delivers.

Tinned Food

The keeping time of tinned food is often misunderstood. If a tin is perfectly sealed and there is no rust on it then the contents will be safe to eat for far longer than the number of years given below. But it probably won't taste very nice because the acids in food gradually eat into the lining of tins and acquire a metallic taste. British tins are now all steel, lined with tin, with no lead in the seam, so this may do you no harm. But lead-seamed tins from abroad may not be so harmless. Acid food

WARNING Tinned food only keeps because the air has been kept out. Once air gets in it is just as likely to go bad as any other food. BEWARE of all the following:
● tins with dents - especially dents on the seam
● those which have signs of rust on the outside
● any even slightly domed at the end (these are already going bad)
● any which smell odd.

in poor tins has a relatively short life. One of the problems is that you seldom know when it was packed. Heinz tins are an exception. Look at the top row of the numbers stamped in the end. The first three figures tell you which day of the year (out of 365) it was packed, and the last figure is the last figure of the year. So 0028 would be 2 January 1988, and 3658 would be 31 December 1988.

Once a tin is opened, tip the contents into some other container. Aided by air, the food will interact with the lining quite quickly.

Keeping Times of Tinned Food

The following times are for an average kitchen cupboard.

Food	Time	Comments
Most tinned food	2 yrs	In perfect conditions in a British climate. In hot damp climates tins rust rapidly.
Prunes, rhubarb	1 yr	The high acid content makes them a special case.
New potatoes, most fruit	18 mths	Fruit in its own juice keeps as long as fruit in sugar syrup.
Milky foods	12-18 mths	Milk may go thick and caramelize. It should be safe if it tastes normal.
Solid meat e.g corned beef, fish in oil	5 yrs	WARNING Tins of pasteurized meat weighing over 1 kg (2 lb) only keep for 9 months and should be kept chilled.

VEGETABLES

Although water is mainly used as the cooking medium, most vegetables are better cooked with a minimum of water, as in a microwave, and are excellent cut up small and stir fried in the Chinese way, or emerge beautifully from long slow cooking in oil in the Mediterranean style.

Variety in vegetables is not just a matter of how they are cooked; how they are prepared also makes a great difference. It was a professional cook in France who first taught me that a finely sliced Salade Niçoise, in which one can have all the flavours mingled evenly in one mouthful, is quite unlike a coarsely chopped one. There is a place for coarse chopping, but if you are interested in what texture does to flavour try taking a lettuce and some French dressing. Tear part of the lettuce coarsely, slice another part in half-inch slices and chop the last section in shreds thinner than a matchstick. Dress them and eat them separately and you will have three different salads from the identical ingredients. And the flavour of every vegetable we cook is equally affected by its preparation.

The timings in this section are intended to be guidelines. They cannot, alas, be gospel because a lot will depend on the variety of the particular vegetable, how old it is, how large you cut it, how much water you use, or how you space it on the dish for microwaving. Often vegetables are cooked for *far* too long. This wastes the vitamins in them and the cost of the energy. See how briefly you can cook each vegetable you prepare and still have it tender enough not to be a salad. For the most goodness and best flavour cook all vegetables until only *just* tender when poked with a fork.

The lid must be left off the pan when members of the cabbage family are cooked. It may seem logical to keep lids on to shut smells in, but that isn't what happens. The smell from the cabbage family is produced by acids which they release, and when the lid is on these smelly acids become more and more concentrated each time they condense on to the lid and drop back into the water - and the smell becomes equally concentrated. But if you leave the lid off the smell wafts away in its weakest form. The other big smell causer is simply overcooking them. This family need very brief cooking indeed.

One of the most useful tricks when cooking many vegetables is to drop them in boiling water and cook them fast until three-quarters done, then drain them and chill them *rapidly* with cold water. After that they can wait until you need them - later that day - and be simply tossed in butter for long enough to heat them. This gives a brilliant green to most green vegetables, and is a boon if guests are coming.

Key

Months in heavy type show the peak season when prices are normally lowest.

Microwave times are for an oven of about 650 watts set at 'high', and for 450 g (1 lb) unless otherwise stated.

To 'top and tail' a vegetable is to cut off just enough to remove the stalk and any spiky or hard bit at the other end.

N/A = Does not apply.

Vegetable & Best Season	Buying	Preparation	Basic cooking method	Microwave	Comments
Artichoke - Jerusalem **January**	They should be plump and not too knobbly.	Peel thinly, dropping into acidulated water. Leave whole or cut in halves or quarters.	Boil/steam 15-40 mins. Purée for soup. Serve with sauce, but not plain.	10-12 mins	Stain hands - wear gloves. Delicious puréed as cream soup with nutmeg and milk.
Artichokes - Leaf/Globe **July**	Choose them fat and fleshy with no browning of the 'leaves'.	There's no need to mutilate the lovely double-pointed leaves by cutting. Invert in salted water for a while to remove wildlife. De-stem.	Cook in boiling salted water for 25-50 mins. Drain when an outside leaf pulls away easily and its fleshy base is tender.	Put 2 artichokes in 2 tbsp salted water. Cover, cook 5½-8½ mins. Stand 3-5 mins.	Serve hot with Hollandaise sauce, or butter melted with black pepper and a dash of vinegar. Or cold with vinaigrette.
Asparagus **May, June**	The best is plump but not woody; the very fine sprue is cheap and tasty, but inelegant.	Pare off any woody outside near the base. Trim the bottoms, rinse off any dirt.	Tie in portions with white string. Wrap foil round tips of bundles. Boil, lying down, 10-40 mins according to size and age.	450 g (1 lb) in 2 tbsp water. Cover and cook for 5½-6 mins. Stand for 3 mins.	The foil round the tips allows you to cook them on their sides without the tips breaking.
Aubergine **All year**	One of the few vegetables in which bruises do not taint the other flesh.	Slice 0.5 cm (¼-½ in) thick, sprinkle with salt, leave in a colander to drain 1 hr.	Pat dry, dip in egg beaten with a little milk. Then in flour. Deep fry until golden.	Only with other vegetables.	Combine best with other vegetables, but are very good fried like this.
Avocado Pears **All year**	They should be just yielding to the touch, not soft or brown.	Only cut open within an hour of eating or the air browns them and the flavour spoils.	Eaten raw all year.	N/A	Leaving the stone in an uneaten half and covering it with cling film makes it keep a day without spoiling. Rubbing the cut surface with lemon juice stops browning, but alters the taste.
Beans - Broad **June**	The smaller, the tastier. Pods should be plump.	If only little-finger-thickness or smaller, cut in lengths like French beans; if big, shell.	Boil 5-10 mins according to age. Cook young ones simply in butter.	4 tbsp water 5-10 minutes. Stand 3 mins.	White sauce with chopped parsley goes well with boiled ones. In extreme old age remove their little coats. Cooking the herb savory with them improves the flavour.
Beans - French **All year**	They should be very slim and snap crisply if fresh.	Top, tail and string if necessary; leave whole or cut in short lengths.	Drop into boiling salted water 6-8 mins or steam; they should be slightly firm to bite into.	450 g (1 lb) in 4 tbsp water 7 mins. Stand for 5 mins.	Dress with melted butter or garlic butter, &/or toasted almonds.
Beans - String **Late summer**	Buy only when slim and tender. They must snap easily, and have no fibrous layer.	Top, tail, string and slice finely on a diagonal.	Boil in salted water until *just* tender, 4-10 mins.	450 g (1 lb) in 4 tbsp water. Cover and cook for 6-8 mins. Stand for 3 mins.	When young they need nothing but a hint of butter; when fibrous not worth eating.
Beetroot **All year**	If raw, check that the roots aren't broken and there is 5 cm (2 in) of stalk on still. Small are best	Rinse gently.	Put them in plenty of boiling water with 1 tbsp salt for 1 kg (2 lb) beetroot, simmer 1-2 hrs. Or bake in a low oven 2-4 hrs.	450 g (1 lb) in 6 tbsp water. Cover and cook for 23-25 mins. Add more water if needed.	They are cooked when the skin comes off easily. Baking gives better flavour. Small beet very good with white sauce. Eat in 2 days once cooked.

Vegetable & Best Season	Buying	Preparation	Basic cooking method	Microwave	Comments
Broccoli **May**	The flowers must not be yellowy and the leaves should be perky.	Strip the woody skin off thick stems. Wash.	Stand in boiling salted water until the stems are almost done. Then lie them on their sides till done, 8-12 mins. Or slice stems and divide heads and stir fry.	450 g (1 lb) in 3 tbsp water (florets to the centre). Cover and cook for 5-7 mins. Stand 3 mins.	Stores badly. Cook within 1 day unless close wrapped. *Do not put the lid on when cooking or it will smell.*
Brussels Sprouts **November, December, January**	Check they have no flies or mould, or yellowing.	Cut a fraction from the base; remove bad leaves. Cut an X in the base.	Drop into boiling salted water and boil 5-10 mins until *just* tender.	450 g (1 lb) in 2 tbsp water. Cover and cook 7-9 mins. Stand 3 mins.	*Do not put a lid on the pan or they will smell.*
Cabbage - Green or White **All year**	Check open cabbages for flies and other nasties.	Cut out the hard core and slice as you wish. Rinse in salted water.	As sprouts but briefer, or stir fry 6-10 mins.	1 medium, sliced cabbage in 1-2 tbsp water. Cover, cook 8-13 mins. Stand 3 mins.	Cook with *no lid on the pan,* and keep it crisp. Finely shredded, it may only take 3 mins.
Cabbage - Red **All year**	It should be shiny and crisp-looking.	As white cabbage, above.	It can be boiled, as white cabbage, and then tossed in butter with a little fresh root ginger, but is usually given long slow cooking with vinegar and spices.	As white cabbage.	Though seldom used as a salad it is just as good as white cabbage and much more decorative.
Carrots **June, July**	Many slim carrots taste like soap; small rougher-looking ones are often excellent. Taste before you buy: they should be sweet and full of flavour.	Very young carrots just need a scrub, top and tail. Older ones need scraping and slicing.	Drop into boiling water with a pinch of sugar for 6-10 mins. Or cook slices very slowly in butter, with a tbsp of liquid.	450 g (1 lb) in 2 tbsp water, and a pinch sugar. Cover and cook 6-7 mins if sliced, 7-8 mins if small, whole. Stand 3 mins.	Young carrots are sold in March, April and May. Dress with butter and chopped parsley. If big and woody only fit for slow casserole.
Cauliflower **September**	A fresh cauliflower has a crunch in its eye.	Soak in cold salted water. Cut off the base and leaves; divide into even florets unless you need it whole.	Drop into boiling salted water and boil for 10-15 mins or steam, or boil 4 mins, drain, stir fry 3 mins with coriander or chillies.	450 g (1 lb) in florets, in 2 tbsp water. Cover and cook 7-12 mins.	Whiten with a little lemon juice in the water. To cook whole and perfect wrap in muslin so you can lift it out. Good with cheese sauce. *Put no lid on the pan* or it smells.
Celeriac **January, February**	Choose ones which are firm, plump and not too dirty.	Peel with a potato peeler. Put in acidulated water immediately.	Dice, boil until tender and purée with potatoes. Or shred, blanch and mix with mustardy mayonnaise or cut and cook as chips.	Diced as carrots.	Lemon juice in the water when cooking keeps it white. At its best in a salad.
Celery **All year**	The tastiest celery has some earth still on. Failing that, look for crispness and whiteness.	Wash, remove brown areas and slice in 1.5 cm (½ in) slices for boiling or halve lengthwise for braising.	Boil in salted water 10-15 mins, or braise 1½ hrs, onion, carrot, and a little bacon moistened with stock.	450 g (1 lb) in 3 tbsp water. Cover and cook 7-10 mins sliced or 12-15 mins halved.	Boiled celery is best smothered in cheese sauce.

Vegetable & Best Season	Buying	Preparation	Basic cooking method	Microwave	Comments
Chicory (Belgian Endive - the cigar-shaped vegetable) Not June or July	Those which are green may be bitter.	Wipe dust off with a cloth; don't wash. Remove any brown parts.	Boil still done. Better baked in a covered dish with butter at gas no 3 or (160°C) 325°F about 60-75 mins.	450 g (1 lb) sliced with 1 oz butter. Cover and cook 7-12 mins. Stand 5 mins. Stir once while cooking.	Very good with cheese sauce. Sliced finely in salads, it goes well with orange. Slice with a stainless steel knife; other steel gives it a metallic taste.
Courgettes July, August, September	The slimmer, the better - within reason.	Rub any dirt off under a tap. Top and tail; slice like bread.	Drop in plenty of boiling water. Drain as soon as the water returns to the boil, toss in butter, or sweat in butter, or stir fry.	They tend to taste bitter when micro-waved.	Have a natural affinity with tomatoes and garlic. Very good finely sliced in salads.
Fennel Summer	Look for compact fat ones, not those which are long.	Rinse, remove any brown parts and quarter.	Boil in salted water 10-15 mins. Or bake with butter in foil parcels 20 mins at gas no 6 or (200°C) 400°F.	2 heads, halved lengthwise, in 4 tablespoons of water or broth. Cover and cook 15-18 mins.	Best with a cheese sauce. Also a lovely salad vegetable.
Kohl Rabi November to April	Best very small - larger than a tennis ball they are tough.	Cut off stalks and root. Drop in boiling water, bring back to boil and cook 2 mins. Transfer to cold water and peel. Dice in 5-mm (½ in) cubes.	Boil in salted water 4 mins, or steam 7 mins.	As carrots.	It goes well with cheese and with ginger.
Leeks January, February	Slim leeks have the best flavour.	Cut off the root, trim off the dark green and brown parts in layers. Slit half-way down or slice in 2.5 cm (1 in) lengths. Soak them in water, stirring and changing the water till no more grit.	Drop into boiling salted water, 7-10 mins until just tender, not sloppy. Or stew whole very slowly in oil with seasonings.	450 g (1 lb) sliced in 4 tbsp water or 25 g (1 oz) butter. Cover and cook 6-10 mins. Stand 2 mins.	They need a cheese sauce or melted butter with a dash of boiled vinegar and black pepper.
Mange-touts May, June	They should be crisp and very small, with no bulging peas.	Top, tail (and string if necessary).	Drop in boiling salted water. Cook 1-3 mins.	Rinse, cook covered in film for 1 min.	Must be quite crisp. Dress with butter.
Marrow Late summer	The younger, the better; a fingernail should scratch the skin easily when young.	Cut off stalk and rough end. Peel very thinly. Halve, scoop out the seeds, cut in 2.5 cm (1 in) slices.	Drop into boiling salted water and drain when just *beginning* to look translucent. Or steam. Time varies with age.	1 medium-sized in chunks with 25 g (1 oz) butter. Cover and cook 6-7 mins. Stand 5 min. Cover young halves, cook 8-10 mins. Stand 5 mins.	When very young drain and serve with butter and black pepper; when older with white, or cheese, sauce.
Mushrooms All year	The tighter the better, unless you want big flat ones for frying.	Rinse off any dirt. Don't peel unless from a field. Slice or leave whole.	Toss in butter with a hint of salt for 5 mins. Add a touch of garlic or white wine or herbs if you like.	225 g (8 oz) whole in 25 g (1 oz) butter. Cover, cook 2-3 mins. Stand 2-3 mins.	If sliced mushrooms in advance lemon juice squeezed on will keep them white.

Vegetable & Best Season	Buying	Preparation	Basic cooking method	Microwave	Comments
Onions **All year**	Avoid any that are sprouting or have a musty smell.	Cut off the root.	Bake in a moderate oven 1-1½ hrs according to size. Or steam 30-40 mins.	4 medium-sized, dotted with 25 g (1 oz) butter. Cover and cook 9-12 mins. Stand 5 mins. Turn at half time.	Best with white sauce.
Parsnips **September, to April**	Small ones are most tender.	Top and tail, and remove any bad or woody parts. Peel thinly. Quarter length-wise or cut in chunks.	Boil in salted water for 20-30 mins or roast with a joint, like potatoes - but watch them: they can cook fast.	450 g (1 lb) quartered in 6 tbsp water and a nut of butter. Cover and cook 8-16 mins. Stand 3 mins.	If boiled mash with plenty of butter and cream, seasoning well. If roasted take them out when nicely golden and return to the pan when the meat is almost done.
Peas **All year**	Only worth shelling peas if they are young and the pods fairly slim and very green.	Shell, removing any with maggots.	Drop into boiling salted water with a pinch of sugar, add 2-4 nicer pods, to improve the flavour. Boil 5-15 mins according to age.	450 g (1 lb) in 1-2 tbsp water and a pinch of sugar. Cover, cook 6-8 mins. Stand 3 mins.	Even better stewed in butter with chopped lettuce (dark outer leaves are fine) and a hint of onion.
Pimentos **All year**	Avoid any with soggy bits or mould: it can taint the whole vegetable.	If you have to clean them don't wash until the last minute as water makes some go bitter.	Grill until the skin is black; peel off under a cold tap. Remove the stalk and seeds. Also stuffed, unpeeled	2 whole stuffed. Cover and cook 6-7 mins. Stand 5 mins.	Grilled peppers excellent tossed in oil and garlic or cold with French dressing.
Potatoes **All year**	Look for unblemished ones of a suitable variety (page 119).	Only peel if you intend to mash them. Otherwise scrub well.	Boiling in salted water takes 15-30 mins according to size. Jacket potatoes take 1-1½ hrs at gas no 7 or (220°C) 425°F. For roasting boil for 5 mins first. Drain, then cook with the joint, basting with hot fat	Two 175 g (6 oz) in jackets. Pierce, cook 6-9 mins. Stand 5 mins. 450g (1 lb) peeled, quartered in 7 tbsp water. Cover, cook 7-10 mins. Stand 5 mins. New, in roasting bag with 25 g (1 oz) butter, 5-6 mins. Stand 3 mins.	New in May-July.
Pumpkin **September to November**		Remove the skin, seeds and woolly centre. Dice.	Steam 30 mins or roast in butter and lemon juice for about 1 hr.	Diced with 1 tbsp water 4-6 mins, stand 5 mins.	It makes a beautiful basis for soup, but turns sour quickly.
Salsify **May**		Top and tail, scrub well.	Boil in salted water about 30 mins. Drain and peel. Cut in lengths and toss in cream and Parmesan or dress with vinaigrette when cold.		

Vegetable & Best Season	Buying	Preparation	Basic cooking method	Microwave	Comments
Spinach **March to July**	Spinach should be lively and squeak as the leaves are pressed into a bag.	Swirl in plenty of cold water to rinse off the dirt. Discard yellow leaves or parts of leaves. Tear out any large ribs.	Put in a large pan, add a little salt and put the lid on. Cook gently with no extra water until tender.	450 g (1 lb) with no added water. Cover and cook 6-8 mins. Stand 3 mins.	Place in colander and cut slightly to release its excess water. Toss it in a pan with butter or cream and a hint of pepper and nutmeg.
Swedes (those with yellow flesh) **January**	Let them not be too big or they become woody.	Peel and dice.	Boil in salted water for about 20 mins, until tender. Drain and mash well, with butter over a low flame so they dry in the mashing. Season.	450 g (1 lb) diced in 4 tbsp water. Cover and cook 9-15 mins. Stand 3-5 mins.	An underrated vegetable - except by the Irish.
Sweetcorn **July to October**	Pull back the silk and check the grains are small, plump and pale yellow.	Strip the green husk and silk. Cut off the stalk and point.	Drop into boiling *unsalted* water - salt toughens the grains. Cook for 5-6 mins, or more if old.	2 ears in 4 tbsp water. Cover and cook 5 mins. Stand 5 mins.	Drain, serve and let each person roll them in butter, salt and pepper, before chewing the grains from the cob. Cooking a few of the surrounding 'leaves' improves flavour.
Sweet Potatoes **August**	Buy whole, unbroken ones.	Wash them gently.	Boil whole in salted water, or peel and roast like potatoes, or bake at gas no 5, 190°C (375°F) for about 45 mins - until soft when poked with a skewer.	450 g (1 lb) whole baked. Pierce and cook 5-6 mins.	If plain boiled, serve with butter; if roasted, sprinkle a little brown sugar on.
Turnips **April to June**	They should be very small - large ones have a woody underskin.	Peel, dice.	Boil in salted water 6-20 mins according to age; toss in butter and herbs.	450 g (1 lb) diced in 2 tbsp water. Cover and cook 6-15 mins.	A young turnip is delicate and delicious; an old one coarse and best reserved for stew in very small amounts.

★ With keeping, some of the natural sweetness of a tomato vanishes. To restore it add a pinch of sugar to tomato sauces and other dishes made with chopped tomato.

★ If you have a surplus of green tomatoes when the season ends, those which are sound, and have a stalk attached, will sit happily on a warm window ledge and ripen, to provide deliciously fresh tomatoes in the winter months.

More information

The British Trout Farm Association, P.O. Box 189, London SW6 5LY Tel: 01 736 1659 - has leaflet giving trout farms which sell to the public.

Tate and Lyle, Enterprise House, 45 Homesdale Road, Bromley, Kent BR2 9TE Tel: 01 464 6556 - advice on using sugar.

The Vegetarian Society of the United Kingdom Ltd, Parkdale, Dunham Road, Altrincham, Cheshire WA14 4QG Tel: 061 928 0793 - RC, M£L, M, B, HC. Handbook of 'wholefood'.

Women's Farming Union, Crundalls, Matfield, Tonbridge, Kent TN12 7EA Tel: 0892 72 2803 - has information leaflets on farm shops, and pick-your-own.

For delicious recipes go to any book by Elizabeth David or Jane Grigson.

Delia Smith's Cookery Course, BBC Publications, 3 vols, paperback

Leith's Cookery Course, Fontana, 3 vols, paperback

Jane Grigson's Vegetable Book, Penguin

John Tovey, *Feast of Vegetables,* Century

The magazine *The Grocer* publishes a list of cash and carry outlets. Some require evidence of a business need - e.g. that you run a shop or guesthouse.

Drew Smith and David Mabey, *The Good Food Directory,* Consumers Association/Hodder and Stoughton - lists shops selling good quality foodstuffs.

Potatoes

Potatoes are a very underestimated food. In 1860 William Cobbett, the author of *Cottage Economy*, was instructing gardeners that there is 'an infinite variety of sorts'; and suggesting they follow the growing methods of Lancashire as 'potatoes are grown to perfection by the Lancashire people' - which is still true today.

There still are a wide variety of sorts, and the names must, by law, be written on their bags. It's worth asking what you are buying, as potatoes differ just as much in their cooking qualities as apples do. To try making a salad with floury potatoes or mashing waxy ones is asking for disappointment, though, of course, how well a potato performs will depend on how well it is cooked. Even the waxiest potato will break up with overcooking.

The best uses for the major potatoes are:

Home Guard/Portland Javelin - boiled, salad

King Edward, Desirée, Maris Piper - all bar salad

Maris Peer - boiled, roast, chips, salad

Pentland Crown - best baked

Ulster Sceptre - boiled, chips, salad

Wilja - boiled.

The vitamins and minerals in the potatoes boil out into water, but there is a limit to how much that water can absorb. So cook them in water which only just covers them. Better still - steam, bake or microwave them. If you have potato water use it for gravy or as the liquid in soup.

- The most nourishing part of the potato is just under the skin, and the skin itself is splendid roughage. To save work *and* be healthier leave potato skins on and just scrub them well. Even chips can be made with the skins on.
- New potatoes cook best when put into boiling water, but maincrop potatoes cook more evenly if put into cold water and brought to the boil - unfortunately, this destroys more vitamins than putting them into boiling water, so you have to choose between texture and food value.
- Always store potatoes in the cool and the dark.
- When potatoes go green, that area tastes unpleasant and contains a poison called solanine. Cut out all the green parts - the rest of the potato will be safe to eat, though I wouldn't give it to a child. (If you've just eaten a green potato don't worry: it isn't a strong poison, just one we are better off without.) Sprouting potatoes are also poisonous once the sprouts are growing but the budlike beginnings should do no harm.
- Don't worry if a potato or a potato crisp has a pinkish-purple patch on it. This is just a natural vegetable colour similar to that in red cabbage.

DRINK

Aperitifs and friends • Wines from Australia to Spain •

This chapter can only dip a toe into the vast sea of information which exists on drink of all kinds, and especially on wine. One of the great difficulties of writing about the major wine producing nations is to strike a balance between them. I have found that even the most expert tasters are by no means unanimous in their judgements. And nowhere is this more true than in responses to the newer wine regions, such as Australia.

The same vines are used in Australia and California as in France, but differences in soil and climate can greatly alter the result. In hot climates grapes ripen faster and this changes the flavour. Also in these countries the vines are still young - and the youth of a vine comes through in the wine. How much pleasure you get from the newer wine countries may depend on how much you resist the temptation to make comparisons.

It would be crazy to reject a cheap and charming Australian Riesling simply because it lacked the sophistication of its European namesakes. But equally it would be a pity to forget the virtues the old wine countries offer, at far more reasonable prices than might be supposed, if you buy from a wine merchant who knows his stuff.

However, these regions are changing too. European wine making has been undergoing a quiet revolution and introducing increasingly modern techniques. These have not enabled the great wines to excel themselves, nor have they managed to turn every red Bordeaux into a Château Lafite. But they do allow wine makers to cope better with problems caused by bad weather or their own inabilities. So sows' ears are turned into silk purses.

APERITIFS AND FRIENDS

Aquavit

Aquavit or schnapps is found (with varied spellings) throughout northern Europe. The basis can be potatoes or grain, flavoured with caraway seeds, herbs or citrus peel. Like vodka, it should be served freezer-cold, not just fridge-cold, in very small glasses and is the ideal accompaniment to rich fish like herring served as a first course or canapé.

Brandy and Armagnac

Any spirit made from distilling fermented grapes can be called brandy. Unfortunately, it's not easy to tell from the label whether a bottle will be good, bad or indifferent. For example, Italian and Spanish labels fly in the face of reason by awarding more stars the *lower* the quality; Greek brandy may need 5 stars before it begins to be drinkable, and the French allow stars to be used any way a maker pleases. For quality, Cognac is undoubtedly the safest; for flaming the Christmas pudding you can get by with the Greek fire water Metaxa.

French Brandy

The finest Cognac comes from the chalky soil around the sleepy town of Cognac at the centre of the area confusingly called Grande Champagne.

Much of the quality of Cognac is due to the double distillation and the exclusion of the first and last liquor which is produced. It is then aged in Limousin oak, with sugar or caramel added as necessary, before being carefully blended with other Cognacs to create the style of the particular 'house'.

Armagnac comes from Gascony, home of Dumas' musketeer d'Artagnan. For Armagnac, wine is distilled and then aged in casks made from local oak so sappy it can scarcely be sawn. The sappiness speeds the ageing of the liquor which lies in it and, like Cognac, it only matures in the wood not after bottling. The result is less strong than Cognac, but is dry with a mellower flavour and more fruit. Really old Armagnac is a beautiful spirit with a full but delicate bouquet. Store it upright so the alcohol does not attack the cork, at about 12°C.

> If anyone offers you a Cognac which is 'early landed' try it. This is Cognac which was brought to Britain in casks and has matured in the moist British climate where the evaporation is low, so the Cognac is said to develop a special character and charm: but I have yet to taste it.

Reading the Label

A Cognac may be described as 'Grand Champagne' or 'Fine Champagne' on its label, provided at least half the blend comes from the Grand Champagne area. If a label names Bas Armagnac, Haut Armagnac or Ténarèze - Armagnac is from that area alone. But if it simply says 'Armagnac' it is a blend.

Cognac/Armagnac	
3 star	at least 3 years or more in the wood
VSOP (Very Special Old Pale) or VO	at least 4 years or more in the wood
Extra, Napoleon, XO Réserve, Vielle	at least 5 years or more in the wood
Hors d'age	25 years or more in casks

★ If you want to check the quality of a Cognac or Armagnac rub a little between the palm of your hands (clean and free from soap or scents) and smell it. The warmth of the skin brings out all the qualities the tongue would find if you drank it.

Serving Brandy

The big balloon-shaped glasses are said to have come about because that shape can be knocked on its side without spilling. And such glasses should never be filled so high that the glass cannot lie on its side.

Connoisseurs, however, say that the vast balloons allow the aroma of the brandy to get lost and recommend small balloons. Any adequate glass with an in-curving rim which will allow you to savour the bouquet is ideal, and a good brandy is to be taken very slowly.

Marc

Marc is made from the debris left after grapes have been pressed for wine. It is a very strong colourless spirit, with more fire than flavour. You'd probably be more grateful for being brought it by a St Bernard than for being offered it after dinner. It goes by national names: *grappa* in Italy, *pisco* in Peru, and so on).

Calvados

Calvados, the distilled cider of Normandy, has such a reputation as a digestive that the term 'trou Normand' is applied to it, to show that even if you were full it would make a hole in your stomach ready for the next course. After being distilled twice over, it is aged in oak for up to 25 years. This creates a beautiful dry drink with a lovely appley scent which is most welcome after a heavy meal, whether or not it makes a hole.

More information

James Long, *Cognac and Other Brandies*, Century

Gin

Gin! Gin a drop of Gin!
When, darkly, Adversity's days set in,
And friends and peers
Of earlier years
Prove warm without, but cold within.
Thomas Hood, 1799-1845

By the end of the seventeenth century gin had become such a great 'comforter' that in some areas there were gin factories at the end of every street and alcoholism became so rife that gin production was banned for 30 years.

Gin has only become really respectable quite recently. Thomas Carlyle called it *'Liquid madness sold at tenpence the quartern'* and a music hall song early this century contained the surprising line 'too many double gins give ladies double chins'. Gin as we know it today seems to have been first made by Franciscus de la Boë, a professor of medicine at the University of Leyden in the seventeenth century, from rye spirit distilled with juniper berries, the name gin being an abbreviation of the Dutch name for juniper berries - *jiniverbes*.

London gin dates back to the eighteenth century for, when the ban on gin making was lifted and distilleries set up over the artesian wells in Clerkenwell and Goswell. Gordon's Gin was the first of these distilling companies and is now the last to retain offices on its old site in the Goswell Road.

Gin is now made from some varied cereal grains and redistilled with juniper and other herbal flavourings such as coriander seeds or orange peel.

London Gin is the classic gin, Plymouth gin is perhaps a touch more highly flavoured and the gin from Holland has a most distinct flavour which may well be more like the first gin ever made.

Pink Gin

Pink gin is a controversial mixture. One classic method is to put several dashes of bitters in a glass, swirl them round, discard the surplus and add a measure of gin and iced water to taste.

Driver's Pink Gin

Driver's is a teetotal 'pink gin' of bitters, ice and slimline tonic. Being dry, it is one of the few drinks that is easy to stick to until the drive home.

> *Gin is adulterated with water, sugar, cayenne, Cassia, cinnamon, grains of paradise, sulphuric acid [!], coriander seeds, angelica root, calken root, almond cake, orris root, cardamom seeds, orange peel, and grey and white salts, and is 'fined' by alum and salt of tartar. The best way is to purchase the unsweetened gin, for the sweetening is employed to disguise the flavour of the various adulterations. If you examine gin through a clean glass it should have no tint, either of a bluish or yellowish cast. The cheap gins should be avoided, and only the respectable dealers should be resorted to.*
> *Enquire Within, 1856*

Liqueurs

Liqueurs are one of the excellent things in life which have not yet been regulated, stamped and made subject to international definitions and restrictions. There is no official description of what is and is not a liqueur. The French call sherry a liqueur wine; we wouldn't, and *vive la différence*. We all know what we mean even if the officials don't.

Liqueurs may only be occasional delights, but they are exceedingly old ones. As long ago as 800 BC Egyptian masons carved pictures of stills into their bas-reliefs, and many of today's liqueurs stem from the praiseworthy efforts of monks in earlier centuries to make their herbal remedies more acceptable. Indeed, at Chartreuse, high in the mountains of the Haute Savoie, they still use a secret recipe to produce a medicine linked to the liqueur. (It is apparently much sought after by those whose horses have ailments and - having tasted it - I am happy for the horses to have it.) But it was not for their medicinal properties that they became all the rage in the *belle époque*, and again in the 1960s, when liqueurs on ice enjoyed a sudden revival.

Whatever their status, most liqueurs are basically a spirit which has been infused with some flavouring and sweetened and the traditional time to serve liqueurs is after meals. In Holland, however - which is probably the greatest liqueur drinking country in Europe - they like to serve liqueurs in the early evening in V shaped glasses like miniature cocktail glasses. But there are those who say the ideal glass is a small balloon shape which will hold the bouquet or 'nose' as the trade like to call it.

Whatever the glass, most liqueurs improve with chilling and last through many pourings.

Many liqueurs are very good in coffee, topped with cream which has been poured on to the back of a spoon held close to the surface of the liquid, so it floats on the top. Each combination of coffee and liqueur has its own name in the restaurant business. Among the best combinations are Gaelic Coffee (Irish whisky), Prince Charles (Drambuie), Monks' (Bénédictine), Calypso (Tia Maria), French (Cognac).

Madeira

As fewer and fewer meals are now lingered over, fortified wines have faded into the background of our drinking consciousness. It is a pity. Port, Marsala and Madeira were hugely popular in earlier centuries and we are missing something by ignoring them.

Madeira has a curious story behind it. The lush little island of Madeira off the coast of Africa produced a wine that was sold as ballast for ships - to be drunk only in emergencies. Brandy was added to the acidic brew to stop it fermenting further on the long journey, across the equator and back, to the far-flung British colonies. The British discovered that wine which was scarcely drinkable at the start of the journey, matured richly in the heat of the ship and could be sold for high prices on their return.

Madeira used to be sent on long voyages before sale until they learned to mature it by 'cooking' it - either by passing hot pipes through its container or by leaving it in barrels stored at the uppermost levels of wine lodges to be baked by the hot Madeira sun. This is still the process and the result is a distinctive toasted caramel taste quite unlike any other wine. It may stay in casks for years but it ages even better in bottle and can be full of life even after 100 years. It was a favourite with Winston Churchill, who used to paint on Madeira, and he is said to have held up a glass of Bual and remarked, 'Do you realize that this wine was made when Marie Antoinette was still alive?'

Buying Madeira

The first thing to look for is the grape variety; each grape has its own particular flavour, and the types of Madeira are named after them, so there is no problem here. Each one can be produced in various grades - dated soleras, straight vintage or blended wines, such as 3-, 5- or 10-year-old reserves. The difference between solera and vintage is that the vintage is the product of only 1 year and is simply left to age whereas with the solera method there is a sequence of barrels each older than the next. Wine is drawn off for bottling from the oldest, and the barrel replenished from the next oldest barrel, which in turn is replenished from its neighbour, and so on down the line. By one of the minor miracles of wine making, when young wine is mixed with old it grows up more quickly and takes on the maturity of the old wine it is with. So, although not vintage, the solera Madeira will be mature. Therefore, the date on a solera bottle is the date of the barrel from which the wine was drawn (i.e. the oldest).

Bual is a rich fairly sweet dessert Madeira with a tawny-brown tone.

Luscious, soft flavoured, dark brown and mellow, **Malmsey** is the sweetest Madeira of all and fruitier than Bual.

Sercial is the driest Madeira and has a deep golden tone and a lightness and sharpness which makes it an aperitif rather than a dessert wine. It is also excellent with a soup such as a game broth, or clear consommé.

Verdelho is pale amber with a soft, full, almost nutty, flavour and drier than any except Sercial. To be drunk either before or after a meal.

Storing and Serving

Madeira is probably the world's most indestructible wine. It needs no special storage and even when opened it will keep for months without spoiling.

As aperitifs, Sercial and Verdelho are best chilled for an hour or two in the refrigerator, but Bual, Malmsey and Verdelho are better after dinner at room temperature. Serve it in relatively small quantities in in-curving wine glasses.

Marsala

I was compiling *Pasta for Pleasure* - my book on regional Italian pasta cooking - when I first discovered the delights of Marsala. A Sicilian restaurateur was horrified to find that I didn't already know and love a drink which had, he told me, been created by the English. With true Italian hospitality he insisted I must taste bottle after bottle and, though some say it's an acquired taste, I found it a taste remarkably easy to acquire.

In fact, it was the British passion for port, sherry and Madeira which, in 1760, persuaded John Woodhouse, a shipper from Liverpool, to keep his eyes open for a wine which would rival them. He found what he was looking for at the western tip of Sicily: a distinctive dry light wine which is highly alcoholic.

Taking his cue from the makers of sherry and Madeira, Woodhouse adapted the wine to British palates, adding *vino cotto* - wine 'cooked' and reduced by two-thirds to give it a bitter-sweet flavour - and fortifying it with local brandy to stabilize it for the sea voyage. By 1773 he had enough confidence to ship the first 8,000 gallons to Liverpool, and it was an immediate success - aided and abetted by Admiral Nelson, who proclaimed it 'fit for a Lord' and bought it for his ships.

By the end of the nineteenth century Marsala was fashionable throughout the Western world and Sicily was exporting as much as 4 million litres a year. But fashions change and now even those who know the *name* Marsala usually associate it with cooking Marsala, and with those misleadingly called 'Special Marsala' - travesties, flavoured with eggs. Like Falstaff, serious wine drinkers can do without *'pullet-sperm'* in their brewage.

Fortunately, those beverages may no longer be labelled Marsala, and the regulations on making Marsala proper have been tightened up. It's all part of a new bid to restore it to its rightful place as one of most interesting, and certainly the most versatile, fortified wines.

Types of Marsala

In a country which has had more governments since the war than there have been years you can't expect a little thing like the labelling of wine to be simple - and it isn't. The following categories have to meet different legal requirements, and some would say that *vergine* is better than *superiore*, which is better than *'fine'*. But keep trying different types and makes until you find the one you like.

Marsala vergine is made without the addition of *sifone* (a blend of sweet wine and wine alcohol) or *vino cotto*. It is gold or light amber and always dry, and ageing is often by the solera method (page 123). *Vergine* or *vergine soleras* is at least 5 years old, but at over 10 years old it can carry the word *Stravecchio* or *Riserva*.

Marsala superiore has a minimum ageing time of 2 years for *superiore*, and 4 years for *riserva*. It can be *secco* (dry), *semisecco* (medium dry), or *dolce* (sweet). Confusingly, these words *may* appear on the label but they don't have to. And on any made before the new laws you may find the following initials instead: SOM - Superior Old Marsala; LP - London Particular; GD - Garibaldi Dolce.

Marsala fine is often darkened with *vino cotto*. The minimum ageing time is 1 year, and it is usually sweet rather than dry. Sometimes labelled IP (Italian Particular) because it was originally created by the English for the Italians. A basic *fine* can't be classed as a fine Marsala, but it makes an inexpensive and cheering tipple.

The dry *vergine* Marsalas not only make excellent aperitifs but are also very good indeed with clear soups, and other first courses which favour a very dry wine, and partner certain cheeses beautifully. In the 1850s they were even drunk with fish. *Superiore* is an easy-going, sociable drink which you can serve with a rich dessert, or sip happily for hours as you linger over coffee, nuts or *petit fours*, or simply sit by the fire. And if the

pleasure tempts you to a glass too many, I'm told it is kind to the head next morning.

The best tend to come from companies, like De Bartoli and Pellegrino, which have not been absorbed into larger enterprises.

Its fall from grace has left Marsala free from the drinking etiquette and (let's face it) snobbery which surrounds most other wines. This includes the correct temperature. Serve it as you like - though chilling often brings out the excellence of the best and has the interesting effect, on the less well made, of muting the alcohol and making it appear better balanced than it really is.

Port

Wars, trade treaties and market forces seldom combine to create something great: port is the striking exception. Hostilities between Britain and France meant French wine was banned from our shores. So when, in 1703, Britain signed a treaty with Portugal containing favourable trade terms Portuguese wine became the obvious substitute. The trouble was that one of the wines on offer - that of the Douro valley - was big but so rough that elderflower juice was added in an attempt to improve it. An English jingle of the time ran:

> *Mark how it smells. Methinks, a real pain*
> *Is by its colour thrown on my brain.*
> *I've tasted it - 'tis spiritless and flat ....*
> *But fetch us a pint of any sort,*
> *Navarre, Galicia, anything but Port.*

The inspired solution was to add brandy to the wine in the cask, so stopping the fermentation at a point which left it sweet and full bodied: precisely the wine to tickle the sugar-loving British palate. It was a huge success and the flourishing port trade was operated by the British families whose names still appear on bottles.

The right to make port was established as belonging solely to the Douro region, making it one of the world's oldest designated wine areas.

Over 5 main varieties of grapes combine to give port its character and depth of colour, and some are still pressed by foot, in the time-honoured way. Then, long before the pressed liquid has finished its fermentation, it is pumped out into vats containing 1 part of brandy for every 4 parts of port. This stops the fermentation and holds the sweetness in the wine ready for ageing.

Ageing and Keeping

It always needs to be aged for some while, either in wooden casks or in the bottle. Wood ages it much faster but the final result is slightly less fine than bottle ageing. This is why the very best wines of the very best years go to make vintage port, which is aged mainly in the bottle.

Vintage port, Crusted port and Single Quinta port are all aged in the bottle. So you either need to buy them when they have reached maturity or keep them in a cellar until that age is reached. These wines will spoil if kept at the wrong temperature.

All other port will get little better with keeping, but

it can be kept for several years without spoiling and isn't fussy as to storage temperature - within reason. The exceptions are a few Late Bottled Vintage (LBV) ports (see below), such as Warre's, which are not filtered before bottling, and continue to mature in the bottle.

Keeping Opened Port
Once a bottle of port has been opened its life span depends entirely on its type. Port which has been wood-aged will keep happily for a month if it is tightly corked. Vintage port will spoil rapidly so it should be drunk the day it is opened. Other bottle-matured port should be enjoyed with equal speed.

Labelling
Port labelling is a mess. It is perfectly legal to sell a stripling like 3-year-old port as 'Vintage Character' because no set age is established in law. And elegant names, like 'Superior' or 'Special' are given to liquids which may be only a cut or so above a ruby. Under EEC law, only port made in Portugal can call itself port.

Types of Port
With the law failing so dismally to set a scale of quality, the first step to buying a good port is to go for a good name. This isn't necessarily a heavily advertised name, and advertising can be less a sign of quality than of quantity.

Experts like to make neat divisions between port which is aged in wood and port which is aged in bottle. But I'm going to stick my neck out and list the different types of ports in a rough order of quality, regardless of how they got there. Do remember that the quality of two different makers will vary.

Ruby port is the least sophisticated member of the family and is blended from several different wines and aged in casks for about 3 years before bottling.

Ordinary **tawny port** is not to be confused with old tawny. Basic tawny is made like ruby except that the wine used in its blending is chosen for its lighter style. So, tawny is browner, paler, nuttier and drier.

White port is an exceedingly popular aperitif, in France especially. It is made entirely from white grapes and fortified, to make a dry aperitif disconcertingly close to sherry.

Late Bottled Vintage (LBV) is wine from a very good vineyard in a single year which wasn't quite good enough to declare a vintage. Unlike vintage port, it is allowed to mature in the wood for 4 to 6 years before bottling. This hurries it along and it is sold ready to drink at once, with a label which shows the vintage and the year it was bottled. Whether LBV is better than Vintage Character port or vice versa is debatable.

Vintage character port is a blend of several good ports, matured in oak casks for 4 to 5 years before being blended together. It has no date on its label.

A **crusted port** is a blend of several different vintages which are matured for 3 to 4 years in the wood, and then aged in the bottle. The character of the port affects the time it takes to reach its peak, but it should not be drunk for 3 years after bottling and most crusted port

is at its best after 5 to 10 years. From 1987 it became compulsory to put the date of bottling on the label. Crusted port throws down a deposit in the bottle.

Old tawnies are a blend of high quality, stylish, full-bodied wines aged in wood until they mature to a deep amber colour and have a fine, delicate, almost nutty, flavour. Old tawnies are sold ready to drink and the standard ages at which they may be sold are 10, 20, 30 and 40 plus years old. There are also old tawnies, such as Dow's delicious 'Boardroom', which are bottled specially at an in-between age. These can be good value although they don't state their exact age.

Quinta is Portuguese for farm and a **single quinta port** is port made with top quality wine from a single farm within the growing area of a major port shipper. In a vintage year this wine would be used for vintage port, but in a non-vintage year this lighter wine, which matures faster, is produced and kept by the makers until ready to drink. The labels always carry the date the wine was made and the words *Quinta do* (or *de*)... They will go on maturing if you keep them. but being lighter in style than most vintage port they should not be kept for much more than 15 years and many should be drunk before that.

At its incomparable best, **vintage port** is one of the very great wines, but it can be made only in a year which produces wine of exceptional quality: strong, rich and so dark it is almost black. This happens only about 1 year in 3, and each shipper is free to declare his own vintage year. Vintage port is created from a blend of several vineyards on a single estate and spends only 2 to 3 years in the cask before being bottled. It is then put straight on to the market, although it is quite unfit to drink and needs to age gently in its bottle for 14 to 30 years.

It requires a proper cellar and the same conditions as red wine (page 132). In storage, it must always be kept on its side with the label uppermost, as a crust of sediment forms on the underside. It therefore needs decanting (page 131).

If you need vintage port for a meal buy it a day or so ahead and let it stand, so the sediment which was shaken up in travelling can fall to the bottom.

Vintage Years
Nobody is entirely sure just how good a vintage year will be until the port is mature. This means there is initial uncertainty about how long any vintage port should be kept. In a truly great year which produces a big full-bodied port it will mature far more slowly than in a lighter year which produces merely a very good port. And the more slowly the port reaches its peak, the longer its mature life will be. The other factor in the keeping time of a vintage port is the way it was made. Some houses make lighter ports which mature faster.

In general, Cockburn, Dow, Graham, Fonseca, Taylor and Warre produce port which matures slowly. Croft, Offley, Quinta do Noval, Sandeman and Smith Woodhouse produce port which matures faster.

Vintage Years

In all the drinking dates given below a fast maturing port may be ready sooner and its prime of life will end sooner.

Vintage	Comments	Drink
1945	A superb vintage still going strong	now to 2000
1947	A light .vintage now past its best	no more
1950	A light vintage now well past its best	no more
1955	Still very good but won't keep for longer	asap
1960	A good year but now getting past its best	asap
1963	One of the very great classic ports	now to 2000 +
1966	An underrated year, therefore good value	now to 1992/7
1970	A big year also underrated	1990 to 2000 +
1975	A light but fine year in some houses, especially Fonseca	Now to 1992
1977	Probably one of the greatest years of the century	2000 on and on
1980	A Cinderella year much underrated. Too soon to predict its life span.	1995 +
1983	Too soon for predictions but don't drink before	1998/2003
1985	Seems likely to live longer than 1983	2000 + +

Serving Port

Port goes well with certain cheese, but it is a mellow contemplative wine which is at its best drunk slowly, after the main eating is over, accompanied by the gentle cracking of nuts. It doesn't have to wait for the dried nuts of Christmas.

Traditionally, it has always been served at cool room temperature, but chilling is essential for white port, and does great things for a fine old tawny.

Port is often served in rather small glasses. Port afficionados deplore them and say that to appreciate the bouquet port must be served in in-curving red wine glasses, filled only a quarter or a third full.

> In literature one sometimes comes across references to a pipe of port. Those who order one must be prodigious drinkers for a pipe contains 534 litres which is about 56 dozen bottles.

More information

Ben Hawkins, *Rich Rare and Red,* International Wine and Food Society

Rum

Nobody knows how rum got its name but there are some colourful possibilities, such as the shortening of rumbustion, meaning a big noise. Originally it came from the West Indies, the spirit being made from the sweet, slightly cloudy liquid which comes from crushed sugar cane. By the eighteenth century it had become the standard drink of the British navy, and gave the language the useful term 'groggy', which originally meant too full of rum to be good for much. However it was adding lime juice to the rum ration which kept sailors free of scurvy and gave them the nickname 'limeys', and it was also the standard 'anaesthetic'. So it had practical uses as well as drawbacks.

Rum is also made in America, Australia, South America and Indonesia and varies considerably in colour and flavour according to its origin. It is usually 70 per cent proof, and in Britain it must, by law, be 2 years old. All rums combine well with pure fruit juice for a long drink, and dark rums are good in coffee and for cooking.

Sake

Sake should be kept in a cool place and drunk fairly soon, as it is loses its quality with keeping. The Japanese make it from rice which has been fermented and then matured in wood. Colourless and very faintly sweet, it is served warm in tiny cups and is usually only 12 to 16 per cent alcohol by volume. To warm it, stand the bottle in a jug of hot water just before serving.

Sherry

> *The next that stood up*
>   *With a countenance merry*
> *Was a pert sort of wine*
>   *Which the moderns call sherry.*
>   *Bacchanalian Sessions*, 1693

Despite all the advertisements which try to make it sound an amusing little tipple, a good sherry is an elegant, even austere, drink which needs to be chosen and drunk with care. Hugh Johnson has rightly described a fine sherry as 'an expression of wine and wood as vivid and beautiful as any in the world', but it is a beauty not everyone enjoys.

The Origins of Sherry

Sherry takes its name from Jerez in the sunbaked chalky southern tip of Spain which points towards Africa. Here the vines grow low against the ground to evade the wind from Africa and draw water from deep in the sub-soil. Originally, sherry was just one of the heavy, sweet wines which were produced all around the Mediterranean in the fifteenth century and even as far afield as the Canary Isles.

In Shakespeare's day such wines were all called 'sack'. The word probably came from the Spanish *sacar* - to draw out - rather than from *seco* (which is often asserted) as *seco* means dry and sack was always sweet. So for a long time sherry was sherry-sack.

*A good sherris-sack hath a two-fold operation in it.
It ascends me into the brain; dries me there all the
foolish and dull and crudy vapours which environ
it; makes it apprehensive, quick, forgetive, full of
nimble, fiery and delectable shapes; which, deliver'd
o'er to the voice, the tongue, which is the birth,
becomes excellent wit.*

Sir John Falstaff, King Henry IV, Part II,
William Shakespeare

With time the sack was dropped and sherry achieved
the remarkable feat of constantly keeping pace with the
fashion in wine, becoming drier and more sophisticated
as the public demanded it. It was also fortified with
brandy to help it travel. Despite occasional upheavals
between England and Spain, it has managed to keep its
popularity through 300 years. Pepys fortified himself
with it before a tricky speech and Victorians considered
it the 'genteel' drink to offer to visitors.

By law, only sherry made in the Jerez area can use
the name 'sherry'. Until late in 1987, sherry-style drinks
like 'Cyprus sherry' could be sold. However, we seldom
came across bogus sherry quite as bad as one Charles
Dickens described:

*Cloudy fluid served up by shabby waiters in vinegar
cruets to disconsolate bachelors at second-rate
restaurants and miscalled sherry.*

Sherry Making

The fermentation and creation of sherry is still one of
the most unpredictable processes in the wine industry.
The liquor is aged in oak barrels and one of the curious
and fascinating features of sherry is that, just as Stilton
owes its green veining and consequent flavour to a
mould which occurs naturally in the area around Stilton,
so there is a rare yeast in the air of Jerez which gives
sherries their particular flavour by consuming the sugars
and other substances and dramatically altering the
chemical composition of the wine.

It is a capricious little yeast and does as it pleases,
growing a thick white coating (called *flor*) on the surface
of some barrels and leaving others alone - nobody
knows why. And it cannot be made to grow where it
doesn't choose to: which is why, even in Jerez, no two
butts of sherry taste quite the same - even if they come
from the same pressing.

The extent to which the *flor* grows determines
whether a sherry will be *fino*, *amontillado* or *oloroso*.
But fortification with brandy can stop the *flor* growing
and blending, and ageing with the solera system (page
123) can create sherries which are consistent.

Types of Sherry

All sherry is fundamentally dry and sweet grape juices
must be added to make it medium dry, medium sweet
or sweet. But even dry sherry may be slightly sweetened
for the British market.

The big divide in sherry is between *fino* and *oloroso*.
As it matures in barrels, sherry will usually develop into
one or the other.

Fino is is the most elegant of sherries, and created by
a thick coating of *flor*. A *fino* can be drunk young and
fresh and is sold simply as *fino*. A good example would
be the Gonzalez Byass Tio Pepe. It does not improve
with storage and is dry, light and delicate.

Amontillado has been allowed to age for at least 8
years in barrels and gained a deeper, more intense
flavour. The *flor* dies naturally after 2 to 3 years - which
means that a *fino* can be converted into an *amontillado*
by adding brandy to kill the *flor*. A really good
amontillado combines dryness with an intense richness
of flavour.

> Confusion surrounds the word *amontillado*. In
> Spain it relates to *style* of sherry and roughly
> means 'a sherry in the style of the Montilla
> district'. Among commercial sherries in Britain it
> is often used simply to indicate *sweetness* and
> any medium sweet sherry may be called
> '*amontillado*', but *amontillado* can be dry.

Oloroso sherry is made without the yeast on the
surface. *Oloroso* means 'fragrant' in Spanish and, as
you'd expect, *olorosos* are softer and fuller, darker and,
in a sense, fruitier. But it isn't always sweet; there is
also *oloroso seco*, which is dry.

Manzanilla comes only from the area of Sanlucar de
Barremeda. Its special flavour is said to come from the
sea, but it could be due to the unusual strength of the
flor which grows in this part of the region. Plain
manzanilla on a label means manzanilla *fina*: a dry
aromatic drink. There is also a manzanilla *pasada*; a
very special sherry which is long aged and deep amber
but crisp and dry.

Cream, **Milk**, **Golden**, **Full** and **Amoroso** are all
commercial terms added to the name sherry when
oloroso sherries have been sweetened, and often
darkened for the British market.

Serving Sherry

It is best not to decant sherry as letting air in can harm
a fine light sherry. But a decanter does no harm to a
darker sweeter sherry and shows its colour off better
than a bottle.

Dry sherry is best *lightly* chilled to about the
temperature of a cool cellar (about half an hour in the
fridge). A sweeter sherry is better at room temperature,
but the best temperature of all is the one you enjoy.
Good *fino* sherry should be drunk the day it is opened.

A less dry *oloroso*, on the other hand, is not ideal
before a meal as its fullness will dull the appetite, but
is an excellent dessert wine to go with nuts and even
with cheese, and if the bottle isn't finished by the
evening's end no matter, for the darker sweeter sherries
can be corked and will keep for several weeks.

More information

Julian Jeffs, *Sherry*, Faber and Faber

Tequila, Mezcal and Pulque
These three drinks are made only in Mexico. Tequila is not made from cactus, as people often assert, but from the agave - which has a rosette of leaves similar to a yucca. It is from the heart of the plant, which is rather like a pineapple, that the spirit is made. When new, tequila is as clear as water but the better qualities are matured in oak for several years and take on a pale golden tinge. Sauza is the best-known brand and if you see a Sauza marked *hornitos* or one that is pale gold try it neat for a taste as pure and clean as any drink you will ever find. You are meant to suck a segment of lime and take a little salt before swigging your tequila. Good theatre, but it never seems to improve the taste, and at 40° proof it is a drink to sip rather than swig.

Pulque is the fermented sap of the agave, and is not a spirit. Mezcal *is* made from cactus. It is a rough thing but much used to tease tourists, for, by tradition, it has a fat caterpillar soaking in the bottom of the bottle. (Mexicans insist on calling it a worm - but it is clearly a caterpillar.) This is no accident: certain caterpillars are a great delicacy in Mexico.

Vermouth
Vermouth is a mixture of wine and herbs strengthened with pure alcohol, and named from the German *wermut* - for the herb wormwood (*Artemisia absinthia*). It is still made in the foothills of the Alps, which have provided the flowers and herbs for it since the eighteenth century. The infusions are blended, chilled to precipitate any impurities, and then pasteurized and aged.

People often make too much of nuances in drinks but with vermouth the reverse has happened. It attracts about as much connoisseurship as orange squash. Different vermouths do, however, taste very different.

Serving Vermouth
All vermouths can be served with ice and a twist of lemon peel, or can be lengthened with soda, and the dry white is the essential side-kick in a dry martini - though my mother, who was young in the days when martinis were too, insists on using half dry white, half sweet white, plus the usual proportion of gin to make the most dashing martini I know.

Unopened vermouth will keep for years, once opened it will only keep for months.

Whisky, Whiskey and Bourbon
It's a pity we never think of this complex, intriguing spirit by its original name. *Uisge beatha* (water of life) was the romantic Gaelic name for it, so whisky it became. Odd though it may sound, medieval Irish monks are said to have brought the art of distilling to Scotland.

Making Whisky
Traditionally, malt whisky is made by soaking barley in water for about 48 hours, then spreading it out, in a golden carpet, on concrete floors in a warm place to germinate and produce enzymes. This allows the starch to be changed into sugar which can ferment to make

alcohol. Called malting, it is a very similar process to that which gives malt bread its distinctive flavour. Nowadays most malting is done less artistically in drums. To stop the germination the barley is then dried in kilns traditionally fired by burning peat, whose smoke is allowed to permeate the grains - the 'peat reek' - giving it the distinctive peaty flavour. Whether a distillery uses only peat and for how long it dries the grain can greatly alter the final liquor. The malted barley, plus a certain amount of unmalted cereals, is then crushed with boiling water before being fermented and twice distilled. Finally, it is put into sherry casks or American oak casks to mature for at least 3 years, but it can mature in casks for as long as 15 years.

There is a distinct lack of legislation controlling whisky. For example, there appears to be nothing to say at what age a blended whisky may call itself 'old'. But only whisky made in Scotland, to approved methods, may be called Scotch whisky. All others may only say 'whisky'.

Types of Scotch Whisky
The big divide in Scottish whisky is between blended whisky and single malts.

Blended Scotch Whisky
Blended whisky may be a mixture of as many as several dozen malt and grain whiskies from different distilleries. This is a process which relies on a blender sniffing a sample of single malt or grain whisky in a tulip-shaped glass and telling, by nose alone, what qualities it will bring to the blend.

Scotch Single Malts
A single malt is what whisky drinking is really about. Made purely from malted barley distilled in a single distillery, single malts are individualists with great variations in flavour and personality. Just why they vary so much in flavour is something of a mystery but no single malt is likely to be sold at under 8 years old but 12 and 15 years are the usual ages and can be as much as 50 to 60 years old.

Well-known single malts include names like Glenlivet, Glenmorangie, Glenfiddich and Talisker.

However, one has the curious name of 'Sheepdip' - rumour has it that it was named so that vets who needed a warming nip while lambing, could get the invoice past the revenue as a business expense. But the Gloucestershire firm at whose behest it was created insists that it was so named purely to honour a Gloucestershire tradition by which farmers have always called whisky 'sheepdip'.

Whisky Areas
Although each distillation has its own special character, they can be roughly divided into groups according to where they come from. Highland malts are those made north of a line from Dundee to Greenock, the home of Glenlivet, and tend to be light but full flavoured. The lowland malts are to the south of that line, and most of them are used in blended whiskies. The Mull of

Kintyre produces a highly individual single malt with a strongly smoky flavour. Islay whiskies vary from the pungent, almost oily to the smooth and are often added to blends to give them extra depth.

Irish Whiskey

Irish whiskey uses the same process as Scotch with a few variations, and is distilled in sherry casks for at least 5 years - 12 years for a high quality blend.

Canadian and American Whisk(e)y

Wherever the Scots and Irish emigrated, whisky began to be made. Canadian whisky is often called 'rye', although the main grain used to make it is maize with only a certain amount of wheat and rye, and it is aged in oak for at least 3 years.

American bourbon is made from 51 per cent maize grain and must mature for 2 years in charred oak barrels. The charring is said to impart its distinctive taste, which can be more agressive than Scotch. If a bottle says 'Straight Bourbon' it is unblended; all other Bourbon is blended. There is also a 'Rye Whisky' which must be 51 per cent rye. Then at the bottom of the market is 'Corn Whiskey', which is often immature and not to be recommended.

> By convention Scotch and Canadian whisky is spelt without an e, Irish and American whiskey has an e.

Serving Whisky

Mixers can perfectly well be added to blended whiskies. Whether you drink a fine whisky neat or add ice or water is entirely a matter of taste.

WINES

Major Grapes Used in Making Wine

Key ● red ○ white ◑ rosé

Vine	Quality/Style	Keeping Potential
Cabernet Sauvignon (grape ●, wine ●)	A great claret (Bordeaux) grape. Big, almost muscular flavour, high in tannin - which makes immature Cabernet Sauvignon mouth-puckering stuff. Its wine is often softened by blending with grapes such as Merlot.	Usually long. It takes time for the tannin to reduce and reveal the rich dry flavours beneath.
Chardonnay (grape ○, wine ○)	The great grape of white Burgundies (Chablis, Macon etc) and an important element in champagne - Blanc de Blancs are 100 per cent Chardonnay. Crisp, dry style. Best with not more than 30 minutes chilling.	Often oak matured. Can be long-lived and take a while to mature.
Chenin Blanc (grape ○, wine ○)	The main Loire grape, making soft rich wines in the Touraine, such as Vouvray, also used for Anjou whites.	Can be good.
Gamay (grape ●, wine ● or ◑)	The grape behind Beaujolais. Light fruity, undemanding. Also used in Touraine (Loire).	Months to a few years.
Gewürztraminer (grape ○, wine ○)	Makes distinctive wines with a strong muscat bouquet, and spicy flavour, such as those of Alsace.	A few years
Grenache (grape ●, wine ● or ◑)	The main grape of Rioja. Also important in Midi and Rhône Valley. Makes a strong, highly perfumed red, or some very good rosé in California.	Variable, can be very long.
Kerner (grape ○, wine ○)	A relatively new cross between Riesling and Trollinger grapes. Not as subtle as Riesling but fruity and full-flavoured with a good acid level.	

Vine	Quality/Style	Keeping Potential
Merlot (grape ●, wine ●)	Often combines with Cabernet Sauvignon in claret, and in wine of the Médoc. Full, generous and soft without flabbiness. Typical Merlot wines are St Émilion and Pomerol.	Yes, but needs less than Cabernet Sauvignon.
Müller-Thurgau (grape ○ wine ○)	A cross of Riesling and the Sylvaner. Light, flowery white wine, low in acid, with a slight muscat flavour. Often rather average, but can be excellent in sweet wines, but may lack acid and balance. The main grape of Germany.	Usually needs to be drunk young.
Pinot Noir (grape ●, wine ● or ○)	The grape of the great Burgundies and used for much champagne. At best subtle and full of nuances, not always fruity but with sweet overtones. Seldom makes good wine outside France. Often given local names e.g. Italy (Pinot Nero), Germany (Spätburgunder)	Varies greatly with the year and location.
Riesling (pronounced Rees-ling) (grapes ○, wine ○)	The classic of Germany and Alsace. An unmistakable perfume, like early summer; flowery, delicate and fresh. Can make subtle wine, with a beautiful balance between sweetness and acidity, fruity but with none of the heaviness that often suggests.	Spends little time in cask but often repays bottle age.
Sauvignon Blanc (grape ○, wine ○)	Makes Loire wines like Pouilly Fumé, and Sancerre. Also in some white Bordeaux. Often described as like 'cat's pee on a gooseberry bush'. Highly acid, strong grassy/green in aroma, almost smoky flavour. Very variable, from delicious to thin. Not at its best in hot climates.	May keep well but often to be drunk young.
Sémillon (grape ○, wine ○)	The great feature of this grape is that it gets botrytis (see page 134). 'Rotting' grapes are hand selected for making the great Sauternes of Bordeaux. Superb deep intense flavour. Also soft dry wines.	Very long, from a good year.
Sylvaner (grape ○, wine ○)	A rather bland grape with little acid, fresh dry wine. Essentially for table wine. Grown more for quantity than quality.	Best drunk young.
Syrah or Shiraz, (grape ●, wine ●)	The major black grape of the Rhône. Big dark wines with distinct cigar box bouquet, such as Hermitage.	Long.

More information
Jancis Robinson, *Vines, Grapes and Wines*, Mitchell Beazley

General Information

Amounts of Wine
Wine should be poured so that the glass is not more than half full. Then its bouquet can be caught in the glass.

a half bottle yields   3 glasses of 125 ml (4·5 fl oz) each

75 cl (1½ pt)
bottle yields   6 glasses of 125 ml (4.5 fl oz) each

a litre bottle yields   8 glasses of 125 ml (4·5 fl oz) each

The amount of wine drunk *per person* increases with the number of people at the table - as there are more hands to reach out and start the wine circulating. For 4 people you need 2 to 3 bottles. With 5 people you may well drink 4 bottles, and after 6 you may as well reckon a bottle a head, for safety. But if half the people are staying 'dry' to drive home the whole picture can alter dramatically.

There are, of course, larger bottles. Among them are some delightfully colourful characters.

Magnum = 2 bottles
Double Magnum - Bordeaux = 4 bottles
Jeroboam - Champagne = 4 bottles
Rehoboam = 5 bottles
Methuselah or Imperial = 8 bottles
Salamanazar = 12 bottles
Balthazar = 16 bottles
Nebuchadnezzar = 20 bottles

Containers can be deceptive. On the whole, wine boxes, tetrapaks, tettabriks and screw caps are signs of low quality wines. But some of the better wine boxes contain perfectly good quaffing wines. And some bottlers put identical wine into both screw-top and corked bottles and sell them at different prices to different markets.

Bordeaux   Burgundy   Alsace

Champagne   Rhine/Mosel   Bocksbeutel

Choosing Wine

The simple way to choose good wine is to have a good wine merchant or follow the columns of reliable wine writers. There is also the *Sunday Telegraph Good Wine Guide* which reports each year on the reasonably priced wines of most of the major supermarkets and wine chains. There is no way you can totally predict quality from a label but you can look for pointers to what may be a good bottle. There are some factors:
- the grape variety
- the age of the vines (old are best)
- the soil the vines are grown in
- the weather that year, in that area
- the method of making (who made it)
- how the wine is stored.

An ordinary vineyard can lie next door to a great one, and be almost the same on the first four factors above.

So knowing where the great wines are grown can be a good start to finding a less famous neighbour which may have a lot going for it.

Once you have an idea what the wine made from predictable varieties of grapes tastes like you can, to some extent, predict the flavour of the wine, though not its quality. Luckily, wines from countries like Australia usually put the name of the grape on the bottle. If, for example, you line up five bottles of Cabernet Sauvignon (a classic black grape), from different places, you won't have five identical flavours, but if you try a little of each you will soon spot what all the bottles have in common. The next step is to discover the way the same grape tastes different when grown in different climates or on different soils, or when used in different ways, and the wines begin to fall neatly into place. Jancis Robinson's lighthearted book *Masterglass* (Pan) is an ideal introduction to the art of comparing wines.

Decanting

Decanting has three uses. A decanter makes drink look attractive - especially whisky. It lets you conceal a bottle of unusual origin from snobbish friends, and it allows you to separate a fine bottle of wine from its sediment. Fine mature wines like vintage port or a 20-year-old claret need to be decanted, but with great care. This is how the head of Dow's Port - one of the great port houses advised me to do it.
- Fill the decanter to the brim with water (not hot water, it may crack) to get rid of any old stale smells.
- Tip out the water and shake out any drops.
- Rinse the decanter out with some inferior port/wine to get rid of the water (if you aren't a port shipper you may want to skip this and just let the decanter drain upside down in an airing cupboard).
- Drape a clean piece of butter muslin, moistened and wrung out (he uses cheap port to moisten it), inside a clean (odourless) funnel in the neck of the decanter.
- Set a lamp at the level at which you will be pouring the bottle so the light will shine through it.
- Pour the bottle very gently into the funnel, through the muslin, watching to see when the deposit is in danger of coming out and stopping before that moment. This usually means leaving the last 1½ inches of a vintage port.

Glasses

There is only one shape which does justice to wine: the tulip. This is because the in-curved shape holds the bouquet of the wine and, as smelling is a large part of tasting, this really does make a difference. For sparkling wines and champagne the tall slim tulips have the added advantage of holding the fizz; whereas the dish-shaped champagne glasses allow the bubbles to vanish into the air at a disastrous rate. Within the tulip form variations of size and shape aren't important. Nor does it matter if you serve every wine from sherry, through red and white to port in the same basic wine glass - provided that the glass is a good shape and size to start with. The nuances of shape are more to do with etiquette than winesmanship.

Keeping Wines

Wine is not like a tin of soup: it is a living thing which will alter according to how it is treated. It needs to be kept in a place which is free from strong smells, in the cool and dark, without vibrations (such as trains) and with the air neither too dry nor too moist. The ideal temperature is about 10°-14°C (50°-56°F), but for short term storage wine can cope with anything between 5°-15°C (40°-60°F) provided the temperature doesn't chop and change. So a partitioned cardboard wine box on its side in a cool place is far better for your wine than a smart rack hung high on a kitchen wall.

Any wine bottle with a cork needs to be stored on its side. The wine then keeps the cork moist and expanded and no air gets in to spoil the wine. It also means that the cork is easier to remove: it is said to take four times the pull to remove a dry cork.

★ Get wine bargains by the dozen - almost all wine shops give a discount that way.

Length of Life

Wines vary enormously in their length of life. Some are at their best when very young and rapidly go over the hill, becoming flat and dull. Others are slow developers: continuing to taste utterly foul for years but, with time, developing a fullness and beauty of flavour which only an expert could have guessed from their early showing.

The longer a wine takes to mature, the longer it usually stays at its peak. A big beautiful Sauternes may take 10 to 15 years to reach its best but may drink well for more than as long again; one of the greatest Italian reds can take 50 years to mature. At the other extreme, new Beaujolais can be over the hill in 3 months.

Unfortunately, there are few rules on how fast wine matures. But broadly speaking, the better the year, the bigger the wine, and the bigger the wine, the longer it takes to mature - if it's capable of doing so. This means that any table on how long to keep wine gives only average lengths which need to be adapted for the bottle concerned.

Labelling and Additives

Alcohol is one of the few exceptions to the EEC rules on listing ingredients on food and drink labels. This is due to be changed in around 1992; however, some new wine countries *do* insist on ingredients appearing. If you see some chemical listed on such a label don't assume it has more chemicals in than its European counterpart. Chemicals certainly are added to some European wine - the Austrian anti-freeze scandal was only an extreme example.

Serving

The big divide is between wines that need to be chilled before serving and those which need to be opened ahead of time to 'breathe' so the oxygen can give a finishing touch to their maturing. White wine doesn't need to breathe at all, nor does Beaujolais. Most red or rosé wines do.

The general rule is that red wines need to be opened 1 to 2 hours before they are needed. But it is better to know the wine and/or taste it and judge what it needs. The right amount of oxygen brings a red wine to its peak; too much makes it die a little. If you have a poor wine and need to knock the corners off it in a hurry pour it into a jug and leave so that a large surface of wine is exposed to the air. You can then return it to the bottle for serving. But be warned: the wine will become oxidized and dull far more quickly this way, so it is not a trick to try on an old precious wine or on one from which you hope to keep half for the next meal.

The bigger a wine, the longer the breathing time it needs. Most of the big Italian reds need 2 to 3 hours and Portuguese reds may need longer. A 20-year-old Colares from Portugal may even benefit from being opened the day before. However, a very old and delicate wine may need to be served the instant it is opened: air will only take it over the top.

Wine Problems

Corked wine isn't what it sounds like. It's not corked if a few bits of cork land in a glass. A truly corked wine betrays itself by smell, giving off a distinctive odour with a hint of chlorine, reminiscent of a swimming bath - though, of course, much fainter. If wine has this smell just recork it and return it to whoever sold it to you.

That corkiness isn't the only peculiar smell which can emanate from wine. A badly made wine can give off a musty smell. But a bad smell doesn't have to mean a bad wine. Occasionally, the pocket of air at the top of a good wine turns nasty. If this has happened the smell will vanish when the bottle has been open a while, and the wine can be drunk.

Sometimes a cork will have tiny white glistening crystals on the bottom. The crystals are called tartar, but there is nothing bad about them. They are formed by the mineral salts which the vine drew from the ground and are most likely to be found if the grapes were left long enough on the vine to become deeply sweet.

Temperature

The precise temperature for wine is a matter of your personal preference but, in general, the more full-bodied the red wine the closer to room temperature it should be and the sweeter a white wine the more you chill it. So, once opened, set red wine in a warm room for an hour or two to warm gently. But don't hurry it along exposing the bottle to sudden heat. It will change - but *not* in a way that is any improvement.

Very big reds	18°C (65°F)
Fairly heavy reds	16°C (60°F)
Rosés, light reds, new Beaujolais	Refrigerate 10°-13°C (50°-55°F)
Dry sherry, tequila, Marsala, *vergine* and rum	about 1 hr

Dry white wines	10°C (50°F) 1 hr	
Sparkling wines and champagne	7°C (45°F) 2 hrs	
Sweet dessert wines, old tawny port	6°C (42°F) 2 + hrs	
Vodka	very cold - 2 hrs in a *freezer*	

Overchilling white wine simply kills it. Indeed, some people would say that the temperatures I have given for champagne and white wine are too low and spoil the flavour. It is a matter of taste.

But chilling champagne is not just a matter of flavour. Only when it is well chilled is it possible to open champagne without it frothing out. Gas expands as it warms and when warm the pressure of the gas in a champagne bottle is the same as in the tyre of a double decker bus.

Wine with Food

People tend to talk as if there were hard and fast rules as to which wines go with which foods: there aren't. The rule of thumb is white wine with white flesh (whether fish or fowl), red wine with red flesh (meat or game). But nobody should worry a jot if their preferences spit in the eye of convention. A few guidelines are given below. Do bear in mind that sauces are every bit as important as the main ingredient. The wine which will go with white fish cooked with a subtle cream sauce is not the same as that which will suit cod with a powerful sauce of tomatoes and coriander. So go by the dominant flavour not the main ingredient.

Asparagus and artichokes tend to make wine taste metallic. Muscadet just about works, or try sherry. May be best without wine.

Beef or lamb (roasted) are the perfect foils for a really good red Bordeaux, or a first rate Rioja or Cabernet Sauvignon from other regions, provided there is no mint sauce to kill them.

Beef casseroles: the simple rule is the bigger the dish, the bigger the wine. Big Provençal stews with black olives and bags of flavour need a drink as hearty as they are. I'd favour a big Portuguese or Australian red, or possibly one from Italy.

Cheese: people disagree more over what wines go with which cheeses than over any other area of wine and food. Whatever you serve, someone will probably love it and someone loathe it. On the whole, the very rich fatty cheeses are best with white wine, and it can be surprising what they go with. A wine merchant insisted I try Roquefort with a Sémillon. I was sure a powerful blue cheese and a sweet muscaty wine would be disastrous. I was wrong and he was right. Port is the classic with Stilton, although I prefer port with nuts, and Burgundies are usually recommended with Brie and its relatives. In fact, the common factor for wines with cheese is not colour but fruitiness.

Chinese food: rumour has it that Hong Kong is one of the world's biggest importers of Cognac because the Chinese drink Cognac with their food. It does go rather well. So does the Japanese rice wine, *sake*.

Curry: there may be some curries which are improved by wine: I have yet to find them. Nor do curries enhance wine.

Fish (white) and shellfish: Muscadet is a good choice: most fish needs a clean fairly dry white with a bit of body to it.

Fish (oily): with smoked fish you may find that a wine based on the Sauvignon Blanc grape is good. Oily fish tends to coat the palate and make wine hard to enjoy, so another solution is to drink a very dry *fino* sherry instead of a conventional wine, also some assertive whites could work.

Game: Hugh Johnson puts it perfectly when he says: 'Drink (very) good red Bordeaux with unhung game, (very) good red Burgundy with any game which has been hung.'

Game soup and other broths: sherry is the drink for this, or possibly a dry Marsala, or Madeira, and put some in the soup too. Even a simple soup from a turkey carcass is very good like that. (The exception is mutton broth, which has too sweet a flavour to need the addition.) An old colonial tip is to put medium dry sherry in a rinsed-out Worcestershire sauce bottle with several dried red chillies. The chilli flavoured sherry can then be shaken into broths to add a little interest.

Liver or kidney need fruity reds, whether from Burgundy or the newer wine areas.

Meat pâté or terrine are usually rich and need a fairly full bodied red with a bit of tannin to cut through this. It could be a good red from Bordeaux, or perhaps from Portugal or a younger wine country. But one of the traditions of gastronomy is the serving of sweet white wines with *pâté de foie gras*.

Oysters Champagne is the classic accompaniment, but a good Chablis is just as perfect.

Pasta: the wine which goes with pasta is decided entirely by the ingredients of the sauce. But drink Italian wines with genuine Italian recipes. There is a character which marries perfectly with the cooking.

Pork: some people favour a clear clean wine like a Chardonnay with pork, others a Rhine wine. Either way it must have enough body to stand up to the meat. Some wines taste a bit watery and acid when faced with its richness. The wine for veal is the same.

Poultry The flavour of poultry varies hugely with how it is cooked, and whether it is chicken or duck. With roast duck, or duck in a heavy sauce, a fruity Burgundy would probably be the answer, with a light chicken dish an elegant white would be better. Duck and goose are rather good with a well-balanced Rhine wine: the sweetness is good with these birds and the acidity cuts through their richness.

Puddings are a problem. Fruit salad is too acid to go with any wine. Fruit tarts are less disastrous but, even so, some say these need Calvados not wine. While chocolate manages to kill almost any drink you put with it. Some gourmets favour Cognac with chocolate though a good Armagnac is almost nicer. And anyone who has a liqueur to serve might end the meal on a chocolate pudding and serve the two together. The really easy puddings to match are the soft creamy ones like syllabub, which can be drunk with a sweet wine like Beaumes de Venise. It is a sickeningly rich combination but there are times when that is just right.

Salad: Vinegar ruins the taste of wine, so it is to be avoided if possible. A French dressing made with lemon juice instead is less antagonistic.

Vegetables and vegetable soups: aren't always as happy with wine as you might expect. When meat and vegetables combine few people will notice, but for a soup it can matter. Carrots are decidedly better with white wine than red, tomatoes need really big gutsy reds without too much breeding; cabbage is easy going, but potatoes go with everything.

Steven Spurrier, *Écoles du Vin*, Century
Hugh Johnson, *Wine*, Emblem
Hugh Johnson, *World Atlas of Wine*, Mitchell Beazley

Wine Terminology
The wine terms covered here are those most commonly used. Others are defined in the text.

Blending: mixing two or more wines together
Botrytis cinerea: (noble rot or *pourriture noble*) is a mould which penetrates the skin of ripe grapes and sucks the moisture from them, so the flavour and sweetness become concentrated.
Brut: the driest of the standard grades of champagne or sparkling wine.
Chaptalization: the adding of sugar to wine to aid fermentation. Originally done in bad years when the grapes hadn't had enough sun to develop their sweetness, but it can be used simply to push up the alcohol levels.
Climat: used in Burgundy for a particular vineyard.
Clos: at one time this was a vineyard enclosed by a wall, but it is now used for any wine estate.
Crémant: usually means a wine with less fizz than is usual for champagne, but more than in a wine which is simply *pétillant*.
Cru Classé: literally 'classed growth'. In 1855 wines in the Bordeaux region were grouped according to *price*, into 1st, 2nd and 3rd class. These classifications remain and others, such as *cru bourgoise* have been added. Not all wines show their class on the label: Château Lafite doesn't, Château Latour does and they are both *Premier Cru*. And the price of a wine in 1855 doesn't always denote its quality today, some '2nd and 3rd class' wines then could be first rate now.
Fermentation: the process by which the sugar in basic fruit mush or juice is converted into alcohol by yeasts.
Secondary fermentation (malo-lactic fermentation): the stage when malic acid is converted into lactic acid and carbon dioxide - which makes the wine less acid.

Fortified wine: any wine to which strong alcohol was added to stop fermentation.
Méthode Champenoise: the method of making champagne which produces bubbles through secondary fermentation in bottle. Only wine made by this process within the Champagne region of France can be called 'champagne'; all other wine made the same way can only be called '*méthode champenoise*'.
Must: the juice extracted by pressing grapes.
Oxidation: the reaction - for good or ill - when air gets at wine.
Pétillant: a term used to describe wine with a faint hint of fizz which leaves a tingle in the mouth, but the fizz is usually so faint you can't see it.
Racking: the process of moving wine from vat to vat leaving behind any deposits.
Tannin: a natural substance, drawn largely from the pips and stalks of grapes during pressing. It helps wine to keep well and highly tannic wines age longest.
Terroir: an area within a vineyard which has particular characteristics affecting grapes grown within it.
Tête de Cuvée: on a label means that the wine was drawn from the best vat.
Ullage: oddly this means either the air space between wine and cork, in a bottle, or the practice of topping up wine in a barrel to stop air getting at it.
Vinification: turning grape juice into wine.
Vin ordinaire: a cheap wine of no known origin.
Vintage: this has two meanings. It is either the annual harvest; or it can mean 'of a very special harvest', as in vintage port, when only in the best years do the shippers 'declare a vintage'.

Australian Wine
It has taken Australia a long time to live down the image it created by setting up wineries with names like Warramate, and calling wine Kanga Rouge and Sally's Paddock. That bottles bearing the name Seaview (not a boarding house but a wine company) and with a label so nautical that it shouts yo-ho-ho and a bottle of rum ever leave the shelves is a credit to the open-mindedness of the wine-buying public. But they do. And rightly so. Australia is offering wines which are good value for money. So, it's not surprising that Australian wines have become the biggest thing to hit British wine importing in a long while. Australia has much to offer. But don't expect Australian wines to taste like European wines made with the same grapes: they don't. Australian reds are big fruity up-front wines often full of tannin and character, but tend to lack the elegance, restraint and complexity of French wines. Among the whites there are also good things, especially some very well made Chardonnays. You may need to pay rather more for an Australian white than for a red to get the same degree of complexity.

Buying Australian Wine
You can't organize Australia neatly into regions, as you can France, and say one region makes big reds, another

light whites and so on. Each winery is likely to grow several different types of grape and will often make two whites and two reds in very varied styles. In Australia there is no kudos in estate wines so most producers buy in their grapes from growers who may be quite distant. This means that the grape type is the best clue to the style of a wine.

Labelling
Australian wine labelling is controlled by Australian law on food labelling but any company uses more or less whatever wording it pleases. In Australia the wine growers often use terms, like Chablis. But, under EEC rules, Chablis can only be used for wine from that region of France. So, for Europe, the Australians have had to drop such names. This leaves the following clues to what a bottle may be like.

The year - 'vintage' may be added. It doesn't mean it's necessarily a high quality 'vintage' wine; it's just a way of trying to make the date it was made look smart.

Grapes - by Australian law, for a blended wine, the first grape named must be the major proportion, the next greatest comes next and any un-named grapes used in the blend must not be more than 15 per cent of the total. But EEC rules only allow 2 grapes to be shown.

State and region - not always there.

Name - all kinds of names like 'Chairman's Selection' are just marketing gimmicks - but so are many European wine names.

Name and address of makers and importer - some bottles also mention any additives and some makers add a thumbnail description of the wine, such as you might find on a supermarket shelf.

Laying Down Australian Wines
Although Australian wines are usually drinkable even when young, some deserve to be laid down. Much depends on the year and the quality, but most Sémillons are better for 2 to 3 years in the bottle and some repay 15 or so. The very best reds, epitomized by the Grange Hermitage from Penfolds, also mature beautifully over as long as 30 years.

The problem is finding a good Australian wine at the right age. Most of it is drunk young and, as one wine merchant put it, 'There's a lot of infanticide where Australian wine is concerned.'

Picking a Good Year
In Australia most wines are made everywhere, and the weather may vary between areas, so it's more difficult to pick the best years for wine than it is in France. This means that you really do need a wine merchant who keeps tabs on the quality of the different vineyards.

Who Makes What Where
Australian wine being relatively new, and lacking very obvious regional styles, it can be hard to know what to buy. So here is a quick guide to names worth looking

for. It doesn't, of course, mean that only these names are worth drinking. Nor does it mean that wine by these names will always be good but it should stack the odds in favour of the bottle being enjoyable. Where a producer excels at particular types these are mentioned.

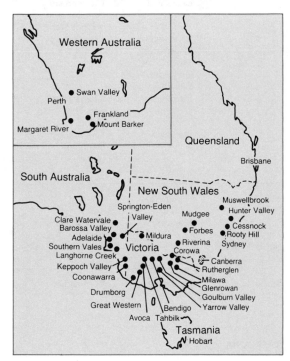

SOUTH AUSTRALIA

Area	Producer	Grape Variety
Adelaide Hills	Petuluma - a big name but a small winery	Chardonnay Cab. Sauv. Botrytis Riesling
Pathaway/ Keppoch	Lindeman's Hardys Sepelts	
Coonawarra famed for its Cabernet Sauvignon	Mildara Lindemans Wynns Redmans Brand's Laira Rouge Homme	Cab. Sauv. Cab. Sauv./Shiraz Cab. Sauv. Shiraz
McLaren Vale	Hardy Château Reynella Geoff Merrill Andrew Garrett	Sémillon Pinot Blanc Sémillon/Cab. Sauv.
Barossa Valley The best of this area age well.	Orlando Seppelts Penfolds Wolf Blass Hill Smith Yalumba Peter Lehman	Grange Hermitage

NEW SOUTH WALES

Area	Producer	Grape Variety
Hunter Valley	Robson	Chardonnay Sémillon
	Lake's Folly	Chardonnay
	Tyrells	Sémillon and Pinot Noir
	Rosemount	Chardonnay
	Lindeman's	
	McWilliams	
	Hungerford Hill	
	Wyndham Estate	
	Petersons	Chardonnay Sémillon Shiraz
	Rothbury	Chardonnay Sémillon Shiraz
Mudgee	Huntington Estate	
	Montrose	Chardonnay
Very good wine but little in UK - yet		Shiraz Sauvignon Blanc
Riverina	De Bortoli	Botrytis Sémillon

TASMANIA

Piper's River	Piper's Brook	Chardonnay Pinot Noir
	Heemskirk	Chardonnay
	Moorilla Estate	

VICTORIA

Great Western	Best's	
Milawa	Brown Brothers	
Echuca	Tisdall	Chardonnay
Avoca	Taltarni	Shiraz and Cab. Sauv.
Yarra Valley	Yarra Yering Yarraburn	Cab. Sauv. Shiraz
Central Goulburn Valley	Chateau Tahbilk	Marsanne
Rutherglen	Bailey's Campbells Stanton and Killeen Morris	All make liqueur muscat

WESTERN AUSTRALIA

Area	Producer	Grape Variety
Margaret River	Vasse Felix	Cab. Sauv.
	Moss Wood	Chardonnay Cab. Sauv. Sémillon
	Cape Mentelle	Cab. Sauv. Sémillon
	Cullens	Chardonnay Cabernet/Merlot
	Leeuwin's - winery of high prestige	Chardonnay Cab. Sauv.
Swan Valley	Houghton	Chardonnay Cab. Sauv.
Often late released ready for drinking.	Evans and Tate	

More information

James Halliday, *The Australian Wine Compendium*, Angus Robertson

Halliday's *Australian Wine Guide*, Angus Robertson - an exhaustive valley-by-valley briefing

Thomas K.Hardy, *Pictorial Atlas of Australian Wine*, Grape Vision

Australian wine is well stocked by Oddbins and Peter Dominic and the following wine merchants offer a very large selection on mail order.

Alex Findlater, 77 Abbey Road, London NW8 0AE
Tel: 01 624 7311

Ostlers, 63A Clerkenwell Road, London EC1M 5NP
Tel: 01 250 1522

Bulgarian Wine

In 1987 Bulgarian Cabernet Sauvignon was the most popular red wine in Britain. When any wine sells in huge quantities it is usually a bad sign. For once it is not. Bulgarian Cabernet has been selling on its very low price in relation to its quality - and some of those who import from other countries have been muttering darkly about dumping and huge subsidies. The Bulgarians deny this and murmur that labour costs are very much lower. However, their tactics have been impeccable.

While meeting its target of popularity Bulgaria was busy passing laws on quality control and creating more elegant wines which bear the words '*Controliran Region*'. There are still only 6 on the market, but the Cabernet Sauvignon (claret style red) is, once again, much better than one would expect for the price, and the Chardonnay (crisp white) has been well rated by tasters. These are now in major wine chains, and in Harrods.

The Cabernet varies according to where it is grown, the heaviest coming from Plovdiv in the south, which also produces a very full flavoured wine, rather like a Rioja, from the traditional Mavrud grapes. In contrast, the Cabernets of Suhindol and Svishtov in the north near the Danube have had less sun and their style is lighter.

Labelling Bulgarian Wines

Strict laws on the labelling of its wines mean you can very easily tell what grade of wine you are buying by how much information you get on the label. They don't class their wines as I have done, but my method simplifies their subdivisions.

Top grade:	can say 'Controliran Region' where it was made e.g. Svihtov, Oriahovitza; the type of grapes used; the year it was made; and it can say 'Estate Bottled'. It may also carry the word 'Reserve'.
Second grade:	can say where it was made; possibly the grape variety; the year it was made. It may also carry the word 'Reserve'.
Third grade:	can give the grape variety; the year it was made (if red but not if white).
Basic grade:	says 'Mehana' (bistro) and is blended from different grapes and regions.

'Reserve' is exceptionally good for its particular type and grade and has been aged in barrels for a set period.

Under Bulgarian law all grape varieties used in making a wine must appear on the label, regardless of how small the percentage is. And to be classified as 'Controliran' approved the grapes must all come from a small defined area, the cultivation and vinification techniques must be approved, and the final wine must meet set standards. White wine must then spend 2 years in barrel and red wine 3.

The word 'region' in 'Controliran Region' is a misnomer; at its largest it is usually a group of vineyards.

Keeping Bulgarian Wine

The keeping quality of Bulgarian wine is largely unknown but Bulgarian Vintners assures me that wine from the traditional Mavrud grape is very slow to mature and may need as long as 15 years in cellar. If you want to experiment with laying down some of the others, 1980 and 1983 were good years for Cabernet Sauvignon and Gamza.

Californian Wine

You Americans have the loveliest wines in the world, you know, but you don't realize it. You call them 'domestic' and that's enough to start trouble anywhere.

H. G. Wells

That quote from a publicity hand-out from Californian vineyards fails to say whether H. G. Wells himself was speaking or whether he put those words into the mouth of a flatterer. There is no way that the wines of America are lovelier than those of France - not as a generality that is. What is true is that there is more to American wine than a Paul Masson carafe.

Wine has become California's new gold. Consistent sunshine makes 'every year a vintage year', and the soil offers a cross section of the best wine growing soils of Europe. The result is what has been described by one wine writer as an 'artesian well of sensationally good vin ordinaire'. They have also planted most of the great European grape varieties and used a combination of modern technology and diligent research into traditional methods to produce some wines of very high quality.

However, the best wine is at least as expensive as comparable wine from Europe. And even using the classic grapes there is a distinct Californian style - which you may or may not enjoy.

Reading California Labels

California doesn't divide wine into regional wines, table wine and so on. In America they may use generic terms taken from France - such as Chablis - to describe a style of wine. For Europe they can't, nor can they use invented names unless they are approved and registered with the EEC. Some names are registered; but the rest use the grape variety and basic descriptions like 'Dry Red Wine'.

If a particular grape is named on a bottle of American wine you know that 75 per cent of the wine is made from it. As Americans tend to plaster the back label with everything except the brand of the corking machine you can get any other information you need from there.

If there is less than 75 per cent of a single grape you will simply find a very basic description or an approved name. Don't think that wines not sold by the grape variety are less good. Some of the best wine is being made with blends of several grapes which complement each other.

Choosing California Wine

One of the easiest ways to find a reliable wine is to go by the area and the winery. On the whole, Napa Valley is the prime area, Sonoma also makes good wine, and some of the finest wine of California is said to be coming from Monterey County. Though not all their wines are good. Among the most reliable wine making companies are Robert Mondavi, Beaulieu Vineyards, Trefethen, Clos du Bois, Firestone and, for a really fine Cabernet Sauvignon, Heitz; for white wine, Château St Jean. There is a new trend for producers to attach the name of a vineyard to some of their finest wines, so this too is something which could be an indication of quality.

Vintages and Keeping

It is difficult to predict the keeping qualities of California wines. Most of the whites are ready after 1 to 3 years, but 20 years of wine making is too short a time in which to discover how the best wines mature.

Bob Thompson, *Webster's Wine Tours: California, Oregon and Washington,* Simon and Schuster

The Wine Institute of California, Premier House, 10 Greycoat Place, London SW1P 1SB (written requests only)
California wine can be obtained by mail order from **Alex Findlater and Co Ltd,** in London or Suffolk (see page 136) or **Christopher's,** 19 Charlotte Street, London W1P 1HB Tel: 01 636 4020.

French Wine

Whatever competition she may face on value for money among the cheaper wines, France has not been toppled from her pinnacle as the home of some of the greatest - perhaps *the* greatest - wines in the world. Trying to write about French wine is like trying to describe the ceiling of the Sistine Chapel - which angel does one start with? For angels there are among the wines of France. Archangels even - remarkable thought-provoking mouthfuls which linger on the memory months and even years later.

As truly great wines come my way only slightly more often than archangels I find it impossible to write about French wine without a tinge of annoyance - not because of my lack of good fortune in this matter, but, because it is the best, possible substitutes are ridiculously hard to find. There has been little attempt to name and label French wines so as to make it easier for the consumer. This section is therefore about a few of the basics for those who feel daunted.

Names can't always be taken as a guarantee. In a few areas - notably Bordeaux and Champagne - it is possible to choose a wine, from a good year, by a particular château or wine house and be pretty sure what it will be like, particularly if you are prepared to pay the price for a wine of note.

However, this is by no means true in most wine areas. In Burgundy, for example, the name is usually attached to the area of land *not* to the individual grower. So a famous wine may be made by as many as 30 different producers. Among them will be good, bad and indifferent wine makers, yet all their bottles can say Gevrey- Chambertin or whatever name applies. So the only way to be sure of a good wine is to find a good wine company and take good advice.

What's in a Name?

Wine is grown in distinct regions, but so far as the name on the label is concerned, it is often a case of boxes within boxes. There are a few individual regions, such as Champagne, making just one style of wine, but usually there is an overall region, such as Bordeaux, which is divided into areas each known for a wine of a particular style; then within those areas there are individual vineyards.

Claret, for example, is all the varied red wine which comes from Bordeaux. There is no area called claret, but you may find wine with claret on its label. Graves on the other hand is both an official wine making region (AOC) and a style of white wine. We tend to feel it must be our fault when French wine labelling is somewhat puzzling but it is confusing and puzzling. The only thing to do is to accept it. (See also Wine Terminology on page 134.)

Labelling

The French have four categories. The rules are these - starting at the bottom.

Vin de table is usually blended wine from assorted regions, or different countries. The label must have:
- the name and address of the company which bottled

it, even if only as a post code
- the volume
- the alcohol content (as from 1989)
- if it is a blend of wine from several EEC countries it must say so.

Vin de pays (this must appear on the label with the region of origin) is better quality table wine and must come from a single region of France. The label must have the same compulsory information as a *vin de table*. It *may* also have the following:
- the name of the producer and his estate but may not say 'Château' or 'Clos'
- grape variety (not common)
- vinification methods (rare)
- brand name.

Vin délimite de qualité supérieure (VDQS) (on the label). VDQS wines slip neatly into place if you think of them as Very Drinkable Quaffing Stuff. They must come from particular vineyards and there are strict controls on the exact area these wines cover, the grapes which are used, the minimum alcohol content and so on. The label has the same compulsory and optional information as a *vin de pays*, but it *may* also give:
- the name of the estate or château where it was made
- the name of the château or clos where it was bottled
- the vintage year
- information on quality.

Appellation d'origine contrôlée (AOC) means that the wine conforms to the strictest definition of where it comes from and how it was made. It only applies to wine which has been made within one of the areas noted for fine wines and defined by tradition and by law.

On the label it will say '*Appellation*' and '*Contrôlée*' on either side of the region which has the right to call itself AOC. There are degrees of excellence in this. If a wine says '*Appellation Bordeaux Contrôlée*' it just means it was made within the Bordeaux region; if it names a small area within that region the chances of it being a good wine are rather higher, and if a single château or vineyard is AOC it is something very special.

As there is no copyright on château names, make sure the château is within the right AOC region. For example, there could be lots of Château Latour around France, but there is only one from the AOC region of Bordeaux. In Beaujolais, which has far fewer châteaux than Bordeaux, they use terms like *climats* and *village* to define more precisely the area from which the wine comes, and so you need to look for the right combination of village or *climat* and AOC region.

Even between AOC châteaux there are degrees of excellence, so to allow you to spot the prime wines the French also have quality designations which can be shown on labels. At the top of the tree come the *Cru* wines: great wines from distinguished vineyards. You would expect these to be standardized from region to region. They aren't. However, the main systems are as follows, starting with the very best:

For Bordeaux
Premier Grand Cru Classé
Grand Cru Classé
Grand Cru
Cru Bourgeois

For Burgundy
Grand Cru
Premier Cru + village on
the label
Deuxième Cru
Appelation Village

The word *'superieur'* added just means there is more alcohol content than is usual for that wine.

French Wine Regions

As **Alsace** has, since 1743, alternately belonged to France and to Prussia its wines are understandably 'un-French'. It is, for example, the only region to sell its wine by the grape names rather than district or site, although 25 high quality vineyards are also allowed to be named.

Alsace produces dry full bodied whites which go well with rather rich food. Its fruity Rieslings and Gewürztraminers have become increasingly popular and some Alsatian wines now carry the *Grand Cru* designation. They can also carry the words *'selection de grains nobles'* if they have been late harvested and selected for botrytis, so not all the white is dry.

Bordeaux is the greatest of all the French wine making areas. This is the home of claret (whose bottles always have shoulders) and home of some of its greatest names - Château Lafite, Châteaux Latour and Mouton-Rothschild. A third of France's AOC wines (page 138) originate here and it has no less than 12 *Premier Grand Cru Classé*, and 70 *Grand Cru Classé* wines in its Médoc area. However, the term *'Grand Vin de Bordeaux'* (great wine of Bordeaux) doesn't necessarily mean the wine is great: it is - misleadingly - allowed on any Bordeaux.

Nobody knows what makes Bordeaux such a superb area for wine making. However, modern wine making techniques have made it possible to produce more good wine - even in unfavourable years.

Most wine here is a blend of at least two grapes, and that produces the subtlety of many of its wines. The permitted grapes for red wine in this region are Cabernet Sauvignon, Cabernet Franc, Merlot, Malbec, Petit Verdot (a grape which gives colour and freshness) and occasionally Carmenère. White wine uses only Sauvignon, Muscadelle (which gives an opulent bouquet) and Sémillon.

The Areas of Bordeaux

Within Bordeaux there are 18 to 25 different areas (depending how you count them). This is not the place to go into all of them, however, it is perhaps worth mentioning some:

Médoc, Haute Médoc and **Graves** form a continuous strip down the south bank of the Gironde River. They hold within them some of the greatest château wines of France (such as Margaux) and noted ones like St Julien and Pauillac. They all produce delicate, elegant reds which age beautifully. Graves also produces the best white wine of Bordeaux and, tucked into the southern end of Graves, like the stone in a peach, are the quite separate areas of **Sauternes** and **Barsac,** famous for sweet, deeply fragrant white wines such as Chateau Yquem which, at their best, have an exquisite

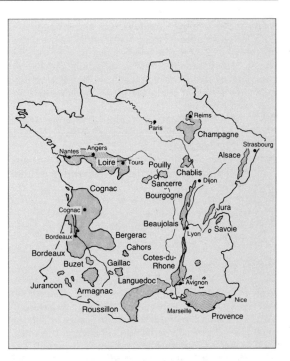

lusciousness. Though the Barsacs are perhaps more interesting as they have a hint of dryness curiously mingled with the sweetness. The best wine of this area needs time to mature and can be laid down for many years.

Entre-Deux-Mers is a large area which takes its name from its position between two stretches of water - the Garonne and Dordogne rivers. It produces attractive light whites from Sauvignon grapes. Lunchtime wines rather than anything serious.

St Émilion is a big area of red wine making. Less distinguished than Médoc and Graves, it makes big, handsome wines with a lot of appeal. The fact that they are sometimes called 'the Burgundies of Bordeaux' gives an idea of their character. And they often suffer less in a bad year than other areas of Bordeaux.

Pomerol is a neighbour of St Émilion, but it produces elegant red wines which are easy to enjoy and have a shorter life than many Bordeaux reds: 3 to 5 years according to the vintage.

Burgundy (Bourgogne) If Bordeaux is the King of France's wine areas, Burgundy is Queen. It isn't a compact area like Bordeaux, but a scattering of regions strung out down the Sâone like misshapen pearls. The structure of the wine industry is also different from that in Bordeaux. Few wines are described by the name of a great château, but the best vineyards may be on privately owned estates (*domaines*). And it is one of the characteristics of the area that wines carrying a single *'village'* name may be made by as many as 30 producers. So the Chambertin 'vineyard' is in fact a parcel of land divided between some 50 growers.

The wine tends to be fruity and rounded, with a strong bouquet, and both red and white often repay keeping. There are over 100 *Appellation Contrôlée* wines in the area but, in addition to those fine wines, Burgundy also produces - or at least sells - a great deal of table wine. I emphasize sells because much of the table wine sold by Burgundian *négociants* (wholesalers) in fact comes from other parts of France - and at one time used to come from as far afield as Sicily. The wine here has four classifications.

- At the top of the tree are *Grand Cru* wines where only the name of the vineyard appears on the label (e.g. Montrachet).
- Next come *Premier Cru* wines which show the name of the parish and the name of the *cru* (e.g. Nuits-Saint-Georges-Les-Porets).
- Below that are *village* wines which show just the parish on the label (e.g. Nuits-Saint-Georges).
- At the bottom are those which only own up to the region and simply say Bourgogne.

The Grapes of Burgundy

The two great grapes of Burgundy are Chardonnay for white wine and Pinot Noir for red wine. Indeed, the experts say that the only place in the world that Pinot Noir is at its best is in the section of France which lies roughly between Fixin in the north and somewhere near Chalon in the south (this lower point is disputed). The other important grapes of Burgundy are Aligoté, which provides some distinctive whites, and Gamay - the grape of the Beaujolais and red Mâcon.

The Areas of Burgundy

Chablis is known for dry elegant whites most associated with Chardonnay grapes, but as the demand for Chablis has grown, there has been an incentive to elevate *petits Chablis* (minor Chablis) to a higher status than they deserve. It is even said, in the wine trade, that three to four times as much 'Chablis' is sold as actually exists in the area. True or not, quality and price are particularly closely linked: cheap Chablis is unlikely to be good.

Côte de Nuits, a chalky area, produces many of the most important wines of Burgundy: among them famous reds like Nuits-Saint-Georges; Gevrey-Chambertin - favourite wine of Napoleon, and Le Musigny - known as the wine of velvet and lace. Also the Domaine de la Romanée-Conti which produces what some claim to be the best red wines in the world. There are also some excellent whites, and its great reds repay longer keeping than any other wines of Burgundy.

Côte de Beaune is a mixed region which produces big beautiful white wines, such as Montrachet, Meursault and Corton Charlemagne; it also has very good reds such as Volnay, Beaune and Pommard, which are lighter and mature faster than the reds of the Côte de Nuits.

Côte Chalonnaise has reds very similar to its neighbour Côte de Beaune, and is an area to watch as its wines are increasingly good.

Mâcon's most famous wine is Pouilly-Fuissé, a pale green-gold wine with a lovely bouquet and freshness. There are also fruity easy-going reds made with Gamay and Pinot Noir, sold as Passtoutgrains. Mâcon *villages* are always dry, fruity and white, and best drunk young.

On labels the name of the village is added to the name of the region e.g. Mâcon-Vire.

Beaujolais is a granite area lying at the southern end of Burgundy which has risen to fame with the trend towards light, undemanding wines. The best Beaujolais villages include Morgon, Fleurie, Juliénas and Moulin-à-Vent. All these can age for 5 years; other Beaujolais should be drunk young.

Beaujolais Nouveau (new Beaujolais) is wine which has not undergone its secondary fermentation. It cannot be sold before the third Thursday in November and continues until 14 December. If you buy some from a poor year drink it before January is out - it goes downhill rapidly. However, a good year will mature in bottle for its first year. In fact, shippers are - quite legally - given labels with which they can relabel their unsold stock of Beaujolais Nouveau as simply Beaujolais, after December 14.

Champagne is made partly from black grapes but the grapes are pressed in a way which minimizes the contact with their dark skins. This explains why champagne made entirely from Chardonnay grapes is called 'Blanc de Blancs' - white (wine) of the white (grapes). Apart from this, blending is a feature of the champagne industry and some of the best champagne is made from as many as 40 different wines. Pink champagne is made by adding red wine to the blend: the only French rosé made by blending wine of both colours.

You will get much better value if you avoid the names which are heavily advertised. Some of the champagne sold by top supermarkets is actually the same as that sold for several pounds more by the big names and among the unknowns a couple of names which offer good value are Bruno Paillard and Palmer.

The **Côtes du Rhône** is the area every holiday maker, bound for the south of France, unwittingly drives through on the Autoroute from Vienne to the Côte d'Azur. In the south near Orange is where you find Châteauneuf-du-Pape, the region's most famous wine: a big, powerful, yet refined red that is unusual in being made from vines which have grown knee-deep in stones which hold the heat at night and speed the ripening of the grapes. It is also remarkable in being made from a blend of no less than than 13 grape varieties. Nearby you find the heavy fragrant natural sweet wine Beaumes de Venise and, in the area of Lirac and Tavel, rosé wines of a distinctive orangy pink.

The soil and climate change down the length of the region, and the wines with them. Cornas, to the north near Valence, produces big purply reds and elegant whites, and farther north again are made two of the great reds of the area: the Hermitage (the better of the two) and Crozes-Hermitage, both needing a very long time to mature. To drink rather younger look at Côtes-du-Rhône *villages* such as Cairanne, Vacqueyras or Gigondas.

The winding valley of the **Loire** is one of the coolest wine growing regions. The grapes do not ripen as deeply here as in the south and retain a certain acidity, which creates wines with a lightness of touch. At the mouth

VINTAGE CHART

★★★★ EXCEPTIONAL VINTAGES: 1921, 1928, 1929 ★★★★									
VINTAGE	Red Bordeaux	White Bordeaux	Red Burgundy	White Burgundy	Côtes du Rhône	Alsace	Pouilly s/Loire Sancerre	Anjou Touraine	Beaujolais
1945	★★★★	★★★★	★★★		★★★				
1947	★★★★	★★★	★★★		★★★★			★★★★	
1949	★★★★	★★★	★★★★		★★★			★★★	
1955	★★★	★★★	★★★	★★	★★★			★★★	
1959	★★	★★★	★★★★	★★	★★	★★★★		★★★★	
1961	★★★★	★★★★	★★★★	★★★	★★★	★★★		★★	
1962	★★★	★★★	★★	★★	★★	★		★★	
1964	★★	★	★★★	★★	★★	★★			
1966	★★★	★★	★★★	★★	★★★	★★★			
1967	★★	★★★★	★★	★★	★★★	★★★			
1969	★	★	★★★	★★★	★★	★★		★★	
1970	★★★★	★★	★★	★★★★	★★★★	★★		★★★	
1971	★★★	★★	★★★	★★★	★★	★★★★		★★	
1973	★★	★★	★	★★★		★★★		★	
1974	★	★★	★★	★★		★		★	
1975	★★★★	★★★	★	★★	★★★	★★		★★	
1976	★★★	★★★	★★★	★★★	★★★	★★★★		★★	
1977	★	★	★	★★		★		★	
1978	★★★	★★	★★★★	★★★	★★★★	★		★★★	
1979	★★★	★★	★★	★★★★	★★★	★★★	★★	★★	★
1980	★	★	★★	★★	★★	★	★★	★	★
1981	★★★	★★	★	★★	★★	★★★	★	★★	★★
1982	★★★★	★★	★★	★★★	★	★★	★★★	★★★	★★
1983	★★	★★	★★	★★★	★★	★★★★	★★★	★★	★★★★
1984	Some outstanding wines in an average year								

Average & Medium vintage ★	Good vintage ★★	Great vintage ★★★	Exceptional vintage ★★★★

These appreciations are based on averages, the exception proves the rule

Copy of the chart drawn up by the Compagnie des Courtiers Jurés Piqueurs de Vins de Paris.

of the river you find Muscadet: dry, clean, light and excellent with fish - then Muscadet de Sèvres-et-Maine. The best Muscadets are those which are *sur lie:* these have spent only one winter in the vats and have been bottled in March straight from the vats which contain the *lie* (lees) - the deposit from fermentation. Its neighbour Anjou is best known for its summery rosé and Saumur for a sparkling white. Vouvray, beyond, produces a Cinderella wine which, most of the time, is simply a pleasant white, but once in a while can turn into something exquisite, firm and delicate and with a delectable honey tone.

Across the river, Chinon and Bourgueil produce dry light reds best drunk lightly chilled. Further up the valley, away from the rest are Sancerre and Pouilly-sur-Loire - homes of Pouilly Fumé, light white Sancerre and also Manitou Salon, which is still little known and exceptionally good value.

Most Loire wine should be drunk when 1 to 2 years old, though the Chinon reds may improve over 3 or 4 years - or even longer after a hot summer. The big exception is Vouvray which, from a good year, can keep as long as 25 years, becoming deeper and more honeyed with time.

Provence is associated especially with rosé, and the general level of other wines is bistro rather than dinner. However, there are little vineyards tucked away which produce some remarkably good wine, both red and white, and the dry rosés of Provence are being appreciated more and more.

The **Languedoc Roussillon** area sweeps round the Mediterranean coast from Arles down to the Spanish border. It used to be known as the wine vat of France, producing vast quantities of bouncing plonk; dry, woody reds and soft whites and rosés. However, it has its share of AOC and VDQS wines and, although it is not rated as one of France's important areas, it has seen the success of other areas and is busy pulling up its socks. It has become an area to watch and has some charming little wines like Clairette de Bellegarde.

More information
Graham Chidgey, *The Wines of Burgundy*, Century
The *Macdonald Guide to French Wines*
Pamela Vandyke Price, *Champagne*, Century
Pamela Vandyke Price, *The Wines of Bordeaux*, Century
  Wine & Food from France, Nuffield House, 41-46 Piccadilly, London W1V 9AJ Tel: 01 439 8371

German Wine
It is a shame that people's first contact with German wine is so often with a bland, inoffensive, blended wine marketed by a big brand name. German wine reaches perfection in Rieslings of exquisite fragrance, full of nuances balanced to create a wine that is quite simply luscious. There are also complex wines from slatey soils, with a hint of steeliness behind the fruit, elegant and sophisticated. However, we expect wine to be for drinking at meals, whereas often German wines are at their best alone.

The other difference between German wine and other wine is that German vines are affected by the weather far more than those in warmer regions.

This means that German wine makers may go to extraordinary lengths to get the very best from their unpredictable raw material, sometimes treating each batch of grapes differently, with a resulting maze of unrecognizable names on the bottles - often with superb wines within. But also a lot of poorly balanced wine is produced, some too sweet, some too acid, and so on. It is this which goes into some of the inexpensive blended brand-named bottles of no real character.

Labelling
Most of the key clues to what you will get in a bottle of German wine are all on the label, if you know how to read it. The important factors are the grape, where it was grown, when it was grown, how it was processed, and what quality the wine is thought to have reached. If 85 per cent of the wine is from one grape its name can be on the label. To the really knowledgeable the most important factor of all may be the particular vineyard, but to know all the little vineyards of Germany is a lifetime's work.

Quality Marks
The marks indicating quality are very simple.

Deutscher Tafelwein is totally West German table wine. (This is not to be confused with *Tafelwein* - West German table wine blended with up to 25 per cent of wines from other EEC wines.) *Deutscher Tafelwin:*
- can name a region but only in a modified form (Mosel not Mosel-Saar-Ruwer and may claim a district of origin (Bereich) but not a village name (Grosslage)
- must reach 5 to 6 per cent natural alcohol before sugar is added to aid fermentation

Landwein (country wine) is very similar.

Qualitätswein bestimmer Anbaugebeite (or QbA) is quality wine from a specific region (*Gebiet*) and is subject to official quality controls which are indicated in a test number on the label. Its rules are as follows.
- Sugar may be added to aid fermentation.
- It can be a blend from several vineyards producing wine of a certain style.
- It must name its region of origin (*Gebiet*).
- It can name its vineyard (if 85 per cent of the grapes were grown there).
- It can say if it is estate bottled or is bottled by the grower, or give the vintage.

Qualitätswein mit Prädikat (or QmP) covers all top quality, natural, unsweetened quality wine, and is strictly controlled and must carry a test number.
- It can give every detail of where it was made.
- The grapes must be approved varieties and be from a single area (*Bereich*).
- It may give the vintage one of the following names which indicate the grapes' harvesting and potential alcohol level.

Kabinett is made from fully ripened grapes harvested

at the normal time, and is elegant and mature.

Spätlese comes from grapes harvested at least 7 days after the usual harvesting date for the particular grape. Spätlese ranges from bone dry to full and rich.

Auslese is particularly elegant and is made from fully ripe grapes carefully selected and separately pressed; the result is usually medium sweet to very rich.

Beerenauslese is made with selected overripe grapes affected by botrytis (noble rot) which gives an intense honey-like flavour and a mature, fruity wine with a very distinct nose and taste.

Eiswein is one of the curiosities of Germany. It is wine made from grapes of Beerenauslese age and quality which have frozen on the vine and are hand-picked and pressed while still frozen to produce a wine of extraordinary fruitiness and concentration.

Trockenbeerenauslese comes from selected grapes left to shrivel on the vines, giving a wine with great concentration and a fine style.

These also give you some idea of its sweetness. Germany is currently ultra-sensitive about its wine being described as sweet and its wine authorities tend to deny the sweetness of wines which are undeniably so. A pity, as Germany has excellent wine which really *is* dry.

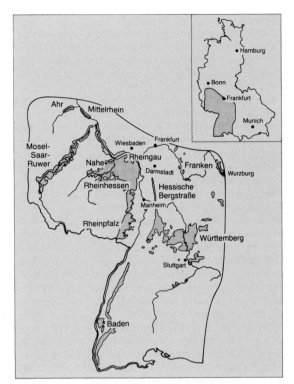

Vines
Although Germany does make red wine almost all the exported wine is white. Riesling used to be the most widely planted vine in Germany. It still holds the crown for quality, but in volume it has been ousted by the more prolific Müller-Thurgau. The other vines grown for white wine are Sylvaner, Kerner, Gewürztraminer, Rulander (Pinot Gris), Scheurebe and Morio-Muskat (a very flowery muscaty wine). Red wine is seldom exported and only a tiny amount produced.

Where the Wine is Made
Germany plays stacking boxes with the names of the areas where wine is made, establishing large areas and then dividing and subdividing them. The basic division is into 11 wine producing regions, or *Anbaugebiete*, whose names can be found on most labels. All of them are clustered along the banks of the Mosel and Rhine rivers and their tributaries.

Each region has its own characteristics, but in Germany there are often sharp changes of soil, even between different sections of the same vineyard, and the steep slopes of the river valleys where most of the vineyards lie constantly meander, so each section catches the sun at different times. These variations can even create marked differences in the flavour of two wines made from different sections of a single vineyard.

Whether you regard the unpredictability this produces as fascinating or infuriating is a matter of temperament. Either way, it needs to be borne in mind. But not all the regions sell to Britain.

The **Baden** occupies the fringes of the Black Forest facing Alsace, and a tiny area round Lake Constance. It is not Germany's most distinguished area and relatively little

Baden wine reaches Britain. However, Ortenau, near Baden Baden, has some famous wine houses which produce fine Riesling (called Klingelburger in that area), Traminer and Rulander wines. And Baden Baden also has excellent carafe Riesling, called 'Mauerwein'.

If you you see a German label on a flagon-shaped bottle, like Mateus rosé, you know instantly that it's from **Franconia**. Germans like to call it 'masculine' wine. It is often drier than most other German wines, fuller bodied and a touch flintier. One of the remarkable features of Franconia is that its wine has kept for extraordinary lengths of time without spoiling. According to reports, wine made here in 1540 was found to be still drinkable in this century.

The Germans regard the terraced vineyards flanking the steep slopes of three key rivers as a single area and wine is labelled **Mosel-Saar-Ruwer**. The region is a mass of small vineyards dominated by Riesling grapes which draw a certain flintiness from the slatey soil, especially in the Saar area, which gives the wine a clean clear finish. The wines have high natural acidity but are fresh, light and well balanced.

The Saar area is cold and the quality of wines here varies immensely from year to year. In a warm year the wine is superb, in a cold one it can be undrinkable. The most outstanding estate is Wiltingen Schwarzhofberg - but look for that *hof* in the middle; the overall name for the whole Saar area is the same but for the *hof*. The Ruwer is a mere stream off the Mosel River, and the tiny vine growing area around it is as variable as the Saar. But when conditions are right its wines are Germany's most delicate; gentle yet infinitely fine and full of subtlety.

The **Nahe** is a slightly terraced region above the River Nahe, with three totally different types of soil. The two *Bereichs* are Schlossböckelheim and Kreuznach and there are very good growers within both. The wine is white and delicate.

Rheingau is the *crème de la crème* of German wine areas and its major growers include a prince and a bevy of lesser nobles. To the north the Taunus mountains protect it, and the width of the Rhine at this point reflects the sun on to the vines, giving the area a uniquely mild climate which can even grow figs and lemons in the open. It includes the Hochheim district, which gave its name to hock, as well as good Mosel regions. Riesling vines excel, producing wines of great elegance and balance, but at the extreme west Pinot Noir grapes are used to make that rare thing - an interesting German red wine - Assmannshausen.

Rheinhessen lies south of Rheingau and the best known wine of the region is light, fruity Liebfraumilch. But there are a few very good vineyards and bottles carrying the *grosslage* name of Rehbach, near Nierstein, are well worth looking out for.

The **Rheinpfalz** (or Palatinate) was an important wine area in Charlemagne's time, and the good climate favours techniques using late gathered grapes to produce richly sweet wine. Some of the regions wines, by producers like Bürklin-Wolf, can be excellent but much of its output is simply table wine.

Regions within Regions

Each of the wine regions above is subdivided into smaller areas, and yet smaller ones. And these may appear on the labels. They go like this.
- The regions (*Anbau Gebeit*) are divided into districts (*Bereich*).
- Each *Bereich* is divided into *Grosslagen* which are groups of vineyards which go by a collective name.
- The individual vineyards (*Einzellagen*) which make up a *Grosslage* are often named after a local landmark - such as a hill.

The snag is that the 1971 legislation which set up this structure chose names for quite ordinary areas which are either identical to, or almost indistinguishable from the names of very fine individual vineyards.

Styles

Certain names are associated with certain styles of wine, but they are not quite as they used to be.

Liebfraumilch no longer comes strictly from Rheinhessen, but has become a generic term for a medium sweet style from Nahe, Rheinhessen, Rheingau or Rheinpfalz.

Hock was once the wine from the Rhine town of Hochheim. Under EEC rules hock is now a generic term for any *Deutscher Tafelwein* from the Rhine, and any quality wine from one of the 8 Rhine regions.

In 1856, when the first edition of *Enquire Within* was printed, it was fashionable to dilute German wines with mixers of one kind and another. There are instructions for lemonade and Rheinish or Moselle wine mixed with water and the author gave this recipe for 'Summer Champagne':

> *To four parts seltzer water add one of Moselle wine (or hock), and put a teaspoonful of powdered sugar into a wineglass of this mixture; an ebullition takes place and you have a sort of champagne which is more wholesome in hot weather than the genuine wine known by that name.*

Seltzer water was a naturally sparkling mineral water from Weisbaden in Germany. Any of today's fizzy waters would probably stand proxy, but I wonder whether the recipe is not a trifle heavy with the water.

Words Used on Labels

Aus eigenem Lesegut: from the producer's estates
Diabetikerwein: diabetic wine (max 4 g. unfermented sugar per l.)
Edelfäule: botrytis (noble rot)
Eigene Abfüllung: estate bottled
Erzeugerabfüllung: estate bottled
Halbtrocken: semi-dry
Perlwein: carbonated wine
Rotwein: red wine
Schaumwein: sparkling wine
Schillerwein: rosé wine from mixed red and white grapes
Seewein: lake wine
Sekt: sparkling wine (with quality controls)
Trocken: dry
Weinkellerei: winery
Weissherbst: rosé wine from red grapes
Weisswein: white wine
Winzergenossenschaft: cooperative

Vintages

As German wines vary so much from one small area to another it is almost impossible to give set vintages but, of recent years, 1976 and 1983 have been the best.

German Wine Information Service, 114 Cromwell Road, London SW7 4ES Tel: 01 244 7558
Hugh Johnson, *Atlas of German Wines*, Mitchell Beazley

Italian Wines

Italian wine is like the Italians: individualistic, assertive and unpredictable. One of the best minor wines I have ever drunk was one I tasted when, after many flight delays, I tumbled exhausted into a Sicilian café just as it was closing for the night. With typical Italian generosity the owner stayed open and, hearing that I was writing about Italian food, gave me a bottle of his best wine - an astonishing brew, the colour of dilute red currant juice. Maybe it was the jet lag that made it taste ambrosial, or maybe it was one of the small unsung miracles of Sicily. I shall never know, for I was certain that I would never forget its name as long as I lived - and I did. I mention it only because it is typical that his best wine should have cut clean across all my preconceptions as to how wine should be. That is true of all Italian wine. It is disastrous to take to it the expectations created by French wine or to drink it with most French food. It is totally distinctive.

It has had time to gain its individuality: six centuries before Christ the Etruscans were making wine in the areas where Florence and Rome stand today, and even had a wine god - called Fufluns. And Italian wine making was so successful that in his *Natural History* of AD 70, Pliny was able to say - with perhaps some partiality - that 154 BC was the year in which Italy became the greatest wine growing country in the world.

Today, according to Burton Anderson in his excellent book *Vino*, Italy produces more than a fifth of the world's wine and accounts for more than a third of the world's exports. Unfortunately, Italy is seen as a place for popular wine rather than for good wine. It is, however, making some very good wines indeed, which deserve to be better known. They range from deliciously fragrant whites to full bodied concentrated reds.

Labelling
The revolutionary regulations passed by the Italian parliament in 1963 laid down three categories, but one was abolished by the EEC, leaving two, plus three EEC categories for typical local wine.

DOCG - *denominazione de origine controllata e garantita* (controlled and guaranteed denomination of origin) wines come from a highly select group of areas producing high quality wines under conditions of rigid quality control which specify the area, the grapes which may be used and how the wine must be made. Barolo, Barbaresco, Vino Nobile di Montepulciano and Brunello di Montalcino were the first four to be nominated, and there has been no rush of others to follow them, though Chianti and Albana di Romagna have just been added.

DOC - *Denominazione di origine controllata* (controlled denomination of origin) wines must come from one of over 200 designated zones, use grapes designated for the area and their production must conform to set rules. *Classico* on a DOC wine means it was made in the heart of the production zone.

Vini tipici (equivalent to French vins de pays characteristic wines) is a relatively new category, used for a wine typical of a certain area and type of grape - and these may be given on the label.

Vini da tavola con indicazione geographica (roughly, table wines with an indication of where they come from)

Vini da tavola (table wines).

Strictly speaking, the first three are quality wines, and that is the order of quality, and all the rest are mere table wines. But, with the Italians, nothing is ever quite that simple. Wine makers must put forward their wine for DOC status, and some makers of excellent wine just don't feel the letters are worth the hassle. Other very good wines use combinations of grapes which the bureaucrats never listed as permissible for DOC wines. So, some wines bearing only *vino da tavola* on the label can be as good as DOC wines, and better.

Some makers try to make up for this confusing situation by providing the consumer with extra information on additional labels. For example, producers' associations may place a seal near the neck of the bottle bearing the name of the association -

Example of a French wine label

① CHATEAU DES TOURS ②
1970
MONTAGNE-St-ÉMILION ③
④ Appellation Montagne-St-Émilion Contrôlée
LOUIS YERLÈS, PROPRIÉTAIRE ⑤
A MONTAGNE (GIRONDE) ⑥
⑦
IMPRIMÉ EN FRANCE ⑧

① The grower's château or vineyard.
② Bottled within the château.
③ The sub-region, of the St Émilion area, from which it comes.
④ Shows the area is AC.
⑤ The name of the château owner.
⑥ The French 'county' of origin.
⑦ The village within the Montagne AC wine area.
⑧ Made in France.

Example of an Italian wine label

① GAUDIO AMILCARE
1980 ②
③ GRIGNOLINO
DEL MONFERRATO CASALESE ④
⑤ denominazione di origine controllata
imbottigliato nella zona di produzione da ⑥
⑦ GAUDIO AMILCARE
BRICCO MONDALINO - VIGNALE MONFERRATO (AL) Italia ⑧
0,75 lt e ⑩   R1 N 20/ AL   ⑨ 11,5% Vol.

① Producer.
② The year of harvesting.
③ Type of wine.
④ Area of production.
⑤ From a DOC region.
⑥ Bottled where it was produced.
⑦ Name of the bottler.
⑧ Where it was bottled.
⑨ Alcohol content.
⑩ Quantity in the bottle.

consorzio - its symbol and a number. The best known of these is probably the black cockerel which has always distinguished Chianti Classico.

Recognizing Italian Wines

An Italian wine label can give a whole sequence of information which may or may not help you to know the type of wine you are buying. There are far too many DOC zones, and wines, in Italy to go into each. So it's more useful simply to consider the wines which are worth looking for.

Some Italian White Wine

Frascati is one of the few wines which tastes exactly like its name. Volcanic soil creates a pale golden wine, fresh without being acid, round but not sweet, full of flavour but still light. It is made in lots of small villages and wineries in the area near Rome and the standard isn't uniform. To find the best you need a good wine merchant.

Moscato d'Asti is lightly sparkling, only slightly sweet and full of soft flowery muscaty fruit. Not great or gorgeous but perfect with strawberries on a warm day. It is made by several wineries but Fontannafredda's can be charming and reasonably priced.

Soave is so well known that it is often bought. Look for the word '*classico*'. That way you stand a far better chance of getting a good wine, without youth it has nothing.

If you are looking for an inexpensive wine, try something from **Sicily**. Though legend has it that Bacchus first made wine here, it isn't one of the very distinguished areas, but its hot climate makes grape growing easy and produces wine in vast quantities. Most of it is shipped out in bulk tankers and Sicilians mutter darkly that it's funny how France 'produces' more wine than she has vines for. That leaves the better wine to be sold in bottles, and in my experience it is quite hard to find a bad Sicilian table wine. If you want to play safe, Corvo, Tonino and Regaleali Nozzo d'Oro are names you may find.

Types of Italian Red Wine

Barolo, the great red wine of Piedmont is often claimed to be the king of Italian wines. It's a deep wine with a beautiful bouquet and huge flavour, which normally needs 10 years of ageing, and a good vintage may live for 25. It needs big Italian flavours to go with it.

Barbaresco is another big red wine from Piedmont. Drier than Barolo, it also needs considerable ageing.

The lovely hilly landscape which formed the backdrop to so many Rennaisance paintings is excellent vine country and Tuscany can claim 3 out of the 6 DOCG wines: **Chianti, Brunello di Montalcino** and **Vino Nobile de Montepulcino.** All three are big red wines and the Nobile in particular is an aristocrat which needs long ageing to smoothe its tannin to velvet. The Chianti is an elegant classic which becomes finer with age. Look for a famous estate like Frescobaldi.

In Lombardy the DOC area of Valtellina has a useful 'family' of wines. They go by the splendidly literary names of **Inferno, Grumello** and **Sassella.** They need 6 to 12 years to mature and are lovely round wines not as distinguished as their Piedmont relatives but very worthwhile.

Recioto Amarone is one of the gems of the area near Venice and takes its name from the fact that it is made with the grapes from the upper rim of each bunch (the *orecchie* - ears). They produce this most distinguished dry velvety red.

There are so many varied wines in Italy that the only way to get to know them is to treat them as a voyage of discovery, travelling the shelves - if not the territory - to discover the ones you like. Michelangelo said of a dry white wine of Umbria that it 'kisses, licks, bites, thrusts and stings' - how many countries can claim even one such piquant seductress?

Keeping Italian Wines

Almost all Italian white wines need to be drunk within 1 to 2 years, the exceptions are the very sweet dessert wines, some of which will keep as long as 20 years. The reds are a different story and the rule is simple: the bigger the wine, and the more tannin when young, the longer it will need in bottle. The following times are recommended by the Italian wine authority and are the average for the wines concerned. Those from a poor year will be ready sooner; those from a good year may need longer.

Vines

It took two Italian professors 5 substantial volumes to describe all the grape varieties of Italy (compare this with the eight major vines used in West Germany). They entitled the work *Principi vitigni da vino coltivati in Italia* (*principal* vines cultivated in Italy for wine making) which suggests that minor ones remain undocumented. And Gianni Bonacina's 3-volume encyclopaedia of Italian wines lists 3,811 different wines made from this army of vines, though some make the number closer to 5,000. So this is a maze it is better not to venture into.

Words Used on Italian Wine Labels

abboccato: a sweet rather mild wine
amabile: medium sweet
annata: year of the vintage
ascuitto: dry
bianco: white
cannellino: sweet or medium sweet
cantina (cantine): wine cellar or winery
co-operativa viticola: wine co-operative
dolce: sweet
fattoria: wine growing estate
imbottigliato dal produttore all'origine: estate bottled
imbottigliato dal viticoltore: estate bottled
imbottigliato nella zona di produzione: bottled in the production zone (but not estate bottled)
infiascato in zona d'origine: put in flasks where it was grown
infiascato (or *imbottigliato*) *nello stabilimento:* put in flasks (or bottles) on the producer's premises

invecchiamento: ageing
liquoroso: a dessert wine fortified with alcohol
passito: wine from dried and semi-dried grapes
pastoso: medium sweet/mellow
profumato: heavily aromatic
rosso: red
secco: dry
semi-secco: medium dry
uva: grape
vendemmia: year of vintage
vino frizzante: slightly sparkling
vino liquoroso: sweet wine with 16-20 per cent alcohol
vino rosato: rosé
vino santo: an amber wine from grapes slightly dried between harvesting and pressing
vino spumante: sparkling
vino vecchio: wine aged 1-2 years beyond the legal minimum for its type (but younger than one marked *riserva*)
viticolore: wine grower
vitigno: grape variety

The terms *vecchio, stravecchio, riserva* and *riserva speciale* mean that the wine has been aged in barrel or bottle for a set time, which varies according to its type.

Wine from Italy, 37 Sackville Street, London W1X 2DR Tel: 01 439 2991
Burton Anderson, *Vino: the Wines and Winemakers of Italy,* Papermac - the perfect book to read before visiting if you want to drink well on a visit to Italy.
Nicholas Belfrage, *Life Beyond Lambrusco,* Sidgwick and Jackson

New Zealand Wine

New Zealand wine is one of the interesting, slightly unknown quantities of the wine trade. It's a bit like a child who has done great things at 'O' level and everyone is waiting to see how it will do in 'A' levels and university. 'Very promising - should do well' is what is being written on its reports at present. As yet, there isn't a lot of it about, but it is beginning to appear on the shelves of major supermarkets like Sainsbury's and it is also to be found from specialist wine merchants like Alex Findlater (page 136).

Although The Mission vineyard was established back in 1851, wine making in a big way only began in the early 1970s. So wineries are still learning which vines do well in what regions and learning the craft of wine making, but anyone who likes watching the development of something new could get a lot of pleasure from following New Zealand wines as they evolve.

Grapes

New Zealand is growing the top European varieties and they still give the stalkiness to the wine which is typical of young vines.

When bringing wines into Britain, New Zealand is governed by rules laid down by the EEC so grape varieties have to be declared on the label, but those representing under 15 per cent need not be mentioned. So some of the Cabernet Sauvignon/Merlot blends will seem to be simply Cabernet.

Area and Wineries

New Zealand already has designated wine growing areas which are accepted by the EEC but, as yet, the wineries are not well enough established for it to be sensible to talk about the characteristics of the individual areas, although Auckland does tend to produce better reds than whites and as an area, Hawkes Bay is outstanding. In the list below I have given some of the wineries worth looking out for. Among names you may find on the shelves, Montana and Cooks are big companies which have wine from all over New Zealand.

Designated Area	Wineries	Comments
North Island		
Gisborne	Matua Valley Wines Delegat's	light clean whites mainly from Chardonnay
Hawkes Bay	The Mission Brookfields Ngatarawa Te Mata Matua Valley Wines Delegat's	Probably the best Cabernet Sauvignon, with Merlot sometimes added. Also Chardonnay and Sauvignon Blanc
Henderson Valley Huapai Kumeu	Cooper's Creek Nobilo's	Cabernet and Merlot but some good Chardonnay and Gewürztraminer
Waimauku Matua Valley	Matua Valley Wines	Prize-winning Cabernet Sauvignon
South Island Blenheim	Corbans Hunter's Cloudy Bay	This region has dried river beds with good soil, and extremes of heat. Chardonnay, Sauvignon Blanc and Riesling do well. So Sauvignon Blanc is wood-aged to produce a *fumé* style wine. Prize-winning Sauvignon Blanc
Nelson	Weingut Siefried	Chardonnay and a Botrytis Riesling

Margaret Harvey (Fine Wines of New Zealand, P.O. Box 476, London NW5 2NZ Tel: 01 482 0093) will advise and supply mixed cases.

Portuguese Wine

Portugal isn't a country for great wines but it does have the sort of wines which most of us can both enjoy and afford. The best known are, of course, Mateus rosé - which hasn't looked back since Sachaverell Sitwell publicized it in the *Sunday Times* in 1951 - and *vinho verde* - one of the lightest, freshest wines for a hot day, and more fun than a lot of the fashionable Sauvignon Blancs. However, the great undervalued wines of Portugal are her really good reds which are full of body. Good partners for steak and joints, and very much to the British taste. The problem is picking them.

Portuguese wine labelling has always been vague and somewhat insular, with each region setting its own controls and doing its own thing. Now it is having to be unified and brought within the rules of the EEC, and this is not proving an easy process. As I write nobody is entirely sure what will and will not be approved.

At the same time the Portuguese wine making industry is in a state of flux. Vast EEC subsidies are being used to grub out old poor quality vines; new methods are being used to produce new styles of wine for the international market, and areas which have been sleepily producing good quaffing wine for the local population are suddenly realizing that making good wine can be a very profitable exercise.

At present most of Portugal's wine is made with traditional Portuguese grapes, but Cabernet Sauvignon and Merlot are starting to move in. Whether Portugal will manage to marry the best of the old with the best of the new, and to boost her overall standards without losing her beautifully idiosyncratic bottles only time will tell. But, for the moment, Portuguese wine is still relatively undiscovered and reasonably priced.

Labelling Portuguese Wine

In the current confusion two words stand out as being worth looking for: *garrafeira* and *reserva*. It is impossible to say whether one is better than the other as their application has never been very precise, and some producers have chosen to label their best wine *garrafeira*, while others have preferred *reserva*. In principle, however:

Reserva may only appear on the label of a wine of outstanding quality in a vintage year. In theory, it could appear on a red or a white wine. In practice, it is usually on a red.

Garrafeira may only appear on the label of a red wine of outstanding quality which has matured in casks for 2 years and for at least 1 year in bottle, and it is generally a wine with long keeping potential. As the law currently stands, it need not necessarily be entirely from one region, let alone one vineyard. The Portuguese blend even some of their best wines and see nothing wrong with doing so.

Either designation can be applied to any first class wine; it does not have to come from a designated area or have been subject to rules as to grapes or anything else. It has yet to be seen whether the EEC wine rules can accommodate either of these designations.

Classifying Portuguese Wine

Portuguese wine has 4 categories which may appear on the bottle.

Região Demarcada *(defined regions)* are areas set by the Portuguese government which have exclusive rights to make wines of a certain type, from specified grape varieties, and carrying a particular name. With any luck the EEC will accept the areas already designated. These are:

Algarve	Colares	Bucelas
Carcavelos	Madeira	Dão
Douro	Vinho verde	Moscat el de Setubal
Bairrada		

The labels of wines from these areas must give the vintage and the maker and say 'Região Demarcada' followed by the name of the region. The bottles also bear a long strip of paper, like a seal which runs up and over the cork (not to be confused with sealing wax seals applied by certain producers.

Vinho Regional *(regional wine)* covers 5 good wine making regions, which are not yet thought to produce quite such good wine as the *demarcada* regions. The division is arbitrary. Some of the good vineyards within these areas can produce better wine than some in the *demarcada* category. This means that small subdivisions are important and it looks as if under EEC rules these will probably be the names to look out for. The regions and their subdivisions are:

Região do Alentejo	Portalegre, Borba, Reguengos, Redondo, · Vidigueira
Região das Beiras	Lafoes, Moimenta da Biera/Tavora, Pinhel, Tarouca, Lamego, Castelo Rodrigo
Região de Estramadura	Alcobaça, Arruda, Alenquer, Cartaxo, Gaeiras, Torres, Azeitão, Arrabida
Região de Tras-os-Montes	Escostas da Nave, Valpacos, Vila Real, Chaves
Região do Ribatejo	Almeirim, Cartaxo, Chamusca, Santarem, Tomar, Coruche

★ If producers don't show any of these names on the label all is not lost - the producer's address, which is often on the label, should give it.

Vinho de Mesa Regional *(regional table wine)* are table wines and 85 per cent of the wine must come from a single defined wine making area. The regions allowed to make this wine are given above for 'regional wine'.

Vinho de Mesa (*table wine*) can be blends of wines from several regions. This doesn't have to mean that they are cheap and nasty. Some *Vinho de Mese* could be dignified as *garrafeira*, if the EEC can be persuaded to allow it.

Producers
In any of the maze-like labelling systems which beset the wine industry it can be useful to have a few reliable names to head for. These may not make the best wine but at least you can be sure it will be above a certain standard. Among those which stand out in Portugal are Caves Velhas, Sogrape, Fonseca and Beira Mar.

The Regions
Alentejo is not yet demarcada but likely to be. Its red wines are generally considered better than its whites and tend to be big plummy wines, quite high in alcohol. The cooperatives Borba, Redondo, Vidigueira and Reguengos are all said to produce the best quality.

Algarve is better known for its tourism than for its wine - and rightly so (**Carcavelos** too). Its production is small and there are better areas to import from.

Bairrada is a prime area and is dominated by the Baga grape which produces big fruity red wines which one nineteenth-century wine writer described as being a 'match for three men - one to drink it and the other two to support him afterwards'. Its wine can take as long as 20 to 30 years to soften and mature. These reds are easily recognized, as they are sold in claret-shaped bottles (with shoulders). The region also makes heavy, spicy whites.

Bucelas is a tiny area and only one firm makes wine here - Caves Velhas. The wine is a light fresh white, similar to Chablis, which is good with fish.

Colares is an extraordinary area, so sandy that vines are planted in exceedingly deep trenches. It is noted for its red wines which need to mature slowly to acquire the deep richness which makes them ideal with game. The white wine tends to be disappointing.

Dāo is one of the biggest wine producing and exporting regions, with production dominated by co-operatives. You seldom find *quintas* or single estates on Dāo labels, but the wine is remarkably consistent. If you like one bottle you will probably like the next from a different firm.

The region has its own strict regulations. On the whole, the Dāo reds are far better than the whites, with a smoothness which comes from slow fermentation. The best recent years have been '70, '80, '83 and '85, but '71, '74, '76 and '78 were all good.

Ribatejo is not a demarcated area but worth looking out for. It is the home of some of Portugal's best *garrafiera* wines. Among the producers to look for are Carvalho, Ribeiro of Ferreira, Caves Velhas.

Setúbal is the home of Moscatel de Setúbal. Rated one of the world's best dessert wines it is fortified and needs long ageing to reach its prime. The 20-year-old is the one to buy. This area is also the home of good basic reds and of a few wines of *garrafiera* quality.

Vinho Verde is both a region and a style of wine which is made there. It is a most confusing name for one of Portugal's most distinctive wines. Literally, it means 'green wine', but green not in colour but in the sense of youthfulness, for, contrary to popular belief, *vinho verde* can be either red or white. It is deliberately made to drink in the year following the harvest and, instead of tasting rough and immature, it is dry, light and delicate with a faint natural fizz. Go for a bottle with Quinta, Solar or Palacio on the label. It will have been made by a small vineyard and is likely to be a more fragrant wine than the *vinho verde* of a large cooperative.

> If you have been wondering where Mateus rosé is made the answer is that it originally came from Vila Real but its production has spread to several other regions. So it has no real location.

Keeping Portuguese Wine
The wine with the briefest life is *vinho verde*, which must drunk before the next harvest, but all Portuguese white wine is best drunk within 1 to 2 years. The sole exception to this is white wine from Colares which usually needs to be aged for 4 to 5 years. Most Portuguese red wine is big with quite a lot of tannin and needs several years to age, and Bairrada and Dāo will often need 10 years in cellar. The Colares red is even bigger and is quite likely to reach its peak after 20 years and may go on for a long while after that.

Words which Appear on Labels
adamado	sweet
adega	cellar
aguardente	brandy
branco	white
clarete	rosé
colheita	vintage
doce	sweet
espumante	sparkling
maduro	matured
quinta	farm or estate
sêco	dry
tinto	red
vinho	wine

Vintages
If a year is good in one part of Portugal it is usually good in most. The very best years have been: '66, '70, '75, '80, '83, '85. An exception is '78 which was excellent in Bairrada but not elsewhere.

Portuguese Government Trade Office (Wine Division), New Bond Street House, 1-5 New Bond Street, London W1Y 5AP Tel: 01 935 6140

Jan Read, *The Wines of Portugal*, Faber and Faber

Spanish Wine
Occasionally one encounters a wine which has the velvety smoothness of brushing a face of a pansy against one's cheek. One such was a Rioja bought for me in New

York by an Englishman who had lived long in Spain and knew what to look for. It is one of the qualities of a fine wine to linger long in the memory.

I mention that wine simply to show that not all the best Riojas (pronounced Ree-oka) are kept in Spain, nor is it the mere table wine which is so widely sold. So far as most people are concerned Rioja *is* Spanish wine, but unfortunately it is suffering from its own success. In 1986 Britain imported 17 times as much Rioja as it had 10 years earlier, inevitably much of it being from the more commercial vineyards - with a predictable fall from grace.

Recently there has been a revolution in Spain's white wines and cold fermentation in stainless steel has replaced the traditional wooden casks, to produce a new style of wine. The wineries of Rioja, Navarra La Mancha and Penedés are leading the way in this. In the hands of some of the better makers this technique has produced whites with a totally new delicacy and freshness, but some of this generation are also thin and lacking in appeal.

Labels on Spanish Wines
The labels which currently appear on Spanish wines follow the rules Spain herself has set. But as I write these are being reviewed by the EEC, so things could be about to change.

There are 30 named Spanish wine areas (*denóminacion de origen*) - equivalent to the French *Appellation Contrôlée* - and each area has its own organization (*consejo regulador*) which sets the rules for that particular area.

Rioja Labels
Rioja is the most important red wine and a long established board of control sets strict standards.

The **Gran Reserva** Riojas are only made in the very best vintages and must spend 2 years in casks and 3 years in bottles, or vice versa, before they leave their maker. They age beautifully.

The **Reservas** are only made in a good harvest and must be aged in cask and bottle for a total of 4 years before being sold.

A Rioja marked **'Vino de Crianza'** or **'Con Crianza'** must spend a year in casks and not be sold until it is 3 years old.

Sin Crianza is just a basic Rioja with no special standing. Rioja can also be white; it is one of Spain's only really drinkable white wines and two names to look for are Marqués de Murrieta and Monopole.

Catalonia - Penedés and Carra
The best known wine of Catalonia is probably Freixenet - the black-labelled champagne-style white which undercuts the cheapest champagne by a couple of pounds. But the wines which everyone is admiring are the red wines produced by the Torrés winery, such as the prize-winning Torrés Gran Coronas Reserva Black Label made from Cabernet grapes. This house also has well-made inexpensive wines like Tres Torrés Sangredetorro and Coronas, and various others with Coronas in the name. The best need 3 to 4 years in bottle.

Castilla-Leon
The great wine of this region of old Castile is the red wine of the *bodega* called Vega Sicilia, which some claim to be Spain's greatest red wine. It is aged for 10 years in oak before being bottled and sold as Vega Sicilia, but part of any vintage is bottled earlier and sold as Valbueña. Vega Sicilia also happens to be Spain's most expensive wine.

Navarra
Navarra, which nestles close to Rioja, used to produce the favourite wine of Catherine the Great of Russia. Today it seems to be producing the favourite Spanish wine of my local wine merchant. These are not the big reds of old, but fresh cold fermented whites, and fruity rosés which appeal to the British palate. Chivité is a good *bodega* to look out for.

Vintages
Very good and very bad years - those in brackets are bad.

Penedés red 67, (68) 70, (72) 73 74, 78, 80, 81, 82,
Penedés white 66, (72) 73, 75, 77, 78, 81, 82, 84,
Rioja 70, (71) (72) (77) 81, 82, 85
Navarra 78, 81, 82, 83, 85

Words which Appear on Labels
año	year
blanco	white
bodega	cellar/winery
cepa	the variety of wine or grape
clarete	a light red wine
cosecha	vintage
criado y embotellado por...	grown and bottled by...
dulce	sweet
elaborado y anejado por...	made and aged by ...

embotellado de origen	estate bottled
engarrafado de origen	estate bottled
espumoso	sparkling
rosado	rosé
seco	dry
tinto	red
vendimia	harvest
viña or *viñedo*	vineyard
vino de cosecho propria	wine made by the proprietor
vino de mesa	table wine

Jan Read, *The Wines of Spain*, Faber and Faber
Jan Read, *Wines of Rioja*, Sotheby publication
Wines from Spain, 22 Manchester Square, London W1M 5AP
Tel: 01 935 6140

Home-made Wine

Some may feel that mention of home-made wine has no place alongside serious grape wines. I disagree. Nobody pretends that apple crumble is *haute cuisine* but very good it is, and life would be the poorer without such pleasures. The same holds true of home-made wine.

Having fond memories of childhood sips of rhubarb champagne, I had intended to include a list of organizations to join if you wanted to find out about making home-made wine. Alas, although wine is made all over Britain, my researches have failed to reveal a suitable organization. Instead I refer you to some books which, I am told by a wine-making enthusiast of many years standing, could set you on the road. I list them in order of sophistication, starting with those most suited to a beginner:

C. J. Berry, *First Steps in Wine Making*, Argus Books
Bryan Acton and Peter Duncan, *Making Wines Like Those you Buy*, Argus Books
Bryan Acton, *Recipes for Prize Winning Wines*, Argus Books
Bryan Acton and Peter Duncan, *Progressive Wine Making*, Argus Books

Being lured as much by the romantic nostalgia of wine making as by the results I have a soft spot for a charming little book by Molly Harris, who plays Martha in 'The Archers'. Called *A Drop o' Wine*, it makes wine making sound as easy as it truly is. The wines don't pretend to be like those you buy; the very essence is that you can only enjoy them by making them, so there are recipes for 'Bramble tip wine', Crab Apple wine, Parsnip wine and even - though it stretches the imagination - Parsley brandy.

A Few Tips

★ One thing which books never seem to tell you is that new corks will only go into a wine bottle if they have been well soaked in hot water first. Put them to soak in a jug, then you can keep them below the surface of the water by putting a cup in the top.
★ If you don't have a cellar where corks can blow off in safety, as the wine continues its fermentation, buy a demijohn with an airlock.
★ Two tips which Molly Harris gives are that you can make perfectly good wine with dried yeast, and that if a wine comes out too dry you can put it right by adding ½ fluid ounce of glycerine to each pint of wine.
★ When wine is being made it needs to be in about the same temperature that you would like to work in - the mid-sixties Fahrenheit - but not in full sun or it will fade.
★ To decant wine, or indeed beer, from a large container into bottles you will need a length of plastic tubing. To transfer the liquid out you simply put one end of the tube in the liquid - being careful not to let it go down into any sediment at the bottom. Then suck the liquid up the tube (not hygienic, but traditional and effective). Pop your thumb quickly over the end, so the liquid is held in the tube, and put it into a bottle which is standing lower than your main container. Spills always happen, so it's useful to stand the bottle in a bowl. It also helps if you can have the whole of the container higher than the bottle.
★ Keep metal away from wine - plastic and glass are better. Keep flies away too, especially the tiny fruit flies which like nothing better.
★ Wine making equipment *must* be well sterilized, each time, before use with camden tablets (from chemists).

You don't have to scour the country for the basics for wine making. Most of what you need can be found at the larger branches of Boots, and Self-Sufficiency and Smallholding Supplies (see under Mail Order in Domestic Matters) has most of the others by mail order.

Ginger Beer

Wine is by no means the only drink you can make at home. The 1856 edition of *Enquire Within* was rich in recipes for home-made drinks; among them the recipe for ginger beer, which I include because one never can find a recipe when in the mood to make it. The quantities are large but can easily be halved or quartered.

> *White sugar, twenty pounds; lemon or lime juice, eighteen (fluid) ounces; honey, one pound; bruised ginger, twenty two ounces; water, eighteen gallons. Boil the ginger in three gallons of water for half an hour, then add the sugar, the juice, and the honey, with the remainder of the water, and strain through a cloth. When cold add the white of one egg, and half an ounce of essence of lemon; after standing four days, bottle.*

Home-made beer can also be an interesting thirst quencher but I can only endorse the words of my predecessor - although he does somewhat overemphasize the difficulty.

> *The brewing of home-made drinks has to a very great extent gone out of late years, even in country places; and therefore we have little inducement to occupy our limited space with the lengthy directions necessary to constitute a practical essay upon brewing. To those who wish to enter on this practice, without any previous knowledge, we would advise their calling in the aid of some one practically acquainted with the process for the first operation. By so doing they will save themselves a great deal of trouble, disappointment and expense.*
> *Enquire Within*, 1856

Domestic Matters

Cleaning • Clothing and Shoe Care •
Equipping a Home • Laundry, Stains and All That
• Mail Order • Pests •

CLEANING

I shall never forget a friend of mine returning aghast from a stint as an au pair in Germany and recounting how she had been made to scrub the trunks of the trees nearest the house. In contrast, when Katherine Whitehorn wrote an article about how to be a bit of a slut, and sweep the dirt under the carpet, she was showered with letters from women who felt they could now own up to being less than perfect housewives. However, sluttishness is no modern development. This piece of advice appeared in the 1856 edition of *Enquire Within*.

> *Never put away plate, knives and forks, &c. uncleaned, or sad inconvenience will arise when the articles are wanted.*

Most of us are far too busy to keep a house *perfectly* clean - unless we employ someone else to do it. Between slobbishness and tree scrubbing there is a happy medium. But the art is keeping everything at the level with which *you* feel comfortable, not trying to conform to some mythical norm of what a good housewife or househusband would do.

The essence of cutting down work is to know exactly what to use for what. So I have tried to deal with every type of surface that you might possibly want to clean and give the fastest and safest way to clean each. In choosing the methods and products to use on fine surfaces I have been advised by those working in museum conservation departments. However, if a valuable object may need special treatment, any museum with fine objects and furniture will advise you.

Choosing Cleaning Products

You will find very few brand names here. This is either because there is very little to choose between one brand and another or because there are good reasons for not recommending one.

I have a private passion for science and technology, which makes me a natural audience for the latest miracle product. Yet I keep coming back to so-called 'old-fashioned' basics because they get faster and better results. I realize that it is hard not to have a sneaking worry that one is somehow doing second best. This isn't surprising. Multi-billion pound industries have spent fortunes making us feel like that. But if you feel guilty using basics remember it's big brother from the chemical industries whispering in your ear, not common sense.

> Used correctly, basics like paraffin, ammonia, white spirit, acetone and turpentine are often better than many branded products. But such chemicals should not be breathed in, and some people can develop an allergic reaction to some of them. This reaction may not occur at first, but acute sensitivity can develop after repeated exposures. So rubber gloves should always be worn when handling these — or other — household chemicals and the windows should be open.

> If you are still tempted to use modern spray-on cleaners, the Friends of the Earth (see Free Time) has a list of those which won't destroy the ozone layer.

Saving Time and Money

The greatest time saver is to make more use of the cheapest and, arguably, the most powerful and versatile chemical we have in the home - H_2O - water. Experts in the top public health laboratory in Britain say water is better than most disinfectants at removing harmful bacteria from surfaces. What's more, leaving water to work away quietly will halve the general cleaning. So, fill dirty pans with water the instant you empty them, leave little pools of water (or wet sponge cloths) on top of awkward marks and stains - on cookers, work surfaces and floors, and soak clothes which need to be washed.

> I do *not*, of course, suggest that you soak clothes which should not be soaked (page 186 onwards), or use water where it could cause damage or an electrical hazard.

The other great saver is to stop using all the products you don't need to use. Every new product not only costs money but also time, when you fetch it from the cupboard.

Basic Equipment

While far too much is often spent on cleaning products, far too little tends to be spent on basic equipment for cleaning jobs. Half the homes in Britain are probably washing up with one washing-up implement, be it brush or cloth. Cleaning is done so often that whoever does it deserves the best equipment the household can afford.

The minimum kit for washing up is a washing-up brush, a looped scourer (for egg and substances which clog other scourers) and an abrasive nylon pad. A bottle brush is a good idea too. There should also be an old abrasive pad for cleaning surfaces like the stove, and perhaps soap-filled pads for bringing up metal or getting stubborn stains off pyrex. In any kitchen there should also be *two* wiping down cloths - one for the kitchen surfaces and the sink, and another for the floor. A cloth which has been used for wiping the floor should *never* be used on anything to do with food preparation or washing up. To put it frankly we all walk on pavements which animals have used as lavatories. We walk traces of that on to our floors. To wipe the floor with a cloth and then wipe the kitchen surface is to transfer such substances to our food. Not a pretty thought.

When it comes to ordinary household cleaning there is an equal need for good equipment. Not only is a vacuum cleaner essential but it is almost as necessary to have a small hand-vacuum, such as a Dustbuster or one like a plastic can on wheels with a long trunk, such as that made by Rowenta, which will clean stairs easily and get up on to curtain tops or into corners. Besides an ordinary duster, a long-handled furry or feathery duster saves a lot of stretching and bending, and instead of cleaning basins with soft cloths, which make hard work of it, use one of the nylon abrasive pads sold for saucepans (but don't use the abrasive side on taps). And keep old toothbrushes for getting into all the awkward places.

With the right equipment and the right products cleaning takes very little time: with the wrong ones it can be a great waste of time.

Disinfecting and Sterilizing

We are bombarded by advertisements which tell us that product X or Y kills germs. That is only part of the story.

Sterilization kills all known germs (viruses, bacteria). For true sterilization you need to heat something to 121°C (249.8°F) for at least 15 minutes with enough liquid to create steam: just possible in some pressure cookers. (Dry heat sterilization in an oven needs 160°C (320°F) for 45 minutes.) The only other method practical for the home is burning - you needn't worry that it will release germs into the air: the particles will be sterile.

Any disinfectant only kills a certain *range* of germs and under certain conditions, and it won't usually kill the spores (see above right). Bleaches, for example, kill

a wide range; phenolics (Dettol, Izal and so on) vary in their effectiveness with the particular formulation and pine disinfectants tend to be fairly limited.

Contrary to what advertisements would have us believe, the *most* effective way to disinfect anything is simply to use water. Germs wash off. What's more, spores, which are not killed by chemicals, are removed by thorough cleaning with hot water. Use a good detergent on most surfaces, and washing soda (with rubber gloves on) where there is grease. The only place in most homes that needs regular disinfectant is the lavatory — as you can't wash it with hot water.

Regular Cleaning

The counsel of perfection is to clean almost everything every day, and clean one room very thoroughly every week. It makes for a marvellously clean house and a dreadfully dull life. The counsel of sanity and efficiency is to clean certain key areas, like the kitchen and basins, every day and then do all the others in rotation according to where you live, how much the rooms are used and how clean you like things to be.

Adhesives

To peel off a self-adhesive label put a piece of foil over it, iron it lightly with a hot iron and peel it off while still warm. The same method works for sellotape. If the label is on the outside of a plastic container just fill the container with the hottest water it can stand, wait for the heat to act on the glue, and peel the label off. If a residue of glue is left it can usually be removed with methylated spirits. But beware of using this on some fabrics or on wallpaper (see A Roof Over Your Head).

When young, Blu-tack will roll off most surfaces if gently rubbed, but it gets cantankerous in its old age and refuses to budge. At this stage if you roll the tacky side of masking tape over it, it will usually come away. But on wallpaper the masking tape may take the paper with it.

Alabaster

Alabaster is often mistaken for marble. In fact, it is far more fragile and dissolves in water. It is not porous like marble, but it is far softer. Use a perfectly clean dry duster, or if moisture is essential, a rag *just* moistened with a *very little* white spirit.

Armour and Arms

Both armour and all kinds of armaments which are purely for display, need to be cared for as to their metal, with moving parts oiled with a fine oil such as WD40. Keep them in rooms which are free from damp.

Bakelite and Celluloid

If you live in a old house with bakelite light switches the best cleaner is Duraglit metal polish wadding. This is just as effective on celluloid. Remove every trace with a soft cloth.

Baking Tins

If baking tins become encrusted with burnt-on food you

can soften the whole crust to a removable state by boiling the tins in a pan with a good handful of washing soda. The worse the dirt, the longer the boil; leave very dirty ones in the pan to soak overnight after boiling. But don't use soda in or on an aluminium pan as it will pit it.

Baths

It is sheer masochism to use an abrasive cleaner on a bath. Once you remove the glassy surface with the abrasive the bath becomes twice as hard to keep clean. Instead install a big bath-cleaning brush and a bottle of thickish washing-up liquid in the bathroom. This means each person in the family can put a little washing-up liquid on the bristles, scrub round the tide mark and splash the soap off with the remaining water before it runs out. So that's *one* job the 'houseperson' doesn't have to do.

To clean an already grimy bath, paraffin can make short work of both tide-marks and limescale. It also does a good job on taps. But it leaves a dreadful smell which needs thorough rinsing.

To treat an even greasier bath fill it with hot water and add several cupfuls of washing soda. Swish it around to dissolve it and leave it overnight. Next morning brush it out with a stiff bath brush.

Stains on a Bath

You can buy products to remove bath stains, but I find they work no better than home remedies, and cost more.

The brownish crusty deposit which forms if hard water lies round a plug hole, or drips from a tap, can be removed with hot vinegar and salt. Apply it with an old toothbrush, leave it to work for at least 15 minutes, then scrape it off with the end of the toothbrush handle. Don't be tempted to scrape it with metal or you will scratch the bath surface and make it harder to clean next time. On bad stains you may need to repeat the salt and vinegar several times. This mixture can also be used to remove water deposits from shower coils.

Rust marks can usually be bleached out with a mixture of salt and lemon juice or lemon juice and borax. Leave the paste in little heaps over the stain and keep remoistening with lemon juice for a day or two or rub rust stains on white baths with a little hydrogen peroxide.

Blinds

Festooned blinds need to be regularly vacuumed with a trunk-style vacuum cleaner. When spring cleaning they need to be dry-cleaned or washed - according to the fabric.

Roller blinds which can't be washed can be cleaned by rolling a ball of dough across them which you have made from flour and water. It needs to have the texture of pastry, so it leaves no trace behind.

To clean Venetian blinds run an L, made from a crust of new bread, along each slat, replacing it when it becomes too dusty. Alternatively, wear a pair of old cotton gloves, moisten them and run the slats between your fingers.

Bolts

Give unused bolts a slide each time you clean whatever they are on. Once a year they also benefit from some graphite or a drop of penetrating oil (watch that it doesn't drip on to pale wood, fabrics or carpets). Apply this to French windows at the end of summer; then they won't be immovable by spring.

Books

Both heat and moisture are enemies of books and friends of the moulds and insects which can destroy them. The ideal temperature is about 15°C (60°F) with low humidity and a good circulation of air. Store them with their spines outwards, unless they are too big to put on any shelf, in which case they are best lying flat. If they need protection use acid-free board (see page 171).

To dust books, brush the pages clean with a dry shaving brush, or run a vacuum nozzle over, while holding them closed. But be careful with nozzles near good books; it is easy to scratch and damage them.

For fine leather bindings I was given this recipe by one of Britain's top book restorers. Take equal quantities of *pure* lanolin (from a chemist) and neatsfoot oil (from a saddler) and mix them together over warm water until they form a smooth cream. Apply this once a year to leather bindings, with a clean soft cloth, rubbing it gently in and polishing it off. The mixture can be used over the gilding and is just as good for leather desk tops as for books.

If you spill water on a book you can usually stop the paper distorting by patting it dry immediately and drying it at once with a hair dryer.

Brass and Copper

Brass and copper need different types of cleaning and different degrees of shine according to where they are. Modern brass of no value can be cleaned with any brass polish, but Solvol Autosol - a chrome cleaner from auto-accessory shops - is recommended by some conservationists, and cleans my brass faster than any other brass cleaner.

If brass knobs and handles on valueless objects, such as modern front doors, need a thorough polish, make a cardboard shield with a hole cut out to the exact shape of the metal and slip it over to protect the paint. There is also a strong argument for saving all this work and lacquering them (see below).

Brass on Fine Furniture

Where brass is on furniture don't attempt to bring it up to a fine shine with metal polish. To do so is to risk permanent damage to the wood, and antique furniture with brass ornamentation is not meant to look as shiny as a row of horse brasses. A regular rub with a clean fabric duster or polishing glove is all the care it needs. If handles are deeply dirty they can be removed and cleaned before being carefully replaced in exactly the same positions. Label each one as you remove it (marked 'top left' etc.).

Lightly tarnished brass and copper can be cleaned with Goddard's Long-term Silver Cloth, but keep a separate cloth for each metal, and a third for silver.

If inlay is deeply tarnished it can be cleaned with infinite care by rubbing with powdered charcoal, or fine oil and whiting (see page 171), on the end of a cotton bud or 0000 wire wool (000 is too coarse and will scratch the surface). Take care the wood is not rubbed at all, and be constantly aware of the danger of removing, or blunting the definition of fine patterning in the metal. Tarnish is infinitely preferable - and diminishes the value of an antique far less. Once a shine is achieved you can polish both the wood and the metal with Renaissance Wax (see page 171), a special polish developed for museums which will retain the shine.

Verdigris
Verdigris is a greenish deposit on brass or copper. A wipe with neat ammonia will remove it instantly. Rinse the ammonia off afterwards and dry the metal.

Very Tarnished
If brass or copper, of no value, is tarnished to almost black wipe it over with hot vinegar and salt (the proportions don't much matter). This will lift deep tarnish with amazing speed, but wipe it off before it dries on the metal, or you will put petrol-blue stains into the brass which are very hard to remove.

The other danger with salt and vinegar is of causing 'bronze disease' in which the metal weakens so badly that it can even fall apart. It is rare but can be triggered by any chloride - such as salt or washing soda. So this is not a treatment to use on the family heirlooms.

Another treatment for deeply tarnished brass and copper, which can even be used when rust has set in, is a solution of citric, tartaric or oxalic acid. The amount you need to use depends on the state of the metal. Start with about 15 g (½ oz) in ½ l (1 pt) water, and use hot water if you want to boost the effect, as all acids are more active when hot. Simply swab the solution on to the metal (out of doors or with floors well protected) - without getting it on yourself or near children and pets. Then leave it for a little while to eat off the tarnish, and rinse it off. If the strength is right it will reveal yellow metal and even remove ancient rust. From there, polishing is a relatively easy job.

Lacquered
Acrylic lacquer can cut down on cleaning but it's important to choose one which both goes on easily and stays on well, but comes off easily once the first breaks in its surface appear. One of Britain's top experts on metal conservation recommends Ercalene (see page 171). Most lacquers will come off with either acetone or methylated spirit. But these will damage polished furniture, so brass handles must be removed before you strip them.

Bronze
Bronze needs the utmost care. It has recently been realized that water can harm bronze and there is the additional risk that chlorides in many cleaning fluids can trigger bronze disease (see Brass). It can also be damaged by numerous other substances and it should not be washed, polished or cleaned with spirits.

Polishing is especially harmful because it removes the patination which is an essential part of its character. Just brush it clean *very* occasionally with a very clean soft brush, and carefully use a cotton bud to remove the dirt from the crevices.

Brushes

Hairbrushes
It's amazing how often people forget to wash their hairbrushes. Most just need soap on a nailbrush, but real bristle hairbrushes need more care. Put a teaspoon of washing soda and a few drops of ammonia in a basin of warm water and tap the bristles gently in this, *without* getting the roots of them wet. Rinse in the same way, and dry, bristle down, away from direct heat.

G.B. Kent and Son Plc (London Road, Apsley, Hemel Hempstead, Herts HP3 9SA Tel: 0442 51531) - will rebristle old-fashioned hairbrushes.

Shoe Brushes
The clogged polish will float off shoe brushes if you just stand the tips of the bristles in white spirit. Pat the brush up and down in the spirit, then stand it on thick newspaper to drain before rinsing the spirit out in water and washing-up liquid - without getting the wood wet or the bristles will loosen.

Cane, Bamboo, Rush and Coconut Matting
These are all easily discoloured by soap. Instead, they should be scrubbed with strongly salted water then with clear water. However, with coconut matting there is a slight risk of a tide mark. So do a test patch first where it won't show and let it dry totally.

If they have become greasy add a few drops of ammonia to the water. If yellow scrub it with a solution of ½ teaspoon oxalic acid in 500 ml (1 pt) water and let it dry naturally. But keep the acid off your skin and away from pets and children. If any marks remain try removing them with methylated spirit.

Chair seats in cane or rush which have sagged should be washed equally on both sides, so that they tighten up evenly.

The experts in the National Trust find that rush matting lasts longest if it is kept moist. This means that on wood floors in dry houses it needs to be watered several times a week.

Carpets

Care
In the first few weeks of a new carpet's life it should be vacuumed as little as possible (some say not at all for 6 weeks) so as to allow the weight of people to bed the fibres together. This is especially true of wool carpets.

The biggest danger to carpets is grit, which can cut into the pile. So, after the first weeks any carpet should be vacuumed regularly, using an upright cleaner for velvet piles, but a plain suction cleaner for loop or shag piles (the brush type roughs them up and spoils the surface).

To remove the dust left round the edge of a room by an upright hoover by far the easiest tool is a small battery-operated cleaner like the Dustbuster, which is also invaluable for stairs, crumbs and cars. Failing that, use a trunk-style vacuum or put on a pair of old rubber gloves (of the soft rubbery sort) and brush with your fingers. This is less tiring than using a hand brush and raises less dust. Rake very long piles with a pile rake.

Stair carpets easily wear through on the edge of each step. To avoid this, move the carpet a few inches up or down each year - or even every 6 months, if it's well trodden. Loose carpets in rooms can also be turned round so the wear is distributed more evenly.

★ Rub a burn instantly with a cut potato to minimize the damage. The only way to remove the brown mark is careful clipping with nail scissors.
★ Dents in carpets will usually vanish overnight if you leave an ice cube on them, but wool responds much better than man-made fibres.

Static in Carpets
Any carpet with a high proportion of man-made fibre is liable to get a build-up of static from the friction of feet; and static attracts dust. To cut this down spray the carpet with an anti-static spray (see page 171 or use about 4 to 6 tablespoons of water with 1 tablespoon of fabric softener in a plant sprayer. Fabric softeners vary in strength.

You can also use a clean duster wrung out in this mixture for dusting acrylic and perspex, which also have static problems.

Soot
Carpets should be *very* well covered before a chimney is swept, but if soot does fall on a carpet immediately sprinkle it thickly with salt and leave it for half an hour before you vacuum it up.

Sweeping Carpets
When sweeping a carpet the dust flies up and lands straight back again. To stop this sprinkle the carpet with slightly damp salt or tea leaves - but if these are too damp they could leave tea stains.

Washing
The **British Carpet Manufacturers' Association** (Royalty House, 72 Dean Street, London W1V 5HB Tel: 01 734 9853) publishes leaflets on carpet care. It recommends using a shampoo meeting the British Standard BS4088, but says there aren't many which do.

I find a shampoo called 1001 removes spots beautifully. But I can't guarantee its safety or effectiveness on all carpets. Some tool hire companies hire out machines which spray shampoo into the carpet and suck the water and dirt back out again. Some are astonishingly effective and easy to use, and save a great deal of time.

> WARNING Whatever the shampoo, all carpets must be treated with a minimum of liquid. Foam-backed carpets may rot if they get too wet and other kinds may shrink dramatically.

Carpet dyes are very prone to misbehaving. So always test any shampoo or stain remover on an off-cut or on a patch of carpet which won't show, and let it dry thoroughly before using it where it would matter. Never use soap, ammonia or bleach. If you use a dry-cleaner-style spot remover, let it dry *totally* before using carpet shampoo, and vice versa.

With any shampoo only use lukewarm water and the recommended amount: extra will just leave a deposit in the carpet to attract dirt. Apply it with a soft-bristled brush - stiff bristles rough up the pile - spreading on the *foam* rather than saturating the pile, and ending with strokes which leave the pile in the right direction. Do not walk on the carpet while it is wet or put furniture on it. It is at its most fragile then and furniture may have hidden metal under the feet which would leave rust stains. If it *has* to stand on it put a small piece of strong plastic under to prevent this - but weight on damp carpets will leave a bad dent.

The **Carpet Cleaners Association** (126 New Walk, De Montfort Street, Leics LE1 7JA Tel: 0533 554352) will supply a list of members in your county. They must have taken courses in cleaning carpets and upholstery and in spot removal. The association will take up complaints.

Chamois Leather
A chamois leather needs to be washed with pure soap, as detergent would remove the natural oils and harden it. Rinse it clean and squeeze the water out without wringing. Hang it to dry away from sunlight or direct heat, and wiggle it gently from time to time as it dries, stretching it slightly in each direction, so it becomes soft and pliable, otherwise it will dry stiff as a board. But don't overdo the pulling or it will tear.

Never be tempted to store a chamois in a plastic bag as it will quickly become slimy and useless.

China and Porcelain
The cleaning of ordinary household china is covered under washing up (page 167), but with old china and porcelain ornaments it is always wisest to assume they are very vulnerable. Never rub at stains with anything hard - not even bristles on a brush - or use strong chemicals. And to dust intricate china wear clean cotton gloves and, holding it firmly in its place dust it with the gloved fingers.

When it needs spring cleaning be very careful. Some ceramics, such as biscuit ware, are totally unglazed. This means they should only be wiped and may need expert cleaning if the dirt is ingrained. Gilt should also be wiped very carefully, *not* washed, as the gilding may come off.

For glazed china which is very greasy some experts recommend washing with Synperonic N first (see page

171) and, if this fails, wiping it with a mixture of equal amounts of white spirit and water with a teaspoon of Fairy Liquid per pint.

It is perfectly safe to hang china, with the hangers which have sprung holders, provided the hanger is the correct size and that plates with cracks are not hung, lest the pressure break them completely. A small square of chamois leather should be put under the clips, to prevent damage to the rims. Pieces of chamois can also be put under the feet of china and porcelain which might scratch a polished surface. Unlike felt, chamois won't leak dye if it becomes damp.

Chrome

Most of the floor and wall cleaners have some ammonia in and this cleans chrome excellently. On stubborn marks use a little neat household ammonia on a damp cloth - but don't breathe it in and do have the windows open wide. If you lack ammonia and the taps are marked, try paraffin or toothpaste. For an extra shine use Solvol Autosol (see page 171), rub it off with a clean cloth and finish with a chamois leather.

Water with a dash of ammonia is good for removing traffic film from chrome on cars, but don't splash it on to the paint. It shouldn't do any harm, but who knows what they will put into paint next? Or use Solvol Autosol.

Cigarette Ash

It was in a little bar in Assisi, just near the tomb of St Francis, that I discovered how to clean ashtrays. The barmaid used a dry pastry brush to remove every trace of ash. Unless some cigarette has left a tarry patch a dry brush is far more effective than washing and doesn't release the smell the way water does. (You do not, of course, use the brush for pastry.)

Clocks

Old clocks should be kept away from extremes of heat or humidity and guarded from dust. You can't stop daily dust falling on them but you can encase them in protective plastic before doing any dust-raising job in their vicinity.

If it stops, a clock of any real age needs a clock repairer used to old clocks. Any museum specializing in fine furniture should be able to give you the name of someone suitable, or contact the Victoria and Albert Museum in London.

Cloisonné

If you use either water or metal polish on cloisonné there is a danger that the moisture will get down the cracks and lift off the delicate enamel. The only possible cleaner for it is a silver polishing cloth, but be extremely careful that the cloth doesn't catch on any corner of metal and pull it out of place.

Computers

The greatest enemy of a computer is any kind of liquid spilt over the keyboard, as it will trickle down into the works. Dust and static electricity are also bad. So the doors of the disk drive need to be kept closed and if there is a man-made fibre carpet in the room which might generate static electricity the carpet should be regularly sprayed with anti-static spray.

The best cleaner for the screen is anti-static spray and a soft cloth. Any good liquid cleaner can be used on the plastic casing of the various parts of the computer - provided a dust-free cloth is used and absolutely no moisture is allowed into any cracks.

Dust under the keys could, eventually, stop them working and a small tool for removing the keys is sold by some computer shops. But first unplug the computer and make a plan of the keyboard. Each key has a spring and if this is sticking remove and clean it, or put in a new one from the manufacturer.

> Computers vary: *before cleaning a keyboard like this ask the makers whether it could do any damage to their machine.*

Cooker Cleaning

Burners

If the area round burners has burnt-on food cover the areas with a cloth wet with detergent and leave it an hour. It will then be much easier to clean.

Glass Doors

Washing-up liquid is all you need to remove minor splashes on the glass doors of ovens. But if the dirt is tougher paint stripper which contains methylene chloride is rather effective. But wear rubber gloves and keep it away from pets and children, and all other kitchen surfaces. Rinse it off well, too.

Ovens

The easy way to clean an oven is to wipe it out every time it is used. But few of us manage such perfection. Proprietary oven cleaners are usually more expensive than caustic soda, even when it is their only ingredient. So one may as well use caustic soda and save money. Treat it with *great care* as it can damage other finishes in your kitchen and do serious injury especially to eyes. *Store it well out of reach of children:* they could make the fatal mistake of thinking it was sugar.

Put 1 tablespoon of caustic soda into 500 ml (1 pt) of hot water in a plastic bucket or large pyrex container. *Put the soda into the water, NOT the water onto the soda.* Wearing thick rubber gloves, swab the whole inside of the oven with this mixture. If there is a risk of any dripping on to the floor cover it with plastic before you start work and keep children and pets away. Leave it until a test patch wipes clean with a plastic saucepan scourer. Time is the vital element; only with a filthy oven will you need a stronger solution of caustic.

When the caustic has softened the dirt, wipe it off with a plastic scourer and *rinse the inside well*. You don't want a residue of caustic dripping into your food. Finally, wipe the inside of the oven over with 1 tablespoon of bicarbonate of soda in ¼ l (½ pt) of water. This makes the oven easier to clean next time.

★ If you have a drop-down oven door avoid having to turn upside-down by checking the roof with an old mirror.
★ Soaking oven shelves overnight in water with washing-up liquid and a good dash of bleach makes them far easier to clean.
★ If something spills over in the oven, or on top, sprinkle salt thickly over it, then it won't burn on so easily. This is more effective with some food than others, but always worth a try.

Drains
It pays to treat drains well: cleaning them when they clog up isn't a pleasant job. So, nothing solid should ever be put down any ordinary drain. That includes not only vegetable rubbish and tea leaves but also liquid fat which will harden in the pipe.

From time to time, pour some neat, or slightly diluted, bleach down the plug holes of basins and sinks and leave for about 3 minutes before rinsing well. This will clean off grease and old scum. Or half fill with very hot water, add a handful of washing soda and when it has dissolved let the water out. With metal sinks you can be even more drastic and use soda and boiling water. (*Don't do this if the drain might be blocked by ice or the pipe may burst.*)

Drains Outside
If an outdoor drain becomes blocked you may need to use the solution of caustic soda used for stripping wood (see A Roof Over Your Head). If that fails you either have something nasty blocking it or you may have tree roots growing into it.

Either needs professional attention. Look in the Yellow Pages under Plumbers and Drains, and in Thompsons under Drain Clearance. Dyno-Rod can be found in most areas of Britain. They cover all types of problem.

★ The easiest way to clean waste disposal units is to drop in a lot of ice cubes, and switch on. The cubes will scrape off any deposit as they go round.
★ To clean heavy iron outdoor drain covers put them on the edge of a bonfire for just long enough to remove the slime and debris.
★ If you have a drain on to which a washing machine regularly disgorges fluff and fabric you can keep it clean by just attaching the foot of an old pair of nylons to the bottom of the pipe. *But* do remove the stocking and throw it away at *very* regular intervals. If the water can't get out because the stocking is full the washing machine will either break or overflow all over your home.

Dustbins and Kitchen Bins
The quickest way to clean metal (*not plastic*) bins is to place lightly crumpled newspaper in and (at a safe distance from anything which might catch fire) put a match to it. Plastic dustbins and waste bins should be cleaned with a solution of water and bleach - at the strength recommended on the bottle. Keep a pair of rubber gloves just for this job.

It was an American friend who had trouble with marauding racoons, who taught me that to keep animals out of bins you just need to sprinkle a little ammonia inside the lid. Even racoons beat watery-eyed retreat.

Enamel
The enamel used on enamel boxes should never be washed, as the water may get into minute cracks and lift off the top layers. Just wipe it with a dry cloth. See also Cloisonné, page 157.

Finger-marks
Remove finger-marks from gloss paint by using a little white spirit on kitchen roll - but be careful with old or unusual paint as white spirit may soften it.

Fire Tiles
It was a housewife in Cheshire who wrote to tell me that her mother had always cleaned glazed tiles around the fire with soapy water and wood ash. It works beautifully and almost instantly removes burnt-on dirt which soap and water alone won't touch. But it must be wood ash: coal ash could scratch the glaze.

Floor Mops
You wouldn't think that anything would want to eat a floor mop, but some bacteria like nothing better. That's why sponge mops tend to go squishy and fall apart long before they are worn away. To stop this you need to rinse the mop after use in a phenolic household disinfectant such as Dettol or Boots Pine Disinfectant. But don't try to kill the bacteria with bleach or chlorine, as these will damage the sponge.

Floors

Dents
Dents in any kind of floor are just dirt cups so fill them in. First, scrape every bit of dirt and grime out of the dent. Then drip candlewax into the dent - you can use children's wax crayons to colour the wax to the right shade. (Just warm the wax and a piece of crayon together in the bottom of a washed-out tin over some hot water.) Having dripped the wax into the hole quickly wipe and scrape off any excess while still warm. Finally smooth it perfectly with wire wool. This can easily last for several years.

Polishing Wood Floors
Whether wood floors need polishing very much depends on their type. Plain boards which have been stripped may be much better sealed with a strong polyurethane sealer. Equally, some very old floors which have never enjoyed a high polish hardly need one. When floors do need polish it can be kept to a minimum if you wipe them over with a wool cloth impregnated with equal parts of malt vinegar and paraffin. This removes dust and leaves a shine with a minimum of work. Then, floor polish only needs to be used two or three times a year.

Sealed Floors
Floors such as cork and wood sealed with a strong polyurethane sealant only need sweeping, but extra stubborn dirt can be washed off. As the seal is shiny there seems little point in making work by polishing them.

HOW TO REMOVE STAINS FROM FLOORS. -
For removing spots of grease from floorboards, take
equal parts of Fuller's Earth and perlash, a quarter
of a pound of each, and boil in a quart of soft water;
and, while hot, lay it on the greased parts, allowing
it to remain on them for ten to twelve hours; after
which it may be scoured off with sand and water.
Enquire Within, 1856

Stone

Porous stone should never be washed with soap as it
will absorb it and gradually become slippery and
dangerous when damp. Instead, use water containing
a little ammonia or washing soda.

If grease has left an immovable mark cover the patch
with a paste made of Fuller's Earth (from a chemist) or
Sepialite (see page 171) and oil of eucalyptus. Cover it
with pierced cling film and let it stay there until the top
cracks, then pull it off. Some of the oil should have been
absorbed by the mixture, but it may take several
applications to clean it entirely and not all grease marks
can be fully removed.

Sweeping Floors

The old practice of throwing used tea leaves on floors
before sweeping has fallen into disuse. But it is worth
remembering if you are moving home and have a floor
to clean before carpeting. Failing tea leaves, even grass
clippings will keep the dust down to a less choking level.

Tiles

If builders have failed to clean off all the cement scum
after fixing you can remove it with Quarry Cement
Remover. Many builders' merchants and tile shops sell
it, but you can also get it from **Dennis Ruabon** (Hafod
Tileries, Ruabon, Wrexham, Clwyd, North Wales LL1G
6ET Tel: 0978 843484.) Otherwise, a sweep and wipe
over with a mop (with a touch of washing-up liquid for
glazed tiles or, for quarry tiles, Quarry Clean - also from
tile shops), is all the care they need. Traditionally, when
quarry tiles are new, linseed oil is wiped over them and
left to sink in - try it on a spare tile and see if you like
the effect. I don't.

Vinyl

Strong alkali will gradually draw the plasticizer from
vinyl and make it shrink and crack, and some
proprietary floor cleaners are alkaline enough to cause
long-term damage. Manufacturers of vinyl floorings
recommend using a little neutral washing-up liquid and
a touch of vinegar instead. But do avoid being generous
- a soapy coating will make it dangerous when wet.

Vinyl is just as vulnerable to chemicals such as bleach,
hair dye, paint thinners, fabric dyes, photographic
chemicals, nail varnish and varnish removers. All will
either stain or dissolve it. There is no cure for such
marks, but surface marks, such as those produced by
black rubber heels, can be removed with a fine metal
scouring pad, sold for saucepans.

Vinyl doesn't really need any polish and, if you like
the look of polish, go gently. Even with only two coats

a year the edges will become yellower than the middle.
When you can't bear this, remove it with ½ cup of
ammonia in 4 l (1 gallon) of cold water plus a dash of
washing-up liquid. Wipe it on to the floor. Leave it for
5 minutes to bite into the polish, then remove it with
a cloth and a looped nylon saucepan scourer. The alkali
of ammonia could damage the vinyl so rinse it
afterwards with a cup of vinegar in 4 l (1 gallon) water.

Flower Vases

Flower vases quickly build up tide marks. If they don't
come off with water and detergent fill the vase with
water, add a good dash of bleach and leave it for a
while. The dirt should simply vanish. Rinse well
afterwards.

> Bleach could harm old or fragile containers
> and should not be used on them.

Freezers and Refrigerators

Both refrigerators and freezers can build up a mingled
smell which is as unattractive as that muddy brown
paint one produced as a child by mixing every colour
together. To remove it: first wash the plastic with warm
water, then go over it with a cloth wrung out in a strong
solution of bicarbonate of soda and water.

To keep the smell down put some lumps of charcoal
at the back of a shelf, changing them every few
months.

Fungus and Mould

If fungus grows on walls or window frames where
moisture collects it will wash off. There are fungicides
which you can buy to stop it returning, but a solution
of bleach and water will deter it as well as anything.
But do wear rubber gloves and do a test patch to see
that the bleach doesn't cause the paint to fade.

If a bread bin or crock grows mould, or the bread
goes mouldy quickly when stored in it, wash it out well,
then wipe it all over inside with neat vinegar.

Gilt

Gilt on a deeply carved mirror seems so gloriously
substantial that it is hard to realize that the layer of gold
is so thin that if you held the gold leaf edgewise it would
be invisible. This means it is very easily removed by
cleaning. To make matters worse, there are two types
of gilding - water-based and oil-based - and only the
very expert can tell which is which. This means that,
as one museum conservator put it, 'I cannot warn people
too strongly against even attempting to clean gilding
themselves.' Even dusting very old gilding can dislodge
loose areas.

Nor can you assume that your local gilder is
necessarily the person to go to if an antique gilt frame
needs repairs.

Gilders fall into two camps: those who restore the
old and add a minimum of new gilt - which keeps the
value of the piece - and those who save themselves time

by just putting new gilding over everything - which can halve the value of the object.

Those warnings do not, of course, apply to modern gilding on plain picture frames, which stand up to dusting, and even to a damp cloth, without a murmur. But a more elaborate frame may be real gilt however modern it is, so age isn't always the guide.

Glass and Crystal

Crystal chandeliers are made so they can be taken down in sections for cleaning - which is a long job. So one chandelier owner devised the following method.

Instead of taking the chandelier down, put on clean cotton gloves, stand on a tall ladder with a bucket of water containing a dash of washing-up liquid (though Synperonic N, page 171, is even better) and a dash of vinegar and wet your gloves with the solution. Hold each section of chandelier firmly in place with one hand while you run the finger of the other hand over it to clean it. Obviously, it takes a good deal of dexterity to do this without falling off the ladder or accidentally unhooking and dropping a section of the chandelier.

Decanters and Fine Glass

Glass is not a single substance. Its composition varies with the period and the maker, so it is never safe to assume that a treatment which works for one piece will work for another.

The first step in the care of decanters is not to leave small dregs of alcohol lurking in the bottom or they will dry to a nasty stain. Relatively new alcohol stains can often be removed by soaking them in neat malt vinegar. Older stains are very hard to remove, and can be impossible. *Do not, under any circumstances*, use a denture cleaning tablet. Such tablets may clean some glass, but they are capable of etching other glass to a cloudiness which is far worse than any stain in the base could possibly be.

If vinegar fails to remove a stain try tearing newspaper into *tiny* pieces and dropping it into a decanter filled with water, and leaving it overnight. This sometimes does the trick. Then rinse it out and dry it carefully. Failing that, some museum experts claim that potato peelings may do the trick.

Glass can also be clouded by the fluorine in water if a decanter is washed and the stopper put in before it is totally dry. The fluorine then condenses on to the inside of the glass and etches it. The cloudiness can only be removed by using formidable acids to eat away the inner layer of glass. Some of the top makers of cut glass will do this job - especially if they made the decanter.

The best place to dry a decanter is upside-down in an airing cupboard - quite a few have slats spaced widely enough for the neck to slip down between them. But be *very* careful or you might find that the neck is knocked off.

★ The only way to undo glass which has stuck is to use the fact that glass expands when it heats. If two glasses are stuck one inside another fill the inner one with iced water. Then stand the outer one in warm water and gradually increase the heat of the water until the inner one can be lifted out.

A Stuck Stopper

If a ground glass stopper has become stuck, put a little penetrating oil round the neck and give it a few hours to seep in. If the stopper can't then be removed you need to heat the neck of the vessel while keeping the stopper cool. Running warm water over the neck, or wrapping a warm towel round it may work - but heating thick glass too suddenly may crack it. So move gently from warm to hot. If the stopper still won't come out, try tapping the stopper all round, gently, with a wooden spoon. Vibrating the glass like that usually works - though if you do it too hard it will chip.

Windows and Mirrors

You can clean sheet glass with a host of substances, but quite the worst is the thick type of cleaner which leaves a deposit around the edge. One of the fastest ways to clean slightly dirty glass is simply to rub it over with a damp newspaper and dry it with a dry one. The printing ink does great things for the glass - if not for your hands.

If glass is really dirty wash it with water in which there is some ammonia (use rubber gloves) to cut the grease of the atmosphere, or just use a little washing-up liquid. Rinse it clean with water containing either vinegar or methylated spirits. To give it an extra good shine polish it dry with a chamois leather. Mirrors, and pictures with gilded frames, need a little care (see Gilt).

★ If the glass is marked with hair spray remove it with methylated spirits.

Pictures

The glass on most pictures can be cleaned like a window. But there is an exception where chalk and pastel drawings are concerned. Rubbing the glass can set up an electrical charge which will draw the tiny particles of loose pastel off the paper and on to the glass, clouding it and spoiling the drawing. Just give glass over pastels a slow gentle wipe.

Iron

Obviously water and iron make poor bedfellows. But once rust does set in it can be removed with citric acid. An alternative cleaner is paraffin and 000 wire wool. Whatever you use bear in mind that iron can be fractured quite easily.

Ivory

The great thing with ivory is to curb one's enthusiasm. It should age to a gentle cream. Trying to keep it looking like new will only damage it. All over it there are hairline cracks into which water can seep - so washing it can have disastrous results in the long term. Blow the dust off it, and when it really *has* to be cleaned use a little methylated spirits on a cotton bud. Using a duster on carved ivory risks catching and breaking it on a loose thread, and the methylated spirits should be colourless (see page 171) as there is a slight risk of the colour staining the ivory. If you are cleaning piano keys be very sparing, any excess may soften the glue which sticks them on. To clean an ivory comb use methylated spirits on dental floss.

Horn and antlers, whether on knife handles or on trophies, should be treated like ivory.

> BEWARE Some books suggest using bleach, lemon juice or peroxide to clean ivory. Any one of these may seem to do no harm, but they burn ivory and, in time, it will become powdery and dull.

Jade
Jade is an easy-going substance. Treat it like glass but avoid using anything which might scratch it, as the surface is quite soft.

Jewellery — General Points
It is easy to clean most jewellery at home but it takes a little care and you need to consider both the type of setting and the gems which may be set in it. Anything you wear often may need cleaning every week, but once a month is often enough.

Check old jewellery to see whether it is closed in behind the stones. If it is, *don't* wash it. At one time, foil was used to back stones with this type of setting, and if the foil is washed it can permanently discolour and ruin the piece. All you can do to clean this type of setting is give it a rub with a clean chamois leather or Goddard's Long Term Silver Cloth.

Pearls, ivory and certain types of inset in jewellery need special treatment - see below before you start cleaning.

For open settings the basic method is to have washing-up liquid and warm (not hot) water in a bowl (not a wash basin - any stones which come loose will go down the plug hole). Put the jewellery in and leave it a little, then brush it clean with a soft bristle toothbrush. If settings have become clogged with soap pick out the soap carefully with a toothpick. (You may find that methylated spirits help remove the soap more easily.)

Rinse the jewellery very well and dry it with a hairdryer or fan heater set to cool. Strain the washing-up liquid through a very fine nylon sieve and check whether any stones have fallen into it. If they have it is a very good thing; any stone which falls out with this gentle treatment would soon have been lost in the street.

Fragile Stones
The fragile stones you are most likely to find in jewellery are opals, turquoise, pearls, coral, jet, amber and emeralds. Pearls and emeralds are special cases (see below); all the others can be washed with soap and water, but not subjected to anything stronger.

Acrylic Jewellery
Acrylics aren't as tough as their modernity might make you suppose. Treat them like fragile stones.

Emeralds
Emeralds look as hard as diamonds but they are more prone to flaws than other precious stones. To disguise these flaws some countries soak their emeralds in a fine green oil which seeps into the cracks and conceals them perfectly - so perfectly that even an expert can't always tell a flawed stone from a perfect one without testing it. The danger is that if you soak an emerald in washing-up liquid - or, indeed, wear it for washing up - you may draw out the oil and reveal a hidden flaw. So leave cleaning to the professionals.

Gold and Platinum
Gold or platinum is often much dirtier than it looks. If you have anything which is plain gold - with nothing set in it - try dropping it in methylated spirit for 3 minutes - not longer. Then remove it, brush any loose dirt off with a soft bristle toothbrush and rinse it. It should look entirely different.

Opals
Opals are a curious combination of silica and water and will craze and lose their colour if they get too dry. So they must be kept well away from heat, and are best left uncleaned or wiped with a piece of silk. If they become dull and scratched they can be repolished professionally.

Pearls
Tradition has it that pearls lose their lustre if they aren't worn at fairly regular intervals. But they are also extremely vulnerable to acids of all kinds, including the acid in some people's skin; these will eat into them and dull them. Wipe them with a piece of silk after you take them off, to avoid the risk of skin acids staying on them and never apply perfume and hair lacquer after you put them on.

Silver
Professionals often clean silver jewellery with silver dip - if it has nothing set in it - the advantage being that no polish lodges in the cracks. But a jewellery designer I know prefers to use a soft toothbrush and toothpaste. It works extremely well and is always to hand. See also page 165.

Kettles
A kettle which is encrusted with hard water deposits uses up more fuel than a clean one. Furring can be kept to a minimum by putting a seashell inside to attract the scale. But to remove scale which has formed, less than half fill the kettle with equal parts of vinegar and water, and bring it to the boil. The mixture will rise up dramatically as it heats, so *don't overfill it*, and be ready to turn it off the instant it looks as if it might overflow. Leave it to work on the scale before rinsing it out. Do this regularly so there is never a heavy deposit to remove. Once the inside is very coated it will take a lot of applications to remove all of it. (There are also branded products to descale kettles, but they aren't cheap.)

IMPORTANT: Read Jewellery — General Points before using these methods.

Kitchen Ranges

An old cast iron kitchen range which is the one surface on which you can use quite a stiff wire brush, and don't have to use the finest wire wool. For cleaning liquids avoid water (see Iron, page 160) *totally* and stick to paraffin or methylated spirit. There are no secrets to bringing a range back to life - it is sheer hard work. But they can look wonderful when finished.

Lacquer

Lacquer ranges from the sublime to the shoddy. Fine antique lacquer is so fragile that even white flour can scratch it, and a drop of water can eat into its surface. Clean it as little as possible and then only with an immaculately clean silk cloth. However much care you take, the surface may become tacky with age. There is no way to prevent or reverse this.

Cheap modern lacquer is scarcely related and you can clean it with a damp cloth, but avoid cleaners which might scratch it.

Lampshades

Hard lampshades of glass, plastic or other substances should be cleaned according to what they are made of - bearing in mind that water should not be used unless the shade is removed from the electrical fitting. Glass shades need ammonia in the water if they are very dirty.

A fabric shade can be washed *if* the trimmings have been attached with waterproof glue and the fabric is washable. First vacuum or brush off any loose dust, then dip it in pure soap dissolved in lukewarm water. Hold it upright or - if it must lie on its side - move it from side to side. On its side the weight of even a little water may make it stretch or tear.

If a fabric shade isn't washable you may wish to risk using a spray-on dry-cleaner if it is too dirty to use without it.

Lavatories

Urine Stains

The most effective lavatory cleaner is undoubtedly bleach. It kills germs, and gets rid of the yellow deposits which some other cleaners allow to build up. It likes time to work, so pour it in and brush it round before going to bed. (If you have young children who might go to the loo alone at night, do it in the morning while they can be kept elsewhere.) For a neglected loo repeated bleaching is the only answer. Use the new bottles of thick bleaches which get up under the rim, or the smell will stay.

Hard Water Stains

The stains on lavatories can sometimes be due to hard water constantly trickling from an inefficient cistern. Use the treatment given on page 154. If that fails to shift them paint on a solution of 1 teaspoonful of oxalic acid in half a cup of hot water and leave it to work. Wearing rubber gloves, scrape it with a hard plastic edge, and repeat. Not a nice job, but then a stained loo isn't lovely either.

Marble

Marble may look as strong as a rock, but in fact it's rather fragile. *The cleaning of valuable marble should be left to a conservator* and it should simply be dusted with a *perfectly* clean duster.

Marble's complex structure of crystals can be broken down internally by a hard knock, and even using water on it can draw out iron in its composition and slowly cause rust stains. Research, with electron microscopes, suggests that water may also encourage the growth of bacteria which slowly discolour it. Of course, people do have marble floors which are washed, but they are most common in dry countries, such as Greece, where moisture seldom lingers. And, as the staining is very gradual, it has only recently been realized that water is responsible for the long-term discolouration.

Marble is also vulnerable to spirits and to acids. A scent bottle or drink will eat into marble and leave a mark as rough as sandpaper. To polish this back to smoothness is a very long job, using wet and dry paper and may be best left to an expert.

If mundane marble is so dirty that you have to use some sort of moisture then white spirit is less harmful than water. If it needs even more thorough cleaning one expert in marble conservation recommends Solvol Autosol, obtainable in car accessory shops. You rub it on in small areas with a small, clean rag and remove any residue with white spirit.

To prevent stains getting into marble so easily wipe on a fine wax such as Renaissance Wax (see page 171). Immediately wipe off any residue and polish it up. Finally sprinkle it with *pure* talc (from a pharmacist; not any old talc which could have additions which would harm the marble) and brush off the surplus.

★ Marble will draw moisture out of cement, and with it chemicals from the cement which can ruin it. Cement should never be used in installing marble. It is equally vulnerable to stains from metal pins used to hold it in place. The only metal which is totally safe is stainless steel - and then only certain types. Before installing marble take advice from a knowledgeable museum conservator.

Stains on Marble

Don't try to remove stains from any marble you value - any stain removal can spoil its surface.

If you spill ink on ordinary marble immediately cover it liberally with salt. This should absorb the ink. Then brush it off, or vacuum it up. Sour milk left on the stain may bleach it out over several days, and much will depend on the type of ink. Treat it afterwards with Sepialite (see page 171), as below.

Brown and grey iron stains can often be bleached out with repeated applications of salt and lemon juice. Finally, draw the salt and lemon out of the marble by covering the area with a thick layer of Sepialite mixed to a stiff paste with water. Leave it until the surface is cracking then pull it off.

For felt-pen marks apply a paste of Sepialite mixed with colourless methylated spirits. Cover this mud pack with cling film with holes pierced in it - to slow down the evaporation rate - and peel it off as above. It will usually take several applications to remove a stain.

Red wine, tea and coffee will all come out with repeated applications of hydrogen peroxide - applied with a paint brush so it only covers the stain. Don't use bleach.

Mattresses

A new sprung mattress needs special care in the early weeks to make the springs and fillings bed down evenly. For the first two months it should be turned over one week and rotated head to the foot the next. In that way all the springs will settle evenly.

Any mattress needs daily airing. Throw the covers off the end on to a chair, so the moisture of the night can blow away. Every few months, vacuum the mattress with a nozzle for fine fabrics, or brush it clean.

Mattress covers are stained by water. Even a leaky hot water bottle can leave a stain which looks like something much nastier. So it is always advisable to put a plastic sheet on any bed occupied by a young child lest it spill something in it.

If a mattress does get wet immediately turn it on its side, so the wet doesn't drip through and rust the springs, and mop the wet up rapidly. Sponge the area with a clean cloth, or use a suitable dry-cleaner if it is a dry stain (see Stains). Leave it on its side until it is totally dry.

Foam Mattresses

Foam mattresses must have a ventilated base or condensation will collect on the underside and the mattress may rot.

Futons

Instead of being left flat a futon should be loosely rolled up each day, so the air can circulate and the moisture dry out. If you spill something on a futon mop the liquid up at once and wipe it with a damp cloth. If necessary, apply a suitable remedy then leave it to dry.

Microwave Ovens

The insides of microwave ovens need to be cleaned regularly as you can't bring them up to scratch with caustic in the way you can an oven with an enamel interior. See stainless steel page 165.

The base of the oven and particularly the mechanism for turning the food need to be kept spotlessly clean, so it can turn easily: microwave motors burn out surprisingly easily if a strain is put on them. It is also important to keep the seal round the door clean so it closes properly; use the same cleaner as for the stainless steel.

Oil Lamps

Only a smoke-coated chimney can mar the soft beauty of the light from an oil lamp, but luckily the chimney is easily cleaned. For reasons which are unexplained, washing a chimney makes it more liable to crack. Wipe it out with newspaper instead: the printing ink helps to remove the soot.

The wick should be soaked in vinegar when new and left to dry, then it will be less liable to smoke, and trim it straight across at each lighting.

Ormolu

True ormolu is brass, or bronze, coated with gold, but some ormolu is gold over zinc, and what seems to be ormolu can sometimes be lacquered brass. Neither should be washed or rubbed hard. Dust it lightly with a soft brush: any polishing may remove the surface metal and ruin it. This means that china and glass with ormolu mounts cannot be washed. Instead, wipe them clean without letting water touch the gold.

Paintings and Pictures

There is only one rule: *don't* clean anything unless it is so dreadful there isn't a hope of it having any value. Scarcely a year passes without someone finding that some neglected drawing or painting is a lost masterpiece.

If an oil painting really is totally valueless you can try cleaning it by wiping the surface gently with a clean rag dipped in dilute household ammonia. If it has any value ask a professional museum restorer to advise you.

Any pictures which are on paper are at risk from damp, insects and too much light. They should be kept away from extremes of all kinds and insects must be dealt with rapidly.

Paths

When green algae form on paths they can be cleaned off by rinsing the area with a fairly strong solution of bleach, such as 1 part bleach to 6 parts water, or with a special product such as ICI's Moss Gun. Leave the chemical on for an hour or two while keeping children and pets inside. Then remove the algae with a very strong jet of water (bounce-off may bleach your clothes). If necessary, scrub the stones with a stiff brush to get the green right off. I find bleach best but the snag is anything you have growing beside the path may die. However, the Moss Gun is also for moss in lawns so if you have stones inset into grass it can be used there without damage to the grass.

Pewter

Sharing, as it does, the colour of silver, it is tempting to expect pewter to have at least some of its sheen. But it is a mixture of tin and other metals and shines with difficulty. Just make the most of its soft sheen by keeping it dust-free and rubbing it occasionally with Goddard's Silver Cloth. Work *round* the circle of a goblet or tankard to produce the best effect. For display you can keep its sheen by polishing it with Renaissance Wax (page 171). But, if the surface of any valuable pewter becomes powdery and white consult a conservator at once. It may have pewter disease and need special treatment.

Don't rub it on the inside: pewter absorbs smells, so polishes can make it impossible to drink from. That would be a shame, for pewter holds the cold. So if you wish to drink cool wine in a hot garden chill a pewter mug in the refrigerator with the wine: a tradition begun by the ancient Romans who also used cool pewter goblets when they slaked their thirst under the sun.

But rinse wine, and any other drink out of pewter as soon as possible because it is very vulnerable to acid. Oak contains very strong tannic acid which it releases into the air and tankards which have stood too long on oak have been known to lose their bases and pewter must not be kept in an oak drawer or cupboard.

> Those who feel tempted to polish vigorously should bear in mind that the difference in value between a piece of pewter with its touch marks in perfect condition and one with them rubbed off can be thousands of pounds.

Plastic Laminates
The laminated surfaces in kitchens need more care than they appear to. To chop food directly on them, or scour them with an abrasive cleaner is to convert an easy-care surface into one which won't look good whatever you do. Stick to thin liquid cleaners, use a chopping board and don't put a very hot pan on the surface or there may be a permanent scorch mark.

Laminates are also stained by clothes' dyes and the colourings on some food labels. Some come out if you leave a pool of washing soda and water over the place for a few hours; others vanish under a pool of lemon juice - but a few shift for neither.

Porcelain Washbasin
The fastest way to clean a basin is to use a cleaner, with no foaming agent, and a saucepan scourer which has sponge on one side and a rough surface on the other.

Rust stains can be removed from porcelain washbasins by leaving a paste of cream of tartar and water to work on them. See also China and Porcelain, page 156.

Pillows
Pillows need daily plumping up by shaking them vigorously and pushing the sides towards the middle several times. This separates the filling and disperses the moisture which has gone into the pillow during the night and keeps them fluffy.

Record Player Heads
Dirt on a stylus distorts the sound. The professional way to clean it is to use equal parts of distilled water and isopropyl alcohol (from a chemist). Put this on a fine brush and brush the stylus with it, very lightly, from *the back towards the front* - any other direction may bend the stylus.

> Treat isopropyl alcohol with great care. It can etch a mark into anything.

Records
Almost every method of cleaning can result in a badly damaged record - and that includes some methods I have heard advocated on the radio. They should *never* be washed - invisible traces of dye can run into the tracks and distort the sound. Nor should they be wiped - this forces dirt off the tops of the tracks and deep into them.

According to scientists in the record industry, the safest way by far is to use an anti-static gun sold by top record shops. Quite a long way behind, is an anti-static cloth. But *don't* wipe the record with it - that just pushes the dirt into the delicate grooves. Instead, rotate the record on a turntable while holding the cloth so it only *just* touches the surface.

If you don't have an anti-static cloth put a clean fine cotton handkerchief in a box with some wet tissues - but not touching them. The moisture will slowly evaporate out of the tissues and condense on to the handkerchief. You can then use it like the anti-static cloth, but the effects won't last so long. A dry anti-static cloth can be moistened in the same way.

No amount of cleaning will do much for a neglected record, so hold records only by the edges, put them away immediately after use, and - most important of all - when putting them away, or taking them out, open the sides of the sleeve so the record doesn't rub against the paper. It is the friction of going in and out of the sleeve which creates most of the static which draws dust on to a record.

Warped Records
If a record warps slightly put it between two perfectly clean sheets of glass in a warm airing cupboard. If the warping isn't too severe the warmth and the slight pressure will flatten it out.

Rugs and Mats
The first essential with mats and rugs is that they don't present a hazard. Rugs on top of carpets can be kept close to the carpet by putting the hook side of a piece of stick-on velcro under each corner. The hooks then mesh into the carpet and hold it firmly. Mats on polished surfaces should lie on a non-slip underlay.

Shaking rugs damages their edges, but most rugs can be vacuum-cleaned, provided the strength of the suction is suited to their age and fragility. An ordinary hard-wearing rug will benefit from an extra thorough clean on some days: vacuum three times - front, back, front. Strong rugs also benefit from being placed face down on dry grass (not newly cut) - or ideally snow - and beaten.

Most mats and rugs can be spot-cleaned and shampooed like carpets (see page 156) but fine rugs normally need to be dry-cleaned (see page 171) so ask about when buying. Oriental rugs should only be cleaned after expert advice as their dyes are unpredictable.

Modern rag-rugs can be sometimes be washed. But there is always a risk that even if the rag part washes beautifully the strings on which it is woven may shrink.

Only wash a rug if you are prepared to take the consequences if it goes wrong. Beat and/or vacuum the rug very well to get it as clean as possible - grit could damage your bath. Dissolve some pure soapflakes in a pint of hot water in a bath. Half fill the bath with cold water and immerse the rug. Leave for several hours or overnight. Then press the water through until a lot of dirt has come out. Drain and rinse in cold water again and again until it is entirely clear. (Very dirty rugs may need two soapy soaks to reach this stage.) Press out as much water as you can. Lift it carefully, supporting it well, and spread or hang it to dry in a clean place outside, away from direct sunlight.

Fur rugs are cleaned like fur (see page 172).

Silver and Silver Plate

There is absolutely no need to acquire a glow of sweat and virtue rubbing away to bring silver to a shine. It can be cleaned with silver dip. This acts on the oxides which are tarnishing the silver, whereas polishing rubs away a little of the silver itself. So dipping is the method silver experts prefer.

But silver dip is only for solid silver, not plate, and don't dip items into it if they have non-silver decoration like ebony or ivory knobs.

To make your own put a plate-sized sheet of aluminium kitchen foil in a saucepan with water and a handful of washing soda. Heat this up and drop the silver in for a minute or two - until the tarnish and stains are just off (don't leave it for a long time). Remove and rinse it and rub with a long-term silver cloth to put a sheen on it.

If the silver cloth is not enough, the fastest effective polish is a mixture of whiting (see below) and methylated spirits. Use it just as you would any other metal polish. If you lack methylated spirits mix the whiting with water and a few drops of ammonia. Rinse the silver afterwards and dry it carefully.

> Whiting is a fine white powder sold in old-fashioned hardware stores, but more easily found in the south of England than in the north. It is made by Blanchard's (page 171).

How far you should go in the matter of removing tarnish is a matter of dispute. Some museums leave old silver looking as if it was made yesterday. It seems a pity. A hint of tarnish in the crevices brings out the design. However, intricate silver is best cleaned with a soft brush to prevent the polish lodging in it.

Black stains on Silver

Black stains caused by acid should be rubbed with salt and lemon juice. Stains made by salt come off most easily if rubbed with the whiting mixture plus salt. If that sounds like the mythology of the 'hair of the dog' just try for yourself. But do rinse both off afterwards and watch out for scratching with the salt - it is a remedy of last resort. Another curious interaction is that if an egg spoon becomes darkened by egg, dipping it in the water in which an egg has cooked will clean it.

★ If you want to make your own polishing cloth mix 4 teaspoons of whiting with 2 tablespoons of household ammonia

and 3 cups of water. Soak a piece of towelling in this, wring it out, let it half dry and store it in a plastic bag.

Storing Silver

Silver has several enemies: rubber, salt, ink, acid, air and light. Exclude all of them and silver will keep its shine for a remarkably long time. You can buy Tarnprufe bags (see page 171), made of a fabric which is impregnated with a substance which will prevent stored silver from tarnishing. These are very much better than storing silver in plastic bags. For, although plastic keeps out the air there is a risk of tarnish from air already in the bag.

Having polished silver, put on cotton gloves and rub it once more to remove any traces of finger acids. Wrap each piece well in special dark, *acid-free* tissue paper (page 171). (Don't wrap it in baize. Baize gives off hydrogen sulphide which tarnishes silver, as do many of the linings of presentation boxes. And *don't* use rubber bands. The chemicals released by rubber can penetrate the paper and eat into the silver, leaving marks which can never be removed.) Either wrap all the tissue-covered pieces up together in more tissue, or put them in Tarnprufe bags.

If silver is on display in a cabinet its tarnishing can be reduced by putting a Carosil capsule (page 171) in the cabinet. These are used by some museums, but are only effective if the cabinet is kept closed.

Silver Plate

Silver plate is a thin layer of silver on base metal, such as copper. It is far more fragile than solid silver because the layer can be rubbed off. Polish it no more than is really necessary.

A product, called the Silver Solution (page 171), puts a thin layer of silver on to silver plate which clings by a chemical interaction. It can be used on worn cutlery and seems too good to be true. The snag is the silver, wears off more quickly than it would if it had been electroplated. This means you have to keep using it again and again which is far from cheap.

> The Silver Solution makes the buying of plate far more risky, as a piece may look perfect, yet simply have the thin layer of silver provided by this solution. So beware.

Silver Gilt

This is a thin layer of gold over silver. It needs no polishing, just washing when dirty, and it should be treated gently, not rubbed.

Stainless Steel

The smooth sheen of stainless steel is easily damaged by even a nylon scouring pad, let alone anything more abrasive. It must only be cleaned with a cloth dipped in a thin liquid cleaner, such as Sainsbury's All-Purpose Liquid Cleaner or in water with a dash of ammonia. I find these more effective and less expensive than products made for stainless steel.

Steel

Antique steel needs to be checked carefully before you start to clean it: engraving or gilding could be ruined by the wrong treatment. If anything intricate is found check the best mode of cleaning with a museum conservator. For ordinary steel, which just needs a slight clean, use Solvol Autosol chrome cleaner (from car accessory shops) which is mildly abrasive and effective.

Steel rusts easily, but the rust comes off with paraffin. If necessary, put small objects in a bath of paraffin for 24 hours, or lay a rag soaked in it overnight on a larger surface. But it can't remove the pitting which rust causes.

To bring up a shine on steel, use 000 or 0000 steel wool (coarser will scratch it) lubricated with paraffin or turpentine. To produce a smooth sheen work to and fro in straight lines always in the same direction, *not* round and round. For knives, see page 168.

Steps

If steps *have* to be scrubbed despite the cold, put salt or methylated spirits in the water, then it won't freeze into lethal ice before it dries. Use a tablespoon of either for each 500 ml (1 pt) of water.

Stoves and Grates

Cast iron isn't as tough as you'd suppose and shutting a door or lid too hard can fracture it. Water is another risk, as it is liable to trickle through the design and rust the inside where there is no enamel. It is far better to clean vitreous enamel with a cloth moistened in white spirit (when the fire is *out*) or with 000 wire wool if it becomes grimy. But don't touch the panes with this.

To get the black lead finish on old-fashioned stoves and grates you need a product called Zebrite (see page 171). Thin it to a cream with white spirit, then paint it on with a cheap paint brush - when the stove is *out* - and leave it for 24 hours to dry. Then buff it up with a soft shoe brush kept specially. A messy job, but thank goodness we don't have to make our own.

> *Blacking is now always made with ivory black, treacle, linseed or sweet oil, and oil of vitriol. The proportions vary... as paste or liquid blacking is required ...*
>
> *Enquire Within, 1856*

Tortoiseshell

Tortoiseshell is easily clouded by water or sunlight. If it becomes clouded it can be reburnished professionally. And one of my *Supertips* readers wrote to tell me that she has restored tortoiseshell by rubbing in a product called Vitapointe, sold for dry hair. Hair and tortoiseshell are very similar substances so this isn't too suprising. In fact, they are so alike that customs men test for real tortoiseshell by scraping off a fraction and burning it: if it smells like burning hair it's the real thing. What can't be predicted is whether Vitapointe could make clouding worse in the long run.

Upholstery

The fabrics on chairs and sofas vary in the type of care they need, which makes some far better suited to a family than others. Before you buy ask the retailer what care is necessary. If he doesn't know ask him to find out - and if he won't you should go elsewhere. Having obtained instructions on how to clean any cloth, follow them exactly.

Cotton and Wool Upholstery

Regular vacuuming, to remove the surface dirt, is basic, and many can be cleaned with either a dry-foam upholstery shampoo or with a dry-cleaner aerosol. Whatever the fabric, don't think that the zips on cushion covers are there so you can take them off and wash them.

★ If you lack a vacuum cleaner for upholstery, put a damp sheet over it and beat it. The sheet should catch the flying dust.

Dralon Upholstery

If you fit arm covers over upholstery make sure they are lined with calico. If Dralon rubs on Dralon, the pile underneath may be damaged by the friction.

Vacuum working against the pile one way, and return the opposite way. If you spill anything mop it up with a clean, white cloth as soon as possible. You may then be able to remove any stain by wiping it gently with lukewarm water and an appropriate amount of 1001 dry-foam upholstery cleaner. First, test, on some part that won't show, that this has no effect on the colour. (You could have bought a Dralon look-alike which might react to it. If it seems alright work very gently without getting the upholstery too wet or rubbing the pile too hard.

Leather Upholstery

Leather has several different finishes and the correct treatment depends entirely on the particular finish. Suede is easily recognized. An aniline finish looks and feels as soft as skin, with no real shine on it. Both these are easily damaged by every kind of stain because they have no coating to seal them. It may be possible to protect them by using one of the leather sprays designed to prevent dirt penetrating shoes. But check with the manufacturer of the furniture. Once stains have formed they need expert treatment unless you want to risk trying some of the methods given for leather clothes (see page 172).

Pigmented leather feels firmer and has a shine to it, but there is an intermediate finish called semi-aniline. To test which you have, moisten a white tissue and press it against some hidden part of the leather - but not a seam. If it produces a dark patch the finish is semi-aniline and needs careful handling, like aniline.

Pigmented leather is quite tough, but it can still be stained by grease, so keep anything oily well away from it. Dust it regularly and if it looks dirty wipe it over with a cloth wrung out in warm water and pure soap (not detergent). The cloth must not be wet or water may trickle through a seam and get on to the back of the leather, which will shrink and distort. In a centrally-heated home pigmented leather needs to be treated 3 times a year with Connolly's Hide Food or with the mixture given for books on page 154.

Loose Covers

Whether loose covers should be washed or dry-cleaned will depend on the fabric (see Washing, pages 185), but only wash them if you are *sure* they are both washable *and* preshrunk, and even then put the covers back on the chairs while still quite damp and let them dry like that. Then they will stretch to size. You may be able to iron them while still on the chairs (if it is tough, old-fashioned upholstery) or you may have to take them off.

Tapestry and Embroidery

These should be treated very gently and not cleaned with water, upholstery shampoo or dry-cleaning aerosols. Plain tapestry (needlepoint) can *only* be vacuum-cleaned each week, very gently, with a nozzle vacuum attachment *without rubbing at the surface* to keep the dust from sinking in. Embroidery which is fixed in position (as in chair seats) may be more fragile and can only be vacuumed if it is sturdy and has no beads or other ornaments which could be pulled off. Otherwise you may just have to go over it very gently with a baby's hairbrush.

If needlepoint or woven tapestry (or embroidery of any age or value) needs more thorough cleaning only a few highly specialized cleaners know how to do so without damage. The Royal School of Needlework (see page 171) will clean and repair needlepoint and embroidery, and woven tapestry can be cleaned by Pilgrim Payne and Co Ltd (see page 171). Removing tapestry from chair seats is a tricky job which should be done by an expert upholsterer or by the School of Needlework itself.

Plastic

Leather-look plastic and vinyl dislike fierce heat, so keep them a respectable distance from both fires and radiators. Detergent, polish or spirit cleaner make the plastic go hard and crack. Instead, wipe with warm water and pure soap, and rinse it off afterwards. There is also a product called 'Son of a Gun', made by STP for simulated leather vinyl car seats. On car seats it does a remarkable job and it could be worth asking the maker of any vinyl-covered suite whether it could be used on it.

Vacuum Flasks

Vacuum flasks can be cleared of smells with the bicarbonate of soda mixture given on page 159. Smells can also be removed by leaving a crushed egg-shell in water in the flask overnight.

Wall Cleaning

Distemper and Whitewash

Both distemper and whitewash are impossible to clean. The only solution is to repaint.

Vacuum fabric-covered or wallpapered surfaces with a battery-operated vacuum cleaner or trunk extension, or tie a clean towel around a broom and brush the walls with this: arm-aching but effective.

One of the best substances for removing small marks from wallpaper is a piece of fresh bread. It is damp enough to ease marks off, and soft enough not to rub the surface as much as a rubber. When I was on BBC Television, I discovered it was even used by the BBC design department.

Some marks will come off with a soft eraser, but you have to be very careful not to leave a pale patch. So, work from the centre, feathering the edge with small outward strokes.

Grease is almost impossible to remove, but putting blotting paper over the stain and ironing it may reduce it. You can also try spray-on dry-cleaner - but do a test patch somewhere it won't show.

Grubby patches, such as those around light switches, on a non-washable wallpaper, can sometimes be cleaned by a gentle rub with a cloth moistened with ammonia. But ammonia could affect the dyes in the paper, so do a test patch - where it won't show. And don't rub so hard you destroy the surface of the paper.

Tiles

Wall tiles can be washed with a foam-free floor and wall cleaner or with a paint cleaning mixture. If grouting has gone grey you may be able to improve it with a little bleach (wear rubber gloves). But see A Roof Over Your Head.

Vinyl Papers

Vinyl papers can usually be wiped with any detergent, but don't get the seams wet and wipe the paper over afterwards with vinegar and water.

Washing Paint

Walls must be washed from the bottom upwards. If a trickle of water runs down over a dirty lower section it leaves a line which you may never be able to remove.

There is no point in using fancy products for cleaning paint. Almost all of them contain foaming agents, so you use one bucket of water to wash the wall and three to rinse the suds off - which is crazy. It is far easier to use a basic mixture such as ½ cup ammonia, ¼ cup vinegar, and ¼ cup washing soda. Another version is ½ cup vinegar, 1 cup ammonia, ¼ cup washing soda. Either goes in a gallon of water. Both mixtures are powerful cleaners, which should only be used wearing rubber gloves and with the windows open, as ammonia is not good to inhale. But both mixtures will cut through dirt on walls with ease. And you can use small quantities of them to keep walls routinely clean.

Washing up

Washing up is a rare skill. The skilled washer-upper makes sure everything is washed in order of cleanliness - greasiest last. They also wash everything - except cutlery - one at a time to avoid bangs and chips.

By the old kitchen rules, glass comes first, followed by cutlery, china, dishes and pans. They are rinsed in hot water containing a good dash of vinegar to remove the soap.

If the handles of good knives don't have visible pins to hold them on keep both the handle and the junction out of the water. Until quite recently, the handles of good knives were stuck on with a glue which comes unstuck in hot water and, though they won't fall out in an instant, the glue will swell and the handle will gradually push away from the cushion of the blade which it rests against, and become loose.

★ If raw egg, blood or flour are washed with hot water the heat cooks them on to the surface and makes them harder to remove. All three should be rinsed off under a cold tap, then washed in hot water afterwards.

★ Cutlery dries with spots on if it is left lying on a draining board, but put it on end in any container and it may dry spotless.

Glass

As vinegar counteracts the alkali in washing-up liquid, a dash in the rinsing water will give glass a better shine.

When washing fine glass make sure any central tap is turned out of the way and put a folded tea towel or a pad of foam rubber in the bottom of the basin. Then an accidental knock won't cause a chip. Avoid having the water too hot, otherwise immersing a thick piece of glass may lead it to expand at different rates in different parts, and cause it to crack. Wash one piece at a time, never leaving anything soaking in the water - lest someone else 'helpfully' drops something in.

Gilding is damaged by strong cleaners, so it is best to wash gilded glass in pure soap.

Glass should be dried in the opposite way to everything else: you hold the cloth still and turn the glass against it. That way, you don't risk wringing a glass off its stem.

Stainless Steel

Stainless steel which is regularly washed in a machine tends to develop a murky coating. Drop it in soapy water with a couple of tablespoons of bleach per pint of water. Leave it to soak until the coating brushes off easily. Then brush it clean and rinse it well. Wear rubber gloves and keep the bleach off everything around - including your stainless steel sink. Paradoxically, some sinks react badly to it.

Steel Knives

Steel knives, which aren't stainless, need to be hand-washed and dried straight after use or they become rusted and pitted. If that has already happened use a butler's trick: put some scouring powder on the end of a moist cork and rub this hard up and down the blade and the stains will vanish.

Tea Stains

China which is stained with tea can be cleaned effortlessly by soaking them for a few hours in water and washing soda. The stains then wash off. Or use salt, or bicarbonate of soda instead - though they are slightly less effective. Gilding can be damaged by any of them, so gilded china must not be soaked. It can be carefully rubbed with salt to remove stains from the places where there is no gilding.

Washing up Bad Food

If food in a container has clearly gone bad or may have food poisoning bacteria in it throw the food away (preferably straight in the dustbin or down the lavatory. Wash it very thoroughly *after* all the other items, rinse it in the hottest possible water and leave it to dry in the air. *Don't dry it up.* Then soak the washing-up brush or cloth in bleach for a while. If it is a pan of food, you can be doubly careful by boiling water in it with the lid on for half an hour, then washing it.

Drying-up cloths can transfer bacteria from one surface to another. So virtue and laziness always go hand in hand: the most hygienic method is to rinse everything in hot water and let it dry in the air, without drying it up.

Wooden Boards and Bowls

Wash wood up immediately after use - it is easily damaged by soaking and if food is allowed to dry only a soak will remove it. If flour has been used rinse the board in *cold* water or the flour will cook on to the surface. Salad bowls don't even need washing; simply wipe the inside out with kitchen paper. That way the dressing oils the wood.

Aluminium Pans

Don't fill a very hot pan with cold water - the base of aluminium is likely to distort.

Aluminium will dissolve in acid. This means traces of aluminium end up in any acid food you cook in them (see Food), but if you want to clean a blackened pan boil up a few rhubarb leaves, then let the acid liquid stand in the pan until the metal gleams. Then wash it very well, for rhubarb leaves are poisonous. If you don't have a vegetable garden substitute 1 teaspoon of cream of tartar for each ½ l (1 pt) water. For really shiny pans use a soap-filled metal pad.

Burnt Pans

There is no need to chuck out burnt saucepans or throw away hours of your life scouring them. All you need is salt, and patience.

Put in enough water to cover the burnt area, add a handful or so of salt (the amount really depends on the size of the problem) and boil it up for a while. Then leave it overnight. If it isn't soft enough to scrape off with the plastic end of a washing-up brush add more salt and boil it up again. With severely burnt pans you may need to repeat the whole process on an underlayer which the salt couldn't reach.

When deposits are burnt on to the outside of a pan you can boil them up in a larger pan, but clean small areas with neat salt on a damp cloth.

Enamel Pans

Enamel will crack with sudden changes of temperature and will also stain if strongly coloured food is left in it. To remove - or reduce - such stains fill the pan with water and boil it up with a handful of washing soda.

Frying Pans

A heavy iron frying pan should be 'seasoned' when you first have it, then food will be less likely to stick to it. To do this you cover the bottom with salt and rub it in to the metal, then heat it thoroughly. Repeat this twice, then wipe it clean without washing it.

Cleaning frying pans is a waste of time. Food is far less likely to stick if you avoid scouring them. So simply pour the surplus fat into some newspaper or into a container for the birds (it may block the drain if you tip it down the sink), then brush out all the debris and remaining fat under a hot tap immediately after use, without resorting to soap.

★ Milk is less likely to stick if you rinse the pan with water first. Then fill it with hot water the moment you empty it, to make it easy to clean. Do the same for any pan which has had egg in it.

Non-stick Pans

To scour non-stick pans is to remove the surface and throw away your money. Filling them with hot water immediately after use stops the food sticking and removes the need for rough treatment. Then just wash them with soap and water. Unless the manufacturer advises otherwise cover any stain with water and add two tablespoons bicarbonate of soda and 125 ml (¼ pt) vinegar for each 250 ml (½ pt) water. Boil this up for 15 minutes and the stain should have vanished or be ready to wipe off. If it hasn't, try again. Rinse the pan well, and rub in a drop of cooking oil.

Smells Which Won't Go

Occasionally a pan seems to hold the smell of food most unpleasantly. To clear this fill the pan with water, add a good dash of vinegar and boil it up. The smell will disappear.

Fill smelly plastic containers with water, add 2-3 teaspoonfuls bicarbonate of soda for every 500 ml (½ pt) water and leave this overnight. The smell should go completely. If it doesn't, repeat using more bicarbonate.

Woks

Woks can be washed in the normal way, but after drying them do as the Chinese do. Put a drop of oil in, heat it and rub it well all over the inside with a piece of paper. This prevents the surface rusting.

Washing-up Machines

Although all the following are kitchen or tableware, they cannot be put in a washing-up machine without damage or serious risk of damage:
- wood items other than wooden spoons
- good-quality glass and lead crystal
- very thick glass
- china with gilding
- bone-handled knives.

If any glass is repeatedly washed in washing-up machines it may develop cloudy patches. This is called etching and according to Lever Brothers there is no known cure.

Smelly Washing-up Machines

As washing-up machines become old they develop a smell which is then passed on to what they wash up - making cups unusable. There are products made to remove this and those I have tried do improve things. But also clean the machine out thoroughly, removing any debris caught in traps and filters.

Waste Bins and Baskets

In an ideal world, people would only put paper in wastepaper baskets, but families are seldom like that. Put an unwanted plastic carrier bag across the bottom of every bin and basket. Clean bins out according to what they are made of.

Wood Furniture

Wood furniture divides into three groups: oiled wood, modern varnished wood, and old furniture finished with wax or French polish.

Carved Wood

In Yorkshire they have the charming tradition of using a whole duck's wing, with its sweeping fan of feathers, to dust tricky surfaces. Less elegantly, you can use a decorator's dusting brush.

Oiled Wood

Tropical hardwoods, such as teak and afromosia, have a very high resin content and oiling is all they need, or like. You can buy oils sold as 'teak oil' or you can use boiled linseed oil, which is cheaper and smells just the same. Just put a little on a ball of cotton wool, wrap a rag around it and rub. You want a thin layer going right into the wood. If it is left on the surface it will interact with the air and form a hard sticky layer which is very nasty.

Varnished Wood

Modern varnished wood can be wiped with a damp cloth and have the occasional lick of polish if old age has dulled its shine. It needs no more than that. If stains start showing in the wood, the varnish has flaws which are allowing liquid to seep through. The only solution then is to remove the varnish. Most have no solvents and have to be sanded off, but check with the maker.

Polished Wood

Caring for polished wood is a lot easier than most people imagine. The main essential is never to let anything hot or wet stand on the surface, and never to write on it with a biro without several layers of padding.

Goodness knows what puritan mythology put the word out that wood had to be constantly polished and 'fed', but it simply isn't true.

It is impossible to feed wood. All polish does is make it look nice and stop moisture getting out. But enough is enough, and extra polish is as unnecessary as wearing two mackintoshes. Wood, which already has a polish, need only be polished twice a year. The rest of the time just rub it over with a clean duster. If a cotton velveteen duster is used the surface is far less likely to develop an unwanted bloom, but you don't have to work as hard as the Victorian ethics of the first *Enquire Within* suggested.

> *The cleaning of furniture forms an important part of the domestic economy, not only in regard to neatness, but also in point of expense. The readiest mode indeed consists in good manual rubbing, or the essence of elbows, as it is whimsically termed . . .*
>
> *Enquire Within,* 1856

Since polish hardly ever needs to be used there is no need for 'time-saving' aerosols. In fact, there is every reason to avoid them. In *Supertips* I warned against their use, but the conservator of the National Trust puts it even more strongly. 'The surface can acquire a slight milky look. No remedy has yet been found. It is IMPOSSIBLE [her capitals] to remove this aesthetically objectionable film without first stripping and then resurfacing the object.'

There is another aspect. When we look at anything we really see the light reflected from it. No two surfaces absorb and reflect the light in quite the same way, and part of the beauty of old furniture is the special way in which old wax polish reflects the light. To varnish it, or to use a different type of polish, is to alter this subtle quality for the worse.

For good furniture Antiquewax is a perfectly good polish, or the recipe used at one of the top museums has the advantage of being more resistant to finger marks than most polishes. Take 2 parts beeswax, to 4 parts paraffin wax, and 4 parts carnuba. (A hardware shop should have beeswax; a pharmacy the other two.) Melt these in a basin over hot water (*not over a flame as they are inflammable.*) Stir them together and stir in about four times their combined volume of *real* turpentine to make a cream. Apply it *very* sparingly (a common fault is too much polish and too little elbow grease) and leave it to dry for several hours before polishing. Treat carved wood like shoes and use a brush to apply the polish and another to remove it. This stops the polish clinging in the dips.

Cleansing

If furniture has a bloom on it, like a grape, it means the atmosphere has left its mark. Wipe it over with a cloth wrung out in warm water and a very good dash of vinegar, drying as you go.

Reviving

Some furniture either cannot or should not be revived - notably old oak and very early furniture and anything with inlays. However, when plain old mahogany furniture, finished with shellac or French polish, has dirty patches where finger dirt has built up it can be vastly improved with reviver. This is a recipe used by restorers and little known to anyone outside the business. Take 2 parts pure turpentine, 2 parts methylated spirits, 2 parts malt vinegar and 1 part raw linseed oil. Put them all in a bottle and shake well as you use it, for it separates easily.

Put some on a ball of cotton wool and test it on a small area which won't be noticed. If the surface of the wood is French polish or shellac a shine will begin to show through. If you work right through the dirt and fail to reveal a shine the surface is wax. It is far safer to give wax to a professional to clean as inexperienced cleaning could cause dirt to enter the wood itself. A third possibility is that it will have no impact at all. If so, you probably have a case of oxidized linseed oil - and that is a suitable case for experts as it is incredibly tough.

On French polish do realize that all DIY treatments carry a risk, and that furniture of any real value is best left to experts. Work very carefully, doing a small area at a time, and never leave drops of the mixture to eat into the surface. Keep changing your cotton wool, or you will just shift the dirt from place to place. From time to time look at the whole object. No old furniture should look like new, keep the differences between the edges and the flats of the wood which speak of its use. It is far better to do too little than too much. The patina of years cannot be replaced, but you can always do more tomorrow.

Damaged French Polish

If French polish on a valueless piece of furniture is badly marked the best course may be to remove it. But it is important for a good piece to have its original finish.

French polish can be totally removed with methylated spirits. You need to work carefully, constantly taking fresh pieces of rag so you don't rub it into the grain.

The ability of meths to 'melt' French polish also means it can sometimes be used to blend out a scratch. This is delicate and tricky and should *not* be attempted on furniture you value. You slightly moisten a very small ball of cotton wool with methylated spirits, wrap a piece of clean cotton rag around it and rub it across the scratch extremely carefully so as to blend it into the rest of the polish. Work very smoothly across the surface; pressure will imprint the weave of the rag on the polish.

Water Marks on French Polish

Miracles seldom happen, but the ash and oil treatment for the white marks on French polish is as close as you are likely to get. On dark wood simply mix cigarette or cigar ash with a little vegetable oil and rub it firmly in until the mark vanishes. If the mark doesn't go it isn't French polish. There is no way you can remove stains from polyurethane coatings.

If the water mark is on French polish on a pale wood rub with an oily Brazil or metal polish wadding - but there is a risk with any proprietary product that the formula will be changed and damage a surface it isn't designed for.

> Some people claim that oil and salt is the mixture to use, but this may scratch the polish. Ash is easily obtained from any pub.

Marquetry

Marquetry is one of the most vulnerable forms of decoration. The thin sections of wood are stuck on to a much thicker base; so heat and moisture can produce different changes in the two and make layers lift off. Furniture with marquetry needs to be positioned very carefully, so it isn't near a fire or radiator. It should also be kept away from windows, as some of the colours may fade very quickly in bright light.

Avoid polishing marquetry, and never use reviver or any other oily substance on it. Instead, dust it with a very soft brush - a duster could catch a corner which had risen slightly.

Oak

If light oak gets very dirty scrub it using a teaspoonful of ammonia in 1 l (2 pts) of water. Wipe off the wet, leave it to dry totally, then sprinkle it with French chalk from hardware shops or Frank Joel (see top right) — and dust off any excess.

Dark oak is usually very old and its original finish may well contribute to its value. Before allowing any would-be restorer to strip it down and resurface it, talk to the Victoria and Albert Museum conservators. Some restorers have very little knowledge about *when* they should renovate.

Pine

Pine is porous and soaks up stains like blotting paper. The only way to avoid this altogether is to seal the surface with polyurethane. But there is no pretending that the surface really suits the character of pine unless it is modern. It may be better to leave an old table bare and just scrub it and bleach off any stains with lemon juice.

A pure wax polish really looks best on pine furniture, of any age. But one has to expect every last drop of water to mark it. Once a polish is achieved it needs no more polishing than other wood (see above) and a wipe with a cloth moistened with white spirit removes water marks from the wax as well as anything.

Positioning Furniture

The two enemies of wood are sunlight and dryness. Central heating is a modern invention which antiques were not designed to withstand. Use humidifiers in every room or have plenty of plants around (though *not* on the antiques) so their earth gives off moisture or tuck saucers of water out of sight in odd places.

Sunlight will bleach dark wood. If a piece is near sunlight do make sure that nothing ever stands on it for very long or you will be left with a dark mark where that section of wood wasn't bleached by the sun.

The National Trust Manual of Housekeeping (Hermione Sandwith and Sheila Stanton, Penguin) gives ideal temperatures and humidity for most types of fine objects.

The Museums and Galleries Commission Conservation Unit (7 St James's Square, London SW1Y 4JU Tel: 01 839 9340) has a register of conservators and will give you names in your area.

The Victoria and Albert Museum (Cromwell Road, London SW7 2RL Tel: 01 589 6371) can put people in touch with conservators around Britain. Its experts will also advise on conservation. Speak to the appropriate department *before* taking objects to them.

Frank W. Joel (5 Oldmeadow Road, Hardwick Industrial Estate, Kings Lynn, Norfolk PE30 4HL Tel: 0553 760851/2) supplies materials used in conservation, such as Sepialite, Renaissance Wax and Synperonic N, in domestic quantities by mail order. Books on care and restoration of fine objects.

Atlantis Paper (Gulliver's Wharf, 105 Wapping Lane, London E1 9RW Tel: 01 481 3784) - stocks many of Frank Joel's items, and has acid-free papers and boards - also mail order.

Blanchard, Martin & Simmonds Ltd (237 Walworth Road, London SE17) - makes whiting.

W. Canning Co Ltd (Unit C, Greatham Road Industrial Estate, Bushey, Watford, Herts WD2 2JB Tel: 0923 37621) makes, and will supply, the brass lacquer Ercalene. A London stockist is **T.A. Hutchinson**, 88 St John Street, London EC1 4EH Tel: 01 253 3186

Connolly Brothers (Wandle Bank, London, SW19 1DW Tel: 01 542 5251) restores leather upholstery.

Meech Static Eliminators (140-144 Clapham Manor Street, London SW4 6DA Tel: 01 622 4555) makes anti-static sprays.

Picreator Enterprises Ltd (44 Park View Gardens, London NW4 2PN Tel: 01 202 8972) sells small quantities of unusual cleaning materials and substances used in conservation, by mail order only.

Pilgrim Payne & Co Ltd (Park Street Works, Latimer Place, London W10 6QU Tel: 01 960 5656) specializes in dry-cleaning furnishings, including woven tapestry and fine carpets. Runs a delivery postal service.

Royal School of Needlework (Apartment 38, Hampton Court Palace, Surrey KT8 9AU Tel: 01 943 1432) will clean and repair needlepoint and other embroidery. Ring for an appointment - security at Hampton Court prevents the admission of unexpected visitors.

Sheffco Ltd (70-78 York Way, London N1 9AG) Tel: 01 837 1211 for stockists of the Silver Solution.

The Tarnprufe Co. Ltd (68 Nether Edge Road, Sheffield S7 1RX Tel: 0742 553652 makes Tarnprufe bags, cutlery rolls for storing silver without tarnishing, Carosil capsules and silver cleaning mitts. At branches of John Lewis and good silversmiths.

Vitreous Enamel Development Council (VEDC) (New House, High Street, Ticehurst, Wadhurst, Sussex TN5 7AL Tel: 0580 200152) tests cleaning materials for vitreous enamel and will supply a list of safe cleaners.

CLOTHING AND SHOE CARE

Brushing Clothes

Removing every speck of dust and fluff from clothing makes an enormous difference. If a clothes brush fails, wrap sticking plaster or sellotape round your hand several times - sticky side out - and run this over the garment. It will often pick up fine hairs brushes leave behind. Running wetted hands over a garment can also be effective.

★ If a garment doesn't have a button where you need it or one falls off at the last minute, a small piece of double-sided sticky tape does duty. But don't use it on delicate fabrics, velvet or corduroy.

Feathers

If large feathers need to be cleaned they should be wiped gently with a clean soft brush dipped in white spirit, and allowed to dry in the air. Small feathers, such as you find in a feather boa, can be dipped into pure soap and water and well rinsed, then fluffed up gently with a hair drier.

Fur Care
This is not the place to go into the rights and wrongs of wearing fur. There are furs in lots of cupboards whose original four-legged owners are long past being able to wear them. And, in my view, it is adding insult to injury for those coats not even to be decently cared for.

Wet is the big enemy of fur - especially modern fur, which is thinner skinned than the old kind. Once wet gets through to the leather backing it can stiffen and wrinkle it. A wet fur should be shaken dry as soon as possible and hung in an airy place *away from heat*. A doorway in a centrally heated house is ideal.

The less fur has to be cleaned the better. So, if possible wear a scarf at the neck to keep make-up off it. If you do get make-up on it very gently work Fullers Earth - for brown fur, or magnesium carbonate - for white (both from a chemist) through it with your fingers. Once it is worked in, leave it for not less than 30 minutes and then shake it out. (The old-fashioned method was to work in warm bran and this is still fine for a thick old fur. These methods can also be used for greasy stains. Any other spots and marks can often be removed by gently wiping - in the direction of the fur - with a damp cloth. But it mustn't be wet.

Unless you wear it constantly a fur should only need professional cleaning every 2 to 3 years.

Fur coats can become sadly bare at the edges while the main part is still perfectly good. A good furrier can usually put this right quite inexpensively. Furriers often advertise in the glossy magazines. Get comparative prices: some companies quote three times as much as others and look at their workmanship. There could be a reason for a low price.

Putting furs into cold storage obviously keeps pests off but it is expensive. However, fur cannot be kept in plastic or it gradually dries out, changes colour and splits. To protect it against moths make a cotton bag rather longer and wider than the garment. Put the closed end of the bag at the bottom and bind the open end *tightly* round the neck of a coat hanger. Moths won't go through cotton to get to the fur. The snag is that woolly bears will (see page 206). So you may have to choose between the damage done by keeping fur in plastic and the damage these creatures will do. Keep the coat in a busy cupboard - insects prefer quiet - and inspect the coat each month. Look for any little twist in the fur - it means a moth has made a nest for its young who will soon come out to dine.

Glove Care
In gloveless days the niceties of glove buying tend to be forgotten. A perfectly fitting kid glove should feel too tight when you put it on, and you should need to ease each finger down over yours by gently stroking it with finger and thumb from tip to base.

You are less likely to tear the seams of new gloves if you take my grandmother's tip and put them in a warm place before wearing.

You can get some of the dirt off pale gloves by rubbing them with a pale India rubber, and wearing the gloves and rubbing your hands through warm flour will also remove some of the dirt. Dark suede which has flattened can also be restored with one of the rubbers made for rubbing suede - but go very lightly.

I never feel a washed glove looks quite as good as it should, but you can buy glove shampoos for certain brands of gloves. Leave doeskin gloves unrinsed, as the soap helps to keep them supple and press all gloves dry between towels and dry away from heat.

The 1856 edition had the following instructions for washing kid gloves, and if you have no glove shampoo they are as good as any.

> *Have ready a little new milk in one saucer, and a piece of brows soap in another, and a clean cloth or towel folded three or four times. On the cloth, spread out the glove smooth and neat. Take a piece of flannel, dip it in the milk, then rub off a good quantity of the soap to the wetted flannel and commence to rub the glove downwards towards the left hand. Continue this process until the glove, if white, looks a dingy yellow, though clean; if coloured, till it looks dark and spoiled. Lay it to dry; and old gloves will soon look nearly new. They will be soft, glossy, smooth, shapy and elastic.*

You can substitute any pure soap for 'brows soap', whatever it was and, whatever the method, gloves should be wriggled at regular intervals as they dry, or they will not dry soft at all.

Hats
Grease on the fabric band inside a hat comes off easily with a drop of hair shampoo on a soft brush. Wipe the shampoo off with a damp cloth afterwards. Or use a spray-on dry-cleaner - but keep it off the parts that show. Greasy leather bands can be cleaned with saddle soap - it won't get the grease out but it will let you wash off any surface grime.

Felt and velour hats need to be brushed, with the nap, with a soft brush, and if they get out of shape hold them in some steam, press them to shape again and let them cool, supported by crumpled paper if necessary.

Pale straw hats can usually be brushed clean. But a real straw hat, such as a boater, can be scrubbed with a little lemon juice and left in the sun if it becomes dingy.

Leather Garments
The labels on leather can be deceptive. Leather garments sometimes say they are 'washable' when they are merely spongeable. However, some suede is genuinely washable - if you follow the maker's instructions perfectly. Some shiny leather responds well to saddle soap or being wiped with milk - do a test patch where it won't show.

Any leather with a shine usually resists stains extremely well - but wipe off grease or oil fast as it could be absorbed and mark it. Other marks usually come off with a lightly damped cloth. The real danger is from scratches, so avoid excited pets.

Suede or leather with a dull sheen will be very vulnerable to stains unless you treat it with a spray-on protection and leather protector, but it is best to ask the makers of the garment whether such a spray can safely be used on their particular leather.

If suede starts to become flat rub it with another piece of suede of the same colour. The special rubbers sold for cleaning suede are also useful but use them gently and be very chary of rubbing suede with metal suede brushes. They tend to rough up the surface and produce what the trade calls 'feathering', i.e. loose floppy bits which make the suede look decidedly tatty.

Leather needs expert dry-cleaning and even then it changes colour. So any set must be cleaned together - whether all the parts need cleaning or not.

Baggy Leather
Baggy leather isn't as easily cured as baggy cloth. So hitch up skirts and trouser knees and avoid over-bagging them. However, a *little* steam can somewhat reduce the bagginess of leather - but do check with the maker before you try it as it could be very harmful to certain leathers.

Don't hold leather close to a strong jet of steam from a kettle spout; just let it be in the clouds of steam above. Then lie the garment flat and smooth it gently to shape with your hands. Some experts go so far as to iron the leather but amateurs could wreak havoc on the skins, so I don't recommend it.

★ Some people suggest putting leather in the freezer to remove bags. *Don't.* Certain finishes will be permanently destroyed by very low temperatures.

Handbags
Handbags need to be treated like leather garments, except that you can occasionally give them a very sparing shine with a colourless shoe polish. But do rub it off very well, or it will transfer grease to your clothes.

It really isn't practical to dye large leather items, but handbags and shoes are perfectly possible. There are two kinds of dye - the kind which sinks in and the kind which you paint on to the surface. Of the two, the first looks far better and stands up to bending and rubbing, so it can be used on soft leather handbags as well as on shoes. Alas, the good range of colours is in the paint kind. But you will get the best result if you paint the dye on, in several thin layers, with a soft artist's brush.

★ Acetone or white spirit will condition shoes ready for most dyes.

Storing Garments
If garments are going to be put away for any length of time - even from spring to autumn - clean them first. Everyone sweats more than they think and perspiration left in a fabric will create permanent stains unless it is removed while still reasonably fresh.

This even applies to a wedding dress which has been worn only once. After all wedding dresses tend to be worn at long intervals - to say the least of it. After it has been cleaned store it in a large box lined with acid free tissue paper (storing fabric in plastic bags for any length of time will cause white to yellow). Keep it in a cool dry atmosphere.

If you are storing any other clothes for more than a few weeks it is also wise to prepare for the worst. You may think you haven't got moths or woolly bears but you can't be sure they won't fly in through the next open window. So if anything is being stored it should be protected against them - see Pests.

★ It is thrifty to mark the back of any pair of tights before putting them on; then all the snags made by the backs of the heels stay on one side and the other side remains respectable.
★ Putting washed tights or stockings in a bag in the fridge and freezing them before removing and drying, does seem to give them more strength to stand up to the snags of life.
★ If a ladder begins to run the best way to stop it is with nail varnish. The second best is with the soft side of a cake of soap.
★ When I was in my teens tights hadn't been invented and the popular joke was that a girl always carried an aspirin and could use it for one of three things - to cure a headache, to hold between the knees (as an infallible contraceptive) or to put in suspenders when the 'button' went. It still works for suspenders and headaches, and most restaurants keep some.
★ If a zip becomes stiff, and isn't clogged with its two great enemies - salt and loose threads - it probably needs lubrication. Run a 2B lead pencil up and down the teeth several times, then raise and lower it, until it runs easily. Better still, use the powdered graphite sold for locks - being careful not to mark pale fabrics.

Shoes

Buying Children's Shoes
Children's shoes can be one of a parent's worst headaches. Children want to look good from a remarkably early age and it can be almost impossible to find shoes which are good for the feet and fashionable. There may be a straight choice: either the child suffers from less stylish shoes for a few years or from bad feet for many years. And the choice is the parent's, not the child's - for the parent is paying. I know they kick up a dreadful fuss, but it is not a fashion decision - it is a medical decision.

While a child's feet are growing the bones are still soft and can be damaged by the wrong shoes, even if they don't hurt. A child's feet must be carefully measured in both length and width before shoes are bought. (Clarks, Start-rite and K Shoes all make children's shoes sized in both directions). On average, children's feet grow a whole size every 6 to 12 months, so new shoes need to be 16 mm (⅔ in) too long to allow for growth. Because they need this extra room, children will slip forward in their shoes unless there is support over the instep.

The backs of the shoes should fit lightly but firmly, without cutting into the ankle bones, and the right toe room is as important as the right length. Shoes which press down on the toes or draw them together will, in time, cause corns and distortion. The line down the inner side of the foot needs to be almost straight and the leather of the toe shouldn't touch the child's toes underneath. High heels are also damaging. They throw the weight on to the ball of the foot and can permanently damage a child's feet. Tight stockings can be as harmful as tight shoes. Avoid stretch socks if possible or else buy stretch socks a size larger than the makers specify. On non-stretch socks a foot which will comfortably go right round the knuckles of someone's clenched fist should fit their feet.

The barefoot children of the Victorian poor have made people link bare feet with poverty. But, in fact, a child who goes barefoot wherever it is safe and warm enough will grow up with healthier feet than one who is always shod. After all, feet were not designed to wear shoes. On uncarpeted floors bare feet are much safer than socks, which could slip on polish.

The **Children's Foot Health Register** (84-88 Great Eastern Street, London EC2A 3ED Tel: 01 739 2071) - is a register of the shops throughout Britain which have staff trained to fit children's shoes, offer children's shoes in four widths and in both half and whole sizes. The list is free with a sae (9in x 6in).

The **Shoe and Allied Trades Research Association** (SATRA House, Rockingham Road, Northants NN16 9JH Tel: 0536 410000) - produces leaflets on shoe care.

Buying Adult Shoes
Adult feet need no less care and shoes should only be bought if they are comfortable. For those with unusual feet - very large, small, wide, narrow or different sizes - this is easier said than done. However, the **Disabled Living Foundation** has a list of those who supply all these needs as well as others supplying special shoes for certain handicaps. It also has a footwear advisor who will discuss problems.

Complaints about Shoes
Complaints about footwear should first go to the shop, then the local Trading Standards Officer, and if that fails to the **Footwear Distributors' Federation,** Commonwealth House, 1-19 New Oxford Street, London WC1A 1PA Tel: 01 404 0955. But they can only deal with complaints about members of their federation.

Caring for Aniline Leather Shoes
If a shoe isn't suede but isn't very shiny ask whether it is aniline leather. This easily absorbs dirt. So ask the shop whether the shoes can be sprayed with a leather protector to keep out dirt and wet. Even so, treat them carefully. If aniline leather does get muddy, wipe it with a cloth barely damped with cold water. Allow the leather to dry and clean it with a recommended cream.

Caring for Fabric Shoes
Shoes made of fabric and rubber are sometimes so well bonded together that they will stand up to a spin in the washing machine - but they might fall apart.

If fabric shoes get muddy, let the mud dry before trying to remove it. Then brush it off with a clothes brush. There are shampoos designed for fabric shoes but they sometimes lighten the colour. So it's best to test their effect on the tongue, if the shoe has one. White canvas shoes can be cleaned with whitener. For dyeing fabric shoes check with Dylon, page 183.

Caring for Leather Shoes
Leather shoes should be polished regularly and kept with shoe trees in, so folds don't form too deeply.

If mud gets on to leather shoes let it dry, then brush it off carefully with a stiff brush and gently sponge off any that remains using as little water as possible. Let them dry completely before polishing with a matching polish designed for the purpose. The easy way to make sure you don't apply too much polish is to use one soft brush for both putting it on and taking it off.

Caring for Plastic, Patent and Wet-look Shoes
Patent, plastic and other wet-look shoes should be sponged clean and wiped dry. To give patent a good shine rub it with a little vaseline, or milk or even face cream. Genuine patent leather easily creases and may crack when worn if it is not properly stored. Patent shoes need shoe trees, (or a wedge of paper in the toe and a springy stick to keep the shape) and vaseline over the surface, to keep them flexible.

Caring for Suede and Nubuck Shoes
Spray suede and nubuck shoes with a protective spray when brand new. It makes these leathers look good for very much longer. Dirt is best brushed off with a stiff *bristle* brush - those metal brushes sold for suede risk making the nap too rough and causing the long straggly bits. But if suede gets shiny it is sometimes possible to remove the shine by gently using a metal brush or a little fine sandpaper *very* carefully.

★ Leather shoes which pinch can be stretched by applying a branded leather stretcher to the inside. It also helps to rub the tight place with the end of a broom handle on the inside when the leather is warm.

EQUIPPING A HOME

Auctions Anyone furnishing a home with limited funds should consider buying at auctions. They offer great bargains and great fun. It's a myth that if you so much as scratch your nose the auctioneer will think you have put in a bid for thousands. The truth is that you may have trouble catching the auctioneer's eye if you aren't a face they are used to.

The catalogue of any good auction house will have a page giving all the rules and conditions, and it is advisable to read this before you buy or sell through them.

In some salerooms prices fluctuate with the season, dropping in January and in mid-summer. They may also vary with what is being sold where. Very large pieces of furniture sell badly in cities, but better in the country, for example. Despite the eagle eyes of dealers, there are good things to be had - not so much antiques as comfortable chairs that someone else was tired of, or perfectly good curtains that didn't fit new windows, good linen sold after a death and so on. However: the law is far less strict about auctions than about other types of sale (see under Law). For this reason they can be a very bad source of electrical goods.

Buying at Auctions

Every auction has a viewing day when you can wander round at leisure, poke and prod the goods judiciously, check that there really is pine under the ghastly paint and look for stains on the beds. The catalogue lets you see how the object has been described and what its lot number is. A 'lot' can be a single object, a set of objects which go together or a random collection of junk.

Porters are great sources of help and information and will say what they think a lot will go for. A porter will also bid for you if you ask him to, but you must tell him the maximum you are prepared to bid, and ask him not to bid above that sum. Allow for the fact that if he gets the item you will be expected to tip him suitably, and you will pay a 'buyer's premium' on top of the bid price, of about 10 per cent. This applies whether you bid or a porter bids.

If you want to bid yourself, you can ask what time the lot is likely to come up. Get there earlier in case the sale goes faster than they thought. To bid, simply make a clear movement with your hand or catalogue so the auctioneer can see it. He will look at you as he accepts your bid, then turn to look for a higher bidder. You can bid again whenever you want.

If you find you have accidentally bid for something you didn't intend to, tell the auctioneer *at once* - then they can usually put the item back into the sale. If you have bought something you will be asked for your name and address and often a deposit while the auction continues. At the end of the sale you pay for the item. You then arrange to remove it within a reasonable time. If it's a house sale this is usually within 24 hours.

Selling by Auction

If you want to sell anything in an auction, ring a sale room that sells similar items and ask if they might be able to sell yours. If there are a lot of items the auctioneer may visit and decide. The auctioneer will usually expect you to get the goods to the auction, but some companies will arrange free collection; others collect and charge for it. The goods are then likely to be put into a sale within 2 to 3 weeks. You can choose whether you give the auctioneer a 'reserve price' below which the goods may not be sold, or whether they simply go to the highest bidder, however low the best bid. The auctioneer takes a percentage of the selling price. It can be as much as 17 per cent, and is unlikely to be below 10 per cent. Usually, the less valuable items attract the higher percentage.

There are no rules as to what happens if an item is unsold, but the policy of some auction houses is that if there was no reserve or a reserve recommended by the auctioneer there is no charge and the owner can take them away or put them in the next auction. But if the seller puts a reserve on which is higher than the house recommends and the goods aren't sold there is usually what they call a 'buying-in fee'. This fee should be discussed when you set the reserve on your goods.

Finding an auction

Most auction houses publish an auction calendar but the main source of information is the *Antiques Trade Gazette. Antique Collector* also gives regular information on the better auctions and house sales and the *Daily Telegraph* lists auctions in its Monday editions; *The Times* lists them on Tuesdays, and the *Independent* may have them on Fridays. Auctions should also be listed in your local papers.

Complaining about Goods

If something you have bought isn't good enough (see under Law) your first step is to complain to the head of the company which sold you the item, The Office of Fair Trading (see below) suggests you stop using the goods and complain immediately.

● If you write keep a copy of the letter.
● Get proof of posting.
● Do not send receipts or guarantees, only photocopies.
● If you ring keep a note of the name of the person you speak to.
● Have your facts clear before you ring.
● Note what you say and what they say.
● Note the date and time of your call.

The shop ought to collect the faulty goods but you may do better to take them back and see the manager. If they really are faulty he or she should refund your money or replace them. If this doesn't happen see Law.

Help and Information on Complaints

Reading the pages on consumer law will give you a good idea of what your entitlements are. The useful leaflet 'A Trader's Guide' from the **Department of Trade** (Room 207, Gaywood House, 29 Great Peter Street, London SW1P 3LW) telling traders just how they must treat customers who have a complaint is a good-eye opener for customers too. On top of that, the **Office of Fair Trading (OFT)** (Room 310c, 15-25 Bream Buildings, London EC4A 1PR Tel: 01 242 2858) has clear, readable leaflets on every aspect of consumer rights and special versions for Scotland and Northern Ireland. However, the OFT cannot deal with complaints.

A complaint always leads to one of the three Cs - compensation, compromise, or a claim in the courts. If you want to avoid the courts then one possible route to compensation may be to get the company's trade association to insist that it sticks to a professional code of practice. The OFT has leaflets on these which the local Citizens' Advice Bureau should have - and is itself another source of advice as are Law Centres.

If you think the law has been broken the Trading Standards Officer may be able to take up the case. Infuriatingly, the section of a local council which houses this useful person has no unified name across the country. If you tell the council switchboard the kind of help you are looking for, you should be given the right people. Or the OFT has a list.

If a trader has broken the Criminal law on trading, the officials may take the matter up directly. If it is a breach of civil law they can advise you on your rights, and perhaps draft letters or put you in touch with relevant trade associations. They may even act as middle men and help you and a trader to agree a solution. However, if you buy something from a company in a different borough you must contact the seller's local Trading Standards Officer, not your own. The exception is when the work was done in the buyer's area - as with installing double glazing.

The **Consumers' Association** has a Personal Service (Freepost, 14 Buckingham Street, London WC2N 6BR) to which you can subscribe separately from the *Which* magazine. The association will advise subscribers on their rights, help them take action, and take up complaints with retailers and manufacturers if necessary. It will also help with taking a case through the county court.

Disposing of What You Don't Need

Under a public health act local authorities are obliged to remove household refuse from your home. But they generally take 'household refuse' to mean the daily rubbish. If you want to get rid of objects which are too big to go in a dustbin, the council will normally send the refuse department to collect them - at a price. Ring and ask for an estimate or take them to the council tip yourself; dumping them is usually free.

If you need to dispose of rubble and wood, skips can be hired through companies in the Yellow Pages. The company then removes the rubbish with the skip.

Disposing of Throw-Aways via Charities
A directory called 'Waste Not' can be bought from the **Charities Aid Foundation,** 48 Pembury Road, Tonbridge TN9 2JD Tel: 0732 356323. It tells you the throw-aways collected by most major charities - from postage stamps to furniture - and where you should take or send them. It also gives addresses of organizations which can tell you how to recycle anything from cans to sump oil. The directory isn't expensive and its price helps charity, your local library should have it — or get it if you ask.

Bottle Banks
If you want to find your nearest bottle bank, your local council should be able to help you. If it can't, there may be one just across a borough or county border. The **Glass Manufacturers' Federation** (19 Portland Place, London W1N 4EH Tel: 01 580 6952) will tell anyone where to find the nearest bottle bank and has leaflets on the importance of recycling. (Don't ask about sheet glass; it's for the glass tableware industry.)

Car Boot Sales
Car boot sales are advertised in the local papers and usually anyone who has something to sell can take it along in his or her car, pay the entrance and parking fee and sell. There are rumours that the law on this may be tightened up. So ring the organizer's number when you see a sale advertised and see what the rules are.

Waste Paper
Waste paper can fetch considerable sums if you have enough of it. My children's primary school used to have a paper dump where parents took stacks of old newspapers. A waste paper merchant cleared the lot when enough had built up. It cost the parents nothing except a few minutes of time and raised very considerable sums for the school.

Doorstep Selling

If someone arrives at your home, or rings suggesting he or she should visit, the key question is 'what do you get from letting people come in and talk which you wouldn't get any other way?' The answer is usually *nothing* - if so, don't let them in. It is all too easy for people to pose as members of legitimate companies and enter your home under false pretences. So the rules for protecting yourself are these.

- Before letting people in check that they have documents which show they do represent a legitimate company.
- Be suspicious if they talk about benefits for your children - they are just playing on your love to make cash for themselves.
- Don't believe those who say you have been chosen for a prize. If it involves you paying a penny, it's just a con.
- Never let anyone 'advise you on security'. The police will do this for free and *they* aren't casing your home.
- Don't believe any sob stories, or any claims to special expertise.
- If you haven't already looked at, *and priced,* similar items in the open market, don't buy. Ask the seller to go away and say you will ring him.
- If anyone wants payment in advance, don't buy.
- Don't trust offers of special terms or discounts unless they are made in writing - and don't believe those who say they will send them in writing.
- Wait until you are absolutely sure of the identity of the company and the salesperson before signing anything.
- Check that the product carries a guarantee.

Remember home selling is so successful because we are all used to being polite to people in our own homes. So it is far easier for sales people to talk us into something we don't want than it would be if we were in a shop. Sales teams are trained to play on this fact.

The **Direct Selling Association** 44 Russell Square, London WC1B 4JP) - operates a code of practice and will help you to resolve complaints.

The **Radio, Electrical and Television Retailers' Association** (**RETRA**) **Ltd** (address, see page 182) - produces a leaflet setting out an 18-point code of practice for its members.

Equipping a Kitchen

Gadgets are fun, but if you want to cook well - with reasonable speed and efficiency - it is essential to have the right tools, and that starts with a good knife and the most versatile pan you can find. Below I cover the basics without which it is hard to cook well unless you are one of those people who can cook good food on an open fire with a few sticks and a knife.

General Equipment

Balloon whisk: a loop whisk (balloon whisk) is the secret of smooth sauces and gravies (see Food). A medium size in stainless steel is most versatile. If you don't have a blender or your gadgets go wrong this whisk will also stand in for beating eggs, and making cakes or mayonnaise.

Chopping block: hygiene experts say wood, being porous, allows bacteria from contaminated food - such as raw chicken - to be passed to cooked food - such as ham. So, instead of wood, they recommend polyurethane or plastic-laminated blocks. To me there is something comforting about the sound and feel of knife on wood. If you feel the same and can run to two boards, I suggest a polyurethane one for raw meat and a good wooden block for everything else. Avoid chopping boards with seams. Once wet the wood will swell, stretching the grooves, and that loosens the joints so they fall apart.

Colander: choose one with holes which rice won't dive through, and large enough to sit over a saucepan and double as a steamer. Avoid plastic.

Electric kettle: jug-shaped kettles use the least energy and those with a soft rubber grip handle which separate automatically from the base are safest.

Grater: the classic is 4-sided stainless steel.

Jug: an accurately marked pint-sized measuring jug. Pyrex are the most useful as you can also stand them in boiling water to heat, or cook in them in a microwave.

Kitchen scissors: the best can be bought with left-handed grips as well as right ones. Wilkinsons make a very simple sharpener for theirs - a boon as kitchen scissors blunt easily.

Knives: a good knife - which will last almost a lifetime - costs less than a tank of petrol and makes cooking a great deal faster and more efficient. But a blunt knife or a poor blade can double the time for any job. Nowadays you no longer need to buy expensive chef's knifes. The knife I have from the moderately priced 'Professional' range of Kitchen Devils is better than its Sabatier equivalent. Whatever the brand, look for a firm blade with no sideways bend to it - which is really sharp and can be sharpened. It should feel comfortably heavy and well balanced in your hand. The minimum number is two: a small sharp one for dealing with fruit and small vegetables, a larger one for meat and larger vegetables. But the more sophisticated your cooking is, the more knives you need.

★ Have a small stainless knife for fruit. An ordinary steel knife can react with the acid in fruit and give it a sharply metallic flavour - which is why old cookery books say fruit must be cut with a silver knife.

Lemon zester: takes strips of zest off in seconds for cooking or garnishing (a nice optional extra)

Palette knife: if you are icing cakes with smooth icing this is essential and there is a world of difference between using a cheap stiff one and using an expensive flexible one.

A knife is only as good as the sharpness of its blade. So a steel is essential. Using one is very easy if you use the method which has been in my family for generations. It isn't conventional, but it works, and you won't cut yourself.

Hold the knife and the steel so they form an X almost parallel to the floor, with the blade on top with its hilt close to the steel. The blade shouldn't lie flat against the steel but be at a *very slight* angle to it. (If you think about the shape of the edge that you want to put on the blade the correct angle will be obvious.) Now, hold your left hand still and move your right to the right - and very *slightly* away from you. Keep the blade and steel lightly but firmly in contact as the length of the blade slides up the steel. Repeat this with the blade under the steel.

The blade will need to caress the steel 5 or 6 times but don't over-sharpen - once the edge is good, stop. It takes a little practise but even doing it slowly and hesitantly will improve the edge, provided you have the angle of the blade right.

Potato peeler: the kind which twirls on its handle removes the thinnest layer, and leaves the most goodness, as the minerals and vitamins are concentrated under the surface of many vegetables.

Spatulas: a wooden one is invaluable for scrambled eggs and sautéeing, a plastic one for scraping out bowls fast. Don't get rubber: it softens in contact with garlic.

Water purifying jug: is needed if you live in an area in which the water tastes of chemicals. But the first essential is surely to be able to have a decent cup of tea or coffee, and this is impossible with chemical flavoured water. You don't need an elaborate or expensive version: the very simple Crystal jug does the trick.

Pans

The pans you need are decided by the kind of food you cook. So, before buying, think how you would like to cook - then buy what suits you. Below are some points to think about. They aren't the last word but they may give you something to disagree with.

It is easy to get trapped into the 'three bears' concept of saucepans. But though a small, a medium and a large pan may sound sensible it often isn't. Big ones give you a choice of how much food you will cook; small ones limit you. The large base also makes better use of the heat from your burner, and saves fuel. The basic minimum is probably one small one which pours well - for sauces, scrambled egg, and heating milk - say 750 ml (1½ pt) - plus two or three large ones for vegetables. It has not been proved that aluminium has ill effects on the brain but, as long as the slightest question mark hangs over this, I cannot advise anyone to buy aluminium. Lightweight enamel is often cheap and practical but it chips easily. Having a yen for the traditional, I would like to say that a good-quality steel pan with a heavy copper bottom, or a heavy enamelled cast iron pan, was by far the best answer. I can't. They may be more stylish and chefly, but modern glass pans cook as well, are easier to keep clean than stainless steel and let you see at a glance if the water is getting low. Yet they are a fraction of the price. Finally, the largest size is at present too small for cooking foods like pasta which need a lot of space. So you may need to buy a really big pan in steel or enamel as well.

On a budget that stretched to luxuries I would also have a little electric pan called Le Saucier, which thermostatically controls the heat of the pan and stirs it at the same time - the nearest thing to having a spare pair of hands that I have yet found.

Pans v Casseroles

Before opting for too many conventional saucepans stop and think about the type of food you like cooking. If you are short of space or money it may be better to buy casseroles, in glass for thrift or in heavy enamelled cast iron for looks, instead of saucepans. It is perfectly reasonable to heat a portion of frozen peas in the bottom of a casserole, but you can't bring a saucepan to the table with a stew in it. Very wide, relatively shallow casseroles are more useful than tall narrow ones.

Frying Pans

The best frying pans have heavy bases. The cast iron ones don't look glamorous but are hard to beat. Don't even consider a frying pan with a base of less than 23 cm (9 in): bacon won't lie flat in it. Good frying pans get better and better with use, provided you only rinse them - see page 169.

A useful second frying pan is a proper copper omelette pan with a tin lining. It really is easier to make a good omelette in this. The ideal size is 24 cm (9½ in) across the top.

Deep Frying

More fires are started in homes because of chip pans than from any other single cause. Therefore the only type to have with safety is an electric one which keeps the heat below danger level and has a locking lid. When there is a good filter this also makes frying almost odourless. They aren't cheap - but neither is having your home gutted by fire.

Microwave Pans

A microwave doesn't need special pans. You can cook in pyrex or in any china or pottery which will take the heat of the food. In practice, not everyone has suitable containers of the right size with no metal on them. If you have to buy for a microwave useful items are classic white soufflé dishes - which are multi-purpose and can now be bought with glass lids for microwave cooking; and a pyrex ring mould - which heats food evenly and will also cook cakes.

Slow Cooker

Anyone who likes casserole cooking and has to be away from the home much should consider getting a slow cooker. They are exceedingly cheap to run and allow you to prepare a casserole at breakfast time and come home in the evening to find it ready. The largest size takes a good-sized chicken.

Mixers and Food Processors

Food processors and mixers aren't totally interchangeable. For kneading bread, or mixing large quantities of Christmas pudding or terrine a big mixer, like a Kenwood, is almost essential. For chopping meat and other food very finely, liquidizing soups, or shredding, grating or slicing vegetables, food processors have the edge. Unless you will only be cooking for two, buy the biggest processor you can afford. The containers can't be filled with liquid, so to liquidize several servings of soup you must do batch after batch if you have a small one - which is tedious and time-wasting.

Choosing a Freezer

There are only two golden rules:
1   All freezers take more than you'd think from looking at them.
2   Once you start using one you will fill it however big it is. Choose the biggest you can afford, and fit in to the space available. Think carefully about where you put it. Freezers must have air space around them, and the cooler the air, the less the temperature changes when you open the door, and the lower the running cost.

For efficiency there is nothing to choose between upright and chest freezers, but an upright with drawers is by far the most convenient, as one hunk of food never blocks another. Whatever the type, make sure it has a 'fast freeze' control if you want to freeze food from fresh, or you won't get good results. The value of automatic defrosting is more dubious. It is pleasant to be spared the chore of scraping off ice and emptying a freezer. The snag is that the temperature is likely to alter at each defrost, which isn't good (see freezing under Food).

Buying a Microwave

All microwaves look small and cook more than you'd think, but there is one severe limitation: many have a turntable which ensures even cooking, but it does mean that the corners are dead space and you can cook rather less at a time than if the food was still. Therefore, unless you will only use it for one or two people, buy the biggest you can afford.

A few foods, such as bread or meringues, don't cook well by microwaves alone. So the most useful ovens are those which combine both microwave and convection. Convection cooks the food with hot air, at the same temperatures as any electric oven, and produces much the same results. So the combination ovens allow you to cook food quite normally but cut the cooking time by zapping it with the occasional burst of microwaves.

You can also buy microwaves which incorporate an electric grill, so you can quickly brown the food as well as microwave it, for the great weakness of a microwave is that it doesn't brown. Bosch has even incorporated a microwave function into a conventional oven, and doubtless other makers will follow.

Microwaves will go on improving for some while yet. So it will pay to look at as many models as possible before buying. Whatever the extras, the basic points you need to check when buying are as follows.

- Wattage - see A Roof Over Your Head.
- The range of settings - 5 is ideal.
- What is the maximum number of minutes it can be set for? It is annoying to have only short periods on an oven which includes convection.
- What is the minimum time for which it can be set, and does it increase in convenient steps?
- Does it tell you when it stops? A tone which tells you is very useful, but hear it before you buy - some are ear-splitting.
- If it combines convection what temperature steps can it be set at?
- How easy is it to work? Some have such sophisticated controls that it is hard to remember the sequence you need.
- Do they have a helpline on which you can phone a domestic scientist if you are having problems?

This last point is important. Cooking with microwaves is easy, but anyone can take a few days to adjust and some instruction books are none too clear. So it is useful to have someone to call. Sharp go one better and not only have home economists you can phone (061 205 2333 and 01 493 7077 if you have a Sharp cooker), but also give a microwave cooking course to anyone who buys one of their microwaves. Other manufacturers may do this, but my enquiries have failed to find one, though Panasonic will loan you a video.

Furnishings from Shops
If you are paying for anything you have an absolute right to make sure it is what you want and has been properly made - in fact it would be crazy not to. It isn't rude to check goods carefully - the shop buyers (if they know their job) do it to the makers, and you can do it to the shops. But it has to be done politely and without damaging the goods.

If you find any faults, change it for another sample or make - and check that one as carefully - *or* ask for a reduction. Shops are often glad to get rid of items which might otherwise linger until the sale, and you may get a bargain - provided the fault is one you can remedy. Remember shops bargain down the price with their suppliers, so there is no reason why you shouldn't do the same to them. I have obtained reductions in the snootiest shops - and they didn't even seem surprised. But, of course, if you do get a reduction you may not be able to change the goods if any other faults develop.

Beds
As we spend a third of our lives in bed, bed buying deserves a bit of thought. Try them out (shops expect this and there should be protectors to stop your feet dirtying the covers). Don't just lie neatly on your back - beds which feel perfectly comfortable like that may seem rock-like on your side. Try every position - within reason. And if you are buying a double bed see it isn't so soft that you roll together.

Alas, this isn't a guarantee against it forming a valley. One way round it is to buy the type of twin beds which clip and zip together to make a double. Identical beds are often made with different firmness of mattress. So you can have a firm mattress for him and a soft one for her - or vice versa - if you wish.

Somehow word has got around that it is a good idea for everyone to have a 'hard' bed, sometimes called an 'orthopaedic' bed. This is a misunderstanding. The bedding industry insists there is no such thing as an orthopaedic bed. It is just a misleading name for a hard bed, and hard beds *aren't* necessarily good for you. What is needed is a bed which, when lying on your side, will let the shoulders and hips sink in far enough for the other areas of the body to be well supported with the spine in a straightish line. Only then is strain avoided at every point. So what most spines need is not a hard bed but a supportive bed. This is not to say that a hard bed may not relieve pain from certain conditions, but we don't all walk with crutches just because they help those with broken legs. And you can *get* backache from sleeping on a bed which is too hard.

Bed Sizes
Small single 90 cms x 190 cms (3 ft x 6 ft 3 in)
Standard single 100 cms x 200 cms (3 ft 3 in x 6 ft 6 in)
Small Double 135 cms x 190 cms (4 ft 6 in x 6 ft 3 in)
Standard Double 150 cms x 200 cms (5 ft x 6 ft 6 in)
Queen 165 cms x 200 cms (5 ft 6 in x 6 ft 6 in)
King 180 cms x 200 cms (6 ft x 6 ft 6 in)
Super King 215 cms x 215 cms (7 ft x 7 ft)

Though the sizes are standard the names aren't: So buy by size not by name. You can have a bed made, for a price, to any size you wish.

Mattresses - Foam
The options for mattresses are foam or springs. Foam is non-allergenic; usually lighter than springs (useful if you need to move the bed much); doesn't usually need turning (useful for the elderly); and won't absorb general dampness in the way other mattresses will - good in weekend cottages, and caravans.

The best foam mattresses have layers of different densities but it can be difficult to judge the quality of a foam mattress. The unpredictability can make springs a better buy.

Mattresses - Sprung
There are two aspects to the comfort of a mattress - the outer layers and the springs inside. For outer layers fleece wool and dacron, or white cotton felt, are expensive but good insulation while hair is expensive

but greatly increases the comfort. Recycled fibres and coir fibre or thin foam are less good. Pocketed springs with separate coils, each in its own cover, stand up best to the stress of two sleepers in a bed and sag least but comfort will also depend on the number of springs and the thickness of their wire.

Children don't need expensive beds but they do need ones with mattresses which will support them properly - not old sagging ones. And it is dangerous to put them into bunk beds until they are old enough to be sensible - that is *at least* 5 years old.

The National Bedding Federation Ltd (251 Brompton Road, London SW3 2EZ Tel: 01 589 4888 - has leaflets on beds but do not deal with bedding.

Alternatives to a Normal Bed

> BEDS FOR THE POOR - *Beech-tree leaves are recommended for beds for filling the beds of poor persons. They should be gathered on a dry day in the autumn and perfectly dried. It is said they smell grateful, and will not harbour vermin. They are also very springy.*
>
> *Enquire Within*, 1856

Nowadays people may not be that spartan, but they are often tempted to make their own boarded bed. Before doing so why not consider buying a futon? Futons are Japanese mattresses made entirely of layers of blown cotton (or wool and cotton). They suit those with certain allergies, are remarkably comfortable to sleep on (especially the type with wool in) and actually *like* to be rolled up during the day, which makes them ideal for children's rooms. There is nothing wrong with sleeping on the floor in a well-heated vermin-free house, and it is time it lost its bad name.

Or you can make a bed area on top of a structure of drawers, shelves, record space - or whatever suits you. You can find the nearest futon stockist from the **Futon Company,** 10-12 Rivington Street, London EC2 Tel: 01 729 0670.

Bedding

The average person releases ½ pint of sweat during the night and this can either linger in the air round the body or be absorbed by the bedding and evaporate into the air on the other side. Since natural fibres absorb more moisture they are better to sleep in than man-made ones.

> BED CLOTHES - *The perfection of dress, for day or night, where warmth is the purpose, is that which confines around the body sufficient of its own warmth, while it allows escape to the exhalations of the skin. Where the body is allowed to bathe protractedly in its own vapours we must expect an unhealthy effect upon the skin. Where there is too little ventilation escape, insensible perspiration is checked, and something analogous to a fever supervenes; foul tongue, ill taste, and lack of morning appetite betray the evil.*
>
> *Enquire Within*, 1856

Blankets and Underblankets

Pure wool blankets are warmer and last longer than any other, but those with mixed wool and acrylic have the advantage of being moth-proof. Avoid rayon and cotton mixtures if you can. Their artificially-created fluff weakens and rubs off in washing.

Any bed is much warmer with a blanket under the bottom sheet, but the underblankets which make a really big difference are the new ones which look like sheepskin. Two good ones are Woolrest (which refunds your money if you don't sleep better) and Brinkhaus. They are a luxury, but ideal for someone who needs extra warmth and might forget to turn off an electric blanket.

Woolrest stockists from 101 Kew Road, Richmond-on-Thames, Surrey TW9 2PN Tel: 01 940 8352; Brinkhaus see below.

Duvets

A good duvet should last 20 to 25 years, and you need it to be at least 45 cm (18 in) wider than the bed, but at least 250 cm (100 in) wide for one adult, 295 cm (118 in) for two people, whatever the width of the bed.

Duvets work like double glazing. We each generate about 100 watts of heat an hour and the air trapped in the filling makes a barrier between the warmth of the body and the air outside. The usual rule is that 4.5 tog is a very lightweight duvet, 9.0 tog is a medium weight and 13.5 tog is extra warm. On the whole, you get what you pay for and it is only worth going for a cheap filling if that is all you can afford, or you know children will ruin it so soon it needs to be disposable.

The various qualities of down and feather fillings can be confusing, but they go like this:
- goose/duck down with feathers - need only have 51 per cent down
- 'pure' white goose/duck down, piroshka or eider down - BSI set minimum down content of 85 per cent.

The Piroshka down is from live free-range geese and so is the eider down. The eider duck uses its down to line its nests, and the down is gathered from these when the birds leave them. So no harm comes to the birds from either of these.

For those who are allergic to feathers, but dislike duvets of man-made fibre, **Brinkhaus** (Dean Clough Industrial Park, Dean Clough, Halifax W. Yorks HX3 4AY) makes them with fillings of wool, cashmere, silk or camel hair - at a price. They also make wool-filled pillows.

In man-made fibres there have also been big improvements. The closest to down, in my view, is Quallofil.

Pillows

The fillings of pillows are almost identical to those of duvets in range and quality. Goose feathers are stronger than duck feathers and keep their bounce longer, ordinary feather pillows are usually poultry feathers which are naturally straight and have to be curled to give them bounce - which means they uncurl in time and give a flat heavy pillow.

British Standards Institute (BSI) Labels

The British Standards Institution is an independent organization financed by government and industry. Its expert committees set the standards which products should meet for reliability or safety. Only in matters of safety are manufacturers *compelled* to meet it on BSI standards. But for a manufacturer to put a BS number on a product which does not meet the BS standard is a breach of the Trades Descriptions Act. However, they do appear on the labels of goods which have not been BSI tested. For example: BS 1970 simply shows that the manufacturers think their hot water bottle conforms to the standard set for hot water bottles.

But a manufacturer can apply for a BSI label for a particular product. It is then tested by the BSI and, if it passes the tests, it is issued with one of the following marks, and repeatedly checked from then on.

The kite mark shows the product meets the general standards set by the BSI, and that production has also been checked by inspectors.

This is the Safety Mark indicating that the goods have reached a safety standard. It may or may not have reached other standards.

If a shopper finds faults in a product bearing the kite mark or safety mark and is not able to sort the matter out with the retailer or the manufacturer the BSI Certification and Assessment Department will take up the complaint and test the item to see whether or not it does meet the set standard.

If a product carries one of the two labels above the BSI will investigate any complaint about the product.

The following label may also occur on other products:

BEAB

This shows that electrical appliances have been tested by the British Electrotechnical Approvals Board and meets BSI standards for safety and durability.

Foreign manufacturers can use a BS number on a product if it meets the right standards and they can also apply for a kite mark.

British Standards Institution, Certification and Assessment Department, Linford Wood, Milton Keynes MK14 6LE Tel: 0908 220908

The Which Book of Consumer Law, Consumers' Association, Hodder and Stoughton

Carpets

Most carpets are blends of different types of fibre. Those which flatten easily are the ones most likely to develop curious shading where two sections flatten in opposite directions.

Fibres used in Carpets

Acrylic fibre looks like wool but has far less bounce and gets grubby more easily, but some liquid stains come off easily.

Nylon is mixed with other fibres to lengthen their life. But it flattens and soils more easily than wool. It also collects static and an anti-static spray may be needed.

Polyester is strong but lacks bounce and only takes light use.

Polypropylene flattens easily and is usually used in looped piles.

Rayon is a cheap fibre which flattens and gets grubby easily.

Wool is the best fibre. It keeps its bounce, and doesn't attract dirt. A high-quality blend is 80 per cent wool, 20 per cent nylon; it gives the bounce of wool with the strength of nylon.

Look for the Carpet Manufacturer's Associations Carpet Performance Rating on carpets. Choose the higher grades, of the six, for areas which get a lot of wear and only use the lighter ones in rooms such as bedrooms.

Checking a Carpet

Carpets need very thorough checking if they are to give you decent wear.

● Check what it is made from - if you find the woolmark, it means the carpet must have 915 grams of wool per square metre and a decent depth of pile.
● Bend it backwards and see how close together the tufts are. The closer the tufts, the longer it is likely to last.
● Look to see if the colour goes right down the length of the tufts. Printed-on patterns may wear off.
● If there is a foam or fabric backing try to peel it off. You shouldn't be able to without considerable difficulty.
● Try tugging and twisting some tufts. If they come out they will do the same in use.

★ It can be less wasteful to buy one width than another, so calculate the quantities in more than one width. The standard widths are 3 ft, 12 ft and 4 m.

★ Protective coatings such as Scotchguard, which are sometimes on the carpet (or fabric) when you buy it, or can be applied by the retailer, can make a dramatic difference to the ease with which a carpet can be kept clean and stain-free.

Fitting carpets

Shops will fit for free. If not the **National Institute of Carpet Fitters** (Wira House, West Park Ring Road, Leeds LS16 6QL Tel: 0532 743721) will give you the name of a fitter in your county who meets certain standards, and if you have a complaint the Institute will refer it to the British Carpet Technical Centre.

Electrical Goods

The British Electrotechnical Approvals Board (BEAB), (Mark House, The Green, 9/11 Queen's Road, Hersham, Walton-on-Thames, Surrey KT12 5RN Tel: 0932 244401) is the independent organization supervising the safety testing of most types of electrical equipment destined for British homes. Products which reach the established British standard are awarded a BEAB certificate. But, since November 1985, two safety marks have been used on electrical equipment:

1 an updated BEAB approved label for products tested and approved by the BEAB
2 a BEAB/CCA label for products tested and approved in other EEC countries.

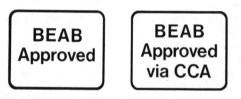

If you have trouble with a BEAB Approved appliance the BEAB will investigate your complaint and, if necessary, withdraw the manufacturer's licence. But the CCA label shows that the BEAB had no hand in the testing. So, if a fault arises, the grievance must be taken to whichever authority gave its approval, or to the manufacturer.

With electrical goods there are very big differences in the way seemingly identical machines perform and last. *Which* magazine is essential reading to get value for money and is in public libraries.

There are advantages in buying from a shop which is a member of **RETRA**. A single code of practice for electrical goods has been agreed between **The Association of Manufacturers of Domestic Electrical Appliances** (AMDEA House, 593 Hitchin Road, Stopsley, Luton LU2 7UN Tel: 0582 412444) and **the Radio, Electrical and Television Retailers' Association (RETRA)** (100 St Martin's Lane, London WC2N 4BD) and the Electricity Council. Under this code:

● if you order goods and pay a deposit you will be given a refund if they aren't delivered on time
● if during the guarantee period the retailer is unable to repair it within 15 days you will either be lent another until yours is ready or the guarantee will be extended by the amount of time you are without your equipment
● if you move to another area your retailer will try to arrange for another RETRA member to take over the servicing arrangements under the guarantee
● you should be offered a service call within 3 working days and told if a minimum charge will be made
● you should be advised of minimum charges for repairs and if possible given the cost of the work needed
● most repairs should be guaranteed for 12 months (3 on some smaller items).

RETRA also deals with complaints against members but it does not have an arbitration scheme. Instead, complaints can be put to an conciliation panel.

Fabrics for Furnishing

Fabric looks so simple it hardly seems worth checking for faults: it is. Go over it carefully then ask about its washability and whether it has been treated in anyway - e.g. against spills. Check that it is suited to the job you want it to do. Material not designed for curtaining may fade quickly in the light. Finally, get them to write down how much shrinkage you should expect. Keep that statement in case the shrinkage is worse but, if in doubt, have material laundered before it's made up.

Furniture and Fittings

If you are furnishing a home, carry with you small samples of the carpet and curtain material, paint or whatever else you have already chosen whenever you go shopping. You may find the very thing you think you need to complete the room just when you haven't got them with you to check the colour.

Before you buy anything check it carefully for size, comfort, wearability and any other features which matter - **never** assume the maker must have got it right.

National Association of Retail Furnishers Ltd (17-21 George Street, Croydon, CR9 1TQ Tel: 01 680 8444) operates a code of practice on the sale of furniture. Under the code they will attempt conciliation between a shop and a dissatisfied customer. They will also arrange for independent arbitration.

Children's Goods and Toys

The British Standards Institution has set safety standards for toys and children's goods which are designed to protect children from a wide range of dangers. Those goods which meet the safety standards will carry a BSI number and/or label (see page 181). If you only buy goods which carry a BSI label it will ensure the cot doesn't have bars so wide the baby's head will get stuck, that the harness really will stop it falling from the pram and that the materials being used won't poison a child - as some old-fashioned materials used to.

More information

If you can't find a particular light fitting in the shops, send an accurate description or a photograph to the **Decorative Lighting Association** (Bryn, Bishop's Castle, Shropshire SY9 5LE Tel: 058 84 658) and they will usually be able to put you in touch with the manufacturer.

The Lighting Book by Deyan Sudjic (published by Mitchell Beazley) - is a useful guide to what you can do with lighting.

The Design Council (28 Haymarket, London SW1Y 4SU Tel: 01 839 8000) - has a design index covering most household items, from fitments to tin openers and can put you in contact with their manufacturers.

The Crafts Council 12 Waterloo Place, London SW1Y 4AU Tel: 01 930 4811 - has a register of craftsmen all over GB.

Curtain Net Advisory Bureau (68 Knightsbridge, London SW1X 7LN) covers terylene curtaining and has free leaflets with good ideas on how to use net in blinds and curtains.

The Home and Contract Furnishing Textile Association (c/o Manchester Chamber of Commerce, 3rd Floor, 56 Oxford Street, Manchester M60 7HJ Tel: 061 236 3210) - will supply leaflets on the care of furnishing fabrics. However, they no longer offer arbitration if you are dissatisfied.

LAUNDRY, STAINS AND ALL THAT

Dry Cleaning

Cleaners need to be chosen very carefully, as certain fabrics need chemicals which only a few cleaners use. The trouble is that there are more dry cleaners than there are fully trained and experienced staff to run them. So, taking clothes or furnishings to the cleaners is no guarantee that they won't be harmed.

Some protection is given by using a member of **The Association of British Laundry, Cleaning and Rental Services Ltd (ABLCRS)** Lancaster Gate House, 319 Pinner Road, Harrow, Middx HA1 4HX Tel: 01 863 7755. Its code of practice covers laundry, cleaning, repairing and dyeing - but not laundrettes or coin-operated cleaning machines. Among other things, its members don't limit their legal liability to negligence or restrict compensation to some multiple of the cost of cleaning - which is a common ploy with non-members. If something does go wrong, and the cleaner doesn't give you satisfaction, the ABLCRS runs an arbitration service. Failing that, you have a right to pursue your claim through the small claims court.

The ABLCRS also runs a Dry Cleaning Information Bureau covering both dyeing and dry cleaning. It is at the ABLCRS address but the number to ring for advice is 01 863 8658.

If you have something fragile it is worth telling the dry cleaner that it *is* special (they may send it to head office) or paying for a special dry cleaner.

If you can't find a suitable dry cleaner locally **Pilgrim Payne and Co Ltd** (address page 171) will accept cleaning by post from all over Britain, and **Jeeves of Belgravia** 8-10 Pont Street, SW1 Tel: 01 235 1101 operates a world-wide postal service. You would not expect this service to be cheap - nor is it. And check on insurance in transit.

Coin-operated Cleaning

Before using a coin-operated dry cleaning machine check the care label inside each garment carefully (see page 184). Some of them mean that clothes can only be cleaned in special solvents, which are not likely to be used in such machines.

If you have problems, and the launderette is not being reasonable, write to the **National Association of Launderette Industries** (Guardian House, 92/94 Foxberry Road, London SE4 2SH Tel: 01 692 8622) with the details. They will encourage the launderette to sort it out and, if that fails, suggest suitable arbitration.

Dyeing and Colouring

You can now dye most fabrics and use a whole range of techniques - hot, cold and washing machine - and combine dyeing with painting the fabric. It's a marvellous way to convert old summer clothes to new but you can't:
- dye acrylics
- dye wool or silk in a washing machine

- cover patterns with dye
- cover stains and marks with dye (but you can cover them with fabric paint)
- dye anything a really perfect black
- remove the colour from polyesters before dyeing them
- dye drip-dry fabrics
- dye waterproof fabrics.

The colour mixing in dyeing is just the same as in painting. If you have a yellow T-shirt and dye it blue it will come out green; dye it red and it will come out orange.

How to Dye Successfully
- Weigh the garment while dry and note the weight.
- Remove all dirt and stains before dyeing.
- Choose the right dye for the type of fabric you are dyeing.
- As the existing colour will combine with any dye you start by removing the colour - unless the colour combination will produce what you want. A Dylon product removes the colours from most fabrics which aren't fast dyed (but don't use it on polyesters).
- Use exactly the recommended amount of dye, water and fixing medium for the *dry* weight of the fabric.
- Have the dyeing vessel large enough for the fabric to be moved about in it, or the dye won't get to the folds.
- Make sure the water is the correct temperature for the type of dye you are using.
- Have enough water to cover the fabric totally.
- When dyeing two items which need to match, but can't be dyed together, you must make sure that there is no variation anywhere in the process. All quantities must be precisely measured and exactly the same amount of time taken for each stage.

> After most dyes a washing machine has to be cleaned out with the longest hottest wash, plus bleach and soap powder. So don't dye in a washing machine unless you are prepared to do this.

★ Adding some very dark blue dye to black dye gives a darker result.

Dylon International Ltd (Worsley Bridge Road, Lower Sydenham, London SE26 5HD) has a consumer help-line on 01 650 4801, and leaflets.

Laundry

Whatever the instructions, it is far better to wash or dry clean clothes and other items gently before they get really dirty, rather than leave them until they need a good seeing-to. The more gently any item can be treated, the less it wears the fabric.

This section covers the washing and ironing of most fabrics which are encountered. However, nothing written here is intended to overrule any instructions which are supplied by the manufacturers of garments or furnishings. My information is for times when no label has been used. Any instructions on labels should always be followed to the letter - if they aren't you will have no come-back if the garment or furnishings shrink, run or are otherwise spoilt.

International Textile Care Labelling Code (ITCL)

More and more fabrics now carry the international textile labelling code, which is as follows.

Shows it must not be washed - this *doesn't* mean it can be dry cleaned.

Shows hand washing is needed.

Shows it can be machine washed at the programme which uses this temperature.

Shows that household (chlorine) bleach such as Domestos can be used.

Shows household bleach cannot be used.

This means it can be ironed, one dot means use a cool iron (120°C), two dots means a warm iron (160°C), three dots a hot iron (210°C).

Do *not* iron - the fabric would be harmed.

Can be dry cleaned in all solvents.

Dry clean in perchloroethylene, or white spirit, or solvent 113 or 11.

Dry-clean with care, not in a coin-operated machine. This is found on velvet, acrylics and some woollens.

Dry cleanable in white spirit or solvent 113, but needs special care in the cleaning process.

Do not dry clean.

Improved by tumble drying.

Do not tumble dry.

How Hot Do They Mean?

Here is how to judge whether you are providing the right temperature for a fabric when you hand-wash it:

100°C	boiling - as if straight from a kettle
95°C	just off boiling
60°C	hotter than hands can bear
50°C	as hot as hands can stand
40°C	comfortably warm
30°C	cooler than the hands

Ironing

There are only 4 things to remember when ironing:

- have the iron as hot as the fabric will stand - and no hotter
- keep the iron moving all the time - or the fabric will scorch
- have the fabric evenly damp all over - spray it if necessary
- order your ironing so a part you have done is never creased in smoothing another part.

On the matter of dampness there really is no substitute for taking off the line when it is just right and ironing it then and there. At the right degree of dampness any fabric irons twice as well in half the time.

The most bizarre information on 'ironing' clothes that I have ever found is this entry in the first edition of *Enquire Within*.

> SOAP MAY BE DISUSED, or nearly so, in the getting up of muslins and chintzes, which should always be treated agreeably to the oriental manner; that is, to wash them in plain water, and then boil them in congee or rice water: after which they ought not to be submitted to the operation of the smoothing iron, but rubbed smooth with a polished stone.

Ironing Pleats

If you simply iron knife pleats you will find that the underfold of the pleat imprints a line on the upper surface which spoils it. To avoid this have a piece of plain white card and slip it into the underside of the pleat, covering the underfold. Then when you iron you have a flat surface to press on.

Order of Ironing

On some garments the order in which they should be ironed is obvious, but blouses and shirts often seem to puzzle people. The best system I know is this:
Collar - ironing from the points towards the centre, **shoulder** and **yoke, cuffs, sleeves** (ironed flat, except on a woman's shirt which would be spoilt), **back, fronts** then button up alternate buttons, fold and re-press the upper part of the **front**.

★ If fabric is too dry a plant sprayer moistens it fastest.
★ The best way to damp over-dried fabric is to splash it with warm water, roll it up tightly and leave it for a few hours.
★ If the thermostat on an iron isn't working test it as irons were always tested before thermostats were invented: spit on it. You can tell by the fizz whether it is cool, medium or hot.

> Why is the flat iron hotter, if the saliva runs along it, than if it adheres till it is evaporated? Because, when the saliva runs along the iron, the heat is sufficient to convert the bottom of the drop to vapour . . .
>
> *Enquire Within*, 1856

Pressing

Pressing is to a garment what a face lift is to a star - it takes the years off. The first essential is an immaculately clean white cloth - such as a piece of old cotton sheeting. Putting the cloth between the iron and the garment avoids making shiny iron marks.

Mild pressing can simply be done by using a steam iron to iron through this dry cloth. That may be enough for very light fabrics. For heavyweight, wet the cloth under a tap, wring it dry and place it on the garment where you wish to press it (unless the fabric is averse to water). Iron the cloth slowly with a fairly hot iron.

Pressing to Remove Bagginess

If you want to press bagginess out, lay the baggy area out flat (open trouser legs out sideways not front to back). Then work from the outer edge of the bagginess towards the centre pressing it repeatedly through a damp cloth until it flattens. Then remove the cloth and place a sheet of clean brown paper on the garment. Iron the paper thoroughly all over and it will absorb the moisture from the cloth and make it hold the pressing better. Make the baggy bit the last part of the garment which you press. Then let it lie in place until cool.

Pressing in Pleats or Creases

If you need to put in a perfect pleat or crease deal with any bagginess first, then fold the fabric *exactly* on the crease line (see above, Ironing Pleats). Press with the damp cloth method and, as you remove the cloth, replace it with the 'banger' described in Crafts. Let the fabric cool, then move to the next section of the crease.

Starching

The modern spray-on starches are slower than traditional starch and the floor ends up like a skating rink. The best way to starch anything is to use a powder starch, which you mix with either hot or cold water as a final rinse. Nothing could be simpler.

The strength recommended on the packet usually produces a pleasant crispness. However, to make the front of a dress shirt really stiff make a solution 3 to 4 times stronger. I find the best way to starch a dress shirt with a stiff front is to dip the whole thing in starch at normal strength, spin it dry, then use a clean pastry brush to brush the extra strong starch very well on to both sides of the cuffs, and front. The detached collar can then be dipped in what remains. If it still feels too soft when it begins to dry, yet more can be brushed on. Iron the stiffened areas while still quite damp. At this stage the starch will try to stick to the iron, so use a hot iron and work swiftly, starting on the inside.

Stiffening Lace

Lace is seldom stiffened nowadays, but stiff lace may return to fashion. The Edwardian way to stiffen it was to pour 250 ml (½ pt) of boiling water on to 30 g (1 oz) of gum arabic, stir until the gum dissolved and dip the lace in this *once it was cool*. The strength was varied to suit the lace and it was finally ironed under white tissue paper.

Washing in General

The first job with washing is always stain removal (pages 193 to 201). If you wait until afterwards you may well find the washing process has set the stain so you will never be able to remove it.

After stain removal comes soaking. Almost any washing, bar wool and fine fabrics, is the cleaner for a soak in ordinary washing powder in a bucket of water overnight.

Hand-washing is simply a matter of squeezing soapy water (see the individual fabrics for temperatures) through the material until all the dirt seems to be out, rubbing it against itself where necessary to get the dirt to shift (if the material will take rubbing.) The vital final stage is to get the soap out by squeezing it through the garment until the water remains perfectly clear on the last rinse.

Faded Garments

When garments fade there are three possible causes: the dye has run, the garments have spent too long in the sun (on the line or on the wearer), or there is a build-up of soap which is masking the colour. This last can be helped by putting a dash of white vinegar in the final rinsing water, as it helps to get rid of the soap. Fading received more hazardous treatment in the past.

> BLACK REVIVER FOR BLACK CLOTH - *Bruised galls one pound, logwood two pounds, green vitriol half a pound, water five quarts. Boil for two hours, and strain.*
>
> Enquire Within, 1856

Fabrics which Run

You can reduce the chances of a fabric running by soaking it in a solution of salt and water. Use a tablespoon of salt to 500 ml (1 pt) of water. It may not make it totally fast but it should improve things.

Fragile Fabrics and Lace Curtains

Fragile fabrics are usually best left unwashed or handed to professionals, but if you find you need to wash something fragile this is the method used by many museums. It can very well be applied to lace curtains which may have been weakened by sunlight to a point where they cannot support the weight of water.

Fold the material carefully into a manageable rectangle or square. Then tack all the layers together with big loose tacking stitches. Soak it overnight - if it will take soaking - in warm soapy water; using pure soap not detergent. Drain and press the water out of it flat against the bottom of a basin. Put it in fresh warm soapy water and press the water very gently through it, then drain and rinse it in the same way until the water is clear. If the fabric is lace put a couple of tablespoons of salt in the final rinsing water to give it a little crispness. Dry it flat, on towels, in the shade.

Very Dirty Garments

If you have trouble with greasy overalls (for heavy motor oil see page 198) or white shirts or sheets which teenagers have forgotten to change, soak them overnight in a bucket of hot water to which you have added half a cup of ammonia. (Mix the water and ammonia before soaking the garments). Ammonia will fade coloureds, so this is a method for whites only.

Limited patches of dirt, like a dirty line around a collar, can be spot-treated by rubbing on a block of Fairy soap before washing, and if necessary going over it with a nail brush.

★ To hang a garment on a hanger on a washing line use two hangers, with the hooks facing opposite ways. Then it won't blow off.
★ If you put too much soap in and a washing machine overflows with suds, pour in vinegar or fabric softener.

Lever Brothers Ltd (Consumer Advice Service, Lever House, 3 St James's Road, Kingston upon Thames, Surrey KT1 2BA) will deal with all kinds of queries about washing.

How to Wash Almost Everything

Acetate

Acetate is a cellulose fibre and must be handled gently when wet. Wash it by hand in cool water or on ITCL programmes 6 or 8; avoid wringing it, and don't give it more than a brief spin. Iron it with a warm iron while still damp.

Acrylics, Modacrylics and Orlon

Acrylics have a nasty tendency to crease and go flat and saggy. They need the greatest care to prolong their decent life. You *can* wash them at ITCL 6, but they last longest if washed and rinsed by hand in cool to warm water, without rubbing or even very hard squeezing. To reduce the static use fabric softener in the last rinse. Give them a *very* short spin, and put acrylic pullovers flat on a towel to dry or they will stretch dreadfully. Ironing over patterns will flatten them, but iron stocking-stitch lightly through a damp cloth and leave the garment in place on the ironing board until it cools.

Antique Fabrics

Antique textiles present a whole range of problems which need to be seen before the best treatment can be recommended. Most museums which contain furnishings have a textile expert who will advise you. However tempted you may be, *don't* try to clean antique fabric without taking advice. Even an antique fabric which looks quite sturdy may fall to pieces the moment you wet it or crush it during washing or dry-cleaning.

Blankets

Blankets should be treated according to what they are made from. Spin them well and hang them *over*, not from, a washing line.

Brocade

Brocade used once to be silk, by definition, but it's now made in a wide range of fabrics; cotton, viscose, polyester, acetate and a variety of blends. Treat it according to the fibre from which it is made - some will need dry-cleaning. Don't iron it too heavily, and allow for the fact that it frays easily. Velvet brocade is a luxury cloth and needs to be dry-cleaned by a cleaner who knows his stuff.

Broderie Anglaise

As broderie Anglaise is pierced and embroidered white cotton, or poly-cotton, treat it like these fabrics, unless it is used to trim more fragile fabric. But don't put it in a washing machine with garments which have exposed hooks and eyes which can catch and tear it, or let the tip of the iron catch in a hole. If necessary, iron through white tissue paper.

Buckram

As buckram is a made for stiffening it is heavily dosed with size. If it is washed this comes out and it becomes a very sad affair. Dry-clean only. Press with a hot iron - if necessary - through a dry cloth.

Bunting

Nowadays bunting is usually cotton, but old bunting was often wool. In either case, the fabric frays easily and the colours are likely to run. Woollen bunting needs to be hand washed as wool. Cotton bunting can be washed by hand or in a machine, as cotton - bearing in mind the risk of colours running. Iron accordingly.

Cambric

Cambric was once the great fabric for cotton petticoats. It's a cotton like that used for handkerchiefs - in fact, some handkerchiefs are cambric. It takes a hot cotton wash and can be starched successfully. Iron with a hot iron while rather damp.

Candlewick

I'm told that candlewick takes its name from the fact that originally the wicks of candles really were used to decorate the cotton. Today the fluffy nap is either pure cotton or - more often - cotton and some synthetic fibre.

It really needs tumble-drying to refluff it - unless it has a foam-rubber back, as some bath mats have. If it can't be tumble-dried shake it well before hanging it out and try to choose a windy day, so the wind tumbles it into softness. Using a fabric softener when washing it also helps. Candlewick fades easily, but dyes just as easily - especially in a machine.

Canvas or duck

Canvas can normally be washed in a machine like cotton, but it is so stiff it needs a machine to itself. It is usually more practical to scrub it with block soap and a stiff brush, then dowse it well with water to get all the soap out. Watch out for decorations, like leather buckles on canvas handbags, which may react badly to water.

Cashmere

You'd think any wool from a mountain goat would be hard-wearing, but cashmere is far more fragile than lambswool. Some experts say it should be dry cleaned, but I have found that after being dry cleaned several times cashmere loses its bounce and starts to bag like an old acrylic, whereas with careful hand-washing it seems to stay perfect for years. Treat it as wool (page 192), being exceedingly careful and avoid pressing it or do it very lightly.

It easily forms little balls on its surface. Good haberdashery departments sell a small device for removing these and it keeps cashmere and angora looking new far longer.

Cheesecloth

Cheesecloth is cotton and takes a hot wash - although it may shrink. It is naturally a crinkled fabric and isn't usually intend to be smooth, so it is usually best to tug it flat in all directions when wet and leave it un-ironed.

Chiffon

Silk chiffon needs dry cleaning and so do most synthetics, but nylon chiffon may be washable. Avoid pressing it if you can; hanging creased chiffon up in a steamy room will often smooth it instead. However, if you have to press it, do so very lightly with a cool dry iron. Heavy ironing will over-flatten it and take away its character.

Chintz

Chintz is really any flowery cotton furnishing fabric, but glazed chintz is a finely woven flowery fabric with a shiny surface. It may have been sized to stiffen it slightly or glazed with a resin. It is best to ask the manufacturer whether it can be washed or it must be dry cleaned. It is often inclined to shrink and washing can make it loose its crispness and deprives a glazed chintz of its sheen. In the old days this was restored by starching the fabric in water that included grated candle wax. It was then ironed on the right side with a special glazing iron. Modern washable chintz simply needs a hot iron when rather damp.

Ciré

The ciré seen most often today is nylon ciré, used for thin showerproof rainclothes. Ciré means 'waxed' in French and, as it's a treated fabric, you need to avoid removing the dressing. So sponge it instead of washing it, let it drip dry and only use a cool iron through a dry pressing cloth.

Corduroy

Corduroy is usually pure cotton but its colour is very inclined to run and its nap easily picks up fluff from anything else in the machine. Check the pockets carefully - a tissue handkerchief washed with corduroy can be disastrous. And turn the garment inside out so the nap won't pick up the fluff which may be in the machine. Wash it on ITCL 2 or 5 according to the depth of colour, or by hand. Iron it on the wrong side, with a fairly hot iron, while still damp.

Cotton

Cotton can be washed at a wide range of temperatures, and some white cotton will even stand boiling - but it needs hot water to get out the soap, and some dark shades run easily. Use ITCL 1, 2 or 5 (page 184) or wash it by hand. The exceptions are good clothes which always look better for hand washing and may have interlinings which make dry cleaning essential. Cotton calico shrinks considerably.

Most cotton can be starched (see page 185) and pure cotton is far easier to iron than the fabrics from man-made fibres. But you must iron it when damp.

Madras cotton needs to be washed entirely alone as the dye usually bleeds massively. Spin it dry and hang it out at once or the dye will transfer in patches all over the garment.

★ If someone has a cold, soak their cotton handkerchiefs overnight in a solution of salt water - 1 tablespoon to a 500 ml (1 pt) of water. This removes the catarrh.

★ Cotton viscose is often used instead of pure cotton jersey, see viscose (page 191).

Crêpe de Chine

Crêpe de Chine was originally a Chinese silk with a crêpe texture. Some polyesters now imitate this so well it is extremely hard to tell the difference. But, if the label is no guide, 'dishpan' hands can be: any pure silk fabric will always catch slightly on hands if they are even a little rough; polyester will slide smoothly over them.

Crêpe de Chine in man-made fibres is handled as for the fibre. The safest bet with silk crêpe de Chine is to have it dry-cleaned, as the colours run easily and it can be hard to iron it so it looks perfectly smooth without flattening the texture of the crêpe and making it look a little tired. However, some people do wash it successfully (see page 191) and crêpe de Chine underwear obviously has to be washed. But this is not something to try, with top garments, unless you are prepared to risk spoiling them. Use a warm iron when almost dry.

Cretonne

This hard-wearing cotton fabric washes well, and takes starch (though it seldom needs it). Use a hot wash and hot iron while damp (see page 184).

Curtains

The washability of curtains depends on their fabric and on their lining and interlining. Most interlinings and many fabrics are not washable so should be dry cleaned. Cotton curtains with cotton linings can usually be washed, but check with the manufacturer. They will almost certainly be less robust than they seem. Sunlight and chemicals in the air eat into curtains - especially the linings - and a curtain can go into a washing machine, looking normal, and come out as strips of rag having fallen apart at every fold. Unless you are *certain* that the fabric hasn't been weakened in this way it is far better to wash curtains by hand.

If there is any risk that the curtains will shrink - and there usually is - undo the hems of the main fabric before washing.

Start by soaking washable curtains overnight in plenty of cold water in the bath (having first removed all curtain hooks). Drain and rinse. Press all the water out, then run a bath of hand-hot water and a good detergent. Let them soak in this for an hour and then squeeze the water through them without twisting or pulling, until all the dirt is loose. Drain and rinse until no more soap or dirt comes out. (Really dirty curtains may need two washes with soap). Press the water out and leave them sitting in the bath a while for more to drain down. Press again (so as not to handle them with too much weight of water in). Spin dry in a machine. Carefully open them out and hang them *over*, not from, a washing line, so the line runs across their width. Iron with a hot iron while rather damp, working up and down the curtain to minimize shrinkage - and hang before they are fully dry, closing them across the window so the air can get to them.

Damask

The damask you are most likely to find in the home is in the form of double damask dinner napkins. Old damask will be cotton or linen, and take a high-temperature wash and a hot iron. If you want beautifully crisp damask, iron it when thoroughly damp. If ironed when too dry it will be limp and miserable no matter what you do. Unlike linen, overdried damask will iron well after being damped, tightly rolled and left a while. Iron it on the right side to give it a sheen. Modern damask may be part viscose and need less heat (see Viscose, page 191).

Denim

Treat denim as cotton but expect shrinkage, unless it is pre-shrunk, and keep it away from other items until very well faded, as it runs repeatedly. Iron when rather damp.

Dralon

Dralon is washable at a low temperature but if it is attached to chairs see page 182.

Duvets

Duvets in man-made fibres can be washed in a large washing machine but use only one third the usual amount of soap powder and wash at 40°C. Then give it 4 to 5 rinses, before spinning it for not more than 30 seconds at a time - if necessary keep switching the machine off. Man-made fibre duvets can then be tumbled dry in warm - not hot - air, until the cover feels dry. Then give it 24 hours' airing to let it dry completely. For feather duvets, see Pillows.

Embroidery

Embroidery needs care, as you have to consider both the background cloth and the threads used on it. Any embroidery on canvas should be dry-cleaned, so should embroidery on silk, and old embroidery needs expert attention. The Royal School of Needlework (page 171) will advise over the phone on the cleaning of embroidery, tapestry and beadwork, and also runs a cleaning service. The items can be taken in or sent by registered post. There is no standard price but they will send an estimate.

White cotton or linen embroidered with *white cotton* thread can be washed in fairly hot water, without rubbing. Stains can be soaked out in bleach - at the dilution recommended on the bottle - provided the fabric is not very old or delicate. Whether you can machine-wash stronger items depends on the nature of the stitches - most stitches are vulnerable to being pushed out of place in the rough and tumble of a machine, but the type with a cut-out design edged with buttonhole stitch usually survives it well. Only you can judge.

Coloured embroidery may run. First take a very damp piece of fabric (white silk lining material is ideal), place it over each of the colours in turn and iron it. If even one colour bleeds on to the silk the item must be dry cleaned. If none of the colours run you should be able to hand-wash it. Use pure soap flakes and cool water at about 30°C (86°F). The less it is handled the better, so soak it first for an hour or two. Then squeeze the soapy water through the material, by pressing it with a clean sponge, disturbing the sewing as little as possible. *Never rub.* Rinse in water of the same temperature using several changes until it is completely clear. Let all the water run out and gently press the embroidery out against the bottom of the sink. Spread it out on a towel and roll it up quite firmly to remove more water. Then spread it on a fresh towel to dry, out of direct sunlight. Iron it while still rather damp.

To iron embroidery which has a raised pattern, pad the board with two layers of blanket, and cover it with a sheet. Then iron the embroidery face down. If the embroidery has a pierced design use a pressing cloth lest the iron rip it.

Fringes on an embroidered shawl are the very devil if they are washed loose, and the tangle they get into can be indescribable. Before washing, tie the threads together in small bundles with white thread or plait small groups and tie the ends. Press the soapy water carefully through each group or they will be less clean then the rest. Before drying the shawl, unplait them and lay them out smoothly.

Felt and Baize
Felt and baize cannot be washed as they may shrink seriously. Dry clean both.

Flame-retardant Fabrics
These are usually fabrics treated with a flame-retardant finish, so it is extra important to follow the washing instructions *exactly* or the finish could be removed.

Flannel
Flannel used to be only a high-quality wool fabric but today it is often partly man-made, and may be totally man-made for school uniform. Strictly speaking, man-made flannels are treated as for the fabric and wool flannel is dry cleaned. However, if a son of mine had white wool cricket flannels I would wash them very carefully (see page 185), but if the care instructions don't say they can be washed you will have no come-back if they shrink.

Georgette
Georgette is dry cleaned or washed and ironed according to its fibre. Check the care label. If you decide to wash silk georgette - which is really a job for an expert - you may have problems; it crinkles up and has to be carefully ironed while quite wet and pulled to shape.

Lace
> Blond lace can be revived by breathing upon it, and shaking and flapping it.
> *Enquire Within*, 1856

Would that it were that easy. Lace ranges from robust modern lace in synthetic fibres to fragile old lace which needs special treament. Very old and fragile lace is best taken to the Royal College of Needlework (page 171). Robust modern lace can be washed or dry cleaned according to what it is made from. Slightly older lace deserves gentle treatment. Use pure soap, *not* detergent, and with very fine lace use distilled water at every stage.

Let it soak for ten minutes in the warm soapy water before washing. The washing method then varies with the strength of the lace. A piece which won't tangle and is not strong enough for handling can be put in a large jar (even a big plastic sweet jar from a sweet shop) with the soapy water and shaken vigorously. A larger piece which is not too fragile can be put in a pillow case. You then squeeze the suds through the pillow case without handling the lace. More fragile lace, or any which would tangle, is better pinned out on a polythene-covered board, and covered with a layer of net. Then gently brush suds through it with a soft brush and rinse it by pouring water over it.

After rinsing old lace, pat it gently dry with a towel and put it in shape to dry flat. To get it perfectly to shape you may need to pin it out on a softboard covered with polythene. Use *stainless steel* pins and put them between the threads *not* into them. Finally, it should be ironed with a warm iron through white tissue paper - so the point of the iron cannot catch and tear the lace. For lace curtains see Net, page 190.

Today we might not go along with simmering a lace veil, but in other respects these instructions from the 1856 *Enquire Within* can hardly be bettered.

> *TO WASH A WHITE LACE VEIL. - Put the veil in a strong lather of white soap and very clear water, and let it simmer slowly for a quarter of an hour. Take it out and squeeze it well, but be sure not to rub it. Rinse in two cold waters with a drop of liquid blue in the last. Have ready some very clear weak gum arabic water, or some thin starch, or rice water. Pass the veil through it, and clear it by clapping. Then stretch it out even, and pin it to dry on a linen cloth, making the edge as straight as possible, and opening out all the scallops, and fastening each with pins. When dry, lay a piece of muslin smoothly over it, and iron it on the wrong side.*

Linen
Linen is very easy so long as you pander to its needs. It likes a hot wash (barring deep shades) and a very hot iron. But to iron up well it must be very much wetter than cotton need be - not dripping but very damp. Then it comes up beautifully without effort. If you let it get too dry before ironing it, it is the very devil and responds neither to damping nor to steam irons. Re-wet totally and re-dry to the right point. The ironed surface tends to shine, so iron it on the wrong side if you don't want this.

Be careful: there are also linen-look fabrics which are cotton and polyester, which need lower temperatures of both water and iron.

Loose Covers
The fact that a cover is loose does not mean the makers intend you to remove it for washing. Most loose covers shrink dreadfully when washed and must be dry-cleaned. If you are putting new loose covers on a chair

wash the material before the covers are made up. Then you have guarded against the worst of the shrinking. Even so, when you wash the covers after use avoid very hot water and put the covers back on the chairs while they are still rather damp. In that way they won't end up smaller than the chairs. You can run an iron over them both before you put them on the chairs and when in place - if whatever is underneath will take the heat.

Milium

Milium is a trade name for an aluminium coating sometimes found on the linings of coats and curtains. If you are making up curtains with it place the metallic side to the inside. It can usually be treated like cotton, but check the maker's instructions.

Net and Tulle

If the washing instructions say nothing to the contrary one would expect net to be washable. It can be made of all kinds of fibres. Cotton net may go sad if not ironed while still quite damp, and is best starched. Nylon net keeps its spring well if washed in cool water. But I did discover that to help the tutus of the ballerinas in Covent Garden stand out perfectly the wardrobe mistresses run a circle of crinoline wire through a net casing on one of the middle layers about half way from the body.

Net Curtains

The secret of keeping terylene net curtains white is simply to wash them often. Ingrained yellowing is hard to remove but Dylon's product for whitening curtains does make a difference. They are best washed by hand using soap powder or detergent and warm - not hot - water. Give them an overnight soak in a warm soapy solution. Rinse until the water is totally clear and then hang them to drip dry *without* spinning or wringing. Re-hang while still damp but, if necessary, iron them lengthwise with a cool iron first. Nylon net is treated in the same way (see nylon, below).

Nylon or Polyamide

Nylon absorbs dye very easily but loses it easily too. Beware of washing dark colours with light. White nylon can be washed at ITCL 3, but coloured nylon at 4, or hand-wash in medium hot water and give cool rinses. Using fabric conditioner in the final rinse will reduce static. Avoid wringing or over-spinning and drip-dry if possible. Iron with a very cool iron as it melts easily. Grey nylon can be whitened with Dylon's curtain whitener (see page 183).

Organza

Silk organza can be washed as silk, unless the label says dry clean only. Polyester organza must be dry cleaned, and viscose organza can be gently hand-washed in warm water, and ironed with a warm iron when slightly damp.

Permanent Pleating

Permanent pleating is usually heat set in a man-made fibre. So heat can unset it. Stick to low temperatures, wash it by hand and drip dry.

Pillows and Duvets

Using an underslip or pillow protector keeps a pillow cleaner much longer. When it does get dirty there are several options. Down and/or feather pillows and duvets can be dry cleaned, but unless they are done by a company which removes the filling and cleans the cover and filling separately (an expensive process) the cover may not look very clean. Alternatively, they can be washed but this is very much at your own risk, as makers don't recommend it. I do, however, find it is very successful. One risk with washing is that some pillow ticking - especially on cheap pillows - is treated on the inside to stop the feathers coming through. After washing, the feathers may come through more easily.

To wash a pillow soak it overnight in a bath of lukewarm soapy water (pure soap not detergent). Wash it in the same way next day, putting a few drops of ammonia in the water, and rinse it in the same temperature until the water runs clear. Spin dry with a series of brief spins and then either tumble it dry - by itself so there is plenty of space - at a low temperature or peg it to the bottom of a wire coathanger and hang it to dry in a warm place. The secret of getting it to come up well is to plump it up as often as possible.

Pillows with synthetic fillings are washed as duvets, but until quite recently they came up incurably lumpy. Mercifully, the better modern fillings such as Quallofil seem to have got over that fault.

Polyester, Polyamid or Polyester and Cotton

Have you ever wondered why polyester or poly-cotton sheets, which are so beautifully crease-free at first, gradually need more and more ironing to be presentable? The answer is that they are finished with a resin which makes them resist creases, but this resin very slowly washes out. The other reason is that at a temperature of about $70°/80°C$ the molecules of polyester mysteriously change their structure and acquire the ability to 'remember' the shape they were in at that temperature. So, if they are scrunched up in a washing machine at the time they will ever afterwards try to return to those creases. For polyester the rules are:
- wash and rinse it at $60°C$ or less
- don't wash dark and light colours together or they may run
- a full or partial tumble-dry fluffs it up and cuts down creasing, but it should not be overdried and should be removed from the dryer the instant it finishes or it will crease in the folds it ends in.

Poplin

Poplin is washed according to the fibre and is usually cotton or poly-cotton. Proofed poplin may not be washable - check the instructions.

Quilting

Quilting ranges from the most robust nylon quilted dressing gown to heirloom bed quilts. Handle ordinary quilting according to the fibre.

Bed quilts need to be dry-cleaned, by a skilled cleaner, or washed with great care, according to the fabric. The problem is to get one clean without disturbing the layers. So if it is washed it must be done gently by hand in a bath. On old and valuable quilting take advice from a museum textile department.

Sailcloth
Sailcloth is usually cotton or polyester and cotton. Treat it accordingly, but strong colours may run.

Satin
The care of satin depends both on the fibre it is made from and on the quality of the cloth. Satin in man-made fibres usually washes beautifully. Silk satin underwear can often be washed as silk (below) but a satin used for top garments will usually need to be dry cleaned.

Seersucker
Wash seersucker according to the fibre, but drip dry and do not iron or the bubbles will flatten out.

Silk
Silk varies hugely in its washability, but it always needs careful handling. It is usually best to dry clean the following types: silk taffeta, chiffon, brocade, georgette and organza (but see also by name above); also printed scarves and ties. And, whether it says so or not, silk which rustles must never be washed as washing will remove the metallic dressing which gives it the stiffness.

Some silks which appear to wash beautifully are tricky to iron well. Some silks are even difficult to dry clean and need very skilled handling. If any silk looks out of the ordinary it is worth using a specialist cleaner.

Silk takes up dye easily but releases it just as gladly. So it is always risky to wash patterns, and each item should be washed alone. To test if the dye will run wet a corner which won't show, place it on a piece of white fabric or kitchen roll and iron it with a warm iron. If no dye comes off it shouldn't run in washing. Wash silk by hand, not in a machine, using very cool water and pure soap, squeezing the liquid through it. It must never be rubbed, scrubbed, bleached or boiled, and can take only very brief soaking. Nor should you rub on block soap to treat a dirty area: it may develop a pale patch at that point.

Rinse it very well at the same temperature, and put ½ cup of white vinegar for every 4 l (1 gallon) of water in the final rinse. It gives silk the feel which old-timers in the cleaning trade charmingly call 'scroop' - a certain crispness. Then roll it in a towel and press out the moisture. Hang it to dry away from heat or direct sunlight. Tumble-drying is not good for it.

Silk needs skilful ironing if it is not to look shabby. It must be evenly damp all over. Garments never dry evenly so let it dry then put it in a plastic bag with a few tablespoons of water, close the bag and leave it for a few hours to moisten evenly. But don't leave it longer and keep it in a cool place (like the fridge) or mildew could set in and this is virtually impossible to remove. Iron it on the wrong side with a warm iron while still decidedly damp.

This method of washing and ironing will suit most silk underwear, some slub silk, and some crêpe de Chine. Slubbed and ribbed silks need a damp pressing cloth over them or they may be roughed up. Shantung is an exception: it must be ironed when dry and damp ironing can mark it.

White crêpe de Chine, which has been frequently dry-cleaned, may become too yellow to wear long before it is out of fashion - let alone worn out. At this stage to risk washing it is no loss but you can't use bleach on silk and I was hesitant to use any strong chemical. However, having tested Dylon's Super White on just such a shirt I found that, though it didn't bring it up like new (it never claimed to), it did restore enough whiteness to make the shirt wearable again. It claims to work on any silk, and on wool and nylon.

Terylene
A polyester fibre, see Polyester.

Ticking
Ticking is closely woven cotton made to keep feathers in pillows. Wash it as cotton and iron when damp. The traditional way to make it more feather-proof still works: you rub the inside well with beeswax (from good hardware stores or by mail from Frank Joel (page 171).

Ties
Ties look harmless enough but any tie cut on the bias (with the threads not running straight up and down the tie) will usually twist irreversibly when wet, and the interlining is prone to shrinking. Leave ties to professionals if you possibly can. If you really can't do that tack all the layers together before you even try any extensive spot cleaning.

Tricel and Triacetates
Tricel and the triacetates are made from acetate fibres which wash well and won't shrink or stretch. But they are best hand-washed in warm water without wringing and should be left to drip dry. Iron them with a warm iron. Tricel velour is an exception and can have a brief spin.

Velvet, Velour and Velveteen
Velvet is very variable; most good-quality velvet can only be dry-cleaned, but versions such as jersey velvets in man-made fibres wash well. Follow the care label religiously. This is not a fabric to gamble with.

Velveteen normally washes like corduroy, but check the care label.

Viscose
Viscose is made of cellulose from wood pulp and waste cotton, which makes it sound tough, but it isn't, and needs tender treatment. Whether on its own or in a blend, hand-wash in water hot enough to have your

hands in comfortably, drip dry (or spin *very* briefly) and use a warm iron.

Viyella

This is traditionally a combination of lambswool and cotton and needs to be treated like wool. There is also pure wool viyella and pure cotton viyella - the latter being more robust.

Waterproofed Fabrics

Fabrics which have lost their waterproofing - or which were never waterproof when they should have been - can be waterproofed at home. **Nikwax** (Durgates Industrial Estate, Wadhurst, East Sussex Tel: 0892 88 3855) makes waterproofers for just about everything from thin nylon to quilting.

Wool and Angora

Wool has three enemies: heat, rubbing and water. All woven wool is normally dry-cleaned, but most knitted wool can be either dry-cleaned or washed - unless the care label says otherwise.

Knitted garments are almost always better washed by hand than in a machine, though blankets can usually be washed safely in a machine with a wool programme.

The secret of keeping wool soft is to use water which is almost cold - for both washing and rinsing - and handle it gently without rubbing. So dissolve the soap thoroughly in 1 part (1 pt, 1 l or whatever) of hot water, then add 3 parts (3 pt, 3 l etc) of cold water. Let a single woollen item soak for 10 minutes in this and then wash it by gently pressing against the bottom of the basin, lifting *slightly* and pressing it down again. Rub spots gently with a cake of Fairy soap and press this extra soap through the wool with the finger tips. But never rub wool or it will mat and felt.

When the dirt has come out, drain the basin and press the surplus water from the garment before lifting it out (lifting very wet wool stretches it). Rinse in several changes of water, *the same temperature as before*, until no more soap comes out and the water is quite clear. Some people like to use a fabric softener for wool. Alternatively, 1 to 2 teaspoons of glycerine in about a litre of cool water makes a softening final rinse without the synthetic smell.

Press out as much water as you can and then spin the water out with a fast spin in a machine, one garment at a time, before lying it out flat on a clean towel to dry. Heavy jumpers should always be dried lying flat like this, or they will stretch out of shape. But a lightweight garment can be hung on an inflatable hanger after a thorough spin. If you have no inflatable hanger simply thread the legs of a pair of tights down each armhole, pull the body of the tights through the neck and peg both this and the two feet, to the line. This avoids the marks which are made if you peg the wool itself to the line. (Incidentally, men can pop a drip-dry shirt inside the pullover and peg it in the same way.)

Whatever the method, wool must be kept out of the sun and away from heat until dry - a tumble dry is disastrous.

If you can't spin wool, lie it out flat on a towel and then roll the towel up like a Swiss roll. If two people take either end of the towel and twist in opposite directions the water can be wrung out without any harm to the wool. Or, if you're alone, walk on the towel.

The less knitting is ironed the better. But it seldom needs it if it has been laid out flat. If it does, use a cool iron on the wrong side, through a slightly damp cloth.

> I started by saying that woven wool should only be dry cleaned. However, my artist son sometimes covers his clothes with so much paint and charcoal that I am loath to present them to a dry cleaner. I wash his heavy pure wool tweed trousers in totally cold water and pure soap, spin them dry, hang them in the shade and press them carefully. They look like new. I *don't* recommend washing woven wool; it could well ruin it, but if a garment which has no interlining is past cleaning by any other method it could be worth a try, *if you don't mind the risk*. But do stick to cold water and pure soap.

Skin Curing

It has always seemed to me a great shame that the beautiful fur of the rabbits which hang outside butcher's shops should be thrown away. It seems almost insulting to waste. With that in mind, and memories of a muff of rabbit skin which I had when very young, I have tried to cure skins, but it has never worked well. So, as I feel the old skills should be cherished, I turned, for this book, to the Women's Institute - always an excellent source of practical information. What follows are methods recommended by a member.

The methods can be used for rabbit, goat and lamb skins, and were given to the WI member by one Miss Mendel, who described them as 'trusted and tried methods' and said the dry method was the easiest. They also carry a note that: 'It must be borne in mind that this is a craft requiring practice and care, and sufficient time devoted daily to the instructions given below. Otherwise, failure must inevitably follow.' The best skins for curing are from rabbits of 6 to 8 months old, and that the skins of those under 4 months , or 'summer skins' are not very suitable. (Alum is sold by chemists.)

Skin Dressing - Dry Method

Skin the animals (not more than 24 hours after killing for a tame rabbit), and remove the inner skin from the pelt as soon as possible. Pin the skin out on a large board with drawing pins, in a good shape, with the fur underneath. Rub well in 2 teaspoons of salt and 2 teaspoons of alum mixed together. Remove it from the board and fold it in quarters, fur side out. Leave for 3 days, then wipe and scrape it well on the inside. Hang it on a line, fur side out, so it dries slowly. For 3 weeks or more scrape, pull, stretch and rub it daily, treating it as if you were washing it, to keep it soft. Also brush the fur. If you can rub some oatmeal in during this process it helps to absorb moisture and whiten the skin, or rub it with pumice. At the end of 3 to 4 weeks it should be cured and soft.

The vital point is that the skin must not be allowed to become hard. Once hard, it is very difficult to get it soft again. The skin side can be rubbed to and fro over a chair back to soften it.

> The recipe says only a small quantity of salt and alum is needed and gives that amount, which is very much less than in the next recipe. Perhaps the amount depends on the size of the skin. I would suspect that if too little is used to treat the whole skin, parts will become rotten, but I may be wrong. I would also suggest leaving it in the coolest place possible, well protected from flies - though the recipe does not say so. And the line must be somewhere cool and shady.

Wet Curing for Skins

Put 2 lb of bran in 1 gallon of water. Fold the skin, fur side in, and immerse it in the water for 1½ to 2 days in summer, 3 in winter. Hang it over a line, fur side out, for about an hour to dry. Take it down and rub in 57 g (2 oz) of alum, and 85 to 113 g (3 to 4 oz) of salt for small skins, making sure it goes right to the edges. Fold in quarters, fur side out, and leave to pickle for 1 day (see note above). Check it and rub in more salt and alum if needed, fold and leave for 1 more day. Scrape out all inner skin. Hang it on a line, fur side out. Let it hang for 2 to 3 weeks daily, stretching and rubbing it as for the dry method above. Brush the fur clean.

Skin Curing Especially for Lamb Skins

Remove any loose fat and skin from the skin. Place in cold soft water for 24 hours, changing the water very frequently. Drain the skin and put it on a board, fur side down. Rub in a dressing made of 1 large tablespoon of salt, 45g (1½ oz) of alum boiled together for 3 minutes in a pint of water, and used while still warm. (Don't let the dressing get on the fur.) Fold the skin in half and leave flat for 24 hours. Repeat the dressing and folding and leave 24 hours more. Hang the skin over a line to dry *very* slowly; as it dries it must be repeatedly pulled, rubbed and stretched, as for the dry method above, until soft. Put the skin fur side up and wash the fur well with warm soapy water *without getting the soapy water on the skin.* When totally dry rub the skin down with pumice or glasspaper.

Stain Removal

Stain removal is one of the trickiest of subjects to explain because so much depends not only on what you do but on how and when you do it. The same method used by two different people on the same stain can produce two quite different results simply because one person was too rough or too impatient. Fabrics can also be unpredictable: I rubbed a little pure soap on a tiny grease spot on a pale-grey pure cotton jumpsuit. It should have been the ideal treatment but the material was so poor that the dye faded instantly from the area, making a brand-new garment unwearable. It's impossible for me to guarantee that any of the following methods are safe, and it's important to read my warnings before attempting to remove a stain.

Of course, when fabrics respond badly to methods which should normally be perfectly safe you can claim against the makers, but it's a hassle to *prove* that you didn't do the wrong thing and money hardly makes up for the loss of a garment you enjoy wearing.

> The great thing is that once you get used to removing stains you begin to know automatically which type of substance will do the trick on other surfaces. Often it is a matter of alkalis acting against acids and so on and it helps if you look for these relationships. You don't need even 'O' level chemistry to do this, just be prepared to observe and experiment. After a while you may find that, like me, you almost delight in seeing a stain for the sheer satisfaction you will get in beating it.

Rules of Stain Removal

Rule 1: *Act at once.* Forget anything your mother told you about saying 'Don't worry, it doesn't matter a bit', and letting a stain sit there. People feel far less embarrassed at having spilt something if they can see it removed before it creates a permanent mark. So get the surplus substance off the surface immediately.

- Scoop up solids with an implement which lifts them out of the fabric without scraping at it.
- Mop up liquids instantly - with a clean light-coloured cloth. (Beware of dyed paper napkins: they will shed dye.)
- Put a clean cloth under the stain, and press between the top and bottom cloths.
- Either get the stained item to a suitable dry-cleaner before the stain dries, keeping it in a plastic bag *en route* with cloths to stop the stain touching other areas, or treat it yourself - *first reading the warning and rules below.*

> *Do not attempt to remove stains from the following fabrics. They are too delicate to clean at home:* silk chiffon, most brocade, watered silk, any silk with a rustle to it, silk jersey and velvet or lurex (unless marked as washable).
>
> Silk often has fragile dyes which may become blotchy with stain treatment. Carpet dyes are also fragile and may fade.

When you try to remove a stain yourself rather than use a professional dry-cleaner, you risk damaging the item in question. It is very easy to misjudge the make-up of a fabric and use the wrong method on it, or to be slightly more rougher than you intended to be and damage the surface. The following methods are tried and tested by me, and work well, or are recommended by top authorities, but please realize *there is no guarantee they will not do damage in your particular case.* Do *not* attempt it unless you accept the risk involved. Remember if you take a tricky stain to an expert and there is a disaster you can usually claim against the firm. If you cause the disaster you have no claim on anyone.

Rule 2: *Always test any method of stain removal on a patch which won't show or on a spare piece of fabric or carpet unless you are* **sure** *the fabric can take it.*

Rule 3: *Suit the treatment to the surface the mark is on.* Treat wool like wool, acetate like acetate and so on, wherever you find it.

Rule 4 *Bear in mind the structure of the item.* You can't push stains through a carpet or upholstery in the way you can through loose cloth, and you must be *very* careful not to over-wet the surface or you may damage any carpet backing, padding or even interlining in a garment. Expect all underlayers to be more fragile and more likely to shrink than any surface fabric. Keep mopping up the liquid with clean white tissues between applications.

Rule 5: *Almost all surfaces are fragile.* You can damage the individual threads with rubbing and create a permanent mark even though the stain itself is removed. Go gently: dabbing not rubbing. A professional technique for stain removal is called '**tamping**' which is tapping the cleaning solution patiently through the cloth, again and again, with the tips of the fingers, or a clean cloth. It looks as if it is having no effect, but little by little it is.

Rule 6: *Start at the edge of the stain and work towards the middle,* so you go from clean to dirty, not vice versa. And, if possible, work from the back of the fabric to push the stain out the way it came. Wherever possible have a thick cloth under the stain and keep moving it as it absorbs it.

Rule 7: *Give any remedy time to work.* Gentleness and infinite patience are vital. Many good methods take a day or more to work.

Rule 8: The distinction between fabrics which are washable and those which 'dry-clean only' isn't very helpful. Most dry-cleanable fabrics can be moistened with *very cool* water, without harm - think what the rain would do if this wasn't so. This means cold and lukewarm water can be used in stain removal on some 'dry-clean only' fabrics. How risky it is will depend on the particular fabric so do a test on a patch which won't show. (See also the warning above.) Upholstery is an exception - nobody expects it to get rained on, so any water may damage it.

Rule 9: *Don't switch from method to method without giving any single one a decent try.* And never switch from a water-based to a spirit-based method - or vice versa - without letting the fabric dry *totally* or you may cause shrinking and felting. This means you can't dry-clean a garment until it is totally dry after stain removal. Nor should you wash it while a spirit-based cleaner is still moist.

Rule 10: *Don't use any cleaning substances, or methods, without realizing - and accepting - their limitations and dangers (see above and below).*

Acetone
Acetone should be avoided. It will melt fabric containing cellulose acetate; so it harms Tricel, Dicel and all their relatives. Beware too: some fabric has just the occasional acetate thread supplying a particular colour or texture. Instead of acetone, use amyl acetate, (from chemists) which removes the same stains without this risk - but it may make some dyes bleed.

Ammonia
Household ammonia will bleach certain dyes and must *never* be used on fabrics containing wool. Use from a few drops to a teaspoonful in 250 ml (½ pt) of water. Only increase the strength if a tough stain will budge no other way, and you are prepared to risk damage to the fabric. If a stain won't move with 1 part ammonia to 3 parts water, ammonia probably isn't the answer. Avoid breathing its fumes, have the windows open when using it, and wear rubber gloves.

DANGER: Nothing which has ammonia on it should be bleached, or vice versa, without thoroughly removing whichever chemical was used first.

Bleach
Bleach can only be used with total safety on white cotton and linen, or on pale-cream-tones of those fabrics - if you don't mind making them lighter. Even then it must *not* be used on crease-resistant, drip-dry, piqué or embossed fabrics. It will fade coloured cottons and actively damage silk, wool and man-made fibres (unless they say they can be bleached). Never let undiluted bleach touch fabric or it may burn a hole in it. Mix the water and bleach, stir well, and then submerge the fabric. Move the fabric in the bleach so it is evenly exposed. Soak no longer than is necessary.

Hydrogen Peroxide

Hydrogen peroxide is a mild bleaching agent sold by chemists in various strengths. Buy '20 volumes', and use 1 part of this to 6 parts water. Do not use it on flame-resistant fabrics or on nylon. But, unlike bleach, it can be used on wool and silk.

Methylated and other Spirits

Methylated spirits, lighter fuel, petrol and any other spirits are all used neat, but they can make some dyes go blotchy and create a permanent mark at the rim of the spirit. In the dry-cleaning trade they call this a 'sweal' - see feathering, below. They will also damage fabrics such as those which are rubberized or made of cellulose acetate - see acetone, above. Only use when unavoidable, and then do a test patch first where it won't show.

NEVER USE A SPIRIT OR BRANDED CLEANER WHILE SMOKING OR IN A ROOM WITH ANY FLAME BURNING - EVEN A PILOT LIGHT.

Proprietary Cleaners

Branded dry-cleaning fluids, such as Beaucaire and Dab-it-off, should only be used on fabrics recommended by the instructions. Even then there may be a risk of a 'sweal' (see methylated spirit above). You can lessen the risk of this by 'feathering'. This is making little strokes out from the centre so you don't leave a neat ring.

Pure Soap

Pure soap is a product which *says* it is pure soap. This usually means a block soap made for washing clothes, or pure soap flakes (trickier to use), or a pure soap liquid or powder made for washing wool. You can't assume that bath soap doesn't contain some substance which is bad for dyes.

Vinegar

Stick to white vinegar or you may get brown staining. But do not use it on any acetate or triacetate fabrics.

WARNING: Any remedy in this chart could damage some fabrics

When All Else Fails

If a stain is resolute, and the fabric won't be damaged by boiling water, stretch the material *tightly* over a heat-proof jug or bowl, with an elastic band, placing the stain in the middle. Pour boiling water from a height on to, and through, the stain until it vanishes. It may help to have some pure soap on the stain before pouring on the water or to rub on some powdered borax. Several kettles of water may be needed.

If you use any water-based method of stain removal, finish by tamping clean water through the area and repeatedly mopping it dry, to remove all trace of the ammonia, borax or whatever else was used. Finally press the area dry with clean cloths.

Basic Stain Removing Kit

If you keep the following in the house you will be able to cope with most stains: glycerine, oil of eucalyptus, borax powder, pure soap, 1001 carpet shampoo, white vinegar, household ammonia, white spirit, Fuller's Earth and possibly an enzyme washing powder. As you can see, the ingredients are very cheap and will keep indefinitely.

★ Enzyme detergents break down protein. So don't use them on fabrics made of protein, such as silk or wool.
★ Any stain can be removed more easily when softened. Old stains which are to be treated with a water-based treatment can be softened by rubbing in glycerine and leaving it for an hour or two.

Adhesives

With adhesives you don't have a lot of choice: if a glue needs strong chemicals to remove it you either use them, and risk spoiling certain fabrics, or decide to live with a glue stain. There simply aren't safe alternatives.

Many glue manufacturers will supply a solvent for their adhesive - if one exists - but the following immediate remedies were suggested by the glue manufacturers themselves. In all cases, work the suggested solvent into the glue, and let it have time to take effect. Then try to mop the stain off with a clean cloth. Follow the rules for stains (pages 193-195).

Adhesive	While Still Wet	Once It Has Dried
Araldite/Epoxy Resin	Very tough to remove. Scoop off surface adhesive before it can dry. Apply Arco Cupran (page 201), or cellulose thinners.	Either of the instant remedies can also be tried on dry resin - give them time to work or use commercial paint stripper.
Evostik Resin W	Easily removed when wet; far harder when dry. Scoop off surplus and sponge off with a clean wet cloth. Make sure it is out of the fabric as well as off.	Try leaving water to soak into it (e.g. a moist sponge on top of the mark). Try to tamp it off once it softens.

Adhesive	While Still Wet	Once It Has Dried
Evostik Impact II	Apply Evostik cleaner (if you keep it). Try paint stripper, or white spirit mixed with washing-up liquid.	Extremely hard to get off once dry. Try Evostik cleaner, but it may fail. (See 'wet' remedies, left).
Supaglue	Put anything it gets on to in water for a long time - including skin.	It's a forlorn hope but try soaking in water.
Tile on Wood (Polycell)	Get it off fast - using water.	Amyl acetate.
Tile Grout (Polycell)	Water.	Hydrochloric acid (e.g. some patio cleaners) but use with great caution and expect damage to fabrics.
General Purpose Filler (Polycell)	Water.	Water.
Frame Sealant (Acrylic), Silicone Bath Sealant, Ready-mixed Filler, Coloured Tile Grout (Polycell)	Water.	Paintbrush cleaner.
Unibond, Copydex	Water.	Dry-cleaning fluid such as Beaucaire or Dab-it-off.
Polystyrene Coving Adhesive, Unistik Contact Adhesive, Unilast Gap Filling Adhesive	Water.	Trichlorethylene or amyl acetate (or acetone, but see page 194).
Woodworking Adhesive, Waterproof Fix n'Grout	Water.	Paintbrush cleaner or possibly white spirit.
Waterproof Woodworking Adhesive, Fire Cement (Polycell)	Water.	There is no solvent for it.
Cork Tile Adhesive, Multipurpose Flooring Adhesive	Water.	White spirit.
Cerafix PVA Adhesive	Water.	Amyl acetate or acetone (see page 194).
Waterproof Tile Adhesive	Water.	Amyl acetate or possibly white spirit.
Bitumen and Bitumen Gutter Sealant	White spirit.	White spirit.
Prit, Gloy, Copydex Child's Play, Solvite	Water.	Water.

Ballpoints and Biros

The chemistry of inks varies with the maker, so results are unpredictable. Red ink is always extra hard to remove and may be impossible (see page 190). The following methods may shift blue or black marks.

- Tamping pure soap and lukewarm water through the stain again and again with a clean cloth underneath.
- Spray on hair lacquer then press out the stain and the lacquer with a clean cloth. (This can work marvellously on light nylon).
- Tamp with methylated spirits. If the stain is on plastic you can wipe it off with this, but a little of the plastic

WARNING: Any remedy in this chart could damage some fabrics

WARNING: Read pages 193-195 before trying to remove any stain

will come off too - so go gently. The same applies to shiny leather but the dye may be affected.
- Tamp with hot or sour milk, or soak washable items in it.

Beer
Beer leaves a brown mark, which can be hard to remove, if allowed to dry. Having mopped it up, sponge with lukewarm water, or with 1 part white vinegar to 5 parts water (not on acetate or tri-acetate). Lacking this, clean it off with soda water. Wash, or soak, washable fabrics before they dry out, and use carpet shampoo on carpets. On acetate and tri-acetate use 1½ teaspoons of borax in 250 ml (½ pt) lukewarm water.

Dried stains may be treated with methylated spirits or the branded spot remover K2r.

Beetroot
Having mopped up all liquid, tamp with lukewarm water containing 1½ teaspoons of borax per 250 ml (½ pt) of water. If necessary add a few drops of ammonia.

Some people swear by gin or vodka on beetroot. I have yet to try it, but I do cherish the tip which I was sent by the mother of a 3-year-old. He rubbed ripe pear on a beetroot stain and so enabled her to wash it out with remarkable ease - a method I have tested with equal success.

Bird Droppings
Scoop up the dropping and sponge off any stain with pure soap and water, the borax solution given under Beetroot, or a carpet or upholstery shampoo, such as 1001. If the laundry on the line was dive-bombed, relaundering should do the trick, using an enzyme powder if necessary. But if the bird has been eating berries the stain bleach may need peroxide, or see 'When all else fails' (page 195).

Blood
Beware of heat: even hot water sets the protein in blood and the stain may then be impossible to remove.

Having mopped up all the surplus, treat bloodstains with *cold* salty water while still wet. Soakable fabrics can be left to soak. Tamp others repeatedly - if necessary using a little pure soap too. Once the stain has almost gone wash carpets with carpet shampoo and cold water. Wet stains should come out quite easily, but once blood dries it is tough to remove. Soak in an enzyme washing powder and cold water or apply cold water and ammonia but wash the stain out with cold water before laundering. Remove any soap or ammonia with clean cold water.

Chewing gum
Don't dab at it - the gum will be pressed in. Remove any large lumps - unless on a corduroy or velvet pile which will come off with it. Then use a spray-on hardener sold by **G.E.Holloway and Sons** (page 201) as directed and break it off in flakes. Failing that, put the fabric in a plastic bag in a freezer. When hard pick off the brittle gum, wiggling the fabric to get it out of

the weave. When every trace is removed wash or dry clean. If breaking hardened chewing gum threatens to take the pile off velvet or corduroy hold the back of the fabric over a steaming kettle spout (beware of burning yourself) and see if picking the chewing gum off when very soft is any better. You may then be able to freeze it again and remove the last traces safely.

Chocolate or Cocoa
Scoop up as much as possible with a spoon, or mop up the liquid. Then work glycerine into the stain and tamp it with lukewarm water and pure soap. Remove the soap by tamping with clear lukewarm water. The borax solution for beetroot is another method.

Coffee
Get coffee out while wet: it is difficult to remove once dry. Having mopped it up, tamp glycerine into it. Give this a few minutes to work then tamp it out with lukewarm water and pure soap. On suitable fabrics use a teaspoon white vinegar to ¼ l (½ pt) water.

Cosmetics
Cosmetic stains can often be lifted off the surface of leather by dabbing it *lightly* with the sticky side of sticky tape. But be careful not to pull off the leather's surface. They wash out of fabrics.

Creosote
This is a nasty one. Take 'dry-clean only' fabrics to an expert. On washable fabrics you may be able to remove the stain by soaking it in glycerine, then tamping with soap - or by applying oil of eucalyptus.

Curry
There are usually two main elements to a curry stain: fat and turmeric. Turmeric gives the yellow colour and is the harder to remove. Applying glycerine at once may stop the stain setting. Then rinse washable fabrics in lukewarm water. On dry-clean only fabrics tamp the stain with the borax solution given for beetroot. On carpet sponge on the borax mixture and leave it for 15 minutes, then sponge the mixture out and shampoo as usual. It may be necessary to apply hydrogen peroxide or bleach - if it will take them.

Dyes
Since I wrote *Supertips* a lot of people have written to asking how to remove the dye from garments which they have put into a washing machine with something which has run. Washing the item without letting it dry first helps, but to remove all the dye you have to resort to bleach - if it was a white fabric which will take it - or to a dye remover, such as that sold by Dylon. This will also remove the original colour of the garment. You then have to dye it back. Alas, there is no product clever enough to remove selectively the dye you don't want and to leave the original one.

Splashes of dye can be treated with methylated spirits or with ammonia and water.

WARNING: Read pages 193-195 before trying to remove any stain

Egg

If fabric can take it, the best treatment for egg stains is the old-fashioned mixture of lukewarm water and a few drops of household ammonia or a solution of enzyme detergent. A safer mixture is 250 ml (½ pt) water with 1½ tsps. powdered borax tamped through the stain.

Excreta (human or animal)

How badly this stains will depend greatly on the diet of the depositor, so what will remove a stain on one occasion may fail on another.

Scoop it out of the fabric, or carpet - a paint scraper is ideal for this. Get as much as possible out by wiping very thoroughly with tissues. But be careful not to rub so hard you break up the texture of the carpet or fabric. Shampoo a carpet immediately with a carpet shampoo such as 1001 - doing a test patch first if you haven't used it on the carpet before. Put suitable fabrics to soak in enzyme detergent and lukewarm water. Tamp the stain out of 'dry-clean only' fabrics with lukewarm water and pure soap.

There are now products which claim to use harmless bacteria to 'eat' the stains and smells from such accidents, and so remove them. 'Odour Eliminator' seems to do the job. Some pet shops stock these products, or contact the manufacturers **Veterinary Drug Co** (Common Road, Dunnington, York YO1 5RU Tel: 0904 488444) for stockists.

Fats and oils

When fats and oils are really thick soap simply can't penetrate them, so first you need to thin them down with a finer oil. The best is oil of eucalyptus (from chemists). Dab off as much oil as possible - without smearing it - with a clean tissue. Then tamp with oil of eucalyptus on a clean cloth until the oil begins to shift. It can then be washed out, tamped out with water and soap, or removed with a dry cleaning fluid, according to the fabric.

If you have no eucalyptus oil and do have a dry-cleaning fluid, or even lighter fluid, these may loosen the grease or oil - or may even remove the stain entirely. But they are more likely to affect the dye. In the last resort, heavy oil and grease can be thinned by working in poultry dripping before washing.

If colourless fats or oils have stained leather or upholstery warm some Fuller's Earth (from a chemist) or potato flour, put a heap of it over the mark and cover immediately with foil and a cloth to keep the warmth in. Leave it for 24 hours. If the stain has lessened try repeated applications of fresh powder. There are also branded grease removers for leather; fabric upholstery may respond to a cleaner like K2r and so may some wallcoverings.

Fruit and Fruit Juice

Mop up as much as possible with a white cloth or tissue, or pour over dry starch and let it absorb as much of the stain as possible, then brush it off. Press glycerine into the stain to stop it setting. Then press tepid water

and borax or pure soap through the stain until it vanishes. Once it is allowed to dry it will be far harder to remove. But in this case apply glycerine, leave it an hour and then tamp as above.

Stubborn stains may need to be bleached out or removed with hydrogen peroxide, or with lemon juice and salt as for rust. If that fails try 'When all else fails' (page 195) applying borax before pouring on the water, or use dye remover (page 197).

Grass stains

Grass stains are among those deceptively simple stains that can frustrate the best of efforts. Nothing is guaranteed to remove them but the following remedies are the most likely to be successful. A soak in mild bleach (as directed on the bottle). Tamping with glycerine, leaving a few hours, then tamping with pure soap and lukewarm water; or tamping with methylated spirits or with the ammonia solution.

Hair Lacquer

Hair lacquer should really be applied before dressing as it stains some fabrics. Remove the marks by tamping with 1½ teaspoons of powdered borax in 250 ml (½ pt) of lukewarm water.

Ice Cream

Ice cream should sponge off but treat chocolate ice cream as for chocolate, and real fruit ices as for fruit.

Ink

Serious staining, such as a pen leak in a jacket pocket, is best taken to a professional cleaner - see also Parker Pens below.

However, it is fascinating to drop an inky handkerchief or shirt into a pan of hot milk and watch the blue ink flow out of the fabric and into the milk. This can be tried with any black or blue non-permanent ink and fabrics which can't be soaked in milk can be tamped with it. If milk fails some inks will come out with salt and lemon juice, others with ammonia and water. Yet others will need alternate tamping with ammonia and pure soap. If these methods fail you may find that tamping with methylated spirits works. It will be more effective if heated over a bowl of hot water (without a flame). But some brands won't come out totally.

Red ink is an eosin dye which is almost impossible to remove except by using methylated spirits or a product such as the dye remover given for felt-pen ink.

Ink on Carpets

Instantly put salt liberally on top. Salt absorbs liquid and will draw the ink out of the fibres. Once the salt has absorbed the free liquid, vacuum or sweep it off very carefully without spreading the stain. Then treat it with hot or sour milk to loosen the ink. Finally, shampoo with carpet shampoo or the milk will smell.

Ink on Leather

Ink on leather may come out if dabbed immediately with

milk, but it may take a lot of dabbing and there is a risk of the milk leaving a grease mark in some types of leather.

Felt-pen Ink

Felt-pen inks vary enormously. Some will come off if treated like blue ink. Red felt pen can react like red ink, and permanent markers may need drastic treatment which is likely to remove the dye. The two possibilities are to tamp it with petrol (which may make the dye run), or to rub in a product called ReDuRan designed to remove industrial dyes from the hands (see page 201). The latter will remove both the felt pen and the dye of the fabric - but you could wash the whole garment, get rid of any remaining dye with Dylon's dye remover and re-dye it.

Parker Pen Co Ltd (Service Department, P.O. Box 6, Newhaven, Sussex BN9 0AX Tel: 0273 513233) has solvents for its inks and information.

Iodine

Mop up the stain, and tamp immediately with pure soap and the water and ammonia mixture.

Jam, Ketchup and Similar Substances

The problem with these substances is that you may be dealing with a natural fruit colour or a food dye or both. If marks don't wipe off with lukewarm water, try tamping with the borax solution for beetroot, or with methylated spirits. Or soak washable fabrics in the borax solution.

Lipstick

Place a pad of tissues or towelling under the stain. Dab with oil of eucalyptus. Let this soak into the stain. Blot off the lipstick and repeat. If necessary, leave the oil in overnight then blot up all loose lipstick and tamp with pure soap and water as hot as the fabric will stand - or on 'dry-clean only' fabrics omit the soap and water and dry-clean afterwards. The effectiveness of the treatment varies with the make, but the eucalyptus may totally remove the stain.

White cotton handkerchiefs with lipstick on will boil or bleach clean. Occasionally eucalyptus fails, in which case try glycerine or surgical spirit - though the latter may shift dye.

Mascara

Waterproof mascara stains should be tamped with oil of eucalyptus then with soap and lukewarm water. Other mascara stains can have soap and water straight away. If these fail, tamp with ammonia.

Mildew or Mould

Mildew on fabrics is decidedly to be avoided as it is one of the hardest stains to remove. The most reliable method is still that recommended in the *Enquire Within* of 1856.

Take soap, and rub it well [into the stain]; then scrape some fine chalk [white blackboard], and rub

it also on the linen. Lay it on the grass. As it dries, wet it a little, and it will come out in twice doing.

The author was an optimist, give it 2 days of soap, chalk and sunlight before you try the alternative - which is to tamp it with 10 per cent hydrogen peroxide - which may harm delicate fabrics.

Mud

The secret with mud is never to try to remove it until *totally* dry. Then brush it off. Working on it while wet just pushes it into the fabric.

Nail Varnish

Nail varnish remover may contain acetone (see page 194).

Paints and Lacquers

Artists' paints should come off using the same methods as for household paints but Winsor and Newton make Win-sol, a paint remover for their paints (from art shops).

Water-based paints can be washed off with water and pure soap if you catch them while wet. Wet oil-based paints and lacquers come off quite easily with white spirit, turpentine or paraffin and on the whole these do not shift dyes - though check all the same. Then remove all trace of these substances.

Once paint or lacquer has dried you have a far tougher job on your hands - and there is always a risk that any substance which shifts dry paint will also shift the dye of whatever you are cleaning. Oil-based paints and lacquers will come off quite miraculously with a hand cleaner called Cupran. Amyl acetate will shift cellulose paints, and tamping with equal amounts of ammonia and turpentine mixed together will sometimes shift other paints, so will paintbrush cleaner/restorer.

Perfume

If perfume stains it is because the alcohol in it has affected the dye of the fabric. This cannot be cured.

Perspiration

Perspiration varies with the body's health; sometimes being acid, sometimes alkaline. This makes removing perspiration stains a matter of trial and error. Tamp acid stains with ammonia, alkaline stains with lemon juice. But go carefully lest these shift the dyes and don't be surprised if the stain won't budge. Perspiration can damage dye and nothing can reverse that.

Plasticine

Remove as much as possible, with your fingernails. Either use hot water and soap or a branded spirit stain remover to dissolve the deposit - according to the fabric.

Printing Ink

A friend of mine in Fleet Street rang me in despair one day asking how she could remove printing ink from a favourite summer skirt. The answer was a solvent such as Dab-it-off. But put a thick pad of clean tissue underneath and work very carefully as such a dark stain is easily spread and very easily leaves a sweal so it needs careful feathering, and immediate dry-cleaning once the stain is out.

Rust
The ease with which rust stains come out of light cotton or linen makes them almost a pleasure. Simply put the fabric in the sun (first catch your sun) and sprinkle a good heap of salt on the rust mark. Then pour over enough lemon juice to moisten both salt and fabric. Leave it in the sun, moistening it with more lemon until the rust mark vanishes. It may take a few hours or a couple of days, depending on the mark. But you don't need to *do* anything except moisten and wait. I have used this successfully on pale-cream pure silk - but with anything other than white cotton or linen there is a risk that the lemon will leave a stain or bleach the dye.

NB This method of removing rust works just as well for rust marks on wood. And it will work without the sunlight, though more slowly.

Scorch Marks
How a scorch mark should be treated depends entirely on what it is on. On man-made fabrics a scorch is normally a lost cause, as some of the fibres melt. On cotton or linen a surface scorch may simply wash out, may respond to tamping with hydrogen peroxide, or may fade if rubbed with lemon juice and left in the sun. On wool you may be able to brush off the burnt fibres. On delicate fabrics try applying a paste of water and magnesium carbonate (from a chemist) and leaving this until totally dry, then brushing it off.

Scorch marks are also a prime target for folk remedies. Among the oddest are Brown Windsor soup, and the following curious mixture: 60 g (2 oz) of Fuller's Earth, 250 ml (½ pt) vinegar, 2 to 3 chopped onions boiled together, applied when cold, and brushed off when dry. And my very early edition of Mrs Beeton has that same recipe plus ½ oz soap and 1 oz dried fowl's dung. So if all sane remedies fail you may like to try these. Some people still swear by them.

Shoe Polish
Tamp repeatedly with white spirit, blotting up the liquid and colour as it loosens. Remove the white spirit with pure soap and water or 1001 Carpet Shampoo if necessary.

Tar
Tar comes off quite easily with eucalyptus oil (this can be used safely on people and animals). Put a good pad of tissue under the fabric and dab with white tissues well saturated with the eucalyptus oil, throwing each tissue away when it has traces of tar on it. Continue until no more tar sits on the surface. To get the last traces out of the fibres tamp pure soap and water through until it comes clean.

In the absence of eucalyptus, petrol and lighter fuel will both remove tar - more hazardously.

Tea
If a tea stain has glycerine rubbed into it the moment it is spilt it should be very easy to remove by tamping with pure soap and lukewarm water. If a stain has dried, leave glycerine to soak in for several hours before trying to remove the stain. Tamp with the borax solution for beetroot. Lemon juice or acetic acid will also remove tea stains but these risk creating a new stain in some fabrics.

Tipp-Ex
I tracked down the cure for liquid tipp-ex at the request of a friend who tipped a bottle down a navy blue dress. Instantly scrape off as much as possible - without pressing it into the fabric or damaging the threads. Tamp the remainder with white spirit, with a cloth underneath, until it has all been removed.

Urine
If a puppy, kitten or child puddles on a carpet mop it up *instantly* and squirt the patch well with soda water. Re-mop, repeat and re-mop. If the puddle is caught before it dries and enough soda is used as an antidote there should be no stain. Failing soda, use Perrier or any mineral water.

Vaseline
Don't let vaseline encounter heat before you try to remove it: it can fix the stain for ever. Vaseline can be tamped out with turpentine before you wash or clean the fabric.

Wax from Candles
Leave wax well alone until hard. If it is in carpet, remove as much as you can with your nails. If possible chill the wax in a freezer, then break it off in pieces. (Wiggle the fabric to get the particles to fall from the weave). If it is in carpet, remove as much as you can with your nails. Then place the fabric between two sheets of absorbent paper and iron with a hot iron (moving the paper) to remove as much wax as possible. But keep moving the paper so the wax is absorbed by a clean section, and be careful not to let a fragile fabric or carpet overheat. Wash in the hottest water suitable for the fabric, or dry-clean. (If necessary, apply paraffin, to thin the wax, before washing.)

Wine
The great thing about a red wine stain is that nature has provided the natural antidote: white wine. Unlikely as it may sound, the best way to prevent red wine staining is to pour white wine over it before it has time to dry. Just mop up the surplus red wine (making sure you don't in your haste do as I once did and grab a brilliant red paper napkin with loose dye). Then pour enough white wine over the stain to wet the stain nicely. Mop that up and you may well find the stain has almost gone. If it hasn't, keep washable fabrics moist until you can put them in to soak. If you have no white wine, mineral water will sometimes do the trick, and so may tap water but less surely.

WARNING: Read pages 193-195 before trying to remove any stain

Old red wine stains can be soaked with white wine before washing, or you can rub glycerine into the stain and leave it for several hours before washing. If that fails the only solution may be to tamp the stain with equal parts of water and hydrogen peroxide.

White wine simply leaves a sticky stain which will wash or dry-clean out without trouble.

> Despite what is often said, red wine should *never* be doused with salt. On some fabrics this may prevent a stain but on others it will set it permanently - this isn't a good risk to take.

More information

G.E. Holloway and Son (Engineers) Ltd (12 Carlisle Road, Colindale, London NW9 0HL Tel: 01 200 0066) make a chewing gum remover and an anti-static spray.

ARCO (P.O. Box 21, Waverley Street, Hull HU1 2BJ Tel: 0782 46015) sells ReDuRan and Cupran and will supply by mail on request. Their industrial hand cleansers also remove stains from the skin.

MAIL ORDER

Mail order is covered by at least three different acts, but these only say how things *ought* to be, and give you rights in court when things go wrong. They don't *stop* things going wrong and, at best, getting redress is time-consuming.

Every year companies simply vanish with the customers' money, or supply goods far inferior to those promised. Order only from well-established companies, with a good reputation, or from those covered by one of the consumer protection schemes. On the other hand, good companies do save you the hassles, and travel costs, of conventional shopping and sometimes offer savings.

The safest are often those belonging to one of the mail order trade associations, which have codes of practice to which members must conform, and will arbitrate if you are dissatisfied. Members' catalogues must carry a statement that they conform to this code. Even then, keep an exact record of all the details you would need to supply if you had to make a complaint (see page 202).

Mail Order Trade Associations

The **Mail Order Publishers' Authority** (1 New Burlington Street, London W1X 1FD Tel: 01 437 0706) covers mail order books and records. Its code of practice includes the following clauses.

- You don't have to pay return postage on 'free approval' items.
- If you undertake a long-term contract you may cancel it after 12 months or if prices rise more than was expected.
- Despatch dates must be given if you pay in advance.

The **Mail Order Traders' Association** (25 Castle Street, Liverpool, L2 4TD Tel: 051 236 7581 or 051 227 4181)

covers the major catalogues and has a code of practice that includes the following.

- The catalogue must give a clear statement of prices, credit terms, and conditions of trade.
- You have a right to cancel any order up to the moment it is despatched.
- If you return goods within the set time limit your money must be promptly refunded in full, provided you have taken 'reasonable care' of them. Get proof of posting.
- Money must be promptly refunded on goods returned because they are unsatisfactory.

The **National Newspapers Mail Order Protection Scheme Ltd (MOPS)** (16 Tooks Court, London EC4A 1LB Tel: 01 405 6806) was created to protect those who buy through an advertisement asking for 'cash with order' which appears in a national newspaper. It has a central fund to repay those who lose their money through advertised goods failing to be delivered when an advertiser ceases to trade. However, it only covers part of the cost of goods paid for by credit card, totally excludes certain types of goods (e.g. plants and food) and only covers advertisements accepted for the MOPS scheme. In practice, that means an awful lot of advertisements in the national press are not covered. So do look for the MOPS symbol on press advertisements - it shows the advertisement is covered by the scheme. And if you often buy from advertisements get the leaflet spelling out all the MOPS rules from the address above.

Under MOPS *you must claim within 3 months of the advertisement appearing.* Write to the advertising manager of the paper which carried the advertisement, sending details of the advertisement, plus the date of your order, evidence of payment and the correspondence about the order. They do not accept photocopies. But keep photocopies in case the originals get lost in the post, and ask the post office for proof of posting (free).

Obtaining or Cancelling Mail Order Catalogues

The **Mailing Preferences Service**, Freepost 22, London W1E 7EZ (Tel: 01 734 0058) works two ways. If you *dislike* mail order you can get them to delete your name from the mailing lists of all their members. But if you *like* mail you can ask them to put your name on their members' lists. But you can't say you want to be on some lists but not on others.

Terms and Conditions

The code of practice of the Advertising Standards Authority covers all printed advertisements. This means the advertisement should be truthful (Note: *should* is not the same as *is*) and that, if money is paid in advance, it should be refunded in full (not as a credit note) if the goods are not delivered within a set time (usually 28 days) or if they are returned undamaged within 7 days.

Payment

The terms of payment vary greatly and need to be looked at very carefully. The golden rule is, if a company doesn't lay out its payment terms so you can understand them, don't buy from it. See also Credit, under Law.

Complaints about Mail Order

Any complaint could end up going to court, *so if you have to make any complaint keep copies of every letter from or to you, and make notes on every phone call - with the date.*

If goods don't reach you within 28 days, you should complain to the company. With this, or any other complaint, write to the department first and if that fails write to the Managing Director.

The next two steps are interchangeable. You could either write to the appropriate trade association or you have a choice of public bodies to turn to - a Citizens Advice Bureau, a Consumer Advice Centre or the local Trading Standards Officer or you can take advice from a local law centre or legal aid solicitor on whether you would be likely to win in court. Such claims can be taken to the small claims court without much cost, but it is always worth getting advice before embarking.

If you sent money in advance for something advertised in the press and never received it because the company went bust, you may be able to get your money back under the MOPS scheme (page 201) by contacting its secretariat. But not all such advertisements are covered by the 'Readers' Protection Scheme'. For example, classified advertisements aren't covered, nor are those for which you didn't send money in advance.

Whoever you complain to will need to know:

- your name and address
- the date of the order
- how much you paid
- the trader's name and address
- the address the goods should have gone to
- the full details of the goods ordered
- what form the payment took - e.g. cheque
- whether you have a receipt or acknowledgement of the order.

Mail Order Companies

I have selected the following mail order companies, and those which appear in various sections of this book, because they sell unusual goods which may be difficult to get any other way, or sell a particularly good selection of goods which may be hard to find if you live far from a major city. However, I have not tested them all and they carry no 'Moyra Bremner warranty of good trading' - whatever that would be.

Animals

Abbot Bros (Thuxton, Norwich, Norfolk, NR4 0QJ Tel: 0362 850220/850309) do an unusual service sending mail order animals such as lop-eared rabbits or tame ferrets by train.

Books

The Good Book Guide (91 Great Russell Street, London WC1B 3PS Tel: 01 580 8466, day or night) is a worldwide mail order business offering any book in print - including paperbacks. You don't have to join to buy from them but if you want you can subscribe to their magazine which reviews some 3,000 of the latest books each year, and this also gives you preferential rates. There is also a children's list.

HMSO Books (P.O.Box 276, London SW8 5DT Tel: 01 211 5656 for enquiries; 01 622 3316 for orders) - not the sexiest of publishers but they publish beautifully illustrated art books often based on museum collections, as well as the ordnance survey maps and official documents.

Camping Equipment

Rentatent Ltd (Twitch Hill, Horbury, Wakefield WF4 6LZ Tel: 0924 275131) sells ex-hire camping equipment, direct and by mail order. See also Pointnorth Ltd, below.

Childbearing and Caring

Mothercare Ltd (Cherrytree Road, Watford, Herts WD2 5SH Tel: 0923 33577) offers the Mothercare range of maternity and children's gear.

National Childbirth Trust (9 Queensborough Terrace, London W2 3TB Tel: 01 221 3833) sells a selection of hard-to-find items like nursing bras.

Clothing

Hopscotch (Poolbridge Workshops, Blackford, Wedmore, Somerset BA28 4PA Tel: 0934 713336) - sells ready-cut kit clothes to sew yourself, for women and children.

Laura Ashley (page 203) - also sells clothes by mail order.

Fabric

Limericks Linens Ltd (117 Victoria Avenue, Southend-on-Sea, Essex SS2 6EL Tel: 0702 343486) - though it sells household linens and pillows, is here because it sells hard-to-find fabrics such as pure cotton sheeting in colours, calico, ticking, or butter muslin.

Pointnorth Ltd (58 High Street, Cemaes Bay, Anglesey, Gwynedd LL67 0HL Tel: 0407 711030) - has all the fabrics for making soft luggage, tents, groundsheets and so on, plus the zips and fasteners to go with them, and even patterns. They also make to order.

Russell & Chapple Ltd sells a most unusual range of items-artists'canvasses and wooden stretchers, bunting, webbing, boat and car covers, stage cloths and druggets, a range of hessian in good colours which is excellent for walls or cheap curtains. Direct from the shop or mail order.

Flowers

The best way to send flowers is to look in the Yellow Pages for a florist which says Interflora or Teleflower. There is little to choose between them: both have high service charges on top of the cost of the flowers themselves, and both will send flowers overseas as well as within Britain. If your Yellow Pages is mislaid, or you want to complain, the head offices are:

British Teleflower Service Ltd, 146 Bournemouth

Road, Chandlers Ford, Eastleigh, Hants SO5 3ZB Tel: 0703 265109

Interflora, Interflora House, Watergate, Sleaford, Lincs NG34 7TB Tel: 0529 304141

Household

Anything Lefthanded Ltd (65 Beak Street, London W1R 3LF Tel: 01 437 3910) sells kitchen and other equipment for the left-handed. Send three 2nd class stamps for the catalogue. There is also a shop at this address.

David Mellor (4 Sloane Square, London SW1W 8EE Tel: 01 730 4259) - has a good range of stylish high-quality kitchen equipment. Catalogue charged for. (CC Access)

Divertimenti (68-72 Marylebone Lane, London W1M 5FF Tel: 01 935 0689) has a very good range of kitchen equipment from an expensive catalogue.

Fast Feathers (36a Canaan Lane, Morningside Road, Edinburgh EH10 4SU Tel: 031 447 9044) - sells feather cushions, pillows and bolsters and also converts eiderdowns into duvets, and does alterations to continental quilts. You can also buy their cambric cases to fill yourself.

Habitat Designs Ltd (P.O.Box 2, Wallingford, Oxon OX10 9EU Tel: 0491 35511) - sells almost anything in the Habitat range and they will send it anywhere in the world - or in Britain. (CC Storecard, Visa, Access, Amex)

Lakeland Plastics (Alexandra Buildings, Windermere, Cumbria LA23 1BQ Tel: 09662 2255) (CC) - sells plastic bags, containers, clingfilm, microwave cookware, freezer items.

Laura Ashley Ltd (Mail Order Customer Services, PO Box 19, Newtown, Powys, Wales SY16 4BR Tel: 0686 622116) (CC Amex, Access, Visa) - sells the company's range of furnishings, furnishing fabrics and papers. These include a good selection of trimmings such as gimp, braid, bias binding, and herringbone webbing - often in 'hard to find' shades. You can order made-to-measure curtains, and any item can be sent as a gift. (Catalogue charged for.)

Lawsons (Bury St Edmunds) Ltd (1a St Andrew's Street South, Bury St Edmunds IP33 1SF Tel: 0284 753304) - sells freezer materials: heavy weight plastic bags, moisture-proof paper for interleaving, freezer tape etc.

Rarespares Ltd (Appliance House, St John's Road, Banbury, Oxon OX16 8HY Tel: 0295 51568) - holds spares for electrical appliances from 89 manufacturers and will send them anywhere in the world. It specializes in appliances which stand on the floor, but has some parts for smaller items like toasters and kettles. (CC)

Siesta Cork Tile Co (127 Cherry Orchard Road, Croydon, Surrey CR0 6BE Tel: 01 680 1250) - sells discount priced cork tiles for floors and walls, including seconds with colour blemishes.

Party

Barnums (67 Hammersmith Road, London W14 8UZ Tel: 01 602 1211) is a shop for carnival and party novelties (also mail order) such as masks, disguises, glow in the dark make-up, wedding bunting and balloons printed to order.

Photographic

Techno Mail Order Shop (9 Hampton Farm Industrial Estate, Hampton Road West, Feltham, Middlx TW13 6DB Tel: 01 898 9934) is the mail order arm of a chain of specialist photographic shops with good prices.

Bonus Film Express (P.O.Box 100, Borehamwood, Herts WD6 2AZ Tel: 01 953 9911) - develops and prints.

Bonus Photo (address as Bonus Film Express) - is a different company in the same business.

Photo Post Express (Argyle Way, Stevenage, Herts SG1 5BR Tel: 08894 76571) - develops and prints.

Rope

If you don't live in a nautical area rope can be hard to find but W. R. **Outhwaite and Son** (Town Foot, Hawes, N Yorks DL8 3NT Tel: 07697 487) sell ropes of every kind.

Smallholding and Self-sufficiency

Smallholding and Self-sufficiency Supplies (Little Burcott, Nr Wells, Somerset BA5 1NQ Tel: 0749 72127) will sell you all those things you can never find: sheep shears (excellent for grass trimming), kilner jars, wine-making equipment, spares for oil lamps, and so on.

Spices and Herbs

Fox's Spices (Aston Cantlow Road, Wilmcote, Stratford on Avon, Warwicks CV37 9XN Tel: 0789 66420) offer spices, including hard-to-find items like vanilla pods plus their own unusual blends of mustard.

Herb Society (77 Peter Street, London SW1P 2EZ Tel: 01 222 3634) - M£L, M, Inf, L - will advice on growing and using herbs.

Stationery

Conservation Books (228 London Road, Earley, Reading RG6 1AH Tel: 0734 668611) - offers a wide - and attractive - range of stationery from recycled paper, plus readdress stickers with a reminder to save trees (which makes re-using envelopes look like virtue not parsimony).

Wine

Bordeaux Direct (New Aquitaine House, Paddock Road, Reading, Berks RG4 0JY Tel: 0734 481711) - is one of a family of wine clubs run by the *Sunday Times*. There is no commitment to buy.

Christopher's (19 Charlotte Street, London W1P 1HB Tel: 01 636 4020) - has mail order wine and a wine club with discounts.

The Wine Society (Gunnels Wood Road, Stevenage, Herts SG1 2BG Tel: 0438 314161) - requires membership but there is no obligation to buy.

See also Drink.

Xmas Specials and Charity

Web Ivory Ltd (Queensbridge Works, Queen Street,

Burton-on-Trent DE14 3LP Tel: 0283 66311) has information on all charities that do mail order, whether for Christmas or other times.

Charity Christmas Card Council (49 Lambs Conduit Street, London WC1 Tel: 01 242 0546) - can give you the addresses of charities selling Christmas cards.

General

★★ Those carrying this mark do a Christmas catalogue, possibly with cards.

Camphill Products (Botton Village, Danby, Whitby, N.Yorks YO21 2NJ Tel: 0287 60424) is a charity for the handicapped which offers handsome engraved glass, pottery, wooden toys, etc.

Empire Stores (18 Canal Road, Bradford, W Yorks BD99 4XB Tel: 0274 729544) - has household and garden goods, men, women's and children's clothes including fashionable items.

Freemans (139 Clapham Road, London SW9 0HR Tel: 01 735 0366) - has household, electrical and garden equipment, plus clothes for men, women and children - including some young and trendy items.

Grattan PLC (Anchor House, Ingleby Road, Bradford, W Yorks BD99 2XG Tel: 0274 575511) offers a wide range of household, linens, electrical, casual clothes for adults and children. After sales service. 7 day a week local telephone order lines.

J. D. Williams & Co Ltd (P.O. Box 285, The Dale Street Warehouse, Manchester M1 8BA Tel: 061 236 9911 for orders); 061 236 4488 for service) sells some men's wear and household goods but mainly clothes and shoes for women. Emphasis on large sizes, up to 26, and wide shoe fittings.

John Moores (Kershaw Avenue, Crosby, Liverpool L70 2TT Tel: 051 928 6611) sells furniture, electrical goods, toys, bed linen, men's and women's clothing for the younger age group.

Marshall Ward (Home Shopping Department, Devonshire Street North, Manchester M60 6EL Tel: 061 273 7171) offers quite stylish clothing for adults and tots to teens, electrical, furniture, carpets, linens, kitchen equipment and toys. (CC)

National Trust (address page 000) sells mainly gifts, clothes and stationery.

NSPCC Trading Co Ltd (P.O.Box 39, Burton on Trent, Staffs DE14 3LQ Tel: 0283 66311 ★★

Oxfam Trading (Murdock Road, Bicester, Oxon OX6 7RF) ★★ Tel: 0869 245011, 9 am-5 pm weekdays or 0869 245017 at other times) sells mainly clothing, household, gifts and stationery.

Save the Children (SCF Trading Department, 17 Grove Lane, London SE5 8RD Tel: 01 703 5400 for information, orders to P.O. Box 19, Hayle, Cornwall TR27 6SF Tel: 0736 753343) ★★ mainly gifts.

York Archaeological Trust (United House, Piccadilly, York YO1 1PQ Tel: 0904 646411) sells unusual Viking-style silver jewellery and some gifts.

Unirose (125 Askew Road, London W12 9AU Tel: 01 749 9735).- specializes in gifts such as chocolates, drink or - for romantics - single red roses.

PESTS

Ask someone if they ever have pests in their garden and they will cheerfully admit to greenfly, blackfly and goodness knows what else. Ask them about house pests and they will probably change the subject. House pests are seen as a sign of dirt and bad housekeeping, and it is rather shameful to admit to them. It is time this myth was exploded. Pests may well come into any house because they sense there are delicious things to eat there, or be brought in on something you buy - that is no reflection on anyone. Cleanliness has nothing to do with their *arrival*, only with how long you let them *stay*. Not letting them stay is what this section is all about.

The first edition of *Enquire Within* instructed readers to exterminate beetles with the deadly delicacy of red lead mixed with sugar and flour, to kill cockroaches with oatmeal and plaster of Paris (which presumably constipated them to death) and to deal death to ants by putting quicklime into their nests. In comparison with that today's insecticides seem positively benign.

Suitable products and the companies which make them are listed at the end of this section.

Controlling Pests outside Britain

Most of what follows concerns pests within Britain. When travelling overseas it is worth remembering that creatures which do not carry disease in Britain can do so in many hotter climates. So *far* more care should be taken to avoid insect bites. Carry with you an effective, broad-spectrum, insect killer or repellent (see page 211), and in certain areas use a product like Deet to keep pests away (from MASTA).

Using Professional Pest Control Companies

If you have pests in the house which could be a health hazard your local council has a duty to do something about them. Contact the local Environmental Health Officer and see if the pest comes within the council's guidelines.

If it doesn't you may need to call in a pest control company. They use chemicals which are not available to the general public. The trouble is you have no way of telling what they are using. This means that only reputable companies should be used. Most reputable companies belong to the **British Pest Control Association** (King's Buildings, Smith Square, London SW1P 3JJ Tel: 01 828 2638) which will provide a list of them, if you send a sae. It also sells an A to Z of household pests which includes some of the rarer ones. Its members keep to a code of practice set up between the government and the association.

Why DIY Pest Control May Also Be Needed

Insects often lay their eggs in deep cracks - out of reach of the chemicals used by pest control companies. How soon these eggs hatch will vary with the temperature, but they can often hatch after the effectiveness of the pest control treatment has worn off - though this obviously depends on the life of the spray. This means that most insects will need more than one treatment to eradicate them.

> All insect sizes given below are for adults.

Ants (garden ants 3 to 5 mm)

Ants don't deserve to be thought of as pests. They may be unwelcome visitors, but in Britain the major ant is the black garden ant and, as one expert put it, 'They are cleanly little things which keep their houses tidy, follow each other along clean paths, and don't feed on anything dirty.'

The only ants likely to be a health hazard are the minute pharaoh's ants. They like moisture and are not choosy where they find it. In hospitals they have been found on anything damp, however nasty. They can make several inaccessible nests in a house and may need professional clearance, but some councils will deal with them (see page 204).

In the tropics ants can present a different hazard entirely. A phalanx of soldier ants is a formidable, and almost unstoppable, army, which will even kill pets and babies in their path. For this reason alone, a crying baby should get prompt attention in such countries.

Black garden ants home in on the smell of sweetness. So, the best course is simply to keep all sweet foods in closed jars, and put some strong-smelling substance - like a little ammonia on cotton wool - at their entry hole to put them off. As they only wander into houses on a seasonal basis, this is often enough. But if you *must* kill them there are two approaches. Either you kill the workers who have come to scavenge or you destroy the nest. There are plenty of ant sprays and powders (see page 211) to kill ants which invade. To destroy the nest you can resort to old-fashioned methods and either pour boiling water on it or spread sugar and borax powder (from a chemist) where the ants walk, or use a branded product based on borax. The workers then take the borax back and feed it to those in the nest, and so poison them. Then they have no young to scavenge for.

Bats

Bats are not pests at all. In Britain they are timid harmless creatures which are protected by law and should be cherished as the friends they are. The stories about them getting in hair are totally unfounded; and they help us by keeping down midges and night-flying garden pests. They are also quite enchanting.

Bed Bugs (round, mahogany-coloured 6 mm long)

Bed bugs are about the size of a ladybird but flatter - hence the nickname 'mahogany flats' - though, as they can drink five times their weight in blood, they aren't flat all the time. They lurk in the cracks in a bed, and in the wall around it and in folds in the mattress. As they feed on human blood a bed makes a perfect dinner

table - though you occasionally find them in padded chairs. They don't transmit infection, but they do leave very itchy bites. (A flea bite has a red spot at the centre and a halo of paler red, whereas a bed bug bite leaves a hard white swelling.)

Fortunately, insecticides have made bed bugs extremely rare in Britain, but if you do find any the council should fumigate. If you are travelling rough, and might meet them, carry an insect spray (see below). Spray it into any cracks and folds or, as they only come out at night, keep the room dark for a while, then hunt them with a flashlight. If you lack a spray, leaving the light on all night will reduce their activity.

Use an aerosol against beetles based on permethrin (page 211) which is approved for use in the kitchen and let the bed dry totally before sleeping on it. (If you can check that the product will be safe to sleep on, it is wisest to do so.) In the old days methods were more deadly:

AN EFFECTUAL LIME FOR THE DESTRUCTION OF BUGS. - Two ounces of red arsenic, a quarter of a pound of white soap, half an ounce of camphor dissolved in a teaspoon of spirits rectified, made into a paste of the consistency of cream: place this mixture in the openings and cracks of the bedstead.
Enquire Within, 1856

Bees

Bees are, of course, friends not foes. If you need to get one out of the house, empty a match box, half open it and slip it over the bee. Then close it gently, you can then release the bee outside.

Biscuit Beetles 'Drug Store Beetle' *Stegobium paniceum* (red-brown, smoothly oblong, $2 \cdot 0 - 3 \cdot 5$ mm long)

This beetle looks very like a furniture beetle and has a remarkable ability to bore holes, and endure a quite extraordinary diet. It has a special liking for red pepper, and in chemists' shops used to live in poisons like strychnine and belladonna. In the absence of such deadly delicacies, it will take up residence in almost any kind of dried vegetable - flour, bread, cereal and packet soups are favourites - and it will eat through containers to get to them. It will also bore through books - even going from end to end of a shelf and eating through lead and tinfoil if they get in the way. These beetles will also walk round the screw threads of screw-on lids, if there is room, so about the only sure way to exclude them is to put foodstuffs in glass jars with ground glass lids which fit exactly.

Unpleasant as they are, these creatures aren't dirty and are no danger to health. If dry food contains them you can bake it in a closed container for 1 to 1½ hours at gas no 4, 200°F (100°C). This will kill the beetles, their eggs and grubs and you can then eat the food - if you want to.

To get rid of them either heat treat all dry food, as above, or throw it away. *Remove all food from the food cupboards*, and use a pirimiphos-methyl- or permethrin-based insecticide which is approved for use near food (see page 211) spraying especially in cracks. Place some appealing bait - like a biscuit - on each shelf, to encourage the insects to walk across the sprayed area to get to it (having told the household not to eat the biscuits). Leave the food off the shelves until you have removed the insecticide (see page 210). There may be unhatched eggs in cracks, but how often you need to repeat is unpredictable, as hatching times depend on temperature. The total life cycle is 7 months and the creatures move about both in the early stages as grubs and as mature beetles.

A very similar beetle, called the cigarette beetle, gets into coriander and caraways seeds - and tobacco. Use the same treatment.

Carpet Beetles or Hide Beetles Dermestidae (usually 2-4 mm but up to 12 mm)

The larvae of carpet beetles (commonly known as woolly bears) do millions of pounds' worth of damage in Britain every year and can also be a health hazard. They can carry human parasites, and even carry anthrax. There are some 50 types with slightly varied food preferences, one kind enjoying the larder, another preferring the wardrobe, but they all live on dry animal proteins - wool, leather, fur, dried meat and fish. The most voracious kind (Anthrenus) will even eat cotton and synthetic fibres if protein is on them - as in a food stain. These creatures leave neat round or oval holes which are well spaced. They can also eat into wood, and there is one record of a wooden ship sinking because these creatures peppered it with holes, having been attracted by its cargo of dead penguins.

They may be brought into houses in birds' nests, fly in through a window, or walk down water pipes from the loft. The larvae look like tiny furry caterpillars, similar in size to the adult beetle.

It is the larvae which do the damage not the beetles, but if you see either I cannot counsel you too strongly to take immediate action. A female lays about 100 eggs at a time, and in a warm house there is no closed season on egg laying. How fast they hatch will vary with the temperature; at 17-23°C (60°-70°F) it could take several months, and the cycle can extend to years if it is very cool. So, since eggs hidden in crevices may not be killed by spraying, it could take monthly treatments to get rid of them.

This is not a pest for which you can call in the council, but private pest control companies will spray against it. A good spray leaves a film which will kill any carpet beetle or woolly bear which crosses it for some while to come - but ask for how long any treatment will be effective. You may also want to take action yourself, and there is quite a lot you can do.

- The beetles are likely to lurk in cracks such as between the skirting and a fitted carpet. Thorough vacuum cleaning will remove some of them, but the eggs are cemented in place.
- Dry-cleaning kills beetles, eggs and larvae.
- Temperatures *below* -18°C kill beetles, eggs and larvae (most domestic freezers run at around -18°C and go below this when on fast freeze - but check your instruction book).
- Powder insect killers for beetles can be used between

skirtings and fitted carpets, or in cracks in floorboards (see page 211).

- Insecticide aerosol sprays against beetles can be used on surfaces and to get into cracks in wood in cupboards and drawers (page 211).
- Liquid pesticide sprays for household beetles can be used (page 211).
- Borax powder, from chemists, kills the beetles.
- Washing (see page 156) kills them.
- They often get into houses via birds' nests in lofts or dead vermin there, so use a permethrin smoke generator (see page 211) in lofts. (If I were moving home, I would use one in every room before I moved in, to reduce the chance of pests being left by the previous occupants. Insect powder between the floor boards is an additional safeguard - especially if put there just before laying the carpet, so it has no time to degrade in the sunlight.)

Obviously, the action you take will depend on what you are trying to treat. Putting tiny things in plastic bags in the freezer is the best option for things which won't dry-clean well (such as real fur toys or padded hangers). Leave them at fast for 24 hours but don't overfill or the temperature won't go low enough.

Borax down right round the edge of the carpet, or in other likely places is one the oldest, cheapest and possibly one of the safest insecticides, but it is not as quick or as effective as modern ones.

All fabrics which could be eaten by them should be washed, dry-cleaned or deep chilled, and then kept in tightly closed plastic bags until *at least* a year has passed with no sign of them. But don't think you can starve them out - they can live without food for 10 months.

Cockroaches (1 - 4·5 cm long - in Britain)

If you have a nose for such things you can detect cockroaches just by sniffing. They have a characteristic odour which also taints the food they crawl over. In Britain we have the black Oriental variety, the smaller German type, and the big (rare) American ones. All three emerge by night, and are easily distinguished from other beetles by their long, waving feelers.

They seek warmth and moisture, and often live in sewers, drainpipes and round lavatories, carrying disease-causing bacteria in their gut and on their feet - causing food poisoning.

They breed abundantly and the time to get rid of them is when you see *one*. However, they are not easy to get rid of as they may keep re-emerging from drains and also take up to 4 months to hatch. So repeated spraying is needed to kill new generations. Use one of the sprays for cockroaches on page 211. In confined places where the powder would not be disturbed, the old-fashioned method is to sprinkle borax round the cracks where cockroaches might appear. A cup of borax in 4 litres (1 gallon) of water can also be used to wash the floor. But it should not be used if pets and children will crawl on the floor. As cockroaches need to be eradicated with all speed there is an argument for using both old and new methods.

Fleas

There are two aspects to the behaviour of fleas: where they feed and where they breed. Most fleas will travel and feed on several different types of animal, but will only breed on one or two.

The human flea will live and feed on animals like dogs, cats and some wild animals, but it only *breeds* on people or pigs. Man can also be bitten by fleas from cats, dogs, hens, pigeons and certain rats - each of which have their own type of flea but these fleas won't *breed* on man. Cat and dog fleas won't live for long if they have only people to feed on - although it may be unpleasant while they are making up their minds.

It is easier to keep fleas down if one knows how they live. Any time a cat or dog goes out and about it is likely to pick up fleas. These rapidly breed in the fur and little pearly white eggs are deposited everywhere it goes. These hatch into tiny grubs which eat the droppings from adult fleas. Then comes a chrysalis stage, in which they can sleep for months but hatch into fleas the instant they sense the warmth and vibration of a mammal nearby. This is why you can get bitten looking over empty houses.

Obviously it is better for animals not to have fleas but you could wear yourself to a frazzle trying to keep animals totally free of them. So some moderation is needed. However, the risk of worms needs to be remembered. Cat and dog tapeworm eggs are eaten by flea larvae and are then present in the adult flea. In grooming itself an animal can eat the flea and so get tapeworms. A child at the crawling stage can get tapeworms too, as the larvae can easily be on its hands. But the only disease carried by fleas is plague - and there are very few places where that is a problem.

Fleas don't like dryness so they are less of a nuisance when central heating is on. But the biggest enemy of fleas is the vacuum cleaner. Regular vacuuming of all the places where flea eggs, grubs and excreta could lurk will normally stop them becoming a problem. But if you move into a house which has had animals you can expect it to have fleas looking for a host, and dinner will be on you. If you simply suspect there may be fleas you could use a smoke generator in each room or use one of the insect sprays (see page 211), but if you *know* it is infested you can call in the council.

Flies

Blowflies (8-12 mm)

The really nasty flies are the blowfly family: bluebottles, greenbottles and the grey flesh fly are the main ones in Britain, and are easily recognized by their brightly coloured metallic bodies. They are among nature's refuse collectors, being attracted by dead flesh, excreta, garbage and pus. So they are usually swarming with bacteria (on average 27,000 germs per fly). It is the smell of meat or fish which attracts them into houses and they will immediately land on food to lay eggs and feed. They then spit on it and suck it up when the spit has predigested it. In addition they leave constant droppings and these habits make them a common cause of food

poisoning. Kill any blowfly you see - a rolled-up newspaper is as good as a fly spray. More importantly, keep meat and fish covered all the time and if you see a blowfly land on it immediately slice off that surface and throw it away. If meat is found with blowfly eggs on, it has clearly been heavily contaminated and the whole thing is best thrown away. The eggs are oblong and white and easily seen.

Keep dustbin lids tightly closed, so they have nowhere to breed near you, and if necessary spray the insides of dustbins, or bags, with a fly killer.

Fruit Flies (3-4 mm)

These are tiny flies which are drawn to rotting fruit or any kind of fermentation. Tradition has it that if they fall into wine they turn it to vinegar overnight. My experience confirms this, but an expert on the subject insists that it is the other way about: they are drawn to vinegar, and I must have been drinking dreadful wine. Either way, keep vinegar, wine and pickles covered if these tiny creatures are about. They do no harm apart from falling in.

Horseflies (Clegs, Breeze flies, Greenheads, Deer Flies) (6-10 mm)

Horseflies are similar in size to a bluebottle, with iridescent eyes, and are rather good-looking - for flies. However, they are particularly to be avoided because the females feed on people and their bites can leave very painful swellings. They can home in on their victim at the remarkable speed of 31 mph - so swat quickly. They breed in damp and marshy areas, and are only occasional visitors to houses.

Houseflies (grey 5-7 mm)

Houseflies are a drab grey and like decaying vegetable matter. However, they can still carry disease - especially in hot climates. A fly spray will work against both these and blowflies, and there is a block which gives off fly-killing vapour (page 211). But prevention is best and since flies home in on food through its smell, the old-fashioned system of having strong-smelling plants on the window ledge also makes good sense.

Hornets

Hornets are like super-wasps with super-stings - so they are definitely to be avoided. They live in hollow trees but one may stray into a house. Kill it with fly spray - or open the windows and wait for it to go.

Lice

It is said that after St Thomas à Becket died his body was seen to 'boil' with the seething mass of lice which left his body as it cooled. The body louse has probably died out in Britain, but two others remain: the head louse and the pubic louse (crabs). The head louse varies in colour from dirty white to greyish black as, rather cleverly, it adapts to the colour of hair it is on. Head lice are only found on the head, but pubic lice can also infest other hairy parts, and even the eyebrows and eyelashes.

Head lice don't restrict themselves to dirty people or dirty hair. Anyone can get them, and school epidemics are common, probably because children put their heads together and tumble about. Crab lice can be caught in sexual intercourse, or possibly from shared towels, bedding and lavatories.

In theory, all lice can transmit infections like typhus and trench fever. In practice, the body louse is the one which does so. This is worth remembering when travelling in the tropics. Even in Britain, lice leave nasty itchy bites which may lead to other problems like impetigo. So they need prompt treatment.

Any chemist will sell you an anti-louse preparation, but they are meant to be used as directed by a doctor. A good shampoo lotion will kill both the eggs and the adults. But the little white egg cases (nits) may still be left sticking to the hair. You can remove them with a very fine-toothed metal comb.

Anything which might carry lice - bedding, towels, hats and so on must also be thoroughly cleaned or washed. Hats can be sprayed with an insect spray containing permethrin (see page 211); once the creatures are dead, expose the inside to the sun for a few days to neutralize the chemical.

Mice *Mus musculus* (body 79 mm, tail 78 mm)

If you have mice the first thing you may notice is droppings: oblong pellets like plump tea leaves. These are dirty enough, but the really nasty thing about mice is that they have no sphincter on their bladder, so as they run across your food and china they leave a steady trickle of urine, which you don't see. And both rats and mice can carry a family of diseases called leptospiroses. The best known of these is Weils disease which is a serious and sometimes fatal illness. The main victims of these diseases are those whose work takes them into sewers, ditches, and so on. But they are not the only people who catch them.

Mice can also do a great deal of damage. Their teeth never stop growing, so to keep them short a mouse has to spend much of its life gnawing. In the process it could gnaw an electric wire and cause it to spark and start a fire. So mice within the walls can be dangerous.

As they are nervous creatures, and keep to the edges of rooms, traps or other mouse killers should be put round the skirtings, having left unbaited nibbles in the same places on previous days - this also applies to rats. The main mouse killer used to be warfarin, but many mice are resistant to this. One effective alternative is made by Sorex (see page 211) and, among other ingredients, contains enough vitamin D to disrupt their metabolism. However, this doesn't mean it is harmless to pets and children - use it only as instructed and *clear it up before they enter the room.*

Instead of making the bait inconspicuous, as modern manufacturers do, the 1856 *Enquire Within* recipe included phosphorus and said:

Small portions of this mixture may be placed near rat holes and, being luminous in the dark, it attracts them, is eaten greedily and is certainly fatal.

Mites (disc-shaped, pale and 0·2 - 2 mm long)

The main mite to infest man is known as the itch mite, or scabies mite, which burrows into the skin. Most of the burrows are on the hands and wrists, so they are easily seen. These mites are the cause of scabies. They are caught by close contact with someone who has them, but are unlikely to be detected until 3 to 4 weeks later - when the itching begins. Several creams kill the mites and severe and unusual itching should be taken to a doctor in case this is the cause.

Other mites occur in food, especially cereals, and look like mobile white insect eggs. The best prevention is to keep all foods based on cereals in a dry place, as they need humidity to thrive. You could kill them in the food by baking (see biscuit beetles, page 205) but it will taste of mites, so it is better to throw it away. If you feel they are in the cupboard itself, remove the food and treat with a spray based on pirimiphos-methyl (see page 211).

Mosquitoes (under 1 cm)

In hot climates mosquitoes carry diseases like malaria and yellow fever and the parasitic worm which causes elephantiasis. The type that spreads malaria is Anopheline which sticks its bottom up when resting; the yellow fever type sits level. We do have Anophelines in Britain but, they only carry malaria if there are people they can get it from. Mosquitoes need water for their larvae to breed, so get rid of standing water (even rainwater in an empty can will breed them) or put a little fine machine oil on the water to block the tiny tubes which the larvae thrust up through the water to breathe. Adults can be killed with a fly spray, but swatting is all that is usually needed.

Moths

There are five slim, white- or brown-winged moths, all with a wing span of 12 to 22 mm, which can wreak havoc in fabrics. They lay their tiny white eggs on any suitable surface, and it is the emerging larvae which eat fur, wool and feathers - and especially favour areas stained with sweat or urine. They also thrive in opened bags of blood fish and bone fertilizer, or in flour or grain. In the house they leave a trail of ragged interlinked holes and partly eaten fibres.

Traditionally drawers were made with cedar bottoms, as moths and other insects were thought to be discouraged by the smell of cedar. Herbs or moth balls were put between clothes for the same reason.

When linen is well dried and laid by for use, nothing more is necessary than to secure it from damp and insects; the latter may be agreeably performed by a judicious mixture of aromatic shrubs and flowers, cut up and sewed up in silken bags, to be interspersed among the drawers and shelves. These ingredients may consist of lavender, thyme, roses, cedar shavings, powdered sassafras, cassia lignea, &c. into which a few drops of otto of roses, or other strong scented perfume have been thrown.

Enquire Within, 1856

Scientists don't agree on whether female moths are put off by strong smells but if you put anything which is free from moths in a tightly closed plastic bag it is safe, and paper is just as effective - provided it has no holes in it. So blankets can be stored in several layers of newspaper, firmly sealed at all joins with sticky tape. There are mothproofing sprays but any gaps in the mothproofing will be vulnerable.

If you find moth eggs or grubs wash or dry-clean the item - if it isn't past use. Treatment as for carpet beetles (page 206) but any likely fabric which is being stored over winter, or for longer, needs protection.

> Although extreme cold will kill moth eggs and grubs - the temperatures used in most fur stores only keep them dormant. So eggs laid the previous season will hatch when you bring the furs home. (see page 172.)

Rats Rattus norvegicus (body 230 mm long, tail 200 mm) Rats carry harmful bacteria and distribute them through their urine and droppings, and through their fleas. They can also bite and, having the same teeth problems as mice, do considerable damage to almost anything they can get their teeth into. In Britain the most common rat is the brown rat. It is more aggressive than the black ships' rat, and the female will even take on a man in defence of young. Though rats are resistant to it in some areas, warfarin is still the recommended poison. If rats seem resistant consult the Environmental Health Officer about another rodenticide. DO NOT LEAVE ANY RODENT KILLER WHERE PETS OR CHILDREN COULD GET AT IT.

Red Spider Mite
These are tiny scarlet garden mites which sometimes hibernate in the house. They do no harm but stain the walls if you squash them. Use fly killer.

Silverfish (silver, carrot-shaped, 12 mm)
Not only are silverfish *not* a health hazard but, in the opinion of one expert on insects, they make excellent pets. They will be very happy in a jam jar and fed on flour. They are, he says, 'to be pitied and loved' because they are as old as the dinosaurs but failed to evolve very far. So they get stranded in dry slippery places, like wash basins, because their feet have just never learnt to cope with shiny surfaces.

They like damp nooks and crannies close to kitchens, coming out at night to feed on starch. They are not a health hazard, but it is unpleasant to have insect life in food. They also eat the starch from old wallpaper pastes, and from bookbindings - which makes them an expensive pest in libraries of old books - and may sometimes eat fabrics.

Keep all starchy foods in jars and boxes, and make the area as warm and dry as possible. They do not survive for long in such conditions. Traps can be set for them by putting down small jars, containing a little flour, with rough-surfaced adhesive tape over the

If you are trying to keep rats out bear their quite remarkable athleticism in mind. According to Norman Hickin, in his book *Pest Animals in Buildings* (published by George Godwin) rats of one kind or another can achieve the following feats:
- enter an opening larger than 1.25 cm square
- climb vertical and horizontal wires and cables
- climb vertical pipes 4 to 10 cm in diameter
- climb the outside of pipes up to 7.5 cm in diameter
- crawl along any pipe or conduit
- jump vertically 1 m from a flat surface
- jump horizontally 1.2 m on a flat surface
- jump horizontally 2.4 m from a height of 4.5 m
- drop 15 m without being killed or seriously injured
- burrow vertically into earth to 1.25 m deep
- climb ordinary brickwork to the first floor
- climb vines, shrubs, trees, telephone wires and power lines
- swim 0.8 km in open water against a substantial current
- dive through plumbing traps
- gnaw through lead or aluminium sheeting, and cinder blocks.

It makes you wonder why nobody organizes a rat pentathlon.

outside. They will then be able to climb in, but their inadequate feet will prevent them from climbing out. If you must kill them use one of the insecticides for crawling insects on page 211.

Spiders
Goodness knows how the dislike of spiders started but it is quite unnecessary. They may not be exactly pretty, but I doubt if they like the look of us much either - and British ones never attack us, unprovoked, as we attack them. In Britain we should regard them as friendly fly-catchers and let them be. (Incidentally, they aren't insects - insects have six legs, spiders have eight.)

In hot climates, spiders should be given a wide berth; some have venom 15 times as potent as rattlesnake venom. (But, as they inject you with very much less, you are far less likely to die of a spider bite than of a rattlesnake bite.) They tend to hide in heaps of timber, in clothing left hanging in sheds and so on, so avoiding them only needs sensible precautions.

Ticks
Both people and pets can pick ticks up on walks. A tick must never be simply pulled off, as it will leave its mouth parts behind to create a nasty sore. Instead, cover the body with cotton wool soaked in ether or chloroform

or smear the body with paraffin or vaseline. After a while it will loosen its grip and can be removed.

Prevention is much better than removal, as ticks occasionally carry disease. And even in parts of Europe, they carry diseases which can be fatal. When walking in a potential tick area (especially central Europe) tuck trousers into socks, and wear long sleeves and a wide-brimmed hat. If there is a major risk from them use a repellent like Deet (from MASTA) on clothing.

Wasps (usually 1-1.5 cm)
Wasps are scavengers, and none too fussy where they walk so they should be kept off food. Don't try to shoo them off: flailing arms may provoke them to sting. Trap them in a jam jar with sweet water or beer in the bottom. Cover the top with paper and push holes in it with a pencil, so they can go in easily but not out.

Some councils will deal with wasps' nests, some won't. Wasps take a fresh nest every year, and do no harm to a building. I had one in the roof above my bed one year and the wasps vanished peaceably at the end of the season. However, if the nest is a nuisance, and has only one entrance, you could either block it with Polyfilla or spray with fly spray designed for wasps. Take care, a spray not designed for wasps may provoke them to sting and if you block, or spray into, one hole when they can get out of another they may well leave the nest and attack.

There is often confusion between wasps and hoverflies. Hoverflies are gentle harmless creatures which should never be killed as they feed on aphids. Being totally unable to defend themselves, they are camouflaged to look like wasps. To tell which is which look at the shape of the tail end: a wasp is pointed, a hoverfly is round. Also look at their flight: hoverflies hover like helicopters; wasps don't.

Woodlice (grey with segmented armour, 5-20 mm long)
Being related to crabs and lobsters, woodlice like it moist and are a warning that somewhere is damper than it should be. They do no harm at all.

Woodworms Wood-boring Beetles (usually 2-3 mm long)
Woodworms aren't worms at all: they are beetles. They fly into houses in the late summer and take up residence in any wood they can find. The most common type makes a neat hole about the size of a pin head. You will often find these holes on old furniture. Look for signs of fine dust on or near the mouth of a hole. If you see it, the beetles are very much alive; if all the holes look old and dark, and there is no dust, they may all be dead.

Prevention is much better than cure. New timber going into a house should be painted or sprayed with any woodworm killer. Furniture should be treated with a branded woodworm killer made for furniture - Cuprinol and Rentokill each make one - but check it

will suit the situation (some cannot be used on polished surfaces) and be very thorough. Exposed rafters can be treated with a permethrin smoke generator (see page 211).

Death-watch beetles live in the heart of hardwood timber, but come out on fine days; they look like an ordinary woodworm but are 7 to 8 mm long and get their name from an eerie series of clicks they emit to attract a mate.

Choosing Pesticides
Today's insecticides are not as poisonous as the old ones and some - not yet on the retail market - should be totally harmless to man. However, it is still the opinion of one of the authorities in the field that 'all conventional pesticides are potentially toxic.' One reason for this is that the safety of any chemical can depend on what it is mixed with. Something which isn't normally absorbed by the skin might be absorbed if put with a particular propellant. And a minor ingredient could produce a reaction while the main ingredient produced none. This means we have to choose insecticides carefully and use them sensibly - not simply assume that if they are on sale to the public they must be safe whatever we do.

Certain chemicals turn up in product after product. One such is permethrin (and related substances ending in 'thrin'). Permethrin is a synthetic relative of the long-established insecticide pyrethrum, which comes from a plant in the chrysanthemum family. Both kill the vast majority of insects as soon as they touch them. The World Health Organization's reports suggest that they are remarkably safe for man. They are also odourless and will not give a flavour to food, whereas organophosphates like pirimiphos-methyl may do. However, there have been some allergic reactions by those with asthma. So it might be wiser for asthmatics to keep out of a room in which these are being used.

How to Use Insecticides (or Pesticides)
Don't be tempted to use garden sprays in the home. In 1985 a law made it illegal to use pesticides other than as directed on the container - which means it is illegal to use garden chemicals on house pests. The law also made it necessary for all household pesticides, and their instructions, to be approved by the government.

Unfortunately, few directions give much guidance on the situations you meet in the home. Before spraying insecticide I want to know how soon I can safely put the bag of flour back on the shelf, or whether a baby or a pet can safely play on a sprayed carpet the same day. I have yet to find a container which gives any guidance on such things.

What's more, when I tried to find someone in the ministry who knew the answers I was told that manufacturers are not asked about situations like that. Nor did the manufacturers have more detailed answers.

If you want to use insecticides safely work out exactly where and how you would like to use them and write to the makers and ask some very detailed questions. If enough people ask how soon the baby may crawl on the carpet, they may realize there are real problems and print some informative leaflets to go with their products.

Some pesticide strips are made to be hung in a kitchen and some sprays say they are safe near food and people. But unless you have other advice from the manufacturer - via the container or a letter - the following minimum precautions will do no harm.

- Read the instructions and follow them precisely.
- Always keep pets and young children away when using pesticides and keep them off the surfaces for *at least* 24 hours.
- Wear rubber gloves when using a pesticide and a face mask so you don't breathe it in.
- Don't use insecticides on or near food unless the makers say it is safe.
- Before spraying any fabric, carpet or other fragile surface (e.g. polished wood) try a test patch somewhere which won't show if the chemicals cause staining and leave it for 24 hours.
- When the insecticide has done its job wash down the surface with plenty of water (wearing rubber gloves) before putting food on it.
- Don't smoke or have naked flames when spraying. Some of the propellants can catch fire.
- Never transfer insecticide into any other container or leave it where children could get at it.
- Throw left-over insecticide down an outside drain.
- Clean out containers very thoroughly if they have been used for mixing insecticides

As the sixteenth-century poet Thomas Tusser wrote in his *Hundreth Good Pointes of Husbandrie:*

Take heede how thou laiest the bane for the rates,
Lest thou poison thy servant, thyself and thy brats.

Both water and sunlight break down many household insecticides and make them harmless. You can use this fact to your advantage. If you want an insecticide to keep on working, shut out the light. If, you want to get rid of the chemical, put it out in the sun. Equally, washing down empty kitchen shelves which have been sprayed will usually make them safe to put food on - once they are dry.

★ A neat way to de-bug a single item is to spray the inside of a plastic bag, let it dry, then put the item into it, close the top and leave it for a day or two. The creatures walk on to the plastic and die. A black bin liner is best as most household nasties move about most in the dark.

★ All insects - fleas, lice and so on - are killed by being soaked for a short while in water at over 60°C. As that is the temperature for minimum-iron fabrics in most washing machines it is easy to de-bug anything which is washable.

Most insecticides are in spray cans. There seems no point in getting rid of bugs while ripping up the ozone layer. If you want to avoid this check the cans against the ozone safety list published by Friends of the Earth (See under Free Time).

Pest Control Companies
I make no claim to be an expert on insecticides. The following list is of some of the companies and their products recommended by those who should know.

On many pesticides you will see Gamma-HCH as one of the ingredients. This is a technical name: it is better known as lindane, the chemical which kills bats.

Ashe Consumer Products Ltd (Ashetree Works, Kingston Road, Leatherhead, Surrey KT22 7JZ Tel: 0372 376151) makes Coopers Mothproofer and Coopers Ant and Crawling Insect Spray.

ICI (Woolmead House, Woolmead Walk, Farnham, Surrey GU9 7UB Tel: 0252 724525) makes Waspend - an aerosol based on pirimiphos-methyl (an organophosphate) for use against flying and crawling insects. It also makes Ant Killer Dust, also based on pirimiphos-methyl. It will also kill other insects which crawl over it.

Octavius Hunt Ltd (Dove Lane, Redfield, Bristol BS5 9NQ Tel: 0272 555304) - makes a Permethrin Wood Treatment Smoke Generator. It is sold specially for woodworm, but it will kill many other insects in the area. Not widely distributed, contact the company.

PBI (Britannica House, Waltham Cross, Herts EN8 7DY Tel: 0992 23691) makes Kybosh, a permethrin-based aerosol against most flying and crawling insects. Also Anti-ant - a powder based on pyrethrum sold for killing ants. But if other insects walk across it, they too will die.

Rentokil Ltd (Felcourt House, East Grinstead, West Sussex RH19 2JY Tel: 0342 833022) has a wide range of chemicals for insect control and good information leaflets.

Sorex Ltd (St Michael's Industrial Estate, Hale Road, Widnes, Cheshire WA8 8TJ Tel: 051 420 7151) makes Sorexa CD - a mouse killer, which kills mice which resist Warfarin.

Synchemicals Ltd (44-45 Grange Walk, London SE1 3EN Tel: 01 232 1225) make Nippon Liquid Ant Killer - based on borax, and Nippon Ant Powder - based on permethrin which will also kill almost any other insect that walks over it. Also Py Garden Insect Killer, based on natural pyrethrum, is also authorized for use on most house pests and suitable for large areas.

More information
British Pest Control Association (Alembic House, 93 Albert Embankment, London DE1 7TU Tel: 01 582 8268) is the professional body of companies making pest killers and carrying out pest control, and its members must keep to a code of practice. The association will give you the names of pest control companies in your area and answer queries. It also sells a good booklet on pest control.

A Roof Over Your Head

Building and Maintenance • Changing Places • DIY • Painting and Papering

BUILDING AND MAINTENANCE

Building, alterations and decorations cover an immense range of work; from getting a painter to repaint your front door, to building a whole house. The aim of this section is to show how you could use the different professions which are involved, what you can expect and how you can get the best possible job for your money.

Advice from the Experts

Architects and Their Role

Whether a building job needs an architect depends on the work to be done and the other skills available in your area. There are firms which specialize in certain jobs - loft conversions or conservatories, say - whose package deal may work well if you don't have special needs. (But compare several companies.) Some builders do a very good job without an architect, though their design skills are likely to be limited and if you have strong ideas about design, a surveyor may prove to be what you need (see page 226). But an architect may provide imaginative solutions and save worry - if not money.

Building a house, or buying one and having alterations done to it, is one of the few areas in which something is purpose-made to your needs. So be very clear about what these are. Suppose you want an extension - one storey or two? Using measures for energy saving or not? And so on. Only when you know exactly what you want will you be able to find the best person to create it for you.

Finding an Architect

The easy way to find an architect is to approach one of the architects' organizations, listed on page 213. If you take pot-luck through Yellow Pages check his qualifications and watch out for the catchword 'architectural'. Legally 'architect' is reserved for someone qualified but there is no law against anyone calling themselves an 'architectural designer' even if they never studied architecture for a day. To check if someone really is an architect ask the **Architects Registration Council of the United Kingdom**, 73 Hallam Street, London W1N 6EE Tel: 01 580 5861. However, this is *not* an organization through which to *find* an architect.

The RIBA recommends that, before choosing an architect, you visit several, ask about fees, look at photographs of previous work, note some addresses and ask for names and addresses of former clients as references. Then speak to some former clients.

Paying an Architect

The first consultation is usually free. Any work he does thereafter may need to be paid for - whether or not you decide to use him - even preliminary sketches.

Fees are usually a percentage of the total cost of the project, and payable in stages. There are no set fee levels; it is entirely negotiable between you and the architect. Get a note of what he will charge, and what he will do for it, in writing. Check also what extras are outside the fee. For a start, VAT is extra.

A leaflet from the RIBA explains all the details. But remember: each time you change your mind while work is in progress you pay for the privilege and if you cut the building cost by doing some yourself the architect's fee may still be based on what a builder would have charged.

The Responsibilities of an Architect

1. Drawing up a preliminary design for the client to approve.
2. Designing a scheme to the client's budget.
3. Submitting the design for planning approval.
4. Drawing up the specifications to meet regulations and putting them before the authorities.
5. Advising on grants towards the cost.
6. Assisting in finding a suitable builder.
7. Architects do not supervise building sites daily but they should make regular checks. And your instructions to the builder should be given through the architect.

Using an Architect - Caveat Emptor

When using a professional we usually think we are paying them high fees to take the load off our backs and do the thinking for us. The truth is even the best architect (or doctor or lawyer) has his/her mind nine-tenths occupied with the needs of other clients. You are the only one able to give undivided attention to yours.

Don't be carried away by pretty plans; try to imagine

it all in three dimensions. One major architectural firm managed to design a large NHS hospital without lavatories. So take nothing for granted.

The codes of conduct of some professional associations are more concerned with preventing architects from poaching each other's clients than with ensuring client satisfaction. And the arbitration only covers a narrow band of complaints and may also be limited to written evidence only (see the leaflet 'Having a Problem' from RIAS). So if things go badly wrong you may need to take it to court.

More Information

The Architectural Association, 36 Bedford Square, London, WC1B 3ES Tel: 01 636 0974 is both a school for architects and an association. Being a *member* of the AA does *not* indicate that someone is a qualified architect.

The Royal Incorporation of Architects in Scotland (RIAS), 15 Rutland Square, Edinburgh EH1 2BE Tel: 031 229 7205 publishes a directory of architectural practices detailing their specialities. It also has advice leaflets and an advisory service.

Royal Institute of British Architects (RIBA), 66 Portland Place, London W1N 4AD Tel: 01 580 5533 has an advisory service and free list of architects suitable for a particular project; vg L, Rg.
Householders' Action Guide, Consumers' Association

Builders and Decorators

The building and decorating business is full of cowboys just itching to take you for a ride. You can only protect yourself by using firms with a good reputation locally or ones which are members of established trade associations. This won't guarantee that you are totally satisfied but at least - in most cases - they won't *intend* to do a bad job. And if they do, you may be protected by an established system of compensation. Whatever the job, avoid using anyone who comes uninvited to your door or rings up offering services. On the whole, a good firm doesn't need to.

There are several organizations which you can use to avoid the cowboy companies. The **Building Employers Confederation (BEC)**, 82 New Cavendish Street, London W1M 8AD Tel: 01 580 5588 is the largest. Its members are vetted by local committees, and must have been trading for a reasonable time and keep to a code of conduct. On all jobs whose cost falls between set limits (check the current limits) they must also offer the BEC guarantee scheme. Under this, for 1 per cent extra on the contract, the client is covered against poor work or a company ceasing to trade. It also covers damage to the work which is in progress, and structural defects for 2 years. Even if you don't take up the guarantee you can still complain to BEC. However, BEC cannot *insist* that a member satisfies a client.

In some areas, builders are less likely to join BEC than the **Federation of Master Builders**, Gordon Fisher House, 33 John Street, London WC1N 2BB Tel: 01 242 7583. This has a National Register of Warranted Builders. To be on the register a builder need not have any qualifications or reach any set standards, but they do have to be approved by other members in their area. Their

warranty scheme is very similar to that offered by BEC. In Scotland the comparable organization is the **Scottish Building Employers Federation** (13 Woodside Crescent, Glasgow G3 7UP Tel: 041 332 7144) - a professional trade association with a code of conduct and a disputes procedure if things go wrong. There is also the **Scottish Decorator's Association** and the **National Federation of Painting and Decorating Contractors**, 82 New Cavendish Street, London W1M 8AD Tel: 580 5588. **Interior Decorators' and Designers' Association**, 45 Sheen Lane, London SW14 8AB Tel: 01 876 4415/6 has a list of interior designers.

Contractors

Estimates, Quotations and Contracts

If the job is simple enough to need no drawings or survey, you can approach contractors direct. But don't approach anyone until you really do know what you want. The charges may be different if you so much as change the brand of paint, let alone if you swop from paint to paper or want a wall in a different place. Always ask a contractor if he will give a free quotation and specification. And ask for references and find out his qualifications.

Any contractor will normally give you an estimate of what the job will cost. But this is just a guess and is *not binding. Always* get a *written* quotation (some firms call them estimates, but once in writing they are legally quotations) pricing all the work item by item. It should also show whether VAT will or will not be added. Compare several before deciding which firm to use.

Having chosen a firm, tell them that you are interested in them doing the work, subject to you approving the contract. They should then send you a written contract clearly showing what work is to be done for what price. For example if a room is to be painted it should mention washing down or burning off old paint. *Nothing* that you would like to have done should be left out. It should also show:

- whether materials are included in the total price (they may not be)
- whether any sub-contractors will be used
- who will be liable if there are problems
- the completion date
- what cancellation rights you have - if any.

Check the small print in any contract carefully before signing; that's usually where the sting is. You may want to insert a clause that the quoted price may not be exceeded without your agreement. And you can ask for a penalty clause by which they lose money if the job isn't completed on time; the builder may or may not agree. The changes should be written into a new contract and sent to you. If you don't like the contract you can say so and find another firm - provided you have done nothing which committed you in law. If you want to accept the contract do so in writing, and refer to it by date - then you have proof of which version you accepted.

> Part of the value of using advisers like surveyors or architects is that they are used to dealing with such contracts and know what should and should not be agreed.

Grants and Permissions

A good builder should be able to tell you what permissions are needed for the work you propose. Don't be tempted to build without permission. If the council discovers unauthorized building it has a right to make you take it down at your expense. And when you sell your home the buyer's solicitors will have to check on whether the proper permissions were obtained.

Organizing the Work

- Ask which work has to be done first - so you can clear the rooms concerned.
- Find out how they plan to dispose of rubbish - so the method suits you as well as them.
- Agree details like lavatory and coffee-making facilities for the men.
- If constant radio music is your idea of hell discuss whether men can be sent who can work without it.
- If you don't want anyone to smoke, get them to agree to this.

These details can create problems if they aren't sorted out at the start.

Inspecting the Work

If you have used a surveyor or architect you should inspect the work when it is finished. Go over it with a fine tooth comb *alone*. Don't just look at things, try using them - flush the loo, check that the immersion heater heats, check the workmanship everywhere, and so on. Make a note of every single problem. Then go over it again with a representative of the building firm, and ask for them to be put right. If you are asked to sign a 'satisfaction note' and you haven't yet done this check, or are in any doubt about any aspect of the work, it is best not to sign it.

If you think that materials used for you were incorrect and need to prove it, the **Building Research Station** (Buckhall's Lane, Garston, Watford WD2 7JR Tel: 0923 676612) will carry out tests, for a fee.

Payment

In principle, payment should only be made for work which has been done, and done properly. But contracts can be structured so payments are in stages, or a firm may need a small sum on deposit if something has to be purpose-made. This should *never* be large or be given to a firm you don't know and you should always get a written receipt on paper *printed* with the company's name and address.

Never pay the final bill until a week or so *after* all the work is done. It sometimes takes a few days for faults and omissions to show up, and during that time

do try out everything they have installed - even if you don't *need* to use it.

Timing

Even if your contract doesn't give a completion date, firms have a legal obligation to complete a job in a reasonable time. If they don't, you should write giving a date by which they must finish and saying you will cancel the job if this is not kept to.

The Building Centre, 26 Store Street, London WC1E 7BT Tel: 01 637 1022 has a permanent exhibition of building items and an information service (9.30 to 17.15 on weekdays and 10 to 16.00 on Saturdays.) If you want to know who makes a particular building product ring the enquiry service on 0344 884999.

Genuine Period Brick Co (Clawddnewydd, Nr Ruthin, Clwyd LL15 2NB Tel: 08245 285) supplies bricks to match old buildings. Delivery is wide.

The **Building Conservation Trust,** Apartment 39, Hampton Court Palace, East Molesey, Surrey KT8 9BS Tel: 01 943 2277 has a permanent exhibition showing how different types of fault need to be repaired in houses of all periods. (Open 9.30 to 17.00, Sundays till noon - bar Christmas and Easter. Last admissions 16.15.) The trust will also suggest people who can advise and help with particular problems.

The Society for the Protection of Ancient Buildings (37 Spital Square, London E1 6DY Tel: 01 377 1644) will advise on all problems affecting very old buildings.

Judith and Martin Miller's, *Period Details* (Mitchell Beazley) shows exactly which doors, cornices and so on, should be in houses of different periods, and also has a directory of useful specialist firms.

Surveyors

If you are about to do any major alterations or extensions a surveyor can be the ideal middle option, provided you don't need the creativity of an architect. Use a fully qualified one with the letters FRICS or ARICS. A surveyor can do most of the practical tasks an architect would do (page 212). Discuss precisely what you would and would not like him or her to do and find out the costs. The Royal Institution of Chartered Surveyors (RICS) sells a booklet called 'The Conditions of Engagement for Building Surveying Services' (phone 0256 55234) which explains in detail what you can expect.

For jobs like valuations and surveys the charge is normally a flat fee. But if a surveyor takes charge of building work for you, the fee will be a percentage of the cost of the job, and 10 to 13 per cent is usual.

Different surveyors specialize in different fields, and it is essential to chose someone who is experienced in your type of job. The RICS will give you the names of surveyors in your area. The rules about choosing an architect apply here too (page 212) and, as always, personal recommendation is the best route.

Problems and Complaints

The RICS has a strict code of conduct and a scheme for the protection of the client's money in the event of a surveyor being dishonest.

If you have any complaint about a chartered

surveyor, or about a firm in which at least one partner is a chartered surveyor (as in some estate agents), send the full details to the Professional Practice Department of the RICS. The Institution will investigate and the surveyor can be reprimanded or expelled from membership. It will not, however, deal with cases which need to go to law.

The Royal Institution of Chartered Surveyors (RICS) (12 Great George Street, Parliament Square, London SW1P 3AD Tel: 01 222 7000) has leaflets on every conceivable topic related to property.

Damp

The key point about damp is that there is always a reason for it, and it should be cured quickly before it causes rot. The most likely causes are:
- lack of a damp course in an old house
- a faulty damp course
- soil or debris building up above the damp-course (it should be 15 cm (6 in) below the damp course
- a fault in the roofing
- loose flashing round a chimney or on a flat roof
- a blocked gutter making excessive water pour over brickwork
- building mortar and other debris that dropped into the cavity wall and now form a bridge by which water can travel to the inner wall
- a leaking downpipe or gutter
- blocked airbricks, so normal damp doesn't evaporate
- cracked brickwork or failing mortar
- condensation.

The first step is to find the cause and do something about it. Built-up soil can be removed, blocked drains and airbricks cleared. If gutters and drains are blocked you may be able to unblock them yourself; sometimes the block is at the bottom of the downpipe.

A leaking gutter or downpipe can be mended with a gutter and drain sealant which can now be squeezed straight from an applicator into the problem area.

If damp comes in through gaps round windows or doors these can easily be filled by injecting a polyurethane foam filler (sold in canisters) and a mastic used to seal on the outside and protect the polyurethane from weather.

Condensation is a special problem. The cure for condensation in general is better insulation (see pages 217-218), more warmth and more ventilation. However, selective insulation can increase the problem. For example, windows may suffer greatly if the walls of a house have been insulated but there is no double glazing. The only solution here is to double glaze (see pages 219-220).

Abundant moisture on the windows doesn't, however, prove the house has rising damp or anything worrying like that. It forms because the moisture given off by human bodies (several pints a day) and by cooking or paraffin heaters will land on any cold surface, and the glass is the only cold surface around.

Dampcourses
Serious problems like a faulty dampcourse or roof are best treated swiftly by professionals. Anyone can spot a crooked wall, but how many of us can tell a proper chemical dampcourse from a botched job? This makes. the installation of dampcourses (along with wood preservation) a prime area for the operations of rip-off merchants. Official estimates are that about £150 million a year is spent on these two treatments and less than half that money is paid to those actually qualified to do the work. So use a member of the **British Chemical Dampcourse Association (BCDA)**, 16a Whitchurch Road, Pangbourne, Reading RG8 7BP Tel: 073 57 3799 which will supply a list of members.

All members of the association must use trained staff to carry out surveys, use products approved by the association and give reports which are honest and free from exaggeration. They must also carry proper insurance covering such things as errors or omissions or the failure of the dampcourse within a specified time. Finally, they must check that the householder is insured for aspects for which he or she is liable. Many companies also offer a guarantee protection scheme, through the Guarantee Protection Trust (page 225). As this is an industry where companies do come and go, it could be useful. Not all BCDA members use the trust, so ask when choosing a contractor. For this it is worth getting several estimates.

Electricity

Dating Your Wiring
Most houses built or rewired after the early '60s have a ring circuit. On this all the sockets are 13 amp and the plugs match them. The older radial system had a range of plugs supplying 15 amp, 5 and, occasionally, 2 amps, often with round pins. If you have any sockets other than those which take big flat-sided pins you don't have a ring circuit, and your wiring is probably more than 30 years old and needs replacing. (Though the reverse isn't always true; having new plugs doesn't always mean the wiring behind them has been renewed, so do check.)

Electricity boards will test the wiring of a home and report on what faults need to be put right. They charge according to the size of the property. The Institute of Electrical Engineers recommends that wiring should be checked every 5 years, and the insulation on wires is not expected to last more than 20 to 25 years and can perish sooner.

Appliances and Sockets
It is very important that the total wattage of the appliances isn't greater than the plug can safely carry. Check the wattage on the back of appliances before putting them on an adaptor. A socket of:

15 amps can safely carry 3,000 watts in total
13 amps can safely carry 3,000 watts in total
 5 amps can safely carry 300 watts in total
 2 amps can safely carry 60 watts in total

WARNING: Electricity can kill. Always turn supply off at the mains before doing any electrical work.

The big gap between the capacity of 5 and 13 amp sockets may look odd, but the fittings for the lower amps are made differently. So they are far more likely to overheat and cause a fire at high wattages.

Charges for Electricity

Two separate charges are made on every bill:
- the standing charge is for supplying the service and is the same however much electricity you use.
- the amount of electricity used is measured in units, and priced at a rate per unit. When the Electricity Boards make price changes it is the price per unit which alters.

Electrical Installations

The trouble with electricity is that its hazards are hidden. Some 3,000 fires a year are caused by faulty wiring, yet anyone can call themselves an electrician and put your life at risk. Use a fully qualified electrician. The **National Inspection Council for Electrical Installation** Vintage House, 36-37 Albert Embankment, London SE1 7UJ Tel: 01 582 7746 (admin) 01 735 1322 (technical)) is concerned with consumer safety and its list of properly qualified contractors is in public libraries. Unlike the lists of many trade associations, those on the list are *not* simply members of an organization, but have been approved by the council as reaching a required standard. Approved contractors should display the NICEIC sign.

The **Electrical Contractors' Association of Scotland** (23 Heriot Row, Edinburgh EH3 6EW Tel: 031 225 7221/2/3 or Freephone 8490) sets a code of practice for its members and operates a complaints procedure.

The **Electrical Contractors' Association** (ESCA House, 34 Palace Court, Bayswater, London W2 4HY Tel: 01 229 1266) only has members with 3 years' training and other credentials. If a member fails to complete a proper job it will be completed by another member.

The **Institution of Electrical Engineers** Savoy Place, London WC2R 0BL Tel: 01 240 1871 publishes the IEE Wiring regulations for electrical installations.

Electric Gadgets

Anyone setting up home should really look round some of the major exhibitions and see what technology is on offer. Here are just a few of the things to look out for.
- Plug-in lighting sockets for ceilings and walls which allow you to remove the fittings. (They have a lock so they won't fall.)
- Brand new neat 2-pin plugs for appliances which use very little electricity - e.g. turntable, tape deck, amplifier. The pins plug into a small adaptor.
- Remote controls which plug into a ring main to allow you to turn on appliances in other rooms.
- Timer devices of all kinds.
- Thermostats which can run each radiator or fire at a different temperature.
- Dimmers which are part of table lamps; others which attach to the cord of a lamp or are on remote control.
- Light sensitive mechanisms which will draw curtains and switch on lights.

- Lights which can be switched on with a remote control.

★ If you decide to install a new boiler control be systematic. There will be getting on for 20 wires inside. Unless you label each wire *as you take it out of the old mechanism* the chances of placing it correctly in the new one won't be good.

The **Design Centre Index** should be able to give you the names of manufacturers, but the following companies are a start. Any firm which stocks their latest products should have a good range.

Drayton Controls (Engineering) Ltd, Chantry Close, West Drayton, Middx UB7 7SP Tel: 0895 444012

Home Automation, Pindar Road, Hoddesdon, Herts EN11 0ET Tel: 0992 460355

Smiths Industries Environmental Controls Co Ltd, Waterloo Road, Cricklewood, London NW2 7UR Tel: 01 450 8944

Superswitch, Houldsworth Street, Reddish, Stockport SK5 6BS Tel: 061 431 4885

How Much Electricity We Use

If you've ever wondered about the cost of running a light bulb or electric appliance the calculation is very simple. A unit is simply 1 kilowatt of electricity being used for 1 hour (kWh). The power of any piece of electrical equipment is given on it in either watts (W) or kilowatts (kW). So the calculation is this:

1 kilowatt plate warmer x 1 hour of use = 1 unit used
2 kilowatt fire   x 1 hour of use = 2 units

1 kilowatt is just a way of saying 1,000 watts, so: 100 watt bulb x 10 hours of use = 100 x 10 watt hrs = 1,000 watt hrs = 1 kilowatt = 1 unit used. Equally: 10 bulbs of 100 watts x 1 hour = 10 x 100 x 1 watt hrs = 1,000 watt hrs = 1 kilowatt = 1 unit used. Or: 8 bulbs of 60 watts x 2 hours = 8 x 60 x 2 = 960 watt hrs = almost 1 unit used.

Once you know how many units an appliance uses you just multiply that by the cost per unit and you have the cost of running it for that length of time. So, if electricity costs 5.5 pence a unit, then running a 1 kilowatt fire for 1 hour would cost 5.5 pence, but running it for 3 hours would cost 5.5 pence x 3 = 16.5 pence.

Fires can use a lot in a quarter. For example, a single 2kW fire used for 5 hours an evening during the winter months would use 1,800 units of electricity - costing over £100 - against roughly £18 worth for a colour TV.

Wattages vary from one manufacturer to another, but those given below are the average wattages and consumption.

Appliance	Wattage	Use	Units
Cooker	12,000	average wk's family meals	17
Coffee percolator	750	75 cups	1
Dishwasher	3,000	a full load - cold fill	2

Appliance	Wattage	Use	Units
Drill	250 - 500	2-4 hrs	1
Electric } over blanket } under	150 - 350 60 - 120	1 week 1 week	2-3 1
Extractor fan	75	13 hrs	1
Food mixer	120 - 700	4-25 hrs	3
Freezer	300	1 day	1-2
Hair dryer	350 - 800	3 hrs	1
Heated rollers	500	20 heat-ups	1
Heaters - convector	1,000 - 2500	2 hrs	2-5
- fan	2,000 - 3000	30 mins	1
- oil-filled radiator	500 - 2500	2 hrs' warmth	1
- radiant bars	500 - 3000	20 mins	1
- storage	2,000 - 3000	a wk	approx 45-75
Iron	1,250	2 hrs	1
Kettle	2,000 - 3,000	12 pts - boiling	1
Lawn mower	250 upwards	3 hrs	1
Microwave oven	600	8 chicken pieces	1
Plate warmer	1,000	1 hr	1
Radio	5 up	200 hrs	1
Refrigerator	100	1 - 1½ days	1
Slow cooker	80-170	8 hrs	1-2
Spin dryer	300	5 weeks	1
Tape recorder	25 - 75	24 hrs	1
Television	80 B&W 100 colour	6 - 9 hrs	1
Toaster	1050 - 1360	70 slices	1
Tumble dryer	2500	4kg (9lb)	2½
Vacuum cleaner	500	2 hrs	1
Washing machine	2,500	weekly wash for four	5
Waste disposal unit	250	50 lb waste	1

Meter Reading
If any meter isn't read - for example, you are out when the reader calls - you get an estimated bill instead. Any inaccuracy will then be adjusted on the following bill, but some boards let you send in your own reading. There are basically three kinds of meter - dial, digital and those showing a special night rate. To read them:

Dial - write down the figure indicated by the pointer on each dial, ignoring the red dial. If the pointer is between two figures write down the lower one. Don't forget that adjacent dials are numbered in opposite directions.

Digital - write down the numbers shown, from left to right, ignoring the last figure shown as 0.1.

Digital with night rate, for Economy 7 (white meter tariff in Scotland) - there are two rows of figures. Read the top row from left to right as for 'Digital' above to get the night rate units. Then read the bottom row in the same way to get the units at the normal rate.

Paying for Electricity - Who Pays
The person who applies for electricity to be supplied is legally responsible for bills being paid. So, whether sharing a flat, co-habiting, or married, beware of being the only one who signs that letter or you could be left holding the bill. If problems have been caused by the desertion of a partner who applied for the electricity, the Board may pursue that person for the money.

Paying for Electricity - Easy Payment
Boards have a duty to get their bills paid promptly. They offer varied schemes said to make payment easier for customers. The Electricity Council (see Organizations) has a free leaflet on these, but most involve paying in advance. So it could be wiser to budget for such bills by saving a regular sum each week or month, in a bank or post office account which pays interest. Those in financial difficulties should approach the board *before* they get behind with payments *and tell them of any special circumstances.*

Paying for Electricity - Disconnection
Although they cannot disconnect for a bad debt on an appliance, boards have a right to cut off supplies if electricity bills, or security deposits, have not been paid. However, they say they will not disconnect old people *who are unable to pay* between 1 October and 31 March. And extra time may be given if Social Services have been contacted or if someone in the household is ill or handicapped in any way.

Energy Saving and Insulation
A lot can be done to reduce heat loss and cut fuel bills. But before you start any insulation work, find out about the grant situation from your local authority or from the Department of Energy Information Office. If you are handicapped or elderly ask relevant organizations.

It also pays to take a look at the facts about what will and will not save you money. There are actually two aspects to energy saving - the need to save world energy resources, and the need to save money on your own energy bill. So far as the first is concerned, any measures which save energy are good news. But to save money you need to save more on energy than the installation costs in the first place - and that means spending wisely.

- The best value for money is a 10 cm (4 in) jacket for a hot water cylinder. It should pay for itself inside a year. Choose one to BS 5615. But a new tank should have a factory fitted one to BS 699, 1566, or 3198. If you already have a jacket on the tank put the new one under. Two insulations are better than one.
- Inexpensive draught strips are also a good investment and easy to apply yourself. Draughts can account for 15 per cent of your heat loss. But have enough ventilation in any room where there is a fire which is not electric; all flames need air.
- The next best value is to insulate your loft with at least 100 mm (4 in) insulation. Up to 25 per cent of your heat may go out through your roof, so this should save you at least £50 a year on your heating bill. This means that if you install it yourself - which is very easily done - you should be saving money within 2 years. (But wear a face mask and gloves when installing insulation; it is better not to breathe it in.) And if your current insulation is 30 mm (1¼ in) or less you may be able to get a local authority grant to help you increase this (but check *before* you do the work). The insulation you use should be to BS 5803.
- Cavity wall insulation is the next best value. About 40 per cent of British houses have cavity walls and a lot of heat can be saved. It needs professional installation but it should pay for itself in 5 years - or even less on a detached house in an exposed position. But see page 215 on condensation.
- Double glazing is the *least* cost effective form of insulation (unless you do a nifty DIY job). In one Consumers' Association report on double glazing they found that double glazing costing £1,250 would save £22 to £25 a year in heating bills. So if fuel costs were static it would be about 50 years before the windows began to pay for themselves. Of course, fuel costs aren't static, but nor does double glazing last forever. That doesn't mean double glazing is always a waste of money. At DIY prices the same windows could have been double glazed for £250. So, allowing for a rise in fuel costs, the windows would be earning their keep in about 7 years. It also reduces condensation on the glass. And it may reduce the risk of burglary. But remember a window a burglar can't break is also one you can't break in a fire. On factory sealed units look for the kitemark and BS 5713. If you haven't got double glazing, put a lining and interlining on your curtains - it makes a real difference.

Insulation Work

If you use contractors discuss any estimates in detail and make sure they plan to insulate to the thickness you want. To insulate cavity walls you need permission from the council. The main danger of cavity wall insulation is that when not done correctly the insulation can act as a bridge for damp. Any contractor should hold an Agrément Board Certificate which shows that his work and materials meet certain technical standards or have British Standards Institution (BSI) registration which allows those they approve to use BS 5618 on their letterhead if they meet the standards of the BSI code of practice.

Another way of insulating walls is to put some type of cladding on them. This is not a cheap process. So it is really only suitable for adding to a home if existing cladding needs to be renewed anyway.

Draught Proofing Advisory Association Ltd, External Wall Insulation Association, National Association of Loft Insulation Contractors and **National Cavity Insulation Association** - all at P.O.Box 12, Haslemere, Surrey GU27 3AN Tel:0428 54011 and give the names of contractors.
British Board of Agrément, P.O.Box 195, Bucknalls Lane, Garston, Watford, Herts WD2 7NG Tel: 0923 670844. Also has lists of approved installers of such things as roofing and chimney lining.
Enquiry Service, British Standards Institution, Linford Wood, Milton Keynes MK14 6LE Tel: 0908 220022
Department of Energy Information Division, Room 1312, Thames House South, Millbank, London SW1P 4QJ Tel: 01 211 6811
Monergy Saver, Freepost Newcastle-upon-Tyne NE1 1BR or Tel: 0800 234 800 - contact this address to find out if there is a local neighbourhood action group which will insulate the home of someone elderly or disabled.
Energy Savings With Home Improvements, Consumers' Association book

Fire

Fire is a far bigger hazard in most homes than we realize. Ordinary foam upholstery, which has not been modified to prevent it catching fire, can fill a room with lethal smoke and go up in a sheet of flames in just over 2 minutes from the moment a lighted cigarette or spark falls on it. And in that almost unbelievably short time the fire can become so fierce that the room is impossible to enter. You and your family are much safer with old-fashioned chairs with old-fashioned fillings or with the truly fire-resistant foam. As it burns, the other kind gives off fumes which kill.

The Department of Trade and Industry has leaflets explaining the labels found on upholstery.

Fire is one of the most preventable accidents. There are general hazards which are easily avoided and, on top of that, each room has its own special hazards. How does your home score for fire risks?

Fire Safety in the Home

Some of the most important safety precautions are the easiest.

- Have enough ventilation for boilers and open fires to burn safely. Too little air could mean a build-up

of poisonous gas, or the gas going out and leaking dangerously.
- Shut all doors at night so that if a fire starts it will spread more slowly.
- Have gas and electrical appliances serviced regularly and stop using anything if you even suspect it isn't in perfect working order.
- Fit smoke detectors to BS specifications.

If a chip pan catches fire:
- DON'T try to move it.
- DON'T put water on it - it will make this type of fire much worse.
- Put a lid on it fast to smother the flames.
- No lid? - Smother the flames by dropping a thick damp cloth over.
- Leave the pan 30 minutes before touching it.

If a chimney catches fire:
- Throw water on the fire in the hearth. The steam from that should rise up the chimney and put the fire out.
- Phone the fire brigade - even if you think the fire is out. It may not be.

FIRE SPREADS IN SECONDS - only try to put it out if it's very small. Otherwise LEAVE THE ROOM FAST and shut the door.
FORGET VALUABLES.
GET EVERYONE OUT OF THE HOUSE FAST.
DIAL 999

In the *very* early stages use a home fire extinguisher, throw water on - except on a chip pan - or smother the flames with anything which shuts out air. Once furnishings are well ablaze the fumes could make you unable to get away. Just shut the door on the room and get out *fast*. YOU MAY HAVE ONLY 2 MINUTES BEFORE THE FLASHPOINT when the whole room is full of flames and it spreads to other rooms.

Paraffin Heaters
- Paraffin heaters need plenty of air but should never stand in a draught or where they could be easily knocked over. Nor should they be near curtains or furniture.
- Keep the wick trimmed and having filled the stove wipe off all surplus fuel with lavatory paper and throw the paper down the lavatory.
- If possible, store paraffin in a cool place away from the house - such as a shed.

Paraffin heaters are now designed so that they will put themselves out if they are knocked over. To be safe they should carry a BS number. They should be checked regularly by any shop which carries a Paraffin Heating Advisory Council sticker.

Glass and Glazing
Double glazing is an area in which companies tend to spring up looking for quick profits. To join the **Glass and Glazing Federation (GGF)** (44-48 Borough Heath, London SE1 1XB Tel: 01 403 7177) a company must have traded for 2 years. No qualifications are needed, but members must conform to the Federation's code of practice as well as the British Standards and Technical Trade Standards. This is not a very great guarantee of satisfaction. However, the GGF also provides a fund which safeguards the client's deposit - up to a certain level - if a member goes out of business before the job is finished.

Double Glazing
Before embarking on double glazing check how much (or little) energy it will save (see page 218). It isn't necessarily the best way to spend your money, but read the GGF leaflets.

How well it retains heat or shuts out noise depends on the type of glass, and the width of the gap between the two panes. Effectiveness increases with the gap. The GGF has produced the following table.

Heat Loss in U Values

	Exposure to Wind		
	Sheltered	Normal	Exposed
Single Glazing	5.0	5.6	6.7
Double Glazing 3 mm airspace	3.6	4.0	4.4
5 mm airspace	3.3	3.6	4.0
6 mm airspace	3.2	3.4	3.8
8 mm airspace	3.1	3.3	3.7
9 mm airspace	3.0	3.2	3.5
12 mm airspace	2.8	3.0	3.3
20 mm airspace or more	2.8	2.9	3.2

A gap of 20 mm (¾ in) gives about as much heat insulation as you will get, but sealed units, with an air space of only 6 mm(¼ in), which it may be possible to install yourself may well be the best value. For good noise insulation you need 100 mm (4 in) or more.

Double Glazing - Safeguards
In double glazing there are highly trained salesmen who telephone uninvited and ask to come and tell you about their product. The wise answer is 'no'. This isn't usually the best way to buy. You need to shop around and compare prices and styles. If you let them talk to you, check your rights (see Law) before you sign anything. And it might be best not to sign at all if the company isn't a GGF member. Their representatives must carry a GGF card.

Safety

A British Standard has been set for glass in vulnerable areas so that it is either unbreakable or breaks safely. Two kinds of glass meet the standard:

1 Toughened glass
2 Laminated glass

Use these wherever there is low level glass, or a glass section to a door, and in wet areas, such as round a shower. A GGF leaflet gives the thicknesses and types of glass which can safely be used.

Heating and Plumbing

Anyone can call himself a plumber, so when having heating or ventilation installed, or plumbing done, there are benefits in using a member of one of the trade associations below. They don't all provide the same protection for the client. So check what safeguards a particular association offers under its code.

Members are sometimes covered by a guarantee under which if they cease to trade or work is unsatisfactory, and complaints to the company prove fruitless, the association will take up the complaint and the problem may be put right by another member, free of charge. The work of any job a member does is guaranteed for 12 months.

Before Using a Contractor

Before you even see a contractor, look into the pros and cons of gas, oil, electricity or solid fuel, and if possible read up the latest developments in the field and talk to the advice organizations for each fuel. Things change rapidly and the perfect solution could be something you have never considered.

Even when using members of an association, always get at least 3 estimates. In an emergency ask about the call-out rate, the hourly rate and other charges. These can vary hugely.

Getting estimates from 3 firms lets you pick their brains. But before a contractor can advise you or give you an estimate you must agree:

- the rooms and areas to be heated
- the temperature they need to be heated to
- the number of air changes assumed for each room or area
- the type of house insulation to be used and whether the contractor will be involved in this or not.

Using a Central Heating Contractor

All those agreed facts should be restated in the central heating quotation the contractor gives. It should also show his terms of trading, conditions of payment and guarantees, plus the following information - which looks complex, but is just basic, logical and essential.

Heat generator - fuel type, heat output, make, type, location.
Fuel storage - capacity, site.
Pump - type, location, how it can be isolated for maintenance.
Controls - on the main generator, room controls, hot tank controls, control of hot water temperature.
Hot water tank - size, type, insulation, material, location, whether gravity fed or pumped, immersion heater back-up type and rating etc.
Heating elements - (radiators) make and type, number, position in each room, responsibility for painting.
Towel rail(s) - size, type, make.
Linen cupboard - method of heating if not from the hot tank.
Cold water tanks - location, connection to mains, size, overflow arrangements, insulation, means of isolation.
Pipework - size of pipework, materials, position whether on surface or concealed, position of stopcocks and valves, type, thickness and extent of insulation.
Electric wiring - description, position, whether on surface or concealed.
Building work - who does what in relation to: accommodation and ventilation for the heat generator, adaptation of existing chimneys or construction of new, provision of storage for fuel, lifting and replacing floor coverings, disposal of rubbish and rubble.

Check all these points are as you want them and ask about anything you don't understand. Misunderstandings can be expensive.

The **Heating and Ventilating Contractors' Association** (ESCA House, 34 Palace Court, London W2 4JG Tel: 01 229 2488) or Home Heating Linkline 0345-581158 (charged at local call rates) or 01-229 5543 for Londoners. Branches in Edinburgh and Belfast. Inf. Ad.

The **National Association of Plumbing, Heating and Mechanical Services Contractors** 6 Gate Street, London WC2A 3HX Tel: 01 405 2678/9 - insists members must show technical competence. Code of practice, warranty scheme and gives details of members.

The **Scottish and Northern Ireland Plumbing Employers Federation** 4 Walker Street, Edinburgh EH3 7LB Tel: 031 225 2255 - covers plumbing and domestic central heating, has a code of practice and will arbitrate. It also offers warranty and insurance schemes.

The **Institute of Plumbing** (64 Station Lane, Hornchurch, Essex RM12 6NB Tel: 04024 72791) is for individual plumbers. The members must 'satisfy the institute regarding their workmanship'. The Institute's directory is in public libraries.

★ If you simply want to refurbish a tired looking bath - or make it match a new basin - it can be resurfaced. **Renubath** (248 Lillie Road, London SW6 Tel: 01 381 8337) isn't the only company which does this but it is one of the most established.

Gas as Fuel

The great thing that gas has in its favour as a fuel is immediacy. Whether it's for a boiler, a sitting-room fire or a burner on a stove, there is no time lag while the element warms up. Its other asset is price, although those who have to rely on bottled gas may find it expensive.

Gas showrooms now try to show more appliances working, and should be able to tell you where you can see any appliance, as computer links are being installed.

Many gas boards have 'Home Service Advisers' who will visit customers in their homes and specialize in helping families with budgeting problems, and in advising the elderly and handicapped about adaptors which may make gas appliances easier to use.

Balanced Flues

The balanced flue allows gas to be used in rooms which don't have a chimney. The air the boiler needs to burn safely is drawn through a pipe in an outside wall and the fumes are released through a parallel pipe into a 3-inch flue which goes up the outside wall. Appliances with this system are often called 'room sealed'.

Gas Central Heating

The days of vast gas boilers are long gone. They can be hung on walls, tucked into cupboards or even put at the back of a fire, with a gas fire in front of them. And, like fires, they no longer need the chimney or large flue they used to require. The one essential is that they have enough air to burn safely. One of the most interesting developments is the condensing boiler which allows you to heat water almost instantly when you need it - and can give considerable savings. Gas is probably the cheapest fuel for central heating.

Gas Fires and Room Heaters

You can buy gas room heaters as radiators, as conventional gas fires and in the form of imitation solid fuel, and they no longer have to have a chimney behind them. The efficiency varies - ask about the cost of any heater in relation to its heat output.

Anyone wanting the homeliness of an open fire without the work of tending one might consider one of the gas fires which imitate coal or logs. I'm not crazy about fakes, but if any fakes work these do. Some of the early fires were very inefficient as heaters, giving out only 12 per cent of the gas as heat. That has changed: the gas board now has a selection of these fires which are 45 per cent efficient and the newest Glow-worm Derwent is 90 per cent efficient. That is even better than the usual radiant gas fires which are only about 70 per cent efficient.

Gas Stoves

It is much easier to cook well on gas than any other fuel, as you can turn the heat up or down or right off with no need to think ahead. This makes it ideal for both burners and grills. As oven heat, it has advantages and disadvantages

> Astonishing as it may seem, imported gas appliances do not have to reach such strict standards as those made in Britain. There are imported gas stoves on sale in Britain with lids which close without automatically shutting off the gas and others which do not have proper insulation between the oven and the outside of the door and could burn those who touch it or even the handle.

Installing Gas

Gas isn't available everywhere, but if you live within 25 yards of a suitable gas main British Gas must normally supply you. If you live farther from a main than that they can choose whether they supply you or not. If you decide to be connected up for gas the first 30 feet of pipe in a public highway are laid free, and so are the first 10 metres of pipe not in a public highway. Any other pipework is charged for according to how far it has to go and how easy it is to lay.

Gas fittings without a built-in flue must have enough air to let them burn - or they could go out and the gas leak could be dangerous. This means that if you are having a gas fire fitted in an existing fireplace the chimney should be swept first, and the flue checked.

By law, gas appliances may only be installed by 'a competent person' and there is a heavy fine for breaking this regulation - DIY fanatics would not normally be considered competent.

Members of the **Confederation for the Registration of Gas Installers (CORGI)** (CORGI HQ, St Martin's House, 140 Tottenham Court Road, London W1P 9LN Tel: 01 387 9185) are assessed for competence and committed to observing gas safety regulations, must be fully insured for public liability and their work is subject to spot checks. However, this organization doesn't act as a conciliator in disputes. Regional offices are listed under 'CORGI'.

Reading a Meter

Gas meters show how many cubic feet of gas have been used. If you want to know what the bill will be, the easiest way is to obtain a free 'Gas Cost Calculator' from your local Gas Consumers' Council. If you don't have one, use the calculation given below.

- If your meter has a row of figures, like a milometer in a car, read only the white figures.
- If you have dials only read the row with black hands. Write down the figure which each hand is on or has just passed, keeping the figures in the same order - from left to right - as the dials.

The difference between the final number now and the last time you read it will be the number of cubic feet of gas you have used. To convert this to therms you multiply it by what the gas board calls the 'calorific value' of your gas. This is on every bill, but is usually between 1008 and 1040 BTU (British Thermal Units). You then divide the answer by 1,000 and that gives you the number of therms you have used. Multiply that by the price per therm and you know the worst.

The standing charge for gas varies slightly from area to area if you have a credit meter (the usual kind). Then the therms are charged at a flat rate. On a coin-in-the-slot meter the standing charge is lower and the therms cost more for the first 39 therms, then the price per therm goes down.

★ The mathematics of that means that, for an approximate figure, you can take the figure you read off your meter minus your last reading.

★ If you find the calorific value on your bill is in megajoules, this is just a different type of measurement for the same thing. 37.6 megajoules = 1008 BTU and 38.8 megajoules = 1040 BTU.

Safety with Gas

The first *Enquire Within* had little to say about safety, but there was the occasional useful warning such as: *Do not tamper with gunpowder by candlelight.*

None of us would be so crazy - even were we in the habit of keeping gunpowder around - but gas is a far more dangerous substance than people often realize. If it collects in any quantity the smallest spark can set it alight and a quantity of gas catching fire creates an horrific explosion.

If you think a gas appliance isn't working properly STOP USING IT IMMEDIATELY and call a qualified fitter through your gas showroom or CORGI (see page 221). But don't wait for gas fittings to go wrong. For safety:
- gas appliances must be serviced regularly
- chimneys and flues must be checked and kept in good condition
- gas appliances must have enough air in the room to burn safely
- don't use a second-hand gas appliance without having it checked by someone from the gas board. Half the accidents from faulty appliances are caused by second hand ones.

★ Fires also have a silent and invisible risk: carbon monoxide poisoning. All fires with flames use up oxygen as they burn and give off carbon monoxide. If there is too little fresh air in the room the carbon monoxide can build up to dangerous levels. Each year 200 people in Britain die from this. If you feel sleepy in a room with a fire carbon monoxide could be the reason. Let air in and have your appliance and the ventilation to it checked by experts.

Gas Consumers' Council (6th Floor, Abford House, 15 Wilton Road, London SW1V 1LT Tel: 01 931 0977) is the major body for gas consumers. You should contact your local office of this council.

Society of British Gas Industries 36 Holly Walk, Leamington Spa, Warwicks CV32 4LY Tel: 0926 34357 is the trade association of manufacturers. It doesn't deal with complaints but it will tell you were to find a particular company or pass on a letter of complaint to top level management.

Gas Marketing (Benn Publications, Sovereign Way, Tonbridge Kent, Tel: 0732 364422) is a trade magazine which covers the latest developments in appliances, and often surveys appliances.

Oil as Fuel

Compared to gas, oil is relatively little used as a fuel (apart from in rural areas) but anyone who needs information on it can contact the **Domestic Heating Department,** Room 0545, BP Oil Ltd, Victoria Street, London SW1E 5NJ Tel: 01 821 2468.

If you smell gas:
1 DON'T LIGHT ANY KIND OF FLAME and DON'T SWITCH ON THE LIGHT - switching on a light causes a small spark in the switch which could set the gas on fire.
2 Open windows and doors to let the gas out.
3 Turn off any appliance which has accidentally been left on. If it is a minor leak and that solves the problem leave it at that. Otherwise:
- Turn the gas off at the meter. There should be a large handle on the pipe - swing it down so it runs parallel to the floor.
- Call the gas board immediately - they run a 24-hour emergency service.
- If you cannot turn the gas off and there is a very strong strong smell, or the smell continues to be very strong even after turning it off, get yourself and others out of the building *fast* and call the police.

Solid Fuel

Solid fuel has more scope than appears at first sight. There are now solid fuel boilers which look like sitting room fires but double as a boiler, heating hot water and radiators in other rooms. And if you already have a central heating system an open fire which also heats water can be linked into the system to provide more options and less dependence on a single fuel.

Looking After Solid Fuel Appliances

The snag is that solid fuel appliances need looking after and flues must be kept clear, and brushed out every month. If there is a throatplate at the top of the firebox it must be taken out and cleaned once a month too. One of the most important jobs is to make sure that the flue or chimney is swept at least once a year. And, of course, an open fire has to be emptied and relaid each day - although this isn't true of stoves.

★ Having riddled a stove to get the ash into the ash pan, give it time to settle. Carry the ash drawer with a damp cloth draped over. Then it won't float all over the room.

Safety with Solid Fuel

- All open fires (and radiant heaters) should have a fire-guard and if there are young children around this guard should be fixed so they can't move it.
- By law if a child under the age of 12 (7 in Scotland) is allowed into a room with an unguarded fire, and is badly burnt, the person responsible can be prosecuted.
- To burn properly - and safely - fires also need a certain amount of air. A room should not be too draught free. If you have double glazing air vents may be needed.

One piece of advice in the 1856 *Enquire Within* is just as good today as the day it was written.

Another consideration as far as economy is concerned is ... to buy at the proper season; for there is with every article a cheap season and a dear one; and with none more so than with coals: insomuch that the master of a family who fills his coal cellar in the middle of summer, rather than the beginning of winter, will find it filled at less expense than it would otherwise cost him; and will be enabled to see December's snows falling without feeling his enjoyment of his fireside lessened by the consideration that the cheerful blaze is supplied at twice the rate that it need have done had he exercised more foresight.

The difference in rate is less than double, but summer coal is certainly cheaper.

Wood

In a stove, where sparks are contained, the type of wood is less important than in an open fire, where certain wood, such as poplar and sweet chestnut, can be a real danger. But the amount of heat a wood gives out and the speed at which it burns varies considerably from wood to wood.

When I was compiling *Supertips to Make Life Easy* I was sent a traditional country rhyme appraising the burning qualities of different wood. On checking it with experts on timber, I found it was totally correct. Ash is the best wood for burning, beech and oak are good but the derided poplar, for example, gives out little more than half the heat of the same weight of oak.

Warm - The Real Fire Heating Association (P.O.Box 35, Stoke-on-Trent, Staffs ST4 7NU Tel: 0782 44311) is a trade association for manufacturers, importers and retailers of fires and appliances using any solid fuel, and can tell you where to find a particular make or see what is available. It also has useful leaflets on fuels and which stoves need conversion in Britain.

The Solid Fuel Advisory Service (Hobart House, Grosvenor Place, London SW1X 7AE Tel: 01 235 2020) sponsors Real Fire Heating Shops all over Britain where real fires are displayed. And its service includes a free home visit to discuss your needs. It will also advise on maintenance.

The **National Fireplace Council** (at the same address) which publishes a catalogue of fireplaces by a large range of manufacturers.

The **National Association of Chimney Sweeps** (address as WARM), will give you the names of the nearest sweeps among its members and deal with a complaint if you can't sort it out. Its sweeps should give you a certificate after sweeping saying when it was swept and reporting on the condition of both the appliance and the chimney.

If there are faults in your chimney the **National Association of Chimney Lining Engineers (NACLE)** (address as WARM) members specialize in relining existing chimneys.

Kitchens

If you own a home, improving its kitchen really does make it more saleable. The choice in fitted kitchens gets wider every year, and the number of companies offering to install them increases equally. However, it is one thing to sell a set of units, and another to have the skilled men to install it perfectly. Before buying, ask for the names of previous customers and talk to them, and see the kitchens if they'll let you.

Another protection is to use a member of the **Kitchen Specialists Association** (P.O.Box 123, Horsham, W Sussex RH13 8YU Tel: 0403 41259.) It doesn't *guarantee* the abilities of its members, but they work to a code of practice registered with the Office of Fair Trading.

There is far more on offer than the average fitted kitchen company suggests. German companies, especially Leicht, have been coming up with some brilliant ways to make the most of space. They are great sources of ideas and a few of these kitchens simply stand against the walls - so you could take it with you when you go. (A point to ask about when buying a house. Imagine buying a house for its kitchen and finding it had vanished.)

If you enquire carefully you will find that a few of the more stylish kitchens on the market are suitable for DIY fitting (though nobody rushes to tell you this). You might find that fitting them yourself would cost no more than having a far less interesting kitchen installed professionally.

> Before buying any system measure and check whether the cupboard in which you plan to put plates will take a full-width plate, and that the drawers are deep enough to take a decent spatula. More than one company has made fittings too small for such things.

Leicht Furniture Ltd, Leicht House, Lagoon Road, Orpington, Kent BR5 3QG Tel: 0689 36413
Ideal Home Book of Kitchens, IPC

Roofing

Roofs and roof spaces really ought to be checked from time to time. You don't have to be a professional to see if a timber is sagging, to smell rot or to notice an attack of woodworm.

★ If you have climbing plants make sure no tendrils go near the roof. The most delicate-looking shoot can lift a roof tile with its little finger. Window cleaners will often chop off invasive bits which are too high to be reached without a long ladder.

Flat Roofs

In theory, flat roofs can be made as weatherproof as any other roof. In practice, the layers of bitumen-covered felt, which cover flat roofs, all too easily leak in time, and the flashing which links the roof to any adjoining wall may let trickles of water through when the wind blows under it.

In particular, over kitchens and bathrooms, the heat and condensation may make the roof surface distort and leak. Condensation can also cause the timbers of the roof to rot, and this risk increases if the roof is insulated from underneath. The only safe way to insulate is to place insulation over the bitumen, which isn't always satisfactory. So heat loss is another disadvantage.

However, if you do buy a house with a flat-roofed extension, or build one, don't dream of making a terrace out of it without checking it has the right timbers - or it won't take the weight.

Roof Repairs

Roofing repairs are usually best left to professionals, unless you have a great deal of skill and a head for heights. Standards for roofing are laid down by the BSI and the **National Federation of Roofing Contractors** (15 Soho Square, London W1V 5FB Tel: 01 734 9164) will supply a list of experienced contractors. They also give technical advice on roofing, and will arbitrate on disputes between one of their contractors and a member of the public. But not all NFRC contractors offer a guarantee. Check this before engaging them.

Security

In 1985 700,000 homes were broken into in England and Wales, and 3 cars were broken into every minute. Most of the burglars aren't skilled criminals but simply dishonest people (or young people) making the most of an opportunity. The first step to crime prevention is blocking the opportunity. You don't need sophisticated burglar alarms to do that, just a few basics - strong locks, spy holes, light in the right places and a bit of thought.

Burglar Detection

Burglar detectors are becoming more sophisticated all the time, and anyone buying a new house should look into the possibilities early on. For example, you can buy a computerized system which controls the central heating, fire warnings and burglar alarms or wire-free alarm systems which can be switched on from a control pad. At the other end of the scale, you can buy small devices which will howl if their beam is interrupted, and lights which switch on if anyone passes them. New products in this field are coming on the market all the time. Check with some specialist suppliers before you decide what to have.

A burglar alarm which meets the British Standard for burglar alarms (BS 4737) may bring down your insurance premium. Unfortunately, many of the alarms which you can fit yourself don't meet this standard. That doesn't mean they are no good. Some could be very useful as a deterrent. There are lights for using on back paths and dark doorways which automatically switch on when the daylight falls below a certain level, and switch off again when it increases.

And, for your personal safety, there are now lights on remote control systems which you can switch on from your car, and garage doors can be opened in the same way.

First Security Group, Fleet Mill, Minley Road, Fleet, Hants DU13 8RD Tel: 0252 622100

Modern Alarms, (259 City Road, London EC1V 1JE Tel: 01 251 1616) - makes varied alarms and those with computerized heating controls.

The National Supervisory Council for Intruder Alarms (Queensgate House, 14 Cookham Road, Maidenhead, Berks SL6 8AJ Tel: 0628 37512) is the professional association of those who install home security devices of all kinds and the members must have 3 years' experience in the business and conform to a code of practice. The association will give you the names of members in your area.

Marking Your Belongings

Marking your belongings can make them not worth stealing. It can also increase the chance of you getting them back if they are stolen. Mark them in an area which cannot be removed or erased. The police recommend marking with your postcode plus house number. But they warn that expert advice should be sought on marking antiques and items of much value.

- An ultraviolet pen can write on surfaces like silver - but the burglar won't see the marks. However, it wears off and needs renewing every 6 months. (Ask the crime prevention officer at your police station where you can buy these pens.)
- Some surfaces can be safely scratched with a sharp-pointed tool or nail - obviously not for anything of value.
- A fine drill can be used to engrave the marks.

Precautions against Burglary

No time is too brief for a burglar. Always lock up completely even if you think you'll only be gone a minute, and don't leave downstairs doors or windows open while hoovering or watching television upstairs. Every police area has a crime prevention officer who will advise - free of charge - on your particular security needs. Major lock and security companies will too.

- Fit security deadlocks on all doors (see Locks, page 239) - many other locks are very pickable. To be safe a front door must have a lock which can be deadlocked when you leave so that only a key will open it. Then nobody can break a pane of glass and undo it. It should carry the number BS 3621. This only applies to locks with a large number of key variations, so someone else's key is unlikely to open your lock.

> For locks of this type new keys are often supplied only by the manufacturer and only then if the request comes with the owner's signature. If you buy a house, find out if this applies and get a letter from the previous owner telling the lock company that you are the new owner, and send this with your signature. When you do this, ask how many keys have been issued for the lock. Then check if you have them all. If you haven't it would be wise to change the lock at once.

- Fit locks which stop the windows opening wide enough to admit a burglar. This isn't hard to do yourself and gives a great sense of security. Get expert advice on how narrow an opening to leave.

I once saw a fireman, in full gear, go through a fanlight I'd have thought too small for a child.

- Fit a chain or similar device so no stranger can push in if you open the door.
- Fit mortice security bolts on vulnerable doors inside and out, and use them when away from home.
- Fit a peepholes in doors so you can see who is outside.
- Install lights over porches and back paths which automatically switch on.
- When out at night have lights on timer switches so they occasionally go on and off.
- When ordering new keys by post get them sent to a friend at another address - then, if they are lost, nobody identifies them with your home.
- If you have an answering machine leave a message on it suggesting you are busy and not able to take the call, not that you are out.

Master Locksmiths Association (13 Parkfield Road, Northolt, Middx UB5 5NN Tel: 01 845 1676) will supply the names of locksmiths. Its members must be properly qualified and abide by a code of ethics. If a member's work is not satisfactory the association will take it up.

Safes
Before installing a safe, talk to your insurance company. There are likely to be rules as to which safes will allow a reduced premium. The main types are free standing, under-floor and wall-fitted. Some of the under-floor safes would be quite easy to fit yourself, and there are concealed safes which look like part of ordinary household fittings.

Timber Treatment
The problem which is most likely to need treatment is dry rot. The fungus causing it is *Serpula lacrymans*. The name comes from the little droplets of water, like tears, which you may see near the mould. You too may weep at the amount of demolition which treating this fungus may take, but at least you can save yourself the tears which might follow from using an unqualified contractor to treat it. You can recognize the mould very easily as it drapes itself in soft cloud-like formations across the wood it destroys.

As timber treatment is a field which is full of unqualified operators, use members of the **British Wood Preserving Association (BWPA)** (Premier House, 150 Southampton Row, London WC1B 5AL Tel: 01 837 8217.) They have to reach a set standard, their work is subject to spot checks, and the association will look into complaints against members and try to resolve the problems. However, any firm can go out of business and the 20- to 30-year guarantees then become worthless. To avoid this, if you pay a small one-off fee to the **Guarantee Protection Trust** (P.O.Box 77, 27 London Road, High Wycombe, Bucks HP11 1BW Tel: 0494 447049) your guarantee from a BWPA member will be insured for 20 years. And if the original firm goes out of business any remedial work will be done by another firm.

WARNING: It is illegal to kill or injure a wild bat, but some timber treatments can be fatal to them. If you find bats where you wish to treat timber, contact the Nature Conservancy Council (see Free Time).

Timber Research and Development Association (TRADA), Stocking Lane, Hughenden Valley, High Wycombe, Bucks HP14 4ND Tel: 0240 24 3091 - provides lists of those making timber-frame housing, and some thought-provoking leaflets on the structure and problems of timber frame housing.

CHANGING PLACES

Buying a Home
The only really easy home purchase is when a tenant who has lived in a property for 3 years uses a right to buy it, which this confers. But at least there are moves to make ordinary home buying easier. The trend is towards large companies bringing all the facilities under one umbrella. For example, Legal and General now offer a service called *Home Move* which does conveyancing through a subsidiary and puts clients in touch with estate egents and mortgage sources. But whether you will get as good a deal on each lot of fees as you would if you shopped around is something to check. Ring Freefone 0800 010181 or write to P.O.Box 142, London W3 0TZ, but by the time you read this there are sure to be other companies doing the same sort of package.

Some building firms provide a house, carpets and fitments. This may make house buying a lot easier, but nobody should be deceived into thinking these extras are free, and if you want to move soon after buying you may not get as much as you paid for the house as all those goods will then be second-hand.

Companies offering an all-in package are likely to be members of the **National House Building Council (NHBC)** 58 Portland Place, London W1N 4BU Tel: 01 637 1248 or 5 Manor Place, Edinburgh EH3 7DH. The telephone hotline (031 226 7115) also has list of developers building sheltered accommodation and old people's housing. The NHBC sets standards for new buildings built by members and gives a 10-year warranty on them. If you are wanting a mortgage on a new house the lender may well want to know whether it was built by a NHBC member, and there could be problems if it wasn't. The NHBC also sells publications on topics like 'Disputes over Defects'. Its 'new homes hotline' on 01 935 7464 will tell you which builders are building the type and price of home which you want - anywhere in Britain.

Estate Agents
Normally, finding a property is a matter of getting your name on the books of as many likely estate agents as possible. Try to find one person in any office who has a real interest in finding you precisely what you want.

A quick way to get to know the market is through Homelink: you brief a Homelink member of the

National Association of Estate Agents, or the head office (see right) with the details of what you are looking for, and where. Then they arrange for a Homelink member in that area to send you details of properties.

Surveys

Before buying a house which is not brand new it is usually worth getting an independent survey. This will tell you what defects you will need to remedy if you buy. The normal procedure is a written report. But those on a tight budget can ask the surveyor whether he can reduce the fee if he just tells you on the phone. If you make accurate notes that may be enough. Or a member of the IVSA (below) will do a standard valuation and report, for a lower charge than a full structural survey.

Those on an even tighter budget can adopt another strategy. Many firms which do work on woodworm and rot, or deal with damp courses, will check a house for these faults - which are some of the most expensive to put right - and give a free estimate of the cost, if they find them. This is not as good as a full survey and it won't tell you whether the roof needs tiling or the bricks pointing. But it is better than no survey at all.

If a mortgage is being taken out, the bank or building society will insist on the property being surveyed by a surveyor of their choice. This is to make sure the property is a sound security loan. It is not as detailed as a structural survey, but it may give some guidance and most mortgage companies will now let the purchaser see the report.

The Incorporated Society of Valuers and Auctioneers (ISVA) 3 Cadogan Gate, London SW1X 0AS Tel: 01 235 2282 is a society for qualified estate agents, surveyors, property valuers and property auctioneers. Its members must conform to a professional code of conduct.
The Royal Institution of Chartered Surveyors, see page 214
The Building Societies Association (see Money) - has a very useful range of leaflets on house purchase.
Timber and Brick Homes Information Council, Stanhope Place, London W2 2HH Tel: 01 723 3444 - has information on houses of this type and who to buy them from and leaflets on DIY in a timber and brick home.

Conveyancing

Legal checks are needed to convey the property from one owner to another (see Law).

Land Registry

Most of the land in Britain is registered with the Land Registry and has a registered owner. One of the duties of the solicitor doing the conveyancing is to check the region's Land Registry to see that whoever is selling the land is the rightful owner, and the boundaries of the land being sold are correct. For this a form must be completed, requesting a search and asking for office copies of the registration, and the Land Registry makes a search and sends the results, free of charge, within a day or two.

If the purchase is going ahead, the Land Registry must transfer the land into the buyer's name. Those who are trying DIY conveyencing must arrange this themselves,

and the Land Registry publishes a series of free, if heavily worded, leaflets on how to do this. There is a set charge based on the value of the property.

HM Land Registry, 32 Lincoln's Inn Fields, London WC2A 3PH Tel: 01 405 2504

Selling a Home

Estate Agents - Who Sells What for What

Estate agents are mainly working for the sellers of the property, and advise them on the price to ask. Nobody has to take that advice, and it is also up to the owner to decide which items will be left in the house as fixtures and fittings.

Estate agents vary greatly in their efficiency. Before putting a property into the hands of one, make out you want to buy a property and see how well they perform. They should also belong to a professional body (below), so that your money is safeguarded.

The estate agent who succeeds in selling the property takes a percentage of the price as commission. There is some variation from region to region, but the main possibilities are these:

Sole agency	Only one agent is instructed, but the seller can still sell the property privately. May be the lowest commission.
Sole selling rights	One agent has exclusive rights to sell. So if the seller sells it privately the agent still gets the commission.
Multiple agency	Several agents are asked to sell the property and whoever succeeds gets the commission. This may bring more buyers but the commission may be higher.
Joint agents	Two or more agents co-operate. The commission is usually more than for sole agency, but less than for multiple agency
Sub-agents	The main agent allows a sub-agent to offer it too and they agree to share the original commission.

Estate Agents - Complaints

Estate agents must act within the Estate Agents Act 1979, which comes under the local Trading Standards Officer and the code of conduct of their professional association - if they belong to one.

If the estate agency concerned does not satisfy you, when you complain, take the matter up with the General Secretary of the National Association of Estate Agents. They also sell a simplified guide to the 1979 Act.

National Association of Estate Agents Arbon House, 21 Jury Street, Warwick CV34 4EH Tel: 0926 496800

Selling by Auction
For an auction to be effective the property has to be advertized and the cost of this is borne by the seller. One key advantage is that purchase by auction is binding. There is none of the delay and uncertainty connected with other forms of sale. Read the ISVA leaflet - see page 226.

Points to Remember when Selling a Home
- Don't allow in callers off the street, they could be burglars - or worse.
- Ask the estate agent always to send a representative with would-be buyers.
- Make the place look, and feel, good.
- All light fittings must work.
- Cupboards must be tidy enough to look spacious if opened (a pre-move clear-out may do the trick)
- A well-kept garden (try to sell at its best or have photos of it in full bloom)
- Make the place look attractive with pot plants and flowers.
- If any room has dreadful decorations (as teenagers' may) painting it white could pay off handsomely.
- Make it smell good.

Finally, remember that a cross or distracted viewer is unlikely to buy - and radio, television, music, children and pets all constitute a distraction. Turn them off, or corral them as best you can.

Letting Property
If the mortgage has not been paid off you will need permission, to let, from the mortgage company. And do get legal advice on the type of tenancy to offer. It makes a big difference to how easily you can get back the use of the property if you need it (see Law). You also need to make an inventory of the entire contents, and prepare a suitable tenancy agreement.

Never be tempted to make an informal arrangement to let to someone. Friends may be totally trustworthy, but a son, lover or relative might move in with them and then decide to stand on their 'rights', and if there was nothing to show they didn't have those rights you would be stuck with the undesirable relative.

If you find a tenant yourself, ask for references and take them up. An estate agent will do most of the work for you - for a commission. But, if they will be collecting the rent, make sure they are a member of a professional association and that a bonding certificate protects both the tenant's deposit and the rent.

Renting Property
Before renting property, check the terms of the tenancy carefully. Better still, get a lawyer to check them. A few of the possibilities are in Law. Also see what outgoings there will be and check with the rent control office to see whether a fair rent has ever been set for the property, and whether the rent being asked is the same - or at least in proportion, if it was some time ago. Then, get an inventory of everything in the place and check that everything the landlord says is there is there. If it isn't, say so at once.

Council Accommodation
The housing departments of local councils have a certain amount of freedom as to the policies they adopt. You normally have to go to the housing department and apply for a house, and are usually expected to have lived in the area for anything from a week to 5 years depending on the authority.

Some councils *must* put you on the list if you fit the terms of those who are allowed to have council houses. Other councils may refuse to have someone on the list, if they wish. How soon you will get a home will partly depend on your place in the queue and partly on how you score. For example, you might get points for each child, more for a child with a handicap, and so on.

Buying a Council House
Under the 'Right to Buy' scheme a tenant can buy the council house he or she is living in. There is a large discount on the price depending on how long you have lived there, or have been a tenant in any other property in this scheme, such as those belonging to:
- District Councils
- London Borough Councils
- new town development corporations
- non-charitable housing associations

★ The leaflet 'Your Right to Buy Your Home' (from the Citizens' Advice Bureau) gives a long list of other tenancies which would count in your favour.

To buy you must have lived in such a property for at least 2 years and the discount rises in stages, with each year after that to a maximum discount of £35,000.

Tenants of charitable housing associations aren't entitled to buy but they may be able to get help with buying a house or flat on the open market.

For those who can't quite afford to buy there are schemes for part renting - part buying, or a landlord may accept a deferred application. A good option as the price and terms of the sale don't rise while you save up to buy.

Those who want to buy should ask their landlord for a 'Right to Buy Claim Form' (RTB1) and hand it in personally - and get a receipt - or use recorded delivery. It is important to have that date because it sets in train a legal timetable in which the landlord has to make certain responses within a certain time. And if he or she fails to do so it is very much in the tenant's favour.

The steps in purchase are clearly laid out in the DoE booklet.

Buying a Council House You Don't Live In
A few councils are operating schemes in which they sell empty council houses to first time home buyers who live in the borough but *aren't* living in accommodation which entitles them to buy. These properties are sold to those thought to be in greatest need.

Moving From Council Accommodation
One of the more astonishing aspects of bureaucracy is that council tenants must get permission from the council before they can so much as swap houses with

another council tenant. However, since 1984 it has become harder for councils to refuse.

Locatex Bureau (P.O.Box 1, March, Cambs PE15 8HJ Tel: 0354 54050) describes itself as a 'non-profit making exchange bureau for local authority and housing association tenants'. It only deals with exchanges from one area to another, but will arrange 3- and 4-way exchanges as well as straight swaps.

The **Tenants Exchange Scheme** (P.O.Box 170, London SW1P 3PX) is a government-backed system for helping people to move if they live in council, or housing association property. It is purely for those who need to move to similar accommodation in another area for a definite reason, such as to take up a job offer, or be near an elderly relative. In addition to existing council tenants, those high on the waiting list, or with a pressing need, will be considered for this scheme.

Complete one of the forms provided by the Exchange and send it in, so your details can be circulated. Also go the housing department each month and look to see if a likely swap is on the list. If you spot one, write direct to the people concerned. If both you and they favour a swap you must then get written permission to move, from the department from which you rent the accommodation. As bureaucratic wheels grind slowly, it can take a month or two. Surprisingly, nobody has a *right* to move, so give yourself the best possible chance by clearly stating *why* you need to move, on your first application.

Housing Associations

Housing associations form a middle way between private rented property and council housing. Some are totally independent, some are linked to organizations such as MENCAP; and others are essentially co-operatives in which people convert property for their own use. What they all have in common is the fact that they are non-profit making, so rents are relatively low.

Your local CAB should be able to tell you what associations there are in your area. Failing that, **Housing Associations Liaison Project** (HALO) (11a Apollo Place, London SW10 0ET Tel: 01 352 0909) has lists of housing associations all over Britain, and HALO runs a scheme to help people in properties to swop with those in other areas. Directories on housing for the elderly and those with special needs should be in a public library.

SHAC (**The London Housing Aid Centre**), 189a Brompton Road, London SW5 0AR Tel: 01 373 7276. It offers advice and help with any type of housing problem.
Marion Cutting, *A Housing Rights Handbook*, Penguin.
Housing Year Book, Longman - lists all local authority planning departments, statutory and voluntary housing associations, aid and advice centres.

Moving Home

There are those who say the only advice on moving is a four-letter word: don't. But, both professional removers and those who have been much-moved seem to agree that the following points are the ones to remember if you want to emerge victorious.

Moving Everything Yourself
The cheapest option is obviously to move everything yourself. Some car hire companies (in Yellow Pages) not only hire out vans, but also the tea chests and other equipment. But check your insurance - it could prove very expensive in the long run if anything is damaged.

★ To move a long case clock the golden rule is 'weights, pendulum, pendulum, weights'. Which means that to avoid damage, you first remove the weights, then the pendulum - and put them back in reverse order.

Being Removed
Removals firms range from vague hippies with vans and free time, to experts bulging with bladder wrap and a fixed determination to take over totally. The more valuable the goods and the farther you are going, the more expert the removers need to be. Asking an inexperienced firm to negotiate your goods through the complexities of shipping and foreign customs is likely to be more trouble than it's worth.

● The best remover is one recommended by at least one friend who has done a similar move. Or if you have valuables to move, local antique dealers often know the good firms. Failing that, or for overseas moves, use a remover who is a member of The British Association of Removers (BAR) (below). If the remover goes bust while your goods are in transit another member finishes the job without extra charge.
● To move you abroad make sure they will give a door-to-door service. Some only do door-to-port - which can leave your goods standing in some dock.
● Get at least 3 estimates.
● Before getting estimates, list *everything* you want them to move - including the garden tubs, and the things in the loft. Also list everything you *don't* want them to move (whatever you will move yourself, or you've agreed to leave as fixtures and fittings). Then give each firm the same *written* list - if you rely on telling them, it's odds on you'll vary it, so the estimates won't compare.
● Indicate which items will need special treatment, most removals men can't tell Ming from Marks & Spencer's. (But bear in mind the risk of burglary if you do this with a fly-by-night firm.)
● If you are wondering about moving some of it yourself, or packing some things but letting them move them, make out two different lists. Then ask each firm for comparative estimates. But choose the items carefully: insurance won't usually cover anything not packed by the removers.
● Don't be tempted to get a lower estimate by 'forgetting' to tell the companies awkward facts about the new address. It's far better to tell them the worst - whether it's parking problems or low doorways. If you don't they have a right to breach the estimate and charge you more - and by then it's too late to negotiate.

Insurance While Moving
If you have a household policy your valuables are·

usually only insured while in that house. And you can't assume that your goods are automatically covered in transit by the removals firm. Many are only insured for a few pounds *per cubic foot* of space taken up by the goods - regardless of their value.

1 You can extend your household policy but this risks a loading on your policy, in future, if there is damage.
2 You can ask the removers to get insurance quotes, giving them an overall valuation plus a note of items of special value. They usually charge for this, but the charge may be hidden in the premium they quote.

Make sure the insurance covers any time in store or in customs; this may not be automatically included. And check the terms. Confidence in cover for £100,000 could be a touch misplaced if you can only claim up to £200 for *any one item*.

Whom to Notify of Your Move

The following need to be notified before the minimum times given here.

Accounts: in all shops with which you have an account - late payment could cost you interest.
Bank: all banks you have dealings with.
Car registration: write to the Driver Vehicle Licensing Centre, (Swansea SA6 7JL) giving details of your car and registration.
Credit cards: as accounts above.
Dentist: you don't need to deregister.
DHSS National Insurance: write to DHSS Newcastle Central Records Office (Longbenton, Newcastle-upon-Tyne NE98 1YX) giving your full name, date of birth and national insurance number.
DHSS benefits: tell your present office and ask them to notify your new office.
Doctor: deregister if you are moving out of the area.
Electricity board: at least 3 days before, and ask for a reading on the day, and *sign on with the board for your new home*. The electricity will be disconnected, if nobody has signed on as a new user.
Football pools: inform your collector or notify them on the coupon.
Gas board: at least 3 to 4 days' notice that you want the meter read on the day of the move, and notify the gas board at your new address of the day you are taking over. Ask for a reading that day there too.
Hire purchase: notify every company.
Hospital or clinic: if receiving treatment.
Income tax: the address on your tax forms.
Insurance: house, contents, car and yourselves, at least 7 days before or you may not be insured.
Mail: arrange for mail to be forwarded. There is a sliding scale of charges according to how long you wish it to continue. But one fee covers everyone in the family - if the surname is the same.
Mail order: any company you use.
Pensions: ask the Post Office.
Personal giro: ask the Post office.
Professional advisors: accountants, lawyers, stockbrokers.
Rates: departments of both areas.
Schools: as soon as possible.
Standing orders: tell any companies you pay.
Stocks and shares: write to the company registrar of all companies in which you hold shares.
Subscriptions: to magazines, clubs etc.

Telephone: give a week's notice to each end and arrange for the bills to change names on the correct day, and for your new phone to be connected.
Traders: cancel milk papers, etc.
TV licence: ask at the Post Office.
VAT office: if you pay VAT.
Water board: at each end.

Preparing for the Move

You can never do too much too soon. All the little jobs take far longer than might be thought. Throw away everything you don't need to take. Drain the lawn mower, and so on. Also:

- Eat the freezer down - completely, if you can. It is a myth that it should be moved when full: it is not designed to carry the weight. If you leave a small amount pack it round with crumpled newspaper to keep in the cold and mop up the drips. If a freezer has to be stored, prop the door slightly open, as mould will flourish inside if it is not running.
- Find out from the vendors of your new home exactly where everything is - fuse box, water heating, stop cocks. You'll never need a hot bath more than on the day you move.
- Agree whether they will leave essentials like light bulbs.
- Make an exact plan of your new home on graph paper and cut out outlines of the furniture. Then you can tell if something won't fit.
- Allocate each room a letter of the alphabet, and put a matching letter on to every item for each room. Either go ahead and label the doors accordingly or give the removals men a floor plan.
- If goods will be going into store put 'Keep Forward' notices on everything you will need earliest.
- Check the instruction books of appliances. Some need to be secured with special braces and you may need to obtain them.
- If you can leave children and pets elsewhere on moving day do so. Moving can be murder - you don't want to commit it too.

  If you have to move with children in tow it helps to lay in a treat for each child. You won't have time to give them attention, and there is nothing like lack of attention to bring out the worst in a child. So fool them. Pre-record a story on tape for young ones, buy a book or absorbing toy for older ones, and some treat foods so they don't feel left out. Get the television out of the old house last and into the new one first, with a good video or two at the ready - if possible.
- Prepare a separate box with everything for the moving day (loo paper, washing bag, towel, passports, dog food, etc - if they apply) plus tea, coffee, an electric kettle, sugar, UHT milk, plenty of mugs - removals men work best on a constant stream of praise and refreshments. Label this box 'NOT TO BE REMOVED' - and take it with you.

On the Day

The removers should pack everything - unless you arranged otherwise - then unpack it and put it in place.

Check it for damage before they leave and show any damage to the foreman immediately - you have very little come-back otherwise.

★ Before moving out, check the meters and make a note of the reading, just in case the boards don't get to them.

British Association of Removers (BAR), 277 Grays Inn Road, London WC1X 8SY (Tel: 01 837 3088) - can give you the names of removers who are expert on anything, from moving goods to Australia to cosseting the family heirlooms.

Pickfords Removals Ltd, Marketing Department 492 Great Cambridge Road, Enfield, Middlesex EN1 3SA Tel: 01 367 0045 - have free leaflets on most aspects of moving.

DIY

This section covers the basics of do-it-yourself which the average person can easily tackle. It also deals with repairs which any home is likely to need. In the course of this I have tucked in as many tips and short cuts as I possibly could. For it's often the little details that make the difference to doing a job well and easily.

But first, a word of caution. In Great Britain 3 million people a year seek medical aid after accidents in the home, and many die from their injuries. Many more are hurt but deal with it themselves. Women are the most vulnerable, perhaps because they spend more time in the home. The most common cause of accidental death is someone over the age of 75 falling; fire comes second. But they aren't the only people who get injured. Two prime causes of accidents to active adults are:

- failing to use a circuit breaker on jobs which could damage an electric flex
- chemicals catching fire on their own when overheated. These include petrol, oil, paraffin, certain polishes, adhesives and aerosols. Keep such items away from direct heat or sunlight.

Abrasive Papers

People talk about sanding a surface but, strictly speaking, there is no such thing as sandpaper. The real situation is this.

- The sandy-looking paper most of us call sandpaper is 'glasspaper'. It's for smoothing wood, and the grades range from extremely coarse to very fine.
- The black paper, often called 'wet and dry', is coated with silicone carbide. This can be used dry or slightly damped. It is particularly used for smoothing down metal and paint - such as in car body repairs. It leaves a sludgy mess behind which you need to wipe off. There are also sponges coated in silicone carbide which are ideal for shaped surfaces and very good for giving a key to paint.
- Emery paper is also black but is very tough and only used for smoothing metal. Great for rust removal.
- The grey-green flour papers are the finest papers of all. They are used in jewellery making.
- For belt sanders there are cloth-backed abrasives in two weights. X weight, in grades 24 - 320, is the heavier and stronger; J weight, in grades 60 - 400, is more flexible.

Sanding Techniques

The trick is to use finer and finer papers until you have a perfect surface. With a piece of planed wood, for example, you might start with a 50 or 60 glasspaper. Then move to an 80, then a 120 before painting. But if you were going to varnish or polish the wood you would go on to use finer papers still.

> It is never wise to breathe in the particles created by sanding, and a mask should be worn. After using a chemical stripper, the wood dust will have the chemicals in it and very shiny or very old paint may well contain lead.
> It is also advisable to wear goggles. A sander can always dislodge a loose fragment and send it flying into an eye.

If you have to sand by hand wrap the paper round a cork block (DIY shops sell them). This makes sure that a large surface is in contact with whatever you are sanding and the cork has enough give not to press the debris from the paper into the surface below it. A wooden block does just that and may create scratches on the very surface you are trying to smooth.

When choosing an electric sander the same rule applies and the softer the pressure, the smoother the finish you can get, but the more slowly it will work.

★ To unclog a piece of sandpaper put the back of it against the edge of a table and drag the paper to and fro across it - to open the grain.

English Abrasives Ltd (Home Sales Department, Marsh Lane, Tottenham N17 0XA Tel: 01 808 4545) will tell you the nearest stockist of any paper you can't find.

Bath Gap Sealant

Sealing the gap between wall and bath, with one of the silicone rubber sealants, is one of those jobs which look so easy it is tempting to try to do it in an odd moment. Don't. The filler sets very rapidly and you must get the whole job done at once. It also takes considerable care to get a perfect result. First clean the area, scraping out any old filler thoroughly.

Rub the area well with methylated spirits: any traces of soap will stop the filler sticking properly. Then run masking tape along the bath and the wall where you want the edges of the filler to come (unwanted sealant is much harder to remove than you might think). And, if the gap is very big, stuff it with a twist of paper. Or, use an expanding polyurethane filler foam to fill it below the bath level.

Choose a time when you won't be interrupted and have some cling film and some washing-up liquid to hand. If you are interrupted put cling film tightly over the sealant. It hardens by absorbing moisture from the air, so shutting out the air keeps it soft for longer.

Starting at a corner, push, rather than pull, the sealant, evenly in a continuous bead. *The instant* it is all the way round, smooth it to shape with a finger dipped in washing-up liquid (which acts as a smoothing fluid and stops it sticking to your finger), and remove the masking tape *at once*.

> There is a limit to how wide a gap these sealants will fill. Very wide gaps are better covered by a special plastic sealing strip, shaped rather like the curved cornice between a wall and a ceiling. You stick this on with a special waterproof adhesive. Cut the corners at a 45 degree angle (see page 261), butt them perfectly together, and fuse them with a special adhesive, so no water can get through.

Carpet Laying

Provided you can cover the area without having to make seams, carpet laying is rather easy. Standard widths are 3.66 m (12 ft), 4 m (13 ft) and 4.57 m (15 ft). Very little carpet is now made in the old 91 cm (36 in) and 69 cm (27 in) widths, so seams are seldom used.

Tools

To lay a carpet you need:
- Stanley knife
- kneekicker - hireable
- hammer
- staple gun (optional)
- bolster (a tool) - for grip strips only - hireable
- hacksaw - for grip strips only
- gripper strips - if being used
- nails
- double-sided tape - for foam-backed only
- metal strip or carpet to protect it at doorways
- 2.5 cm (1 in) carpet tacks - if tacking it down.

★ Carpet should not be laid over plastic/vinyl tiles. They gather condensation and the carpet will eventually become mouldy and smelly.

Preparing the Floor

The first essential is to have a flat surface to put the carpet on. Concrete must be given a smooth surface as for tiles (page 237). If the surface is already smooth but dusty you can either use the levelling compound to stop the dust or go over the concrete with Unibond. Floorboards must be made level (page 236) or covered with hardboard as for tiling - page 237.)

An amazing amount of dirt and cold comes up through gaps in floorboards, so it's a good idea to fill any big gaps between them. If the gaps are extremely wide you may find soaking twists of brown paper in wallpaper glue and laying them into the gaps is easiest. If you are going to sand the floor you can leave the filler a little proud and sand it smooth.

Under the Underlay

Put a layer of thin cardboard called 'felt paper' on the floor before putting down a foam-backed carpet or rubber underlay. It provides another layer of insulation and means there is no risk of the carpet or underlay sticking to the floor - a nuisance if you want to replace the carpet or take it with you when you move.

Planning the Fixing

Foam-backed carpet can be stuck down with double-sided tape. For non-foam-backed carpet you can turn the edge under and hammer in tacks at intervals. This is cheap and very easy. Or you can fit gripper strips which are thin lengths of wood with nails all tilting at an angle towards the wall. The carpet is then hooked over the nails and held down by them. This sounds easy but, in my experience, is far harder than using tacks.

Seaming

Sewing a seam is tougher on the hands than you'd think possible. Luckily, one seldom needs to do it unless moving a carpet from one room into another and needing to patch odd corners.

Use a curved needle and linen thread, and wear tough leather gloves with a thimble inside. The technique is then to put the two edges right side to right side and oversew them together. Check the tension of your stitches to see they will hold the two edges firmly, but still allow the carpet to open flat.

There are tapes which can be used to hold carpet together, or you can use a strip of hessian and a PVA glue. Many people find these perfectly good, but I personally feel that the only tape which makes a totally satisfactory seam is the one professionals heat weld to the carpet.

Underlay

Foam-backed carpet needs no underlay; all other carpets do. Rubber underlay is considerably better than felt. If you can't afford it you might consider contacting a company that does contract flooring and see if you can buy their offcuts when they do a big job. Good quality rubber underlay can be pieced together like a jigsaw with adhesive carpet tape on the fabric side, and is none the worse for it.

Carpet Repairs

If a carpet has a stain which can't be removed, or a burn, a neat patch may be less noticeable. Unless the carpet has a pattern in it that you want to follow, mark a neat square exactly on the grain of the carpet. Stick a skewer in the centre of this and hold it up off the underlay as you cut an X in the centre of this so you can get your hand in. Hold the carpet up firmly and cut the square out neatly with a Stanley knife. Place the piece on top of an offcut of carpet, match any pattern exactly and cut out the new piece. Push a circle of strong fabric through the hole and smooth it out under it. Apply carpet adhesive to either the carpet or the fabric - whichever is easier. Press the carpet on to it. Put adhesive on the patch and press it into place.

★ It's a good idea to keep any decent-sized pieces of waste carpet. If you stain the carpet in the room you can test stain removal methods on them. You can also use them to patch the carpet if necessary. And if there is an area which gets a tremendous amount of wear or dirt, putting a section of the same carpet down as a mat is far less intrusive than a mat of a totally different sort. If you want to do this, coat the back with PVA adhesive to stop the edges fraying.

Carpet Tiles
Carpet tiles are laid on a plain smooth surface just like vinyl tiles (page 236), and the planning and laying are organized in the same way. They usually have the non-slip direction of each tile shown on the back. If so they should be laid so the arrow alternately points forwards and sideways. This stops them gradually creeping if the wear is more in one direction than another.

Rugs
If the rugs are on top of a carpet, you can stop them curling up by putting self-adhesive velcro on the corners of the underside - using the hooked half of the velcro.

The best way to stop a rug sliding is to put a rubber underlay under it, or you can buy anti-slip strips to put on the back of rugs. Alternatively, use the foam type of stick-on draught excluder or - on a rug of no value - coat the back with a PVA adhesive (letting it dry very well before putting the rug on the floor). If the corners turn up on a hard floor use a double-sided tape at each corner.

China Repairs
Broken china and glass can easily be repaired with epoxy resin such as Araldite. The snag is that the resin turns yellow, so no amount of care can stop a yellow line showing on glass. For earthenware which is not going to be used and washed up - such as a display plate - it is better to use Durafix or Evostick Resin W. Araldite can run into the body of the earthenware and create a stain.

When using Araldite the greatest possible care must be taken to leave no glue on the surface, and to prevent it getting on gilding or lustreware.

For a really good result have everything to hand before starting. First try matching the pieces together to see how they fit. Make sure that the surfaces are totally free from grease by wiping them with acetone, or methylated spirits. Let this dry. Then piece the object together using the sharpened end of a matchstick to apply no more glue than will *just* cover the surfaces. But if some does ooze, carefully wipe it off with a little methylated spirits while it is wet, without pushing the pieces out of true.

If a small piece is missing it can be rebuilt by mixing a little kaolin powder (from a chemist) into the Araldite or adding a suitable powdered clay to the glue for pottery or earthenware. This can even be tinted to match with ground artists' pigments, but these are expensive. Powder colour will work at first but the colour will slowly change over time.

The firmest way to hold the pieces in place is with gummed brown paper tape: it tightens as it dries, and by moistening it you can take it off without tugging at the break.

While it dries the object must be very well supported. Use anything which works - such as plasticine or clay. You can stand a plate on its edge in a biscuit box of moist sand - with the mended section uppermost. Cups and bowls are usually best resting on their rims.

When the glue is firm but not totally hard, wet and remove the tape, pare off any surplus glue with a razor blade, and wipe it clean with methylated spirits or acetone, *without* letting any run into the joint.

There are, of course, special china mending cements. The ceramics conservation unit of a major museum recommends Ablebond (from Frank Joel, page 171). This is very strong but hard to use. If you want advice on mending fine china or other objects invisibly, the restoration departments of museums are usually extremely helpful.

> *The white of an egg, well beaten with quicklime, and a small quantity of very old cheese, forms an excellent substitute for cement, when wanted in a hurry, either for broken china or old ornamental glassware.*
>
> Enquire Within, 1856

The Ceramic and Glass Conservation Group (c/o **The United Kingdom Institute for Conservation,** 37 Upper Addison Gardens, London W14 8AJ Tel: 01 603 5643) - answers queries; lectures, demonstrations, newsletter, booklists.
Judith Larney, *Restoring Ceramics*, Barrie and Jenkins
Nigel Williams, *Porcelain Repair and Restoration*, Colonnade/British Museum Publications

Door Problems

Door Trimming
If a door has to be shortened to fit over new flooring take it off its hinges. Turn it upside down, rest it on the flooring, upright against the frame, and mark the amount it stands above the lintel. Most people then mark a line so the door will be about 0.5 cm (¼ in) shorter, to allow for the fact that the weight of the door will have pressed a carpet down. But on a hard floor where draughts are a problem you may want simply to cut to the door side of the line.

If you have any doubt about your ability to keep the saw totally vertical - so both sides of the door are cut to the same amount - clamp a length of thick wood along the line on the upper side of the door. Then keep your saw against it. For tips when sawing (especially veneer) see page 261.

If you miscalculate and a door is too long, an electric sander is the best solution. Failing that, hang the door, put a sheet of sandpaper under the point which is too long and swing the door to and fro over it while standing on the ends of the sandpaper. Gradually raise the sandpaper by putting newspaper underneath. Not quick, but at least it has a better chance of hitting the spot than hand sanding with the door off.

Squeaking Hinges
Most squeaking hinges can be cured by applying powdered graphite (from locksmiths), penetrating oil

or thick washing-up liquid. Suit the lubricant to the type of door. (Graphite is also a safe cure for squeaking piano pedals.)

Sticking Doors
Doors will stick when they expand in wet weather or when coats of paint build up and enlarge them. But first check the hinges, a loose screw can let the door lean away from the lintel and stick on the other side. If excess paint has built up the paint will usually be scratched where the door scrapes. The place can then be sanded down, to allow room for fresh coats of paint.

Sliding Doors which Fall Out
If a hardboard sliding door falls out it is usually because the lower edge has worn down and allowed the door to drop low enough to fall out of the upper rail. The solution is to glue used matchsticks at intervals along the bottom of the door with wood glue. I have sliding doors which have run perfectly on them for 6 years, so it's not just a temporary solution.

Drawers which Stick
A drawer which sticks can usually be cured by rubbing a candle or a cake of soap underneath its runners. If this doesn't cure the problem the wood may have swollen at the sides and this area needs sanding down until the drawer enters cleanly.

Electric Appliances

On the whole, electric appliances are best left to experts. However, the law of nuisance dictates that they only break down when you have the greatest possible need for them. And if, for example, the video fails on Christmas Eve you may be less worried by the gamble of damaging it than by the prospect of the entire family fighting over which film to watch.

Improving Radio and Television Reception
The insides of radios and televisions are not designed for DIY and it is safest to leave them alone. However, if reception is poor there may be quite a bit you can do without touching the inside.

The Department of Trade and Industry (see Organizations) has a booklet 'How to Improve Television and Radio Reception' and the BBC produces a leaflet on how to get the best out of stereo radio.

> If you have pets which sit on the television, or if you ever put anything on it, or above it, which might shed leaves, petals or fluff (especially a Christmas tree), the debris which gets down through the little slits could well cause reception problems. It could also cause a fire. The television should be cleaned out regularly by a professional and nothing which sheds should sit on it.

> WARNING: Any DIY on an electric appliance is risky. You might accidentally cause expensive damage, and its guarantee may cease to be valid. Only attempt repairs if these are risks you are prepared to take.

Refrigerator Door Seals
If the seal ceases to work on a freezer or refrigerator it is usually extremely easy to replace it yourself. Most seals are held in place with a few cross head screws and the manufacturer's service centre should be able to tell you whether there are any snags and be able to post you a new seal if there aren't.

Tape Recorder Troubles
Three faults commonly afflict tape recorders: crackle on the tape, unclear recording and play back, and the tape getting tangled in the machine. Crackle could be a duff, or ancient, tape or a loose microphone lead at the time of recording. You can test this by making a recording and wiggling the lead. A new cable, or a professional repair, should cure it.

Fuzzy sound is likely to be caused by dirty heads. Clean the heads with head cleaner or methylated spirits on a clean lint-free rag, *without* letting any meths get on other parts of the machine.

BEFORE WORKING ON THE INSIDE OF A TAPE RECORDER UNPLUG IT FROM THE ELECTRICITY SUPPLY.

If a tape gets wound into the works of a machine the chances are that it's a 120-minute tape. These tapes are much thinner than the others, as so much more has to be packed into the cassette, and they tend to cause this problem. (This makes them a bad buy.) Their thinness also means that if they do get tangled you have to be very careful or bits will break off and stay in the machine. Instead of tugging hard at the tape, work in light jerks teasing and wiggling it into unwinding without breaking. Often it helps to use tweezers.

Video Failure

BEFORE YOU DO ANYTHING UNPLUG BOTH MAINS AND VIDEO LEADS INCLUDING THE CONNECTION VIA THE TELEVISION.

If playing back a video gives a very poor picture or nothing but white crackle on the screen the head may need cleaning.

If you have the type of video in which a section rises up to take the tape, remove the cover to this small section (it's usually held on with a couple of screws). If the video isn't of this design, you may need to remove the whole top. The head is a metal disk with a rim the depth of a video tape. Rub the edge of this head with a freshly laundered handkerchief, slightly dampened with methylated spirits until it looks spotless, without touching that part with your fingers - finger oils could make the picture worse. Even if the rim doesn't look dirty give this treatment a try. Dirt which is invisible to the naked eye can make a difference. But *don't* be tempted to rub it with anything rougher than the cloth. A scratched head would be a useless head. Then replace the cover and try it.

> It is important to use a clean cloth, *not* tissue or cotton wool because if tiny fragments came off and got stuck in the machine they could do damage.

Washing Machine Troubles
There are few things more annoying than a washing machine failing with a full load locked inside it. But the solution could be quite simple. Many modern washing machines have a kind of mechanical 'appendix' for catching things which shouldn't have been in the machine in the first place. When this catches something the machine may automatically switch off, fail to empty, overflow or whatever its whim is. This appendix is usually in the front of the very bottom of the machine, often behind a slim panel which can be opened, provided you have absolutely no fingernails or don't mind losing those you do have.

First check your instruction book carefully to see if your machine has such a device. If it has, there should be instructions on exactly how to get at it and free the offending object. The machine will then work again.

If the machine has simply gone off, check the fuse in the plug and the fuse on the fuse board before calling out the repair company.

Washing-Up Machine Troubles
If a dishwasher ceases to wash well there may be trouble with its rotary arms. A common problem is something caught under them so they can't rotate on the central pillar. Try wiggling them. They may come free. If that isn't the problem they may be dirty inside or the holes may be blocked. If not, you need to remove them. The instruction book may tell you how. If it doesn't, only you can tell whether you want to take the risks involved in working on the machine without the maker's blessing.

If you want to go ahead, there is often a screw top to the pillar which unscrews in the reverse direction to a normal screw. Or there may be a metal clip which is sometimes very hard indeed to replace.

If water leaks from under a dishwasher or washing machine it is always worth pulling it out and checking the hose. Often it is only held on with a screw-up ring and a new hose can easily be put on. With call-out charges as high as they are, this is money well saved.

Electrical Work

Extending a Flex
The best way to make a flex longer is to remove it entirely and fit a new flex the right length. But if you need to make a temporary extension, the only safe way to do it is with a flex connector. This has metal connectors, into which you screw the flexes, within a

plastic container which insulates them. The important point when wiring it is that the blue wire *must* lead directly to the blue wire and the brown wire lead directly to the brown one. You should also use the same type of flex at both sides of the junction.

> TO JOIN FLEXES WITHOUT USING A PROPER FLEX CONNECTOR IS TO INVITE A FIRE. To put the joined flexes under a rug or mat is doubly dangerous.

Fuses
There are fuses inside square-pinned plugs and on the fuse board of the house. If a single electric appliance fails the first thing to check is whether the plug has fused. This is just a matter of unscrewing the central screw in the plug to open it, prising out the oblong fuse and replacing it with another.

Use the fuse recommended by the maker of the appliance. Failing that, there is no danger in using 13 amp fuses for everything, and you can certainly do so if you want to. *But* the whole role of a fuse is to act as a buffer when things aren't quite right. If you have a 5 amp stereo, and put a 13 amp fuse in its plug it will work perfectly - but if there is a power surge (which can happen) the 13 amp fuse fails to block it and the stereo could be damaged. But a 5 amp fuse would break, cutting off the electricity and the stereo would be safe. So using the right fuse for the appliance can be a useful protection.

The Electricity Council says that the easy rule is to use a 3 amp fuse for all appliances below 700 watts - the wattage is given on the back of any appliance. However, some appliances, such as televisions, create a brief power surge as they are switched on and a low amp fuse may fail rapidly. For them a 13 amp is more practical.

> Electric blankets *must* be fitted with the fuse recommended by the manufacturer (usually 3 amp) *not* with a 13 amp fuse.

★ If you replace a fuse and the appliance still doesn't work check the fuse by putting it in the plug for a light and seeing if the light works with it in. Fuses can be duff.

Fuses on the Consumer Unit (Fuseboard)
If several lights or sockets cease to work a main fuse has probably gone. The solution will be found on the main fuseboard, which is usually near the meter and probably in the garage, or a cupboard of some sort. There are three types of fuseboard:
- circuit breakers with either buttons or switches
- cartridge fuses - for which you need cartridges of the right amps
- fuses taking fuse wire - for which you need the correct fuse wire.

WARNING: Electricity can kill. Always turn supply off at the mains before doing any electrical work.

Circuit Breakers

The trend is towards circuit breakers. The great thing about them is that to restore the electricity you simply TURN OFF THE FUSEBOARD, press the button which has snapped out, or switch a switch from off to on, CLOSE THE COVER and SWITCH THE BOARD ON again. (For safety it is important to stick to this order.) If it immediately switches off again there is an electrical fault which must be put right.

In addition to the ordinary circuit breakers, some homes now have what are called RCDs (residual current devices). These switch off the current the instant there is an imbalance between the live and neutral wires anywhere on the circuit. This could save your life. So, if a house is being rewired it will be safer if you ask for a circuit-breaker-style of board with an RCD. But get expert advice on its fitting.

> If you don't have this type of board use a plug-in circuit breaker for all outdoor jobs and any which could cut a flex.

Repairing Cartridge Fuses and Wired Fuses

FIRST SWITCH THE FUSEBOARD OFF. Some boards seem to have several switches, on and around them. Switch them *all* to off and you won't go wrong.

The fuses need to be pulled out of the board to check them, and they can be devils to get out. They may be colour-coded which should give you a clue which to look at.

5 amp - white - will be for lighting circuits
15 amp - blue - will be for an immersion heater
30 amp - red - will be for the ring circuit of the main sockets and cooker or shower
45 amp - green - will be for the cooker or high-powered shower

Cartridges are easy to replace but when these blow they don't show it - and it takes a special meter or continuity tester to check them. To find the culprit try a new cartridge in each fuse in turn, switching the board back on and checking whether things are working again after each one. Start with the fuses with the most likely amp. To replace the fuse you simply unscrew the fuse carrier, fit the new fuse and screw it up again firmly. DON'T FORGET TO CLOSE ANY COVER BEFORE SWITCHING ON AND TO SWITCH OFF THE FUSEBOARD AFTER EACH CHECK.

On the oldest kind of fuse a wire runs either across the top, or through a little ceramic channel down the centre and is held by a screw at either end. Look for a fuse in which this wire is broken. Then unscrew one screw to release the old wire. Wind a new wire of the CORRECT AMP (the amps are marked on the cards of wire and on the back of the fuses or on the board) round the screw and screw it in. Thread the wire from one screw to the other, wind it round the second screw and screw it in firmly - without making the wire too taut. Replace the fuse. CLOSE THE COVER TO THE BOARD BEFORE SWITCHING ON.

NEVER mend a fuse with anything other than wire of the right ampage. Using heavier wire allows the cables in the house to overheat. More than one family has been burnt to death that way.

A blown fuse can be a warning. If a fuse blows again the moment you mend it there is a serious fault. Try to remember which appliance you switched on just before it blew the first time. Unplug it and see if this solves the problem. Even if the fuse doesn't blow immediately it's a good idea to find out why it blew. Are you running too many appliances off a single socket and overloading it? Is the wiring in a plug or fitting causing a spark? Fires are caused that way. If any fuse blows twice in a short period call an electrician: it is cheaper than a burnt out home.

★ Many fuseboards, infuriatingly, give no indication of which fuse belongs to which part of the circuit. Having found the culprit write a label saying which lights or points that one belongs to and stick it on the fuse box above that fuse.

Flexes and Cables

Unless you are a competent electrician it is safest to leave the hidden cables alone and confine yourself to the flexes and fittings which show on the room-side of the wall.

All flexes look much the same and it's tempting to think that the small differences don't matter much. They do. It can be dangerous to use the wrong flex for the job.

Choosing the Right Insulation on a Flex

The safety of a flex depends on its being insulated correctly for the job. If a flex will be taking a lot of wear it is safer to use a heavier flex than the appliance demands. The main types of insulation are these.

Parallel twin PVC	clocks
Light duty PVC	televisions, food mixers, table lamps, hairdryers, refrigerators
Light duty PVC (85°C)	hanging lights
Ordinary duty PVC	washing machines, tumble dryers, kettles, slow cookers
Rubber (60°C)	plate warmers or electric frying pans etc
Rubber with braid outside	irons, toasters, some room heaters
High temperature rubber 80°C	immersion heaters, storage heaters

WARNING: Electricity can kill. Always turn supply off at the mains before doing any electrical work.

If an appliance has had a 3-core flex the replacement flex *must* also be 3-core. 2-core flexes should only be used when the makers say they are correct.

★ A 0·5² mm flex for a hanging light will hold up to 2 kg (4lb 6oz).

Rule 1	Rule 2
You can safely put a 3-pin plug on a flex which has only 2 wires.	It is *not* safe to put a 2-pin plug on a flex with 3 wires

Wiring a Plug

Plugs are extremely easy to wire provided you do it *exactly* like this. The instructions are for a standard 13 amp plug. But the basic method and position of the wires is just the same for any 3-pin plug. But do bear the following rules in mind.

Colours of Wires and What They Mean

	Live	Neutral	Earth
EEC and modern British appliances	brown	light blue	green and yellow
Major cables and old British appliances	red	black	green
Appliances in America	any colour	white or grey	green

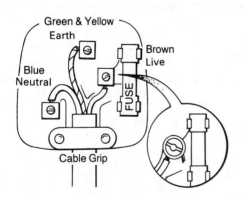

Green & Yellow Earth
Brown Live
Blue Neutral
FUSE
Cable Grip

The correct wiring is shown in the illustration. The easy way to remember which wire goes where was taught me years ago by an electrician. With the flex towards you brown and red - which both have the letter R in - go to the Right. Blue and black - which both have the letter L in go to the Left. And green for grass grows up. Alas, it doesn't work for American colours.

If there is no green or green/yellow wire just put the other wires in their correct places and make sure the empty screw for the earth wire is screwed in firmly so it won't fall out, or it could fuse the plug.

To wire a plug you need a screwdriver and something to strip the wires. Wire strippers are easiest, but nail scissors or a sharp blade will do, if used carefully.

1 Undo the large screw in the centre which holds it together, and remove the back.
2 Undo the two screws which hold the small bar at the bottom in place. Sometimes there is a V-shape in plastic instead.
3 Tuck the flex under the bar and decide how much of its outer coating you must cut off (if it isn't already stripped) to let the inner wires reach the 3 contact points with ½ cm to spare. Remember the outer coat of the flex *must* be under the bar, so the flex can be held firmly in place.
4 Cut back the flex coating to the point you have marked, without cutting into the coating of the inner wires.
5 Cut the core wires so they are ½ cm longer than they need to be to reach their contact point and strip about 1.2 cm (½ in) of coating off the end of each. Then twist the little wires inside neatly together.
6a If the wires are to be inserted into holes in the pins fold the bare section neatly in half and squeeze it to a compact end - this holds firmly. Loosen the screws in the pins, and insert the wires, placing the colours exactly as illustrated. (You may have to take the fuse out to get at one. Just push it out of its clip with a screwdriver.) Tighten the screws to hold each wire firmly.
6b On some plugs the wire is put between two brass discs held down with a screw. For this type don't fold the ends but coil each into a little circle, so the screw will go through the centre with the discs holding it down firmly all round.

Finally, when the wires are in place, screw the grip firmly down over the flex. Check that the fuse is correct. Then screw the back on.

Flooring

Floor Tiles

The following method is for laying cork or vinyl tiles. For ceramic tiles see page 259.

Preparing a Wood Floor

To lay cork or vinyl tiles you need a perfectly flat surface so lay sheets of hardboard on to the boards and then lay the tiles on top. Tiles shouldn't be laid on new boards as there will be movement while they settle down. Old boards need to be made flat by knocking down any protruding nails and sanding down any edges that stand up, or they may buckle strangely as the weather changes. To condition hardboard brush the rough side over with about ½ l (1 pt) water for every 4 sq m (approx 4 sq yds) and leave it for about 5 days in the room where it will be used.

WARNING: Electricity can kill. Always turn supply off at the mains before doing any electrical work.

When you have done this nail the board to the floor, rough side up, cutting it carefully to shape (see ★) with a fine saw to fit exactly round obstacles like radiator pipes. (If it only fits roughly the tiles have no support at the gaps and may break off with wear, leaving an ugly hole and a dirt trap.) Nail the boards down firmly but not too hard or they will be pulled down into dips as they warp with age.

> If you are laying very thin vinyl tiles it may be better to put the hardboard smooth side up or the roughness will eventually show through the tiles.

★ To cut hardboard to shape easily cut a pattern of the floor in newspaper, lay this on the board, mark round it and cut the hardboard to shape.

Preparing a Concrete Floor

Few concrete floors are perfectly flat: the answer is to cover the floor with a self-levelling compound, but this is one thing I haven't tried myself. You mix it according to directions, pour it on the floor, let it find its own level and spread it gently with a plasterer's trowel so it covers the entire area. Then let it set and dry completely (usually 24 hours).

Marking the Tile Positions

Mark the mid-point on each wall, at skirting level. Stretch cotton twine from side to side of the room between each pair of marks, and nail it into the floor or skirting base at the mid-points on the wall. Check with the corner of a newspaper that the strings cross at a perfect right angle (square corner). If necessary, adjust them until they do. Rub chalk along the underside of each string, lift and ping the string against the floor to leave a straight chalk mark.

Place a row of glueless tiles from the string to the wall. If a gap of less than 6 cm (2½ in) is left you will have a fiddly border of small pieces at both sides of the room. Adjust the position of the string and place a line of loose tiles right across the room and check you haven't created an annoying border on the other side of the room either. Repeat in the other direction.

Laying the Tiles

Start tiling from where the strings cross. If the tiles aren't ready-glued spread the recommended adhesive for the tiles evenly over about a square metre (yard) of floor. Put the first tile in place, with its two sides exactly against the angles of the chalk line. Butt the next one *exactly* against it, with no gap at all, and one edge against the line - lowering it into place on the glue, not sliding it. Repeat, working away from the centre in each direction.

The easy way to cut part tiles for the edge is to place a tile *exactly* on top of the last whole tile. Put another tile partly on top of it but with its edge resting against the skirting. Hold the stack firmly and mark the line of the edge of the top tile on the one under it. Cut the

tile along the line with a Stanley knife (it helps to have a block of wood to cut on). Then glue it in place against the wall.

When tiles have to be fitted round awkward shapes either use a profile gauge (from an ironmonger) or fit the corner of a newspaper in the angle formed by the laid tiles and slash and cut it until it is exactly the shape the tile needs to be. Place this on the tile, mark the outline, and cut it out. For safety put an X on the upper side of the paper to avoid turning it over by accident.

Finishing Off

Vinyl tiles need no sealant, and most cork tiles are sold with a polyurethane coating. However, those that have no coating need to be sealed. First, let the adhesive dry throughly. Then make any edges and corners totally flat with fine glasspaper. Wipe the floor over with white spirit to remove the dust. Apply 3 coats of polyurethane varnish, according to instructions.

Replacing Damaged Tiles

The golden rule when replacing tiles is *never* to lever a tile out by the edge. As most tiles are stuck down with either a bitumen or rubber solution there's a good chance that heat will soften the glue. So put a piece of kitchen foil over the tile and iron it with a hot iron, *giving plenty of time for the heat to penetrate*. While it's still hot stick something sharp into the middle of the tile, and see if you can lever it up by the centre. Normally a tile will come out quite easily. If it won't come up remove it with a hammer and chisel. Work from the centre out to the edges, being careful not to damage the surface under the tile. Make the surface smooth and clean. Spread glue on a replacement tile, and press it into place. Varnish when dry, if necessary.

Hardwood Flooring

The square sections of hardwood which imitate parquet are usually called wood mosaic panelling and are made in 46 cm (18 in) squares. They are laid very much like vinyl tiles (page 236). Use graph paper to work out exactly how you will place them for minimum wastage. But do buy enough, on another batch the wood could look slightly different.

The floor surface needs exactly the same preparation, and marking up as for vinyl tiles. But the wood squares are much harder to cut than the vinyl, so position the strings so that on two sides of the room the sections come exactly to the edge, leaving a 12 mm (½ in) expansion gap at each edge to allow the wood to move. So cut yourself a strip of wood 12 mm (½ in) thick, and place this against the wall when fixing the squares nearest the edge.

Use a fairly fine toothed tenon saw (page 261) to cut the wood and a bitumen adhesive to stick it down. If you mark it with bitumen remove it *at once* with white spirit.

The small gap all round the room is then filled with a strip of cork. The doorway needs to be finished with a threshold strip of matching wood, which can be shaped to come level with the flooring in the next room.

Before the bitumen is completely dry, check the floor for any edges that stand up. Place a wood block over them and hammer it to press them down. Let the flooring dry completely. If necessary, sand any corners or edges that aren't perfectly smooth. Remove the dust, wipe down with white spirit and varnish with a polyurethane varnish made for floors.

There's no need to rip off an existing skirting. You can buy lengths of small in-curving beading - rather like a plain ceiling cornice - which can be put up against the skirting on top of the edge of the parquet to hide any small gaps. It's a good idea to prime and undercoat this before fixing it. And if the wood is unvarnished give it all its coats of polyurethane varnish before you fix this beading.

Sheet Flooring

Buying

Most sheet flooring today is vinyl and the choice is between the flat and the cushioned kinds, but there are no standard widths for either. The cushioned kind is softer to walk on but it will become dented if you put heavy furniture on it - such as a kitchen table. It also has a fairly short life. Flat hard vinyl lasts longer.

Sheet flooring will wear quickly if the floor under it is uneven. So prepare the floor as for laying floor tiles (page 236). Then, if the flooring is to be loose laid, cover the floor with felt paper, leaving a bare margin.

Meanwhile leave the flooring in a warm room to relax - cold sheet flooring may crack as you unroll it. Plan how to lay the flooring to avoid the seams being at the door or anywhere else which gets a lot of wear. You also need to avoid having a narrow strip of flooring which will lie badly. (A sketch of the room to scale, on graph paper, can help.)

Laying Sheet Flooring

A lot of the vinyl flooring now on the market is designed to be laid loose and stay flat. This makes it very easy to lay. Check the measurements of the room in several places - few rooms are perfectly even. Take the longest measurement and cut the flooring 10 cm (4 in) longer. If you are laying more than one sheet make sure you cut the lengths so any pattern will match.

Lay the flooring in place, with one edge nicely against the wall or fittings. Lay the next length overlapping. Vinyl is inclined to shrink slightly, and linoleum stretches. So leave it just like that for a few weeks - you can walk on it meanwhile.

When it's ready to trim start by getting rid of the overlap. The pattern may be one which needs to match exactly, in which case it is best to seam it edge to edge and cut the excess off at the outside of the room. Other patterns will only match if you overlap and cut them.

To cut an overlap, line up the two layers so the pattern will match at the seam if you cut through both layers. Hold it firmly in position with plenty of masking tape. Double check that the pattern hasn't shifted out of true and that the flooring still reaches the edges of the room. Try to choose a cutting line where the design

will hide the seam. Then cut through both layers with a Stanley knife against a long steel rule.

Having cut the seam, use one side of strong double-sided tape, or whatever tape the manufacturer recommends, underneath to hold the two sections together. Fix it to one half, then place the other carefully on top, making sure the seam is closed tightly.

Next, trim off the surplus at the edges. If the flooring is flexible you can simply press it into the angle of the wall with a metal rule and cut along it with a knife. Where it has to go round bends cut lots of slashes from the edge of the flooring down towards the floor. This allows it to take on the shape - but be careful not to cut too far. If the flooring is harder have a ready-made newspaper pattern of the room to place on top of it and cut round.

Start by cutting the flooring to length or width - whichever has the least complicated outline - measuring and cutting carefully and allowing a little extra on the second edge. Then trim off the excess - when you are sure it really isn't needed. For this, hump the flooring up in the middle of the room. Finally, use a tube of seam sealant to close seam entirely and make sure there is no trap for dirt or water.

Most flooring will lie perfectly smooth and unmoving, but it is even better to fix it under the edges with double-sided tape, and sheet flooring which needs to be stuck down can now be fixed with the recommended adhesive.

★ Keep off-cuts in case you need them for repairs or to test stain removal methods.

Repairs to Soft Vinyl Flooring

Scratches, dents and cigarette burns are the most common damage. On soft flooring there is nothing you can do about any of them. The best repair is to cut out a section of floor along any strong lines in the pattern - very easy with a tiled pattern. Cut a matching section from your offcuts and stick it in place with flooring tape on the back, then seal it with seam sealant.

Repairs to Hard Vinyl Flooring

Major damage to a harder sheet flooring can be repaired in the same way, but it may not hold so well, and on a plain floor the repair may show more than the mark.

Burns can be made less noticeable by rubbing them with fine wire wool until the brown section vanishes - though this leaves a dip.

Scratches which show up pale against darker plastic can be toned down with shoe polish, but a better method can be to melt a candle and children's wax crayons together to get the right colour, then drip this into the dip and smooth it off. Make the dent spotlessly clean and, having dropped in the wax, smooth it with a finger while still hot and use a blade or wire wool to make it perfectly level. Wax fillings I inserted are still invisible after five years of heavy wear.

Glass Buying

The cheapest place to buy glass is usually a specialist glass merchant (listed under Glazier in the Yellow

Pages). The standard sizes are 3 mm, 4 mm, 5 mm, 6 mm and 10 mm. On small windows 4 mm is enough but if the panes are large or very exposed 6 mm or even 10 mm would be better. And glass which is low or where someone might easily break it should be safety glass.

Any glass merchant will cut glass to size for you, but you can cut it in just the same way as a glazed tile (page 258), and if a small amount has to be removed from an edge it can be broken off with pliers after the glass has been scored.

Locks

Maintenance
The best substance for keeping locks, bolts and everything else of that sort running smoothly is an annual dose of powdered graphite from a locksmith. This may well loosen a jammed lock.

Oil should not be used on locks because it attracts and holds dust, and this will jam the lock. However, it is sometimes impossible to get the graphite into a lock - for example, if a car door is jammed. In this case use penetrating oil which is graphite suspended in fine oil. It does, however, carry the same risk of dust collection as any other oil.

Changing a Rim Lock
If you have a rim (surface mounted) lock it is very easy to change it yourself. The vital thing is to remove the lock and take it to the shop with you. Then you can be certain the new lock will fit in the same holes. The other important point is that many of these locks have a connecting bar which has to be cut to length for the thickness of each door. This is the only part of installing a new lock which needs a special tool. But, if you have the old lock with you to show the correct length, ask the shop to do this for you.

To remove the lock simply unscrew every screw you can see and remove them all. Sometimes they may be very long and act almost like bolts within the lock, so they may take a little pulling out. Putting in the new lock is simply a matter of screwing them in again. However, the connecting bar often has to be set at a particular angle if the lock has a deadlock system. So check the instructions on this.

★ Don't throw the old lock away, put it in a bag with all its keys. Next time you lose your key and feel a burglar could use it you simply put the original lock back again - and so on, *ad nauseam.*

Nails and Nailing
There is a lot more to nails than appears at first sight. The range of shapes and sizes is extraordinary and using the right one for the job can make it far easier to get good results.

Pick a hammer with the right weight of head for the job - and for you. The heavier the nail, and the tougher the surface, the heavier the head. Strictly speaking, different shapes of hammer are meant for different jobs, getting the weight right matters more than the shape. On wood use the finest nails which will hold it, and

place oval ones so the oval runs the length of the grain, to avoid splitting.

When joining two pieces of wood together the nail needs to be 3 to 4 times as long as the depth of the upper wood. There is always a risk of splitting the grain if nailing near the end of a plank or if two nails are placed in a line along the same grain. If necessary, near the end of a piece of wood, drill a hole, slightly smaller than the nail, before driving it in.

Nailing down into the end grain of wood is largely a waste of time. If a proper joint can't be made use plenty of good wood glue (the end grain also absorbs glue) and then use fine joinery nails to hold the glued sections firmly in place.

★ To insert a short nail without hammering your fingers hold it with tweezers or put Blu-tack, putty, clay or chewing gum round it.

★ To avoid denting the wood if you miss, push the nail through a piece of cardboard (corrugated is good). Tear it off before the final - careful - blow.

Removing Nails
You can remove a nail with the split end of a claw hammer, or with pincers, and tacks can be lifted with a tack lifter (a V-shaped notch sometimes found at the end of other tools). The most powerful of these is the hammer but the pincers are far better for getting a grip on a tricky nail. Both are used with a rolling movement, not by pulling upwards. To protect the surface from denting by either tool, slip a wallpaper scraper under them before levering.

PAINTING AND PAPERING

Painting

With painting, as with anything else, the right tool for the job makes a great difference.
- Rollers are fastest but bad for gloss. They don't leave as smooth a surface as pads or brushes, and foam rollers tend to spray paint around but are good on textured surfaces: the deeper the pattern, the deeper should be the pile of the roller.
- A large paint pad covers the area rather faster than a brush and leaves a better surface than most rollers.
- A 10 cm (4 in) brush is slowest but easiest to clean, and produces the most reliable finish. You will probably need one to get into awkward corners anyway.
- Spray guns can be hired. They are very quick in a bare room and good for awkward shapes like louvred doors but they can clog and splutter, inject the skin with paint dangerously, and the fiddle of thinning the paint and cleaning the spray eats into the time you save.
- It takes skill to get a good result. And, unless you have a very large area to cover in an empty house it is hardly worth using one, but wear a face mask and have plenty of fresh air in the room, if you do.

★ Tie a piece of string across the paint tin from handle to handle. Then you can wipe off surplus paint without getting the rim clogged up.

Awkward Places
- A very small radiator roller is the easiest way to paint the wall behind the radiator.
- A roller with an extension handle is the easiest way to cope with a ceiling which is out of reach.
- A large paint pad firmly anchored to a broom handle will paint high walls you can't otherwise reach; it will also get into corners where the roller can't go.
- With care you can use the long-handled radiator brush to do the angle between ceiling and wall which rollers and pads can't handle.

Skirtings
The important tool here is called George. This is a useful curved piece of metal with which you can shield the flooring while painting the very bottom of the skirting.

★ Choose professional quality paint brushes with split ends to the bristles; they produce a smoother finish.

Cleaning Brushes, Rollers and Pads
Brushes used with water-based paints should be washed *immediately* after use - the paint can dry rapidly. *Don't* leave them in deep water, or when the wood dries the bristles will be loose and shed all over your paint.

After being used for oil-based paints, brushes need cleaning in white spirit, turpentine or turpentine substitute, paraffin or brush cleaner. Once clean a brush should be washed in soapy water, rinsed well and dried. Then it should be left to dry completely with a piece of paper wrapped round the bristles and held with a rubber band to hold the bristles in line.

If a brush becomes hard the commercial brush restorers will do a very good job of cleaning it if you give them time.

★ To avoid bristles becoming bent through brushes standing on them drill a hole through the wide part of the brush handle when you buy it. You can then stick a skewer through the hole and hang the brush in the jar.
★ If you don't want to clean brushes used for oil-based paints because you'll use them next day, put a few drops of white spirit in a polythene bag, pop the brushes in and close the bag tightly round the handle.

Rollers hold a lot of paint, so roll as much as possible out on newspaper. Dismantle the roller and remove the sleeve, wash out water-based paints as for a brush. Oil-based paints are most easily cleaned out in a strong polythene bag with some white spirit. In case it dries stiff, put the cleaned sleeve back on and let it dry on the roller.

Paint pads can be cleaned like brushes but don't leave them soaking in spirit; if you do they may fall off their handles.

Many of the the chemicals used in DIY, such as white spirit and methylated spirits, can set up severe allergic skin reactions in some people. It is not unusual for someone to use these chemicals for years without trouble and then become sensitive to them. Unfortunately, the skin trouble may persist for a long time and even be permanent. Wear protective gloves when using any solvents and have plenty of fresh air so the fumes are not breathed in.

Getting Ready to Decorate

Cracks
Despite the phrase about papering over the cracks, they need to be filled in and sanded smooth for both paint and paper.

Brush and scrape the loose particles from any cracks. If they are wide, undercut them slightly, so they will hold the filler. Most cracks indoors can be filled with an ordinary filler. But outdoor cracks need an exterior filler, and very fine cracks need the very fine ready mixed filler. Until you have used it you may not believe how perfectly a hairline crack can be filled. It saves a lot of sanding later if you wipe the surplus off with a damp cloth or tissue, or the end of a damp paint brush, while it is still wet. When it's really dry, sand the surface perfectly smooth.

If the wall has moved and created a slight 'step' use an electric sander to remove the step and make the surface level. This creates an immense amount of dust and protective covers are needed over everything.

Paint Types

Primers
Primers provide a buffer between a bare surface and the covering paint. Most surfaces can be treated with an All-Purpose or Universal Primer, but some need special primers (pages 242-245).

Surfaces which have been painted before don't need primer - unless patches are bare. If it is suitable, use a quick drying acrylic primer, then you can do the next coat the same day. But when any primer is dry, rub it lightly with fine abrasive paper and wipe the dust off with white spirit.

Undercoats
The undercoat both blots out the colour underneath and provides a base for the top coat. If an unusual primer has been needed, or you will be using a liquid (as opposed to non-drip) gloss or an eggshell finish on wood, an undercoat is a good idea. But it's often quicker just to apply the topcoat until the effect you want is achieved. If you do use an undercoat, put oil-based undercoat with oil-based topcoat, water-based under water-based - but it doesn't have to be the same brand.

Topcoats

There are now so many names like vinyl, acrylic and silthane it's hard to tell what paints are suitable for what.

The situation is far simpler than it seems. The big divide in paints is between those which are oil-based and those which are water-based. If you want to know whether a paint is one or the other look at the instructions. If you can thin it with white spirit it is oil based, if you thin it with water it is water based.

Gloss Paint and Satin or Eggshell Finish

Gloss paint is oil based. Liquid gloss and non-drip gloss are both made for indoor use. The non-drip is easier to use. There is also exterior gloss. Gloss paints are intended for use on wood and metal but can be used on other surfaces. The less shiny oil-based paints, like Eggshell or Satin, are used in the same way as gloss and on the same materials.

Emulsion Paint

Emulsion is a water-based paint. Modern emulsions are usually vinyl based and, unlike the old-time emulsions, wash well. The important difference between them is usually the degree of sheen. None of these paints has the really matt finish of distemper and old emulsions, but aim for the paint with the least sheen. Plaster is seldom dead flat and the more sheen a paint has, the more every bump and line shows.

★ Paints vary enormously in density and sometimes a brand which seems expensive will cover in 1 or 2 coats what a cheaper brand will cover in 2 or 3.

WARNING: Teething toddlers bite anything hard they can lay their jaws on. Before painting anything which might be bitten by a toddler make sure the paint is not toxic. A primer containing lead must NEVER be used for anything a child might bite as lead can poison children. By law, any primer containing lead must say so on the tin, so if it doesn't say that, your primer will be all right. Most ordinary paint shouldn't be harmful to children, but it might be wise to check with the maker. There are also special nursery paints on the market.

Special Paints

There are special paints available which it may be worth knowing about. The major paint manufacturers are listed on page 248 and will tell you whether they make a certain paint, and give the nearest stockist.

Microporous Paint or Varnish

The idea of microporous paint is to allow wood which has not fully dried out to lose its moisture through pores in the paint instead of lifting the paint off. This may make the finish last longer on new wood but there is no advantage to using this over old paints.

Rust Repellent Paint

Iron drainpipes sometimes stain the walls of houses and spoil the effect of a pale paint finish. This paint is devised to stop rust stains forming.

Textured Surfaces

Before applying a textured surface, think twice. You can conceal an uneven wall just as well with a textured paper and the paper is far easier to remove when you tire of it.

If you still want a texture the best option is to go for one which can be removed on a backing paper. Brolac's Tartaruga, for example, has a special backing paper which allows it to be peeled from the wall with the upper layer of paper. Or line the walls with lining paper before putting up the textured surface.

Water Repellent Paint

This is a clear liquid which can be applied to exterior bricks to stop them absorbing moisture. It can also be used on stone, plaster and other surfaces.

Stripping Paint

There are four ways to strip paint and varnish - sanding, caustic soda, proprietary strippers, and heat. For removing French polish see page 243, and varnishes on metal may come off with acetone - but always do a test patch first in a place where it won't show if the chemical and metal interact badly.

Burning

Burning is often the fastest and cleanest method of removing old paint. Modern electric heat guns are exceedingly easy to use, and work excellently. Make sure you have somewhere safe to put it when very hot. On the floor it is all too easy to put a hand or foot on it - very nasty indeed. And check that there is nothing which might catch fire in the area. The heat gun is far less likely to scorch wood than a flame, especially if you keep it moving, but it can crack glass if pointed at it.

Have plenty of air in the room, as the paint may give off harmful fumes. Start at the bottom of the paint so the heat rises to the rest of it. Play the heat gun over the paint until it can easily be scraped off with a suitable scraper, such as a combination shave hook which is especially good for moulding, or a stripping knife. Be careful not to make gouges in the wood as you scrape.

Caustic Soda

This is the cheapest way of removing paint. You need an area out of doors and a water supply.

Safety

Before using caustic soda get into old clothing and put on wellingtons, thick rubber gloves and goggles. Caustic burns slowly. If you have a hole in the rubber gloves you may find a neat patch of skin has been eaten away. It is therefore extremely dangerous to eyes. Keep pets and children indoors.

> If caustic does splash on to skin wash it off with plenty of water AT ONCE.

Mixing Caustic
Have a plastic (not metal) bucket of water (it is made more powerful by hot water) and add a few tablespoons of caustic soda to 2 gallons of water, then stir with a stick. The strength you need depends on the paint. Apply a little, leave it for 10 minutes and if the paint isn't reacting add a little more caustic to the water and test it again.

> WARNING: NEVER *put water on to soda.* It can cause a violent reaction in which the soda erupts like a volcano giving off very strong fumes which are dangerous to breathe, and possibly splashing into your face.

Using Caustic Soda
- Brush the liquid on with an old plastic washing-up brush or something similar. (It will melt the bristles of a paintbrush.)
- Leave the chemical to work until the paint looks very soft and puckered; don't rush it - washing it off before it has time to penetrate makes extra work.
- Remove the paint with water, either using a jet of water from a hose or a brush and bucket of water.
- You may need to repeat this several times. Be careful not to roughen the surface of the wood when getting off the last fragments of paint.
- Go over all bare wood with water containing a good tablespoon of vinegar per pint. This neutralizes the caustic.

You can also make a plastic bath of caustic and dip small items in it. But this can dissolve the glue at joints and it may not be easy to put them together again. Caustic may also cause colour changes in wood, and very strong caustic can cause small black spots.

Proprietary Strippers
There are several brands of stripper which can be used. Nitromors even makes one for polyurethane varnish - which has always been the hardest surface of all to remove - but I have yet to test it. Some strippers come in paste form, some as liquids. Before buying one for indoors, check how the stripper needs to be removed. Some have to be washed off with a lot of water, others only need to be wiped off with spirit.

Give the chemical plenty of time to penetrate deep into the paint before you try to remove it. It should scrape off as in burning, using the same tools. For intricate moulding or carving, a friend of mine gets excellent results by applying a paste stripper, wrapping it in cling film or plastic and leaving it overnight. The wrapping stops the paste drying out, so it goes on working for hours. In the morning the paint peels out of the tricky bits in nice chunks.

> WARNING: Keep these strippers off the skin and out of the way of pets and children. Work with the windows well open as the fumes may make you feel ill.

Removing Gesso
Gesso, the white chalky substance which was used as a basis for finishes earlier this century, is especially hard to get off. Getting water into it is the secret, and wrap it in wet newspaper and keep wetting the paper for hours so the gesso gradually becomes sodden.

Preparing Varied Surfaces for Painting or Papering

Aluminium
Rub aluminium down with a fine wet and dry but use white spirit instead of water. Wipe clean with white spirit. Then prime with a Metal Primer containing zinc chromate.

Anaglypta and Supaglypta
Anaglypta and supaglypta need no preparation before emulsion, but the first coat is usually thinned - check with the paint or paper manufacturer. Before an oil-based paint, whether eggshell or gloss, these papers need a coat of acrylic primer/undercoat. All this applies whether the pattern is in paper or blown vinyl. A sheepskin roller is often best.

Bare Wood
Before painting or varnishing, wood which isn't perfectly smooth must be sanded down (see page 262). Make sure all dust is removed with white spirit. If screws or nails show on the surface place another nail on top and hit it lightly. Failing that, the heads need to be coated to prevent them rusting. A dab of metal primer and a touch of gloss, when that dries, is ideal. (In an emergency you can even use clear nail varnish, but sand it afterwards to give it a key.)

Go over all knots with Knotting, using 2 coats on very resinous wood to stop the resin coming through.

Prime with a an Aluminium Wood Primer (especially on resinous woods) or All Purpose Primer, using 2 coats

> Some woods are not ideal for painting. Teak has natural oils which make it retain paint and varnish poorly. On oak it will begin to crack and flake far sooner than on other woods. For exterior sills it is simpler just to oil them occasionally with linseed oil. Columbian pine exudes resin from its entire surface, not just from knots. It is best left unpainted, but if you must paint use aluminium primer first.

on the endgrain, as this is far more absorbent. *After* the first priming, fill cracks and dips with an all purpose filler. Or use extra fine, ready mixed filler on very fine cracks. Sand the filler smooth when dry and prime.

Brick, Concrete, Stone, etc
First treat any sign of mould or lichen so it isn't spread to other areas (see mould, page 244). Remove and replace loose mortar or cladding and fill all cracks. Brush down and remove all signs of dust or loose particles. If there is a chalky or dusty surface use a sealer. Get advice (see page 248) as it needs to be thinned to suit the surface trouble.

Cane and Wicker
Clean old cane by scrubbing with sugar soap. Dry it out *completely*. Apply an All-Purpose Primer, thinning it enough to avoid clogging up the weave. Then use a gloss or eggshell paint or the spray paint on page 248.

Chalky and Powdery Surfaces
For distemper and whitewash see below. Other chalky surfaces can be treated with a stabilizing solution, which penetrates the surface and binds it in place. Use the same treatment before papering. Manders, Sandtex and Crown all make one.

Creosote
If wood has been treated with creosote the creosote will stain the paint. But the older the creosote is, the fewer the problems. Smooth the wood (see page 262). Then apply 2 coats of aluminium primer. If the top coat can be dark it obviously reduces the chances of stains being too unsightly.

Damp Walls
Neither paper nor paint will cling to a damp surface. Once the damp has been cured you can prevent any stains showing through your new paint by first applying a damp resisting composition.

If it is impossible to cure the damp it may be necessary to put up an inner wall on battens, with room for air to circulate behind it. If the problem is condensation a layer of sheet polystyrene on the walls usually prevents this. Let the polystyrene dry for several days before cross-lining (page 250), and then either paint or paper on top of that. But see page 244.

Distemper and Whitewash
Distemper is an old-fashioned finish which produces a creamy paste if you rub it with a damp cloth. Before painting or papering you must get rid of it. It may wash off, but it is often on lining paper. If so, strip the paper. If you scrub it off and get back to bare plaster, give it time to dry. Then paint it over with a stabilizing solution which will bind the powdery remains together. Treat whitewash the same.

Emulsion Paint
Before painting or papering, emulsion paint must have any rough or flaking areas sanded down to a smooth firm surface. Ideally, it should be rubbed lightly with wet and dry paper to give a 'key' and washed down with Sugar Soap. The sponge pads with a sanding surface are ideal as they let you wash and sand in one; all you need do then is rinse. Take extra care with the washing anywhere that there might be grease on the walls, as paint will not hold over grease, and start at the bottom. For cracks see page 240.

French Polish
The French polish must be totally removed or it will dissolve into the paint. A paint stripper will do this. So will methylated spirits. The latter is the best method to use if, instead of painting, you want to bring the wood to a natural shine with wax.

Galvanized Metal
New galvanized metal resists paint and it will flake off. The traditional way of making it possible to paint galvanized metal is to let it weather for 6 months to 1 year, but experts recommend using one of the following methods to give it a surface which will take paint.
1 Go over it with white spirit and 00 wire wool, then paint it with a primer containing calcium plumbate (this contains lead, so beware).
2 Treat it with Mordant Solution (from builders' merchants supplying the trade), use white spirit to degrease any areas which don't go black. Then prime with an all-purpose primer.

Gloss Paint
If the surface is good, just rub it down lightly with a fine wet and dry paper (about 320) to give a 'key', and wash it with Sugar Soap. But any paint which is loose or raised should be rubbed down until the surface is smooth, then finished off with fine wet and dry.

If much paint is loose or flaking it will need to be stripped (see page 241). Rub down all bumps and 'steps' to give a smooth surface. On metal check for rust and if necessary rub back to bright metal with wire wool or abrasive paper, and prime with an anti-rust primer. For cracks see page 240.

> Remember: if the undersurface is rough you don't stand a chance of getting a glassy smooth topcoat. Paint *won't* smooth out the dips; it will sink into them.

Before papering gloss paint give it a key, then wash it to remove any gritty bits and cross-line (page 250) before putting up the main paper.

Gutters and Drainpipes
All types need to be thoroughly cleaned of dirt and debris and, if possible, flushed out with water. But don't use anything abrasive on asbestos. Check that there are no leaks at the seams, and repair as necessary. Treat as for the material they are made from.

Hessian

Hessian must usually be completely removed - treat it like wallpaper, but try to get at one corner so it can pull off in sheets. Then wash the wall down well to remove all traces of fabric.

Before painting over hessian remove all dust. Cover it with a thin coat of cold water size (similar to wallpaper paste. This may stop the paint filling up the weave.

Iron

Iron needs great care. If there is a solid coating of paint don't tamper with it. Just rub it with sandpaper, wash it down and paint it. If there are flaws or rust, rub it back to good paint, or to bright metal. Wipe clean with spirit and prime within an hour with an All-Purpose Primer or an anti-rust primer based on zinc phosphate, if there is no rust yet, or one based on zinc chromate if there has been rust.

If the outside has been painted with bitumen it needs a good coating of Aluminium Primer to act as a barrier between the bitumen and the topcoat. Then use any oil paint. However, the primer won't prevent the paint cracking as the bitumen moves. To avoid cracking you can use a paint like Berger's Weathercoat No 1 (not 2 or 3), although the colour range is limited.

Lincrusta

Lincrusta is made with linseed oil. First, get rid of surface grease by wiping it down with white spirit. You can then apply an oil paint or an All-Purpose Primer. If you want to use emulsion paint apply an oil-based undercoat first. (See also page 241).

Linoleum

Most paint isn't good at standing the wear and tear of feet, but if you move into a place with old linoleum it will take paint well. The lack of wear in the paint won't matter if you just use it round the edges. Remove any wax or polish with white spirit and a rough nylon scouring pad. Scrub with detergent and then use an all-purpose primer, undercoat, and an oil-based paint.

Masonry Paint

The first job is to sand off all loose, bubbling or flaking paint, rubbing smooth. On a powdery surface a stabilizing solution must be used.

Mould or Lichen

If there is mould or lichen, treating it must be the first job, or surface preparation may just spread it. Apply a fungicidal liquid according to instructions while wearing gloves and goggles, and keeping it off other skin surfaces. Leave it for the recommended time (usually 24 hours) and then scrub off. (Paper must be stripped afterwards). If the growth is severe 2 treatments may be needed.

When dry, the surface can be made good and papered or painted with mould resistant paint.

It is also possible to wash the surface with 1 part of household bleach to 5 parts of water. Leave this for 48 hours and then rinse it off.

Nicotine Stained Paint

Nicotine has remarkable powers of penetration, and the yellowing will slowly seep through and stain new paint and even pale-coloured paper. To stop this, wash the surface *very* well with Sugar Soap, and rinse thoroughly. Apply an aluminium primer or alkali-resisting primer - which should be in shops supplying the trade. On top, use an oil-based paint.

Plasterboard

Before papering, plasterboard must be painted with a primer, so you will be able to strip the paper without the water damaging its surface. It should then be cross-lined. Apply a primer sealer before oil-based paints, but emulsion can be applied direct.

Plaster

New plasters vary greatly in their drying times - some can take a year. Ask the plasterer how long it will be before you can paper over it. If you paper too soon the moisture in the plaster will make it stick badly. Fully dry plaster only needs a layer of wallpaper paste to stop it absorbing the paste from the back of the paper.

Before painting, fill any holes or cracks, rub down, dust off the surface. Emulsion paint can be applied directly to the plaster, with the first coat thinned according to instructions. For the first year it should not be painted with an oil based paint. Instead, use a cheap contract emulsion from a builder's merchant, such as Covermatt. The cheaper emulsions are porous enough to let the moisture come out of the wall.

Plastic (PVC)

Stiff plastic of the type used in window frames and drainpipes can easily be painted. Wash with detergent to remove any surface grease. Rub lightly with a *fine* abrasive paper to give a key and paint with gloss paint.

Polystyrene

Polystyrene can have paper applied directly to it with wallpaper paste, but not with any solvent based glue. Before painting, wash it with hot water and washing-up liquid. When totally dry paint it with any emulsion.

> Oil based-paints must *not* be used on polystyrene as it increases the danger from them in a fire.

Putty

Pick out and replace any old or cracked putty or water will seep under your new paintwork. Apply an all-purpose primer.

Radiators

Rub any rust spots back to bright metal with wet and dry paper or wire wool and coat it with Universal Primer. If a new radiator is in good condition simply wipe it with white spirit to remove any grease, apply an oil-based undercoat and give this a 'key' with wet and dry paper when totally hard. Oil-based paint is the recommended topcoat, but painting with modern vinyl emulsions is no great risk. But you must expect it to get dirty and need repainting more often.

Textured Surfaces

Before papering, textured surfaces have to be stripped. A few are applied to double-backing paper and the top layer will peel off. Others are on lining paper - which means a tough paper-stripping job. Those put straight on to the plaster or paint may respond to steam stripping or paint stripper. If you know the make of the finish, write to the manufacturer and ask how best to remove it. Before painting, clean it as best you can, then use a primer sealer.

Tiles

Polished quarry tiles won't take paint well. If tiles have no wax on, wash them clean with Sugar Soap. Allow them to dry completely - the joints take longest - and apply a primer sealer (2 coats on the joints improves the finish). An oil-based paint is probably the best coating but emulsion should work if the priming is good.

Woodstains

There is always a danger that woodstain may seep through. Contact the advisory service of the company which made the stain or the paint you plan to use.

Problems with Paint

Crazing is likely to happen if a coat of paint isn't totally dry before the next one is applied. Surface crazing can be rubbed down and repainted. Deep crazing needs complete stripping.

Gloss paint goes **dull** if it gets damp before it has time to dry. Repaint in better weather.

Efflorescence is an almost frothy white deposit which comes out from under the paint and pushes it off the wall in crumbly pieces. Don't wash the area. Putting water on the plaster will only increase the problem. Instead sand down and leave it bare until the salts have stopped appearing, wiping the area with equal parts of vinegar and water. When the salts no longer appear, sand off any remaining crystals, prime and repaint.

Flaking and blistering happen when one coat of paint isn't sticking to another, because gloss paint has not been rubbed down or because of moisture or grease between coats. Sand down to a firm surface and repaint.

Trouble-Free Painting

- Before painting with gloss, wipe surfaces down with white spirit.
- Don't wear any clothing which has fluff, or it will fly on to the paint.
- Stir all paints - except jelly paints - well before use.
- Flick the dust from new brushes before using them and break them in on undercoats.
- Before using a paint pad, brush it hard with a stiff brush and wash it in soapy water, with a nail brush to get rid of surplus fluff.
- To save time cleaning up afterwards put the roller

tray in a bin liner bag and close it at one end loosely enough for the bag to dip down into the tray. Fill the tray with paint on top of the bag.
- Paints give off fumes which are bad for you. *Always* work with the windows open.
- Never try to paint when moisture will land on the surface soon after. So don't paint outside late into the day when dew is about to start or steam up the kitchen just after decorating. In time it will flake off.
- Don't paint when a surface is hot.
- Put an open paper bag by the telephone, then you can stick a painty hand in before picking it up.
- Stretch a section of old tights firmly across a large jar or clean empty tin, with a rubber band and pour the paint through the tights.
- Fix a section from a pair of tights across the top of the paint can so it dangles in. Pressing your brush down against the nylon will force the paint up through it.

★ When painting a ceiling cut a small slit in an old sponge, and stick the handle of the paintbrush through the slit. The run-back is absorbed by the sponge and doesn't proceed down your hand and arm.

★ Wear an old hat when painting a ceiling - one always puts one's head against the ceiling sooner or later.

★ If you wear spectacles put a smooth layer of cling film over them before painting ceilings. Then splashes won't get on the lenses.

Method of Working

If a whole room is being painted the basic order is ceiling, walls, gloss paint on doors, windows and so on. You start high and work down and start near the light and work away from it.
- Brush up and down, then across a square and finish by going up and down. Keep the edges of each new square thin.
- With a roller you need to have the paint in a roller tray and apply in a big W-shape, then roll crosswise, then up and down.

All the final strokes should be in the same direction. And work so that you are never going over the edge of another patch after it has begun to dry. This means working up and down a long wall, not along it, and the same with a ceiling - and working fast in hot weather.

Panelled Doors

No two experts agree on the 'correct' order in which to paint the sections of a panelled door. Having a system, and working fast enough to prevent any paint drying before you go over it from another direction, are all that matters. Remove door handles and anything else on the door before you start. But make sure one handle is left in the room lest the door slams.

Pipes

Hold a sheet of cardboard between the wall and a pipe when painting it. Be extra careful if painting near brick as the paint will never come off. Outside a house paint the pipes first with exterior gloss paint, let them dry totally, wrap polythene round them and paint the walls.

Radiators
There are very small rollers, on long handles, for getting behind radiators. These are by far the easiest way to paint the wall there.

Windows
★ Windows easily get paint flecks on them. Protect them - just before you get to them - by placing a sheet of wet newspaper flat against the glass. It clings perfectly.
★ Textured glass which may get splashed can either have newspaper held over it with masking tape or be brushed with slightly diluted washing-up liquid.
★ If you want to cut down the time the windows must be open you can make paint dry more rapidly by adding Liquid Dryer to it. This is a product only sold in shops for professional decorators and is used very sparingly; 1 teaspoon well stirred into a litre of paint is enough.

If you have a steady hand and patience it is less work to use a proper cutting-in brush to paint a window frame near the glass than to apply masking tape.

If you apply masking tape, place it exactly where the edge of the paint should be, and remove it while the paint is wet or the paint may peel off with it. Avoid using other tape - it won't come off the glass easily - and don't use masking tape on a window in full sun on a hot day: it seems to fuse itself to the window.

Include any edges which will show from whichever side you are working (inside or outside) when the window is open. Over putty go $\frac{1}{16}$ in on to the glass to stop moisture running behind it. Windows need to be painted early in the day and left open to dry for as long as possible. Long after paint is dry to the touch it will stick to another layer of paint.

Marks and Stains
★ If you splash paint on to carpet or furnishing clean it off *that instant.* Water-based paint will come off with water. Oil-based paint needs white spirit - but first *always* test a little of the spirit on a patch of carpet, or fabric, which won't show if a mark is made.
★ If splashes of emulsion paint get on to gloss, a little methylated spirits will sometimes take them off.

On Stopping
★ When you finish with paint clean the rim of the tin with a cloth dipped in white spirits, put the lid on firmly and store upside down - then the skin forms on the bottom, not the top.
★ Paint the lid of any tin of paint with its contents before storing it. Then you know exactly what shade is inside.
★ The easiest way to store a small quantity of left-over paint is to pour it into a jam jar. Make sure the screw ring has no paint on it, close and store upside down.
★ If you want to leave brushes uncleaned overnight you can drop them in enough water just to cover the painty section. Both oil-based and emulsion paints stay flexible under water.
★ One of the neatest ways to clean a brush with spirit is to put a little spirit in the corner of a strong plastic bag. Then pop the brush in. It uses far less spirit and you can rub it into the bristles with your fingers through the bag, without getting your hands dirty.

One way of getting rid of the smell of paint is to put dishes of sliced onion round the room. But don't eat the onion.

Special Effects and Decorative Finishes
If you are tired of the look of a room, but the paint is in perfectly good condition, you can simply clean the walls impeccably and change the whole effect by adding a decorative finish. You can also use sponging and ragging to conceal any unevenness in a wall or simply use the matt emulsion glaze to give shiny emulsion the really matt look which is such a deliciously subdued foil to certain styles of furniture.

Using any of the following techniques is enormously satisfying but it does take practice to achieve really expert results. Try a technique on a loo wall before embarking on the sitting room.

Important Basics
● Cracks must be perfectly filled. Even use very fine filler to close the hairline crack between two sections of wallpaper or lining paper.
● The basic paint on the wall must be as perfect as if you planned to do no more painting.
● Start work with plenty of hours ahead. Leaving a wall half done can create an edge of hard colour which will spoil the effect.
● Assemble everything you need before you put a drop of paint on the walls.
● Work quickly. The edge of the previous bit of painting must always be wet when you join on the next section: work up and down a wall not along it. For broken finishes like ragging, avoid laying on the sections in a neat band. Instead, have bulges and indentations.
● For techniques where flat paint is applied and then broken up while wet, work with someone else if you can. It reduces the risk of a line where paint has dried before you could get to it.
● The paint drying too quickly will be your biggest problem. Turn off the heating, avoid working in very hot weather, and don't use a fast drying paint.
● It is easiest to get a professional result if you choose shades which are fairly close in tone: say, a cream base coat, with soft apricots, or even close tones of two different colours such as blues and greens. But the stronger your colours, the more perfect your work needs to be.
● Be sure to mix enough for the whole room. It will be almost impossible to match it exactly on a second mixing.
● The linseed oil in glaze makes it increasingly yellow as it dries. So, pale blues can turn greeny, pale pink goes orange. Follow the instructions on the tin very carefully and use as little glaze as possible when working with colours which might be spoilt by yellowing.
● When using paint and glaze add the glaze to the paint, *not* vice versa. Like any rule, this one can be broken. If you want glowing transparent autumn tones - apricot, orange or brown - you can achieve

this by mixing a little artist's oil paint, of the shade you want, into the glaze.

- If you have put a delicate decorative finish on woodwork and want to make it stand up to wear, coat it with several coats of polyurethane varnish, just as if it were wood. But you may have to varnish all the woodwork to match.

★ There is no problem about painting over either the oil paint glaze or the emulsion glaze when you want to redecorate the room.

First Stage
The room must have been painted with at least two coats of the base colour in either emulsion paint or an oil-based eggshell. Whichever was used, stick to the same type of paint for the decorative finish.

All the finishes here need to be thinned. Oil-based eggshell paint must be thinned with white spirit, water-based emulsions with water. Add the liquid slowly, mixing well between each addition.

A slightly see-through effect is needed for all of them, but a colour wash will use the thinnest paint and paint for dragging will usually be the least thinned. The trick is to make it thin enough but not so thin it trickles down the wall. For the best effect, oil-based paint should be made more manageable by adding Radcliffe's Oil Scumble Glaze.

★ Radcliffe also makes an Emulsion with a high sheen, with moderate sheen or very matt which can be used to protect your finished walls and make them wipeable, without changing the colour.

Colour Washing
Colour washing can be done with either water-based emulsion paint, or with an oil-based eggshell finish, or by adding colour and white spirit to Radcliffe's Scumble. It is a deliberately patchy effect with brushstrokes in paint thinned until semi-transparent.

First, see the Basics above, and complete the First Stage, having the paint very thin. For an average room use a 100 mm (4 in) brush, but in a tiny loo you might prefer a narrower one. Start at the top in a corner and have only a little paint on the brush, to avoid runs. Brush quickly and roughly, using short individual strokes going every way so some cross and reinforce the colour, and others don't quite cover the base coat. Let this dry totally. You can leave it at that or end with a coat of special emulsion glaze.

Ragging
There are two completely different methods of using rags to create a finish: ragging on, and ragging off. Ragging off is often called rag rolling.

Ragging on is the simpler of the two, and it is easiest to get a really good effect if you use two different tones on top of your base colour. You use the folds of a piece of fabric to print their pattern on the wall. Any plain cotton fabric will do. But have plenty of it, as you need a new cloth whenever the one you are working with is too saturated and a change of weave to some other fabric will show.

Read the Basics on page 246, then complete the First Stage. Crumple a rag up into a loose shape, dip it lightly in the paint, take the excess off on the side of the paint tray then dab away. Keep your arm loose and constantly alter the angle you dab at. Otherwise the rag will produce a dreary set of identical marks like a set of cat's paws walking up the wall.

When this coat has totally dried you can go over it with another tone, or emulsion glaze as for colour washing (see above). If the effect is too heavy you can also fade the colour slightly by going over it with a coat of the base paint diluted until it is thin and milky.

An oil-based paint is best for **ragging off** (rag rolling) and you can use all kinds of rags. Some people prefer chamois leather, and you can even get a very crisp effect with a crumpled plastic bag.

Read the Basics (page 246) and complete the First Stage. Then, working systematically from one of the corners, paint a patch of wall with the diluted paint and immediately roll a crumpled rag across it - so it lifts the wet paint off in uneven patches. Leave about 30 cms (12 ins) from the edge unragged, (you do that bit when you roll the next patch) to give a smooth join. Keep repeating this on neighbouring patches of wall, so the ragging covers the entire surface. Constantly open and re-crumple the rag, and discard it when it ceases to pick up paint well. When this coat has totally dried a second decorative colour can be applied in the same way. The rags can be washed out in white spirit and re-used, and if you use a chamois it is constantly rinsed in spirit as you work.

Sponging
Sponging is one of the easiest methods to use successfully, especially if you use two shades rather than one. You need a big natural sea sponge with a fairly open texture. Read the Basics on page 246 and complete the First Stage. Have your colour in a paint tray. Dip the sponge *lightly* in it, dab any excess off on a piece of newspaper. Dab the wall lightly at fairly close intervals to produce speckled clouds. Keep turning the sponge so the outline isn't always the same in any one direction, and don't press too hard or you will have a big splodge. When dry, go over the same area with a darker or lighter shade. If some areas become too heavy the base coat can be sponged on to correct the weight of colour.

Stencilling
Stencils are a very effective way to make a wall look unusual and several companies now sell stencils (see page 248). First paint the wall. Let it get very dry indeed - to stencil sooner is to court disaster. (Or thoroughly clean your existing walls). Spray the back of the stencil with a light coat of the spray mount used for mounting photographs. Let this dry. Coat it again. When it is dry it will have a tacky surface which will hold the stencil against the wall but allow you to remove it easily. A heavy stencil may need a few pieces of masking tape too, but beware of pulling the paint off.

★ Before you try stencilling the walls, experiment on some large sheets of paper until you get just the effect you want.

Use a spirit level and plumb line to place the stencil perfectly on the level or upright. Press it against the wall and stencil carefully. Use subtle colour combinations rather than sharp contrasts, in oil-based paint, emulsion paint (matchpots provide small quantities) or even artists' acrylics, with a small piece of fine-textured synthetic sponge, or a stubby stencil brush.

A lot of professionals use car spray paint for soft effects. An even better option may be the new range of Oakey HomeStyle (see right) silk finish polyurethane spray paints in DIY shops. Before spraying, mask the wall with newspaper and the room needs to be *very well ventilated*. You should also wear a proper protective mask, and car spray should not be used by someone who could be pregnant.

★ When spraying, you can get colour variations either by having several stencils and opening up different sections of the pattern on each, or by closing sections of the pattern with pieces of paper or masking tape.

★ To mitre the corners of borders, use a set square to draw a faint pencil line at 45° from the wall. Lightly place a piece of wide masking tape so it masks the wall on one side of the line. Stencil up to and just over it, and remove the tape. Let the stencilling dry totally, then put the masking tape to mask the stencil side of the line and stencil in the joining section. The pencil line will rub out when the paint is dry.

If the final effect looks a little sharp and hard you can soften it by thinning the paint you used for the walls until it is very milky and put a very light wash of this over the top.

The stencils used for walls can just as easily be used for fabric, so walls and curtains or cushions can have the same motif. Caroline Warrender (below) sells paint for fabric stencilling. Tips for using stencils on fabrics are:
★ Only use cotton.
★ Wash and iron the fabric first.
★ Stencil a piece of paper and try positioning it on the fabric to find the best spacing for the design. Then use tailor's chalk to mark out all the positions for the edges of the stencils over the whole of the fabric.
★ Attach the material firmly to a board with drawing pins before you attempt to stencil.

Ploton Ltd (273 Archway Road, London N6 5AA (08.15-16.00) Tel: 01 348 0315) - sells the special materials for finishes and for gilding. It also sells artists' materials (mail order in Britain and overseas).

Carolyn Warrender (91-93 Lower Sloane Street, London SW11 4NR Tel: 01 730 0728) - is a shop with lovely stencils, plus all the materials for using them. (Mail order in Britain and overseas.) Inexpensive and tempting catalogue from P.O. Box 358, London SW11 4NR Tel: 01 622 8275 - (cheque or credit card).

The Home Ideas Department of Libertys (Regent Street, London W1R 6AH, Tel: 01 734 8323) - has stencils.

Laura Ashley (page 203) - does a range of stencils.
Information line on **Oakey Home Spray Paint** Tel: 01 801 2368
Alex Davidson, *Interior Affairs: the Decorative Arts in a Paintbrush*, Ward Lock
Jocasta Innes, *Paint Magic*, Windward/Berger
Lyn Le Grice, *Art of Stencilling*, Viking

Berger Cuprinol, Petherton Road, Hengrove, Bristol BS99 7JA Tel: 0272 836110 (also covers Brolac paints)

Crown Paints Advice Centre, P.O. Box 37, Hollis Road, Darwen, Lancs BB3 0BG Tel: Freephone 6067 (for advice) 0254 74951 (for information on stockists)

Manders Paints Ltd, P.O. Box 9, Old Heath Road, Heath Town, Wolverhampton WV1 2XG Tel: 0902 871028

ICI, Wexham Road, Slough SL2 5DS Tel: 0753 31151

International Paint, Customer Services, 24-30 Canute Road, Southampton SO3 A5 Tel: 0703 226722

Polycell Products Ltd, Consumer Services, Broadwater Road, Welwyn Garden City, Herts AL7 3AZ Tel: 0707 328131

Sandtex, Axo Coatings (decorative department) 99 Station Road, Didcot, Oxon OX11 7NQ Tel: 0235 815141

Papering and Wallcovering

When I first started to paper walls there was little choice. Now there is an enormous range, and Crown has even given dreary old anaglypta a new look by creating anaglypta Victorian and Edwardian cameo friezes, art nouveau dados and even one paper which looks like Renaissance Spanish leather. These could be a boon to anyone trying to restore a period house on a budget.

Even now the selection of papers in vinyl and washable finishes is nothing like as good as the range in those which are not washable. An almost forgotten solution is a product called Gard. This is a milky fluid which can be painted on to any ordinary paper. It dries to a clear washable finish and lasts remarkably well.

Wallpaper: to Strip or Not to Strip

If a wall is papered you can often paint over it very well, especially if the faint seam lines are filled with extra fine filler. The exceptions to this are flock papers, the shiny types of vinyl and washable papers. (The soft blown vinyls used in anaglyptas are a different matter.) The paint may go on perfectly well but it may not last. The other snag is that some ordinary papers bleed if you paint over them. Test these with both water and spirit, for colourfastness.

If you are going to paper the wall, the counsel of perfection is to strip off all the old paper and get back to a clean bare wall. But, in some houses paper has been laid layer upon layer over the years until now they seem almost held up by these papiermâché walls. However, if you do paper over, your paper will only be as firm as the weakest underlayer. The other disadvantage is that you will have to manipulate the placing of your seams so none of them come exactly over any previous ones. Tricky if you are centring the paper over the fireplace and the last person did too.

★ On vinyl-coated paper get your nail under *just* the vinyl coating and carefully tear it away. If it comes off smoothly - leaving the backing paper in good condition, and well stuck to the wall, the manufacturers say you can treat this as lining paper and put your new paper over it. But not all professional decorators are happy about using it as lining, especially if the top paper is heavy.

How to Strip Wallpaper

For large areas it's well worth hiring a steam stripper (below). There is a certain childish pleasure in ripping great strips off a wall, but it palls quite quickly and, when doing it by hand, you are left tearing and scraping long after it has ceased to amuse.

> If there is any mould on wallpaper it should be treated (page 244) before you start stripping, otherwise the washing will just spread the spores even further.

If you haven't dealt with any vinyl coating (see the tip on page 248) do so. Other papers need to be thoroughly scratched. Buy or hire a tool called a perforator for doing this, or slash them with an old Stanley knife blade or scratch it with several metal skewers held with their ends level.

> Once paper starts falling it is very easy for the perforator or Stanley knife to become hidden - but they could cause a very nasty accident if stepped on. It is best to clear the floor *totally* before starting to strip, and *put any dangerous tools in a safe place.* Then protect every inch of floor and furniture: stripped paper is very messy.

A **steam stripper** can be dangerous. People have been seriously burnt from using them incorrectly. Make sure that the machine is supplied with full instructions on basic use and safety precautions *which are legible* - not covered with other people's wallpaper. Avoid directing the steam plate at your skin, especially when stripping a ceiling, but you can also get burnt by a whoosh of steam shooting out if you open the tank while it's very hot or pour water on to hot elements when it has boiled dry. So the basic precautions are these:

- Stand it on a level surface.
- Don't fill the tank too full.
- Don't allow the hose to get a kink in it, or pressure could build up.
- Check the water level every 30 minutes - having first turned the tank off and given it time to cool.
- NEVER open the tank when it is fully hot.
- If you accidentally let the tank boil dry, let it cool before adding water.

The right-handed will find the fastest method is to start at a bottom-right-hand corner. Then the steam rises and loosens paper above and you can scrape off the paper with a wallpaper scraper in your right hand as you move the steamer to the left.

> WARNING: Stop stripping instantly if you see unpainted plasterboard under the paper. Water or steam is likely to damage it. On plasterboards you can only paper over the paper.

For **hand stripping** sponge the paper over to make it thoroughly wet. Adding products such as Polypeel or washing-up liquid helps the water to seep in, and the hotter, the better, but Liquid Polypeel will work with cold water. Wear rubber gloves with these products.

Wet the paper thoroughly, and go and have a cup of something while the liquid works. There is no point in scraping away until it has. Once soggy, start scraping at it with a wallpaper scraper and keep sponging as you go. Trickling water down behind loose paper speeds things up.

Finally give the wall a good wash to remove all the bits and pieces and leave it clean and smooth. If the surface under the paper is firm it is ready to be painted. If not treat it appropriately.

Essential Tools

Papering takes more equipment than painting, but it lasts for years.

- Paper hanging brush.
- Large scissors (wallpaper will blunt dressmaking scissors dreadfully).
- Paste brush.
- Long metal ruler - a metre is good.
- Coiled steel measure for measuring walls and paper.
- Plumb line - a penknife on string isn't bad.
- Large table - you can buy a fold-up papering table.
- Seam roller.
- White loo paper to remove surplus glue.
- Bucket for wallpaper paste.

Ladders, pasting tables, scaffolding for stairwells and so on can be hired.

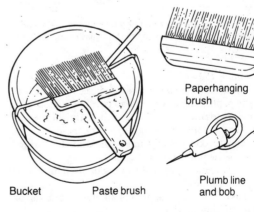

Paperhanging brush

Plumb line and bob

Bucket

Paste brush

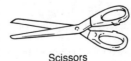

Scissors

Trimming knife

Seam roller

Applying Wallcoverings

The maker's instructions should always be followed. My suggestions are only for when wallcoverings lack them.

Wallcovering	Method	Comments on Hanging
Anaglypta and Supaglypta	Use all-purpose or heavy-duty paste but with a fungicide if the paper is vinyl. Don't roll the seams and be careful not to stretch or flatten.	Vastly improved of late. Can be painted with emulsion, even when in blown vinyl.
Flock	Use fungicidal paste and keep it off the surface at all costs.	Take care not to flatten when smoothing, and don't roll the seams flat; press with the brush.
Foil paper	Use fungicidal ready-mixed paste.	Easy but the shine highlights bumps in the wall. May lift at seams in steamy rooms.
Grasscloth, Silk, Woolstrand	Use ready-mixed adhesive. Silk often put up head to tail.	Fragile but easy on a flat surface. Very tricky at overlaps and round obstructions. Needs skill.
Hessian: paper-backed	Use ready-mixed adhesive.	Easy to apply, but paste needs soaking in for a while.
Hessian: not paper backed	Use heavy duty or ready-mixed adhesive.	Easy but needs meticulous care, see page 253
Lincrusta	Crown Lincrusta Glue, ready-mixed or all-purpose adhesive.	Cross-lining first is essential, using all-purpose adhesive. It is not overlapped at angles. Fill gaps with putty.
Ordinary wallpapers	Use any wallpaper paste.	Handprinted papers may not be colour-fast; check before putting up.
Vinyl	Use heavy-duty paste with a fungicide. On overlaps glue with Vinyl Overlap or Copydex.	Usually very easy to hang. Use a sponge to smooth the self-glued kind.
Washable papers	Polycell Plus suits most, but suit the glue to the weight of the paper. Make sure edges and corners are well stuck down or they curl off.	These are papers with a film of plastic. They can be wiped but not scrubbed.
Woodchip	Hang with ready-mixed heavy duty paste.	Hard to cut at the top and bottom, and tears easily. Don't paint until the glue is thoroughly dry, 1-2 days

★ When hanging any paper on fairly new plaster use a ready-mixed adhesive. It is less likely to rewet the plaster and therefore sticks better.

Using Lining Paper

In theory, all walls are best cross-lined (see right), before you hang paper, and a wall in bad condition should be lined before painting with one called finished extra white. The benefits of lining paper are these.

● It helps to conceal any unevenness in the surface (use the heaviest weight).
● It stops the main paper shrinking or stretching over any unevenness.
● It makes the top paper less likely to bubble or develop glue marks.
● It lessens the risk of shrinkage and joint gaps.
● You can use special pitch-coated lining paper on surfaces inclined to be damp.
● 'Cotton' lining paper can be used to cover wood and conceal serious problems - but it's expensive.

In practice, on a sound emulsioned wall a paper will often go up perfectly without any lining. So lining can be a lot of work for very little benefit. However, not lining is taking a gamble.

Under paint, lining paper runs from floor to ceiling. But, if you will be wallpapering over, it runs the other way - from wall to wall. This is called cross-lining. Use the same glue that you will use for the paper or heavy paper may pull the lining off. Let it dry completely before papering over.

Buying Wallpaper

Wallpaper widths are not totally standardized, but most paper is 52 cm (21 in) wide and the roll is 10.05 m (33 ft). Mercifully, very few papers are untrimmed now. Untrimmed paper needs a special trimming machine to trim it correctly and this will mean using a professsional decorator with the machine and the expertise. When buying any paper certain points are worth checking.

● Is the paper the usual width and length? Those based

METRIC WALLPAPER CALCULATOR (No. of rolls needed for walls)												
Wall height from skirting in metres	Measurement round room in metres (including doors & windows)											
	10	11	12	13	14	15	16	17	18	19	20	21	22
2.0 m to 2.2 m	5	5	5	6	6	7	7	7	8	8	9	9	10
2.2 m to 2.4 m	5	5	6	6	7	7	8	8	9	9	10	10	10
2.4 m to 2.6 m	5	6	6	7	7	8	8	9	9	10	10	11	11
2.6 m to 2.8 m	6	6	7	7	8	8	9	9	10	11	11	12	12
2.8 m to 3.0 m	6	7	7	8	8	9	9	10	11	11	12	12	13
3.0 m to 3.2 m	6	7	8	8	9	10	10	11	11	12	13	13	14
3.2 m to 3.4 m	7	7	8	9	9	10	11	11	12	13	13	14	15

on fabrics are often in fabric widths.

- Are the edges ready trimmed or will it need trimming?
- Do all the roll numbers match? On different print runs the colours may vary.
- Will the shop take back any unopened rolls if you overbuy? Many will.
- What is the depth of the pattern repeat? When calculating the number of rolls needed you will need to allow for the wastage this causes on every length.

Although it's almost impossible to calculate the exact amount of paper needed, the chart above* gives you the rough calculation. To be safe add the depth of the pattern repeat to the height of the wall you will cover, use that as the height of the wall when reading the chart and allow for error.

* I am indebted to Laura Ashley Plc for this chart.

Hanging Wallpaper or Lining Paper
Papering can only be done after all the paintwork (doors, windows, ceiling, etc) has had its last coat of paint and is thoroughly dry.

If you are papering the ceiling, start there (page 253) but don't paper a ceiling unless it will really pay dividends: it's tricky and exhausting. For walls one traditional place to start is beside the main window, or the central strip over the fireplace. But I suggest unpractised paperers start wherever is least noticeable - then the less perfect parts won't catch the eye.

Choosing the Paste
Choose a paste suited to the type of wallpaper. Follow the wallpaper manufacturer's instructions on wallpaper paste or see page 250. If a vinyl paper comes ready-pasted there is no need for any other glue.

★ To avoid having a nasty bucket to clean out afterwards put a bin liner in the bucket and fix firmly with masking tape.
★ Tie a string across the bucket tightly from handle to handle, so you can wipe the brush against it.

Preparing the Paper
Check your rolls so you can see how patterns will match, and that there is no colour variation in plain

ones. If there is a large pattern decide where you want to place it in relation to features in the room. A big pattern should always be centred over a fireplace, its height will dictate the positioning of all the other lengths. If so, measure and cut that length of paper and (if you aren't starting papering at that point) match the patterns of all other pieces to this before cutting. The fabric cutting rule of 'measure twice, cut once' applies here too.

Each drop needs to be the length of the wall plus 10 cm (4 in), always cut the strip of paper before pasting, so you can match the patterns before you cut.

Marking a Guide Line
Door edges and windows are seldom as upright as they look. So, hold the top of a weighted string against the top of the wall where you want your first seam to come. Let it hang freely. When it hangs unmoving, get someone to hold it firmly at exactly that point while you draw a line beside the string.

Gluing
Papers vary in how they need to be treated. Ready-pasted paper is put in a trough of water for a set time. This works best if you roll the paper up, leave it in the water until half-time and then roll it the other way (in the water) - otherwise there are often dry patches. Read the instructions carefully. Ready-pasted sounds like an easy option but you are handling messier wetter paper than in any other method.

Where there are no instructions, you can assume you are meant to do the following. Spread out the paper so the edge just sticks out beyond the edge of the table. Paste that side and the centre thoroughly (make sure there are no lumps of badly dissolved glue). Shift it so the other edge sticks out beyond the table and paste that section. Quickly fold it in loose Z-shaped folds.

Support it well as you take it to the wall. Put the top edge above the top of the wall by about 5 cm (2 in), with it exactly beside the upright line. Use the paper hanging brush to smooth the paper on to the wall upwards and downwards, unfolding the lower layers once the top is in place. Work carefully away from a single point or you will trap air in pockets.

★ Smooth quickly and lightly: if the brush is used heavily it will stretch the damp paper - especially on a paper with a raised pattern.
★ If you like a slippy surface to work against, or the wall is lined, put a coat of size or thinned wallpaper paste over each section of wall before hanging the paper.

Trimming the Top and Bottom
Once a length is in place use the brush edge to push it right into the angle of the top of the wall. Fold the surplus down, making sure the fold is *exactly* at the top of the wall. Pull the top of the paper away from the wall and cut off the surplus - cutting not *on* the fold but immediately above it gives the best fit. Brush it back into place and repeat at the bottom.

Repeat, making sure the seam is perfectly edge to edge, without the slightest gap, and matching the pattern at the seams *exactly*. Roll each seam flat with the seam roller unless the paper has a raised pattern. Wipe off any excess paste gently with clean white loo roll but don't rub hard: the surface can be surprisingly fragile.

★ To reduce the risk of tears in the paper, when cutting to shape or width, measure and draw the cutting lines on the paper when dry, apply the glue, and cut when the stiffness goes.

Papering Corners and Bends

At corners measure the distance from the edge of the previous length of paper to the corner, at the top, bottom and middle. Cut to the *greatest* width plus 4 cm (1½ in) for going into a corner, or plus 8 cm (3 in) for going around one - trim it once in place so only 2.5 cm (1 in) is left.

Brush the paper right up to the corner, then hold it firmly while you push it into or around it with the brush. For the next length mark an upright line, as before, a suitable distance from the corner and position the paper against it. (Keep any pattern motif at the right level.) Brush it into place on the wall and over the underlap (using special glue for vinyl) and trim off the surplus overlap, from this top layer, in other places.

★ Professional paperhangers often place a strip of wood *firmly* down the corner and tear the surplus top paper off with a quick *downward* movement. Done correctly, this leaves a softer edge than cutting and the overlap becomes invisible when dry. Of course, it only works with paper.

★ If a bubble of air under the paper won't smooth down, pierce it with a hypodermic needle, where it won't show, and suck the air out, smoothing it with the brush as you do so. If you discover a bubble after the paper has dried inject a little thin glue under the paper.

Papering Round Doors

Measure up and cut an upside-down L-shaped paper to hang, which overlaps the frame by 4 cm (1½ in) (if there is that much spare) at the top and side. Proceed as for a corner, cutting a diagonal to the angle of the door frame. Crease and cut off the surplus where it meets the upright door frame. Then smooth the section above the door into place and do the same at ceiling and skirting.

Papering Round Windows

You hang paper round windows with projecting frames as you would round doors. Those inset deep into the wall - with a reveal - need other treatment. The conventional method is to paste a section of paper over the centre of the top of the window, bending it round the angle and into the upper part of the reveal. Paper the two small sections of the upper part of the reveal which are usually to either side of it, then the sides of the reveal, and then paper the wall to each side matching the paper to the central strip.

Papering Round Radiators

Getting round the brackets which hold radiators on the wall is done by measuring carefully from the edge of the last paper to the bracket and making a slit up the paper from the bottom to the point which will touch the top of the bracket. You may also need to cut a hole

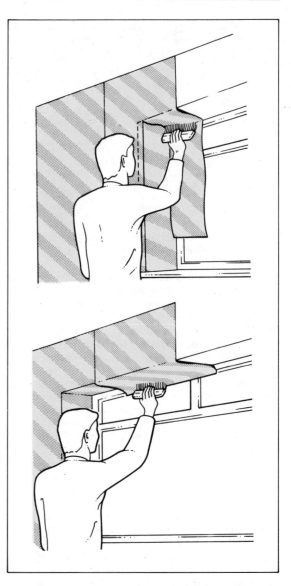

out of the paper to fit round the bracket. Then brush both halves into place - one of the little rollers sold for applying paint behind radiators is ideal.

★ If a radiator is hot the lower paper rapidly dries. Turn off the radiator long before you reach that point in the room.

Papering Round Switches and Sockets

Turn the electricity off at the mains, remove the front plate and paper just under its edges, with a hole carefully cut in the centre. But foil papers must not go under the plate lest they conduct electricity.

Papering Round Light Fittings

For lights it is best to switch off at the mains and remove them. Make an X in the paper and push the wires through, then trim off surplus paper which will come under the fixing (keep foil *well* clear of electric wires). Immovable ceiling roses are treated like light switches.

★ If you find a section of papering hard to do quickly, *don't* leave the under layers folded up against each other. Once they begin to dry together you can say good-bye to that length of paper. Unfold them and let them hang. If paper starts to stick to the wall at the wrong point you can usually pull it off without damage - especially if you sized the wall first.

Papering a Ceiling

Unless a room is remarkably low you will need two stepladders and a plank running between them. You also need a third step ladder (preferably with a platform top) or spring-loaded pole with a papering platform (which can be hired).

Ceilings are normally papered with the paper running *across* the ceiling as you look at the main window. But paper across the shortest distance: vast lengths of gluey paper can have a life of their own.

Establish a line to start from by measuring back from the wall a paper's width minus 2.5 cm (1 in), at intervals across the ceiling. Draw a straight guide line joining the marks. Measure, paste and fold the paper as for a wall (page 251) adding the same allowance to the length. Push it well into the angles. If the walls are not to be papered, fold and trim the surplus as for the bottom of walls. Otherwise, simply trim the ends to run 2.5 cm down the walls and cut a slash in the corner so it can overlap neatly.

Papering Stairwells

The secret of papering a stairwell is to have a really secure working platform. Do size the wall, this buys you extra time in which to manipulate the extra long paper.

Preparing Friezes

Friezes can make a tremendous difference to a simple paper. If a room is too high you can improve its proportions by taking the wallpaper only up to where the picture rail would be. But do use a spirit level to mark the line for the frieze.

You can also take friezes down the wall in stripes or all round the edge of the paper like braid. When joining two sections of frieze, match the patterns exactly. Use special adhesive over vinyl.

★ Keep your offcuts of wallpaper. If a stain is made on the paper, which can't be removed, or a child scribbles on it, you can sometimes cover a mark completely.

★ If you put an ordinary paper over a greasy patch on the old wallpaper the grease is likely to betray you by working its way through to the front of the new paper. To stop this put a coat of paint over the grease spots. In a kitchen you probably won't be able to find all the small spots, so stripping really is necessary.

Fabric Wallcoverings

Hessian and Felt - on Backing

Paper-backed hessian is usually 52 cm (20½ in) wide, felt is 79 cm (31 in) wide and there is less wastage than with paper as you can buy it by the metre or in very long rolls. Backed fabric can be treated like unbacked

hessian (see below). The only difference is that some is put up edge to edge, not overlapped.

Felt can be very heavy. Put it on a cardboard roll (fabric shops and carpet shops throw them away). The ends of the roll can then rest on a pair of flat-top steps.

With any fabric keep the glue off the front or remove it the instant any gets on.

Decorative Felt - Unbacked

Decorative felt is made in a marvellous range of colours and produces the slightly muted acoustics that one associates with very expensively furnished rooms. It is, however, exceedingly wide - 183 cm (6 ft) - and heavy, which makes hard to handle. Put it on a roll and treat it like the paper-backed version above. It helps to have someone to turn the roll while you glue it down as it can be unwieldy.

Apply a coat of size to the wall, and let this dry. Then put heavy-duty ready-mixed adhesive (the less spare moisture there is, the better) on the wall, and roll the felt against it, with a paint roller, through a piece of polythene. Otherwise, treat it like hessian (immediately below).

Furnishing Hessian

Ordinary furnishing hessian is remarkably easy to put on walls. It is very inexpensive and usually sold in several weights. The width can be 91.5 cm (36 in), 102 cm (40 in), 114 cm (45 in) 137 cm (54 in) or 183 cm (72 in), but the plain corn-coloured shades tend to be in the wider widths and the best colours in the narrow ones. It is a fraction of the price of the backed kind (see left) but won't totally conceal the colour of the wall behind, so either use lining paper or first paint the wall.

● Iron the lengths of fabric before you put them up. Pressing them against the wall *won't* remove the creases.
● Apply the paste to the wall.
● Use a paint roller to press the fabric in place.
● Take care to keep the weave on the straight.
● Overlap the seams by 2.5 cm (1 in).
● Leave all surplus at the top, bottom and round fittings and also the seam overlap - *untrimmed* until the hessian is *totally* dry - in case it shrinks.

Once dry trim off the surplus at the top and bottom with a sharp blade cut through the mid-point of the seam overlap from top to bottom. *Very carefully* pull off the surplus (if threads aren't properly cut it will cause fraying, so be ready with nail scissors). Put glue under the two edges and use a seam roller to press the edges perfectly flat. (Have plenty of spare blades to hand: cutting against the wall blunts them very quickly.)

You could apply any fabric which was heavy enough not to let the glue come through and would stand up to being slashed at the overlap. But man-made fabrics' behaviour will be unpredictable.

B. Brown (Holborn) Ltd (Warriner House, 32-33 Greville Street, London EC1N 8TD Tel: 01 242 4311) - sells wall felt by the yard plus hessian, suede and metallized PVC.

Plumbing

Air Locks
If some of the radiators in a central heating system are cold while the rest are hot, there is probably an air lock. Air locks can also cause a hammering sound in the pipes when a tap is turned on; or the water may come out in fits and spluttering starts.

Curing Cold Radiators
Place a washing-up bowl or bucket under the end which has a small square socket. Insert a radiator key into the socket and turn it very carefully until you can *just* hear a hissing sound or a drip of water comes out. *Stop* the instant either of these happens and let all the air come out until seeping water follows it. Let the water drip a little, until you are sure no air comes with it, and then screw the valve in tightly again. If more than one radiator is cold you may need to do this to each. Do this with someone else around. The thread to these valves is very short and it's extremely easy to turn it one turn too many and have it shoot out under the pressure. The scene as one tries to stem the spurting water with one finger while desperately stretching for the out-of-reach valve with the other hand is worthy of farce, but it's far from funny when it happens.

Alterations to Plumbing
Alterations to a plumbing system, other than replacements and repairs, are controlled by law. Each water authority has its own bylaws covering things like stop cocks and tank sizes. There are also building regulations which must be complied with. If you break any of these regulations you could be prosecuted, fined heavily and held liable for any damage which results - and water in the wrong place can do an awful lot of damage. So check the bylaws.

Frozen Pipes
Pipes in a loft must be properly insulated to avoid freezing (page 218), but they can freeze elsewhere in the system if taps are left dripping in icy weather. So make sure the washers are working before the winter comes and, when conditions are bad, keep the plugs in all the basins, then if someone does leave a tap dripping it won't spell disaster.

The best way to avoid freezing is to keep the house at least one degree above freezing. If you are away it is usually cheaper to run the heating at this minimal level than to pay for the damage from burst pipes. NEVER PUT UNATTENDED HEATERS IN THE LOFT TO KEEP THE PIPES WARM.

Dealing with Frozen Pipes
The first sign of a frozen pipe is usually that a tap won't run. If any part of the *hot* water system is frozen there is a risk of explosion if the boiler is left on: so TURN IT OFF. Check first in the loft: the insulation may have fallen off a pipe making it easy to spot a culprit. Look carefully: if there is no sign of a crack thaw it *gently* with a hot water bottle draped over it, a towel wrung in very hot water, or a hairdryer, starting at the end closest to its outflow. NEVER USE A BLOWTORCH. Have a bucket ready, and know just where your stopvalves are - you could be wrong about that crack. If there is even a slight chance that pipes feeding the hot water system could be frozen call a plumber. Plumbers are cheaper than explosions.

Frozen outflow pipes are harder to get at. If there is no access pouring hot water down may clear them, but you may need to do this repeatedly, draining the water through the trap under the basin after each attempt.

Dealing with a Burst Pipe
1 Wrap the pipe tightly with something waterproof and put a bucket underneath.
2 Turn off the boiler.
3 Turn off the appropriate stopvalve - or all stopvalves.
4 Flush the lavatories to drain the system rapidly.
5 Also run the *cold* taps - saving the water in buckets, basins and saucepans. You may need to wash, cook, and use the lavatory before the pipes are repaired.
6 *Don't* turn on the hot taps or the water cylinder may collapse if part of the hot water system is frozen.
7 Switch off the immersion heater.
8 Call a good plumber or use a pipe repair kit.

How Plumbing Works
Every building is slightly different but the fundamentals of plumbing are always the same. It is worth locating and labelling each stopvalve some wet Sunday. Then you can act faster in an emergency - and, if disaster strikes while you are out, whoever is home has a sporting chance of dealing with it. BEFORE DRAINING DOWN ANY SYSTEM REMEMBER TO TURN OFF THE BOILER.
- In the pavement, garden or forecourt there will be an external stopvalve which belongs to the water authority. Turning this clockwise cuts off the water to the entire building.
- Hidden inside the house (e.g. the cellar, or under the stairs) there will be another stopvalve. Sometimes this turns off all the cold water, sometimes only the kitchen tap - in which case, the other cold taps must be fed from a storage tank near the roof and there should be another stopvalve on a pipe coming down from it (try the airing cupboard).
- If you turn off all these stopvalves and run all the water out through the taps you will drain most of the system - and modern plumbing systems usually include drain cocks, near the stopvalves, from which you can drain any remaining water. There will also be drain cocks on the boiler and the hot water tank.

Jammed Stopvalves
If a stopvalve jams try grasping it with the longest handled pliers or wrench you can find, and then turning - the extra leverage the long handle gives may do the trick. Applying penetrating oil may also help.

Knocking in the Water System
Air which causes knocking in the pipes needs to be

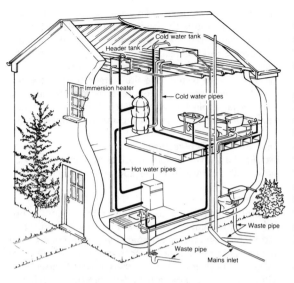

forced out. The standard way to do this is to take a short length of garden hose pipe and 2 Jubilee clips (screw tight rings). Fix one end of the hose to the cold tap in the kitchen (or any other tap fed directly from the mains) and another to the hot, turn on whichever tap in the house seems closest to the knocking, then turn on both the taps linked by the hose. This should force the air out of the system.

Lavatory Blockage
A blocked lavatory can often be cured by using a sink plunger as in sinks (see right). Another method which may work is to take a bucket of water and pour it from as great a height as you can manage. But watch out - if this fails to shift the blockage the water may overflow on to the floor. If you think the blockage may be just round the bend, there is a bendy drain clearer you can thrust through it. Failing that a distasteful option is to bale the loo out and (in rubber gloves) try to reach it - a piece of thick wire bent to a hook can help, but go carefully or you scratch the glaze of the lavatory. If all these fail, it's a job for a professional.

Lavatory Cistern Problems

Overfilling
If a lavatory cistern overfills, lift the top off the cistern and check inside. The ballcock which should float on the water and shut the water valve may have sprung a hole and taken in water, so it no longer floats. Flush the loo and keep the bar in the cistern held up to stop water entering. Unscrew it from the end of the bar and empty it. Dry the ball and mend the hole with a suitable waterproof glue before replacing.

The other possible cause is that water deposits have built up round the hinge where the bar moves up and down. Scrape off the deposits with a screwdriver or use a bath or kettle scale remover (first checking that none of the components of the cistern are substances on which that chemical shouldn't be used.)

Occasionally, the trouble may be that the washer in the cistern needs replacing. As there are numerous different designs it's a job for a plumber. But you can watch what he does and do it yourself next time - on some cisterns it's a simple job.

Poor Flushing
Loos flush badly when the plunger action, which connects to the handle lever, isn't dead above it. If a flushing is poor, open the top of the cistern and look at the bar which connects to the handle. A chain or rod will be hanging from it. If it can be moved, move it until the rod or chain hangs straight down from it - not at an angle. Then tighten the nut on the bolt holding it in place. Occasionally, in modern plastic cisterns, the whole mechanism inside tilts over. Shoring it up with strong wire will keep it running if you don't mind a Heath Robinson interior to your cistern.

Plumbing Maintenance
- Never empty fat, tea leaves and vegetable scraps down a sink. In time they will form a solid block which is very tough to shift.
- Replace the washers on taps, and on ballvalves in cisterns, as soon as they start to drip - one drip a second can waste 400 gallons a year. Because of this some water authorities offer a free re-washering service. Check with the phone number on your water rates.
- Turn each household stopcock briefly off and on once a year. If they aren't turned regularly they may become immovable.
- Turn radiator valves once or twice a year to stop them locking.
- Having turned a radiator full on, turn it back a half turn - then the valve won't stick to the top and lock it at 'full on'.
- Have the boiler serviced regularly.
- Check the water tank annually for corrosion - brown or white patches - and call a plumber if you spot any.
- Clean out the gutters at least once a year and check that the down pipes are working.

Sinks and Basins Which Won't Drain
The best time to deal with a blocked sink is when the water starts draining slowly, not when it blocks totally. It is often possible to clear the pipe just by using a sink plunger (a stick with an inverted rubber cup on the end). As water is going out, put the plunger over the outlet and use it to 'stamp' on it repeatedly. If you lack a sink plunger, a rubber ball which will squish down and cover the whole outlet will do, or even a dense sponge.

If that doesn't work, the trap under the basin needs to be cleared. The trap is a U-bend, or other shape, between the pipe leading down from the basin and the pipe leading into the waste system. It should be attached to these pipes by large nuts. Put a bucket underneath then use a long-handled wrench to unscrew both nuts. Wiggle the trap part until it parts company with the pipes, and clean it out with a hook of wire and by flushing water through. Brush the screw threads to get any dirt and deposit off and then oil them with penetrating oil before screwing the trap back on. Be *very* careful not to cross thread the nuts. It is easily done.

Tap Troubles

If a tap drips the washer usually needs changing. Taps basically divide into those which can be changed without turning off the water supply and those which can't. If you are having any building done it's a good idea to ask the plumber to show you how the washer should be replaced on the taps you have chosen and ask him to tell you the size of washer needed for each tap. Then write to the manufacturers of the tap and ask to buy some suitable washers. At present all new taps have to be sold with washers which meet water board standards for safety. But, amazingly, washers bought loose do not have to meet these standards and some are not as safe as they should be.

Leaking Spindles

If a tap oozes water round its middle, or at the top, it has a leaking spindle. You don't have to turn the water off. Just get at the tap mechanism - as for ordinary washers below. The nut at the very top of the tap mechanism is the gland nut: tighten it. If this fails to cure the leak, undo the nut and replace the gland packing. On old taps this may be string covered in vaseline - so you can just make that. Newer ones will need an O-ring or a washer. Then screw it up again.

Replacing Mixer Tap Washers

The washers on mixer taps are usually in the domed ring which sits at the base of the central tap section. Just undo this - it may be held by a small screw - and replace them. There is no need to turn off the water.

Replacing Ordinary Washers

Turn off the supply at the stopcock. Turn the tap full on. As taps come in various designs you need to adapt what follows to suit the tap you have. If there is a big knob to turn the tap on there may be a screw to undo in the top; then you can remove it. Others come off if you continue to turn them after the tap is full on. Round the middle of a conventional tap - or of what is revealed when you remove a knob - there should be a large nut. Use an adjustable wrench to undo this - protecting any chrome by wrapping a cloth round it first. If it is stiff you may need to hold the rest of the tap with another wrench so as not to strain the pipework. Lift off the tap mechanism and the washer is at the base. Replace it, undoing any nut which holds it. Wipe down any screw threads, smear them lightly with oil or vaseline to make them easy to undo next time, and reassemble - keeping the tap full on. Turn the water on again and only turn the tap off when it has come through.

Replacing Supatap Washers

Supataps don't need to have the water turned off. The tap mechanism hangs from the end of a curved pipe which rises from the basin or sink. For these you just turn the tap on slightly, then use a spanner to undo the nut which is above the body of the tap. Turn the tap until it comes free. Then press the end of the tap on a flat surface and the inside should pop up. Lever out the washer which is shaped like an outsized drawing pin. Replace it with a new one the same size. Put the tap back by reversing the procedure. If this doesn't cure the leak, the anti-splash device which holds the washer may need replacing. This you can do in the same way.

Shower Hose Replacement

Provided a shower is turned off its hose can simply be undone at the nuts at either end and replaced at will.

Repointing

Repointing neatly is a touch harder than it looks, but Polycell now makes a pointing mix to which you just add water, which at least spares you the worst of the mixing - although it is not an economical option for large areas. Try pointing, at first, where it won't show. You will need a small diamond-shaped pointing trowel, and a hawk to carry the mortar on. You can make a hawk by screwing a bit of broom handle on to the centre of a piece of plywood or hardboard.

Scrape the loose pointing *very thoroughly* with a hooked piece of metal, and if necessary use a masonry chisel. Then brush out the dips very well.

If you need to make your own pointing mix 1 part of lime, 1 part of cement with 6 parts of builder's sand - tell the merchant what it's for so they give you the right kind. The amounts are by volume not weight. Mortar dries fast: don't mix more than you can use in half an hour. The trick is to add just the right amount of water. If there is too much it trickles down the wall and leaves marks which are extremely hard (or impossible) to remove. Add the water a little at a time, mixing very well. It should be wet enough not to crumble and dry enough not to slide off the trowel or trickle if the trowel is tilted.

Standing to the left of the area (if you are right-handed), press the mortar carefully into the dips; keep it off the bricks as much as possible, and trim off any excess with the tip of the trowel. Work a neat square about a metre each way. If the first mortar is becoming hard you can use an old brush to brush any surplus off the surface. Look to see what shape the other mortar is. Smooth to shape carefully with whatever will give the shape you want.

★ If you find that the mortar has stained the bricks you may be able to get the stains off by rubbing them with another piece of brick.

Screwing

Screwing is such a simple job that it's easy to suppose anything goes provided the screw looks long enough to hold the two parts together. This isn't quite the case. Having the right screw for the job and using it in the right way matters.

Buying Screws

The right screw has to be chosen for its thickness

(gauge), its length, what it is made of, its head type, thread type and coating. This is the order in which the description of screws appears in catalogues.

★ If you have screws and need to check their gauge, measure across the screw head in sixteenths of an inch, double the number and subtract 2. That is the gauge number.

Situations Needing Special Screws

Several materials react chemically if a steel screw is in them. Oak, for example, contains a lot of tannic acid. This may have made it the perfect wood for galleons but it reacts with the ordinary steel used for most screws, and creates blue stains in the wood. Afromosia and idigbo will also be stained by steel. So only brass or stainless steel screws can safely be used in these woods.

Brass isn't strong enough to screw into hardwoods without breaking. First screw in a twin steel screw, then replace it with the brass one. On metal there can also be interactions, particularly between steel and aluminium alloy - which will rapidly corrode and become hard to move. The rule is to choose a screw in the metal you are working on.

★ In a damp atmosphere ordinary steel will rust. If you will ever want to remove the screws, use aluminium alloy, brass or stainless steel instead.

Inserting a Screw in Wood

Ideally, a screw should be inserted into a hole drilled to take it. If you lack a drill, a bradawl is a lot better than nothing. It's a cheap tool because it's simply a shank with a tapered screw thread at the tip and a crossbar handle, like a basic corkscrew, and it's made in several sizes. You screw it into the place where the screw should go to start the hole.

When joining two pieces of wood together you need to drill two different widths of hole. In the upper section of wood drill a 'clearance hole' the same width as the screw. In the lower section, where you want the screw threads to bite, drill a 'pilot' hole smaller than the screw. How much smaller depends on the wood. On hardwood it should only be a little smaller, on softwood it should be quite a bit smaller.

★ For a screw with a countersunk head also drill an inverted cone to let it sink into the wood.
★ When drilling a series of holes mark the correct depth on the bit with a band of masking tape above that point.
★ To mark two pieces of wood at exactly the same point for drilling and screwing find the correct position on one. Make a small hole with a bradawl. Rest a ball bearing or gravel chip on this dip. Place the other wood in position on top. Protect the wood with a wallpaper scraper and strike a firm hammer blow on top. A matching dent will appear on the underside.
★ To cure a loose screw remove it, insert a Rawlplug and replace it. Otherwise, matches or other slivers of wood can be glued into the hole and left to dry, then the screw replaced. Place them so the pressure will be against the long grain of the wood, not pushing the grain apart or the wood may split.
★ If you don't have a Twinfast screw and need to screw into chipboard you can use any screw without risk of the chipboard crumbling if you drill a hole slightly larger than the screw, and glue in a wood fibre Rawlplug. When it has set, the screw will hold perfectly.

★ It is impossible to screw up into hardboard. Always organize things so you can screw down through hardboard into a thicker base.
★ Ratchet screwdrivers work best if treated with powdered graphite (from a locksmith), not with oil.
★ All screws go in more easily if the tip is rubbed in beeswax polish. They will also be easier to remove.

Inserting Screws in Walls

Making the Hole

In theory, you can make the hole by hammering a Rawltool in as you turn it, or with a hand operated bit and brace. But a Rawltool will only work on certain types of wall and, as tools are so easy to hire or borrow, it seems masochistic to do it with anything but an electric drill. And some surfaces can only be drilled this way. Use a masonry bit and, if possible, have a drill which will go to a lower speed for working on hard surfaces. As you work, keep withdrawing the drill to pull out the debris, and have a newspaper under to catch it.

> WARNING: When you drill into a wall it is always possible that an electric wire may be hidden in the plaster. There are little battery-operated gadgets which light up if you run them over a wall which has a wire in it. If possible, use one to check the place where you plan to drill. Failing that, protect yourself by wearing rubber gloves and rubber-soled shoes as you drill.

Securing the Screw

Screws only fix into walls if they have something to bite into, such as a Rawlplug or filler compound. Both fibre plugs and plastic ones work well, filler is more of a nuisance. There is also a greater risk that the moisture in it will make the screw rust immovably.

Choose the plug to suit the screw. In some brands of plug one size covers several gauges of screw; in others the sizes must match. Moulded wallplugs with ridges on the outside are less likely to break the screw or crack the wall than smooth-sided extruded plugs.

The hole you drill should be the same size as the plug you plan to use. If the hole is the right size the plug should push home with a few taps of a hammer, but it must not be loose.

★ If you plan to screw the screw right in, so the smooth part of the shank will enter the plug, use a size larger plug and suit the hole to this. Otherwise the wall may crack.
★ If a Rawlplug is too long for the screw cut off the inner end before inserting it.

Screwing into Cavities

If you want to fix something on a thin wall with a cavity behind it is not impossible. There are some splendid devices, such as cavity toggles, for doing just that.

The big question is how much weight the wall will stand. Before hanging anything of any weight on a thin surface check what it is made of. Then ask the manager of a timber yard to advise you on the load it can carry.

Screw Removal

If a screw is firmly stuck, there are several ways of tackling it. A power drill with a screwdriver attachment is the easiest. Failing that, put a strong screwdriver in place on the screw, tilt it at a slight angle and give it a few sharp blows with a hammer to shift the screw in the direction in which it should turn. If this fails try some blows straight down to shift it in its bed.

If you happen to have an open fire an old-fashioned but effective trick is to hold the tip of a red hot poker against the end of the screw and make it very hot. This makes it expand and when it cools down it should be looser in its bed. If all else fails, the head of the screw can be drilled off.

Squeaking Stairs and Boards

If a stair creaks the quick and easy way to repair it is to put an L-shaped bracket underneath to support it.

Squeaking floor boards are usually cured by puffing French chalk between two boards which are creaking against each other, or by nailing the loose board down.

Tiling

Ceramic Wall Tiles

Buying

The standard sizes of factory-made British tiles are 150 x 150 mm (6 x 6 in) and 115 x 115 mm (4½ x 4½ in) and they usually have little knobbly bits at the edges called spacer lugs. There are also imported tiles in all shapes and sizes.

Beware: standard factory-made British tiles are easy to cut to shape: not so some Continental hand-made tiles. They often look marvellous but use other clays which may refuse to break neatly where they are cut. Some may need an expensive, and potentially dangerous, rotating cutter to go through them: expect a lot of hassles and wastage.

★ The smaller tiles are slightly thinner. Some people think this makes them easier to cut. In fact, the reverse is true. It is far easier to cut the heavier tiles without breaking them in places where you don't want them to break.

What You Need

cement spreading knife or trowel	battens
notched cement spreader	masonry pins
spirit level	grouting
	pincers
	carborundum stone

tiles - including some with curved edges to use at the top and or sides.
tile cement - waterproof if the tiles will be in a wet atmosphere, like a small bathroom, otherwise ordinary tile cement is fine.
tile cutter (one of the simplest and most effective is the Cintride tungsten-tipped tile cutter)

★ Check that all the tiles come from the same batch or there could be large colour variations.

★ Even if all the tiles are from the same batch there may be small variations in colour. To avoid these showing start by mixing up all your tiles, both within a single box and between boxes. Small variations from one tile to the next won't show but a block of tiles a shade lighter than the next would.

Stage 1

- Use a spirit level to find the lowest point on the floor (or bath or whatever the tiles are above).
- Mark a point exactly one tile's width above this.
- Using a spirit level, draw a line, from that point, round the area to be tiled and *perfectly on the level*.
- Use masonry pins to fix battens in place with their top edge *exactly* on the line.

Stage 2

There are two rules for how to position the tiles; sometimes they work hand in hand; sometimes they fight. Only you can see which is the most important in a particular room.
- The central tiles should be at the mid-point of the wall.
- There should never be an awkward break in the pattern or a cut tile at a point which will hit the eye as you enter the room.

Bearing these rules in mind, use a plumb line to mark a vertical line where the edge of the last whole tiles will come at one side and fix an upright batten with its edge at the line.

Stage 3

Spread tile adhesive to cover 1 m (1 yd) square in the area close to the two battens. Scrape a notched spreader firmly across the adhesive, pressing it against the wall, to leave a series of even ridges. Line up a tile carefully against the two battens and press it firmly in place. Line up another tile carefully beside it and press it firmly in place. Continue this process until the entire square of cement has been covered.

★ If the tiles have no lugs provide a space between the tiles by putting two matchsticks sticking out between them, and do this between each pair of tiles.
★ If you want to include heavy items like soap dishes scrape off the cement where they should be, put an ordinary tile lightly in place with a couple of pieces of tape going behind it and sticking out above and below. Then, when all the tiles are *totally* dry and solid, pull out the spacer tile by the tapes, spread cement on the back of the soap dish, scrape it into ridges as on the wall, and press it into place. Then secure the tile with masking tape to the firm tiles to either side of it. Only grout when this fitting is dry.

Stage 4

To cut a tile to size:
- measure the exact size it needs to be, top and bottom
- mark this on the glazed side and, using a straight edge, run a tile cutter firmly down the glazed surface on this line
- place the cutting line exactly resting along the length of a pencil
- snap the tile by pressing on its raised ends.

On L-shaped cuts pincers can be used to nibble off the tile in sections after marking and scoring. If you have to cut a U shape to go round a small pipe you can mark the curve with the tile cutter, then drill a series of holes, within that curve, with a masonry drill. These should allow you to break off the small sections neatly.

Rough edges can be smoothed with coarse glass paper or a pumice or carborundum stone.

★ To drill a hole in a glazed surface, without the drill sliding, make a small mark on the glaze with the tip of the tile cutter. If you have the wrong sort of cutter for that, put a piece of sticky tape or elastoplast over the spot instead. Once the tip of the bit is in, make a wall of plasticine or Blu-tack round the hole and put a little paraffin inside this to oil the bit as it sinks in.

Stage 5
Remove the battens and fit the lowest row of tiles, cutting or filing them to size as necessary.

Stage 6
Leave the tiles to dry for 24 hours, then fill in the gaps between the tiles with grouting. Press it well into the gaps and smooth the surface with the round end of a stick. Wipe the grout off the surface while still moist.

★ At one time all grouting was white. Now you can buy it in all kinds of colours. As white grouting always greys with age it makes more sense to choose a colour if it suits your tiles.

Old grouting can become dingy and dull. Scrub it clean with detergent, then paint it over with a product such as VersaTile. The white version will bring old grouting up to white; the coloured versions can be used to create a checked effect. If you use such a product, put plenty of newspaper down underneath. The process involves washing off the surplus and it sticks to everything it falls on to.

Ceramic Floor Tiles
The method for ceramic floor tiles is almost the same as for walls but bear in mind the following.
- You need to start with a perfectly flat floor. This is easiest to create with hardboard nailed on top of a smooth wood floor (see page 236).
- The adhesive needs to keep a little give in it.
- Put battens on the floor, along one end and up one side to form a *perfect right angle*.
- The thickness of the tiles can make them hard to break.

Replacing Broken Tiles
Damaged ceramic tiles are very easy to replace: you simply break them up with a hammer. The pieces will fly dangerously so wear glasses or goggles, and be doubly safe by fixing a sheet of strong plastic across the top with masking tape. Once a tile is broken it can be levered free. Then sand down or chip off the remains of adhesive, or the new tiles will stick out.

Cork Tiles
Cork tiles are easy to fix on a wall. Draw an upper guideline with the help of a spirit level and fix them to the wall with a heavy duty wallpaper adhesive. There is no need to use contact adhesive - as some books suggest - and it makes it hard to remove them without damaging the wall. They can be cut using a steel rule and a Stanley knife.

Mirror and Metal Tiles
Mirror tiles are attached with adhesive foam pads. If the wall isn't smooth, you can get the tiles to the same level by stacking the pads one on top of the other. They are cut by scoring down the line with a glass cutter and pressing as for ceramic tiles (page 258).

The soft metal of metal tiles can often be cut to size with kitchen scissors.

Polystyrene Tiles and Sheet Polystyrene
Polystyrene tiles are often used to conceal a poor surface. Some fire authorities are not keen on their use. They are now made with a flame-retardant material, but even flame-retardant is not the same as flame proof. They should be reserved for rooms with radiators rather than fires, or stoves.

Polystyrene tiles are centred on the ceiling as for floor tiles, and fixed it with heavy duty wallpaper adhesive over the entire back of the tile - you'll find the ready-mixed form is strongest. Work away from the points where the lines cross, butting the tiles carefully against each other.

Polystyrene sheeting is sometimes recommended to reduce condensation in a room, as it provides a warm surface which the moisture won't settle on. It is put up just like wallpaper, but without pressing.

★ Some fire authorities feel polystyrene ceiling tiles are so dangerous they will not allow them in offices - yet we can still buy them for our homes. The danger is that, if flames reach polystyrene and it catches fire, flaming droplets will fall over other parts of the room, spreading the fire rapidly and giving off poisonous fumes. There are now polystyrene tiles available which have been treated to make them less of a fire hazard, but the fire brigade say even treated tiles are not entirely free from risks.

Tools

FAMILY TOOL CHESTS - Much inconvenience, and considerable expense might be saved, if it was the general custom to keep in every house certain tools for the purpose of performing at home what are called small jobs, instead of always being obliged to send for a mechanic and pay him for executing little things that, in most cases, could be sufficiently well done by a man or boy belonging to the family, provided the proper instruments were to hand.
Enquire Within, 1856

Obviously, the tools you need vary with what you want to do. Whatever you buy, it is worth choosing a really good quality. A good tool will last a lifetime. A poor one will disappoint you from the first day. A bad workman doesn't blame his tools: he buys bad ones.

Electric Drills

An electric drill is vital if you plan to do anything which needs you to put screws into anything harder than softwood. Which type of drill you should choose depends on how much you will use it and what you will use it for. The key points to look out for when buying a drill are simple.

- A hammer action is really a must for concrete or masonry.
- The lower the speed a drill will run at, the thicker the bit it will take. So at high speeds the outer edge of large bits would go so fast they would overheat.
- If you think you will ever want to use the drill as a power screwdriver (useful for those without muscular arms), it must be able to drop down to very low speeds. But a drill loses power unless it has 'torque' control too. So look for those two features together. And - a point it's easy to forget - if you might want to use it for taking screws *out* it must be able to go in reverse.

Bits and When to Use Them

To get good results it is vital to have the right bit for the right job. For large holes in wood there are big flat bits but for most holes in wood there is a conventional bit with a twist designed to cut a clean hole and shunt the debris out at the same time.

A masonry bit has a flat carbide section at the tip. This helps the drill's hammer action bite into hard surfaces. Metal needs a completely different sort of strength and the whole bit must be made of high speed steel (HSS). Many metal bits are chrome vanadium instead of HSS. They may be a bad buy as the metal loses its edge fast and could distort in use. HSS, on the other hand, can - at a pinch - be used as an all-purpose bit. For glass or tiles you need a tile bit with an end like a small trowel.

More Information

Black and Decker, Westpoint, The Grove, Slough, Berks SL1 1QQ Tel: 0753 74277 - information and service centre.

Martek Ltd, P.O. Box 20, Redruth, Cornwall TR15 2UF Tel: 0209 219911 - makes a bit sharpener which claims to be able to sharpen even HSS bits. The bit manufacturers are less convinced, and I have yet to try it.

Hammers: choose a small to medium claw hammer with a hickory handle. The claw is useful for taking out nails, and the hickory handle is the best wood for any hammer. Hickory has long fibres so it can take the vibration of the hammer without risk of the head coming loose, and it feels less jarring to use.

Saws - see right

Screwdrivers: Three screwdrivers are vital: a small electrical screwdriver, a medium sized screwdriver for X-head screws and a decent sized ordinary screwdriver - about 6 mm across the tip and 26 cm long, with a wide 'cabinet' handle which makes it easier to tackle tough screws.

Shavehook

A combination shavehook is ideal. The varied shapes of its sides fit most situations.

Sharpening Tools

Tools which need to keep an edge, such as chisels, should be sharpened on an oiled carborundum, and (ideally) finished on an oiled arkansas stone. There is, however, an art to making a blade really sharp on a stone which takes a little practice. A chisel, for example, needs to be rubbed to and fro while held at an absolutely steady angle of 30 degrees to the carborundum. If you are doing a lot of woodwork and don't find this easy you can buy a honing guide to keep it at this angle. Sharpening is an art which is well worth practising, as sending tools off for sharpening is a time-consuming business.

The secret of keeping the carborundum and stone in good condition is to lubricate them, with the cabinet maker's mixture of neatsfoot oil and paraffin in equal parts, for other oils clog up the stone and make the particles of steel stick to it. If, however, you have either a stone or carborundum which has already been spoilt by such oils it can easily be restored by simply putting it on a sheet of blotting paper in an oven which has just been turned off. If this doesn't put it in good heart it needs regrinding. You can regrind it by simply putting some silver sand and water on a sheet of glass and rubbing the carborundum on this until the surface is restored. (Neatsfoot oil is sold by shops selling horsey sundries.)

If you lack a carborundum, any nice piece of sandstone will sharpen a steel knife, and in some parts gravestones were often used for the purpose.

★ To see at a glance which screws and nails you have, put each kind in a different screw-top jar.
★ To store the jars neatly make a hole in the centre of each lid and use a screw to fix each lid to the underside of a shelf.
★ If tools have to be stored unused for a while give the blades a smear of 3 in 1 oil to keep off rust. If you have no oil, vaseline is better than nothing. The exception to this is a ratchet screwdriver which should be treated with graphite not with oil.
★ To be safe the distance from wall base to ladder should be not less than ¼ the height of the ladder. On soft ground there should be a plank under it.
★ If you want to make life easy for yourself buy tools, such as spanners and wrenches, with the longest handles you can find. The laws of physics dictate that the longer the handle, the less effort it takes to lever with them.
★ Smooth the path of a metal plane by rubbing a candle on the underside. On an old wooden one use linseed oil.

Types of Saws

'Trim the plastic to length with a tenon saw', the double glazing instruction says blithely. Most of the time one can work out what is meant by a term because only a tool of a certain kind could possibly do the job. That is not so when it comes to saws. There is nothing in the look of a saw that gets up and shouts at you that it's a tenon saw rather than a hacksaw. So here is a brief run-down on saws, for those who are not yet on first-name terms with them.

Buying
Saws vary greatly in quality: one in tempered steel is a 'hardpoint saw', meaning it should keep its sharpness.

The blades of panel and tenon saws are graded by the number of points they have to the inch (they have defied metrication). A saw with 10 points to the inch is called a ten-point saw. Panel saws range from 7 to 10 points to the inch, tenon saws from 10 to 13. The fewer teeth there are to the inch, the faster it will probably cut, but the more roughly it will do so.

Care
Saws should be hung up somewhere dry and after use a saw should be wiped clean and given a light coat of any machine oil, but this is best wiped off before use on wood or it will make oil marks.

Hacksaws: are rather what they sound like: general purpose saws for hacking through metal. So a hacksaw is a plumber's saw. The blade can be changed. Suit the size of the teeth to the thickness of the metal: the thicker the metal, the coarser the teeth. But don't use fine teeth on very soft metal or it will stick in them.

A panel saw or handsaw is the classic wood saw with the large blade. It is made to cut through planks of timber up to 2.5 cm (1 in) thick. But it can easily handle jobs like cutting the bottom off a door. It's a thoroughly useful saw.

A tenon saw is made for finer jobs on wood, such as cutting joints. The strut of metal along its upper edge prevents it bending and makes exact cutting possible. A useful size is a 30 cm (12 in) with 12 points to the inch.

Coping saws are made to cut shapes in wood, such as a U-shape round a radiator pipe in a floor board. The thin blade is detachable, so you can cut a hole in the middle of a piece of wood by drilling a hole and threading the blade up through it before attaching the blade to the saw.

Confusingly, there are also coping saws made for metal, which look almost identical. The difference is that the blade of the wood saw can be turned at an angle - which often makes it far less awkward to cut a curve. If you are buying a coping saw make sure you get the right one.

A fretsaw is part of the same family as a coping saw, but the blade can only handle relatively light jobs.

A padsaw is essentially a long thin knife with a saw edge where the blade should be. It's a weak saw of last resort, but the only one which can saw a keyhole - after you've drilled the main hole, of course.

★ Having marked a line to cut along, cut just to the unwanted side of it. Cutting *on* the line will leave the wood a blade's width too short.
★ To saw easily only press on the saw stroke *away* from you and try to saw with a steady rhythm.
★ To make a panel saw slip better rub the blade with a candle.
★ To stop wood gripping the saw, and making it hard to move, put a wedge of wood in the saw cut to open it up.

★ If it's hard to saw a straight line clamp on a batten with its edge on the line you want to saw and keep the side of the blade against it.
★ To stop thin ply whipping about when you saw, clamp battens to it.
★ If you have to saw across the grain of a veneer - as when shortening a veneered door - it's easy to avoid the jagged tears in the veneer which sawing can cause. Just score through the cutting line on both sides of the door, very deeply with a Stanley knife, before sawing.
★ You can buy a block of wood, called a mitre box, which has slots at 45°. To cut wood to this angle you just clamp it in the box and slip your blade into the slot and saw. You will then cut a precise angle with ease.

Wood
The trend recently has been towards leaving wood unpainted. In response, wood finishes have greatly improved. You can now buy polyurethane varnishes without the glaring plastic shine of the old ones. There are also microporous varnishes which allow the wood to dry out through invisible holes in their surface, and non-drip varnishes which help you make a smooth job of it. Many also claim to stretch with the wood instead of cracking.

For rough wood there are now wood preservatives which act as a base coat and save the need for creosote, and Timbercolours which will stain garden sheds or fences to shades which blend with the garden. The stains for indoors include translucent colours as well as wood shades. There are also new products which claim to arrest rot and firm up wood which is going soft.

Buying Timber
The most important point about buying timber is to buy from a timber yard, *not* a general DIY shop - unless it is really well-stocked. A good timber yard will offer a bigger and better selection and instead of having to buy ready-cut wood to the size the makers decided, you can buy ready-cut wood to the exact size you need. If you have no good timber yard near you, **Fitchett & Woollacott** (Willow Road, Lenton Lane, Nottingham NG7 2PR Tel: 0602 700691) supplies good planed timber and will deliver orders over a certain value (only £30 as I write) anywhere in Great Britain. In pine it is well worth buying the joinery quality, ordinary white pine is extremely soft, and good for very little.

Man-made Boards
Among the man-made boards the newest and best is called MDF. This is essentially a wood pulp bonded with glue under pressure. It looks uninviting and sounds worse, but it is extremely strong and will take screws like wood. A friend of mine who is a first class cabinet maker says it will even make dovetail joints.

Chipboard is light, cheap but it breaks easily if asked to carry a load with too little support, won't take screws well and tends to crumble at the edges.

Blockboard is very different and made of long chunks of wood sandwiched between two layers of veneer. The best type is called lammin board. Blockboard's great fault is that the chunks aren't always bang up against each other and if you cut it down a gap you can be left with a useless edge of two pieces of veneer with no filling. However, if you are making book shelves to rest on wall brackets, it's cheap, strong and the veneered sandwich can be matched with a stick-on veneer edging strip. So you can make a strong set of shelves, which don't have to be painted, for far less than the price of a set of flimsy ready-made shelves from a DIY shop. A timberyard will cut boards to the size you need.

Polyurethane Varnishes
If a plain pine table needs a coat of varnish to protect it from the assaults of family life polyurethane is ideal. It is also the one to choose if the varnish rubs off a modern piece of furniture, or a decoratively painted piece of furniture needs a protective coat.

But if the furniture has any antique value at all polyurethane should *never* be used. To put a modern finish on an old piece is to ruin its value. There are also practical considerations that should make you pause.

Applying Varnish
Varnish is no different from applying paint except that, being transparent, it is less forgiving. The wood must be prepared in just the same way but the surface sanded even more finely (down to a 150 paper). For outside it is wise to start with a wood primer which doubles as a preservative. Do include the parts which don't show - like under the legs of garden tables and chairs, which is where moisture is most easily sucked up.

The varnish is then put on just like paint but it is even more important that the surface is *perfectly* dust free, and to get a good finish you must work in a warm place. Give it even more time to dry than the makers suggest, so you have a really hard finish and rub down lightly with very fine wet and dry paper (about 180). This is vital as the first coat of varnish brings up little 'hairs' on the wood which will forever spoil the finish if not removed. But don't rub hard. For a really perfect finish give it a light rub down after each coat with an even finer wet and dry - say 220 down to 320.

The success of any wood coating depends partly on the wood it covers. Oak, for example, has very strong tannins and any varnish applied to it is unlikely to last more than 2 years - if that. It is very much better to leave oak bare and rub in linseed oil. Some of the very resinous woods such as teak, afromosia or Canadian pine can also present problems and lift the varnish. Afromosia, teak, mahogany, rosewood and iroka can all be given linseed oil instead of a varnish and several sparing coats of this will gradually build up quite a good shine as the linseed oil oxidizes and becomes hard and shiny. Use 1 part linseed oil and 1 part turpentine mixed together. But be careful not to leave trickles as they will be hard to remove.

Rot in Wood
The most damaging fungus is **dry rot**. Despite its name, dry rot starts when spores from the air germinate on damp wood. The spores will germinate anywhere which is dark, has still air, timber with 20 per cent moisture and a temperature of about 20°C (68°F). Unfortunately, if the other conditions exist the fungus can even attract moisture to the wood to give it the damp it needs.

Dry rot needs drastic - and usually professional - treatment the instant it is found, as it spreads fast. Timbers must be cut back to 60 cm beyond the last point of rot. Plaster that has fungus on has to be removed, and all surfaces in the area have to be treated with a fungicide.

Wet rot is really any rot other than dry rot and the essential difference is that wet rot can only live if the wood is naturally wet. When you take away the source of moisture it dies. The treatment for wet rot is to remove the rotten wood and stop the source of moisture.

Rot Prevention
Prevention is a matter of treating all timbers with a combined fungicide and insecticide which will stop the rot growing on it. These should be applied after wood is cut to shape, so all cut surfaces are covered. Immersing the wood is often the easiest method. However, many of the chemicals used for such treatments can be dangerous if you breathe them in or get them on your skin. Wear clothing and rubber gloves which stop the chemicals touching you. Also use a good face mask when spraying, and have as much air going through the area as possible.

Even with treated timber you should guard against conditions which encourage rot. Damp should not be allowed to enter and leaking roofs, gutters, poor damp-courses and so on should be put right.

Wood Furniture Repairing
When repairing furniture it is vital to suit the treatment to the age of the furniture. Totally permanent glues like Araldite, which cannot be undone, should never be used on wood furniture. But modern wood glues, which are very strong and easy to use, are fine for gluing most modern furniture. However, they should not be used for repairing old furniture; the old glues which are on the furniture could react with the PVA wood glue and make a very unsatisfactory join. Also, if one part of a piece of furniture comes loose the chances are other parts will follow suit. Eventually, the best repair may be for an expert to undo all the joints, clean them and re-build the whole piece. If one section has been repaired with a modern style of glue it would make this difficult or impossible.

For old furniture buy an animal glue such as Pearl Glue or Comet Glue. Good DIY shops sell them or you can get them by mail order from shops which supply furniture restorers. But Comet smells particularly foul.

Pearl Glue comes as little brown granules and needs to be heated over simmering water. Only heat very small quantities, as melted glue will go bad if stored for long.

The effectiveness of any furniture mending depends on the two surfaces being held really tightly together until the glue is dry. If the inner tube and string clamping suggested below won't suit what you have to mend it is well worth buying a G-clamp.

Broken Legs and Struts
When wooden chair legs, struts and table rails break they normally do so at a long sloping angle. The repair is simply a matter of applying a good wood adhesive, placing the two sections exactly together and clamping them tightly with a G-clamp.

If the angle is short, the repair won't be strong enough and the strongest method is to drill a hole down the centre of each piece (like coring an apple) and glue in a strong piece of dowelling linking the two. This can only be done if you have drilling equipment which will let you line up both sections at exactly the same angle to the drill.

Loose Crossbars
The crossbars which hold the legs of old chairs together often come loose. To fix them scrape the old glue out of the hole and off the end of the bar. Check how well the two sections now fit. If the fit is loose you will need to slide a sliver of matching wood into the hole where it won't show. The piece from one of the rolls of self-adhesive veneer for edging shelves is often ideal. But it must be placed against the long grain of the hole, so there is no risk of the extra pressure splitting the wood. Apply a good wood glue and insert the crossbar. Use an inner tube 'clamp' to hold the legs together. Failing that, wet some cotton string, and wind it as tightly as possible between the legs, padding them where it might cut in, for cotton twine tightens as it dries. It can be drawn tighter still by inserting a stick and twisting it, then propping the stick so it can't untwist.

★ A free and effective way to clamp many types of repair is to have wide rings cut from a section of inner tube. Any tyre company will give away inner tubes in a whole range of sizes and you just cut them with a sharp blade and wash them in detergent. But do be careful where you put the clamp. In the wrong place it will open the break, not hold it tight.

Uneven Legs
If any piece of furniture has one leg slightly shorter than another make a paste with a little sawdust and a good glue. Put a thick sheet of paper on a hard floor and have the furniture by it. Put a little heap of the paste on the bottom of the uneven leg and press it down on to the paper until the legs are all perfectly even. Trim off any paste that shows, let it dry, then tear the paper off.

Veneer
Veneer has a tendency to lift as the wood under it swells and shrinks with the weather. If a corner comes up it should be stuck down with all speed or it will soon be broken off in dusting. It is usually a job best left to a professional: the wrong glue could disrupt the other veneer around it.

However, if you are prepared to risk the damage you could do if you get it wrong, it may be possible to stick it down with one of the mild glues given on pages 195-196. But this can only be done if the veneer still fits in the space it has risen from, and any glue which gets on to the surface of the furniture must be wiped off immediately with a moist rag. A piece of thin paper should then be placed over the veneer and a book or two placed on top to hold it down as it dries.

Weak Corner Joints
The angles round the frame of a chair seat, or of a table, often become loose with age. If there is a plain right angle inside each corner it can be strengthened by gluing in a block in the shape of a right-angled triangle from which the apex has been trimmed. On modern chairs of no value you can simply use a purpose-made metal L.

More information
Dennis Young, *Repairing and Restoring Antiques*, Peerage Books - covers antiques and fine objects of all kinds, not just wood furniture.

General Tips
★ To keep air out of a quick dry paint, while you have a cup of tea, cover the tin with cling film - it's quicker than hammering on a lid.
★ New bricks will age fastest and blend with an existing house if you brush them with milk.
★ Sashcords on windows run more smoothly if you rub soap on the part which passes over the wheel.
★ When filling cracks in walls have a wet paintbrush to hand. Having smoothed the filler, brush it with the paintbrush. It will have a smoother finish and need less sanding.
★ To make polystyrene accept paint more easily brush it over with wallpaper paste and let this dry.
★ If you are using more than one tin of paint there is no guarantee the shades are identical - especially if the paint has been made with one of the new mix-in-the-shop colours. Before painting tip all your paint into a bucket, stir well and return it to the tins. Then all the wall will match.
★ To plaster a dusty wall after alterations, or apply new pointing to an area where it hasn't held well, brush the surface with a PVA adhesive like Evo-bond. When this dries, it sticks the dust to the wall and gives the plaster or rendering something to grip onto. Check the dilution with the makers.
★ Never lean a ladder against a gutter. Some gutters collapse from rust, others from lack of natural strength.
★ If rendering on walls has large flaws, all loose and flaking material must be brushed out and the gap filled with a mixture of 1 part of masonry cement to 5 parts of soft sand. Use two coats, and smooth the last coat level with the old rendering.

THE FAMILY

Family Matters • Education to Sixteen • Education Sixteen to Ninety • Retirement and After

Of all the subjects in this book none is bigger, or perhaps more important, than coping with a family. It is a topic which is impossible to cover in anything like the detail it deserves in less than a whole book. In child rearing, for example, it has only been possible to write about a few of the key problems which most often worry parents. In isolation what I say may seem fragmentary or superficial. I would rather take this risk than have a reader turn to my pages, with a crying baby and find not a word to help them. But, being trained in teaching and psychology, and a parent of long standing, I am powerfully aware that neat solutions and easy answers are not part of the currency of child rearing. Each child is different and can only be raised in the context of its own particular character and needs. No solution works for every child, nor would it be right to apply it to every one. Lacking space to give caveats all I can do is offer suggestions and leave my readers to judge whether they seem worth a try in their particular circumstances.

While this section was being written the government was still putting its Education Act through parliament. Many of the features were already known and unlikely to be changed, so you will find them in what follows. However, one of the curious features of the Act is that it gives the government a remarkable amount of leeway to make future changes without putting them before parliament. Those changes are impossible to predict but any parent would find it useful to follow the education pages of the press to be up on the latest developments which may affect their children.

However, this is not a section solely on children. It also covers the less shifting sands of starting a career, returning to work, and coping with retirement and the incapacities of old age.

FAMILY MATTERS

Adoption and Fostering

All local authorities deal with adopters in their area. The book *Adopting a Child* by the **British Agencies for Adoption and Fostering (BAAF)** (11 Southwark Street, London SE1 1RQ Tel: 01 407 8800) lists all private and state agencies offering babies and/or children, or libraries should have the Social Services Yearbook which lists approved adoption societies.

Having found which agencies would suit you, write to each giving all the details about yourself (and your partner) - including your racial group and religion - and saying whether you want a newborn baby or will accept one slightly older. There are very few normal, healthy British babies available and some agencies have so many parents already waiting that they even close their lists. Most agencies expect adopters to be:

- married for over 3 years - but not for more than 10
- in good health
- definitely unable to have a child themselves
- over 21 (by law) but in their 20s or 30s
- of the same race as the baby.
- Some agencies may have religious requirements.

Adopting an older child is a totally different situation. Agencies are mainly concerned to find the right placing for a child with a particular problem. So those who wouldn't stand a chance of adopting a baby may be welcome to adopt a child. Apply to your Social Services Department and to any other agencies near you in the BAAF book (left).

You can also widen your choice by using the exchange service of BAAF which puts would-be adopters in touch with suitable children all over the country. It produces a book called *Be My Parent* which gives details and photographs of children needing parents. BAAF will tell you where you can see the nearest copy.

That isn't the only route to a child: **Parents for Children** (222 Camden High Street, London NW1 8QR Tel: 01 485 7526/7548) is a voluntary adoption agency which finds adoptive parents for school age children usually with problems or disabilities. It places London children with people living within 100 miles of London.

The Cost of Adopting
It is illegal for an agency to charge for offering a child for adoption. To formalize the adoption you shouldn't need a solicitor, so it will cost very little. And, if you are adopting a child with special needs, the agency usually pays this. Once the child is yours it becomes a drain on your income, just like any child, but children with special needs may be eligible for a special allowance.

BAAF (left) has an excellent range of books and leaflets. **Harmony** (22 St Mary's Road, Meare, Glastonbury, Somerset BA6 9SP Tel: 04586 612) offers advice and counselling for mixed race families, whether by marriage or adoption, and links up members in similar situations. RC M£L, M, G. sae.

Through **Parent to Parent Information on Adoption Service (PPIAS)** (Lower Boddington, Daventry, Northants NN11 6YB Tel: 0327 60295) adoptive parents help and advise would-be adopters on where and how to find a child to adopt, based on shared experience. Support group RC, Opt.M£L, S, M, L, B, G, sae

The Post-Adoption Centre (Interchange Building, 15 Wilkin Street, London NW5 3NG Tel: 01 284 0555 9.30-5.30 Thursday to 8pm) provides professional advice and counselling for adoptees, adoptive parents and those who gave children for adoption.

Hedi Argent, *Find me a Family*, Souvenir.

WARNING: The vast majority of children who are offered for adoption are those genuinely in need of a home. But every now and then a child is put into care because a loving family is overwhelmed by misfortune for a while. Occasionally mistakes happen and a child is offered for adoption despite the fact that it has loving parents who will want .it back as soon as a temporary crisis is over. It would be wise for anyone intending to take legal custodianship or adopt a child to talk first to the child's parents and see what the real situation is. Few acts could be crueller than to deprive parents for ever of a child they want. And a child who is not reunited with its parents may always feel rejected and unloved.

Fostering

Those who want to become foster parents should apply to their local social services department. The National Foster Care Association will put you in touch with other foster parents who can tell you more about fostering. It really means looking after a child as if it was your own for any period of time from a few weeks to a few years.

Couples who wouldn't be allowed to adopt a baby may be given one to foster. But most of the children put out for fostering are older children with problems. Moreover, those who do the best job are those who, instead of capturing the child's love for themselves, try to keep the links with its natural family going (if this is reasonable). It takes immense generosity of spirit to do that, but if bridges are built with the family it could mean that the foster parents become part of the child's extended family for ever.

Those who want to foster should talk to BAAF (page 264) and to local authority agencies, and children's homes like Dr Barnado's. Foster parents should be able to obtain money to cover the cost of caring for the child.

The National Foster Care Association (Francis House, Francis Street, London SW1P 1DE Tel: 01 828 6266/7) has information on all aspects of fostering. RC, M£M, M, L, B.
A Guide for Parents with Children in Care, Parents' Aid, 66 Chippingfield, Harlow, Essex

Birth of a Brother or Sister

Think for a moment how you would feel if your husband or wife left home one day saying he or she would be back soon, stayed away for several days and came back unexpectedly in the arms of a lover. That is roughly what a young child experiences when a mother goes off to hospital and returns with a new baby. The child first feels deserted and then is faced with a rival. It's amazing more toddlers don't turn to infanticide. But, being upset, they are often demanding just when their mother has quite enough on her hands with the demands of the baby.

- Tell the child/children about the coming baby but don't make too much of it being someone to play with. Newborn babies are poor playthings and you don't want to add disillusionment to the other feelings.
- Before you go away record bedtime stories, and chats, on tape so your child can hear you talking to it when you're away.
- Try to ring home at least once a day and talk to the child, if it is old enough to find presents have little presents hidden round the house and each day give it the clue to finding one. They can be tiny - they are just to show you thought about it.
- Don't return home carrying the baby. Let your partner carry the baby, so you can hug the child.
- Don't buy a present for the child to give to the baby, buy a present for the baby to give the child and don't leave it out when people bring a present for the new baby.
- Once you are home don't let the baby overwhelm any special time you used to have with the other child. Try to give it some time with all your attention each day - maybe just before bed when your partner can deal with the baby if it cries.
- Don't let the child hear you saying adoring things about the baby which might put it in the shade.
- Let the child play a part in caring for the baby and *praise* what it does.
- Don't let any change in an older child's routines - such as weaning from a bottle, toilet training or moving to a big bed - happen as the new baby arrives.

Child Battering

Few parents can swear that never for a moment have they wanted to hit one of their children exceedingly hard or post a screaming baby out of a window. Those that have been spared these feelings may well have been spared the circumstances which can make a parent that desperate. In most parents such feelings are fleeting moments which are instantly controlled and suppressed. To have these emotions from time to time is not unnatural: to feel you have to give in to them is. And it is just as dangerous to attack a child with cruel and violent words as with fists.

Where to Get Help

If you feel that you may batter your children, or have already done so, you need to talk to someone about it. Don't be so ashamed of the feelings that you can't ask for help. Talking about them will make you far less likely to do whatever you fear you may do.

If there is no one among your friends and family phone one of the organizations which help. **Parents Anonymous** (9 Manor Gardens, London N7 6LA Tel: 01 263 8918) offers a helpline for parents who feel they may attack their children physically, sexually or verbally. The Samaritans (in your phone book) will also help you, so will the NSPCC (page 283), and OPUS (page 283).

You don't *have* to give your name and address - even if they ask for it - so you can talk without the risk of your children being put into care.

You can also ring these lines if someone in the household is already battering a child. The people on any of these lines can tell you how to get help, or you can go to your doctor.

Child Care while Mothers are Away or Working

There is a desperate shortage of childcare facilities for the children of parents who go out to work. The organization which is campaigning for this to change is **The National Childcare Campaign Ltd** (Wesley House, 4 Wild Court, London WC2B 5AU Tel: 01 405 5617), but there is still a long way to go. **The Working Mothers Association** (23 Webbs Road, London SW11 6RU Tel: 01 228 3757) is a pressure group which lobbies for the facilities needed by working mothers and sells a *Working Mother's Handbook* designed to help mothers cope with some of the practical problems which they face when working and bring up a family. Its local groups have information on local child care, help organize local child care provision, and provide links between working mothers so they can pool problems and solutions. It is also producing a 'nanny kit' for those who want to know how to employ a nanny. M£L, M, G, Ad, inf. (See also page 281.)

Childminding
More children go to childminders than to any other form of care while parents are at work. Children over 5 can be looked after by anyone the parent chooses, but, by law, anyone who looks after a child under 5 in their own home (as opposed to the child's home), for cash or kind, must be approved by the local authority and properly registered. Some childminders are excellent but don't be too impressed by registration. Some minders do attend courses but they do not have to be trained *in any way* and there are no national guidelines on standards. A minder is simply visited by the social services department to see if she seems suited to looking after children and that her house is clean, and the house may be checked by the fire brigade. She also has to sign a declaration that she is in good health and that neither she nor any member of her family has been convicted of an offence against a child or had one taken into care.

If you want to find a childminder you can ring the local social services and ask whoever is responsible for childminders to let you have a list of those in your area.

This may well be more depressing than cheering, in some areas there are several hundred childminders and most of them have no vacancies. So it could take an awful lot of calls to find a place.

You may well find it better to contact the **National Childminding Association** (8 Masons Hill, Bromley, Kent BR2 9EY Tel: 01 464 6164) which campaigns for proper recognition and standards of childminding and is in touch with local groups of childminders who tend to know who has vacancies and who hasn't. It recommends good childminding practices, runs training courses, and has published a book for the parents. So it could be a route to committed childminders who have learnt about what a growing child needs.

In most areas minders are registered to look after 3-4 children under 5, including their own. But they may also look after over-5s out of school. There are no set hours or rates, although the NCMA does issue guidelines.

The fees normally cover everything the child eats or uses (paint, paper) while there. And before taking on a minder you need to agree not just fees and hours but the sort of food she will give, how she would punish a child, and her approach to things like play, toilet training, bad language and masturbation. If her views on these things run opposite to yours you could have a very confused child. You also need to agree what will happen if she or the child is ill - minders don't normally look after sick children. Having agreed the details put as much as possible in writing and both sign it. Those who cannot afford the full amount may be able to get the social services to pay part and minders can get free milk for each child using form WF/DN 15.

Children will settle most easily if they visit the minder with their mother several times before being fully left. At these times they can then get used to their mother leaving them alone with the minder for gradually increased periods, starting with only a few minutes out of the room, and a good minder should encourage this. (See also Absent Parents, page 271.) When a child is left it is essential to give the minder the following information:
- parents' address and phone numbers at home and work
- address and phone number of another person to contact in emergency
- the name and address of the child's doctor
- details of child's age, immunizations, allergies, etc.

Nursery Care
There is absolutely no obligation for local government to provide any kind of schooling or care for the under 5s - unless they have special needs which cannot be met at home. However, some boroughs do have nursery schools or day nurseries. Responsibility for them may be split between the education department and social services. So, if you want to know about everything on offer for under-5s in your area, contact both.

Day nurseries are run by nursery nurses and operate from 8.30 to 6.30 on weekdays. So they will cover the hours when you might be at work.

Nursery schools or **nursery classes** attached to a

school, are run by trained nursery teachers - so they are likely to give a child more stimulation - but they only open from 9.00 to 15.30, and they keep to term times and normally take children from age 3 upwards. To get a child into one you put its name down at birth.

Private nurseries and **nursery schools** can employ more or less whoever they like but they usually run only during term time and often take children only in the morning *or* the afternoon.

Pre-school play groups are set up by mothers for mothers. Any group of mothers can set one up, and employ staff they choose, provided the premises are approved by the local authority. However, the groups usually meet only 2 to 3 times a week. They are a good way to get a break, but they don't meet the full needs of the working mother.

The Pre-School Playgroups Association (61/63 Kings Cross Road, London WC1X 9LL Tel: 01 833 0991) is an association of such playgroups. It links parents both through playgroups and mother (or father) and toddler groups and tries to help parents to understand their chidren and help them to develop. In some areas there are special opportunity groups for the handicapped. It is an excellent source of information on the needs of young children. RC, G, B, L, F, V, HD.

Scottish Pre-School Playgroups Association, 16 Sandyford Place, Glasgow G3 7NB Tel: 041 221 4148/9 has details of how to set up or find pre - school playgroups.

British Association for Early Childhood Education (Studio 3/2, 140 Tabernacle Street, London EC2A 45D Tel: 01 250 1768) is a charity for those interested in nursery education. Good leaflets M£L, M, G, B.

Choosing a School for the Under 5s
Check any school or nursery to which you plan to send your child. The key points to look for are much the same as in a primary school (see page 289), but there should be more messy play with water, paints and plasticine.

Workplace Nurseries
In many ways, the ideal solution is a workplace nursery as the children spend the minimum time away from you and you are spared extra travel and hassles. A few colleges and some companies have them, and the organization which can help you persuade an employer to start one, is the **Workplace Nurseries Campaign** (Room 205, Southbank House, Black Prince Road, London SE1 7SJ Tel: 01 582 7199). Trades unions may also have information. See also WEA, page 306.

Older Children Outside School Times
There is a serious problem over the care of school age children after school and during the holidays. If you have turned to this page wondering at what age you can safely allow a child to come home from school to an empty house, I have to disappoint you. There are ages below which the law would frown on a child being alone, but there is no school age at which anyone can say that a child can be *safely* left alone, day after day, in the late afternoon and through the holidays.

Children can be divided into 2 age groups: those too young to be left to take themselves home and cope alone, and those who are old enough to get up to no end of mischief if they have too little supervision. Children who have long unsupervised gaps between the end of school and a parent's return have the freedom to sniff glue, take drugs, make love while under age and commit crimes.

Obviously some children in their teens are well able to cope alone for an hour or two after school and can be counted on to behave well. But it is never safe to assume that *every* child can be left alone like that. Even within a single family one child may be quite safe alone and another may not. Bear in mind how a child would cope if something went wrong. Suppose that in making tea they burnt themselves - could they handle it? And, safety and delinquency aside, many children need the support of coming home to an adult if they are to cope with the stresses of school.

One solution is provided by the **National Out of School Alliance Ltd** (Oxford House, Derbyshire Street, Bethnal Green Road, London E2 6HG Tel: 01 739 4787/7870). This is a charity which helps in the setting up of schemes, of all kinds, to look after children after school. It can put you in touch with existing schemes or help you to set one up. The local authority should also have information on centres to which children can go after school.

In some areas there are clubs and other voluntary organizations for children to go to between school and the end of the adult working day. But in most places there is a yawning gap between the care that is needed for children out of school and what is available, and it will be some while before parents who are school governors hold enough sway to make schools provide the facilities which are needed after school hours. Meanwhile, it may be necessary for them to go to relatives or to a childminder for far longer than you might imagine - until you think about what they could get up to alone.

Child Development
One of the burdens of parenthood is that it is almost impossible to avoid comparing your child with the next one and wondering whether its behaviour and achievements are normal or advanced for its age. This means that parents are very quick to spot that a child isn't developing quite normally and a mother shouldn't be afraid to take a child to the doctor if she feels something is wrong, but if nothing is found amiss don't worry yourself sick about the oddness or slowness of your child. Keep on doing all the things which give the child a chance to learn and develop and remember that children aren't standardized products, each has its own pace for everything it does and that it is the pace which is right for it. One friend of mine has a daughter who refused to crawl or stand until over 2. This odd behaviour remained a mystery but she grew up not only physically normal but extremely brainy.

Having watched my own children and a multitude of their friends from nappies to employment I have to tell you that:

- there are no 'normal' children - every child is different
- slowness and even failure at any stage are no indication that a child won't do brilliantly as an adult, nor, alas, do the swift walkers and primary school stars always go on to great things.

However, since parents *will* make comparisons, here are some guidelines as to what that totally mythical animal, the normal child may do.

1 month:	grasps a finger tightly
6 weeks:	smiles back at you, gurgles
2 months:	a baby lying on her tummy can lift her head
3-4 months:	reach out and touch an object, roll around but not over, can stop her head lolling about
5-6 months:	begin to make sounds like Da-da or Ma-ma (but they have no meaning)
6-7 months:	briefly sit unsupported
8 months:	sit securely without support
7-9 months:	slide across shiny floors on its tummy
9-10 months:	master crawling, pull herself to standing by holding on to the furniture, say a real word - and mean it
10-12 months:	clap hands, begin to help to undress herself
13-15 months:	stand without holding on, systematically bang a drum
15-18 months:	begin to stand up from sitting, start walking - unsteadily, put big bricks on top of each other, play will be more deliberate
20-24 months:	slide downstairs feet first on its tummy (if taught to - safer than trying to walk)
2-3 years:	go up and down stairs, begin to draw (not just scribble), undo screw tops, and turn door handles, jump up and down, kick a ball (roughly), thread large beads on a shoelace, undo large buttons, manage some dressing and undressing
3 years plus:	manage buckles on shoes, cut with scissors

From this point a child learns to do such a multitude of things that it is impossible to list them.

★ If your home is warm there is no need for a tiny child to wear shoes. Bare feet are much less likely to slip when learning to walk.

★ If a child is ill he or she may slide back a few stages but will soon catch up when well again.

> Do keep a diary on your child if you possibly can. One of my biggest regrets is that I failed to keep up the one I started on my children. Early motherhood is so engulfing that one feels one will never forget the day they .... but one does, totally. And the children forget too. It is a great loss. One of the loveliest things one can have is such a diary and - to judge from my children's response to my fragment - it is something the children will find fascinating too.

Crying

Anyone with a crying baby has all my sympathy: few things are more exhausting. If it's your first child you may be wondering what you are doing wrong. The chances are the answer is 'nothing'. Some babies cry and some don't. So if you are sure a baby isn't hungry, wet, dirty, sore (nappy rash is very nasty), or windy, and hasn't got a nappy pin sticking into it, the physical problems are solved. That doesn't mean a crying baby is being naughty. It should *not* be left to cry to expand its lungs, that is an old wives tale with *no* truth in it.

We all know that, as children and adults, we have had times of feeling downright lonely and miserable. There seems no reason why babies can't too. Think of the cosy, unvarying security a baby knew in the womb, lulled by the never-ending beating of its mother's heart. Then compare it with the world full of quietness and sudden strange sounds and cold air and new sensations which a baby has to adjust to. It isn't really surprising if a baby feels a bit lost and miserable is it? And it's important that the baby is quickly comforted and reassured.

Predictably the things which soothe a crying baby are those which restore some of the sensations it had in the womb: rocking, being held close and warm, rhythmical sounds, the smell of its mother's body. When I was in Africa where black mothers carry their children constantly on their backs I never once heard a child cry, and probably the best solution for a tiny crying baby is to wear a harness which lets it ride on your back like an African child - tiring, but probably less so than for ever picking it up to comfort it. (See also page 282.)

Crying and Anger in Older Children
The British often react as if crying was a bad thing. It can be, but it needn't be. One of the important roles of a parent is to help a child to accept and understand its own emotions, and feeling sad is one of them. If a child wants to blub over a minor hurt it does no harm at all to give it quick sympathy and then distract its attention and encourage it to be braver. But children do experience real grief and loss - even if it is only the death of a much-loved pet - and at these times a good parent will help a child to release the pain inside it and let it cry. It is heartbreaking to hear a child weeping, but adults have to be strong enough to bear that and not say 'don't cry' and not try to distract it until they feel the *child itself* is beginning to be ready to end its tears. Meanwhile, they should just give quiet comfort and support, and expect the grief to come back from time to time.

Exactly the same thing applies to anger. Not all the emotions a child feels are good or comfortable. It may be desperately jealous of its brothers and sisters and have moments of hating its parents. These feelings can only be handled well if they are acknowledged and perhaps talked about. Yet so often parents force a child to fake emotions, saying to one who has not yet got over a row - 'Come and kiss mummy then' which rides rough-shod over the child's real feelings. It's far better to say gently, 'You're still angry with me, aren't you?

Do you want to talk about it or would you like to be by yourself for a while?' That shows that the child's anger is accepted and understood (children can be very frightened of their own feelings) and that the parent will let the child decide how to handle it in its own time. The parent also needs to give children opportunities to discuss ugly feelings once the worst is over. This helps a child understand itself and other people.

Death in the Family

People are sometimes embarrassed about telling a child about death. But it is important that a child grows up feeling at ease with the world, and everything in the natural world is born, grows and dies. If a child can see the loss of human loved ones in the context of the whole order of nature, death will seem less strange and less alarming. This is something which can be touched on lightly when dead-heading flowers or going for a walk in autumn. Children find patterns comforting and the patterns of nature can be a useful anchor.

If someone known to a child dies it may have more impact on a child than you'd expect. Young children go through a stage when they feel the whole world revolves round them and at this stage a child feels all powerful and can very easily believe that the bad thoughts it had about the person concerned - which may easily have included wishing they'd go away for ever - caused the death. Similar feelings can afflict an older child if it has been brought up with religious views which suggest it can do harm by having bad thoughts.

So give any child a good reason for a death that is totally unconnected with the child. For example, you could say that granny was old and very tired so she asked God to be very kind and take her to heaven to rest and God took her there. That way death isn't expressed as something nasty which has been done to granny by a bad child or anything else, but as a positive release.

If a child finds it hard to get over a death or wets its bed for a long time after it or has real problems of any other kind it is worth bearing in mind that it may be blaming itself and feeling dreadfully guilty. If so it may need professional help to get over these wrong ideas.

> It can be very hard to tell a child that someone is dying but children should not be lied to. If you pretend to a child that someone who is dying is just going away for a little while they will never feel safe when people go away because they will have learnt that those who 'go away' don't come back. It is far better for them to be told the truth about one death than imagine a score of deaths whenever those they love go away.

When there is a death in the family it can sometimes be easier to talk to a professional comforter by ringing the Samaritans or some other helpline, than to express grief to friends and family. Whatever means you choose it is important not to hold grief in.

The organizations related to conditions which can be fatal, which are in the medical section of this book, often have support groups for families both during the time leading up to a death and after it. But the following organizations are concerned with grief from varied causes and also support the bereaved in the practical problems which come with any death.

The Compassionate Friends (6 Denmark Street, Bristol BS1 5DQ Tel: 0272 292778) offers direct support, through its county secretaries, and creates parent-to-parent links for those who have lost a child of any age. There are special groups for those whose child has died from murder or suicide. M£L after that, M, L, G, RC,.

Cruse-Bereavement Care (126 Sheen Road, Richmond, Surrey TW9 1UR Tel: 01 940 4818) now offers counselling, information, and contacts with others to those suffering from any kind of bereavement. M£L, M, G, L, Ad, inf.

The National Association of Widows (NAW) (First Floor, Neville House, 14 Waterloo Street, Birmingham B2 5TX Tel: 021 6438348) provides an advice service by widows for widows and is also a pressure group. G, L, s.a.e.

War Widows Association of Great Britain (17 The Earl's Croft, Coventry CV3 5ES Tel: 0203 503298) helps war widows and their families, champions their cause to government and keeps them in touch with new legislation, allowances and pension rights. It also may also be able to help with accommodation. RC, M£L, M, L, RG, some A.

Discipline

The first thing to sort out where discipline is concerned is whether or not a child is really being naughty. A friend of mine found her 4 year old twin grandchildren busily covering her newly-painted white front door with a thick layer of mud. Being a forebearing woman she held her fire and asked them what they were doing, and they solemnly replied that they had almost finished painting it. The distinction between paint and mud isn't as clear to a 4 year old as it is to us.

Misunderstandings like that happen with children all the time and if they aren't to feel the adult world is most unfair it pays to stop and wonder - and ask - *why* a child is doing what it is doing. Experienced parents don't need to, they can see at a glance whether the 4 year old poking hairpins in the electric socket is trying to learn about sockets or planning to wire up the baby. The look on the face becomes unmistakable.

When a child is very young it can't tell you why it does what it does. The only solution is to get into a habit of trying to see things from the child's viewpoint. That doesn't mean being a martyr to your child but, once you understand the reasons for a child's behaviour, it is a lot less annoying. If you know that a child pouring water out of the bath on to the floor is discovering that water falls (for all it knows it might fly) you can talk about the matter, explain firmly that the bathroom floor isn't the place for this experiment, and provide a suitable alternative. That way you are spared the mess and the child goes on learning. But if you just get angry and say it is naughty you are teaching it that learning about the world is a bad thing to do. A tiny child who learns that cannot be expected to do well in school, can it?

At the same time children feel more secure and more loved if they have a framework of sensible rules and parents who won't let them do anything they like. Children even appreciate the rules which they kick against and protest at, as it lets them know where they stand. Some modern parents prefer to be 'a friend' to their child and avoid setting rules; this can be very cosy and is great for the parent's delusions of youth but it can leave a child confused. Children can find their own friends, finding parents is much harder.

Punishment or Reward?

Studies which have been done with animals show that all animals learn better when they are rewarded for doing the right thing than when punished for doing the wrong one. There is no reason to think the human animal is an exception.

Many parents think of punishments as smacks and rewards as treats. In fact it is the parent's love, attention and approval which is the greatest reward a child can have and the withdrawal of attention and approval is the greatest punishment.

Yet one of the greatest - and most natural - pitfalls of parenthood is to ignore a child who is quietly doing something good and give it attention the moment it is bad. Thus neatly teaching it that it gets the reward of your attention for bad behaviour, but not when it's good. It's wise to revise this. The other great reward is getting its own way. The key to stopping a child behaving badly is to make it very unsatisfying and unrewarding for the child. This takes almost superhuman strength, but it is possible. Just. Most of the time.

Every battle lost prolongs the war, so the sooner a child knows it can't get away with murder the better life will be for all of you, however, a fine line must be drawn. Despite the fact that even a delinquent toddler can reduce an adult to a gibbering wreck children don't feel powerful. A balance has to be struck: guidelines must be tight enough to maintain order and make a child secure but not so tight, and so inflexible, that the child feels it has no hand in its own destiny. Parents who say no and change it to yes when a child screams and frets are just letting it down, but ones who can *never* be persuaded to change no to yes when presented with a *reasonable* argument (as opposed to an aggressive one) just make a child feel helpless, and that can make it very hard for it to succeed at other things.

> No relative should ever withdraw love or threaten to withdraw love as a punishment. Nothing a child does deserves such cruelty.

- Have clear rules, but not too many of them.
- Try to notice when a child is behaving well and give it attention and praise (even quick attention like saying it is good or clever, plus a quick smile, hug or kiss is often enough).
- If a child is naughty punish it immediately (delayed punishment confuses a young child as it can't work

out what it is being punished for). Usually all you need do is say it is being naughty, get cross and then put a distance between you and it. If you are giving it attention, and it behaves badly, leave the room saying you don't like being with it when it behaves like that. If the child wasn't getting attention, give it even less by banishing it to its room, or putting it there. Ignore it for a while, then say it can only come out if it behaves. If it doesn't behave put it straight back and ignore it for longer. If it comes out sooner and says it's sorry and shows it intends to be good, accept it.

- If a child is being bad and you tell it to stop and it doesn't, make a firm threat, such as 'If you do that again we will go home' (assuming it is enjoying being where it is). There is an age - usually between 2 and 4 years old when children are determined to find out where the lines are drawn and have to test such situations. If you want peace from then on you *have* to do what you have said you will do (so if it misbehaves at the zoo do avoid saying that if it does that again you will throw it to the lions). Carry out your threat even if it spoils the day for everyone (you should have thought of that before).
- Don't let yourself be worn down by repeated grizzling. If you've said it can't have a second ice cream stick to it, or you will just train it to grizzle - which will be a rod for your own back. If it goes on at you put space between you and the child - if it's safe to do so.
- Sometimes a child is just generally vile without doing anything you can easily punish, or you may be somewhere which means punishment can't be given - like out to tea with friends. In this case a severe telling off once you get the child alone may be enough, but if the behaviour was bad enough to warrant actual punishment stop the child having some treat - saying it is because he or she behaved badly. A very young child will need to miss the treat almost at once or it won't seem fair (no bedtime story, no ice cream for supper or whatever), a child of 8 plus can, if need be, understand a punishment several days later. So you can let the rest of the family stay up to watch a special programme but not the naughty one.

Obedience

You can use a child's imagination - which is very powerful - to foster obedience. One of the most useful tricks I ever learnt for bringing up very young children was counting to 5. You tell a child to do something and it doesn't you say - in a voice which suggests trouble may be on the way - 'I'll give you until I count 5'. You then start counting slowly, out loud - rather as if pretending to be a giant. Most children will do nothing for 1, 2 and 3, so start moving towards them in a giant-like manner (it needs to be half in play, half serious). By 4 most children will rush in giggling alarm to do what they've been told to do. A child of spirit or at a very rebellious stage will stay put. Give it space to be defiant, by saying 'four-and-a-quarter, four-and-a-half, four-

and-threequarters' in a voice which gets more and more mock threatening. Most children will comply *just* before 5. The great thing about the method is that it allows a rebellious child to rebel harmlessly by not going until the last moment, and allows you to get obedience without anger or punishments. But children do grow out of it. If a child won't budge by 5 grab it and carry it off to do what it ought to inflicting some harmless 'punishment' like tickling it or holding it upside down - and don't try it again, the child is too old for the method.

To Smack or Not to Smack
Smacking does great things for parents: it releases all the pent-up emotion that an exasperating child can rouse in the adult breast. Unfortunately it does very little for the child and can do real harm. It should be avoided if possible and kept to the very minimum if it can't be avoided. However, there may be a case for using it if your child does something very bad when it is impossible to use any other serious punishment. For example if it puts its life in danger by running across a road you might grab it and give one sharp wallop on its bottom. The very fact that you *don't* normally smack your child will make it realize that this is something you feel very strongly about. You also need to explain *why* you feel so strongly.

Dr Haim G. Ginott, *Between Parent and Child*, Staples Press
Dr Christopher Green, *Toddler Taming*, Century
Dr Miriam Stoppard, *Baby Care Book*, Dorling Kindersley

Divorce
Parents thinking of divorce sometimes wonder whether they should hang on until a child reaches a certain age before they break up the marriage. Children need both their parents (or whoever else they have learned to love) at every age, so there is no good time for dividing a child from one of them. There may however be especially bad times. Some psychologists would say that one of these is in the pre-school period, between about 18 months and 5 years. This is because children have a self-centred view of the world and haven't yet realized that other people have their own lives which are quite unconnected to them (the child). As they think the whole world revolves round them they also tend to think they *cause* much of it to happen.

This means that if a parent leaves a child of this age it may believe that the parent has gone away because it is a bad or unlovable child. If a child gets this idea it can be a dreadful burden to it and lead to very severe depression and all sorts of behaviour problems. At this age telling it something different doesn't help much as it can't yet grasp the complexities of relationships and the feelings of early childhood bite deep, so even learning the truth later in life doesn't always lift the sense of unworthiness and guilt.

Effects of Not Seeing Parents
It is not unusual for lawyers and well-meaning friends to suggest that the parent with whom the children aren't living should make a 'clean break' and cut himself or herself off from the children. The idea is that this will allow them to make a new start with some step-parent and save pain on both sides.

There are some parents who are so violent or corrupt that their children may be harmed by them. But in normal circumstances all the evidence suggests that not seeing a parent is very bad for the children. Love does not conveniently dry up and if children have learnt that when they loved and trusted their father or mother, he or she was capable of deserting them *totally* they are not going to find it easy to love and trust again. Indeed it could make it hard for them to trust a member of the opposite sex in marriage either.

However hard it may be for the adults, the children should see as much of the distant parent as possible and that parent should make it very clear that he or she still loves them and misses them, and takes a real interest in them. This shouldn't just be a matter of the statutory weekend outing but also of occasional phone calls and doing things with the children which they specially enjoy - whether it's kicking a football with them or going to the seaside. It should also mean taking an interest in the things they do, and turning up to sports days and school plays. It doesn't mean giving the children expensive presents or letting them get away with murder so as to gain favour - which is trying to bribe and corrupt them and that is quite unworthy of any decent parent.

If this is to work, the partner who is looking after the children needs to be very careful not to criticize the other parent to the children. This is a huge temptation, but one consolation is that if the other parent really is a ****** he or she will soon reveal it, and the children won't need any telling. And if he or she isn't as bad as you think, but just failed you, you will have avoided having your children think badly of you for slagging off someone they love. So you gain either way.

> Just how important both parents are to a child was shown by a study done by psychologists in Cambridge in which they showed that children aged 5-9, whose fathers are simply away from home more than usual because of their work, were less obedient and more likely to be unpopular at school and to have temper tantrums.

Kathleen Cox and Martin Desforges, *Children and Divorce*, Sheffield Psychological Service, 9 Newbound Lane, Sheffield.
Ann Mitchell, *Coping with Separation and Divorce*, Chambers
   The National Children's Bureau (page 283) has a booklist on children and divorce.

Handicaps
On average, 20 mentally-handicapped people are born in Britain every day and other handicaps swell the total number tragically. In some it shows at once, in others it is only revealed gradually; an IQ of 50 usually divides

severe mental handicap from moderate handicap. The most common is Down's Syndrome which affects 30 per cent of severely handicapped people and results from an extra chromosome disrupting development from conception onwards. German measles (rubella) during pregnancy is another common cause, see In Sickness. Poor nutrition, smoking and drinking during pregnancy can also cause mental handicap, as can lead absorption.

Bringing up a handicapped child presents special problems which cannot be covered here, but many of the organizations on page 282 will advise you, and have excellent books and leaflets.

The Law and Handicaps

In general the law which applies to the average citizen also applies to the handicapped. But within many acts of parliament there are special clauses relating to the handicapped - for example, clauses concerning their employment. Mencap (see above right) publishes a complete list of relevant acts, grouped according to which aspect of life they affect.

When They Grow Up

Though parents may want to care for their handicapped children for as long as possible, they have no legal obligation to house and care for any child after the age of 18. From then on the social services have a duty to provide accommodation and care. Many parents feel guilty about asking for this, which is a pity. Of course, the handicapped should have every possible loving care: every human being, handicapped or normal, has an equal right to live - as opposed to exist. But caring for a handicapped child can deprive the rest of the family of their rights to love and care, and make it impossible for the parents to have a marriage which offers any real fulfilment. So in every decision about the care of the handicapped it is not their needs alone which have to be considered. For the sake of the rest of the family, there can sometimes be a strong argument for residential care. Moreover, the adult handicapped often want independence and adult relationships which they cannot have at home.

In practice, leaving home may mean the adult handicapped are put in a mental handicap hospital. However, their needs are beginning to be understood and there are some excellent units with special housing, and even facilities for married couples. Meanwhile the gap is filled by voluntary organizations. Mencap, for example, runs family-sized homes for the mentally handicapped. It also manages inherited money for a handicapped person, and parents can contribute a specific sum to Mencap which will ensure that, after their death, their handicapped child will be regularly visited by a voluntary helper who will take a personal interest in his or her welfare.

The Camphill Village Trust (Delrow House, Hilfield Lane, Aldenham, Watford, Herts WD2 8DJ Tel: 092 76 6006) provides communities where those over 21 live, work and gain training which may lead to outside employment. There is a long waiting list - apply at 18 years old.

National Autistic Society (274 Willesden Lane, London NW2 5RB Tel: 01 451 3844) advises parents and runs schools and centres. M£L, MG, L, Adv.

Royal Society for Mentally Handicapped Children and Adults (MENCAP) (123 Golden Lane, London EC1Y 0RT Tel: 01 253 9433) has 500 affiliated local groups which provide practical help and advice. Many run pre-school playgroups, youth clubs, and holiday schemes. RC, M£M, S, ChS, F&F, M, L, B, V, F, E, G, H, Rg, Res, A, C, legal, Ins, HD.

Helping at Home

There are all kinds of practical reasons why children should help in the home but the most important one is probably that they need to learn the trade-off between rights and responsibilities. As they get older they gain more freedoms and privileges, helping is the flip side.

The best time to teach children to help in the home is when they are under 5. At that age everything is a game and an achievement. A child will *love* making wet patterns on a kitchen floor with a mop and will easily learn how to do it quite thoroughly, or be fascinated watching the bubbles go down the basin after helping you clean it out. And a simple skill, like brushing dust into a dustpan properly helps it to co-ordinate. Skills learnt at this age will stay for life - even if they lie dormant a while.

> NO DANGEROUS CLEANING FLUIDS MUST BE USED WHILE YOUNG CHILDREN ARE HELPING. If they see you using them they may, one day, try to use them alone.

As a child gets older it can begin to take responsibility for certain jobs. For example, a 4-year-old can easily lay the table for tea. By starting with a job like this the consequence of not doing it follows naturally without nagging or punishment: until the table is laid the child can't have tea. Extra jobs can be added as a child gets older and they should - as far as possible - be linked to the child's needs, for example:

- from 5 a child can feed its own pet - if reminded - unless it's a horse
- from 6 a child can make a bed with a duvet
- from 7 a child can put its dirty clothes in a laundry box, put away clean clothes and clean its shoes
- an 8-year-old can easily make a proper bed
- a 9-year-old can dust and vacuum its own room at least once a week
- a 10-year-old can help dry up
- a 12-year-old - of either sex - can sew on its own buttons
- a 12-year-old can hand wash its own smalls or special jumpers
- a 13-year-old can do most basic mending, if taught
- a 14-year-old - of either sex - can iron some of its own clothes. Unless it genuinely has something important to do - like work, not play - any child over 10 can also help clear-up and wash-up any meal it eats.

I don't suggest that children should come home from a long day in school and wade through homework only to be faced with a heap of washing and ironing. But they should learn to do the small quick jobs themselves and not expect a hard-pressed parent to do them, and during the holidays they can easily do rather more, though grade the amount of work to the age.

Of course, children will try to foist the whole lot on to their parents - especially in adolescence. But the secret of getting kids to help is never to do the jobs they leave undone. If you have said 3 teenagers should clear Sunday lunch and wash up and find they don't do it, make it clear that no other meals will be served until they *do* clear it. If they should have ironed something and didn't, let it stay unironed. Sooner or later they will need that garment to go out in. They may decide to go out in it unironed, and you will wince at what people will think. Just grit your teeth, sooner or later your scruffy son in the shaming unironed shirt will meet a girl he wants to impress and ironing skills will suddenly emerge.

To some people all this will seem old fashioned, but it has benefits for the child as much as the parent. Children who clean their own rooms have more privacy than those who don't and when they leave home they have at their fingertips all the skills they need to look after themselves. This is no small advantage. However, it does assume that the parents are hard working too. You can scarcely expect a child to do its own cleaning while its parents lead the life of Riley.

Putting Toys Away
Putting toys away is the first job children do. It can be one of the games you play with a child - while very young putting bricks into a bag is as much fun as taking them out. Of course, parents have to do the lion's share in the early years, but if children always help tidy up protests are far less likely. And when a child fails to put away something *it was well able to* just remove it from the toy stock. When the child next wants it you say it can't have it because it didn't put it away. The child will be very cross and you can then say it can have it to play with if it puts it away this time. If the child agrees, it gets it. It then needs to be reminded to put it away and if it fails a second time it should be without it for several days and be told why. But do be reasonable in *how* you expect things to be put away. Demands for excessive order can be counter-productive.

★ Children seldom do one jigsaw puzzle at a time. To make putting away easy allot a different letter of the alphabet to each puzzle and put it on the back of every single piece, plus the number of pieces in a puzzle - so if puzzle A has 36 pieces A36 is written on every piece. Then you just count all the As into the same bag.
★ Most jigsaw puzzle boxes break - keep puzzles in the plastic nets fruit is sold in.
★ Make it easy for children to put toys away: have big containers to put things in. Plastic bowls and baskets can stack in a corner, big 'shoe' bags will hang from hooks under a bookshelf, plastic sweet jars can stand on the floor or have their lids screwed to the underside of a shelf.

Illness
A child can become ill either for physical reasons or for mental ones and if worried or upset may very easily make itself vomit: I was so miserable at boarding school that I often used to throw up on the last day of the holidays. I wasn't putting it on; my body was simply reacting to my desire to stay at home. Lots of children do that.

When a child becomes ill for mental reasons what it needs most is love and attention, so this is no time for brushing it off with a few brisk words about it being all in the mind. At the same time it is not a good idea for a child to learn that it can evade life for very long by being ill. So the best approach is to give plenty of love and attention while making it clear that there is a definite limit to how long it can last.

When a child is ill with some infection it is likely to be bored, fretful and return to more babyish ways and need more 'mothering' than it does usually. You can more or less judge how fast a child is recovering by how good it is. A very sick child is usually very good, and the better it gets the more restive it becomes. When it ceases to be listless give it plenty of things to do. Televisions, radios and tape recorders can be a boon but don't forget some old-fashioned play things too. There is nothing quite like a stiff dough of 2 parts flour to 1 part salt and a little water, which a child can pinch and punch and generally vent its frustration upon.

Illness in Hospital
Illness is stressful for everyone, and for a young child hospital doubles the distress. It is taken into a strange place, and surrounded by people it doesn't know, who wear peculiar clothes and do things which are often unpleasant and sometimes painful. What's more a child under 5 has no real concept of time and, if its mother leaves, it may feel deserted for ever. The distress this can cause should not be underestimated. Children should only be admitted to hospital if they cannot be properly nursed at home, and in hospital they need a parent with them as much as possible.

Since 1961 the National Association for the Welfare of Children in Hospital, which I helped to found, has, with the aid of enlightened members of the medical profession, campaigned for parents to be allowed to stay all day and all night with children who are very young and for free visiting for older children. In the best hospitals it is the norm, and parents have a right to ask for this, and to use every persuasion to obtain it. It is also important that children are nursed in children's wards, not with adults, and that they have an opportunity to play. That said, parents have a duty to help, not hinder, the staff.

If hospital staff don't understand children's emotional needs they may say that parents should not visit as 'it upsets the child'. This is frankly poppycock. Children don't cry because their parents *come* but because they *go*. And it's a strong argument for them staying all the time, not for their staying away. But if they do have to go - and those with several children may have to - then at least the child knows that they cared enough to come and has been able to express its sense of loss by crying when they leave. This is far better for a child than sitting alone feeling deserted and rejected with no outlet for this sense of loss. Evidence shows that the unvisited young child, who gives no trouble and stays dry-eyed, takes longer to recover from illness, is often deeply depressed and has severe behaviour problems on leaving hospital. Whereas those who have their parents with them recover quickly and have few problems afterwards.

If parents cannot stay with a young child in hospital they should not be surprised if it is difficult for a while when it returns home. Some children cling, or wet their bed, or suck their thumb, as they did in babyhood. Others appear to be saying 'you rejected me and now I'm going to reject you' and go for aggression and disobedience. This calls for a delicate balance between rejecting it still further, or letting it get away with too much. Give it lots of love and attention, plus harmless things to get aggressive with - hammering toys, drums, finger paints - and a chance to talk about being in hospital and say it was cross and hurt. And, when you feel exasperated, think how you might feel towards your husband if he walked out on you - the child is feeling much the same.

There are enormous problems for parents who have several children if one of them is in hospital, and it can be very difficult for a mother to know where to give her time. She should talk to the doctors about this. Some hospitals have play groups which the other children might be able to attend while she was visiting the sick child, she may also be able to leave tape recordings of bedtime stories, so even when she has to leave, the sick child doesn't feel totally deserted.

National Association for the Welfare of Children in Hospital (NAWCH) (Argyle House, 29-31 Euston Road, London NW1 2SD Tel: 01 833 2041) is a pressure group and information source on the needs and rights of children in hospital. It has 70 branches, RC, M£L, ChS, F&F, M, L, B, G, HD, sae *Children in Hospital - an action guide for parents*, NAWCH/Consumers' Association
James Robertson, *Young Children in Hospital*, Tavistock

Safety

Each year new products come on the market to make life safer for children. But most home safety depends not on how many gadgets you have but on how careful you are about doing basic things safely. This quiz will give an idea how safe a child is in your home.
1 Is your medicine cupboard lockable or too high up for a child to reach even on a chair?
2 Do you dispose of medicines in the dustbin?
3 Do you keep all chemicals in their original containers, and where children cannot get to them?
4 Do you turn saucepan handles back, out of reach of children always, sometimes or never?
5 Do you ever put hot drinks in places where children could reach them?
6 Are any sharp tools or knives in places where children could get them?

7 Are there bars or anti-thief locks on upstairs windows to stop them being opened by children?
8 Would you put a gate at the top of the stairs to prevent toddlers falling down them?
9 Are matches and lighters kept where children could reach them?
10 Do your electric plugs have 'sleeves' on all but the tips of the plugs?

Score 1 for each yes to questions 1,3,7,8,10; and 1 for no to 2,4,5,6,9. For question 4 score 2 for always; 1 for sometimes. Congratulations if you scored 11; 7 to 11 you are reasonably careful; under 7 and it's time to think about being more careful.

Those who teach their children 'family' safety rules, like 'don't go to such and such a cupboard it has poisons in', tend to forget that visiting children haven't learnt the same rules. Large numbers of children are injured, and even killed, in other people's homes. It may be easier to warn children against hazards, but it is safer to remove the hazards - then nobody's children get hurt. But teach them safety as well: other people may not be so thoughtful. Children may even come to grief visiting grandparents, who have long ago forgotten that bleach or weedkiller in a lemonade bottle can be dangerous.

★ If you keep used plastic bags, tie a knot in the top of each so children aren't tempted to put them over their heads.
★ Don't give pillows to babies. They don't need them and they could be smothered by one.
★ Kiddi-proof, Boots and Mothercare sell plug covers which will prevent toddlers pushing hairpins into sockets or plugging appliances into them.
★ Children underfoot in a kitchen can be a danger. If a kitchen is small enough for children to be a hazard have a gate on the kitchen door. Then children can see in but not come in. Children who grow up with this arrangement accept it happily.

The Royal Society for the Prevention of Accidents (ROSPA) (Cannon House, The Priory Queensway, Birmingham B4 6BS Tel: 021 200 2461 - L, B, F), produces a booklet on this. Another by the **Child Accident Prevention Trust** (28 Portland Place, W1N 4DE Tel: 01 636 2545) called 'Keep Them Safe' gives details of equipment for child safety. The Department of Trade and Industry (see Organizations) has leaflets on general safety in the home.

Sex and Children

It might be convenient if children were, as the Victorians believed them to be, innocent about sex until adolescence stirred. They aren't. A child's body is its first plaything and it will naturally explore its whole body, not leave patches untouched. If you see your child 'playing with itself' don't be shocked or cross. It is totally normal, and does no harm, and you should not make it feel that there is something bad about touching those parts of itself. The Almighty didn't make dirty bits and to suggest to a child that some parts of its body are worse than others may make it harder for it to be a responsive sexual partner when adult. But a child does have to learn that there are some things it doesn't do *in public*: picking its nose, and handling its private parts are two of them and they should both be treated in the same, matter of fact, way.

Exploring other Children

Children are curious about everything and other children's anatomy is no exception. It is a good idea to explain to a toddler that boys and girls are made differently, as soon as it has had any chance to see the opposite sex. Some children who aren't told get quite worried and think a girl has had a penis chopped off (and worry about losing theirs) and a little girl I knew scratched herself raw trying to find one, believing it was hiding. Children can be told that little girls have a secret place in their tummies, like their mother has, which means they will be able to carry a baby in there. Then they know that each sex has something special. The more matter of fact a parent can be about such things the less likely a child is to spend much time taking down the knickers of other children, but the more secretive or shocked you are, the more it will be fascinated and curious. Most children do go through a brief phase of this but calling them to food will usually distract them from the game.

The Facts of Life

The time to tell children the facts of life is when they ask, and this is not a question to brush aside. If you ask them questions to find out what they want to know and tell them simply and honestly it is very easy to explain. Don't worry about them being too young, they will forget anything they can't understand, and ask more questions as they get older. But if they haven't asked by 6 or 7 it is time to manoeuvre an opportunity. You could, for example, ask if they have ever wondered how they were made, and whether they would like to know. If you don't tell them they will be told in the playground and it is much better for them to get the basics from you, not learn a lot of nonsense. The very young child only needs the basic anatomical facts but, even at this age, it can be put in the context of love and caring. Then as they get older they can be told a little more, to suit their curiosity and age and parents can talk about the morality of sexual behaviour and about contraception. A child should have clear guidelines as to what is, and is not, acceptable behaviour long before it will be tempted to experiment sexually - by 12 in many children. And girls should know about periods before they happen - which can be as young as 10 years old.

Homosexuality

Adolescents usually get crushes on members of their own sex. Whether it's a teacher, or a pop star or a sports star this is very normal and should be accepted without comment or teasing. It is also quite normal for a child to get emotionally attached to a friend of their own sex. In some children this remains an unfulfilled love which never has any physical expression beyond holding hands, in others there may be a certain amount of homosexual activity. This can be very hard for parents to take and the big worry is that the child is going to be homosexual for life. And even a deeply liberal parent

may worry about AIDS and regret the possible loss of grandchildren which that would entail.

However, loving one's own sex is a normal stage in adolescence, which affects most children. Even if a child has indulged in full homosexual behaviour it does not mean that he or she is 'a homosexual' and the child should *not* identify itself as one. In some people attraction to the opposite sex doesn't develop until the 20s, so even if this behaviour extends into the student years the die is not cast. But it would be wise to talk seriously to the child about the risks of AIDS. It can be pointed out that as heterosexual love can include saying 'no' homosexual love can too.

The big danger comes if parents accuse a child of being a homosexual, or it feels ashamed and cut off from friends who are less drawn to their own sex. This can mean that he or she feels cut off from the opposite sex and it may then be impossible to build that type of relationship, if and when it is wanted. If a child never grows out of loving his or her own sex the parents have no choice but to go on loving the child and to accept its sexual choice, however hard this may be.

Sexual Abuse of Children

The sexual abuse of a child is any sexual activity which abuses the trust a child places in adults. It is not only *what* is done but the *spirit* in which it is done which matters.

Since the huge publicity about fathers abusing their children some parents have become nervous about perfectly normal activities like fathers bathing their daughters or romping around tickling them, or about kissing and hugging. These are an important part of showing love and there is no need to worry. But if, while playing quite normally with children, a parent or *any* adult finds that they (the adult) are getting any kind of sexual stimulation out of it *that is the moment to stop.* Those games should *not* be repeated and nor should any others which have a similar effect.

It is all too easy to move from the seemingly innocent to the not so innocent. What's more, children are very quick to sense an adult's mood, we all know that even a very young child knows a loving hug from a phoney hug, and it is just as quick to spot the sexual hug and feel alarmed by it. It may not be able to say *what* is wrong but it will know that *something* is. And it will know this long before an adult has behaved in a way which is actually assault - and be upset.

How Do You Tell if a Child is Being Abused?

If a child is sexually abused it is likely to show in its behaviour. It may not be easy to pin down the difference between a child who is disturbed because of sexual abuse and one who is upset in some other way, but these are some of the signs to look for.

The abuse will probably be a terrible secret which it can tell nobody. Carrying such a secret can be a barrier to friendships and to reasonable responses to adults (it, quite rightly, thinks adults don't understand how it feels, and loses trust and respect for them). So it may seem in some way cut off from all those around it.

It may behave in sexual ways which are quite odd for its age - either directly or in play with dolls, or in what it draws - or may masturbate openly, or be sexually aggressive.

There may be almost any kind of behaviour problem: bedwetting, nightmares, loss of appetite, unexplained pains, depression or learning problems - though all these could have other causes.

A child may be 'good' but seem watchful and uneasy in the presence of a particular adult, or of adults in general, when it wasn't like that before.

Preventing Sexual Abuse
It is important for parents to trust a child's dislikes. If a child says he or she doesn't like some adult babysitting, or putting them to bed or bathing them the child may have a very good reason which it simply can't explain. When I was 12, I asked my parents not to put me in a situation where I had to undress in front of a particular woman. Even at that age I couldn't say why, and it seemed silly to say I was confused and frightened, so they dismissed my fussing. As an adult I recognized that she was lesbian. If a child *is* just fussing it does no harm to indulge them. If it has sensed something is amiss distress has been avoided. That doesn't, of course, mean that any adult a child takes a dislike to should be suspected of sexual abuse - he or she may just have cold hands or bad breath.

There are now campaigns which help to train children not to talk to strangers and to say no to those who tell them lies about taking them to Mummy. However, the sad truth is that children are far more at risk from someone they know than from strangers. It may be the milkman, the postman, a lodger or one of their own family. And it isn't restricted to those who lack the education or intelligence to understand the damage they may be doing. But you can make them less likely to suffer an attack.

- Tell them they must never go off with any stranger and arrange a code word with them, so that if you are ever unable to fetch them the person you send will say that special word. It needs to be one they won't forget - like the name of their favourite doll - and only you and the child should know the code.
- Don't let young children be out by themselves.
- Don't let young children use public lavatories alone.
- Don't let anyone babysit or take care of a child without checking them out carefully.
- If children are old enough to come home alone from school or to go to the shops alone arrange a safe route and explain why it is important to stick to it.
- Tell children that if *any* adult ever hurts them or tries to do anything which they dislike, or find frightening, they should forget all the normal rules and scream, bite, scratch and defend themselves in every way possible.

You can do all this without talking about sex or alarming a child. All it needs to know is that some adults get bad feelings which make them hurt children even though they are kind at other times.

Traditional stories can be a help. It was my own daughter who pointed out to me that Little Red Riding Hood was a marvellous story for teaching a child that people aren't always quite what they seem and that if any kind and familiar person suddenly begins to behave in big, bad ways, which are not like their normal selves, a child should keep very calm and be very sensible and get away fast to its mother. The great thing about using a story like this is that it allows you to distinguish between the kind normal person who is usually in evidence, and the bad one who emerges when the adult gets in the grip of a perverted sexual drive.

What to Do if a Child Talks about It
It is seldom easy for a child to talk about anything which is deeply upsetting and, if a child even begins to say something which suggests it has had a bad experience - of any kind - the most important thing an adult can do is simply *listen*. It needs to feel that it has the adult's attention and that *nothing* will interrupt. If its first attempts to talk are brushed aside because you need to make a meal, watch TV, or leave the house, it may not get up the courage to speak again. If necessary miss the train to work, and burn the dinner.

Whatever the child tells you keep calm, and let it feel you can cope and will support it. Children very seldom lie about these things, so *believe it* and gently encourage it to tell you more. A child who has been abused may well feel very guilty and needs to be reassured that it is not to blame for what has happened. It will also need to get the burden off its chest, so don't say anything which suggests it should not talk about what has happened. Sometimes the incident may be distressing but relatively minor, but if something illegal has happened you should ring one of the organizations given below and discuss the best course to follow.

The important thing is to protect the child and prevent it ever happening again but, however horrifying the situation may be, don't forget that a child is quite capable of divided feelings. It may love a particular adult when that adult is being normal and be terrified and repulsed by them when sex overwhelms them. What the child may want, therefore, is to get rid of the 'bad' part of the adult but keep the 'good' part. So getting a close relative, especially a father, sent to prison may not always be in the best interests of the child, and may leave it with a burden of guilt which it will find hard to handle. In a situation like this the child's needs must come first and it should not be separated from a non-molesting parent.

Help and information
Childline 0800 1111 is a free helpline for abused children.
Incest Crisis Line (Tel: 01 593 9428, 01 422 5100, 01 890 4732) is run by people who were child victims of incest, and offers telephone support and counselling for adults and children.
In Support of Sexually Abused Children (P.O.Box 526, London NW6 1SU Tel: 01 202 3024) provides a crisis line for the non-abusing parent.
Kidscape (82 Brook Street, London W1Y 1YG Tel: 01 493 9845) offers advice and information to parents worried about the risks of child abuse.

Mothers of Abused Children (Tel: 0965 31432) is a help line for mothers.

NSPCC (67 Saffron Hill, London EC1N 8RS Tel:01 242 1626) has leaflets and advice for parents worried about the problem.

Survivors of Incest (c/o South London Woman's Centre, 55 Acre Lane, London SW2 5TN Tel: 01 326 0333/274 7215) is a help line for those who have suffered from incest.

Sleep

The Sleep a Child Needs
There is no set amount of sleep a child must have at a certain age, but most tiny babies sleep most of the time. Then the morning and afternoon periods shorten little by little, and after a while the morning sleep can be dropped.

How early children should go to bed is a tricky issue. Children need quite a lot of sleep if they aren't to be irritable and difficult in the day - and parents need a decent break in the evenings if they aren't to be the same.

Television and working mothers have pushed back the hours and people now spend more time enjoying their children than they used to.

But you can have enough of even a very good thing and parents with a sense of self-preservation set bedtimes so that they get enough time to rest and enjoy each other. You can put tinies to bed at 6 to 6.30 and have any child under 10 in bed by 8 at the latest with a clear conscience - if it suits your family. If you stagger the bed times, letting them go to bed 15 minutes later each birthday you have a structure which will allow you to give each child some undivided attention at bed time. If children are difficult, lack of sleep may well be the cause, so try putting them to bed earlier.

Some experts say that for children to feel secure and sleep well they need to sleep in only one place. For some children this may be true, but it is convenient if children grow up knowing that they can sleep safely anywhere. Until they were well into primary school I used to take mine out with me and they would sleep on any spare bed anywhere and stay nine-tenths asleep when I carried them in their sleeping bags to the car and back into their own beds. Most children will adapt to almost anything if you start it young enough.

Getting Children to Bed
If children are told to stop playing a good game or watching the television in order to go to bed you make bed the thing which takes them away from the fun. (The same happens if bed is used as a punishment.) If children are enjoying themselves make them stop a little before bed and tidy up. Then bedtime is the nice time they escape to from boring tidying.

If a tiny child refuses to go up to bed turn off the lights in all the other rooms, but leave a light on in its room. Children, like moths, head for the light. (But don't do this unless it's safe.)

Getting Children to Sleep
One school of thought says that if a child wakes at night a loving parent will sacrifice his or her sleep to care for

it and if this means you are dropping with exhaustion for the first years of a child's life that is the price of parenthood. Others - of whom I'm one - say that the most important thing a parent can do for its child is survive with reasonable sanity. Excessive loss of sleep, combined with a tired and naughty child, can drive the gentlest to the brink of child battering.

There is good evidence that most children wake from time to time at night. Some wake and go quietly to sleep again, others wake and cause mayhem. I firmly believe that many of the latter do so because they have learnt that bad behaviour bring rewards. Suppose you woke in the night and, experimentally started yelling, and people you loved rushed in with glasses of wine and plates of food and hugged and kissed you or got you up and took you to a party. Might you not be tempted to do it again next time you woke?

That said, everything a parent does has to be suited to the age and development of the child. A baby who cries for food is doing what it has to do and should not be left to cry (page 268), nor should any tiny baby be left to cry even if there is no obvious reason for the crying. Equally a slightly older child may be genuinely frightened or wake from a nightmare and need swift attention and a good deal of comforting. So may a sick child or a child when there has been some sadness or upheaval in the family.

If a child hears you going to a new baby in the night it may - quite reasonably - fear that you love the baby most and need to be given extra love and reassurance. But tell the child how clever he or she is to be able to sleep through the night, when the baby can't.

There is a world of difference between these reasons and the crying of a child who wants attention and holds a family to ransom with its screams. If you stop to think you will know whether your child really needs your love and attention or is being a tyrant. It is the child who is just trying it on who must not be rewarded. But if you expect the child to control itself, you need self-control too. You can't get a child up from its bed to play because you came home late, or allow it down so you can show it off to visitors and then expect it to sleep the next night when you want it to.

> Some very restless handicapped children may need a sedative to sleep, but it is not wise to give any child a sedative without consulting a doctor.

Helping Babies and Children Sleep
There are many ways you can stack the odds in favour of a child going to bed when you want it to and either sleeping or staying quiet. There will be times when some - or even all - of them won't work. But they are always a step in the right direction and the secret is to find a method and stick to it.

★ Tiny babies should lie on their tummies to sleep, or lie on their side. But don't always lie them on the same side.
★ A baby's body loses heat very easily during sleep, so the room should be at about 24°C (75°F).

★ 2 to 3 is the worst age for sleep problems - try to survive until a child is 4 or more.

It is more restful for parents if babies get used to sleeping in their own room, but a baby or toddler can sleep anywhere and it may be less stressful to have a baby asleep in a crib under the table or beside your bed, than screaming in its room. Some babies seem to need to be slowly weaned from constant human company (which they had in the womb) just as they need to be slowly weaned from the breast or bottle, in which case gradually have it sleep a little farther from you as the weeks and months pass.

- Small babies often sleep better to gentle sounds. Research suggests that the tapes of a human heartbeat help, so does quiet gentle music of almost any kind.
- Babies may sleep better if quite firmly wrapped in a shawl.
- Small babies will fall asleep when rocked.
- If you find a baby is having trouble getting to sleep in the evening wake it earlier from the afternoon sleep. (However, it is very restful for mothers if some afternoon nap is kept up for a good number of years. If the routine is never broken a child will sleep or play quietly for an hour each day, giving its mother a much needed break. A child who rests in the afternoon is usually calmer and easier to get to bed in the evening too.)
- Be reasonable, don't expect a child to lie quietly with nothing to do. Give babies interesting (and safe) dangles above their heads so they can pat them and make them move, but nothing which it can throw out of the cot or it may scream until you pick the missing object up. Give toddlers safe and comforting toys in their bed, and let older children have things they can safely and quietly play with in their room.
- At any age a child sleeps best in the dark (unless it wants a little light), in a bed which is warm (a hot water bottle sees to this but only use water at bathwater temperature, from the tap - a bottle filled from a boiling kettle can burst and scald a child).
- If you find a child gets your attention by climbing (or falling) out of a cot put the mattress in a play pen and put it to sleep there. Then it can't hurt itself and has more room to play.
- Make bedtime a cosy, comforting ritual in which the child calms down and gets more attention than usual. Bath and play with it, put it to bed and read it a story or sing it nursery rhymes. (Children are often soothed to sleep by having their forehead stroked or their face or head very lightly tickled.)
- If a child cries go to it at once and find out what the matter is and try to sort it out with the child in its bed (not picked up - unless it clearly needs comforting) - or at least in its room. Bringing the child to join the rest of the household is a reward to avoid if you can.
- Some children sleep best with a nightlight and many need the door ajar so they don't feel alone. There is no need to be quiet: normal noise makes a child feel safe.

If a child wakes and cries at night most psychologists say *don't* take it into your bed. A parent's bed is quite the nicest place for a child to be so if you do that you have given it the best possible *reward* for crying - it can cause awful problems. Children in bed have been known to wreck their parents' sex life, and a single mother is setting the scene for bitter rivalry between the child and any man she ever shares a bed with. This does not, of course, mean that it *always* causes problems or that a child can't have a cuddle in bed at other times. And sometimes a child will go to sleep happily alone in its parents' bed and can be carried to its own bed when they turn in.

When a child reaches the age when it comes down for drinks it may be genuinely thirsty. Let the child have an unrewarding drink - plain room temperature water and if it's hungry give it a plain slice of brown bread - no butter, no jam, no nothing. If it protests say it can't have anything else as it would be bad for its teeth - which is perfectly true. Then take the child *straight* back to bed. The next night put a mug of water and some bread in its room. You may then find it will call or come down on a new pretext. Then you know it is attention seeking. If it has a good reason for needing more attention give it. If it doesn't, explain that enough is enough.

Once you know a toddler is just trying it on firmness is the only answer. Make sure it has plenty to play with safely in its room. Then put it firmly back and tell the child it *must* stay there but can sit and play quietly on its bed if it isn't sleepy. This is when a battle of wills starts. If it tries to leave its room pick it up and put it into bed that *instant* (don't tell it to go - carry it). If it screams or throws a tantrum tell it very firmly to stop - then leave. Let it cry for several minutes - by the clock - then go in and coolly calm it down. If necessary pick it up for long enough for the tears to ebb, then put it to bed saying it is being very silly and that it doesn't matter how much it cries it must still stay in its room.

There are hyperactive children who seem to need so much activity that they simply can't handle being alone, and they may also be crying babies in the first 4 months. Part of the trouble seems to be that in the first year or two of childhood their desire to *do* things far exceeds their ability to play constructively. My first child was like that and I know how hard it is to handle. There is no choice but to give such children attention until they reach the age when they can occupy themselves. Often they are very intelligent and, with a bit of encouragement, can learn to read at a remarkably early age and then spend hours with books. Meanwhile I suggest you cling onto the thought that Mrs Mozart had a tough time too: you could have a genius on your hands.

Then put it in bed and leave. If it cries again repeat the treatment leaving it to cry for rather longer each time. Sooner or later the child will realize that if it cries nothing nice happens - and peace will reign - provided you never waver. But you *must* pretend to be *very* cool and calm during all this. The message the child has to get is that you are a rock. You love it and can be counted on to be there if it is genuinely upset, but if it is trying to push you around you can't be moved. (See Discipline.) This method can be used for children who won't settle at night, for those who wake during the night and for those who insist that if they wake early the rest of the house must too. But it is only for the child who *wants* attention, not for the one who *needs* it.

Step-Parenting

One of the great, hoped for, consequences of divorce is a second marriage. But unless you divorce in the first dew of youth you are likely to find that almost all your potential partners are divorced too - so a posse of children may be part of the package. There has been a tendency to think that, provided neither side takes exception to the other, step-parenting is much like any other kind of parenting. The experience of more and more couples shows this simply isn't so, in fact, in the words of one experienced counsellor to step-parents 'the emotional minefield is quite terrifying'. Some people say this is why one in every two second marriages break up, and it can certainly be a contributory factor.

- The step-parent may have to handle huge pressures from ex-husbands and ex-wives - this can happen even if the step-parent played no part in the break-up, and is even more likely if they *were* the cause. It is a very restrained ex-partner who manages to never say a word against someone they feel is the cuckoo in the nest.
- The step-parent who has his or her own children has to struggle to treat both step and natural children equally, *and* not let any joint new arrival be unduly favoured as the non-problematic child of the family.
- The step-parent who has no children can easily feel that the stroppiness which afflicts most adolescents is hostility towards him or her as step-parent. They then meet imagined hostility with actual hostility and before they know what's happening it's practically pistols at dawn.
- Most little girls instinctively flirt outrageously with their fathers, and have another phase of playing up to them sexually in adolescence. The child is just practising for adulthood, just as it practised bouncing a ball, and means nothing by it but it can sorely try the patience of a mother (and tempt some blood fathers). But when the 'father' has only been acquired by marriage the situation is potential dynamite. It takes a lot of maturity for the adults to defuse it.
- When children are being brought up by two sets of parents, there are bound to be conflicts of standards, to which there are no easy answers.
- A couple may have conflicting expectations of their roles. For example, a mother who has been worn down by trying to discipline sons on her own, may suddenly expect her new husband to lay down the law. While he, not yet having gained their affection, may - quite reasonably - be wanting to tread a little gently for a while. She feels unsupported (and lacks one of the key things she looked for in marriage), he feels bullied when she nags him about it and suddenly romance seems out of the window and the children seem to have pushed it out. So both parents are fed up with them. The children then feel that the marriage has made their parent less loving and then they *really* start to raise mayhem.
- Another stumbling block can be that step-parents often feel they ought to love their step-children. It would, of course, be lovely if this emotion could flow sweetly over them with the confetti. It doesn't. Nor is there any reason why it should. Actively disliking a prospective partner's children has always seemed to me a good reason for not marrying a man, or woman. But (love at first sight aside) to expect more than a glow of goodwill in the early stages of any relationship, with child or adult, is not common sense. With gentleness, honesty and goodwill, love will have a chance of growing, but those who feel they have to fake love, or expect to *be loved* immediately may make the real thing impossible. Children detect the phoney like a geiger counter picks up radiation. And they don't trust it.

Being a Step-Child
About a million British children have step parents and it's every bit as hard for them as for their parents - and probably harder. The adults have at least chosen the situation, the children have had it thrust upon them. Even if they have managed to go through infancy without hearing a single story about a wicked step-mother, the idea of being landed with a new relative isn't necessarily pleasant. Why should a child even like, let alone love, someone just because one of their parents does?

Nor does liking the step-parent always smooth the path. Relationships are complicated and children often look for people to blame when things go wrong in their lives. If they blame their mother for the fact that their father left (and they may well do so, whether she was much to blame or not) they may well find it much easier to take their anger out on her new partner (whom they aren't afraid of losing) than on her. So behaviour may not be what it seems.

All children go through periods of depression and misery in adolescence - it's the hormones moaning - and they usually think their family are being lousy to them. A child with a step-family isn't necessarily any more miserable than any other, but he or she has to hand a ready-made fantasy that everything would be different if only their real mother or father was there. And in a job lot comes resentment against the step-parent who is wrongly seen as being the cause of their adolescent dumps. Then the step-parent, who may be doing his or her very best to be tolerant of a less than easy child feels wrongly disliked and a vicious circle of genuine resentment is started.

All that is before you even consider what the arrival of a new baby may mean to the other children in the family. For children aren't slow to realize that a child which belongs to both parents may have an edge in the popularity stakes. The trouble is that mother nature got it wrong when she programmed children's behaviour. When a child feels unsure that it is loved you might expect it to behave in ways which are extra lovable - like a cat does. Instead it does the reverse and is usually naughtier, noisier, and less appreciative and affectionate. It may also wet its bed, and even steal. Understandably, parents and step-parents may react to the bad behaviour rather than to what is causing it and so the child feels even less loved.

The Solutions
The examples I have given are only a random selection of the friction points which can arise in step-families. Every family is different but there is one thing families with problems all share: you can't solve them unless you are prepared to remove the layers of misunderstanding by talking about them. It isn't always easy to start doing this within the family itself. So some people may find it is easiest to talk to a counsellor at the **The National Stepfamily Association** (162 Tenison Road, Cambridge CB1 2DP Tel: 0223 460312 - 2 pm to 5 pm and 7 pm to 10 pm most days). This is an organization for step-parents which offers telephone counselling, has local groups where step-parents can exchange problems and solutions, leaflets and courses on how to be a step-parent, and generally tries to help people over the hurdles. M£M, M, A, G, Ad. but you don't have to join to use the confidential telephone counselling service.

Maggie Drummond, *How to Survive as a Second Wife*, Robson
Elizabeth Hodder, *The Step-Parent's Handbook*, Sphere
Brenda Maddox, *Step-parenting*, Unwin
Ann Mitchell and Christine Richard, *Children in the Middle*, booklet from the Stepfamily Association

Toilet Training
It used to be thought that you could train a child to be clean and dry well before it was 18 months old. Science has shown that what really happened was that the *child* trained the *mother* to put it on the pot at the times when it was most likely to perform anyway - such as just after a meal. But believe me it isn't worth making the big issue of toilet training which used to be fashionable, all it does is make work for the mother and upsets for the child.

The truth is that no child begins to have control of its bowel and bladder until it is at least 18 months old and the sensation of being about to go, and the act of going, don't get clearly linked in a child's mind until around 2 years old. By all means pop a baby on the pot after meals if you want to avoid the occasional dirty nappy, but don't leave it there for long and don't expect it to become the slightest bit trained.

The easy way to start bowel training is just to put a child on the pot for a minute or 2 - not longer - after every meal from the age of 18 months or 2 years old. Don't tell it what to do, just let it sit a little while.

Usually nothing will happen. No matter, it has got used to the pot - so far so good. But one day, on the laws of chance its bowels will move as it sits there. This is the moment to make the child feel it is the cat's pyjamas. Praise it warmly and say it is a big boy like daddy or a big girl like mummy and give it a big kiss. There's nothing a child likes as much as pleasing.

Don't expect it to repeat the miracle, but try to notice how long after a meal it usually 'goes' and time the pot sitting to around that time, giving more praise each time. Once the idea is established you can suggest a child tells you when it wants to go. Once again praise it when it does.

Staying dry comes harder and later because the sensation isn't so strong. Start training when your child can stay dry for a couple of hours during the day and obviously knows when he or she is going. That may be any time between 2 and 3 years old.

If you leave rubber pants off, a child may well be more likely to notice wetness - especially if you open a door or window and let in a gust of cold air. If it remarks on being wet change it and tell it how you are making it comfy in a 'nice dry nappy or pants' - but *don't* reverse this and say wet or dirty nappies are bad. Comfort is the issue not virtue or cleanliness. Once a child dislikes being wet you can offer it a pot as a way of solving the problem. If a child does manage to tell you it wants to go it will only know at the very last minute. Act swiftly, but if it sits down too late don't be cross, *sympathize* and say it will work better next time. You, the pot and the child all need to be on the same side. It's not a question of you imposing cleanliness on an unwilling child, but if a child does go in the pot praise it warmly.

★ Don't expect a child to be dry or clean at night until it is well established by day.
★ Never get cross with a toddler for accidentally failing to get to a pot in time. Even once it is trained it can easily be so absorbed in what it is doing that it simply doesn't notice it needs to go. Clearing up after it may be a darned nuisance but it wasn't naughty.
★ Don't worry about the age at which a child is trained, choose a time when the child is ready and it suits you. If it's a bother to get it out of thick winter clothes, wait until early summer and train it when it can be out of doors in pants without plastic.
★ Don't let speed of potty training become a race between you and the next mother. However much others boast they are only showing that they care more about using a child to boost their own ego than about letting it mature in its own time - and *that* isn't much of an achievement.
★ If a child seems frightened of a pot and doesn't want to sit on it sit on it yourself (fully dressed) to do something nice like read a story or play with the child. Once you've done this a few times sit on the floor to read the story with the pot beside you and suggest it as a good seat for the child to get close. Once it's used to sitting on it fully dressed go on from there.
★ Don't be surprised if a child who is ill or upset wets or dirties its pants or its bed. We all know that in the heat of battle grown men can lose control - why should we expect less of a toddler when it finds life hard? Put a rubber sheet on any bed a child occupies until it is well past the years of risk. Long after they stop wetting they smuggle drinks to bed and spill them, so it's all to the good.

Bed Wetting

Any child may wet its bed occasionally until about 6 years old. It may dream it is on the lavatory and go in good faith, or its bladder may not warn it properly, or it may be too frightened of the dark to go along to the lavatory and fall asleep still wanting to go - with predictable results, or it may have had too much to drink before bed and been too heavily asleep to wake. The obvious solutions are restricting drinks before bed, leaving a light on so it can go to the lavatory without fear or having a pot under its bed.

There are also children who become dry and then suddenly start bedwetting and keep doing it night in night out. It creates a mountain of washing which can be very hard to tolerate and may go on for years. There is a wide gulf between doctors and psychologists as to why this type of bed wetting happens. The truth is nobody really knows. However, it often follows a deeply upsetting experience - such as someone in the family dying, or the parents divorcing - and the psychologists who say it is a substitute for weeping may not be wrong. Certainly it is a complete waste of time to try to stop a child doing it by punishing it. It won't work. There are all kinds of devices which claim to cure it by waking the child as it goes, but the truth is that there is only one certain cure: time. The time may seem endless, but no bed wetter ever reached 21 still wetting the bed. It has to stop. Meanwhile the child needs to feel well loved and supported.

★ Don't worry about the child lying in the urine. It isn't pleasant, but if you go in and change the sheets when you go to bed you make twice as much washing and double the chances that you will feel overwhelmed and angry. It is far more important for you to keep calm than for the child to keep dry.

Where to Get Help

If you are in a hurry to find help of any kind the agencies listed below can help you find the sort of person you want quickly. Some specialize in temporary help in emergencies. Some cover straight domestic work, others cover nursing and there are some who can provide people for jobs like animal or house sitting, or accompanying children to stations. Agency charges and terms vary considerably and one way to by-pass an agency fee on a nanny is to get one through a training college - most of which make no charge. The snag is that the nanny may only be available at the end of the summer term.

The classic route to help in the home is an advertisement in the magazine The Lady, (39 Bedford Street, London WC2E 9ER Tel: 01 379 4717). It appears weekly on Thursdays and an advertisement must be handed in 8 days in advance. Through it you can find anyone from a cleaner to a butler trained in martial arts.

If you are not in a hurry, you may find it cheapest to use local advertisements. Make your advertisement reasonably precise. It is far better to have 2 applicants who are right for the job than 10 who aren't, so give the key details. Vague wording like 'Help needed with two lovely children in Hampshire' could get you Mary Poppins or Dracula. And, having asked for 2 references, follow them up - there is no guarantee the references aren't invented.

There is not anything to be gained in economy by having very young and inexperienced servants at low wages; they break, waste, and destroy more than an equivalent for higher wages....

Enquire Within, 1856

Agreeing the Job Details

Before you take anyone on come to a firm agreement about pay, hours, conditions, and give them a written list of exactly what you expect them to do. If you don't see eye to eye, drop them then and there. Taking on someone who has any doubts about their role, or whom you have doubts about, creates more problems than it solves. Having agreed the work before they start, arrange that you will discuss it again at the end of the first week. That way you both have a forum for change.

★ If someone will be looking after an elderly person - who may have certain things they do and do not like to be helped with - list what those things are in some detail. This cuts down the friction which easily happens with the elderly.

The following information provides broad guidelines, it is not hard and fast and although the salaries were right for 1987 - they will have risen by now; however, the comparative levels should be constant.

Au Pair and Au Pair Plus

An au pair is 17 years old or more, is usually from abroad, and lives as part of a family. She is *not* a domestic servant, but she should be prepared to share the household jobs with her hostess, and help look after the children, for about 5 hours a day. The pay and conditions are set by the Department of Employment, and adjusted with the cost of living, so they need to be checked with the DoE. But, as I write, an au pair should have her own room, full board and about £25 to £30 a week, and she must have 5 consecutive hours free time a day, 3 to 4 free evenings, and 1 free day. As an au pair plus a girl is paid about £30 to £35 a week and works about 6 hours a day for 6 days a week. Au pairs may not be capable of coping with children alone.

Mother's Help

Mother's helps and nannies have traditionally lived in, but more and more live out and fit into the schedule of a working mother.

A mother's help can cope with the children alone, if necessary, and does light housework. However, she is not qualified to care for a very young baby. She normally works 5 full days, plus some baby-sitting and has 2 free days a week. The pay is about £40 to £75 a week - living-in.

Nanny, Nursery Teacher or Governess

A nanny should be qualified or experienced and able to take total charge of children. She does everything a mother would do when on duty, but does no housework except that involved in caring for the children. A nursery teacher or governess cares for children from the age of 2 upwards and whereas, in theory, a nanny is mainly concerned with the children's physical needs, this role involves more emphasis on manners and mental stimulation. All these jobs attract £60 to £150 a week with 1 to 2 free days. See also the 'Nanny Kit', page 269.

Housekeeper, Domestic, or Maid
A maid or domestic may do all the household cleaning, cooking, washing and ironing, with 1 to 2 free days and be paid £60 to £100 a week. A housekeeper is expected to do those jobs, or supervise others in doing them, and to run the household, with 1 to 2 free days and receive about £60 to £150 a week. None of these is expected to look after children as well.

Butler
Butlers can be obtained to cover a lunch or a dinner as well as for full-time work. You are unlikely to find one for under £10,000 a year, full-time. Butlers do no heavy cleaning or child care but they do an enormous range of other jobs, from serving food to looking after their master's clothes. Hours tend to be flexible and open to negotiation but they usually have 1½ days off a week.

Organizations
The following organizations serve all parts of Great Britain unless otherwise stated.

Babysitters Unlimited and London Domestics Unlimited (London House, 271-273 King Street, London W6 9LZ Tel: 01 741 5566(baby) 5868(domestics) provides experienced or qualified babysitters and daily helps, plus party helpers and Cordon Bleu cooks. London only.

Bligh (24 Chancery Lane, London WC2A 1LS Tel: 01 405 7061) specializes in Australian and New Zealand nannies and mother's helps, plus some companions to the elderly.

British Nursing Association (82 Great North Road, Hatfield, Herts AL9 5BL Tel: 07072 63544) provides both nurses and professional carers.

Care Alternatives (206 Worple Road, London SW20 8PN Tel: 01 946 8202) provides unqualified staff or nurses to look after the elderly or disabled by day or night.

Childminders (9 Paddington Street, London W1M 3LA Tel: 01 935 2049/9763, London and the home counties) a babysitting service, using experienced sitters. Also supplies ironers and domestic help.

Consultus, (17 London Road, Tonbridge, Kent TN10 3AB Tel: 0732 355231) supplies nurses, midwives, maternity nannies, nannies, mother's helps, cook housekeepers, companion housekeepers, proxy mothers to cope with families, and helpers for the elderly.

Country Cousins and Emergency Mothers (10A Market Square, Horsham, West Sussex RH12 1EU Tel: 0403 210415) specializes in short-term help in emergencies. Helpers live as part of the family and will stand in if a mother is ill, or if an elderly or handicapped person needs care. They also live in with pets while owners are away and escort people to airports, trains, etc. Salaries similar to a housekeeper's.

Homesitters Ltd (The Old Bakery, Western Road, Tring, Herts HP23 4BB Tel: 0442 891188) supply responsible retired people to house sit, and care for the pets, while owners are away.

Kensington Nannies (49-53 Kensington High Street, London W8 5ED Tel: 01 937 2333) for qualified nannies.

The Nanny Service, (9 Paddington Street, London W1M 3LA Tel: 01 935 6976/3515) supplies mother's helps, daily and live-in nannies, and temporary nannies, also maternity nannies.

Occasional and Permanent Nannies (15 Beauchamp Place, London SW3 1NQ Tel: 01 225 1555 (24 hours answerphone)) supplies nannies, mother's helps, maternity nurses and babysitters, here and overseas.

Universal Aunts (250 Kings Road, London SW3 5UE Tel: 01 351 5767) supplies a multitude of personal services. In addition to temporary and permanent staff and helpers of every kind, they have people who will house sit, pet sit, dog walk, shop, cook, take people sightseeing, meet people from stations and airports, and even queue for visas, mend your clothes or witness your marriage.

UK and Overseas Domestic and Au Pair Agency Ltd (87 Regent Street, London W1R 7HF Tel: 01 439 6534 or 01 437 6424) supplies every type of live-in staff from au pairs to butlers recruiting both in UK and abroad. Also finds overseas jobs for British staff/students.

Ivor Spencer School for Butlers (12 Little Bornes, London SE21 Tel: 01 670 8424) supplies both part-time and full-time butlers in Britain and overseas.

Training Colleges for Nannies:

Chiltern Nursery Training College, 16 Peppard Road, Caversham, Reading, Berks RE4 8LA Tel: 0734 471847.

Norland Nurse Training College Ltd, Denford Park, Hungerford, Berks RG17 0PQ Tel: 0488 82252

Princess Christian College, 26 Wilbraham Road, Fallowfield, Manchester M14 6JX Tel: 061 224 4560

Sources of Help

BM Cry-sis, (London WC1N 3XX Tel: 01 404 5011) provides help and support for the parents of crying babies.

The Children's Society (Edward Rudolf House, Margery Street, London WC1X 0JL Tel: 01 837 4299) runs many projects to help families, including such things as centres to try to help families stay together and sheltered accommodation for adolescents.

Church Army, (Independent Road, Blackheath, London SE3 9LG Tel: 01 318 1226) is an evangelistic organization (C of E), offering counselling, advice, and support on most human problems regardless of race or creed. RC, M, L, V, G, Rg, Res, A, HC, HD, sae.

Exploring Parenthood (41 North Road, London N7 9DP Tel: 01 607 9647) has discussion groups where parents can learn more about parenting and exchange ideas with each other and with doctors, therapists and psychologists. National courses for parents, plus brief workshops on specific topics, like step-parenting, or child development. Will also run a workshop for groups of parents anywhere on a subject of their choice, if invited. Members get access to a hotline and three confidential sessions. M£M, RC.

Family Welfare Association (501-505 Kingsland Road, London E8 4AU Tel: 01 254 6251/4) offers support to those facing problems of any kind - bereavement, loneliness, unemployment, difficulties over housing or education, and accommodation for the elderly. It also makes grants to those in serious need, and has a useful book list.

Gingerbread see General Clubs in Free Time.

Home Start (140 New Walk, Leicester LE1 7JL Tel: 0533 554988) uses volunteer visitors to support families with young children through difficulties and crises, and reduce the isolation often experienced by parents of young children. RC.

Meet-a-Mum see General Clubs in Free Time.

The **National Children's Bureau,** (8 Wakley Street, London EC1V 7QE Tel: 01 278 9441 and **Voluntary Council for Handicapped Children)** is an information source with a library and excellent book lists on most of the topics which can affect a child.

National Council for One-Parent Families (255 Kentish Town Road, London NW5 2LX Tel: 01 267 1361) gives free confidential advice for single parents (unmarried/divorced/bereaved) of both sexes by phone or post 9.15 am - 5.15 pm, plus leaflets and books on all aspects of single parenthood. Closed Wednesdays and weekends. Pressure group welcoming non-single parent members, RC, M£L-M, sae appreciated.

National Society for the Prevention of Cruelty to Children, (67 Saffron Hill, London EC1N 8RS Tel: 01 242 1626) is on call 24 hours a day - see your phone book. Reports of child neglect, cruelty or abuse are totally confidential - names are never revealed. Children are not always taken from the family. There are also counselling for parents in distress, playgroups, day-care centres, grants for families in crisis, and support through family centres, plus referral to other supportive organizations. Pressure group on child cruelty issues. Parent Care Club for NSPCC supporters offers substantial discounts on children's goods by leading brands. RC, ChS, L, M.

The National Toy Libraries Association (68 Churchway, London NW1 1LT Tel: 01 387 9592) provides information and advice about the 1,400 toy libraries around Britain. Also some special advice on toys/aids for the handicapped. RC, M£L.

Organizations for Parents under Stress (OPUS) (106 Godstone Road, Whyteleafe, Surrey CR3 0EB Tel: 01 645 0469) provides help by parents for parents whenever parenting seems hard and is the umbrella and contact point for organizations like Parents Anonymous, and Family Contact Line. Offers local groups, befriending, drop-in centres, and in some areas a 24-hour help line.

National Marriage Guidance Council - Relate (Herbert Gray College, Little Church Street, Rugby, Warwickshire CV21 3AP Tel: 0788 73241) offers counselling to couples, both married and unmarried, regarding difficulties in the relationship. You pay what you can afford. Some centres offer sexual therapy. Listed in local phone books under 'Marriage' or under 'Relate'.

Shelter, (88 Old Street, London EC1V 9HU Tel: 01 253 0202) offers advice, support and housing for the homeless.

The Soldiers' Sailors' and Airmens' Families Association (16-18 Old Queen Street, London SW1H 9HP Tel: 01 222 9221) assists the families of those who are, or have been, in the forces with problems of any and every kind. RC.

Students' Nightlines exists in most universities and polytechnics. Those in trouble or distress can ring for a chat - usually between 8 pm and 8 am. The lines aren't manned by experts, just by those who take the time to listen and try to help. They are also an information source on anything from what's on at the local cinema to what to do about VD. The universities take it in turn to act as national co-ordinator, but the number should be available through the students' union.

A library may have the Mental Health Foundation's directory called 'Someone to Talk To' which lists the numbers of help lines of all kinds.

EDUCATION TO SIXTEEN

Home and School

Preparing a Child for School
Imagine how you would feel if your nearest and dearest got you up early one morning, put you into big and unfamilar clothes and then took you by a strange route and led you into a vast building full of scores of other people - most of whom were much larger than you and making a lot of noise - and then walked out on you. I, for one, would find it alarming and be pretty cross - wouldn't you? Yet that is what an unprepared child experiences when going to primary school for the first time. And it doesn't help that the child probably can't tell the time, so its mother saying she will be back at 3 o'clock doesn't let it count the hours. It doesn't have to be like that.

- It will be much easier for a child if it has been to some kind of playgroup, can cope with other children and knows that if its mother goes she also comes back.
- Dress the child in the new uniform around the home from time to time, so it feels as if it belongs, and try to give it enough wear to make the fastenings easy for the child to undo alone, or it may be defeated and wet itself, which is a horrid humiliation.
- Good primary schools often let children visit the school with their parents before they are due to start. If the school doesn't normally do this you could offer to help in a class for a day while bringing the child with you. (Don't worry that you don't know anything about teaching, extra hands are always useful.)
- Take your child to functions like sports days or nativity plays. Then talk afterwards about how it will be able to be an angel or run races when it's at a big school.
- Try to teach your child to read its own name before it goes to school, then it will easily find its own peg and find other possessions in school. If it can't manage this, sew something distinctive, like a coloured ribbon inside its coat and use a biro to draw a picture inside the top of each wellington. Then it will be able to find its own clothes.
- If you are allowed to stay with your child on the first day or two of school do so. If you aren't, know this beforehand and explain to the child that you will have to leave but that you will be back in the afternoon, and plan with it a special celebration tea for the end of the first day so it has something to look forward to.

Whatever you do, all the new experiences of school are demanding and a child may be very tired for the first few weeks. It's a good idea to avoid doing too much after school and to cherish it a little. Put it to bed rather earlier than usual, until this phase passes.

Transferring to Middle or Secondary School
Transfer to a new school is both exciting and stressful for most children, much as taking a new job is for an adult. Adults usually get some immediate benefits out of the stressful experience, such as better pay. It is no bad thing to blunt the edge of the child's change-over in a similar way, with a pocket money raise the first

week and by giving a deliberately celebratory air to shopping for school equipment. But beware of buying your child anything which is of outstandingly good quality. It may make it harder for your child to lend to others.

Parents also need to express confidence in the new school, even if it wasn't their first choice, but they shouldn't tell false tales of how much fun it will be. It could make the child feel they are deeply out of touch.

As with starting primary school the child is likely to be far more tired than usual for a few weeks, which could mean that instead of flopping it will be tetchy and obnoxious. There may also be difficulties in settling down to the business of homework. It will help if a routine is established from early on.

> Children usually have exaggerated ideas of how much grown-ups - especially parents - know and understand. This can lead them to think a grown-up must *know* about an unfair (or perverted) teacher or about bullying in the school. It's a good idea to explain to a child, from primary school onwards, that you aren't able to tell what happens in the school and that you want them to tell you if they are ever upset or worried about anything.

Teaching at Home
There are three aspects to teaching at home: teaching a child totally at home because you have an objection to schooling, teaching a child at home because illness or absence abroad makes it impossible to attend school, and simply boosting what is done in school by doing a certain amount yourself. The reasons, and the age of the child, will affect what you teach, but there are certain principles which apply to all teaching whatever the age of the child. Those I briefly cover below.

Should Parents Teach their Children?
Many teachers lack confidence and feel threatened by the thought of children being taught by their parents. After all, if any old parent can teach, what price the teacher's training and experience? This is very understandable, but it is not only a good idea for parents to teach their children, it is essential. And I speak as a teacher.

The best and easiest time for anyone - child or adult - to learn anything is when they feel like doing it. Yet teachers simply aren't there in the vital early years and even the best teacher with the smallest class cannot notice and stimulate the special interests of every schoolchild every day. And with children there is more to learning at the right moment than just pleasure. They are marvellous learning machines and a confident child keeps pushing back the frontiers of his or her achievements, step by step, always progressing to the next thing which can *just* be managed. You can see them doing it physically: walking along the tops of walls as soon as they are sure of level ground. They also do it

mentally, unerringly choosing the next activity they are ready to master. If we can follow a child's leads and teach it what it wants to know the child is learning what it is ready to learn. Which means it learns quickly and easily. It doesn't matter a jot whether the activity is officially 'right' for its age, where learning is concerned what a child *wants* to learn *is* right for that child. If it points to words at 1 year old, and asks what they are, it wants to read - so teach it. And if stacking bricks is its great delight, give it bricks to stack. The child is the best judge of what it needs to do.

A child learns more between birth and 5 than at any other time in its life - and its parents are the main teachers, even when they don't realize it. This doesn't mean that if you are educating your child at home you sit there waiting for it to take an interest in nuclear physics. Adults have to try out topics and ideas on children and see which ones they latch on to. Only if you play them music will you discover whether they enjoy it. If nothing excites them, and you are educating a child entirely at home (page 287) some basic teaching will do no harm at all if it's done the right way.

Teaching in the Early Years
People often forget just how much a child needs to learn. Stop and think for a moment about what the world must be like to a new baby who doesn't yet know up from down, hard from soft, and has no idea why it is lying on a blanket one minute, in water the next. Somehow its immature brain has to make order out of the extraordinary chaos that must seem to surround it.

Teaching it about the world starts the moment you first hold it and it learns the feel of your body. From then on it needs lots of varied experiences to help it sort the world out. There's proof that the children most likely to do well in school are those who were given lots of stimulation in early childhood. You may not be able to make your child a genius, but what you teach it from birth to 5 can make the difference between it being a success or a failure for the rest of its life.

Talk to it from the very first so it learns language - but use normal English, there's no point in giving it the extra work of learning both gee-gee and horse. Whether in pram or crib it needs something to focus its eyes on and things to touch so it can learn to co-ordinate hand and eye to touch them. Give it something which will swing if it touches it or make a noise, but make sure everything it is given is safe for it to chew. Babies are also learning what is edible.

It would take pages to explain all the things you can do to help a baby and toddler learn, but knowing what to do is half instinct, half imagination. If you try to see the world from the child's point of view and realize all the things which are new and strange, and all the skills it doesn't have, you will soon work out what a child needs. The great thing is to remember that a child is learning from each thing it does. To a child *all* play is learning. Once you see how hard it works at it and how quickly it will latch on to each new experience, being a parent becomes much more interesting. To us a child with a rattle is just a child making a noise. To a baby it is a discovery at least as important as learning to drive is to an adult. It learns that such a sound exists and - far more important - it learns that it has the power to make sounds with something other than its own voice.

A young child doesn't need expensive toys to learn about the world. A wooden spoon tied to the side of a cot, and a row of empty, brightly painted, cotton reels hanging above it, which swing when touched, give it just as much to learn from as anything you can buy. (But keep them out of chewing distance.) Pictures from magazines can decorate its wall and give it new shapes to look at. As it gets older, saucepans and wooden spoons make great (if ear-splitting) drums, water and sand teach it vital lessons about the amount which a container will hold - which is important in mathematics. Newspaper is just as good for early attempts at painting as any art paper.

In all this don't expect a child to stay clean, tidy and quiet. To think that a 'good' child is one who is like that is to misunderstand childhood. A child who is really developing its brain regards every day as a series of experiments and experiments are messy. Half the art of parenthood is setting up situations where the mess can be limited to places where you don't object to it. The other half is learning to answer questions. Children have an uncanny knack of asking questions at quite the worst moments, but however many they ask, or however odd they may seem no parent should ever get cross with a child for asking. To do that is to tell a child to stop thinking - and the quick route to a child who won't learn in school either. If you don't know the answer say so, and perhaps try to find it out together.

The Basics of Teaching a Child
If you start to teach your child anything - reading, games, music or mathematics - there is one basic rule which always applies whatever the age or ability of the child. The child must enjoy it and get satisfaction from it. Many adults use teaching children as an excuse to show the children how big and clever they - the adults - are. Thus making the child feel small and unable to do things. To teach you must leave your own ego behind. All teaching must be designed to make the *child* feel big and clever and it should feel more confident and more successful with each new thing it learns or tries to do. So play down your own prowess, make some mistakes yourself, and laugh about them - so failure isn't a bogey man.

At the same time keep the child's risks of failure to a minimum. This means that each new task you ask it to do should always be just a little step up from what it has already mastered, so it is within its ability. If it can read 10 words give it those 10 to read, then add 1 more. When it can read 11 words, add 1 again. Don't try to rush it by leaping from 10 to 15 in a burst of parental pride - unless the child shows you that it wants to learn faster. This doesn't mean the child has no challenges, it means the challenges are always the right size for it. Only a bad rider tries to take a young horse over hard jumps before it has mastered basic ones, and we should use horse sense with children.

It is because teachers now believe in keeping failure to a minimum that you may see that some mistakes in your child's homework are not corrected. If a child makes a lot of mistakes and every single mistake is pointed out it is very discouraging. So good teachers often correct only the mistakes a child can learn from - at that moment.

If you watch children you will see they will learn to bounce a ball, and for a few days they bounce it everywhere, revelling in this achievement. Then suddenly they begin throwing it against the wall and catching it. They've learnt, they've practised and they've moved on. Copy this pattern and make the practice a pleasure. All kinds of learning games can be invented to do this. But watch the child. Stop just *before* the child has had enough, so it is hungry for more next time.

If you want to teach any creature to do something you link learning with reward. To a child learning is itself rewarding (unless it's taught badly), but it is doubly so if an adult (especially one it loves) praises its achievement. Children grow intellectually on a diet of praise and encouragement the way a plant grows on fertilizer. Whether you are teaching it to do up its own shoes or to read give it plenty of love and praise whenever it even *begins* to get something right, and largely ignore mistakes - except where a slight explanation is essential (to help them, not to satisfy the parent's ego). Don't be afraid that praising a child for getting things a little bit right will take away its incentive to do even better. Children, like adults, can take praise till it's coming out of their ears and still be glad of more. When did *you* ever find that you were praised so much that you gave up trying? Nor will it get big-headed, it's the child who doesn't really feel good enough who is most likely to boast.

The Pitfalls of Home Teaching
The most common pitfall is that parents naturally want their child to succeed, and even shine. The temptation is to push the child, forcing it to work when it should be playing, getting impatient when it makes mistakes and so on. This is not only nasty for the child but a bad way to get results. The parent who makes learning unpleasant is actually teaching their child *not* to learn. And so is the parent who *always* has to know best, and win at every game, and who chooses to lecture rather than discuss. It is also worth remembering that each child has its own sequence and its own pace. You can never expect it even to follow the pattern of its brothers or sisters.

If you are teaching a child something and ever feel impatience or anger rising *stop teaching that instant* and leave it a day. Once a child links learning with your anger, it will switch off its brain faster than you'd think possible. There are only three reasons why young children fail and make mistakes - the adult has given it an unsuitable task, the adult has gone on for too long, or the adult has taught it in the wrong way. In all three cases the child deserves no anger.

All that may seem very soft. It isn't, it's plain time and motion study. The only quick way to teach anyone anything is to use their eagerness and fuel it with satisfaction.

The second pitfall is the one of trying to channel children into one's own interests. Every child differs, but inside each is the ability to be deeply interested in something, and one of a parent's greatest roles is to introduce each child to the widest possible range of experiences and when it shows an interest in one, feed that interest.

The final pitfall which teachers, rightly, fear is that of parents imposing on children outdated and damaging methods which will make them thoroughly confused. Reading and mathematics are the two subjects most vulnerable to this. It is pointless for parents to use methods which conflict with those used in school even if they think that modern methods are daft. It is easy enough to ask a child to show you how its teacher does a certain type of sum or gets it to read words or go and ask the teacher. Any parent who makes it very clear that they ask in a spirit of co-operation, so that they can help their child by the 'right' method, should find teachers only too happy to explain.

There are also methods of teaching young children which don't cut across any systems. Geraldine Taylor is a teacher who runs courses all over the country, showing parents how to teach their children. She can be contacted via **Central Bristol Adult Education Centre** (189 Newfoundland Road, St Pauls, Bristol BS2 9NY Tel: 0272 556415). Other information from Education Otherwise - page 287.

Teaching a Child to Read
The moment you first sit a child on your lap and show it the pages of a book you are starting to teach it to read. Even if the book only has pictures it is learning that books have interesting things in them. That's important, so a child should be shown picture books from a few months old, and read stories as soon as it will begin to understand them. And children who learn rhymes learn to read faster.

When you show them pictures avoid the temptation to name letters of the alphabet which are often beside them. Learning the alphabet does more harm than good. When we read we use the *sound* of the letters not the names (you only need the alphabet to look things up in dictionaries and telephone directories). But if you've already taught your child the alphabet don't worry, it will get over it.

There are all kinds of reading systems and they all work. If a child is under school age the method which is least likely to clash with anything a child later learns in school is simply to teach it to recognize whole words. Children do this very easily. You show it the word cat and you say cat quite normally, not c-a-t. Teach it with ordinary letters - e.g. cat - *not* capitals and the younger the child the larger you should write them. With a pre-school child a couple of inches high is ideal. Put each

word on paper and make the first words it learns ones which are important to it - its own name, mummy, daddy, its pet or whatever. When it can recognize a lot of nouns you can start adding other words like is, and, here, and build them into sentences. With an older child modify this to its interests, and if it prefers to read from a book let it do so.

At any age it doesn't matter if the word is quite long, children recognize a house just as easily as a table and, with the whole word method of teaching reading, size makes no more difference to words than it does to objects. They can be written large on sheets of paper and a good game to play is to put 2 or more words down (according to the stage the child is at) and ask it to find a particular word and pick it up. You can then praise each word it picks up correctly, and make much of counting how many it got. This game can be used for quite advanced readers using quite a lot of words and 'racing' them to find one - the child must win most of the time.

★ I have found that when reading is done by recognizing a word and picking it up, rather than saying it, any child can do it - even an autistic child or one with a speech problem.

Once a child can read a few words on paper you can pick out those same words in the books you read to it, and let it read the words it knows - or make a book with a story about itself. Before long it is reading whole pages. This means that if a child is a slow reader you can read books to it which are right for its age - and let it read the words it knows from them - rather than condemning it to the humiliation of books which are too young for it. Once a child can read quite well you can, for example, point out the way words like sand, hand, land all have 'and' in, and you and the child can start looking for patterns and playing with letters and building words with them - and spelling is born.

Even if you have time for nothing else do get your child to read to you a little, once it starts learning at school, and praise its efforts. Research shows children learn far better if they have this encouragement.

Teaching a Child Maths
The first blessing a parent can bestow on its child's mathematical ability is never to let it hear you say you hated maths or were bad at it. Then it won't expect it to be a bogey.

Children have all kinds of things to learn before they can do sums. They have to learn the language of maths. We take the words for granted but a child has to learn what numbers are and what things like roundness are. It's so easy to play counting games with a toddler's fingers and toes and to say 'look at that big *round* ball', or that *square* red brick - not just big ball or red brick. It also needs to learn about more and less. In the bath it can have plastic containers of different sizes and pour water from one to another. Gradually it will grasp the fact that what fits in one won't always fit in another. When it has a slice of bread you can say you will cut it in half, or in quarters and do so. Later on it can do the cutting. Take it shopping and let it hear you using money and later help to get coins from your purse. And, when a child starts to add up, and you can change the rules of dominoes instead of matching 2 to 2 and 4 to 4, match the dots so they add up to 10.

All those things sound very simple - but they are the basic mathematics it will use all its life, and the child who learns such things has a great foundation for maths in school.

> Modern maths teaching in schools can look like nothing but play. There is method in this. The new maths teaching lets children learn about real situations and then transfers this learning to numbers on paper. It is no good chanting the times table before you have grasped that 'three twos are six' actually means that it you have 3 bags of apples, with 2 in each bag, you have 6 apples.

British Association for Early Childhood Education (Studio 2-3, 140 Tabernacle Street, London EC2A 4SD Tel: 01 250 1768), RC, (formerly the Nursery School Association) M£L, M, G, L, B.

National Association for Remedial Education (2 Lichfield Road, Stafford ST17 4JX Tel: 0785 46872) is an organization for teachers of those with with learning difficulties, but some of the publications

The National Library for the Handicapped Child (Blyton Handi-read Centre, Lynton House, Tavistock Square, London WC1H 9LT) helps and advises parents of handicapped children who have reading problems.

Laurie Buxton, *Maths for Everyman*, (aimed at parents who don't like maths and would like to help their children)
Do You Panic About Maths, Heineman Educational
Glen Doman, *Teach Your Baby to Read*, Jonathan Cape
Any book by Michael Holt on maths teaching is worth reading
Dr Roger Morgan, *Helping Children Read*, Methuen
Geraldine Taylor, *Be Your Child's Natural Teacher*, Penguin

Bypassing Schooling

By British law a child must be educated, but education is not defined as schooling. All the relevant Education Acts say that parents have a duty to see that a child is educated according to its needs and that Education Authorities must as far as possible see to it that children are educated in accordance with their parents' wishes. The parents rights are also enshrined in the United Nations Declaration of Human Rights which says:
● everyone has the right to education
● education shall be directed to the full development of the human personality
● parents shall have a right to choose the kind of education that shall be given to their children.

Equally, the European Convention for the Protection of Human Rights and Fundamental Freedoms says: '...the state shall respect the right of parents to ensure such education and teaching is in conformity with their own religious and philosophical convictions.'

At the same time parents can be taken to court, and a child put in care, if an LEA believes the education they

give is not adequate. So parents who intend to educate their children themselves would be well advised to talk to others who have tried it and know what the authorities accept or quarrel with.

Education Otherwise (25 Common Lane, Hemingford Abbots, Cambs PE18 9AN Tel:0480 63130) is for those who want to educate their children themselves, and provides mutual advice and information. Links to the US counterpart. RC M£M, M, L, B. Guide to parents' rights.

Home Education Overseas

Parents who have to go abroad for their work may find themselves needing to keep their children abreast of British education so that they can return to it - if only with the right examinations to get into further education. The major organization which provides parents with what they need to achieve this is the World-wide Education Service (WES). It is an arm of the Parents National Educational Union which has several schools around Britain, and its Home School service provides an education programme by which a parent can teach a child at home with the postal guidance of a WES tutor, who is a qualified and experienced teacher. Its courses include a nursery education course for 3 to 5 year olds, designed for parents or nursery teachers, and a course for 5 to 13 year olds, plus single subject courses for children who are attending a local school abroad which lacks certain vital subjects.

The courses show a parent how to teach a child, as well as offering a course of what to teach it, and provide assessment and references which can be offered to future schools. Older children need to use one of the open learning schemes leading to exams (see page 307).

World-Wide Education Service (WES), Strode House, 44-50 Osnaburgh Street, London NW1 3NN Tel:01 387 9228

State Education

Describing the British education system is a bit like shaking hands with an octopus: there is no obvious point at which to start. Nor does it make it any easier that it is currently undergoing such a shake-up that this particular octopus keeps waving its tentacles about just when you try to grasp one. What follows is the state of play as I write, but new legislation is in the pipeline and it is anybody's guess how it will fare in parliament. So, before taking any major educational step, it would be wise to double check that nothing important has changed since this was written.

> What follows concerns England and Wales. Please assume that all references to the DES include the Education Department of the Welsh Office. Scottish Education is covered on pages 293 to 294.

Authority and Where it Lies

The school system is supervised by the Department of

Education and Science from offices topping a row of shops in Waterloo. The other bodies involved in education are the education departments of the local authorities (LEAs), the churches and other voluntary bodies who have schools within the state sector, the governing bodies and the teachers.

One of the key issues at present is how much control and influence should rest with the Department of Education and Science (DES) (and the Education Department of the Scottish Office) and how much with the other educational bodies. Neither the 1944 Education Act, which is still the foundation of the system, nor the Act which followed it gave the DES much power and its role has been to fund the universities (via the University Grants Committee), control the educational building programme, and accept or reject LEA plans for school reorganization. It is also the court of appeal for disputes between parents and local authorities.

Until recently the DES created national policies, through changes in legislation, but did not administer them or play any part in what was taught. This has changed and is still changing. The 1986 Education Act set rules relating to specific subjects like sex education, and by the time you read this, we may have a national curriculum, which would put the DES firmly in the driving seat.

Government Departments Involved in Education

The Manpower Services Commission (MSC) (an arm of the Department of Employment) is playing an ever-growing role in courses for those over 16. So government is also involved in what is happening to the older age groups without being restricted by the DES-LEA relationship.

At the other end of the age range social services departments, which come under the Department of Health and Social Security, provide day-nurseries, and certain educational facilities for the mentally handicapped.

Finally the Department of Industry has been involved in the introduction of computers in schools, and provides training at Information Technology Centres, and industry itself is now being brought in to sponsor City Technology Colleges. So the whole framework of education is changing.

Local Education Authorities

Almost all the 105 education authorities of England and Wales are simply branches of local councils. Each is run by a Director of Education or Chief Education Officer and an education department. The elected councillors of the county or metropolitan councils influence decisions via an Education Committee. But only half the members of the Education Committee need be elected councillors, and it includes members co-opted for their expertise. The 1944 Education Act makes LEAs responsible for the moral, spiritual, mental and physical development of their communities by ensuring that 'efficient education...shall be available to meet the needs of the population in their area'. This means the LEAs must provide the schools and colleges for their area,

recruit and pay teachers, and provide equipment, materials and back-up services. The Education Committee is responsible for seeing that this is done, and for approving the day-to-day running of the education system in the authority.

LEA Funding

Education usually eats up more than half the total budget of any local authority. The money spent by LEAs comes from 4 sources:

- a share of the rate support grant (which is paid by central government to the local authority)
- grants from central government made directly for educational purposes (for which LEAs can apply)
- money from local rates
- money raised by the authority, for example through evening classes

The latest education act will enable LEAs to charge parents for special activities which have always been free - such as individual music lessons and some out-of-school activities.

LEAs' Duty on Meals

An LEA may provide meals and break for children in their schools, but it has no duty to do so, and may charge what it wishes. The only exception, at the time of writing, is that it must make 'appropriate provision' for free meals for the children of those on certain state benefits.

LEAs' Duty on Transport

LEAs must provide free transport to and from school where they think it necessary. In practice this means they normally provide it if the child is at their nearest state (or voluntary) school and if they live more than walking distance away. However, 'walking distance' is 2 miles for those under 8 and 3 miles for those over 8.

You will notice that this means that if parents choose a school which is not the one nearest to them this could leave them with the travel costs. In practice LEAs vary considerably in how generous they are, some charge pupils for riding on a school bus if they don't have an automatic right to be on it.

Choosing a State School

Since the 1980 Education Act, parents have had the right to choose the school their child goes to, and the Local Authority must try to send the child there if it can. This applies at every age and situation, and includes not only all ordinary state schools but all voluntary maintained schools. Parents can even apply for a school in a neighbouring authority, or for a place in a state boarding school.

To give parents a foundation for their choice the LEA must make available them the following information free of charge. Interested parents can either read it in a public library or have it sent to them.

- The LEA policy on primary and secondary education.
- The LEA policy on admission and appeals.

- A list of the schools.
- The arrangements for school meals and transport.
- Details of arrangements for general education welfare.
- Policies for children with special needs.
- How they identify children with special needs.
- Arrangements for Welsh language teaching (Wales).

The following information must be sent free of charge by the school itself if you ask for it:
- the curriculum
- the arrangements for making subject choices
- the details of how the school is organized
- its policy on discipline
- its policy on school uniform
- a list of the main activities outside the school curriculum
- its policy on public examinations
- the most recent examination results.

Once you know which schools you are interested in you can ask the head teachers whether you can see round each. This is not a privilege. It is something you have a right to do - at the school's convenience.

How to Check Out a School
In any school, if the teachers assign a child or two to show you round it is a very good sign. It shows the school has nothing to hide and is prepared for you to quiz the children. Do so: children will tell you far more than teachers.

Don't just wander round looking, take time to sit and listen quietly. Ask the head if you may sit in on some classes - and pick different age groups and subjects. If you find the teachers boring your child may too.

Try to talk to other parents. The gaggle found outside most schools at the end of each school day will be more than willing to talk about their children's education.

If you can see into the playground stand outside and watch at break-time. You will soon see whether children play happily, or gang up on the weaker children and you may be able to tell whether they get up to other mischief.

In primary schools look for:
- children who seem to be enjoying themselves without excessive noise
- lots of evidence of creative activities - models, paintings
- children responding willingly to the teacher
- a library with books children would *want* to read
- equipment they can climb and play on outside.

Ask:
- how mathematics, reading and writing are taught
- whether you may stay and help in the class if your child needs you in the first few days
- if they have family grouping
- do children keep one teacher as they go up the school or do they get a new teacher as they move up a form (the latter means that if they don't get on with one teacher they have a chance with another)
- what facilities there are for science and music
- about the policy if a child develops learning difficulties
- what the arrangements are for school meals
- about the qualifications and experience of the teachers
- the policies on any issues you care about - sex, religion, etcetera
- about the policy on homework
- about the parent-teacher (home and school) association
- what equipment they have for teaching children about computers or for teaching foreign languages.

Listen to *how* the head replies as well as to what is actually said. Do you have the impression that he or she really wants you to know and likes parents being involved? Or are you just a necessary evil?

In secondary schools ask:
- about the range of subjects which can be taken at GCSE and at AS and A level
- how flexible they can be over odd combinations of subjects at GCSE or AS or A level
- whether any tutor is assigned to keep a particular eye on a pupil's welfare throughout the years in school
- about the number and qualifications of teachers in key subjects, especially mathematics and science
- about the policy on remedial teaching
- about the policy on homework
- about the policy on discipline and how much the children help to run the school
- what punishments are given (having first read what they put in writing)
- about the policy on foreign languages - which do they offer and what methods and equipment do they use
- what facilities they have for practical subjects like design and metalwork
- what facilities are there for computer studies and what are the qualifications of the teacher
- what part music, drama, art and sport play in the life of the school and also whether practical subjects like cooking and child care are open to all pupils - and both sexes - or only to girls or those who aren't academic. A good school should find time for all these *and* get good exam results.

The information the school puts out should show you how well pupils have done in public exams. Ask about any facts which aren't clear.

Absorb the atmosphere of the place: is there a feeling of reasonable order or do the classrooms feel as if they could erupt at any minute? Are the children polite and confident, or over-polite and nervous, or sloppy and rude? Do the teachers seem to care or is there a feeling that they are time-serving?

More information
Felicity Taylor, *Choosing a School*, ACE (page 299)

Getting a Place at the School you Want

As you'd expect, good schools have parents queuing up to get their children in, so most schools have some kind of points system. However, LEAs vary in what points they give to which criteria, and voluntary schools (see page 293) don't have to follow their LEA's rules. Some give high points to the children who live nearest, most give them to the brothers and sisters of those already at the school, others to those in greatest need, and so on. Some schools will explain their system, some won't. But voluntary schools may give priority to those belonging to the church which founded them - which may look like racial discrimination, even though it isn't.

★ In case early application scores points, get your child's name down well ahead of time. You need to apply for some primary schools when a child is 2.

Most LEAs expect applications for places to be in by the end of January for the following September, but this varies and the education department concerned will tell you how to apply. If you are asked to give a second and third choice do so, it won't reduce the chances of getting a place in the first choice school, and if that is full your child may go to your second choice.

> It's politic to write and thank the head of any school you have visited, and say how much you enjoyed the visit. You can also tell the head of the school you have chosen that you hope he will be able to accept your child (he or she may have no say - but who can tell). To the other heads include a let-out clause - unconnected with how the school is run - such as you are not sure how easy it would be for your child to get to the school by public transport. You could find your child is allocated to one of these schools instead of to your first choice and there's no point starting your relationship with the head as one of the parents who rejected the school.

If Your Choice is Refused

If the authorities refuse to give your child a place in the school you want they must give their reasons. If you are unhappy about this arrange to see the officials concerned, or write to them, as soon as possible. Explain why your child needs to go to that school and ask them to reconsider. If you think that some report by a previous school or by some official has influenced the decision you can ask to see any reports on your child. You don't have a *right* to see these, but they might let you and there may be aspects which you can explain. For example, a child may have been through a period of bad behaviour when upset by a family problem.

★ Until recently all schools closed their books when 80 per cent full. It is now government policy for schools to fill to the brim, even if it means other schools having too few pupils to be worth keeping open. So if the authorities say the school is full ask how full. If it has vacant places which it is refusing to fill you can point out that this is not DES policy.

If talking to the authorities doesn't work you have a right of appeal. The documents from the LEA *must* tell you how and where to appeal. Check them carefully as there may be a time limit as little as 14 days. Appeals are in writing and you should give your reasons for wanting the school of your choice. You can:

- say why you don't like the school which has been allocated
- say why you aren't convinced by the reasons given for refusing a place
- add anything else which helps your case.

You will then be sent a note of the date of the appeal hearing. You can ask for a different date, if you have a good reason for this. But tell them at once. You then need to prepare what you will say. Find out all you can about the admission arrangements in the area and the school they want to send your child to, and be sure to take with you your original letter and notes of everything you want to say, and any evidence you need.

> Once a child is attending the disliked school the LEA has a case for saying that it obviously *can* get there and has settled in. So, in practice, parents who keep their child out of school while fighting this battle are more likely to win. However, they must - by law - see that the child is being educated in a suitable manner at home. If they fail to do that the child could be taken into care and sent to school.

In theory, if your appeal is turned down you can appeal to the Secretary of State for Education at the DES (see Organizations) setting out your case clearly and concisely. Those in Scotland write to the Secretary of State for Scotland at the Scottish Office, those in Wales to the Secretary of State for Wales at the Welsh Office. In practice, you haven't much chance of getting the decision reversed, but if the procedure was unfair in any way get your local councillor to complain to the local ombudsman. (The ACE booklet *School Choice Appeals* gives some useful advice on preparing an appeal and explains the rules - so you can tell if they were broken.)

> It is impossible to predict what the admissions procedure will be for schools which decide to opt out of their LEA and be responsible to the DES. Nor has there been any indication of how a parent could make such a school a first choice and pick ones within the LEA as second and third choices, since this would not endear them to the LEA.

Compulsory Schooling

An LEA must educate a child from the beginning of the term which follows his or her 5th birthday and a pupil must stay at school until the end of the spring term if their 16th birthday is between 1 September and 31

January, or until the Friday before the last Monday in May if their birthday is in the rest of the year. Between 16 and 19 schooling is optional but if a pupil wants more education the LEA has a duty to provide it.

Curriculum

As I write, the government is in the process of establishing a set curriculum for schools. If government has its way, 3 core subjects will be taught from the age of 5 to 16: English, Mathematics and Science, plus Welsh for those in Wales, and 7 foundation subjects - history, geography, a modern language, technology, art, music and physical education.

Nothing very revolutionary, so you may be wondering what's new and whether the subjects will have to be taught for a set number of hours or follow some other rigid rule. I have been assured that nothing of the kind is planned, and that schools will be free to teach what else they like in the time left over from those subjects. Whether this will stifle the pioneering innovation which has always been such a feature of the best of British education is impossible to tell until the system has been running a while.

What may, however, change is how subjects are taught. HMI proposals for foreign language teaching set pretty firm guidelines. If they are followed there will be far more listening to the language as it is normally used, far more speaking, and far less translation, until a pupil reaches the more advanced levels.

The government also wants all pupils to have testing and assessment at the ages of 7, 11, 14 and 16. The idea will be to compare them with the 'normal' achievement for their age. Nobody is yet very clear about what will be done if a child isn't up to standard but it seems there are no plans to make children retake a year.

Discipline in School

Normally systems of punishment in schools are laid down by the local education authority and then heads put them into practice. It is therefore the LEA which normally decides issues like whether school uniform will be worn, although it is often the head who sets strict rules on how children may behave when wearing that uniform. Parents do not have a right to ignore such rules but they are entitled to know the discipline guidelines set by a LEA and if they don't like them they should lobby their local councillors and the board of governors.

Supporting the School

Teaching groups of potentially riotous children is essentially a conjuring trick which depends on the children not seeing too clearly how easily they could topple the whole set-up. If parents want their children to learn anything it is vital that the children behave in a disciplined way - and they won't if they feel the teachers don't have the backing of parents. So, *for the child's sake*, parents must seem to back the school whenever possible.

However, teachers aren't saints: sometimes they behave badly and make the wrong decisions. A parent who supports teachers, even when they are clearly behaving stupidly or being seriously unfair looks to a child like someone who is on the side of authority and not of what is right - and that is not a position a child respects. So, support has to be tempered with a little caution. If a teacher behaves badly a parent may be able to sort it out by talking to the teacher (if it's appropriate) or help the child understand that the teacher may have had a good reason for a wrong action.

Punishments

The usual range of punishments which a school may give are such things as not taking part in activities which are specially enjoyed, doing extra work, or staying in when others play. Some schools go farther and have special rooms to which children are sent if they upset their normal class.

No matter how difficult a child is, corporal punishment is now illegal. So banning a child from school (exclusion) has become the final punishment. The 1986 Education Act set out the step-by-step procedure which has to be followed if a child is excluded. And exclusion covers any situation in which a child is told to stay away from school, whatever the LEA calls it.

There are 3 kinds of exclusion: **fixed** exclusion usually only covers a few days, so **indefinite** exclusion is more serious, and **permanent** exclusion the worst of all. Under the 1986 Act if there is a fixed exclusion:
- a parent must be told immediately
- the LEA and governors *only* need to be told if a child is excluded for a total of more than 5 days in any term, or will miss a public examination.

If the exclusion is indefinite or permanent:
- the parents must be told immediately *and* given the reasons for it
- the LEA and governors must always be told.

What a Parent can Do

The steps a parent can take are quite complicated but the basics are as follows.
- Ask the head to tell you why the child was excluded and what type of exclusion it is (it's best to ask in writing but a phone call is better than nothing).
- Ask to see the head and discuss it. It may help to take someone with you. If the school has been unreasonable try to take a parent governor.
- If that fails write and tell the Chief Education Officer that you want to appeal against the suspension.

In all this, make sure you keep any letter you write and replies you get.

An independent panel may hear your appeal, and the reasons given by the governors. Normally no written evidence is used on either side, but you should plan what to say and it would be good to have all the letters with you. The independent appeal panel can reject an appeal, but if they approve it the head must either take the child on a date set by the panel, or permanently exclude the child. If the head opts for permanent exclusion the ball lands back in the LEA court: it must place the child in another school or provide it with home tuition. In some areas LEAs tend to forget this and leave a child out of school for long periods. They are breaking the law and you should remind them of that.

Anyone who feels the appeals procedure wasn't properly run can complain to the Local Ombudsman through a local councillor, and may even complain to the Secretary of State - though this is not likely to get results.

The Advisory Centre for Education (page 299) has a detailed briefing on what a parent can do about exclusion.

Parents' Role in State Education

The 1986 Education Act made big changes in the role which parents can play in the state education system. Before the Act a school of 300 to 599 pupils, for example, would have 26 school governors, half of them appointed by the local authority and likely to toe the party line. Today that school would have only about 16 governors: the head teacher, 2 other teachers, 5 co-opted governors from the local community, 4 parents, plus 4 appointed by the local education authority. (See also Scottish education, page 293).

An annual general meeting of parents elects parents to the board. Since the governing body is the watchdog of how a school is being run this is a distinct step forward.

The Role of School Governors

The act has altered the functions of the governing body, and given it more power in relation to both the curriculum and the way money is spent. With the head and the LEA it also has a new obligation to ensure:
- the presentation of opposing political views when political issues arise in the classroom
- that where sex education is taught it should encourage moral values.

The governors must also be given, by the LEA, a financial statement about the cost of running a school and may be given a sum to spend on books, equipment and so on, under conditions set by the LEA, and with the head's approval. The snag is that nobody knows what happens if they fail to balance the books.

Governors' Duty to Report to Parents

The Act says that the governors are answerable to the parents and must submit an annual report to them each year containing the following:
- the names of governors and who appointed them
- the name and address of the chairman and clerk
- a summary of what the governing body has done that year
- a financial statement from the LEA
- details of how the governors spent any money allocated by the LEA
- details of any gifts to the school
- details of outside exam results (secondary schools)
- describe what has been done to improve the school's links with the community
- give details of any information the governors have

on sex education
- details of the annual general meeting (AGM).

An AGM must be held within 2 weeks of issuing the report. The meeting is open to all parents of children registered at the school, plus the head, the governors and anyone the governors wish to invite. The meeting gives the parents a chance to discuss how the governors, head and LEA have acted during the past year, and it can pass resolutions, but only if the number of parents present is equal to 20 per cent of the pupils on the school roll. The governors *must* consider these resolutions and pass resolutions related to them.

The exact working will take some time to shake out, but already there is more emphasis on explaining things to parents. However, parents are also being called on to do more for the school in terms of fund raising.

Opting Out

Under the Act schools may decide to opt out of their local education authority and take their funds not from the local authority but from central government. And if enough parents want the school to opt out the governors *must* consent to it.

Learning to Govern

Under the 1986 Act, all local authorities must run free training courses to help governors understand what is expected of them. The NAGM (below) also runs training courses and the Open University has a course called 'Governing Schools' which is designed to help school governors understand their role and the system within which they have to work. It could be of interest to any parent now that there is more interaction between teachers and governors.

Any parent who is well-informed on changes in education is obviously in a stronger position when discussing what should happen in a school. The education section of the *Guardian* is published on Tuesdays, the *Independent* runs one on Thursdays, and *The Times* has a weekly *Times Educational Supplement* - which is sold separately from the paper. See also ACE.

Advisory Centre for Education (ACE) (page 299) has a leaflet summarizing the 1986 Education Act and a briefing on how to be a school governor under the Act.

Community Education Development Centre (CEDC) (Briton Road, Coventry CV2 4LF Tel: 0203 440814) promotes community education and runs courses for parent governors.

European Parents Association, Den Abt 64, 2151 Vlimmeren, Belgium.

Home and School Council (81 Rustlings Road, Sheffield S11 7AB Tel: 0742 662467) publishes newsletters and literature to foster home and school links.

The National Association of Governors and Managers (NAGM) (81 Rustlings Road, Sheffield S11 7AB Tel:0742 662467) organizes very good courses for governors and potential governors. It also supplies useful leaflets, including a 'School Governors' Guide', 'Modern Maths Explained' or 'How to Help a Child at Home'.

National Confederation of Parent Teacher Associations (48 Hamerton Road, Northfleet, Gravesend, Kent DA11 9DX Tel: 0474 60618) is a federation of parent-teacher associations (often called Home-School Associations) attached to schools all over Britain. Area officers have information on local issues and on matters like education law. Its publications cover numerous aspects of schooling and child rearing which would interest parents.

Parent Teachers Association of Wales (Tolgoed, Pen-y-Lon, Mynydd Isa, Mold, Clwydd, CH7 6YG Tel: 0352 4652) is a federation of the associations in the eight Welsh LEAs.

Scottish Parent Teacher Council (30 Rutland Square, Edinburgh EH1 2EW Tel: 031 228 4726) encourages partnership between parents and teachers and publishes booklets and a newsletter.

The Schools
State schooling divides up a child's schooling in several different ways. Some LEAs use one, some another, but many of them have several different systems operating at once. These are some of the options:

5 to 7 or 8 - primary or infant school
5 to 11 - primary education
8 to 11 - junior school
8 to 12 or 9 to 13 - middle school
11 to 18 - chosen by selection - grammar schools
11 to 18 - *not* chosen by selection - comprehensives
16 to 18 - VI form college

The system is made more confusing than it need be by the fact that some authorities seem to dislike the term 'middle school' and have two stages of primary school or two stages of secondary school.

The government has now thrown in a wild card in the form of City Technology Colleges, which will normally cater for 11 to 18 year olds, across the full range of ability in their area, and be registered as independent schools - yet charge no fees.

Voluntary Schools
About 1 in 3 of the state schools in England and Wales are voluntary schools. Most of them are Church of England and Roman Catholic schools, but there are 3 types of voluntary school. In all of them religious instruction is in the hands of the voluntary body.

Many are **aided schools** in which a voluntary organization (e.g. a church) appoints most of the governors (who in turn appoint the teachers), and pays for external repairs and extensions. The LEA pays for all the running costs, from salaries to internal repairs.

In **controlled schools** the building was originally set up by a voluntary body but the LEA pays all the costs, and a smaller proportion of the governors are appointed by the voluntary organization. And, in practice, the governors have considerable say over the appointment of teachers.

Special agreement schools, are ones in which an LEA agrees to contribute to the building of a voluntary school, but most of the governors are from the voluntary body.

Assisted Places at Independent Schools
The 1980 Education Act encourages fee-paying schools to take a proportion of children from families who cannot afford the fees. The parents then pay according to their income and the difference is paid by the DES. The schools select the pupils for assisted places, at any age, and many of them are for places in the A level years. The Department of Education and Science has a list of schools taking part in this scheme. You get it from Room 3/65, Elizabeth House, York Road, London SE1 7PH Tel: 01 934 9211 and need to apply to the school for a place and take the entrance examination in the usual way.

The scheme has limitations. A child can only benefit from it if it has, at some time, attended a state school for at least 2 years, and the state contribution only covers tuition, and expenses such as travel and uniform, not boarding costs. However, some schools don't ask boarding fees (or full boarding fees) from these pupils.

Specialist Schools
There is a short list of music and ballet schools, such as the Royal Ballet School, and the Wells Cathedral School, for which pupils may get state aid with fees.

State Education in Scotland
In education, as in most things, Scotland is a law unto itself. The normal pattern is for children to attend co-educational primary schools from the age of 5 until 12. There are no voluntary schools but denominational schools (mainly Roman Catholic) are a major feature of the system. Scotland is also one area where village schools still remain. After 12, state schools are comprehensive, even though some still call themselves grammar schools, and take a child through the next 6 years. At the primary stage teachers have been free to teach whatever curriculum they like but schools are guided in the secondary curriculum by the Consultative Committee on the Curriculum.

The LEA sets a catchment area for each primary school and children have been expected to attend the school in their area, and all move on to a single secondary school. But now parents can ask for their child to go to another school, even in some other LEA, and the LEA must agree unless there is good reason not to. If an LEA refuses, the parents can appeal to an independent committee and from there to the sheriff.

The assisted places scheme (see left) operates in Scotland as it does in England. The rules on special education are also the same as for England. For information on parental choice and assisted places in Scotland write to the **Scottish Education Department** (Room 4/10, New St Andrew's House, St James' Centre, Edinburgh EH1 3SY Tel: 031 556 8400), but write to the Department at Room 209, 43 Jeffrey Street, Edinburgh EH1 1DN for information on education for children with special needs.

The most radical feature of Scottish education is likely to be the degree of parent power. The government proposes to set up a school board for each school. Each board will have a majority of parents, plus some staff and members of the community, and will gradually take over the administration of the school. This means that if these boards become law Scottish parents will have very much more power than other British parents.

Scottish Parent Teacher Council (30 Rutland Square, Edinburgh EH1 2BW Tel: 031 228 4726) is the umbrella for parent-teacher associations in Scotland but parents may also join individually. It is a good source of information.

Independent Schools

The term independent school covers those, for children of all ages, which are not state run. They range from well known public schools - which are, of course, private - to private nursery schools.

Parents tend to think that what their child needs is a 'good school' and the suggestions on choosing a state school (page 288) apply just as much to the private sector, but it isn't as simple as that. Independent schools vary greatly in what they offer and in how they handle the children. Some put huge emphasis on academic achievement, others on sport, others on the arts. Some expect uniform of almost military neatness, others use home clothes and are extremely relaxed about tidiness. Yet all of these extremes could be very good schools - though a child who might thrive in one could be a miserable failure in another. What is needed is a school which suits a particular child, which will foster his or her strengths and help overcome any weaknesses. This sounds extremely obvious but it's amazing how many parents focus all their attention on the qualities of the school and none on the qualities of the child, or assume that because a school was good for them it has to be good for their son. If in doubt it can be worth using an educational psychologist to assess a child's potential before deciding on schools. Sometimes children who fail to shine in junior school can be very able indeed.

Nursery Schools and Kindergartens - see page 266.

Preparatory Schools
These schools usually take children from 7, 8,or 9 to 11 or 13. Most belong to the Incorporated Association of Preparatory Schools (IAPS). To join this association a school must be inspected and approved by HMIs - so it is some guarantee of quality. The classes tend to average 10-12 pupils, and each school usually takes 80-150 pupils in all, either for boarding or day school, or a mixture of both. Their aim is mainly to prepare children to enter public schools through passing the Common Entrance examination, which may require subjects which can't normally be obtained at that age in a state school. However, even when they are the junior half of a public school, attending one may not guarantee a child a place in the senior school - or even give it a better chance of getting in, though it may do. It can be just as effective - and far more convenient - to have a child at a prep school nearer home. Because good prep schools are the easiest route to the public schools, the best are overwhelmed with applications and it is wise to get a child's name down soon after birth.

Senior Schools
Senior schools range from excellent top-flight public schools - for which the term independent is increasingly used - down to establishments which are, quite simply, a racket. Nobody should be deluded into thinking that all private schools are necessarily better than all state schools. Some are undoubtedly better than many state schools, but they are not better than all of them. Many private schools are, in fact, a good deal worse than many state schools and may lack facilities which are basic in the state sector.

Unless you plan to send a child to a school which is so well known and respected that its standards are beyond question, consult an impartial organization like Gabbitas, Truman and Thring or ISIS (page 295) over the choice of school. If you don't you could be paying through the nose for very little.

To get into an independent school your child must usually be able to pass an entrance examination and you must be able to pay the fees. The exams for the best schools are very tough indeed but most give scholarships for academic ability or for skill in certain subjects like music, and these reduce or kill the fees altogether for those able to win them. There may also be scholarships for those in special categories such as the children of clergymen. But to get a scholarship you usually need to apply for it. The *Independent Schools Year Book* notes scholarships and assisted places beside each school, and Gabbitas, Truman and Thring's book *Which School* also has information on these. The other possibility is an assisted place - page 293.

Boarding Schools
In the private sector you can find boarding places for children as young as 5, but the normal age to start boarding prep school is 7. Although public schools are known for being boarding schools there is no need to start that young, some pupils don't board until 13, and others go through the whole of their private education as day pupils.

There are fierce arguments for and against boarding education, and the issue is too big to cover here. But, there is no evidence whatever that sending a child to boarding school when young helps it to stand on its own feet - in fact rather the reverse. Second, parents should not underestimate the difficulty of keeping close to children, and having a real influence on their development, once they go to boarding school. Some do manage to stay close but when you only see your child for a quarter of the year you are bound to have less chance to maintain links than if your child comes home each day. So it takes more effort on both sides.

Senior Schools - How to Get In
The majority of senior schools are single sex and boarding, with day and co-educational schools a small minority, but more and more boys' schools admit girls to study A levels. Although entrance is by a competitive examination, and possibly an interview, many schools will only allow a certain number of children to sit the examination and may close their books several years before. So, for safety, applications to day schools - for which demand far exceeds supply - should be made by the time a child is 5, and for boarding schools at least 3 years before the exam.

Entry to girls' schools is usually by a Common Entrance examination at 11. Some boys' schools also have entry at 11, usually through their own examination, but for the majority entry is via Common Entrance at 13 - a standardized exam with the pass mark varying from school to school. For a child from a state school there may be practical problems. Common Entrance has compulsory papers in English, Maths, French, History, Geography, Scripture and Science, at a very high standard for the age of the children. Children who have not been to a preparatory school may not have covered the syllabus. This can be remedied with good coaching, but it may take at least a year. However, some very good schools take a broader view and base entry on a school report and personal interview.

★ Old Common Entrance papers can be obtained from **C.E.Publishing Ltd**, Ashley Lane, Lymington, Hants SO4 9YR

Unusual Schools
Within the independent sector there are schools which are totally unlike the rest - music schools, stage schools and so on, and others, such as the Steiner Schools, are unusual in their total attitude to education. Steiner schools take children from 4½ to 18½ and offer an education which is decidedly alternative. Parents make contributions, instead of paying set fees, and the emphasis is on the whole person and the spiritual and emotional life of the child as much as its intellectual development - which means they rarely take examinations which might gain entry into university. Quite separately there are special Steiner schools for the maladjusted and handicapped.

Steiner Schools Fellowship, Kidbrooke Park, Forest Row, E.Sussex RH18 5JB Tel: 0342 82 2115

What Does Private Education Offer?
The state *v.* private school argument is complex. I have taught in both sectors and the overwhelming advantage which the private sector offers is simply - variety.

If state schools were as quirky as private schools, and parents could choose a school with marvellous music for a musical child, and one with great rowing for a rower, and so on, the private sector might well be struggling. While sending a child to a state school may mean having the authorities place it in a school which will make it a square peg in a round hole parents may feel that the state isn't the ideal option for certain children. And if the DES uses the new curriculum to put a strait jacket on teachers in the state sector this may increasingly be so.

Gabbitas, Truman and Thring Education Trust (6 Sackville Street, London W1X 2BR Tel: 01 734 0161) provides free information and advice on all types of education in the private sector, including tutorial colleges, schools for special problems or abilities, some further education, finishing schools overseas and schools in GB where foreigners can learn English. It can also recommend educational psychologists who will assess a child's ability. They also publish a wide range of books including a guide to independent further education.

Independent Schools Information Service (56 Buckingham Gate, London SW1E 6AG Tel: 01 630 8793) publishes a book on over 1,300 independent schools, and has information on school fees insurance schemes, and on how grandparents can help with fees and has a list of schools which offer assisted places.

Your local LEA will hold a list of all independent schools in your area, as well as the state schools.

Special Needs
Dyslexia and other Reading Problems
There used to be a bad joke that if poor children couldn't read they were stupid and if rich ones couldn't read they 'had dyslexia'. That isn't the case. Any child who finds reading and writing much harder than other subjects may be dyslexic. But caught reasonably early no reading problem need be a permanent handicap to an able child. Even dyslexics can get degrees in subjects that need a lot of reading and writing.

Defining Dyslexia
Dyslexia simply means 'difficulty with words' but experts apply it to a particular type of reading difficulty and suspect that there may be a physical problem in the brain which scrambles certain messages. This may be inherited or, for example, be caused by lack of oxygen to the brain during birth. Whatever the cause a dyslexic child's ability in reading and writing isn't what you'd expect for its intelligence.

To diagnose dyslexia takes professional testing, but if your child is over 8 and more than one of the following applies you ought to have tests done soon. Don't wait and hope he or she will 'grow out of it'. Does he/she:
- find reading much harder than other subjects?
- find writing much harder than other subjects (except reading)?
- manage to do some hard things in maths but get muddled on basics?
- read or write b for d, or 29 for 92 or confuse dab with bad?
- have trouble telling left from right, yet manage things which are much harder?
- sometimes write words with letters jumbled?
- have a bad sense of direction?
- have more trouble tying shoe laces, and ties than is usual for his or her age?

You can ask the school to arrange for the local educational psychologist to do tests or you can contact the organization on page 296 and see a psychologist privately. If dyslexia is officially diagnosed it usually means that extra time is allowed for taking public examinations - and a dyslexic may well need this.

There are also children who don't show the classic muddles of dyslexia but do find reading and writing far harder than they should, given their intelligence. In my experience these children sometimes have quite big emotional problems too. But the cause can just as easily be a practical problem like temporary deafness caused by ear infections or a family upset or spell in hospital just when it should have got to grips with reading. So dyslexia is by no means the only reason why a normal child may be a slow reader.

What to Do if a Child has Reading Problems
If a child is diagnosed as having dyslexia it has a 'specific learning difficulty' under the Education Act and the school should provide remedial teaching. There are also private classes in some areas which the BDA (see right) should be able to put you in touch with, but if a child isn't attending such a class parents can do a lot to help any slow reader.

In helping a child with reading problems you need to realize that it has two difficulties: the actual learning difficulty, and the sense of frustration and failure at finding it lacks basic skills which children who are no brighter have mastered. The longer this has gone on the more the child will have grown to hate and fear the tasks which humiliate it - namely reading and writing. So the first block to overcome is usually a refusal to risk the humilation of failing, by trying. This means it *must* start with reading it can succeed with quite easily.

Parents who are tolerant can help a child to overcome these feelings (though probably not if the causes are emotional). Those who have to see their children achieve may need to avoid trying to help; the child will feel their annoyance when it fails - even if they keep their mouth shut - and this will humiliate the child still further.

Those who feel they could help their children can try the methods I have given for teaching a child to read on page 286. They are the ones I devised when I specialized in teaching reading. I found they also worked with slow and dyslexic readers. Those who consult experts may find they are given different advice and should then follow it: it is important to follow *one* system. However, I am alarmed to find some experts say words should be broken down as much as possible when teaching dyslexics. In my experience dyslexics can learn to recognize *whole* words quite easily but when words are broken down the end may be scrambled with the beginning. This matches their behaviour in everyday life. Even the most dyslexic never confuse a chair with a table, but ask them to sit on the left arm of a chair and they may well sit on the right.

So, for the sake of dyslexic children, I'm going to stick my neck out and suggest you should be very cautious about breaking down words, and get any expert who suggests it to give some very good reasons for it.

★ Some children who write b for d and so on get them right when typing. Typing also allows their work to look much more grown up. This gives them a great feeling of achievement and also makes it easier for teachers to mark the *content* of their writing. As children like reading their own work it also gives them practice at reading normal print. So a typewriter - or even a computer with a printer - can be a big boost.
★ If possible get a teach-yourself typing course and encourage the child to learn to touch type - then it will make fewer mistakes, work faster, and have a skill other children don't have - another confidence booster.
★ Computer games where the child has to make something move around the screen are valuable for smoothing out its left/right confusion.

★ Computer games which ask the child to type in words, are a good incentive to reading and writing.
★ If a child can't read well it will never want to do so unless it learns to enjoy books. So it is doubly important that it is often read to and that the books are ones which *really* interest and excite it. Don't worry about whether they are literature or not. But don't just read to the dyslexic child while the others read to themselves or it will just feel humiliated. Make reading an activity which is part of family closeness and love.

An adult who thinks they may be dyslexic can ask to be tested by the psychology service of the Manpower Services Commission, and may be able to attend a dyslexia clinic. Or testing can be arranged through the organization below.

British Dyslexia Association (BDA) (98 London Road, Reading, Berks RF1 5AU Tel: 0734 668271) provides referral to sources of help, information, advice, seminars, conferences, lists of suitable schools/clinics. M£M, S, ChS, F&F, M, L, B, E, Rg, C, HC, HD, sae.

Gifted Children
Only the least sensitive would deny that a severely handicapped child needs special help. Sadly the severely gifted child is less fortunate. Few people realize that the child who thinks in ways which nobody around can understand, and has interests the rest of a class can't share, can be just as miserably isolated as a child with crippled legs. So the isolation and frustration of gifted children is hardly given a thought, and to suggest that there should be special teachers to meet the needs of such children seems like indecently heaping educational riches upon those already rich.

Psychologists estimate that one child in every hundred has exceptional gifts. For some this is remarkable intelligence, which may show in early talking and reading, for others it may be a talent like music or mathematics which will develop later. But a gift can be a very mixed blessing. Only the most understanding parents and teachers find the energy to meet the child's endless quest for new information. It is hard for a child to have 10 sums returned covered with corrections, but it is at least as discouraging when a child who has eagerly completed the entire book in an evening is rounded on by a teacher irritated at having a whole term's homework schedule destroyed at a stroke. Yet this does happen. Worst of all, the interests of gifted children seldom match their age so they become the odd ones out, and may be ridiculed for their strange hobbies and use of long words. So, partly out of a need to conform, partly out of frustration, many drop out and become unhappy misfits or even delinquents.

Any parent whose once quick and responsive child becomes difficult and starts getting bad results at school, or throws temper tantrums which it should long since have outgrown, should wonder whether the child may be far more able than has been realized. Parents shouldn't judge the child by themselves: most of the best minds of history didn't have very exceptional parents.

Nor should they expect them to seem like geniuses. Albert Einstein was considered 'slow' in class and Ramanujan Ayangar, one of the greatest mathematical geniuses of the past 100 years, was dismissed as unteachable. And there are still cases of brilliant children being classified as subnormal because they are so off-beat there seems no other explanation. Their ability to think in ways others don't, can even make them think up such complex answers to intelligence tests that they get them wrong. So an average child may get higher marks than a brilliant one.

In Russia and China such children are seen as a national resource and given every encouragement in special schools. Here in Britain there is little provision for these children. In theory schools have a legal obligation to provide each child with education to suit its ability. Where gifted children are concerned this has yet to be tested in the courts. Some local authorities do try to provide for the very able, but most pretend they do not exist.

As long as the state fails to fulfil its obligation to educate these children according to their needs, the best option for some may be a scholarship, or assisted place, into the private sector - though only the very best schools will offer what they need, and they will still be in a tiny minority.

Gifted Children's Information Service (21 Hampton Lane, Solihull, W.Midlands B91 2QJ Tel: 021 705 4547) is run by an educational psychologist who provides assessment and counselling (for a fee). It also publishes teaching packs, and computer programmes, to use with gifted children. vg B, Inf.

Joint Educational Trust (JET) (38 Hillsborough Road, London SE22 8QE Tel: 01 693 7159) places and finds scholarships for children when their abilities or family circumstances create special needs not matched by a family's ability to pay.

The National Association for Gifted Children (NAGC) (1 South Audley Street, London W1Y 5DQ Tel: 01 499 1188) is a pressure group which allows parents to meet for mutual support and has clubs where gifted children can get together. M£L-M, G, V, Ad, excellent list of books and leaflets, sae.
Peter Congdon, *Helping Children of High Intelligence*
R.Povey, *Educating the Gifted Child*, Harper & Row
A. Stevens, *Clever Children in Comprehensive Schools*, Pelican
U. Axline, *Dibs: In Search of Self*, Pengiun - a real insight into the problems of being gifted.

Handicapped Children or Children with Special Needs
Handicapped children, and those who have special problems - such as dyslexia or speech difficulties - are now called 'children with special educational needs'. The 1944 Education Act rule that children must be educated according to their needs and abilities applies as much to them as to any others.

The 1981 Education Act came out against this and said that as far as possible handicapped children should be educated in ordinary schools if it was 'reasonably practicable', but authorities have been free to do what suited them.

Assessment of Problems
If a child under 2 has problems talk to your GP or clinic. If *you* want an assessment made of its mental or physical abilities the authorities have a duty to give one, but if anyone suggests your child should be assessed you can refuse. If a problem is found you should be able to get special equipment under the health service and special toys from toy libraries.

If a child aged 2 or more seems to have a problem it should really be assessed at least a year before starting school at 5. This gives time to sort out the best possible schooling. The rules of the 1981 Act are these:

- if parents want an assessment it cannot, unreasonably, be refused
- the authorities have a duty to identify children who will need special schooling and at this age parents must allow assessment (or appeal against them) and take the child along
- parents must be told their child will be assessed and have 29 days in which to write asking that no assessment be made, giving their reasons
- when a child is assessed they have a right to be there and to give evidence of its abilities and problems
- if the LEA decides the child has no special needs the parents may appeal to the Secretary of State for Education
- if the LEA decides a child does have special needs it must send the parents a draft statement and the professional advice it was given
- a parent who disagrees with any of the assessment of the child has 15 days in which to say so and ask to see an official
- a parent who still objects to what has been issued must be told to appeal and where they can get help

A child will be assessed as needing special schooling mainly on the advice of an educational psychologist. If you feel your child has been incorrectly assessed, for example you think it is deaf but bright and the LEA has classed it as unintelligent, you need evidence on your side. It would help if you could get another educational psychologist to assess your child and present that, independent, view to the LEA or appeals board. Organizations catering for those with particular disabilities may be able to help you find a suitable psychologist. Most are listed elsewhere in this book, but if your child has a rare disorder which I haven't covered the **Voluntary Council for the Handicapped Child** (8 Wakley Street, London EC1V 7QE Tel: 01 278 9441) will send you a complete list of such organizations - for a large sae. Or write, with an sae, to the **Independent Panel of Special Education Experts** (12 March Road, Tillingham, Essex CM0 7SZ Tel: 062 187 781) which helps parents get a second opinion. **The Advisory Centre for Education** (page 299) has a good booklet giving all the details about what happens at an assessment and how to appeal.

- the parent then appeals to the local appeal committee which can either dismiss the appeal or ask the LEA to reconsider its statement
- if the appeal is dismissed a parent can appeal to the Secretary of State for Education
- all children classed as having special needs must be re-assessed at between 12½ and 14½.

How Long Does Assessment Take?

The time an educational assessment takes varies with the problem, but a child may need to see as many as 6 different people at different times and this takes at least 3 months and can take as long as a year, from start to finish. If you ask, the LEA *must* tell you who suggested the child should be assessed and who will do the assessing - and how - and show you all reports which have been made on your child. You also have a right to know about any case conferences on your child and can ask to be invited to them.

The LEA must also give you full details of their policy on educating children with special needs and on any schools to which they might send your child.

Where Will a Child be Educated?

If the LEA says a child has special needs it will also say what it plans to do about them. In principle the parents of a child with special needs have just the same right to choose a school as they would for any other child, but there is seldom a choice between different schools catering for a particular problem. If there is, or if a child is allocated to a special school and the parents would rather it attended a normal school they can appeal against the decision in the same way as against any other school choice (page 290).

What Education is Best for a Child?

If you have a child with special needs and are wondering whether it would be bettter in an ordinary school or a special school there is really no easy answer. So much depends on the handicap, on the child, and on the facilities it will and won't have in either establishment. I suggest you contact any organizations for the handicap your child suffers from (see In Sickness) and talk to other parents in the local branch. They will be able to say whether enough money has been spent on integrating the children into normal schools or whether the equipment will be much better at a special school. The **Centre for Studies on Integration in Education** (840 Brigh Road, Purley, Surrey CR2 2BH Tel: 01 660 8552) was set up by the Spastics Society to encourage LEAs to absorb handicapped children into normal education and also has a lot of information on what is being done in different areas.

The schooling provided locally by LEAs isn't, of course, the only option. There are a few boarding places in the state sector and you also have a right to educate a handicapped child at home (page 287), or find it a place in an approved independent school. If the LEA approves the placing - or even chooses it - it may pay the fees and you can certainly ask for this.

When You Move

If you leave the area in which a child has been assessed as having special needs it may take a little while for you to get information on how the new area educates children with such needs. So write and ask well in advance. The assessment can be transferred from one area to another, but if you don't want it transferred you can ask the new area for a fresh assessment. The new authority may still see all the old reports and may be influenced by them, but this does give you a chance to muster new evidence and argue your case again.

Speech Problems

The situation on speech therapy is complicated. Logically speech is part of education, and some LEAs *do* include it in their duties. But the law is unclear on who is really responsible for it so some authorities pass the buck to the DHSS which usually employs the therapists. The DHSS has no obligation to act fast as speech problems aren't fatal. There is, in addition, a national shortage of speech therapists. If your child has this problem you should ask for it to receive therapy and be prepared to lobby very hard until it gets it. The earlier it gets help the better. The **Association for All Speech Impaired Children (AFASIC)** (347 Central Markets, Smithfield, London EC1A 9NH Tel: 01 236 6487) has an inexpensive leaflet on educational facilities for children with this problem and other leaflets and reading material which will help parents both to get their entitlements and to help a child with this problem.

Terms Used in Education

CBVE - competency based vocational education, aimed at making those of 16 plus competent in skills needed for particular jobs. Once competence is achieved they stop the course.

CDT - Craft Design Technology: a new course which combines practical skills in these 3 areas and now has its own examination at GCSE and A-level.

CTCs - the new 'City Technology Colleges' which the government is planning to set up in urban areas to give a secondary education heavily based on technology.

Family groups - a group of unrelated children of different ages who work together. The idea is that the older ones help the younger ones and, in doing that, learn new skills themselves.

HMI - Her Majesty's Inspectors. These inspect the standard of education in schools and colleges and report to the Secretary of State for Education and Science.

Setting and Streaming - ways of grouping children of similar ability so they learn together. In streaming, children are sorted into classes by general ability and stay in those classes for all subjects. This is quite rare nowadays. In setting, children belong to mixed ability classes, and learn most subjects in that class. But for certain subjects, such as maths or foreign languages, they split up into different groups (sets) according to their ability.

TVEI - Technical and Vocational Education Initiative. This was a specially funded drive in which groups of schools and colleges have been trying to organize the curriculum for 14 to 18 year olds to make it more relevant to adult working life. It is now part of a national scheme.

Publications Despatch Centre (PDC) (DES, Honeypot Lane, Stanmore, Middx HA1 7AZ Tel: 01 952 2366 ext 503) will supply a list of free publications by the Department of Education and Science and a catalogue of priced and unpriced publications by Her Majesty's Inspectorate.

Welsh Office Education Department (Information Division) (Gown Buildings, Cathays Park, Cardiff CF1 3NQ Tel: 0222 825111) will send a list of its publications on education.

Scottish Education Department - page 293.

Department of Education for Northern Ireland, Rathgael House, Balloo Road, Bangor, Co. Down BT19 2PR Tel: 0247 466311

Advisory Centre for Education (ACE) (18 Victoria Park Square, London E2 9PB Tel: 01 980 4596) is an educational charity, pressure group, and information centre for state education. Free advice by letter and phone (2 pm - 5.30 pm) on every aspect of schooling. Bulletin for members, M£L, L, handbooks on key topics, plus *Education A-Z* on where to look up information on education.

Campaign for the Advancement of State Education (CASE) (via ACE above) is what it says - a pressure group. M£L-M, M, L.

EDUCATION: SIXTEEN TO NINETY

Career Advice

The most important, though sometimes neglected, issue in deciding a course to take after school is what career it will lead to. Ideally everyone would get independent career advice at fourteen, before deciding which exams to take, as it is all too easy to close doors by having the wrong combinations of subjects, but the tendency is to give advice a stage later.

Free Advice on Jobs

The LEAs must provide a career advice and information service for all pupils in full-time education at every educational establishment (except a university). The careers officers are also meant to help pupils find a job, and a new computer network on careers is being set up to help with this. The LEA service is in the phone book under the local education authority or under Careers Service. Advice may also be available from Jobcentres and the advice centres of the Manpower Services Commission (MSC).

Career Occupational Information Centre (COIC), Room W 1103, MSC, Moorfoot, Sheffield S1 4PQ Tel: 0742 704563 sells a remarkably good range of publications, from those giving job information for teenagers to others with ideas on how an adult can retrain or a housewife take up a career. Many of them should be in a school careers library but to buy books write to 'Sales Department, Room W1103' above. There are also COIC bookshops in many major towns and London boroughs - well worth a browse.

The careers advisory service for school leavers is run systematically by local education authorities, but there is no nationwide educational and careers advice service for adults. Instead there is piecemeal provision by assorted bodies and some areas are far better provided for than others. The **Educational Guidance Services for Adults Centre,** Christopher House, 94 London Road, Leicester LE2 0QS Tel: 0533 542645 has compiled a leaflet listing the addresses throughout Britain.

Private Advice on Careers and Training

Sheer pressure of numbers means that it is impossible for the state advice services to assess someone's abilities and aptitudes in great depth, and a good private assessment may be worthwhile, if it can be afforded. Such assessments are not cheap, but can stop a square peg drifting into a round hole and being miserable - and unsuccessful - for ever more. The problem is in knowing how good an assessment centre is. Check several before booking and choose the one which offers the most.

Any worthwhile centre will give a battery of tests which will take at least a morning and a psychologist should spend a good while discussing the results with the client and pointing out the options they suggest. Most companies use standard psychological tests, so there is not likely to be much difference between them on that score. The important difference is the skill with which each psychologist relates the results to the client's personality and sums up their suitability for the jobs which their abilities would allow them to do. This is impossible to assess from the outside, but you can ask whether they provide information on courses in the careers they suggest, and whether they also advise on finding a job in that field, making job applications and handling interviews.

The companies below are a starting point for enquiries, but their presence here should not be taken as a sign of recommendation, as it has not been possible to vet them all. Unfortunately most private career guidance centres are clustered in London and the rest of Britain is very ill served.

Career Analysts (Career House, 90 Gloucester Place, London W1H 4BL Tel: 01 935 5452) offers a very thorough careers guidance service for all ages from mid-teens upwards.

Career Counselling Services (46 Ferry Road, London SW13 9PW Tel: 01 741 0335) uses a combination of tests, interviews and self-evaluation writing and drawing exercises.

Career and Educational Counselling (Tavistock Centre, 120 Belsize Lane, London NW3 5BA Tel: 01 794 1309) is part of the Tavistock Institute of Medical Psychology. It offers career advice for all ages. (Also in Bristol and Cambridge.)

Independent Assessment and Research Centre (57 Marylebone High Street, London W1M 3AE Tel: 01 935 2373) offers vocational guidance from teens to middle age, and guidance on children, aged 7-14, with educational problems.

National Advisory Centre on Careers for Women (8th floor, Artillery House, Artillery Row, London SW1P 1RT Tel: 01 799 2129) is an educational charity advising girls and women of all ages for a low fee. Books on careers for women by mail order.

Vocational Guidance Centre (15 Piccadilly, Manchester M1 1LT Tel: 061 832 7671) offers advice for all ages from mid-teens upwards.

Other Sources of Information on Careers

There is a mass of free information available on almost any career. Almost every professional body or trade association has a helpful booklet or leaflet. So do many less obvious organizations, for example, the Countryside Commission has a booklet on careers in conservation. These booklets are normally free and very informative, and usually detail the qualifications which are needed or the in-service training which is provided. The addresses of many such organizations are in this book. If they aren't your library will have a directory.

Certain publishers have large ranges on career and educational opportunities and a good bookshop should be able to show you their booklists or give you their address, so you can get their list yourself. Among them are Kogan Page, Longman, Hobsons Press and Careers Consultants. This last covers topics like finding jobs overseas or running your own business. Local libraries should also have a good range of such books and reference librarians are usually good at finding the right ones to solve a particular problem.

Careers A-Z, Collins/Daily Telegraph
An A-Z of Careers and Jobs, Kogan Page
The Job Book, (ed. Denis Curtis), Hobsons
John Morrison, *A Positive Future*, Hutchinson
Thelma Barber, *Careers and Jobs Without 'O' Levels*, Hobsons
Ruth Miller, *Equal Opportunities - a Career Guide*, Penguin
Juri Gabriel, *Unqualified Success*, Puffin/Penguin
Occupations 19.. (updated annually), MSC
Scottish Handbook of Adult and Continuing Education, Scottish Institute of Adult and Continuing Education (SIACE), 30 Rutland Square, Edinburgh EH1 2BW Tel: 031 229 0331
British Qualifications, Kogan Page, lists all the different types of qualifications you can obtain in Britain.
Higher Education in the United Kingdom, Longman, is updated annually. Lists all the places which offer diploma, foundation, degree and/or post-graduate courses in a subject, and the duration of the courses.
Andrew Paton and Martin Good, *Second Chances - The Annual Guide to Adult Education and Training Opportunities*, National Extension College
The Directory of Further Education CRAC (vast, in libraries)
Second Chance in Scotland: A Woman's Guide to Education and Training, (ed. Lesley Hart), SIACE

Examinations

Exams offer little unless they provide a key to something else, be it entry to further education or a job. With GCSE (and Scottish Standard Grade) being a 2-year course the time for a child to start thinking about what it wants to do after 16 is now pushed back to the early age of 13 to 14. The new, broader, approach provided by AS-levels may smooth out some poor choices, but it may not cope with all of them. A book which provides useful pointers is *Which Subject? Which Career?* by the Consumers Association and Hobsons.

GCSE

GCSE (and Scottish Standard Grade) is intended to be just what it sounds like: a cross-breed created by mating GCE O level with CSE. The offspring is an examination which the breeders in the Department of Education hope will give every child some proof of their achievement at school. It will be taken at around the age of 16 and the appeals system is similar to that in the box above right, but is to be reviewed.

The Scottish exams are not identical to those in Britain. The Standard Grade, of the Scottish Certificate of Education, replaces the old 'O' grade and has the same 7 levels of award as for GCSE (but numbered 1-7, not ordered alphabetically), 7 simply shows the course was completed. The Scottish Higher remains unchanged and very different from A-level, since it covers more subjects and those who have done very well at the previous exams often take it in one year. There is also a prestigious Certificate of Sixth Year Studies (CSYS) which can be taken by those who pass Higher in the first year and wish to stay on another year. If a candidate's results are far less good than would have been expected, an appeal can be made. In which case the papers will be re-marked and the pupil's usual school work looked at.

The New System

The avowed aim of the new system is:
- to make pupils feel that their work in school is valued
- to show what pupils *can* do, not what they can't
- to provide a unified system for every school
- to have general criteria applying to all subjects
- to foster practical skills and the application of both skill and knowledge to real-life situations.

At the end of a 2-year course the children take an examination which is marked by an outside examiner, in just the same way as GCE or CSE.
- Where all pupils can't do the same task, different exercises are set for groups of different ability. There are also 'differentiated' exam papers (page 301).
- There are changes in approach. English language, for example, now includes practical materials like writing letters and instructions.
- There is a new emphasis on talking and listening, in both English and foreign languages. To pass English pupils must now reach a certain grade in spoken English as well as written English.
- In science the new emphasis is on scientific methods, and the syllabus contains more practical work and less learning by rote. The application of science, and its impact on the environment, is also emphasized.
- Work done during the 2 years is assessed by teachers and counts towards at least 20 per cent of the marks. (Usually special projects rather than the entire body of work for the year, and maths is exempt from this until 1991.) Independent assessors check that the marking doesn't vary from school to school.

The amount of work assessed varies from subject to subject, but children will always be told whether a piece of work is counting towards their exam or not.

How Grades Compare

CSE	O Level	GCSE	O Grade	SCOTLAND Standard		
	A	A	A	credit	1	100 - 77
	B	B	B	general	2	76 - 65
1	C	C	C		3	64 - 50
2	D	D	D		4	49 - 40
3	E	E	E		5	39 - 30
4		F		foun-dation	6	29 - 20
5		G			7	

Those who fail to reach the minimum standard for grade G will be ungraded and won't get a certificate. Everyone else will.

Differentiated Papers
The idea behind differentiated papers is that there might, for example, be 4 papers each slightly harder than the previous one. Each pupil would only take the 2 which suit his or her ability. Both the papers which are taken and the standard reached in them give the final mark. So, for example, those who take papers 1 and 2 can get grades G up to E - depending on how well they do them. Those who take 2 and 3 can get grades F up to C. But only those who take - and do well in - papers 3 and 4 can get grades A and B. Pupils are likely to be taught in separate groups; streaming by any other name.

Stepped Papers
Stepped papers assume that all the pupils may be in the same class and will sit the same papers. But within each paper there will be different grades of question. It will be like mental mountain climbing: everyone will answer the questions on the lower slopes and they will then climb to the upper slopes of the harder and harder questions according to their intellectual muscle.

How it Will be Administered
The examination will be administered by 4 examining groups in England and one in Wales working to nationally agreed criteria and the Secondary Examinations Council (SEC), which is an independent authority, will monitor all aspects of the examination so as to maintain a uniform standard across the country.

CPVE (Certificate of Pre-vocational Education)
CPVE is a course which is designed to provide a bridge between school and work or further training for work. It is for pupils of 16 plus who aren't able to take A or AS levels, and the course can be taken either in school or in various types of college. The standards for CPVE courses are set by City and Guilds and BTEC.

It is divided into 10 areas:

basic maths	social skills	science and
problem solving	creative	technology
practical skills	development	
social and	personal and	information
economic	career	technology
talking and	development	
writing		

The course places more and more emphasis on skills which will lead to a job or job training as pupils get farther into it. It also includes 15 days of work experience and additional studies like community activities or even a GCSE course. Pupils are able to steer the course towards their own interests and, instead of taking an examination, are continuously monitored. At the end they are given a certificate in three parts:

1 A profile report which assesses their ability in the 10 areas, and says what vocational modules have been completed and gives assessements of their communication skills.
2 A summary of their work experience and how it went.
3 A portfolio of work they have done.

A and AS Levels
A levels were unchanged by the upheavals in the examination system, so pupils will usually take from 1 to 3 subjects, which they study in depth, over 2 years. But, as before, the very able will be allowed to take more than 3 subjects and to take them in a year.

The new development has been the introduction of AS-level as a parallel examination for those of the same age and ability. AS courses are designed to take about half as much work as an A level, but reach the same intellectual standard. The aim is for pupils to take 2 AS levels in place of one of their A levels. So they can study more subjects, and choose ones which complement or contrast with their A levels. For example, a scientist could do two sciences at A level, plus an AS foreign language and an AS in economics. The grades and standards for AS are exactly the same as for A level and the first AS examinations will be in the summer of 1989.

According to the government, universities and professional bodies have adapted their entrance requirements to take account of AS level. The Council for National Academic Awards accepts 2 AS levels as equalling one A level (at the same grade) for entrance to DipHE and first degree courses, so do UCCA, and the Civil Service. However, there may be some variation as to *how many* A levels may be replaced by AS levels and universities may expect an A, rather than AS, level in the subject that someone is applying to read.

The A level marking system has also been revised. Grade C now covers a wider range of marks, and grade N introduced, which means someone has narrowly failed, but doesn't count as any grade of GCSE. Any mark below N is U, unclassified.

Records of Achievement
By 1990 all pupils should be given a Record of Achievement when they leave school. This will be a summary of what a pupil has achieved in all aspects of his or her school life. This can then be shown to potential employers or training schemes.

Getting into Further and Higher Education

To get a place on most courses you simply apply to the institution which is running the course. However, for courses in higher education - degrees etc. - you normally apply via one of the following admissions bodies.

The Art and Design Admissions Registry (Pen House, 9 Broad Street, Hereford HR4 9AP Tel: 0432 266653) covers BA Hons and BTEC HND courses in art and design. Application forms are available from early February and must normally be in by mid March. Information on courses.

Central Register and Clearing House (3 Crawford Place, London W1H 2BN (no phone)) covers B.Ed degree and DipHE courses, while the Graduate Teacher Training Register, at the same address, covers the Post Graduate Certificate in Education. All forms and booklets are available from September the previous year.

Polytechnics Central Admission System (PCAS) (P.O.Box 67, Cheltenham, Glos GL50 3AP Tel: 0242 526225) covers admission to all polytechnics and certain colleges for first degree courses, except art, design, and teacher training and has a 'Free Guide for Applicants'. Apply between 1 September and mid-December a year ahead - but late applications are usually accepted until May. Most offers are made by March. Polytechnics have a clearing procedure similar to that used for universities and in the run-up to the final allocation of places PCAS has a 24-hour hotline for vacancy information on 0272 21771. Newspapers like the *Sunday Times* often publish vacancy lists too. For polytechnic courses which don't lead to first degrees you often need to apply direct to the college concerned.

UCCA

The **Universities Central Council on Admissions (UCCA)** (P.O.Box 28, Cheltenham, Gloucestershire GL50 1HY Tel: 0242 222444) processes applications for admission to full-time first degree courses at all the universities in Great Britain except the University of Buckingham. The following is only a rough guideline on possible procedure - it is essential to check the 'Notes for Candidates' in the UCCA handbook as the rules change remarkably often.

Even within one subject different universities vary considerably in what they offer and what they require from applicants. Before filling in an UCCA form read some of the following:

University Entrance: The Official Guide - in most libraries

Scottish Universities Entrance Guide, Scottish Universities Council on Entrance, 12 The Links, St Andrews, Fife KY16 9JB

University and College prospectuses and handbooks - free from them

How to Apply for Admission to a University - free from schools or from UCCA

CNAA Directory of First Degree and Diploma of Higher Education Courses - free from CNAA

Application Procedures

Applications for university places should reach UCCA about a year before the applicant wants to go up to university - check the UCCA handbook for closing dates. The actual closing date is some while later. The UCCA form allows for several universities to be chosen, and different courses may be applied for at different universities.

> Applications for Oxford or Cambridge also need applications direct to them and their deadline is usually far earlier than the general UCCA date, so this should be checked in good time. (See right.)

A few people are offered unconditional places on the strength of their past results. If you accept one of these offers you are committed to that university.

Most will be offered places at some of the universities they have applied for, provided they obtain certain grades in the exams they are about to take. The grades required by these conditional offers will vary with the university but a candidate must reply, through UCCA, within a set time and is limited to one firm acceptance and one insurance acceptance. *Fill up every section of the UCCA form; blanks are counted as refusals.*

The August exam results are sent direct to UCCA by the boards, and from there to the universities. They then decide whether or not to confirm their conditional offers, and may confirm a place even when the set grades have not been reached.

Some people will be rejected by all their universities, but this still leaves three routes to a place. The candidate or the school can write directly to some other university, quoting his/her UCCA number, and applying for a course, or CAP, or Clearing can be used.

Continuing Application Procedure (CAP)

In January, under the Continuing Application Procedure (CAP), UCCA asks candidates to choose four more universities and sends their application to one of these which still has vacancies in the candidate's subject. If these applications lead to a conditional offer the procedure is the same as above.

Clearing

If there are no courses with spaces, or the candidate is refused by the CAP universities too, UCCA will automatically suggest an application for a place through Clearing in August. Anyone whose grades were too low for their conditional places to be confirmed is also able to use Clearing. This system allows someone to be considered for *any* course for which they have appropriate qualifications, though their preferred universities and regions are taken into account.

Clearing shouldn't be seen as a dumping ground. Some very good universities are short of applicants for certain courses. However, some Clearing offers aren't made until the university term has almost started - so stay in Britain until term begins.

Scholarships and Awards

Scholarships and Awards
The scholarships offered by universities are given in their prospectuses and it is up to a candidate to apply to the universities for these. Industrial sponsorships may also be available and UCCA has a free leaflet on combining these with an application.

Oxbridge
Both Oxford and Cambridge require applications direct to them *and* via UCCA.

Cambridge Inner Collegiate Applications Office, Kellet Lodge, Tennis Court Road, Cambridge CB2 1QJ Tel: 0223 333308–information on colleges and you either apply here or direct to the colleges between March and mid-October a year before.

Oxford Colleges Admissions Office, Wellington Square, Oxford OX1 2JD Tel: 0865 270207, has information and forms and handles all applications between 1 September and mid-October the year before.

Information Sources

Education from sixteen upwards covers a wider range than any other part of the education scene. At one end there are basic literacy and numeracy schemes, in the middle ground there are courses in hobbies, leading to basic examinations, and in the upper reaches there are courses on professional skills and graduate and postgraduate work.

There has been a government drive to fit higher and further education more closely to employment, and create new training and retraining opportunities. As a result education from sixteen onwards is in something of a turmoil. The neat divisions between school, and after school, have become blurred, and the same pre-vocational courses are being offered in schools and in colleges. The division between student and adult education has also become almost non-existent as educational institutions have increasingly focused their courses towards the workplace, so that initial training and adult retraining are happening side by side.

Even the universities are developing new courses to update adult employees in skills needed in business and industry, and links are being formed between companies and universities which provide advanced courses in leading-edge technology (see page 307).

At the same time Open Learning schemes now cover most subjects, from basic skills through to postgraduate work, and the old rigidity of the British system is beginning to break down in favour of a modular system in which achievements on one course can be counted towards another, and people can move from one discipline, or one institution, to another without having to treat education like Monopoly and return to GO.

There are more schemes than ever to help people train, retrain or extend their training. The local Job Centres and the Area Division Offices of the Manpower Services Commission are the places to find out about aspects of funding which fall outside the usual provision of grants.

If you are thinking about entering further or higher education things are now so fluid that you may well find almost anything. Below are some of the possible sources of information and help.

The Art and Design Admissions Registry, Pen House, 9 Broad Street, Hereford HR4 9AP Tel: 0432 266653 has information on most art and design degree courses.

The Education Counselling and Credit Transfer Information Service (ECCTIS) (P.O.Box 88, Walton Hall, Milton Keynes MK7 6DB Tel: 0908 368921) is a free computerized service giving information on courses in further and higher education leading to qualifications of any kind. ECCTIS will answer personal queries, but computer links to Prestel in public libraries and local careers offices allow you to delve the database directly. If you know what you want to study, and the sort of qualification you want, ECCTIS can produce details of all the suitable courses either in your area or throughout Britain. It also has credit transfer information, but it won't answer open-ended questions about what you could do.

Higher Education Information Service (HEIS) (Middlesex Polytechnic, Trent Park, Cockfosters Road, Barnet, Herts EN4 0PT Tel: 01 368 1299) gives free information on undergraduate courses and DipHE, BTEC and Higher Diplomas throughout Britain. Answers queries and produces a computerized list of undergraduate places outside the university sector.

The Manpower Services Commission (MSC), has information on the ever-changing schemes, grants and career opportunities. The address is in the phone book.

Materials and Resources Information Service (Maris-Net (Ely) Ltd) (Bank House, 1 St Mary's Street, Ely, Cambs CB7 4ER Tel: 0353 61284) has a computerized information service on training and education, including a database of open learning courses for both the employed and unemployed.

National Institute of Adult Continuing Education (NIACE) ((England and Wales) 19b De Montfort Street, Leicester LE1 7GE Tel: 0533 551451) is an information source on virtually any type of course available to those over eighteen, but does not give personal advice. It sells a useful book *Residential Short Courses*. There is a separate body for Scotland - the **Scottish Institute of Adult and Continuing Education (SCIACE)**, 30 Rutland Square, Edinburgh EH1 2BW Tel: 031 229 0331

Network Scotland Ltd, (74 Victoria Crescent Road, Rowanhill, Glasgow G12 9JQ Tel: 041 357 1774) offers advice and information to those of any age who have left school. It covers education and training opportunities throughout Scotland, in both the public and private sector, including facilities for the handicapped. And it also publishes a very clear directory of Open Learning opportunities in Scotland.

Outward Bound Trust, (Chestnut Field, Regent Place, Rugby, CV21 2PJ Tel: 0788 60423/4/5) offers personal development opportunities for 16 to 25-year-olds through short courses in adventure sports (climbing, sailing, etc), and city challenge courses in which they help with the old and handicapped, but some funded places, RC, A, T, HD, sae.

Committee of Directors of Polytechnics (Kirkman House, 12-14 Whitfield Street, London W1P 6AX Tel: 01 637 9939).

Scottish Community Education Council, (Atholl House, 2 Canning Street, Edinburgh EH3 8EG Tel: 031 229 2433) is a quango concerned with community education - youth clubs, evening classes, and other communal activities - which will give information on this aspect of education, and also has some publications.
See also page 304 to 308.

The Education Year Book, Longman
David Dixon, *Higher Education - finding your way*, HMSO
Brian Heap, *How to Choose Your Degree Course*, Careers Consultants

John Pratt and Tyrell Burgess, *Polytechnics: a Report*, Pitman
Directory of First Degree Courses, CNAA, see right
Compendium of Advanced Courses in Higher and Further Education, from the Regional Advisory Council for London and South Eastern Region, Tavistock House South, Tavistock Square, London WC1H 9LR Tel: 01 388 0027
Graduates and Jobs - HMSO (looks as the job prospects following different types of degree)
Making the Most of Higher Education, Consumers' Association and Hodder & Stoughton
Opportunities in Higher and Further Education for Mature Students, CNAA
The Polytechnics Courses Handbook - lists all polytechnics courses
Scottish Handbook on Adult Education in Scotland, from SIACE
The Student Book, Papermac
University Entrance 19..: The Official Guide, Sheed and Ward

Organizations behind the Courses

Further and higher education is constantly changing and new courses and new organizations are being created all the time. Therefore the following rundown on the organizations behind the courses can only be a guide to *some* of the main opportunities in the field of further education. For a survey of everything in the field consult ECCTIS (see page 303).

BTEC

Business and Technician Education Council (BTEC) (Central House, Upper Woburn Place, London WC1H 0HH Tel: 01 388 3288) approves courses and awards qualifications in subjects allied to agriculture, business and finance, computing, construction, design, engineering, catering, leisure, public administration, caring, and science. They are designed for those in, or preparing for, employment. Courses last 1-3 years depending on the level and whether they are full or part-time. Many professional bodies recognize BTEC courses and BTEC National awards can gain entry to many degree courses. BTEC also administers City and Guilds courses in schools and colleges.

To find out what courses are available in any area contact BTEC, but applications for a place on a course should be made directly to the institution running it. Many are organized so that people can teach themselves in their free time. You register with an institution which runs that course then have the support of tutors who assess your work and teach key classes.

Qualifications

BTEC courses can lead to these qualifications:
- certificate of Pre-Vocational Education (CPVE) at 16+
- BTEC First Certificates and Diplomas - no formal qualifications are needed to study for these but the student must be 16 or over, and have left school
- BTEC National Certificates and Diplomas - most of these need 4 'O' level/CSE grade 1 passes, or equivalent GCSEs, or a BTEC First Certificate, or CPVE 'with appropriate attainment', and the student must be at least 16

- BTEC Higher National Certificates and Diplomas - students must be 18 years old and hold an appropriate BTEC National Award of suitable A-level passes
- BTEC Continuing Education Certificates and Diplomas - these courses are designed for those over 21, and they may be admitted because of experience instead of paper qualifications
- Students who successfully complete short study courses, or individual units of study, receive a Certificate of Achievement.

City and Guilds

The **City and Guilds of London Institute** (46 Britannia Street, London WC1X 9RG Tel: 01 278 2468) provides syllabuses for examination and certification throughout the British Isles. Most are linked to industrial occupations but range to hobbies like photography and gardening. They are taught in schools, colleges of further education, approved training centres, and adult institutes.

They are structured so that students can gain practical qualifications in ascending steps. This means that the length of courses varies from a term to several years. Successful students gain certificates or records of achievement, and licentiateships (LCG) at the higher levels. In Scotland, equivalence has now been established between some City and Guilds and SCOTVEC certificates (see page 306). Details of the courses are in the *C & G Handbook* and the *Candidates Guide*, and in a clear series of leaflets.

There are no age limits for most courses and, although prior qualifications may be recommended, entry is at the discretion of the colleges. Courses usually start in September, and exams are usually held in December or in May-June.

It is also possible to prepare for many City and Guilds exams at home, but entry to the examinations must be through the local examinations secretary at a centre where City and Guilds courses are taught, and the closing date for entry may be as much as 8 months before the exam. Grants may be obtainable.

CNAA Courses

The **Council for National Academic Awards (CNAA)** (344-354 Gray's Inn Road, London WC1X 8BP Tel: 01 278 4411) approves degree, degree equivalent, postgraduate, and DipHE courses in colleges and polytechnics, not in universities. It grants more degrees than any other British institution.

Unfortunately, because traditional academic qualifications have always rated more highly than practical ones, CNAA courses have often been seen as second-class citizens. However, they can be a very good option and, unlike most university degrees, they include sandwich and modular courses, and often lead to job-related qualifications.

CNAA also covers a wide range of postgraduate and post-experience courses particularly in technical and business subjects. The CNAA directory gives all the entry requirements.

CNAA Degrees - Entry Requirements
The minimum requirement must be broadly equivalent to 5 GCE passes, and 2 A-levels, but different colleges may require specific subjects or set higher standards. And in some subjects further education courses may provide alternative (or essential) qualifications. For example a one-year art foundation course may be required for an art degree, or BTEC or SCOTVEC qualifications alone could gain entry to some degree courses and polytechnics have scope for considerable flexibility over who they accept. And, as the CNAA's free guide *Opportunities in Higher Education for Mature Students* shows, qualifications may be different for mature students, and relevant experience may be accepted instead of exam results.

Degrees - Credit Accumulation and Transfer Scheme
This is a new CNAA scheme, commonly known as CATS, designed to introduce more flexibility into higher education. Under it, a student wishing to take a course at a polytechnic, college or university may be able to gain credits for previous work. If, for example, someone has done a year towards a degree then had to drop out, that first year may gain exemption from part of a new course. Equally, this system may allow someone to put together a very personal course of study based on units taken from several different courses.

The system is still finding its feet, but to use it apply to the CATS Unit at CNAA. They can explain it in detail and, for a fee, will assess applicants and advise them of their 'credit rating'. There is a plan to include work experience, so this is worth asking about. (It will be interesting to see whether they count bringing up a family as creditworthy experience towards teaching or child psychology.)

Diploma of Higher Education (DipHE)
The DipHE is a qualification obtained after a 2-year course equivalent to the first 2 years of a degree. So entry requirements for DipHE courses are similar to those for degrees. It is accepted in its own right by some employers or it can be the first step towards a professional qualification, - or count as a 2-year credit towards a suitable degree.

Getting on a CNAA Course
It's wise to start about 18 months before you want to attend a course. The *CNAA Directory of First Degree and Diploma of Higher Education Courses* lists the colleges and polytechnics where each subject can be studied. Next, get the prospectuses of those which interest you and decide where you want to go. In Scotland you then apply to those institutions for a place. In the rest of Britain (with some exceptions) you should apply through one of three bodies *at least a year before you want to start the course*. However, gaps do occur at the last minute and it is always worth trying to get in, even at the start of term.

Henley
The Henley Management College (Greenlands, Henley-on-Thames, Oxfordshire RG9 3AU Tel: 0491 571454) runs a range of post-experience management courses including some which cater for open learning.

The Industrial Society
The Industrial Society (Peter Runge House, 3 Carlton House Terrace, London SW1Y 5DG Tel: 01 839 4300) runs over 2,000 short courses and seminars a year, all over Britain. Besides covering traditional management skills these include starting up a business, using women employees more effectively, and how to cope with the stress of running a home and a job. Courses are also created at short notice to meet special demands, so if the course directory hasn't got what you want, ask. It also publishes a range of books on business skills, including guides to employment legislation designed to help both sides understand their rights and obligations.

Open University
Having pioneered the mass availability of open learning the Open University has a substantial range of courses and study packs, and aims for both for personal and professional development. In addition to degree and similar courses, there are modules on technical subjects, postgraduate-level courses on such topics as manufacturing, or the industrial applications of computers, and short courses focused on home life such as one on 'The Growing Child' and another on 'Planning for Retirement'.

Its Open Business School has the blessing of the British Institute of Management and has already been used by many of Britain's biggest companies. It offers short courses, lasting 12-30 weeks, which can be combined to give a Diploma in Management. The courses cover topics such as international marketing, women into management, accounting for managers, and starting your own business, and use multimedia techniques - tapes, television, books, assignments and residential weekends - to create a training package which can be fitted into the day of those who work full-time.

No qualifications are needed to start most OU courses, but some other higher level study may count towards an OU qualification, and equally some OU credits are now accepted towards qualifications in other institutions. On some short courses, if you look at the material and realize you can't do it you can return it and have your money back provided you do so within a set time (check the brochure). So decide *fast*.

Fees range from about £10 to several hundred pounds. There are regional offices in most county towns or contact the student enquiry office at **The Open University** (P.O. Box 71, Milton Keynes, MK7 6AG Tel: 0908 653231) which publishes informative booklets.

The Open College
The Open College (P.O. Box 35, Abingdon, Oxfordshire OX14 3BR Tel: 0235 555444) is the place to apply if you want information about vocational training. Most courses are intended for those who want to improve their business or technical qualifications related to specific types of work and lead to qualifications such

as those of SCOTVEC or City and Guilds, or to credits towards them. But there are also courses related to private life. So the vast selection of courses, listed in the college's Open Book range from those on how to do business in China to DIY car maintenance.

Like those of the Open University, Open College courses are taught by a combination of text, tapes, television (Channel 4) and written tutorials using materials provided by the college. Students also have access to local Open College centres, often within existing educational institutions, where they can join and get advice, information, tutorial support and practical training. But if you live somewhere remote and want to join contact the **National Distance Learning Centre,** Parsifal College, 527 Finchley Road, London NW3 7BG Tel: 01 435 6479.

You can enrol any time and the charges vary from around £20 to several hundred pounds but it may be possible to be funded by LEA grants, Government training schemes, or an employer.

Royal Society of Arts (RSA)

The Royal Society of Arts Examinations Board (RSA) (8 John Adam Street, London WC2N 6EZ Tel: 01 930 5115) is not what it seems to be. Its original title was 'The Royal Society for the Encouragement of Arts, Manufacturers and Commerce' and it pioneered commercial and technological examinations in Britain. Today its examinations and assessment schemes range from shorthand and typing to business studies. The emphasis is on real life needs, and LEA grants may be available for more advanced courses.

The RSA publishes a very clear guide to the range of courses, but you apply to the institutions teaching them. Previous qualifications are seldom needed.

Many RSA schemes are offered at three levels - Stage I, II or III - and the more advanced ones lead to certificates and diplomas. There is also a Certificate of Continuing Education designed for those returning to work, and taught in some adult institutes.

University of Buckingham

The University of Buckingham, Hunter Street, Buckingham MK18 1EG Tel: 0280 814080, is the only university in Britain which is totally outside the system. Its degrees are awarded after 2 years of study. Students work four 10 week terms each academic year, which starts in January. There is no closing date.

It offers both undergraduate and postgraduate courses and the bias is towards those which have some links with business or industry: business administration, law, languages, economics, computer science, and biological science. An unusual feature is that all students who aren't fluent in two languages take a language as part of their course, whatever their main subject.

Apply direct to the university, not through UCCA. Students are accepted on the basis of their potential as well as their achievements, and mature students may be judged on their work achievements as well as on their academic qualifications. Students can obtain the usual LEA mandatory grant plus a grant towards one third of the cost of fees, and some bursaries are available from the university for those who need them.

Scottish Vocational Educational Council (SCOTVEC),

Hanover House, 24 Douglas Street, Glasgow G2 7NG Tel: 041 242 2000, is responsible for administering the Scottish National Certificate which was introduced in 1984, and the Higher National Certificates and Diplomas. The main areas covered include technology, science, agriculture, business and public administration, information technology, secretarial studies, art and design, food and hotel work. The courses are available in most forms, from full-time school work to open learning via registration with appropriate colleges. The National Certificate is now modular, so a student can build towards it module by module as time and work allow, and the courses can be found in further education colleges, central institutions, schools and other centres.

Workers' Educational Association (WEA)

The WEA, Temple House, 9 Upper Berkeley Street, London W1H 8BY Tel: 01 402 5608/9, is a voluntary movement to spread adult education and increase individual development. It is a democratic organization in which the members decide what they will learn and how they will learn it. Classes are taken by professional teachers and lecturers and cover topics like history, women's studies, arts, music, or social sciences. There is great emphasis on enjoyment and involvement.

The courses are usually 1½-2 hours a week for 10-24 weeks, and are funded by local and central government and, to a lesser extent, by fees. Many of the classes have child care facilities attached, so mothers of young children can attend. The address of the nearest WEA classes should be available from your local library, or from the head office above.

Youth Training Schemes (YTS)

These government-backed schemes are designed to introduce school leavers to work and give them a basic training in the process. They are taken on as trainees by an employer, in a field they are interested in, and given in-service training with a guaranteed number of weeks 'off-the-job' training as well, plus paid holidays. All 16 year olds have a right to 2 years of YTS if they wish, those over 17 are entitled to 1 year. As it is a training programme rather than employment the weekly money is not as high as the wage for a similar job. There is no guarantee of a job at the end but qualifications are designed to make job finding easier. The local careers office or Jobcentre has the details.

Specialized Information Sources

Adult Education

Adult education is usually associated with evening classes in pottery or French. In fact it covers every level up to higher degrees, and adult is usually defined as over 18. Make enquiries with your education authority in midsummer as many courses get booked up and only those who apply early on the first day get in.

Degrees and Professional Qualifications

All the usual degree courses are open to any adult but anyone who lacks the right set of exam results should look at polytechnics. One person in three attending a polytechnic is a mature student, and polytechnics have more leeway than most for discounting exams, and counting your life experience. They also offer a vast range of other full-time, part-time and sandwich courses leading to degree equivalent qualifications, diplomas, certificates and professional qualifications.

Adult Literacy

Most public libraries have information on where to obtain help with basic skills in reading, mathematics and spoken English. Failing that, the following organizations can give advice.

The **Adult Literacy and Basic Skills Unit** (ALBSU) (Kingsbourne House, 229-231 High Holborn, London WC1V 7DA Tel: 01 405 4017) directs people to their nearest source of help. ALBSU may be able to direct would-be helpers towards a suitable organization.

Reading and Writing Help Service (Room 208, Bryson House, 28 Bedford Street, Belfast BT2 7FE Tel: 0232 322488) covers Northern Ireland. See also **Network Scotland** - page 303.

Ex-offenders and Others

The **Apex Trust Employment Resource Centre** 1-4 Brixton Hill Place, London SW2 1HJ Tel: 01 671 7633 is a charity which provides advice, and training for those who face special problems in the job market - such as ex-offenders.

Open Learning and Distance Learning

Open learning covers all levels of education, from the most basic to postgraduate, but most forms of open learning are open to those who lack the qualifications to enter conventional courses. This is one of the exploding fields of education but essentially it comes in three kinds:

1 Some organizations, such as the Open University, exist purely for open learning.
2 Some conventional examining bodies are now structuring their syllabuses and materials so that people can follow the courses without attending an educational institution.
3 More and more educational institutions are becoming aware that not everyone who wants to study can enrol as a full-time student. So they are letting people enrol, and use facilities like libraries and special tutorials, while doing most of the course at home.

The best way to find type 3 is often to ask local educational institutions whether they would let you study that way. The other types have information points.

The **Council for the Accreditation of Correspondence Colleges** (CACC) (27 Marylebone Road, London NW1 5JS Tel: 01 935 5391) is the body which officially inspects such colleges. It is very much safer to stick to correspondence courses which are CACC approved and accredited. CACC will send you a brochure listing approved courses or tell you whether a particular course is accredited. If you are dissatisfied with a correspondence course complain to CACC.

The **Co-ordinating Committee for Distance Learning Schemes for Vocational Further Education** (Hanover House, 24 Douglas Street, Glasgow G2 7NG Tel: 041 248 7900) is the information source on taking SCOTVEC courses. For distance learning related to BTEC courses contact the main BTEC address.

The **College of the Sea** (The Marine Society, 202 Lambeth Road, London SE1 7JW Tel: 01 261 9535) offers a vast range of correspondence courses to those at sea.

London University (Senate House, Malet Street, London WC1E 7HU Tel: 01 636 8000) has a scheme for external degrees without attending a course. However, it offers only single degrees and diplomas identical to those taken by full-time students. Write to the Secretary for External Students.

National Extension College (18 Brooklands Avenue, Cambridge, CB2 2HN Tel: 0223 316644) - courses range from hobbies, and how to study effectively or use a computer, through GCSE and A levels, to courses preparing for the Open University.

The BBC issues a publication three times a year called *Learning at Home*, listing its educational programmes (from BBC Education, Villiers House, London W5 2PA). Local radio stations also have education programmes and the station manager has information on them. For education programmes on independent radio or television write to the Education Officer at the IBA and ask for the booklet *Resources for Adults*. Both the BBC and ITV publish rather good books so it's worth asking for a publications list too.

See also Open University page 305 and Open College page 305 and Henley Management College page 305.

A Directory of Open Learning Opportunities in Scotland 19.. free from **Scottish Council for Educational Technology**, Dowanhill, 74 Victoria Crescent Road, Glasgow G12 9JN Tel: 041 334 9314

Second Chances from the COIC (page 299).

Open Tech Directory - usually in Jobcentres and MSC offices.

Overseas Courses

Central Bureau for Educational Visits and Exchanges (Seymour Mews House, Seymour Mews, London W1H 9PE Tel: 01 486 5101) provides information, advice, help and a list of courses for British people who want to study abroad and for foreign students who want to study in Britain.

Postgraduate Courses

Most universities offer postgraduate courses. The *Directory of Postgraduate and Postexperience Courses* is free from CNAA (page 304). Don't be discouraged, it is oddly organized and the course you want may seem to be non-existent. Further searching will probably reveal it. Failing that, try ECCTIS (page 303).

Jupiter Consortium Ltd (The Brunel Science Park, Professional Development Programme, Brunel University, Uxbridge, Middlesex UB8 3PH Tel: 0895 73504 or 01 943 3685) was set up to provide industry with information on postgraduate courses in technology management at the leading edge of development, and identify gaps in the system. It has compiled a unique guide to such courses and, though not set up to advise the public, will give information on what courses are available in this field and where they can be found.

Postgraduate business courses are offered in many universities, but two which specialize in this field are:

London Business School, Sussex Place, Regents Park, London NW1 4SA Tel: 01 262 5050 and **Manchester Business School,** Booth Street West, Manchester M15 6PB Tel: 061 273 8228

Private Sector Courses
Many subjects such as secretarial work, dance training, or beauty therapy are covered by colleges operating outside the state sector. The Department of Education and Science no longer inspects and approves such courses, but an accreditation scheme is operated by the:

British Accreditation Council for Independent Further and Higher Education (Middlesex Polytechnic, Bounds Green Road, London N11 2NQ Tel: 01 368 1299) which can supply the names of approved colleges.

The Conference for Independent Further Education, (c/o Colonel J.L. Parks, Lovehayne Farm, Southleigh, Colyton, Devon EX13 6JE Tel: 040 487 241) is a group of colleges which have banded together to maintain standards and they will supply a list of members and their courses.
The Directory of Independent Training and Tutorial Organizations (DITTO), Elizabeth Summerson and Maureen Davies, Careers Consultants Ltd.

Teacher Training
Teacher training is scattered between colleges of education, colleges of higher education, polytechnics, and training colleges in subjects such as drama. A postgraduate teaching qualification from a university is another option.

The Graduate Teacher Training Registry (3 Crawford Place, London W1H 2BN Tel: 01 402 5317) is the place to contact for information on entry to any 1-year postgraduate course in teacher training (PGCE).

Advisory Service on Entry to Teaching, General Teaching Council for Scotland, 5 Royal Terrace, Edinburgh EH7 5AF Tel: 031 556 0072
In Ireland apply to the Department of Education.

Further and Higher Education in Scotland
The distinctive feature of Scottish universities is that ordinary degrees need a 3-year course, but Honours degrees take 4 years and many degree courses in subjects like medicine take 5 to 6 years. Entrance is through the same system as for any other university in Britain.

Scotland has, as yet, no polytechnics. Instead its colleges of higher education bear the uncharismatic title of central institutions - which is, perhaps, why one has applied to be called a polytechnic. Information on their courses is in a handbook from the Information Office, **Paisley College of Technology,** High Street, Paisley PA1 2BE. But applications for places should be made to the individual colleges. Information on further education is from the LEAs.

Unemployment and Retraining
Replan is a government programme to encourage the setting up of courses for those who are unemployed. There should be a REPLAN officer in your region, who you can talk to. Or write to REPLAN for information on courses c/o NIACE on page 303.

There are threshold schemes in certain skills which allow someone unemployed to gain experience while receiving a very low wage. For example **The National Computing Centre Ltd** (Oxford Road, Manchester M1 7ED Tel: 061 228 6333) will take on suitable, but unqualified and unemployed, school leavers and give them a ten-month training in computing. The Jobcentre and MSC should know about Threshold schemes.

An MSC retraining scheme which operates nationwide to retrain members of ethnic monorities who are unemployed is run by **Lancashire Industrial Language Training Unit** (54-56 Blackburn Road, Accrington, Lancashire BB5 1LE Tel: 0254 393316).

Commission for Racial Equality Elliot House, 10-12 Allington Street, London SW1E 5EH Tel: 01 828 7022 also has information on training schemes.
Guy Dauncey, *The Unemployment Handbook,* National Extension College
Nice Work if You Can Get It as above.

Handicapped Students
The Warnock Report described the provision for handicapped students as 'confused, patchy, and inadequate', and recommended better, more co-ordinated, provision. However, the take-up on the courses which do exist is patchy, with some classes closing for lack of interest, while others in the same area are oversubscribed. Those looking for a course would do well to look at every possible option: a good deal is available but it takes a little finding. Many of the charities specializing in a particular handicap have education advice services. There are also general sources of information:

National Bureau for Handicapped Students (336 Brixton Road, London SW9 7AA Tel: 01 274 0565) gives advice and information, plus useful books and leaflets on courses, support services and educational options, most are free to handicapped students. RC, M£L, S, F&F, M, L, B, EI, Rg, C, HD, sae.

The Open University (page 305) has a special adviser for handicapped students. The OU Students' Association also helps and it has a fund to provide handicapped students with equipment they need for studying, if they can't afford it.

The Scottish Centre for the Tuition of the Disabled (Queen Margaret College, Clerwood Terrace, Edinburgh EH12 8TS Tel: 031 339 5408) arranges volunteer tutors for handicapped people in Scotland who need special help.

Vocational Qualifications
The major problem in choosing a course leading to a qualifications for a particular job is that there are about 300 examining bodies in Britain, each setting independent syllabuses leading to an assortment of awards and qualifications. So it has been almost impossible for any layperson to tell which qualification was better than another. That is changing. Now there is a new stress on giving people skills which an employer will want, and qualifications which an employer will recognize. The **National Council for Vocational Qualifications** (222 Euston Road, London NW1 2BZ Tel: 01 387 9898) has been given the job of simplifying the system and creating a coherent framework for such courses throughout Britain. Courses are being assessed and adjusted so that those of different examining bodies

give equal qualifications, and they are then given NCVQ accreditation. The organization already has the best overview of vocational qualifications.

Women and Further Education
Women with children can have special problems in finding courses they can combine with the demands of a family. The open learning schemes, given elsewhere, can be ideal but some women may be desperate to get out of the home. Fortunately, colleges are becoming more aware of the needs of women, but they vary enormously. *Women Returners Network Directory* by Ruth Michaels, published by Longman, lists all the courses which will suit women who are having to combine study with bringing up children, including those which have creches, and gives useful contacts and addresses for more information.

RETIREMENT AND AFTER

There are very few areas in which the elderly are different from anyone else, so most of their needs are dealt with in the rest of the book. However they do suffer one special handicap: society's expectation that they will not just clock-up birthdays but become fragile, slow-witted, stiff (in mind and body) and generally ill. This may be the case but, unless there is some specific mental or physical illness, it isn't a necessary part of old age. In the Far East you see elderly people sitting cross-legged on the ground. Yet all they did to achieve this suppleness was never *stop* sitting on the ground.

Essentially the secret of making the most of old age is simply to keep on doing whatever you did when young, and if possible do things you never did before. The route to making the best of being old starts at about forty, and think of old age as a time for winding up, not winding down. By then all your responsibilities should have shifted to other people's shoulders and instead of wrapping yourself in cotton wool you can really begin to live in a carefree way and do all the things you never had time for.

Giving up Work
To give up work suddenly after a lifetime structured by its routine can be a terrible shock. Nor is it just a matter of habit. If you have devoted yourself to your job you may have hung your whole identity on your role at work, you may *be* a bus driver, an accountant or whatever that role has been. To you this may be even more 'you' than your name or your role as husband, wife or parent. To cease to have that job can feel like ceasing to exist in the real world. This problem has to be tackled head on.

Moving from Work into Retirement
Good employers may now let people work a gradually decreasing number of days a week, so they can become used to the freedom. It is well worth enquiring about. Even if a company isn't doing it already the personnel

officer might be persuaded to give it a try. Of course, the temptation may be to give the utmost to the job right to the end, working longer than ever - as if to prove that retirement isn't necessary whatever the rules say. The sad truth is that this is most unlikely to win the admiration and appreciation it deserves and may leave you doubly stranded on retirement day. Long before you retire try to find new roles which you can enjoy and in which you can feel that you matter to other people and have something to contribute.

If you have to retire on the dot and want to keep on working and earning it may be possible to find a new job. **The Pre-Retirement Association** (19 Undine Street, London SW17 8PP Tel: 01 767 3225 - M£H, L, G, B sae) has a list of organizations which find employment for the retired. A similar list can be obtained from the **Scottish Retirement Council** (212 Bath Street, Glasgow G2 4HW Tel: 041 332 9427) which also runs courses on retirement, which are paid for partly by local government, partly by the individual's firm.

> Do check what your earnings will do to your pension. Sometimes people can lose more than they earn. If that is the problem, or you don't want to earn money, voluntary organizations and many of the clubs and associations I have listed elsewhere are crying out for helpers. Now that more and more women are working, those who are retired are needed by the voluntary services as never before.

The Time of Your Life: A Handbook on Retirement, Help the Aged (Tel: 01 253 0253).
Henry Miller, *Countdown to Retirement*, Hutchinson Benham, gives food for thought.
The Open University (page 305) has a course on preparing for retirement.

Fun in Old Age
Retirement is also the time to learn new skills and take up new interests. The adult institutes are already full of canny pensioners making use of the bargain rates at which they can attend classes. In a few areas this is being taken one step further and adults are attending classes in ordinary schools. This provides an even larger range of classes, fills schools which have falling rolls, keeps teachers on their toes, and makes it far harder for the young to mess about or get violent in class. It seems such an excellent idea that I feel one really constructive thing pensioners could do is press to be allowed to study in schools.

There is also the **University of the Third Age (U3A)** (Langton Close, Wren Street, London WC1X 0HD Tel: 01 833 4747) which has learning centres for the elderly all over Britain. And don't forget that if you have no first degree there is no age limit to mandatory grants to university, and that many courses are based on open learning which allows you to do the work in your own home, often with the help of tapes or TV.

If anyone suggests that you can't learn so well when you get older ignore them. The only time the brain loses its ability to learn is when you stop asking it to.

Housing in Old Age

Away from it All?

People often dream of retiring to a place by the sea or in the country. There is something to be said for selling a family home which is too large, moving to a smaller place and using the difference in price to provide a better income. But research suggests that people should look around very carefully before choosing a new area, and shouldn't wait until retirement before they move. Old age is a time when friends are needed - even if it's only to do the shopping when you have a cold. The elderly should also think very carefully about how near they should be to their nearest and dearest. There is no surer way to strain a relationship than by moving too close and no way to guarantee loneliness more than by moving so far it is an expedition for them to reach you.

Carrying on in Your Own Home

Wherever someone elderly lives, the ideal situation is for them to be able to stay in their own home until they die. Luckily technology is making this easier. There are now alarms which can be carried constantly which allow someone to get emergency help by telephone even if they have fallen and cannot reach the phone itself, and some will automatically call for help. This is likely to be an expanding field, so check with the Disabled Living Foundation to see what is available.

Those who want to stay in their old home may be able to get grants to make it more suitable. If it's too big the best answer may be to convert part of it into accommodation which can be rented out. If it's the right size but difficult to get about in, aids can be added or rooms switched around to make it more suitable. Either way the timing of this needs careful thought. Once your income has dropped after retirement you may be able to get a grant for such work, even though you would not be eligible for a grant while working.

If it is simply a matter of insulating a home to keep heating costs down **Neighbourhood Energy Action** (2-4 Bigg Market, Newcastle upon Tyne NE1 1UW Tel: 091 261 5677) may have a local branch which can get this done at minimal cost. If it's a matter of making other improvements Age Concern has a fact sheet on where the elderly can get financial help. **The Anchor Housing Trust** (Oxenford House, 13-15 Magdalen Street, Oxford OX1 3BP) has a fact sheet called 'Staying Put', and Help the Aged (page 313) has a leaflet on grants for insulating your home. For certain jobs the DHSS may even pay the interest on a bank loan to get the work done.

Janice Casey, *Housing in Retirement*, Age Concern
Moving Home in Retirement by Shac/Anchor Housing Association from SHAC, 189a Old Brompton Road, London SW5
Safety in Retirement, ROSPA (see page 274)
Where to Live in Retirement, the Consumers' Association

Housing and Widows

Not all widows are elderly, but the vast majority are and, at any age, the fear which many widows share is that if a home is rented or mortgaged in the husband's name they will have no right to live there once he is dead. This is not the case, a widow has a right to continue to live in what was her home. However a widow may be faced with too much home and too little income or a widower find the family home too large to manage.

The worst time to make a decision to move is when suffering from the grief and shock of a bereavement. Once that is over there are plenty of solutions. If the home was rented a smaller place can be found, and some of the organizations on page 313 can help. If it is owned some of the options given above may apply, or selling it may provide enough spare capital to give a better income. Don't forget that if a house was bought from a council it may be possible to sell it back to the council, and continue to live in it paying a rent which is lower than the mortgage repayments - or the council may be able to help with mortgage repayments. These are only some of the possibilities. For a full survey read the excellent Halifax Building Society leaflet *Home Help for Widows* (which is nothing to do with home helps in the domestic sense) from NAW (page 269), and talk to your local Citizens Advice Bureau.

When Living Alone is Too Much

When living alone becomes too much for someone elderly, the first thought may be to look for an old people's home or a nursing home. But it is no small thing to give up independence and the possessions of a lifetime and accept life among strangers. It is all too easy to be over-protective and rush an old person into a home when they seem frail and then discover this was only due to a temporary illness. It may well be better for someone to live 5 happy years wearing themselves out coping at home, than live 10 miserable ones mourning for their lost freedom. Even if they become quite infirm it may be possible for them to stay at home with the right help.

Local authorities vary hugely in how much assistance they will provide to help someone manage in their own home. Here are some of the services which should be available. If they are provided, even an elderly person with quite a severe disability may be able to have the pleasure of staying in their own home for longer.

- Meals on wheels.
- Visiting chiropody.
- Bathing by a district nurse.
- Physiotherapy visits.
- Laundry service, including incontinence supplies.
- It may be possible to have a nurse get them up in the morning and then return to put them to bed at night.
- Social services will also install aids like handles by a bath, a raised lavatory or a second stair rail.
- If social services don't provide a home help it may be possible to get a supplementary pension to cover the cost of paying for help.

Some authorities produce good booklets listing their services so ring and ask. Otherwise ask the duty clerk at social services how you get each of these services, and whether there are any others. GPs, and charities such as the Red Cross and St John's Ambulance may also be able to help you.

However, it has to be said that even under the most efficient local authorities, someone elderly may find themselves alone for too long at weekends. Some of the agencies which offer carers are on page 282 and local agencies are listed in Yellow Pages under 'nurses'.

Leaving Home
Once someone elderly decides to leave their old home the possibilities are:
- more suitable ordinary accommodation - possibly from a housing association at low rent
- a purpose-built house or flat with a warden on call nearby, as the most basic kind of sheltered accommodation
- a self-contained room in a private home for the elderly to which they take their own furniture
- a room in a state-run home for the elderly
- a room in a state or private nursing home or hospital
- they can live with their family.

Low Rent Accommodation
Low rent accommodation only solves one problem, but it may be the most pressing one in early old age. The Pre-Retirement Association (page 309) has a list of housing associations which rent reasonably priced accommodation to the elderly, and local councils may be a source of other names. **The National Association of Almshouses** (Billingbear Lodge, Wokingham, Berks RG11 5RU Tel: 0344 52922) has a list of all the organizations which administer almshouses.

Sheltered Accommodation and Nursing Homes
Building sheltered housing for the elderly is a field which is still finding its feet, and those considering such accommodation may find it revealing to read a report by the **Centre for Policy on Ageing** (25-31 Ironmonger Row, London EC1V 3QP Tel: 01 253 1787) called *Growing Old Together*.

Imperfect though some sheltered accommodation may be, it's much in demand and to get a place in a block of private flats with a resident warden you may need to put your name down several years before. The same goes for rooms in sheltered homes for the elderly run by charities. Some of these will care for someone who becomes ill while a resident, but will not take on someone who is already infirm. So, you may need to get your foot in the door while still spry. If you once worked for a large organization find out whether it has any links with sheltered accommodation. Quite a few large institutions help charitable organizations and in return can recommend ex-employees for places.

State-run Sheltered Accommodation
Unfortunately state run sheltered schemes are quite rare, and the standard option is what the officials call 'Part 3 Accommodation' in a local authority residential home, run much like a state hotel for the elderly. Usually the personal possessions which can be brought into these are very limited and many local authorities only accept those who already live in the area, so it can be difficult to move a relative closer to where you live.

Local authorities charge a set weekly fee and state benefits may help. The details are constantly changing but Age Concern and Counsel and Care for the Elderly (page 312) have good information leaflets on everything you need to know and will also help and advise.

Where People Fall Between Two Stools
Unfortunately there's a crying lack of accommodation for those who can't quite manage alone but aren't ill. Even to get into Part 3 accommodation you have to pass a fitness test. The catch is that some elderly people fail this test but are not ill enough to be accepted by a state nursing home or hospital. So they are refused a place in a home *and* in a hospital.

The Caring Trap
Some people may want to have an elderly parent to live with them until they die, and take on the responsibility gladly. But nobody should take on an elderly relative believing it is just a step towards state care. Once an old person is living with you it is likely to be for the rest of their life.

If an old person can't manage alone it is far wiser for one of the family to go and live in with them, until the matter is sorted out. You have only to show that you *can* take them in for the council to rule that they don't need to look after the old person because you can. It doesn't matter that you are caring for them at the price of giving up work and squashing the children into one bedroom. Once a council has shifted the burden on to the family it tends to stay there.

Families have no legal obligation to house any relative over the age of 18, so if you refuse to look after an elderly relative the state *must* find a place for them - if necessary by assisting with the cost of care in the voluntary or private sector. It isn't easy or pleasant to take things that far but it may be the only way if you can't cope with caring for them.

Looking After Someone Elderly
There are undoubtedly some wonderful old people who have lost their physical strength and need looking after but unfortunately, there are also many who through mental illness, or deterioration, are little more than a shadow of the person they once were. Those who care for them face a special problem of grief and alienation. They should not feel guilty if they find it hard to handle. To have someone you love look at you with eyes which no longer recognize you, or behave in ways of which their old self would have been ashamed, is a heartbreaking experience which is becoming familiar to more and more families as medicine swells the numbers living to a ripe old age.

Looking after an elderly person is at least as tying and tiring as looking after a small child. There is also the emotional upheaval of reversing the roles - having someone you once relied on relying on you. This can bring with it anger and guilt which is compounded by the fact that if someone becomes deaf you cannot talk to them without raising your voice, and may feel angry simply because you are shouting.

If an old person has ceased to enjoy life, the carer will sometimes resent the seemingly pointless burden of caring and wish the old person were dead. To feel this, even occasionally, about someone you love, or even about a helpless stranger, is not easy to handle - yet almost every carer feels it at some time. It may help to read about how other people have experienced it.

Dr Brian Long, *Coping With Caring*, Mind publications (from MIND, see In Sickness).
Mace, Rabins and others, *The 36-Hour Day*, Age Concern/ Hodder & Stoughton
Jenny Pulling, *The Caring Trap*, Fontana - a carers story.

Coping with Caring
Any carer needs to get as much practical help as possible to lessen the burden. Some local authorities offer far more help than others, but it is worth trying any or all of the following (but see also page 310):
● a good family doctor should be able to refer you to other help if you talk frankly - don't put a brave face on it and don't be fobbed off with pills.
● some areas have an incontinence advisor - ask a GP
● the family doctor should be able to arrange for a district nurse to come and do the medical chores
● a community psychiatric nurse can help to nurse the mentally ill at home
● some health authorities will admit an old person to hospital while the carer has a holiday
● if an old person is leaving hospital, the hospital social worker should put you in touch with help
● some areas have day centres and day-care centres and the elderly are collected from home and returned
● residential homes may take the elderly for a couple of weeks to give the carer a break
● social services departments may arrange holidays for the old and infirm.

You may be able to get help from the voluntary services. Some social services departments have volunteer organizers who can put you in touch, or contact your Council of Voluntary Service, Rural Community Council or Citizens' Advice Bureau.

National Council for Carers and their Elderly Dependants (29 Chilworth Mews, London W2 3RG Tel: 01 724 7776) is an invaluable source of advice, and support. RC, M£L, M, G, L, pressure group.

Nursing Homes and Other Residential Care
One of the best sources of detailed information on private and voluntary residential and nursing homes for the elderly is the charity **Counsel and Care for the Elderly** (131 Middlesex Street, London E1 7JF Tel: 01 621 1624 - 10.30 am - 4 pm). They inspect every place they recommend and try to match a person's individual needs

to the home they suggest, unfortunately this service *only covers Greater London*. However, they provide some grants to elderly people, of limited means, anywhere in Britain, and their advice service on problems related to old age is open to anyone.

The **Elderly Accommodation Counsel** (1 Durward House, 31 Kensington Court, London W8 5BH Tel: 01 937 8709), covers the whole of Britain and ranges from slightly sheltered housing to hospices for the terminally ill (though cancer hospices aren't a feature). You fill in a form and the computer prints out addresses which match your needs. There is a nominal fee for names and addresses of about 6 organizations, but those who are hard-up can get free information. However, the accommodation is not inspected.

Be wary: some agencies take fees from the nursing homes so they are not unbiased, and many do not inspect the homes they recommend. A better first source of information is the Registration Officer for Residential Care Homes at the local social services department, or the Registration Officer for Private Nursing Homes in the District Health Authority. These departments inspect and register residential homes and nursing homes, and you may be able to find out if any would particularly suit you or your relative's needs. If someone is being discharged from hospital the Hospital Social Worker may be able to suggest some.

Do inspect any accommodation, or nursing or residential home before accepting a place - the quality varies from excellent to disgraceful and even places which are recommended may change hands.

Homes for the Elderly - What to Look For
A home should be a home in the best sense of the word. It should also be registered with the authorities and if the registration isn't displayed ask to see it. It isn't easy to do a thorough assessement of a home in a brief visit. So the following list gives points to look for: they come from Age Concern and Counsel and Care for the Elderly, plus some of my own.
● Is the atmosphere attractive and welcoming?
● What are the other residents like? Would the person concerned get on with them?
● Do the residents have their own rooms or must they share?
● Can people bring personal belongings, like ornaments and small pieces of furniture?
● Do the bedrooms lock, and is there a place to lock away valuables?
● Is there a telephone the residents can use and does it take both outgoing and incoming calls?
● What level of care does the place offer - will they help with washing or dressing if necessary?
● What is the food like? Can residents make their own snacks or drinks? Do they provide for special diets?
● Is is warm enough?
● What is the daily routine? How rigid is it? And will it suit the person concerned?
● Can people go to their rooms whenever they wish?
● Are there free visiting hours and can the residents see their visitors in private?

- What activities go on there? Can the residents continue their hobbies?
- Are residents involved in the running of the home?
- Do residents keep their own GP?
- Is the home clean and safe? Look in the kitchen and the bathrooms.
- Are there aids in the bathroom and lavatory? Like a bell in case of trouble?
- How are medicines given and what records are kept?
- Under what circumstances would a resident be asked to leave?
- What are the fire drills and when was the last practice?
- Will a pet be accepted?

Abbeyfield Society (186-192 Darkes Lane, Potters Bar, Herts EN6 1AB Tel: 0707 44845) sets up houses all over Britain, run by resident housekeepers, in which elderly people live together. Each with their own furnishings in their own room, at a reasonable rent. RC.

Friends of the Elderly and Gentlefolks Help (42 Ebury Street, London SW1W 0LZ Tel: 01 730 8263) has a long history of running homes for the elderly.

Grace Link (Mrs Gould's Residential Advisory Service for the Elderly) (Upper Chambers, 7 Derby Street, Leek, Staffs ST13 6HN Tel: 0538 387524 Link line charged at local rate Tel: 0345 023300) advises on residential homes in southern England, excluding self-catering accommodation, and the homes are inspected. Small refundable fee.

Mobility in Old Age

Car drivers should check the rules for holding a driving licence in old age and be careful not to drive when taking certain medicines.

Those who need to use a walking stick should have one the right length. The top needs to be about 8 cm (3 ins) up the wrist when the arm is hanging straight down by the side.

Wheelchairs for indoors, whether hand or electric powered, can be supplied free by the NHS provided a doctor recommends it. Electric wheelchairs for outside are not supplied by the NHS but, by law, can be driven on the pavement at up to 4 mph. Get their details from The Disabled Living Foundation which also has them on view in London for those who book an appointment.

Personal vehicles are now made to carry the disabled or elderly short distances. They are usually electric and range from sturdy glorified tricycles to rather natty miniature cars which are so much fun that I long to possess one. They need to be bought privately and may all be driven on the pavement without a licence at up to 4 mph. But larger vehicles like electrically-assisted pedal-powered cycles and tricycles driven at up to 15 mph must go on the road, though they can be used without a licence or helmet. The Disabled Living Foundation has the details.

Safety and Old Age

Many old people are at special risk from their own forgetfulness, from being unsteady on their feet and from lack of money to have things seen to, and relatives need to think about their special needs.

- Is the wiring old and dangerous? (They may be unable to pay for renewal.)
- Are the stairs a hazard - torn carpet, poor lighting, weak banisters? Better no carpet than a broken leg.
- Is the kitchen arranged so that nothing heavy can fall from a height?
- Are the handles of kettles and pans able to be held safely by arthritic hands?
- Are rugs on non-slip backings?
- Are there trailing flexes that might not be seen?

Finally, is there a phone wherever they might need to call for help? If not installing a phone line could be the best Christmas present they could have.

Warmth in Old Age

Cold is a special hazard for the old. It is not simply a matter of poverty. Any old person is at risk. With age, the ability to notice changes in temperature diminishes - just as eyesight and hearing diminish. So even those who can afford to heat their home properly may still die of hypothermia through just not noticing how cold the room has become. And once someone's temperature falls below a certain level he or she will simply fall into a deep, and fatal sleep. For safety the elderly need heaters with timers and thermostats so they will automatically be kept warm enough. The elderly should aim for a room temperature of 21°C (70°F).

Keeping warm is also a matter of keeping in the warmth which the body makes: lots of layers of warm loose clothing, which trap the air between them are warmest, especially if at least the inner ones are wool. The old-fashioned idea of a shawl or rug is very cosy (especially with a hot water bottle under), but modern science can even go one better. Camping shops sell large thin sheets of foil-coated plastic, often called Space Blankets. They are for wrapping round mountaineers to help them survive cold, as the foil reflects back heat. They make granny look a touch like a space man but are cheap and work wonders wherever you need to keep the cold out. More information from Help the Aged.

More information

Age Concern - England - 60 Pitcairn Road, Mitcham Surrey CR4 3LL Tel: 01 640 5431; **Scotland** - 33 Castle Street, Edinburgh EH2 3DN Tel: 031 225 5000; **Wales** - 4th Floor, 1 Cathedral Road, Cardiff CF1 9SD Tel: 0222 371821/371566; **N. Ireland** - 6 Lower Crescent, Belfast BT7 1NR Tel: 0232 245729 - It exists to 'help elderly people by every possible means'. Local groups, listed as Age Concern in the phone book, offer help, advice and information, plus useful leaflets on benefits, medical services, and residential care and so on.

DPS Consultants (Dodds Lane, 27 Preston Street, Faversham, Kent ME13 8PC Tel: 0795 531472) runs pre-retirement counselling courses, which are usually paid for by an employer. They cover the whole range of problems experienced by those who retire from senior and middle management.

Help the Aged, (16-18 St James's Walk, London EC1R OBE Tel: 01 253 0253 or Freepost, London EC1B 1BD) has free advice and information leaflets. Advice Line: 01 250 3399. Food Line: 01 253 0253. Heating Line: Freefone 0800 289 404.

Free Time

Active Games • Board Games and Others • Cards • Party Games for All Ages • General Clubs • Hobbies and Sports • Marriage and Dating Agencies • Music, Drama and Entertainment • Gardening • Houseplants

ACTIVE GAMES

In this section you will find the basic rules of the sports and games you may suddenly want to play with family and friends. It is designed to fill the gap when you can only half remember how to play something, and no official rule book is to hand, or when you know how to play but can't recall the dimensions of the court or area of play - as can happen with croquet. Those who want to know the full rules for match play, or seriously take up any of these sports and games, should consult the official bodies listed in Hobbies.

Boules (petanque) (2 - 6 players)
There are several versions of boules but, in Britain, petanque is probably the most popular - often with sets brought back from French holidays. A set comprises several metal balls (boules) somewhat larger than a tennis ball, and a very small ball called a cochonnet. You need a flat expanse of ground, and a boule is thrown underarm, with it under the hand as it comes forward. The aim is to get your boules as close as possible to the cochonnet - or knock the other team's boules away from it.

Two teams play against each other. With one or two in a team each player has 3 boules; with more each player has 2 boules. A coin is tossed to decide who throws the cochonnet. That person then draws a circle 36-50 cm (14-20 in) across, stands in it and throws the cochonnet 6-10 m (20-30 ft), and not nearer than 50 cm 50 cm (1 ft 8 in) to an obstacle. Then a member of his team stands in the circle and throws a boule as close to the cochonnet as possible. Someone from the opposing team then throws from the circle, trying either to get his boule even closer or to knock the opponent's boule farther away. Once the first two boules are in place, whichever team has a boule *farthest* from the cochonnet continues to play until someone places one nearer or they run out of boules. Then the other team plays all its boules.

The British Petanque Association says 'the winning team gets as many points as it has boules better placed than the best of the losing teams'. So if team A has 3

boules nearer than the nearest one of team B, A gets three points. For the next game the circle is drawn where the cochonnet previously was, and the first team to total 13 points in a series of games wins.

Croquet (2 or 4 players)
Correctly played croquet is nothing like its P. G. Wodehouse image. Far from being a lackadaisical game for idlers, it is a daunting game of strategy in which you try to get your own ball through a sequence of hoops, while ruining your opponent's chances by deflecting their balls.

It is played on a lawn using 6 hoops, a central peg and wooden mallets, and 4 balls. Four players play as two teams, each person having one ball; blue and black opposing red and yellow. Two players use two balls each, blue and black versus red and yellow.

The aim is to get the ball through all 6 hoops, in the right order, twice over - once from each direction. Whoever does this first wins - no matter how many strokes it takes. Alternatively, a game can have a time limit and the winner be whoever scores the most points in that time. Score one for hitting a ball through a hoop, and one for hitting it against the peg at the end - so 13 points is the maximum for each ball in a round.

Toss to start; the winner either chooses to play first *or* picks the colour of ball(s) she will play. The first stroke of each ball is taken from one of the baulks (see diagram opposite).

- To get all balls in play the sides play alternately, playing one ball at each turn.
- Each player keeps to her own ball(s).
- The sides play alternately.
- *Within* each team the players need not play alternately; whoever has a ball in the most advantageous position at any turn plays, even if it means one player, in a team, monopolizes the game for turn after turn.
- A basic turn is one stroke with one ball — but the exceptions are the very essence of the game, and a skilful player can extend a single turn to reach right to the final peg.

The exceptions are as follows.

1 If a ball goes through a hoop the player may play 1 more stroke.
2 If the ball hits one of the other three balls (a roquet) the player may have 2 more strokes. These *must* be a croquet shot and a continuation stroke.

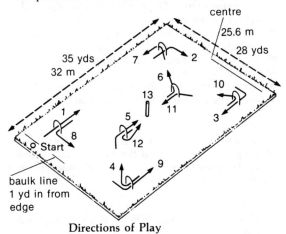

Directions of Play

Croquet Shot After a Roquet
The player picks up her ball and puts it so that it touches the ball she roqueted. Then she strikes her ball so the other ball moves. Failure to make the other ball even wobble is a foul and the player's ball is replaced where it was before.

Having been roqueted, a ball cannot be roqueted again in that turn - unless the player's ball goes through a hoop first. Going through a hoop restores the right to roquet any of the three balls.

Continuation Stroke After a Roquet
This is an ordinary stroke, played with the ball just used in the croquet shot. If, during this shot, another ball is roqueted, or it goes through a hoop, the rules for these apply all over again.

Out of Bounds
If a ball goes over the boundary line a player can place the ball a yard (about a mallet's length) in from the boundary at the place where it went off, and play continues.

Fouls
The striker must not:
● touch the head of her mallet with her hand
● kick or hit the mallet on to the ball
● rest herself or the mallet on anything while making a shot
● move a stationary ball, which is resting against a peg or hoop, by hitting the peg or hoop
● strike the ball with anything but the face of the mallet
● touch any ball which is in play with any part of her anatomy (except to put it in position for a croquet shot)
● hit a ball, which is resting against a hoop or peg, towards that hoop or peg
● hit the ball twice in any ordinary shot.

A foul must be called before the next stroke is played. The penalty is the ending of the player's turn with no points scored.

Darts (for any number of players)
There are various games which can be played with darts and a darts board. What follows is the standard game.
1 The board is hung so its centre is 5 ft 8 in (173 cm) from the floor.
2 The throwing line in international championships is 7 ft 9¼ in (237.5 cm) from the board, for both sexes. But many pubs have lines farther away from it, and the players agree on a line before play.
3 Play can be by individuals, pairs, or teams of any agreed number.
4 Either toss to start or throw and see who gets closest to the bullseye.
5 To start scoring a player must get his or her dart inside the outer rings - that dart is scored, but darts played prior to that dart have no score.
6 In team play scoring starts for the whole team when one member of the team gets a dart inside the outer rings.

The starting total is 301 or 501, or 1,001 - and the players agree which they will use. Scores are deducted from the total agreed.
● A dart in the inner bull scores 50.
● A dart in the outer bull scores 25.
● Darts in the sectors score according to the sector.
● Darts in the outer double ring score double the score for that sector; in the inner double ring they score treble.
● Darts outside the outer double ring score nothing.

Traditionally, in pubs, if someone wants to join a game he offers to 'chalk' (write up the score) for the other players on the blackboard. He will then play the winner of that game.

The winner is the first player to reach exactly zero. But zero may only be reached by throwing a double. So, if a throw would bring the score to one, or take it past zero, that throw is not scored, and the turn ends.

Eight Ball Pool (for 2 players or 2 teams)
Pool is played on a pocket billiards table, using a white cue ball and 15 other balls. The balls can be given numbers from 1 to 15. The key ball is black, which is number 8. There are also spot (or yellow) balls numbered 1 to 7, and striped (or red) balls numbered 9 to 15. It can be played by two players or two teams, and the order of play with each team doesn't vary.

Aim
The aim is to pocket the 8 ball first, having first pocketed all the balls of a particular group. This group is decided by the opening play. To start the balls are arranged in a triangle, as illustrated, with the 8 ball on the spot. You toss a coin to start. The winner decides who will make the first shot ('the break').

The Break

The first player plays the cue ball from anywhere within the 'D', aiming for any of the balls in the triangle. The aim is to pocket a ball, or make at least 2 balls hit a cushion (the padded sides of the table). If they fail to do this the game is restarted with the balls back in the triangle. This time the other player (or team) begins and the previous team forfeits a turn - so their opponent has two consecutive turns.

If a ball is pocketed as the result of a break that type of ball (e.g.striped) becomes the type which the player or team must play for throughout the game, and the other side is automatically allotted the other type.

If a player pockets balls of both types, on the break, he/she can choose which to play for.

Bad Breaks

- If, in pocketing the first ball, the cue ball is also pocketed, or any other foul stroke is made, then the ball doesn't count in deciding which balls will be played for.
- If a player pockets the 8 ball on the break the game must be restarted by that player without any penalty - even if there was a foul.
- If no balls are pocketed on the break, but it is still a valid break, then turns alternate between players/teams until a ball is pocketed.

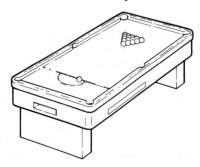

Play

The cue ball is always played from where it comes to rest. A player's turn continues until he fails to pocket a ball on any shot, or commits a foul. Once a player has pocketed all the balls of his group he can then try to pocket the black into any pocket, and so win the game.

Fouls

The penalty for a foul is loss of the next turn, and on the first shot of the following turn the opponent can hit *any* ball on the table without a penalty. The fouls are:

- pocketing the cue ball
- hitting the opponent's balls before your own
- failing to hit any ball with the cue ball
- playing a jump shot (where one ball leaps over another)
- hitting the 8 ball with the first impact of the cue ball while your own balls are still on the table
- pocketing an opponent's ball
- striking the cue ball twice over in a shot

- striking the cue ball with anything but the tip of the cue
- balls landing off the table (these are respotted on the 8 ball spot or as close as possible without touching another ball on a direct line between the spot and the centre of the 'D'. But for this the cue ball is replayed from anywhere in the 'D'.)
- touching any ball (except to respot it or position the cue ball when required by a foul)
- not having at least one foot on the floor
- playing out of turn
- playing before the balls have come to rest
- letting the cue touch balls other than the cue ball.

Snookering

A player is snookered when his way is blocked, so he cannot play a legal shot. If this happens as the result of a foul shot then the usual foul shot clauses apply but also the cue ball can be played from the 'D'.

Loss of Game

A player loses the game if he or she does any of the following:

- pockets the cue ball when potting the black
- pockets the 8 ball before pocketing all the balls in his/her group
- pockets the 8 ball in the same shot as another ball, except after a foul, when only the 8 ball and the other team's balls are on the table
- if he doesn't try to play some ball of his own group.

Snooker (for 2 players, 2 pairs or 2 teams)

Snooker is played on a standard billiards/snooker table. The players use 15 red balls, 6 coloured balls and 1 white cue ball.

Basics

1 Toss to start and set up all the red balls in a triangle, as shown in the diagram, and the coloured balls are set up on the spots marked on the table.
2 Pairs and teams play as for singles, with turns alternating between the sides.
3 Within each side they play in the same order throughout the game. *Throughout the game only the white cue ball can ever be struck by the cue.*
4 In any turn a player must first aim to hit a red ball - unless there are no red balls on the table.
5 If a player fails to pocket a ball at any stroke his or her turn ends.
6 Apart from the first break of the game, the cue ball is always played from wherever it came to rest in the previous player's turn. (The only exception to this is when the cue ball has been pocketed, in which case it is played from the semi-circle.)
7 Players must always have at least one foot on the floor (i.e. not lie on the table).

Play

1 The first player puts the white cue ball within the marked semi-circle, and plays it so it strikes any red.

2   If a red is pocketed the player continues his 'break' by attempting to pocket any non-red ball.

3   If a coloured ball is pocketed the player now tries to pocket a red. This sequence of red and coloured balls alternates as long as there are reds on the table.

4   If the cue ball comes to rest against a ball, which is *not* the next type to be played, the stroke must be played without even wobbling the ball that the cue ball touches, otherwise a penalty score is awarded to the opponent as in penalty scoring.

5   If the cue ball comes to rest against the type which *is* due to be played the player may play a ball of either colour next, or even miss, without incurring a penalty.

6   Red balls which are pocketed stay in the pockets.

7   Coloured balls which are pocketed are *immediately* put back on the spot they occupied at the start of the game (respotted) - even in the middle of a break.

8   The player who pockets the last red ball may then try to pocket *any* coloured ball, and this is respotted. After that the balls must be struck by the cue ball - and pocketed - strictly in the order of their value, starting with the lowest. At this stage, coloured balls are *not* respotted.

9   The winner is whoever has the highest score at the end of the game. If there is a tie the black is brought back into play and the first to score from it wins.

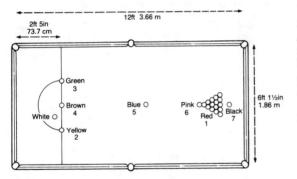

Scoring

Each correctly pocketed ball is added to a player's score as follows.

red = 1	brown = 4	pink = 6
yellow = 2	blue = 5	black = 7
green = 3		

Fouls and Penalty Scores

After any 'foul shot' a player loses his turn (keeping his score up to the shot before the foul) and a penalty score is awarded to his opponent. Fouls are as follows but the minimum penalty is 4:

- If a cue ball is pocketed 4 is added to the opponent's score.
- If the cue ball fails to hit a ball its value is the penalty.
- If the cue ball hits the wrong ball (e.g. red, when it should be coloured) the penalty is the value of the correct ball.
- If the wrong ball is pocketed the penalty is the value

of whichever ball is higher (between correct and pocketed).

- Simultaneously hitting or pocketing 2 balls, other than 2 reds, the penalty is the value of whichever is higher.
- Pocketing 2 balls in one shot, the penalty is the value of the higher of the two.
- For pushing a ball, jumping it over another or playing it out of turn the penalty is the value of the ball hit.
- For forcing a ball off the table the penalty is the value of the 'on' ball or the ball which was hit, whichever is higher.
- For playing 2 successive reds the penalty is 7 points.

Respotting Balls

- An illegally pocketed coloured ball is respotted *immediately*, whatever the stage of the game.
- If a coloured ball can't be replaced on its spot, because another ball has rolled on to it, the coloured ball is put on the vacant spot with the highest score.
- If all the spots are covered the ball goes as close as possible to its spot (without touching another ball) and on the shortest direct (imaginary) line between its spot and the top cushion. The only exception to this is if there is no space between the covered spot and the top cushion in which case the ball must be placed in a direct line to the bottom cushion.

Snookering

A snooker is when a shot is blocked because a ball which must not be hit is directly between the cue ball and the ball to be hit next. However, the shot must be played, and the usual penalty is scored if the player misses or hits another ball first.

If that situation arises because the previous player fouled the above rule does not apply, and any ball on the table may be played. If this ball is pocketed it scores 1 - except if there are no reds on the table. In that case it takes the score of the ball which the 'snooker' prevented him from playing.

More information

John Pulman, *Tackle Snooker*, Stanley Paul

Table Tennis (2 or 4 players)

The standard ball is white or yellow and 38.2 mm (1½ in) in diameter. The racket can be any size, provided it is a single piece of wood, and covered with a sheet of rubber. To win a player, or pair, must score 21 points. But if the score reaches 20 all, winning then requires a 2-point lead. A match can be one game, the best of 3 or the best of 5.

To start toss a coin; the winner either decides who serves first *or* picks his/her end.

Serving

The server lightly tosses the ball, from waist level using a flat hand, and hits it so it bounces once on the serving side, and once on the opponent's side. At the moment of striking the ball, for service, the bat must be behind the end of the table.

Service changes to the other player or pair after every 5 points. But, once the score reaches 20 all, opponents serve alternately. In singles this is simple. In doubles there is a set order of service and of play.

- The server always stands at the right-hand side of the table.
- The serve must travel diagonally across the table, starting by touching the right-hand section on the server's side.
- The sequence of service in doubles is this:
  A to T
  T to B (A and B having swopped sides)
  B to S (S and T having swopped sides)
  S to A (A and B having swopped sides)

Play for Singles and Doubles
- On a return the ball must cross the net without bouncing on the returner's side.
- A return which touches the net or supports is still good if it lands on the opponent's side.
- The ball *must* bounce once after crossing the net.
- The ball may *only* bounce once before being returned.
- Players change ends after each game, and also when the score reaches 10 in the final game.

The sequence of play in doubles follows a strict order in which the players on each side take the returns alternately, as follows:
  A serves to T
  T returns service
  B must take T's return
  S must take B's return
  A takes the return from S, and so on.
Points are scored when:
- an opponent fails to hit the ball
- an opponent breaks any of the rules of play
- an opponent strikes out of sequence in doubles play.

A let is a rally which doesn't result in points and the serve is retaken. This occurs when:
- the ball touches the net or supports during service, and still lands correctly
- a ball is served when the receiver isn't ready and has *not* attempted to hit the ball.

More information
Reginald Moore Ed., *Official Rules of Sports and Games*, Kaye and Ward

BOARD GAMES AND OTHERS

In this section you will find the rules for some of the most popular family games, from chess to tiddlywinks. Mah Jong and Go I have reluctantly had to omit as they are far too complex for a book of this sort. Games like Monopoly, Scrabble and Trivial Pursuit are also omitted because if you have all the pieces you need you almost certainly have the rules.

Backgammon (2 players)
This is an excellent game which can be played with or without a gambling element. It probably came to Europe from the Middle East, as a primitive board suggests it was played in Sumeria in 2600 BC. When it was introduced in the eleventh century it took both nobles and commoners by such storm that both Church and state tried to suppress it as an immoral time-waster. For centuries it remained immensely popular with the upper classes, and only the eighteenth-century craze for cards ousted it from fashion, upon which it became a favourite game with the clergy.

Before starting play, each player places her 15 pieces on the board as shown below. To start, each player throws one of the two dice. (It is customary to call the dice score at each throw.) The highest starts, using the two numbers just thrown. Thereafter they play alternately, throwing the two dice each time. The dice dictate the number of points the pieces may be moved. For example, throwing a 4 and 6 allows you to move one piece along 4 points then on 6 points (or vice versa), provided either the 4th or 6th points are free, or move one piece 4 points and another 6 points - moving in your own direction of play. If a double is thrown the potential moves are doubled. So double 3 allows you to move any variation of four 3s. You may not land on a point occupied by 2 or more of an opponent's pieces; but you may cross it at any stage of the journey.

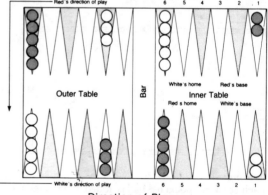

Direction of Play

A single piece on a point is a 'blot'. An opponent may land on it and place it on the central bar. It can only be brought into play by its owner throwing a number corresponding to a free point (i.e. an empty point or one with only one of the opponent's piece's, or any number of the player's own) in his base. For this reason, tactics tend to concentrate on 'making points' (placing 2 of one's pieces safely on the same point), and in trying to land on one's opponent's 'blots' and remove them from the board.

When you have all your pieces home you can 'bear off' pieces from the points the dice allow. So a 5 and 2 allow one piece to be removed from point number 5 and another from point number 2. Or moves to the value of 5 and 2 can be made, or one piece removed and another moved. If a 6 is thrown and there are no pieces on the 6 point a piece is removed from the next highest point - and so on.

The winner is whoever bears off all his pieces first. A hit is when the loser has also reached the bearing-off stage. A gammon is when all the loser's pieces are not yet home. A backgammon is when the loser still has a piece in her opponent's home table.

Gambling at Backgammon
The players first agree a stake, and place the doubling die on the bar, with 64 uppermost. If the loser has managed to bear off one or more stones she only pays the agreed stake. If the loser has all 15 men on the board she plays twice the stake. If she has any on the bar she plays three times the stake. If doubling has taken place the same rules apply but to the doubled stake.

If a player feels he is at an advantage he can double the basic stake. His opponent can either stop the game and pay the stake first agreed or agree to double and continue. The doubling die is then put on the bar with the 2 uppermost and the control of it passes to the doubled player so the other cannot double again. If he in turn feels likely to win he can redouble - to 4 times the original stake. And his opponent has to pay up or agree - and so on.

The National Backgammon Players Society, 27 Moorfield Road, Manchester M20 SU2 — M£H, age 18+, G, competitions, also events for under 18s.
Oswald Jacoby, *The Backgammon Book*.

Battleships (2 players)
As a child, I inherited an ancient board for battleships drawn out under a sheet of yellowed perspex. It looked as if it dated from the First World War and must have had very different connotations then.

Each player needs 2 sheets of ordinary squared paper and a pencil. On each paper draw a big 'board' ten squares by ten, and labelled A to J across and 1 to 10 down. Each player then labels one 'board' 'Enemy Fleet' and the other 'Home Fleet' and marks in his fleet on the home 'board' as follows:

The Fleet	Squares Filled
1 battleship	4 per ship
2 cruisers	3 per ship
3 destroyers	2 per ship
4 submarines	1 per ship

Take turns, to call out a square (e.g. D5). If your opponent has no vessel on the square he says 'no'; if there is a ship on the square he calls 'hit'. Tick X on your enemy fleet 'board' so you can see what is where. To sink a ship you must hit all of its squares, and each player must say when a ship is sunk. The winner is whoever sinks all the enemy ships first.

Chess (2 players)
Chess is said to have been invented by an Indian philosopher, in the sixth century AD and it reached Europe between 700 and 900, becoming an essential skill for travelling minstrels.

It is played on a board of 64 squares, using 16 pieces.

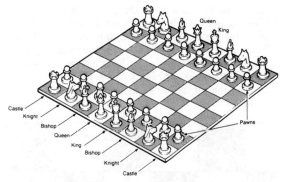

The Pieces on a Chessboard

One player takes 2 pieces, a white and a black piece, switches them around behind his back and holds his hands out. The other chooses, and accepts that colour. Have a white square at the lower right-hand corner of the board. White makes the first move.

The object of the game is to achieve a position from which the opponent's King could be captured. When someone sees that their next move will achieve this they must say 'check'. The opponent must protect the King, or it is 'checkmate' and the game is over. During play an opponent's piece may be taken off after a move which lands the capturing piece on the same square.

Each type of piece is allowed a different type of move, as follows. Only the Knight may hop over other pieces - whichever side they belong to. Obviously, the greater the scope for movement, the more powerful the piece: it is seldom worth sacrificing a powerful piece to capture a low one.

Piece	Moves	Takes
King	One square in any direction, including diagonally	As it moves
Queen	Any number of squares in any direction, including diagonally	As it moves
Rooks/ Castles	Any number of squares forward or backwards or at right angles	As it moves
Bishops	Any number of squares forward or backwards on a diagonal	As it moves
Knights	An L-shaped move, 2 squares one way and 1 to the side, travelling in any direction except diagonally. To do this they may hop over other pieces	As it moves
Pawns	Only move forward. Each may move 2 squares on its first move. But only 1 square otherwise	Takes on a diagonal

Three Special Exceptions
1 *En passant:* if in moving two squares forward, on its first move, a Pawn lands *beside* an opponent's Pawn it may be taken just as if it had moved one square and landed diagonally to it. The winning Pawn is put on the square the victim would have occupied had it only moved one square.
2 If a Pawn reaches the opponent's back row it may be

converted into *any* piece the player wishes.
3 Castling is a double move made in a single turn to place the King in a less vulnerable site. A Rook and a King must be in their starting positions with no pieces between them. The King moves 2 squares towards the Rook. The Rook moves to the square next to the King on the far side - jumping over the King to do so.

Castling

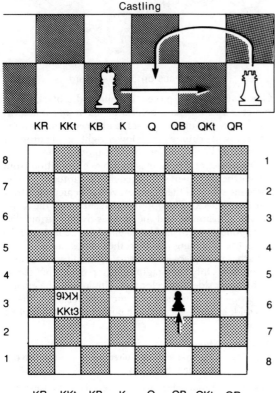

Chessboard Notation

Each square is named after the column name and row number of the *colour which is playing*. So each square has two names, as in the example. The piece moving is named first, then the square of its own colour on which it moves. So P-QB3 means a pawn does the move shown. X means 'takes'.

Standard Notation
Chess pieces are named after the Queen's or the King's side of the board. Pawns are named according to the piece they stand in front of.

British Chess Federation, 9a Grand Parade, St Leonard's-on-Sea, East Sussex TN38 0DD Tel: 0424 442500 — players of all standards are welcome, though few have facilities for child players.

Dice

Liar Dice *(4 or more players, gambling)*
This is one of several versions using 5 poker dice. Throw one dice each - highest starts. You also need to agree what stake will be lost for each call or challenge which proves false. *Throughout the game the dice throws are*

concealed from everyone except the person throwing.

The first player throws all 5 dice, then calls their value - e.g. 'a pair of fours, a pair of aces, and a two'. The call can be true or any part of it can be a lie and all 5 dice are called at each call. The concealed throw is slid to the next player, clockwise, who may rethrow all or part of the throw keeping them all concealed. Whatever is thrown, the call *must* be higher than the previous call, and so on round the table. Each player may say the person before was lying, upon which the throw is revealed. If it was a lie the liar loses a chip to the challenger; if it was correct the reverse happens. Play starts again with all 5 being rethrown. The possible calls, in ascending order, are as follows:

- one pair
- two pairs
- three of a kind
- low straight - i.e. 1-2-3-4-5
- high straight - i.e. 2-3-4-5-6
- full house - i.e. three of a kind, and a pair
- four of a kind
- five of a kind

In all pairs and runs 6s would win over 5s, and so on. Aces are high. If you don't want to play for money let each person have three chips and, having lost all their chips, they are out. If you are playing for money, chips have an agreed value.

Poker Dice *(5 players or less,)*
Roll to decide who starts, as in liar dice. Each person has 2 throws per turn. On the second you can rethrow all 5 dice, or just some of them, or leave the first throw unchanged, and not throw a second time. A note is made of the throw thus achieved. The highest throw wins, using the rank order given in Liar Dice. Two equal throws are settled by a play-off.

More information
Skip Ferry, *Complete Book of Dice Games*, Hart (New York)

Dominoes *(2 or more players)*
One type of domino set takes the numbers up to six, the other up to nine. The sixes version has 28 pieces, and the nines 55. The rules vary widely, so agree them before play starts. Here is one version.

Place the pieces face down and shuffle them. Take 5 pieces each (7 with few people and/or a large set). Stand them on edge, so the other players can't read them. Whoever has the highest double puts it down, then takes another piece. Each player plays one piece in turn and picks up a replacement. The pieces are played by placing a 4 dot against another 4 dot, and a 2 dot against a 2 dot - and so on anywhere on the table. All the pieces are placed end on except the doubles. Doubles go at right angles to the main line and can be added to at both ends and both sides. When someone cannot match any piece on the board either the turn is missed or the player must take a piece without playing - which makes the game more interesting.

Whoever gets rid of her pieces first wins. If pieces are left, but nobody can play, the winner is whoever has the lowest total of dots. In a series of games the winner of each game subtracts her dot total from the total for all the other players. This gives her score for the game. The first to total 100 is the overall winner.

Draughts (Chequers) (2 players)

Draughts is played on a chequerboard, with 8 squares each way, and each player has 12 men. You can either win by capturing all your opponent's pieces or by surrounding them so they cannot move.

Place the board with the white square at the bottom right-hand corner. Decide who will play which colour as in chess (see page 319). The men are placed on the 12 dark squares nearest each player. Dark always starts play. The players make one move each, alternately.

1 A basic move is one square diagonally forwards.

2 To capture an opponent's piece it must be diagonally next to yours, with a space on the far side. You then jump it, taking the jumped man as you do so. You can use one move to take as many as are available in one journey, zigzagging if necessary.

3 A man that reaches the farthest row on the opponent's side becomes a King (a spare man being placed on top). It can then move diagonally forwards or backwards at will.

Play with any piece ends when a player removes his hand and a piece may not be touched if it is not going to be played.

If a man could have been taken, but wasn't, an opponent should say so and the player replace the man he has moved and make the move that would take the other man. This stops a player avoiding taking an opponent if it will put his man in a vulnerable position. In tournaments this now replaces the 'huff' rule.

Nine Men's Morris (2 players)

A seemingly simple, but very intriguing, game which dates back to the Bronze Age. It can marked out on earth or sand and played with stones.

Each player has 9 pegs. Each alternately puts one peg anywhere on the board until all 18 pegs are in place. After that, at each turn, a player can move one peg to the next hole along the lines on the board.

The aim is to get 3 pegs in a row along one of the lines on the board. This entitles a player to remove 1 of his opponent's men from anywhere on the board, except where it is part of a line of 3 - unless no other men are available. Once a player has only 3 men he may move to *any* empty hole on the board. The winner is whoever reduces an opponent to only 2 men, or makes him unable to move.

It is not usually permitted to break and re-form a line of 3 on successive moves, but some people allow this.

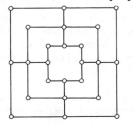

Roulette (any number of players)

Roulette is an eighteenth-century game, which had its heyday in the casinos of a hundred years ago. Players bet on a certain number or chance on the table. The croupier calls out 'Rien ne va plus', - no more play - to end the betting and the wheel is spun so a ball tumbles between red and black numbered pockets. When it stops the ball settles in a pocket - and those who bet on that number win. The rest lose their money.

The numbers are dotted about and the European has 37 pockets, but the American 38 including a 00.

The board, on which bets are placed, has no effect on play and is simply designed to make it easy for the croupier to see who is betting what. The players put their chips (counters indicating their bet) on their chosen number(s) or colour. There are two designs - European and American. The options are almost the same, but the European version uses French terms. To place one's chips on each is to bet as follows:

How Bets can be Placed	Potential Win
Rouge (a red diamond) - red will win	even money
Noir (a black diamond) - black will win	even money
Pair - an even number will win	even money
Impair - an odd number will win	even money
Manque - a number 1-18 will win	even money
Passe - a number 19-36 will win	even money
En plein - stake on a single number	35-1
À cheval - stake on line between 2 numbers	17-1
Transversale pleine - on 3 numbers in a horizontal row	11-1
En carré - on 4 numbers in a square block	8-1
Transversale simple or sixaine - 6 numbers in 2 horizontal rows	5-1
Colonne - on a vertical column of 12 numbers	2-1
Colonne à cheval - on two adjacent columns	2-1 on, or 1-2
Douzaine - on 12 numbers, either 1-12, 13-24 or 25-36. Stake on first dozen, second dozen or third dozen	2-1
Douzaine à cheval - on two adjacent dozens	2-1 on, or 1-2

Solitaire (1 player)

Solitaire is said to have been created by a French nobleman, during his imprisonment, and makes a particularly good pastime for someone confined to bed, as it doesn't require the flat surface needed for patience.

With any game of solitaire you are trying to get all the men off the board except one, leaving that piece in a position which you decided at the start - such as the centre. There are various types of board, but the traditional one is octagonal with 37 holes in it. A move is always to jump another man and remove the jumped man from the board, and the standard lay-out is to fill all the holes except that in the centre.

Anyone who is bored with the basic form can try playing so as to leave a chosen pattern.

Spillikins (Pick-a-sticks, Jackstraws) (2-5 players)

You need a set of spillikins. These are fine straight sticks marked in different colours, with pointed ends. Draw lots for the order of play. The last player then holds the spillikins in a bundle with the points just touching the floor and lets them fall in all directions. The first player removes as many spillikins as he can, but the moment another player spots movement in a stick which an opponent is not trying to remove she calls out and the player's turn ends. This continues until all the sticks have been removed. The person with the most can be the winner or you can allot different scores to type colours before play starts.

A player may not attempt to move one spillikin, fail and try another, but may use a spillikin she has already drawn to help move another; in some versions she may only do this if the spillikin is a certain colour.

More information
R.C. Bell, *Discovering Old Board Games*, Shire
Official World Encyclopaedia of Sports and Games; Paddington Press.
Waddington's Illustrated Encyclopaedia of Board Games, Pan.

CARDS

Card Games
This is not the place for a treatise on card games for card addicts, such as bridge or canasta. They deserve books to themselves. It is just a selection of some of those games which are amusing enough to pass a wet afternoon, and can be learnt fast enough for beginners to enjoy them.

For most card games there are no definitive rules, so these versions may not be your versions. They are fun for all that.
- A pack needs 52 cards covering 1-10, jack (knave), queen, king, ace, in each of four suits - hearts, clubs, diamonds and spades. The joker, if there is one, is removed unless otherwise stated.
- Any pack which is used must be well shuffled.
- Play always starts with the player on the dealer's left, unless otherwise stated.
- Numbered cards normally score their face value, and court cards score 10. Aces can be 1 or 10 according to the game - 'aces high' means they score 10.
- To 'cut' you each take a group of cards from the stack; the one showing at the bottom is your card. Highest wins.

Black Lady (3-7 players, easy)
This is a simple version of Black Maria. The aim to get the *lowest* score in a series of games. Queen of spades = 30. Hearts score: ace = 11; jack, queen, king = 10. Other hearts have face value. No other cards score.

Cut to deal - highest deals (aces high). Deal the whole pack - if the number of players won't divide into 52 exactly remove some 2s before dealing.

Players look at their hands, choose 3 unwanted cards and pass all these at the same time, to the player on their left (queen of spades may not be passed). Then play starts.

The first player places any card face up in the centre. Each player in turn places on it one card of the same suit (the number sequence doesn't matter). Someone with no cards of that suit follows with a card of any suit.

At the end of the round, whoever placed the highest number of the opening suit takes that trick and places it on the table in front of them. They then place the first card for the next round - choosing any card they wish.

When all the cards have been played the score is totalled. All hearts in someone's hand or in their tricks are counted against them, as is the queen of spades. However, having *all* the hearts *and* the queen of spades is a grand slam: it scores zero - and 125 penalty points are given to each of the other players.

Cheat (3 players upwards - very easy)
The aim is to get rid of all your cards first. Ace is both high and low, so it can be followed by a king or a 2.

Deal the whole pack — add packs so everyone has 8 or more cards. The first player puts down 1, 2, 3 or 4 cards face down in the centre, calling what has been played (e.g. 'three 9s'). This call may be true, but it can be as false as the player wishes.

Each player in turn then plays 1, 2, 3 or 4 cards on top of the first ones, calling truthfully or untruthfully, but the call must always be the next number above or below the previous call (i.e. three 9s could be followed by 8s or 10s).

After a call anyone can say 'Cheat' and turn over the cards just called. Cheaters, who are found out, must take all the cards in the centre, but if the call was correct the challenger picks them up instead. This continues until someone has no cards left - and so wins.

Pelmanism (2-6 players - a memory game)
Cut to start - highest starts. Place a shuffled pack, face down, in rows, to form a rectangle. Each player in turn then turns up 2 cards, so everyone can see them. If they match (e.g. two black 6s, two red kings etc) the player takes them. If they do not they are turned face down again. This continues until all the cards have been removed, and whoever has the most pairs wins. In another version making a pair gives another turn.

Poker (3/5-7, ideally 5 to 7 players - easy to play, hard to play well)
There are numerous versions of poker. Anyone playing a serious game or for high stakes should read up on it in a book by a card expert: it is easy to lose a lot of money - especially if your companions play an unfamiliar version.

A chip value is agreed before the game starts and so is a maximum stake. The player on the dealer's left puts a chip on the table in front of her. This is the ante. (Hence the term 'to up the ante'.) The second player puts up chips - called a straddle. These, plus all the later stakes, form the 'pool'.

The dealer gives each player 5 cards, face down. Aces are high. Players decide whether their cards are good enough to play with - if not they can drop out. The third player 'speaks' first. She can drop out or put up a stake of twice the straddle (i.e. 4 chips). The other players in turn can throw in their hand, or stay in by putting up chips which either equal the stake of the previous player or double it. Those who put up the ante and straddle can throw in their hand (losing what they put up) or raise their stakes to the appropriate total. Stake raising round the table continues until nobody wishes to go further.

Those in the game can keep the 5 cards they have, or try to improve their hand by giving 1, 2, 3, 4 or 5 cards back to the dealer, who places them at the bottom of the pack before dealing replacements. (Changing 4 or 5 cards is slightly mad, but it is not against the rules.)

The betting then starts with the third player. In turn each player may throw in their cards (and lose their stake), say 'check' and remain in without increasing their stake, or raise their stake by any amount within the limit. When everyone is at 'check' all the players show their hands and the best hand takes all the stakes.

An alternative ending is that checks are not allowed. When two players remain either may raise her stake to equal that of another player and say 'see you'. Her opponent must then raise her stake, to avoid being seen, or show the hand. The higher hand wins.

The strength of the hands, in descending order, plus the odds against most being dealt in the initial hand, is as follows:

Royal straight flush - ace, king, queen, jack, 10 of one suit
Straight flush - king, queen, jack, 10, 9, or any lower run of 5 in a suit (of two straight flushes the higher run wins) (64,973:1)
Fours - 4 cards the same - e.g. 4 fives (higher cards win) (4,164:1)
Full house - 3 cards the same, and 2 cards the same - eg 3 nines and 2 fives (of two full houses that with the higher 3 wins) (693:1)
Flush - 5 cards of the same suit - e.g. jack, 9,7,6,3 (of two flushes that with the highest card wins, if these are the same the second card decides it) (508:1)
Straight - 5 cards in number sequence, of varied suits - the highest first card wins, two equal cards split the pool (254:1)
Threes - 3 cards the same, plus 2 odd ones (46:1)
Two pairs - e.g. 2 kings, 2 sevens, plus an odd card - highest pair wins (20:1)
One pair - e.g. 2 jacks, plus 3 odd cards (15:11)
Highest card - 5 assorted cards - the highest card wins

Pontoon (Vingt-et-un) (3-7 players)

The aim is a hand which makes 21, or just under. Ace = 1 or 10; court cards = 10; others at face value.
1 Whoever cuts the pack at the highest card becomes banker. He then deals one card to each person, himself included. Everyone puts up a stake (according to how good their hand looks). If the banker holds a good card (e.g. ace, court card, 10, 2) he may want to tell everyone to double their stakes.
2 A second round is dealt, face down. Anyone who now holds a 'natural' - cards adding to 21 (i.e. ace plus court card or 10) - must reveal it. The banker then pays 3 times their stake and they will take the bank at the next game.

3 The banker offers another card — each player may:
● 'buy' a card (for not more than his original stake),
● 'twist' - have a card dealt face up,
● 'stand' and take no card, provided his cards total 15 or more.
4 This proceeds until up to 5 cards each, but having twisted a player may buy no more cards. A player may not buy a fifth card if his hand totals 11 or under. If, at any point, someone's hand adds up to more than 21 they must say they are 'busted' and lose their stake.
5 The banker turns his cards face up and adds 1, 2 or 3 cards to it, in turn. At any point the banker can stop and say he will pay anyone with a higher hand - e.g. with a 6, 4 and 9 the call would be 'pay 20 and 21'. The players then reveal their hands. The pay-out is as follows:
● hands equal to the bank or lower lose their stake
● hands higher than the bank and under 21 are paid their stake
● hands of 21 are paid double their stake
● five cards totally under 21 get double their stake
● a hand of three 7s gets triple its stake.

If the bank is 'busted' it pays out a stake to everyone still in. If the banker has 21 or 5 and under, he gets single stakes from anyone with the same and double stakes from everyone else.

★ If someone has a pair they may say 'split' and make two hands by placing a bet on the second hand equal to their first stake, and the banker deals a second card to each hand. The player then plays the two hands separately.
★ If there are several naturals the one to the dealer's left has priority. If the banker has a natural he shows it and each player pays him twice their original stake - except a player with a natural who only pays the original stake. The game ends there.

Racing Demon (2 to 4 players, fast and competitive)

Use old packs, one pack per person - they will swiftly get dog-eared. For scoring each must look different.

Each person deals 13 cards face up to their left, and places 4 cards face up in a row beside them. On the word 'Go' everyone starts to play, as if playing patience. The following moves are allowed.
● Turn over the cards in your hand in threes.
● Put aces in the centre.
● Build on anyone's aces in ascending order, (2,3,4 etc.) in suit, using cards from the pile of 13, from the row of 4 or from the remaining cards as you turn them over.
● build on your own row of 4 in descending order, alternating red and black, using cards from the 13, from other rows or from those you are turning over.

The first person to get rid of all the 13 cards in that pile wins and calls 'out' - and all play stops. Each person's score is the number of cards he or she has in the middle, minus the number left from their stack of 13.

Rummy (2 to 6 players, very easy)

Rummy has at least five variations. This is a basic version. Ace is 1, court cards 10. Others at face value.

Deal 10 cards for 2 players, 7 cards for 3-4, 6 cards for 5-6. The remaining cards are placed face down, with the top card face up beside them. Each player in turn picks up a card - from the face-up or face-down stack - and then discards one face-up.

The aim is to make sets of 3 or 4 cards (i.e. 10s or 3s or kings) or to make runs of 3 or more (i.e. 2,3,4,5,) or Q,J,10,9,8 in the same suit. Both sets and runs are allowed in the same hand.

The first person to get all his cards into sets or runs says 'rummy' and shows the hand. (A card cannot appear in a set *and* a run.) The game then stops and any cards in the other players' hands which are not in a set are counted against them. The person with the lowest score, after an agreed number of games, wins.

The Shop Game (4 up - the more the merrier, 1 to 2 packs)

Despite its title, this is not just for the very young - I learnt it from someone who played it, between practices, as a rowing Blue. Each person is dealt an equal number of cards (odd ones left over are set aside) and they are left face down in front of each player. Starting at the left of the dealer, each person in turn announces what shop they are (any shop they wish). They only say it once and nobody may name anyone's shop during the game.

Going round the table each player turns up one card from his hand. If there is already another card of that number/type on the table, of any suit, each owner must name a product sold in the other's shop. Whoever is slowest takes all the upturned cards in front of the other player and puts them at the bottom of his own hand. Once a product has been called it cannot be used again by any player. The first to get rid of all cards wins.

Whist - Knock Out (2 to 6 players, very easy)

The dealer cuts, and the card revealed is trumps. He then deals 7 cards to each player. The first player places a card in the centre. The next player follows with any card in the same suit, or trumps it with a card from the trump suit. (If they can do neither they discard a card on to the heap.) At the end of the round whoever placed the highest trump wins and takes that trick. If there are no trumps the highest card in the initial suit takes the trick. This continues until all hands are used up. Whoever has the most tricks wins that game; those with none are out.

Each successive game is played in the same way, but with one less card per person per game. At each game the winner of the previous game can choose trumps *after* having seen her hand. Anyone who fails to get a trick in one game becomes 'doggy' in the next and is dealt only one card. But 'doggies' may pass in any round and play nothing. If they again fail to get a trick they become

'blind doggy' and are not allowed to look at their one card before playing it. If they again fail to get a trick they are out. If a doggy or blind doggy gets a trick they get the same number of cards as the other players on the next round.

More information

Hubert Phillips, *The Pan Book of Card Games*, Pan

Patience

Aces and Spaces (1 pack)

This sounds very simple, but it may surprise you.

Lay out 4 rows of 13 cards, face up, from left to right, to use the whole pack. Remove the aces and place one to the left of each of the four rows (position them to make it easier to get the patience out). You may now move any card into any space *provided* it is the same suit as the card to the left of the space, and one higher than that card. Try to get each of the 4 suits, started by the aces, in correct order reading from left to right.

Demon (1 pack)

Place 13 cards in a stack to the left, all face down except the top card. And lay 4 cards face up in a row.

Place 1 card, face up, above the 4. This card decides what cards will be built on to get the patience out. If a 10 is placed there each of the other 10s will be placed beside it, as they show up, and each of these will be built on in suit in ascending order (i.e. 10, jack, queen, king, ace, 2, 3-9). The 4 cards face up at the start are built on in descending order (red, black, red, black) with cards from the pack, or with ones from the top of the 13 to the left, or by moving cards from one row to another. Any card may go into an empty space in this row. Turn up the remaining cards in threes. When a run through these produces no result place the top card to the bottom (this may be done only twice before being out) and run through again.

Klondike (1 pack)

This is one my daughter taught me. How hard it is depends on the number of cards you choose to turn over in the pack. One variation is that you go through once in threes, once in twos, once one at a time. Another to go through them only once — in ones.

Place 1 card face up to the left; put 6 cards face down in a row to its right. (Call them rows 1-7.) Place a card face up on row 2, and one face down on 3, 4, 5, 6, 7. Place a card face up on row 3, and one face down on 4, 5, 6, 7. And so on until each row ends with one card face up.

Rules of Play

- You may move face-up cards from one row to another placing them on top of one another, in descending order (7, 6, 5, etc.), alternating red and black. But if a space opens you may only fill it with a king.
- Any ace which comes up immediately goes to a row above the seven. And aces are built on in ascending

order (ace, 2, 3, 4) in suit.

- The cards remaining in the pack are turned over in threes, and the top card can be placed, as appropriate, on any row or ace pile. Once the top card of the three has been played the one beneath it may be played too - and so on.
- The patience is out when all the cards are stacked on the aces of their suit in correct order.

PARTY GAMES FOR ALL AGES

Games tend to evolve, gathering regional and family embellishments and alterations. So I don't pretend my versions are the 'right' ones (if such exist), and I apologize to anyone who is frustrated by failing to find their favourite game here. Use these versions as a starting point for your own additions. They range from the simplest games for toddlers, to those designed for teenage and adult parties with dancing. But there aren't really any neat divisions between children's games and adult ones. Barring the self-consciousness of adolescence, most games can be enjoyed by almost anyone, if the mood is right. I know of some middle-aged intellectuals who scored a hit by giving a birthday party for adults, complete with party tea, children's games and going-away presents. So, I've given the lowest possible age for each game, but only set an upper limit when physical or emotional developments dictate a ceiling (Granny had better not play musical bumps). I have marked each game 'out', 'in', or even 'out/in' according to their potential.

Some 'outdoor games' can be played in a large (damage-proof) room; some 'indoor' ones, such as musical bumps, are rather better on grass. It is purely a matter of practicality. Games marked 'travel' can also be played in transit if those near you can stand it, though some games may need advance preparation like carrying paper and pencils.

The minimum number of players is given: + after means more can play ; + + means it would be *better* with more. How many more will vary with the size of the room, the age (and unruliness) of the players. Most find 12 children at a time enough, unless they are very, very good.

Organizing Games at Children's Parties

Organizing games takes all one's attention, so have a helper to handle distractions - children bent on destruction, mothers who come early or leave late, or tinies with over-excited bladders. There is no faster recipe for chaos than leaving a group of children in mid-game while you escort one desperate infant to the loo.

The other factor to bear in mind is the order of the games. Children arrive noisy and energetic or shy and withdrawn. Either way, start with games that release both energy and inhibitions - preferably one which late-comers can join. They need to work off enough restlessness to sit still and eat. Those after tea should be calmer - some children throw up when over-excited. For your sanity, punctuate the proceedings with games which enforce silence - I recommend Beans and Straws and Kim's Game.

Treat it like a military operation. Everything you need for each game must be *totally* ready in advance, and to hand. And prepare the territory as if for an invasion - remove everything which might get damaged, lock every door they shouldn't enter and keep the keys.

The rules for some good games are given below but don't forget Chinese Whispers, I Spy, Pass the Parcel, Musical Bumps and Chairs, Shipwrecks, Treasure Hunts, Wellie Throwing and Egg and Spoon Races — none of which need rules from me.

Prizes at Children's Parties

If a prize is given for any game it is essential to give one for *every* game, or there are hard feelings. Ideally there should also be some team games in which the winning team each get a prize. That way every child should win something. Unfortunately, some mothers use the size of the prizes to compete with other mothers. This is cruel to the less well-off, and brings out the worst in children. One answer is to establish a truce between mothers by agreeing a no-prize rule, or a severe limit to the value. Failing that, hide wrapped prizes in an improvised bran tub of shredded newspaper in a big box. Let each child pick its own prize which you immediately put in a bag labelled with its name for it to take home. That rules out any comparison of prizes while the party is in progress.

Alphabet Game (6 up, nos 3+, in/out/travel)

Decide on a topic - say food or pop singer's names. Then the first person says one beginning with A, the next person one beginning with B, and so on, in turn (e.g. apple, banana, custard, etc.). If you can't think of one you are out.

Apple Bobbing (5 up, nos 2+, in/out)

Tie long strings firmly to the stalks of as many apples as there are players. Hang them, at mouth level, from a swing frame, doorway, or French window lintel. Each player stands in front of an apple and on the word 'Go' starts to eat their elusive apple - without touching it with their hands. The first to finish and hold it in the teeth wins. Or have clean buckets of water with apples in. (Leave the stalks in if you want to make it easier, remove them if you don't.) Part of the fun is watching, so have two 'sittings'.

Baby Face (15 up, nos 8 + +, in)

Each guest gives you a photograph of themselves as a baby (name the backs instantly). Display each with a number, and keep a list of which is who. Everyone has to list the babies by name; whoever gets most right wins. In groups which don't know each other play Star Face, naming photos of well-known people.

Balloon Dancing (10 up, nos 10+ +, in)

Disco dancing goes on while a balloon is patted from

person to person without touching the ground. If the balloon hits the ground the person who lets it fall is out, or pays a forfeit.

In another version a balloon must be held between each couple while they dance. They are not allowed to touch each other (or the balloon) and must keep time to the music. Start with an easy tempo and make it progressively harder. Those who drop it are out, but it is hilarious to watch.

Beans and Straws *(3 up, nos 2+, in)*
Give each player a drinking straw and an empty jam jar, and scatter small dried haricot beans, or split peas, on the floor. On 'Go' they collect beans by sucking them, one at a time, on to the end of the straw and dropping them into their jar. Touching them is not allowed. Whoever gets the most within a set time, wins.

Boom *(4 up, nos 4+ in/out/travel)*
Count round the group *fast*, the first person saying 1, the second 2, and so on up & up. But whenever a number has a 4 in it (e.g. 4, 14, 24,) the person says 'boom' instead. Anyone who says the wrong number or fails to say 'boom' at the right time is out. You can replace any number with 'boom'. Try 1 as 'boom' for giggles with older children.

Botticelli *(14 up, nos 6+, in/out/travel)*
A game for players of equal knowledge or some will feel put down.

One player 'becomes' a well-known person, and tells the rest his or her initials. Everyone else in turn asks a question designed to reveal who the person is being. If the initials were J.C. this might be 'Are you a famous actress?' The person being questioned isn't allowed to say 'no'. They have to think of an actress with those initials and their reply must be 'No, I am not Joan Collins' (or whoever). If they can't manage this the questioner gets a second turn in which he may ask a general question such as, 'Are you male or female? - yes or no answers to these are allowed. If the questioner thinks he knows who the person is he can ask directly, e.g. 'Are you Julius Caesar?' If right he now takes the celebrity seat, if wrong he misses a turn. An easier version is to use only one initial not two.

Charades *(10 up, nos 8+, in)*
Two groups are formed. Each goes away and prepares to act out - with or without costumes - a long word or proverb, or the title of a book, film or play, for the other group to guess. First, the actors say whether they are doing a word, proverb or title - and whether of a book, film or play. The title is then acted out syllable by syllable, or word by word. Each scene *depicts* one syllable or word, and that syllable or word is also mentioned at least once. (If 'seasons' was in the title either the whole word could be acted or there could be one scene about the sea and another about sons.) Then, in the final scene the whole word, phrase or title is acted out and said at least once. The group which is guessing may try to guess the word or phrase at the end of each

scene - and the charade ends if they guess the whole title. But no clues are given. At the end the group may confer before guessing the complete word or phrase - and in some families only a set number of guesses are allowed. Then this group acts their charade.

The Chocolate Game *(4 up, nos 4+, in/out)*
Everyone sits on the floor in a circle. A plate is put in the centre with a large bar of chocolate, plus knife and fork. Also in the centre are a wellington boot, funny hat, pair of gloves (oversized for the players) and false nose. The players throw a dice in turn. Whoever throws a 6 must don the costume and eat as much chocolate as possible, *with the knife and fork*, while the others throw the dice. When a 6 is thrown that person stops eating and the thrower takes his place. This continues until the chocolate is eaten. (Have some spare chocolate for those who never got a turn in the middle.)

Consequences *(6 up, nos 2++, in/out/travel)*
Each person has a pen and a very long, narrow piece of paper. A series of 'facts' will be written down and, after each, the papers folded, to conceal the writing, and passed on. Then at the end you all take it in turns to read out the paper you have. The order of what is written is this:
1 a man's name - famous or invented
2 a woman's name - famous or invented
3 the place where they met
4 what he said to her
5 what she said to him
6 what he gave her
7 what she gave him
8 what the consequences were
9 what the world said.

Dictionary Games *(7 up, nos 6+, or 2, in/out/travel)*
One team looks up a difficult word in the dictionary and each of them gives a definition for it - only one of which is correct. The other team confers and guesses which is correct.

This can also be done in reverse, with one team picking a difficult word and the other team having to give the correct definition. Or one person reads out a definition and the others each write down the word they think it refers to. On holiday it can be played with two languages - providing painless learning.

Donkey *(3 up, nos 4+, in/out)*
A large picture of a donkey (with no tail, but a dot where it ought to start) is displayed on a surface which will take drawing pins. Each player in turn is blindfolded and given a large fabric tail with a drawing pin through the upper end. She then tries to pin the tail on the right spot. The pin hole is marked with her initials and whoever gets closest to the tail dot wins.

Feeding Time *(6 up, nos 4+, in/out)*
Pairs sit opposite each other cross-legged (on a washable floor or outside). One is given a *large* bib and has his hands tied behind his back. The other is blindfolded and

has a spoon and some messy or hard-to-manage food (e.g. jelly) which, on 'Go', they must feed to their partner. The first couple to finish wins. The best part of this is watching, so do two 'sittings'. This is an end-of-party game. The mess is so memorable that my adult children still fondly recall the party for which I invented it.

Fish Blowing *(3 up, nos 4+, or team, in)*

You need a shiny floor and identical fish outlines cut from newspaper. The players stand behind a chalked line with a fish in front of them, and there's another line chalked some way down the room. On 'Go' they blow their fish down the room. The first fish to cross the line wins.

For the team game half of each team stands behind each line. The first person in each team blows the fish until it crosses the opposite line, the next blows it back and so on, until the last player crosses the line.

The Game *(Dumb Crambo)* *(10 up, nos 10+, in/out)*

Two teams each make a list of song/book/film/play titles which they would like those in the other team to act. Each person in turn is given his title by the opposing team and then has to mime it for the rest of the team to guess. The whole title can be acted or the words or syllables acted in any order.

The actor is allowed to make the following signs to help his team understand. The team then call out what they think each sign means and the actor may nod or shake his head or repeat the sign if they are wrong.

- Put hands together, as if praying, and open like a book = book title.
- A dramatic gesture while opening mouth = song.
- Use two hands to outline the shape of a theatre curtain = play title.
- Hold one hand up to the eye, like a lens, and wind with the other = film title.
- Hold up spread fingers to show how many words there are in the title.
- Hold up fingers to show which word in the title they are about to act (e.g. 3 fingers is third word).
- Hold up fingers (as above), then place them on the forearm to show how many syllables the word has. Then place them on the forearm again to show which syllable of the word is to be acted (e.g. 2 fingers in the air, then 2 on the forearm, then 1 in the air and on the forearm says 'I'm going to act a 2 syllable word starting with the first syllable').
- Describing a circle with both hands means you will act the whole phrase. You may also act a word which sounds like one in the title, in which case you first tug your ear.

The team call out the word or syllable they think is being acted (or even the whole title) as soon as they have a clue and the actor can nod, shake or even make beckoning signs if they are getting close.

Some families set a time limit, and time each performance - the fastest team winning - but most just play it for the fun.

Grandmother's Footsteps *(4 up, nos 5 +, in/out)*

The players gather at one end of a room with just enough space to move, all facing a 'Grandma' a little bit in front of them. 'Grandma' moves down the room, doing curious movements, which the others have to copy while trying to creep up on her. 'Grandma' can turn round at any time and anyone seen moving is out. The first person to touch 'Grandma' is the winner. With young children, just creeping up is enough, and Grandma can stand in one place.

Hangman *(7 up, nos 4+, in/out/travel)*

Each in turn says a letter of the alphabet, chosen so that it could make a word. Someone who says a letter which completes a word is out - even if a longer word would have been possible e.g. p,a,r,T (Y). The rest then start on a new word. At their turn anyone may challenge the previous player if they suspect him of saying letters which wouldn't make a word. If he can't name a real word he is out.

Islands *(4 up, nos 10+, in/out)*

Small, well-spaced islands are marked on the floor with chalk, or created with objects. While the music plays everyone dances or bounces about. When it stops they must get on an island. Anyone at 'sea' is out. At each turn an island is rubbed out, or made smaller. The last person in wins. If you like you can operate an 'only one person per island' rule. (Beware of islands which might slip on a polished floor.)

Jigsaw Treasure Hunt *(4 up, nos 1+, in/out)*

A picture is cut up (preferably after being pasted on thin cardboard) and the pieces hidden all round a room, or a garden. The players then have to look for the pieces and form them into a picture. A time limit can be set if you wish, or it can be played in teams and a different 'jigsaw' hidden for each team - each being numbered, or given a colour on the back, to avoid confusion.

Kim's Game *(Memory Game, 5 up, 2+, in)*

Between 10 and 25 small objects are placed on a tray - according to the ability of the players. The players each have a pencil and paper, and form a circle. The tray is put in the centre, and they have a minute (in silence) to look at it. Then it is removed while each person lists everything they can remember. The best list wins.

Knees Tease *(mixed ages, nos 10++, in)*

The teenage or adult males go out of sight and bare their legs, then parade across a stage or doorway which has been curtained so only their lower legs and knees can be seen. The rest guess which legs belong to whom - either jointly or on paper.

Knees Up *(10/12 up, nos 18++, in)*

Everyone dances, and when the music stops the girl has to sit on her partner's knees with her feet off the floor. Those with the girl's feet on the ground, or who fall over, are out. The last pair in is the winner.

Matchboxes (4 up, nos 8++, team, in/out)
Each team leader is given the outer section of a matchbox. On 'Go' the team leader places the matchbox on her nose and, using the nose only, passes it to the next nose in the team and so on. The first team to get it to the back of their line wins. A dropped matchbox is picked up and replaced on the nose of the person passing it.

Variations: An orange is held between the chin and the collar bone, and passed - the Orange Game. A round balloon is passed with the knees - the Balloon Game.

Matchbox Treasure Hunt (4 up, nos 3+, out)
Each player has a matchbox and has 2 minutes to put into it as many different types of things as they can find. The one with the greatest number wins.

Matching Pairs (5 up, nos 10++, in/out)
This is a good ice-breaker at parties where people don't know each other. Make a list of pairs, chosen to suit the ability of the players (e.g. cup/saucer, bread/butter for young children; Rod/Stewart, David/Bowie for teens; Bonnie/Clyde, Laurel/Hardy for adults). Write cup (say) on one piece of paper, saucer on another, and so on. As each guest arrives you pin one of these on their back, without them seeing it, and tell them they have on their back half the name of a household object (or a film duo, pop star or whatever) and they must pair up with whoever has the other half. Anyone can ask any question they like but the only permitted answers are 'yes' or 'no'.

If you want this to lead to dancing, write the first half of each pair in black and the second in red. Then give blacks to males and reds to females. If you want it to lead to team games you can plot balanced teams by listing in advance who ends up red and who black. The pairs then split for the team games.

Murder (8 up, nos 6+, in)
Take as many cards from the pack as there are players, making sure they include a jack and an ace. Each person draws one. Whoever gets the ace is the detective and the jack is the murderer. The detective goes away into a lighted room, with the door shut, while the lights are put out in the rest of the house (or just one room) and all the other players move about in the dark. The murderer chooses a victim and taps him three times on the shoulder. The victim must then count to 10, scream and fall to the ground, dead. When the victim screams the players must stop exactly where they are. And on hearing the scream the detective puts the lights on and goes round noting people's whereabouts. Then they sit down in the same room while the detective cross-questions them. Everyone must tell the truth except the murderer. When ready the detective may accuse someone of being the murderer. If the detective is wrong the murderer goes free; if he or she is right the murderer must confess and pay a forfeit.

Two classic Victorian forfeits were 'Kneel to the wittiest, bow to the prettiest, and kiss the one you love

the best', or 'Laugh in one corner, cry in another, sing in another and dance in another.' But it can be anything to amuse the group and tease the person paying it.

Noisy Animals (4 up, nos 8++, in)
This game can be an end in itself or a way of setting up pairs for some other game. But you need a room in which nobody will knock anything over in the dark. List animals which make distinctive noises (e.g. pig, donkey), having half as many animals as there are players (if you run out just repeat some). Secretly allot each animal to two different players. Nobody must know what anyone else is. Switch off the lights and tell everyone they must make their animal's noise, and pair up with whoever else makes it. But they must go silent on finding their 'twin'. Switch on the lights when you can only hear two people. The last two noisy animals have to pay a forfeit when the lights go on.

Obstacle Race (3 up, nos 4+, out)
This one needs play, not party clothes, and shoes should be removed first if there is water (most children won't unless you tell them to). An obstacle course is constructed from anything you can lay hands on - planks balanced on bricks, plastic garden cloches to wriggle under, boxes and barrels to crawl through, a paddling pool to splash through, and so on. The players have to negotiate the course in the shortest possible time. The fastest wins. You can add complexity by making them get from one obstacle to another in different ways. One can be run, another hopped, another skipped and so on. Or you can add a ball to kick or hit from A to B. One of the best parties I ever went to was costume obstacle croquet.

The Paper Game (5 up, nos 4+, in/out)
There are two versions: one for younger children, another for disco and adult parties. Young children are each given a sheet of newspaper, and bounce around, to music, holding it. When the music stops they must fold it in half and stand on it. This keeps being repeated and those falling off are out. Adults have one sheet of newspaper per couple and they dance while the music is on, then fold it and stand on it. Either way, the last one(s) in win.

Question and Answers (12 up, nos 6++, in/travel)
Everyone has a pencil and two pieces of paper. Each person in turn asks one question, to which everyone - including the questioner - must secretly write an answer. When everyone has had a turn, each person puts their name at the top of their paper. Then all the papers are handed to the organizer, who numbers them and reads out each list of answers in turn. Everyone then guesses, and writes down, who they think each list of answers belongs to. The organizer then says who each list really belonged to and the person who identified the most lists wins. This can only be played by people who know each other, and the idea is to ask questions with revealing answers. So it can be dynamite in the wrong hands. If there are delicate relationships, temperamental

teenagers or dodgy marriages in the group, and/or people foolish enough to ask upsetting questions, it is best avoided.

Shopping (3 up, nos 2++, in/out/travel)
The first person says, 'Aunt Julia went shopping and she bought a pound of apples' (or anything else). The next person repeats exactly what the previous person said and adds one thing to the shopping list. And so on, in turn, with people dropping out whenever they make a mistake in the list. Quarrelsome children may need an arbitrator who notes the purchases in order.

Simon Says (3 up, nos 3+, in/out)
The players stand facing 'Simon'. 'Simon' calls out instructions which the players must *only* follow if the words 'Simon says' precede them. (e.g. Simon says, 'hands on head'. Simon says, 'left leg up'. 'Stand up'.) Anyone who stood up would have been out. Little children get muddled quite easily; older ones need the instructions to be very rapid. The last one in wins.

The Singing Game (7 up, nos 3++, in/out/travel)
You go through the alphabet, each person singing a song whose title or first line starts with that letter - or, at a pinch, any line starting with the right letter. So 'Roxanne' could be followed by 'She Loves Me' and so on, with those who can't think of a song dropping out.

Squeak Piggy Squeak (7 up, numbers 6+, in)
One person is chosen as piggy and stays alone, while the others go and dress up, disguising themselves with cushions, false beards, etc. Then they go into a room on all fours and the lights are put out. Enter piggy on all fours. Piggy tries to catch someone and guess who they are. He may feel them, and say 'Squeak Piggy Squeak' at which the caught person must squeak. If he can't guess them correctly, in one guess, they go free. If he is right they become piggy. Disguises are swopped, out of piggy's sight, before carrying on.

Team Drawing (4 up, nos 8++, in/out)
Make a list of things which must be drawn - suited to the ages of the players, for example a cup is easy but 'happiness' is hard. The two teams are in different corners of the room with pencils and lots of sheets of paper. Each sends a player to the organizer, to get the name of something to draw. The player then draws it as fast and as accurately as she can and the rest of the team have to guess what it is. Once they guess correctly the next member of the team comes up. The first team to guess their whole list wins.

Team Tie Ups (7 up, nos 12++, in/out)
Each team stands in a circle, and one person is given a long piece of string on the end of which is tied a spoon (at my daughter's college they used a kipper, but I don't recommend it). On 'Go' they thread the spoon *down* under their clothes, and pass it to the next person who threads it *up* under their clothes, and so on. The object is to get every member of the team linked and the two ends of string tied together in the least possible time. Some people play it by threading the spoon down, or up, the *next* person's clothes - but that is up to you.

Word Making (7 up, nos 2+, in/out/travel)
A very useful game because it needs no preparation and produces silence. Choose any really long word, with a wide range of letters in, and ask them each to write down as many words as they can make from the letters in the word. The one with the longest correct list wins (exclude proper names if you wish).

GENERAL CLUBS

The following clubs and organizations, for both children and adults, welcome members and/or fund raisers, but are not linked to any hobby. The head offices will usually put you in touch with your local branch. Clubs for specific hobbies are found in the following section, and many of the voluntary organizations and charities to be found throughout this book welcome helpers or fund raisers. Most of the faiths listed in the religion section also have clubs and societies.

Boys Brigade, Computer and Business Centre, P.O. Box 94, Glasgow G1 2RH Tel: 041 332 3430 — M£Var, Rg, G, ages 6-18, A

Girls Brigade, 168 Bath Street, Glasgow G2 9TQ Tel: 041 332 0936

City Women's Network, Ferrari House, 258 Field End Road, Eastcote, Middx HA4 9NB Tel: 01 868 6653 — M£H, A, forum for senior professional women within the Greater London area only.

Gingerbread, 35 Wellington Street, London WC2E 7BN Tel: 01 240 0953 — for solo parents of both sexes. G, M, L, A - children welcome, mutual help, Ad and Inf on problems such as housing, benefits, law etc, pressure group, sae.

Girl Guides Association, 17-19 Buckingham Palace Road, London SW1W 0PT Tel: 01 834 6242 — runs Brownies (age 7-10), Guides (10-14) and Rangers (14-18). Lone guide postal scheme for those who can't reach a group. A, emphasis on self-reliance.

Meet-a-mum Association, 3 Woodside Avenue, South Norwood, London SE25 5DW — support and company by mother for mother - including those with post-natal depression, one-to-one contacts and G, sae.

Mensa, Freepost, Wolverhampton WV2 4BR Tel: 0902 772771 a club for the bright. M, A, Disc.

The Mother's Union, The Mary Sumner House, 24 Tufton Street, London SW1P 3RB Tel: 01 222 5533/4/5 — worldwide organization of clubs for Christian women (a few men now join). Emphasis on traditional Christian values, and on service. A, toddler groups, pram service, discussions, supportive holidays for parents under stress. Also runaway children can phone them and they will pass on the child's message to home.

National Association of Boys' Clubs, 369 Kennington Lane, London SE11 5QY Tel: 01 793 7987 — for boys and young men (mainly 11-19). Clubs for almost every activity - sport, drama, etc. - and special projects relating to unemployment, drugs and other youth problems.

National Association of Women's Clubs, 5 Vernon Rise, King's Cross Road, London WC1 9EP Tel: 01 837 1434/5/6 — an educational charity coordinating 620 affiliated women's clubs covering a wide range of activities.

National Federation of Gateway Clubs, 117 Golden Lane, London EC1Y 0RT Tel: 01 253 9433 — varied leisure activities for the mentally handicapped, helpers welcomed.

National Federation of Women's Institutes, 39 Eccleston Street, London SW1W 9NT Tel: 01 730 7212 — not the fuddy-duddy organization it sounds. It covers both town and country and provides every conceivable activity from jam and gym to political lobbying. Own adult education college. M£L, M, A, L, B, HC, HD, sae.

National Federation of Solo Clubs, Room 8, Ruskin Chambers, 191 Corporation Street, Birmingham Tel: 021 236 2879 — clubs for the single, widowed, divorced or separated of both sexes aged 25-65. Aims: to relieve loneliness by social activities and group holidays at home and abroad, sae.

The National Women's Register, 245 Warwick Road, Solihull, West Midlands B92 7AH Tel: 021 706 1101 — international, autonomous linked groups of 'lively minded women' meet to discuss topics other than house and home. M, L, RC, M£L.

National Playing Fields Association, 25 Ovington Square, London SW3 1LQ Tel: 01 584 6445 — campaigns for the preservation and increase of open spaces and play facilities. RC.

The National Union of Townswomen's Guilds, Chamber of Commerce House, 75 Harborne Road, Edgbaston, Birmingham B15 3DA Tel: 021 455 6868 — open to all women. It aims to improve life for women and broaden their education. Monthly meetings. Activities range from arts, crafts and sports to political debates and lobbying on international issues. RC, M£L, M, A, HD, T, HC, G.

Network, 25 Park Road, London NW1 6XN Tel: 01 402 1285 — for women in business and the professions. M£H, Rg, M, A, seminars.

Polite Society, 18 The Avenue, Basford, Newcastle-under-Lyme, Staffs ST5 0LY Tel: 0782 614407 — campaigns for more courtesy and consideration everywhere. M£L, M.

Rotary International, Kinwarton Road, Alcester, Warwicks B49 6BP Tel: 0789 765 411 — aims to link men (not women) in service and fellowship - but membership by invitation. M, G, RS.

The Scout Association, Baden-Powell House, 65 Queens Gate, London SW7 5JS Tel: 01 584 7030 — for boys aged 6-15½, both sexes 15½ onwards, no upper age limit A, Ins, HD, HC, B (addresses of local troups at libraries).

United Kingdom Federation of Business and Professional Women, 23 Ansdell Street, London W8 5BA Tel: 01 938 1729 — aims to help working women use their full potential in society. M£Var, M, Rg, G, Inf.

Women's Royal Voluntary Service, 234 Stockwell Road, London SW9 9SP Tel: 01 733 3388 — for both men and women who would like to use their free time to help others. Members do community work such as Meals on Wheels and toy libraries.

Youth Clubs UK, Keswick House, 30 Peacock Lane, Leic LE1 5NY Tel: 0533 29514 — numerous G, HD, social and other activities for both sexes 11-25. Scheme for the young unemployed.

Youth Hostels Association, Trevelyan House, 8 St Stephen's Hill, St Albans, Herts AL1 2DY Tel: 0727 55215 — has adventure activities, good value accommodation all over Britain and overseas. All ages. RC, M£L, Rg, G.

HOBBIES AND SPORTS

Hobbies are a booming business; there's an association for everything, from dowsing to egg guilding or bicycle polo. To cover every organization would take a whole book, so this section just gives the key associations for the most popular activities and a few off-beat ones thrown in to titillate the palate, plus the names of specialist directories which give those I couldn't mention. There is no separate section for children because the vast majority of clubs welcome anyone who is keen enough, however young or old.

Some of the organizations given are associations of totally separate clubs; others are parent bodies with their own branches. Either way, they will tell you the nearest club you can join.

Organizations for activities covered elsewhere in this book, such as animal care, are under the activity, and clubs linked to no *one* hobby are in the Clubs section (see page 329).

If you want to find Chickens' Lib or anything else the *British Directory of Associations*, is in most public libraries. But if you want to take up a sport I haven't listed, like tchouk-ball, one of the following organizations is sure to have the answer.

British Sports Association for the Disabled, Hayward House, Barnard Crescent, Aylesbury, Bucks HP21 9PP Tel: 0296 27889 - the co-ordinating body for sport for those with physical limitations. RC.

Sports Council, Information Service, 16 Upper Woburn Place, London WC1H 0QP Tel: 01 388 1277 - open 9 am-5 pm (Mon-Fri). Information on the usual sports clubs, associations and residential and holiday courses.

Angling
National Anglers' Council, 11 Cowgate, Peterborough PE1 1LZ Tel: 0733 54084 - NB for all types of angling. L, HD.

National Federation of Anglers, Halliday House, 2 Wilson Street, Derby DE1 1PD Tel: 0332 362000 - NB for coarse fishing (i.e. fresh-water fish other than salmon). G.

National Federation of Sea Anglers, 26 Downsview Crescent, Uckfield, East Sussex TN22 1UB Tel: 0825 3589 - covers this fast-growing sport. M£V, A, diary, Rg, G, Ins, HD, Fest, Comp, sae.

The Salmon and Trout Association, Fishmongers' Hall, London Bridge, London EC4R 9EL Tel: 01-283 5838 - M£L, M, A, HD, G, HC
Magazines include: *Angling Times, Angling Mail, Sea Angler* and *Trout and Salmon.*

Antiques see Fine Arts

Archery
The Grand National Archery Society, 7th Street, National Agricultural Centre, Stoneleigh, Kenilworth, Warwickshire CV8 2LG Tel: 0203 23907 - M£V, A, HD, G - will teach beginners, and it is best not to buy equipment without advice, sae.

Astronomy
The British Astronomical Association, Burlington House, London W1V 9AG ONL Tel: 01 734 4145 - M£M, H, M, Lib, loan.

Athletics
Amateur Athletics Association, Francis House, Francis Street, London SW1P 1DL Tel: 01 828 9326 - From 11 upwards. A, B, HD.

Backgammon see page 318.

Badminton

The Badminton Association of England, National Badminton Centre, Bradwell Road, Loughton Lodge, Milton Keynes MK8 9LA Tel: 0908 5688227 - M, L, B, A, HC, G, Ins.

Ballooning

British Balloon and Airship Club, PO Box 1006, Birmingham B5 5RT Tel: 021 643 3224 - M£M, M, B, EI, Rg, A, 18+ only, instruction, sae. Spectators welcome.

Baseball

British Baseball Federation, The Lido East Park, Holderness Road, Hull HU9 2DR Tel: 0482 76169 - G, HC, Comp.

Basketball

English Basketball Association, Calomax House, Lupton Avenue, Leeds LS9 6EE Tel: 0532 496044 - B, E, L, Rg, G.

Billiards

The Billiards and Snooker Control Council, Coronet House, Queen Street, Leeds LS1 2TN Tel: 0532 440586 - covers 5,000 affiliated clubs. Average club membership £ML, B, L, Rg, A, sae.

Bird Watching

British Trust for Ornithology, Beech Grove, Station Road, Tring, Herts HP23 5NR Tel: 044 282 3461 - M£M, M, Lib, surveys.

The Royal Society for the Protection of Birds, The Lodge, Sandy, Beds SG19 2DL Tel: 0767 80551 - M£M, M, L, G, HD, L, RG, A, F, H, sanctuaries, club for under 16s, M, A, HC.

Scottish Ornithologists' Club, 21 Regent Terrace, Edinburgh EH7 5BT Tel: 031 556 6042 - M£M, M, G, vg Lib, B, A.

The Birdwatchers' Yearbook, Buckingham Press - lists all bird clubs and sanctuaries.

Bowling

There are two types of bowling.

British Tenpin Bowling Association, 114 Balfour Road, Ilford, Essex Tel: 01 478 1745 - M£L, F, Comp.

English Bowling Association, Lyndhurst Road, Worthing, W. Sussex BN11 2AZ Tel: 0202 22233 - linked to county associations. Spectators welcome. B, L, A, HD.

English Bowling Federation, 62 Frampton Place, Boston, Lincs PE21 8EL Tel: 0205 66201 - covers bowling-green bowling.

Bridge

English Bridge Union, 15b High Street, Thame, Oxon OX9 2BZ Tel: 084 421 2221, Scottish Bridge Union, 32 Whitehaugh Drive, Paisley PA1 3PG Tel: 041 887 1903, Welsh Bridge Union, 19 Penygraig, Rhiwbina, Cardiff CF4 6TD Tel: 0222 611 652, Northern Ireland Bridge Union, Mar Lodge, 9 Upper Malone Road, Belfast BT9 6TD Tel: 0232 668279 (evenings) - links hundreds of clubs promoting Duplicate Contract Bridge through club events and magazines. Ages about 9 to 100.

London School of Bridge and Club, 38 Kings Road, Chelsea, London SW3 4NB Tel: 01 589 7201 - the school offers 7-week courses for all levels, from absolute beginners upwards, for fees. M£H, country members half price.

Mollo and Gardener, Bridge for Beginners, Pan

Camping and Caravanning

The Camping and Caravanning Club Ltd, 11 Lower Grosvenor Place, London SW1W 0EY Tel: 01 828 1012/7 - M£M, M, G, HD, Ad, Ins, Disc, A, foreign touring service, Ins, sae. Sites, club for 12-17.

The Caravan Club, East Grinstead House, East Grinstead,

West Sussex RH19 1UA Tel: 0342 26944 - M£M, L, Ins, sites, foreign touring service, courses, breakdown service.

Canoeing

British Canoe Union, National Watersports Centre, The Elms, Adbolton Lane, Holme Pierrepont, Nottingham NG12 2LU Tel: 0602 817412 - M£L, M, L, H, EI.

The Canoe Camper (see Camping and Caravanning Club above).

Caving

National Caving Association, c/o The White Lion, Ynys Uchaf, Ystradynlais, Swansea SA9 1RW - 300 clubs in Britain, including cave diving. Rg, 18+ only, sae.

D. Judson, Caving and Potholing, Granada

Chess see page 319.

Coin Collecting

British Association of Numismatic Societies, c/o Department of Numismatics, Manchester Museum, University of Manchester, Oxford Road, Manchester M13 9PL Tel: 061 275 2661 - links local groups, HC, slide hire.

Magazines include: Coin and Medal News and Coin Monthly

Conservation

British Association of Nature Conservationists, Rectory Farm, Stanton St John, Oxford OX9 1HF Tel: 0867 35214 - RC, M£M, M, some groups, sae.

British Trust for Conservation Volunteers, London Ecology Centre, 80 York Way, London N1 9AG Tel: 01 278 4293/4/5 - volunteers undertake conservation tasks all over UK. RC Opt.M£L, M, H travel paid, training for the unemployed.

Coastal Anti-Pollution League, c/o Marine Conservation Society, 4 Gloucester Road, Ross-on-Wye HR9 5BU Tel: 0989 66017 - RC, M£L, booklet on beach conditions useful for holiday-makers, sae.

Council for the Protection of Rural England, 4 Hobart Place, London SW1 0HY Tel: 01 235 9481 - M£L, M, G.

Flora and Fauna Preservation Society, c/o Zoological Society of London, Regent's Park, London NW1 4RY Tel: 01 387 9656 - dedicated to international wildlife preservation. M£M, M, meetings, talks, B, A.

Friends of the Earth, 26-28 Underwood Street, London N1 7JQ Tel: 01 490 1555 - RC, M£L, M, L, B, G covers conservation worldwide, workshops, sae.

Greenpeace, 30-31 Islington Green, London N1 8XE Tel: 01 354 5100 — tries to prevent the destruction of the natural world. M£M.

London Wildlife Trust, 80 York Way, London N1 9AG Tel: 01 278 6612/3 — London wildlife surveys, conservation campaigning for threatened species — until last year there were bee-orchids in Brixton. RC, M£LM, M.

National Federation of City Farms, The Old Vicarage, 66 Fraser Street, Windmill Hill, Bedminster, Bristol BS3 4LY Tel: 0272 660663 — RC, M£L, M, L, G, A, C, HD. Also city gardens, sae.

National Trust — see page 333.

The Nature Conservancy Council, Northminster House, Peterborough PE1 1UA Tel: 0733 40345 — has an Inf sheet on bodies concerned with wildlife and the countryside. L, B, posters.

The Royal Society for Nature Conservation, The Green, Nettleham, Lincoln LN2 2NR Tel: 0522 752326 — RC, M£L— M, excellent M, G, A, B, HD, weekends, Watch club for junior members, sae.

World Wide Fund for Nature (formerly World Wildlife

Fund), Panda House, Wayside Park, Godalming, Surrey GU7 1XR Tel: 0483 426444 — devoted to conserving and protecting habitats, rainforests and wetlands, and promoting sustainable development whilst maintaining biolgical diversity worldwide Mot Var, A, Ad, E, Ed, F, G, Inf, L, M, RC, sae.
Anthony Chapman, *The Countryside and Wildlife for Disabled People*, from RADAR (see In Sickness).
Environmental Directory, Civic Trust — lists national and regional organizations concerned with amenities and the environment.
Edward Goldsmith, *Green Britain or Industrial Wasteland*, Polity Press
Nigel Hildyard, *The Macmillan Guide to Britain's Nature Reserves* (£30), Polity Press

Cricket

National Cricket Association, Lord's Cricket Ground, London NW8 8QN Tel: 01 289 6098 — covers 52 county organizations, F, A, L, non-playing members £L, holiday courses for juniors. Not exclusively for men.
The association recommends a 4¾ oz ball up to the age of 14, and the following bat sizes for different ages.

Age	Bat size
6+	3
8+	4
11+	5/6
13+	6/Harrow
14+	Harrow
16+	Full size

Women's Cricket Association, 16 Upper Woburn Place, London WC1H 0QP Tel: 01 387 3423 M£L, non-playing members welcome — including men, Rg, Year Book, international links.

Croquet

The Croquet Association, Hurlingham Club, Ranelagh Gardens, London SW6 3PR Tel: 01 736 3148 — links 180 UK clubs. M£L—M, L, B, E, G, Rg, HD, long sae (see page 316).

Curling

Royal Caledonian Curling Club, 2 Coates Crescent, Edinburgh EH3 7AN Tel: 031 225 7083 — M£L, M, G, Comp.

Cycling

British Cycling Federation, 16 Upper Woburn Place, London WC1 0QE Tel: 01 387 9320 — NB for cycle racing and cycling clubs. Handicaps, such as blindness, via the Tandem Club Liaison Officer. Racing only from 12+. M£L—M, B, E, Rg, Ins, HD, sae.
Cyclist's Touring Club, Cotterell House, 69 Meadrow, Godalming, Surrey GU7 3HS Tel: 04868 7217 — has useful Information for touring in the UK and overseas. M£L—M, M, L, E, EI, T, HD, Ins, routes.

Dancing

British Ballet Organization, Woolborough House, 39 Lonsdale Road, London SW13 9JP Tel: 01 748 1241 — will put people in touch with nearest teacher, for ballet or tap. B, L.
English Amateur Dancers Association, 14 Oxford Street, London W1N 0HL Tel: 01 636 0851 — covers all types of ballroom dancing and competitions.
English Folk Dance and Song Society, Cecil Sharp House, 2 Regents Park Road, London NW1 7AY Tel: 01 485 2206 — M£L—M, L, B, TR, E, A, G, sae.

International Dance Teachers Association, 76 Bennett Road, Brighton BN2 5JL Tel: 0273 685652/3 covers most dance, plus dance-exercise.
National Association of Teachers of Dancing, Suite 2, 56 The Broadway, Thatchem, Berks Tel: 0635 68888 — as above.
Royal Scottish Country Dance Society, 12 Coates Crescent, Edinburgh EH3 7AF Tel: 031 225 3854 — welcomes everyone interested in traditional Scottish dancing. M£L, M, B, L, E, cassettes, records, G, A, some HD, sae.
Scottish Council for Dance, Moray House, College of Education, Cramond Campus, Cramond Road North, Edinburgh EH14 6JD Tel: 031 336 5836 — an Inf source on dance, in Scotland.
The Society for International Folk Dancing, 16 Devere Walk, Watford, Herts WD1 3BE Tel: 0923 221696 — has about 40 local groups, some within LEA adult classes. M£L, B, TR, R, weekend courses, sae.
C.W. Beaumont, *Complete Book of Ballet*, Putnam
Mary Clarke and David Vaughan, *The Encyclopaedia of Dance and Ballet*, Pitman

Drama

British Theatre Association, Darwin Building, Regents College, Regents Park, London NW1 4NW Tel: 01 935 2571 — caters for both amateurs and professionals. M£H, M, HC, Inf, C, Dis on theatre tickets, grants, dialect tapes and records, world's largest drama library, scripts and sets. Playwrights' script reading service (for a fee), workshops and courses.
National Operatic and Dramatic Association, 1 Crestfield Street, London WC1H 8AU Tel: 01 837 5655 — links clubs for amateur opera and drama. Loans vocal scores, and pantomime scripts. M.

Embroidery - see page 385

Fencing

Amateur Fencing Association, and Ladies Amateur Fencing Union, The De Beaumont Centre, 83 Perham Road, London W14 9SP Tel: 01 385 7442 — M£L—M, M, L, B, E, G, Rg, A, some HD, Ins, spectators, sae. Doesn't need great fitness. PGL and Butlins do some fencing holidays.
Modern British Fencing, Thetford Press

Film Making

Institute of Amateur Cinematographers, 63 Woodfield Lane, Ashtead, Surrey KT21 2BT Tel: 03722 76358 — for film and video enthusiasts. M£M, M, G, F Lib, V, TR, Comp, Fest, Ins, sae.

Fine Arts

Antique Collectors' Club, 5 Church Street, Woodbridge, Suffolk IP12 1DS Tel: 0394 385501 — M£M, vg M, NG, B, auctions listed in magazine, worldwide.
Georgian Group, 37 Spital Square, London E1 6DY Tel: 01 377 1722 — for lovers of Georgian architecture and decorative arts. M£M, A, G, weekends, courses, private views.
National Art Collections Fund, 20 John Islip Street, London SW1P 4JX Tel: 01 821 0404 — helps retain works of art in UK. RC, M£M, M, A, private views, art tours, also under 30s group, sae.
National Association of Decorative and Fine Arts Societies, (NADFAS) 38 Ebury Street, London SW1W 0LU Tel: 01 730 3041 — M£M, M, NG, A, vis., lect., H, Disc. Also young NADFAS for age 8+.
National Heritage: The Museums Action Movement, 9A North Street, London SW4 0HN Tel: 01 720 6789 — M£M, M, museum handbook, private views.

National Trust, 36 Queen Anne's Gate, London SW1H 9AS Tel: 01 222 9251 — RC, M£L-M, M, free entry to all NT houses and gardens - and handbook. Working holidays for volunteers aged 16+. Young National Trust for children. Numerous events.

Old Water-colour Society's Club, Bankside Gallery, 48 Hopton Street, London SE1 9JH Tel: 01 928 7521 — M£M, M, A, Disc, sae.

The Thirties Society, Basement Flat, 18 Comeragh Road, London W14 9HP Tel: 01 381 9797 — campaigns for the preservation of the best post-1918 architecture and design. M£L—M, M, A, T, sae.

Victorian Society, 1 Priory Gardens, London W4 1TT Tel: 01 994 1019 — M£L—M, G, A, preservation society.

The British Art and Antiques Directory, Ebury Press — lists antique dealers, specialist societies and courses on all aspects of fine arts.

Flower Arranging

National Association of Flower Arranging Societies, 21 Denbigh Street, London SW1V 2HF Tel: 01 828 5145 — G, Rg, L, M, H.

Flying

Aircraft Owners and Pilots Association, British Light Aviation Centre, 50a Cambridge Street, London SW1V 4QQ Tel: 01 834 5631 — M£H, age 17+, M, B, L, Ins, International links, Inf.

British Gliding Association, Kimberley House, 47 Vaughan Way, Leicester LE1 4SE Tel: 0533 53105 — clubs teach gliding and hire out the planes. Age 16+ for solo flights. B, A, L, E, HD, HC.

British Microlight Aircraft Association, Bullring, Deddington, Oxford OX5 4TT Tel: 0869 38888 — microlight aircraft (an off-shoot from hang gliding) offer relatively low-cost powered flight. 17 - 75. M£H, M, Rg, sae.

Folklore

The Folklore Society, c/o University College London, Gower Street, London, WC1E 6BT Tel: 01 387 5894 — M£M, M, Lect.

Football

The Football Association, 16 Lancaster Gate, London W2 3LW Tel: 01 262 4542 — 42,000 clubs under county FAs. Res courses.

Genealogy

Federation of Family History Societies, The Benson Room, Birmingham and **Midland Institute**, 7 Margaret Street, Birmingham B3 3BS Tel: 021 236 3591 — M, B, G, Ad, sae.

Guild of One Name Studies, Box G, 14 Charterhouse Buildings, Goswell Road, London EC1M 7BA links those researching a particular surname — it could be yours. M£L.

Society of Genealogists, 14 Charterhouse Buildings, Goswell Road, London EC1M 7BA Tel: 01 251 8799 — M£H, B, access to the society's collection of parish registers and directories. But the services of a professional genealogist are obtained via the **Association of Genealogists and Record Agents**, 1 Woodside Close, Caterham, Surrey CR3 6AU

Golf

The Golf Foundation, 57 London Road, Enfield, Middx EN2 6DU Tel: 01 367 4404 — RC promoting golf among the young. A, F, V, M.

The Ladies Golf Union, 12 The Scores, St Andrews, Fife KY16 9AT Tel: 0334 75811 — link point for over 2,000 clubs.

Royal and Ancient Golf Club, St Andrews, Fife KY16 9JB Tel: 0334 72112 — governing authority for golf.

Gymnastics and Acrobatics

British Amateur Gymnastics Association, 2 Buckingham Avenue East, Slough, Berks SL1 3DZ Tel: 0753 32556 — responsible for gymnastics and sports acrobatics. M, L, B, E, A, G, HD, Int. Comp. sae.

The British Slimnastics Association, 14 East Sheen Avenue, London SW14 8AS Tel: 01 876 1838 — dedicated to 'the whole person approach to fitness' Classes. M£L, M, L, B, A, tapes, seminars.

Handball

British Handball Association, Handball House, 32 Grove Place, Bedford MK40 3JJ Tel: 0234 213597 — has 87 affiliated clubs. All abilities welcome, spectators too. M£L, B, L, Rg, NB.

Hang Gliding

British Hang Gliding Association, Cranfield Airfield, Cranfield, Beds MK43 0YR Tel: 0234 751688 — M£H, Ins, B, M, A, T, legal, 16+ only and averagely fit, sae. Links 44 local branches, but hang gliding needs tuition and equipment costing several hundred pounds. Non-flying members very welcome.

Hockey

All England Women's Hockey Association, Argyle House, 29—31 Euston Road, London NW1 2SD Tel: 01 278 6340 — Links 966 local clubs. L, B,V, A, Rg, Ins.

The Hockey Association, 16 Northdown Street, London N1 9BG Tel: 01 837 8878 — links some 800 clubs, with average membership fees £L—H, A, B, L, Inf on holidays.

Jigsaw Puzzles

The British Jigsaw Puzzle Library, 8 Heath Terrace, Leamington Spa, Warwicks, Tel: 0926 311874 — a postal loan service (callers only by appointment) for jigsaws which suits the puzzles to the taste of the borrower. Membership 3 months, 6 months or 1 year, sae with enquiries. No children's puzzles.

Kites

Kite Society of Great Britain, 31 Grange Road, Ilford, Essex IG1 1EU Tel: 01 478 6668 — M£L, M, some G, Inf, Disc, international festivals.
Ron Moulton, *Kites*, Pelham

Lacrosse

All England Women's Lacrosse Association, 16 Upper Woburn Place, London WC1H 0QJ Tel: 01 387 4430

Land Yachting

British Federation of Sand and Land Yachting Clubs, 23 Piper Drive, Long Whatton, Leics Tel: 0509 842292 — links 20 member clubs M£H. Land yachts at £150 and range from the DIY to the tailor-made. L, A, Int. Comp, HD, sae.

Magic

There is no national organization for amateur magicians, but a public library may know of a local club.

Marquetry

Marquetry Society, The Barn House, Llanon, Nr Aberystwyth, Dyfed SY23 5LZ Tel: 097 48 581 — M£L, M, G, A, Comp, sae.
Ernie Ives, *Marquetry for Beginners* (from the Marquetry Society)

Martial Arts

The British Judo Association, 16 Upper Woburn Place, London WC1H 0QH Tel: 01 387 9340 — G, HD, G, HD, sae.

Martial Arts Commission, 1st Floor Broadway House, 15/16 Deptford Broadway, London SE8 4PE Tel: 01 691 3433 — NB for all martial arts teaching, except judo. Inf, B, Ad. If using a club not found through MAC, ask to see the instructor's MAC licence. Anyone can set up as a martial arts teacher, and unqualified instructors are a danger to their pupils.

Military History

British Model Soldier Society, 22 Lynwood Road, Ealing, London W5 1JJ Tel: 01 998 5230 — M£L, G, M, Comp, Auctions, age 12 to 100+, covers models, serious military history and military memorabilia.

Military Historical Society, National Army Museum, Royal Hospital Road, London SW3 4HT Tel: 01 730 0717 — M£L, M, some G, A, visits to battlefields, sae.

Models

International Plastic Modellers Society, c/o 9 Pretoria Road, Gillingham, Kent ME7 4ND Tel: 0634 53759 — M£L, M, G, A, Comps, Ex, all ages, sae.

Model Power Boat Association, c/o 489 Canterbury Way, Stevenage, Herts SG1 4EQ — M£L, M, G, Rg, A, HD, Ins, Comp, regattas.

Motorcycling

Auto-cycle Union, Miller House, Corporation Street, Rugby, Warwicks CV21 2DN Tel: 0788 540519 — covers all types of 2- and 3-wheel motorized sport, G, all ages from 6, send 9×6 in sae for starter pack of Inf.

Motor Sports

RAC Motor Sports Association, 31 Belgrave Square, London SW1X 8QH Tel: 01 235 8601 — NB for all motor sports, from cars to karting, issues licences. Link for local clubs.

Mountaineering

British Mountaineering Council, Crawford House, Precinct Centre, Booth Street East, Manchester M13 9RZ Tel: 061 273 5839 — M£L—M, M, L, B, F, HC, HD, T, Ins. Most courses are for 16+, some for those 50+.

Music

Amateur Music Association, c/o Music Department, City of Manchester Education Committee, Medlock Junior School, Wadeson Road, Manchester M13 9UR Tel: 061 273 3094 — has Inf on local music societies, HD.

British Association of Barbershop Singers, c/o Martin Anderson, 72 High Kingsdown, Bristol BS2 8EP Tel: 0272 273286 — M£H, 45 British clubs, men only, but there is a Ladies Association of British Barbershop Singers at this address.

British Music Information Centre, 10 Stratford Place, London W1N 9AE Tel: 01 499 8567 — Inf source on 20th-century (classical) British music.

National Association of Choirs, John Robbins, 21 Charmouth Road, Lower Weston, Bath BA1 3LJ — will refer people to their nearest choir.

National Federation of Music Societies, Francis House, Francis Street, London SW1P 1DE Tel: 01 828 7320 — a reference point for all kinds of music societies, and provides wide-ranging help to societies which join it.

See also Opera and Drama, page 336.

Marianne Barton ed., *British Music Yearbook*, Rhinegold - lists music teachers, amateur choirs and orchestras; *British Music Education Yearbook* - lists festivals, competitions, courses, etc.

Netball

All England Netball Association, Francis House, Francis Street, London SW1P 1DE Tel: 01 828 2176

Orienteering

British Orienteering Federation, Riversdale, Dale Road North, Darley Dale, Matlock, Derbyshire DE4 2HX Tel: 0629 734042 — orienteering is competitive navigation on foot - a purposeful form of jogging. 150 affiliated clubs. Competitions are divided by age, starting at 10. M£L-M, B, L.

Know the Game Orienteering, (£1.50 from the federation above).

Events listed in *Compass Sport* magazine.

Parachute Jumping

British Parachute Association Ltd, 5 Wharf Way, Glen Parva, Leics LE2 9TF Tel: 0533 785271 — for the fit aged 16-50, non-participating associate members also welcome. A, B, HD, M, L, G.

Parascending

British Association of Parascending Clubs, 18 Talbot Lane, Leicester LE1 4LR Tel: 0533 530318 — like parachuting - except that you start on the ground and go up (then down) after being towed by a landrover or speed boat. Links some 70 properly insured member clubs. Equipment is provided. Fitness to fly is decided by each instructor - but this association uniquely has a blind president. M£H, M, L, Ins, HD.

Petanque

British Petanque Association, 8 Maddoxfield Way, Botley, Southampton SO3 2DW Tel: 048 92 4112 — M£L, NG, RG, L B, E, HD, age 14+, rule book.

Michael Haworth-Booth, *The Game of Boules*, Farall

Photography

The British Society of Underwater Photographers, 29 Sandown Close, Blackwater, Surrey Tel: 0252 878265 — M£M, M, G, A, Comp, sae.

The Camera Club, 8 Great Newport Street, London WC2H 7JA Tel: 01 240 1137 — M£H, M, min age 18, Disc, courses, use of darkroom. No branches.

Royal Photographic Society, The Octagon, Milsom Street, Bath BA1 1DN Tel: 0225 62841 — M£H, M, awards, Ex, special interest groups but not local clubs.

There are masses of local photographic clubs - you can find them through the local library.

Peter Rowlands, *Underwater Photography*, Macdonald
P. Schulke, *Underwater Photography*, Prentice-Hall

Poetry

The Poetry Society, 21 Earls Court Square, London SW5 9DE Tel: 01 373 7861/2 — Inf on competitions and festivals, poetry magazines, workshops, evening classes, poetry bookshop, readings and criticism, for a fee. Linked to about 40 poetry bodies M£M.

Racketball

British Racketball Association, 50 Tredegar Road, Wilmington, Dartford, Kent DA2 7AZ Tel: 0322 72200 — M£L, M, handbook, EI, Comp.

Radio
Radio Society of Great Britain, Lambda House, Cranbourne Road, Potters Bar EN6 3JE Tel: 0707 59015 — the organization for radio hams. L, B, F, T, EI, Ad, licensing Inf, Ex.

Rambling — see Walking

Riding — see Animals

Rowing
Amateur Rowing Association, 6 Lower Mall, London W6 9DJ Tel: 01 748 3632 — covers 480 clubs. Ages 8-80+. L, A, B, HD.

Rugby
The Rugby Fives Association, 12 Alexandra Cottages, Hardings Lane, Penge, London SE26 7JJ Tel: 01 659 4159 — linked to 40 local clubs, M£L, sae. Main cost — the beer afterwards.

Rugby Football Union, Rugby Road, Twickenham TW1 1DZ Tel: 01 892 2452 — covers numerous local clubs for children and adults, average local membership £10 - £20, L, Rg, V, HC, some HD, refereeing courses and opportunities.

Running
Road Runners Club, 40 Rosedale Road, Stoneleigh, Epsom, Surrey KT1Y 2JH Tel: 01 393 8950 — M£L, M, G, Ins, Comp.

Sailing
Royal Yachting Association, RYA House, Romsey Road, Easleigh, Hants SO5 4YA Tel: 0703 629962 — covers sailing craft of every size, including windsurfers. Links to some 1,500 independent clubs. M£L, B, L, EI, E, T, A, HD, Ins, great discounts. Could be worth joining even if you don't sail.

Shooting
The Clay Pigeon Shooting Association, 107 Epping New Road, Buckhurst Hill, Essex IG9 5TQ Tel: 01 505 6221 — NB + or target shooting with a shotgun. M£M, LC, A, L, B, HD, Inf, 17+.

National Rifle Association, Bisley Camp, Brookwood, Woking, Surrey GU24 0PB Tel: 04867 2213/4 — covers clubs for most types of shooting. Gun ownership is restricted (see under Law), but most responsible people can get licences. Approx M£M, M, A, Ins.

Skating and Roller Skating
National Skating Association of Great Britain, 15 - 27 Gee Street, London EC1V 3RE Tel: 01 253 0910/3824 — covers skating, roller skating and ice hockey. M£L-M, L, B, A, tests.

Skiing and Ski-bob
The English Ski Council, Area Library Building, The Precinct, Halesowen, W Midlands B63 4AJ Tel: 021 501 2314 — has 60-70 local clubs. M, B, A, Inf, sae.

The Ski-bob Association of Great Britain, 10 Brierholme, Hatfield, S Yorks DNY 6EH Tel: 0243 512418 — Inf on ski-bobbing (essentially a bicycle on skis), M£L.

Snooker — see Billiards.

Squash
Squash Rackets Association, Francis House, Francis Street, London SW1P 1DE Tel: 01 828 3064/5/6 — M£M, M, handbook, G, Ins, priority bookings for squash events. Also BUPA discount.

Women's Squash Rackets Association, 345 Upper Richmond Road, West Sheen, London SW14 8QN Tel: 01 876 6219 — M£L, A, some HD, Ins, B, L, coaching, Comps - Int and UK, sae.

Stamp Collecting
The British Philatelic Federation Ltd, 107 Charterhouse Street, London EC1M 6PT Tel: 01 251 5040 — M£M, but local clubs cost much less. Links to clubs specializing in certain typ stamps. Its yearbook is a mine of information on stamp collecting, including numerous magazines.
Stanley Gibbons, Stamp Collecting: How to Start
F. J. Melville, rev. A. R. Blair, Stamp Collecting, Hodder and Stoughton

Surfing
British Surfing Association, G5, Burrows Chambers, East Burrow Road, Swansea, West Glamorgan SA1 1RF Tel: 0792 461476 — M£L, M, L, EI, A, some HD, Ins, B, L, G, sae, A.

Swimming and Diving
Amateur Swimming Association, Harold Fern House, Derby Square, Loughborough LE11 0AL Tel: 0509 230431 — links swimming clubs and sets standards for instruction.

British Sub-aqua Club (BSAC), 16 Upper Woburn Place, London WC1H 0QW Tel: 01 387 9302 — M, EI, E, Ins, local M£M—H and includes BSAC fee. Members can usually dive with overseas branches when on holiday. Tuition free. Age 14+, and reasonable fitness and swimming ability.

National Association of Swimming Clubs for the Handicapped, St George's House Drive, Brighton, East Sussex BN1 6FL Tel: 0273 559470 — gives referral to numerous local clubs. L, B, Ins, A, EI.
Pat Besford, Encyclopaedia of Swimming, Robert Hale & Co
Good leaflets on swimming with various medical problems from: Sport for All, Aquatic House, 1 Birmingham Road, West Bromwich, West Midlands B71 4JQ.

Table Tennis
English Table Tennis Association, 21 Claremont, Hastings, East Sussex TN34 1HF Tel: 0424 433121 — linked to 6,000 independent local clubs.

Tennis
Lawn Tennis Association, Queen's Club, West Kensington, London W14 9EG Tel: 01 385 2366 — LTA, M£M, M, Ins, HC, E, A and Disc on major tennis events. Numerous affiliated clubs, with membership fees £5 — £150, offer lessons and facilities.

Walking and Rambling
Backpackers Club, c/o Eric R. Gurney, PO Box 38, 7-10 Friar Street, Reading, Berks R63 4RL Tel: 04917 739 — for all who backpack - on foot, wheel, or canoe. M£M, M, L, EI, A, HD, Ins, Ad, Inf, sae.

Ramblers Association, 1/5 Wandsworth Road, London SW8 2XX Tel: 01 582 6878 — M£M, A, G, M, L, H, guides.
If you feel your walker's rights are infringed contact the Pedestrians' Association. Address as for Ramblers Association, or Tel: 01 735 3270.

Yoga
The British Wheel of Yoga, 1 Hamilton Place, Boston Road, Sleaford, Lincs NG34 7ES Tel: 0529 306851 — NB for yoga classes.

MARRIAGE AND DATING AGENCIES

A lot of career and social situations make it very hard for people to meet others to go out with - let alone marry. As a result more and more people are using marriage and dating agencies, and lonely hearts columns. There is even an agency for people who just want companionship from their own sex.

Lonely hearts columns are found in various publications, but one of the most established and respectable is probably the personal section of the *New Statesman*, Foundation House, Perseverance Works, 38 Kingsland Road, London E2 8DQ Tel: 01 739 3211.

Most agencies ask a set fee for a given number of introductions, or for a year, or both — often plus a lump sum, from each person, if a marriage results. But they vary considerably in the number of introductions, the types of people, the regions of Britain in which they have a good selection, and the thoroughness of the vetting. So check the details of several before you sign on with one.

There are two professional bodies to which such agencies belong. The larger is the **Association of British Dating Agencies** (29 Manchester Street, London W1M 5PF, no phone). Its members must conform to a code of conduct which, among other things, says that:
- members must give clients a realistic number of introductions
- all information from clients is strictly confidential
- the agency must state whether it limits membership to those who are unmarried and, where this limit applies, ask for a signed statement of freedom to marry.

The **Society of Marriage Bureaux**, 124 New Bond Street, London W1 Tel: 01 629 9634 — is much smaller and its code of conduct stipulates that:
- a client will only be accepted after an interview
- a client's name and address will not be given to anyone without their consent
- the client's descriptions will not be published in any media
- they will only accept clients who are genuinely free to marry.

The professional organizations may be able to give you the addresses of marriage and dating agencies which serve your area. These are just some of the main ones.

Dateline (23 Abingdon Road, London W8 6AH Tel: 01 938 1011) is a dating agency which uses a computer to match its members. It claims that 2,500 new people join it each month, and the questionnaire finds out who wants dates and who is looking for a serious relationship.

Hedi Fisher Introductions (45-46 Chalk Farm Road, London NW1 8AJ Tel: 01 267 6066 (24 hrs), 01 485 2916) — claims to cater for middle, upper, and professional class clients looking for marriage or a stable relationship, mainly in the south.

Katherine Allen Marriage and Advice Bureau (3 Cork Street, London W1X 1HA Tel: 01 949 3050) A marriage rather than a dating agency. All clients are interviewed and evidence of

singleness is required. Clients are mainly managerial and professional.

The Marriage Bureau (Heather Jenner) Ltd, (124 New Bond Street, London W1Y 9AE Tel: 01 629 9634) is a long-established company and introductions are based on a form and personal interview.

Old Friends (18A Highbury New Park, London N5 2DB Tel: 01 226 5432) is an agency for friendship rather than dating, and not limited to the opposite sex. Mainly for age 40+ who are finding it hard to meet new friends.

MUSIC, DRAMA AND ENTERTAINMENT

London

Agencies for West End Theatres

Tickets can be bought direct from the theatre or through the agencies given below. *But* agencies can add as much booking fee as they like to the price of a ticket, and £1 to £2 *per ticket* is low. It may be more convenient to book through an agency but you usually pay for the convenience. Mark-ups vary with the show and not every agency covers every theatre. Here are some of the better ones.

First Call, 01 240 7200 (24-hr CC booking, low fixed booking fee)
Group Sales Box Office, 01 930 6123 (discounts for group bookings)
Keith Prowse, 01 741 9999 (many shows without a booking fee)
Lashmars, 01 493 4731 (controlled booking fee)
Omega Bookings, 01 836 3962 (discounts for group bookings)
Ticketmaster, 01 379 4444 (24-hr CC booking, some shows with no booking fee)

Transport

Society of West End Theatre (Bedford Chambers, Covent Garden Piazza, London WC2E 8HQ Tel: 01 836 0971) has leaflets and information on aspects of the London theatre scene, including leaflets on the public transport mini-bus service which runs from theatreland to Waterloo and Victoria.

Those who prefer to travel by car can use the scheme whereby those visiting the Albery, Criterion, Wyndhams, Whitehall, Piccadilly or Donmar Warehouse can book a space at the nearest NCP car park when they book their ticket and get a discount on the cost of parking on presenting a voucher from the theatre.

Entertainment in London

Most theatre ticket offices are open from 10 am until the start of the evening performance. Tickets paid for by credit card often need to be picked up about 45 minutes before the performance. Cut-price tickets are sold, for the same day, in a booth in Leicester Square after 12 am for matinées and from 2.30 to 6.30 pm for evening performances. They are half-price + 80p, for cash only.

Many theatres offer:
● reduced price seats at afternoon performances for senior citizens, if seats are available, on production of a special card. To join this scheme write to Senior Citizens Scheme, Society of West End Theatre (address above).
● reduced price seats for students just before the show, if room. Sixth-formers may also join the scheme. Write to Society of West End Theatre (left).
Other theatres may be able to assist those with wheelchairs. For information ring 01 388 2227/8.

Greater London Arts (9 White Lion Street, London N1 9PD Tel: 01 837 8808) has information of general arts activities and shows on the fringe.

Outside London

Festivals and Festival Theatres
There are so many excellent festivals that I can only give a selection from - not of - the top festivals in Britain. Among those left out are unique events, such as that at York where they perform the medieval mystery plays, which only happen every few years. The full range of festivals can be found in *Arts Festivals in Britain and Ireland* (Rhinegold), and a free leaflet giving the details of more than 25 major festivals can be obtained, from November for the following year, on written request from the **British Arts Festival Association** (23 Orchard Road, London N6 5TR).

Information on amateur music festivals can be obtained from the **British Federation of Music Festivals** (198 Park Lane, Macclesfield, Cheshire SK11 6UD Tel: 0625 28297). Amateur theatre, poetry and dance festivals can be traced through the organizations given in the Hobbies section.

Aberdeen International Youth Festival (July/August), Town House, Aberdeen, AB9 1AQ Tel: 0224 642121

Aldeburgh Festival of Music and Arts (June), Aldeburgh Foundation, High Street, Aldeburgh, Suffolk IP15 5AX Tel: 072885 3543 (box office) or 072 885-2935 (information) - also music at other times of year.

Bath International Festival (May/June), Linley House, 1 Pierrepont Place, Bath, Avon BA1 1JY Tel: 0225 62231

Belfast Festival of Arts (November), Festival House, 25 College Gardens, Belfast BT9 6BS Tel: 0232 667687

Brighton Festival (May), Marlborough House, 54 Old Steine, Brighton BN1 1EQ Tel: 0273 29801

Cambridge Festival (July), Cambridge Festival Association Ltd, Mandela House, 4 Regent Street, Cambridge CB2 1BY Tel: 0223 358977

Cheltenham International Festival of Music (July), Town Hall, Imperial Square, Cheltenham, Glos Tel: 0242 523690 (bookings from May)

Cheltenham Festival of Literature (October), Box Office as above (bookings from early September)

Chester Summer Music Festival (July), Swanston West, Whitchurch-on-Thames, Oxon RG8 7ER Tel: 073 57 2466

Chichester Festival Theatre (April-September), Oaklands Park, Chichester, W Sussex PO19 4AP Tel: 0243 781312 (bookings near the opening date)

City of London Festival (July), City Arts Trust, Bishopsgate Hall, 230 Bishopsgate, London EC2M 4QH Tel: 01 377 0540

Edinburgh International Festival (August), Edinburgh Festival Society, 21 Market Street, Edinburgh EH1 1BW Tel: 031 226 4001 *also*

Edinburgh Festival Fringe Society (August), 170 High Street, Edinburgh EH1 1QS Tel: 031 226 5259

Festival of British Music (June), Barbican Centre, Silk Street, London EC2Y 8DS Tel: 01 638 4141

Glyndebourne Festival Opera (May-August), Lewes, East Sussex BN8 5UU Tel: 0273 812321 (bookings in January, but some returns nearer the date)

Harrogate International Festival (August), Royal Baths, Harrogate, N Yorks HG1 2RR Tel: 0423 62303

Malvern Festival (May/June), Winter Gardens, Grange Road, Malvern, Worcs Tel: 0684 892277 (bookings from February)

The Mayfest (May), 46 Royal Exchange Square, Glasgow G1 3AR Tel: 041 221 4911

National Mod (Gaelic Festival, October), An Comunn Gaidhealach, 109 Church Street, Inverness IV1 1EY Tel: 0463 231226

Perth Festival of the Arts (May), The Round House, Marshall Lane, Perth PH2 8NU Tel: 0738 38353

St Magnus Festival (June), Strandal, Nicholson Street, Kirkwall, Orkney KW15 1BD Tel: 0856 2669

Shrewsbury International Music Festival (July), Tourist Information Centre, The Square, Shrewsbury Shropshire 5YI 1LA Tel: 0743 50761 (from June)

Stratford upon Avon Festival (July), Civic Hall, 14 Rother Street, Stratford upon Avon, Warwick CV37 6LU Tel: 0789 67969

Swansea Music Festival (September), Civic Information Centre, P.O.Box 59, Singleton Street, Swansea, West Glamorgan SA1 3QG Tel: 0792 468321 - information on the Swansea Festival Fringe (October) is at the same address but Tel: 0792 476666

Three Choirs Festival (mid-August), Honorary Festival Secretary, 38 Bridge Street, Hereford HR4 9DQ Tel: 0905 613988 (bookings from mid-March)

Regional Arts
The regional arts associations are the best people to tell you about the arts in their areas. Most have a mass of activities and some publish a free arts diary like a small magazine; others have an arts newspaper, and regions like the south west have so much going on that there is a commercial publication which covers the events.

The local tourist boards have excellent information on every aspect of the visual arts in their area, and the regional arts associations will be able to tell you about 'friends of' schemes which allow you to support art galleries, and gain entry to their private views, or to have priority bookings for theatres and concerts. Around Manchester, for example, there are more arts organizations that you can befriend than in London.

Buckinghamshire Arts Association, 55 High Street, Aylesbury, Bucks HP20 1SA Tel: 0296 434704

East Midlands Arts, Mountfields House, Forest Road, Loughborough, Leics LE11 3HU Tel: 0509 218292

Eastern Arts Association, Cherry Hinton Hall, Cherry Hinton Road, Cambridge CB1 4DW Tel: 0223 215355

Lincolnshire and Humberside Arts, St Hugh's, Newport, Lincoln LN1 3DN Tel: 0522 33555

Merseyside Arts, Bluecoat Chambers, School Lane, Liverpool L1 3BX Tel: 051 709 0671:

Northern Arts, 9-10 Osborne Terrace, Jesmond, Newcastle upon Tyne NE2 1NZ Tel: 091 281 6334/4363/7213

North West Arts, 4th Floor, 12 Harter Street, Manchester M1 6HY Tel: 061 228 3062

Scottish Arts Council, 19 Charlotte Street, Edinburgh EH12 4DF Tel: 031 226 6051:

South East Arts, 10 Mount Ephraim, Tunbridge Wells, Kent TN4 8AS Tel: 0892 41666

Southern Arts, 19 Southgate Street, Winchester, Hampshire SO23 9DQ Tel: 0962 55099

South West Arts, Bradninch Place, Gandy Street, Exeter EX4 3LS Tel: 0392 218188

The Welsh Arts Council, Holst House, 9 Museum Place, Cardiff CF1 3NX Tel: 0222 394711:

West Midland Arts, 82 Granville Street, Birmingham B1 2LH Tel: 021 631 3121

Yorkshire Arts, Glyde House, Bradford, West Yorks BD5 0BQ Tel: 0274 723051

The Welsh National Opera Ltd (John Street, Cardiff CF1 4SP Tel: 0222 464666) has no permanent theatre. For details of venues contact this address.

The Royal Shakespeare Company, Stratford upon Avon, performs at both the Royal Shakespeare Theatre and the Swan Theatre. Bookings for both are through Tel: 0789 295623/295655

GARDENING

This section is designed to offer a few solutions to the most common gardening problems. A wonderful range of plants is available to those who venture beyond the inadequate gardening sections of many DIY stores. So, wherever possible, I have suggested sources of plants, seeds, information and advice. The nurseries chosen either have an established reputation or a list of special interest. That they will live up to these is something I cannot guarantee.

Planning a Garden

It is very much the fashion to have clumps of shrubs, or independent shrubs, upon grass-plats: people must follow their own taste; but, in my opinion, nothing is so beautiful as a clear carpet of green, surrounded by shrubs and flowers, separated from it by walks of beautiful gravel.
William Cobbett, *The English Gardener*

Good gardens are about surprises. A garden you can see all in one glance may look beautiful but is no more interesting than a story to which you already know the ending. So even the smallest garden should be given at least one hidden corner which has to be discovered. And paradoxically, cutting off part of a garden from view makes it seem bigger, not smaller.

The British climate also needs to be considered. Most of the time we are looking out of the windows. So that should be the point from which the garden looks best - especially in winter. This means having some choice winter flowering shrubs and early bulbs close enough to enjoy them.

Another secret is tailoring a garden to meet your circumstances. There are two sides to this. The first, and most neglected one, is fitting it to your lifestyle. If you are busiest in late March, beds full of roses, which need pruning at that time, will be either a burden or a disappointment. The lay-out of a garden can make a vast difference to the amount of time you need to spend on it.

Plants need to be spaced so they will have room to achieve the beauty of their form, but there is something gentle and restful about a garden in which the plants are allowed to touch and, so to speak, put their arms around each other.

At the same time a garden has to be practical. A garden of any size without space to burn rubbish or make compost is like a house without a bathroom and lavatory. But these necessities need to be incorporated so that they don't spoil the view, and so does any garden shed. If they are planned for from the start it is easy enough to tuck them behind a hedge or decorative trellis which adds to the design. See also Lawns, page 343.

Choosing Plants

The wrong way to buy plants is to walk round a garden centre, see a pretty flower and be seduced. The right plant should:

- like the soil
- like the amount of sun or shade you can offer
- like amount of moisture, or lack of it
- be hardy enough for your garden
- look good with the plants around it
- provide flowers and foliage when your garden needs them
- fit into the space below ground as well as above it (see Law on tree roots).

Quite a few plants can produce allergic reactions, mainly as very nasty rashes. If you have been gardening and develop an unexplained rash the following plants are the most common cause:

Bamboo	Euphorbia
Marrow	Tomato
Hyacinth	Cucumber
Rue	Geranium
Chrysanthemum	Primula
Daffodil	Courgette
Conifer	Hogweed
Hellebore (Christmas Rose)	Rhus
Runner bean	

Tubs, Pots and Boxes

Plants will grow in almost anything provided it will hold soil and has drainage holes at the bottom to let out water. In Greece houses are often brilliant with flowers growing in old tin cans. Whether it's a window box or a tin can, place it where you intend it to stand. Put flower pots in saucers for better watering and raise other containers slightly on pieces of tile so water can run away. Put about 2·5 cm (1 in) broken flower pots, old china, stones or bought coarse gravel in the bottom through which water will drain easily. Top with John Innes No 2 potting compost. Plant anything which will fit into the container when fully grown - an increasing numbers of shrubs and roses can. Water and fertilize regularly and protect them from frost by wrapping a plastic sack round with straw, hay, or even polystyrene granules between the sack and the tub.

> Few things are more cruel to a plant than to under-water it. Under-watering causes roots to grow towards the surface and so makes it harder for it to reach the moisture deep down in a dry season. A small shrub needs at least a gallon of water at a single watering in dry weather, and a large shrub needs as much as 4 gallons. Herbaceous plants need enough water to penetrate 30 cm (1 ft) into the ground. So douse areas thoroughly.

More information

Beth Chatto, *The Damp Garden*, Dent
Beth Chatto, *The Dry Garden*, Dent
The Good Gardener's Guide, Consumers Association - lists good nurseries both by area and by speciality, with detailed information on what each offers. Invaluable to anyone planting up a garden.
Penelope Hobhouse, *Colour in Your Garden*, Collins
Christopher Lloyd, *The Well Chosen Garden*, Hamish Hamilton
Diana Saville, *The Illustrated Garden Planter*, Penguin - groups plants by their use.
Allen Sawyer, *The Plant Buyer's Directory*, Ebury Press - gives plants grouped by flowering season

Visiting Gardens

There is no better way to get inspiration than seeing what other people have achieved. At almost any time of the year you can visit the gardens open for charity or see the Royal Horticultural Society gardens at Wisley. There are also some fine gardens attached to major nurseries.

National Gardens Scheme, 57 Lower Belgrave Street, London, SW1W 0LR Tel: 01 730 0359 - lists numerous private and National Trust gardens, in England and Wales, which open for charity, in a guide published each February.
Royal Horticultural Society Garden, Wisley, Nr Woking, Surrey GU23 6QB Tel: 0483 224234 - open to everyone (not just members) every day except Sundays and Christmas Day. Nov-Jan 10.00 to 16.30. Feb-Oct 10.00 to 19.00 or sunset - whichever is earlier. Sundays are for members only.
See also **Cottage Garden Society** and **Garden History**

Society, page 368 and the **National Trust**, page 333.
Historic Houses, Castles and Gardens, Papermac.
Good Gardener's Guide, Consumers' Association - says which nurseries have gardens to view.
Tourist Boards often have information on gardens in their areas.

Bulbs, Corms, Tubers and Rhizomes

Few plants give such good return on money, space and labour as bulbs. For a few pounds you can have splashes of colour all over an average garden, even in the bleak months of the year. There are tulips, frothy alliums, and elegant creamy galtonias for flower beds; early snowdrops, daffodils and nodding fritillaries to go in grass; the beauties of colchicums, bluebells and tiny cyclamen to clothe the bare patches under trees and shrubs. There are bulbs for every size of garden, from towering lilies for shrubberies to miniature bulbs for sink gardens. Once in, most *prefer to stay in* and pests and diseases are rare. Even hyacinths can be freed from their potted imprisonment to naturalize into glorious drifts in a southern garden.

> Throughout this section 'bulb' will usually include both bulbs and corms.

Look at some species varieties. For example, species crocuses offer a far softer range of colours than the gaudy basics, and species tulips will happily naturalize when others must be lifted or risk disease. Get a catalogue from a good bulb specialist, to see how much is available. They withstand postage well.

When buying bulbs, corms, tubers and rhizomes plumpness is a good sign. They should also have no sign of mould or disease. Choose lily bulbs which are small to medium-sized, as they establish better than larger ones.

Planting for Indoors

Plant bulbs in pots 2½-3 months before you want them to flower. Place stones over the holes of a largish flower pot, to allow good drainage. Make some John Innes No 1 potting compost thoroughly damp (if the container has no drainage holes use bulb fibre). Three-quarters fill the pot. Position the bulbs so the noses of large bulbs just rise from the compost, and smaller ones are just covered, and fill in firmly with compost or fibre.

Put them in a cool, dark place - under a black bin bag in the garage, say - for 2 months, out of reach of mice and rats. Keep them damp - but don't overwater. When an inch (2·5 cm) of shoot is showing put them in a cool room until buds show - early warmth can make them budless.

Planting Outside

Dig the hole *at least* 3 times the total length of the bulb from top to bottom. To plant bulbs thickly, stagger them and plant some deeper. Deeper planting also lets you adjust their flowering time; if planting is too shallow

CHOOSING BULBS FOR THE GARDEN

Planting times

a = autumn	g = when in leaf	N = November	
ea = early autumn	O = October	Mar = March	
sp = spring	S = September	M = May	
ls = late summer			

Soils

r = rich soil	a = any good garden soil
p = peaty	wd = well drained
nd = not dry	c = needs a cool position

Colours

r = red	p = pink	o = orange	b = blue
w = white	c = cream	y = yellow	m = mauve

Positions

s = likes sun	S = full sun essential
ss = prefers semi-shade	/ either option tolerated

	Planting Time	Colour	Soil	Situation	Jan	Feb	Mar	Apr	May	Jun	Jul	Aug	Sept	Oct	Nov	Dec
Allium (ornamental onion)	a	pmy	r	S					X	X	X	X	X			
Anemone (wind flower)	a	rwbmp	c	s/ss		X	X	X	X							
Chinodoxa (glory of the snow)	a	b w	nd	s		X	X									
Colchicum (naked lady, meadow saffron)	s	pm	r wd	s	X	X							X	X		
Crocosmia (montbretia)	a	oy	wd	s						X	X	X				
Crocus	a	wymbc	a	s	X	X	X	X					X	X	X	
Cyclamen	g	pwm	pwd	ss	X	X	X			X	X	X		X	X	
Dahlia plants (dormant tubers)	M/J A/M	rpmyw	rwd	S							X	X	X			
Fritillary	S/O	m	rwd	ss				X	X							
Galanthus (snowdrop)	sp	w	a	ss		X	X									
Galtonia	a	w/c	a	s							X	X	X			
Gladioli	Mar–M	por	rwd	s					X	X	X					
Hyacinthoides (bluebells)	a	b	a	ss					X							
Hyacinthus (Roman hyacinth)	a/g	pwm	nd/wd	ss					X							
Iris	a	lybmw	rwd	S	X	X	X			X	X					
Leucojum (summer snowflake)	ea	w	rnd	ss					X	X						
Lilium (lily)	O/sp	pwoyr	wd	ss						X	X	X	X	X		
Muscari (grape hyacinth)	a	wb	a	s					X	X	X					
Narcissus (and daffodil)	S/O	yc	a	s		X	X	X	X							
Ornithogalum (star of Bethlehem)	a	w	a	s				X		X	X					
Scilla (squill)	a	b	a	s				X	X							
Tulips	O/N	proy	r	s				X	X	X	X					

X means a reasonably hardy variety of that bulb flowers in that month. But if you choose any *one* variety of a particular bulb it may only flower for one of the months given. Of course, hardiness depends on general conditions as well as temperature.

bulbs may lack the water and food they need and fail to flower. However, irises with rhizomes must be planted so the upper surface is visible, for the sun must ripen them to produce the next year's blooms. Only the grandest, such as lilies, should hold court singly. To give a natural effect, throw bulbs and plant them where they fall. In tubs and window boxes use John Innes No 2 rather than soil. For planting times see the calendar, page 364.

★ Colchicums are often called autumn crocuses. This confuses them with the crocuses which flower in autumn; a different family entirely. Count the stamens - crocuses have 3; colchicums have 6.

★ Plant colchicums where their coarse leaves, which come after the flowers, will be hidden.

A difficulty arises over cyclamen. Some say these fragile ballerinas like their tubers only *just* covered with soil; but a top supplier advises 5-10 cm (2-4 in) in very open soil with plenty of leaf mould and light shade. Once planted, they resent disturbance.

★ If you can't decide which is the top of the cyclamen tuber and which the bottom (a common problem) plant it on its side - it will sort itself out.

Dahlia tubers should be planted about 10 cm (4 in) deep, but plants should be planted according to their soil level. Space all dahlias according to their final size - their width will be about a half to three-quarters of their height. Put a stake in the hole as you plant them - adding it later risks piercing a tuber - suiting the thickness to their final size. A large dahlia needs a really thick stake.

Feeding and Care

Bulbs prefer a rich well-drained soil and those which like semi-shade enjoy leaf-mould. If the drainage is poor, tuck a little sharp sand at the bottom of the hole before planting them. They can then be kept happy with a dressing of bone meal in autumn and dried blood in spring. They also need to be watered in the months after flowering, if these months are dry, and given a liquid feed high in potash. Daffodils look tidier if you break off the seed head but are best left to die down, with no tying or fuss. Grass should not be cut until the foliage of any bulbs in it yellows. If you remove green leaves bulbs can't store up the food for next year's flowers.

Pests and diseases are mercifully rare. The biggest problem is narcissus fly and this can be treated with a proprietary insecticide. Tulip fire is relatively rare and far less likely with bulbs which are deep planted. It can be treated with an anti-fungal powder.

Storing and Propagating

Most bulbs don't like being lifted and stored but, if you have to lift them, put them in a cool airy place and brush them clean when dry. Then store them in straw in a cool dry place.

Large-flowered gladioli won't stand frost. Lift and store them in the autumn, as above (small-flowered gladioli will naturalize happily, unless conditions are very cold). Conventional tulips need to be lifted, but species and hybrid tulips can be left to naturalize provided the plant is cut off at ground level and removed when it yellows. Otherwise, disease may develop.

When daffodils, alliums, crocuses and montbretia form large clumps dig them up, just as the leaves have died, and gently divide them. They can then be stored in a cool place or replanted immediately.

Irises with rhizomes should be lifted after flowering, when they become crowded. Cut the leaves in a neat fan 10-15 cm (4-6 in) long - remove dried-out rhizomes and replant the young ones facing towards the sun, with their roots firmly down under them, and the top of the rhizome exposed.

Lift dahlias as the first frost wilts them. Cut the stems to 10 cm (4 in). Leave them upside down for a few days in a cool, airy place, brush off the soil, dust with fungicide and store in a cool place in dry peat. (You may just get away with leaving them in the ground if you cover the ground with peat and heap bracken or straw over it. Keep this down, with angled sticks or bean netting pegged over. Whether they then live or die will depend on the season, the coldness of your soil, and how far north you live.)

Companies supplying bulbs by mail order:
Avon Bulbs, Upper Westwood, Bradford-on-Avon, Wilts BA15 2AT Tel: 02216 3723 - a wide range of bulbous plants.
Walter Blom & Sons Ltd, Coombelands Nurseries, Leavesden, Watford, Herts WD2 7BH Tel: 09273 72071 - a wide range, but particularly tulips.
Broadleigh Gardens, Barr House, Bishops Hull, Taunton, Somerset TA4 1AE Tel: 0823 286231 - many bulbous plants, foliage plants, Californian irises.
Kelways Nurseries, Barrymore, Langport, Somerset TA10 9SL Tel: 0458 250521 - irises, peonies and daffodils are the specialities, but also other bulbs and border plants.
Philip Tivey and Sons, 28 Wanlip Road, Syston, Nr Leicester LE7 8PA Tel: 0533 692968 - dahlias and chrysanthemums.
Brian Matthew, *The Year Round Bulb Garden*, Souvenir Press Martyn Rix, *Growing Bulbs*, Croom Helm

Herbaceous Plants (Perennials)

Herbaceous plants are among the showiest in the garden, but they have the unfortunate habit of dying down each winter, leaving their site empty but for a few desolate stalks. A border mixing shrubs and herbaceous plants conceals this.

When they die in the centre dig the clump up in autumn or spring, split it in half, using two forks back-to-back if necessary. Remove dead and over-woody sections, split into manageable sections and replant. But some plants - generally those with fleshy roots, such as peonies - resent this disturbance.

Choosing Herbaceous Plants

The 20 plants on the following pages are among the easiest to grow and the least demanding, while being showy in either flower or foliage.

The flower is the poetry of reproduction. It is an example of the eternal seductiveness of nature. Jean Giradoux

Choosing Herbaceous Plants

Plant	Appearance	Flowers	Support	Soil	Position	Height
Alchemilla mollis (Lady's mantle)	Neat pale-green leaves with frothy greeny flowers.	July	No	Dry or moist	Shade	45 cm (18 in)
Anemone japonica (Japanese anemone)	Rose-coloured anemone flowers on tall stems.	Aug/Sept	No	Any humus	Sun or shade	45-80 cm (18 in - 3 ft)
Aster varieties (Michaelmas daisy)	Clusters of delicate daisy flowers in pinks and mauves - new varieties are bigger and better.	Sept/Oct	Maybe	Any	Sun	25-90 cm (10 in - 3 ft)
Campanula persicifolia (Persian campanula)	Delicate papery bells in white or mauve on firm stems.	May/July	No	Moist	Sun	90 cm (3 ft)
Chrysanthemum indicum varieties	The florist's style chrysanthemum in singles and doubles in every shade.	Sept/Oct	Maybe	Rich loam	Sun	60-90 cm (2 - 3 ft)
Chrysanthemum maximum (Shasta daisy)	Clumps of neat dark foliage throwing up numerous big white daisies with yellow bosses.	July/Aug	No	Loam	Sun	50-80 cm (18 in - 2½ ft)
Dianthus varieties (Garden pinks)	Like small carnations on fine stems with heady scents above grey green foliage.	June on	No	Well drained loam	Sun	15 cm (6 in)
Gaillardia (Blanket flower)	Bold daisy-like flowers.	July-Sept	Yes	Light well drained	Sun	60 cm (2 ft)
Gypsophila	Clouds of tiny white flowers on grey green stems.	Aug/Sept	Yes	Any deep	Sun	1 m (1 yd)
Hellenium	Daisy-like flowers in yellow or bronze.	July-Sept	Maybe	Any	Sun	80 cm (3 ft)
Helleborus varieties (Christmas rose)	White and greenish white anemone-shaped flowers borne in the worst weather.	Jan-April	No	Prefer rich moist loam	Shade or semi-shade	30-60 cm (1 - 2 ft)
Hemerocallis varieties (Day lily)	Clusters of big satiny trumpet-shaped flowers above strap like leaves, in yellows, reds and oranges.	July-Sept	No	Any	Sun or semi-shade	60-80 cm (2 - 3 ft)

Choosing Herbaceous Plants

Plant	Appearance	Flowers	Support	Soil	Position	Height
Hosta varieties	Handsome spade-shaped glaucous leaves with delicate understated mauve flowers.	July/Aug	No	Moist	Shade or semi-shade	45-75 cm (18 in to 2 ft 6 in)
Iris germanica (Bearded iris)	Sculptural fans of flat leaves above which rise big beautiful flowers in every possible colour.	June	No	Any well drained	Sun	75-100 cm (2½ - 3 ft)
Lupinus polyphyllus (Russell hybrid lupins)	Tall spikes for numerous pea type flowers in almost every colour. Eye catching.	June	Maybe	Light loamy	Sun	60-80 cm (2 - 3 ft)
Papaver orientalis (Oriental poppy)	Dramatic silken poppies in scarlet, salmons and pinks with silky black stamens.	June	Yes	Dry light	Sun	75 cm (2 ft 6 in)
Peony officinalis	Big silky cabbagy flowers in ruby, pink or white varieties.	June	Yes	Rich	Sun or semi-shade	46-76 cm (1½ - 2½ ft)
Phlox paniculata (Garden phlox)	Flat panicles of satiny flowers in pinks, reds and mauves and white.	July - early Sept	No	Well drained loam	Sun or semi-shade	80 cm (2 ft 8 in)
Pyrethrum	Bold daisy-shaped flowers in pinks and crimsons.	May/June	Yes	Loam	Sun	60 cm (2 ft)
Sedum spectabilis (Ice plant)	Fleshy glaucous leaves and flat wine red heads of tiny flowers massed together.	Aug/Sept	No	Any	Semi-shade	20 cm (8 in)

More information

Beth Chatto Gardens, Elmstead Market, Colchester, Essex CO7 7BD Tel: 0206 222007 - unusual herbaceous plants.

Blooms of Bressingham, Bressingham Gardens, Diss, Norfolk IP22 2AB Tel: 037 988 464

Scotts Nurseries, Merriot, Somerset TA16 5PL Tel: 0460 72306

See also, **Sherrards**, page 362; **Kelways**, page 341; **Hilliers**, page 362

Brian Davies, *The Kingfisher Guide to Garden Plants*, Kingfisher

Lawns

If you haven't got a lawn stop before you create one. In country gardens you can limit the lawn area with careful planning, and small town gardens may be far more manageable - and just as attractive - with good paving, bricks, tiles or even gravel. It costs more to lay these, but you don't have to buy a mower or edge trimmers and they will never need so much as a teaspoonful of fertilizer. If you *are* laying a lawn remember it will probably be the largest single thing in the garden. This visual domination means that its shape dictates what the whole garden will look like. A strip of straight-edged lawn creates a garden like a green railway line. Curve it and introduce hidden surprises and you can make a small garden seem big, and a big one charming. Make shapes with a long rope or hosepipe before deciding how the lawn should be.

Creating a Lawn

November to March is the best time to prepare for a lawn. Clear the ground, removing deep weeds and rubble. Dig it thoroughly, adding peat, compost or leafmould to improve it. Also add coarse sand if the ground is heavy: waterlogged ground encourages numerous lawn problems.

Level it carefully with a rake and the edge of a long plank, and roll it *lightly*. Then leave it for a month or, better still, all summer. If necessary, use a systemic weedkiller to eradicate problems, such as bindweed.

Seeding a Lawn

The grass family is enormous and the best of the new grass mixtures give strength and limited growth and a compact look. But many grasses professional lawnsmen use are not sold to the general public. Instead, outdated grass seed is often offered. Even well-known companies sell mixtures based on coarse agricultural ryegrasses which, in the opinion of one turf expert, are not suitable 'even for low quality football pitches'.

The best lawn grasses are only sold in large quantities. But gardening clubs and those prepared to buy 25 kg or more might find it useful to obtain the inexpensive leaflet 'Turfgrass Seed' from the Sports Turf Research Institute (opposite). It lists grasses used by professionals and analyses each for shortness of growth, summer greenness and compactness - plus seed merchants who may sell them. A lawn needs a combination of grasses. For a family lawn which will withstand reasonable wear but look fine-leaved and uniform a good mixture is:

50 per cent turf type (not agricultural) perennial ryegrass
20 per cent smooth-stalked meadow grass
20-25 per cent red fescue
5-10 per cent bent

If you pick varieties in the 'Turfgrass Seed' leaflet which score As or Bs for low growth and compactness (density), you should be able to create an impressive lawn which needs a minimum of maintenance. The fescues, which score A on growth, only grow 5-6 inches in a full season. Or pick varieties recommended by a *Gardening Which* trial.

Grass seeds like warm ground. So, sow from late August through September, or April-May, according to the weather, when the soil is damp, not wet. First rake in 60 g (2 oz) of Growmore per square yard, or an autumn lawn food, even if it's spring. Then sow evenly, allowing 40-50 g (1½-2 oz) of seed per sq m (sq yd).

★ Just weigh it out once, put it in an old yoghurt carton and mark the level on the carton for future batches. Sow half across the square and the other up and down it.
★ If you are vague about the size of a square metre (or like to be exact) make a yard wide 'railway line' with two long strings and place yard-marker sticks across.

Rake the seed in *lightly*, water regularly and don't walk on it. With this much seed bird theft should be no disaster, but re-sow bare patches after 8 weeks. When the grass is 5 cm (2 in) high, roll it *lightly* (e.g. pull a mower over it without mowing) and mow *very* lightly next day. Keep *just* trimming the tops until it's established, but don't use it for 3 months, and go easy for a year. Don't use weedkiller until it's grown up.

Creating a Lawn with Turf
Turf creates a lawn faster, but the grass is less. Check it carefully before you buy. The best time to lay is October or November - though you can still lay until February. Place a plank against the lawn edge. Stand on the plank and lay the turfs against it, butt them closely together. Place the plank on the turfs - your weight will firm them. Lay against the previous row - but stagger the joins, like bricks - and cut turfs to shape

with a half-moon lawn edger. Water it, and leave it unmowed and unwalked on for 4-6 weeks. Then treat it very gently for several months, never letting it dry out.

Lawn Care and Maintenance
Mow grass, if it's growing, when it needs it. If the weather is very mild there's no point in letting the grass get long just because it's December. Mow to a shorter length for well-fed luxury lawns made from fine grasses. Most family lawns will be better if mown to a longer length.

Have the blade set high for the first mow or two, and leave *short* clippings on the lawn; they keep it healthier. Long clippings, however, must be removed as they kill the grass.

Feeding
Each mowing takes goodness away from the grass. So, unless the lawn gets something back, it will slowly decline. In the spring and early summer it needs nitrogen. In tests by the Consumers Association, home-made lawn sand, Growmore or sulphate of ammonia all compared well with branded lawn foods costing more. There are several recipes for lawn sand, but theirs was 1 part ferrous sulphate:3 parts ammonium sulphate:20 parts sharp sand, applied at 140 g per sq m (4 oz a sq yd). For Growmore and sulphate of ammonia use about a handful to the sq yd. All three need only be applied in spring and perhaps again in summer. The ferrous sulphate in the lawn sand will also deter moss.

Lawns also need humus and, as they like acid, a scattering of fine peat in autumn is good. (If the soil is clay use 2 parts peat:1 sharp sand.) Apply enough to cover well without stifling the grass. This isn't essential, but you get a better lawn. Add potash too if you can.

Problems in Lawns

Bare Patches
Prick the earth all over with a fork. Sift on a thin layer of good soil. Water it, and sow and treat it like a new lawn.

Brown Patches
Brown patches can be caused by urine from bitches, vixens, spilt oil or petrol, leatherjackets (daddy-long-legs' larvae) eating the roots, and certain diseases. Spike the area well to improve the drainage and discourage leatherjackets, and - if the patches are persistent - water with Benylate against diseases, or apply an insecticide to kill the leatherjackets.

★ To catch leatherjackets water the grass in the evening, and cover it with a plastic or a tarpaulin. Next morning the leatherjackets should be on the surface ready to be removed.

Bumps and Troughs
It is easier to fill in dips than remove bumps. So start by sifting soil into any dips, so it almost covers the tips

of mown grass. When it grows through sift on some more, and repeat until the hollow is level.

For bumps, make shaped slits straddling the bump. Cut away under the grass roots, roll it back level the soil, roll back the turf, firm and water it.

Disease
Treat red thread, which causes pinkish patches with sulphate of ammonia. Fusarium, a disease causing yellowy brown patches on lawns, can be treated with Benylate.

Fairy Ring
This is a ring of fungus which releases nitrogen, and makes the grass a deeper green, but will kill it in time. Use a fungicide.

Generally Poor Condition
A lawn which is well past its best can be renovated. In late summer rake it very well, removing moss and matted grass. Fertilize as page 344. In September sow with a fine turf-type ryegrass at 20-25 g (1 oz) to the sq m (yd). If you can't get a top professional seed go for Hunter - a variety which is available to gardeners. If necessary you can mow over it with a rotary mower (until it reaches blade height), but not with a hover. Next spring mow it in gently, setting the blades high at first.

★ For moles there is no sure cure, except enlisting a mole catcher, or a rodent officer from the local council. It is variously claimed that garlic, mothballs and slices of lemon down their holes, or *Euphorbia lathyrus* planted at intervals, deter them.

Moss
Moss is worst in shade or when drainage is poor. To keep it at bay rake the grass regularly, spiking it to let the air in, and feeding it well. There are also moss killing granules and sprays which will kill moss for a season. But unless you get rid of the cause it will come back.

Weeds
Weeds should be little trouble if a lawn is mown regularly. If you use a lawn weedkiller apply it immediately after mowing, and at the next mowing leave the box off so the clippings lie on the lawn. They should *not* be composted. Mowings after that can usually be composted, unless the manufacturers say otherwise, but cannot be used as a mulch.

Slime
This is found when the ground is waterlogged and compacted, especially under trees, and is a coating of algae. Unless the cause is cured it will keep returning. Improve the drainage by major spiking; scatter coarse sand or fine gravel on the area and brush it into the holes; cover it with peat and sand and re-sow.

Lawn Watering
Lawns should not be watered every day - even in a drought - it encourages a shallow root system. Instead, water more thoroughly less often. A lawn needs about an inch of rainfall a week. Put an empty jam jar within the spray area and move the hose when the jam jar holds an inch.

Lawn Mowers
There is no one mower which has all the answers. If you must have stripes rotary mowers do the best job. But the fast, efficient, petrol-driven ones are heavy to turn, and the starter cord is often an invitation to back trouble. The electric ones are slower and have all the hassles of the electric flex, without the ease of movement you have with a hover. To make up for this, some, such as the Qualcast Concorde range, have a lawn-raking attachment which makes very short work of one of the worst jobs in the garden.

If you simply want an easy life a hover, *with* a box which collects the grass, has the edge. It will cut a swathe through long grass and nose neatly under the unstaked shrubs which tumble across its path. It also feels effortless. The disadvantages are that the sward never has quite that brushed-velvet finish, there is no weight to roll out bumps and you have to contend with the cable.

Whichever you buy, do get a machine that is large enough. There is no point in marching 30 times the length of your lawn if you can cut it in 20 with a wider blade.

★ The cable from electric lawnmowers is easier to control if you put it over your shoulder. But it is wise to use a circuit breaker.

Lawnmower Care
Clean a lawnmower well at the end of the season and send it to be sharpened, and overhauled if it needs it. If it doesn't come back with oiled blades use an old-fashioned cotton-headed dish mop to apply oil - then your fingers won't get cut. Cover the engine with a large paper sack to keep out dust and leaves. But turn the motor over every few weeks in winter, then it will be easy to start in spring.

Sports Turf Research Institute, Bingley, West Yorks BD16 1AV Tel: 0274 565131

Pests and Diseases
Skill with these has two aspects - reducing the vulnerability of the plants, and attacking the pests and diseases before they get a hold. One of the more unlikely methods of doing this was put forward in the first edition of *Enquire Within*: to get rid of grubs in fruit trees and bushes it advised that a fire should be built in the orchard:

> so that the smoke may blow among the trees, you will destroy thousands; for the grubs have such an objection to smoke that very little makes them roll themselves up and fall off.

Reducing Vulnerability
● Good feeding and watering make strong healthy plants more able to withstand attacks of any kind.
● Choose varieties which resist disease.

- Burn any dead material so it won't harbour trouble.
- Encourage the natural parasites of potential pests.
- Grow companion plants (see page 348).

Snails are particularly fond of bran; if a little is spread upon the ground, and covered with cabbage-leaves or tiles, they will congregate under them in great numbers, and by examining them every morning, and destroying them, their numbers will be materially decreased.

Enquire Within, 1856

Nipping Trouble in the Bud
- Check plants regularly and pick off any diseased leaves, or remove the first signs of caterpillars by hand.
- At the first sign of trouble introduce any biological controls which are available.

Or

- Decide at the start of the season that you will use chemicals and plan your spraying programme before trouble starts. Many pests have life cycles in which

it is essential to catch them at a particular stage if they are to be killed. Whitefly, for example, has 5 stages and is only vulnerable to pesticides in 3 of them. By hitting pests at a vulnerable stage you can often stop trouble quickly using a minimum application. But if you let a pest get established, you may need to spray again and again to get results.
- Most diseases are fungal. There is usually a three-way choice; cross your fingers and hope it won't spread, destroy the plant or spray.

Before resorting to sprays read what Dr Stefan Buczacki (page 368) has to say about using garden sprays for particular problem. Some are very good, but he is decidedly pessimistic about the effectiveness of chemicals on certain problems - you could just be using up your leisure for very small returns.

Treating Pests and Diseases

Problem	Natural Method	Chemical Method
Aphids	Introduce or encourage ladybirds and hoverflies. Hoverflies like bell- and daisy-shaped flowers and adore buckwheat. One hoverfly larva will eat 1,000.	Spray with pirimicarb (Rapid) (designed not to harm bees, ladybirds or lacewings).
Blackspot	Buy resistant rose varieties. Remove and burn affected leaves. Hard prune the following year to remove infected wood.	Spray with 'Roseclear' (designed not to harm bees, ladybirds or lacewings).
Canker on fruit trees	Cut out infected area or cut off the branch and burn it. Use a wound seal on the cut.	Spray new trees with benomyl, but established canker may resist it. If so, burn the tree.
Carrot root flies	Delay sowing until May to miss one generation of flies. Sow very thinly (thinning attracts them). If you must thin, remove thinnings and water to damp the smell. Have a string soaked in creosote (but not dripping) stretched above the row. Plant onions next to carrots and pull thin carrots. In winter clear the ground totally and put mothballs down.	Not well controlled by chemicals, but apply bromophos or diazinon granules to seed drill, then in August/September drench the soil in a solution of trichlorpon.
Caterpillars	Pick them off by hand on sight, and crush all eggs. Most effective when done early.	Spray with an insecticide such as HCH or permethrin (Picket).
Clubroot	Apply lime before planting and improve soil texture: it is worst on poorly drained acid soils. Use a long rotation and burn affected plants immediately. Scrub tools with hot soapy water.	There is no known cure for this. Dipping plants in a clubroot dip before planting may help.

Problem	Natural Method	Chemical Method
Codlin moth	Use the pheromone trap 'Trappit' (page 348) to catch the males from mid-May, so they fail to mate. Encourage tits: they eat the caterpillars.	Spray with permethrin (Picket) or fenitrothion about mid-June, after blossoming, and again 3 weeks later - *before* damage is seen.
Earwigs	Stuff straw into flowerpots and upturn them on sticks. Burn the contents each morning.	Treat plant with malathion or HCH.
Eelworm	Burn all infected plants - bulbs, fruit, onions, phlox, etc. Keep those plants off the soil for 3 years.	None.
Fireblight	This disease is subject to statutory control; it is widespread south of a line from Preston to Hull. But you need not destroy the plants, and only nurseries need notify the Ministry of Agriculture. It is caused by a bacterium. Prune out and burn infected branches to below the staining. Treat the cut with a bacterial paste and sterilize tools afterwards.	There is no chemical treatment.
Leaf miner	Remove and burn affected leaves. Get rid of groundsel and sowthistle, which may harbour the pest.	Spray with Lindex or Symbol 2.
Mildew	Remove affected leaves and burn them.	Spray with buppirimate and triforine (Nimrod I) or propiconazole (Tumbleblite).
Onion root fly	Plant carrots by them - the scent of carrots masks the onion scent. The pupae overwinter in the soil. Dig well in autumn.	HCH helps but can contaminate the onions. Apply bromophos, diazinon or chlorpyrifos granules before sowing.
Silverleaf (a silvery sheen to leaves of plum trees with a mauve fungus on dead branches)	Wood must be sawn off by mid-summer and burnt. Sometimes the problem clears itself up. If not, dig up the tree and burn it with as much root as possible. Treat as fireblight.	There is no chemical solution to silverleaf.
Wilt in seedlings (the lower stem blackens and they bend)	Start with clean compost and a clean greenhouse or propagator and you shouldn't get it.	Drench the soil with Cheshunt Compound, or a fungicide containing benlate or mankozeb at the first sign of trouble.
Woolly Aphid	A natural parasite of woolly aphids called *Aphelinus mali* is now established in southern England. Avoid using chemicals if it may be present. Prune out severely infected wood. Grease bands can be applied in September and left until spring.	Systemic insecticides like dimethoate or formothion or contact insecticides like malathion or HCH.

★ Some insecticides are formulated to be harmless to bees. If using any others don't spray until evening, then the bees will be out of harm's way.

Treating Problems in the Greenhouse

Problem	Natural Method	Chemical Method
Mealy bugs	Introduce the Australian ladybird *Cryptolaemus montrouzeri* which eats these and scale insects. Or swab off with cotton wool and methylated spirits.	Their coating resists contact insecticide. Use a systemic such as formothion.
Red spider	Introduce a mite called *Phytoseiulus* which eats them.	If you spray, change the chemical regularly as they rapidly become immune.
Scale insects	Swab off with meths on cotton wool.	Easily killed with a contact insecticide in the early crawling stage. Once attached use a systemic such as formothion.
Slugs	Create slug pubs by sinking yoghurt cartons or saucers filled with beer slops (free from pubs) at intervals in the soil; or put bran under cabbage leaves and seek and destroy those that collect each morning.	Slug pellets - there is also a slug and snail powder which claims to be totally harmless to birds.
Whitefly	Introduce the chalcid wasp (*Encarsia formosa*) which eats them. Grow some nasturtiums nearby to keep whitefly or greenfly off tomatoes.	Spray with permethrin every 7 to 14 days.

Pest predators only control pests once they have bred and built up numbers. Not all domestic greenhouses have the right conditions for this, and they may walk out through the ventilation without doing their job. Natural Pest Control (see below) sells them, but check if they suit your situation.

Biological controls are nothing new. In ancient times the Chinese fostered the ants which ate destructive insects, and even built bamboo bridges so the ants could cross from one tree to the next.

Companion Plants

It has long been thought that some plants protect others from pests and diseases. The scientific evidence for this is, on the whole, lacking. But it's hard to believe that anything would be passed down for centuries if it had no truth in it. Some traditional pairings are:

● sage to keep away cabbage whites
● savory to keep blackfly off broad beans
● cabbage near celery to ward off leaf miner
● French marigold near cabbage to ward off cabbage whites
● nasturtiums with tomatoes against whitefly and greenfly
● garlic with roses against whitefly and greenfly.

★ Bird damage to fruit can be prevented by throwing an old net curtain over any small bush. Birds get entangled in cotton but not in curtains.

★ If mice are prone to pinch the pea seeds or crocus corms tuck holly leaves round these as you plant them. Mice hate pricked noses. A less charming method is to taint the seeds by rinsing them in a weak solution of paraffin.

More information

The **British Agrochemicals Association**, 4 Lincoln Court, Lincoln Road, Peterborough PE1 2RP Tel: 0733 49225 - has a consumer information service with free and low-cost leaflets.

Fisons Horticulture, Paper Mill Lane, Bramford, Ipswich IP8 4BZ Tel: 0473 830492 - the consumer information service for both Fison and Murphy.

ICI Garden Products, Woolmead House East, Woolmead Walk, Farnham, Surrey GU9 7UB Tel: 0252 724525 - has a consumer information service with useful booklets.

Natural Pest Control, Watermead Road, Yapton, Barnham, Bognor, Sussex PO22 0BQ Tel: 0243 553250 - supplies predators to control insect pests.

Steele and Brodie, Stevens Drove, Houghton, Stockbridge, Hampshire SO20 6LP Tel: 0794 388698 - sells the pheromone trap 'Trappit' for male codlin moths.

The Royal Horticultural Society (see page 368) has a list of companies supplying insect predators.

Stefan Buczacki and Keith Harris, *Collins Guide to Pests, Diseases and Disorders of Garden Plants*, Collins

Propagation

Most plants will root if you pick the right part of their anatomy. They usually root best by the type of tissue which makes up the biggest portion of their structure. So trees root from hardwood cuttings, plants with big tap roots do best from root cuttings, and fleshy leaved houseplants root best from leaf cuttings. Whatever the cutting, take plenty as some always fail.

To a professional gardener the divisions between stem cuttings, green-wood cuttings, soft-wood cuttings and semi-ripe cuttings are subtle and important, but the method is broadly as follows.

Shoot Cuttings

- Take 8-10 cm (3-4 in) shoots.
- Remove all but the top 2-3 leaves, and shorten to just below a leaf joint.
- Dip shy rooters in hormone rooting powder.
- Push them into pencil holes in a moist mixture of equal parts sand and peat.
- Stand the pot in a plastic bag, with sticks to keep the bag off the leaves. Close and place on a north- or east-facing window ledge.
- Wipe out excess condensation.
- Repot individually and harden off when roots form.

> Geraniums are an exception. Leave the bag off and don't water: they like it dry. Harder wood and cuttings in a greenhouse or frame can also do without the bag.

Hardwood Cuttings

In winter take newly ripened wood from a shrub or tree, cut to 13-25-cm (5-10-in) lengths, cutting the tops at an angle and the bottoms straight across. Dig a trench in some fertile soil, insert the cuttings a hand's span apart so only the top 2-3 buds show. Fill in the soil and firm it. Water for 9 months and then transplant.

Root Cuttings

These are just 5-cm (2-in) lengths of thick root which are placed in compost and allowed to sprout. Lie them on their sides and *don't* use rooting powder on them - you need shoots not roots. Try this with oriental poppies, acanthus and phlox.

★ When carrying cuttings from other gardens blow up the plastic bag, like a balloon and tie the neck tightly: the moist air will cushion the cuttings against knocks.

★ The purpose of plants is reproduction. If we frustrate by dead-heading many will flower week after week in their attempts to produce seeds. With others dead-heading produces more next year. So it pays dividends.

★ If you have a hanging basket which is too high to water easily, just lob ice cubes in. If you include fertilizer in the ice cubes put that ice tray in a labelled plastic bag - fertilized gin and tonic is no joke.

> To find fertilizers and grow bags based on organic materials contact the **Henry Doubleday Research Centre** (page 368). Fertilizers based on cow manure can be obtained from **Stimgro Ltd**, Bridge House, 97-101 High Street, Tonbridge, Kent TN9 1DR.

Layering

Find a young, flexible, fast growing shoot near the ground - on the sunny side of the shrub. Prepare the ground under it with slow release fertilizer, such as bonemeal, adding sharp sand and organic matter to give a potting compost texture. Dig a short trench some 15 cm (6 in) deep, as shown.

Make a slash on the underside from just below a leaf node, up towards the tip to the centre of the stem. Insert a used matchstick into the slit and brush on hormone rooting powder, for hard-wood cuttings. Remove leaves below soil level and peg it down with strong bent wire. Cover and firm well in. In about 18 months the plant should be ready. Cut it carefully from its parent a few weeks before potting it up and only lift it if the roots seem well established.

More information

Philip McMillan Browse, *Plant Propagation*, Mitchell Beazley

John Innes Potting Compost

Even the best soil isn't ideal for growing seedlings and potting up, so a special mixture is usually recommended, the most popular being John Innes No 1 or 2. Although John Innes compost is available commercially, anyone can make it themselves if they can buy the basic ingredients. The recipe was devised at the John Innes Research Institute and made freely available as a contribution to the war effort in the Second World War. The basic mixture is:

3 parts granulated peat (e.g. sphagnum moss peat)
7 parts loose medium loam (stacked a year and sterilized if possible)
2 parts coarse lime-free sand.

The fertilizer used with this is made by mixing:

2 parts hoof and horn meal
2 parts by weight superphosphate of lime
1 part by weight sulphate of potash.

> The measuring container will be far larger for the basic mixture than for the fertilizer.

John Innes No 1: mix 110 g (4 oz) of the fertilizer mixture to 8 gallons of the basic mixture. This is used for potting delicate plants. Also add 20 g (¾ oz) of ground chalk or limestone to each 8 gallons unless you will be planting lime hating plants.

John Innes No 2: add 8 oz of the fertilizer, and limestone as above. This is used for most plants.

John Innes No 3: a rich mixture using 12 oz of fertilizer and is for well-established plants.

Pruning

Pruning depends on:

- the type of plant
- its particular variety within that family
- the conditions in your area
- how long the plant has been established.

Why Prune?

The main reasons for pruning are:

- The leading bud in a shoot is always dominant and will take the lion's share of the food available to that twig or branch, leaving side shoots to get the leftovers. Only by removing the leader can you stimulate side shoots. As many plants flower or fruit on new wood, this gives twice the crop.
- To stay healthy some plants need to throw up new shoots from the base. They will only do this if others are cut out from the base - or fairly near it.
- Vigorous plants grow so thickly that branches may die back if the plant isn't given air. Pruning gives it air without spoiling the shape - nature may not be so careful.
- Leaving dead or unduly old wood on a plant fosters pests and diseases.
- Shortening stems reduces the risk of the wind rocking the plants and loosening the roots.
- Pruning newly planted shrubs almost immediately often helps them to establish. (With container grown plants only prune in the correct pruning season.)
- Some shrubs and trees just need to be kept to a good shape or prevented from getting out of hand.

How to Prune

If disease and die-back are to be avoided the first essential is to have really sharp secateurs and (if needed) a sharp saw which won't bruise the stem, drag at the bark or leave rough pieces standing up.

- Pruning cuts must be *just* above a growing point (bud or eye) and must slope away from it.
- On woody branches the buds may not show. So, cut dead wood back to a healthy branch at a neat angle.
- Cuts which are more than 1 cm (½ in) across must be painted with a 'wound paint' to fight possible infection.
- To decide where to cut, look at the shape of the whole plant.

How Much to Prune

Evergreens seldom need pruning. With deciduous shrubs, the amount of pruning needed varies greatly according to the individual plant. Buddleias, for example, need to be cut right back to within a few inches of the growing point of the branch. This looks like a massacre, but by July the long arching branches will have returned, whereas unpruned it will become a straggly mess. Most shrubs need less draconian measures. When in doubt remove one third of the oldest growth to ground level on shrubs and climbers over 3 years old. But it is far better to find out their exact needs; even roses don't conform to the rules you might expect. Pruning stimulates growth, so the more vigorous the rose the less harshly you prune.

The importance of meeting each plant's needs holds good not just between families - shrub roses needing less pruning than bush roses - but also between individual varieties. For, like people, even roses within a single family have their own strengths and weaknesses to be considered before you cut. Learning to understand their personalities can be one of the most satisfying aspects of gardening. Anne Countess of Rosse, who created Nymans and Birr Castle attributes her success to 'love ... of plants and motherly understanding of their whims'.

When to Prune

To know when to prune you have to know the habits of the plant in question. The nursery you bought it from should be happy to tell advise you. However, trees and shrubs can broadly be divided into two groups -

those which flower or fruit on last year's wood you prune soon after flowering, to give it a full year to grow those flower buds.

those which flower or fruit on this year's wood you have to prune a little earlier the same year - or prune so late the previous year that no growth will occur after pruning.

Fruit Pruning

Fruit pruning varies greatly with the type of fruit. However, for most fruit, pruning is light for the first year, then in the following years a third to a half of the length of the main shoots is removed. When trained on walls many types of fruit benefit from having unsuitable side shoots removed between July and September.

Rose Pruning

This subject needs the details found in the book recommended opposite. What follows is simply an outline. On all roses:

- Cut dead or diseased wood away to where the stem looks healthy.
- Cut to an eye which points outwards in a suitable direction. Cut immediately above the eye at 45°.
- On types which develop mildew or blackspot cut out enough wood to let the light get to all the leaves when they develop.
- Halve the length of any blind shoots - those which have no bud at the end when others are flowering.

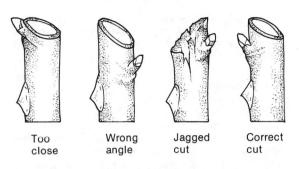

Too close   Wrong angle   Jagged cut   Correct cut

Pruning a Hybrid Tea Rose

- Dead-head to the first outward pointing leaf below any divisions for the flowers.
- Most roses are grafted on to the roots of wild roses. Any shoots thrown out from *below* the rootstock (the point from which the main shoots spring) are suckers of the wild rose type (the leaves have more sections). Remove them on sight, or they will take nourishment from the main shoots. If you cut them they will produce *two* suckers for every one. Instead, dig back to where they come from and tear them roughly off.
- Burn the prunings immediately or they can harbour disease.

> When planting new roses cut the first few inches from the stems and trim off any bruised or broken roots before planting.

Floribundas

The first spring cut all stems back to 15-23 cm (6-9 in) from the ground. When spring pruning in following years:

- cut new shoots by only a third
- cut year-old wood 15-23 cm (6-9 in) long
- cut older wood 10-15 cm (4-6 in) long
- completely remove stems crowding the centre.

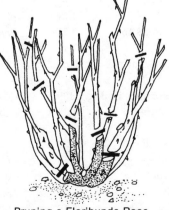

Pruning a Floribunda Rose

Hybrid Teas

Cut back in March to about 15 cm (6 in) the first year. In other years cut vigorous stems to 23 cm (9 in), the rest to 15 cm (6 in) and cut out branches which crowd the centre.

Climbers and Ramblers

Climbers and ramblers fall into several groups and the pruning needs more detail than there is space for here, but the book recommended below gives it all. Dead-head by cutting back the flowering shoot to 3-4 eyes.

Species and Shrub Roses

Hybrid musks, rugosas, gallicas, moss and damask roses, China roses and Bourbons are not pruned for the first year but need some pruning in February or March after that, and some also need summer pruning. This is usually light but varies considerably with the type.

More information

Christopher Brickell (Director General of the RHS), *Pruning,* Mitchell Beazley - few books manage to be totally clear and very comprehensive. This is both.

Seeds

Preparation for Sowing Outside

- Dig over the area and remove weeds.
- Rake the soil until fine, but not dusty, removing debris.
- Tread firm and rake in phosphate fertilizer.
- Draw lines to mark where the seeds go.
- Draw drills (minute trenches) in the soil with a stick if the seeds will be sown in lines.
- Sow thinly (1-2 cm, ¼-½ in, apart is ideal).

★ Mix very fine seeds with fine sand to make it easier not to sow too thickly.
★ To get seeds off to a moist start, mix them into some wallpaper paste. Put it in a plastic bag, cut a very small corner off the bag and squeeze the seeds and paste out along a row as if icing a cake.

Golden Rules for Success

- Sow seeds when the temperature will never be above or below the levels they need for germination (page 352).
- On average sow them not more than 1-2 times their

own depth - unless otherwise instructed on the packet.

- Keep them watered but not sodden.
- Thin out the seedlings at 1 in high or if 2 true leaves.

★ Mark out the edge of each flower you are seeding, with a channel filled with sand then you can see which seeds are where.

Seed Sowing Inside

- Fill a seed tray with *moist* seed compost - garden soil contains weeds and bacteria (but if you want to use it you will get better results with 1 part of peat:1 part of sharp sand:6 parts of soil.
- Don't sprinkle fine seeds too closely, and place pea or similar seeds 2·5 cm (1 in) apart. Cover (as above).
- Cover the tray with glass or cling film, then with paper to block the light and place in a warm position.
- When the first shoots appear remove the paper and place the tray in full light.
- When the shoots become tiny plants remove the glass or film.
- When just large enough to handle, transfer to another seed tray a couple of inches apart.
- Plant them out when well established and the weather is warm enough.

★ The trays can be anything with drainage. If you have nowhere to plant seeds inside big polystyrene boxes discarded by fish markets can be used as a cold frame outside.

★ Try sowing seeds in compost in a half-round gutter in a greenhouse or propagator. For transplanting you just remove the gutter end and slide the seedlings off with the minimum of disturbance.

★ Store seeds is in a concertina file. If each section is allotted a month, or half month, you can allocate each packet to the month for sowing. For succession sowing move it on through the file after each sowing.

Problem Seeds

Certain seeds will only grow successfully when given special treatment. Those which will not transplant usually say so on the packet. If seeds need to be pre-chilled sow them in small trays or pots and put them in the salad section of a domestic refrigerator (about 1°C, 33°F) for 3-5 weeks. If you haven't got room for that pop the sealed packet in there for the 3-5 weeks before sowing.

For marrow and courgette seeds and others of this family counteract the strait-jacket of their tough little coating by making a small nick in the edge and soaking them in lukewarm water for an hour or so.

Parsley is a slow germinator, but is improved by a soak in hot water a few hours before sowing. The old saying is that whoever can make parsley grow wears the trousers in the household.

Flower Seeds - Shelf Life and Germination

I am indebted to the seedsmen Thompson & Morgan for the following tables. These show their research findings on the conditions needed for successfully growing the most popular flowers and vegetables from seed. Storage times are, of course, for quality seeds, packed in foil and kept in a cool even temperature. Seeds in an open packet may keep less well, but they are usually best in a screw-top jar in a cool dark place.

Sowing and Storing the Seeds of Flowers

Flower	Storage Time in Years	Ideal Germination Conditions		Factors Affecting Germination	Days till Germination	When to Sow
		°C	°F			
Ageratum	2	21°-24°(70°-75°)		Needs light	10-14	*Sp*
Alyssum	3	18°-24°(65°-75°)		Needs light	7-14	*LW/ESp*
Antirrhinum	2	18°-24°(65°-75°)		Needs light	10-21	*Sp*
Aster	2	18°-21°(65°-70°)		Pre-chill perennial asters for 2 weeks	10-21	*Sp*
Begonia	nil	21°-27°(70°-80°)		Don't cover with soil; put plastic over seed box	15-60	*LW/Sp*
Cactus	nil	24°-27°(75°-80°)		Sow uncovered in furrows in box	5-180	*Green*
Calceolaria	nil	15° (59°)		Above this temperature less germination	14-21	*Green*
Coleus	2	18°-24°(65°-75°)		Indoors only in good light	10-20	*LW/Sp*
Cyclamen	1	13°-16°(55°-60°)		Above this temperature germination may stop	30-60	*LW/Sp* or *LS/A*
Dahlia	nil	18°-21°(65°-70°)		Keep compost moist	5-20	*Sp*
Delphinium	nil	10°-13°(50°-55°)		Less germination above this temperature	14-28	*LW/Sp*
Dianthus	2	18°-25°(65°-77°)			14-21	*LW/Sp* or *LS/A*

Flower	Storage Time in Years	Ideal Germination Conditions		Factors Affecting Germination	Days till Germination	When to Sow
		°C	°F			
Geranium	1	22°-24°(72°-75°)			3-21	*LW/Sp*
Gloxinia	nil	18°-24°(65°-75°)		Don't cover seed; keep moist; put plastic over box	15-30	*Green*
Impatiens	2	21°-24°(70°-75°)		Needs high humidity	21-30	*Sp*
Marigold	3	21°-24°(70°-75°)			5-14	*Sp*
Nicotiana	2	21°-24°(70°-75°)			10-20	*Sp*
Pansy	1	18°-24°(65°-75°)		Pre-chill for 2 weeks	14-21	*LW/Sp* or *LS/A*
Petunia	1	18°-25°(65°-77°)		Germinates best at the higher temperature	10-21	*Sp*
Primula - indoors	nil	13°-16°(55°-60°)		Higher temperatures reduce germination	20-25	*Green*
Salvia	1	18°-27°(65°-80°)		Pre-chill 3 weeks	10-14	*LW/ESp*
Sweet peas	2	13°-16°(55°-60°)		File or soak seeds	10-20	*LW/ESp*
Wallflower	3	18°-24°(65°-75°)			10-14	*LSp/ES*
Zinnia	1	21°-27°(70°-80°)		Sow in individual pots	10-24	*Sp*

ESp = Early Spring	*S* = Summer	*A* = Autumn
Sp = Spring	*LS* = Late Summer	*LW* = Late Winter
Pre-chill - see left	*Green* = sow in a greenhouse	

Vegetable Seeds - Shelf Life and Germination

Vegetable	Storage Time in Years	Ideal Germination Conditions		Factors Affecting Germination
		°C	°F	
Artichoke	1	13°-18°(55°-65°)		
Beans - French	1	24°-27° (75°-80°)		Won't germinate below 51°F
Beans - broad	1	21°-24° (70°-75°)		Germination from 41° to 90°F
Beans - runner	1	24°-27° (75°-80°)		Won't germinate below 51°F
Beetroot	4	open ground		Germination from 45° to 80°F
Broccoli	3	21°-24° (70°-75°)		Germination from 41°-90°F
Brussels sprouts	3	21°-24° (70°-75°)		Germination from 41°-90°F
Carrots	3	open ground		Germination from 45°-80°F
Cabbages	3	21°-24° (70°-75°)		Germination from 41°-90°F
Cauliflowers	3	21°-24° (70°-75°)		Germination from 41°-90°F
Celery	4-5	10°-18° (50°-65°)		Only those temperatures work
Celeriac	4-5	10°-18° (50°-65°)		Only those temperatures work
Chard	4	open ground		Germinates from 45°-80°F
Chicory	3	open ground		
Chinese greens	3	21°-24° (70°-75°)		
Corn salad	2	open ground		
Courgettes	4	24°-27° (75°-80°)		Won't germinate below 56°F
Cucumbers	4	24°-27° (75°-80°)		Won't germinate below 56°F
Curly endive	3	open ground		
Gourds	4	24°-27° (75°-80°)		Won't germinate below 56°F

Vegetable	Storage Time in Years	Ideal Germination Conditions		Factors Affecting Germination
		°C	°F	
Kale	3	21°-24°	(70°-75°)	Germination from 41°-90°F
Leeks	1-3	21°-24°	(70°-75°)	Germination from 45°-75°F
Lettuce	3	open ground		
- butterhead				Won't germinate above 77°F
- crisphead				Won't germinate above 85°F
Marrows	5	21°-24°	(75°-80°)	Won't germinate below 56°F
Mange-touts	1	open ground		Germination from 41°-90°F
Melons	4	21°-27°	(75°-80°)	Won't germinate below 56°F
Onions	1-3	21°-24°	(70°-75°)	Germination from 45°-75°F
Parsnips	nil	open ground		Germination from 45°-80°F
Parsley	1	open ground		
Peas	1	open ground		Germination from 41°-90°F
Pimentos	1	21°-27°	(75°-80°)	Only above 60°F
Radishes	4	open ground		Germination from 41°-90°F
Spinach	1	open ground		
Spinach beet	4	open ground		Germination from 45°-80°F
Sweetcorn	1	21°-27°	(75°-80°)	Only above 51°F
Tomatoes	4	21°-24°	(70°-75°)	Only above 51°F
Turnips	1	open ground		Germination from 41°-90°F

Those marked 'open ground' must be planted directly into their final site when the temperature is right for germination. The rest can, in theory, be started in a greenhouse or out of doors, but the temperature needed for germination may make an outdoor site unsuitable at some times of the year - or, indeed, at all.

Mail Order Seeds

Chiltern Seeds Bortree Stile, Ulverston, Cumbria LA12 7PB Tel: 0229 56946 (CC) - its quirky dimensions make this the most irritating catalogue in the business, but their selection is good and includes many British wild flowers.

Suffolk Herbs, Sawyers Farm, Little Cornard, Sudbury, Suffolk CO10 0NY Tel: 0787 227247 - a very unusual, ecology-minded list with flowers for butterflies and cottage gardens.

Thompson & Morgan, London Road, Ipswich IP2 0BA Tel: 0473 688821 (CC) - includes many unusual seeds. They also publish a magazine with advice and information on growing from seed.

Unwins Seeds Ltd, Histon, Cambridge CB4 4LE Tel: 0945 588522 (CC)

Soils and Fertilizers

There are three important qualities to soil:
● the size of the particles
● the extent to which it is acid or alkaline
● its richness in a whole range of plant foods

The ideal soil is a loam with a good balance of clay, sand and humus (organic matter). Put a few spoonfuls of your soil in a tall glass container, add water, shake it well and wait to see what layers it settles in. Humus will largely float and provides many plant foods. Sand will go to the bottom and clay will sit on the sand. Sand has large particles; clay very fine ones. But the extent to which the clay sticks together into 'crumbs' varies

according to whether it is acid or alkaline. How well it 'crumbs' dictates how fast water drains away. This, in turn, makes it a cold or warm soil.

All those factors determine the kinds of plants which will do well. To try and make a plant which likes warm well-drained soil thrive on clay is like trying to make an alligator thrive in the Arctic.

Acid v Alkaline

Soils range from the very alkaline soils on chalk and limestone, to very acid peaty soils - though not all peat is acid. Most plants grow less well in acid soils because vital foods are locked up by the acid. There are simple kits to test what you have. They give a pH value between 0 and 14. Where soil is concerned a pH below 6 is acid, 6-7 is neutral and above 7 is alkaline. Soil testing is interesting but looking at neighbouring gardens and seeing what thrives will tell you as much.

When soil is too acid the usual cure is hydrated lime, but it is almost impossible to increase the acidity of alkaline soil. The amount of lime you need to apply depends on the type of particles as well as on the degree of acidity. Clay needs considerably more liming than acid sandy soil. But go carefully; too much lime will stop plants growing just as effectively as too much acid, and some vegetables take exception to it.

Soil Types

Type	Particles	Effect	Fertility	Action
Clay (heavy)	Very fine, particles stick together.	Holds water and is slow to warm in spring. Hard to dig.	Usually good.	Add lime in autumn to bind the particles. Add compost, manure, leaf mould and sharp sand.
Loamy	Fine and coarse mixed.	Half way between clay and sand - the excellent middle way.	Usually good.	Just because it's good don't neglect it. Every soil needs compost or manure.
Chalk	Fine.	Alkaline, but the soil is sticky and unpleasant to handle. Plants yellow from lime-induced chlorosis.	Usually poor.	Needs very large amounts of humus to reduce both alkalinity and stickiness.
Peat	Fine to medium.	Often acid, and waterlogged, but plenty of humus.	Fair, but too acid for many plants.	Add lime to reduce acidity if it is acid.
Sand (light)	Very coarse, open soil.	Water drains very fast, but it warms quickly in spring. Easy to dig.	Poor. Plant food quickly washed from the soil.	Often needs lime against acidity. Add compost, manure or leaf mould to hold moisture.

Topsoil v Subsoil

Topsoil is the fertile layer of soil into which humus has decomposed over the centuries. Deeper down is a less fertile layer but builders sometimes take - and sell - the topsoil. If you need to buy in topsoil remember a cubic metre weighs about 1 tonne. You will need a layer at least 30 cm (1 ft) deep. So 1 tonne will cover an area 3×3m.

Fertilizers, Conditioners and Mulches

Different chemicals have quite specific effects on plants, and these dictate when to use them. But a balance between the chemicals may be needed before plants can use them properly.

Nitrogen boosts plant growth and leaves. So use it during the growing period - especially in spring - and on leaf vegetables. Not at flowering time. Lack of it produces stunted plants with pale or bluish leaves.

Potassium stimulates the production of flowers and fruit, so use it when those are being made - usually summer and early autumn. Lack of potash produces potatoes which cook badly and have black patches, and can give a burnt look to fruit tree leaves.

Phosphates increase root development and maturity - use when planting, on root vegetables, and generally.

Calcium is needed to make cell walls.

Hungry plants may need some 'fast food', for example, liquid tomato fertilizer will bring on most flowers and fruit rapidly. Branded fertilizers always give plant foods in a set order, e.g. 1:2:3 means 1 part nitrogen:2 parts phosphates:3 parts potassium (or 1N:2P:3K). Fertilizers should be dug or watered in.

All soil needs to have organic matter added to it to keep the texture healthy and open. In nature what came out of the ground is returned to it. Our tidy gardens deprive the soil of its natural roughage and we need to make good the loss. Earthworms play a vital part in keeping the soil open, and save us digging, but they need humus to live and work for us. The more compost you add, the happier the earthworms are and the more there are to do your digging.

Applying organic matter as a mulch saves even more work: it keeps down weeds and holds in moisture; as the worms will gradually drag it underground it also adds humus to the soil. Hoe, water and apply a layer several inches thick in April or May and don't disturb it during the growing season.

Wood ash is a useful source of potash though short-lived. Use a good handful of bonfire remains per sq m (sq yd) at any time.

Composted bark and wood chips can be spread as a mulch an inch or so thick under shrubs and trees. They look good and work very well. But they have no food value and bacteria will take nitrogen away from the plants to break them down. So nitrogen fertilizer *must* be used on the bed before they are applied first.

Blood, fish and bone meal is an invaluable general fertilizer combining all the main plant foods. Use a handful or two per square metre a week before sowing or planting and again during the growing season.

Bone meal is high in phosphates with some nitrogen. It releases these very slowly.

Compost contains all the foods plants need and can be dug in or used as a mulch. It also improves the texture of all soils. Compost making is really very easy. Any container with strong sides which allows in air will do - tough Netlon made into a square with four stakes for example - and you can compost anything except:

- food which attracts rats or flies.
- matter which decays very slowly, such as paper
- branches, twigs and very woody stems
- diseased matter
- invasive weeds such as bind-weed or couch grass: they may not be killed.

Vegetable matter rots because of bacteria which are in the soil on your weeds anyway - but add some earth if the heap is mainly mowings. These bacteria need moisture - so moisten it if you add dry matter. And those which produce compost with a nice earthy texture need air. (Without it other bacteria take over producing a stinking sludge.) Given these conditions, any heap of garden refuse would rot in time. But to speed up the process use sulphate of ammonia or a proprietary activator, like Garotta, on every hands' depth of debris. The traditional additive was slops, for urine is an excellent activator, so if you do run out of chemicals...

The heap can be any size but cover it with dark plastic, or an old carpet weighted with bricks, to keep in the heat. Start a new heap each year, or when the bin is full, leaving the other until it almost resembles soil before spreading it.

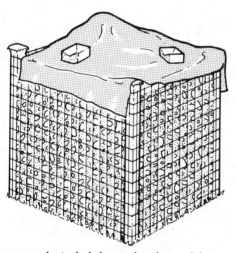

Leaves can be included or make a heap of their own, or just put them in vegetable nets or well-perforated refuse sacks, with some activator, and let them rot by themselves. They can be dug in or used as a mulch before other compost is ready.

Dried blood is high in nitrogen and also contains potassium, sodium, calcium and phosphate compounds, and releases these quickly into the ground. Use about 50 g (2 oz) to the square m (sq yd).

Fish manure is now hard to find but is an excellent general fertilizer. Use 100 g (4 oz) a square m (sq yd).

Green manure is a term used for plants grown on bare ground and then dug in. Apart from leguminous plants, which fix (store) nitrogen from the air, they contain nothing which wasn't in the soil they grew on, but they do improve the texture and they allow fertilizers which might have been washed from light soil to be retained for future plants. The best green fertilizer is probably comfrey.

Growmore is a general inorganic fertilizer containing all 3 plant foods.

Hair, feathers and hoof and horn meal all contain nitrogen which they release very slowly. They can be dug in or added to a compost heap.

Horse and other manure is a mixture of animal waste and whatever was used as litter. The litter is the snag. Bacteria need nitrogen to break down substances like straw, and especially wood shavings. Until these have been broken down, putting manure on a bed will *take vital nitrogen away* from the plants, not add any. Unless you have room for a manure heap, only buy manure when well rotted. Use a barrowload of horse manure to about 12 sq m (12 sq yd) either dug in or as a mulch. Other animal and bird manures usually contain less litter but some are very strong. Apply them when well decomposed, and in lower concentrations.

Lime reduces the acidity of soil; it also provides calcium. It binds clay into clumps. Add it in autumn, not in spring, and if clay is very acid use gypsum in preference to lime.

Seaweed conditioners do break down clay - but they don't work miracles.

Seaweed manure is very valuable, though low in phosphates. Use a barrow load for 10 sq m (10 sq yd) and add bone meal to make up the phosphates.

Sedge peat is especially useful for improving the texture of soils, helping it to hold moisture without becoming heavy, and is slightly acid. Applied as a 2·5-5 cm (1-2 in) mulch on shrub borders; it also combats weeds.

Spent hops improve soil texture and add nitrogen. Use a bucketful to a square m (sq yd).

Spent mushroom compost is an excellent mulch which helps the soil hold water and improves its texture.

Sulphate of ammonia is high in nitrogen and a dusting round plants will boost them in the early spring. But using it in the compost heap and then spreading the compost is even better.

Sulphate of potash is alkaline and rich in potash. Apply 100 g (4 oz) per square metre (sq yd).

Shrubs, Trees and Roses

Shrubs and small trees are too often the also-rans of a garden, yet they deserve the place of honour. Nothing, except bulbs, outshines them in a labour-saving contest. Many of the most beautiful need no pruning, tying or tending. Though they may each play prima donna in their flowering time, they are also the back-drop against which the rest of the garden is acted out, and for a garden to look good through the dog days of winter there should be a *far* higher proportion of evergreens than are usually planted.

It takes time for shrubs and trees to grow into these roles. Most good catalogues give the final height and width of each shrub but, if they only give the height, a rough guide is that most shrubs are slightly wider than their height, and most trees narrower. It is all too easy to over-buy and plant shrubs according to their initial size, rather than the final size. This means none will develop their proper form and some will eventually have to be removed, which is a wasteful exercise. And shrubs, like people, are only easy-going when they are happy.

For mail order choose a reputable nursery but when picking them yourself look for:
- a strong straight trunk on trees
- even growth in all directions
- branches which are free from disease or wounds
- a well-developed root system - if you can see it
- maturity - mature shrubs establish better than young fleshy ones.

Buying Climbers
With climbing plants bear in mind which way the wall faces. Most have distinct preferences and good garden catalogues list climbers according to which aspect they prefer. The range of possible plants, for any wall, is a lot wider than the prevalence of climbing roses would suggest and it's well worth looking at some of the lesser known options. The ground must be deeply fertilized, as it may be hard to get at again, especially if it is set in paving.

Buying Roses
In the 1970s if you wanted a sturdy, heavily scented rose you had to turn to old varieties. That is no longer true. Nurseries like Le Grice have now bred sturdy, disease-resistant roses with the heavy scents. There are also new ground-cover roses and low growing roses for small areas. The range of possibilities has never been so wide. Don't buy from the meagre range in many garden centres until you have looked at some good catalogues (below).

If you are searching for a particular rose you loved and lost, the Rose Growers Association (page 368) has a pamphlet to help you find it.

Planting Trees, Shrubs and Roses
For the best time to plant see the Gardening Year, page 364. Planting at the right time is essential for bare-rooted plants, and an advantage even for container grown ones. If you plant shrubs and trees in a dry spell it will take a *lot* of watering to make them thrive.

Dig the ground thoroughly, if possible a month before planting. Water container-grown plants regularly while they wait to be planted and an hour before planting. If they have arrived bare-rooted and you can't plant them immediately, because of cold or wet, heel them in. For this put the roots of bare rooted trees in a trench, with them lying on the ground, cover the roots with earth and tread it firmly.

To give the plant a good chance you need a hole which is deep enough to repeat the old soil level, with the roots comfortably spread out to their tips.

A small tree	needs a hole	50cm (18in) deep
A tree 2·8m (9ft) high	needs a hole	1m (3ft) wide
Taller trees	need a hole	1·4m (4ft 6in) wide
Shrubs 50cm (18m) high	need a hole	60cm (2ft) wide

Mix half the soil with an equal amount of peat or compost, plus 2-3 handfuls of bonemeal per barrowload or use one of the planting mediums, such as Fisons Greenleaf, which retain the moisture in the soil and make it easier for shrubs to establish. These can replace the soil and peat mixture or simply be used close to the roots. Having made the hole, work half a bucket of manure or compost into the next 25 cm (9 in) of soil.

Stand the plant in the hole and check that its soil surface line will be just below soil level. Lift trees and shrubs by their root ball, then their roots won't be torn. If it is bare-rooted check that the main root goes straight down, and the roots can fan out. Deepen or fill as necessary. Recheck the depth, and hammer in a sturdy stake about 12 cm (5 in) from the trunk of anything with a tall main trunk. Place it on the side from which the wind mainly blows (look at trees nearby to find this) and hammer it well in before planting the tree.

Some plants hate lime and love acid. The most common lime haters are: azaleas, rhododendrons, lupins, magnolias, camellias, heathers, lithospermum, gentians, styrax. On soil which is not acid enough their health and happiness can be improved by putting peat into the planting hole and by regular applications of a plant food which contains sequestered iron.

In dry weather water the base of the hole well. Check a bare-rooted plant and cut off any broken or bruised sections of root. Spread bare roots out, or centre a root ball, in the hole and fill in gradually with the soil and peat and tread it gently in as you go, disturbing the pot shape of container grown plants as little as possible. Leave a slight dip on the surface, and water this unless the soil is wet.

Tie the tree to the stake with a plastic tree strap just below the branches.

★ When fences need to be treated to prevent them rotting use Cuprinol not creosote. Creosote can injure plant shoots for a long time after it is applied. Before erecting the fence, stand the bottoms of the supporting posts in a large can of waste sump oil (from a garage) for a few weeks to protect the wood against underground wet.

Good Shrubs

No boy will face a holly hedge of any degree of thickness.
William Cobbett, *The English Gardener*

The following list gives 25 shrubs and trees which have a lot to offer almost any garden, yet demand a minimum of care and attention.

Most are hardy, but those living in the colder regions may not be able to grow all of them. Between them, they provide a range of flowers and foliage to give interest in every month of the year. But which will grow best will depend on your soil and your situation, or you may find you prefer a different member of a family to the one I have given. This is just a starting point for exploration.

Trees and Shrubs Through the Year

| E = evergreen | ✱ indicates that no pruning is needed |

Name	Description
Amelanchier	A compact fast tree covered with a froth of white blossom in spring, with brilliant scarlet leaves in autumn, plus tiny crimson berries if soil and weather suit it. Grows almost anywhere.
Azalea many varieties E ✱	The dwarf evergreens of this family are ideal for the front of any moist lime free border. Providing a brilliant display when in flower and a nice cushion of evergreen leaves afterwards.
Buddleia 'Lochinch'	Not the prettiest shrub but graceful, undemanding and beloved by butterflies. Prefers slightly dry soil and sun. Fast growing. Cut right back in March.
Camellia japonica varieties E✱	Camellias, with their glossy leaves and rosette-like flowers are so lovely they look difficult to grow. In peaty soil and semi-shade nothing is easier. But the flowers go brown if early sun strikes them. Not totally hardy so best on a sheltered wall.
Chamaecyparis Lawsoniana varieties E✱	These conifers are indispensable in any garden. They offer a wide range of colours, from the golden yellow of *lutea* to the blue green of *Ellwoodii*, and their conical shape gives height to any bed they are used in.
Choisya ternata E✱	This Mexican Orange Blossom produces masses of sweet scented flowers and attractive foliage in any good soil, though it prefers sun. Remove dead wood after March flowering.
Cytisus scoparius varieties ✱	The most upright of the garden brooms. A spectacular smother of pea-like flowers. Long green stems all winter. Likes any not too wet soil, and sun or semi-shade.
Euonymus 'Emerald Gaiety' E✱	Very easy going shrub with silver and green glossy variegated leaves. Will thrive in any soil and in tubs. There is golden variegated form too.
Forsythia varieties	Too common to need recommending, but nothing else provides quite so much colour in early spring. Grows almost anywhere. Prune overcrowding straight after flowering.
Genista lydia ✱	This has the same flowers as a broom but it makes a low mound of glowing gold, in light soil and sun. Totally trouble free.
Hydrangea paniculata 'Grandiflora'	The hardiest of all hydrangeas and very striking with huge conical heads on elegant arching stems. Cut last year's growth by half each spring.
Magnolia loebneri 'Leonard Messell'	A magnolia with a cluster of deep pink star-like flowers and a warm well-drained peaty soil. Hardy and trouble free.

owering colours	Jan	Feb	Mar	Apr	May	Jun	Jul	Aug	Sept	Oct	Nov	Dec	Size
white				✕									6 m × 5 m
red yellow white pink				✕	✕	✕							1 m up × 1 m
blue							✕	✕					2 m × 1.8 m
hite pink red		✕	✕	✕									1.5 m × 1.5 m
													1.2 m up × 50 cm up
white			✕						✕				1.8 m × 2 m
gold lemon eam ruby red					✕	✕							1.5 m × 1.5 m
													60 cm × 80 cm
yellow		✕	✕										2 m × 2.4 m
gold					✕	✕							60 cm × 80 cm
eamy white fade to pink								✕	✕				2 m × 1.8 m
pink				✕									3 m × 1.8 m

Name	Description
Mahonia aquifolium 'Charity' E✷	One of the most handsome evergreens. An imposing plant, with toothed leaves and sprays of lily-of-valley-scented flowers. Dislikes waterlogged soil and prefers semi-shade. If leggy prune after flowering.
Malus (crab apple) 'John Downie'	An attractive tree with spring blossom and scarlet orange fruit which make excellent jelly. A good combination of fruit and beauty.
Osmanthus delavayi E✷	A plant to grow for its scent, though the handsome dark green leaves are a good foil for other flowers too. Any sunny well drained soil.
Philadelphus varieties (often wrongly called Syringa)	Free-flowering, heavily scented shrubs which are trouble free in any well drained soil, in sun or semi-shade. Thin out old wood after flowering, if crowded. Charming flowers.
Pieris 'Forest Flame' E✷	Eye-catching shrubs for lime free soil, with rosettes of new leaves a clear red and panicles of waxy flowers. Choose a sheltered semi-shade position with moist soil — cold wind scorches new growth.
Prunus (Flowering Almonds Cherries and Plums) varieties most	No other flowering tree matches the profusion of prunus blossom in spring — with cherries especially. They like sun and some are small enough for town gardens. *Subhirtella autumnalis rosea* is a good one for winter blooms.
Pyrus salicifolia 'Pendula'	A charming weeping tree with slim silver-grey leaves but inconspicuous flowers. Trouble free and unfussy, its colour, size, and shape make it a good foil for other plants, in a small garden.
Rhododendron yakusimanum hybrids E✷	If the soil is lime free and moist this king of shrubs flourishes untended. When happy some grow to vast size, but these are dwarf hybrids to suit an average garden, in beds or in tubs. Flowering depends on having enough water the year before and on dead-heading before seeds form.
Rhus cotinus 'Royal Red'	A beautiful foliage plant with striking wine-red leaves from spring to autumn, but it must be pruned to 2–3 'eyes' in March to get the best effect. Easily grown in sunny well-drained soil.
Rosa Hybrid Musk	It was a Frenchman in 1904 who created the first of these delightful, under-used shrub roses. They form hedges or dense tumbling mounds which are smothered in heavily scented densely petalled blooms in May and June, and will flower on until September if dead-headed. But they flower in such profusion that this dead-heading is lengthy. Buff Beauty excels in scent, colour and form.
Rosa bourboniana	The Bourbon roses of the last century may have been ousted from most gardens by the hybrid tea, but not deservedly. Large, almost cabbagy, fragrant blooms and an easy going habit which needs no pruning, except removing dead wood makes them an excellent buy.
Senecio greyi E✷	A mound of attractive grey-green foliage, invaluable in vases, and daisy-shaped flowers make this New Zealand shrub invaluable. Not *very* hardy nor very tolerant of wind. If straggly in old age prune after flowering.
Viburnum tomentosum 'Mariesii'	This is, admittedly, too wide for many gardens. But when the full length of its tiered branches carries its flat white heads of florets, the cascade effect is so ravishing it cannot be excluded from this list. Unfussy as to soil or site. Or for winter flowers there is Bondnantese Dawn. A quite different type of viburnum but just as valuable.

flowering colours	Jan	Feb	Mar	Apr	May	Jun	Jul	Aug	Sept	Oct	Nov	Dec	size
lemon	✕	✕											1.8 m × 1.5 m
pink & white				✕	✕								5 m
white				✕									1 m × 1 m
white						✕	✕						1.8 m × 1.5 m
white pale-pink cream			✕	✕	✕								1.8 m × 1.5 m
pink white			✕	✕	✕		also Autumn						3 m up × 3 m up
													3 m × 2.5 m
white pink red apricot mauve yellow					✕	✕							1 m × 1 m
													1.8 m × 1.8 m
white pink apricot yellow red					✕								1.2 m × 1.5 m
pink white crimson						✕	✕						1.5 m × 1.5 m
yellow						✕	✕						1.2 m × 1.5 m
white					✕	✕							2.1 m × 3 m up

Wall Supports

It pays to prepare a wall for a climber well before the plant needs the support. The cheapest supports are vine-eyes, screwed into drilled holes, with wires stretched between them. But for plants like clematis, attach Netlon to the vine-eyes. If inserting a lot of vine-eyes is a problem sink two long bamboo poles into the ground near the wall and only insert vine-eyes near their tops. Lash the tops to them with wire and tie the Netlon between them. A more attractive option is trellis, but the lack of air behind the climber will increase the risk of mildew.

Mail Order Trees, Shrubs and Roses

Hillier Nurseries (Winchester) Ltd, Ampfield House, Ampfield, Romsey, Hants SO51 9PA Tel: 0794 68733 - offers trees, shrubs and some hardy perennials.

Notcutts Nurseries Ltd, Woodbridge, Suffolk IP12 4AF Tel: 039 43 3344 - has a range of trees, shrubs and roses, and one of the most informative catalogues in the business.

J. O. Sherrard and Son Ltd, The Garden Centre, Wantage Road, Donnington, Newbury, Berks RG16 9BE Tel: 0635 47845 - a large range of shrubs and roses

Scotts Nurseries (Merriott) Ltd, Merriott, Somerset TA16 5PL Tel: 0460 72306 - includes an unusually large range of fruit.

David Austin Roses, Bowling Green Lane, Albrighton, Wolverhampton WV7 3HB Tel: 090 722 3931

R. Harkness & Co Ltd, The Rose Gardens, Hitchin, Herts SG4 0JT Tel: 0462 34027 (will export) - roses

Peter Beales Roses, London Road, Attleborough, Norfolk NR17 1AY Tel: 0935 454707

John Mattock Ltd, Nuneham Courtenay, Oxford OX9 9PY Tel: 086 738 265

Le Grice (Roses) Ltd, Norwich Road, North Walsham, Norfolk NR28 0DR Tel: 0692 402591

Brian Davis, *The Gardener's Illustrated Encyclopaedia of Trees and Shrubs*, Viking - all the facts a gardener really needs plus excellent photographs. Invaluable.
Fred Roach, *Cultivate Fruits of Britain*, Basil Blackwell - a classic, and substantial, survey of the whole field including many almost lost varieties.
Brian Vines, *Trees for Small Gardens*, Pelham

Tools

> *If anybody will have a piece of cabbages, and will dig between the rows of one half of them twice during their growth, and let the other half have nothing but a flat-hoeing between, that person will find that the half which has been digged between will, when the crop is ripe, weigh nearly, if not quite, twice as much as the other half.*
>
> William Cobbett, *The English Gardener*

The essential tools are those given below, plus a trowel and lawn edging shears. To them you can add all kinds of extras - like rakes, cultivators, hedge trimmers and so forth - which your particular garden demands.

Good tools last for years; bad ones drive you mad for years. Handle each before you buy. Go through the movements you'd use and check that it suits *you* - and anyone who may use it. Wolf Tools use a special system which allows a selection of heads (for hoes, cultivators, rakes, etcetera) to be clipped firmly on and off handles

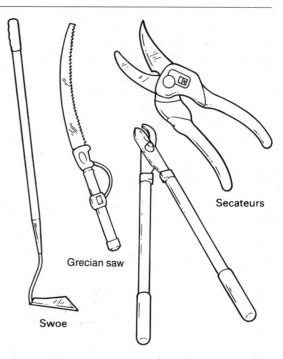

Secateurs

Grecian saw

Swoe

Long-handled secateurs

in a range of lengths. So nobody of any height needs to get backache from using the wrong length of handle and there are less handles cluttering up the garage or shed.

A **fork** and **spade** tend to be bought as a pair. But the spade has to be lifted with a weight of earth, whereas a fork does not. So it may be less back-breaking to have the spade slightly smaller.

There are three major types of **hoe**: the Dutch, the draw and Wilkinson's the Swoe. The easiest to use in a small garden are the Swoe and the Dutch hoe, with the former having a decided advantage round roses and shrubs.

If you buy a **rake** choose one with prongs which spring smartly back into place if you pull them back slightly. If they bend it will be useless in no time.

Every garden needs a **rubbish carrier,** but in small gardens it is most convenient to have a vast bag or a dumper sheet with handles. If you have to buy a barrow, the ball-wheel Ballbarrow is hard to beat. The same company makes a plastic **roller** which is weighted by putting water in, so you can adapt it to light or heavy rolling.

★ To save back strain: face your wheelbarrow in the direction you intend to go *before* you fill it, then you never turn it fully laden.

If you have any small branches or very thick rose or shrub stems to cut through, a curved-bladed **Grecian saw** is essential. The best I have used is by Wolf Tools (see opposite) and can be attached to a short handle for using on roses or to a long one to reach up to branches.

Buy the very best **secateurs** you can afford: cutting plants with inefficient ones just causes them to die back.

Those with curving blades are least likely to cause bruising.

If you have thick branches to cut buy long-handled secateurs too. The less strong you are, the longer the handles should be: by the rules of leverage the longer the handle, the less effort you have to put in. Wilkinson Sword now make some at over 61 cm (2 ft) long and the extra inches do make a difference. Tree-lopping versions of such secateurs will even reach right up to small branches. Wilkinson Sword (see below) have an approved list of companies which sharpen them and run a postal sharpening service.

There are some very sophisticated bits of equipment among today's **watering kits**. They include meters which will turn a tap off once a set amount of water has been delivered, hoses which roll flat as tape for easy storage, hoses for laying round the garden to release a gentle trickle from end to end, and sprinklers which will spray a set pattern to match the shape of your flowerbed. The possibilities get better all the time.

Tools last best if scraped clean and wiped with an oily cloth after use, then hung up in a dry place.

Wilkinson Sword Ltd, Sword House, Bridgend, Mid Glamorgan, Wales CF31 3YN

Wolf Tools, Ross-on-Wye, Herefordshire HR9 5NE Tel: 0989 67600 - will provide a list of stockists.

Vegetables

It is most miserable taste, to seek to poke away the kitchen garden in order to get it out of sight. If well managed, nothing is more beautiful...

So wrote William Cobbett in *The English Gardener* in 1845. Not everyone would agree with him. But one way of bridging the gulf is to sow some of the more unusual and decorative vegetables in the borders with the other plants. Tall roses make no objection to being interplanted with dwarf French beans, the occasional courgette is rather attractive between shrubs and some of the smaller vegetables, like those below, can be tucked into any border.

New vegetables are coming on the market each year and some long-standing kinds are less cultivated than they deserve to be.

Corn salad: a favourite in other parts of Europe this produces small leaves with a most distinctive flavour late in the season. Easily grown in a mixed border.

Kohl-rabi: a tasty vegetable which is happy in poor dry soil where other vegetables may sulk.

Land cress: a splendid substitute for watercress which thrives in ordinary soil and grows like a weed.

Rocket: has slightly peppery leaves much loved by Italians. A delicious addition to salads which can be grown in any flower bed as you only pick a few leaves at a time.

Swiss chard: an easy form of spinach with a big central rib which can be cut out and cooked separately.

★ When growing sweetcorn plant it in blocks; it is wind pollinated and pollination may not be good in a single row.

Cloches and Cover-ups

Vegetables only grow when the day-time temperature is comfortable (comfortable for vegetables that is) - about 6°C (43°F). Only by keeping out the elements can a gardener buy extra time and raise crops which like it hotter than the average British summer. If you don't want to buy cloches make wire arches, covered with strong polythene, stretched tight and weighted. Lakeland Plastics (page 203) sell a kit by mail order. Make a ventilation hole at either end to suit the length of the tunnel.

★ When the weather is cold protect plants in the greenhouse by covering them with newspaper.

Winter Storage

Onions: can be stored in old nylon tights knotted to keep each onion separate and hung in a cool dry place. They will keep through the winter.

Marrow, pumpkins, vegetable spaghetti: can be hung in netting or spaced on shelves in a cool, dry place and will keep 2 to 4 months.

Potatoes: must be stored in the dark and cool - but not below 4°C (40°F) as frost changes their chemistry unpleasantly. A big paper sack from a frozen food wholesaler is ideal.

Carrots, swedes, turnips: can be left in the ground if it is covered with straw and polythene, but may be attacked by pests. They may be stored in a box of slightly moist sand in a cool place.

Beetroots: store in sand as above.

Brussels sprouts, cabbage, leeks: can be left growing until harvested.

★ An old trick for getting early crops is to tilt the bed against a wall at a 40° angle towards the sun. You remove the topsoil, create an angled bed with subsoil or rubble and cover with topsoil.

More information

Tony Biggs, *Vegetables*, Mitchell Beazley
Kenneth A: Beckett, *Growing under Glass*, Mitchell Beazley

Weed Control

The old saying that one year's seeding is seven years' weeding has been proved to be scientifically correct - and that's assuming you don't slack during the seven years. But though seeded weeds are the most numerous, they are by no means the worst.

New Gardens

Anyone with a brand new, uncultivated plot is well advised to spend the first year just getting rid of any serious weeds. Once you have plants in place it can be impossible to remove weeds which multiply with long underground roots. While the earth is bare you can repeatedly dig and remove the roots; or use a systemic weedkiller though the least decorative method is one of the most effective: cover the ground with black polythene, or an old carpet, for 6 spring or summer months. Ideal for those who have moved into a house with carpets they hate, though it may not endear you to the neighbours.

Seeded Weeds

To keep weeds to a minimum have well-fed healthy plants which are fairly close planted. Where there have to be spaces, such as around roses or shrubs, the ground can be mulched or use ground cover plants to fill in gaps.

For vegetables peg down sheets of black polythene, cut slits in it and plant the seedlings through the slits - or run strips of polythene between seeded rows. Make sure the ground was watered first and put down slug pellets before you lay the plastic or slugs will decimate the careful rows.

★ To avoid introducing new weeds let any container-grown plant stand for several weeks before planting and remove the weeds which emerge.

Troublesome Weeds

Regrettably, sometimes chemicals are the only answer. Some of the weeds listed here cannot be removed from among established plants in any other way.

Dandelions Dock Sorrel	These can be dug out, but may re-grow if any of the tap root is left. Use a systemic weedkiller based on glyphosate (Tumbleweed).
Bindweed, Couch grass, Creeping thistle, Ground elder, Horsetail, Stinging nettles	Hand weeding these creeping roots is depressingly like pruning: remove one shoot and you get two. Repeated digging on bare ground may remove them. Otherwise a systemic weedkiller is the answer. Use glyphosate (Tumbleweed) or Fisons' Killer for problem weeds. Apply these when there are several leaves showing but the top growth isn't enormous, and repeat the application at least once a week for 3 weeks. It works slowly. It also needs 6 hours without rain, after you apply it, as it is absorbed slowly.

The Gardening Year

This calendar gives a sequence of jobs. They must be shifted, forwards or backwards, to suit the weather in any year and the climate of each area.

	JANUARY	FEBRUARY	MARCH	APRIL	MAY	JUNE
BULBS CORMS AND TUBERS	Check pot grown bulbs. Bring indoors those ready to flower.	Plant alliums, anemones and tigridias. Also snowdrops in the green, or divide clumps. Bring pot-grown bulbs indoors if ready.	Feed with general fertilizer. Plant galtonia, and schizostylis, montbretia and gladioli. Enjoy the display and plan additions.	Plant dormant dahlia tubers 6 in deep in warm areas if mild. Plant freesias and gladioli. Dead-head narcissus and tulips. Leave foliage as it is.	Plant gladioli early, then crocosmia and agapanthus, also dahlia tubers. Lift tulips, if need be, after flowering.	Move any that need to be moved. Keep gladioli well watered. Tie up dahlias as they grow.
CLIMBERS	Prune wisteria.	Cut Jackmanii clematis to 1 m (3 ft) near end of month. Thin weak wood in summer bloomers. Prune wisteria.	Cut back Jackmanii clematis, as February, if not done.	Remove very old stems from roses.		Tie in new shoots.
FRUIT	Apply tar-oil emulsion to fruit trees to clean them of insect eggs and moss - on a dry day. Prune apples when the weather is frost free. Plant bare-rooted trees.	Prune fruit trees and feed with general fertilizer like Vitax Q4. Spray peaches, almonds and nectarines against peach leaf curl. Plant.	Last chance to plant bare-rooted trees and bushes. Spray against apple and pear scabs as buds open.	Spray gooseberries and strawberries every 2 weeks against mildew. Remove blossom from first-year trees to let them build their strength.	Hang a pheromone trap in apple and pear trees to catch coddling moths before they lay eggs for maggots. Treat gooseberries with Benlate against mildew. Put fruit protection under strawberries.	Thin excess fruit from branches after June drop. Net soft fruit against birds. Spray gooseberries against mildew every 2 weeks. Root strawberry runners. Spray apples against red spider.

Oxalis — This leaves little bulbils which sprout fresh plants. A systemic weedkiller may be the only way to get rid of it.

Creeping buttercup, Brambles — Both these send out runners which root avidly, and only relentless digging will get rid of them. Otherwise buttercups may need glyphosate and brambles a brushwood killer.

★ Shepherd's purse, in particular, should be kept clear of vegetable patches as, it belongs to the brassica family and can harbour clubroot.

Using Weedkillers
The great drive of the chemical companies is towards weedkillers which are highly selective and only kill particular types of plant. But the main types of weedkillers are these:

Contact weedkillers, such as paraquat, kill any foliage they touch.

Residual weedkillers contain chemicals which do not break down quickly, so they will stop weeds germinating. These are used on drives and stone paths. They can be selective or non-selective. Some non-selective forms, such as sodium chlorate, dissolve easily in water and leach both downwards and sideways through the soil, putting at risk plants growing nearby - and their effects last for 6 months. Such chemicals are to be avoided unless there is no alternative.

Systemic (translocated) weedkillers are put on the foliage of deep-rooted weeds, and sink into the plant, and travel through the whole system. But it may take several applications to make a tough weed die. Both selective and non-selective ones exist.

★ Never increase the dose of a weedkiller to make it work faster. The doses are scientific; if you add more or less you will make it work **less** well.
★ If you need a funnel for weedkiller cut the top from a plastic squash bottle, just below the 'shoulders', for one you can use and throw away.

Margery Fish, *Ground Cover Plants*, Collingridge - a marvellous introduction to ground cover.

JULY	AUGUST	SEPTEMBER	OCTOBER	NOVEMBER	DECEMBER
Water dahlias and gladioli. Mulch dahlias with compost or manure and tie up. Plan bulb order for autumn planting.	Plant autumn crocuses, colchicums and Madonna lilies. Begin to plant narcissus (daffodils). Protect dahlias against earwigs.	Plant spring bulbs and corms, hardy lilies and bulbous irises. Lift dahlia tubers once frosted. Disbud dahlias for larger blooms. Plant bulbs in pots for indoors.	Plant tulips, winter aconite, anemones and spring bulbs not yet in. Plant narcissus in bowls for Christmas. Lift dahlias once frosted. Lift gladioli.	Plant tulips. Bring bulbs in pots into cool room in week 4. Lift dahlias. Feed with bonemeal.	Finish planting tulips.
Prune long new wisteria growths to 6-7 buds. Tie in new growths.	Tie in new growths. Prune wisteria if not done. Prune rambling roses after flowering.	Tie in new growths. Prune climbing and rambling roses.	Tie in new growths.	Hard prune outdoor vines after leaf fall. Prune wisteria.	Hard prune outdoor vines if not done. Prune wisteria. Plant. Protect tender ones with bracken or straw at roots.
Prune currants after fruiting. Root strawberry runners.	Layer blackberries. Spray gooseberries and strawberries against mildew. Summer prune as needed. Cut raspberry canes to ground level after fruiting. Plant new strawberry beds.	Prune off surplus shoots on wall-trained trees and prune fan shapes from mid-month. Prune raspberries and gooseberries. Order fruit trees for autumn/winter planting. Fit grease bands in week 4 against winter moths.	Plant soft fruit canes and fruit trees. Spray apple trees against canker. Spray peaches, almonds and nectarines. Prune fan-trained forms. Order for winter planting. Cut out fruited raspberry canes, tie in new canes.	Prune apples and pears after leaf fall. Apply insecticide against woolly aphis. Cut out canker on fruit trees. Plant new trees from now on.	Plant bare-rooted trees. Finish pruning - if frost-free.

It is only to the gardener that time is a friend, giving each year more than he steals Beverley Nichols

	JANUARY	FEBRUARY	MARCH	APRIL	MAY	JUNE
GREENHOUSE	Clean out and disinfect. Plan spring sowing. Sow sweet peas and begonias.	Sow summer bedding plants such as tobacco plants and lobelia near end of month. Sow tomatoes.	Sow half-hardy annuals. Sow tomatoes here or on a window ledge. Pot on early sown tomatoes.	Sow tomatoes, marrow. Sow courgettes and sweetcorn from late in month.	Sow sweetcorn, pumpkin. Spray for pests if necessary. Root cuttings of herbaceous plants and shrubs.	Shade the sunny side. Pot on as needed.
HERBACEOUS PLANTS	Take root cuttings or hardwood cuttings as needed.	Divide and replant established clumps. Top dress with complete fertilizer.	Plant from mid-month. Lift and divide established clumps.	Plant until mid-month. Put supports in place. Feed with blood, fish and bonemeal.	Divide and replant clumps of primroses and polyanthus. Plant out. Stake tall plants.	Take cuttings of phlox and dianthus. Move and divide bearded irises after flowering. Dead-head regularly.
LAWNS	Sweep up leaves, cut and repair edges.	Spike 5 cm (6 in) deep all over with a fork to let in air and improve drainage.	Rake off leaves. Mow lightly to 3 cm (1¼ in) if growing. Apply moss-killer if it's needed. Roll.	Mow weekly (1¼ in). Roll if bumpy. Prick and reseed bare patches. Feed.	Mow twice a week, to 1·5-2·5 cm (½-1 in) long. Fertilize or use combined weedkiller and fertilizer.	Mow twice a week, to 1·5-2·5 cm (½-1 in) long. Water in dry weather.
ROSES	Find manure ready for mulching.	Plant. Prune hybrid teas, floribundas and standards and any others if newly planted - in warm areas.	Plant. Feed early with fertilizer such as Vitax Q4. Prune hybrid teas, floribundas and standards and any newly planted. Lightly prune shrub roses. Spray with fungicide.	Spray every 2 weeks against blackspot and mildew. Mulch when warm enough with compost or manure. Prune hybrid teas and floribundas in cold areas.	Spray against greenfly. Spray fortnightly against diseases. Mulch as April.	Spray fortnightly against diseases. Feed with balanced fertilizer. Dead-head. Water if dry. Liquid feed.
DECIDUOUS SHRUBS & TREES	Plant if weather mild.	Plant if weather is mild. Give slow-release fertilizer e.g. bonemeal. Prune forsythia after flowering. Take hard-wood cuttings.	Plant if weather is mild. Prune many summer flowering shrubs and feed with balanced slow release fertilizer.	Prune early spring flowerers. Mulch.	Prune winter damaged branches, and privet hedges. Dead-head winter flowering heathers and mulch with sedge peat.	Take cuttings of those which flower early. After flowering prune those which flower on year-old wood.
EVERGREEN SHRUBS & TREES	Choose sites to receive these later, possibly dig the holes - but cover to prevent water logging.	Dress area with slow fertilizer as above. Take cuttings of conifers and place in cold frame.	Cut out any winter damage. Shake off snow before it breaks branches.	Good time for planting. Prune if needed, unless in flower. Mulch.	Dead-head azaleas and rhododendrons. Prune winter-damaged branches.	Dead-head azaleas and rhododendrons.
SOWING - FLOWERS OUTSIDE		Risk some perennials in a cold frame - say lupins and hollyhocks.	Sow hardy annuals, like sweet peas, from mid-month if weather good.	Sow annuals like sunflowers. Plant out violas, lobelia, alyssum if frost is over.	Sow hollyhocks in position. Sow annuals. Sow biennials in boxes. Plant out half hardy bedding plants. Sow perennials.	Sow calceolaria and cineraria, for pot plants next winter, in a cold frame.

JULY	AUGUST	SEPTEMBER	OCTOBER	NOVEMBER	DECEMBER
Layer carnations. Root semi-hardwood and pelargonium cuttings. Sow biennials and perennials. Spray against whitefly.	Fumigate at night against pests and diseases. Don't let dead leaves lie about. Sow cyclamen. Pot fuchsia cuttings.	Sow pansies, viola, godetia and clarkia. Remove shading from the glass by mid-month. Prick out earlier seedings in trays.	Pick the last tomatoes and cucumbers. Wash and disinfect throughout. Allow corms to die down, dry and store corms.	Fumigate against pests and diseases.	Check and tend over-wintering plants.
Divide bearded irises, cutting leaves by half, replant. Dead-head.	Sow in seed beds for planting out next year. Dead-head. Spray against mildew Divide and replant irises as July.	Dead-head. Plant early season flowers from mid-month. Divide and replant irises if not done. Position plants seeded in the spring.	Plant until mid-month. Position plants seeded in the spring. Lift, divide and replant large clumps. Take cuttings of shrubby ones.	Mulch well with manure. Cut back dead growth if you wish. Tuck dead leaves and slug pellets over tender subjects under twigs in week 4.	Put slug pellets near hellebores. Tie the tops of kniphofias together to keep out wet.
Mow twice a week, to 1·5-2·5 cm (½-1 in) long. Possibly feed as in May. Water when dry.	Mow twice a week, to 1·5-2·5 cm (½-1 in) long. Use combined weedkiller and fertilizer if needed. Water when dry.	Rake lawns to remove dead grass and moss. Spike to let air in. Mow to 2-3 cm (¾-1¼ in) once a week. Autumn feed and dress.	Rake off leaves. Mow to 2-3 cm (¾-1¼ in) once a week if mild. Autumn feed and possibly top dress if not done in September.	Rake off leaves. Mow if mild and grass still growing to 2-3 cm (¾-1¼ in).	Clear blown leaves.
Spray fortnightly against diseases. Liquid feed once if not in June. Water if dry. Dead-head.	Spray fortnightly against disease. Spray for aphids if necessary. Dead-head. Water if dry. Remove suckers.	Spray fortnightly against diseases. Dead-head. Remove suckers.	Spray against diseases until mid-month. Prepare beds for planting. Remove suckers. Dead-head. Cut bushes to half in windy positions.	Best time for planting if bare rooted. Plant from containers. Prune climbers which flower more than once. Prune tall bushes to reduce height by half in windy areas if not done.	Clear away dead leaves to reduce risk of mildew and blackspot next year. Disinfect soil with Jeyes fluid.
Trim hedges. Lightly prune those which need post-flowering pruning. Trim broom. Feed with liquid general fertilizer.	Trim hedges. Take cuttings of elderly shrubs. Pot up. Place in greenhouse or on cool window ledge. Prune some early flowers.	Plant container-grown plants. Order bare-rooted plants for planting in winter. Take semi-hardwood cuttings.	One of the best times for planting.	Best time for planting. Prune beech and hornbeam hedges.	Remove snow from branches after heavy falls. Plant if weather good enough.
Dead-head rhododendrons. Feed with a general fertilizer.	Layer rhododendrons and azaleas to propagate.	Good planting time. Take cuttings for cold frame.	Good time for planting.	Plant heathers.	Remove snow from branches after heavy falls - especially from conifers. Plant if weather allows.
Transplant biennials.	Sow spring flowering annuals such as Iceland poppies and antirrhinum.	Plant out polyanthus seedlings. Plant out biennials such as wallflowers in flowers' sites. Sow hardy annuals on site.		Plant out pansies, sweet Williams, and violets. Put cloches over autumn-sown hardy annuals.	Plan planting for next year. Note the results from this year.

	JANUARY	FEBRUARY	MARCH	APRIL	MAY	JUNE
VEGETABLES	Set early potatoes to sprout. Plan the sowing for the year. Sow peas and early broad beans. Also shallots in the warm areas.	Cover ground with polythene or cloches to warm it. Sow Brussels sprouts, leeks, and lettuce under cloches at end of month in warm areas. Sow broad beans, plus possibly early carrots, cabbage and onion in warm areas.	Put cloches over soil to warm it. Sow spinach, beet, radishes, spring onions, leeks, broad beans, Brussels sprouts, sweetcorn onions. Sow lettuce, and carrot under cloches - week 4. In the south plant asparagus.	Sow radish, cauliflower and lettuce. Sow parsnips from late in month. Plant out courgettes under cloches. Plant out brassicas. If late, sow courgettes in window ledge and runner beans in pots. Transplant brassicas (cabbage family).	Sow winter cabbages, from week 3. Sow Chinese cabbage and swedes week 4. Plant outdoor tomatoes. Sow French, runner beans and parsnips. Transplant brassicas large enough to handle. Thin as needed.	Sow cauliflower, courgettes, marrows and chicory in weeks 1 and 2. Sow beetroot, French beans, kohl-rabi and early peas. Plant out courgettes, tomatoes, cabbages, sprouts. Spray blackfly. Thin seedlings.
SUNDRY	See to lawn mower. Fork empty beds. Tidy up. Shake snow off shrubs.	Prepare wall supports for wall plants. Shake snow off shrubs.		Hoe weeds down. Keep new planting well watered.	Water new plants. Mulch. Plant window boxes, hanging baskets and tubs.	Keep hanging baskets moist. Water garden when dry.

Cottage Garden Society, 15 Faenol Avenue, Abergele, Clwyd LL22 7HT Tel: 0745 832059 - promotes cottage gardening, has a 'find a plant service' helping members find old plants. M£L, A, Ad.

The Garden Centre Association Ltd, 38 Carey Street, Reading, Berks RG1 7JS Tel: 0734 393900 - tries to maintain standards in garden centres and has an inspection policy. Its members conform to a helpful code of practice and check the rules.

Gardens for the Disabled Trust, Church Cottage, Headcorn, Kent TN27 9NP Tel: 0622 890467 - M£L, M, Inf for disabled gardeners, grants, Ad.

The Garden History Society, 5 The Knoll, Hereford HR1 1RU Tel: 0432 354479 - M£M, M, Lect, H, Visits. Pressure group for preservation of historic gardens.

The Good Gardeners' Association, Timber Yard, Two Mile Lane, Highnam, Glos GL2 8BR Tel: 01 449 7944/04352 305814 - an international association dedicated to organic gardening. M£M, M, B, Disc, sae.

Henry Doubleday Research Association, Ryton Gardens, Ryton-on-Dunsmore, Coventry CV8 3LG Tel: 0203 303517 - promotes and researches organic gardening. Provides mail order seeds, organic fertilizers and pesticides. M£L, M, Ad, Inf, B.

The Herb Society, 77 Great Peter Street, London SW1 2EZ Tel: 01 222 3634 - promotes all aspects of herbs. M£L, B.

National Association of Allotment and Leisure Gardeners Ltd, Hunters Road, Corby, Northants NN17 1JE Tel: 0536 66576 - has some 1,500 societies around Britain. They also obtain bulk buys of seeds, chemicals and garden sundries which can considerably cut the cost of gardening. M£L, M, A, Disc, legal.

The National Trust for Scotland, 5 Charlotte Square, Edinburgh EH2 4DU. Tel: 031 226 5922 - will plant a tree or shrub to commemorate someone.

Royal Horticultural Society, 80 Vincent Square, London SW1P 2PE Tel: 01 834 4333 - Britain's premier gardening body. M£H, M, B, Ad, Lib, free entry to the gardens at Wisley and summer flower shows.

Rose Growers Association, 303 Mile End Road, Colchester, Essex CO4 5EA Tel: 0206 8440088 - has an inexpensive leaflet called 'Find That Rose' listing over 2,000 roses and which nurseries sell them.

The Soil Association, 86 Colston Street, Bristol BS1 5BB Tel: 0272 290661 - is an international organization to promote organic gardening, market gardening and farming. It sets standards for commercial producers. Members can obtain a list of those members who produce organic food commercially, but anyone can obtain the paperback they publish giving sources of organic produce. M£M, M, B.

The Woodland Trust, Autumn Park, Dysart Road, Grantham, Lincolnshire NG31 6LL Tel: 0476 74297 - will plant trees to commemorate someone, and promotes the protection of woodland.

Christopher Brickell ed., *The Royal Horticultural Society's Concise Encyclopaedia of Gardening Techniques*, Mitchell Beazley
Dr Stefan Buczacki, *Gardeners' Questions Answered*, Collins
Gertrude Jekyll, *Wood and Garden*, Papermac
Christopher Lloyd, *Foliage Plants*, Penguin
Christopher Lloyd, *The Well-Tempered Garden*, Penguin
Alan Titchmarsh, *The Allotment Gardener's Handbook*, Penguin

Drying Flowers

There is something very satisfying about preserving some of the blooms of summer against the bleak days of winter. A great mystery is sometimes made out of the business of drying flowers, but very few demand special techniques, and some, like teasels and honesty, even dry themselves in the flower bed if you are prepared to leave them there - a policy for which tits reward you with a fine display of acrobatics as they rootle out the seeds from the teasel heads.

Below are the main methods, and some of the plants you can use them on. But experiment: sometimes two different methods bring out totally different colours in the same plant.

The flowers or leaves must be picked when *dry* and in *perfect* condition, and usually *just* before they are fully open.

JULY	AUGUST	SEPTEMBER	OCTOBER	NOVEMBER	DECEMBER
Early on sow beetroot, calabrese, chicory, Chinese cabbage, winter radish, autumn spinach, spinach beet, kohl-rabi, lettuce. Liquid feed tomatoes.	Sow spring cabbage, Brussels sprouts, kohl-rabi, winter radish, lettuce, endive, spinach, turnip. Cut back artichoke stems after heads have gone.	Sow winter lettuce under cloches. Plant out cabbages, spring greens and Savoys. Ripen off onions under cloches. Lift carrots in warm areas and store. Harvest and store most of your crops.	Plant out spring cabbages, cauliflowers and lettuces in a cold frame. Lift root vegetables. Sow corn salad, winter radish and spinach. Lift and store carrots in cold areas. Start winter digging.	Lime soil which grew brassicas. Plant garlic. Protect globe artichokes with bracken or straw. Protect lettuce with cloches. Sow early broad beans in warm areas. Prepare chicory for forcing.	Protect globe artichokes as November.
Water when dry	Water when dry.	Keep weeds down. Tie plants against autumn winds. Rake up leaves.	Rake up leaves and store for leaf mould.	Protect tubs with plastic wraps round straw, leaves or bracken.	Treat algae on paths and steps. Sweep up leaves. Order seeds and plants for spring.

Cool Air Drying

Tie the stems firmly in small bunches and hang them in a cool, dark, airy place. This is the method to use for any plant with seeds which might ripen and burst from their anchors if in the warm. If plants don't lend themselves to bunching fill a big container with perfectly dry sand and stick the stems in this. But don't use this for heads which may droop as they dry.

Hot Air Drying

For hot air drying hang bunches in a hot dry place, such as an airing cupboard, or above a boiler (but not if they could cause a fire hazard). This removes the moisture before a flower has time to fade. So it keeps the colours of flowers far better than using cool air.

Preserving in Glycerine

For this method pick twigs in summer when they have lost their youthful tenderness but are still perfect, with the sap rising in them. They will fail to take up the glycerine properly later in the season.

You need 1 part glycerine (from a pharmacy) to 2 parts hot water. Mix the water and glycerine and put the mixture in a tall narrow container which will allow the liquid to come 4-5 in (10-13 cm) up the woody stem. Put the stems into this mixture and leave this somewhere dry and not too light. When any sweatiness appears on the surface they are ready; hang them up in a paper bag to await use.

Preserving in Borax

Drying flowers in borax is an excellent way of preserving flowers. Some do go brown, but others stay astonishingly true to their summer colours.

Put an inch of household borax (from a pharmacy) in a box, place the flowers on it, sift over more borax to cover the petals in a deep layer, then put the box in a warm airing cupboard. The best way to immerse the flowers in the borax varies with the shape of the flower.

Daisy shapes can be stood on their faces with only a relatively short stem left, while delphiniums need to lie on their sides. Some may even prefer to be hung so they dangle in it.

Leave the flowers in the borax for 10 days, until the petals are dry enough to have a slight rustle. Support them underneath as you lift them very carefully from the borax. Use an artist's brush to brush off the borax. Then store them carefully in a cardboard box out of reach of dust. (Borax is a fairly mild chemical but, as always, keep it away from children and pets and wash after using it.)

Pressing

For pressing flowers and leaves all you need is a big book or a well-trodden rug on a dry floor. The rug method is ideal for ferns and larger flowers. Put newspaper under the rug, spread the ferns on it, put more newspaper on top, and cover it with the rug until the leaves are dry and pressed. For flowers use clean paper lest they take up the newsprint.

Book pressing is ideal for small flowers like pansies. Put them between paper in the pages of a big book, and weight it with more books.

Both methods are lovely for children. There is the fascination of flowers almost miraculously preserving their colour and it takes only a touch of glue for even the least artistic to produce an attractive picture.

Special Exceptions

Bullrushes easily burst into fluffy seeds. To prevent this, spray them very well, with a strong-hold hair spray, hang them in a cool place, until totally dried. Use this for any seed head which may not hold.

Iris foetidissima needs a different cosmetic treatment: use a dab of clear nail varnish to glue on its brilliant orange berries just as they show.

Physalis (Chinese lantern) need to be picked before they seem ready. That is just when the *first* lantern turns orange. They will all gain brilliant colour as they dry.

For **honesty** wait until it is fully dry, then rub each disc-shaped seed case to remove the dull outer coating and reveal the silvery disk within.

Plants to choose

Cool Air Drying	Warm Air Drying
Acanthus	Clarkia
Achillea	Delphinium
Acrolinium	Eryngium
Alchemilla	Gypsophila
Allium	Sedum
Anaphalis	**Borax Preserving**
Artichokes (globe)	
Cow parsley	Cornflower - blue
Fennel	forms
Golden rod	Dahlia
Grasses and rushes	Delphinium - the best
Gypsophila	method
Delphinium	Montbretia
Eryngium	Parsley
Helichrysum	Rue
Honesty	**Glycerine**
Hydrangeas	
Nigella seed heads	Beech
Poppies - seed heads	Box
Physalis	Camellia
Rhodanthe	Eucalyptus
Rushes	Fatsia
Sedum	Ferns (variable)
Many seed heads	Garrya
Stachys	Love lies bleeding
Statice	Mahonia
Teasels	Nigella

Arranging

Push large stems into dry sand, which weights the container as well as supporting the flowers. For lighter sprays in cottage-style arrangements simply make a lattice of sellotape across the vase. Formal arrangements need the support of *brown* oasis held in position with wire or by a pin holder.

Wiring Flowers

Florist's wire can replace the stem. Good garden centres and flower shops sell it; so do flower arranging societies.

For flowers such as helichrysum a gauge such as 210 mm works well. The wire can either be pushed up through a hollow stem, or it can be pushed down through the flower - won't show. The trick is to bend the very tip of the wire into a tiny hook, so that when you pull it down to hide it, it will not pull out completely.

HOUSEPLANTS

Being drawn from different climates all over the world, houseplants demonstrate even more vividly than garden plants the huge diversity of plant preferences. Among them are plants which love heat, hate heat, want jungle conditions, prefer a desert and abhor the light. To get the best from them mimic the conditions they originally came from. Describing individual plant needs is outside the scope of this book. What follows are general points which houseplants have in common and the information needed to choose one to suit your situation.

Cleaning Houseplants

If dirt and dust accumulate it stops them breathing through their leaf pores. So they need to be kept clean.

Cacti, hairy-leaved plants and succulents: brush the dust off with a soft paintbrush and give cacti a wash and brush-up with clean water and a shaving brush.

Large smooth-leaved plants: brush dust off gently with a brush or duster, wipe with damp tissue or a product made to clean and shine the leaves.

Small smooth-leaved plants: brush off dust as above, shower *gently* but thoroughly or wrap a plastic bag firmly over the soil and, holding this in place, swish the leaves in a bath or bucket of tepid water.

Botanical Names	Common Names
Agapanthus	Blue African Lily
Aucuba	Spotted Laurel
Bromeliads	Urn Plants
Calceolaria	Slipper Flower
Chlorophytum	Spider Plant
Dieffenbachia	Dumb Cane
Fatsia	Castor Oil Plant
Hedera	Ivy
Impatiens	Busy Lizzie
Iresine	Chicken Gizzard
Maranta leuconeura	Prayer Plant
Monstera deliciosa	Swiss Cheese Plant
Myrtus	Myrtle
Pachystachys	Lollipop Plant
Pelargoniums	Geraniums
Philodendron scandens	Sweetheart Plant
Philodendron hastatum	Elephant's Ear
Sansevieria	Mother-in-Law's Tongue
Santapaulia	African Violet
Solanum	Winter Cherry
Spathiphyllum	Peace Lily
Syngonium	Goose Foot Plant
Thunbergia	Black-Eyed Susan
Tolmiea	Piggyback Plant

Conditions for Houseplants

As houseplants are hijacked from their native environment, it is only thrifty to choose plants which can be happy in the positions we provide. There are plants for almost any environment - except sitting on a television or next to a gas stove. Televisions get hot and plants don't like having their roots cooked and gas creates fumes which certain plants cannot tolerate. But the position they like isn't always the one we might choose for them. Pricey azaleas, for example, are far better suited to a loo than a sitting room.

★ If you want to check the relative light at different points in your rooms set a manually operated camera for a very fast film and using its light metre, compare the f-stop setting you would need at different points in the room.

Ideal Conditions for Houseplants

★ Means the plant is very easy to care for.

Sunny window ledge or very close to a sunny window facing south	Very close to an east or west window	Bright light but no direct sun (e.g. a little way into the room)	A fair distance from a sunny window or in a dull room	Right away from a window but in daylight

Average central heating but using humidifiers to keep the air moist in summer and winter

Pilea (winter) Anthurium (winter) Citrus Impatiens (winter) Kalanchoe (winter) Poinsettia (winter)	Croton, Coleus, Dracaena Palm, Capsicum, Ferns (if under 23°C, 72°F) Dieffenbachia (winter) Hypoestes, Hippeastrum Impatiens (winter) Kalanchoe (summer) Iresine, Pelargonium Pilea (winter), Sansevieria★, Saintpaulia, Spathiphyllum (winter)	Anthurium (summer), Aphelandra, Bromeliads★, Begonias, Caladium, Dieffenbachia (summer), Gloxinia, Impatiens (summer), Peperomia, Maranta (winter), Poinsettia (summer), Pilea, Sansevieria★, Schefflera, Scindapsus, Syngonium-variegated, Spathiphyllum (summer)	Cyperus, Fittonia, Maranta (summer), Monstera, Philodendron, Sansevieria★, Schefflera, Syngonium - all green	Ficus elastica★, Sansevieria★

Rooms heated to over 15°C (60°F) all year & _dry_

Cacti and succulents, Zebrina★, Nerium	Chlorophytum★, Ficus elastica, Decora★, Zebrina★			

Rooms usually at 10°-15°C (50°-60°F) and slightly cooler at night

Cacti and succulents★ Beaucarnea	Asparagus★, Chlorophytum★, Calceolaria, Coleus, Celosia, Solanum, Yucca, Ficus (tree type)★, Spathyphyllum (winter), Thunbergia	Azalea, Chlorophytum★, Cyclamen, Hedera★, Aucuba, Fatsia★, Hydrangea, Primula, Vines, Ficus (tree type)★, Spathyphyllum (summer)	Aspidistra★, Fatshedera★, Fatsia★, Hedera helix★, Helexine★, Tolmiea	Aspidistra★

A very cool room, around 5°C (40°F) to 10°C (50°F) in winter

Carex, Fatshedera (winter)★, Agapanthus	Carex, Fatshedera (winter)★ Cacti and succulents★, Heliotropium, Myrtus	Acorus, Aspidistra★, Aucuba, Carex, Fatshedera (summer)★, Ophiopogon, Clivia, Saxifraga★, Tolmiea	Aspidistra★, Aucuba, Tolmiea	Aspidistra★, Tolmiea

Feeding

Houseplants need more food during the growing period than during the dormant months - which are usually October to March.

Don't feed at all for 2-3 months after repotting. If you have used a potting compost there will be enough food in the soil. Whatever food you use, follow the maker's instructions exactly and, if the soil is dry, water first then apply the fertilizer. Overdosing a plant, or giving fertilizer on dry soil, can burn its roots.

★ For thrift use a general liquid fertilizer, such as Liquinure, _carefully_ diluted to the right strength for a very small quantity.

Pests and Diseases

If pests strike, you can try getting rid of them by putting a plastic bag over the soil, to hold the plant in its pot, and swishing the leaves in cool soapy water (pure soap not detergent). See page 345 for other natural methods.

There are good houseplant insecticides. Fisons now produce an aerosol spray which can be used on succulents - which many such can't. Take the plant out of doors to spray it, and only use sprays made for houseplants.

Common Problems	Cause
Brown tips or edges to leaves	Dry air Bruising from handling
Brown and yellow tips and edges	Any fault in culture can cause this; look for other symptoms
Curling leaves which fall	Less heat than it needs More water than it likes Draughts
Dull, lifeless, faded leaves	More light than it likes Red spider mite Dirt on the leaves
Flower buds falling	Drier air than it likes Less water than it needs Less light than it needs Shock/Insect damage
Flowers wilting fast	Less water than it needs Less light than it needs Drier air than it likes More heat than it likes
Flowers failing to be made	Less light than it needs Drier air than it likes More food than it needs Too much room in the pot
Leaves falling off suddenly	Shock - quite common on being moved, also if moved from shade to sun Much less water than it needed
Little or no growth - in winter - other times	Normal Less food than it needs Less light than it needs Less water than it needs.
Lower leaves drying and falling	Lack of light or water More heat than it likes
Rotting stems	Disease, fostered by more water than is needed - especially in winter
Rusty or reddish streaks on amaryllis	A bulb mite - destroy the bulb
Slime on the pot	Too much water is lingering
Spots on the leaves - dry light-brown - soft dark-brown - cream or white - like blisters	Less water than it needs More water than it needs The water was too chilly for it Spraying leaves which dislike water on them Disease
Variegated leaves turning plain green	Less light than it needs
White crust on the pot	Hard water Overfeeding

Common Problems	Cause
Wilting leaves	Too little water More sunlight than it likes More heat than it likes Drier air than it likes Pest damage Water not draining properly
Yellow leaves - which stay on - which fall	Hard water when it dislikes it Calcium in the compost when it dislikes it Old age of leaf - quite normal More water than it likes Cold draughts

Potting Up

Repotting is only necessary when a plant outgrows its pot. If the roots are a closely felted mass on the surface it is pot bound. This doesn't always mean you should put it in a bigger pot. Some plants flower best that way. So check. To repot take a pot only one size up.

Watering

Most plants will accept water from above or below, but cyclamen, African violets and gloxinias object to the top of their compost being wet, so they must only be watered via the saucer. Either way, use room temperature water and check the saucer 30 minutes later and throw away any water which is lying there. Sitting in water can kill then.

Most plants like their soil to be *just* moist all the time. But azaleas, for example, like to be positively wet. Dunk them every day in a bucket up to their compost level, leave for an hour and drain. In contrast, Swiss cheese plants like to become rather dry between waterings. Check on each plant's special preferences.

There are several ways to keep plants happy while you are away on holiday. How long they last depends greatly on the weather and the type of plant. In summer move plants into a cool room, but if you are turning down the heating in winter find them a warmish one. In summer a bathroom is often ideal.

● Put plastic in the bath (to keep it clean), then a thick layer of wet newspapers or bath towels. Water the plants and stand them on the wet surface.
● Put a thick layer of peat in the bottom of a container much bigger than the plant pot. Stand the pot on the peat and fill round the sides with peat. Water so the peat is moist right through.
● Push a length of material into the hole on the base of a pot, as a wick. The pot then sits on the lid of a carton full of water and the wick goes through a hole in the lid and into the water.
● Stand a bucket of water higher than the plants. Tie pieces of string to the bucket handle so that one end goes to the bottom of the bucket and the other goes down to a pot plant.

Kenneth A. Beckett, *The RHS Encyclopaedia of Houseplants*, Century
Dr D.G. Hessayon, *The House Plant Expert*, PBI

CRAFTS

Basic Sewing • Crochet • Embroidery and Tapestry • Knitting • Knots • Patchwork • Soft Furnishing

BASIC SEWING

This section is designed to fill in some of the gaps left by patterns, and to explain the basic techniques and stitches, plus the key methods used in mending. There isn't space for a complete sewing course, only for the problems which occur most often.

Bias Strips

Making bias strips for binding or for enclosing piping cord takes a great deal more fabric that you might suppose. Buy generously, or use newspaper to work out the amount you need. Either:

- Take a square or rectangle of material and fold in a triangle as illustrated. Pin and cut along the fold. Sew the triangle to the other end.
- Draw lines, parallel to the angle you have cut, the width you need. Cut the strips out.
- Machine your bias strips as illustrated.

Or fold fabric selvedge to selvedge, and seam - so you have a tube. Cut round the tube at a precise diagonal (fold the fabric to mark this) until you have a long diagonal strip which can be cut to the width needed.

Button Sewing

Basic Buttons

I once had a friend whose husband's buttons never seemed to stay on for two days together: his wife sewed the buttons on without a shank. Unless you want to make a career of resewing buttons give each one a shank. When you draw the first thread through there should be about ½ cm of thread between the button and the fabric (*more* on a thick garment, like a coat). This starts the shank.

Hold the button between your first two fingers, *keeping the shank as long as before*. When you have done enough stitches to make the button secure, wind

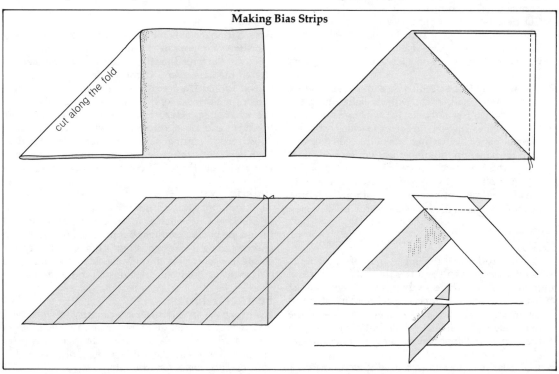

Making Bias Strips

cut along the fold

the thread several times round the shank, between the button and the garment, then finish the thread off with several small tight stitches into the back.

★ If a button has to take a lot of weight on a heavy coat, use a small flat button on the inside to take the strain. This is sewn on as you sew on the upper button, so the thread goes through its holes when it goes to the back of the fabric. It lies flat against the cloth with no shank.

★ An old tailoring trick is to have a block of beeswax, from a hardware store, and rub the thread across it. For a waxed thread will last far longer.

Buttons on Soft Fabrics

Soft fabrics, such as jersey which may be pulled by a button, can have a smaller reinforcing button put on the inside (as above). You can also support a button by putting a circle of leather cut from an old kid glove on the inside or face the button edge with tape or ribbon.

Buttons in Space

If you have to sew a button on a yawning gap in a child's shirt don't despair. Just sew it on to a length of matching strong tape. Then pin the tape on the inside of the hole, so the button goes through it, and hem in place.

Chiffon, Tulle, Net, Mohair

Fine fabrics need special handling.
- If transparent fabric needs an ordinary flat hem, allow twice the hem you think you need. With the turn-in the full depth of the hem, its edge comes on the fold and no line will show against the light. Chiffon, however, needs a rolled hem and tulle normally needs no hem at all.
- Cut these fabrics out with very sharp scissors or it will be tricky to get a straight line.
- You have to tack these materials as pins fall out. Have the fabric resting on a table to prevent it going out of shape.
- Sew with the finest needle you can and set a loose tension and small stitch, with a slight zigzag for machining chiffon and tulle, to allow for stretching.
- If fine fabrics won't slip through a machine use strips of tissue paper to give the seam body. Whether you need the paper on top, underneath or on both sides varies with the fabric. Afterwards tear off the paper. If you don't have tissue paper, newspaper will do the job - but newsprint may come off on the fabric.

★ On chiffon pin from the seam out towards the allowance: or pin holes may show in the body of the fabric.

Collars

For a collar to lie well the upper layer of fabric must be slightly larger than the lower one - it has to travel a little bit farther. There are two ways to ensure this.
- When pinning the upper layer (and its attached interfacing), match the true outer seam line of the underside with a line about 3mm (⅛ in) closer to the edge on the upper fabric (tapering to nothing at each collar point).
- If a collar is to have a fold, fold it along the neck

fold, tacking the raw edges together. If the collar is then sewn in place it should lie perfectly.

Darning

Darning is rather unfashionable. But there is something rather satisfying in keeping a beloved jumper going with a judicious darn or two.

★ Shrink darning yarn before use as it might shrink in the wash. Ten minutes in a steamer over boiling water should do the trick - but don't get it wet. Dry it thoroughly before using.

★ You can double the life of a jumper by sewing leather elbow patches on it while it's still fairly new (it is much harder to sew them on to the curve of an old and stretched sleeve). Good haberdashers sell ready-made leather patches which wash well and are ready perforated for sewing.

Dutch Darning

By far the best form of darning is Dutch darning, in which the darning thread follows the path of the knitting wool - as in Grafting page 393. It is very easy when the knitting is just thin. But for a hole you need to thread a knitting needle through each row from one side to the other, and sew over it, then sew the stitches into the row above. This is considerably trickier. Darn well into the area which is unthinned. Stop each row at a different point so that there is no hard edge and match the wool perfectly, then the repair will be almost invisible. But do use a round-ended needle.

★ The trick for threading a needle with darning wool is to fold the wool over the needle. Pinch it together firmly and slide it off the point of the needle, then push this flattened loop through the eye.

Standard Darning

Basic darning is only a little faster than Dutch darning and shows far more. Use a round-ended needle, which won't cut the threads, rather than a darning needle, and stretch the area over a darning mushroom. Take the thread to and fro across the gap using little running stitches at either side of the hole, and going well beyond the weak area. Keep the threads parallel and close together, and leave a little loop when you return, to allow for pull during wear. When the hole is filled go back *across* it in the same way, but run the needle over and under the threads it crosses - like weaving.

Elastic

The traditional way to **insert elastic** into, say, a pair of knickers is to stitch it to the eye of a bodkin and thread the bodkin through. But pinning on a safety-pin and threading it through is much quicker. To **replace elastic** just sew or pin the new elastic to one end of the old, then just pull out the old, pull in the new.

Feather Fillings

Feathers have an extraordinary capacity to work their way through fabric. Only very closely woven fabric, such as pillow ticking, will frustrate them. An extra precaution is to rub the inside of the fabric throughly with beeswax before stuffing it.

If you have to transfer feathers from one pillow to another be prepared for them to fly. One way to avoid this is to make matching openings in the two pillows, sew the two openings mouth to mouth and push the feathers through from one to the other. A faster way was devised by an ingenious manageress of a bookshop in the Midlands. She cleaned her vacuum cleaner, removed the bag from it, attached a pillow in its place and sucked the feathers out of the old container - with an extension nozzle - straight into the new one.

Hems

The techniques for finishing a hem vary according to the type and thickness of the fabric, and whether the hem is on a fairly straight line or round a curve. But before sewing, trim the hem allowance so that an even amount will be turned up all round.

★ Full skirts drop where they are on the bias. So hang them up for a few days, to drop, before the hem is put up.

Human anatomy is much less even than we might suppose. For the best hemline, wear the garment and the shoes you intend to wear with it, and get someone to mark an even distance up *from the floor* with tailor's chalk, and a long ruler.

Easing Fullness
If a skirt is full, extra fabric has to be eased in - binding should be attached first.

1 Run gathering threads round the upper edge of the hem. Draw them up so the turned-up edge fits perfectly. Pin it down. Tack it in position. Press the edge in place. This is a good method when there is only a little extra fullness to be lost, and on wool you may find that pressing makes the easing perfectly flat. The hem can then be herring boned (see right).
2 Pin up the hem, matching seams to seams and also matching the straight of the material (i.e. the vertical weave). Take lots of tiny 'darts' to ease in the fullness between the pinning. Pin, press, and sew them down.
3 A very slight amount of extra fabric can be disposed of by making your hem stitch a little to the right of where it would normally be. (The left for left-handers.)

Plain Hem

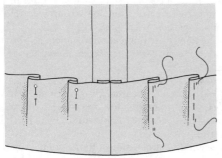

This is a hem for lightweight fabrics. Turn the hem up on the marked line and pin it in place. Trim it even if

necessary. Turn the upper edge in less than 1 cm (½in). Then press and pin it all round, taking darts as shown above if needs be. Perfectionists tack the hem but, at a pinch, you can get away with pinning only - unless it's on a very full skirt or a very soft fabric. Try the garment on, check the hem and adjust if necessary. Hem stitch in place as shown.

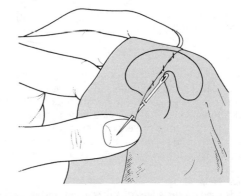

Some people hem most comfortably with the lower edge of the hem towards them; others with the garment towards them. The stitch ends up the same, either way.

Bias-edged Hems
A bias-edged hem suits a fabric which would make a bulky line if it were turned in. Equally, if there isn't enough material to make a decent width of hem use wide bias binding. It should match as closely as possible.

Establish the depth of the hem and trim any unevenness. Open one folded edge of bias binding and pin it along the edge of the hem without stretching or puckering, and machine it along its fold line. Hem like a plain hem.

Herringboned Hem
Herringbone stitch is mainly used for stretch fabrics, as it stretches more than ordinary hemming. It is also good on trouser hems, and moderately thick fabrics which might create a ridge by other methods.

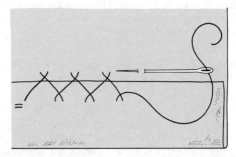

If the edge might fray oversew it. Otherwise pink it. Turn up the hem and pin leaving the upper edge flat, not turned under. Sew as illustrated, being careful not to pull the thread too tight or it will press the hem edge against the right side and form a ridge.

Blindstitched Hem

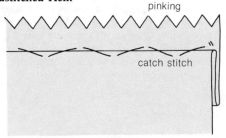

pinking

catch stitch

This is ideal for thick fabrics as the upper edge isn't pressed against the right side, so a ridge is avoided.

Finish the edge as for a herringboned hem (see illustration on page 375), but pin the hem in place 1 cm (½ in) down from its top edge. Tack if necessary. Fold back the fabric and sew as illustrated above, using catch stitch, being careful not to pull the thread too tight.

Rolled Hem

This is used on the edges of silk scarves and is used on chiffon and similar fabrics. Hold the fabric as illustrated for hem stitch and hem it finely, but just rolling the very edge under with your thumb and hemming it down. This is very tricky to do at first, but it gets easier.

Sometimes a tiny edge is turned in and machined down, then rolled by hand afterwards. Try both ways on scraps and see what suits you and your material.

Removing Hem Lines in Tough Fabrics

Margaret Thatcher says that the secret of being able to put hems up or down as fashion demands, is never to press a sharp edge in a hem. She has a point. But if a hem already has a sharp fold in tweed, undo the hem and open it out on an ironing board. Using a damp cloth, and an iron as hot as the fabric can stand, press the fold out as much as possible. Then place a thick piece of old-fashioned white cotton twine exactly along the foldline on the *right* side, and press with a damp cloth again. Remove the cloth and cover the area with the wooden 'banger' described on page 378. When the fabric is cool remove the wood and move on to the next section. The string should remove the dent. But if it doesn't, repeat the process. This time get someone to hold the string taut along the line while you hit it firmly into the line with the 'banger'.

★ To make a doubled thread less likely to twist into knots put a knot in each end separately.

Interfacing

Suit the weight to the fabric and the job in hand, and match the interlining to whether you will wash or dry clean the garment. The stick-on kinds can be useful for quickly made garments, like children's clothes, but the woven interlinings give a more professional finish.

On something like a cuff first attach the interlining to whichever side will be uppermost - then the interlining conceals the ridges created by the seam allowances.

Jersey

The ease with which jersey can be sewn varies with the fibre it is made of. Heavy jersey is easy; fine silk jersey is for the expert or the incautious.

● Use a ball-ended needle - pointed needles can cut the thread and make jersey ladder.
● Use a *very slight* zigzag stitch to give a little stretch to the seam. This prevents the thread breaking when the garment is worn.
● Very fine glove and lingerie jersey may need to be sewn with tissue paper, like chiffon (page 374).
● Hand oversew open seams.

★ Out of the packing it's hard to tell which needles are ball-ended and which aren't. For instant recognition put a dab of nail varnish near the top of all ball-ended ones.

Leather

When sewing leather there is no room for error. You can't pin it and you can't take stitches out without leaving a permanent line. The following instructions are for making soft leather garments. Heavy handbag and belt leather needs a heavy duty machine or hand sewing.

Patterns for Leather

As leather is limited in size you either have to choose a pattern with quite a few seams or be prepared to create seams where none exist. Plan extra seams carefully so they will match up front and back. As you can't unpick leather, the pattern needs to be carefully fitted and altered and if the leather is expensive, make the garment in calico first to make sure it fits perfectly.

Cutting Out Leather

First check the skin for flaws. If it has any, mark them exactly in chalk on the wrong side, so you can skirt round them. Place the pattern pieces on the leather so that any nap will run down the body on all the pieces. Stick them down with sellotape. Draw round the outline with school chalk - tailor's chalk contains grease and may mark leather. Make pencil holes at the marking points on the pattern and mark these points with chalk (or a biro works well on the wrong side). Cut out.

Sewing Leather

Those who can't sew a straight line should draw the seam lines with a ruler on the wrong side. Hold the sections together with paperclips, bulldog clips or sellotape bent over the seam allowance. But be sure to keep all these strictly to the seam allowance, to avoid marks.

To sew it, by hand or by machine, use a special three-sided leather needle - leather clings impossibly to round needles. Choose the smallest one which will handle the thickness, and do a few samples to see what stitch length looks right.

Slit sewn darts open almost to the point, trim to look like seams and stick darts, hems and seams down with a touch of rubberized adhesive - unless the leather is fine enough for this to spoil its softness.

Machine Sewing

Ending Stitching
If it is left unfinished off machine stitching will undo just as much as hand sewing. When you come to the end of a dart, or any section which won't be reinforced with other stitching, sew the stitching back up for 1.5 cm (¾ in) to secure it.

Stitch Size
The size of stitch needs to be altered to suit each type of fabric. On the whole, thicker fabrics need longer stitches, but the texture also matters. So check the stitch on off-cuts of the same number of layers, then pull them open and see how it will look on seams.

Turning Corners
1 Stop just short of the corner.
2 Turn the large wheel, on the right of the machine, by hand, until the needle reaches the exact point you want. Then wind the needle *well into the fabric*. Lift the foot.
3 Turn the fabric until the foot is pointing down the next section. Bring the foot down and machine the next section.

Turning Points

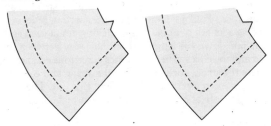

Oddly, you will get a sharper effect by not sewing a point at all. Sew almost to the point. Turn the foot as above. Sew one or two stitches across the point - depending on the length of your stitches. Turn the corner again, and continue.

Exactly the same method is used when a neckline has a faced slash at the centre front.

★ The quick way to change from one sewing thread to another, on a machine, is to break the old thread near the reel, tie the new one to the broken end and pull the new thread through to the needle.

Marking Up Dressmaking
It saves a lot of time if all the markings are transferred to the fabric before the pattern is removed from it. This means you can match one section precisely to another with the minimum of fiddling about.

Where the pattern has a V notch, cut a V sticking out from the seam allowance.

Where there are holes or black dots the method of marking them needs to be chosen to suit the situation: there is no point in spending hours using method (1) on a child's cotton dress.

1 Have a long tacking cotton, on the double, and take a stitch into each marking point, through the paper. In two layers of fabric you leave the ends *very* long. When you unpin the pattern you pull the two layers slightly apart and cut between them, leaving tags of cotton in both.
2 A soft lead pencil marks cottons beautifully and washes out if you aren't heavy-handed with it.
3 You can mark through the holes with tailor's chalk, but it tends to rub off, so sew up soon after.
4 A small spiked tracing wheel used with tailoring carbon paper gives a line of dots on basic cottons.

Matching Stripes (and Other Patterns)
Bold patterns or horizontal stripes or checks have to match at seams if the garment is to look good. This needs forethought when you cut the pieces out, and some careful pinning when you sew it. Buy enough material to shunt the pattern pieces about.

Cutting Out Stripes to Match
When you need patterns to match it is usually safest to cut each piece singly. With the fabric the wrong side up position and pin a pattern piece on to it. Mark on the paper the exact position of any major lines or patterns. Then mark the position of the pattern piece on the fabric with tailor's chalk. Then *turn the paper over* and place it for cutting the other half, using the marks you made on the paper to get a perfect match to stripes or patterns. When you have done this with all the pieces, and are sure that they will all fit on the fabric, cut the first piece of each pattern. Turn the uncut fabric over and place the paper patterns - with the fabric still attached - on the positions you chalked. Match the lines or patterns perfectly, pin in place and cut out.

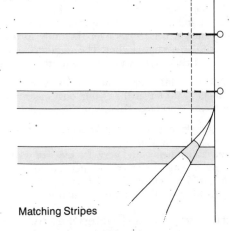

Matching Stripes

Sometimes it is impossible to have stripes or a pattern meeting everywhere. So decide which part will most catch the eye and try to get the best match at that point. Then let the rest look after itself.

Sewing Patterns and Stripes
Books often insist that to get a perfect match you must tack your seams. This simply isn't true. Tacking is much

looser than frequent pinning. You get the best match by using long thin tailoring pins. Roughly pin your seam edge to edge. Then start at whatever point on the seam most catches the eye and exactly match the sections of fabric on the seam line, pinning so the pin is at right angles to the seam. Do this at small intervals all down the seam and machine it immediately. If you have used fine pins, the machine should go over them without breaking the needle.

Moygashel and Linen

These loosely woven fabrics have a dreadful tendency to fray. The only way to prevent this is to oversew the seams as soon as you cut out the pattern pieces. But first work out where you will need to trim them.

Patching Knees

When small boys are at that age when they are all knees and elbows abandon hope of them having decent trousers for everyday and patch them on the inside as soon as you buy them. They may look stiff in front but they will last twice as long without springing a hole. This is no situation for 'cordon bleu' sewing. An iron-on patch is the answer.

★ Once a knee is through you may find enough for a patch inside a pocket. You can then replace it with a different fabric or sew up the pocket.

Pattern Fitting

Check that a pattern fits before cutting it out. It allows you to take a pattern up somewhere above the bottom edge, make a tuck or insert a section (but remember to redraw the seam line so it looks right, a tuck may have produced a stepped effect). If you have to add or subtract from seams it is much better to adjust several slightly than make a big change on one.

Bear in mind that there must always be a few inches extra so the garment flows over the body instead of hugging it like a sausage skin. The standard amounts for a close-fitting style which will skim the body are:

skirt 7.5 cm (3 in) larger than your hip size
bust 10 cm (4 in) larger than your bust measurement
sleeve 5 cm (2 in) larger than your upper arm

For loose styles or sizes over 102 cm (40 in) hip or over, the ease should be greater.

Some adjustments are very tricky. For example, adjusting for uneven or very sloping shoulders. If this is your problem, put in shoulder pads and adjust the thickness to make the shoulders balance.

Plastic and Plastic-Coated Fabric

PVC-coated cotton tends to stick to the machine foot. The solution is just to brush a little cooking oil down the seam line before sewing. But be sure to wash it off with soap as oil hardens some plastic.

Light plastic needs paper on the seam (page 382). Use a long stitch, as the plastic is weakened with every needle hole, and if it suits the situation, strengthen it by sewing in straight tape or seam binding.

Pressing

The most important way to make garments look less home-made is simply the old tailor's trick of pressing each seam as you go along (though not on velvet or other fabrics which cannot be ironed). Use a steam iron on lightweight fabrics. On most wool use a clean, very damp cloth between the iron and the fabric.

Wool fabrics tend to spring up even after pressing. Tailors cure this by using a 'banger' (also called a 'basher' or 'knocker') - a piece of wood about the size of a brick with a flat base. Tailors use a good bit of hardwood, but a chunk of smooth pine is fine. Rest this on the fabric, for a minute or two, immediately you remove the iron: the wood absorbs the steam and you get a perfectly flat result. If an area is obstinate - and the fabric can stand it - bang the seam into docility with it. But it won't cure excess thickness where surplus should have been trimmed off (page 381).

★ To make the two halves of press studs match perfectly sew the male one on first. Rub chalk on its 'nose'. Press this against the other section of fabric. Push a pin up through the chalk mark, sit the female half on the pin, and sew it in place.

Rouleau Ties (Shoestring Straps)

To make the very thin fabric cords used as shoestring straps, cut a strip of material, on the bias, twice the width you want the strap to be, plus a small seam allowance. Fold in half lengthwise, wrong side out, placing a length of twine inside sticking out at each end. Machine down the length, about half way between the fold and the edges. Then sew twice across one end across where the string sticks out. Pull the string and ease the rouleau down over it until it is right side out. Then cut the string off at the end where it is attached.

Seams

Open Seams (Plain Seam)

The basic seam is an open seam. For this you just put the two right sides together, edge to edge, machine down it and press it open. The classic seam width is 1.5 cm (⅝ in). The edges are finished as follows:

Cutting with pinking shears if the fabric won't fray.

Oversewing, by a machine zig-zag or by hand. Hand oversewing is one of the best finishes of all.

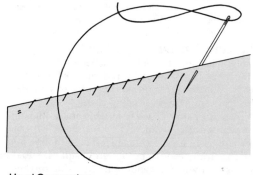

Hand Oversewing

Turning the edge in and machining it down. This suits very fine, firm fabrics like lawn.

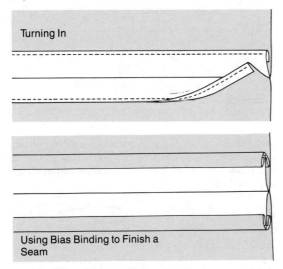

Turning In

Using Bias Binding to Finish a Seam

Self-finishing by trimming one seam allowance short and folding the other round it and hemming it. For very fine and sheer fabrics.

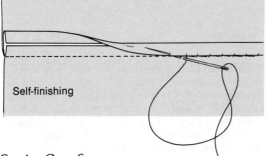

Self-finishing

Curving Open Seams
When an open seam has to go round a curve, slits must be cut in the seam allowance which goes round the longer curve and V-shaped notches cut from the smaller.

Double Stitched Seam (Flat Seam)

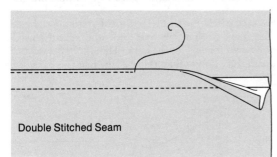

Double Stitched Seam

1 Make this like an open seam.
2 Trim *one* seam allowance to 5 mm ($^3/_{16}$ in).
3 Fold the other seam allowance over it and iron on the right side to get a sharp seam.

4 Fold in the edge of the longer allowance, tack down and machine down from the right side.

When this is used as a decorative seam (welt seam) start by making the open seam so it opens with the raw edges on the *right* side.

Simple Flat Seam
For interlinings just overlap the edges by 1.5 cm ($^5/_8$ in) and machine down them.

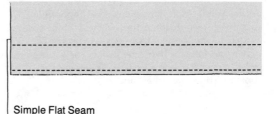

Simple Flat Seam

French Seam
This starts the opposite way to most seams. Pin the *wrong* sides together, and machine down only 1 cm ($^3/_8$ in) from the edge. *Iron the seam open.* Fold along the seam line, *right* sides together. Pin together and machine along the main seam line (having first trimmed off any seam allowance which might stick out through the seam.)

★ This is good for sheer fabrics where a seam will show. Open seams can also be converted into a kind of French seam by folding the raw edges in towards each other and holding them together with a fine running stitch. This is the best way to finish armholes on transparent fabrics.

★ When the initial seam is made like an open seam, but not opened up, as at the edge of a cuff or collar, press *open* the seam as if it was going to be used as an open seam, *then* fold it to its final flat position.

Silk
Silk is easily spoilt by the wrong handling and frays very easily. So work as quickly as possible, and don't fuss over it too much.
● Use fine tailoring pins.
● Use a fine needle (e.g. a machine needle, such as number 70).
● Sew with silk thread, use silk lining material - such as jap silk, and for very fine silk follow the tips for fine fabrics (page 374).
● Finish off raw edges by hand.

Sleeve Insertion
An excellent method of inserting the head of a sleeve smoothly into an armhole is one I was taught to use when tailoring.
1 Turn the sleeve inside out and the 'bodice' right side out. Put the 'bodice' down the sleeve so that the two armholes match.
2 Pin the underarm seams and matching notches.

3 Pin round, with pins at right angles to the seam, easing the fullness over the top of the armhole and pinning at frequent intervals to distribute it evenly. Press on a small ironing board or tailor's ham if this is appropriate. Sew.

Having the sleeve as the top fabric when you machine also makes it easy to avoid sewing in little wrinkles. Distributing gathers evenly is also easier this way.

> With a bulky garment it may be impossible to put the top half down the sleeve. In that case, just turn the sleeve head back as illustrated. Then machine in two operations - sew the top with it turned back like that, then sew the bottom from the other side.

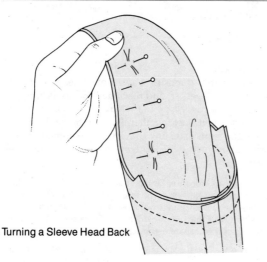

Turning a Sleeve Head Back

Stitches

Backstitch can replace machining - if you can sew straight enough (have a chalk or pencil line). Bring the needle up a stitch length ahead then down through the front of the previous stitch. And so on. The length of each stitch should mimic the size of a machine stitch.

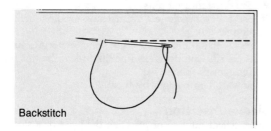

Backstitch

Tacking (Basting) is a long stitch used to hold a seam before it is machined. Chalk a line to sew along or stretch the thread ahead of you and hold it down with your thumb as a guideline. The stitches are each about 2cm (½ to 1 in) long (see above right).

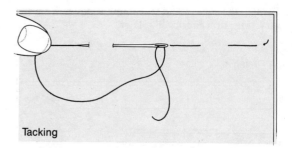

Tacking

Lock Stitch is a *very* long, loose stitch used to hold the lining and interlining to a curtain so that they move as one. Only a thread of the main curtain material should be picked up.

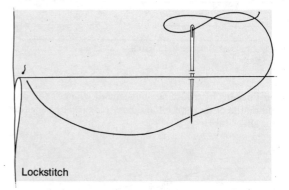

Lockstitch

For **running stitch** (gathering stitch) make a series of stitches each a small fraction of a centimetre long. Do this several stitches at a time by just dipping the point of the needle in and out, until the needle-tip is full. As there is always a risk of a gathering thread breaking put two rows of running stitch very close together for gathering and pull both at once.

Divide the area to be gathered into halves or, quarters, or even eighths and sixteenths, if necessary, and mark the same fractions where the gathering will be attached. Then the points can be matched. When the gathering is the correct length put a pin in and wind the threads round it in a figure of 8 to hold them.

For **stab stitch** you bring the thread up to the right side then, *very* close to where it came out, stab the needle down and through to the back. The stitches at the back are slightly longer than those at the front. It *cannot* be

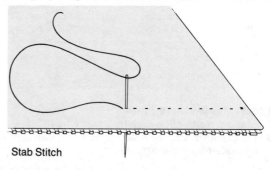

Stab Stitch

done as a single movement, and to do it well you need the shortest, finest needle which will hold your thread.

Tools

Machines
Modern computerized sewing machines can do wondrous things, but only the most dedicated seamstress will use a fraction of them. It should be easy to change the foot and the needle and it is useful if the base plate sticks out like an ironing board end, then you can curve an armhole around it. If a machine can do the following it will do most jobs:

- sew forwards and backwards with easy adjustment of stitch size
- do a basic zigzag stitch in varying stitch sizes
- do a zigzag created by lots of little stitches.

Needles for Sewing Machines
Using the right type of needle makes a difference.

Standard needle: Size 80 (11) for fine sewing. Size 90 (14) for medium weight fabrics. Size 100 (16) for heavy fabrics. Size 110 (18) for thick threads.

Ballpoints are for sewing jersey. Use size 70 (9) for very fine jersey, other sizes as standard. Ballpoints can also be Teflon-coated, to prevent the needle skipping on Lycra. Needles with names like 'Perfect Stitch' are specially ground to get better results on man-made fibres - but an ordinary ballpoint and a slight zigzag copes with most fabrics.

Spearpoint Needles are 3-sided for leather use: size 80 (11) for chamois, size 90 (14) for most clothing leather.

Denim Needles also sew canvas, denim, heavy linen, twill, heavy plastics and imitation leather. Size 90 (14) light denim. Size 100 (16) denim. Size 110 (18) fur fabric or very heavy upholstery. Size 120 (19) canvas.

Needles for Hand Sewing
The most essential tool is a fine needle. Not even an archangel could sew a fine seam with the rapiers which people often use. Strictly speaking, different types of needles should be used for different jobs, but for most dressmaking you can get good results with a no 10 crewel. This is not really correct, but its long eye is easier to thread than a round-eyed needle like a between, it is flexible enough to do good hemming, and long enough to sew on buttons. Even so, a very short, fine between must be used for stitches like stab stitch.

However awkward it feels at first, anyone who intends to sew should learn to use a thimble. It makes sewing much faster and more accurate. It goes on the middle finger and should be metal, as plastic can crack.

Pins
Choose long fine tailoring pins in good steel.

Scissors
Sharp cutting-out scissors, with long blades, are essential for dressmaking. Left-handers who have trouble finding them should write to Wilkinson Sword (page 361 or see page 203.) This company also makes a remarkably effective and inexpensive device for sharpening scissors.

Threads
Use a thread which is the same fibre as whatever you are sewing - or as close as you can get. Man-made fibres are infuriating to thread through a needle. Mercerized cotton is the most pleasant thread for wool, cotton, and blends. For synthetics, and stretch fabrics where the strength of synthetic threads is an advantage, get a mixed thread combining a synthetic core with a cotton coating, such as Coats Duet or Sylko Supreme.

Thick button-hole threads are used for button-holes. The polyester version is widely available, the silk version isn't, but is much more pleasant to sew with.

★ If thread knots during hand sewing put the point of the needle through the loop and gently tug each end of the thread in turn. One of them will pull and allow the slip knot to undo.
★ If you have to use synthetic thread run it through a block of beeswax before sewing to stop it twisting.
★ To thread synthetic thread through a needle, have very sharp scissors and cut it at an angle. The same may work with cotton thread, but if it doesn't, wet it and bite it flat.
★ You can buy needle threaders to make it easier to thread machines; failing that, the finest fuse wire bent to a similar shape will do the job on some needles.

Trimming Bulk
Whenever seam allowances threaten to produce unsightly bulges they need to be trimmed so they lie flat - after you have checked that the sewing is correct, and the fit good. How close you cut must be varied with the type of fabric; those which fray easily need far bigger turnings. A balance has to be struck between leaving bulk and trimming off so much that the seam is weakened - judge each situation on its merits.

If you cut several layers as one there will be a nasty ridge when the area is pressed. To avoid this trim the seam allowances in a series of steps, with the allowance which will be closest to the surface of the finished garment the longest one.

On points the angle of cut should leave the angle of the seams smaller than the corner they have to fit into when it is turned right side out.

Whenever gathering has to be pressed flat, within a small space - such as a waistband - it should, ideally, be trimmed to flatten it.

Velvet, Velour, Velveteen and Corduroy
These vary enormously in handling. Ordinary cotton velveteen and corduroy can almost be treated like any other fabric, but high-pile velvet is probably the hardest of all fabrics to sew successfully at home and may be impossible to press. Beginners should avoid it and even the expert be wary. The only exception is certain furnishing velvet.

Pattern Choosing
It is hard to get a good finish on seams on velvet. So

choose a pattern which has no seams in places which catch the eye. For most velvet avoid patterns which need buttonholes: it may be impossible to make satisfactory ones.

Making Up

All these fabrics must be cut out so the nap runs the same way on all the pieces. This is normally up the body on clothes, but downwards on curtains - so it catches the dust less. But these rules aren't sacred; hold it up and choose the effect you prefer.

Corduroy can be sewn like any other fabric, but all the others in this family need more care. Tack and machine all seams *in the direction of the pile,* and don't have too tight a stitch, or they may pucker. If they still pucker put tissue paper *between* the two layers of fabric. If it still puckers hand sew every seam. Jersey velvet should be treated like jersey (page 382).

★ On velvet use stab stitch for inserting a zip.

Pressing

Some velvets mark permanently when pressed. Experiment on spare pieces of fabric to discover how far you can go - it varies considerably with the composition of the fabric. Try putting a spare piece face up, with the section you are ironing face down over it, so the pile is cushioned. If you can't press it properly at home a dry cleaner may be persuaded to do it for you.

Waistbands

Most patterns tell you to use fabric on both sides of a waistband. On fabric of any thickness sew a length of stiff Petersham ribbon to replace the inside section. This makes the band much less bulky.

★ Most fabrics have a right side and a wrong side. On plain fabrics where the two are similar check the selvedge. The wrong side usually has a less finished edge.

Zips

Basic Zip

● Sew up the seam to a point a fraction above where the base of the zip will come - stop and machine back for 2 cm.
● Tack the remainder of the seam together on the seam line, using rather short tacking stitches.
● Iron the seam open on the wrong side.
● Pin the zip so the top is just below the waistband or top of the opening with the teeth exactly behind the centre of the seam. Tack in place.
● Using a zip foot, machine, turning in the corners as on page 377.

★ For a couture finish sew the zip in by hand using stab stitch (see page 380).

Concealed Zip

For a lapped or concealed zip, sew the seam as above.
● Use chalk or tacking to mark the seam line up each side of the zip opening.
● Tack the other (rear) seam allowance so that the

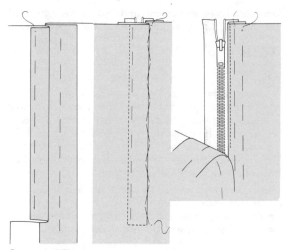

Concealed Zip

folded edge will lap under the other side, by about 3-4 mm, when the marked seam lines meet. Cut the seam allowance to let it lie flat. Press. ★
● Tack the zip as illustrated, and machine with a zip foot.
● Catch the front section so the seam lines meet. Then tack the zip where it lies against it. And sew in, using stab stitch, for the neatest finish of all.

> If machining, leave the ends long where the machining stops at the bottom. Thread the top thread on a needle and take it through to the back and finish it off. Finish off the back thread by hand too.

Replacing a Skirt Zip

To replace a zip in a skirt or dress unpick the stitches holding the zip in place. If unpicking part of the skirt band is too difficult, or you won't be able to resew it, cut the zip off flush with the waistband. (When you sew in the new zip you can't insert the tops tidily under the band. But you can turn them at right angles and sew them down.) Having removed the zip, pull out every scrap of thread from the old stitching. Then insert the zip as in method (1) or (2) above. ·

Inserting or Replacing a Trouser Zip

Sewing a zip in trousers looks very complicated. In fact, it is very easy if you take it step by step. The steps are the same as for a Concealed Zip up to the ★.
● Place the work face up and fold half the garment out of the way so you can tack the zip to the seam allowance on the undersection. Machine it in.
● Put the fly opening in place and lock stitch closed.
● Turn wrong side up and fold the undersection of the garment out of the way so you can tack and machine the free half of the zip to the underlap extension.
● Tack the zip guard (which stops the zip catching where it hurts) and machine it to the underlap extension.

● Turn right side up and machine the curve of the fly.

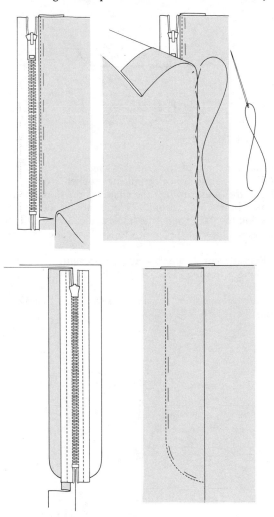

Replacing a Trouser Zip

More information

Ann Ladbury, *Dressmaking with Basic Patterns*, Batsford.
Ann Ladbury, *Fabrics*, Sidgwick and Jackson - An A-Z of
fabrics and how they behave when sewn.

   Clothkits, Lewes Design Workshop Ltd, 24 High Street,
Lewes, Sussex BN7 2LB Tel: 0273 477111. Sells ready-cut and
printed clothes by mail order.

CROCHET

The basic operation in most crochet is pulling a loop
of thread through a loop, or loops, already on the hook.
A huge range of stitches can be produced but you really
need a pattern. So what I have given here are the basics
of how to start, plus the stitches which are used most
often. When I refer to a certain number of 'loops on
the hook', both completed loops and a wind of yarn
round the hook count as 'loops'.

Basics

Unless crochet is being used to edge some existing work
there are usually three steps to starting.
1 A chain is made to the length needed.
2 A foundation row is often used to give firmness.
3 The pattern rows. (In the first row the hook should
   pass under the top *two* threads of the foundation row,
   at each stitch, unless the pattern says otherwise).

Beginning

Have the hook in your right hand like a pen. Attach
the yarn to the hook with a slip knot. Twist the yarn
round the little finger of the left hand, so it emerges over
the back of the finger, passes under the ring finger, and
over the second and first finger. Hold the other end of
thread, which trails from the loop, between the thumb
and second finger of the left hand, and keep the yarn
taut to the ball by lifting your first finger.

   To make a loop you then sweep the hook under and
round the yarn, moving towards you, and draw the
yarn back through the loop made by the slip knot. The
knack is to have the yarn comfortably firm, but not too
tight, and to roll the hook towards you, as you draw
the yarn through. (Left-handers reverse the use of the
hands.)

   For a Chain just keep pulling each loop through the
one before until you have the right number. In counting
stitches the loop on the hook is not included.

Turning Chains

A unique feature of crochet is that each row has a height
which is not related to the thickness of the thread or
the size of hook. So you can't simply stop at the end
of a row and turn to go back. On all but the shallowest
rows you need to add a few chain stitches at the end
of each row, which are carried up the edge of the work.
This 'turning chain' varies with the height of the stitch
to be worked in the following row — which is why
instructions often tell you to put the hook through the
second, third or fourth stitch to start a row, and into
every stitch after that. If you crochet stripes start
working in the new colour at the *beginning* of the
turning chain - or you will have the wrong colour
running up the end of the next row.

Finishing the Work

Cut the thread a few inches away from the last loop.
Slip the thread through the loop and draw it tight. Then
darn the end of thread invisibly with a tapestry needle.

   Crochet in mercerized cotton should be washed when
it's finished and sewn up. Then block it to shape as for
knitting and iron it through white tissue paper.

Increasing and Decreasing

In crochet the methods of increasing and decreasing vary
according to the stitch you are doing, and a good pattern
should give the details.

Joining Yarn

To join new yarn lie the remaining tail of old yarn along
the top edge of the work, with the end of the new yarn

beside it. Then, as each stitch is made, the two are bound in. If you change colour bind in the old colour only, then bind in the new colour on the return row.

Tension

You should work a pattern square to see if your tension agrees with the pattern before starting the work. The size of the crochet hook can be adjusted up or down to alter the size of the work - just as in knitting.

Stitches

Slip Stitch is a very flat stitch.
1 Make a chain of the required length (unless you have some other row to work from).
2 Slip the hook through the nearest stitch of the row you have made, and draw the yarn through both this stitch and the loop on the hook. Repeat into each stitch along the chain for the length needed.

Double Crochet produces a strong close fabric.

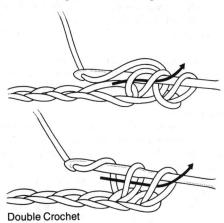

Double Crochet

1 Make a chain of the required length.
2 Slip the hook through the chain, one stitch away, and draw a loop through (2 loops are on the hook).
3 Hook the yarn and draw it through both loops.
4 Repeat 2 and 3 into every loop in the chain.
5 Make a turning chain of 1 stitch at the end of the row.

Half Treble creates a slightly more open fabric.

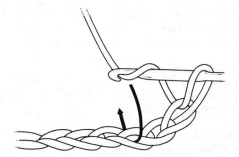

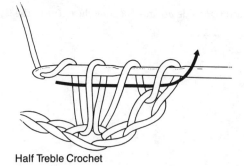

Half Treble Crochet

1 Make a chain of the required length.
2 Twist the yarn once round the crochet hook.
3 Slip the hook through the chain, at the third stitch, and draw a loop through (3 loops are on the hook).
4 Wind the yarn round the hook and draw it through all the loops on the hook - to leave one loop on the hook.
5 Repeat steps 2, 3 and 4 into *each* chain.
6 Make a turning chain of 2 at the end of the row.

Treble follows steps 1, 2 and 3 as for a half treble but into the fourth stitch, then:

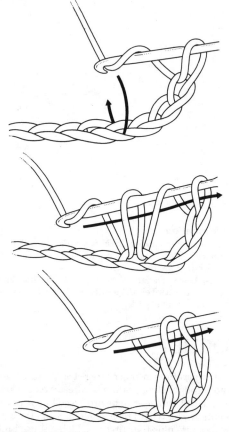

Treble Crochet

4 Wind the yarn around the hook and draw it through all but the last loop (2 loops on the hook).

5 Wind the yarn round the hook and draw it through both loops on the hook.

6 Repeat steps **2**, **3**, **4** and **5** into each chain.

7 Make a turning chain of **3** at the end of the row.

Sizes for Crochet Hooks

The sizing of crochet hooks grew up with the centuries, and the result is chaos. In Britain, they are now measured in millimetres. But crochet hooks tend to travel down the generations, so you may meet hooks using old sizing.

The old British sizing uses two different numbering systems - one for the larger hooks made of aluminium and plastic, and one for the smaller steel ones - and there is a confusing patch where they overlap in the middle. The American sizing uses the same principle but excels itself with two number series and one alphabet series - but they always do it bigger in the States.

The yarns given below will give a reasonably close piece of work, a larger hook creates a lacy effect.

	mercerized cotton						up to 4 ply wool or cotton				double knitting cotton or wool		chunky yarns						
No.	60	60	40/50	20	10	5													
mm	0.60	0.75	1.00	1.25	1.50	1.75	2.00	2.50	3.00	3.50	4.00	4.50	5.00	5.50	6.00	7.00	8.00	9.00	10.00
British	6	5	4	3	2½	2	1	2/0											
British							14	12	11	9	8	7	6	5	4	2	1/0	2/0	3/0
US								1	2	4	5	6	7	8	9	10½	12	15	
US	14	12	10	8–9	6	4	1	1–0											
US							B	C	D	E	F	G	H	I	J	K			P

More information

Sally Harding, *Crochet Style,* Windward - a book that includes Tunisian crochet if you are curious about it.

Pauline Turner, *Creative Design in Crochet*, Batsford — dated designs, but a wide range of stitches and techniques. *Starting Crochet* - a Coats booklet from Coats stockists.

EMBROIDERY AND TAPESTRY

It is high time that embroidery was rescued from the sexist, ageist backwater to which it has been consigned. Even in the 1920s it was considered a good pastime for both sexes and was much favoured by officers in the navy. With the right stitches and the right threads even the relatively unskilled can have a lot of fun, and produce some attractive results - think of the peasant embroideries of Mexico and India. Embroidery with colourful threads is a great wet afternoon pastime for children from the age of 8 onwards. And it does a lot to make them neat-fingered - a Victorian virtue, but one worth having.

Crewel Embroidery

Embroidery can be done on any fabric, from the finest silk or lawn to heavy linen, but it is seldom worth spending time on it unless the material is a good quality natural fibre. Whatever the fabric, you will get a much better result with far less effort with an embroidery frame. The easiest to use are those which have a stand, or clamp on to a table, but even the simplest frame will pay dividends. Place the fabric over the smaller ring, put the larger ring on top, tug the fabric until it is smooth, but not unduly stretched, then tighten the upper ring.

The big divide in threads is between wool and cotton - silk is rare now. Wool wears better, but only suits the heavier fabrics. And **stranded cotton** is much more versatile. It's soft and silky and its six fine strands can be separated. So you can use a single thread for the finest stitches or all six for chunky work, or combine strands of different shades. It suits any fabric, and crewel needles numbers 5 to 8, according to the number of strands. The finer the needle the better

★ If the thread gets twisted let it hang down with the needle on the end and it will untwist.

★ To thread a needle with any springy thread, such as wool, fold it over the needle. Press it between finger and thumb as you draw it off the point of the needle - then thread this flattened loop through the eye of the needle.

★ If you prick yourself and drop blood on your work, chew a small ball of white cotton and use the saliva-filled ball to dab off the blood immediately. It should leave no stain, if you do this quickly.

Copying a Design

● The easiest way to acquire a design is to buy a transfer, place it face down on the fabric, pin it carefully in position (centre it if necessary) and iron it with a fairly hot iron.

● You can place dressmaker's carbon paper on the fabric, pin the design over and trace simple outlines with a tracing wheel.

● You can trace any design on tracing paper, then enlarge or reduce it by the square method given below. Once it is the right size the easiest way to trace a complex design on to light-coloured fabric is to go over the design in black ink. Then place it on a sheet of glass. Fix the fabric carefully over it. Then shine a light up so the design will show through clearly and you can draw it onto the fabric with a pencil or special pen.

- To enlarge or reduce a design draw a grid of lines over it. Take a fresh sheet of paper, the right size for your final work and draw a grid of the same number of squares on this. Then copy the design from one to the other, copying the position of each line and shape in relation to the lines and squares of the grid.

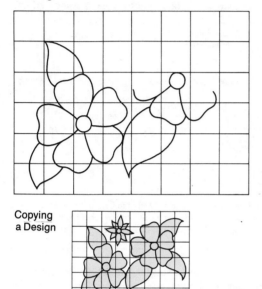

Copying a Design

Embroidery Stitches

Start with a small knot underneath, and finish by taking several stitches into the threads on the underside, or weaving the thread a suitable distance through them before cutting it.

Chain Stitch makes quite substantial lines. Bring the thread up to the right side and take a stitch as shown. Pull the needle through, above it so that the thread forms an elongated horseshoe.

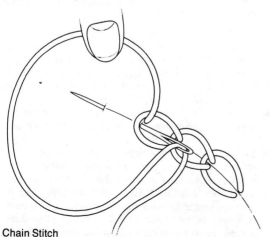

Chain Stitch

French Knots are used as the stamens of flowers. With the needle pointing *up* the thread, wind it several times round. Then push the needle through the fabric, close to where it came out, tighten and pull it through.

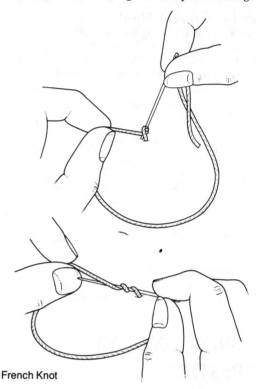

French Knot

Lazy Daisy is an easy stitch for making small flowers. Make a stitch as shown, and pull the needle through, so the thread forms a loop round it. Then push it down, so a stitch straddles the end of the loop. Bring the needle out at the base of the next petal and repeat.

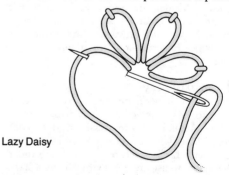

Lazy Daisy

Satin Stitch is hard to do well and always needs an embroidery frame. The thread can lie either straight across or at any angle. But the stitches must be perfectly parallel and close together, so no fabric shows.

For long and short satin stitch the next layer of stitches can either mesh irregularly into the bottom of the row above - or butt exactly on to them - according to whether you want a defined line or delicate shading.

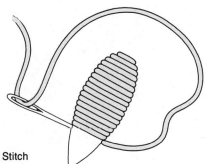

Basic Satin Stitch

Great subtleties are possible if you use your threads cleverly. You can also start by running stitches in the opposite direction to make a padded effect.

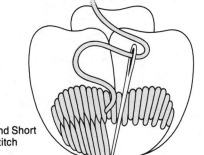

Long and Short Satin Stitch

Stem Stitch is used for lines of stitching. Keep the thread always to the same side of the needle, and make the stitches all the same length.

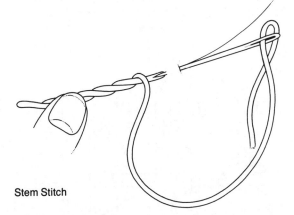

Stem Stitch

Tapestry (Canvas Embroidery, Needlepoint)

Let me say straight away that it is quite incorrect to use the word tapestry for what I am going to write about. Tapestry is a woven fabric picture, such as a Gobelin tapestry, not one sewn with a needle on canvas. But everyone I know calls the canvas type 'tapestry', not the correct names - canvas embroidery or needlepoint. So tapestry I shall call it.

Canvas

The best canvas is called double thread and its threads hold their positions with a minimum of distortion; it also allows you to use tramming if you wish. Of the single thread canvases 'interlock' is the most stable. Ordinary canvas has a tendency to pull out of shape with handling and is best kept for small tapestries which can be quickly done.

Each type of canvas comes in a variety of gauges still based on the inch - so 7 has 7 stitches to the inch. Choose the gauge to suit the object. Chair seats normally use gauges 10 to 14, whereas a handbag needs a fine canvas such as a 17-gauge. You need a piece at least 10 cm (4 in) longer and wider than the design.

To stop canvas fraying at the edges, when you start sewing, make a turned-in hem, of about (½ in) 1 cm, and machine it all round. Draw the exact outline of the canvas on a large sheet of white blotting paper before you start to sew - and keep the blotting paper for blocking.

Copying a Design

Canvases with the designs painted on them are undoubtedly the easiest to work, but you can copy any design you like. Either copy the design on to graph paper, and work from the graph, counting stitches, or trace the chart by putting the design under the canvas and drawing on the threads with a canvas-marking pen (sold by needlework specialists). If you wish to paint in the colours use thinned acrylic paint not oils - oils will slowly rot an unprimed canvas.

Yarn

Four ply tapestry wool is ideal for medium gauge canvas, or 2 ply crewel wool, which you can use double or single, according to the gauge of the canvas. There is also 2 ply Persian wool and perle or stranded embroidery cotton.

The amount of thread needed varies with the stitch and the canvas size, but as a rough guide Coats suggest the following quantities, using tapisserie wool on double thread 10 gauge canvas.

	per 10 m skein	per 13.7 m skein
Tent	29 rows x 30 stitches	39 rows x 30 stitches
Trammed tent	22 rows x 30 stitches	30 rows x 30 stitches
Half cross	38 rows x 30 stitches	52 rows x 30 stitches

Frames

You may be able to get away without a frame, but large ones will distort too much. You can buy special rectangular frames for the job - but they are expensive. To fit canvas on a frame sew heavy tape top and bottom of medium or light canvas. Mark the centre in each edge and attach it accordingly to the instructions for the frame working from the centre of each side. Adjust the frame so the canvas is taut.

A less expensive option is to buy the type of frame made for stretching canvas for paintings, or use an old picture frame, which lets the tapestry just fit within the opening. Match the mid points of the sides of both the frame and the canvas, and attach it top and bottom and then at both sides with drawing pins. Then work away from these centre points keeping an even pull.

Whatever the frame, make sure the canvas is perfectly stretched before you start sewing or the tapestry will never look right.

Needles
You *must* use a blunt-ended tapestry needle in a size which will slip through the canvas without dragging.

Starting and Finishing
Every stitch is done in two movements - down through the canvas, then up through the canvas - and the thread pulled right through on each. Always try to make a downward stitch where there is already some yarn in a hole, as an upward movement roughs it up.

Start with a knot on the *right* (top) side about 3 cm (1½ in) from where you need the thread - the knot can be cut off later when some other stitches have secured the thread leading to it. Then bring the thread up where you need it. When you finish that thread or section bring it to the right side a short distance from the stitching and leave an end until the under-thread has been sewn over. If there is no room run it through the thread underneath, once vertically and once horizontally.

Where colours mingle have a different needle threaded with each, and keep them at the front of the work until you need them. Then run the one you need through the back to where you need it.

Stitches
Tramming is making a series of very long stitches along each row, on the right side of the work, to provide padding over which the tapestry stitches are worked. This makes a tapestry far more hard-wearing, but you can only do this on double mesh canvas. The tramming should match the colour which will be over it and lie along the centre of the close pair of threads. Bring each new tram up through the last square of the one before - then there are no dips where the ends of two threads meet - and make it no more than 4 to 5 cm (1½ to 2 in) long.

Half-cross stitch, on the right side, looks like tent stitch but, as the thread travels a shorter distance on the back, it is less firm. So this should be worked on double thread canvas, or interlock.

Tent Stitch (or Basketweave) uses a considerable amount of thread but wears and covers well - which is why it is the basic stitch for most tapestry.

Upright Gobelin is a stitch which can be worked over 2, 3 or 4 threads - provided the thread is thick enough not to leave gaps on the longer versions.

Order of Work
It is always tempting to start with the bit one likes best, but the correct order, to ensure clear shapes, is first the veins and outlines, then the motifs, then the background.

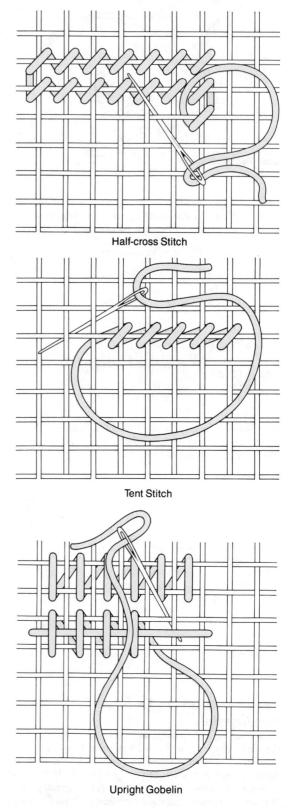

Half-cross Stitch

Tent Stitch

Upright Gobelin

Blocking a Finished Tapestry

A tapestry always needs to be blocked before being made into the finished item. Take a board about 10 cm (4 in) longer and wider than the tapestry. Cover it with the blotting paper on which you drew the outline of the canvas. Then tack the tapestry face downwards on it with drawing pins, about a thumb width apart, stretching it carefully to the size of the original outline (if necessary snip the selvedges slightly to allow for stretch). Damp it well with a sprayer and leave until completely dry - unless the instructions say otherwise. Not easy — so you may prefer to have it done professionally (see below).

Embroiderers' Guild, Apartment 41, Hampton Court Palace, East Molesey, Surrey KT8 9AU Tel: 01 943 1229 M£M, M, G, Lib, A

The Royal School of Needlework, 5 King Street, London WC2E 8HN Tel: 01 240 3186 — will stretch, mount and make up and mend items of tapestry (canvas embroidery) embroidery, and bead work. The shop has an excellent range of materials and equipment and an illustrated mail order catalogue (CC). Classes B.

Dunlicraft Ltd (Pullman Road, Wigston, Leicester LE8 2DY Tel: 0533 811040) has a list of stockists (sae).

Coats do inexpensive booklets covering most aspects of needlecraft. For stockists contact Coats Domestic Marketing Services, 39 Durham Street, Glasgow, G41 1BS Tel: 041 427 5311.

Batsford Encyclopaedia of Embroidery Stitches, Batsford

Thérèse de Dillmont, *The Complete DMC Encyclopaedia of Needlework*, Running Press (USA), — despite Edwardian illustrations, an embroiderer's bible. A book for enthusiasts.

KNITTING

Ancient and soothing, knitting allows you to relax, to save money and watch television all at the same time. It is also blessedly easy, and even someone with two left thumbs can produce *something* which will be a pleasure to wear, if only a straight scarf in a stunning yarn. Complete beginners should see right.

It pays to read knitting patterns with a critical eye. The methods they choose are often those which are quick to explain, rather than those which give the best results. Often little changes, which would improve the finish, need to be made right at the start - like knitting up the first part of a front band with the ribbing.

If things go wrong and you can't make it work, write to the company - big ones have very helpful advisory services.

Alterations

Altering a pattern isn't hard, but careful where you do it. Before changing a shaped section draw it out on graph paper, one square to a stitch, showing the increases or decreases. Then you can see the best place to add or subtract, without spoiling the shape. If the alteration will affect a seam draw both pieces.

To alter a pattern to fit a slightly different size use a larger or smaller needle (see Tension, page 394). But, to make a big change you need more stitches. This is

tricky and takes experience.

When making a child's garment, which you may need to enlarge later, plan ahead. Sleeves are easier to lengthen if you knit down from the top. You can even knit them (and the body) on circular needles, so you have no seam to unpick. This is how jumpers were knitted for centuries in certain parts of Britain. For lengthening either unravel from the bottom, pick up the stitches and knit the extra you need; or cut it at some point, undo a row, then knit on from the unpicked edge and graft the new knitting to the old (page 393). Either method shows least if you put a band of contrasting colour at the join.

Beginners

Knitting is very easy. Any pattern is only made by combining knit stitches and purl stitches. And what looks like gobbledegook on paper will make total sense when you start doing it, provided you go one step at a time. The ideal yarn is a mohair in a stunning colour. Its fuzziness will conceal any unevenness in the knitting, and your pleasure in its colour will keep you going.

Putting stitches on the needle — casting on — is the hardest part for beginners, so if possible get someone else to cast on and do the first couple of rows. If you can't, turn to casting on (page 391), use method 1, which is very easy. Continental knitting is undoubtedly fastest, so, why not start with the faster method? Try knit stitch, then purl. When you can do both, you can knit. For your first garment, choose a textured wool knitted on fairly large needles. It won't take an eternity to finish and from there on it's pure pleasure.

A *left-handed* beginner needs to sit *facing* the person who is teaching them. Then their movements are a mirror image of the teacher's. But constantly having to reinterpret patterns, because they are working in the opposite direction, can get confusing, so it is often better to learn the Continental style of knitting (below) instead. This also gets over the disadvantage of the twist of the yarn being made for right-handed knitting.

The Continental Method

Continental knitting is extremely fast. The needles are held as illustrated and the yarn comes up between the little finger and ring finger of the left hand, across the backs of the three fingers, and once round the first finger. For either plain or purl, the right-hand needle goes through the loop on the left and the needle tip

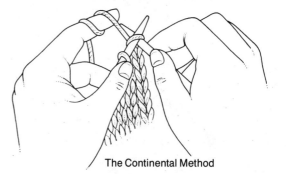

The Continental Method

hooks the yarn back through the loop. The trick is to keep the yarn neither too slack nor too tight, by holding it with the little finger, and to keep the right wrist flexible.

> Almost every country has a different way of holding the wool. If it ends up over the top of the first finger and is controlled by the others suit yourself.

The English Method

The needles are held as illustrated. The yarn goes once round the little finger of the right hand, under the middle two fingers, and over the first finger. When knitting a stitch the right hand slides forward, winds the yarn round the needles, then grips the right needle between thumb and forefinger as it hooks the yarns through the loop. It feels very awkward until you relax.

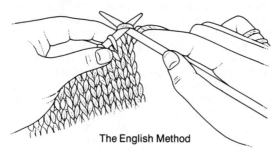

The English Method

Knit Stitch

This is the most basic stitch. * With the wool on the far side of the work, you push the right-hand needle away from you, through the nearside of the loop at the tip of the left needle. Take the yarn under the right needle and up between the two needles. Hold the yarn tight and twist the right needle so it pulls that yarn through the stitch as a loop, then slide the last stitch off the left needle. Repeat from * for each stitch.

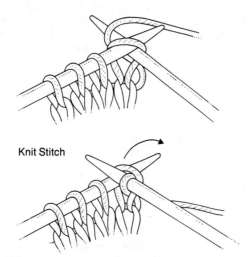

Knit Stitch

> For the Continental method the needle movement is the same, but you use your *left* hand to position the wool.

Purl

To purl, have the yarn at the nearside of the work. Then push the point of the right-hand needle through your side of the stitch on the left needle, with the point travelling to the left. Take the yarn over the top of the right needle, down between the two needles and pull it tight(ish). Then tilt the point of the right needle so it hooks the wool backwards through the stitch on the left needle, and at the same time slide that stitch off. (Continental — see above.)

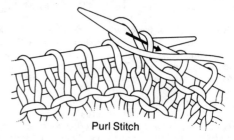

Purl Stitch

General Knitting

Bands and Borders

If a garment has a ribbed welt, and needs ribbed bands up the front, it is neatest to cast on and knit the stitches for the band when you do the welt. Then slip the band stitches on to a safety pin, to knit up later. Work both bands at the same time (using 2 balls of wool). Then, when you make a button hole on one side tie a piece of yarn to the same row on the other, for perfectly positioned buttons.

Button Holes

You need to buy the buttons before making the button holes or you may not be able to find ones which fit.

For a basic button hole, with the slit in the direction of the stitches, knit up to the row on which it will start, then across to where you want it to come. Slip the remaining stitches in the row onto the right needle without knitting them. Join a small ball of yarn to the edge of the knitting. Then knit back with this. Switch to the main ball, repeat so a slit is created where you switch balls. When the button hole is long enough, work across the width of the band using the main ball.

A beautifully neat button hole can be done if you knit a band with a facing. Work to the start of the hole * and break off your yarn, leaving a long end. Join in a contrasting colour - leaving long ends and work across the button hole stitches. Break off the yarn. Join in the main colour ** and knit to the matching hole in the facing. Repeat from * to **. When the facing is folded back, match the contrasting yarn marking the button holes, pull out this yarn and graft (page 393) the front and back sections together, top and bottom.

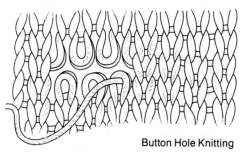

Button Hole Knitting

★ Yarn is dyed in batches. Two different dye lots may look the same in balls, but look very different knitted up. Buy all the yarn you need at the start - the shop may sell out of your dye lot by the time you need some.

Casting On

Different methods of casting on need to be used according to the result you want. But use a slip knot to put the first loop in the needle, and leave a long end which you can use for sewing up later.

It is often a good idea to cast on using needles a size or two larger than you will use for the knitting. Even so, casting on can be uncomfortably tight to knit. A good trick to prevent this is to place a slim needle beside the main needle, then cast on to both needles. (Stop the needles slipping with a twist of sticky tape near the knobs). Then slip out the extra needle and your stitches will be comfortably loose.

The **thumb method** is too sloppy for most edges but it creates stitches which are easily picked up later. You just knot a loop of yarn round the needle and then repeatedly make a loop with your thumb and pick it up on to the needle.

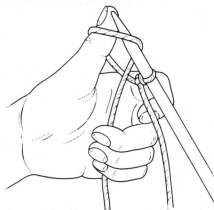

Thumb Method of Casting On

For the **twisted thumb method** turn the loop right round, so the needle goes into what was the front of the loop. This makes a neater, but rather elastic edge, which can be used before ribbing. The stretchiness is an advantage with yarns which lack give, such as cotton or metallic thread.

When two needles are used the basic method is to knit a stitch, using the initial loop, slip it on to the needle,

and knit the next one into that - and so on. A neater edge is given by **double casting on.** Knot yarn round the left needle. Slip the right needle through the loop, knit a stitch and slip it onto the left needle. * Slip the right needle *between* the last two stitches, knit a stitch and slip it on to the left needle, making it comfortably loose. Repeat from *.

Casting Off

Casting off is a job which it is easy to do with a sigh of satisfaction and indecent haste - which can lead to trouble later. Think about the job casting off will do on the garment. Will it need to stretch to let a head into a small neck? Or must it stop a shoulder seam stretching under the weight of a heavy sleeve? Different situations need different approaches, but the basic points are these.

● Cast off on a knit row, if there is one.
● When casting off in a series of steps, slip the first stitch to reduce the stepped effect.
● If you need stretch, use a needle 1 to 2 sizes larger.
● If you don't want firmness or a defined line, where an edging starts, stitches can be slipped on to a holder - to be picked up later, and not cast off at all.

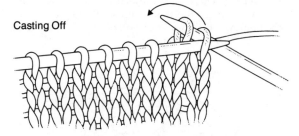

Casting Off

For **basic** casting off, knit the first two stitches, * put the tip of the left needle into the first and lift it over the second, off the end of the needle, and drop it. Knit another stitch and repeat from * to the end of the row. On the last stitch cut the yarn so there is enough to sew up the seam, and slip it through the final loop.

For **stretched basic** start exactly as for basic, but when you lift one stitch over the other keep it on the left-hand needle while you knit the next stitch, and *then* drop it. Hanging on to it like this has the effect of stretching the loop and makes it less likely to have a tight edge.

★ Circular knitting can be done on a circular needle or on 4 double-pointed straight ones. The latter are the most practical for small circles, the former for large ones.
★ Keep tabs on the position of the 'seams' for increasing or decreasing. So, slip a loop of ribbon, or a safety pin over the needle, at the point where they should be. When you reach that point again transfer the marker up to the new row.
★ If a circular needle feels stiff at first put it in an airing cupboard or warm it in a basin of hottish water, and dry quickly, before casting on.

Dealing with Several Colours

The secret of handling **vertical stripes** is to wind several balls and use one for each stripe. At the junction between one stripe and the next, pass one yarn over the

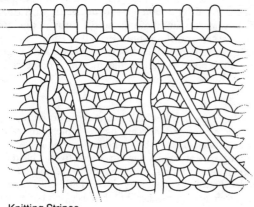

Knitting Stripes

other, linking them neatly together. This technique will result in neat checks with no loops of yarn behind.

On Fair Isle and similar patterns simply carry the yarn along the back for 4-5 stitches, without linking it into the knitting. This is called **stranding**. It's very easy but be careful. If it's too tight it takes all the give out of the knitting. If it's too loose you catch your fingers in it when putting on the garment.

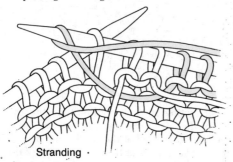

Stranding

In **Weaving** the spare yarn is taken across the top of the yarn being knitted, at each stitch, so it is woven along the back. It's the best method to use if the yarn has to travel more than a few stitches along the back. In any garment the two methods can be used according to the situation. The old Fair Isle knitters would even use two methods of knitting at once, holding one colour in the right hand, English style, and the other in the left hand to knit Continental style. Anything is possible, so long as it works.

Decreasing

Decreasing is done by knitting two stitches together. You will usually get the best results by doing it one or two rows in, as it's easiest to sew up an edge which has a single line of knitted stitches. But first, decide where the decrease will look best. Annoyingly, stitches knitted together always lean to the right. When you want a left-sloping decrease, slip one, knit one and pass the slipped stitch over. If several decreases need to be made in a row knit 2 together at even intervals.

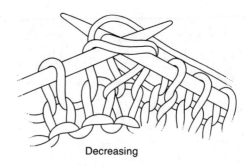

Decreasing

Dropped Stitches

It's worth checking both sides of your work frequently for dropped stitches. If you have dropped one it can be picked up with a crochet hook, for a few rows, so it looks like knitting. Put your crochet hook through the loop at the base of the ladder, hook it onto the 'bar' of the ladder just above and pull it through the loop. Repeat to the top. (Use the same system to repair ladders in heavy tights, but suit the size of the crochet hook to the thickness of the yarn.)

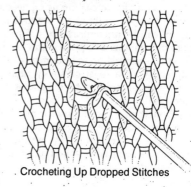

Crocheting Up Dropped Stitches

Elastic

Yarn with little elasticity, like acrylic, cotton and mohair, will quickly lose its shape on ribbed sections and become baggy. You can prevent the problem by knitting in shirring elastic as you knit the yarn. Use a stranding technique (see left) to run it along the back, catching it in every couple of stitches. Or thread it through at the back of the work with a tapestry needle afterwards. You can do this to bought sweaters, preferably before bagging has begun. You can also buy ready made 'strips' of shirring with several rows linked by a fine web - which could speed up the de-bagging of an old jumper.

★ Odd ends of yarn, from joins, should just be threaded on a tapestry needle and woven neatly into the back of the garment, near the seams.

★ If a few stitches need to be held while others are knitted a nappy pin makes a good holder.

Garter Stitch

This is the easiest stitch of all, as every row is in knit stitch. It has a lot of stretch. So, when it is used as a border to other knitting, some patterns suggest using needles one or two sizes smaller. Check the first row

- it often looks much better on one side than the other - and choose the better side for the right side.

Grafting

Grafting is a very easy way of sewing two stocking stitch sections together, so they seem to have been knitted as one. But it can only be used if their final rows have not been cast off. Lie your sections edge to edge. Thread a blunt-ended tapestry needle with knitting yarn and slip the last two stitches off each needle. Then follow the illustration carefully, so you sew together the matching stitches from each needle. The yarn follows the meandering path it would in knitting. Pull the yarn

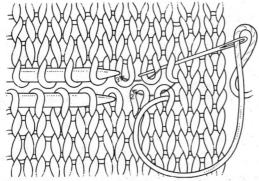

The needle follows the arrows for the next steps 2 3

through carefully so that the 'tension' of your sewn row is exactly the same as in the knitted rows to either side.

Grafting can also be used to join basic ribbing. The easiest way is to graft the knit stitches on one side then on the other. First divide the stitches, on each piece of knitting, so every plain stitch is on one needle and every purl on another.

Increasing

If a number of increases must be made in a row, divide the number of stitches in the row by the number of increases to find how often you should increase one. Then they will spread out evenly across the row. If a large increase is needed above a welt it will look better if you do half of them in a row after the ribbing and the other half in the next row.

There are two ways of increasing. The basic method is to knit into the front of the stitch and, without lifting the stitch off, knit into the back of a stitch. Then slip it off. The other is, on a knit row, to bring the yarn forward under the needle, then pass it to the back *over* the needle before knitting the next stitch. This extra yarn is then treated like a new stitch on the next row. This is used above a hole.

Interesting Facts

There are a number of easy ways of producing fancy effects to jazz up an ordinary pattern. But the more elaborate the stitch the more yarn you use, the stitch also alters the size of the garment. So check your tension using the stitch you plan to use.

Bobbles come in every shape and size, but for a very simple bobble, on a knit row, work until the position

for a bobble. * Knit into the front and back of the next stitch 4 or 5 times before slipping it off. Work alternate knit and purl rows on those stitches for 4 rows. With the purl side facing you lift all the stitches over the end one in turn. ** Continue the original row. On each bobble repeat from * to **.

Cable looks impressive but is quick and easy. It can be done with three strands as a proper plait, or with two as a twist. For a twist using 6 stitches slip the first 3 stitches on to a short double-pointed cable needle (the same gauge as the main needles), put this in front of the work or behind, according to the direction of the twist you want. Work 3 more stitches, with your main needles then knit in the stitches from the cable needle. Continue as before until the next twist is needed. A three strand plaited cable uses the same method with 3 groups of stitches and, every so many rows, one of the groups is slipped on to the cable needle and put either in front or behind, to give the over and under of a plait. The overs and unders can be made often, to produce a tight twist or plait, or a loose one. And the number of stitches involved varies from 2 to about 12.

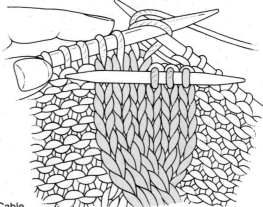

Cable

Eyelet holes for ribbon to be threaded are made by knitting two together wherever you want a hole, passing the yarn over the needle and to the back again, and knitting on from there to the next hole. On the next row the yarn over the needle is also knitted - so you get back to the same number of stitches.

Joining Yarn

It seems inelegant but the strongest way of joining yarn is to knot it on to the old yarn at the edge of a row. Finish off the ends when you sew up.

With shaggy yarn which won't show an extra strand just *overlap* the two ends, by at least 15 cm (6 in) and carry on knitting. This is not as strong as the knotted method and on big stitches yarn could pull loose with wear. You have to judge whether it will hold firmly.

Splicing works for slightly rough yarns or fluffy ones, but is bad on smooth ones. Unravel the last few inches of yarn, so the strands are separated, and do the same to the end of the new yarn - the larger the needle, the farther you must undo, but 15 cm (6 in) is average.

Overlap the two yarns, spreading the strands and matching the strands. Cut through these pairs of strands at different points so the junctions are staggered - long, middling and short. Bring all the strands together and twist them into a single strand, and knit immediately.

★ To check if an end of yarn is enough for a row stretch it across the row and back three times. That much should knit a row using a basic stitch. For fancy stitches allow more.

Knitting Needle Size Equivalents

mm	GB old	US
2	14	0
2¼	13	1
2½	-	-
2¾	12	2
3	11	-
3¼	10	3
3½	-	4
3¾	9	5
4	8	-
4¼	-	6
4½	7	7
5	6	8
5½	5	9
6	4	10
6½	3	10½
7	2	-
7½	1	-
8	0	11
9	00	13
10	000	15
		16

★ To avoid losing your place in a pattern use markers. A kirby grip slid down the edge of a paper pattern does well. Safety pins, or contrasting yarn tied in, can mark crucial points in the knitting itself. For example, you often find instructions like 'knit 20 more rows and then cast off'. Marking the start means that if you forget to turn the counter you aren't lost.

★ When two parts need to match exactly knit both at the same time - using two balls of wool on the same needle. It is far more satisfying to come to the end and know you have done two fronts, than to face doing yet another, and the match is exact.

Moss Stitch (seed stitch)

For moss stitch knit 1, purl 1, knit 1, purl 1 across every row, just as in rib. But in moss stitch a knit stitch comes above a knit stitch, and a purl above a purl - producing a series of tiny bumps.

Picking Up Stitches

First mark off the area into halves, quarters and even eighths. Small safety pins make the best markers - ordinary pins fall out or split the yarn. Then divide the number of stitches to be picked up by the number of sections marked off. With 72 stitches to pick up you would mark the knitting off into eighths and pick up 9, evenly-spaced stitches (72 ÷ 8 = 9) in each section. This gets an even result every time.

Use a needle 1 or 2 sizes smaller than you will use for knitting up the stitches. Hold the edge of the knitting firmly, insert your needle just below the line of casting off. Wind the yarn round the needle, as if knitting, and

tilt it up through the hole carrying the loop of yarn with it. Repeat. (If you just pick up loops from a cast-off edge you get awful results.)

Ribbing

Basic ribbing is, knit 1, purl 1, repeated on every row, with an even number of stitches. So a purl in one row always has a knit above it in the next, and vice versa. Rib welts and cuffs are usually knitted on needles two sizes smaller than the rest of the garment. The basic stitch can be varied by alternating more stitches (eg knit 3, purl 3) but such changes affect the size of the garment - check your tension.

Stocking Stitch

This was originally used for stockings - just as garter stitch was used for garters. It is simply a row of knit stitches, followed by a row of purl stitches, repeatedly.

Tension (gauge)

Tension testing is infuriating. Just when one is longing to get going on some new knitting it stops you. But, over a whole garment someone who knits very tightly or very loosely can change the size by several inches without adding or subtracting a stitch. So failing to check the tension imperils the whole project.

Patterns normally say how many stitches and how many rows are allowed to a given measurement. Knit a square several stitches larger than the measurement given. Put a line of pins down one row and along another and measure from these with a ruler. If there are fewer stitches to the measurement than the pattern says, change to a smaller needle. If there are more stitches change to a larger needle. Either way, keep knitting squares until you get a perfect result. If you do change needles remember to change the needles for the ribbing by the same number of sizes.

★ If you have to unravel work, thread a needle, smaller than the ones you are knitting with, through every stitch in the first correct row below the fault. Then you can quickly unravel back to that point without dropping a stitch.

Yarns

Yarn manufacturers want to sell yarn, so naturally they say their yarns *must* be used to make up the patterns. The truth is that what matters is that the tension is right. If, by adjusting the needle size, you can make a square with the same number of stitches to the cm (in) as the tension the fit will be the same. Obviously, this is most easily done if you buy a yarn of the same thickness as the one given but small changes can work very well.

If you have trouble getting interesting yarns Patricia Roberts, whose designs often use lovely colours and textures, runs a mail order service from 60 Kinnerton Street, London SW1X 8ES Tel: 01 235 4742. So does Colourway, 112a Westbourne Grove, London, W2 5RU Tel: 01 229 1432.

If you buy yarn in skeins not balls, put two dining-room chairs back to back, stretch the skein around them. Wind the yarn round and round several fingers, about a dozen times. Remove it, hold the little bundle between thumb and fingers, so the next winding will go *across* the first lot and *over* your fingers. Keep turning the ball so the yarn winds first one way then another - and always *over* your fingers. This prevents the spring being stretched out by tight winding.

★ Before starting to knit with a ball drop it in a small plastic bag, pull the end of yarn out through the neck and put an elastic band loosely round the opening. This keeps it clean, and stops it rolling about the floor.

★ Yarn which has been knitted up is usually too crinkled to knit with. To smooth it out, make it into a long skein by winding it round the back of a chair, and secure it in several places with loops of yarn. Dip this into lukewarm water, squeeze gently and hang it up to drip dry looped over the neck of a rust-proof metal coat-hanger.

Machine Knitting

It is impossible to cover machine knitting here because of variations in machines. But there are knitting machine clubs and classes all over Britain which practised knitters can join and where beginners can ask advice about buying a machine. Your local library may be able to tell you about them, or see below.

Brother Knitting Machine Division, Jones + Brother, Shepley Street, Audenshaw, Manchester M34 5JD Tel: 061 330 6531
The company runs a telephone advice service for its own machines. It has a list of tutors and classes throughout Britain, and of knitting machine shops which stock their machines.

Making Up

The first thing to do is check that you made the pattern pieces correctly with no faults or dropped stitches. Most knitting then repays some preparation. Some you can just smooth with your hands, others need blocking and pressing. Whatever the method, knitting should be handled *lightly*. Pressing heavily can make a new garment look flat and tired, before it's even worn, and ruin a raised design. Only you can judge the resilience of your yarn and pick the best method to use.

Blocking is pinning knitting to the perfect size and shape. You need an ironing board or padded table (an old blanket covered with a sheet on a kitchen table is ideal). Place the knitting wrong side up, and very carefully pin it to shape and size, measuring and being careful not to pull it crookedly. Insert long tailoring pins, at an angle, at very frequent intervals down the edge (too far apart will give the scalloped edge sometimes used for decorating shawls). Place them between the stitches, not into the yarn itself, or they will damage it. Then use one of the options below and leave the piece pinned out until it is *completely* dry.

● Damp it with a plant sprayer and just leave it.
● Place a damp cloth over it and press it *lightly* with a warm iron - not for acrylics, raised patterns, or fluffy wools.
● Hold a steam iron a few millimetres above it and spurt the steam on to it - not for acrylics or silk.
● Wet a towel with hot water, wring it out *very* well,

and lie it on the knitting while still warm. Then remove it when the yarn has absorbed the moisture and flattened with the weight.

Sewing Up

Before sewing up mark long seams in halves and quarters with safety pins between the stitches. Match these, plus any stripes, when joining up the seams.

Use a blunt-ended tapestry needle for the sewing and, if possible, sew the seams with the ends of yarn left when casting on or off. When you have to start a new thread secure it with several small stitches. If the yarn is too bulky cut several lengths, and separate the strands to make threads of a manageable thickness. Then damp these, twist them firmly and leave them to dry.

Seam Styles

Choose the style of seam to suit the result you want. A long loose coat may need a loose seam to prevent it looking puckered as the garment stretches. But a tight sweater needs firm seams which won't gape as the garment is stretched.

Oversewing is the easiest method and good for ribbing, and wherever you want stretch. Pin the two layers of knitting together, like hands praying. Then oversew, matching row to row. Pull it comfortably tight and it will open into a perfectly flat seam.

For **backstitching** place the pieces as for oversewing but make a seam, one or two stitches in (See Backstitch, page 380). This is the firmest seam. Use it to give firmness to a shoulder seam, for example.

In **invisible seaming** place the pieces side by side with a right side up. Then sew through the loops to either side, as illustrated, drawing the two sides together. This has more give than backstitch and usually produces a neater finish than oversewing.

Invisible Seam

For a straight shoulder seam with no decreases the best method is a **knitted seam**. For this you end the shoulders by slipping the stitches on to a stitch holder. To finish and join them you put each on to a needle, so the needles both face the same direction. Then knit

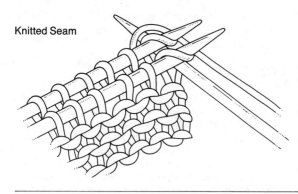

Knitted Seam

a row taking a loop from each needle at each stitch, and casting off the stitches you make as you go along.

Hugh Ehrman ed, *Designer Knitting*, Century Hutchinson - highly original designs.
Shelagh Hollingworth, *Knitting and Crochet for the Physically Handicapped and Elderly*, Batsford - hard-to-find old-fashioned patterns like fingerless gloves.
Michael Pearson, *Traditional Knitting*, Collins - a fascinating history of British traditional patterns with guidelines for recreating them.
Debby Robinson, *The Encyclopaedia of Knitting*, Michael Joseph - a first-rate book on techniques.

KNOTS

I first realized the benefits of knots when I was on the television programme 'Pebble Mill at One'. A researcher and I were knotting grass round an egg for dyeing at Easter. Exasperated at her grass repeatedly coming undone she asked me the knack - the knack was a reef knot. She said that was the most useful thing she'd learnt in ages. So here is a selection of the most useful knots for everyday situations.

★ Pushing through a loop, not an end, in the last stage of many knots makes them easy to undo.
★ If you are ever using rope, a useful rule to remember is that twice the thickness gives 4 times the strength - provided both ropes have the same structure and composition.

Reef

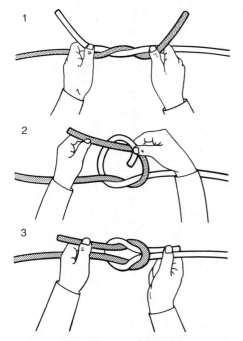

This is the basic knot for tying together two bits of string (tape or whatever) which are the *same* thickness and will have *equal stress* in opposite directions. But it is

a dangerous knot to use if the stress will be unequal.
Hold one end in each hand. Go left over right, and under. Right over left, and under. Pull tight.

Sheet Bend

This is useful when you need to join two bits of string of different thicknesses.
Fold the end of the thicker rope into a loop. Feed the thinner rope up through the loop, round the back of it, then under itself. Pull it tight.

Fisherman's Knot (Water Knot)

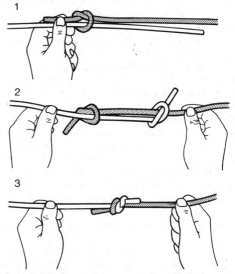

Another knot for joining two lengths of unequal thickness. Not as elegant as a sheet bend, but it works - provided it isn't asked to stand too much strain.
Place the two ropes side by side. Knot each end as illustrated. Pull tight.

Slip Knot (Noose)

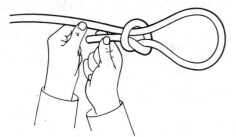

The most basic, and useful, is the slip knot. Make a folded end. Pass the short end over the other, round under it, then down through its own loop.

Round Turn and Two Half Hitches

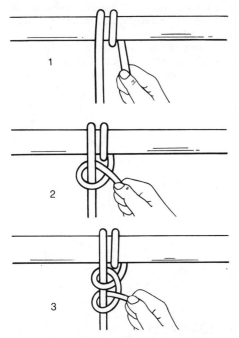

A useful knot for attaching a rope to a ring in a wall - to tie up a washing line, or a horse.

Sheepshank

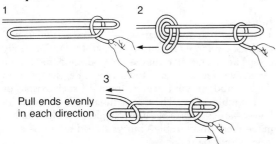

Pull ends evenly in each direction

If you go camping and guy ropes keep slipping, which you don't want to cut, you may be glad to know this. I certainly have been.

Clove Hitch

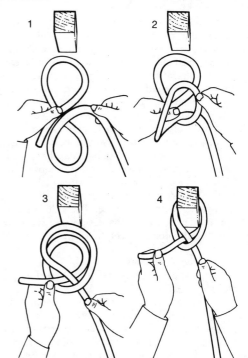

A very easy knot for hitching a rope on to a post. Where you can't drop it over the end you can thread it round to form the same shape, but this is harder.

Lashing

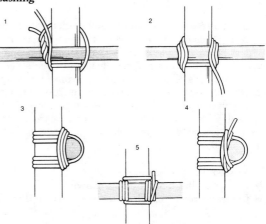

Useful to link two garden canes together. Start with a clove hitch. Wind rope round the front of cross bar, behind the upright, across the front of the other side of the cross bar, and back behind the upright. Repeat several times, pulling it tight. Then wind the rope tightly several times round the ropes, passing between the upright and the cross bar. Tuck the end of the rope under a secure loop and pull tightly.

Bigon and Ragazzoni, *The Century Guide to Knots*, Century - covers a vast range of knots.

PATCHWORK

Patchwork has something for everyone. It is so simple a child can do it, but at its best it can be a folk art. And there is something extraordinarily touching about old quilts in which stitchers have patiently created loveliness out of the scrap fabric of their lives. A really fine old patchwork is a revelation, which could make you itch to start one. There are some good examples in *Patchwork Quilts* by Avril Colby (page 400).

Unlike embroidery, in which you can only take stitches of a reasonable size, you can make patchwork pieces in any size you like. Use big, slap-happy pieces for a quick bedspread for a child, create a fabric mosaic of minute fragments, with years of patient labour. And you can either sew it gently by hand or whizz simple shapes together with a machine. The skill lies not so much in the sewing, as in the design you create with the shapes and colours of the fabrics.

Assembling the Templates

The fabric patches are supported and shaped by paper or cardboard backings. You can buy metal templates for cutting these out. But to make any size and shape you want you only need a protractor, a pair of compasses and a ruler. Even if you day-dreamed through maths lessons patchwork geometry is child's play on graph, or squared, paper especially. Once you have drawn a shape make a master template on firm cardboard for cutting out. For the papers, cut exactly round it, being careful to have sharp corners, but cut the fabric pieces 1 cm (½ in) larger, all round.

Square

There's no need to back square patchwork pieces if you are going to machine them. Mark the template outline with a pencil or tailor's chalk, cut out and machine squares together into strips. When you have several strips, iron the seams open and machine the strips together. If you put half squares at the ends of alternate rows you stagger the seams and get a wall effect which conceals slight inaccuracies. Oblongs can be treated the same way, and both are great for quick quilts for a child's bed.

Five-Sided Figure - Pentagon
- Draw the lines and circle as shown.
- Centre a protractor where the lines meet and mark

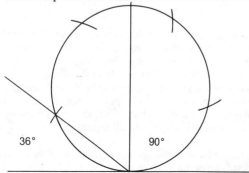

36 degrees. (Have its bottom black line on top of the line along, and the line up its middle on the upward line. Then read round to find 36 degrees.)
- Draw a line from that dot to where the other lines meet at point A.
- Open the compasses to *exactly* the length from A to where that line crosses the circle, at B.
- *Keeping that measurement*, put the compass point where the line crosses the circle and make another mark as shown. Repeat this, round the circle and draw lines, joining them.

Six-Sided Figure - Hexagon

This is one of the most successful shapes and you can vary it with internal triangles and diamonds. It is also very easy to make.
- Use a pair of compasses to draw a circle.
- *Keeping them open to the same extent*, put the point on the circle and draw a curve across it where the pencil touches.
- Move the point to where that mark crosses the circle and make another mark farther on, as above.
- Repeat this until you have 6 marks, then join them.

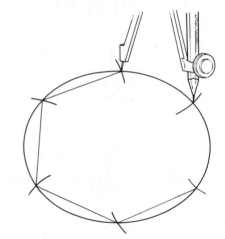

Seven or More Sides

Figures with more than six sides fit together less well and you need to fill gaps with other shapes. Draw them as for five-sided shapes. To find the angle you need, divide 180 by the number of sides you want. So for an eight-sided figure, 180 divided by 8 = 22.

Fabric

The nicest patchworks are surely those in which you can pick out family fragments with nostalgia. But family scraps are fewer than they were, and remnants can be expensive. The answer is to scavenge. Beg scraps from the rag trade in your nearest town - if such exists - or raid jumble sales. They sometimes sell garments in lovely fabrics as rags because a single indelible stain has made them unwearable - but you need to ask as such 'rags' won't be on show.

Almost any fabric can be used, but, apart from log cabin designs, it is easiest to work with similar weights and, on the whole, jersey and man-made fibres look wrong. New washable fabrics *must* be pre-washed - to avoid later shrinkage - and ironed flat before use. This includes any backing fabrics, lining and interlining.

★ It makes it a lot easier to find the next piece you need if you put each shade in a different plastic bag.

Preparing the Pieces

Most patchwork experts say you should use paper, the weight of heavy notepaper, to support the pieces and give them their shape. I find it crushes too easily, so I prefer thin cardboard, the weight of postcards. Card *must* be used for fragile fabrics such as velvet, silk and glazed cotton, which would have needle marks if you tacked them on to paper.

For paper backings you tack right through both the paper and the right side of the patch. For card you just draw the fabric together on the back with long stitches. Either way, if the shape of the piece allows, have the grain running the length of the piece.

Design

Part of the fascination of patchwork is that it has layer upon layer of design, like Chinese boxes which go one inside the other. Do leaf through books like those given on page 400 for inspiration before you embark on your own designs. Then, once you start planning a patchwork with coloured pens on graph paper, you may find the planning almost as pleasurable as the sewing. There is also a lot of pleasure in an informal patchwork which you create at random. Either way, you can be certain that what you make will be unique - and when else can you be sure of a world first?

Sewing Patchwork Together

For sewing two backed shapes together put the two pieces, right side to right side, and use a whipping stitch. Match your thread to the fabric, in both colour and type and use a fine needle.

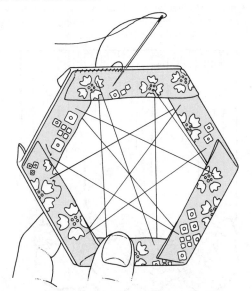

Log Cabin

In log cabin patchwork, instead of using backing papers, measured strips are sewn on to a foundation square 15-38 cm (6-15 in), in the order illustrated, using a fine running stitch. Its effectiveness depends entirely on the skill with which you plan and position the squares. A design takes a lot of forethought. But using a foundation fabric means you can mingle fabrics of different weights, such as silk and velvet, in a way which would be unsatisfactory in other patchwork. Open and smooth each strip carefully away from the centre, pin it down once it is attached, and tack round the outer edge of the last strips.

When all your squares are finished mark the template size in pencil on the back material, so you can sew exactly down the lines. Then hand sew them together or use a machine.

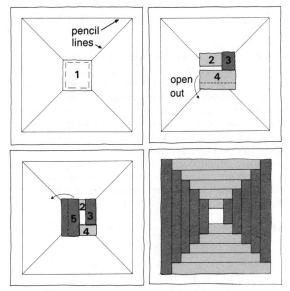

★ Use fine, stainless steel pins; ordinary ones may rust and leave stains.

Trimming and Making Up the Finished Patchwork

● Make sure your patchwork is the exact size you need - you can't cut it down or the seams will open. So, if necessary, sew in shapes to create a straight edge.
● Iron on both sides (unless it is velvet). Then cut the threads holding the papers and remove them. If you don't get them all out they will make nasty balls in the wash. In *Oliver Twist*, Dickens writes of a patchwork quilt which 'rustled' - did thrifty Victorians leave the paper in, to add insulation? If so, they must never have washed the quilts.

Interlining and Lining

Make up cushions, and similar items as you would any fabric, but a bedcover may be better interlined. This gives it a slightly padded look which suits some patchworks admirably, and at night gives extra warmth.

For interlining use an old blanket or a soft, washable

interlining. Cut or seam this to the right size with flat seams, then tack the quilt to it carefully. Use long lines of tacking from side to side in each direction, making sure the quilt lies perfectly smoothly.

The lining can be any pre-washed fabric and there are three ways of joining it - (1) and (2) are fine for thin work, but (3) is best if the interlining is thick.

1 Pin and tack the two wrong sides together, turn the edges in towards each other, so they match, and sew two rows of fine running stitches round the very edge to join them.

2 Pin the two right sides together, and machine or backstitch round the edge, leaving a big enough hole to turn the 'bag' inside out. Then sew up the hole.

3 Start like (1) but, instead of turning in the edges, bind them with long strips of fabric. At the corners make a diagonal fold and sew it flat by hand. Machine or use running stitch along the edge of the binding on the upper side, then fold it over the edge and hem.

Knotting

The patchwork, its interlining and lining need to be held together. Patchwork used to be quilted on, but an easier way to join the three layers is the knotting method used on the 'stobbed' quilts of County Durham in the nineteenth century. To do this take a very short stitch through all the layers. Leave the ends long, tie a reef knot and cut the ends to 1 cm (½ in). You can make these ties either in the centre of patch pieces, with the ends on the right side - or invisibly on a seam with the knots on the wrong side. And you can use matching thread, or a decorative one, such as twisted embroidery thread like Anchor perle cotton.

Knotting Method

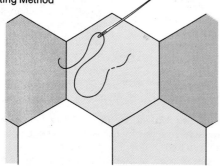

The Patchwork Dog and the Calico Cat (21 Chalk Farm Road, London NW1 8AG Tel: 01 485 1239) is a shop with a mail-order catalogue (CC). Mainly patchwork, but also for embroidery, tapestry and dressmaking, and patterns. Some of their patterns could be very useful for amateur dramatic companies.

Quilters Guild, 38 Woodstock Road, Begbroke, Oxford, OX5 1RG - is an international guild for increasing the understanding of patchwork, quilting and appliqué. You may only join if you do one of these. M&M, M, L, Lib, workshops, Young Quilters 5-18.

Avril Colby, *Patchwork*, Batsford
Alice Timmins, *Patchwork Technique and Design*, Batsford
Fine Patchwork and Quilting, Odori

SOFT FURNISHING

The great thing about making soft furnishings is that it only demands a few, very basic techniques and is nothing like as fiddly as making clothes. Anyone with a sewing machine and a little patience can do it. This section provides the key facts you need to know.

Bear in mind that most furnishing fabric is 120 cm (47 in) wide and some is 136 cm (53½ in) wide. It is prudent to ask whether it is washable or 'dry clean only' before you buy it. Then, having bought it, write to the retailer and ask what shrinkage can be expected and how you should keep it clean. File the reply with the bill and a sample of the fabrics. This may sound calculating, but if the curtains on a large window shrink, several hundred pounds may have been wasted.

Rods and Tracks

Before deciding what curtains or blinds to have, it is worth looking at the tracks which are now available. Some of the unexpected options are - brass rods which bend round bay windows complete, spring-loaded rods to hold up net curtains, tracks for Austrian blinds which incorporate cord holders - and there are even devices which will open and shut your curtains by remote control. Many of the companies also supply ready-made blinds or curtains. If your local shops don't have a good selection some of the big mail order houses do (page 202) or contact the companies direct (page 407).

Blinds

Blinds fit into even the smallest space, and can make the most constricted window look attractive, whereas curtains squashed into tight alcoves can look as if they are playing sardines.

Austrian Blinds

Austrian blinds are particularly good for improving a window which isn't quite as high as it should be, as they look prettiest when only half-drawn up. Hanging them some way above the window, so the upper edge is not quite exposed, makes it look longer.

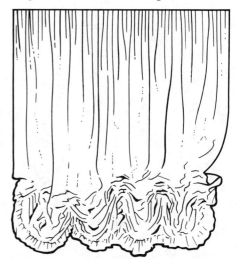

The ruched swags of Austrian blinds have a period air reminiscent of silk frocks, so they look particularly good in glazed fabrics, which catch the light on the folds. But any lightweight curtain material can be used, and they can be unlined or lightly lined.

The blind needs to be twice the width of the space it will fill, plus seam allowances of 1.5 cm (⅝ in) each. For a very full swag, make it two and a half times the width. It looks best slightly longer than the window (say 20-46 cm, 8 to 18 in extra), plus seam allowances and extra inches if the heading stands up, so that a ruched section covers the bottom even when fully let down.

Ideally have a frill either along the bottom, or right round. For luxury, two in contrasting colours and slightly different lengths. You need:

- pencil pleat tape - a fairly deep pencil pleat usually looks best
- plain narrow tape and rings, or Austrian blind tape which has ready-made loops to run the cord through
- cords to draw the blind up
- a special track or single curtain track, plus screw-in rings to carry the cords which draw up the blind
- a cleat or wedge to hold the blind string in position.

★ Before buying a blind kit check the contents carefully: in some the pencil pleat heading is shallow and would not suit some windows.

Making the Blind with a Lining

1 Measure and cut out the material and any lining to exactly the same size. If necessary, seam lengths of fabric together (see Curtains, page 403) but for blinds place a full width in the centre and add equal amounts to either side. Press the seams open.
2 Make and gather the frill (page 407).
3 Pin it on the right side of the main fabric, matching the raw edges.
4 Pin the lining on top - right side to right side. Machine round a seam's width in from the edge, as if making a bag. Trim the gathered seam allowance.
5 Turn the 'bag' right way out, press it to get sharp edges to the seams. Then smooth it face down so that the back and front are perfectly matched with no wrinkles. Tack it like this.
6 Fold over the top 1.5 cm (⅝ in) and pin the heading tape across the top, as on page 404.
7 If you are using plain upright tapes and hand-sewn rings, sew the rings on, 15-20 cm (6-8 in) apart, spacing them exactly.
8 Position the vertical tapes. The maximum effective width for a swag, as it hangs, is 30 cm (12 ins) So: if the blind is twice the width of the window, the tapes should not be sewn on more than 61 cm (24 in) apart. If the blind is two and a half times the width of the window, the tapes must not be more than 76 cm (30 in) apart. The spacing also depends on what figure will evenly divide into the width of the window. Place the first ring or loop of *every* tape 6 cm (2½ in) up from the bottom. Tuck the top under the heading tape and turn the bottom 1.5 cm (⅝ in) under.

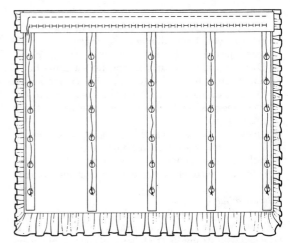

9 Machine across the heading tape, then up each side of the upright tapes. Draw the heading to the final width, and insert curtain hooks. Then thread the cords through the filaments or rings, tying each neatly to the bottom one.
10 Set up your track and space the cord holders to match the position of the tapes. Hang, running the cords through.

You can adjust the way the blind falls by shortening some strings in relation to others. Then tie all the strings together, or attach them to a ring - with the blind fully let down - and have a single cord coming down the side to a cleat.

Unlined Austrian Blinds

Omit steps 3 and 4. Instead, pin a matching bias binding across the bottom of the frill. Then sew on the binding with the frill. Trim the seam allowance on the frill, fold the bias over it and hem it to conceal the raw edge. Press in the sides allowance and conceal it under the side tapes.

★ Weighting the edge of the blind with curtain weights can improve the hang.
★ Where an ugly window really needs concealment use an Austrian blind in the centre and have a swagged pelmet and false curtains to cover the frame.

Roller Blinds

These are the thriftiest, and easiest, window coverings of all. You can make all kind of elaborate bottoms, but they are just adaptations of the basic version which follows. You need: a roller mechanism, a batten for the bottom, a cord and cord holder.

Establish the width of roller which will fit in your window. The blind must be the width of the roller plus 5 cm (2 in). The length is the total of: the measurement round the roller + the length from the bottom of the roller to sill + the material you need to fold up at the bottom 3 cm (1¼ in).

Making

- Fold up the bottom, right side to right side, by the amount you have allowed and machine the side seams just under 2.5 cm (1 in) in. Turn and press.
- Oversew the sides, turn in and herringbone flat.
- Stitch across the pocket to take a batten and across the top to make a tunnel the right size for the roller. Insert the roller and hold the fabric in place on it with drawing pins.
- Open one side seam enough to insert batten. When it's in, screw on the cord holder and cord.
- Roll the fabric round the roller and twist the spring catch in the roller before placing it in the holders.

Roman Blinds

Roman blinds are usually lined, but if the fabric is fairly stiff they need not be. The top has no heading but is attached with strong Velcro to a small shelf. Make them the width of the window, lining them like an Austrian blind, but with a battened bottom - like a roller blind. Use upright tapes and cords, as for Austrian blinds, about 30 cm (12 in) apart.

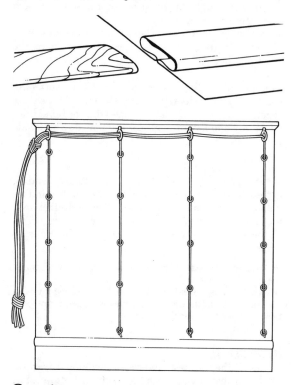

Curtains

Very often the difference between a stunning window and a dull one isn't the cost of the fabric; it's the way it is used. The variations are endless but look at the windows in the context of the whole room.

Curtains can be used to create optical illusions. Taking curtains right across the width of a room can make it seem much wider. If the room is too low, curtain the windows individually, using them to create a series of vertical lines. If the window is narrow for its height

you need enough track to either side to give an impression of a wider window and a dreary window can be given interest by simply framing it charmingly.

Headings

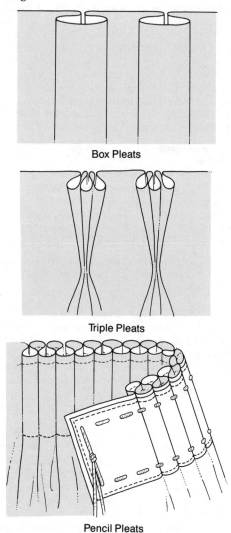

Box Pleats

Triple Pleats

Pencil Pleats

For a hidden heading you only need a very basic Rufflette tape to gather the fabric evenly. For a more elaborate heading the major effects produced by heading tapes are those above, but tapes can also produce smocked and ruffled effects, and there are translucent tapes, for lace and net. There is also a Rufflette tape which allows you to make the curtain and its lining separately and link the two with the curtain hooks. This won't give the same hang as lining in the usual way, but it could be used to put protective lining on a very sunny window. It also means shower curtains can have a fabric exterior and a detachable waterproof lining - so they need not be dreary.

Headings using tape are undoubtedly the easiest to sew, but for a luxury look you need a heading about

13 cm (5 in) deep and most aren't made to that width; also tape is machined on - which shows on the front and slightly spoils the effect. So the most professional finish is given by making the heading by hand.

Measuring Up

It is the width of the track, *not* the size of the window, which decides how wide the curtains must be and the length will depend on where you place the track.

The track always needs to be wider than the window - unless, of course, it is pinioned between two walls.

Normally, if a window is about 90 cm (3 ft) wide, the track needs to stick out 15 cm (6 in) beyond the window *at each side*. If the window is wider you will need proportionately more or the curtains will look too squeezed together when drawn back. Also bear in mind that curtains without pelmets usually stand a little away above the rail, and those on rods usually hang slightly below it.

Curtains need to be *generous*. Whatever the heading, they can't be less than twice the width of the track and to look really good need to be two and half times the width. But check the heading tape instructions - some only work if the curtain is a certain multiple of the track length. To find out how much fabric you need first establish the total length you will need for a finished curtain. The sum is this:

distance from rail to where you want it to end +
depth of hem +
allowance for turning in the upper edge
    2.5 cm (1 in) +
the length of the pattern repeat +
depth of the heading (unless they will hang by
    its top edge) +
allowance for shrinkage ±

                  Total length

★ Most fabric manufacturers say there can be up to 5 per cent shrinkage. That means curtains 2 m (6 ft 7 in) long, could shrink 10 cm (4 in). Also see page 182.

Multiply the length of a curtain by the number of widths of fabric you need to make the curtains wide enough, adding a 6 cm (2½ in) turning at each side of each curtain. Then calculate, and add on, the extra material for a pelmet.

Lining and Interlining Curtains

Lining makes curtains hang better, improves the insulation and protects the curtain fabric from the ravages of the sun, which might fade it in streaks on the folds, and make it fall apart far sooner. Use the measurements for the curtains, bar any allowance for pattern. Choose a good quality cotton sateen or investigate insulated lining. It usually looks best if all the windows have the same lining material.

Interlining not only gives curtains a softly luxurious look but also acts as insulation. So interlined curtains pay for themselves in lower heating bills.

There are several different kinds of interlining. The best is bump, domette is next, and even a cheap interlining is better than none. But interlinings aren't washable, so only interline curtains which will be dry cleaned. Buy the same quantity as for lining.

★ On washing, the curtain fabric and lining material may shrink by different amounts. If you plan to wash curtains, wash both fabrics to shrink them, before cutting out.

Cutting Out Curtains

Spread out a full curtain's length of fabric before cutting. Professionals use a vast table. Lacking that, spread it out on the floor, on one of the big plastic sheets which most DIY shops sell. And the golden rule is check everything twice before you cut or sew.

1 Decide where you want your pattern to come. Some very bold patterns look odd if they are incomplete at the bottom of a curtain.
2 Measure the length you need, positioning it to get the pattern where you want it. Mark it on the right side - first making sure it is perfectly flat and straight. *It is essential for the fabric to be cut straight across, not at a sloping angle or the curtains will never hang properly.*
3a If there is no pattern to match just cut the remaining lengths by measuring.
3b If the fabric has a pattern, place the cut length beside the one you are about to cut. Match the pattern *exactly*, pinning it at key places, then mark the cutting lines. And do this for *each* length. Cut out the lining and interlining to the same size.

Sewing Curtains

Pin and sew the seam lengths 1.5 cm (⅝ in) in from the edge, exactly matching any pattern (see above). Any part widths must come at the outer edge of each curtain. Put small cuts at intervals down the selvedges, as you go, so they don't pucker. Sew the lining in the same way.

★ Try out your stitch length on two spare bits of fabric, face to face. Too tight a stitch will create a gathered seam; too loose will look home-made.

★ Having pinned velvet sew it immediately or the heads may impress dents in the pile.

> For unlined curtains follow the steps below, ignoring all references to interlining and turn in and hem the edge. For curtains lined but not interlined ignore all references to interlining.

1 Iron all the seams open (unless fabric can't be ironed). Doing it at this stage makes a difference.
2 If the interlining needs to be seamed use a simple overlap.
3 Spread the curtain out face down. Place the interlining on it, so the top and sides match and both layers are totally smooth and lying straight. Pin together about 30 cm (1 ft) from the selvedge edge, and turn the interlining back almost at that point and lock stitch. Smooth, pin and repeat at 60 cm (2 ft) intervals, making the last one only 30 cm (1 ft) from

the edge. (Make sure the two layers stay perfectly matched at the top.

4   Cut off the top 2.5 cm (1 in) of interlining. Turn the top of the curtain over the edge of the interlining and tack it, folding in the corners as shown below - 6 cm (2½ in) in from the side - and trimming the excess interlining at the angle.

> This is the point at which professional curtain makers mitre the bottom corners and sew the hem. But to do that you need to be 100 per cent sure that you have every measurement correct and that you won't change the level of the heading tape. The order below allows for error and mind changing.

5   Treating the curtain and interlining as one, turn the side in 6 cm (2½ in). Herringbone this to the interlining using a fairly long stitch (see page 375) and catching both layers of the fold-over, but leave the sides unhemmed to twice the probable depth of the hem. If there is no interlining just herringbone the curtain fabric.

Lining the Curtain

6   Turn in one side edge of the lining by 2.5 cm (1 in) and iron the fold. Make little cuts in the selvedges at intervals. Mark a chalk line down each folded-in side of the curtain 4-5 cm (1¾-2 in) from the edge. Pin one folded edge of the lining down the chalk line and hem it to the curtain. Leave the bottom loose, as on the curtain itself.

7   Smooth the lining across the curtain, pinning the top, lock stitch to the interlining in the same way as the interlining was attached. Turn in the far edge of the lining and hem it to the chalked line of the curtain.

8   Pin the header tape just below the edge and 2.5 cm (1 in) beyond the curtain at either end. Undo and knot the strings on the wrong side at a point just inside the width of the curtain at the central edge as shown. Fold the tape end under just inside the curtain edge. At the other end pull out the strings from the surplus on the *right* side and turn the end under. Make sure there is room to machine without sewing over the strings.

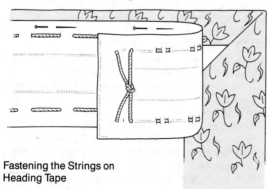

Fastening the Strings on
Heading Tape

Pulling Up the Strings

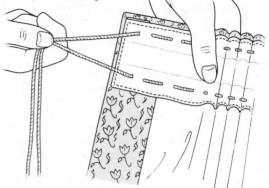

9   Machine up one end of the tape, along the upper edge, and half way down the far end. Then machine down the first end, along the bottom edge, and up the far end. Draw up the heading and insert the hooks not less than 10 cm (4 in) apart.

Making the Hem

10 Pin the curtain and interlining together, slightly above the bottom, making sure neither pulls the other. Turn a little of the interlining back and lockstitch the two layers together.

11 Hang the curtains, decide the hem, pin and re-check. Fold in each corner on a diagonal where the hem line meets the side fold. Iron this and cut along interlining at the fold. Fold it all back into place. Pin down the loose sections of the side-turnings making sure the angled corners create neat mitres with the hem. Herringbone the hem and loose sides. If it isn't interlined, hem carefully so the stitches won't show.

12 Fold the bottom of the lining in towards the curtain so the lower edge is about 5 cm (2 in) above the bottom of the curtain. Fold in its top edge, press, and machine. Finally, hem the loose sections of the lining edges.

★ Ideally weight the curtain by stitching a lead weight, like a button, on to the interlining at each seam in the curtain fabric and at each corner. Or run bead-style weights right along the bottom, securing them at intervals.

Make sure the heading is perfect and hang the curtain. If you are not hanging it from a pelmet board, push the last hook into the ring from the window side, so it curls the edge of the curtain around.

★ For the best hang, adjust the folds carefully and tie strips of fabric round the curtain to hold the folds together - but not crushed - for 24 hours.

Headings without Heading Tape

If you don't want to use heading tape, the top of the curtain can be lined with buckram which is sold for this in various widths. After step **3**, tack it in place along the top and tack the interlining and curtain over it. Then omit 4, 8 and 9 and hem the top of the lining to the curtain. Mark out the pleat positions by measuring them

- allowing about 4 inches flat between each triple pleat. Machine the basic pleat in place, on the right side, and fold and sew it in the triple pleat by hand. Finally, hemstitch a strong tape along the back where the pin-ended hooks will stab in.

Shortening Curtains
Much the easiest way to shorten curtains is to measure them carefully and cut off the excess from the top, then attach a new heading tape. Having drawn a cutting line tack all the layers together very carefully right across the curtain before you cut.

Pelmets
Pelmets divide into hard and soft. In deciding which to use bear the maintenance costs in mind. A soft pelmet can be washed or sent to the cleaners. To get a hard one clean may mean calling in professionals to deal with it.

The size needs to be related to the length of the curtains. A pelmet of less than 15 cm (6 in) looks skimpy; long curtains need considerably more, and the side-drops of elaborate pelmets usually need to be one third the length of the curtain.

Supporting a Pelmet
Some companies make pelmet rails which are linked into the curtain rail. It is probably best to attach substantial pelmets to a shelf which can also carry the curtain rail. A piece of ½ in pine, 15 cm (6 in) deep, supported on L brackets is ideal for the shelf.

Hard Pelmets
1 Design the pelmet you want, cut a pattern in newspaper, and check that it looks right on the window. Don't feel limited to simple shapes, you can do anything that suits the window.
2 Draw the shape on ¼ in ply and cut it out, with side pieces that will cover the sides of the shelf..
3 Seam some interlining, with flat seams, to cover it, plus about 10 cm (4 in) each way. Seam the pelmet material with a full width of fabric at the centre and extra width added to either side - if the shape you have chosen demands it.
4 Use sticky-backed carpet tape on the board to hold the side pieces at right angles. Cover with interlining - cutting slashes if you need to fit it round curves - and use a staple gun or Copydex to attach the fold-over firmly. Let any glue dry.
5 Iron the fabric for the pelmet. Repeat the procedure for the interlining, so it is nicely taut and the design is not pulled out of true. Pull it, pin it and look at the right side before slashing the fixing. Fix with Copydex or a staple gun. Carefully glue on any braid trimmings.
6 Cut out a lining to the shape of the pelmet plus 2 cm (¾ in) all round. Machine a strip of velcro along the top edge, just below the turning allowance. Pin the lining on to the wrong side of the pelmet, turning in its edges, and hem it in place, using a curved needle if need be.

Assembly
Glue the other half of the velcro firmly on to the edge of the shelf above the window.

Screw the curtain rail in place half way back on the board, so the curtains won't brush the pelmet.

Screw two ring screws into the board at each side very close to the wall - to take the end curtain hooks and make sure there is no draught between the window and the curtain.

When the glue is dry, hang the curtains. Then press the velcro of the pelmet firmly against the shelf. It should hold perfectly but you can put a small nail through the side flaps close to the wall.

Soft Pelmets
Soft pelmets are miniature versions of curtains so they must be twice the width of the track. Even an unlined pelmet can have an interesting heading tape, and it is simply made like a very short curtain.

The pelmet is made like a curtain but the lower edge is finished differently. For a pelmet either seam the lining on at the lower edge and fold it up the back to the top, before making the heading, or line it like a curtain, tack the lower edges together and bind them decoratively.

The easiest way to make elaborate soft pelmets with a lot of shaping was devised by a friend in Cambridgeshire. Cut the pelmet shape out of a piece of newspaper with no allowance for gathering. Place it on top of a piece of paper twice its width, which has a long straight edge at the top. Draw vertical lines on the pelmet pattern at 5-cm (2-in) intervals. Cut carefully up each line and space the 'pelmet' out across the under paper, with its upper edges against the top edge. Create precise 5-cm (2-in) gaps between each of the 'slices'. Stick it carefully to the paper underneath and cut it out.

Curtain Ties
There is no magic formula for ties: just use a tape measure to loop the curtains back and see what length you need. They will take more fabric than you might expect and you should allow for this when buying.

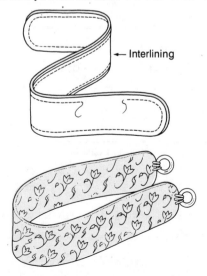

← Interlining

Net Curtains

Net curtains need to be twice the width of the space they will fill. In length they should be the length of the window plus about 18 cm (7 in) for the hem and extra for the top - see the steps below.

Cut out and seam with French seams, having the selvedges at the outside, so they need no side hems.

To hang them on a rod or wire, turn in the top by 2.5 cm (1 in), and by an inch again, pin and iron it. (If you want a frill above the rod make these turn-ins longer). Machine along the bottom edge of this hem. Then make another row of stitches higher leaving enough room to push the rod or the looped end of the wire through without effort.

To hang them on a rail, turn in the top 1.5 cm (½ inch). Attach transparent heading tape as for curtains (page 402).

Hang the curtains and decide on the depth of hem you need. Take the curtains down and fold the bottom edge up by *half* the depth of hem you need. Iron in the fold. Fold it again by the same amount, so the raw edge touches the fold. Press, pin, and machine in place.

Loose Covers

Loose covers aren't hard to make, but they do take a great deal of time and patience. For instructions on making them it would be hard to better those given in the *Which* book on page 407.

Choose a fabric which will take a good deal of wear, such as a heavy cotton, linen union or rep. The rule-of-thumb guide for how much fabric an armchair will need is 5 times the height of its back. But *don't buy* by this; just use it to decide what price of fabric you can run to.

The following measurements are a slightly better guide to how much fabric you will need. They are based on fabric 122 to 137 cm (48 to 54 in) wide, but do remember that if you have a pattern you will need considerably more and that quite small differences in key dimensions could mean that you require more fabric than is suggested.

Cushions

Cushions can be made by anyone with a sewing machine and cutting-out scissors. For the most basic, you just measure the cushion, across the top from seam to seam. Then cut two sides each 4 cm (1½ in) bigger, in each direction, than the cushion. Put them right side to right side, and machine 2 cm (¾ in) in from the edge, leaving one side half open in the middle. Clip the corners, as on page 381, then turn the cover inside out and iron it. Ease the cushion in and sew it up. If you want a zip opening put it in first; and sew the other sides as above.

For a piped cushion you need a good deal more fabric and cotton piping cord. Boil the piping cord for 5 minutes and dry it well or it may shrink when cleaned. Create bias strips of fabric 6 cm (2½ in) wide (see page 373) and sew them over the cord.

Pin the two layers of the cover together, with the piping between them, so that the seam lines match. When you are almost where you started, cut each end of the piping cord so it overlaps well. Pull the casing off it a little way and seam the two ends to fit the size of the cushion. Cut the strands of the cords to stepped lengths, twist them together and bind them firmly with cotton. Close the casing round this and tack into place.

Before sewing the cushion you need to fix the cord to one side of the cover where you will have the opening. Then machine round the rest of the cover with a zip foot, right up against the bulge of the cord. Trim, turn right side out, insert the cushion and hem the opening neatly together. A frill is put round a cushion in just the same way.

Without back cushions in the shape illustrated			
	armchair	2-seater sofa	3-seater sofa
Seat depth	86 cm (34 in)	86 cm (34 in)	86 cm (34 in)
Back height	80 cm (31½ in)	80 cm (31½ in)	80 cm (31½ in)
Back width	77 cm (30 in)	142 cm (56 in)	191 cm (75 in)
Fabric	7 m	10 m	13.5 m

With back cushions				
	armchair	2-seater sofa	3-seater sofa	wing chair
Seat depth	92 cm (36 in)	92 cm (36 in)	92 cm (36 in)	87 cm (34 in)
Back height	82 cm (32 in)	82 cm (32 in)	82 cm (32 in)	114 cm (45 in)
Back width	75 cm (29 in)	150 cm (59 in)	198 cm (78 in)	91 cm (36 in)
Fabric	9 m	14.5 m	16.5 m	6.5 m

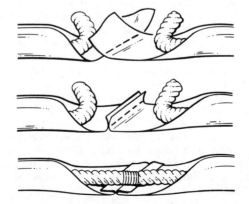

Frills

All frills are made the same way.

- A good frill must be twice as long as the measurements of whatever it will be attached to.
- In deciding the depth of a frill err on the side of generosity. Even a frill on a pillow looks skimpy if less than 8 cm (3 in) deep.
- Most frills need to be made with a double width of fabric, plus hem allowances, so that the fold is the outer edge of the frill.

By folding, find the half, quarter and other subdivisions of its length, until you have it marked into manageable sections. Fold and mark the edge of whatever you will attach it to in the same way, and match the marks.

★ For a frill with a machine-hemmed edge you machine a thin double hem first.

Round Tablecloth

These have become almost too popular, but their great virtue is that they allow you to create a table out of nothing more expensive than a few chunks of supporting wood and a sheet of ply. But the tablecloth costs more than you might think. For example a table 91 cm (36 in) across and 76 cm (30 in) high takes 8 metres of plain 137-cm (54-in wide fabric.)

To make your pattern, stick together a number of sheets of newspaper until you have a sheet rather larger than the cloth you will need. Fold this in half and then into a quarter. Take a long piece of string and tie a pencil to one end. Measure along the string, from the pencil, the distance from the floor to the table top, plus half the width of the table. Push a drawing pin through the string at this point. Push the pin through the folded corner of the newspaper, and hold the pin firm. Then stretch the string to its full length and mark a quarter of a circle. Cut round this pencil mark with the paper still folded.

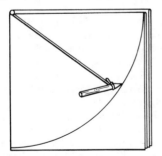

Before cutting out the cloth decide on your hem. Circular hems are hard to sew neatly. There are several other options.

- Bias binding - cheap, easy.
- Fringing of some kind - expensive but stylish.
- Braid - fairly expensive but effective.
- A wide bias strip of some contrasting or toning fabric. Very effective but takes time and fabric.
- A lining, so you make the two as a bag and turn it inside out. Heavy on fabric unless you have an old sheet looking for a home.

Use the paper to cut the fabric for the tablecloth. (Remember the circle has no allowance for seams or hems.) For the most luxurious effect put an undercloth of curtain interlining under the tablecloth.

Bed Linen

It is very easy to make attractive bed linen and you can save a fortune doing so. I buy sheets in attractive colours in the sales and just seam them into something more interesting. The more expensive shops often have king sizes in the sales which are ideal.

Duvet Covers

The most basic duvet cover is made just like the basic cushion cover on page 406, except that you either sew ties (made from the fabric or matching straight tape) along the opening in the foot or sew on a strip with ready-made poppers. Either way, you can finish it in under an hour. For a more decorative cover add contrasting strips of fabric, wide broderie Anglaise strips with ribbon threaded through or put a deep frill right round the edge.

Valance and Frilled Bedcover

For a valance, cut out and, if necessary, seam up fabric to the size of the surface of the bed base plus 2 cm (¾ in) seam allowance all round. Cut strips of fabric the depth of the bed base plus 2 cm (¾ in) seam allowance at the top and 5 cm (2 in) for the hem. Treat these as for frills and seam to the base.

A bedcover with an edge that is gathered from surface level can be made in the same way as the valance. You just increase the length of the frill. Attach to the top - with the pattern side facing the other way - a section twice the pillow's measurement from front to back and 26 cm (10 in) wider, at either side, than the bed.

More information

Antiference Ltd (Kirsch), Bicester Road, Aylesbury, Bucks HP19 3BJ Tel: 0296 82511 - makes brass rods which bend, tracks, spring-loaded net rods, electronic curtain pulls.

Hunter Douglas Ltd, 15-16 Bellsize Close, Walsall Road, Norton Canes Cannock WS11 3TQ Tel: 0543 75757 - makes Luxaflex tapes, which provide some of the more unusual headings, and ready-made blinds.

Rufflette Ltd, Sharston Road, Wythenshawe, Manchester M22 4TH Tel: 061 998 1811 - has a consumer advice service on using heading tapes and blind kits.

Silent Gliss, Star Lane, Margate, Kent CT9 4EF Tel: 0843 63571 - makes blind kits, tracks, electrically operated roller blinds.

Sunway UK Ltd, Grovelands Industrial Estate, Longford Road, Exhall, Coventry CV7 9NB Tel: 0203 361500 - ready-made blinds, including Austrian and festoon.

Swish Products Ltd, Lichfield Road Industrial Estate, Tamworth, Staffs B79 7TW Tel: 0827 64242 - makes blind kits, ready-made blinds.

Soft Furnishings, Designers' Guild, Pan Books
Which? way to make soft furnishings, the Consumers' Association, Hodder and Stoughton

Things Mechanical

Bicycles • Cameras • Car Buying and Selling • Car Driving •
Car Care and Maintenance • Computers

BICYCLES

My own relationship with bicycles ended when a pedal irreplaceably parted company from the ancient frame of the secondhand two-wheeler I had bought as a sixth-former. I would never have looked closely at a bicycle again had not my succession of children required bikes of every type and size, right up to a multi-gear racer. It is to my, now adult, son - whose hobby it is - that I owe most of the information in this section.

Buying a Bicycle

Children's Bicycles
The ideal time to learn to ride a bicycle is when very young, and the best place to buy it is a bicycle shop rather than a toy shop. There are still traditional cycle shops where they take pleasure in guiding a child up through the stages of bicycle riding, and make sure it has the right bike for its size and ability. Such a shop is well worth searching out, and the men in it are usually good at telling the child how to care for the bicycle too - which may be more effective than words from parents.

Ideally, children start with tricycles. Even at this stage there are differences. Good tricycles have ball bearings at the main moving parts, such as the headset where the front wheel turns; cheap ones don't. The cheap ones go perfectly well; the snag comes if they have to be repaired. Those without ball bearings may be impossible or expensive to put right. As tricycles fairly seldom need repairing it's a gamble which is the better option.

From tricycles the next stage is a small bike, with large tyres and a pair of outrider wheels splaying out from the back wheel as stabilizers - so the bike won't easily fall over. It should be possible to remove the outriders when they are no longer needed. Children like the achievement of riding without the stabilizers as soon as possible, but taking them off before the child is steady will just give you the job of mopping up rather more grazed knees.

Small-wheeled bicycles are usually needed until a child is about 12 years old and at every stage the bicycles should be given a critical look. According to those in the business, there's a lot of rubbish around in junior bikes. There are also seductive bicycles which may not be the best ones for the job. For example, children tend to fall in love with the brilliantly marketed BMX bicycles. They are fun for messing about on but aren't designed for flat ground.

Adult Bicycles
The big divide in adult bicycles is between small wheels (20 in or under) and large wheels (around 27 in). Within the large-wheeled group there is a steady gradation from heavy basic bikes to light sporty ones.

The big disadvantage of small wheels is that you have to work harder to go at any given speed. This makes them a poor choice for long distances and for hilly country. The plus side is that the slow speed and small wheels make them easy to use in tight situations, such as heavy traffic.

The greatest advantage of small-wheeled bicycles is that there are fold-away models which can be kept in a flat or carried in a car. There are also ones which collapse even more and can be carried as hand luggage. Before buying any folding bike it is advisable to scour the latest tests on them, in *Which* and in cycling magazines, and check the reports on the folding mechanisms.

Buying Secondhand
Bicycles seem like a natural secondhand buy. They can be, but there are basic precautions which need to be taken:
- Be suspicious of secondhand sports bikes which have been used for over 2 years. The gearing is likely to be very worn and this is expensive to put right. But it isn't easy to recognize worn gearing unless you have seen it before.
- Rotate the wheels while looking at them edge on, so the far side seems to disappear behind the nearside. Then rotate them. If the far side doesn't stay invisible the wheel is buckled and a bad buy.
- Check the brakes: they shouldn't need to travel very far before gripping - to sell a bike with defective brakes is illegal.
- Look at the side view of the line of the main column from handlebars to front wheel. The upper part of the 'fork' holding the wheel should be in line with the column itself. If it isn't the bike has crashed and could be weak elsewhere.
- Check the paint of crossbars near where they join the uprights. Vertical cracks in the paintwork, or rust, also suggest a crash has damaged the frame, which is potentially dangerous.

Care and Maintenance
Bicycles must have a certain amount of care and maintenance if they are to remain safe. A bike which

has been out in the rain should be dried with a cloth before being put away, and if it is being used much it should be checked once a week. The most essential points to check regularly are the brakes.

Brakes
Make sure the rim of the wheel is free of oil and grease, otherwise the brakes won't work. Use spirit to remove any oil or grease you find, but keep it off the tyres. After that there are three parts to having safe brakes:

1   Is the pad correct for the wheel rim?
     With new bikes this is no problem, but you do need to be careful when buying replacement pads and check those on a secondhand bike. Most brakes work by pressing against the rim of the wheel and not all brake pads suit all rims. Having the wrong brake pad may not show in the dry, but in the wet it can be dangerous. Leather pads are bad for aluminium wheel rims but ideal for steel rims. The other possibility for steel is a special composition.
2   Is the pad in good condition?
     Pads need to be replaced when worn by half their full thickness. They are easily replaced but if one end of the shoe which holds them is closed, put it to the front so the block doesn't slide out. Make sure it is positioned so it will pull against the rim not the tyre.
3   Does the cable need adjusting?
     Most brakes work on cables which go down to levers which operate the brakes. As the brakes start to wear you can tighten them by taking up the slack in the brake cable. You do this by turning the barrel screw at the end of the cable housing.

Chain
Since the chain communicates your energy to the wheels it's more important than it looks. It must be kept clean and well oiled, and if it has been used over salted roads it needs to be cleaned immediately or it may seize up.

How often you need to remove and clean it varies with the use. If you do a lot of serious cycling it could be every two weeks; if you only use it an average amount then every couple of months will be enough. On a hub-gear or single-speed bicycle the chain will undo at a spring clip which you can open with a twist of a screwdriver. But you need a pin extractor to undo one of the links on the chain of derailleur gears.

Having removed the chain, use meths, paraffin or petrol and a small scrubbing brush to get off all the old oil and dirt. Replace the chain on the bicycle and rub it well with a light multipurpose oil, such as 3 in 1, on a cloth, back-pedalling it as you do so.

If a chain breaks it can be repaired with a chain riveting tool. With derailleur gears the spring-loading will adjust the tension. With other bicycles you need to adjust the position of the wheel until there is about 1·5 cm (½ in) of play at the mid-point.

Gears
The most basic type of gear is the hub gear with its 3 to 5 ratios enclosed in the hub of the wheel. As they aren't exposed, you don't have to do anything about them unless they go wrong. But if they do go wrong take them to an expert as they are hard to put right. You can, however, make minor adjustments, and will probably need to. To stop gears slipping when you change gear you can re-set them by selecting the middle gear, then undoing the lock nuts beneath the cable connector. When the end of the indicator rod is precisely level with the axle you tighten the lock nuts and the adjustment should be correct.

Derailleurs look more complicated, but are far more amenable to DIY. By shifting the chain between notched discs of different sizes, it can give between 5 and 21 gears, but the most basic adjustment is to tighten the central bolts on the control levers from time to time. More important is to adjust the tension of the cable - especially if you have removed the back wheel. To adjust it you loosen the anchor bolt on the gear changer, pull the cable through and re-set the adjustment screws on the top of the changer until it moves easily from one gear to another. (Note: one screw adjusts the setting for top gear, the other the setting for bottom gear.)

Handlebars and Saddle
These adjust by undoing a quick release lever, or a bolt. Having undone the nut, tap the bolt lightly with a hammer to release the stem. If an old bike is severely stuck try turning the seat or handlebars sideways rather than pulling. Failing that, put penetrating oil round the joint and leave it.

Tyres
Tyres must be kept at the right pressure to steer safely, but you don't need a gauge to keep them correctly pumped. Anyone with a reasonable grip can do it by feel, once they have felt them at the correct pressure. When not in use for any time, bicycles should be hung up with the tyres slightly deflated, so the weight isn't carried by the tyres. Check the tyres regularly for anything which might puncture them. If there is a puncture:

1   Turn the bicycle upside down.
2   Remove the wheel from the bicycle. (With a derailleur you need to put it in gear on the smallest sprocket first.)
3   Lever the tyre off with a tyre lever or a strong teaspoon handle. *Don't* use a screwdriver as it may rip the inner tube.
4   Remove the inner tube. If you can't see or hear the puncture, inflate the tube and slowly rotate it through a basin of water. You will see bubbles coming up from the hole.
5   Dry the tube and mark the puncture site with chalk.
6   Roughen the area round the hole with glass paper.
7   Choose a patch which will fully cover the hole and spread a matching area of tyre adhesive (*not* ordinary glue) round the hole.
8   When the adhesive is almost dry press the patch on firmly.
9   Wipe off any surplus glue and let it dry completely.
10 Dust over the patch with French chalk to stop it

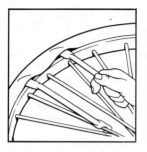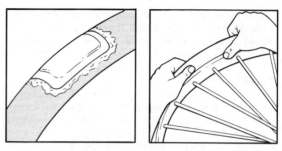

sticking to the tyre.

11 Pump up the tube. Test the repair in water, then deflate it.

12 Check, inside and out, that nothing is in the tyre which could cause another puncture; and that the spokes aren't sticking up on the wheel rim.

13 Push the valve through the hole in the tyre, and slip the inner tube into place before pumping it up.

14 Replace the tyre on the wheel, levering it carefully so as not to pinch the inner tube.

Oiling

To get the maximum efficiency from your bike you can buy special oils for every part of a bicycle - if your interest and pocket allow - but a light multipurpose oil will do the job quite well enough for the average bicycle. If a bicycle is being used all the time it needs to be oiled as follows:

● Pedals - monthly
● Wheel hubs - monthly
● Gears - monthly

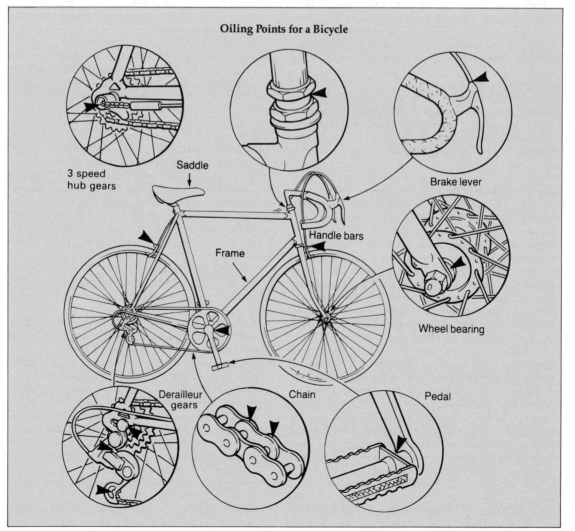

Oiling Points for a Bicycle

3 speed hub gears · Saddle · Brake lever · Handle bars · Frame · Wheel bearing · Derailleur gears · Chain · Pedal

- Brake stirrups - monthly
- Headset and bearings - a light oil monthly (some need only a touch, some quite a bit; check with your manual or a bicycle shop). Turn the bicycle upside down to do this or the oil may drip onto the tyres.
- Brake cable - light oil occasionally.

Fitting the Bicycle to the Rider

For safety, a bicycle must be the right size for the rider. But the less good bicycle shops try to sell children's bicycles by the age of the child. It may be a rough guide but children don't always come in standard gauges. So the actual size of the child is a much better guide. You may need to be firm with the shop about this. When my 12-year-old son was pushing 6 foot, one shop insisted that a 12-year-old must need a child's bike.

To allow for growth you need to buy the biggest bicycle the child can manage. This means that with the seat fully down they should be able just to touch the ground securely with their feet on each side. If you want to buy a bicycle as a surprise you can pretend you are measuring up for trousers.

A rough guide if you see them near a bike they like is that the cross bar of a boy's bike (or the equivalent point on a girl's) should be just below crotch level when they stand beside it.

Adjusting a Saddle

For both children and adults the saddle should be adjusted so the leg is fully stretched when the arch of the foot is over the pedal at its lowest point. The handlebars should then be adjusted to give a comfortable position.

In adjusting the seat and handlebars, there should be *not less* than 8 cm (3 in) of handlebar stem, or seat pillar, inside the column.

Safety

Carrying Children and Luggage

The basic safety rule when carrying children or luggage on a bicycle is not to carry more than half your own weight, or it will be dangerously unstable. For a child's seat alone, fitted on the rear, the weight limit is only up to 20 kg (45 lb) and the seat needs to be carefully attached and guards fitted to prevent a child's fingers getting caught in any part of the bicycle.

Visibility

Cyclists need to do everything possible to make themselves visible. Unless they also drive a car, they seldom realize how easily bicycles blend into the background when a motorist is mainly watching for larger vehicles. A big danger is wearing dark clothing. Reflective diagonal bands, and arm and leg bands all increase visibility and you can now buy some with small lights on. Reflectors on the wheel spokes make a bicycle more visible from the side, and a sticking-out reflector makes it easier to see from behind. And, when buying cycling clothing, choose colours which show up in bad weather and in the dark.

Protection

A good crash helmet protects the skull but leaves the ears clear so you can still hear traffic. It should have a hard plastic shell and a strong foam inner lining. Look for a BS number to be sure it has been tested and approved.

Cycling Proficiency

There is a national cycling proficiency scheme which is run by the **Royal Society for the Prevention of Accidents** (Cannon House, Priory Queensway, Birmingham B4 6BS Tel: 021 200 2461) through local Road Safety Officers. Children from the age of 9 can be given training and road safety tests plus lessons on bicycle care. Contact the above address if you want to know the name of your nearest centre and your council hasn't been able to help.

Theft

Many hundreds of thousands of bicycles are stolen every year, so it is worth taking a few preventive measures.

Note all the details of your bicycle, so it can be identified by the police if it is stolen. In addition to the colour, model and make, there should be a maker's serial number on the frame somewhere. This is vital.

Park it where lots of people are passing, and put the chain through both wheels and the frame. (This deters thieves from stealing parts or sawing through the chain.) Alternatively, use one of the U-shaped shackle locks. These are made of hardened steel and are very effective. They are more expensive than chains, but some carry a year's insurance. As the insurance element in the price is considerably cheaper than most independent insurance, this makes them an especially good buy for those who can't put their bike on a household policy. But the insurance may only cover loss incurred *when the lock was in use* and you may need to *prove* that it was used. Not easy.

Tools

For basic care and repairs, you need a puncture repair kit, 2 to 3 tyre levers, allen keys, a multi-size spanner, chain riveting tool (unless the chain is super-link) and pliers.

More information

Bicycle Magazine does regular reviews of bicycles
Richard Ballantine, *Richard's Bicycle Book*, Pan - a guide to all you need to know about bicycles.

CAMERAS

This section is for those who are wondering about buying a camera, and for those who have one and are not sure how it works.

Buying a Camera

There are basically three types of camera on the market:
1 Cartridge load cameras in which almost everything is automatic and the film comes in a cartridge, so you don't have to fiddle about.

2   Compact cameras in which most functions are automatic, but you load a normal 35 mm film.

3   Single lens reflex cameras, known as SLR cameras, in which ordinary 35 mm film is also used and all or most of the decisions are made by the user, though it may be possible to make them automatic if you wish.

The choice of camera depends entirely on what type of person you are and what you want to do with it. There is no camera which is 'best'. Nor is it reasonable to say that a beginner should start with a very undemanding camera, with a cartridge load, and then move on to something more exacting. Some total beginners would love to be able to take pictures with so little thought; others would hate the lack of flexibility.

If you simply want to be a 'point and press' photographer - as they put it in the trade - then there are any number of cartridge and compact cameras on the market which can produce good pictures with little or no thought.

However, before buying one, do consider what you may want to do with the camera. An automatic is fine for happy snaps on the beach or in the garden. But automatic cameras do have some limitations, so only buy one if you can either afford to replace it with a more versatile camera when you need to, or if you are sure you will never want any of the options it lacks.

When choosing an SLR camera a key point is that some are 'aperture priority' - so you select the aperture setting and the camera selects the shutter speed (both explained below). Others are 'shutter priority' - which is simply vice versa. Some let you select both. The first essential, when buying a camera, is to find your preference between aperture priority or shutter priority. The range is constantly improving, so check out any reports in *Which* magazine and read the magazine *Which Camera* before talking to local dealers. Prices are also variable and can be judged by advertisements; the mail order camera company on page 203 is also a good yardstick. There is no disadvantage in buying at the cheapest price for that model, as the guarantee will be the same whatever the price.

Cameras Explained

The modern camera seems to have passed into the realms of space-age technology, but it is really exactly as it was in the nineteenth century: a box containing film and a hole which lets light onto the film to record an image.

Films vary in the amount of light they need to create a picture. Those which need very little light are called fast films; those that need a lot of light are called slow.

However complex a camera may look, the first thing to get right is the amount of light reaching the film. Without that there is no picture. Two things decide how much light reaches the film:
● the size of the opening letting in light (the aperture)
● the length of time light enters for (the shutter speed).

If you are a 'point and press' photographer with an automatic camera, both the size of the opening (aperture) and the time it stays open (shutter speed) are set for you. If you have an SLR camera you may be able to choose the opening (aperture) or the shutter speed, or both.

As you would expect, the two interact. So if you increase the hole, you can let light enter for a shorter time yet still get a picture. So long as you increase one as you reduce the other, and vice versa, the situation - so far as light is concerned - will always balance out (just as $2 + 4 = 4 + 2$).

Automatic cameras may judge the light for themselves and decide on the size of the opening and how long the

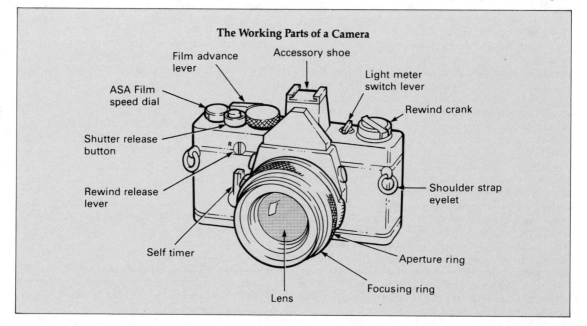

The Working Parts of a Camera

Film advance lever

Accessory shoe

Light meter switch lever

ASA Film speed dial

Rewind crank

Shutter release button

Rewind release lever

Shoulder strap eyelet

Self timer

Aperture ring

Focusing ring

Lens

shutter should be open. On some other cameras there may be simple settings, so you set it for a sunny day, a cloudy day or flash.

Shutter Speed Range

On most SLR cameras the range of shutter speeds is from a 1000th of a second, to 1 or 2 seconds, and there is also a 'B timer'. When set on B timer the general rule is broken and the shutter stays open for however long you hold down the shutter release button.

The shutter speed controls the length of time the film is exposed to the image. What I've said above makes it sound as if it doesn't matter whether you have a fast shutter speed and a large opening (aperture) or vice versa. That is true if you just want to get *an* image on the film. But to get a *good* image you need to balance the two to suit the situation. This is really very simple.

Fast Movement

If a photograph is being taken of a fast moving object, such as a bird or a racing car, then a fast shutter speed is needed to 'freeze' the subject and prevent it blurring. This obviously demands a wide opening (aperture) to give the film enough light.

But suppose you wanted a slight blur, to show its speed. Then you would have the shutter speed slightly slower, so the car moved past the camera while it was still open. With a slower shutter speed you would then use a slightly smaller opening (aperture).

A racing car is an extreme example, but the same would be true of capturing a child running or playing, or even the fleeting expression on someone's face - though the speed could be slower, so the shutter could stay open longer and the opening (aperture) be smaller.

When Close Up

Movement also counts if you want to get very close to something. A flower which is barely trembling in the breeze will look perfectly stationary at most speeds if you photograph it from several metres (yards) away. But the closer you go the more any swaying will show on the picture, and if you plan to fill the whole frame with a single bloom you will need a fast shutter speed to cut out both the tremble of the flower and camera wobble. Here again fast speed will go with a large opening (aperture).

Shutter Speed and Light

If the light is poor, and whatever you want to photograph is not moving quickly (or - preferably - not moving at all) a slow shutter speed can be used. But below a 60th of a second even a slight unsteadiness in the hand will make the picture lose its sharpness, so it is wiser to support the camera on something steady. This doesn't have to be a tripod. Many photographers take excellent pictures, in very low light, by just resting a camera on a wall or a car (with the engine off and nobody moving inside it).

It is the combination of shutter speed and aperture which form the final exposure that will achieve a crisp, light-balanced photograph.

What the Size of the Opening (Aperture) Does

The examples above demanded a particular shutter speed, and the size of the opening (aperture) had to follow from that. But it doesn't have to be like that: the size of the opening also gives different qualities to a picture.

Light Effects

We may think of light as a single entity, but it isn't really like that. For example, if a child is sitting with her back to a window the amount of light behind her will be far greater than the amount on her face. If you simply focused the camera in her direction and adjusted the f-stop by the reading on your light meter (which is what an automatic camera would do) she would come out as a silhouette against a nicely photographed background. To photograph her face you would need to set the f-stop (see below) for the light *on* her face. So you would either take a reading by going close to her or take an overall reading and then open up by one and half to two f-stops. Then she would be properly exposed and the background would probably be rather bleached - which can be very effective.

Effects on Focus

Whenever a camera is pointed at anything it is focused on a particular point (automatic cameras which have 'autofocus' will automatically focus on the first object which occupies a major part of the picture; other cameras have to be focused - see page 415). The point which is focused on (and everything to right and left of it) will look perfectly sharp and clear in the picture. How clear everything else will look depends on the size of the opening (aperture). The rule is:

- the smaller the opening (aperture), the greater the range of distances, behind and in front of the point of focus, which will look crisp and in focus.
- the larger the opening, the more hazy things will look which are behind or in front of the point of focus.

In a non-automatic camera the size of the opening (aperture) is controlled by turning a ring on the lens which is marked in f-stops. The more you close the opening (aperture) the larger the number of the f-stop and each f-stop allows in half as much light as the previous one. The distance which is in focus at any f-stop is called the depth of field.

Pros and Cons of Different Depths of Field

When you use a large f-stop, giving a small depth of field, you have to be far more precise in your focusing, or your subject may be out of focus. But once you get that right the subject will stand out sharply against a softly blurred background - which can be very effective.

If you use a small f-stop, giving a large depth of field, much more is in focus, so you can get away with less precise focusing and do it faster. The penalty is that your main subject may look more of an also-ran, as everything else will be just as clear. It is points like this which make the mysterious difference between a 'snap' and a photograph.

The size of the opening (aperture) isn't the only thing which affects the range of distances that will be in focus. Two other factors play a part: how close the subject is to the camera, and the type of lens you are using. The closer a subject is to the camera, the less depth of field at any f-stop. Different lenses operate within a different range of f-stops and also have different depths of field at the same stops. So, if you focus a standard 50 mm lens, and a 28 mm wide angle lens and a telephoto lens on the same point, and choose the same f-stop the depth of field will vary considerably.

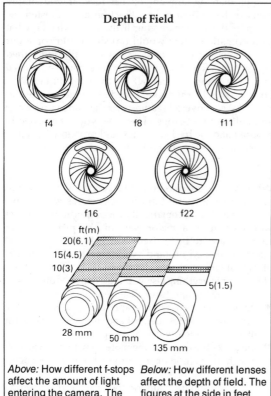

Depth of Field

Above: How different f-stops affect the amount of light entering the camera. The higher the f-stop the greater the depth of field.

Below: How different lenses affect the depth of field. The figures at the side in feet (metres) show the depth of field for each lens.

Film

How It Works

Film works by capturing light in microscopic particles called silver halide. The silver halide is embedded in a gelatin to form what is called an emulsion. Colour film can either be designed to produce negatives, or to produce slides (transparencies). Slide film (also called 'reversal') produces both slides and excellent prints. In theory, film which gives colour negatives is designed for prints, but will also produce colour slides and black and white prints. In practice, amateurs can seldom get slide quality from it. So using slide film usually gives more options.

With both colour and black and white film, the larger the particles, the more sensitive they are to light. So fast film uses larger particles than slow film. This difference in particle size doesn't usually show in the size of print you put in an album (though this will depend on how you took the picture), but if you enlarge two photographs, taken on different speeds of film, the larger particles of the faster film will give the enlargement a grainy look.

Film Speeds

Film speeds are now shown as two sets of figures like this: 125/22° - the first is the ASA number for cameras using ASA speeds, the second is the DIN number for cameras using DIN speeds.

These are called ISO speeds and an ISO speed is always referred to in terms of the number before the slash. So an ASA 125 and an ISO 125 are just identical 'roses' by other names. The main ISO numbers used by amateurs are these:

ISO 50   Film for studio work.
ISO 100   A fine-grained film for using in good light and for fine detail. You can make big enlargements without graininess or loss of definition.
ISO 125   A film for most conditions
ISO 200   A very useful film which allows you to get pictures even in rather poor light. It offers a wide range of shutter speeds and apertures but still allows a good deal of enlargement before the sharpness drops off.
ISO 400   This allows you to take fast moving objects with a fast shutter speed, so you freeze the action. It also lets you take shots indoors, in light conditions which would otherwise demand a flash - ideal for places like temples and art galleries where photography may be allowed but flash is banned. But it isn't suited to very bright sunlight and big enlargements may be grainy.

Whatever the ISO, you can stack the odds in favour of getting a good print by using film such as Kodacolor Gold, which is made to be tolerant of errors and, at any setting, needs a less precise exposure to get good results.

Film Care

Film dislikes heat and humidity. If you buy professional film it should be kept at below 13°C (50°F). Amateur film is more tolerant and accepts room temperatures, but it still dislikes hot sunlight and if you are taking a film or camera to a hot beach or picnic it is best to keep it in an insulated bag (see page 416).

Flash

Using flash allows you to take pictures when the light is too low for the film you are using. Angle the flash so it bounces off some light surface - such as a white ceiling - and down onto your subject. You don't have to be a demon mathematician to spot the point it needs to bounce off.

Flash can only operate within a limited range. This is 1·2 m to 5·5 m (4 to 18 ft) with a normal lens and works best within 2·4 to 3 m (8 to 10 ft), though it will go closer with certain close-up lenses. Objects closer to the flash will look paler than those farther away, so the differences in distance shouldn't be too great.

How to Use a Camera

Inserting Film

For cartridge cameras you just insert the film according to the handbook. With 35 mm you must insert the tongue of the film in the spool to the right and then pull the film spool back to slot in place, so the film stretches across the back of the lens. (Don't worry about this bit getting light on it.) Now use the wind-on lever on the top of the camera to wind on as for 2 exposures. With some cameras you may need to press the shutter button, as if taking a photo, between each wind on, or they will not wind on. Make sure the holes in the film nestle nicely over the little 'cogs' sticking up inside the camera. Then shut the camera. Now wind on *twice* more, looking at the top of the camera on the side where the main film spool is. There is a rewind knob there which will turn if the film is going through properly - as you turn the lever at the other end of the camera. If it doesn't turn open the camera and sort the film out. By winding the film on 4 times you don't lose money. There should still be the correct number of exposures, but by skimping it the film may slip and the whole reel be wasted.

Setting the ISO/ASA

Some modern cameras automatically read a code on the film (called a DX code) which tells them the speed of the film, in which case you needn't make any adjustments at this stage. But most cameras need to be set to operate with the speed of film you have bought. Look for a knob marked ASA or ISO (it doesn't matter which as they are all the same film speed by another name). Set the knob so the number indicated matches the ISO/ASA speed written on the box of film. Sometimes it doesn't say ISO: it just has a figure like 100, 200 or 400 written on it.

Setting the Exposure

On a simple camera this may be done automatically or you may have to judge whether the light is bright or dull, and set it to sun or cloud. Don't go by whether there *are* clouds. It can be cloudy but quite bright - especially if water, snow or white buildings are reflecting the light.

With an SLR camera you will need to check the light meter and turn the ring on the lens to the right f-stop (see page 414), or adjust the shutter speed, bearing in mind the points on pages 412 to 414. If in doubt, on an average day, with a moderately fast film set the shutter speed to 125. This is fast enough to minimize the effects of wobbling hands or any slight movement by your subjects.

Focusing

Simple cameras may give you a choice of close-in (indicated by a head and shoulders silhouette), a few feet away (figures full length) or at a distance (indicated by trees or mountains). Set the control to whichever position is most similar to what you want to photograph.

SLR cameras can have various types of focusing, but the most common is a split field. To focus with this look through the camera and try to look at something (in your picture) with a line in. Turn the focusing ring on the lens until the line is perfectly straight.

Lenses

One of the great advantages of an SLR camera is being able to change lenses. It adds a whole new dimension to taking photographs if you can pop on a wide angle to capture a sweep of scenery or use a zoom to 'get close' to people and animals which would be camera-shy. Most camera shops have a choice of good quality lenses, and if you are going to change lenses it is worth having as good a one as you can afford.

Lens types vary in two ways: how wide an angle of picture they capture, and the distance from the subject at which they operate well. The standard lens offered with most 35 mm cameras is 50 mm. This lens captures the scene very much as the eye would see it. It operates from about half a metre to infinity.

From 50 mm downwards there are the wide angle lenses. These allow you to take in more in all directions. So they are useful for landscapes. The disadvantage is that, in capturing more of the scene than the human eye they distort perspective.

Any camera with a standard lens can work at a distance as close as 1·2 m (4 ft). To get closer, for example to take flowers or insects, you need a macro lens designed to produce sharp pictures with very little distortion when very close to the subject. There are zoom lenses with macro facilities but these are seldom as good as a pure macro.

From 50 mm upwards (e.g. 110 mm, 200 mm to the extreme of 3,000 mm) there are the telescopic and caterdioptric lenses which enable you to capture that lion you daren't get close to, in daredevil pictures which look as if you did (to all but an expert eye). The zoom is the most flexible lens as it allows you to alter the point of focus very quickly, which is perfect when taking anything in motion, so wildlife and sports photographers tend to use these. A 70 or 80 to 210 mm lens is one of the most useful and most widely sold.

Since these lenses exaggerate the closeness of the subject they will also exaggerate camera shake; you therefore need to have the shutter only open for a short time if you possibly can. The rule of thumb is that to avoid camera shake the slowest shutter speed you can use is the number closest to the focal length of your lens (but not less than it). So:

Focal Length	Shutter Speed
50 mm lens	60th of a second
80 mm lens	125th of a second (from 60 to 125 may seem a big gap, but no speed closer to it is above 60)
200 mm lens	250th of a second
400 mm lens	500th of a second

Problem Solving

Blank film It probably failed to go through the camera. (see left).

Bleached and pale pictures Over-exposure. Either you had too slow a shutter speed or the aperture was open too wide. Another possibility is that this was a faster film than the previous one and you forgot to change the film speed to the new ISO (ASA/DIN) setting.

Blobs on the picture You either got something in the way of the lens (such as your fingers) or the lens is dirty.

Blurred picture Either the camera wobbled or the picture was out of focus.

Streaks on the first few shots You pointed the film cassette at the light when loading or unloading it, and a little light got through the slit.

Taking Better Snaps

The rules for taking expert photographs are rather different from those for taking snaps. The following hints are for snaps, not art work.

★ Get in close to your subject. Whatever you are taking should almost fill the frame - a picture of a whole house seldom means much; a shot of a stunning door (or face) can be great.

★ Don't get people to pose. It's far more interesting to catch them unawares with typical (or odd) expressions than to have a row of heads facing the camera.

★ Don't take every picture standing up or sitting on a chair. Try other levels for a change. Children often look better from lower down.

★ Don't be so busy looking at the subject of the photograph that you don't see the curious post in the background seeming to stick out of the person's ear or the dog doing something unmentionable by Granny's foot.

★ If you want to get pictures of people, be patient. Pretend to take pictures until they get tired of paying attention to you and start behaving normally; *then* photograph them.

★ Don't feel you always have to have your back to the light. That makes your victims face the sun, and screw up their eyes; side lighting is usually more effective and kinder.

When You Go on Holiday

- Check the camera over at least a week before leaving.
- Buy spare batteries - sizes which seem standard in Britain may not be obtainable in some countries.
- Buy plenty of film (unless you are sure it is cheaper at the airport or where you are going).
- As heat can seriously affect film, keep it cool. If you will want to take your camera about in a hot climate, put it and your film (plus books but *not* swimming things) in one of the insulated cooler bags

supermarkets sell for frozen food and picnics. *Make sure you don't tuck in anything liquid which might spill on the camera.*

- Keep sand and dust off the camera and *never* open the back when dust or sand are blowing.

More information

Kodak Limited, Consumer Services, P.O.Box 66, Station Road, Hemel Hempstead, Herts HP1 1JU Tel: 0442 61122 - offers help and advice on all aspects of photography, and does good leaflets on topics like how to take pictures or process your own film.

Julian Calder and John Garrett, *The 35 mm Photographer's Handbook*, Pan

John Hedgecoe's Photography Course, Mitchell Beazley

CAR BUYING AND SELLING

The Cost of Buying

A car is probably the most expensive thing you will ever buy - apart from a home. So, before buying one it's as well to tot up the real cost - it comes to a lot more than just the price. To get an idea you need to add up the figures for the following on the car you have in mind:

- the depreciation (an average family car loses about £1,000 to £1,200 of its value in its first year)
- the interest on the money you borrow (or interest not earned if you take money out of the bank and pay cash)
- insurance
- road tax
- servicing
- petrol - miles x price (an average motorist drives 10,000 miles a year)
- parking
- replacement cost of tyres
- an annual MOT test if the car is over 3 years old
- special clothing for a motorcyclist.

Add up the figures you get and divide your answer by the number of miles of motoring you expect to do and you will have the cost per mile - you may find it would be less expensive to take a taxi each time.

★ The figures for a motorbike shouldn't be so daunting, but before buying a motorbike check that the law allows you to buy the type you covet - the post office has a leaflet on this.

New v Used

The moment you take delivery of a new car it becomes a used car and is worth less than you paid for it (unless it is a rare car in enormous demand). The steepest drop in value in the first year is for cars at the top and bottom ends of the price range, but even an average family car can lose over 15 per cent of its value in the first year.

With a used car you get a cheaper car, but you risk buying a car which will have the problems associated with its age and may also have been worn by bad driving and poor maintenance. Some cars are far tougher than others and will give fewer problems in their old age. So the type of car you want is an important

---

Don't let film go through X-ray machines if you can avoid it. The faster the film, the greater risk that it will be harmed by X-ray equipment in airports. Some airport equipment may be safe for film, but a lot isn't - whatever they say. So, if you want to have anything to show for your trip, keep all your films - used and unused - at the top of your hand luggage and take them out before the luggage is X-rayed. The more often film is X-rayed, the more likely it is to fog, so if you are touring you may need to get some processed *en route.*

factor in choosing whether or not to buy secondhand. Similar comparisons apply to motorbikes.

Buying New

When buying a new car or motorcycle you pit your intelligence and judgement against millions of pounds' worth of seductive advertising and brochures. You only get good value if you are forearmed against the blandishments of both, with a knowledge of exactly how well any car lasts, as well as performs. The research is easy. *Which* magazine, from the Consumers Association, does reports on family cars each month (there is no longer a separate *Motoring Which*), plus an annual *Car Buying Guide* which includes user reports from 25,000 people. Back copies should be in your public library. The AA has road test reports on most cars, which are free to members, and good motoring magazines also have reports and tables of new car prices.

If you can pick your timing, buy either early in the year or just after the registration letters change - then the car seems new for longer and you get a better price when you sell.

Comparing Makes

To get the best out of any reports it helps to have a system, such as listing the points you want to look at and writing beside them the facts for each model you are interested in. Here's a useful 12-point checklist of the basics:

1 petrol consumption - town and touring (and grade of petrol)
2 depreciation (some cars hold their value better than others)
3 cost of insurance (the cost rises with the category and it isn't just sports cars which carry a premium)
4 suitability to your type of driving - speed, parking etc
5 number of doors - for young children you need child locks or only 2 doors
6 boot capacity and ease of carrying shopping or luggage
7 cost and frequency of servicing
8 ease of getting servicing done near you
9 maximum speed
10 time taken from 50 to 70 mph (this is usually a realistic figure, whereas 0 to 60 mph tends to be much less so)
11 the real cost of the car, on the road
12 the details of the manufacturer's warranty.

In theory, all the usual legal protections apply to a car as much as to anything else. But in practice, though you can get a company to replace a faulty chair, it is well nigh impossible to get a faulty car totally replaced. So the poor owner is faced with a series of battles over individual repairs. It therefore pays to buy a reliable make - however much fun a car is, it's no fun off the road.

If you do have trouble with a car, and the dealer isn't giving you much joy, get on to the manufacturer. He has a reputation to maintain.

Prices

The car industry has been plagued by over-production for years now. So discounts are rife, as are extras like special deals on servicing - for example, car loans while yours is in dock. But don't buy an amazing bargain without checking out the model - it may be a car which has been given the thumbs-down by a lot of people.

Part Exchange - Pros and Cons

You will usually get a better price by selling your car privately than you will by trading it in. You can then talk down the price of the new car by playing one dealer off against another. However, it is illegal to misrepresent the condition of goods you sell, so if you know the car has a fault it may be best to sell it to a garage, as they may be less put off than an individual. (See also Selling, page 420.) Some companies may offer to help you finance the purchase. See Consumer Law before you accept the offer.

Taking Delivery

On delivery of a car or motorcycle you should be given:
● the pre-delivery inspection checklist - make sure that all the points on it have been properly checked, and no defects found
● the manufacturer's warranty
● the handbook
● the vehicle registration documents (log book).

Buying a Car Abroad and Importing It

Car and motorcycle prices in Britain used to be inflated compared to those on the Continent, and there used to be a clear case in favour of buying abroad. Whether this is worthwhile now depends on the model, the relative strength of the two currencies and how good a deal you can strike - in 1987 the saving averaged 15 per cent to 20 per cent. But you need to be meticulous in your research. Here are some checkpoints:
● Check out the company and choose an established dealer; pick the wrong one and you may well lose your money - they die like flies.
● Check every detail of the specifications in that country. You *can't count on a model having the same ones as it would in Britain*. The name is no guarantee.
● Read the small print about price increases.
● Check that the warranties will be valid in Britain.
● Check the details of the delivery date.

The Consumers Association publishes an 'Action Kit - Importing Your Car' which tells you everything you need to know, and it is well worth getting. Mistakes in this field can cost you dear.

The AA has lists of established dealers, plus a leaflet on how to import and runs an import service which will, for a fee, handle a number of the formalities for you. This applies to non-members as well as members.

★ If you want to buy or sell a special registration number there are several companies which deal in them. One such is **Elite Motors**, P.O. Box 1, Bradford on Avon, Wilts. Check the prices in magazines like *Autocar* before buying or selling.

Buying Secondhand

About 4 million used cars change hands in Britain each year, and it's estimated that one person in ten is dissatisfied with their purchase - that's 400,000 disappointed people a year. If you don't want to be one of them you need to look into any secondhand purchase very carefully.

Preparing to Buy

The first thing to do is put yourself in a bargaining position by talking to the manager of a garage which services cars of the type you plan to buy. Discover its most common faults, and how much it costs to put them right. Make a note of every price so you have something to show a would-be seller when you haggle over the price.

A vehicle must be covered by insurance before you drive it. If you already have car insurance, a phone call to your broker should give you immediate cover so you can test-drive cars. If you aren't insured, arrange cover with a broker before you go out to see a vehicle, so you can insure it in a hurry if you decide to buy.

Dealers

If you use a dealer, for a new or a used car, pick one which is a member of the Society of Motor Manufacturers and Traders (SMMT), the Motor Agents Association (MAA), the Scottish Motor Trade Association Ltd (SMTA) or the Motorcycle Retailers Association (see page 427).

- Dealers must make a pre-sale inspection of the vehicle and give you a checklist of faults they find. Those faults are your responsibility, unless the dealer agrees to put them right. But it is illegal to sell the vehicle if the faults make it unroadworthy.
- Code dealers must check the vehicle's mileage.
- Any claims made must by law be true - but get them in writing anyway - there are liars in this industry as in any.
- A dealer may offer a warranty - but check what it covers and for how long.

However, a car bought from a dealer is unlikely to be a bargain; the same car from an owner-driver should be quite a bit cheaper. If you read the small print you may find the advantages of some dealers' guarantees may not be what they seem at first glance.

Auctions

Auctions are risky for the inexperienced, because you can't drive the car or have it inspected by an expert - and people can, and do, use auctions to sell loads of junk. They may also be used to sell reborn wrecks.

Despite that, auctions can also produce bargains if you really know about cars, and auctioneers are much better to deal with than you might expect. However, your legal protection when buying by auction is limited, because auctioneers may legally opt out of many of the usual sellers' obligations (see page 174). Read the small print in the auction catalogue and on any notices which are up. The rule is *caveat emptor* - buyer beware.

Buying Privately

A vehicle bought privately, through an advertisement or a computer contact, is often the best buy. Car or motorcycle magazines, local papers and *Exchange and Mart* are all good sources of advertisements, and you can also buy by computer (see page 420). However, some of the consumer protection laws don't apply to private sales. A vehicle sold privately need only be 'as described', and this attracts cowboys who pose as private sellers. To protect yourself against these:

- Scan the columns for the same phone number cropping up for more than one car.
- Be suspicious of any number you can only ring between very limited hours (they are probably manning a phone box).
- Don't let anyone bring the car round to you - they may be concealing their true address, and will afterwards melt into the night with your money, leaving you with a dud car.
- Watch for trade terms like 'All good' appearing in 'private' advertisements.
- Make sure the seller's name is in the log book - and distrust any excuses.
- Don't think an MOT is any guarantee of roadworthiness. Cowboys switch licence plates, so a good car is tested while bearing the number plate of the heap of junk they plan to sell you. Then they switch back the number plate so that the bad car appears to have an MOT.

★ If you find a good buy try to pay cash and use this to bargain the price down - most people are tempted by a thick wad of notes.

Checks from Professionals

Even the most honest seller may be unaware of hidden faults in a vehicle, so you can't even buy from your grandmother without risk. It is well worth getting an AA or RAC inspection first, and protecting yourself legally by agreeing to buy it only 'subject to inspection'. Inspection costs money, but it could save you a great deal more. If the seller seems reluctant to have it inspected they probably have something to hide, so leave it alone.

If the inspection shows up faults - but the car is still worth buying - get the seller to lower the price by whatever it will cost to put the faults right. But don't feel that having had it inspected you are committed to buying. You aren't - unless you make some commitment in words or writing.

A cheaper and quicker check - though less thorough - is an MOT. If it doesn't pass you will have avoided buying a dud, and if it passes you know it's roadworthy - for the moment, though it may have non-MOT faults which will soon cause problems. If you tell the centre why you are having it tested they may be prepared to tell you about such faults as well.

Checking a Car Yourself

Before you get to that stage, there are number of checks which should tell you whether it is worth having tested.

First, check the car's log, insurance, MOT and service history (see page 418 for phoney MOTs) - a careful owner should have every receipt. As a precaution, telephone the previous owner and ask who they sold it to and whether it was in any accidents. Then go over the car itself.

Checking the Bodywork

One of the most common causes of cars failing the MOT is rust. Nowadays faults like that can be far more expensive to put right than problems in the engine. So first check for rust, or damage to the body. If it has been patched up and resprayed it will show, unless it was very professionally done - in which case the chances are they didn't spray over rubbish.

- Look carefully at the paint surface against the light. If it has a faintly orange-peel look it has been resprayed.
- Meticulously check all surfaces which aren't painted - including inside the engine; most resprays leave paint traces *somewhere.*
- Go over the surface of the car with a good magnet - where it fails to cling the body-work has been filled, probably after rust. Beware.
- If you don't have a magnet tap carefully over every inch and listen for a change of sound.
- Get under the car and look for rust there too - if you can. And lift the carpets and look for rust under them. Be suspicious of carpet which has been glued down and of areas recently undersealed: both may conceal rust. Rust underneath is costly and dangerous.
- Look for rust on the headlamp reflectors, on some cars a new pair could be expensive.
- Check the chromework for cracks.
- Inspect the join between the bumper and the chassis. If the bumper supports are bent or cracked the car has been in a crash, and could give dangerously at the next impact.
- Don't necessarily be put off by a small dent - it should take money off the car's value but it won't fail you an MOT, and it tells you that the car is honest, not patched up, or, at least, not recently. Just in case it was done earlier it is still worth checking over.

Checking the Interior

- Look hard at the mileometer. If it has been reset the numbers may not be perfectly in line.
- Look at the pedals. On a car which has really done 30,000 miles or under there shouldn't be much wear on the accelerator or the brake.
- Look at the dent in the driver's seat. Unless the owner is very heavy, a car with genuinely low mileage shouldn't show much wear.
- Check that all the seat belts work. Most belts can't be mended and have to be totally replaced - not cheap. And a faulty belt could make it illegal to drive or carry a passenger.

Checking the Mechanisms

- Go round and press the car down to bounce it. If the shock absorbers are in good condition the car will bounce up and rapidly become still. With worn shock absorbers the car bounces for longer. (Try bouncing a new car in a show room first, so you know how it should behave.)
- Before starting the car, open the bonnet and feel the engine. If it is warm the chances are that there are problems they are trying to hide by warming it up first.
- Look at the oil on the dip stick. If it is very dirty the car has been poorly maintained. If it is very thick it may have been filled with thickener to stop rattles in worn crankshaft bearings (often called the big ends). Run your finger round the inside of the hole where the oil goes in - if you feel a muddy substance Fullers Earth has been used to thicken the oil. It means the seller is a tricky customer: avoid the car.
- Look in the radiator: any sign of oil in there means trouble.
- Run the car with the radiator cap off - if there are large bubbles the head gasket may have gone - that could be expensive.
- Start the engine and then look at the exhaust. Blue smoke shows the car is burning oil. This could mean worn piston rings, worn valve guides or that it needs a re-bore - all quite costly.
- With the engine running, cover the end of the exhaust firmly with a *thick* cloth. You should feel pressure build up and then the engine should stall. If it doesn't the exhaust probably has a fault. (NOTE On cars with a powerful engine the exhaust will be hot, and this is not a trick to try with valuable or classic cars with delicately tuned engines.)
- Check the tyres - including the spare tyre. Tyres which are generally worn are just old (try to adjust the price accordingly). But tyres which are more worn on the inner or outer edges suggest problems. The tracking could be out - quite cheap to put right - or the king pins or the wheel bearings may be faulty - both expensive.
- Get someone to work the lights - including the brake lights - one by one, while you check if they work.
- Beware of cars with an engine number which doesn't look quite as it usually does. It may have been ground off and restamped. Thieves buy wrecks to get their papers and then doctor a stolen car to make it fit the credentials. They also buy two wrecks - one ruined at the back, the other at the front and join them together. This is called 'ringing' in the trade, and these cars are clearly to be avoided.
- Find a large space and turn the car on full lock once in each direction, listening carefully - on rear wheel drive cars it will show up any noises in the differential in the rear axle. On front wheel drive cars the constant velocity joint will be noisy.
- On a straight flat *deserted* road check the steering and brakes. To do this set the car on a straight course and take the hands just off the wheel. It should keep perfectly straight unless the road has a heavy camber. Then brake gently. If it pulls to one side the brakes are either incorrectly balanced or the discs are worn.

Discs can be expensive to replace, as you must always replace both sides at once.

The Formalities of Purchasing Secondhand

Before buying a secondhand car look at the log and check that the seller is the registered owner. If he or she isn't, be suspicious and ring the previous owner before any money changes hands. Possessing the registration documents is *not* proof of ownership.

When you pay for the car, *get a signed and dated receipt,* and take the car but leave your name and address.

The seller should keep the log book while any cheque is cleared. Then he or she should tear off the portion at the back, on which notification of change of ownership is given, and send it to the DVLC at Swansea, and send that portion of the registration documents to you. When you get them you too have to fill in a section of the documents and send the whole document to the DVLC address given on the slip - be sure to use the right postcode or it will go to the wrong department.

Selling a Car

If you want to sell a car the options are the same as when buying, but there are some basics to remember:
- If the car isn't fully paid for get the finance company's permission before you attempt to sell.
- Time spent cleaning the car first will pay handsomely.
- Smokers should banish the smell of smoke, or non-smokers may not buy.
- Have the following ready to show any buyer - log book (vehicle registration certificate), MOT certificate and, if needed, service record book or receipts showing the servicing.
- The law on not misrepresenting something you sell applies to you too. If you say it has new brakes, or low petrol consumption and it hasn't you can be prosecuted. So, if the buyer asks for facts to which you don't know the answer, say you don't know - don't invent anything.
- Don't forget to notify the DVLC (see above) that the car has been sold - or the police may be knocking on your door if the new owner is a hit-and-run driver.

Advertising a Car

You are likely to get the best price by advertising, but you need to make sure that you neither break the law nor get ripped off by a dishonest buyer. So here's a quick check list for safety:
- Know the law on selling secondhand goods (see Law) and keep it.
- Don't let a prospective buyer drive the car unless you have *seen* that their insurance covers them to drive your car (you don't want a claim on *your* policy).
- Don't let a prospective buyer drive your car without you (and take a friend too if you're a woman and the buyer is male).
- Don't part with the car until you have cash in hand or have cleared the cheque through the bank. (I know

I said something different in car buying - but whichever you are doing you need to protect *yourself.*)
- Know the going price for similar cars and price it appropriately.
- When the deal is done give the buyer a receipt and ask him or her to sign a paper saying they have bought the car 'as seen and inspected'.

Several guides to secondhand car prices can be bought at newsagents and the prices in *Exchange and Mart* are also a useful guide. But no printed price should ever be taken as gospel; cars can sometimes fetch more, and often a lot less. The condition of the car is one factor and so is the season. Coupés, for example, will fetch much more in spring than in autumn.

Buying and Selling by Computer

Computerized selling is still in its early days, but at least one company offers it for secondhand cars. Cardata is the computerized marriage bureau of the car world, matching sellers with would-be buyers all over Great Britain. It costs a good deal more than the average advertisement in the press, but they will advise you and put the car into an auction at much less than the usual percentage fee if it doesn't sell through them, and offer various perks as well. It may also be a good way to find a type of car which isn't easy to track down - and there is no charge to a buyer. For either service ring 01-205 8000 9 am-9 pm weekdays or until 2 pm on Saturdays.

If you want to buy a car through a dealer ring 01 205 0205. Cardata will - at no charge to you - find the car you want within 24 hours (or so they say). They then give your name and phone number to up to three nearest garages which offer this car.

Selling by Auction

This is likely to bring in the least money but it is a way of getting rid of a car in a hurry, or disposing of one well past its best. But remember, it is illegal to sell a car which is not roadworthy without making this clear.

You usually put the car in on the same day as the auction or the day before, and most auctions charge a small flat fee and then take a minimum commission which is a percentage of the sale price (there may also be a maximum commission). You can set a reserve price, below which you don't want the car to be sold, but a high reserve could leave it on the shelf. Be sure to check the terms of the auction house before leaving your car.

CAR DRIVING

Car Hire

You can hire vehicles of every type, from Rolls-Royces to lorries. Opening times for car hire companies are usually limited to standard business hours, except for branches at places like airports. Just look up 'Car hire' in the Yellow Pages and ring the local offices of a hire company. Anyone who hires will have to pay a deposit which will be forfeited (at least in part) if the car is damaged. Before accepting it check it thoroughly with a company representative and *both* write down any faults, such as marks and scratches.

Children in Cars

By far the safest place for a child is the back of a car, and even if the adult in the front is wearing a seat belt *it isn't safe for a child to be held on that adult's lap.* If an accident happened the shock of even quite a slow-speed impact would fling the adult's arms wide open - however hard they tried to hold tight - and let the child be flung through the window.

Whether or not seat belts are compulsory in the back of a car, a child should always wear one. Being light, a child is more easily flung about than an adult and, if there's a crash, a child becomes an unguided missile, smashing through the windscreen and on to the road - possibly into the path of on-coming traffic. If there are adult belts in the rear seats you can buy booster cushions which raise a child high enough to use them safely in its middle years. Babies should be carried in carry cots, with their head towards the middle of the seat, and carry-cot restraints should be used. Toddlers are safest in special car seats with a safety harness, and when they weigh 18 kg (2½ stone) they need a child's seat belt or an adult belt which can be adapted to children.

Handicapped and Disabled Drivers

Some car manufacturers - such as Ford - give a big discount to anyone registered disabled. Others, such as Volkswagen, only give discounts to those receiving a mobility allowance. The best way for a disabled person to buy a car really depends on their circumstances. There is a scheme run by **Motability** (2nd Floor, Gate House, West Gate, Harlow, Essex CM20 1HR Tel: 0279 635666) which allows handicapped people to use their mobility allowance to buy a car on hire purchase, provided it meets certain criteria. It's useful for those who would find it hard to get a loan from any other source. But it charges interest at commercial rates, and you may be able to negotiate a better deal elsewhere - especially if you are not totally dependent on the mobility allowance. There are also leasing schemes which can be very attractive.

Information on these, and on much else, can be obtained from the **Disabled Drivers' Association,** Ashwellthorpe Hall, Ashwellthorpe, Norwich NR16 1EX Tel: 050841 449 (10am - 3pm) which campaigns on all aspects of mobility and welcomes disabled non-drivers. M£L, M, G, L, Adv, Inf, H, Ins.

Insurance - see the Money section

Learning to Drive

To learn to drive you must have a provisional licence, which you get by filling in a form from the post office and sending it to the DVLC address given on the form. (The provisional licence for a car lasts for life.) You must also be insured, or drive a car insured for a learner driver (see Money).

Professional Instruction

Every professional instructor must be qualified and have a coloured sticker on his or her windscreen saying Department of Transport Approved Instructor. All instructors have to be approved, and your lessons are only as good as the teacher concerned. So you may do as well, and save money, by asking around and finding a particular individual who is good, rather than by opting for a big name.

Motorcyclists can get the addresses of training centres from the following organizations:

British Motorcyclist Federation Rider Training Scheme, P.O. Box 2, Uckfield, East Sussex TN22 3ND Tel: 0825 712896

The National Motorcycle Star Rider Training Scheme, Federation House, 2309/2311 Coventry Road, Sheldon, Birmingham B26 3PB Tel: 021 742 6511

Royal Society for the Prevention of Accidents (RoSPA), Motorcycle Training Scheme, Cannon House, The Priory, Queensway, Birmingham B4 6BS Tel: 021 200 2461

Learning Privately

If someone is learning, or practising, on a private car it must have a white plate 18 x 18 cm (7 x 7 in) front and back, carrying a red L, 10 x 9 x 4 cm (4 x 3½ x 1½ in). They must also be accompanied by a qualified driver.

Applying for a Test

You should have been sent a booklet about the driving test when the DVLC sent you your provisional licence. But if you need to obtain it write to the **Driver Enquiry Unit,** DVLC, Swansea SA6 7JL.

The forms for applying for the driving test are in post offices. How far ahead you need to apply varies with the area; so ask locally. But you may take the test anywhere you choose - it doesn't have to be where you live - provided you send your application and fee to the appropriate Traffic Area Office. They are listed under Transport, Department of, in telephone books, and your local Traffic Office can give you the addresses of those more far-flung. So, if you want to take your test where only cows will challenge your right to the road you can.

The usual delay on getting a test is 3 to 4 months, but you may get tested sooner if you will take a cancelled appointment at short notice.

★ Don't take the test in an automatic car or you will only be licensed to drive solo in automatics. For other cars you would need another driver beside you.

Motorcyclists

Motorcyclists take the test in two parts; the first part being off the road, the next on it. You *must* apply to take the second test within 5 years of taking the first one. However, a motorcyclist's provisional licence only lasts 2 years. If they exceed that time there must be a gap of a year before another provisional licence is obtained. So the test should be taken within that time, and if illness or absence abroad prevents this, surrendering the licence gives you the right to claim the balance of unused time when you wish to.

Problems with Licences

If your licence is lost apply for a duplicate on a form from the post office and pay a small fee. Telephone queries about *driving* licences should be made to the DVLC on 0792 72151 and those regarding *vehicle* licences on 0792 72134.

Advanced Motorist's Test

If you haven't been convicted of a serious traffic offence for 3 years and drive any motor vehicle, or a motorbike of over 200 cc, and think you could be an ace driver, it could be worth taking the Advanced Motorist's Test. If you pass and join the **Institute of Advanced Motorists** (359 Chiswick High Road, London W4 4HS Tel: 01 994 4403 M£L, M, G, B, Ins.) you may be able to get up to 20 per cent discount on your car insurance, plus discounts from some car hire companies. But these advantages only apply while you remain a member of the Institute and you cease to be a member if your licence is endorsed for a motoring offence.

The Institute will put you in touch with the nearest local group which helps people prepare for the test, so you are examined locally by the Institute's examiners.

Learning to Control Skids

Most serious road accidents involve loss of control or a skid, and some motor racing circuits run courses on how to handle these. For example, the **Silverstone Skid School** (Unit 22, Silverstone Circuit, Towcester, Northants NN12 8TL Tel: 0327 857788) has a device which can simulate ice, grease or water by variably reducing the grip of the wheels - and the device happily makes a roll-over impossible. **Brands Hatch Skid Arena** (Freepost, Sevenoaks, Kent TN15 6BR Tel: 0474 853855) runs similar courses using a skid pan. Compare prices and the time you get - it varies dramatically.

Motoring Organizations

Whether it is worth joining a motoring association or not depends very much on the reliability of your car and how much you will use the subsidiary services: some have a lot more to offer than just a breakdown service. They don't all work on the same basis. With National Breakdown, Mondial and Europ Assistance membership covers the *car* for any number of drivers, and they vary on their charges for further cars; the other two clubs cover the *drivers* for any car they drive, and a husband or wife may take out associate membership. They also vary in their strengths and weaknesses. The AA and RAC offer lots of services like car inspections and route planning, whereas a company like Mondial has none of these but its forte is its medical emergency service when travelling overseas.

With any organization, you need to choose the type of membership which suits your needs; some cover only rescue, some repairs and others include breakdowns within a mile of your home. This latter can be important. I once had a car which only seemed to break down when parked overnight - and, foolishly, the one cover I didn't have with my motoring organization was 'home start'. So check exactly what is required.

Automobile Association, Fanum House, Basingstoke, Hants RG21 2EA Tel: 0256 20123 (Head Office) 0256 492004 (Holiday Bookings) 0256 244617 (Insurance Services)

Europ Assistance, 252 High Street, Croydon, Surrey CR0 1NF Tel: 01 680 1234

Mondial Assistance, Church House, Old Palace Road, Croydon CR9 1QB Tel: 01 681 2525

National Breakdown Recovery Club, Cleckheaton Road, Low Moor, Bradford BD12 0ND Tel: 0274 671299 (Admin) 0800 400 600 (Breakdown Freefone)

RAC Motoring Services, RAC House, Lansdowne Road, East Croydon, Surrey CR9 2JA Tel: 01 686 2525

Saving Fuel

It's amazing how much petrol can be saved without doing anything very dramatic. Start with the car. For optimum saving:
- Use the recommended tyre pressure.
- Use the correct oil at the right level.
- Have a clean carburettor which is correctly adjusted.
- Have the timing of the engine set correctly.
- Use the right grade of petrol for the car.
- Don't carry unwanted weight - garbage in the boot, mud under the wheel arches, an unused roof rack.
- The car uses most petrol when on choke so:
    move off as soon as you start up
    park the car so you can move off easily
    push the choke in as soon as you can.
- Drive in top gear as much as possible.
- Don't suddenly speed up or slow down; do everything gently.
- If stuck in a jam turn off the engine.

Starting Problems

- Silence or a faint clonk on turning the key indicates a flat battery (see page 424).
- Engine turns but fails to fire indicates a damp distributor (see page 425) or no petrol.

Weather Problems

Deep Water

If you have to drive through water which is higher than the exhaust the secret is to keep up your acceleration from start to finish. While you accelerate the pressure from the engine forces the fumes out of the exhaust and stops the water going in. But the moment you slow down water will be sucked in and you will stall. Test the brakes, when it is safe to do so, as soon as you are clear of the water, and keep depressing them slightly to dry them out.

Fog

Fog creates optical illusions as well as limiting the visibility, therefore you can't see if someone ahead is stopping. So:
- Leave a far bigger gap than usual between you and the car in front.
- Use your headlights or fog lights, whenever visibility is under 100m (110 yd).
- Clean your headlights, windscreen and rear lights when safe parking can be found.

Slippery Conditions

The secret of driving on snow is gentleness. Treat all the controls as if they were made of glass and avoid any sudden movements. If you find the back of the car is swinging turn your wheel *very gently* in whichever direction the back is going. So if it swings out to the left, turn the wheel slightly to the left. But don't overdo it - overcorrecting a skid can put the car into an uncontrollable spin. Equally, front-wheel-drive cars will tend to understeer, and go straight on at corners. So lift the accelerator and wait for the grip to improve.

Safety Points

- On ice, stopping distances can be up to 10 times more than usual, so keep your distance. On a normal motorway you should be able to count to 2 seconds between the car ahead passing an object and you passing the same object - on ice you should be able to count to 20.
- When you need to brake don't try to do it in one movement, but pump the brake gently up and down (smartly called 'cadence braking', and useful in heavy rain too). Only brake when travelling in a straight line.
- Go steadily in deep snow; slowing down can suck snow into the engine and stall it, and it may be impossible to start.
- *Don't* lower the tyre pressure to give a better grip - that is an old-fashioned technique which doesn't work with modern radial tyres.
- Fit chains for long journeys on snow and ice.
- When travelling in very bad weather carry food, drink, blankets (a space blanket is a good idea too) and a shovel - even in Britain marooned drivers die. If you do get stuck the AA advise you to
  - tie something bright to the highest point of your radio aerial
  - *Stay in your car*
  - beware of running the engine if the snow is blocking the exhaust or the fumes will enter the car and be fatal.
- If a car seems to be dragging, the handbrake may be frozen to the rear wheel. Do not continue driving until this has thawed as, even if you release the brake lever, the brake shoes may be stuck to the drums.
- When moving off on a slippery road put the car in second gear, and let the clutch out slowly to reduce wheel spin.

★ If you can't get a car key into a frozen lock keep warming the key with a lighter or match just before you put it in.

★ Put Vaseline on the front of lights to stop the snow sticking.

★ When you scrape snow or ice from a windscreen wipe it over with methylated spirit straight afterwards - being a spirit, it won't be in a hurry to refreeze. But don't let meths get on the paint of classic cars.

Weather and Road Information

If you need to know the weather forecast for any area you can telephone the Meteorological Office Weather Centres, though they don't give information on the roads themselves. If you are planning to cross the Channel or the North Sea you may find it more useful to talk to a coastguard as they can tell you the forecast and say how the wind direction is affecting their particular stretch of sea. Coastguards also provide information on tides and weather for yachtsmen and scuba divers.

Meteorological Office

Aberdeen	0224 722334
Belfast	08494 22339
Birmingham	021 782 4747
Bristol	0272 279298
Cardiff	0222 397020
Glasgow	041 248 3451
Leeds	0532 451990
London	01 836 4311
Manchester	061 477 1060
Newcastle	091 232 6453
Norwich	0603 660779
Nottingham	0602 384092
Plymouth	0752 42534
Southampton	0703 228844

Department of Transport
Motorway Information

M1 Luton	01 571 6866
M63 Manchester	061 788 7888
M4 Severn Bridge	0272 299299

Coast Guard

Dover	0304 210008
Harwich	02556 5518
Falmouth	0326 317575
Solent	0705 552100

CAR CARE AND MAINTENANCE

Basic Cleaning

- If anyone in the family suffers from car sickness it may help to go over the whole interior, from time to time, with an **anti-static spray** to stop the build-up of static electricity (see page 427).
- **Chrome** is best cleaned with a branded chrome polish such as Solvol Autosol - avoid wire wool which can scratch it permanently.
- **Upholstery** and **carpets** should be vacuumed (the most convenient way is to use a small battery cleaner such as the Dustbuster). Most car fabrics can be shampooed with a good upholstery shampoo. But, if a stain has penetrated the underlying foam, don't expect to remove any smell.
- **Vinyl** and **rubber** can be renovated extremely effectively with a product made by STP which goes by the odd name of 'Son of a Gun'!
- **Leather** should be cleaned with saddle soap (unless otherwise instructed.
- One of the safest and most effective cleaners for **windows** is a tablespoon of ammonia in 500 ml (1 pt) water - but keep this off the paintwork. Rub insects off with one of those ball-like nylon saucepan cleaners that look knitted, but don't let the central metal clip scratch the window. If you need to clean

a windscreen while away from home use wet newspaper - the printing ink helps remove the traffic film.

- **Paintwork** should be cleaned with washing-up liquid and water and polished with a high quality resin wax. Really dirty paint can be cleaned with a product called T-cut, but this can only be used very occasionally as it removes a layer of paint with the dirt. Using Brasso instead works, but it is too abrasive to get really good results.

DIY Maintenance and Servicing

The rising cost of servicing makes car DIY ever more tempting. There are car maintenance classes at many Local Education Authority evening classes and some garages and dealers also do them. But before you get too optimistic about the amount of servicing you will be able to do, check with someone who knows your type of car. Modern cars are becoming more and more difficult to service yourself, as they may need highly specialized equipment. Even so, there are a number of basic jobs which anyone can do with ease on most cars, although I strongly suggest keeping well away from the brakes. A car which won't start is a nuisance; a car which won't stop is a disaster.

You can buy manuals which tell you how to service almost every make of car. Autodata, Autobooks, and Haynes all produce them - and the Haynes manuals are particularly good. Also the spares departments of dealers usually sell the service manuals for their cars. But some makers ban their sale to the public and, as they are written for experienced mechanics, they can be perplexing if you aren't.

Battery Filling

Most modern batteries are sealed units which need no attention, but older ones need regular topping up with distilled water - sold at chemists and motor shops. If your battery doesn't show how much water it needs make sure the plates are covered by a couple of millimetres.

★ Strained through a handkerchief, to remove debris, the water from defrosting your fridge is perfectly good distilled water for car batteries.

Battery Reviving

When a battery is so dead that turning a key doesn't produce even a 'clonk' it may be past help. But if you can raise a faint 'clonk' the battery of a non-automatic car can usually be revived. There are two methods. The first can only be used for a non-automatic; the second can be used on both automatics and non-automatics.

1 For a bump start:
   a switch on the ignition
   b put the car in 2nd gear (not 1st, 3rd or 4th)
   c take off the hand brake
   d press down the clutch and keep it down
   e get the car moving (pushed or downhill)
   f when it is rolling bring up the clutch and the engine should fire.

Once the car engine is firing you must keep it turning over until this has charged up the battery. If it stalls you may have to start all over again, so keep it gently revving if you have to stop.

2 If you have a pair of jump leads:
   a Put a car with a live battery within jump lead reach of the flat battery - but don't let the two cars touch. Each battery has a pair of 'knobs' on it, usually with plastic covers. Remove the covers and look for the + and − signs by them.
   b If there is any doubt about the strength of the working battery, start the engine of that car.
   c Connect each end of the red lead to the positive + 'knobs' on each car. Hold them by the insulated handles and DON'T touch the car body with the end of the lead.
   d Attach each end of the black lead to the negative − 'knob'.
   e Start the car with the faulty battery. As soon as it fires you can uncouple the jump leads, but keep the engine running - revving it slightly if it sounds weak. Then immediately take the car for a drive for at least 20 minutes - preferably without using anything which needs electricity (radio, lights, wipers) - to recharge the battery before switching off the engine.

Not only is it impossible to bump start or tow start an automatic car but they are also tricky to tow. Some manufacturers set strict limits on the distance and speed that an automatic car can be towed without damage so do check the manual first.

> Most car batteries have the same volts, but not all give out the same amount of power. So a low-powered car may not be able to start a high-powered one, though revving the weaker engine very hard may help. Also if you set up the jump leads and leave the small car's engine running for a while it may boost the other battery.

Buying Tools

Good tools are expensive and there is no point in buying even one until you know what jobs you want to do and have checked which tools are needed. Most jobs on modern cars can be done with 11 mm, 13 mm, 15 mm and 17 mm spanners, and on older cars with $7/16$ inch, $5/8$ inch and ½ inch ones. It is usually cheapest to hire tools which are rarely used - Yellow Pages list hire shops.

> Don't even consider doing anything which needs you to get under the car unless you have a proper tripod axle stand and know exactly where to position it for safety. Bricks, wood blocks, jacks and so on may look secure but all of them can collapse and people are killed every year because of this. And always have a car on level ground when working on it.

Changing a Tyre

This is very easy:

1 Get out the spare wheel and check it's inflated (there's no point in proceeding if you put it away flat and forgot to repair it) then put it close to the flat tyre.
2 Double check that the handbrake is fully on.
3 Put bricks or some other blocks under a wheel on the good side of the car.
4 Lever the hub cap off the flat tyre with the end of a screw driver.
5 Loosen the wheel nuts (anticlockwise) with a wheel brace - the old-fashioned sort with a U-shaped kink is useful for the less brawny, as you can stamp on the U if arm force isn't enough.
6 Put the jack in the correct position for your type of car. Not all makes are the same but it will be under the edge of the side - your manual will say where. On soft ground you need to put something firm under it. Make sure it is standing firmly. Then jack up the car - lifting it high enough to let you insert a non-flat tyre afterwards.
7 Remove the wheel nuts - put them where you won't lose them (the hub cap is dodgy; if you step on the edge it will catapult them everywhere).
8 Remove the wheel and put the spare one in its place (you may need to raise the car higher with the jack, as a fully inflated tyre may be larger than you thought).
9 Screw on all the nuts as tightly as you can, working on diagonal pairs.
10 Let the jack down and replace the hub cap.

Damp Distributor

In wet weather some cars are prone to get damp in the distributor. When this happens the engine turns over but it won't fire. The distributor is easily recognized as it has several thick leads joined to it at slightly cone-shaped junctions. To dry it out undo the clips which hold the top on, and either spray WD40 inside or blow it dry with a hair dryer, on an extension lead. Sounds unlikely, but it works. If necessary, dry under the lead junctions too.

★ With an old car which is vulnerable to cold and damp, it is easiest to start it if you have put a blanket under the bonnet overnight. In this case it is ESSENTIAL to leave a corner of blanket sticking out where you can't miss it: leaving it in while driving could cause a fire.

Electrical Parts

If any electrical part stops working look for a broken fuse and replace it, with one of the same amps. Some fuse boxes have labels showing the function of each fuse. But many cars have sequence wiring which means that if a fuse for one part goes, another part may cease to work too. On my Honda, for example, fusing the windscreen wipers immobilizes the windows. If the same fuse blows twice, for no good reason, have the wiring checked; there is probably a fault and that could cause a fire. If a light stops working it is probably a bulb. These are easy to replace.

Fan Belt

It's a good idea to check that the fan belt is taut whenever you check the oil. A loose fan belt will allow the engine to overheat and will stop the alternator working properly, so the battery won't recharge.

The old trick of replacing a broken fan belt with a nylon stocking does work - if you can get it on (engines aren't designed like they used to be) it will get you to the nearest garage, though no further.

Oil Checking

The oil should really be checked once a week. If it gets too low the engine wears faster, and will eventually seize up. Just pull out the dip stick (it usually has a loop you can put your finger through), wipe off the oil at the base, push it fully in again, withdraw it, and check the level. It should be just below the line marked as 'max'. If it needs topping up (and it won't tip in tidily) but you have no funnel, roll up some thick paper into a cone and pour it in down this.

Oil Changing

Oil needs to be changed at least every year. To do it yourself first get a suitable container - larger than the contents of your oil tank. (Buy a Bell Drainer Can which holds 8 l (14 pts) if you plan to do this often).

1 Run the car to warm it up and make the oil runnier.
2 Put the container in place.
3 Undo the drainage plug on the sump and let the oil drain fully into the container.
4 Replace the drainage plug and refill.

If you bought your oil from a garage it may dispose of the old oil. If you bought it (often more cheaply) from a discount shop you should take it to the container for such things in the local authority dump. If it is thrown away anywhere else it can cause contamination.

The filter needs changing rather less often than the oil. On most cars it is a job for a garage, as it can be very tough to remove.

Overheating Engine

If a light on your dashboard doesn't tell you the engine is overheating, your nose should. If you smell something odd, stop and check. If it seems to be overheating DON'T be tempted to remove the radiator cap - the steam it releases will scald you. Leave the engine open and wait for the radiator and engine to cool, *then* look. If the water is low, top it up slowly with lukewarm water to avoid too sharp a change of temperature. If the metal hasn't warped with the heat, all should now be well.

Rust

Rust is one of a car's biggest enemies. And salt is the biggest rust creator. After a cold spell, when salt will have been on the roads, give the car a hose down underneath as well as on top. (Check the brakes afterwards by trying them out when you aren't needing them.) Also lift the carpets and unblock the vent holes in the floor. Whether it is worth having a car rust-proofed really depends on what protection the manufacturer has given the car, how often you are prepared to hose down the underside and whether you live near salt sea air. Wherever you live, don't cover a car in a plastic cover or tarpaulin; this stops air circulating and creates ideal conditions for rust.

Rust in the bodywork can be treated, but you need to let each stage dry out completely before starting the next. So start when you have a series of free evenings or weekends.

1   Use a wire brush and wire wool to remove as much rust a possible, using finer and finer wire wool as you get deeper in.

2   Apply an effective rust treatment such as Trustan, according to its instructions.

3   Allow that to dry completely before applying a filler, such as Isopon.

4   When this has dried completely use a fine sandpaper, and then a flour paper (see below) until it is perfectly even.

The secret of a good finish is to use 3 *thin* coats of spray-on car primer - allow each to dry according to the instructions before applying the next. Use flour paper (the finest grade of sanding paper) to give this a key. Then spray on 3 to 4 *thin* coats of top coat - allowing it to dry between. Don't try to cover exactly the same area with each spray - uneven spraying prevents an edge being created. Make the final coat *slightly* heavier than the others. Then let the paint dry for several days. When it is *totally dry and hard* go over it with T-cut to smooth out any speckles. Finally polish it up.

Scratched Paint

Clean the scratched area well and wipe the scratches with white spirit to remove any oily grime. Use a very fine artist's brush to apply several layers of paint to the scratches, letting the paint dry very thoroughly between each coat. For this start with 4 parts of thinner to 6 parts of paint and gradually reduce the thinner on each coat. When the top coat is totally dry T-cut the area and polish it.

Tyres

The correct tyre pressure is more important than it may seem. The right pressure opens up the tread so its edges grip the road - just what you need in the rain. So it pays to make regular checks and adjust the pressure for heavy loads if your tyres need it - but read your manual to see whether they do need extra pressure and, if so, how much.

There are no fixed rules; it all depends on the tyres - which is one reason why it is important to stick to the tyres the makers recommend.

Incidentally, it is illegal to carry a spare tyre which is not fit for use - for example, with too little tread.

★ Some handbooks have the tyre pressures in obscure places. Having found the pressures, make life easy for yourself by writing them on a sticky label and putting it somewhere convenient, like the glove locker flap.

Water

Water needs weekly checks in summer - it should be almost up to the top. Anti-freeze with corrosion inhibitor must be used all year for cars with aluminium cylinder heads. On other cars add antifreeze before the coldest weather starts - it doesn't have to be removed when the weather warms up. However, it must be chosen to suit the make of car - the wrong one can rot the pipes.

★ Be warned, if you have a high-tech car and a cellular phone is installed badly it can interfere with the electronic systems which control functions like the braking and ignition. So cellular phones need expert installation.

Professional Servicing and Repairs

It is tempting to suppose that, so long as a car goes, all is well with it. Unfortunately, this is a dangerous and expensive view. Regular checks are needed to keep the car safe and prevent unnecessary wear.

Most manufacturers recommend different types of service at different intervals. Their spacing is dictated not just by the design of the car but by the built-in ageing speeds of components like oil and spark plugs. Stop-start town driving is toughest on a car and makes regular servicing doubly important. On modern lean-burn engines spark-plugs usually need attention at around 10,000 miles, and the best lubricating oils need changing after 16,000 to 20,000 miles, so these will set the interval of the shortest service.

Most new cars have a warranty which covers parts and labour for the first year. The mileage may be limited or unlimited, but certain parts, such as tyres, won't usually be covered for fair wear and tear and you will have to pay for basics like oil. Also, this warranty may only be valid if you use an approved dealer and make no changes to the car.

By law garages must use reasonable care and skill and charge an appropriate price. There is also a code of practice established between the Office of Fair Trading and the major motor trade organizations given on page 427. If you go to one of their members they should follow the code. Even so, it pays to take precautions that the work is correct and that bills don't soar. Personal recommendation is the best guarantee of a good garage. Failing that, there may be an advantage in using a garage which is a member of one of the trade associations listed below - though some very good small garages do not belong to them. Wherever you go, you can protect yourself against problems with the following steps:

● At services, agree what will be done, and leave your telephone number and ask them to contact you, and get your approval, before doing anything more than that. This puts a brake on creative servicing.

● For anything more than a service give the garage a written list of what you want done and ask for a *written* estimate covering parts, labour, and VAT.

● Before you leave your car get a definite indication of when the car will be ready, and tell them when you will be collecting it.

- Ask if the work or parts are guaranteed. (Companies following the motor trade's code of practice must guarantee repairs for a stated mileage or time.)
- Get a detailed invoice.
- Under the VBRA code of practice (see right) if work has to be done again because the first lot was unsatisfactory the car's guarantee period must be extended by however many days it is off the road this second time.

If you aren't happy with the work the steps to getting things put right are these:

a   Complain to the manager or garage owner at once, in writing using recorded delivery, and try to get things put right then and there.

b   If you can withhold payment until you are satisfied do so - but write to them saying that you are only withholding it until the job is done properly.

c   If you have to pay, when you know you aren't satisfied, give them a letter saying you are not satisfied with the work and that you make the payment 'without prejudice' - and keep a copy of the letter. This wording means that your payment doesn't harm your right to take legal action if necessary.

d   If the garage refuses to put things right get free advice from a CAB, Consumer Advice Centre or Trading Standards (Consumer Protection) Department, or use your motoring organization to help you. And if it is a dealer get on to the manufacturer - the SMMT (right) has the address.

e   If you used a garage which belongs to one of the organizations listed (right) ask for their help.

f   If the garage is not a member of such an association taking the matter to court is the final option.

If there is a major problem and you plan to take legal action it may be worth getting an independent inspection from a motoring organization. They may also be able to give you free legal advice and even representation (see page 422 and under Law). Or, you can use the complaints and conciliation service of one of the organizations on the right if the garage is a member.

Theft Prevention

It is a nuisance for thieves if a car's windows are marked with its registration number as it makes it harder to disguise. You can now buy kits which allow you to etch the number on to the glass. Some are small electric drills; others are etching fluid, and some companies will etch it for you. So it's worth asking about.

Theft is also far less likely if you avoid parking in side streets, always lock up and leave nothing tempting in full view - apart from the car, that is. But a practised thief can enter a car in seconds. Happily, alarms are getting better all the time. Some of the most sophisticated only react to disturbance *inside* the car - so bounce-off-the-bumper parkers don't set them off. At the other end of the scale, there are devices, like the Krooklok, which prevent a car being driven away but don't stop thieves taking the radio. The price range is from several hundred pounds to under £10. But my favourite story is of the man who found an imitation snake curled up on the passenger seat a most effective deterrent.

More information

Meech Static Eliminators, 140-144 Clapham Manor Street, London SW4 6DA Tel: 01 622 4555 - will tell you the nearest stockist of their anti-static spray.

Motor Agents Association National Conciliation Service, 73 Park Street, Bristol BS1 5PS Tel: 0272 293232 - operates the same code of practice as the SMMT (see below) and offers a similar service for both cars and motorbikes. The **Motorcycle Retailers Association** - this is a division of the Motor Agents Association and complaints about its members go to the Park Street address, above.

Scottish Motor Trade Association Ltd, Customer Complaints Service, 3 Palmerston Place, Edinburgh EH12 5AF Tel: 031 225 3643 - operates the same code of practice as the SMMT and offers a similar service, but mainly deals with complaints about servicing and repairs of both cars and motorbikes. But it does handle complaints about new cars for the few manufacturers which belong to this association.

Society of Motor Manufacturers and Traders Ltd (SMMT), Forbes House, Halkin Street, London SW1X 7DS Tel: 01 235 7000 is primarily for the benefit of its members, but has a consumer affairs department which administers a code of practice, which covers both new car sales and work under warranty. It offers a free conciliation service and, if no conciliation is possible, it offers arbitration - which the customer must pay for, though you may get it back if you win. There is usually no appeal against the arbitrator's decision.

Vehicle Builders and Repairers Association (VBRA), Belmont House, 102 Finkle Lane, Gildersome, Leeds LS27 7TW Tel: 0532 538333 - members of this association follow a code of practice for body work only. If they also do other repairs they are not within the code. It deals with complaints in a similar way to the SMMT.

COMPUTERS

Computers should never have acquired the exalted status they now have. Fascinating and invaluable as they are, even the most advanced have less brain power than a three-year-old. They do, however, score on single-mindedness. The three-year-old uses its brain not only to think but also to do tasks like seeing, hearing and running about, which need incredibly rapid and sophisticated electro-mechanical interactions - we too run on electricity. But the computer just sits there and sends spacecraft to the moon or re-organizes the world banking system - which is very much easier. That's why the space fiction dream of robot servants pandering to our every whim is still, alas, a long way off. It's also why nobody needs to be daunted by them.

To use a computer you don't need to have a clue how it works; you can drive it in blissful ignorance, just as you can a car. But knowing the basics lets you use it with more flexibility and makes you feel like the boss. It also helps you to know what to look for when buying.

Don't let the jargon bother you. To misquote *Alice*, the computer boffins 'only do it to annoy because they know it teases'. And you'll find computer jargon full of little jokes; for example, half a byte (a unit of measurement, pronounced bite) is called a nibble, and the mechanism which carries information is called a bus.

What a Computer Can Do for You

I have been in love with my personal computer for several years now. Seeing my devotion to the thing, people are always asking me if they should buy one. The answer is 'yes' *if* you want to do one of the things which a computer does well. Here are just some of the jobs it can do in the family, or in a home-based business.

- Carry out any kind of written work and allow you to change the text around, correct mistakes, rewrite it, remove words, and then print out a perfect copy, as if you had never made a single error.
- Check what you have written against its own dictionary, and point out any spelling mistakes - whether in a letter, an essay or a professional document.
- Provide you with numerous copies of anything you write, without the expense of photocopies.
- Hold copies of letters on memory, so you can refer back to them without the clutter of paper copies.
- Run educational programmes which help children or adults to learn at home - an increasing feature of 'open learning' programmes.
- Rapidly do any kind of mathematics, from basic VAT calculations to high-flown scientific ones.
- Create a spreadsheet and, at the press of a button or two, do the repetitive financial calculations needed to evaluate stocks and shares, or give a profit forecast.
- Allow you instantly to look at any information you have saved on the computer, without riffling through drawers or searching filing cabinets.
- Create a computer version of a card index system, in which you just tell it which 'card(s)' you want and it instantly shows them on screen or prints them out. For example, it will print out address labels for everyone in a particular category - say those you want to send a Christmas card to, or all your business contacts in America. But it could equally well hold medical records or sermons for different times of the religious calendar.
- Draw and print out graphs and diagrams needed for work or school.
- Play games, ranging from innocent games for children to the most risqué sex quizzes from California, plus unbeatable chess.

That may give you an idea of what they do. To appreciate fully the pleasure of using a computer, and the speed and ease it can bring, you must feel for yourself how swiftly it lets you add up a long column of figures, draw a graph or alter a sentence. And that is quite apart from special applications in the home, by which computers control security and heating systems, turn on appliances and operate fire alarms.

About Hardware and Software

There are two aspects to using a computer - the hardware and the software. The hardware is anything you can see, and kick - the screen, printer, keyboard and the control unit with its chips and disc-drive. The software is the program which tells the computer what to do, and you mainly buy it on a tape or floppy disk.

Hardware and software are usually created by different companies. The hardware gets all the publicity: the software is the important part. Without software the hardware (the machine) is like a severely brain-damaged person - it may be alive but it isn't able to do anything. When we touch something hot a message goes to our brain and it instantly tells the muscles to move away from the heat. In the same way, if you touch a key which means you want to print, the software picks up the message and tells the computer hardware to start printing.

Buying a Computer

Paradoxically the best advice on buying a computer is *don't*. The starting point isn't the computer, it's the software (see above). Without software a computer is as useless as a car without an engine - but most software only runs on a certain group of computers. Don't be seduced by computer companies which claim that their computer can run any one of hundreds of programs, or handle programs of incredible sophistication. You may not *want* to run hundreds of programs, or *need* incredible sophistication. A computer which only runs three programs which do exactly what you want is a better buy than one which runs a hundred which don't. So find the right software first. But be wary of very new programs, they often have teething troubles.

Then, *before you buy the software* find a computer which will handle it efficiently. Good computer companies should be able to demonstrate most programs. But have a go yourself. Computers handle differently, just as cars do, and one may suit you better than another.

Unless you know someone who is getting rid of an almost new machine, in order to have the latest thing, it can be risky to buy secondhand, but new ones are often discounted if you haggle. Choose a dealer with a good track record likely to give good after-sales service. If you are new to computers you may well need someone to explain any points you don't understand - few manuals are as clear as they should be.

Computer Types

Computers can be divided into a series of groups.

Home computers have smallish memories, and run programs from cassette tapes. These are largely used for children's games.

Pocket computers, like the Psion, are scarcely larger than a pocket calculator, and will hold notes, addresses, or any specialized data they are designed for. The best have very sizeable memories and can be linked to a larger computer, so the information can be fed into its memory or printed out on its printer. Psion, for example, has a memory of up to 128K (see page 430) which will hold some 4,000 names and addresses, and has programs built into its microprocessor which are compatible with major data base and spread sheet software for personal computers. But by no means all pocket computers have such facilities.

Micros (sometimes called **Personal Computers**) with upwards of 256,000 units (bytes) of memory, and either twin floppy disks or a hard disk. (The hard disk gives them 10 to 100 million units of memory.) These vary considerably in power, and the prices range from a few hundred pounds to a few thousand. They are the ideal computers to have in the home and can be used for anything, from a game to writing a book, or running a small business. Examples are the Amstrad, the IBM Personal System/2 and the Dec Rainbow.

Mini-computers, whose small name belies their considerable power. Far bigger than a micro, they always have a hard disk, and many millions of units of memory in banks of chips. This power allows a single control unit to run a whole series of screens and keyboards. These are computers for largish businesses - and have a price to match.

Finally, there are **mainframes.** Not the bulky affairs which featured so largely in early science fiction films but still large, and used for jobs like directing robots to assemble cars or controlling the railway system.

The first three types are the ones to go for, but only some of the machines in each range will meet your needs.

Hardware Explained

Computers come in a series of parts, which are explained individually below. In theory, you can mix and match them to suit your needs and pocket. But the personal computer end of the industry is still in its early stages. The general trend is towards standardization, which would allow you to choose different parts from different makes - as you can a hi-fi - but such standardization is yet to come. At present companies are torn between standardizing so people can switch from other systems on to theirs, and trying to be different so nobody can desert their system for another. What's more, even if all the hardware works together, that doesn't guarantee that the software you want will work on that combination of hardware.

So, choose a dealer large enough to have a range of options from different manufacturers, then you can check the compatibility of each part before you buy. As some computer dealers are staffed by young men with more enthusiasm than knowledge, *test* the compatibility, then double check it with each company concerned.

Keyboards - Basic Keys

These are just basic QWERTY typewriter keyboards, with extra keys added. Sometimes keyboards are all in one with the control box or screen, sometimes only linked by a coiled lead. Those with a lead are much less tiring because you can adjust your position to suit yourself. Keyboards also vary in whether their extra function keys are to the right or the left. If you are decidedly right-handed you may find the left-biased keyboards annoying.

The basic character set, which includes symbols as well as letters of the alphabet, is pretty standard. But if you have an off-beat program, or are thinking of buying a little-known computer, check that the keyboard has all the symbols you need. For example, watch out for cheap imported computers with a $ but no £.

Keyboards - Function Keys

The extra keys are important because they can tell the computer to do all kinds of useful jobs, like allowing you to insert words in the middle of a line, or search through a document to find a particular word, or perform a mathematical function. Some computers have far more function keys than others, and it pays to have plenty. It is much easier to touch one function key, for each task, rather than memorize and use a special sequence of ordinary keys - which is what you must do otherwise.

The function keys are usually controlled by the software. So when using a financial program a certain key may instruct the computer to carry out one function, such as adding a column of figures, but when using a graphics package it could tell the computer to make a vertical line of a certain length.

Keyboard Adaptation

Some unusual programs allow you to tell the software to create symbols which aren't part of the usual character set of that program - say accents to put on foreign words. Making these adjustments is an easy job, once you know how, but you need to know which forms to call up, and what instructions will produce the result you want - and this isn't always easy to find in the manual. So, if you buy a program of this sort, ask your supplier to set up these keys for free when they supply the machine. Then watch while they do it - and take notes, so you can change it next time. Failing that, ring the software manufacturer and ask. There will normally be two forms in the program - one to tell the screen to produce the symbol and another to instruct the printer. You need to have the name of each form, so you can call them on to the screen, and know the numbers to insert in the forms to get the symbols you want.

The Mouse

A mouse is a device which can be attached to some computers to allow you to move an arrow easily around the screen and point to anything which is on it. Having pointed to something - perhaps the name of a document - you can then use the mouse to tell the computer to do something to it, like erase it. The mouse only does what a keyboard and cursor can do, but it does do it slightly faster.

Printers

Printers are like electric typewriters, except that instead of the instruction to print a letter going straight from the key to the printing head, it is held in memory until you want a printed copy. There are three main types - daisy wheel, dot matrix and laser. The big differences between them are in the way they get the symbols on to the paper. Like daisy wheel typewriters, daisy wheel printers have each letter at the end of a flexible 'petal'. So you have a choice of typefaces at a moderate price. Dot matrix printers are usually the cheapest. They have a group of tiny pins which are thrust forward to create the shape of a letter or figure as they hit the paper. Like the daisy wheel, they use a typewriter ribbon, but the print quality is less good and the typefaces are usually more limited. Laser printers are in a different league. They cost a great deal more but they can produce almost book quality print, in a vast range of typefaces, at many times the speed of other printers. However, not all software or hardware can drive a laser printer.

The great trade-off is usually between speed and quality. Don't be too impressed by printers working so much faster than typewriters. A typewriter prints as you go along, the printer can only do it after you have finished, and you have to sit there while it does it, to check the paper isn't scrunching up. At the end of a day this can be very tedious unless the machine has a real zip in it. Buy the fastest that has a price and type quality you can accept.

The Screen
The screens (called monitors) vary hugely. At one end of the spectrum (and price range) there are monitors like those on DEC's big VAX machines, designed for industry, with colour rivalling a colour photograph. At the other, there are the single-colour machines used for most word processing and number crunching. In personal computers full colour images tend to be less sharp than single colour ones. So, for writing and mathematics it's best to forget multicolour machines - though it's fun for games and graphics.

Whether you opt for a black, green or orange screen is a matter of taste. Psychologists say that a black and white screen is most tiring to look at and tend to favour orange and black as the most restful. I personally find orange exhausting and much prefer green and black.

The Control Unit
The control unit is the box of works to which all the other parts are linked by cables. If the keyboard, printer and monitor are the arms and legs of the machine, the box is its body, filled with vital organs.

The Microprocessor
The key 'organ' in the control unit is the microprocessor (or CPU - Central Processor Unit). This is the biggest chip in the computer, and the part which does the work. It performs mathematical and logical functions at a speed approaching the speed of light. It is also the middle man which allows information to be held in memory, or sent out to the screen or printer. The better the microprocessor, the more powerful the machine.

Until fairly recently microprocessors were only able to handle 1 unit of information (8 bits) at a time. Now many can handle 2 units (16 bits), and 4 unit (32 bit) machines are coming. The more bits they can handle at a time, the faster the computer. But, microprocessors

are still rather primitive, and their abilities are limited to logical or mathematical functions which are wired in and unchangeable. The thinking robot is still a long way off.

The Memory
The other key 'organ' in the control unit is the RAM (Random Access Memory). These are the chips which accept and hold the computer program when you load it in. If there's a large memory the whole program is put into it when you first start. If the memory is too small for this the computer does a rather smart trick and 'remembers' the key sections and fetches the rest from the disk when it needs them. So the size of the RAM doesn't necessarily limit the power of the program you can run, but a small one really slows things down.

RAM chips also hold work you are doing until it is put on to your storage disk. Some programs automatically put your work on to the disk, almost as you create it; others hold it in memory and only put it on disk when you give a 'save' signal. The snag with the latter system is that in a power cut, your unsaved work is lost. Very annoying. So either choose a computer which has a battery back-up which keeps the RAM going for a while after power is cut off, or a program which automatically saves the work.

The Disk Drive
The disk drive (on machines which operate from disks not tapes) is an electro-mechanical device which spins the disk, and allows a magnetic head to record files on to it or read programs or other data off it, much as with an ordinary tape recorder. You need two disk drives, so that you can copy data from one to the other - either twin drives for floppy disks, or a hard disk plus a drive for a floppy disk.

Hard Disks
The more powerful machines have a hard disk built in. This is actually several disks in a stack, each with a large storage capacity, able to run at many times the speed of a floppy disk. So computers with hard disks are much faster to use. The big advantage of a hard disk is that all your software programs, and all the work you do, can be permanently stored on it. So they are ready to run whenever you switch on, whereas with floppy disks the programs have to be loaded in each time you start up, which makes switching from one type of program to another very tedious.

Unfortunately, hard disks occasionally 'crash', destroying everything on them. So hard disk computers have a disk drive for floppy disks, which can take copies of important documents. Alternatively, you can get a plug-in unit which lets you transfer the data to cartridge tape. This is expensive, as yet, but these tapes can store much more data than a floppy disk.

The Modem
A modem enables one computer to talk to another down a normal telephone line. It does this by converting the computer data into sound waves. But you can only use

it if the two systems are able to work together. Unfortunately, some computer systems have as big a communications gap as an Englishman and a Chinese.

When buying a modem an important point is the speed at which it sends the data down the line (see baud rate, page 433). The faster it is, the more it will cost, but the shorter your computer's telephone calls will be.

Software
'Software' is the term used for a computer program, sold on a floppy disk. The software is the brain of the computer. But it's the brain of a slave. You are the master and tell it what to do, the software decides the best way to do it, and the hardware (page 429) does the work. Some people think that to run a program you have to know about programming. Far from it. That's the job of the people who made it. You use it like you would a record - switch on, put it in place and roll it.

There are usually two parts to software, and these must work hand in hand and be compatible. The operating system tells the computer *how* to do the work, *in principle.* The applications program enables the computer to do a *particular* job, such as word processing or mathematics.

Operating Systems
The operating system runs what you might call the internal office of the computer.
- It organizes the filing system, and keeps an index of everything you create on the disk.
- It controls the movement of all data within the system, inputting it into the memory, for example, or directing it to the printer.
- It stops a faulty applications program from wrongly deleting data which you want saved.
- It also has various utilities which allow you to do jobs like copying a document from one floppy disk to another, or from hard disk to floppy. Using these is often a lot faster than doing the same job via the applications system, so it pays to read your manual and use these.

While the computer is running, the operating system polices operations and does a double act with the applications program, alternating tasks - without you even knowing it. And each applications program is designed to work with a particular operating system.

The best operating systems tend to become standard - in their time - and be used by most of the popular machines and applications programs. However, some applications programs for home computers use little known operating systems which enter on the sidelines. Avoid them for serious applications. It takes hundreds of man years of programming to perfect an operating system. So an operating system from a small company is unlikely to be any match for an established one.

In the early days of home computers Apple used an operating system called CPM which became the standard for most small computers. It was overtaken by the far superior MSDOS (pronounced MSDos and standing for Micro-Soft Disk Operating System) for all IBM compatible machines. But MSDOS has certain weaknesses and is due to be displaced in its turn.

Applications Programs
Applications programs are the software packages which allow you to use the computer for *particular* jobs such as word processing, doing accounts, creating graphs or playing games. And you can switch from one type of program to another just by removing one disk and replacing it with another, or at the press of a button if a computer has a hard disk.

Most modern programs come on floppy disks - thin plastic circles inside stiffer plastic envelopes - but simple programs on basic home computers can be on ordinary cassette tapes played on a tape recorder plugged into the computer.

There are four points to bear in mind when buying software.

1   **Will it run on your computer** (or on one you can afford)? If you don't already have a computer it is better to choose the software first and then find a computer to suit it.

2   **Will it do what you want it to do?** This sounds very basic, but fast-talking salesmen can easily give the impression that any accounts package they have on offer will suit any kind of accounts, or that their word processing package will do what you want, when it will only do part of what you want. If their software has limitations they may tell you all other software has the same limitations. So first write a very specific list of everything you would like the software to do, then go through any piece of software *in detail*, testing it carefully.

3   **Will it do things in the way you want them done?** It's easy to be so delighted with the new box of tricks which a computer program offers that you forget to be critical. Different programs do the same things in different ways - and some ways are much more convenient than others. For example, some word processing software is designed so that you can only make alterations at the bottom of the screen. This legacy from typewriters is very inconvenient because when making changes you can't see the words which will follow what you are re-writing.

4   **Is it compatible with the industry standards?** This is a safeguard for the future. Programs are improving all the time and you may, one day, want to buy an even better program and transfer all your data on to it. You can only transfer data between compatible programs, and the most popular programs become the 'industry standard', so the chances of being able to transfer from one of them is much greater. The current industry standards are D-Base II for database programs, Lotus 123 for spread sheets, and Wordstar for word processing. However, this doesn't mean they are the best. They may be, but conformity and virtue aren't *always* the same thing. I have a little known British word processing program, called LEX, which - when I bought it - could do things almost unheard-of in its competitors.

Using a Computer

Getting Started with Tape

If your software is stored on magnetic tape you just switch on the computer, and it usually loads up the program automatically and brings up a menu from which you can choose what you want to do. The trouble with tapes is that to get at any data on one you have to wind all the way back to the point the tape was at when you stored it - which is very slow. So their main use is for children's games.

Getting Started with Floppy Disks

The golden rule is never work from the original, floppy disk, copy of your software. Take copies and work from those. Then if they get damaged you still have your program. Unfortunately, some companies are so worried about the threat of pirate copies being traded that they have made it impossible to take a copy of their program. Check this out.

If a machine uses floppies the usual routine is to switch on and insert the operating system disk (such as MSDOS) in one of the disk drives. Then press a key to transfer the program to the computer's memory (RAM). This is called booting up - from the term to pull yourself up by your bootstraps.

You then replace the operating system disk with an applications program disk, and press a key or type in a password to put the applications program into memory. The memory may take the whole program or take some and call on the rest from the disk when it needs to. Then a 'menu' will usually come up on the screen listing what the program allows you to do - for example, create or edit a document, or set the printing style. But before you choose you must usually put a document disk in the other disk drive. This is a formatted blank, or partly used, disk which will receive and store the documents you create (see page 433). You are then ready to go.

Getting Started from a Hard Disk

When you use a hard disk you only copy the operating system and the application programs on to the hard disk the very first time you use them. They are then permanently remembered until you erase them. So all you need to do is switch on and type in the name of the applications program you want to work from. When you use the correct exit procedure the work you have been doing is automatically transferred from the computer's memory chips to the hard disk and stored there until you erase it.

Disk Copying

There are all kinds of housekeeping jobs which can be done with just the operating system (e.g. MSDOS). The most important of these is making a second copy of any work you do. Good machines and disks are remarkably reliable but they do have their off moments. They can lose a document, or a whole disk can become unreadable. So it is vital to keep a second copy of everything you do. These are called 'back-ups'. Making

one is just a matter of telling the computer you want to copy a disk. A typical MSDOS instruction would read 'diskcopy a: b:', which means copy the disk in drive A on to the disk in drive B. You then put a spare disk in B and the one you want to copy in A, press a button and wait.

When it copies a complete disk the computer erases everything which was on the disk before. So always start by copying on to a spare disk. Then make a copy on to your back-up disk. Then if the whole process goes wrong, at any stage, you always have one good copy you can use.

A floppy can't hold the entire contents of a hard disk. So when taking back-up copies from a hard disk on to floppies you have to copy them by a certain category, such as documents created that day, or some other criterion, and keep taking a new disk for each group of documents. Alternatively you copy on to cartridge tape which may take the entire contents of a hard disk.

Floppy Disks

Floppy disks come in different dimensions, memory capacities and types and you need to use those suited to your computer. The blank disks which you buy may also need to be set up ready to take data (formatted) either by copying a format disk or through an instruction from the operating system.

Disks are (invisibly) divided into sectors - like a slice through an orange. At first the computer puts the documents you create neatly into the sectors. But, as you erase work, spaces are left. The computer uses these up too. So it may start by putting a document in one sector, run out of space there and put the rest of it into some other. When you run through a long document there may be an occasional pause before the next page comes up; this is probably because the computer is having to scan several sectors to find it. But you can sometimes use the operating system to reorganize the documents neatly into sectors and speed things up.

Floppy disks are getting bigger all the time and some can now take $1 \cdot 2$ megabytes. That means you can put 1,200,000 letters of the alphabet on to one disk - which is an average book. But, whatever kind you have, there is bound to be a better disk tomorrow. And, whatever the size, you need to have enough room for the documents you want to put on it. This isn't simply a matter of having enough space for the document itself. A document on a disk needs what I think of as 'turning space' and, like an oil tanker, it needs slightly more than its own length to 'turn' in. So if you want to create a document some 10,000 bytes long you must have more than 20,000 bytes free. And, if you have a system which automatically creates a duplicate copy on the disk the moment you change the first one, you would need over 30,000 free bytes (see page 427 on bytes) to turn that document.

Tips on Computer Use

Naming Documents

Whatever your software or hardware, think carefully

about what you need from your computer before you start to use it. How quickly it will find and display the information you store greatly depends on how you organize things.

Each document must have a name, and a big time-saver is to put a prefix, such as a number, on the name of anything you create, so that your work is grouped into directories - much as papers of one kind might share a drawer in a filing cabinet. This is almost essential with hard disks. For example, all letters on money matters could start with 5. So if you are looking for a letter you wrote to your bank manager, but have forgotten the letter's full name, you can ask the computer to show you only a list of letters which have names starting with 5 - which speeds things up a lot.

Similarly, document names usually have a suffix, such as .ltr for letters. Create different types of suffixes for different types of documents so essays could have the suffix .ess. Then if you want to delete all your letters but keep all your essays you can give a single command to delete all documents with names ending .ltr, and know your essays will be safe.

Data Bases

Salesmen sometimes make out that all data bases are the same. They aren't. Good data bases can be adapted to take any kind of information you want. It's best not to enter data on to a data base until you are certain the form has been arranged so that you can record and extract information by every single criterion which you might need. Each type of information is called a 'field', so a name is one field and an address is another. A vital field is one which allows you to enter two or three code letters. This allows you to use such letters to mark and extract, for example, the addresses of all those to whom you send Christmas cards, or all customers who need to be billed in a certain month.

Disk Errors

If your computer says there's an error and it can't read a floppy disk, exit, remove the disk and tap it lightly so it changes position in its sleeve. Replace it in the disk drive and try again. This usually solves the problem, though you may need to repeat it several times to do the trick.

Disk Labelling

Obviously every disk must be labelled to show its contents. A useful tip is to write on the main copies in red and on the back-ups in black. Then you can instantly tell which is which and there is far less risk of accidentally erasing documents by copying the back-up on to the main disk when you mean to do the reverse. And, if you have a lot of disks, covering different topics, use a different colour to label each type.

★ One of the most useful adjuncts to all this high-flown technology is an elastic band. Put one round each disk (*in* its sleeve), from top to bottom, as soon as you make a back-up copy. That way all the disks with new work on will have missing bands, and you know instantly which ones to back-up.

Service Contracts and Guarantees

Any computer should come with a year's guarantee. If it doesn't you should wonder why. After that you may be offered a service contract. These can be very expensive, but anyone covered by a contract usually gets attention the day they phone, while those without it may wait a week or so. So, if your computer is vital to you, a contract may be worthwhile whatever the price, and there may be two ways of cutting its cost. They may reduce the price if you agree to take the computer to them and collect it afterwards, or you can take a slight risk and only take out a contract for the two parts of a computer which go wrong most often - the printer and the disk drive. In addition, a lot of applications programs suppliers have a helpline service, if you pay so much a year. Check this when buying any program.

Terms Used in Computing

baud rate the speed at which a modem can send sound waves, carrying computer data, down a telephone line. 300 baud (obscurely known as V21) is about 300 words a minute and 1200 baud (V23) is about 1,200 words a minute.

cursor a small patch of light which shows the point of the screen where you are working.

data anything you create on the computer, whether writing, mathematics or drawings.

debug correct errors in a program (strictly for the experts).

edit change and correct a document which has been created and held in the computer's memory.

index the list of documents which have been created, which is held on the disk of the applications program.

ROM stands for Read Only Memory - i.e. you can get data out but you can't alter what's in there. Predictably, it has passed into slang as a none too kind description of some people's brains.

update an instruction used to change data which is already in the data base. For example, you call an address to the screen, change it, and 'update'. The machine then erases the old address and puts the new one on the disk instead.

LAW

Consumer Law • Criminal Law • Divorce and Separation • Driving and Vehicle Law • Employment Law • Family Law • Household Law • Legal Aid •

Britain operates not one legal system but several. There is one law for England and Wales (which allows Wales special rules over such things as pub opening hours), and there are different systems for Scotland and Ireland.

The biggest divide of all is probably between England and Scotland. No act of parliament prior to 1707 has any force in Scots law - unless it has been re-enacted since. Historically, through its link with France, Scottish law is linked to Roman law in ways in which other British law is not. Since a great deal of law is based on the precedents of decisions made by previous courts, this leads to considerable differences between Scottish laws and those in the rest of Britain.

These historic differences, in turn, affect how parliament drafts legislation for Scotland. So, for example, the law contained in the 1980 Housing Act, which allowed council tenants to buy their own property, had to be separately drafted for Scotland to allow for the differences in property law in the two countries.

Parliament can pass two separate acts, but it is unfortunately impractical to write here the two or three separate legal sections which are needed to do justice to Ireland and Scotland, as well as to England and Wales. I therefore apologize to my readers from both nations for having included less of their law than I would have wished. Unless specific reference is made to Scotland or Ireland, readers in those countries should assume that the law in their part of Britain may be different.

Finally, a word of warning: this section doesn't pretend to be a comprehensive guide to law. Instead, it is designed to provide a broad portrait of how the law operates in the areas which most affect people's daily lives, so that when they approach a lawyer, or an advice centre, they will already have some feel for what they can expect and what their rights may be. But details which could be vital in a particular case have had to be left out. On top of that, law changes fast and new laws will have been enacted since this was printed. So, inevitably, some of the facts here will be out of date by the time you read them. *Anyone planning to do anything which could have legal consequences - such as writing a will - or intending to take any kind of legal action, should not take what they find here as gospel, but should consult a lawyer.*

You don't need to have deep pockets to get legal advice. There are lawyers in most of the organizations given in the following chapters and many of the charities concerned with special issues have lawyers able to advise on their field. Between them these organizations also produce a wide range of useful leaflets and booklets giving legal facts in laymen's terms.

CONSUMER LAW

Banking

There is an implied contract between a bank and its customer that the bank will honour the customer's cheques (if there is enough money in the account), obey instructions and not disclose the customer's affairs to other people. Usually, if a bank pays out a cheque when it should not have done it is liable - for example, if a cheque needs two signatures and is passed with only one. There are, however, various rules which it is worth knowing:

- If a cheque card number is written on the back of a cheque that cheque cannot be stopped.
- If you lose your cheque book and notify the bank immediately the bank is liable for any cheques forged. If you fail to tell the bank *you* are liable.

As soon as a bank knows someone is dead it stops all their cheques (this doesn't apply to a joint account). So if a husband is seriously ill and the wife is financially dependent on him it would be a good idea for him to give his wife a cheque for enough for her to live on for several months, and she would be wise to use it immediately to open an account in her name alone, and not tell the bank of the death until the cheque has been cleared. This may sound hard-hearted, but adding sudden poverty to grief is even harder.

Buying and Selling

Every time we buy something we are making a verbal contract which has two parts. The first part is our offer to buy the goods at a given price; the second part is the shopkeeper's acceptance of our order or verbal agreement to sell them to us. Once both halves are completed, there is a binding contract and we cannot change our minds without risking penalties (such as

This is guidance not gospel: before acting consult a solicitor.

The Courts and Appeals System of England, Scotland and Wales

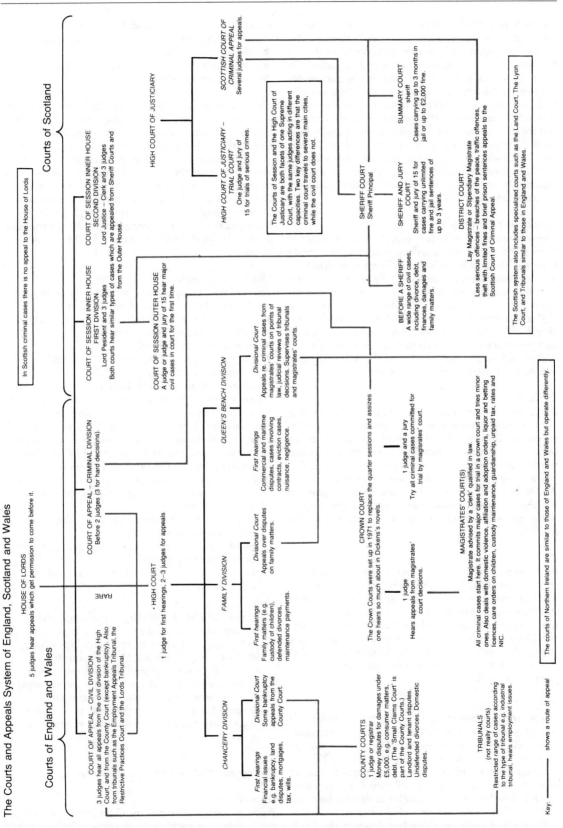

This is guidance not gospel: before acting consult a solicitor.

compensating the shopkeeper), nor can the shopkeeper decide he or she wants to raise the price. With mail order goods the company only accepts the order when it *posts* the acceptance, so the customer is free to cancel the order up to that point. At an auction the acceptance is when the hammer comes down - so if you want to back out speak up *fast* before it strikes. All this means that either side can sue the other for breach of contract and the seller cannot make a customer accept substitute goods. The customer is entitled to her money back if they aren't what was agreed or ordered. However you buy, the legal implication is that the goods are not defective in any way. If they are, see Quality and Safety on standards of goods.

Buying in Your Own Home

There is one very important exception to the rules of buying and selling. If you order goods on cash or credit from a salesman who calls at your home uninvited (e.g. an encyclopaedia salesman) you will normally have 7 days as a 'cooling-off' period, in which to change your mind, provided the value of the goods is over a set sum (£35 at the time of writing). It is also possible that this clause will cover the situation when someone rings up and persuades you to let them come to your home in order to sell you something - but at the time of writing this had not been defined for certain.

Deposits

If you see something you like in a shop and put a deposit on it, to hold it while you look elsewhere, it could be expensive. Deposits placed on goods are usually taken to be a legal contract to buy them. The only way round this is to ask the person who accepts the deposit to give you a receipt saying that the deposit is returnable if you decide not to purchase. The same rule applies to services, but in either case it doesn't hold if the supplier of the goods or services fails to deliver in a reasonable time.

Ordering

If you order goods you may give a date by which you must receive them, and if they don't arrive by that time you can refuse them. If you don't give a date companies still have a legal obligation to deliver within a reasonable time. How long is 'reasonable' will vary with the goods, but 28 days is used for many situations. If goods are slow in arriving you may write to the seller and say that if they have not come within a certain time you want your money back.

Sellers' Obligations

There are two different aspects to the law regarding the sale of goods - criminal offences and civil offences. Criminal offences are prosecuted by officials like the police or (more often) the Trading Standards Officers; for civil offences the consumer herself has to sue. In practice, where a case might fall into either category Trading Standards Officers may try to lighten their own work load by insisting it is a civil offence.

Criminal offences are those laid down in the Trade Description Acts 1968 and 1972 and the Consumer Protection Act 1987. They make it illegal to:
- display misleading prices
- describe either goods or services falsely
- display prices which are not genuine.

The clause on prices in the latest bill covers not only goods but also services, accommodation and facilities. Goods with 'reduced from' notices must have been on sale at the higher price for 28 days during the past 6 months. But, as it is up to the prosecution to prove this was *not* the case, this is not as strong as it sounds. Vague signs saying things like 'up to 50 per cent off' or 'up to £15 off' are also illegal under the 1979 Bargain Offers Order - though even quite reputable shops use them. But if you think any retailer has broken these laws report it to your local Trading Standards Officer, at your council.

Quality and Safety

The civil law acts applying to most new or second-hand goods, and the servicing related to them are:
- The Supply of Goods (Implied Terms) Act 1973
- Unfair Contract Terms Act 1977
- Sale of Goods Act 1979
- Supply of Goods and Services Act 1982
- Consumer Protection Act 1987.

However, nobody should be too confident of the protection given by these laws. The Chairman of the National Consumer Council has described current consumer legislation as 'leaking like a sieve'. What's more, the law distinguishes between goods and services. So the protection you get if you spend £500 on a holiday (a service) won't be the same as you get if you spend £500 on a cooker. However, the following are the key points on goods (and directly related services).
All goods sold must:
a   'correspond with their description' (this applies to both labels and sales talk)
b   be of 'merchantable [acceptable] quality'
c   be 'fit for the purpose' they are sold for
d   be reasonably safe, having regard to all circumstances.

> Clause (a) also applies to secondhand goods, whether they are sold privately or in a shop - so be very careful what you say when selling your car. But if you are buying remember that (c) does not apply to secondhand goods in the same way as it does to new goods, and even on new goods a retail company has a get-out clause if it can prove that it could not 'reasonably have known' that the goods were unsafe.

Buying and Selling - Special Situations

Auctions

Auctions are not governed by all the usual rules. Unlike most traders, an auctioneer *can* refuse to be responsible

This is guidance not gospel: before acting consult a solicitor.

if goods are faulty, but auctioneers must say so in the catalogue or on a sign. However, in some cases, it can be challenged.

Business Purchases
All the rules above apply to someone who 'deals as a consumer' (i.e. not for business purposes) and buys goods of the type used for private purposes. The rules for buying by competitive tender and/or for business purposes are not covered by all the consumer laws.

Credit Notes
The law doesn't recognize credit notes. If a customer has not accepted the goods he is entitled to a cash refund. If the goods have been accepted then he will only be entitled to damages. So a credit note can be either a bad deal or rather a good one.

Exclusion Clauses
Sometimes organizations put up notices which claim they are not responsible for all kinds of things. Sometimes these are genuine warnings to remind people of how the law stands; sometimes they are utterly false exclusion clauses with no basis in law. For example, you may see notices saying that a company is not responsible for any death or injury suffered by someone on their premises. In law they *would* be responsible if the death or injury was due to their negligence, and no amount of notices can alter this. This also applies to 'no refunds' notices on sale goods. In these circumstances, they can refuse a refund if you just change your mind, but if the goods are faulty in any way the notice doesn't absolve them of their legal liability. There is, however, a grey area regarding damage to your goods while in someone else's care - such as a car in a car park or a coat on a restaurant coat rack. Whether you get compensation for loss or damage will largely depend on whether it was reasonable to expect them to take better care, in the particular circumstances.

> When someone is buying for business, not therefore as a consumer, shopkeepers are allowed to insert various exclusion clauses and these should be looked for.

Goods on Credit
The Consumer Credit Act 1974 in some circumstances makes the supplier of credit carry part of the liability for goods meeting the standards outlined above. This means that if you use a credit card, bank loan or HP to buy goods which turn out to be faulty you may be able to sue those companies - but the sum must be over £100 and under £30,000. This may sound crazy but it could be useful if a supplier goes bankrupt, so it is usually worth buying large items on credit.

Guarantees
All goods and services must, by law, reach certain standards and perform for reasonable periods of time. Guarantees can add to the obligations of a company

in relation to its goods and services, but they can never reduce a company's obligations below those set by the law. Guarantees which promise the earth are suspicious - the company may be planning to vanish before they are called on to fulfil those great promises. However, exclusion clauses may be valid if the buyer is not 'dealing as a consumer' (see left).

Despite that, if something breaks down while under guarantee there is no set time limit in law within which the manufacturer, or their agent, must come and put things right. In law they are expected to act within a 'reasonable' time - but a court might think a delay reasonable which a mother of young children with an unusable washing machine might find intolerable.

However, the Association of Manufacturers of Domestic Electrical Appliances and the Electrical and Television Retailers Association both have codes of practice which say that, even if goods are *not* under guarantee, servicing should be available within 3 days (and the service operative should be able to say whether they will call in the morning or afternoon). So, members of these associations can be reminded of this code.

Hiring
In England, Wales and Northern Ireland anyone hiring goods has virtually the same rights as someone buying them. In Scotland there are implied terms under common law which consumers should check before hiring.

Postal Selling
The Unsolicited Goods and Services Act 1971 says that if you are sent goods you have not ordered you may ignore the invoice and keep the goods. If the company fails to collect them in 6 months they become yours. Alternatively, you can write to the sender and say the goods were not ordered and suggest they collect them - if they don't the goods belong to you within 31 days.

A more subtle version is to send leaflets inviting you to inspect a book, or something similar, for 14 days before paying. You order it, and when it arrives you are legally bound to pay for it or return it in 14 days. The company gambles on you either forgetting to return it in 14 days, or being reluctant to pay the postage on the heavy item. But if you do send it back get a proof of posting slip from the post office.

Refusing to Serve a Customer
Anyone supplying goods or services may refuse to serve any customer, provided the refusal is not on the grounds of race or sex.

Stolen Goods
If you accidentally buy stolen goods you aren't guilty. If you buy goods you know, or believe to be, stolen it is a crime punishable by imprisonment.

Telephone Selling
There is a technique called sugging, in which someone rings up and makes out that they are doing simple market research; they then try to sell you something.

This is guidance not gospel: before acting consult a solicitor.

It is not illegal but if you can find out the company's name and address report it to **The Market Research Society**, 175 Oxford Street, London W1R 1TA Tel: 01 439 2585. It is against the society's code of conduct and if a member is engaged in it the Society can penalize them. But there is no redress for the person who has been conned.

Codes of Practice

If a company is in breach of the code of practice of its trade association this does, in a sense, put right on your side. But the code of practice may not be identical with the law. In that case, it is usually best to try to settle the matter by first pointing out to the firm that it is in breach of the code of practice, and say that you will take the matter up with the trade association if they don't satisfy you. If necessary, ask the trade association to sort it out. It may suggest taking the matter to arbitration; this is not the same as arbitration in a court (see Organizations). So discuss these options with a Citizens Advice Bureau or Law Centre. The Office of Fair Trading (in Organizations) has a free leaflet explaining arbitration under codes of practice.

Conveyancing and House Buying

A house or flat is the biggest purchase most people ever make and, to protect the buyer, there are a series of steps which must be taken before ownership is transferred from one person to another - which is all conveyancing is. From the outside, the whole business seems immensely complicated, and is usually left to lawyers, but it is far simpler than it looks and it is possible to do it yourself. For that you need far more information than there is space for here. It is essential to read up on this subject and get every move right (see right). What follows is only an outline of the moves in the game. It is safest to use a conveyancer who is a member of the **National Association of Conveyancers** (2 Apsley Hill, Woburn Sands, Milton Keynes, Bucks MK17 8NJ Tel: 01 549 3636). Members must have several years' experience of conveyancing and keep to a code of conduct which includes professional indemnity insurance.

Gazumping

Those who prefer to leave conveyancing to a lawyer would do well to choose one who does a lot of this kind of work. There is always a risk that the seller will accept a better offer while your conveyancing is being done. This gazumping is legal right up to the moment when contracts are exchanged. So speed counts, and a solicitor who does a lot of conveyancing usually moves faster. So there is less chance of you losing your dream home.

Registration of Property

In England and Wales there are two types of property - registered and unregistered. For centuries ownership of land or property rested on deeds which showed that on a particular date B bought the house from A, then another deed would show that C bought it from B, and so on down the years. Hence the need for the old deed

boxes. Then politicians had the bright idea of keeping a register of who owned what, and there are now Land Registers for each area. The theory was that in due time every property in the land would be neatly docketed. They aren't. So the conveyancer may have to work with either system.

Freehold and Leasehold

A freehold property is totally owned by the present owner - who may or may not also occupy it.

A leasehold property is owned by one person while someone else has a lease (a form of licence) allowing them to live in it rent-free for a certain number of years. This can be anything from 1 year to 99 years and the price of the lease is related to how long the lease runs for. What follows is primarily for freehold property. Leasehold follows a similar pattern, but there are other checks on the clauses of the lease which need to be made.

The Stages in Buying a Property

Whether the property is registered or not the stages in buying a home go like this:

1 You find a place you like and make an offer on it through the agent. You should always say, verbally and in writing, that the offer is 'subject to contract' - or you could legally commit yourself to buy before you have arranged for the money to pay for it.
2 If the offer isn't accepted you negotiate until you and the owner agree a price. The agent may ask for a deposit but in law you don't have to give one. If you do, keep it nominal - and it must be returned to you if the sale doesn't go through, whatever the reason.

> It is perfectly legal for someone to sell you a house which is falling apart: houses are sold 'as seen'. So at this stage it is wise to have a surveyor's report (see page 214) and ask the seller about any guarantees on the property - it may have been treated for damp or dry rot under a guarantee scheme. When there isn't a run on property a surveyor may look at the place *before* you make an offer but, when things are being snapped up, that delay can lose it.

3 A solicitor is instructed to do the conveyancing, or you start yourself (it takes 1 to 6 weeks).
4 At the same time you start to arrange the mortgage.
5 When the mortgage is agreed and the conveyancing done contracts are exchanged. It is legal for a seller to accept a higher price right up to this point, and there can even be a contract race in which several people try to get a property for the same price and whoever completes the legal and financial formalities and exchanges contracts with the seller gets the property. But from the moment contracts are exchanged the two sides are bound by law. On exchange of contracts 10 per cent of the purchase price is usually deposited with the solicitor.
6 A completion date is now set - usually 28 days later.

This is guidance not gospel: before acting consult a solicitor.

This is the date when the whole transaction takes place and you become the owner.

The Steps in Conveying a House

The legal steps in buying or selling a freehold house are as follows. For convenience they are written as if solicitors were involved on both sides. But it is perfectly legal for you to do your own conveyancing.

> The company from which you intend to get a mortgage should be contacted when you start the conveyancing, then all the financial steps are going on parallel with the legal ones and neither (with luck) holds up the other. The mortgage company will use its own solicitor to check the vital facts about the house, but the buyer's solicitor is expected to keep the company informed and send it any documents (such as the evidence of ownership) which come from the seller's solicitor.

1 The seller's (vendor's) solicitor checks the documents on the property by either:
   a looking at the deeds (usually held by the mortgage company)
                    or
   b seeing the land certificate (the Land Registry sends a photocopy).
2 If everything seems correct, and the vendor does own the property, the vendor's solicitor draws up a draft contract and sends it to the buyer's solicitor. (Both the Law Society and Oyez publishing have standard forms for draft contracts.) The solicitor will also send a copy of the registration, if the land is registered, or of any restrictive covenants on an unregistered property.

> Write into the draft contract some agreement about reasonable access to the property between exchange of contracts and completion. Then you can measure up, and so on. Without this you have no right of entry until completion - even if the property is empty.

3 While this is going on the buyer and seller should agree on what fixtures and fittings are included in the purchase price. In law things which are permanently attached to the property should stay. But looks can be deceptive. There are now whole fitted kitchens which look attached but are free-standing and removable - which could be a bit of a blow if you fall in love with the kitchen, and move in to find it empty.
4 The buyer's solicitor reads the draft contract and then:
   a asks the vendor's solicitor about details like boundary fences, mains connections, tenants and formalizes agreement on fixtures and fittings;

   b writes to the local council and asks about any council matters which could affect the property - proposals to develop the area, planning permissions granted in the past and so on (this is called a 'local search' and is done on a standard enquiry form);
   c gets the buyer to sign a copy of the contract ready to be exchanged later.
5 Before contracts can be exchanged, and the buyer committed to the purchase, he or she should be happy about every detail of the following:

   ● the mortgage offer
   ● the surveyor's report
   ● the local authority search
   ● the seller's answers to the questions put to him or her
   ● the information on the ownership of the property.

If there are problems in any of these areas - say the property is in the path of a proposed motorway and might be compulsorily purchased - this is the time to take back the offer and withdraw from the deal. But if nothing bad is revealed the contracts can now be exchanged.
6 The buyer deposits part of the purchase price (usually 10 per cent) either with the estate agent who arranged the sale or with the seller's solicitor. This money comes out of the buyer's pocket, not from the mortgage company and the buyer can always ask the seller to accept less than 10 per cent - at today's prices even 5 per cent is a sum few people would risk losing by suddenly pulling out. For if the deal is dropped now the buyer could forfeit the whole deposit. But the money is held on deposit by the solicitor or estate agent and doesn't go to the seller until completion.

> The buyer should take out insurance on the property (or it should be done by the bank or building society loaning the money). This should date from the moment contracts are exchanged. At that moment the buyer becomes liable if the whole place burns down. A seller would do well to keep his or her insurance up until completion as a double safeguard.)

7 As soon as the money is deposited contracts can be exchanged. This is just what it sounds. The buyer has signed one copy, the seller the other and they swap copies - usually through a solicitor. At the same time, if the property is unregistered the buyer's solicitor will receive an 'abstract of title', which means copies of whatever document(s) prove the seller's ownership.
8 The buyer's solicitor checks the 'abstract of title', if there is one, and asks any questions of the other side which arise from it. Alternatively, he gets the

This is guidance not gospel: before acting consult a solicitor.

seller's permission to contact the Land Registry and check the legal ownership of the property - and asks any questions which arise from that.

9 The buyer's solicitor prepares the draft transfer which legally transfers ownership of the property, and sends it to the vendor's solicitors for approval. (It is only called a 'conveyance' if the land is unregistered). If it's approved a smart copy of it is signed by the vendor (via the solicitor).

10 The seller's solicitor sends a completion statement to the buyer's solicitor saying exactly how much money remains to be paid. This will be the difference on the purchase price, plus any rates which have been paid in advance. If rates are unpaid for the time before the sale they are not the buyer's responsibility.)

11 The buyer's solicitor checks that his or her client isn't bankrupt by getting a certificate to this effect from the Land Charges Department, Drakes Hill Court, Burrington Way, Plymouth PL5 3LP Tel: 0752 779831.

12 Finally, the buyer's solicitor sends a form to the Land Registry (for a registered house) or to the Land Charge Registry (if it is unregistered) to check that while all this was going on nothing happened to alter the status of the house.

13 When the all-clear is given by those final enquiries, and the mortgage company is ready to produce the money, the deal can be struck. This is usually about three months after your first offer to the estate agent. The actual sale (for that is what completion is) usually takes place in a solicitor's office. This is often the office of whoever is acting for the seller's bank or building society (if the seller is still paying off the mortgage). Bank drafts and the titles to the property are exchanged. The estate agent is told to release the keys and in nothing more dramatic than a flurry of paper the ownership of the property has changed hands.

There is no longer a set scale of fees for conveyancing and people other than solicitors are licensed to do conveyancing. Prices tend to range between ½ per cent and 1¼ per cent of the purchase price - and to that add VAT, stamp duty and various expenses.

If that left you wondering why anyone should pay as much for it *The Conveyancing Fraud* by Michael Joseph is a very clear step-by-step guide for DIY conveyancers written by a lawyer, and for a modest fee he gives telephone consultations (Michael Joseph, 27 Occupation Lane, Woolwich, London SE18 3JQ Tel: 01 855 2404). There is also a good section in John Pritchard's *Penguin Guide to Law*.

Alternatively, a middle path is to use a member of the National Association of Conveyancers, 44 London Road, Kingston-upon-Thames, Surrey KT2 6QF Tel: 01 549 3636. Its members are specialists in conveyancing who work outside the solicitor's system, and usually charge rather less. But check that your mortgage company will accept whatever method of conveyancing you choose.

To DIY or Not to DIY
Whether it is wise to do your own conveyancing will depend very much on the situation. A leasehold flat will have all kinds of leasehold clauses which might benefit from a legal eye (though they might not). A new property needs clauses in the contract about the quality of the finished work, which a beginner might find hard to draft.

Any property may have some hidden complication, like an ex - wife's claim to it, which won't show until the investigations are underway. But, when no snags occur, many people find DIY conveyancing of a registered freehold perfectly possible.

For safety, there should be a lawyer acting on the other side, and whoever is doing it should always be prepared to hand the job over to lawyers and let them finish the job if an unexpected snag occurs - and if you've done half the work you may be able to negotiate the percentage accordingly.

Oyez (**Legal Stationery**), 16 Third Avenue, Denbigh West, Bletchley, Milton Keynes NK1 1TG Tel: 0908 71111 - sells conveyancing forms.

Receiving orders for bankruptcy can be viewed at Thomas Moore Building, Law Courts, Strand, London WC2A 2LL Tel: 01 936 6444 and petitions and receiving orders can be searched for via the Land Registry (page 226).

Data Protection

Under the Data Protection Act 1984 you have the right to know what information companies and organizations hold on you. The Data Protection Register, in major libraries, lists all data holders and if you ask for a copy of any data on you a holder *must* send what they have - though it may cost you £10 a time. However, data related to national security is outside the act and criminal, taxation, medical and social work records may sometimes be withheld.'

You can ask for any record to be corrected, and if the holder refuses the Investigation Department of the *Data Protection Registrar* (Springfield House, Water Lane, Wilmslow, Cheshire SK9 5AX Tel: 0625 535777) will take it up and can make an enforcement order. If, however, you want compensation you can take the data holder to court - the Data Protection Registrar has only limited powers to help you.

Drink

Licensing Hours
British law distinguishes between on-licences and off-licences - according to whether the drink is sold to be drunk on or off the premises. The hours for pubs and so on are as follows but a forthcoming bill may abolish the afternoon break and make other changes:

Outside London:	11.00 am - 3.00 pm	5.30 pm - 10.30 pm
Within London:	11.00 am - 3.00 pm	5.30 pm - 11.00 pm
Sundays, Christmas	12.00 am - 2.00 pm	7.00 pm - 10.30 pm
Day & Good Friday:		

This is guidance not gospel: before acting consult a solicitor.

But licensing justices can alter the hours in their district and the licensee may open later or close earlier. There are also special licences for special situations.

a The Supper Hour Certificate for restaurants adds an hour, provided the drink is part of a meal.

b An Extended Hours Order takes the licence to 1 am in restaurants with entertainment.

c A Special Hours Certificate extends the licence to 2 am or 3 am if there is food, music and dancing.

Most of these extensions don't apply on Good Friday, Maundy Thursday or the day before Easter, so illogically you can't dance the night away before one of the major bank holidays.

The licensing hours for off-licences are 8.30 am to the evening closing hour for that licensing district on weekdays. On Sundays the hours are the same as for on-licences.

Measures in Licensed Premises
The quantities for draught beer and cider are 185 or 280 millilitres (⅓ or ½ pt) or multiples of these. At present wine can be sold in any measure the landlord chooses, but spirits may only be sold in the following measures - 24, 28 or 35 millilitres (¹/₆, ¹/₅ or ¼ of a gill), or in multiples of these. The landlord must clearly display a notice saying which measure is being used. The exception is when three or more liquids are mixed together, which could explain the popularity of cocktails - among publicans.

Carafes may only be offered in the following sizes:
metric: 250 ml, 500 ml, 750 ml, 1000 ml
imperial: 10 fl oz, 20 fl oz

Food
Basically, food in shops and restaurants must be fit for human consumption and comply with a whole range of constantly changing regulations on things like additives. If food is off, contains anything it should not or does not contain what the label says it should, complain to the shop and get your money back. You should also complain to the manufacturer. Unfit food in shops and restaurants should be reported to the Environmental Health Department of the local council; and keep the evidence for him or her to see.

Restaurants
Restaurants are covered by the general clauses in consumer legislation and also by some rules designed just for them. The most important ones are these.

● They must display a notice outside, or immediately inside, their door giving the prices of food and drink, *and* any cover charge, *inclusive* of VAT. If they don't you can report them to the Trading Standards Officer. However, menus at the table don't have to show prices inclusive of VAT.

● Service charges must be displayed outside, like the other charges; if they aren't there is no need to pay them, and there is also no need to pay them if the service wasn't worth paying for.

● A restaurant doesn't have to admit you if you are not suitably dressed - even if you have booked.

● You are obliged to pay a restaurant bill, but if the meal was dreadful you can pay what you think is reasonable. Explain why you aren't paying the rest and leave them your name and address. It is then up to the restaurant to sue you for the difference. Pay by cheque or credit card so you had evidence of how much you paid.

● If you book at a restaurant it can be a contract in law, and if you don't turn up you may be liable for a bill. One restaurant successfully sued for the loss when a large party booked and a small party turned up. On the other hand, it's more doubtful that a court will uphold your claim if you sue because the table you booked wasn't available.

● If your clothes are damaged by careless serving you can claim the cost of the cleaning, or of a new garment if it can't be cleaned. They may also be liable for the loss of your property in their cloakroom - even if they have a notice saying they are not liable - provided they are clearly offering to look after it. A coat rack in the body of the restaurant may offer less protection.

Gold and Silver

Standards for Gold and Silver
Both gold and silver are normally mixed with other metals to make them stronger. There are strict regulations on how much of these alloys can be added. The following table shows the usual international standards for gold, and the British standards for silver, in parts per thousand.

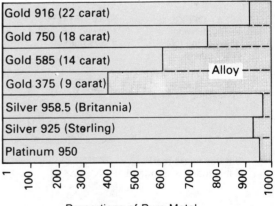

Proportions of Pure Metal

Jewellers normally talk about gold in terms of carats. But, in Britain, since January 1975, gold has had to be stamped with the amount of gold in parts per thousand, and this is common on overseas gold as well. Imported silver may also have its standard number stamped on it, but British silver carries a hallmark which tells you a great deal more.

Hallmarks
The British hallmarking system, dating from 1300, is

This is guidance not gospel: before acting consult a solicitor.

one of the world's oldest forms of consumer protection. By law, anything sold in Britain, and described as gold or silver, must be independently tested at one of four assay offices and stamped with a mark to show that it contains not less than a certain proportion of precious metal. Three different types of approved symbols fall within this system:

1 those used on items made in Britain
2 that used on anything imported into Britain and stamped by a British assay office
3 the mark stamped in certain European countries for export to Britain.

The mark you'll find most easily is the row of four symbols used for solid silver, made in Britain. To work out the date of a piece and where it was made you only have to decipher the mark from left to right.

1

THE SPONSOR'S MARK with the initials of the person or firm which made the articles

2

THE STANDARD MARK showing it is English sterling or Britannia silver

3

ASSAY OFFICE MARK showing which of the four assay offices tested it.

4

DATE LETTER showing the date it was marked.

The usual standard mark for sterling silver is

But this is the mark if it is made in Scotland

For Britannia silver the mark is the same for both England and Scotland but changed in 1975

Before 1975   After 1975

Until 1975 the four British assay offices all used different symbols for the same year - so to date a piece you first had to look up the assay office, *then* the date. On anything made since 1975 the date letter is the same for all four offices.

1975 was also a year of change for the standard marks on both British and imported gold and silver. The books listed at the end will help you to decipher the hallmarks.

EPNS and Gold Plate

These letters stand for electro-plated nickel silver, which means the article is not solid silver but a base metal, plated with a thin layer of silver. But objects in EPNS can still have considerable value if they are very old or attractive.

Gold plate has no distinguishing stamp. Technically, it is very hard to plate an article with anything but pure gold - incredibly thin though that layer may sometimes be. So items which claim 9 carat plating may well be coated in something less than gold.

Buying Gold and Silver

Anything sold in Britain *as* gold or silver has to be hallmarked. If it hasn't got a hallmark it can't be sold as such. But since 1975 it has also been legal for British gold and silver to be exported without a hallmark. The Middle Eastern and American tendency to value newness has meant that more and more silversmiths are exporting their wares unmarked - so no date mark betrays the 'shameful' fact that last year's silver is being used. So lack of a hallmark can't be automatically equated with poor quality.

Nor are hallmarks an absolute guarantee of the genuine article. Until the mid-1970s it wasn't illegal, in Holland, to mark silver and gold with fake hallmarks, and there was a cottage industry at the turn of the century doing just that. 'Dutch gypsy pieces' the London assay office calls them. Your only protection is to get a receipt, with an accurate description of the goods, giving the precise gold or silver standard of the article you are buying. Take no excuses; even a stall should be able to give a signed scrap of paper. You should then have legal redress if it turns out to be a lower quality.

Buying Overseas

Britain is one of the very few places to set official standards for items made from precious metals. Baltimore once had a hallmarking system, but its silver then become so popular that the other silver making centres ganged up and had it stopped. If you are buying abroad remember that in some places they sometimes use pure silver or pure 24-carat gold. Both are so soft you can bend them between your fingers, so they may seem inferior because of their very purity. But in other countries the proportion of gold or silver *claimed* for a particular item may be far higher than the actual content. Heaviness for its size is a characteristic of gold. So some sharp dealers in the Far East make fake designer label watches with lead centres, and cover them with a thin coating of what is laughingly called '90-day gold' - as it wears off then.

This is guidance not gospel: before acting consult a solicitor.

There is no rule of thumb which will tell gold plate from solid gold (without scraping it) or, without chemical analysis, reveal how much other metal has been added. Even the colour of gold is no guide.

London Assay Office, Goldsmiths' Hall, 1-2 Foster Lane, London EC2V 8AQ Tel: 01 606 8975 - has a free leaflet on hallmarking - sae.
Judith Banister, *The Country Life Collector's Pocket Book of Silver,* Country Life.
Bradbury's Book of Hallmarks, J. W. Northend - gives a pocket reference table of hallmarks.
Touching Gold and Silver: 500 Years of Hallmarks, The Goldsmiths' Company.
The Hallmarking Act 1973, C43, from HMSO, gives all the details of changes in marks on precious metals since 1975.

Hire Purchase and Credit

If you buy on hire purchase the goods don't belong to you until you have made the final payment. So it would be illegal to sell them. Under the Consumer Credit Act 1974 this fact must be printed in the contract which you sign. If you buy on credit the goods belong to you immediately.

Whichever way you buy, the company must tell you the cash price of the goods, the rate of interest and the total price *with* the interest. This may well be in writing on a label or on the contract - so read both carefully.

Cancelling an Agreement
Customers can change their minds up to the point when the company approves their application for credit. Those who sign the agreement at home have the usual 'cooling off' period (page 436). If you cancel the agreement within the legal period you should get all your money back bar a £3 fee.

If part-exchange was involved you should get the goods back in unchanged condition within 10 days. Failing that, claim the trade-in value, in cash. You must also keep the company's items in good condition - if they have already been delivered, and allow them to be collected - you don't have to return them physically. (See also Buying in Your Own Home, page 436).

A credit agreement cannot be cancelled once it is in force; an HP agreement can. But you can only cancel an HP agreement if you have paid all the payments up to half the credit price of the goods, and the goods are in good condition. To cancel you simply notify the company and return the goods. But you lose all the money you have spent up to that point, and if the goods are not in good condition you can be liable to pay for their drop in value.

Debt
If a customer gets behind on HP payments the company can reclaim the goods. But first they must give the customer 7 days' notice in which to pay. If you have paid a third, or more, of the credit price, they cannot reclaim the goods without a court order. (See also page 494).

Early Payment
If you pay off the whole amount early you should pay less than the credit price, because interest charges are related to the amount of time for which the money is borrowed. Sort this out before paying it off.

Extortionate Interest
If the interest rate is 'extortionate' you can ask the courts to reduce it. But in deciding whether it is extortionate the courts will look at all the circumstances: a high rate is not always an extortionate rate.

Licensed Lenders
To lend money legally a company must be licensed by the Office of Fair Trading (OFT). If the company isn't registered it is committing a criminal offence, and any agreement is not legally valid - so you don't have to pay it a penny. However, the lender can apply to the OFT for a validation order. This order gives a lender the right to obtain repayments under the agreement. However, the OFT can impose certain conditions. Equally, a court can alter the terms of the agreement and the interest rate. If you want to check if a company *is* registered contact the OFT at Government Building, Bromyard Avenue, Acton, London W3 7BB Tel: 01 743 5566.

They have the public register of lenders and for a tiny fee will tell you whether a company is registered or not.

Refusal of Credit
If any company refuses to give you credit - when they allow credit to other customers - it may be because they have checked with a credit reference agency and been told that you are a bad risk.

If you know of no reason why anyone should think this, there is a set sequence which may enable you to put the record straight. *But the timing is crucial.*
1 Within 28 days of the shop denying you credit ask for the name and address of the credit reference agency they used.
2 The shopkeeper must supply this within 7 days - not to do so is a criminal offence.
3 In reasonable time write to the agency in question and ask for a copy of the file on yourself (there will usually be a small fee).
4 The agency must send the file (if they have one) within 7 working days.
5 You then tell the agency which points are incorrect and ask for them to be altered or removed.
6 The agency has 28 days in which to tell you what it proposes to do.
7 If you are not happy with what they propose you have 28 days in which to send a note of up to 200 words, which must be put on your file, giving your views on the sections you object to. If the agency does not agree to put this on its files you can appeal to the Director General of the OFT. There is a heavy fine for agencies which are unreasonable in their reaction.

This is guidance not gospel: before acting consult a solicitor.

Services not Related to Goods

'Services' covers not only obvious services like car servicing but also such things as holidays. As with goods, the major protection is given to private customers 'dealing as a consumer'. Therefore, if a company agrees to perform a service for a given price there is an implied contract between you, just as there is when the purchase of goods is agreed (page 434). Under this contract you have a right to expect certain things.

- The contractor will use the right materials for the job. This means right in both type and quality.
- He will do a satisfactory job using 'reasonable care and skill'. (Trade associations often have established standards of what is reasonable. So it may be safest to use one of their members.)
- The job he does will be the job you asked him to do. (You don't want him to make a lovely job of taking down the wrong wall.)
- He will take care of your goods (e.g. not scratch your car in servicing it).
- The job will be done 'within a reasonable time'. Reasonable can be a touch elastic, so if you need the job done by a certain date make that very clear right at the start - preferably in writing.

If someone fails on any of these clauses they are in breach of contract and you should be able to claim damages.

Broken Appointments

If you break an appointment with someone supplying a service and so cost them money (e.g. fail to turn up at the dentist) they are entitled to charge you. Equally, if you are taking time off work to wait for the washing machine serviceman explain this to the company when you book the appointment and ask them to be punctual. Then if he turns up in the afternoon when the appointment was in the morning you can claim a nominal sum for the cost of your time and any phone calls you made to his company to trace him. The best way is to knock it off the bill when you pay it, and make clear why you are doing this. The company may try to sue you for the difference but it is very unlikely.

Charges

When the contractor does a reasonable job you should expect to pay a 'reasonable amount'. If a company tries to charge more than a *similar* company would charge for the same job it is not 'reasonable', and you are not bound to pay it, nor need you pay for work you did not ask to be done (unless it would have been impossible to do the work which was ordered without this extra work). This applies only when charges have not been agreed in advance.

If you agree a price in advance you have to pay it, even if you later discover that it is daylight robbery. Equally, if a company gives you a firm quote it is binding on both sides. If the painter finds the job takes twice as long as he planned that is his problem: he can't charge you extra. However, if you are given an estimate

it is only a guideline to the final cost. So it is wise to accept the estimate in writing and say clearly that if any extra work needs to be done, or if, at any point, the work seems likely to exceed the estimate by more than £x (whatever sum you wish) the contractor must get your approval before continuing.

Forgotten Goods

If you forget goods (such as dry cleaning) and leave them with a company for a long time the company should write and remind you. As this is a hassle most have a notice or clause in the agreement they have with you, saying that if goods are not collected within so many months they will be sold. They are entitled to do this. So if you take your tiara to be cleaned, tell your family where it is - accidents do happen and you could die before you can collect it.

Hiring Goods

Hired goods are expected to be in a safe condition. The small print in the hire contract may say the company isn't liable if the equipment kills or injures someone. This disclaimer isn't worth a jot. If the injury was because the equipment wasn't working perfectly (e.g. an electrical fault), rather than due to your negligence, the company is liable. Even so, some lawyers say you should check the small print of any hire contract and delete clauses which you don't think reasonable. But those who hire goods are expected to take reasonable care of them.

Hotels and Holidays

A hotel booking is a contract which is binding on both sides. So the following conditions apply.

- It is legal for hotels to charge a deposit in advance, and they can keep at least some of it if you fail to cancel and don't arrive.
- If a hotel accepts your booking, but has no room when you arrive you can claim compensation. They also have a duty to accommodate you without a booking, if they have room and you aren't drunk, shabby or otherwise inadmissible. But this doesn't apply to small establishments and guest houses.
- The prices, plus VAT, must be displayed near the entrance or in reception.
- If you cancel you may be liable for damages or lose your deposit.
- If you book through a tour operator and the holiday is a disaster - for reasons the tour operator should have foreseen (e.g. the hotel is nothing like its description) you can sue not just for the cost of the holiday but for disappointment too. Usually the sums involved will mean you can use the small claims division of the county court which is cheap and relatively easy. Alternatively, the Association of British Travel Agents (ABTA) runs an arbitration scheme. Unfortunately, ABTA expects the wronged customer to put down a deposit before the arbitration.

For your obligations to pay the bill see Restaurants (page

This is guidance not gospel: before acting consult a solicitor.

441); the difference is that a hotel can retaliate by keeping your belongings, though you will be glad to hear they may not keep your car or your horse. So if you find yourself at a Fawlty Towers, lock your luggage in the car *before* you argue the bill with the manager.

Taxis

Taxis can be one of the thorniest services. But, alas, they *are* within their rights to sail by with the For Hire sign alight and laughing at you. It is only when they are stationary that they must accept a passenger (traffic lights don't count). They can only charge what is on the meter when within the meter area (the radius varies with each city) but they can negotiate any fare they like outside that limit - provided they do it at the start of the journey.

In London there are special rules. If they stop to pick you up they must accept you as a passenger provided:
● you aren't asking them to go outside the Metropolitan Police District
● you aren't asking them to drive for more than an hour or 20 miles
● there are no detours to pick up other passengers.

When Things go Wrong

● When goods or services are unsatisfactory complain to the company which supplied the goods - not the manufacturer. The retailer, in turn, has a claim against the maker. And if they were a gift, the *buyer* must do the complaining. If a fault in the goods causes damage or injury the situation is different (see right).
● If the wrong goods are delivered to you, and you do not 'accept' them in the legal sense, or if the goods do not meet the rules on quality and safety (see page 436) and are judged defective, you can reject them and get your money back. In the latter case, you may also be entitled to compensation for any losses or expenses incurred. You do not have to take a credit note instead. However, if you have accepted the goods you may only be entitled to damages. So a credit note can be less than you are entitled to or rather more, according to the situation.
● Many of your rights in law rest on the issue of whether you have 'accepted' the goods. There are several situations in which the law would say you have accepted them.
  a You say you have accepted them.
  b You keep them for long enough to imply you have accepted them.
  c You do something which implies you own them (e.g. security mark them with your postcode).

Once you have accepted goods you lose your right to reject both them and the contract. But you still have a right to compensation for any breach of the terms of the contract. In either case, you are able to claim damages for any defective state. But beware of those delivery notes some firms ask you to sign which say that the goods are 'received and in good condition',

when you haven't had a chance to inspect, let alone try, them. You may be 'accepting' the goods in law. So sign the note, but cross out the bit about good condition and write 'subject to inspection' instead.

Liability for Injury or Death

Under the Consumer Protection Act 1987 the manufacturer, importer or 'own brander' of a product became liable for death, injury or damage to personal property (worth £275 or more) caused by defective goods. This clause covers electricity, gas and water as well as goods. And under the Act it is no longer necessary to prove negligence when you sue them.

Where to Get Help

If you ask the company concerned to put things right, and it doesn't, there are many sources of help and advice.

If you have used a trader who belongs to a trade association you may be able to get that trade association to take the matter up. In some cases, although your remedy isn't with the manufacturer, it may be possible to persuade a manufacturer to lean on a dealer. Failing that the Trading Standards Officer on your local council (or the council where the goods were bought).

Don't ignore the clout of the consumer programmes on radio and television like 'That's Life'. Anyone can write to them. Law Centres, CABX and some independent advice centres will advise you and have very readable leaflets on consumer law put out by the OFT. Or contact the OFT. You may be able to take the matter to the Small Claims Court (see Organizations) and get a legal remedy.

Which Personal Service, Dept BJJ, 2 Marylebone Road. London NW1 4DX Tel: 01 436 5544 is an advice and help scheme you can subscribe to. It enables you to get written and telephone advice if you have any consumer problems. The service is separate from subscribing to the magazines, but reading *Which* before shopping can prevent a lot of problems.

National Consumer Protection Council, 31 Chestnut Drive, Wanstead, London E11 2TA Tel: 01 989 5569 is a small organization which will advise on consumer problems and take up justified complaints.

Gordon Borrie and Aubrey Diamond, *The Consumer, Society and the Law*, Pelican

Ed. Edith Rudinger, *The Handbook of Consumer Law*, Consumers Association, Hodder and Stoughton.

CRIMINAL LAW

In some families children learn the criminal law with their mother's milk. But for many it is a closed book. It shouldn't be. Ancient rights and civil liberties, such as habeas corpus, which are the pride of the British legal system, are enshrined here. But, like any rights, they only exist if they are used. So we should all know them.

Most of the time the police and the average citizen are on the same side. But mistakes can happen. You may think you will never be on the wrong side of the law, but few things are more distressing than to be arrested when innocent, and find yourself facing the full force of bureaucracy without knowing your rights. When that happens there is no one to help you and nowhere to read them up, and being a prisoner is more intimidating than you can imagine until it happens to you.

Arrest and Before

There is a set sequence of events if someone is thought to have committed a crime. Up to the point when someone is charged the police are free to decide that they have the wrong person, and let the matter drop. The order of events is this:

● questioning
● arrest
● questioning
● detention
● being charged.

In the Street - Stop and Question

The police may stop you in the street and ask you basic questions, such as your name and address. But you have an equal right to ask why they want to know. The police have to give a good reason for questioning someone - even if they only need a name and address. Whatever they say it is not a good idea to get into a debate with them about whether you are, or are not, connected with the offence they are interested in.

Though you are not obliged to stop or to give your name and address in these circumstances, the wisest course is usually to give it with as little fuss as possible. If you are innocent it does no harm, and if you are guilty they will find it out anyway. But some law centres say that while the police are taking down your particulars you should take down theirs - note the officer's number, which should be visible, and ask what police station he or she is from. A policeman who is simply doing his duty will have no objection to giving this, and with a policeman who is throwing his weight about it acts as a polite reminder that he is not above the law.

If the police then want to know more you have the right to refuse to answer any questions without a lawyer. And this is the wisest thing to do.

In the Street - Grounds for Stop and Search

Under the Police and Criminal Evidence Act 1984 a police officer may stop and search someone who is reasonably suspected of carrying:

● illegal drugs
● firearms or other offensive weapons
● protected plants, birds etc
● adjuncts to terrorism
● stolen goods or instruments used in theft.

The 'reasonable grounds' must be more than just a hunch, and must apply to the particular individual. So even if 90 per cent of car thefts were committed by redheads that would not be sufficient reason for stopping a redhead who was walking peaceably down a street.

The procedure for stop and search is laid down in a code of practice, though code lacks the power of law. It says that, before carrying out a search, a police officer must identify himself or herself by showing his or her warrant card (an identity card, not to be confused with a warrant for arrest) and the suspect must be told:

● the police officer's name and police station
● the grounds for the search
● the object of the search
● that, having been searched, they can ask for a copy of the record of the search within a year.

In public, the police may only ask you to remove a coat or jacket and gloves. Further searches must be done in a van or police station. But - amazingly - if you are out of public view the police may go as far as a strip search (by an officer of the same sex) or even an intimate body search, *without having to arrest you first*. However, this can *only* be carried out by a doctor.

The aim of such searches must be to establish whether you are carrying anything which might do harm to yourself or to others, and a police superintendent must authorize the search. However, under the 1984 Act the suspect is not *obliged* to give a name or address and the police may not detain someone in order to obtain a name and address. After the search the suspect must either be arrested or allowed to leave.

Questioning

In law, there is no such thing as 'helping the police with their enquiries'. You are either under arrest or not. If you aren't, you don't have to go to a police station or say anything (apart from giving your name and address). But if you are a vital witness and you refuse to co-operate you could be said to be obstructing the police.

The key point to remember is that, since the tortures of the Court of Star Chamber were abolished in the seventeenth century, a central rule of British justice has been *the right to remain silent*. Nobody has any obligation to say anything (especially if it would harm them) - before, during or after an arrest. Only a lawyer can judge what can and can't be used in a court. So this right to silence should be used until your lawyer is present (see page 447). This applies during general questioning as well as after an arrest. Most of all, lawyers advise that nobody should *ever* admit to a crime, as they may be ignorant of some vital defence which may be lost if they admit guilt to the police. So if the police want to question you, a lawyer's advice is:

● answer *no* questions, except for giving your name and address, until you have seen a solicitor
● keep calm and polite
● don't attempt to bluster, swear or bribe
● if drunk or otherwise incapacitated, say nothing at all except your name and address until you recover.

Questioning of Children - see page 449

Questioning Mentally Ill and Mentally Handicapped

Everything above applies just as much to the mentally ill or handicapped as it does to other citizens. But, in addition, under the police code of practice mentally ill or handicapped people should not be interviewed or

This is guidance not gospel: before acting consult a solicitor.

asked to make or sign a written statement in the absence of an appropriate adult, i.e.:

- the person responsible for his/her care or custody
- the nearest relative
- someone not in the police who is experienced in dealing with the mentally ill or handicapped
- a responsible adult who is not part of the police service.

One of those people should make sure that a lawyer is present before anything is said to the police.

Arrest

The rules on how the police should treat someone who has been arrested are partly laid down in the Police and Criminal Evidence Act 1984 and partly in the police codes of conduct. When making an arrest a police officer must say that someone is under arrest and give the reasons for it - even if the reasons are obvious. They must say the well-worn words about the right to remain silent 'and anything you say ....'. But, they don't need a warrant for most offences. There is a list as long as your arm of offences, such as smuggling, indecent assault, treason and murder, which need no warrant. But the crime doesn't have to be so serious. You can be arrested, without a warrant, for:

- refusal to (or failure to) take a breath test
- obstructing a highway
- being drunk and incapable
- refusal to give a name and address when legally obliged to, e.g. after a car accident
- assault
- certain immigration offences.

On arrest you immediately have vital legal rights.

Your Rights on Arrest

- You can insist on seeing a solicitor in private. You can phone your own or there is a roster of duty solicitors, selected by the local Duty Solicitors Committee, who can be phoned. The police have the number to call and the solicitor's services are free. The duty solicitor may be a better bet as he will be up on criminal law, whereas your solicitor may not be.
- You can telephone a friend or relative (or at least ask for them to be told of the arrest).
- You can refuse to answer any questions (page 446).
- You may see a copy of the correct codes of police practice.
- You may keep all your property (pocket contents etc) unless it could be used for escape.
- The parents of anyone of 16 years or under must be told if their child is arrested (page 449).

Those legal rights can only be delayed by a very senior officer, and only then in serious cases, for example, when access to a phone could allow other members of a gang to be warned. However, the police normally question anyone they arrest, and they may do so as much as they wish - even though you have no obligation to answer. That is their job; silence is yours. They can also search the place where they arrested you, plus anywhere that you live or have a business.

Unfortunately, one of the travesties of British justice is that they may also search you - even if, as in refusing to take a breath test, the search could reveal nothing relevant to the crime. They may also take your fingerprints (however irrelevant) if you are over the age of 10 - and, if they need to, may use reasonable force in doing this. But usually photographs and intimate body samples (urine, blood etc) need written consent, and the samples must be taken by a doctor.

Detention

On arrest, the police must take you to the police station as soon as possible, and in most cases they can only detain you for 24 hours without charging you. For serious offences, such as murder, incest or manslaughter, senior officers can extend this to 36 hours. But they must give the reasons. Any extension is very rare, and can only be authorized by a magistrates' court - at which you can be legally represented. The maximum time you can be held without being charged is a total of 96 hours.

If the whole thing has been a dreadful mistake, or the police behave badly, you may be able to take a case against them for wrongful arrest, false imprisonment or assault. If it comes to the crunch, they can be politely reminded of this.

Charging

The police should charge you as soon as they can. This involves an officer formally reading out the crime you are charged with and giving you a copy, plus a notice of your legal rights. For most offences you would then be released and only come before the courts some months later. But if the police want you to be remanded in custody (i.e. imprisoned until the trial) they can hold you until the next sitting of the magistrates' court. They then have to show that you might leave the country or repeat the offence. Your lawyer will argue for release on bail. If bail is granted it may involve the deposit of money, but usually there are more basic conditions, like checking in at a police station each week.

Assault

Assaults come under the Offences Against the Person Act 1861 and tend to reflect the propriety of those times - which means the law offers more protection than you might expect.

Common assault covers any situation in which someone touches you in an unjustified way. So pushing or slapping are common assault and so is sexual harassment which involves touching or kissing. Common assault isn't a police matter, but you can take out a summons in a magistrates' court against someone who assaults you and that person can be fined, though courts don't like trivial cases.

Actual Bodily Harm

Actual bodily harm covers an assault in which bleeding or severe bruising is caused and this is a police matter. If it is reported to the police, an officer must take a full statement from the victim. If you are prepared to go to court and accuse someone of assault the police should arrest the person concerned. You don't need a witness, but it helps. Unfortunately, so few women are prepared to go to court about being beaten up by husbands and lovers that the police may be unsympathetic in wife battering cases. But any woman who is prepared to use her rights can speak to a senior officer and demand that the law be followed.

Defending Yourself

You may use 'reasonable force' in self-defence. The trouble is that nobody knows how much force is reasonable until the courts decide afterwards. Lawyers say 'use no more than you absolutely have to'. Many people believe that it is all right to use a weapon so long as it is not something *designed* to be a weapon. But, in law, *anything* can be considered to be a weapon if you use it as one. And if, in defending yourself with it, you injure someone the fact that you were not carrying it for that purpose is not a copper-bottomed defence. In practice, the court's decision over whether your force was reasonable will be linked to the provocation, on both sides, and the relative power of the opponents.

If you are attacked make as *much noise as possible* and don't play fair - *go for the vulnerable bits immediately, and hard* - and the police recommend a personal alarm. Many police authorities offer free instruction in self-defence.

Grievous Bodily Harm

Grievous bodily harm involves serious injury and is a police matter in the same way as is actual bodily harm.

Personal Safety

From the press you'd think that elderly women were the most frequent victims of attacks. In fact, some of the worst attacks are on young males, and I personally know of two incidents which resulted in young men, who were well able to defend themselves, being effectively castrated by the boots of gangs. So *nobody* should disregard personal safety. But, while being careful, it pays to seem confident - but not aggressive. Those who look afraid, and those who seem to ask for trouble, are equally likely to get it.
- Avoid walking alone after dark.
- Even with friends avoid dark alleys and lonely roads.
- On public transport keep with several other harmless-looking people.
- Don't wear jewellery where it shows.
- Remember drinking slows your reactions and makes you an easy target.

- Have your keys ready in your hand, so you can let yourself in quickly. If you hold them with the points sticking out through a clenched fist they also make an emergency weapon.
- If you have to walk alone, stick to the middle of the pavement and walk briskly, keeping alert to anything suspicious around you.
- Make life hard for bag snatchers by wearing shoulder bags diagonally, not swinging from your shoulder. And have the flap next to your body.
- Don't advertise the fact that you live alone: enter only initials and surname in the phone book and add an imaginary flatmate to name plates by doorbells.
- Don't invite peeping toms by dressing or undressing in sight of an uncurtained window.
- Keep a whistle and blow it into the phone if you get obscene calls.
- Don't drive with the door unlocked at night.
- Don't get into your car at night without checking the back seat.
- Keep a map so you don't have to stop to ask directions.
- Never give lifts to strangers.
- Don't hitchhike.
- When alone at night carry a personal alarm in your hand and be prepared to set if off. Polycell makes one which can double as an intruder alarm on a door or window - useful when travelling.

Bail

If someone is accused of a crime they can either be 'remanded in custody' - imprisoned until the trial - or released on bail. As remanding in custody is imprisoning someone before they have been found guilty this shouldn't happen unless there are good reasons for it. But in practice the system isn't always as good as it should be.

If a warrant is issued for an arrest the magistrate may put a note on the back saying the accused should have bail. In this case the police *have* to release the suspect after charging him or her, but without this they cannot do so.

Where there is no warrant it is up to the police whether they remand someone in custody or not. They can release them on 'police bail', but if the police refuse bail they must bring the prisoner before the magistrates within 24 hours (48 at weekends and public holidays). The magistrate must then grant bail unless the suspect has previously skipped bail, or the offence carries a prison sentence and any of the following applies:
- there are substantial grounds for thinking it will lead to another offence
- there are substantial grounds for thinking the course of justice will be obstructed
- there has been too little time to assess suitability for bail
- the case has been adjourned for a report to be prepared (e.g. a probation report).

If bail is refused, the magistrate must give her reasons to the accused in writing. The accused will then be held

This is guidance not gospel: before acting consult a solicitor.

in a remand prison and, although this is for 8-day periods, in practice these are constantly renewed until the trial. However, the accused can put forward changes of circumstances and, if bail is still refused, can appeal to the crown court.

The rules for children are different. The police must give bail to those under 14 unless they are charged with murder or manslaughter. And between the ages of 14 and 17 bail can only be denied if they are likely to break bail, defeat the course of justice, are charged with murder or manslaughter, or it is in their best interests.

Bail Sureties

There is no need for any conditions to be imposed or surety demanded, when bail is granted, but in practice they often are. It may be just reporting to the police every few days, or surrendering a passport, but often two people are required to stand surety for an accused. The sureties agree to sacrifice a certain sum if the accused does not turn up at court when required. This money isn't held by the court meanwhile, but the court will check on the person's ability to pay if the need arises.

Burglary

The first rule on burglary is that if you suspect one - either in your own or in someone else's property - phone 999. Don't feel you shouldn't bother the police - it is far less work for them if they can catch a burglar red-handed, and if it's a false alarm they understand. Unless you are very sure that you can tackle a burglar without danger to yourself leave him alone. But note (in writing if possible) every detail which will help to catch him - his description, car or motorcycle number, and so on.

However, if you think you can safely grab a burglar and hold him, you can make a citizen's arrest for this, as for any other crime. All you need do is say you are arresting him. You can use reasonable force in doing this and the rules for reasonable force are the same as for assault, but you have more right on your side if someone has invaded your property.

Children and Crime

At all ages children have the same rights as adults (see page 447), and legal aid is usually available. However, children under 10 cannot be prosecuted, though if they repeatedly behave illegally they may be taken into council care. Between 10 and 14 children can be convicted of crime, but only if the court can prove the child knew what it did was 'wrong'. At 14 children should know the law and can be convicted as if they were adult, and fined and/or sent to a detention centre, or put into care. A child is a 'juvenile' until its 17th birthday, after which it is essentially an adult so far as criminal law is concerned.

The questioning of those between 10 and 17 is a grey area, as the latest act lays down no clear rules. This means they are left to a code of practice. The code of practice says that their parents must be told as soon as is practicable and that a child must not be interviewed, or asked to sign anything, except in the presence of:

- their parent or guardian
- or a social worker
- or another responsible adult who is not a police officer.

The adult concerned should *always* make sure a solicitor is there too - even though some police give the impression that the child is sufficiently protected if a social worker is there. Social workers are not legally trained in criminal law. The only time when the code allows the police to question a child without such adults being present is when some harm might result if there was a delay. Children's fingerprints can only be taken at the age of 14.

What Can Happen to a Child

Children are tried in juvenile courts, which are special sections of the magistrates' courts, unless the case also involves adults. In that case they will usually be tried with the adults, but sentencing will follow the juvenile pattern. There is no set hierarchy of sentences laid down by law. But an informal one does exist and, in practice, persistent offenders progress up a ladder of penalties which are broadly as follows.

Police Caution

Police have discretion to let children off with a caution if they admit to the offence. But an innocent child should *never* admit to an offence just to avoid the embarrassment of a court case. In the long run the court case is far less embarrassing than a criminal record.

A curious side effect of a child being let off with a caution is that any victim of their crime may well lose the right to compensation.

Absolute or Conditional Discharge

If the court decides not to punish the child it can be discharged without any strings attached. Alternatively, the court can leave the child unpunished on condition that it commits no more offences for up to 3 years. If the child reoffends within that period, it can be punished for the original offence, as well as the new one.

Bindover

The parents of children of 14 to 16 years (10 to 13 years if the crime is homicide) can be told to ensure that the child will behave over a given period, the penalty for failure being a fine (surety) of up to £1000 if the child misbehaves.

Fines and Compensation

Parents or guardians can be asked to pay fines and compensation for their children's misbehaviour, and the children can also be fined. Children who fail to pay may be sent to an attendance centre.

Supervision Order

A supervision order appoints an official, such as a social worker or sometimes a probation officer, to 'assist and befriend' the child. And the order can last up to 3 years. Some supervision orders also have clauses about where

This is guidance not gospel: before acting consult a solicitor.

the child must live and ordering it to take part in certain activities for a certain period, or placing it under night curfew. This is sometimes referred to as 'intermediate treatment', being a half-way house between mere supervision and putting a child in care.

Deferred Sentence

If a child can produce evidence that it is turning over a new leaf (for example, it is starting a job or a course) the court may decide to pass no sentence until several months have passed, so that it can see whether the child really has reformed - and make the sentence suit the new situation. The sentence is deferred in this way for a set period of time.

Attendance Centre Orders

If an offence is in legal terms 'imprisonable', or if a supervision order has been broken, a young offender may be ordered to spend a certain number of hours each week at an attendance centre, often run by the police, where it is instructed and kept occupied.

Community Service

This is community social work for up to 120 hours, and it can be imposed on 16-year-olds convicted of an imprisonable offence. If a child breaks the order it can be fined up to £200.

Care Order

Children who commit an offence which could carry a prison sentence can be put into care. This takes the responsibility for the child out of the hands of the parent and puts it into the hands of the local authority. The authority then decides whether the child will be allowed to remain at home (rare), go to foster parents or a children's home, or be put in secure accommodation (effectively a prison unit attached to a community home).

The order usually lasts until the child is aged 18 and the parents have no direct appeal against it - although they can ask their child's lawyer to appeal.

The courts can also order that certain people do not have charge of a child. This is called a 'charge and control condition'.

Custody

The authorities see custody as a last resort, and it is only resorted to after a social enquiry report into what alternatives may be available. It involves sending the child either to a detention centre (the 'short, sharp shock') or to a youth custody centre for a time. Both are juvenile forms of prison but the regimes are different. Those over 15, of either sex, can be sentenced to go to youth custody, but detention centres are reserved for boys aged 14 to 20 on short sentences of up to 4 months. Youth custody can be for 12 months. Unfortunately, children waiting to be placed in a centre may be put into an adult prison for a short time while a place is found for them.

Children can get up to one-third remission for good behaviour.

Sentences for Grave Offences

If a juvenile is convicted of any offence which could carry a sentence of more than 14 years for an adult (e.g. rape, arson, murder) he can be sentenced, in a crown court, to a certain term in custody - which can be as long as a life sentence. These 'Section 53' offenders can be put into secure accommodation, youth treatment centres, youth custody centres or prison. But they can also live in ordinary community homes.

The law on children is different in Scotland from the rest of Britain. In Scotland someone is a child until they reach 16, and up to that age they can fall within the special Scottish system of 'children's hearings'. These hearings are conducted in part by a panel of ordinary people from the area trained to deal with children's problems, and take the place of juvenile courts. They deal both with children who have committed crimes and with those who need care and protection.

The Children's Legal Centre Ltd, 20 Compton Terrace, London N1 2UN Tel: 01 359 6251 - provides a free, and confidential, Ad and Inf service by letter or telephone (2-5 pm weekdays)for young people in England and Wales. It will also take enquiries from adults on issues concerning children, provided it is clear that the child involved would not object.

Justice for Children, 35 Wellington Street, London WC2E 7BN Tel: 01 836 5917 - advises on children and the criminal law and on child care issues.

Courts and Sentencing: A Guide for Young People and their Advisors, Children's Legal Centre

The Police Act: A Guide for Young People, Children's Legal Centre

Drugs

To possess, use or sell an illegal drug - such as cannabis, cocaine or heroin - is a criminal offence, no matter how small the quantity. It is also an offence knowingly to allow any prohibited drug to be kept or used on your property. So if friends start smoking hash at your party you are committing an offence - unless you try to stop them. It is also illegal to sell even small quantities of drugs which can be misused, even if you got them from a doctor.

Drugs are divided into different classes. Trading in Class A - which is used for drugs like heroin - carries the heaviest penalties. But the legal classes are *not* an indication of the dangers of using those drugs. Some of those in Class B are extremely dangerous.

Rape and Indecent Assault

Despite its publicity in the press, rape is a relatively uncommon crime. The law defines it as the 'unlawful carnal knowledge of a female by force or fraud against her will'. (A man can't rape a male; it is indecent assault not rape.) Carnal knowledge is taken to be penetration of the labia (the outer lips of the vagina) by a penis. Full penetration isn't necessary; near penetration may be enough. Penetration of any other part of the body may be classed as sexual assault. Sexual assault and penetration with objects is indecent assault and a serious offence - what follows still applies.

Some women feel it cannot be rape if the man is a

friend or relation, or an ex-lover. It can. A large proportion of rapes are committed by men whom the women know well. Even if a man has slept with a woman at some time it does not give him a right to force her to have sex for ever more.

Reporting Rape to the Police
If a woman wants to see the rapist brought to justice she should go to the police station *in the area in which she was raped, as soon as possible*, without washing or changing her clothes. Her appearance and all the physical traces left by the rapist are vital evidence. She is allowed to have a friend with her throughout her time at the station.

What Happens at the Police Station
She will need to be examined by a doctor, to get evidence of the rape, but she may ask for it to be a woman doctor or her own GP. She will also have to make a statement to the police, but may ask to return and do this the next day. More and more police stations now have special homely rooms and female officers for rape cases. As they may need to keep the clothes she was wearing, they also provide others for her to go home in.

Officially, neither the police nor the courts are now allowed to ask about irrelevant sexual history (except in an appeal case). But old ways sometimes die hard. So, if they forget this, she should remind them of this rule.

Help and Support for Rape Victims
There are Rape Crisis Centres all over Britain offering free, confidential support and help to rape victims. If they are not in the phone book the **Rape Counselling and Research Project & London Rape Crisis Centre** (P.O. Box 69, London WC1X 9NJ Tel: 01 278 3956, office, 01 837 1600, 24-hour helpline, RC, L, B) accepts calls from anywhere in Britain - reversed charge if necessary - and will give you the details of your nearest Centre, anywhere in Britain. Their people don't force victims to go to the police, but they will go with them if they want to, and also stand by them in a clinic or court. There are also Victim Support Schemes, which will send someone to be with a rape victim. The police will contact the nearest scheme if you ask them to.

Aftercare
The medical examination at the police station does not test for pregnancy or venereal disease. There is a pill which can be taken after intercourse to prevent pregnancy, but it needs to be taken as soon as possible afterwards, within 72 hours at the outside (see In Health). A VD check is also wise.

Searches
Phoney Policemen
Pretending to be a policeman is an easy way into someone's home. Even if someone is in uniform ask to see his or her warrant card: any genuine policeman should always carry one and should have no objection to showing it. It should carry the badge of the police district, a photograph, name and rank of the holder and a warrant number. It is just an identity document - a warrant for an arrest is quite different.

Police Rights to Search
Police may enter premises either because a householder allows them to or because they have a search warrant. To get a warrant they must convince a court that a serious offence has been committed and that a search will produce evidence. They are only allowed to force themselves in without a warrant when arresting someone for an offence, searching after an arrest, preventing a breach of the peace, saving life or recapturing an escaped prisoner. But if a search is unjustified and unauthorized the police are trespassers, like anyone else, and can be ejected and sued. But to be justified doesn't mean that you have to be wanted for an offence, or even linked to one.

To get a warrant the police must convince a magistrate that they have been refused access or have been unable to communicate with the householder. Once the police obtain a search warrant the owner of the property has no automatic right to be told a warrant has been obtained or to be present at the search.

If the police want to search your home without a warrant they must explain the purpose of the search, tell you that you don't have to agree and that they may take away evidence. Landlords shouldn't usually permit searches of their tenant's property without a search warrant, and police shouldn't search on this basis.

Limits to Searches
What the police do during the search must suit the reason for it. So, strictly speaking, they can't search for *people* in drawers, but they can look in cupboards. However, the law now entitles them to take *any* evidence related to *any* offence if they think it might be lost, concealed or destroyed (and they may retain it for use in a trial); the exceptions are items:

a subject to legal privilege (e.g. solicitors' letters)
b excluded under the Act (e.g. medical specimens, journalists' confidential notes)
c used in a trade, profession or position of office.

After any search the officer in charge must make a record of the search which will be held at sub-divisional police stations. Warrants must be returned to the issuing court and can be seen by the householder for up to 12 months.

Searches by VAT Officers
VAT officers can enter your business premises at any reasonable time and are allowed to inspect the areas used for the storage or supply of goods. If you are suspected of fraud, they may conduct a full search, similar to a police search, but first they must obtain a search warrant from a magistrate.

Vehicle Searches
Road checks can only be done by uniformed police, but

This is guidance not gospel: before acting consult a solicitor.

the grounds for vehicle searches are the same as for people, and written information on the reasons for the check can be obtained in writing within 12 months. An unattended vehicle can be searched, but the officer must leave a note to say it has been searched, who has searched it and that an application for compensation for any damage caused can be made to the police station.

Sex and Sexual Abuse

In law a boy cannot consent to homosexuality until the age of 21. At 14 he can be convicted of rape or unlawful intercourse if the girl is under 16. Girls and boys under 16 cannot legally consent to sexual intercourse.

The sexual abuse of children involves sexual activities *of any kind* by an older person to a child, and is a criminal offence. Children who are concerned about adults who behave in a sexual way towards them can make a free phone call to **ChildLine** on 0800 1111 and talk to someone who will understand. They don't have to give their name or address unless they want to.

Child abusers who want help should ask their GP if they can see a psycho-sexual therapist; they should not be asked to explain why. A local Rape Crisis Centre may have the details of a local incest or child abuse group.

The Incest Crisis Line, P.O. Box 32, Northolt, Middlesex UB5 4JS Tel: 01 422 5100 or 01 890 4732 or 01 593 9428 - gives support and advice to children or adults regarding sexual abuse of children, by anyone - not just relatives - and nobody is reported to any authority.

In Support of Sexually Abused Children, P.O.Box 526, London NW6 1SU Tel: 01 202 3024 - helps the non-abusing parent.

Kidscape, 82 Brook Street, London W1Y 1YG Tel: 01 493 9845 - has free leaflets, for parents and teachers on how to help children avoid sexual abuse.

Incest Survivors' Campaign, c/o AWP, Hungerford House, Victoria Embankment, London WC2 6PA Tel: 01 836 6081 - can put people in touch with survivor's self-help support groups all over the UK.

Mothers of Abused Children, 25 Wampool Street, Silloth, Cumbria CA5 4AA Tel: 0965 31432

Theft

Theft is defined as dishonestly taking somone else's property and intending permanently to deprive them of it (i.e. not just borrowing). If you suspect someone has taken something you can report it to the police.

Shoplifting

The shop needs to prove that you didn't intend to pay for the goods, so they seldom arrest anyone until they are out of the shop. But officious store detectives may take a change of department as proof enough. If you want to pick goods up and take them to a better light, avoid trouble by asking an assistant. If none can be seen, hold the goods high where all can see them. The elderly and absent-minded might find it safest to pin up their pockets, it is so easy to accidentally slip something into a pocket when you mean it to go in a basket - I've done it more than once when thinking of other things, and

had to go back and pay for them.

Store detectives have no special powers of arrests. They are only making a citizen's arrest and you have all the rights given under Arrest on page 446. You may also protest your innocence, and say you will sue the store for wrongful arrest if they pursue the matter.

But don't let them tempt, bully or persuade you into explanations if there is any risk of you saying the wrong thing. It is easy to be confused and intimidated by people in authority, but stand on your rights, ask to ring a solicitor and say nothing. You don't even have to give the shop your name and address. The policeman can hear the facts on both sides and decide whether to arrest you or not. But if you don't want to speak without a solicitor you can be taken to a police station where they *must* let you see one (see Arrest, page 446). This is safest.

The prosecution is usually brought by the shop, which means that if you're acquitted you can claim damages against the shop for malicious prosecution.

Crisis Counselling for Alleged Shoplifters, c/o NCPC, London NW4 4NY Tel: 01 202 5787 or 01 722 3685; after 7 pm ring 01 958 8859

Victim Support and Compensation

Anyone who has been a victim of crime and is finding it hard to handle can get help and support from members of their local **Victims Support Scheme.** The police have the number of the nearest branch and a member of the scheme will come to the police station to provide support, visit a victim at home, go to court with them, help with replacing vital documents, such as pension books, and simply let the victim talk. This is a free service manned by volunteers, with government backing. Members of the Scheme will also advise on compensation.

In theory, victims of crime can get compensation from criminals for loss and injury resulting from a crime of violence, theft or criminal damage. The reality is a little different. Since 1982 the courts have been able to order anyone convicted of such a crime to pay compensation to their victims. But the victims have to rely on the police or the prosecution asking the court for this. As victims aren't normally told that the culprit is going to be tried they can't usually tell either of these bodies that they would like to receive compensation - so they seldom get it. There are moves afoot to make courts automatically consider compensation in all such cases - so check whether they have just become law. Meanwhile, if you are a victim *ask the police to make a note that if they catch the criminal you want them to ask the court for compensation.*

Those who have suffered from a crime of violence may be eligible for compensation from the **Criminal Injuries Compensation Board.** The Board will only consider claims if:
- the criminal has been prosecuted, or there is good reason why they cannot be prosecuted (e.g. they can't be found or are insane or under age)
- the compensation would be over a set sum (£550 as I write)

This is guidance not gospel: before acting consult a solicitor.

- you reported the crime promptly
- you apply, in writing, within the time limit of 3 years from the injury.

Those who lose a husband, wife, or child under the age of 18, because of crime may also apply for compensation. So may non-relatives who paid the funeral expenses after a death from crime. Application forms are available from the **Criminal Injuries Compensation Board**, Whittington House, 19/30 Alfred Place, London WC1E 7LG Tel: 01 636 9501/636 2812.

National Association of Victims Support Schemes, 17A Electric Lane, London SW9 8LA Tel: 01 737 2010/01 326 1084 (RC)

Wildlife
The Wildlife and Countryside Act 1981 makes it illegal to:

- kill, injure, disturb, or take any protected species, such as badgers and red squirrels
- pick or uproot protected plants, or uproot *any* wild plant.

The lists of specially protected species are long, and range from moths to dolphins. Birds are divided into four groups: pest species, sporting birds, specially protected species and the others. The pest species are:

collared dove, crow, feral pigeon, herring gull, house sparrow, great black-backed gull, jackdaw, jay, lesser black-backed gull, magpie, rook, starling, wood pigeon

Only the pest species and sporting birds may be killed. All other birds are protected, and it is illegal to kill, injure or possess one, or to damage, destroy or steal from their nests.

As the lists in each category are long, the safest course is to harm nothing at all, and treat every plant and creature with consideration. Those who need to know the categories can obtain full details from the **Nature Conservancy Council** (page 331).

Witnesses
Although there's no legal duty, except in respect of terrorism, it makes sense to assist the police and report crime. If you offer to be a witness to a crime outside your area you can always give your evidence to your local police force, when the time comes. But you may have to go to court if the other side wishes to cross-question you, in which case your expenses will normally be paid.

Reporting Crimes
If you think theft is being committed:
1 dial 999 immediately - better a false alarm than an unreported crime
2 note the appearance and distinguishing features of the criminal
3 note the registration number and description of the vehicle used
4 keep watching.

Sources of Help
Justice, 95a Chancery Lane, London WC2A 1DT Tel: 01 405 6018. Campaigns on general issues of justice, and takes up some *serious* cases of injustice - mainly involving imprisonment. Useful publications on aspects of law.
Law Centres - see Organizations.
There are **Police Monitoring Groups** in many areas where relations between the police and the community are not smooth. Those who feel they are being victimized can talk to their local group - a local law centre can put you in touch.
Release (Legal Emergency and Drug Service) Ltd, 169 Commercial Street, London E1 6BW Tel: 01 377 5905. This is a national charity offering a 24-hour emergency service in relation to any legal emergency related to criminal law, or to drug problems of any kind. Its service is totally confidential and it has a list of solicitors all over the UK who are experienced in criminal law.

Your local police station will usually have a crime prevention officer who will come and advise on ways of protecting your property from crime and will know about any neighbourhood watch scheme which you can join.

DIVORCE AND SEPARATION

Divorce
If a marriage breaks down the law is no longer concerned with whom is to blame. There are several ways a marriage breakdown can be dealt with, and each has different effects. Only one rule governs them all: God is on the side of the big battalions (solicitors), and the most ruthless partner gets the best deal. Common sense, right and justice scarcely come into it.

To divorce you *must* have been married 1 year or more, but divorce no longer depends on one of the partners doing something wrong. The only grounds for a divorce are that the marriage has broken down beyond repair - 'irretrievable breakdown' as the lawyers put it. There are five situations in which the court may judge that a marriage is beyond saving, and if one of these can be proved the divorce usually goes through - whether the other person wants it or not.

1 The couple have been living apart for 2 years (or more) and both want a divorce.
2 The couple have been apart for 5 years and one partner wants a divorce. Almost the only grounds for preventing such a divorce are if a woman can show that she would suffer severe hardship - which may be the case if the couple are elderly and funds limited.
3 The husband or wife deserted the other at least 2 years ago. Oddly, this is one of the trickier grounds as, among other things, it involves showing that the partner who deserted did so against the other's will, was not justified in leaving and regards the marriage as dead. Also, any separation order automatically changes it from desertion into separation.
4 One partner has behaved in such a way that the other cannot reasonably be expected to live with them. This is a remarkably broad category. It covers

This is guidance not gospel: before acting consult a solicitor.

In 1, 2 and 3 'kiss and make up' periods are allowed to interrupt the years apart. But the rules are tricky. You can get back together as many times as you like during the 2 or 5 year period provided the *total* time, i.e. the occasions *added together*, does not exceed 6 months. But if they total more than 6 months you go back to square one and are not deemed to have been apart at all. Also, none of the time together is counted as part of the 2 or 5 years. So, if you get together for 3 months, during 2 years apart, you only qualify for divorce 2 years and 3 months after you first parted.

such things as refusing to have children, physical and verbal abuse, drunkenness, drug taking, gross financial irresponsibility and mental illness resulting in impossible behaviour. But it can cover almost anything which the particular person involved finds intolerable, including quite minor sexual perversions, incessant whistling or even non-stop DIY.

5   One partner has committed adultery and the other feels he or she cannot continue the marriage. Courts are remarkably lax in the evidence they require of adultery - it is often enough to prove inclination and opportunity. But if adultery is admitted the courts don't usually hold this against someone in the arrangements over money and the children - although gross examples of adultery may affect the final settlement. The law also allows the couple to live together for up to 6 months (either as a block or in scattered weeks) after the last act of adultery, to try to make it up, without losing the right to divorce under this clause. The partner sueing for divorce can ask the court to award costs against their partner and their lover.

Bringing the Case

When a marriage breaks down most people want to get the divorce over as fast as possible and put that part of their lives behind them. Natural enough, but not always wise. Even good solicitors tend to think of the immediate situation rather than discussing the ifs, ands and buts which may affect the rest of their clients' lives. So you need to be feeling cool enough to think through every detail yourself extremely carefully. Decisions made at this time can affect the rest of your life - perhaps disastrously.

Anyone who is upset by the situation should take as long as they legally can and let the distress subside before embarking on the actual proceedings and agreeing to anything. In your desire to get shot of the whole business you may agree to terms which are not to your advantage. Nobody should assume that the terms are only temporary, because they are bound to marry again soon, or let their solicitor assume that - as they tend to with young and/or attractive women. Life isn't that predictable.

The Cost of Divorcing

You can now divorce without using a solicitor. This looks like a cheap sensible option, and for some couples it can be. It would be misleading to try to explain the procedure briefly, but any county court has a free booklet called 'Undefended Divorce' which explains it. The Consumers Association book *Getting a Divorce* may also be useful. However, it is risky to try DIY divorce if a case is defended, if there are children, or if you want a financial settlement.

Divorce is expensive - and the more the couple fight over the details, the more it costs. However, I cannot state too strongly that it is *essential* to have a solicitor who is experienced in divorce, and the best that you can afford. Cynical though it may sound, if you may ever want a divorce, and need a lawyer for it, start saving now. The picture on legal aid for divorce is patchy. In principle, if your income and capital are below certain limits, you can use the Green Form Scheme to pay for the basic divorce (see page 481). Then if there is a dispute, for example about money, you use legal aid - here too there are income and capital limits, but they are different sums. In either case, the question is - will the lawyer you want do legal aid? The Family Law Act 1987 made it possible for the Rule Committee to set restrictions on legal aid fees. These may mean that very few lawyers in central London will be taking on legal aid divorces in future, but those in less highly paid areas will do better than before from legal aid divorce work. So your chances will depend on where you live.

Arrangements for the Children

In law, there are two parts to the business of caring for the children: legal custody, and care and control. The person who gets care and control (sometimes confusingly called 'actual custody') has the children living with him or her. Whoever gets legal custody (and it can be awarded to both parents) makes the big decisions like choosing their schooling, administering their property (if they have any) or vetoing an under-age marriage. The two responsibilities used to be routinely split between the parents, but nowadays whoever cares for the children usually gets legal custody too. However, the parent without custody does keep some rights. They may oppose the child changing its name, being adopted or going into council care.

If parents can't agree over who has the children the court can ask a welfare officer to investigate and both parents will be visited. The well-being of the children is the key concern in the court's decision - though little notice is taken of what the children themselves want unless they are in their mid-teens. They are usually given to the mother, but the older the children are, the more chance there is that the court will give them to the father, especially if they are all boys. Even with young children, it is not unheard of for fathers to win care and control and claim maintenance for the children from their successful wives. (They have, however, been less successful in claiming maintenance for themselves.)

The access to the children granted by the courts to the parent who loses the children is very variable. It

This is guidance not gospel: before acting consult a solicitor.

may be a vague order for reasonable access, with no definition of what is reasonable, or it may be so precise as to make it very hard for the parent to meet the terms. Precise orders tend to be made when one side asks for them. However, if a parent obstructs the access set by the courts, the courts can be asked to intervene. Unfortunately, some lawyers - who know very little about children - advise their clients not to visit their children. This can be very damaging indeed to the children. However hard it may be for the parent concerned, the access provisions should make it possible to keep up their relationship (see page 271), unless contact could harm the children.

Formalities

When a divorce is granted the court issues a decree nisi; the decree absolute can be applied for 6 weeks later and is normally granted automatically. The divorce is then final and you should obtain a divorce certificate from the divorce registry or the county court which granted the divorce. This proves the divorce.

Money Matters

On money there are no firm rules and nobody should take what follows as any guarantee of what will happen: *every case is different.* But don't be optimistic about the outcome. Divorce is easy; living on the money you have afterwards seldom is.

The application for maintenance can be made when the divorce petition is filed, or those who are separated but not starting divorce proceedings can apply to the magistrates' or county court for a maintenance order. The magistrates' court is very much faster, but the procedure is a little rough and ready. Wherever you go, this is an area in which natural justice and common sense scarcely enter the door. How much you have to live on - or pay out - will depend more on the skills of your lawyer, than on the merits of your case.

First, the 50/50 split is a myth. Some women do get away with murder, but in most cases the wife comes off badly. The courts have enormous leeway in what they award, but in practice they usually play safe and stick to precedent. Traditionally - though some lawyers think otherwise - courts have assumed that a woman needs less money than a man. The rule which they sometimes apply is the one-third rule. This means that the wife gets one-third of the *total* family income - i.e. her earnings and her husband's put together. Maintenance for the children may be added to that - but sometimes the woman is expected to keep herself *and* several children on that one-third. What's more, recent legislation says that women should be encouraged to return to work or to re-train in order to support themselves, even when they are also bringing up the children.

The new emphasis is on what lawyers call 'a clean break', in which a lump sum and/or property is awarded instead of maintenance. This has some advantages, but unless a wife paid for part of the home, she may end up with only one third of the value of that (unless the property is in their joint names). The final catch is that a woman who uses legal aid to fight for her rights has to refund the money, her case cost, to legal aid if she is awarded a lump sum above a certain size. This applies even though she may need that money to house herself and the children. If she is awarded any share in the property she must refund the legal aid whenever that property is sold. A woman should think carefully before accepting a lump sum, as possessing more than a set amount (page 484) would bar her from state benefits.

Tax rules for both payer and receiver also need careful checking. The 1988 budget made large changes. These apply to settlements made after set dates in 1988 - so it is not safe to assume you will be taxed in the same way as a divorced friend.

In some cases, a wife may be allowed to live in the family home with the children until they are 18 (upon which she may be homeless with no stake in the property market). But she is only likely to get this if she stayed in the house and the husband moved out. A tenancy will depend on the terms of the tenancy, but a council house can usually be transferred from one partner to another on a court order.

Money on Re-marriage

The wife's right to maintenance for herself ends if she marries again, and a husband can even apply to stop maintenance if she lives with a man (though in both cases the children's share will continue). A husband can also ask the courts to reduce the maintenance because of a change of circumstances, for example because he wants to remarry and support a second family. Equally, a wife can also apply for the order to be increased, but the court will always look at the joint income of her and her ex-husband, so if she earns money to pay the bills, while waiting for the case to come up, the courts can *reduce* the maintenance because she is earning more than she was when the maintenance was set - and this often happens. However, catch 22 is that failure to apply for an increase of maintenance, when you need it, can be taken as proof of being able to manage on what you get and make it harder to get an increase later.

Maintenance and Death

Maintenance ends on an ex-husband's death. So, although the ex-wife and children can apply for a share of his estate, it is wise (and less costly) to have a legacy to her and the children written into the maintenance agreement in the beginning. It may also be worth including clauses related to insurance. For example, a husband could undertake to pay insurance for the children's education (which will cover school fees whether he lives or dies), or to insure his life with his ex-wife receiving the proceeds if he dies.

Failure to Pay Maintenance

If a separated or divorced husband stops paying legally agreed maintenance the wife should immediately remind him, and send her lawyer a copy of the letter. If maintenance isn't paid there are several remedies. A magistrates' court can be asked to serve an 'arrears of maintenance summons', even if it is only a week late.

This is guidance not gospel: before acting consult a solicitor.

Then both sides have to appear before the court and the husband is usually told to pay up. If he defaults repeatedly an order for 'attachment of earnings' can be made, which means the money is taken out of his earnings, and paid to his ex-wife, before he gets them. But with some occupations a woman on low maintenance may need the court to make the maintenance payable to the DHSS. As income support normally makes up the difference between her income and the set level this means she gets income support every week from the DHSS whether the husband pays or not. But, if a large sum is involved the court can be asked to issue a 'judgement summons', in which the defaulter is brought before a judge. Failure to pay after that carries severe penalties, including prison. The same applies if a woman is paying maintenance to a man.

The Child Poverty Action Group, 1-5 Bath Street, London EC1V 9PY Tel: 01 253 3406 has leaflets on welfare benefits.

Separation

Until divorce proceedings a husband is legally obliged to support his wife and children. An informal separation in which the two simply live apart and agree matters, like maintenance and access to the children, is civilized and thrifty. However, there may be snags. For a start, the Inland Revenue may tax them as married, so until 1990 it could be cheaper to get a solicitor to draw up a formal separation deed. Divorce courts may use such deeds as the basis for future arrangements, so it is very important to make sure that no points are overlooked. For example, a wife should usually make sure she is paid maintenance - however little. If she renounces her right to it, in the deed, the courts may dismiss a claim for maintenance at the time of the divorce. And once a claim is dismissed by the courts she may *for ever* sacrifice her entitlement to it - even if her circumstances change dramatically. Equally, husbands should make sure there is a clause allowing the maintenance to be reduced if circumstances change - or he may never be able to reduce it. It may also pay to check the deed with an accountant before finalizing it, as the wording can affect the tax liability, even on the same sum. (This also applies to payments on divorce.)

When there are religious objections to divorce there can also be a judicial separation. There is no need to show that a marriage has totally broken down.

Both types of formal separation remove sexual rights and remove desertion from the grounds for divorce.

Annulment

Annulments are statements that the marriage was never valid, so a Roman Catholic should be free to marry someone else (provided the Church accepts the annulment). The main grounds are bigamy, that no sex took place - sex *before* the marriage doesn't count, lack of consent, mental illness, venereal disease, or pregnancy by another man at the time of the marriage. But children born in an annulled marriage remain legitimate, even if the marriage was bigamous - provided one parent did not know of the bigamy.

Divorce Conciliation and Advisory Service, 38 Ebury Street, London SW1W 0LU Tel: 01 730 2422 (10 am-5 pm weekdays) - helps to sort out problems between couples who are considering divorce, are involved in divorce proceedings or have been divorced. It also helps them cope with its aftermath, and assists in practical difficulties. For example, separated or divorced parents can sort out disputes regarding the children. The counsellors are not a substitute for a solicitor, but they can reduce the conflict. The service is totally confidential and a 1½ hour initial session costs about £20, though those who are unemployed or not earning may not be charged.

Families Need Fathers, BM Families, 27 Old Gloucester Street, London WC1N 3XX Tel: 01 467 8319 - was originally for fathers who had lost access to their children after divorce, but now helps both sexes.

Gingerbread, 35 Wellington Street, London WC2E 7BN Tel: 01 240 0953 is a self-help and social organization for single parents. The Scottish head office is at 39 Hope Street, Glasgow G2 7DW. Tel: 041 248 6840.

National Council for the Divorced and Separated, 13 High Street, Little Shelford, Cambridge CB2 5ES Tel: 01 254 2080 (after 5.30 p.m.) - gives companionship, support, and is interested in legal issues. The NCDS Trust may be able to assist in cases of hardship, RC, M£L, L, G, A, H, Ad, Inf, sae.

National Council for One Parent Families, 255 Kentish Town Road, London NW5 2LX Tel: 01 267 1361 - helps people cope with the financial and housing problems which may follow divorce, separation, the death of a spouse or becoming an unmarried mother. Advice is free and confidential. Campaigns Ad, Inf, L, B.

National Family Conciliation Council, 34 Milton Road, Swindon, Wilts SN1 5JA Tel: 0793 618486 - is a charity, with local offices, which helps couples resolve the issues which are disputed after a marriage breaks down, especially those concerning the children. In Scotland contact the **Family Conciliation Service (Lothian),** 127 Rose Street, South Lane, Edinburgh EH2 5BB Tel: 031 226 4507.

Principal Registry, Family Division, Room A44, Somerset House, London WC2R 1LP Tel: 01 936 6000 - will supply copies of a decree nisi or absolute to anyone.

Solicitors Family Law Association, (DX 54) 154 Fleet Street, London EC4A 2HX - is a group of matrimonial lawyers who feel it is better to keep conflict to a minimum in family law cases. They will put you in touch with members in your area.

Women's Aid Federation, PO Box 391, Bristol BS99 7WS Tel: 0272 420611.

Burgoyne, R. Ormrod, M. Richards, *Divorce Matters,* Penguin
Divorce: Legal Procedures and Financial Facts, Consumers Association
Which: Guide to Divorce, Consumers Association

DRIVING AND VEHICLE LAW

Drivers tend to feel that most motoring offences are trivial matters. But the law sees them as criminal offences, however trivial they may be. Where they differ from other 'crimes' is that, where cars are concerned, the law isn't concerned with whether you *intended* to commit an offence, only with whether you did so. Luckily, only major offences are put into the criminal records.

For some offences the police must warn you there might be proceedings against you, either at the time or within 14 days or issue a summons within that time.

(This does not apply if the offence played a part in an accident.) These offences are - ignoring certain traffic signs and police signals, most speeding offences, parking dangerously, careless or reckless driving, or aiding and abetting such offences.

Failing to produce documents or take a breath test can be an offence in itself. However, drivers have no obligation to say anything which will be to their disadvantage in an insurance settlement or a court case and, if they are arrested, they have the rights given under Criminal Law, page 446.

Accidents

You *must* stop if you damage another vehicle, a person, certain animals, or anything attached to the land in which the road is situated. If you want to remember which animals you must stop for, the AA suggests the mnemonic 'How Can A Man Drive Past Galloping Sheep' - i.e. horses, cattle, ass, mule, dog, pig, goat, sheep. On stopping you must then give your name and address and the vehicle licence number (plus the name and address of whoever owns the vehicle, if *you* don't) to 'anyone who reasonably requires it'. If someone has been injured you also are required to give your insurance details.

> Allowing an injured animal - of any kind - to suffer unnecessarily could lead to a prosecution for cruelty.

There is normally no need to report any accident to the police. But, if either side fails to meet all those requirements they must go to a police station in person, or to a constable, and report the accident as soon as possible - certainly within 24 hours - and produce any documents which they could not produce at the time. You have, however, 5 days in which to produce the insurance certificate. If the police come to the scene they may well prosecute for reckless or careless driving. The police are likely to require all the documents, as listed above, but in this case you have seven days to produce them.

> If you are involved in one of the accidents listed above and you neither stop and give details nor report it to the police it is an endorsable offence with 4 to 9 penalty points, a fine and possibly disqualification. For you to be 'involved in an accident' you don't have to be damaged. If your driving caused others to have an accident the law says you are still involved.

In an Accident
DO
Stop. Get the other car's licence number if it doesn't stop.

DON'T
Attack or abuse the other drivers.

DO
Take names, addresses, car numbers and insurance details of everyone involved in the accident.

Ask witnesses for their names, addresses, and comments, or note their car numbers.

Note the date, time and place of the accident, and the road widths.

Note *everything* that could have played a part in the accident - light, road signs, weather etc.

Take precise notes of all damage or injuries to all concerned.

Note the speeds everyone was travelling at.

Note whether those in other cars wore seat belts.

Note whether other drivers smelt of drink

As soon as you can, afterwards, write down everything that happened, *in detail*.

Report the accident to your insurance company (there is usually a time limit of 7 days).

DON'T
Apologize or admit guilt or blame.

Move the cars, unless they are causing an obstruction, until you have sketched or photographed all the details of the scene.

Make a statement to the police while you are still shaken up. What you say will be written down and may be given to the other side's insurance company. So just give them your name, address, car number, insurance details, driving licence and MOT papers. Then politely say you will make a statement later.

Call the police unless you want everyone concerned breathalysed - which most forces do automatically. But if an ambulance has been called the police will come anyway.

Leave it to your insurance company to claim from whoever is to blame. Write yourself.

What it costs you will depend on who is at fault. So say as little as possible, and write down as much as possible. However, not saying 'sorry' doesn't mean you have to be uncivilized. You can still express sympathy if you choose your words carefully.

Careless or Reckless Driving
The offence of dangerous driving has been abolished. The offences are now 'reckless', 'without due care and attention' or 'inconsiderate'. 'Reckless driving' is the charge when a driver deliberately, or unthinkingly, drives in a way which creates an obvious risk of injuring someone or damaging property. And you can also be

charged with 'causing death by reckless driving'. Recklessness applies both to the manner of driving *and/or* to the condition of the car. The penalties are heavy fines, 10 penalty points and possibly disqualification and imprisonment.

The term 'without due care and attention' is used when a driver departs from the standard of a competent and prudent driver and, for example, makes an error of judgement or fails to drive with enough care. This charge is often made after minor accidents. It usually leads to a fine and 2 to 5 penalty points. 'Driving without reasonable consideration' is a little-used offence.

Cycling Law

The law for cyclists is much the same as for other road users, and if they ignore a policeman's or traffic warden's signals, or disregard traffic lights or signs, they are in just as much trouble. In some cases, parents can be heavily fined for faults in their children's bicycles, the list of offences includes:

● riding with defective lights - or allowing a bicycle to be used with defective lights - at night or in poor visibility
● riding with defective brakes - or allowing a bicycle to be used with defective brakes
● riding on the pavement
● holding on to another vehicle
● walking a bicycle through red traffic lights (though crossing on a pedestrian crossing is allowed on foot)
● racing when not authorized
● carrying a passenger (apart from a child in a seat)
● failing to give way to a pedestrian
● selling or trying to sell a bicycle with poor brakes.

In addition, a bicycle must have a white light at the front and a red light and a reflector at the back if it is being used after dark. Offences can mean fines up to £1,000.

Drinking and Driving

Random breath tests are not allowed, but a police constable in uniform may stop any vehicle at random - for example, to check that it isn't stolen. Having stopped you for some other purpose, the officer can ask you to take a breath test if there is reason to suspect that you have taken alcohol. This also applies if you have committed a traffic offence while moving (not a parking offence) or been involved in an accident. There are several offences one of which is being 'in charge' of a vehicle while unfit through drink or drugs.

Incidentally, to be a 'driver' you must appear to have the intention of driving. This is a very grey area of law and intention can be widely interpreted. If you think you are too drunk to drive, don't decide to sleep it off in the car, the safest bet is probably to go home by taxi. However, the law is such that there is *nothing* I can tell you to do which will *guarantee* that you will not be prosecuted for drinking and driving if you have been drinking and came by car.

If you are asked to take a breath test it is an offence to refuse to do so. You just blow into a small device and it gives a pass or fail result. If you pass, that will usually be the end of it. If you fail, it isn't evidence of an offence, so you will be taken to the police station and tested on a machine which gives your 'score' on a print-out which both you and the police officer must sign. You must then be given a copy, or sent one at least 7 days before any trial.

The police *must* take two readings, on the machine at the station, and use the lower of the two. The legal limit is 35 micrograms of alcohol in 100 millilitres of breath, but the police *may* let you off with a warning if you have under 40 micrograms. If you are over 35 and under 50 micrograms, and the police intend to prosecute, you have a statutory right to have a blood or urine test as well, if you ask for it. You may take part of the sample to have it independently tested. If your breath registered over 50 micrograms you have no automatic right to such extra tests but they may sometimes be permitted. If these tests are done when you register under 50 micrograms their results are used in court and not the breath test's results. But if you registered over 50 in the breath test, that result is used and *not* any blood or urine tests - even if they are done.

How many drinks will put you over the limit will depend on a number of factors, including your size, weight, sex, state of health and how long you took to drink them. But you could be over the limit with only a glass or two. What's more, the police may prosecute *even if you are under the limit* if they feel your driving was affected by alcohol. They may also enter your home if you are a drink-drive suspect, especially if you have been in an accident involving injury to someone.

If someone has had a drink within the previous 20 minutes they should tell the officer and ask if they can wait a little before taking the test, as excess alcohol may be on their breath and make them fail when they would otherwise have passed.

Those who object to taking a breath test on the street, or cannot do so, will be arrested and taken to the station where they must then take a breath test. Those who cannot do this for medical reasons may be allowed a blood or urine test instead. If a medical problem would make it impossible to take a breath test it's wise to carry a doctor's letter stating the condition you suffer from. The legal limits for these tests are 80 milligrams of alcohol in 100 millilitres of blood, and 107 milligrams of alcohol per 100 millilitres of urine. You should be given part of the sample so you can have it independently tested if you wish.

> Refusing to take a breath test is an offence in itself: maximum penalty, disqualification for 1 year and £400 fine.

If you are convicted of drinking and driving, the magistrate has no choice but to disqualify you for at least a year; you can also be sentenced to 6 months in prison and up to £2,000 fine, unless special circumstances apply to the offence. So if someone binds you hand and foot, pours whisky down you, sits you in the driving seat and sends the car careering downhill

This is guidance not gospel: before acting consult a solicitor.

(as they did in a Cary Grant spy film) you could just hang on to your licence, but this isn't a get-out clause for those who will suffer hardship if they can't drive.

For a second offence within ten years the disqualification is for 3 years plus, possibly, up to 6 months in prison, and/or up to £2,000 fine.

> You can be convicted of being drunk in charge of a bicycle - and the fine is up to £400.

Drugs

Not only is it illegal to drive under the influence of illegal drugs, but it is now known that some medications may reduce someone's driving ability as much as alcohol. The law now says you must not drive under the influence of *any* drugs which might affect your driving. Check with your doctor whether it is safe to drive when taking any medicine.

Though it isn't an offence to drive when ill, doctors have discovered that someone with flu makes driving errors very similar to those made when seriously under the influence of drink. So you could commit a driving offence because you were under the influence of flu.

Driving Licences

The ages for driving licences are broadly these:

16 - moped, invalid carriage, small tractor, small mowing machine

17 - motorcycle, car, large tractor, small road rollers, commercial vehicle under 3·5 tonnes laden

18 - commercial vehicle up to 7·5 tonnes laden, trainee on a heavy goods vehicle (HGV)

21 - all other vehicles

Anyone may apply for a licence provided they can read a number plate at 67 feet in daylight - in glasses if they need them - and don't have any physical or mental disability which makes them unsuitable. Apply, using form D1 from a post office, to the DVLC address on the form. (For any other purpose write to DVLC, Swansea SA99 1AB Tel: 0792 72151.) The provisional licence entitles the holder to drive a car if there is a qualified driver with her and learner plates are visible front and back. Learners on two-wheel vehicles are restricted as to what cc and weight they may ride and have a limited time to pass the two part test. They should read the DVLC leaflet D100.

On passing the test, your licence is normally valid until you reach the age of 70. It must then be renewed every 3 years. At any time you *must* admit to any health problems which might make you unfit to drive. Those with non-British licences, or an international licence, may drive for one year continuously, before having to take a British driving test. But someone who holds a licence from the EEC, Australia, Gibraltar, Hong Kong, Kenya, New Zealand, Norway, Singapore, Sweden or Switzerland may be able to obtain a full British licence without taking a test.

If a policeman asks to see your licence you must either produce it immediately, or take it to a police station of your choice within 7 days - posting it won't do. Driving without a licence or while disqualified attracts a heavy fine plus penalty points.

Epilepsy

The rules on epilepsy are broadly these but check the details with the DVLC at Swansea (page 422).

Those who have had epilepsy may have a licence if they have been free of fits for 2 years or have had no fits *while awake* for the past 3 years. If they already have a driving licence when fits start it must be reported to the DVLC, in which case the licence will be withdrawn if fits occur while awake.

Insurance

As a motorist you must be insured at least against your liability for injuries to other people: third-party insurance. Heavy fines are imposed for failing to do this, plus penalty points, and possibly disqualification. More extensive insurance is optional. Sometimes insurance only covers a particular driver in a particular car, but your policy may cover you to drive other people's vehicles. It may also cover other people to drive yours. Check with your insurer if you don't know which type you have. Usually the wider the cover the more it costs.

Lights and Horns

All obligatory lights and indicators have to be in working order all the time - even if you never drive after dark. They must be used from half an hour after sunset to half an hour before dawn, and there are fines for breaches of any of the following rules.

- Dipped headlights should be used by day if the visibility is very poor.
- Side lights and rear lights must be used at night where there are street lights.
- Dipped or full headlights must be used outside built up areas at night.
- Fog lamps must be used when moving if visibility is seriously reduced but may not be used when stationary.
- Hazard warning lights may only be used when standing still.
- The rear number plate must be clean and illuminated.
- A reversing light must not exceed 24 watts and must have a European Approval mark if fitted after April 1986.
- There are strict rules on the exact position and colour of lights.
- A car may only be parked after dark without lights if:
  you are not within 10 metres of a road junction
  you are parallel to the nearside kerb (except in a one way street) and as close as may be
  the speed limit is 30 mph.
  Otherwise you must use side lights.
- Horns must not be used between 11.30 pm and 7 am.

Motorcyclists

On the whole, any law which applies to a car driver also applies to a motorcyclist, but there are certain differences.

- a moped up to 50 cc can be ridden at the age of 16 on a provisional licence
- a motorcycle can be ridden at the age of 17 on a provisional licence *provided the motorcycle is under 125 cc*
- a full licence can be obtained at the age of 17
- *both parts of the motorcycle driving test must be passed before a motorcycle of over 125 cc can be ridden.*

On top of that the following regulations apply to motorcyclists alone.
- Helmets are compulsory for both riders and passengers.
- It is illegal to carry a pillion passenger on a provisional licence.
- It is illegal to carry a passenger without footrests.
- It is illegal for a motorcycle to tow a trailer.

MOT Tests

Any private car which has been registered for 3 or more years must have an MOT certificate. The registration date is usually the important one, *not* the date of the road tax disc. The police may ask to see it, but if your vehicle is not roadworthy an MOT certificate is not a defence.

Parking

By a rather nasty quirk of law, you can never assume that you have a right to park on a public road unless there is a notice to say you can. The absence of yellow lines doesn't mean a thing - you can still be done for obstruction. There could also be local zoning laws and not knowing about these is no defence. Dangerous parking is liable to a fine, penalty points and, occasionally, disqualification, but most parking offences

only attract a fine.

However, the rules on when you *can't* park are these:
- double yellow lines along the road - no parking at any time (in practice)
- single yellow line along the road - no parking at certain times
- broken yellow lines along the road - restricted parking

Parking on a zig-zag by a pedestrian crossing is a serious offence, even if your car is only slightly over the end of them.

Bicyclists are not bound by the yellow lines, but they can still be prosecuted for a parking offence if their bicycle is on a traffic clearway, in a dangerous place, or on a footpath.

Penalties on Lent or Borrowed Vehicles
The 'registered keeper' of a vehicle is liable for any parking offences which attract a fixed penalty offence involving the vehicle. If someone borrows your car and commits an offence and you receive a 'statutory statement', complete it and give their name and address on the form. Also, get them to sign it before you return it, or you will be prosecuted instead of them. The exception is a hired car. Here the hirer or the hire company may be liable according to the terms under which it was hired.

Clamps
You can be clamped - in clamping areas - for most parking offences which could earn a ticket. To get a car unclamped you must go to the clamping station given on your ticket, pay a substantial fine and return to your car and wait for the van to come and unclamp you. Then you must remove the car. If you don't go back

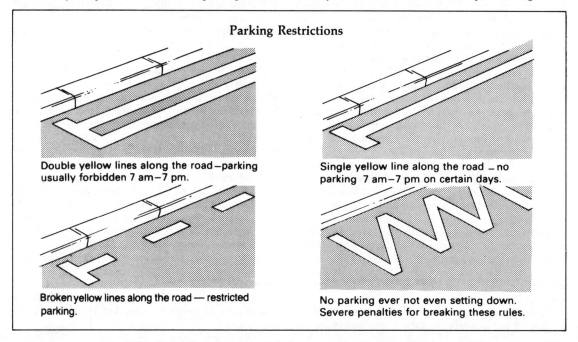

Parking Restrictions

Double yellow lines along the road—parking usually forbidden 7 am–7 pm.

Single yellow line along the road — no parking 7 am–7 pm on certain days.

Broken yellow lines along the road — restricted parking.

No parking ever not even setting down. Severe penalties for breaking these rules.

This is guidance not gospel: before acting consult a solicitor.

and drive it off, you can be clamped a second time. Those who could find this a frequent problem may find it worth joining the **Car Clamp Recovery Club** (P.O.Box 380, London SW1E 5EW Tel: 01 235 9901) which will go and pay a fine or move the car. But even members are charged for the service.

> Cars on meters should not be clamped unless the bay is suspended, the meter was 'fed', or the car has stayed 2 or more hours beyond the time paid for.

Meters
Motorists may not feed meters to add to their initial time, even if that was under the maximum time, nor move their car to another meter in the same group. Staying on a meter after the set time attracts an excess charge ticket and so does parking elsewhere in the same area of meters. Staying longer than the excess charge period makes you liable for a fixed penalty. Failure to pay a parking ticket within the set time (usually 21 to 28 days) or notify the authorities that you wish to contest it, means whoever owns the registration documents will be given 21 days to pay the penalty or request a hearing. If he does neither he will be charged the penalty plus 50 per cent, and administration costs.

Penalties for Breaking the Law

Endorsements and Other Penalties
Conviction for most motoring offences means an endorsement, which is reported to the DVLC at Swansea, plus penalty points. If you total 12 penalty points for various offences in 3 years you automatically lose your licence for at least 6 months unless there are special circumstances. However, someone who has previously been disqualified in the past 3 years will lose their licence for a minimum of 1 year, and two disqualifications will make it a minimum of 2 years. Most offences have fixed penalty points, but some are at the court's discretion. So it can be worth putting your case to the court. Remember, disqualification takes effect immediately. You may not even drive the car home. Fines can also be imposed for all offences, though the courts seldom impose anything like the maximum fine. Serious offences involving risk to others can land a motorist in prison.

Fixed Penalty Tickets
Fixed penalties have been standard for parking offences for a long time, but in 1986 their scope was widened. In situations where you would have been prosecuted before, you may now get a fixed penalty ticket. Basic tickets can be given by either a police officer or a traffic warden. Yellow tickets are given, only by a uniformed police officer, for offences such as speeding, for which a driving licence is also endorsed. You will either have to surrender your licence then and there or take it to a police station. If you are guilty you should pay the penalty within 28 days. If you were not guilty you can

go to court. But just forgetting to pay is expensive: failure to pay within 28 days raises the penalty by half.

Registration Document (Log-Book)
This shows who is registered as having a vehicle, the 'registered keeper', and who has had it before. This is not always the same as who owns it. If you sell or buy a car, or change your name or address, you must notify the DVLC *immediately*. If you own a car and want to know who owned it before you, the facts can be obtained from the DVLC (page 422) which has the records of all registered keepers.

Road Tax
If a car is on the road, road tax has to be paid for it - even if the car won't go. You may apply for road tax at the post office up to 14 days *before* the old disc runs out. You may drive to or from a *booked* MOT test without a tax disc. The tax disc must be displayed at the bottom corner of the windscreen on the nearside. The tax applies to that vehicle only, but if you sell the car before the time is up you can apply to the DVLC at Swansea for a refund - details are available from the post office. Late applications for road tax are always backdated.

Roadworthiness
The police can stop a car *at any time* to check whether it is up to standard on tyres, lights, steering, brakes and other aspects which could affect safety, pollution and noise. But, unless the car has caused an accident, the driver may insist that the inspection is arranged for some other time within the next 30 days.
- All brakes must work within set stopping times.
- The handbrake and steering must be properly adjusted.
- Windows must not be obscured - e.g. by dirt or stickers.
- Lights and reflectors must be clean and working.
- Horn, rear-view mirror, silencer, speedometer, windscreen-wipers, washers and seat belts must all be in good working order.
- The car must not be in a dangerous condition - bent metal could cut someone passing by.
- Any load must be secured so that it cannot be a danger or nuisance.
- Neither petrol nor petrol vapour may leak from the petrol tank - a suitable petrol cap is a must; rags won't do.
- Tyres must suit the vehicle they are on, have at least 1 mm of tread all over, be correctly inflated, be of the same type on the same axle, and have no cut longer than 2·5 cm, or 10 per cent of the tyre width - whichever is greater.

Penalties for breaking these regulations range from a fine to penalty points and possible disqualification for dangerous faults. But some police forces have vehicle rectification schemes in which a minor defect must be put right within a set time and a form to that effect signed by an authorized tester given to the station.

This is guidance not gospel: before acting consult a solicitor.

Seat Belts

It is compulsory to wear seat belts in the front of a car except when reversing; and it is *illegal* for a child under 12 months to sit in the front unless 'suitably restrained by equipment suited to its age and weight' - someone's arms are not enough. If children aged between 1 and 13 are in front and not wearing seat belts the driver can be prosecuted. Pregnant women and the disabled are not exceptions - unless they have an exemption certificate from a doctor saying they should not wear a seat belt for medical reasons. You can find other exemptions in the Motor Vehicles Regulations 1982.

Signs and Signals

- Twin unbroken white lines in the centre of the road - don't cross them even with one wheel, except when essential (e.g. to pass a parked vehicle).
- Unbroken line and twinned broken line in the centre of the road - you can cross if the broken line is on your side and it is safe to do so.
- Diagonal lines within broken lines - it isn't illegal to enter these but you are meant to keep out of them and should only enter them if you can see it is safe.
- A cross-hatched box at a road junction - don't enter it unless you have room to get off it on the other side (unless turning right).

These explanations are not as exact as those in the Highway Code: check it to know the full meaning.

Speeding

The possible speed limits are 30, 40, 50, 60 and 70 mph. If street lamps are under 200 yards apart the limit is 30 mph, unless you see some other speed sign. If the spacing is wider, or there are no lights at all, the limit is 70 mph on motorways and dual carriageways, and 60 mph on single carriageways, unless there is a sign giving some other speed.

For a speeding charge the police must follow you for 3/10ths of a mile, or use a radar check. They often caution for minor speeding, but conviction carries endorsement and 3+ penalty points, plus a fine.

John Pritchard, *The Motorist and the Law*, Penguin - an A-Z of all you need to know in readable form.
The Duffer's Guide to Motoring Law, the AA - a simple guide to basics.

EMPLOYMENT LAW

Conditions of Work

The laws on conditions of work vary greatly with the job, but in shops and offices the key points are these:
- The temperature should not be lower than 16°C (60·8°F) after the first hour - and there should be a thermometer with which to check this.
- There must be adequate ventilation (natural or by air conditioning) and no harmful fumes.
- There should be enough space. However, if you want to know how the law defines overcrowding, I can only refer you to the Offices, Shops and Railway Premises Act 1963, which sets out the rules for shops and offices in this remarkable piece of prose.

The number of persons habitually employed at a time to work in such a room as aforesaid shall not be such that the quotient derived by dividing by that number the number which expresses in square feet the area of the surface of the floor of the room is less than forty or the quotient derived by dividing by the first-mentioned number the number which expresses in cubic feet the capacity of the room is less than four hundred.

The punctuation is theirs; even the Department of Employment has been unable to explain the meaning.

Health and Safety Executive, Baynards House, 1 Chepstow Place, London W2 4TF Tel: 01 229 3456. HSE Publications: St Hugh's House, Stanley Precinct, Bootle, Merseyside L20 3QY Tel: 051 951 4381

Contracts

Any employee signing a contract with an employer is bound by it, but the contract can often be negotiated and adjusted before signature, so it pays to read the small print. Those who have no contract should usually be sent written 'Conditions of Employment' within 13 weeks of starting the job. (This does not apply to part-time and seasonal workers, or to certain jobs, such as public officials and inshore fishermen.) It is very important to check those conditions carefully as you could be bound by them, even if they are less good than they ought to be. The document should give the following:
- names - yours and the employer's
- job title - this need not include a description of the work
- pay-rate, how it is arrived at, and whether weekly or monthly
- hours of work - hours a day, days a week, overtime
- pension scheme - the details or how to learn about them
- sick pay - rules on sick notes, what sick pay you get and for how long
- holiday entitlement - length and pay
- notice - minimum period of notice to leave, on either side
- discipline - any rules, and what happens if you break them
- complaints procedures - who you can complain to if you need to.

Dismissal, Redundancy and Leaving
Contracts may state the minimum notice to be given on leaving or on dismissal. Failing this, the Employment Protection Act 1978 gives the following:
Employed under 1 month - no notice
Over 1 month under 2 years - 1 week
Over 2 years under 12 years - 1 week per year employed
Over 12 years - 12 weeks

The employee should be given written notice of the

reason for the dismissal, if he/she asks for it, but any employer may give wages in lieu of notice, and the rules do not apply if someone cannot work (for example, if in prison or seriously ill). The rules for giving notice to an employer whom you intend to leave are much the same, and in both situations the more senior the position, the more notice is expected on both sides. The rules of redundancy pay are complex but anyone made redundant should enquire about it, and a union representative should be able to help. But it must be claimed within 6 months.

Redundancy is normally considered a fair reason for dismissal - unless someone was unfairly chosen to be made redundant. But in many other situations dismissal may be 'unfair' in law - if you have been employed for 2 years or more. If someone feels they have been unfairly dismissed they can take their case to an industrial tribunal. If the dismissal is judged to be unfair the possible solutions are to - get the job back, be given another job instead, or be paid compensation. Dismissal is not limited to telling someone to go; if an employer behaves in such a way that the employee has to leave this is still dismissal.

Time Off

In industries which have wages councils minimum holidays with pay are laid down. For other industries there is no legal minimum, but - if it comes to it - courts accept that an employee can take a holiday, with pay, of whatever length is normal in that industry. Paid time off is also allowed for union activities, and for civic duties such as sitting on a local council.

Disabilities and Handicaps

Those who choose to register as disabled may be employed under the disabled quota. This says that in a company employing 20 people or more 3 per cent of the jobs must be given to the handicapped. Employers can get special exemptions, for example, if it would be too dangerous. But if a handicapped person feels they have been refused a job because of the handicap they have no legal right to fight the discrimination. For, though there are laws against sex and racial discrimination, we do not yet have a law against handicap discrimination.

Discrimination

The Race Relations Act 1976 made it an offence to treat someone unfavourably because of their race, colour or origins. The Sex Discrimination Act 1975 did the same for both sexes. This means that an employer may not advertise a job in a way that bars any race or sex. Nor may jobs, promotion, housing and so on, go to people because they are (or are not) a particular race or sex. In interviewing people, questions may not be asked of a woman which would not be asked of a man - for example, do you intend to have babies? It is also illegal to treat any race or sex less well than another as regards goods and services.

However, the law does not make *all* sexual and racial discrimination illegal. It is still legal to discriminate in all areas not specifically covered by the acts. For example, verbal abuse is not covered and the acts specially allow discrimination in certain circumstances. For example, racial and sexual discrimination are allowed in jobs in private houses (so nobody is obliged to have a male nanny or a female butler), and sexual discrimination is allowed in businesses employing less than 5 people. Where sex or race is in itself a qualification for a job, discrimination is also allowed. So you *can* insist on a girl modelling women's clothes or a black actor playing a black part. Private clubs may also discriminate in some circumstances, and so may someone letting or selling part of a house in which they or a near relative live.

The Equal Pay Act 1970 lays down that both sexes must receive the same pay for the same work, or for work of equivalent value.

Breaches of these acts aren't handled by the police. If the acts are broken the person who has been discriminated against has to bring a civil complaint, and there are time limits. A case related to sexual discrimination must be started within 3 months if it relates to employment, and 6 months for other areas.

If you have to bring a prosecution under these acts the Commission for Racial Equality and the Equal Opportunities Commission will advise, assist and even represent you in court. And both have forms on which the initial complaint can be set out, and booklets explaining the acts in detail. CAB, law centres and trade unions may also help. Cases not connected with employment can get legal aid (means tested) and in some cases the commissions or trade unions may assist financially.

Commission for Racial Equality, Elliot House, 10-12 Allington Street, London SW1E 5EH Tel: 01 828 7022

Equal Opportunities Commission, Overseas House, Quay Street, Manchester M3 3HN Tel: 061 833 9244

Industrial Tribunals

Industrial tribunals cover such problems as:
- unfair dismissal
- rights related to employment protection
- redundancy pay and rebates from redundancy funds
- maternity rights
- equal pay and conditions for women
- sexual or racial discrimination
- complaints relating to health and safety at work
- rights to pay during lay-offs
- lack of union notification regarding the transfer of undertakings
- exclusion or expulsion from a trade union
- certain aspects of compensation.

The Department of Employment leaflet 'Industrial Tribunal Proceedings' gives full details of what complaints can be heard by a tribunal and gives a simple step-by-step account of each stage. It should be read before applying, as what follows is only a general outline of the procedure. For most cases, the application must be made within 3 months of the offence. However, if the case is being taken through the Equal Opportunities Commission or Commission for Racial Equality, the limit may be 6 months.

Application forms for a hearing by a tribunal are found in Jobcentres, Unemployment Benefit Offices and CAB, and the latter may be able to help you with the application. Either the Equal Opportunities Commission or the Commission for Racial Equality may help with cases in their field. Applications should be sent to the London office, which will forward them to the right regional office. The system in Scotland is almost identical.

The Procedure
A copy of the application for a hearing is sent to whoever the case is being brought against and they receive a form on which they must say whether they will fight the case, and on what grounds. This form must be completed and sent in within 14 days - but if there are good reasons why this was impossible a tribunal may accept it later. If it is not sent in at all you may not usually appear at the hearing, but you are still allowed to settle the case with the applicant before the hearing.

Most cases are sent to the Advisory Conciliation and Arbitration Service before the hearing, and through them a settlement may be reached without a hearing.

The Hearing
Notice of the date is given at least 14 days before and if either side is unable to attend they must tell the tribunal office immediately. A new date may be fixed if there is a good reason for it.

The procedure is informal but like that in any court. Each side may call witnesses and may question both their own and the other side's witnesses, and the tribunal may question all concerned.

Either side may put their own case to an industrial tribunal, but if they want someone to speak for them they can ask a trade union representative or a solicitor to do so. Anyone who needs a solicitor should get the leaflet 'Legal Aid for Civil and Criminal Cases', free from Jobcentres etc (as above), as they may be entitled to aid.

If whoever brings the case is not happy with the outcome he or she may appeal provided there is a point of law which justifies this. The appeal must be made within 42 days to the Employment Appeals Tribunal of the High Court; if that fails you may go to the Queen's Bench Division of the High Court, and from there to the House of Lords.

Central Council of Industrial Tribunals (England and Wales), 93 Ebury Bridge, London SW1 Tel: 01 730 9161/2/3/4/5/6/7
Central Office of Industrial Tribunals (Scotland), St Andrew House, 141 West Nile Street, Glasgow G1 2RU Tel: 041 331 1601 8 am-5.30 pm (admin) 10 am-5.30 pm (court)

Maternity Leave and Allowances
A woman cannot be sacked because she is pregnant. If this seems like the reason for losing your job contact the Equal Opportunities Commission at once (see page 463).

Time Off
All women are allowed paid time off for antenatal care - even part-timers and those in new jobs. But they should tell their employers when they will need to be absent, and show them a certificate proving the pregnancy. However, taking time off for antenatal *classes* is a grey area. It isn't an automatic right, but refusing a woman time for them could be a matter for an industrial tribunal. If this is a problem talk to a law centre or the NCCL (see Organizations). Fathers have no statutory right to time off for the birth, but some employers make it part of the contract.

Alternative Work While Pregnant
If a woman can't do her normal work because she is pregnant (for example, it's too heavy for her) she only has a right to be given another job which is more suitable if she has worked at least 8 to 16 hours a week for the employer for 5 years or more. Or she has worked full-time for the employer for 2 years or more.

Statutory Maternity Pay
Women can also apply for Statutory Maternity Pay (SMP) - which replaces the old Maternity Pay and Maternity Allowance. Key qualifications are:
- you have been employed with the company for at least 6 months by the end of the 26th week
- you earned enough in the last 8 weeks, before entitlement, to pay National Insurance contributions.

There is a flat rate, but if you have been with an employer for 2 years full-time or 5 years part-time you can get up to 90 per cent of your normal pay for the first 6 weeks. Tax and National Insurance are deducted as usual. It is paid for:

6 weeks before the birth
plus 7 weeks after the birth
also for 5 weeks before or after, or split between both periods
_____
Total 18 weeks

To get it: write to your employers at least 3 weeks before you intend to stop work asking for SMP and enclosing your maternity certificate - Form MAT B1. *Write on time, even if you don't have the form;* late claims may be *too* late. Read the DHSS leaflet 'Babies and Benefits'.

> If the pregnancy lasts 28 weeks you are still entitled to SMP after the birth, even if the baby was stillborn. But you may not take SMP from one employer after having started work for another.

Maternity Allowance
Maternity Allowance is paid at a flat rate per week to the self-employed and to those who lost out on SMP because of job changes. It is paid from 11 weeks before

the birth and you can only claim it if you have been paying National Insurance contributions for 26 weeks out of 52 in the period ending 15 weeks before the baby is due. Claim it from 11 weeks before the birth from the social security office.

Badly off women who are not working may be able to get a lump sum Maternity Payment before the birth.

Returning to Work After a Baby

Under the Employment Protection (Consolidation) Act 1978, if you left work to have a baby you can take up to 40 weeks' maternity leave (from 11 weeks before the birth to 29 weeks after), and then get your job back, provided *all* the following conditions apply.

- The company employed 6 or more people when you left.
- You have worked for the same employers for at least 2 years by the end of the 12th week before the baby is due (5 years if you work less than 16 hours a week).
- You work at least until the 12th week before the baby is due (weeks are whole working weeks including Friday).
- You tell your employer *in writing* that you intend to return after the birth, and send the letter 3 weeks before you leave (if you suddenly have to stop work for medical reasons you just have to write to the employer the instant you can).
- You confirm the intention to return in writing 7 weeks after the baby is due (or, the employers may write to you from 7 weeks after the birth asking if you plan to return; if this happens you have only 14 days in which to reply).
- You return within 29 weeks of the birth, having given at least 3 weeks' warning to the employer.
- You give at least 3 weeks' warning of the exact date you intend to return.

Since these letters are vital at least get 'proof of posting' from the post office.

A 4-week period of grace is allowed on either side. So, if your employer isn't ready to have you back, your return can be delayed for up to 4 weeks. And if you are not well you can delay your return for that time - *with a medical certificate* - without losing your rights.

> If you don't know whether you will want to return or not guard your options by following the procedure for keeping your job, but notify your employer the instant you decide you don't want it.

On Your Return

On returning, you must have the same pay and conditions as before - including any pay rises which have occurred in your absence - but not necessarily the same job. But the time you were away from work doesn't count as part of your total time in employment when a pension is calculated.

Rights of Women, 52-54 Featherstone Street, London EC1Y 8RT Tel: 01 251 6577 - is a feminist organization, campaigns and advises on women's rights.

Patents

Whether you are entitled to patent an invention may well hang on how closely it is connected with your work. If you are in a 'position of special responsibility' in a company (linked to the invention) or invent something as part of your normal work, the patent rights will usually lie with the employer. But the employee can ask for a financial deal if the company is likely to benefit considerably.

In other situations, a patent can be granted by the Patent Office to anyone who devises a new product or manufacturing process, or an improvement on an existing one, which is unknown in Great Britain or elsewhere. The patent gives the holder the sole right to make or sell his or her invention for 20 years from the filing of the patent application. But there are certain limitations on what can be patented. Fleming couldn't patent penicillin because it was a discovery not an invention but, ironically, the Oxford team which devised a way of isolating and storing the drug could, and did. Another oddity is that an invention doesn't have to be able to work at the time of patenting: Whittle's jet engine couldn't work when he patented it, but it was capable of working *in principle.*

It is also possible to register designs - for example, a greeting card or a new style of telephone - but to be registered the design must be new and original. Trade Marks can also be registered. However, there is no copyright registration. So if someone wants to prove that they were the author of a particular piece of writing at a certain time they should post a copy of it to themselves by registered post and leave the envelope unopened. Or they can deposit it, in a sealed envelope, with a bank or solicitor and get its acceptance dated on their records. However, there is no copyright to a title or name. I could call this book *Mrs Beeton's Household Management* if I wished.

Institute of Patentees and Inventors, Suite 505a, Triumph House, 189 Regent Street, London W1R 7WF Tel: 01 242 7812 - assists inventors in furthering and patenting inventions and sends a bulletin of new patents, available for development, to industry. M£H, M, meetings.

The Patent Office, State House, 66-71 High Holborn, London WC1R 4TP Tel: 01 831 2525 - has clear leaflets on all aspects of these issues.

Pay

Since the Wages Act 1986 nobody has a *right* to be paid in cash. Whether payment is in cash or by some other method is something which the employer and employees must agree on. They must also agree whether it is weekly or monthly, and agree upon any fringe benefits - and there are no longer legal restrictions on payments in kind to manual workers.

Deductions

All employees must be given itemized pay statements

which show the total earnings, all deductions and the sum paid after deductions. The normal deductions are tax and national insurance, but in some jobs deductions may be made if the employee causes losses (e.g. the till is short or something is broken). In most situations deductions for loss or damage can only be made by an employer if:

a   they are written into the employment contract and the contract, or an explanation of it, was given to the employee before the deduction

or

b   if the employee agreed to them in writing before they were made.

However, there are special situations in which this is not the case, and the law limits the amount which can be deducted, in this way, from the wages of certain types of worker.

Any dispute over deductions or payments which can't be resolved can be taken to an industrial tribunal within 3 months of the payment or deduction being made. In the case of a series of incorrect payments or deductions, this must be 3 months from the last in the series. An employee may also be able to take an employer to court for breach of contract.

Low Pay Unit, 9 Upper Berkeley Street, London WIH 8BYT Tel: 01 262 7278 - information for those on low pay, and their rights.

Sexual Harassment

Sexual harassment is difficult to define but fundamentally it is behaviour of a sexual nature which is unwanted, unreciprocated and causes distress or serious embarrassment. The Equal Opportunities Commission (page 463) is the main organization which advises and helps women with this problem. They like women to contact them fairly early on, but their general advice is this.

● Tell the man to stop doing it - so he cannot claim that you wanted his attentions - and if possible do this in front of a witness.
● Talk to your female colleagues about it - he may be doing it to everyone, but only when each of you is alone. It will be less distressing if you don't feel a sole victim and it is easier for a group of women to put a stop to it.
● Keep a note of each incident, giving what happened and the date.(Don't rely on your memory; notes at the time are better evidence.)
● If necessary, talk to your employer about it.
● If the harassment reaches a pitch which would be sexual assault it is a police matter, and the sooner it is reported to the police the better.

Women Against Sexual Harassment (WASH), 242 Pentonville Road, London NI 9UN Tel: 01 833 0222 deals with queries on this subject. RC, B, Ad, Inf, L.

Trade Unions

When someone joins a union he becomes legally bound by the rules of the union - even though nobody may

bother to show him the rule book. But unions cannot treat their members in a way which is clearly unjust, even if the rules permit it.

Closed Shop
Nobody can be forced to join a union. But employers may legally have an agreement with a union whereby only members of that union are employed. However, this closed shop agreement *must* be voted for by a majority of the staff of the company, and this vote re-taken every 5 years. When a closed shop agreement *is* in force, anyone can be refused a job if they fail to join the union, or lose their job if they are expelled from the union. But there are certain exceptions. Someone can refuse to join if:

● They are already an employee when a union-management agreement is made, or when a new union-management agreement comes into force.
● They have a sincere objection to trade union membership in general, or to membership of the union in question.

Anyone expelled from a union when a closed shop is operating can complain to an industrial tribunal within 6 months. If unfair treatment is proved, they may receive substantial compensation, or the union may be compelled to accept them. But dismissal for non-membership of a union is now unfair dismissal in all circumstances.

Elections
All members of the principal executive committee of a union must be elected by secret ballot and submit to regular re-elections.

Picketing
Picketing is legal provided it only uses peaceful persuasion to try and stop others entering the workplace. But this doesn't mean pickets may break other laws. They may not, for example, obstruct the highway or commit assault. Only 6 people may be on a picket at once and they may only be:

● employees
● ex-employees who lost their job through the strike
● full-time union officers of the relevant union representing those employees.

Strikes
● All ballots to decide on strike action must now be a secret ballot.
● Anyone on strike loses his or her right to be paid. But there is no guarantee that striking workers will get strike pay from their union. It usually depends on whether or not the strike is official, whether the union decides to offer strike pay, and whether it can afford to do so.

★ The issue of money is worth checking before agreeing to strike, since unemployment benefits are not payable to those on strike.

This is guidance not gospel: before acting consult a solicitor.

More information

Companies House, 55-71 City Road, London EC1 Tel: 01 253 9393 - Companies are registered with the Registrar of Companies and the details of any registered company can be obtained from the addresses above for a small fee.

Companies Registration Office, Crown Way, Maindy, Cardiff CF4 3UZ Tel: 0222 388588 Postal Search Section: 0222 380107

Registrar of Companies, 102 George Street, Edinburgh EH2 3DJ Tel: 031 225 5774 - for Scottish companies.

FAMILY LAW

Abduction

It is a criminal offence to try to take a child abroad when you have no right to do so, but once a child is out of British territory it is extremely hard to get him or her back. So prevention is essential. A parent who believes someone may try to do this can ask the police or Home Office to alert all ports and airports: contact C2 Division, 50 Queen Anne's Gate, London SW1H 9AT Tel: 01 213 3102 or 5185.

If a child has already been abducted, the **Foreign and Commonwealth Office Consular Department** (Room 605, Clive House, Petty France, London SW1H 9HD Tel: 01 271 3000) can advise you on what to do. Gingerbread has a group for parents in this situation called the **Children Abroad Self-help Group,** Keighley Gingerbread Advice Centre, 33 Barlow Road, Keighley BD21 2EU Tel: 0535 669752.

Abortion

In England, Scotland or Wales, it is a criminal offence for anyone other than a doctor, or a nurse under his supervision, to cause an abortion. But a pregnancy may be ended, before the 28th week (in practice earlier - see In Health), if two doctors agree that:

1 The mental and physical risk to the mother and her existing children is greater if the pregnancy is continued than if it is ended.

or

2 There is substantial risk that the child will be severely handicapped mentally or physically.

It is not essential to get the father's consent, but the parents of a child under the age of 16 should be consulted. In Northern Ireland abortion law is altogether stricter.

Artificial Insemination by Donor (AID)

Although AID is legal, the law says the baby should be registered as illegitimate - 'father unknown'. There are moves to change this, but meanwhile the husband should be careful to *name* the child in any will, since the term 'my son/daughter' may not be valid. However, the illegitimacy can be 'erased' if the father adopts the child, and a new birth certificate can then be issued. The birth certificate can take two forms. In its long form it shows the child is adopted, but the short version does not (see page 468).

Birth Registration and Certificates

A child's birth must be registered by the set time (page 469). To do this either parent simply goes to the Registrar of Births, Deaths and Marriages and gives them the details of the child, and of both parents - no proof of the birth is necessary. However, if a child is illegitimate both parents must go along if both want their details to appear on the certificate, or the father must send a sworn testimonial. Otherwise the mother registers the birth and only her details appear.

> Babies are registered in the area where they are born. But this can be done via another office if it is more convenient. One nice quirk is that babies born on planes are registered via the Civil Aviation Authority and those born on ships via the Registrar of Shipping and Seamen in Cardiff.

Adopted Children's Certificates

Since the Children Act 1975 adopted people over 18 have had the right to apply to the Registrar General to obtain a copy of their original birth certificate which includes:
- their mother's (and possibly their father's) name, and occupations
- their date and place of birth
- their mother's address at the time.

Those adopted before 12 November 1975 must see a social worker first, but those born after that date are not obliged to do so - though they may if they wish to. The job of the social worker is largely to explain to the adopted child the problems of their birth-parents who believed they would never be able to be contacted after the adoption.

The first step is to obtain an application form from **The General Register Office** (OPCS, Segensworth Road, Titchfield, Fareham, Hants PO15 5RR - an odd address, but correct). The form asks for all the details of the adoption and allows applicants to choose where they would like to see the social worker, if this applies. At the interview they will be given the basic facts, but a birth certificate has to be bought for the standard fee afterwards.

National Organization for Counselling Adoptees and Their Parents (NORCAP), 3 New High Street, Headington, Oxford OX3 7AJ Tel: 0865 750554 - offers self-help counselling for adoptees over 18, adoptive parents and those who have given a child for adoption. Advises adoptees on tracing their original parents. Pressure group for computerized adoption register allowing birth parent/adoptive parent exchange of medical and other non-identifying information, RC, M£L, M, sae.

Copies of Birth, Marriage or Death Certificates

The cheapest way to obtain a birth, marriage or death certificate is to apply to the Superintendent Registrar in the area where the registration took place. That way it costs only about half as much as from the General

This is guidance not gospel: before acting consult a solicitor.

Register office, and is usually much quicker. If you know the area you can find the address of its superintendent from 01 242 0262. If you don't know the area you will have to apply to the **General Register Office** (St Catherine's House, 10 Kingsway, London WC2B 6JP Tel: 01 242 0262), but you can pay a reduced fee and search for it yourself. Either way, you need to give the person's surname, first names, date and place of birth, the father's names and the mother's name and maiden name. A certificate can be either short or long - the latter having more information and costing more.

Family Trees
Those trying to trace a family tree can get a leaflet on what facilities are available from the **Office of Population Surveys and Census** at the above address.

Children

Adoption and Custodianship
The law on adoption was tidied up by an Adoption Act which came into force from 1987. To adopt a child in Britain your home must be in Britain, but this includes those who are not British but live here permanently and British people temporarily overseas. Married couples adopt jointly but if a couple are just living together only one of them may adopt the child - and would keep it if they split up. Someone single may also adopt. Adoption gives the adopters full parental rights and responsibilities for a child, and they must be over the age of 21. If you are related to the child or obtained it through an adoption agency you can obtain an adoption order once the child has lived with you for 3 months; otherwise it is 12 months. If you are considered suitable, and the parents don't veto the adoption, the court will make either an interim order or an adoption order. The adoption order makes you the adoptive parent immediately. The interim order means the child can stay with you for the next 2 years, but you must apply again for an adoption just before that time runs out. All adoptions *must* be done via an adoption agency. The only exceptions are for close relatives, those who have fostered a child for over a year, and those adopting a child from outside Britain. Even these cases must notify their local authority. But, once an adoption order is through, the child is as much yours as if you had given birth to it (see also page 264).

Since 1985 there has been an alternative to adoption called custodianship. This gives someone all the rights of 'legal custody', which means the child can live with them, and be looked after and brought up by them, and they can make all the decisions about its health and education, and even consent to its marriage. If a foster parent gets custodianship the child is no longer in the care of local authority and the local authority cannot make decisions about its welfare - though it can pay a custodianship allowance.

Although being a custodian has many of the rights and duties of a parent, there are the following limits:
● he can't arrange for the child to emigrate
● he may need to get permission even to take the child on holiday abroad
● he cannot change the child's name
● he cannot decide the child's religion
● he has absolutely no right to the child's property
● the natural parents remain the legal parents of the child.

For a child's natural parents custodianship has both advantages and disadvantages. In adoption proceedings their consent would be needed, but this is not always essential for someone to gain custodianship. However, custodianship orders can be changed or ended but adoption is for ever.

Custodianship is often preferred by the courts in certain circumstances. The main ones are when a step-parent, relative or foster parent wishes to adopt a child. A foster parent can also apply for custodianship after looking after a child for 12 months, if the parent consents, or after three years even if the parent objects.

Ages which Matter
A child's rights and obligations increase steadily with its age, although in practice, until the later years, the parents usually act on the child's behalf and the obligation may be as much theirs as the child's.

There are no age limits relating to the following:
● the age at which a child may be left alone, or left to care for other children
● complaining against discrimination because of race or sex
● complaining against the police
● gaining access to personal information covered by the Data Protection Act 1984
● choosing your own religion - though parents can object
● refusing medical treatment - but you cannot *consent* to it until a set age
● opening a bank account - if the bank thinks you can handle it. But an age limit may be set on an overdraft.

The information in this section only covers some of the rights which exist. Others appear in other sections of this book and a full list of rights and duties can be obtained from The Children's Legal Centre (see page 450), to which I am indebted for much of the information opposite.

Children in Care
When a child goes into care the local authority takes on the 'rights and responsibilities' of a parent and has very considerable powers to decide what will happen to it. It can put the child in a home, with foster parents, with relatives other than the parents, and - if it chooses - prevent the parents from even seeing the child. Every care order must be reviewed twice a year. A child may be compulsorily taken into care for a whole range of reasons. These include:
● being beyond parental control and delinquent
● sexual or other abuse by the parents
● the death of both parents

Significant Ages

At Age	A Child Must	A Child May
Birth	pay tax	claim tax allowance
3 weeks	have its birth registered (Scotland)	have a passport (Scotland)
6 weeks	have its birth registered (except Scotland)	
19 weeks		be adopted
2 years	pay a child's air fare	
4 years	no longer live in a brothel	(it can do so until the age of 4)
5 years	start full-time education; pay fares on transport; stop getting free vitamins	be given alcohol at home; see U or PG films (if the manager allows)
7 years		draw money from a bank or National Savings or a building society account; open and use a TSB account
8 years		be prosecuted (Scotland)
10 years		be prosecuted; be convicted of a criminal offence and be put in care for crimes; be sentenced to custody for life for very serious crimes
12 years	pay full air fare	have life insurance; buy a pet; be liable for contracts (girls in Scotland); consent to medical treatment (girls in Scotland)
13 years		get a part-time job for limited hours subject to local restrictions
14 years	pay full fare on buses and trains (half with photo-card on LRT); be responsible for wearing a seatbelt in a car	go into a pub, but not buy or drink alcohol there; be convicted of rape (if male) or unlawful sex with girls under 16; consent to medical treatment (boys in Scotland) have some responsibility for contracts (boys in Scotland)
15 years		open a Giro account - with a guarantor; see a category 15 film
16 years	cease to be on a parent's passport	consent to sexual intercourse (girl); marry with parent's consent; leave school; leave home (Scotland); work full-time if you have left school; get a national insurance number; marry without parent's consent (Scotland); claim income support; some local authorities may let you be a tenant; live in a brothel; join a union; consent to medical treatment; apply for legal aid without a parent's signature; pilot a glider; buy liqueur chocolates; buy fireworks; drive a small mowing machine; smoke in public; have beer, cider or wine with a meal in a pub; sell scrap metal
16½ years		join the armed forces (boy) with parent's consent
17 years	cannot be put in care	become a street trader; hold a pilot's licence; apply for a helicopter licence; be sent to prison
17½ years		join the armed forces (girl)
18 years	pay for dental treatment unless in education; cease to be a ward of court; cease to be in care	vote; take on all adult legal obligations; make a will; buy drinks in a bar; be tattooed; get married without parent's consent; donate your body to science; see a category 18 film; be liable for debt; buy a house; pawn goods in a pawnshop; donate blood; enter a sex shop; buy an R18 video; change your name; place a bet; take out HP without a guarantor
19 years	cease to be automatically entitled to full-time education	
21 years		consent to a homosexual act (males); become an MP or councillor; apply for a licence to sell alcohol

This is guidance not gospel: before acting consult a solicitor.

Voluntary Care

It is often assumed that children *only* go into care because their parents are cruel to them. This is not the case. Thousands of children go into care each year because their mother is ill and their father can't cope, because the father has run off and the mother can't look after them and find work or a new home, or because the family is simply homeless. If parents put a child into voluntary care, they can ask to have it back at any time during the first 6 months.

After a child has been in care for 6 months parents must give 28 days' notice if they wish to remove it - and it is wisest to give this notice in writing. The 28 days gives the local authority a chance to make a 'Section 3 resolution' which will take away the rights of the parents and give them to the local authority - if the authority feels it would be better for the child not to return home. The parents must be told this is being planned; they then have a right to object within 28 days of being told, and take the matter to the juvenile court.

Disadvantages

There are very considerable disadvantages to putting children in care - even briefly.

During voluntary care parents have a right to see their children but the law does not lay down how much access they should have, nor does it compel the local authority to place a child somewhere that the parents can conveniently visit. Lack of understanding may allow social workers and foster parents to put up barriers to the regular and easy contacts between parents and their children which are vital if the children are to continue to feel needed and loved.

They may do this with the best of intentions wrongly believing that, if a child cries after parents have visited, the visits are upsetting it (see Children in Hospital, page 273). But if a parent loses touch with a child this can make it harder to get the child back, as the social services may claim it is settled and happy where it is and may put a care order on it which makes it impossible to remove it from the home.

If you have relatives, it is probably better to ask them to look after the children. Then you can at least see them when you can manage it. But if you think you may have to put a child into care read the '101 questions and answers' put out by Parents Aid before you contact social services.

It may be best to do almost anything rather than allow the social services to take charge of your children. If you put your child into voluntary care the social worker is meant to find a home or foster home which is as close to you as possible, and you are meant to be able to see your child often and to remove it from care at any time you like within the first 6 months, after that you need to give 28 days' notice.

There are also purely practical considerations. For example, if you put your children in care so as to find time to get somewhere decent to live, you will actually make it far harder to get council accommodation. For, by not having the children with you, you will cease to be a priority category, and councils can - and do - say

that as the children are in care there is no need to give you a home. And lacking accommodation, you may find it very hard to get the children out of care.

If a child is fostered for any length of time this also opens the door to a custodianship, or even adoption, application by the foster parent (page 468); if this happens the parent loses the child for ever. In some cases this may be best for the child. But some concerned and loving parents have, through illness, put a child in care as a temporary measure and found themselves fighting to retain their parenthood. Any family should take good advice, from a law centre or one of the organizations below, before putting a child in care.

Parent's Rights

While a child is in care a parent has limited rights and very little say in the child's life.

a A parent can apply to the magistrates' court to have the care order ended and have the child back but this application can only be made at intervals of 3 months or more.

b A parent can apply to the court for an access order if they have been prevented from seeing the child - but only if they have been *totally* prevented. If the arrangements are just bad the only redress is to use the local authority complaints procedure. A CAB or Law Centre should be able to advise on this.

The legal position in care proceedings is curious. In most such cases, the proceedings are defined in law as being between the *child* and the local authority, and parents can only apply for Legal Aid on the child's behalf. However, parents are also allowed to have their own lawyer in court and she may address the court. Neither may be represented at emergency hearings. It is also the child who must appeal, to the crown court, against the decisions of a magistrates' court. But while that is true of most cases there are situations in which parents *can* fight in their own right and get Legal Aid to do so. It is a tricky area and it is important to have good legal advice in such proceedings.

One of the disgraces of British society is that the law is stacked against even good parents and in favour of officials. It is all too easy for parents who put a child into care voluntarily to find that the social services department deprives them of rights - and of their child. With the best of intentions, social workers with big budgets for fostering and adoption and tiny ones for helping families stay together sometimes violate family bonds which ought in the emotional interests of the children to be preserved. And the tragedy for the family is incalculable. But changes are afoot.

The Law Society has set up a nationwide panel of solicitors who will act for parents and/or children in care cases, and are experienced in acting for them. Local advice centres may have the list or you can obtain it from the Care Panel Administrator at the Law Society (see Organizations). The organizations below will also help.

Family Rights Group (6-9 Manor Gardens, Holloway Road, London N7 6LA Tel: 01 272 7308 or 4231; telephone advice 9.30-12.30 Mon,Wed,Fri) offers advice and information, including the views of a solicitor, to those who have children in care or who are involved in child abuse proceedings. RC, M£M, vg L, vg B.

Parents Aid for Parents Separated from their Children (66 Chippingfield, Harlow, Essex CM17 0DJ Tel: 0279 36597) has a guide for families whose children are in care and gives advice and information. It also has a network of groups.

A Voice for the Child in Care (60 Carysfort Road, London N8 8RB Tel: 01 348 2588) fights for a better deal for children in care and for them to have more say in what happens to them. Children who are in care should contact this address.

Place of Safety Order
If the authorities believe that a child is being battered, or in any way abused, a 'place of safety order' can be made, by a single JP. If this happens the child is immediately put into care without the parents or child having any chance, or right, to put their case. A child can also be put into care for 8 days - without a court order - by a police officer, if it is for the child's safety.

Wardship
Local authorities are increasingly making children wards of court. This is a process by which the High Court gives all the parental rights to the court, so no decision about the child can be made without the court's permission. A child can be made a ward of court very quickly. But whoever asked for the wardship must apply for a preliminary hearing within 21 days, this decides whether the child should stay as a ward. If the application is not made wardship ceases automatically. Parents can be legally represented in wardship proceedings.

Once a child becomes a ward of court it may live wherever the court decides, and the major decisions in its life must be made by the court. This lasts until it is 18 unless the wardship is cancelled by the court.

National Association of Young People in Care, 2nd Floor, Maranar House, 28-30 Mosley Street, Newcastle-upon-Tyne NE1 1DF Tel: 0912 612178 - run by and for young people in care, this tries to improve conditions and to give advice and information. Free membership for under 14s.

Rights of Women, 52 Featherstone Street, London EC1 8RT Tel: 01 251 6577 Tuesday, Wednesday, Thursday 7-9 pm - legal advice by phone or letter - *not* to callers.

See also Justice for Children page 450 and Childrens Legal Centre, page 450.

Corporal Punishment
The law allows parents to administer 'reasonable chastisement'. In practice, this means you can smack a child but not do anything which could cause damage or injury. So a clip round the ear - which could damage the ear - would be unreasonable, whereas a smack to the bottom would be reasonable - provided it was not administered with anything which caused bruising. It is a criminal offence to exceed the reasonable limit. Corporal punishment in schools became illegal, under an Education Act, in August 1987.

Education
LEAs must provide children from the age of 5 to 16 with education suited to their 'age, ability and aptitude' (often

called the 'three As'). It isn't easy to *prove* that education fails to meet a child's needs - but parents can fight this in the courts if they feel their children are ill-served by the state system.

Parents must ensure that their children receive a full-time education which meets the 'three As' criteria. Allowing a child to play truant or keeping it at home to help is illegal. This doesn't mean that children must always go to school. But parents who educate their children at home must be able to show that the 'three As' criteria are being met, or they can be taken to court and ordered to send the children to school, and in extreme cases the children can be taken into care (see also page 468).

Dress and Discipline
All schools are allowed, within reason, to dictate how a child will dress and behave in school and on the way to and from school, and punish the child accordingly. Head teachers of state schools may prevent pupils attending school by suspending them, but may not expel them. (See page 291).

The only class from which parents have an automatic right to withdraw a child in a state school is Religious Instruction - if it differs from their beliefs.

Leaving School
Children may leave when they are 16, but they cannot leave instantly.

Those born between 1 Sept - 31 Jan leave at the end of the Spring term
Those born between 1 Feb - 31 May leave at the end of May
Those born between 1 Jun - 31 Aug leave at the end of the summer term

Fostering
The law classes private fostering as any arrangement whereby someone looks after someone else's children - except while the parents are away on holiday. It doesn't have to involve payment. Local authorities must be notified if a child is fostered unless it is done by a relative, or guardian, or is for under 27 days (6 days if the fosterer is registered). Anyone who fosters a child for a year may apply for custodianship (see page 468), and after 5 years of fostering for custodianship (see page 468) may apply to adopt it and a natural parent cannot remove the child from the fosterer while waiting for the case to come to court. (See also Care page 468.)

Grandparents
Grandparents have no automatic right of access to their grandchildren, but they can apply to the courts for access to both legitimate and illegitimate grandchildren. In some circumstances, they can even obtain custodianship.

Illegitimacy
A child is legitimate if the parents were married either at conception *or* at the time of birth (unless they were

legally separated when the child was conceived). Illegitimate children can be made legitimate either by the parents marrying (which allows a new 'legitimate' birth certificate to be written), or the mother and her husband (who is not the father) can jointly adopt the child. Any adopted child is regarded as the legitimate child of whoever adopts it.

Blood tests may be able to show a man is *not* the father of a child, but they cannot prove that a man *is* the father - because a lot of people have the same blood group - so all rights in relation to illegitimate children rest with the mother. However, fathers of illegitimate children have a duty to support them and the National Council for One Parent Families (page 456) has a form which a man can use to make a voluntary agreement to this. If a man doesn't the mother should apply to a magistrates' court for an affiliation order within 3 years of the birth (after that it is too late). As with divorce maintenance, the woman should always stake her claim even if the sum she gets is tiny. Nobody knows what the future holds. Any woman could run into difficulties and, if she has failed to claim, the child may suffer.

There are new tests using chromosomes which *can*, effectively, prove a particular man is the father but they are not normally available. See Child Poverty Action Group (page 456).

Scottish Council for Single Parents, 13 Gayfield Square, Edinburgh EH1 3NX Tel: 031 556 3899

Nationality
The law on nationality changed in 1983. A child is now British if it is legitimate and one parent is British, or it is illegitimate, with a British mother. In these cases it makes no difference if it is born outside Britain. It is also British if its non-British mother or married non-British parents are legally settled in Britain at its birth. The other details of nationality are highly complex and covered by leaflets from the **Home Office Immigration and Nationality Department**, Lunar House, 40 Wellesley Road, Croydon CR9 2BY Tel: 01 686 3441.

The Joint Council for Welfare of Immigrants, 115 Old Street, London EC1V 9JR Tel: 01 251 8706 - will advise and help those with immigration problems.

Sex
A girl under 16 cannot consent to sexual intercourse but - despite the Gillick case - a doctor may advise her on contraception, without her parents' knowledge in certain circumstances. These include being unable to persuade her to tell the parents (or allow him to tell them), believing she intends to have sex anyway, and being convinced of her ability to understand the advice and its consequences. (See also page 275.)

Sexual behaviour of any kind towards someone under-age is illegal.

Step-parents
Step-parents have no automatic rights over a step-child.

This means that if the children are living with a mother and step-father, and the mother dies, the natural father may take the children away - even if he has not seen them or taken any interest in them for years. However, the step-parent can apply for guardianship, custodianship (see page 468) or adoption or ask for the child to be made a ward of court.

Children's Legal Centre (see page 450)
Children, Parents and the Law by the Consumers Association, Hodder and Stoughton

Death and What To Do
When someone dies there are a number of formalities which have to be observed quite rapidly.
1 If organs have been bequeathed for donation the nearest hospital should be phoned immediately - kidneys must be removed within 30 minutes and eyes within 6 hours. However, most organs are only accepted from donors aged under 55 - though eyes are an exception.

If a death has to be reported to a coroner his consent is needed before any organs can be donated. Also, in law, the body belongs to the relatives, not to the person who died. So if they object to the organs being taken or the body going to medical research they don't have to observe this part of a will.

---

2 The dead person's doctor must be told (unless they died in hospital).
3 If the doctor has seen the deceased, within the past 2 weeks, or treated them during their last illness, he will normally give the relatives a free certificate saying the cause of death. Otherwise the death must be reported to the coroner who may order a post mortem.
4 The will must be found, and whoever is responsible for dealing with it must be contacted.
5 If the body has been left to medical research your nearest medical school or, for the south of England, the London Anatomy Office (Tel: 01 741 2198), should be contacted as soon after death as possible. If the body is accepted by them they will send an undertaker to collect it. The medical school will then see to a funeral or cremation within 2 years, and invite the relatives to attend if they wish to.

To find out about bequeathing your body to medical research contact your nearest medical school or (failing that) the London Anatomy Office, P.O. Box 915, London W6 8RP.

---

6 The will must be checked to see if a space has already been paid for in a graveyard.
7 A funeral director must be found and the arrangements made for the funeral - though the date cannot be fixed if the coroner has not yet issued a pink form (see also The Funeral, opposite).

This is guidance not gospel: before acting consult a solicitor.

Every death must be registered with the local Registrar of Births, Marriages and Deaths within 5 days, unless the death has been referred to the coroner. In this case, it cannot be registered until he issues a pink form. Police stations, post offices and other public bodies can give the address of the Registrar's Office and registration is a simple procedure if you take the right papers and information. These are:

- the deceased's full name (including maiden name) and home address
- full details of date and place of birth, and sex
- his or her occupation
- the date of birth of the surviving husband or wife
- the place and date of death
- details of any state benefits they were receiving.
- the doctor's certificate of cause of death
- the dead person's NHS card - if possible
- any war pension order book - if applicable.

Whoever goes to the registrar will also have to give their own details as the informant. The registrar then provides certificates registering the death and allowing a burial, plus leaflets on welfare benefits. The registration certificate then needs to be taken to the DHSS office to obtain the death grant and widow's benefit.

What Happens in Special Cases

If someone dies of an industrial disease, suddenly, in an accident, during an operation, or the cause of death is uncertain, the doctor *must* report the death to the coroner, who arranges a post mortem, and possibly an inquest. Only after this will the coroner issue a certificate permitting the burial and allow the body to be taken away. He will also issue a certificate of the cause of death which will either be given to the relatives or sent to the registrar. If the death occurs abroad it must be registered according to the rules of that country and also with the British Consul there.

Extra Things to be Done

When someone dies a lot of ends need to be tied up and these are some of them.

- Tell any relatives or friends who ought to know.
- Tell the deceased's - bank
  solicitor
  insurance companies
  credit card accounts
  building societies
  stock broker.
- Return any pension book to the DHSS.
- Apply for death grant (and widow's benefit - if applicable).
- Alter the insurance cover on the deceased's car if someone else is to use it.

The Funeral

The cost of a funeral comes out of the dead person's estate. Some banks and building societies will release money for this on production of the death certificate. State benefits may also be available, if the person was eligible, provided an application is made before the funeral is arranged. If there is too little money to cover the cost of the funeral then the executors may be legally responsible for meeting the bill themselves.

It is up to the relatives to decide on cremation or burial. They have no legal obligation to carry out the deceased's instructions as to the type of funeral. A check should be made that no plot has been reserved in any graveyard - it may have been paid for in advance.

Before a burial can take place the funeral director must have either a registrar's certificate for burial, or a coroner's order for burial, plus an application for burial signed by the executor or next of kin, and - if there is one - the deeds reserving a special plot.

For a cremation the funeral director also needs:

- cremation certificates from two doctors
- a cremation certificate signed by the crematorium's medical referee
- an application for cremation signed by the executor or next of kin
- notification from the next of kin of what to do with the ashes
- *if* the death was reported to the coroner, a coroner's certificate of cremation.

Wills

Anyone in England, Ireland or Wales who is sane and over the age of 18 can - and should - make a will. (In Scotland the age is 12 for girls and 14 for boys - and the law on wills is rather different).

If someone who is very old, or of variable mental state, makes a will, it is wise to have a doctor check that the person really knows what they are doing (and make a medical note to this effect), and also to act as a witness.

★ A marriage usually revokes all previous wills, so make a new will as soon as you marry - or divorce.

Almost any high-street solicitor will advise on how to make a will. Charges vary, but if you shop around it shouldn't be expensive. If substantial sums are involved it may also be worth consulting an accountant, so that no more goes to the government on your death than really has to.

Of course, it is perfectly legal to make your own will and since the law changed in 1982 it has been a lot simpler but, even so, mistakes can be expensive and distressing for those whom you wish to benefit. If you want to save money on will making the safest method is to read up the details in the books given below and draw up a very correct draft will and take it to a lawyer for checking. Then legal fees will be cut to a minimum. But don't delay in making one. It is simply not fair to the rest of the family.

Anyone making a will, who will not consult a lawyer, should first read *Wills and Probate* by the Consumers Association (published by Coronet) and the section on wills in John Pritchard's *Penguin Guide to Law*. Words do not mean the same things to lawyers that they mean to you and me. So you can write a will, which seems clear and concise to any ordinary mortal, only to have it mean something totally different in law. What follows

This is guidance not gospel: before acting consult a solicitor.

is only a rough outline of what a will requires, which may be useful background and make it easier to write the draft to take to a lawyer.

- It must be in writing (typed or hand-written).
- It must say that it is the last will and testament.
- It must give the *full* name of the person whose will it is - including the maiden name of a married woman.
- It should be dated and say it revokes all previous wills (even if there are none, this is a precaution).
- The first paragraph should appoint executors (see below), though you don't have to, and they may benefit from the will.
- The pages should be numbered.
- The lines should be spaced so there is no room to insert anything - which is why a will should *not* be written on a form from a stationer.
- It must be very precise. Give the full name of each person you want to leave anything to, if there could be any misunderstanding.
- If you name sums of money make it clear whether it is before or after tax.
- Remember inflation will reduce the value of lump sums. So it is wiser to divide the estate in fractions rather than actual figures.
- Be very specific. If you say you leave 'property' to someone it could mean several things. If you say 'my house 3 Acacia Avenue, SW13 and all its contents' there is no argument - but update this if you move.
- Have a final clause bequeathing 'everything else I own', then there will be no problem over anything not disposed of.
- It must be signed *immediately under the bottom of the last page,* by the person making the will *in the presence* of two witnesses (in Scotland it may be unwitnessed if whoever is making it writes it entirely by hand and signs it).
- If there is more than one page the will maker and the witnesses should sign every page immediately under the bottom line.
- The two witnesses must be adult, sighted and traceable, and neither they nor their spouses may benefit from the will in *any* way - or the gift to them becomes invalid. So *never* witness the will of a relative. Witnesses must sign and give their name, address and occupation.
- Put it in a safe place, such as with a solicitor, and tell those concerned.

If you don't make a will, your property won't go to the state - as many believe - unless you have no close relatives. Instead, it will be divided among close relatives according to rules laid down in law, and your personal representatives will also be those the law decrees (depending what relatives you have). What the law dictates may not agree with your intentions at all, and needs more administration than a well-written will, so dying intestate siphons off money to lawyers when you'd rather give it to those you love.

If you do make a will but leave a husband or wife an unusually small proportion of the estate, the Inheritance (Provision for Family and Dependents) Act 1975 allows them to apply to the court for a reasonable share, and they are likely to get it.

> For a very nominal sum you can lodge your will with the Principal Probate Registry, Somerset House, Strand, London WC2. There is then no risk that it will be lost, though you need to tell everyone concerned that you have done that.

Executors to a Will

An executor (executrix - female) is someone who is appointed in a will, to act for someone after their death and see their wishes are carried out. So they can do things like reclaiming money that is owed, as well as looking after the will. But as they are merely *acting for* the estate they do not have to pay anything out of their own pocket, nor must any of the estate go into their own pockets. They may, however, recover their expenses for doing this job.

If you are appointed as an executor but don't want to act as one you can renounce the position in a letter to the Probate Registry. If there is no executor, trustees or anyone benefiting from the will may apply to the Probate Registry for permission to act as an administrator of the will. But when someone leaves very little there is no need for this and cash, jewellery and small savings can just be divided up as the will instructs.

Appointing professionals - bankers, lawyers or accountants - as executors may not be a good idea. Organizations are much less likely to settle things quickly, or be sensitive to special needs in the family. They may also charge large sums for the work involved *plus a percentage of the estate* - usually 1 to 2½ per cent. Don't imagine banks are the cheapest: they tend to be more expensive than solicitors. There is nothing, however, to stop any appointed layman getting advice from any professional who is needed or even, if the estate is complicated, appointing a law firm to handle things. The difference is that professionals appointed in this way can be dropped if slow or inefficient, whereas if they are appointed as executors you are, frankly, lumbered with them.

Principal Family Registry, Family Division, Somerset House, Strand, London WC1R 1LP Tel: 01 936 6000 - has copies of all wills which were lodged when probate was taken out. Anyone can have a copy.
'How to obtain probate', an explanatory leaflet by the Lord Chancellor's Department
'What to do after a death', DHSS leaflet No 49 from the leaflet unit P.O. Box 21, Stanmore, Middx HA7 1AY
What to do When Someone Dies, Which Books, Coronet
Wills and Probate, Consumers Association, Coronet

Domestic Violence

The Public Order Act 1986 excludes family rows. So verbal assault in the family has no legal remedy - no matter how vicious it is. Physical assault is different.

Not since 1861 has it been legal for a man to hit his wife. So far as the law is concerned it is a criminal offence just as it would be if a man beat up his neighbour. This means that the police have an absolute duty to prevent it happening - if necessary by putting the man in a cell for the night and prosecuting him. It is not correct for the police to say that they can't prosecute if a woman won't take a case against the husband. If they saw the evidence of physical attack that is enough. (See Actual Bodily Harm page 448.)

Unfortunately, the police often treat domestic violence as a special case. However, the courts now offer some protection against domestic violence both for wives and for those living with a man but not married to him. A married woman has three options; a woman who is not married can only use the second.

1   A magistrates' court can make two types of order:
   a   A personal protection order can be made if the court is satisfied that the husband or wife has used or threatened violence against their partner or one of the children, and feels the order is needed for their protection.
   b   An exclusion order may be made, ordering the husband or wife to leave (or keep out of) the mutual home. For this there must have been violence (or threat of it) against the partner, or child, or the terms of a personal protection order must have been broken.
2   A county court can grant several different types of injunction, which can cover a couple who are living together as well as those who are married. These can:
      order a partner to stop molesting the other;
      order a partner to stop molesting a child who is living with the applicant;
      exclude someone from the joint home;
      make one partner allow the other back into a joint home.
3   If divorce proceedings have been started a divorce court can grant broadly the same two injunctions as a magistrates' court.

A woman can represent herself in these applications but it is probably safer to use a solicitor, and Legal Aid is usually available. It is best to use a Law Centre, Women's Aid Centre or CAB, to find a solicitor who is experienced in cases of this sort and sympathetic to the problems. If an injunction is granted then the solicitor should ask for a power of arrest to be attached. This will only be granted if actual bodily harm has been caused to the innocent partner or to a child and the court is satisfied that it is likely to happen again. But it means that if the man breaks the injunction the police can be called to arrest him. Failing this, the woman has to go back to the court and show that the injunction has been breached - power of arrest may then be given, and further breaches of the injunction can mean prison.

Coping with Violence

Wife beating is a guilty secret which often condemns a woman not only to pain and fear but to shame and loneliness. There is no need for any woman to be ashamed or to feel alone. There are men who beat their wives among the richest and most educated as well as poorest and least able. Nor should a battered woman - or anyone else - believe the common idea that women who are battered must have asked for it and must enjoy it. People do not kick cats because the cats enjoy it but because the cat is weaker than themselves and they can get away with the cruelty. Women get beaten up because physical weakness, financial dependence and anxieties about providing for the children trap them with men who are too immature to control their rage and violence, and feel free to break the law behind closed doors.

No woman who is being battered with words or blows should try to handle this situation alone, nor should she ask her children to keep it a secret, both she and the children need to unburden themselves. Being battered brings a woman's spirits so low that she may find it impossible to get away unless she finds support. She should contact her nearest refuge.

There are some 200 refuges for battered women around Britain which not only provide homes to which battered women and their children can escape but also offer a free telephone advice service. They all have different names, so you can't easily find them in Yellow Pages but the telephone exchange normally knows where they are. So ring directory enquiries and ask if they can give you the number of the nearest refuge for battered women. Or ring the 24-hour crisis line of **Chiswick Family Rescue** - Tel: 01 995 4430 - which has a list of all the refuges in Britain. Or write to this organization at P.O.Box 855, Chiswick, London W4 4JF Tel: 01 747 0133 (office hours). This centre will advise and take in women from all over Britain, not just from London.

If you are being battered you may fear that if you leave the man you will be penniless and homeless and have your children taken from you. This isn't so. If you leave a violent man and have no income you will be entitled to social security benefits and under the 1985 Housing Act you will have priority on a council house list.

Elsewhere in this book I say that a woman, splitting up from a man, should try to stay in the home and get him to leave. But with a violent man this is usually impossible and even dangerous. You should first get advice from a refuge, once you have found a place in one you can live in safely and use it as a base from which to find a new home. You only risk having children taken into care if you have nowhere to live while waiting for a council house.

Even if you feel you can survive the beatings it is a terrible ordeal for any child to have to hear, or see, a father beating a mother, and the fear and sense of impotence which this causes a child can scar it deeply. There is no virtue in remaining in a relationship which causes a child such suffering.

This is guidance not gospel: before acting consult a solicitor.

More information

Women's Aid Federation, P.O. Box 391, Bristol BS99 7WS Tel: 0272 420611

Sandra Horley, *Love and Pain: a Survival Guide for Woman,* Bedford Square Press. Written by the director of the oldest refuge for women this has all the facts a battered wife needs to know.

Epilepsy

Some drugs used in the treatment of epilepsy are barbiturates included in the Misuse of Drugs Act. Epileptics using these drugs should carry a doctor's letter about their treatment which can be shown to the police if necessary.

Marriage

If an engagement is broken neither side has legal redress - not even for money spent for the wedding - but wedding presents should be returned. There can be problems if the couple has already bought a house together, and the best safeguard is to put in equal amounts and have it in their joint names.

As recently as 1929 the minimum age for marriage was 14 for boys and 12 for girls. Today it is 16 for both sexes, but under 18 the written consent of both parents must be obtained (or the consent of whichever has legal custody), except when this is not appropriate - for example, when one parent has deserted.

Who Can Marry Whom

The bars on who may marry whom are dictated not so much by consanguinity as by a desire to prevent the social boat being rocked by seductions within the family. It therefore applies even to those people who are adopted or who have divorced and left the family.

You may not marry your:

- brother/sister
- uncle/aunt
- nephew/niece
- son/daughter
- father/mother

The rules on marrying other members of your family, or those related by marriage, are complex and have changed. Consult a lawyer.

Valid Marriage

A marriage is valid only if it has taken place in a registry office or in some other place licensed to register marriages - such as an approved church. Not all churches and temples are registered and some religions have registered temples in Scotland but not in England. So it is always advisable to check the situation. When a place of worship is not registered a registry office wedding must take place before or after the religious ceremony.

The Effects of Marriage

If a woman adopts her husband's name she must get her bank account put into that name and the new signature authorized. But, she doesn't have to take her husband's name. So she can continue to use a passport in her maiden name, or send it in to be changed, as she wishes. Nor does a British subject automatically change nationality on marrying a foreigner - though she may obtain dual nationality. But marriage does change some financial facts.

- A man can be liable for his wife's debts on household essentials.
- If either dies without making a will most of their possessions go to the other.
- Tax allowances change - and *the date of the marriage can affect tax levels* - so talk to an accountant before setting the date.
- State benefits change (and they may also change when people live together as 'man and wife' without benefit of marriage).
- There is also an implied consent to a reasonable amount of sex, it is therefore *legally* impossible for a man to rape his wife, unless there is a magistrate's exclusion order, a separation agreement, or divorce proceedings have started.

However, it is no longer the case that one partner cannot be forced to give evidence, for or against, the other in a criminal action.

Mental Illness

There should be no fear that someone will be 'put away'. The 1983 Mental Health Act says that only those who are 'abnormally aggressive or seriously irresponsible' can be held against their will for any length of time. If a person needs treatment in hospital he is usually admitted as a voluntary patient and can leave at any time - even against the doctor's advice.

The official terms used are 'formal' (i.e. compulsory) admission or 'informal' (i.e. voluntary) admission. When someone's admission is compulsory it always involves the evidence of at least one doctor, and the ease with which they can leave depends on the section of the act under which they were admitted. The relevant sections of the act are sections 2 to 5; the bare bones are these:

Section 2. **Admission for assessment,** at the request of the nearest relative or a social worker. The case must be reviewed every 28 days, and to appeal the patient must apply to the Mental Health Review Tribunal (MHRT) within 14 days of admission.

Section 3. **Admission for treatment,** at the request of the nearest relative or an approved social worker for up to 6 months, renewable for a 6-month period, then annually. One appeal may be made to the MHRT in each period.

Section 4. **Emergency admission,** at the request of the nearest relative or a social worker. Initially for 72 hours, but up to 28 days more if two doctors agree.

Section 5. **Compulsory detention of voluntary patients,** while staff obtain a compulsory detention order. Sometimes the patient's nearest relative can persuade

This is guidance not gospel: before acting consult a solicitor.

the doctors to make an admission voluntary, not compulsory, by offering to take responsibility for the patient should he or she leave the hospital.

Admission under 2 and 3 needs the written recommendation of 2 doctors. Controversially, section 4 only needs a doctor. Those compulsorily admitted must be told which section they were admitted under and given written information about appeals, legal aid and discharge. Legal aid is available for appeals to the Mental Health Review Tribunal (MHRT); but the patient can be represented by a friend instead of a lawyer. Relatives may also discharge a compulsory patient from hospital by giving 72 hours' notice that they are taking charge of them. The doctors can prevent this with a barring notice - against which the relative may appeal to the MHRT within 28 days.

If the objection is not to the fact of detention but to treatment during it, a complaint should be made to the Mental Health Act Commission for the region. The hospital concerned must give the addresses of the Mental Health Review Tribunal and the Mental Health Act Commission to a patient or relative. And Mind (see In Sickness) has lawyers who will advise the mentally ill, or their relatives on their rights in law.

Housing the Mentally Ill

The official trend to 'community care' means that many mentally ill patients are dumped on their families. When someone is violent or otherwise dangerous this can be intolerable. However, families have no obligation in law to house a mentally ill child, or relative, who is over the age of 18. If there is no hospital to care for the sufferer the obligation falls to the housing department. Parents may need to be very firm to have this right enforced, but only when more make this demand will the true meaning of 'community care' be brought home to those who so glibly talk about it.

Rights

Those being treated for mental disorders lose their rights in various ways. For example:
- their mail in and out can be stopped in certain circumstances - but no stop can be put on letters addressed to their MP, the Mental Health Review Tribunal and certain other public bodies
- they may not serve on a jury (even if only under GP treatment)
- they may not vote if compulsorily detailed
- if they are not able to run their affairs anyone suitable may apply to the court to be a 'receiver' (which is essentially a trustee) of their property during the illness. If someone is appointed the patient loses almost all control of his or her financial affairs.

Treatment

The mentally ill can be treated against their will. But there are limits. ECT, hormone implants and brain surgery require the patient's consent (unless he is incapable of giving it) and strict medical approval.

HOUSEHOLD LAW

Animals

Dogs and Nuisance

The law says that dogs must be kept under control, wear collars with the owner's name and address on public highways and not foul the footway. You can bring a private prosecution against owners who allow their dogs to foul the pavement, worry poultry or livestock on agricultural land, and if a dog is deemed to be dangerous it can be put down. But a dog cannot be shot just for *chasing* animals, only for worrying or attacking them - or for attacking a human being.

General Duties and Obligations

Cruelty and neglect are illegal - and abandoning a dog is classed as cruelty. The owner can also be held responsible for its behaviour. If it runs into the road and causes an accident its owner may be sued. But for the owner to be held liable the court must prove that reasonable measures were not taken to keep the dog under control. In the case of a dangerous animal, it isn't enough to take reasonable measures: if the animal escapes the owner is liable for any harm caused even if he did everything possible to prevent the escape. The same applies if an animal of a safe species is dangerous through temperament or special circumstances, and if livestock stray and damage someone's property. So, if your neighbour's cow munches your flower borders you could have a claim.

Importing Animals

No creatures of any kind may be imported into Britain without an import licence from the Ministry of Agriculture, Fisheries and Food, not even your pets. For a licence write to the **Animal Imports Division,** Government Buildings, Hook Rise South, Tolworth, Surbiton, Surrey KT6 7NR. Birds are usually allowed to be quarantined in the owner's home for 35 days. Almost all other animals have to be held for 6 months in a ministry-approved establishment (check with the Animal Imports Division), and the owner pays for their keep. However, owners are allowed to visit their pets and may even ask for a kennels or cattery near where they live - if one exists. Anyone trying to smuggle in a pet is liable to an unlimited fine, and up to a year in prison, and the animal may be destroyed, or quarantined, or sent back to the country it came from.

★ Dog licences are from post offices but to keep a dangerous wild animal you need a licence from your local authority.

Boundaries

Curiously, there is no *legal* obligation to fence your property or to maintain the existing fences, but you may be obliged to under the title deeds. The deeds usually say which fences belong to which house. If not, a fence usually belongs to whoever has the support posts on his side.

If a tree from a neighbour's garden has branches

which overhang your garden you are entitled to cut off the branches at the point where they overhang. But they belong to the neighbour, and it is prudent to ask, in writing, whether he would prefer to chop the branches himself.

The same applies to tree roots, but tree roots present a far greater threat. They can invade water pipes and cause serious problems and the presence of a large number of roots under a house can, in dry seasons, take enough water from the soil to cause subsidence - especially with thirsty trees like willows. So, if a neighbour plants a tree close enough for the roots of the mature tree to threaten your house or drains alert him immediately, in writing, to the potential risks to your property. If you want to know whether it is close enough to cause damage, a rough guide is that trees' roots will stretch as far - in each direction - as the height of the full-grown tree.

Whether a tree owner is liable for damage caused by falling branches depends on why the branch fell. If it was rotten the owner should have noticed; if it was healthy but there was a gale it isn't the owner's fault.

Building

Planning permission is needed for developments of any kind - and the scope is very wide, ranging from change of use to modernization, conversion and some repairs. Those who don't get permission from the district council when they should have done can be made to restore the building to its previous condition - regardless of cost. However, the following can usually be done without permission - but *do check your particular situation*. There's no accounting for by-laws.
- Improvements within a building which do not extend it or change its use (e.g. most replacement windows).
- TV aerials.
- External maintenance - even if it changes the look of the building.
- Demolition - unless it is a listed building.
- An extension falls within set rules:
  a it must not be taller than the house itself
  b it will not stick out beyond the front of the house if this is on a public path or road
  c it does not have direct access on to a classified road
  d it will not obstruct the view of road users
  e it must be not more than 15 per cent of the size of the original house, or 70 cubic metres - which ever is the greater
  f it must not go over an existing drain or sewer.

Obtaining planning permission (or discovering you don't need it) isn't the end of the story.
- If the property is mortgaged you may need approval from the mortgage company.
- If a party wall is affected you may need your neighbour's consent.
- The alterations must not infringe your neighbours' rights to light.
- Leaseholders may have restricting clauses in their lease.

- There can be restrictive covenants on a freehold.
- You may need approval, of sections of the work, under building or water board regulations.

Guns and Crossbows

The law on guns was laid down in the Firearms Act 1968, with additional clauses on imitation weapons in the Firearms Act 1982. Breaking these laws risks both prison and fines.

★ If an imitation firearm is easily converted into a real weapon, and looks like one of the firearms mentioned below, the law on real weapons applies in all respects.

Aged Under 14

Those under the age of 14 may not possess, be lent or use any firearm except in a shooting gallery, in an approved club, or when on private land and supervised by someone over 21.

Aged 14 to 17

No type of gun may be bought under the age of 17. But, this age group can be given or lent various guns, provided they have the necessary certificate from the police. Check with your local police.

Aged 17 Upwards

The purchase and possession of air weapons is unrestricted after the age of 17. Purchase or use of a shotgun requires a shotgun certificate. In certain circumstances, such as when under instruction, on private land or in a cadet corps, shotguns can be used without a certificate. But to purchase, possess or use rifles, pistols, revolvers, short-barrelled shotguns or certain 'dangerous' air rifles you must have a firearm certificate from the police. This involves completing a form and giving references. If the police refuse to grant, vary or renew a firearm or shotgun certificate you can appeal, within 21 days, to the Administrator of the Crown Court.

Crossbows

It is now illegal to sell a crossbow to anyone under 17 and there are heavy penalties for doing so.

Noise

The Control of Pollution Act 1974 covers unwanted noise of all kinds, from barking dogs to grinding factories, as do many local by-laws. Write to whoever is causing the noise saying it constitutes a nuisance and asking them to stop it within 14 days, and have this letter signed by any neighbours who are equally bothered by it. If that fails you can prosecute. The Department of the Environment leaflet 'Noise: What you can do about it' explains what to do. You can also get advice from the Noise Abatement Society.

Noise Abatement Society, P.O. Box 8, Bromley, Kent BR2 0UH Tel: 01 460 3146 campaigns against unnecessary noise of all kinds and assists members in their complaints against it. 24-hour 'hot-line' for reporting excessive aircraft noise 01 633 3001. RC, M£L-H, L, B, F, E.

This is guidance not gospel: before acting consult a solicitor.

Telephone

It is an offence to use the telephone to make calls which are grossly offensive, indecent or menacing, and to cause annoyance, inconvenience or needless anxiety by such calls. But it isn't easy for a victim to *use* this law. So say nothing and hang up. Many offensive callers would like nothing better than to hear you sounding angry or upset, and hanging up stops their fun. If the calls persist get a loud whistle and blow it straight into the mouthpiece of the phone and hang up - very nasty for the ears. Then report the calls to the police. British Telecom may also be able to help by intercepting your calls, changing your number or blocking in-coming calls altogether. Women should list themselves in the phone book by initials and surname only, because first names, or Miss, Ms or Mrs can attract such calls.

However, if the calls are from a particular person who is getting his kicks out of threatening you, think twice before changing your number. It is better to be threatened on the phone than in person - which could be the result if the telephone option is blocked.

Tenancy

The law relating to tenancy needs a book to itself. Act has been added to Act, like children playing hand-stacking, with each one modifying, but not replacing, the last. With private landlords alone there are over sixteen different types of tenancy. Here there is only space to sketch in the main facts, not the multitude of special clauses. It is vital to talk to a lawyer before letting property, and it may be useful before becoming a tenant.

The key question for most tenants is whether they are protected by the Rent Acts. Much will depend on the terms of the written or verbal agreement between the landlord and tenant. However, they may well be protected if:
- they have absolute possession of part of the property - even a room
- they are renting all or part of a home - as opposed to business premises
- they do not receive meals or substantial services
- the tenancy is not for the purposes of a job
- it is not a holiday or company let
- the rateable value of the rented property is within certain set limits
- the rent exceeds two-thirds of the rateable value of the property
- the tenant does not conduct business from the property
- the landlord does not live in the same property (living in a separate flat in the same building may sometimes count as living in the same property and it needn't be the landlord's only residence).

The Acts may give complete or partial protection according to the circumstances, and there are also exceptions for those whose tenancies started before 1974. Before 1974 a key factor in whether a tenant was protected was whether or not the let was furnished. For lets started before that date the rules are rather different.

So someone with an unfurnished flat in the same house as the landlord may well be protected if the let started before 1974.

Rent

Weekly tenants *must* be given a proper rent book, and it is an offence not to provide one. Council tenants must usually pay whatever the council asks, but they must be given 4 weeks' notice of increases. Councils also have a duty to police private tenancies, and if private tenants feel they are being overcharged they can can ask the rent officer (under Rent, in the telephone book) or Rent Tribunal (if the tenant has restricted protection) to decide what is a fair rent. First ask the rent officer if there is a registered rent for the property. If there isn't, check the rents for comparable properties in the area by looking at the rent officer's register of rents - which is open to the public.

Once a fair rent has been registered, tenants may not be charged more - even if they signed an agreement to do so. If the rent officer sets a higher rent than they are paying, it cannot immediately be increased in full, only in stages over 2 years. With certain types of agreement it may not be possible to charge more even if the rent officer sets a higher rent.

Two years is the magic figure when it comes to fair rents. Once a rent officer has set a rent he will not normally review it for 2 years from the date of registration. If it is not reviewed that rent remains in effect, and to charge more to a tenant who is not fully protected is a criminal offence. However, after a tenant leaves, a landlord may let the rent officer know the property is vacant and ask to have the registered rent cancelled - and charge the next tenant more.

> There is no back-dating of rent changes. If the rent is to go up the landlord cannot recover the extra rent for preceding weeks, and if it is to go down the tenant cannot get a refund. The exception to this is if the landlord was charging more than a rent already registered with the rent officer - in which case tenants can be refunded up to two years' excess rent.

Eviction of Owners and Relations

The most important point is that *no one can be evicted from their home without a court order*. With council tenants this also applies to the husband or wife or (if the tenant dies) to any close relative who has lived in the property for the previous year. The same applies with private tenants, but relatives of the dead tenant need only have lived in the property for the past 6 months. Deserted spouses have the same security as the original tenant but on divorce, whoever is not the tenant loses the right to live there - unless the court specifically transfers the tenancy to that person.

Anyone who is being asked to move out or is being harassed by a landlord may be able to get help from the Tenancy Relations Officer on their local council. They should also take legal advice.

Eviction Orders

Both council tenants and private tenants can be evicted with a court order, but councils usually prefer to ask tenants to remedy the situation.

How easily a private landlord can get an eviction order, through an application to the county court, will depend on the type of tenancy and the degree of Rent Act protection it gives. Often tenants are entitled to stay on in the property even after the end of the fixed period tenancy agreed in a contract. Whatever the situation, the case has to be heard and the tenant must normally have at least a week's notice of the hearing (3 weeks in some cases). Common grounds for eviction are:

- serious rent arrears - which the tenant cannot or will not remedy
- damage to the property or furnishings by the tenant or sub-tenant
- the ending of employment which was a condition of tenancy
- the use of the premises for illegal or immoral purposes
- a major breach of the tenancy agreement
- the owner needs the property for himself or his family - but the owner has to prove that without the property he will suffer more hardship than the tenant will in moving, and must normally have told the tenant, from the start, that he might need the property for himself
- the neighbours have been caused considerable nuisance.

All those reasons apply whether the tenant causes the problem or whether someone for whom he is responsible causes them. In some circumstances, the following grounds can also be used:

- a member of the armed forces now needs the property back to live in
- the property is a holiday home
- the property is a retirement home - and needed to retire to, or is needed by a member of the owner's family after his/her death
- the owner previously lived in it and needs to live there again, or has died and vacant possession is needed to sell the house
- the tenant has allowed overcrowding
- the tenant signed a shorthold agreement which is at the end of its term.

> Even when a landlord has a right to take over the property, to live in, there are strict rules on giving notice which the owner must keep to, or fail to regain possession.

Tenancy and eviction are, however, extremely complex areas of law, full of special clauses and exceptions. Both tenants and landlords should see lawyers. In particular, owner-occupiers who need to leave their home, but will wish to return should take good legal advice before letting. It is not easy to ensure that they will be able to get it back and a lot depends on setting up the tenancy in the right way, and giving the right warnings about your possible return, *right at the start*. A landlord may have more rights when letting to a company so this option should be discussed with your lawyer.

If an eviction order is granted the tenant usually has 28 days in which to leave, though the order can sometimes be immediate. If a tenant fails to leave by the appointed date the landlord should ask the court bailiff to eject them - which will probably take another 2 weeks at the very least.

Leaving Voluntarily

If there is fixed-term tenancy the tenant may be committed to paying rent to the end of the tenancy, even if she no longer wishes to live there, but when the tenancy ends the landlord does not have to have written notice of departure. In most *other* cases, the landlord must have written notice giving the date of departure. The notice periods vary with the tenancy:
weekly and monthly tenancies - 28 days notice
3 monthly - 3 months notice
1 year - 6 months notice.

Repairs

In general, landlords have a right to enter their property to do repairs - even against the tenant's wishes - but not for the purpose of improvement, conversions or extensions. Equally, a landlord has an obligation to do certain repairs, especially if a tenant asks for them to be done. But this is a tricky field: which repairs must be done by the landlord and which by the tenant depends on a host of factors - including the type of tenancy, its duration, and the wording of agreements. The most usual situation is the one covered by a section of the Landlord and Tenant Act 1985. Under this a landlord must repair:

- fires and heating appliances
- baths, sinks and lavatories
- gas, water and electricity supplies
- external pipes plus their drains and gutters
- the structure, walls and roof.

If a landlord fails to do these a tenant can ask the county court for an injunction, or a specific performance order, forcing the landlord to do them (legal aid may be available). The other remedy is for the tenant to get the repairs done himself and deduct the cost from the rent. This is legal, but the landlord may then try to evict the tenant for improper payment of rent and the tenant will have to prove he was justified in what he did. So it is very important first to make sure that the landlord *is* liable for the repairs - under your particular tenancy - and to keep ample proof that the repairs needed to be done and cost precisely the sum you have deducted from the rent. Alternatively, have the work done but, instead of deducting it from the rent, sue the landlord for the cost.

This is guidance not gospel: before acting consult a solicitor.

Where there is a health hazard or a lack of basic amenities - such as a lavatory - or such delapidation that the place may be unfit to live in, the local authority has a duty to make the owner put things right. In practice, it may not be quick on the draw - as it could often mean finding money for a grant. If the authority fails to come and inspect the problem you can ask the magistrate's court to order it to do so. If it then fails to act talk to your local CAB, or law centre, lobby your councillors and MP, and don't forget the power of the local media if the situation is really awful.

Services

The maximum rates at which gas and electricity can be resold to tenants are laid down by gas and electricity boards and can be checked at their showrooms.

In certain types of tenancy, landlords may also charge for services such as maintenance, insurance and staff, provided the charges are reasonable. For major outlays, such as roof repairs, there may also be an obligation to consult the tenants.

Squatting

Squatting is trespass (see below). But you may not use force to get the squatters out. If they refuse to go apply to a county or crown court for a possession order. This can be done within 5 days of your application, and the bailiff has to do the evicting - which can take a week or two but may take considerably longer.

Sublets and Sharing

Council tenants may take in a lodger, who lives as one of the family, but this must usually have council approval, or the sub-tenant can be evicted. If a private tenant sublets, the Rent Act protections (if they apply) normally pass on down, and may even pass to a sub-sublet. But much depends on the rights of the original tenant to sublet. Flat or house sharing isn't specially covered by the law. So sharers are usually considered to be sublets. One way round this is to make it a joint tenancy - which means the landlord has to approve both (or all) the tenants, and also approve any who replace them. But it can be argued that a landlord has appeared to approve a new tenant simply by accepting rent - even if the method of rent collection gives him no way of noticing the change.

National Tenants Organization, 142 Falcon Court, Dudley Close, Old Trafford, Manchester M15 5QD Tel: 061 226 9542 - is a pressure group by and for council tenants. M£L, M, L, G, Ad.

Trespass

In normal circumstances the law is on the side of privacy. People can't just barge into someone else's home or garden. If they do, the owner can first ask him or her to leave, and if he or she refuses, as much force as necessary can be used to eject them. The difficulty comes in defining - and proving - that no more force was used than was necessary. So, in practice, using any kind of force could lead to a prosecution for assault.

If someone repeatedly trespasses the best course is to get an injunction from a court forbidding them to trespass; they can then be fined or imprisoned if they continue.

LEGAL AID

What follows immediately below is the Legal Aid system for England and Wales. The system for Scotland and Ireland is on page 483.

Legal Aid is a state-backed system designed to ensure that nobody is deprived of legal advice for lack of money. It is operated by a large number of high-street solicitors and enables people to get help and advice which would otherwise be barred to them. However, it is means tested, and the levels mean that many people have too much money to obtain Legal Aid, but too little to pay the soaring fees of the specialist lawyers needed for certain cases, nor does it cover all types of case. So, Legal Aid is by no means a cure all.

The Green Form Scheme

Legal Advice and Assistance covers any kind of help from a solicitor except being represented in court; a solicitor can even visit you if you are ill and need a lawyer. It includes advice, letter writing, getting a barrister's opinion or preparing a written case to go before a tribunal.

Assistance by Way of Representation covers the cost of a solicitor preparing your case and representing you in a magistrates' court, or certain tribunals. It applies to cases on issues such as adoption or care proceedings, separation, maintenance, or appeals to a Mental Health Review Tribunal.

There is a set figure which Legal Aid will pay for the Advice and Assistance and a solicitor cannot go beyond it without special permission from the Legal Aid office. By the standards of legal charges in some cities, it is a very low sum indeed, and many firms will not work for such a small fee. However, once approval has been obtained from the authorities, the sum for Assistance by Way of Representation is not limited. If a solicitor refuses to accept a Legal Aid case she need give no reason for refusal.

Children are also covered by both parts of this scheme and can, in some situations, apply for it in their own right. But parents usually apply on behalf of those under 16. This is means tested but your means are assessed by lawyers.

Civil Legal Aid

What it Covers

If your solicitor has tried to resolve a problem under the Green Form Scheme and finds it has to go to court you may be able to get Civil Legal Aid. Even if you have too much money to qualify under the Green Form Scheme, it may be worth applying for Civil Legal Aid because the limit here is higher.

Civil Legal Aid covers being represented by a solicitor or barrister in all the courts except the coroner's court, and some tribunals (though it does cover the Lands Tribunal and the Employment Appeals Tribunal); it also includes appeals. However, there are detailed rules which prevent it from covering cases of certain kinds - such as undefended divorces in county courts. An interview, in order to find out whether your case would fall within the rules, can be paid for by the Green Form Scheme - if you qualify financially.

To obtain Civil Legal Aid you complete a form from your solicitor and apply through him. Be very careful how you complete this form. The fact that you need to take a case and lack money doesn't mean the Legal Aid people will give you Legal Aid automatically. Instead, they decide whether it is *reasonable* for you to get such help, and their decision will be based on what you say on the form. If they turn you down you may be able to appeal to the area committee. (See also Means Test, right).

A solicitor may wait until approval for Civil Legal Aid comes through before starting work on your case, because the Legal Aid cannot be back-dated to cover any work done before approval was granted.

Urgent Cases

If you need help urgently a solicitor can apply for Emergency Legal Aid. In suitable cases this can be granted immediately. But to get it you have to pay any contribution you are assessed for, and agree to pay the full cost of the legal work if your long-term application for Legal Aid is refused. This emergency help only covers you until your main application for Legal Aid is granted or refused.

Legal Aid for Criminal Charges

This falls into several parts, but it only covers defence. You cannot bring a criminal private prosecution under Legal Aid.

Duty Solicitor Scheme

The Duty Solicitor Scheme covers the cost of being advised by a solicitor if the police question you about a criminal offence - at the police station or elsewhere. You can use a duty solicitor whom the police will telephone (page 447), or any other solicitor who is prepared to work under this Scheme, and there is no means test on this. There are also duty solicitors at magistrates' courts, or on call, who will advise you free of charge under this Scheme on your first time in court (on this case).

Criminal Legal Aid

The Advice and Assistance clauses of the Green Form Scheme also cover criminal cases. But full Legal Aid covers a solicitor or barrister preparing your case and representing you in court. It also ranges from the initial proceedings right through to every level of appeal. You obtain a form from the court in question, complete it and apply to the court itself. The court has to decide whether it is 'in the interests of justice' for you to have Legal Aid, so a lot depends on how well you present your case on the form.

If the court turns you down you can apply again, as often as you wish, right up to the trial. And you can use the Green Form Scheme to get a solicitor's help in preparing the case, and then represent yourself. In serious cases you can also ask the Law Society to review your case - and tell the court you are doing this.

Overseas Legal Aid

If a British citizen needs legal representation overseas it may be possible, as certain countries are signatories to an international agreement. Under this you can complete a Legal Aid application in Britain and the authorities send it to the equivalent Legal Aid organization in the country in question. You may then be able to get whatever Legal Aid is available in that country - if its officials feel you qualify for it.

The Means Test

All forms of Legal Aid, except the Duty Solicitor Scheme, are means tested. To qualify for Legal Aid *both* your income *and* your savings must be below a certain limit. The limits are set on sliding scales according to whether you are single or married, the ages of any dependants and vital outgoings such as rent, mortgage or maintenance payments. The levels for income, savings and deductions also vary between the different types of Legal Aid, and are regularly changed; so it would be misleading to give them here, but any CAB has them or contact the Legal Aid Head Office (below). However, the authority assessing entitlement varies. The DHSS assesses it for civil cases and the courts for criminal cases and the solicitor himself, for the Green Form Scheme.

It is an offence to declare a false level of income or savings in your application. If you are married, and live with your spouse, and the dispute is not with him or her, then your joint income will be what counts. Income includes all money coming to you from all sources, including child benefit, before deduction of tax and national insurance. Savings include all the obvious things - deposit accounts, building society, investments, post office savings and so on. They also include the value of certain insurance policies if they were realized and any personal effects of substantial value, such as jewellery, furs or antiques. But they don't include your home, ordinary furniture, clothing or the tools of your trade.

Your Contribution

The idea behind Legal Aid is that each person should pay what they can afford, and the state should pay the difference. In practice, this means that even with Legal Aid you could pay a fair sum.

If your savings and income are below the minimum figure all the legal costs are paid by Legal Aid; if they are between the minimum and a set maximum Legal Aid pays part of your legal fees, and you pay the rest. In the case of the Green Form Advice and Assistance this will be a proportion of the set maximum which solicitors may charge under the Scheme. This is usually paid at once. The same applies to Assistance by way of Representation.

With Civil Legal Aid, if you qualify to pay some contribution you will pay a fraction of the fees for the action. If you lose, and costs are awarded against you, you will pay a fraction of the legal expenses of the other side. But this is not an unlimited amount and the court must take account of the circumstances in deciding how much will be paid. You are usually able to spread out your contribution over a year for Civil Legal Aid, or over six months for Criminal Legal Aid. This delayed payment is a mixed blessing, because it means that the size of your contribution will change if your income changes before the whole amount is paid off - and incomes tend to go up more often than down.

The Price of Success
If your legal case results in you gaining financially, by more than a set amount, you will then be better off. So you may well have to repay all or part of the Legal Aid which you were granted. This is called the 'statutory charge'. However, if you gain a house, in which you need to live you don't have to sell it to pay the lawyers. Instead, the Legal Aid office will put a 'registered charge' on the home which means that whenever you do sell it the money has to be repaid. Even then, if you sell the house only in order to buy another one it may be possible to transfer the registered charge to the second house and continue to owe the money.

This statutory charge can make the fruits of success decidedly bitter and the impact it will have on any settlement constantly needs to be considered in deciding the terms which are acceptable. A wife using Legal Aid may be better off getting monthly maintenance - which will not be liable for the statutory charge - rather than a lump sum, which will.

Using Legal Aid
Not all cases qualify for Legal Aid and not all solicitors do Legal Aid work - look for the Legal Aid logo. The

'Solicitors' Regional Directory' in a public library lists what types of cases solicitors handle and whether they do Legal Aid work. Or write to Legal Aid (P.O. Box 9, Nottingham NG1 6DS) stating the type of case involved (accident, divorce, etc.), and the area in which you want to see a solicitor (it might be more convenient to see one near your work than near your home). Charities specializing in a particular problem may also know of lawyers specializing in that field.

If you want to know whether you qualify you can ask the DHSS or, perhaps better, ask a solicitor for a fixed fee interview. If he agrees you will get half an hour's legal advice for a set fee (£5 in 1988) and find out whether your case is suitable and also whether your finances make Legal Aid likely.

The Legal Aid Head Office, Newspaper House, 8-16 Great New Street, London EC1A 3BN Tel: 01 353 7411/4 - will supply legal aid information.

Scotland and Ireland
Legal Aid in Scotland is very similar to the scheme given above, but there are certain local variations. To get the details of Legal Aid in Ireland write to its law society. For Scotland contact the Scottish Legal Aid Board.

Legal Aid Scottish Board, P.O.Box 123, 44 Drumsheugh Gardens, Edinburgh EH3 7SW Tel: 031 226 7061

Incorporated Law Society of Northern Ireland, Legal Aid Department, Bedford House, 16-22 Bedford Street, Belfast BT2 7FL Tel: 0232 246441

This is guidance not gospel: before acting consult a solicitor.

Money
Benefits and Grants • Money Management • Insurance • Mortgages
Pensions • Savings • Stocks and Shares • Tax

It is a great pity that money involves numbers. We deal with money in our pockets every day without a pause. But with larger sums the bogey man of mathematics casts his shadow. As a result, money matters have a reputation for being hard to understand and best left to the experts. This is simply not so. Money matters are actually no more complicated than gardening or DIY. The real trouble is that a mystery has grown up around them and those in the money world have been allowed to develop a language which most of us simply don't know.

Don't let this put you off. If you ask for financial information from anyone, be prepared to ask for an explanation the moment they say anything you don't understand. Don't be afraid to reveal your ignorance. Ask, and keep on asking, until they put it in plain English. There is nothing to be said about money which can't be said in terms anyone can understand, and if the people you are consulting fail to do that it isn't you who is being stupid.

You need to be prepared to do this because never before has the ordinary consumer been faced with such a range of financial services, service companies and opportunities as he or she is today. And for almost every choice there is a pitfall. There are a few rules which could, however, help anyone to hang on to their money a little bit longer.

- Never rush into any financial decision.
- Always get as much professional advice as you can, from several sources - there is more free advice available in this field than in almost any other.
- Go to the reputable sources.
- If anyone telephones offering financial advice, don't even agree to talk to them. They are trained to persuade you to buy a particular type of financial product. You don't need financial advice from those who have an axe to grind.
- Beware of advertisements in newspapers. The law is now stricter than it was. But there are always loopholes. The better the company the less likely it is to take out a small ad. Finding an adviser through a professional body is far safer.
- Beware of advertisements which offer to advise and help you with debts. Many of those who place such advertisements are really offering loans at much higher than normal rates, although, when they talk to you, it may not seem that way. Scores of people have lost their homes by borrowing from such companies (see Debt, page 497).
- Before making any kind of financial decision bone

up on it. Have a look in this chapter. Read *Which* magazine - *Which* now has excellent financial sections each month. Listen to BBC Radio 4's 'Moneybox', which gives first-rate information on personal finance. Check some of the books and leaflets I list. Read the family or personal finance sections of the newspapers. Never take any financial decision without checking the latest facts - the financial world changes daily.
- Don't forget the managers of banks, building societies and other reputable organizations are sources of free advice.

★ Pause for thought before starting a family, and prepare your finances. A survey in the *Sunday Times* a few years ago found that it costs the average parent £66,000 to raise a child to the age of 18, and for many parents it is £164,000. And that doesn't include the difference it may have made to the mother's earning potential.

BENEFITS AND GRANTS

Far too many people lose out on benefits they are entitled to because they don't even try to claim them, and it is often the most deserving cases who go without. They are not gifts from some all powerful state. Rather they are drawn from a rainy day fund which you and your family paid into in taxes and national insurance. Payments can sometimes be backdated *if* there's a good reason why you didn't claim - but not knowing your rights *isn't* classed as a good reason.

There are several dozen different benefits waiting to be claimed. Some are only handed out if you have paid enough in national insurance (contributory benefits) but many don't depend on that. To claim any benefit get a form from your post office and fill it in, or go to your local social security office or Citizens Advice Bureau and ask what benefits you might be entitled to and ask them to help with the forms.

As I write, major changes created by the 1986 Social Security Act are coming into force (in April 1988) and many of the details are not yet available from the DHSS. So, unfortunately, I can't give a thorough briefing on benefits. However, some changes are known and the following benefits are either new ones which have already been announced or old ones which may survive - though possibly under another name and with some modifications.

★ Some benefits can now be paid straight into your bank or building society account if you ask for this.

From April 1988 the time limits for applying for certain benefits - such as widow's benefit, the retirement pension or invalid care allowance - were extended. If you now apply within 1 year of entitlement the payments will be back-dated in full.

Benefits for a Low Income or Unemployment

A whole parcel of benefits for those on low incomes have been renamed and had their rules altered.

A key change is that under the old scheme savings were not counted, but the income from them was counted as part of the total income. Under the new scheme, savings are now looked at too for certain benefits. As I write you are allowed savings of up to £3,000 without it altering the Income Support, or Family Credit which you receive. If your savings are over £3,000 and under £8,000 the rule is the larger the savings the smaller the benefits. And if you have more than £8,000 you may get no Income Support or Family Credit at all. *But do ask* as the figures and rules could change.

Income Support

Supplementary Benefit (SB) has been replaced by Income Support. Like SB you will be able to claim it if you aren't in full-time work and your income is below a certain level. Under the new scheme there are 3 types:

- a low rate for the single and childless under 25
- a basic rate for everyone else
- flat rate 'premiums' for those in special need, such as lone parents, the disabled or elderly (and they can earn slightly more without losing any benefit). Income support may also help to pay mortgage interest or home loans.

Family Credit

Family Credit (FC) takes the place of Family Income Supplement (FIS) and makes larger payments depending on the number and age of the children. To get it you must meet *all* these rules:

- you must have children
- one parent must work at least 24 hours a week (the hours aren't reduced for single parents)
- not have more capital than the limits (see above)
- the income must be below a set threshold. FC is paid weekly at a post office or monthly into a bank account, and single parents will *not* get less than a couple with the same family. But, unlike FIS, it won't entitle the children to free school meals or milk and vitamins. But it does entitle families to free NHS prescriptions, dental treatment and travel to hospital. It is normally paid to the mother.

Unemployment Benefit

Unemployment Benefit is a contributory benefit (see page 484) paid to those who are out of work - but are able to work and available for it. Take your National Insurance card and the P45 from your last employer to the social security office. The rate varies according to whether someone is single or married and according to the number of children they have. Payment starts 4 days after employment ends and lasts for 12 months.

(Anyone who is made redundant after working for the same employer for 2 years (after the age of 18) may also be entitled to redundancy pay from the employer. The amount depends on the length of service, pay and so on, but the law sets minimum sums.)

Allowances for the Unemployed

Anyone who is unemployed and thinking of going on a Manpower Services Commission course should ask whether they would be entitled to an allowance. They should also ask at the Jobcentre about allowances for travel to look for jobs in other areas, and to help them with moving home to take a new job.

Benefits for Illness and Disablement

Where handicap, disablement and old age are concerned there may be benefits both directly for the disabled person and for those who look after them. There are leaflets which give the full range of financial and practical help available to those with disabilities (page 487). These include not only money but equipment and a special rail card. The benefits which may be available include the following, but there are far more benefits than I can list, so do ask a CAB or social security office.

Sickness Benefit for someone who is too ill to work and is not receiving sick pay from an employer.
Statutory Sick Pay (SSP) from your employer - if you have qualified by paying Class 1 National Insurance. SSP only covers 28 weeks at a stretch. After that you may qualify for *Invalidity Benefit*.

For all those you must have paid enough National Insurance. For the following it isn't necessary.
Severe Disablement Allowance
Mobility Allowance is for those almost, or totally, unable to walk - but claim before the age of 65.
Attendance Allowance can be claimed for someone older than 2 years who needs constant care and attention.
Invalid Care Allowance can be claimed by the person who attends someone who needs constant care.

Income Support (see left) is also available for the sick, disabled and handicapped, whether they live at home or in residential care. There are extra payments to the disabled but the sum paid may be reduced if an attendance allowance is claimed. In addition a new fund is being set up to make special payments to the disabled - contact the Disablement Income Group (page 487).

Those who have been in-patients for more than a year were entitled to a resettlement benefit. That has stopped but a loan from the Social Fund may be available.

Victims of Industrial Accidents

Victims of industrial accidents, or illness caused by work, have a set of benefits including special allowances for industrial injuries and for death from industrial accidents, and the rules here changed in April 1987. Since then both Industrial Disablement Benefit and Reduced Earnings Allowance may be claimed in full, one does not reduce the other.

> Any benefit may alter if you go into hospital or residential care. Equally, on leaving hospital there may be special help with fares, appliances or medicines. Ask the hospital social worker to advise you.

Child Benefit

Child benefit is paid tax-free for each child until they leave school. And there is an extra single parent's benefit on one child.

Housing Benefits

If you find it difficult to pay your rent or rates you may be able to get help from your council - although it is no longer available to students in college-owned lets. This applies whatever other benefits you are, or aren't, getting (but see the note below). Under the new rules you can still get 100 per cent of rent, but only 80 per cent of rates. However, the period of housing benefit is now longer, so it's swings and roundabouts.

> Under the old system if you were on Supplementary Benefit the Housing Benefit department was told, automatically, that you might need help. Now you must apply separately for Income Support and Housing Benefit - they do not communicate.

Special Needs

Guardian's Allowance

A guardian's allowance is a tax-free weekly payment to anyone who takes an orphan into his or her family. It can be claimed whether or not you are the legal guardian.

Maternity Benefits

If you have paid enough NI contributions and aren't getting Statutory Maternity pay from an employer you may be able to get a Maternity Allowance for 18 weeks. The rules are complicated, check the DHSS leaflet *before* giving up work or you could lose this benefit.

Social Fund

The Social Fund replaces the old system of single payments, made to those already receiving other benefits, to meet special needs. The key difference is that single payments were given outright to those who could prove a real need for them, but money from the Social Fund will be an interest free loan which must be paid back over a set period. Also, the officials now have far more power to choose who will and will not receive them. Only maternity and funeral payments may be claimed as of right. What's more, the fund has a limit. When the kitty runs dry there will be no money however deserving your case.

Under this scheme there are Budgeting Loans for those on benefits already, Crisis Loans which anyone can claim in a serious crisis, and Community Care Grants to help someone cope in the community - after a long period in care for example. But savings of over £500 will affect the payments.

Widows' Benefits

There are three sources of potential income for a widow - widow's payment, widowed mother's allowance, and a widow's pension. All of them depend on her husband having paid enough National Insurance.

The Widow's Allowance has been abolished and replaced by a **Widow's Payment.** This is a tax free lump sum of £1,000 payable as soon as the husband dies, providing a woman was under 60, or her husband was not drawing a pension, when he died. It should be claimed within 12 months.

On top of that, the Widowed Mother's Allowance or the Widow's Pension are now paid from the time of the death, but the rules on entitlement have changed.

A **Widowed Mother's Allowance** is still paid to those who are pregnant or have at least one child under 19. Claim within 6 months or benefit may be lost.

The rules for the **Widow's Pension** are harder. Those who don't have children and are 44 or under get no widow's pension. Between 45 and 55 there is a sliding scale of widow's pension, and anyone who is 55 or over when her husband dies gets the top rate. A woman's age when her husband dies establishes *forever* the rate of pension she will receive. However, the pension is index linked so the sums she gets will rise with the cost of living. Claim within 12 months.

The **Industrial Death Benefit** (which used to pay a few pence more than a normal widow's pension to those widowed by industrial accidents) will now exist only for those who became entitled to it before April 1988. From then on these widows will only have the same entitlement as other widows.

Anyone whose husband died (or dies) after 5 April 1979 should also be getting his entitlement to an earnings related pension.

More information

The DHSS publishes free leaflets covering each benefit, but the simplest general guide to benefits is called *Which Benefit*. It lists the possibilities and names the detailed leaflets which cover each of them. It should be in post offices, social security offices and Citizens' Advice Bureaux, or write to the DHSS office (see Organizations). Your post office has free stamped envelopes in which to send for free DHSS leaflets. The DHSS also has a freephone number on 0800 666 555 which answers

If you disagree with what the officials decide to give you, ask if you are entitled to appeal. (In some cases you are, in others you aren't.) If you can appeal be sure to write to your social security office *within 28 days of the decision*, and say you wish to appeal. The Citizens' Advice Bureau will advise you on how to do this.

If officials have paid you less than you should have had, you are now entitled to full payment of the money owed you - dating right back to when the mistake was made.

queries about social security benefits.

Scottish Home and Health Department, St Andrew's House, Regent Road, Edinburgh EH1 3DE Tel: 031 556 8400 has leaflets on benefits of all kinds.

War Pensions Branch, DHSS, North Fylde Central Office, Norcross, Blackpool FY5 3TA Tel: 0253 856123 or the nearest War Pensioners' Welfare Office - listed in the phone book under Social Security - has information on benefits for war pensioners.

Disablement Income Group (DIG), Millmead Business Centre, Millman Road, London N1Y 9QU Tel: 01 801 8013 is a pressure group and information source on benefits for the disabled and handicapped. So are many other special organizations found in this book.

Department of Transport (see Organizations) publishes a 'Door to Door Guide' to transport for the disabled which should be in social security offices.

The British Pensioners and Trades Union Action Committee (97 Kings Drive, Gravesend, Kent DA12 5BQ Tel: 0474 361802) will advise and represent senior citizens and widows in disputes about entitlements.

Good booklets are also published by **SHAC** (page 228) or **Child Poverty Action Group,** 4th Floor, 1-5 Bath Street, London EC1V 9PY Tel: 01 253 3406.

Grants

Local Education Authorities throughout Britain give two kinds of grant: mandatory and discretionary. Both are paid to the student termly and cover living expenses, books and travel. They are not intended to cover the summer holiday and students may be able to draw certain social security benefits if they can't find summer work. The fees for the courses are paid, by the LEA, direct to the university.

Mandatory Grants

Mandatory grants are ones the local education department *must* pay to a student who takes one of the courses 'designated' by the Department of Education and Science, provided they meet certain rules. The major 'designated' courses are those leading to a first degree, Higher National Diploma, or a teaching qualification. But these are not the only ones, others - such as sandwich courses leading to qualifications equal to a degree - are also covered. However, there are some curious exceptions: for example, the foundation year of an art degree doesn't qualify for a mandatory grant neither does a first degree through open learning qualify.

Grants no longer vary with the subject, as they used to, but there are other variations. There are 3 rates: one for those who live at home or choose to live in private digs; another for those living in hall and attending a London college or university; a third for those in hall or lodgings elsewhere.

Who is Entitled to Mandatory Grants?

There is no upper age limit on mandatory grants, they are open to anyone who attends a designated course and has lived in Britain for the previous 3 years. However, those who have had lived abroad because of their own or their parents' work aren't usually disqualified.

The greatest risk of losing entitlement to a grant is from having too much income - capital is not assessed. However, various allowances are set against the gross income, and the cut off point for obtaining a full grant varies with the number in the family. Unfortunately the calculations are such that it isn't easy for anyone to work out what grant, if any, they should get, although the main rules of assessment are simple.

- Usually the authorites look at the combined income of the student and his or her parents.
- If the parents are divorced the income of whichever parent has custody will usually be assessed with the student's income.
- If a student is over 25 when the academic year starts the parents' income is not considered.
- If a student has been self supporting for any 3 years the parents' income is not considered.
- If a student has been married for at least 3 years before the course starts the parents' income is not considered but the authorities assess the total income of the couple.
- If a student is married with a dependent spouse and/or child the grant may be increased.

Above a certain ceiling the grant shrinks as the net income rises - though not on a £1 for £1 basis. But even a student who gets no grant at all for living expenses will still have her fees paid.

If a covenant pays money towards a child's education the payments are assessed as the child's income. The money then has lower allowances set against it than if it was assessed as belonging to the parents (see Covenant form IR47). So what is gained in tax may be lost in grant. Also, the budget of 1988 abolished the tax advantages on covenants taken out after 15 March that year.

Discretionary Grants

A local education authority also has the power to give a discretionary grant for any non-designated higher or further education course except those leading to higher degrees. Getting such a grant depends on whether the local authority has the funds, whether you seem to deserve one, and on the suitability of the course. LEAs are unlikely to give grants to attend courses run by private establishments which are not accredited by the DES. So make sure you apply for a well established and accredited course and muster good evidence to support your case.

Although degrees through open learning don't qualify for mandatory grants a LEA may well make a discretionary grant towards books or residential courses within the syllabus - if it is your first degree.

When and How to Apply for a Grant

It is vital to apply for a grant at the right time. You cannot apply before January if the course starts the following autumn. But in some authorities you should apply by March to be sure to have the money for the start of the autumn term. *Don't* wait to be accepted for a course. If you aren't accepted the grant is automatically cancelled. If you wait until you are accepted you will still get a grant, if you're entitled to it, but the money may not arrive until well into the first term - which is no fun.

> LEAs can refuse a grant totally if you apply too late. The latest date on which you may apply is the last day of the first term of a course.

You get a grant application form from a school or from the education authority of the area where you live - in the phone book under the name of the council, then under 'education' within the council numbers. Application procedures vary, but there are normally three stages:
1 You fill in the application form and send it in.
2 If they think your course entitles you to a grant you are sent another form which they use to assess how much money you will get.
3 If you are offered, and accept, a place you complete a 'college acceptance form' and send it to the college. (If your place depends on exam results wait and send this part in only when you have the results.) The college then tells the local authority that you have definitely been accepted. Only after the authority has this in writing from the college will you get any money.

Other Sources of Money

Local authorities aren't the only sources of grants. Industry and various government departments - especially the services - have sponsorship schemes. These are covered in the booklet *Sponsorship 19..* published each year by COIC (Department CW,, ISCO 5, The Paddock, Frizinghall, Bradford BD9 4HD Tel: 0742 704563). There can be distinct advantages in taking this route, as an employer can sponsor a student by up to £2,000 a year without it reducing the state grant. Those who do a period of study overseas may be able to get a grant from the country concerned - it is certainly worth a try, as the grants are usually more generous than British grants.

There are also educational charities and trusts which give grants for specific purposes, such as foreign travel to study a particular aspect of a course. Reference libraries should have the following directories which have lists of charities which tell you what each will support.

Department of Education and Science, Publications Despatch Centre, Honeypot Lane, Canons Park, Stanmore, Middx HA7 1AZ Tel: 01 953 2366, publishes *Grants to Students - a brief guide*.

Scottish Education Department, Haymarket House, Clifton Terrace, Edinburgh EH12 5DT Tel: 031 244 5868 (direct line) - publishes *Guide to Student Allowances*.
Charities Digest, Family Welfare Association
The Grant Register, Macmillan Press
Directory of Grant-making Trusts, Charities Aid Foundation

MONEY MANAGEMENT

Accounts

At one time the choice was simple, you had a current account at a bank for day-to-day money, and some kind of deposit account as a back up. Current accounts didn't pay interest and deposit accounts did. That is no longer the choice. Various 1986 Acts took down the neat fences which had for years penned each type of financial service into its own field of interest and now almost every type of financial institution is behaving like almost every other type. So banks no longer have a monopoly on the cheque book account, building societies are offering hot competition and other financial organizations are in the running.

Looking after other people's money is a highly profitable business, so each new company is trying to offer newer and better baits to get you to put your money with them. Some current accounts now pay interest and there are numerous different types of deposit account, some of which offer the facilities of a current account - including a cheque book.

Accounts for Daily Money

A current account at one of the big four banks (Barclays, Lloyds, Midland and National Westminster) is the most obvious place to put money which you want to use for day-to-day living. But it isn't always the best place, so look at the other options. Some building societies offer current accounts where *they* pay *you* interest. Some offer commission-free travellers' cheques, and some of the other banks such as TSB, Girobank, Clydesdale, Bank of Scotland and so on, have features which the big four lack. For example, as it uses post office counters, Girobank is open post office hours.

This means that *if* you can keep more than one account in reasonable credit you should consider taking the pick of the perks and benefits from several companies by splitting your money between several accounts. A building society paying interest might, for example, be the best place to have a current account, but you might need to have another account in a bank, so you could use the loan facilities.

Financial facts change daily, check the latest figures before making a decision.

Before opening an account with any company tell them your status (a student, for example). Useful questions to ask before opening an account are these.

- Do they pay interest on a current account?
- Do they have any other account which pays interest and allows you to use a cheque book in the usual way?
- Do they offer free banking? If so, what sum must be in the account for services to be free? Would charges be made *the moment* you fell below that sum, or is there a period of grace?
- What is the limit of a cashcard withdrawal per day?
- How often can you have a free bank statement?
- What information does the bank statement give?
- How many branches do they have?
- Can you cash their cheques at any other banks without being charged for the service?
- Do they allow overdrafts? If so, up to what sum?
- What would an overdraft of £200 for 6 months cost in interest? (Giving a set figure for set months makes comparison easy).
- Do they give loans, and if so what for?
- Will you get any perks if you open an account?
- How much do they charge for the following:
  (a) if you are in credit
  (b) if you aren't
    holding an envelope in safe keeping?
    holding a small box in safe keeping?
    a loan of £5,000, and would other sums have another rate?
    issuing travellers' cheques (if you travel)
    issuing foreign cash (if you travel)
    paying standing orders
    bouncing a cheque
    cancelling a cheque
    arranging an overdraft
    extra statements
    credits and debits if you are overdrawn
    direct debits
    money from a cash dispenser
    standing orders
    financial services (other than advice) e.g. buying shares
- What standing charges are there?

Finally, do they have any services specially suited to you? For example, the Bank of Scotland already has computer banking which will give you information and let you pay your bills via a home computer.

Savings and Deposit Accounts
In savings and deposit accounts you have an even wider choice than in current accounts. Every bank has several different types and, on top of that, there are all the building societies, and options like National Savings.

Some people say that as the interest rates only vary by a per cent or two it doesn't matter where you put your money. I disagree. It isn't worth constantly swopping from place to place. But it *is* worth choosing the best rate to start with - provided the account doesn't have any disadvantages which make it unsuitable.

The most likely disadvantages are that some accounts must be kept above a certain sum, and some need long notice of a withdrawal and/or make you lose months of interest on any money you take out before the end of a set time. So the key questions to ask about such accounts are these.

- What is the rate of interest?
- Is a minimum sum needed to open or maintain such an account?
- How much notice must you give before taking money out?
- If money is taken out what interest is lost on it over what period?

Banking and Banking by Any Other Name

Banking is a bit like motoring: you are expected to know the rules, and it is always up to the customer to find out the facts and to keep tabs on their own money.

Goodness knows how bank managers came to be elevated to the status of punishing father figures. A bank is a service industry - like a hotel. It looks after your money just as a hotel looks after you. It should be chosen and used in the same spirit, and the bank manager regarded in much the same way as a hotel manager, not as someone who can tell you what to do. The same applies to building society managers, and others, who offer banking services.

There is no point in banking with any bank because your family has always banked there, or because your husband or wife does. Unless, of course, the family has such a reputation with that bank that it will let you borrow money with the least possible fuss.

If your bank ceases to offer the services you want, or refuses a reasonable request, or charges more than the next bank - *move your account.* You can even move an overdraft if another bank will take it on.

That said, bank managers have the power to grant or refuse loans and overdrafts. If you were a bank manager who would you rather lend to - a customer who ignored you until money was needed, or one who kept you informed of their success and treated you like a human being? So, cultivate your bank manager.

- Don't just visit him when there's a problem. Make sure you meet him (it is seldom a her) and get to know him. Give him lunch if it's appropriate.
- If you get a new job or promotion write and tell him, and say what difference it will make.
- If you get a loan or overdraft let him know what you have achieved with it and thank him.
- If you need money go armed with the facts on why it's needed and the figures on repayment.
- Never run up an overdraft without arranging it with the bank. This shows you have things under control and will cost less.

Cash Cards
The machines which give you cash when you insert a card and punch in a number are both useful and dangerous. The cards are known as debit cards, because

bank computers take the sum straight out of your account, and the number as a PIN number (Personal Identification Number). The snag is that these cards aren't covered by the law. There are moves to change this but, at present, banks can write their own rules and they have written rules to favour themselves. They don't accept that mistakes can happen. So, if money is taken from your account by the machine, they say it must have been done by you or with your knowledge - and they won't refund it. Not even if you can prove that you couldn't have been near a machine at the time.

The moral is *never* tell anyone - not even your nearest and dearest - your PIN number and *never* keep it anywhere near your card. If you can't remember it write it in a way which won't be recognized. Best of all ask to choose your own PIN number (some cards allow this) then choose a number which means something to you but to nobody else. Like your mother's birthday, plus the number of the bus you take. Then you won't need to write it down. If it is lost, ring and *report it at once* (page 492). Then confirm this in writing the same day saying the time of day you rang at and giving the name of the person you spoke to. Then nobody can say you didn't tell them soon enough to stop a withdrawal.

★ Keep a written record of when you use your card. It could be useful evidence if there was a problem.
★ Cash cards are no longer limited to being used in machines of the company that issues them. More and more companies are linking up. If you have a card ask where you can use it.

Cheques

It pays to write cheques carefully. However, what can and cannot be done with a cheque is a matter of banking practice, not law. Incidentally, the payee is the person whose name follows the word 'Pay', and a cheque is not 'legal tender', so if someone wants to refuse a cheque they have a perfect right to do so.

An **uncrossed cheque** doesn't have tramlines up the middle. This is the least safe form of cheque. It can be paid into any bank account, or the payee can get cash for it at the branch it was issued by, provided they can show they are the payee.

A **crossed cheque** has tramlines up the middle and only the person who owns the cheque book can get cash with it. Anyone else must pay it into a bank account. However, it doesn't have to go into the account of the payee. If you wrote me a cheque I could sign it on the back or, better still, write 'Please pay Fergus

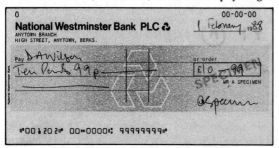

Bremner' and my son could then put it into his account. It would also be legal for him to then sign it and put instructions to pay someone else and it could be paid into that person's account. And so on.

To open a crossed cheque (i.e., make it possible for someone to cash it) write 'please pay cash' between the tram lines and sign it there as well as in the usual place. The payee can then get cash for it at any bank if they can prove they are the person named. So if, for example, someone stole your wallet containing both an opened cheque and a credit card they could easily cash it.

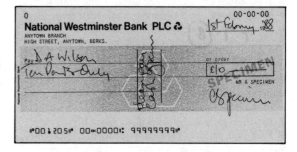

Cheques marked a/c payee only between the tram lines can only be paid into the account of the payee. There is no way the payee can make it payable to anyone else. And if it is stolen, and someone tries to pay it into their account, the bank will still automatically pay it to the person you named or return the cheque to you. So this is the safest way to write a cheque when paying anyone by post.

However you write your cheques it is vital to note how much was paid, and to whom, on the counterfoil. Only then can you easily prove that you did pay a bill, or check that your bank statements are correct.

Banks won't honour cheques which are more than 6 months old but the person who wrote it is liable for 6 years. If you have a cheque over 6 months old keep a photocopy and return the original asking for a replacement.

Cheque Cards and Bounced Cheques

Having a cheque accidentally 'bounce' (be returned unhonoured) is one of the more embarrassing things which can happen. A bank only has a duty to pay out on a cheque if there is money in the account to meet the *full sum*. If you have £50 in the bank and write a cheque for £75 it needn't pay a penny (unless you have arranged for an overdraft). That applies also to standing orders and direct debits. So if you are overdrawn you could find a vital payment, such as a mortgage being bounced and end up with real problems.

One way to avoid this - if you have enough money - is to keep some spare money in a high interest account in the same bank. Then instruct your bank automatically to transfer funds from your high interest account into your current account the moment your current account approaches a set level (whatever guarantees free banking and will prevent vital payments bouncing). In effect, it means you are using a high interest account as a cheque account.

If you write a cheque and your cheque card number is written on the back of it the bank *must* pay whoever the cheque is made out to - provided it is not more than the £50 which the cheque card guarantees - even if you have no money in the bank. But, the number must *not* have been written by you. However, a cheque card doesn't guarantee a forged cheque. (See also Stopping a Cheque, below.)

Forged Cheques
Suppose you write a cheque for £20 and someone alters it to £120 and the bank pays out the larger sum. If you wrote the cheque carefully, so any additions had to look like additions, the bank was wrong to pay the money out on a suspect cheque and they should not take the extra money from your account. But if you left gaps which made it easy for the forger you would be to blame and they would be entitled to debit your account.

However, if your cheque book is lost or stolen and someone forges your signature the law says that your bank ought to know your signature. So if it pays out that is the bank's loss not yours. This applies even if the cheque carries a cheque card number. However, you should notify your branch as soon as you know the cheque book has been stolen. Monday morning is soon enough if you discover the loss at a weekend. If you are away and can't find the number of your branch phone the head office (page 492).

Post-dated Cheques
If the date you put on a cheque is for some time in the future it is said to be post-dated. A bank should only pay out money on, or after, the date on a cheque. This can be a convenient way of paying back money in stages. Post-dating a cheque is also useful if your account is low but you know money will come in on a certain date. But the person you are paying needn't accept it.

Stopping a Cheque
If a cheque has the bank card number on the back it cannot be stopped. If it doesn't, you can ask your bank not to pay the cheque and it *must* do as you say - unless it has already paid out the money so - though it will probably charge you for doing so. It needs the instruction in writing but you can phone and ask for the cheque to be held until your letter arrives. If the bank pays out, when you have told it not to, it bears the cost.

Did you know that if you get on to a bus and only have a £10 note with which to pay the fare the bus conductor can't refuse to accept it? Nor may he or she get back at you by giving you change in dozens of small coins. If you only have the note and there isn't enough change give your name and address and wait for the bill.

Cash is legal tender and, by law, nobody may refuse to accept it in payment. But there are limits to what someone is obliged to accept in small coins. You can pay any amount you like in £1 coins but nobody has to accept:
- more than 20p worth of 2p or 1p coins
- more than £5 worth of 5p or 10p coins
- more than £10 worth of 20p or 50p coins

Services from Banks
The range of services banks can offer was so much expanded by the Financial Services Act 1986 that they are never going to be the same again. Nowadays almost every imaginable financial service can be obtained from some bank somewhere - though a bank won't always be the best place to get it.

Standing Orders
A standing order is a convenient way to pay a regular set sums such as an annual subscription. You just give the bank the details of how much should be paid, to whom and on what date, and they do the rest. This is usually done on a form provided by the company you are paying. There may or may not be a bank charge for a standing order - check.

★ It is very easy to forget about standing orders and go on paying out for magazines which are being sent to an old address. Banks do not always cancel them when you instruct them to. So keep a separate file with the letters which both start and stop them. Then your proof won't get lost.

Direct Debit
A direct debit is an arrangement whereby you give permission for a certain organization to make various charges directly to your account, and authorize the bank to pay them. This can be a convenient way of paying rates month by month, for example, instead of in a crippling lump sum. Unless you have free banking there is usually a charge for each direct debit, so it costs more than writing a cheque yourself. Only reputable organizations may directly debit an account, and if a mistake is made you should be refunded by the company or your bank.

Debit Cards
A debit card is really a cross between a credit card and a cheque book. You give the shop the card and it is handled like a credit card, but instead of being sent to a credit card company, the bill goes to your bank which

Financial facts change daily, check the latest figures before making a decision.

takes the money out of your account within a couple of days. It can also be used to guarantee cheques and to withdraw money. It has the same £50 limit on payments as a cheque card.

Complaining About Banks

If you have a complaint write to the manager of the branch concerned. If that fails write to the Customer Services Department at the head office. In addition there is the banking ombudsman.

The banking ombudsman is a lawyer appointed by a council, and paid for by 19 major banks. His job is to sort out complaints by customers when complaints to one of these banks have failed to get results. He offers a free service as an impartial referee. You can get leaflets on this service by phoning, but complaints must be made in writing. The banking ombudsman is in touch with other ombudsmen and where necessary he may refer a complaint on.

The Office of the Banking Ombudsman (OBO), Citadel House, 5/11 Fetter Lane, London EC4A 1BR Tel: 01 583 1395

More information

Banking Information Service, 10 Lombard Street, London EC3V 9AP Tel: 01 626 8486
The following organizations are among those which offer current accounts and various banking services:
Bank of Scotland, The Mound, Edinburgh EH1 1YZ Tel: 031 442 7777
Barclays Bank PLC, 54 Lombard Street, London EC3P 3AH Tel: 01 626 1567
Clydesdale Bank 30 St Vincent Place, Glasgow G1 2HL Tel: 041 248 7070
Co-operative Bank, 1 Balloon Street, Manchester M60 4EP Tel: 061 832 3456
Girobank PLC, 10 Milk Street, London EC2V 8JH Tel: 01 600 6020
Lloyds Bank PLC, 71 Lombard Street, London EC3P 3PS Tel: 01 626 1500
Midland Bank PLC, 27-32 Poultry, London EC2P 2BX Tel: 01 260 8000
National Westminster Bank PLC, 41 Lothbury, London EC2P 2BP Tel: 01 726 1000
The Royal Bank of Scotland, 42 St Andrew Square, Edinburgh EH2 2YE Tel: 031 556 8555
Standard Chartered Bank, 38 Bishopsgate, London EC2N 4DE Tel: 01 280 7500
TSB Group, 25 Milk Street, London EC2V 8LU Tel: 01 606 7070
Abbey National, Abbey House, Baker Street, London NW1 6XI Tel: 01 486 5555.
Alliance & Leicester, Glen Road, Oadby, Leicester LE2 4PF Tel: 0533 717272
Bradford & Bingley, P.O. Box 2, Bingley, West Yorkshire BD16 2LW Tel: 0274 568111
Britannia, P.O. Box 20, Newton House, Leek, Staffordshire ST13 5RG Tel: 0538 399399
Gateway Building Society, P.O. Box 18, Worthing, West Sussex BN13 2QD Tel: 0903 68555
Halifax, P.O. Box 60, Trinity Road, Halifax, West Yorkshire HX1 2RG Tel: 0422 65777
Leeds Permanent, Permanent House, The Headrow, Leeds, West Yorkshire LS1 1NS Tel: 0532 438181
National & Provincial, Provincial House, Bradford, West Yorkshire BD1 1NL Tel: 0274 733444

Nationwide Anglia, Chesterfield House, 15-19 Bloomsbury Way, London WC1V 6PW Tel: 01 242 8822
Town & Country, 215 Strand, London WC2R 1AY Tel: 01 353 1476
Woolwich, Equitable House, Woolwich, London SE18 6AB Tel: 01 854 2400

Borrowing Money

We are fast becoming a nation of credit junkies. 'Buy now, pay later' is the message many advertisements blare out. In fact it is almost impossible to live today without borrowing - even if it's only a mortgage. In the right circumstances, borrowing can be a very good idea. However, it must be done with caution, and the terms of the loan checked very carefully.

Numerous banks, credit card companies, finance houses and even back-street money lenders are willing to lend you money and they usually word the offers so it looks as if they are doing you a favour. They aren't. *You* are doing *them* the favour. The easiest way to make money is to charge high rates for lending it.

As the law stands there is no limit to the level of interest which may be charged. The best protection which you, the consumer, have against those who want to charge you excessive interest rates is to not to borrow from them (see also pages 494-495).

Safer Borrowing

Before you borrow money check the following points.
- The APR
- Is the interest fixed for the whole of the loan period or will it change as interest rates change?
- Can you get tax relief on the loan? You can get tax relief on the interest on loans from some sources but not from others. How you will spend the money also makes a difference. Ask the Inland Revenue.
- Will the lender be charging a fee for fixing the loan? Even a bank may charge for this.
- Over how long a period may the loan be repaid, and what other options are there?
- Does the lender require any security? The company might ask for your home or an insurance policy as a guarantee. See page 493 on the risks of using your home.
- Will the lender make a charge if you decide to pay off the loan early?
- Will the lender need references?
- Could you get better terms from any other source - have you *really* explored all the options?

It is always hard to keep track of borrowing, but it pays to keep a strict check on it.
- Have a file for all papers related to any borrowing.
- Keep a note of each payment you make and get a receipt if it isn't by cheque.
- If you have problems about repayment write letters and keep copies of the letters.
- If the money you owe is being collected from you, a charge for this may be hidden in your payments. The person collecting the money may not admit to this. Ask the head office if you would pay less if you

Financial facts change daily, check the latest figures before making a decision.

took the money round yourself.
- When you have paid off a loan ask for a statement in writing confirming this.

Your Rights
If you discuss a loan away from the offices of whoever is lending the money, *and* sign the agreement away from the offices, you have a right to a 'cooling off' period. You should be given a copy of any agreement you sign, and it ought to carry an explanation of your cancellation rights. But you should also be sent a separate notice of your cancellation rights. From the day you receive this you have 5 days in which to cancel.

If you do cancel, do it in writing and make sure that you get proof of posting from the post office.

If you decide to pay off your loan early it won't always be as big a saving as you might expect. Some lenders will make a charge for the interest they will lose by the debt being paid early. However, they are not entitled to *all* the interest you would have paid. In the Consumer Credit Act 1974 there is a formula for how much the lender may charge. A Citizens' Advice Bureau or Money Advice Centre will be able to give you the details if you feel you may not be getting your due.

> The government publishes **Consumer Credit Tables** which spell out the cost of loans of all sizes, with a range of interest rates, and for varied periods. The OFT (see Organizations) has a leaflet telling you what tables cover which rates, and the tables can be bought from HMSO (see Organizations). But your public library should have, or get, the table you need. These tables allow you to find the true APR on any agreement you enter into.
>
> The OFT also produces a range of free, readable and very helpful leaflets on borrowing and debt.

Borrowing Money Against Your Home
One of the most dangerous ways to borrow money is to get a loan against the value of your home. Such loans are, of course, offered by banks and building societies on reasonable terms. But many of the finance houses which offer them charge *extremely high interest rates* (though they may be worded to seem lower) and large brokers' fees may be concealed in the agreement. And IF YOU FALL BEHIND WITH THE REPAYMENTS YOU MAY LOSE YOUR HOME TOTALLY. This applies even if the amount you owe is much less than the value of your home, for the home will be sold and the money used to pay off the loan. The stories, given in a 1987 National Consumer Council report, of those who through illness and personal problems, have got behind with their payments and ended up homeless make tragic reading. It could happen to anyone who uses their home as security.

Don't be fooled by the wording. When anyone lending money says it is a secured loan they *don't* mean you are secure: they mean *they* are. Secure in knowing that if you can't pay they can get their money by selling your home. Of course, they do give you any money left over from the sale after taking their capital and all the interest. But the change will be meagre compensation for being made homeless.

> The fact that the home is jointly owned by a husband and wife does NOT prevent a company from selling it to cover a debt taken on by only one of them. There are insurance policies which provide an income if someone becomes sick or is made redundant. Before using your home as security against a loan, it might be wise to take out a policy which would allow you to keep paying at least the interest on the loan if things go wrong.

If you can't meet any loan secured against your home don't panic. The moment you have problems go to a local Money Advice Centre, or a Citizens' Advice Bureau, or even talk to the manager of your building society or bank. Very often simply talking the matter over with someone else will allow you to see how you can cope. If the company is reasonable and decent it should be prepared to extend the loan period. If it is a 'rip-off' company charging you excessive interest it may be possible to get the interest reduced by going to court. But *don't wait*. You should try to find a solution *before* they start moves to take your home.

Choosing Borrowing
A lot of people feel that borrowing is really rather bad. But borrowing has nothing to do with virtue and a lot to do with common sense. If prices are rising fast and it will be cheaper to buy something today, despite the interest on the loan, it is clearly more sensible to buy now and pay later. But if prices are stable and borrowing expensive, you do much better to save up and pay cash. The rules depend on what is happening in the market place. However, it is never wise to borrow more than you can pay back - *even if* you fall sick or lose your job.

Check Trading
Check trading is only found in certain areas. The system is that an agent gives you a trading voucher which you can use at a particular range of shops. The money is then collected from you over a period of weeks, with interest added. *This is a bad way to borrow.* The cost of the loan is crazy: the APR (see page 499) can be as high as 100 per cent. So for every £1 you use for shopping you owe £2.

★ It is illegal for anyone to accept a social security benefit book as security against a loan or debt.

Credit Unions
Credit unions are the best way the ordinary consumer

can spit in the eye of all those who seek to make money out of him or her by charging high rates on money. What happens is that a group of people get together and pay money into a central fund. Members can then borrow from this at a fixed and reasonable level of interest. As money in the fund gathers interest the savers are also paid a certain amount of this each year. This is an excellent way to borrow money if you wouldn't find it easy to borrow from an organization like a bank.

To form a credit union people must have some common bond, such as all working for the same firm, living in the same street or belonging to the same organization. There are strict rules on how such unions must be run. To find out more contact the **National Federation of Credit Unions**, Fifth Floor, Provincial House, Bradford, W. Yorks BD1 1NP or the **Credit Union League of Great Britain**, P.O.Box 135, Credit Union Centre, High Street, Skelmersdale, Lancs WN8 8AP.

Free Money
The best borrowing of all is, of course, interest free, and there are more free loans than you might think. Even if you have money to burn it is crazy to pay on the nail if credit will cost you nothing. Keep your money and use it to earn interest.

Some shops offer interest-free loans to buy goods in their sales. This is an excellent way to furnish a house cheaply, and there really are no hidden snags - unless the prices are higher than elsewhere. The credit is usually interest free for a year. The only cost is whatever your bank charges to service a standing order. If necessary deposit the money with a bank or building society which won't charge too much and will give you interest in the meanwhile.

To use credit cards - but always pay the bill *in full* before the 'pay by' date (see pages 501-502) - can give up to 8 weeks' interest-free money.

Some stores have accounts which are interest free if you pay within a certain time. If you buy at the start of the month that's a month's interest-free money.

Mail order firms sometimes let you pay in stages without charging anything extra. If the prices are no higher this can be worthwhile. But do ask in writing if it really *is* interest free. Some do charge interest, some don't and it isn't always clear in the catalogue.

> Do remember that free loans can turn into expensive loans if you time your repayments badly.

★ Although it *is* possible to get loans for free, be suspicious. If anyone doesn't want money on the nail there may be a snag. Look for the APR. If you can't find one, write and ask to be told the APR - by law you must be told the truth.
★ If you have bought something on credit and it is faulty *don't stop paying*. If you don't keep to your side of the bargain you could lose your rights. So go on paying while you complain.

Hire Purchase
If you buy on credit you own the goods even if you haven't paid off the debt. With hire purchase you don't own the goods until you have paid the whole sum. All hire purchase terms include interest and you should ask what APR is being charged *before* signing any agreement..

Interest Rates on Borrowing
The *relative* cost of borrowing from respectable organizations by different methods remains much the same, even though the actual rates vary. This means that although the following chart won't tell you exactly how much borrowing costs it will let you compare the cost of borrowing money in different ways.

The APR is the *real* cost of borrowing the money for a year (see page 499) and includes not just the interest but also the other costs which are part of the loan, like brokers' fees - it might be better if it were called WICEY - What It Costs Each Year. By law anyone lending you £15,000 or less must give the APR but there are some exceptions. Credit card companies and banks giving overdrafts are among them.

The Comparative Terms of Borrowing

The terms in this chart are NOT those applying as you read they show how loans would probably compare if the bank base rate was 10 per cent.

Type of loan	Minimum	Maximum	Repayment time	APR	Comment
Planned Overdraft	nil	What your bank manager will permit	As agreed with bank manager, usually short	12·5%	Very reasonable interest charges but you may end up with a hefty bank charges bill.
Credit Card	nil	Your credit limit	Indefinite, provided you pay the agreed minimum per month	26·5%	An expensive way to borrow. Avoid it. See page 501.
Gold Card	nil	Varies according to card, may be £10,000	Indefinite	13%	Good value and you aren't running up bank charges.

Financial facts change daily, check the latest figures before making a decision.

Type of loan	Minimum	Maximum	Repayment time	APR	Comment
Bank Revolving Credit Schemes	£180-£300 depending on scheme	Up to 30 times your monthly saving, i.e. £50 a month saved enables you the chance to borrow up to £1,500 at any one time	Indefinite	20%	More than an agreed overdraft, so why use it?
Store Revolving Credit Schemes (Budget accounts)	Around £100	Up to 30 times your monthly saving	Indefinite	35%	Very expensive, even more than credit cards. Avoid it.
Bank or Building Society Personal Loan	Usually around £300	Around £10,000	Within 3 years	20% (business loans cost less)	Usually marginally cheaper than a credit card but almost always more expensive than an agreed overdraft.
Personal Loan from a Finance Company (or Shop)	Usually several hundred pounds	Around £10,000	1 to 5 years	35%	Usually far too expensive, don't touch it with a barge pole.
Using your Insurance or Pension	Around £100 against the value of your insurance plan, several thousand pounds against your pension.	Will be related to the value of your policy. Check with the company.	Subject to terms of policy. May simply be taken from the sum of money due when the policy ends.	Variable	The cost is usually reasonable but it could seriously damage the long-term return on your insurance or pension plan.
Unplanned Overdraft	Nil	Until your bank says stop	To be agreed, usually short.	22·5%	Much more expensive than a planned overdraft. If they will let you run up any overdraft get a planned one - it's much cheaper.
Money Lenders	Any	What they feel like	As arranged	Often over 1,000%	Usually daylight robbery. Never, never use one. They are only the route to far more trouble.
House Mortgage	Usually £5,000	A set multiple of your income	Usually around 25 years	11% over 20 years	Reasonable, usually a good buy but shop around for the best deal.

It's very easy to see from the chart that getting a planned overdraft may be the cheapest option. But banks are no longer the only reliable places to get overdrafts. Some building societies and other forms of legitimate financial organizations are beginning to offer them. This means there is more and more competition. That should mean that they are fighting for customers and competing on interest charges, so shop around.

You don't *have* to borrow from your own bank or building society. You can borrow from any organization you wish.

Loans v. Overdrafts
Loans can be obtained from a wide range of financial organizations, from reputable banks to disreputable money lenders, and the rates will vary according to whom you obtain one from, and also what type of loan you have.

A **personal loan** is usually more expensive than an overdraft, but is for a set time and carries a set rate of interest, which stays the same from the day you sign the agreement. If interest rates are rising this could be to your advantage. If you negotiated a fairly reasonable

Financial facts change daily, check the latest figures before making a decision.

rate of interest in the first place you might end up doing better than by taking out an overdraft, for overdraft rates change from time to time, and you pay the going rate at the time you pay back the money - not the time when you signed the contract.

An **ordinary loan** is also for a set time but the interest rate isn't fixed - the better deal when interest rates are falling.

Mortgage Interest
It is worth remembering that mortgages use the same system as overdrafts, and the cost of your borrowing normally rises and falls with the changes in interest rates. So it's unwise to mortgage yourself up to the hilt in case interest rates rise and you can't meet the payments.

Pawnbrokers
Pawning something is usually a very bad way to raise money. If you need money that desperately, how certain can you be that you will have the money to get your valuables out of hock before the pawnbroker has a right to sell them? Family fortunes have been thrown away by those who always thought they'd be able to get the next object back. Had the objects been sold they would have fetched many times as much and far less would have been lost.

If you do pawn something you should be given a paper telling you how you can get it back. Normally you must repay the sum in full by a certain date. If you can't, you must pay interest on the money, or lose the object you pawned. However, the pawnbroker doesn't have to insure the object and if it gets lost that's your problem. You have no comeback and you still have to pay back the money.

Revolving Credit and Budget Accounts
A budget account is a system called revolving credit and it doesn't go round to your advantage. What happens is that you agree to pay a certain amount to the shop each month - like the old Christmas clubs. Then the shop allows you to spend more than you are paying in, raising your credit level each time you make a payment. The shop doesn't officially charge interest for the credit it gives but it does make service charges. You need to be pretty good at sums to work out what rate of interest those service charges equal. Those who have done the arithmetic have found that they often come to even more than the interest on a credit card - and that itself is too high.

Budget accounts are a wonderful way for shops to induce shoppers to buy from them, and make a handsome profit at the same time. They are a very bad deal for the shopper.

Refusal of Credit
If you are refused credit:
● always try more than one company
● ask why they are refusing you, although they are not always obliged to tell you
● be realistic about your ability to repay - you may be able to obtain a smaller sum.

Most companies use a computerized system of credit scoring, i.e. you must score several points for various factors (such as length of employment with current employer, income, length of time at a current address) and your total must be within an acceptable range.

Many companies use credit reference agencies to check your credit history. If you think you have been turned down on this basis see Law, page 443. If you think you have been refused credit because you are a woman this is illegal - contact the Equal Opportunities Commission (page 463).

Budgeting
Pick up almost any book on personal finance and the author will tell you to write down your income and expenditure and budget carefully. It is good advice - especially for anyone who is getting used to having an income for the first time. Arranging it in columns helps. Split up your possible expenditure into headings such as: food, drink, clothes, travel, entertainment, cigarettes, rent, heat etc., sundries. Then tot up each column at the end of the month.

I was blessed (and also cursed) with a Scots headmistress who used economics lessons to din it into us that the essence of money management was to make choices. We had to write down expenditure, then look at what we had spent our money on, and ask ourselves if we had really had as much value out of spending it that way as if we had spent it some other way. Then if the answer was 'no' she said we should try to stop spending money that way the following month. It was very good advice.

Budgeting for the Broke
It has to be said that all budgeting advice is best suited to those who have enough money and leisure to do it. If one is really hard up searching for the cheapest of everything, and doing every job the least expensive way absorbs so many hours in the day that there seems to be no time to budget. What's more, if one does write it down, seeing how close one is to being broke, or how the debts are mounting, is deeply depressing. I have lived like that and anyone who simply can't face budgeting in those circumstances has all my sympathy. I couldn't either. That doesn't mean letting chaos reign. Some steps can be taken to make ends meet, if not exactly overlap.
● Work out what you can do without. A lot of spending is automatic. Stop buying the things you don't care about so you *can* buy those which matter to you.
● Try to be extra thrifty for a while and build up a small kitty, then use this to allow you to buy larger quantities of items like detergent which are cheaper in bulk. Small quantities aren't always more expensive, weight for weight, but they usually are.
● Only carry a cheque book or credit card if you know you have to buy a single expensive item which you have planned for. The rest of the time carry only enough cash to cover what you really need.
● Work out how much major bills will come to each

Financial facts change daily, check the latest figures before making a decision.

month and transfer that much into a special account in the bank or building society and don't touch it for any other purpose.

- Buy fresh food in markets - if there is one near you - or in inexpensive butchers and greengrocers. Supermarkets are only good value for fresh food if you shop in the last few hours of Saturday, when they are marking food down. But their own brands are often best value for basics like detergents.
- Cut down on cleaning materials (see the chapter Domestic Matters).
- Stop boosting chemists. The average healthy person does not need sticking plaster, antiseptic mouthwash, cough and cold medicines, laxatives, and so on. In Sickness explains why.
- Use energy carefully - see page 217.
- Finally, the most useful step I ever took when I was hard up was to adopt the policy that whatever it was I couldn't afford it. Only if I could convince myself - the following day - that something was totally *essential* would I allow myself to buy it. Making oneself take a day to think can make a lot of purchases much less appealing.

Debt

Few things are worse than owing money and feeling there is no hope of paying it off. If this is your problem the first thing to realize is that you aren't alone: there are people who can help you. More and more Money Advice Centres are springing up: ask your local library. If there isn't a money centre the Citizens' Advice Bureau will help you instead.

However, you may prefer to cope alone. I don't advise it. But, if you want to, the first thing to do is face the problem. You may well feel shaky and frightened and simply want to put the bills in a heap, unopened and pretend the whole nightmare isn't happening to you. Believe me, the worst part isn't the bills, it's what is happening in your head. You can't *really* forget a problem like that. Once you face it you will find that, however bad it is, the situation is less bad than you feel it is.

> Whatever you do DON'T borrow more money to pay off old debts, (unless an Money Advice Centre or similar unbiased advisor says it is the best course).
> And don't sell anything which you haven't fully paid for.

Step 1 Get the leaflet 'Debt, a Survival Guide' published by the OFT (a CAB should have it).

Step 2 Face the bills. The first thing to do is write to each company to which you owe money:
- say you have a problem with paying
- say that you are sorting out your finances
- ask them to give you a short time to do that

Step 3 Add up your income - pay, social security,

pension, any other sources. Ask yourself whether you could get more money. Have you talked to the CAB about what state benefits you could get? If not, do so - whatever the social security office has said.

Step 4 Very carefully add up what you *must* spend each week to live - rent, rates, heat and light, food, travel to work, essential clothing. Add up a separate list of how much you spend each week on items which you could live without, but like to have. Add the totals from these two lists together. If you take that figure away from your income how much is left? If there is nothing left look at the second list and decide what you could give up. It may be lousy to give up cigarettes and drink, if you enjoy them, but the worry of serious debt is probably worse.

If there is still nothing left even if you do without all luxuries you MUST get outside advice - unless you can see a way to increase your income or cut your costs. A new head may see a solution you can't see.

Step 5 If you have some money over (even if only after doing without all luxuries), look at all your debts and how much you are expected to pay per week, month or year - if there is such an arrangement. Write two lists. In list A put those which must be paid to avoid losing your home or your heating - rent/mortgage, rates, gas, electricity, or a loan secured against your home. Put all the rest in list B.

See how you could share out the spare money each week between the organizations on list A. (Leave a little for those in list B and do the same.) Arrange it so that those to whom you owe most get the most. It may mean each gets very little but at least they can see you aren't just ignoring them.

Step 6 Now write and give each of the companies or organizations these facts:
- your income per week or month
- your outgoings on absolute essentials (including a small sum for emergencies)
- your debt to them
- that you wish to pay it off
- how much you are offering to pay off each week. Also tell them *briefly* if there is some good reason why you got into debt (for example if you were ill or made redundant). And ask any public body - council, gas, electricity - if they have any scheme for helping people in situations like this.

> *Make sure the sum you offer is one you can keep up.* It is better to offer a smaller sum and stick to it, than offer more and end up getting behind again.
>
> *Keep a copy of all letters you send and of all replies.*

Usually a company would rather have some money - however little - than go to the hassle of taking you to court or repossessing your furniture. Once they agree to your proposals, set up a system for paying. If you have a bank see if the money can be paid automatically - but make sure you won't be charged for this. If you are paid in cash put the money to pay the debts aside - the instant you get it - into some kind of account on which you don't get charged for putting it in or taking it out.

Once the system is running smoothly you can begin to work out ways to increase your income. There are always more ways to make money than there seem to be at first sight.

Being Taken to Court for Debt
If a creditor threatens you with court you won't end up in a debtors' prison. That was in Dickens's time. Debt is not a crime: it is a mistake. And someone to whom you owe money may not harass or threaten you - with the law or with violence. If they do so report them to the police or the Trading Standards Officer. People need a licence to lend money and they can have their licence taken away if they break the law.

You can get free legal advice from a law centre - your public library or CAB can tell you where to find one. Also solicitors who do legal aid work may be able to give you free advice (see page 481).

Don't wait for legal advice before dealing with papers from the court. Reply within a few days. If you admit to owing the money but need time to pay, you fill in an Admission form, (if you haven't yet been through Steps 1 to 6 above use them to help you fill in the form). If you deny owing all or part of the money, you fill in a Defence form.

The court normally decides that a certain sum must be paid to the other person each month. You *must* stick to that sum. If you can't do that because your situation changes you should *immediately* write to the court and ask for the amount to be changed. If you simply fail to make the payments the creditor can:

- ask for a bailiff to go in and take your property to the value of what is owed (he can't take your partner's property though)
- ask for an attachment of earnings, in which he is paid out of your wages or salary before you get it
- put a charge on your home. This means that if you fail to keep paying off the debt your home can be sold and the money taken from its sale. This can be done even if a home is jointly owned and only one person is in debt.

One way to avoid any of these may be to ask the court for an administration order. In this they look at your situation and work out what you should pay to whom and you then pay the whole sum to the court and the court pays the creditors. This can only be done if your debt is under a set figure.

In Scotland different terms are used but the procedure is very similar.

WARNING: If you agree to act as 'guarantor' or to 'stand surety' for money someone else borrows it means that if they don't pay the money back you have to pay it in full, plus any interest they owe.

If you don't agree to act as guarantor, or sign anything, you aren't usually liable for anyone else's debts. Not even those of your husband, wife or child (but see 'a charge on a home' below left).

Financial Calculations
The way in which interest rates are expressed doesn't always leave you much the wiser. The figures are all there but the real rates can seem oddly unrelated to those which appear on paper.

If the figures aren't totally clear, and you are planning to borrow or to invest, it is well worth working out exactly what the interest rates will really mean. This isn't hard. If you have a calculator it is just a matter of going step by step through one of the calculations below.

As even the mention of anything to do with maths can make some people's minds close up like a poked sea-anemone, I just want to clarify a few terms.

Percentages
The basic thing about percentages is that you pay, or receive, so much in every hundred. If you borrow £200 at 5% interest, you have to pay back £200 plus £5 interest for every hundred. So you pay back £10 in interest.

But that statement above is meaningless. The missing factor is time. And it's here that people can end up paying far more than they expect. If you pay 5% per annum on that £200, you obviously pay £10 a year. But if you pay 5% a *month* you could be paying out £10 × 12 = £120 a year *in interest.*

It is on this that it is easy for people to be caught out. Suppose you were desperately needing money to pay a bill, and your local money lender offered to lend you £300 at 16% interest a year. You hesitate, as the interest sound high, and he says 'I tell you what I'll do, just for you I'll make it ½% a week'. Have you got a bargain? Would you have done better or worse if he had offered 2% a month? (Answers opposite.)

The answers there were based on simple interest, but when compound interest is used - as it is in most business situations - what is owed can mount up remarkably quickly.

Borrowing - Compound Interest
Compound interest is the system used by most organizations which lend money.

With compound interest, if you can't, or don't, pay back money you owe, and don't pay the interest either, that interest is added to the basic debt. For the next time period you then pay interest on the initial bill *and* on the interest. This sequence of paying interest on interest can stack up month by month, making the total year's interest far bigger than the sum you first borrowed. If you ran up a bill for £100 and the interest rate was 10%, and you paid off neither at the end of the first month, the figures would look like this.

Month 2: Your bill was £100 at an monthly interest rate of 10%. You didn't pay, so £10 interest was added £100 = you now owe £110.

Month 3: You didn't pay, so 10% of £110 was added to your bill = £11. This means your bill for month 3 is £110 + £11 = £121.

Month 4: If you don't pay it, 10% of £121 will be added on = £12.10. So your bill for month 4 is £121 + £12.10 = £133.10.

At this rate, if you keep on failing to pay the total bill you will owe £313.84 at the end of the year and £213.84 of that will be interest. Credit card companies don't charge as much as 10% but the sums still mount up. Of course, if you have invested money and the interest keeps being added to the main sum (usually called the principal) it is very good news. The catch is that whereas money is often lent by big organizations on a basis of monthly compound interest, they usually *pay out* interest on a yearly basis.

Answers to the questions opposite.
Over a year the interest on £300 at 16 per cent a year = £48
Over a year the interest on £300 at 2 per cent a month = £72
Over a year the interest on £300 at ½ per cent a week = £78

Calculating Compound Interest on Investments
If you are investing money on a compound interest basis there is a formula for calculating how much your money will have grown by any year you care to name. The formula looks hard but taken step by step, with a calculator, it is easy enough. If the way it is written is unfamiliar look up the Rules of Mathematics (in Facts and Figures) because the order in which you do the calculation makes a big difference.

P - stands for the principal, i.e. the sum you invest
R - stands for the annual rate of interest
n - stands for the number of years it is invested

The deposit grows to P $(1 + R)^n$ but as R is a percentage, you have to put it over 100 before you work with it:
$$P \left(1 + \frac{R}{100}\right)^n$$

So investing £100 at 10% p.a. for 3 years and compounding the interest goes like this:
$$£100 \left(1 + \frac{10}{100}\right)^3$$
which gives £100 $(1 + 0.1)^3$
which is £100 $(1.1)^3$

Powers, i.e the $(1.1)^3$, have to be dealt with first. $(1.1)^3$ is $1.1 \times 1.1 \times 1.1 = 1.331$

So you have £100 x 1.331

So after 3 years the principal has grown to £133.10.

Calculating Simple Interest
With simple interest you only earn interest each year on the basic sum you invested - even if you don't take the interest out. So if you invest £100 (the investment is called the principal) at 10% you get just £10 interest each year, and after three years the £100 invested has only grown to £130.

To calculate the interest you will get by this method over a given period of years you use the formula:

$$\text{Interest} = \frac{\text{principal x rate per annum x period of years}}{100}$$

So in the example above interest $= \dfrac{100 \times 10 \times 3}{100}$

So interest over 3 years   totals = £30

The Annual Percentage Rate (APR)
When you are borrowing money, the interest rate you will pay on it is often quoted in ways which conceal the true amount which you will be paying (see pages 494-495). Consumer legislation has made it compulsory for organizations like building societies and banks to quote you the Annual Percentage Rate - known as the APR, which is the true cost of borrowing over a year. But not everyone who offers to loan you money may keep to the law - and, even when the APR is given there can even be some sneaky tricks to disguise it. A full-page advertisement in the national press by a mortgage corporation recently proclaimed:

Our rate is now 10·8%
(Typical APR 10·25%)

Anyone glancing quickly at that might suppose the APR was lower than the other rate: ·8 looks less than ·25, But they have left out the zero after the 8·-10·80 is the real figure. To see just how different it is to apply these percentages to figures. Borrowing £60,000 at rate of 10·25% per annum would cost £6,150 a year. Borrowing £60,000 at rate of 10·80% per annum would cost £6,480 a year. A difference of almost £10,000 over 30 years. So it's wise to look at quoted APRs very carefully.

Mortgage Repayments
When you take out a mortgage whoever you borrow the money from should tell you, if you ask, precisely what the repayments will be each year. But interest rates change, and when they do it may be easier to work out the figures for yourself than to ask them to revise their figures. Those not mathematically inclined may recoil from the formula. They needn't. If they substitute their own figures for those I give, and follow step by step, it's just like walking up a hill: all you need to do is put

one 'foot' in front of the other - and, with a calculator, the walking is being done for you.

The formula is:
The annual repayment =

$$P\left(1+\frac{R}{100}\right)^{n}\times\left(\frac{\frac{R}{100}}{\left[1+\frac{R}{100}\right]^{n}-1}\right)$$

P stands for the sum borrowed - the principal
R stands for the annual rate of interest
n stands for the number of years the mortgage will run

Suppose you have a £40,000 mortgage so P is 40,000
borrowed at 12% p.a.   so R is 12
with repayments spread over 30 years so n is 30

The first thing you do is replace those letters in the formula with the matching figure. This gives:

The annual repayment =

$$40,000\left(1+\frac{12}{100}\right)^{30}\times\left(\frac{\frac{12}{100}}{\left[1+\frac{12}{100}\right]^{30}-1}\right)$$

First deal with the small fractions inside the brackets i.e. divide each 12 by 100. This gives:

The annual repayment =

$$40,000\,(1+0.12)^{30}\times\left(\frac{0.12}{[1+0.12]^{30}-1}\right)$$

Now do the additions inside the brackets. That gives:

Annual repayments =

$$40,000\,(1.12)^{30}\times\left(\frac{0.12}{[1.12]^{30}-1}\right)$$

The 30s at the top right-hand corners of the brackets are powers. That means the figure in brackets needs to be multiplied by itself that many times. There are tables to give you the answer or you can keep pegging away on a calculator till you reach the answer - but I suggest you keep a note on paper of how far you have got; it is very easy to lose track. In this case it comes to :

Annual repayments =

$$£40,000\times29.96\times\left(\frac{0.12}{29.96-1}\right)$$

Next take the 1 from the 29·96 in brackets, which gives you:

Annual repayments =

$$£40,000\times29.96\times\left(\frac{0.12}{28.96}\right)$$

Divide the 0·12 by 28·96 and you get: 0·0041436

Annual repayments = £40,000 x 29·96 x 0·0041436

Next multiply 29·96 by 0·0041436. Since multiplying a number by anything less than 1 makes it smaller you needn't be surprised that:

Annual repayments = £40,000 x 0·1241422

Multiply these together and you find that

Annual repayments are £4,965·69.

Borrowing v. Using Capital

Anyone who is self-employed or running their own business may find themselves needing to buy a piece of equipment, or a perhaps a car for business use, and wondering what is the best way to finance it. Should you borrow the money at the lowest rate of interest you can find? Or should you use capital which could otherwise be invested to draw interest? As the rate of interest paid to you is usually lower than the rate you pay out when you borrow, it looks at first sight as if the prudent course is to use capital. In fact, it isn't a simple as that.

The interest on the capital is probably taxable at the rate for *investment* income. But the money you pay in interest on a business purchase can usually be set against the taxation on *earned* income. So the cash benefits will vary according to the two rates of tax. The easiest comparison is to find the cost per year on each, once tax is allowed for, *at imaginary rates*, as follows:

In each case the cost allowing for tax =
$$S\times\frac{1}{100}\quad\frac{1-T}{100}$$

Taking some imaginary figures, it works like this.

S - stands for the sum you need to spend - say £4,000
I - stands for the rate of interest per annum - let's say you get 8% if the money is invested, but pay 10% on the money if you borrow it
T - stands for the tax rates - suppose the interest if it's invested is taxed at 30%, but you can set the interest paid on the loan against tax at 28%.

So, with these imaginary figures, *if you use capital*,

the real cost is $£4,000\times\frac{8}{100}\left(1-\frac{30}{100}\right)$

which works out as   £4,000 x 0.08 (1 − 0.3)

which becomes   £4,000 x 0.08 x .7

Financial facts change daily, check the latest figures before making a decision.

Multiply those together and the annual cost of buying out of capital is shown to be £224.

But *if you borrow* the money the real cost is

$$£4,000 \times \frac{10}{100} \left(1 - \frac{28}{100}\right)$$

which becomes   £4,000 × 0.1 (1 − 0.28)

which is   £4,000 × 0.1 × 0.72

Multiply those together and the annual cost of borrowing is shown to be £288 a year.

With these imaginary tax and interest rates it still looks as if it is better to use capital. That isn't necesarily so for two reasons. First, even with both the interest and the tax rates stacked against borrowing, the difference in cost is only £64 a year and a fair proportion of this could be offset by capital growth if you invest your money wisely. Second, borrowing money leaves your capital free for use on other things - like holidays, or medical emergencies - for which you'd be unlikely to get a loan or which you couldn't set against tax.

Paying with Plastic

Used wrongly, paying by plastic can be the road to ruin but it also has distinct advantages.

- You can use your card to order and pay by telephone.
- Used carefully, they give you interest-free loans.
- Credit cards (but not charge cards) give extra consumer protection (see page 502).
- You can pay overseas without the cost and hassle of changing money.
- It allows you to pay for goods costing more than the £50 backed by a cheque card.
- Charge cards have no pre-set spending limit so they are very useful in emergencies abroad when you might need to buy a plane ticket in a hurry.
- With some, you can pay money over and have an account in credit then draw on this for cash when abroad without the hassle of travellers' cheques - and some pay you interest if your account is in credit.
- Some can be used to draw cash in banks or from machines - but watch the charges.
- Some of the perks may be appealing, such as discounts on travel or hotels, or private health insurance, or the use of a lounge at London airport.

Credit Cards v. Charge Cards

Credit cards and charge cards are often confused. **Credit cards** don't charge you for having the card but they do let you repay your debt slowly and charge interest if you don't pay within a certain time. **Charge cards** charge you for having them, and you must pay your bill in full when it arrives. If you don't, they don't demand interest but they do make a 'late payment charge' which increases with your delay, and can make late payment even more expensive than failing to pay a credit card bill.

Access and Visa are credit cards, and all the credit cards in Britain are within one or other of these schemes. American Express and Diners Club are charge cards. Although a charge card may be useful for the traveller, credit cards are accepted at more places than charge cards, and on the whole there seems no point in paying for a service you can get for free. So, for ordinary day-to-day payments credit cards are perhaps better value than charge cards. However, if you are repeatedly *slightly late* in paying, the first angry letter from a charge card company will be cheaper than the interest on a credit card, charge cards score on loans at very reasonable rates via gold charge cards (see page 494) - all gold cards are charge cards not credit cards.

Despite the twinned parents the credit card system isn't uniform. Interest rates vary considerably, according to which bank (or whatever) issues the card: at the last count the cheapest card charged 7 per cent less than the highest. Most banks and major building societies now offer credit cards. Shop around and see who is charging what and what perks and services are offered with each version of the card. The professional associations given in this book have the addresses and you may like to compare charge cards too. Once you know which card you want you just fill in a form to apply, but it will have a credit limit above which you may not spend.

Gold Cards

Gold cards are issued by both charge card companies and banks - for a yearly fee which is considerably more than a normal charge card. And there may be a joining charge in the first year. To get one you need to have earnings above a certain limit - but the limit may not be as high as you'd expect.

For that extra fee you get an automatic borrowing facility that is usually around £10,000, immediate cash drawing rights of several hundred a day and a range of perks (which usually includes a card protection plan). If you are planning to get a gold card, go into the perks carefully as some are far more useful than others. A Midland Bank gold card, for example, includes a free annual consultation with a tax and investment consultant. But with all gold cards the most valuable perk is that the interest rate is remarkably reasonable (page 494) and could certainly save you the cost of the card if you were to borrow several thousand pounds.

How Cards Work

Credit and charge cards can be a blessing or a curse according to how you use them. Once you start using a card you will receive a statement each month saying what you owe. The blessing is that they can allow you interest-free credit for up to 8 weeks. The free loan works like this: you buy something on the first day you have the card. At the end of the month the card company sends you the bill. At the bottom it will give a date by which the minimum payment must reach them - usually 4 weeks from the date of the bill. So you pay up to 8 weeks after you buy. During that time your money could be earning interest in a deposit account, so you could be *making* money on the deal. The trouble is that the loan is *only* free if you pay off the *whole bill* before that date.

If you leave *any* part of the bill unpaid, or are even a day over the due-by date, you start losing money hand over fist. If you don't pay in full by the date you are immediately charged interest on the amount outstanding not just from the 'due by' date but *from the date of the bill* four weeks earlier. And interest clocks up at an alarming rate.

> WARNING: If you draw cash with a credit card the charges on this *aren't* delayed until the 'pay-by' date. Access charges you interest on a percentage basis *from the date it appears on your statement* (i.e. almost immediately). Visa doesn't charge interest but charges a single flat rate fee (1·5% as I write), you pay it in full on the pay-by date. If you don't you also pay interest, as on any unpaid debit.

Credit card companies may let debts go on mounting. You cannot rely on them to put a break on your spending. So the great rule is *never spend more by credit card than you can afford to spend in cash* - then the money is there to pay the bill in full.

Charge cards are different. They expect you to settle your bill in full and may cancel your card if you don't pay up quickly enough.

How to Save at Cards

★ Pay your bill *in full* by 3 days before the last payment date - then you get maximum free credit and never pay interest.
★ If you might forget to pay your bill in time, pay it *the instant* you get it, but postdate the cheque to 3 days before the final payment date. It might be wise to attach a letter saying the cheque is postdated and asking them to hold it until the date.
★ If your credit card company refuses to take a postdated cheque, still postdate it and put the envelope where you can't miss it, and place a big note beside it saying 'Post on...' and a date a week before the money is due.

Interest Rates on Credit Cards

Failing to pay a credit card company is a *very* expensive way to borrow money (see page 494). In real terms the cost of borrowing on a card can be as much as *twice*

the lowest bank lending rate. And some store cards which operate like credit cards charge interest at almost *three times* the lowest bank lending rate. *It is financial madness to borrow at such rates when you could almost certainly borrow more cheaply elsewhere.* Quite rightly, credit card companies have been strongly criticized by the National Consumer Council.

The Law and Your Cards

Credit cards are covered by the 1974 Consumer Credit Act which means that if your card is lost or stolen and then used by someone else, you may only be liable for the first £50 - though some companies set even lower limits. And from the moment you notify the company you cease to be liable at all.

The Act also makes the credit card company have joint responsibility with the retailer for whatever you buy with the card, provided you spend above a certain limit. This can give you extra protection if the article you buy goes wrong. Illogically, charge cards are *not* covered by that act so they give no extra protection.

It is illegal for anyone to charge you extra because you are paying by credit card, and if they have a sign saying they take credit cards they may not refuse them - unless they have an equally large sign saying they cannot accept them for certain items.

Pinpoint System

This is probably the shape of things to come. You feed your credit card into a machine, tap in your PIN number and the machine lets you have the goods you want and the bill is automatically changed to your credit card.

Tips on Using Credit Cards

★ Keep all credit card bills and check them against your account.
★ Paying by credit card when overseas saves you the commission on changing travellers' cheques. However, you could lose out in currency fluctuations. Visa payments in *any* foreign currency are first converted into dollars then into sterling. Neither is done the instant you pay, so a time gap could lead to something costing more than you expected.
★ In some countries there is a trade in the carbons from between the layers of a credit card bill. Numbers can be read on them and used for telephone purchases or forging cards. When travelling it's wise to ask for your carbons.

	Access	**American Express**	**Barclaycard**	**Diners Club**
Address	Southend-on-Sea X, SS99 9BB	P.O.Box 70, Brighton, Sussex BN2 2ZP	Barclaycard Centre, Marefair, Northants NN1 1SG	Diners Club House, Kingsmead, Farnborough Hants GU14 7SR
Queries on statements	0702 354040	0273 696933	0604 234234	0252 513500
Queries on credit and balance	0702 352255	ditto	ditto	ditto
Reporting lost or stolen cards (24-hour)	Number on statement or 0702 352255	01 222 9633	0604 230230	ditto

Financial facts change daily, check the latest figures before making a decision.

★ Don't put cards in a safe deposit box in a foreign hotel. In some countries there is a roaring trade in forged cards, and they are easily 'borrowed' from a safe deposit.

★ On an expensive item it is sometimes worth using credit cards in reverse. Shops pay a percentage of every credit card sale to the card company; so if a shop takes credit cards say you'll pay cash if they discount the goods by 5% (most shops pay 3% to 7% to the card company so they gain by this and so do you).

> *Ready Money will always command the best and cheapest of every article of consumption, if expended with judgement; and the dealer who intends to act fairly, will always prefer it.*
>
> *Enquire Within, 1856*

Shop Cards

More and more shops are offering cards. Confusingly some are run like charge cards and some like credit cards. Check whether interest will be charged if you fail to pay the account in full within the set time. The interest on some shop cards is daylight robbery.

There is no point in getting a store card unless you often shop somewhere, like Marks & Spencer or John Lewis, which doesn't take credit cards. It is just another bit of plastic to carry around and a separate bill to pay. The more cards you have the harder it is to budget.

Most of all, avoid cards which ask you to pay money into an account in order to be allowed a loan later. These are really budget accounts with plastic trimmings. If you have money to pay in anywhere put it in a bank or building society which pays interest. Then you can spend it where you want.

> *Trust not him who seems more anxious to give credit than to receive cash.*
>
> *The former hopes to secure a hold upon you in his books; and continues always to make up for his advance, either by an advanced price, or an inferior article: whilst the latter (who takes cash) knows that your custom can only be secured by fair dealing.*
>
> *Enquire Within, 1856*

Protection Plans

There are several companies which offer 'protection' for your card. You pay a fee and let them have all your credit card numbers. Then if your cards are lost or stolen you just ring the 'protection' company and it notifies all the card companies. Card protection companies claim to offer protection against fraudulent use up to great sums. In fact the benefits are often more to the credit card companies than to you as you can only be liable for the misuse of a credit card up to a small set sum - Access, for example, sets it at £25.

However, frequent travellers may find it convenient to have just one number to contact 24 hours a day, especially as some of the companies will rush interest-free cash to a stranded client. There may also be key tags which will direct your keys back to you, if you lose them, via the protection company - safer than having your own address on them. You can also ask them to hold the numbers of documents, such as your passport,

so if it was stolen you could just ring the company and ask for the numbers. Of course, all this suggests that you go round with the phone number of the protection company engraved on your heart. For how on earth would you find it out if everything was stolen in Bogota?

The following companies offer card protection plans.

Cardwise, Southend-on-Sea, SS2 6BR Tel: Freefone 'Cardwise' or 0702 362999

Card Protection Plan (CPP), 198 King's Road, London SW3 5XP Tel: 01 351 4400

Credit Card Sentinel (UK) Ltd, New Lane, Havant, Hants PO9 2NR - Freefone 'Sentinel' in UK or reversed charges from anywhere in the world to 0705 471234

Credit Card Securities, Morris Court, 40A New Road, Chippenham, Wilts SN15 1HL Tel: 0249 655275

American Express and Diners Club each have their own card registration service.

PLANNING FOR TOMORROW

Until the 1986 Financial Services Act (which began to come into force on 29 April 1988), advice on financial planning and investment was a free for all, with precious little consumer protection. Now *only* authorized firms, which have established their competence, honesty and solvency, may give financial advice. They are authorized by one of the Self Regulatory Organizations (SROs) set up to cover different types of financial planning. Supervised by the Securities and Investment Board (SIB), the SROs both set their own rules and police their enforcement. But *all* firms which give advice must, by law, act in the client's best interests and take account of the client's circumstances and other investments. If any firm fails to do this, first complain to the head of the firm. If that fails, complain to the SRO - the name of the appropriate SRO *must* be given on the firm's papers. The SRO is able to penalize the firm, and it is now possible for a dissatisfied client to take an action in court for compensation - and even get the assistance of an SRO in this. However, if the SRO fails to handle your complaint properly, ask the SIB to take it up, (some SROs are also linked to an Ombudsman). The SIB and the individual SROs have leaflets on how the whole system operates and what the rules are.

Securities and Investment Board, Information Office, 3 Royal Exchange Buildings, London EC3V 3NL Tel: 01 283 2474.

Financial Intermediaries, Managers and Brokers' Regulatory Association (FIMBRA), 22 Great Tower Street, London EC3R 5AQ Tel: 01 929 2711.

Securities Association, The Stock Exchange, Old Broad Street, London EC2N 1HP Tel: 01 256 9000.

Life Assurance and Unit Trust Regulatory Organization (LATRO), Centrepoint, 103 New Oxford Street, London WC1A 1QH Tel: 01 379 0444.

Investment Managers' Regulatory Organization, Centre Point, 103 New Oxford Street, London WC1A 1PT Tel: 01 379 0601.

Financial facts change daily, check the latest figures before making a decision.

Insurance

There are several key rules when it comes to buying insurance.

- Compare what several companies have to offer.
- Read the small print *very* carefully.
- Having chosen a company be sure you know *exactly* what it covers you for and what the terms are.
- Ask if there are any circumstances which would allow you any kind of reduced premium. There are often small clauses which you may already have met without realizing it, which would save you money. But look critically at clauses which give you a reduction - some are totally unrealistic.
- One of the hidden snags about insurance of all kinds is the issue of 'material facts'. If you fail to tell the insurance company anything which *it* thinks is relevant to your insurance, your whole policy may not be worth the paper it is printed on - no matter how much insurance you have paid. And you can't even get a refund. So include every conceivable fact that might possibly be of interest to them. And, if the broker fills in the form, check it before signing and see if all the facts are there. If you don't it's *you* not the broker who will suffer. And if something happens, after you take out a policy, which could alter your standing with an insurance company write and tell them.

It has to be said that even with the greatest care you may not be able to rule out all problems. Someone I know is locked in battle with one of the biggest companies in the land. He claims a lawnmower is a garden tool, they claim it is a vehicle and therefore not covered by a household policy.

Buying Insurance

You can buy insurance direct just by writing to the companies, or you can buy through a broker. It costs the same either way. Brokers advertise in Yellow Pages. But it's usually best to go to one who specializes in a particular type of insurance. You can get the names of specialist brokers in your area from the **British Insurance Brokers Association (BIBA)**, (14 Bevis Marks, London EC3A 7NT Tel: 01 623 9043). Then ask several brokers to see what deal they can get you and insure with whoever does best for you.

If you are diligent you may be able to get an even better deal by searching hard yourself, but the great advantage of brokers is that, if they are any good, they know not only which companies are cheap but also which pay up with decent grace. There's little point in getting a cut-price premium and then finding that getting the company to pay would make getting blood out of a stone seem easy by comparison. So do ask the brokers about this before deciding who *is* offering the best deal.

Claiming on Insurance

With some types of insurance you can claim whether or not it was your fault. If, for example, you drop a lighted match on the upholstery and the house burns down you should still be insured for the house.

Comprehensive car insurance also covers you even if you cause the accident. However, with some types of insurance your claim won't be met if you haven't taken 'reasonable care'. This applies particularly to losing things or having them stolen. But you should never assume you aren't covered. If your policy doesn't make it plain put in a claim and see what happens, insurance is full of small print and for once it might work in your favour.

If you need to claim act fast. You needn't send in all the details but you should phone your insurance broker or the insurance company *within a week* if you can, certainly within a few weeks. Just say you will be claiming and why, ask for a claim form, and make a note of the name of the person you speak to - as a precaution in case they forget to log your claim. If you don't feel up to phoning, someone else can do it for you. If you fail to phone at the right time phone as soon as you can - it is always worth trying, but the longer you leave it the less likely you are to get your money. The same applies if someone else will be claiming against you. *You* must tell your company as soon as you know this is happening.

You must also take steps to see that the damage isn't made worse for lack of attention. For example, you should prevent rain coming in through a damaged roof. But keep the bills as you will need to claim for them.

★ If something is stolen, here or abroad, always report it to the police and get documents from the police to prove you have done so. Otherwise you may have trouble claiming.

How fast the company will expect to receive the form varies with the type of claim. It's wise to write and acknowledge the form when you receive it and ask the company how soon they need it back and whether you should proceed with repairs and claim later.

In any insurance claim the more information you can give the better. If you are claiming on house contents and have valuations or receipts send photocopies of them with the claim form. But, if the values are out of date, your claim should show the current replacement value of every item, plus what deduction you have made if your policy compels you to allow for wear and tear. Calculate this item by item, as different items have different life expectations and this affects what deduction you should make. If something would normally last 10 years, and it's 3 years old you take 3/10ths off the current price.

If you can't face the job of claiming after a major disaster you can ask a loss assessor to do it for you. But he or she will probably charge a percentage of the sum you get from the insurance company (and you can't add the assessor's fees to your claim). Before taking on an assessor, get a written estimate of the likely fees. You can find an assessor through the **Institute of Loss Assessors**, 14 Red Lion Street, Chesham, Bucks HP5 1HB Tel: 0494 782342.

★ Keep a photocopy of your house inventory and of each of your insurance policies at your bank or some other place away from your home. You would need them after a fire.

Financial facts change daily, check the latest figures before making a decision.

Complaining

If you aren't happy with the way your insurance claim is being handled, or if they offer you less than you think is reasonable, first complain to your broker or the branch where you bought the policy. Then complain to the head office, if that fails, contact the **Life Assurance and Unit Trust Regulatory Association,** Centre Point, 103 New Oxford Street, London WC1EA 1QH Tel: 01 379 0444. Or talk to the **Association of British Insurers** (page 509).

You can't complain directly to a Lloyds underwriter. But you can complain to The Manager, Advisory Department, **Lloyds,** London House, 6 London Street, London EC3R 7AB Tel: 01 623 7100.

If all these fail there is **The Insurance Ombudsman Bureau,** 31 Southampton Row, London WC1B 5HJ Tel: 01 242 8613. If the company is a members of the IOB he will investigate (free of charge) and make a decision which the company must follow if you agree. But you are free to reject his decision and take the matter to court. Or, if the other side agrees, you can take the matter to the **Institute of Arbitrators** (Organizations).

Car Insurance

If you drive a car it must be insured. That's official. It is illegal to drive any car unless it has minimum legal cover. This is very limited insurance which *only* pays out to someone else whom you kill or injure while driving. It doesn't cover injuries to you, or to your car or theirs. So don't think that because you only have an old banger you only need minimum cover. If you damage someone else's car it could cost you dear.

Third Party cover only pays out if you kill or injure someone (including your passengers) or damage someone's property (it doesn't have to be a car) while driving.

Third Party, Fire and Theft also gives cover if your car, or its accessories are stolen, or if it catches fire.

Comprehensive Insurance covers third party, fire and theft, but also covers all accidental damage to your car, or to yourself while driving.

The cost of car insurance varies hugely with the cc of the car, where you live, who will drive it (the fewer people, the cheaper), and the company you choose. Shop around. (See also Advanced Motoring page 422.)

A policy may also cover you to drive other people's cars, but it will normally cover only you unless you said you wanted your car insured for other drivers too. Before anyone else who is uninsured drives your car you should ask for their name to be added to the insurance if the insurance doesn't cover other drivers. This can be done - often at no extra cost - for even very short periods. This is where a good broker, who knows you, is useful. If you are changing cars you can also switch the insurance with just a phone call.

No Claims Bonuses

If you make no claims for a certain number of years most insurance companies give a 'no claims bonus' - they reduce your premium, by a set percentage, for each year in which no claim has been made. The more claim-free years, the greater the reduction. However you may lose part of it if you make any claim at all. Normally you go back 2 notches on the scale. So before claiming for a small sum check whether you will lose more in bonus than you are claiming. Some companies allow one broken windscreen a year without loss of bonus, and others allow you to insure against loss of bonus.

Health Insurance

Permanent Health Insurance

The rather ineptly named Permanent Health Insurance (PHI) provides an income each week if you fall ill and are unable to work. There are two possibilities: you can be paid a fixed sum, set at the start; or you can agree a sum which is index linked, so it increases with the cost of living. This last is the better bet. In times of inflation a fixed sum can rapidly become worthless.

Either way the payments will only start when you have been off sick for a certain period - which you set when you take out the policy. The shorter the waiting period the higher the premiums, but companies vary greatly in how short a waiting time they will allow. The cost also varies with your age and whether you agree to payments stopping at retirement age. But women are always charged more than for men.

Choose a policy to suit your circumstances. But if you are employed don't take out PHI without asking your employer how you are covered if you fall ill. Some policies taken out by employers reduce benefits if someone is getting money from elsewhere. It seems dreadfully unjust, but it's allowed.

If you decide you want PHI look at the policies of as many companies as possible and *do read the small print.* There can be all kinds of hidden snags. For example, some will only pay a percentage of your usual income, others reduce what they pay if you get state benefits - and so on.

Personal Accident Insurance

Personal Accident Insurance is just what it sounds. It pays out if you have an accident in the course of your work and can't work.

Private Health Insurance

Whatever your views on private medical care it may be essential for someone who is self employed and might lose a large part of their income if a hospital appointment cropped up at the wrong time. The costs are high and unless you are in such good health that you would rather save your money and take it out of your piggy bank if you get ill, the key to affording private treatment is a good medical insurance policy. Any broker can arrange this but it can be helpful to contact companies yourself and compare the benefits. They can vary considerably and every detail should be checked before you sign on. Some have schemes for preventive health checks - which can be very valuable. Also ask what would entitle you to a discount on the premium. Often being a member of a motoring organization or holding a certain credit card will get one - but a broker may not tell you this unless you ask.

More information

AMI Health Care, 4-7 Cornwall Terrace, London NW1 4QP Tel: 01 486 1266

Bristol Contributory Welfare Association (BCWA), Bristol House, 40/56 Victoria Street, Bristol BS1 6AB Tel: 0272 293742

BUPA, Provident House, Essex Street, London WC2R 3AX Tel: 01 353 5212

Crown Care, Crown Life House, Crown Square, Woking, Surrey GU21 1XW Tel: 04862 5033

Crusader Insurance PLC, Health Care Department, Reigate, Surrey RH2 8BL Tel: 07372 42424

Hospital Saving Association, Hambleden House, Waterloo Court, Andover, Hants SP10 1LQ Tel: 0264 53211

Orion Insurance Co. PLC, Orion House, Bouverie Road West, Folkstone, Kent CT20 2RW Tel: 0303 850303

Private Patients Plan Ltd, PPP House, Crescent Road, Tunbridge Wells, Kent TN1 2PL Tel: 0892 40111

Western Provident Association, Freepost, Bristol BS1 5JY Tel: 0272 273241

Home Insurance (Building Insurance)

If you have a mortgage the mortgage company will suggest firms to go to for insurance, and you may benefit from the buying power of the mortgage company and get cheaper insurance. But you have a right to check other insurers and, if you find a better deal, ask the mortgage company if they will accept it. However, if they do, they may charge you an administration fee for the extra work.

Building insurance covers all buildings and outbuildings, plus most things which are fixed and part of the house and its grounds, including swimming pools, gates, walls, paths and drives. The cover includes most, but not all, of the accidents which could befall a home: flood, fire, subsidence, accidental damage and so on. It also covers your liability to someone injured on your property because you didn't maintain it properly. So if a friend falls through your floor, you're covered.

Exclusion Clauses

Exclusion clauses may mean you can't claim if someone falls through your floor because of dry rot, woodworm and a whole range of similar problems which are specifically excluded. Nor can you claim the cost of the treatment and rebuilding they bring upon your head. And these are by no means the only items which a policy may exclude. So any policy needs to be searched for these traps.

Excess Charges

Policies may have clauses saying you pay the first £XXX of a claim of a certain type. Particularly when it comes to subsidence and landslip.

How Much to Insure For

The essential point to remember is that you insure to cover the cost of rebuilding the house - not its market value. The Association of British Insurers (page 509)

issues a table to guide you, as rebuilding costs vary with the region as well as the value of the house. They are based on square footage. So measure the width and depth of the house, and of all outbuildings, and find the area. Then multiply the area by the cost per square foot in your region. But if your house is unusual in any way you may do better to have the cost of rebuilding estimated by a surveyor. The Royal Institution of Chartered Surveyors (page 214) can give you the name of someone suitable, so can the Incorporated Society of Valuers and Auctioneers (page 226).

If you are buying or selling your home there are strict rules as to who is responsible for insuring it at different stages and these vary between England and Wales, and Scotland. Check with your insurance company and make sure it is never uncovered and your responsibility.

WARNING: One of the more astonishing injustices in the insurance system is that some policies pay out *nothing at all* if you haven't insured for the true value. Others pay out but, if you were underinsured by 20 per cent, they pay out your claim minus 20 per cent. Obviously rising costs can put any policy at risk of this unless it is index linked. *Read the small print very carefully* and go for index linking if you can.

Remember to check these points on any buildings policy.

- Are you covered for the cost of living elsewhere during repairs?
- What is the value of that cover (it's usually a percentage of the sum insured)?
- Are there any clauses whereby you pay the first £X on any claim? If so how much and on what aspects of the claim?
- Is it index linked?
- Does it cover the cost of restoring the building to how it was or does it make it 'as new'?

If you are renting check whether the landlord is paying building insurance and what it covers internally. You may be responsible for insuring the rest.

House Contents Insurance

Insuring the contents of a house covers more than just theft or damage to the objects. It may also cover you if an employee slips on your slippery mat and breaks a leg or your china ducks fly off the wall and peck someone. Contents insurance should also cover a tenant for most types of damage to the building. Surprisingly this type of insurance may also cover personal liability. This is for damage which you do to someone else or their property even if the accident isn't in the house.

There are also a multitude of other risks it can embrace.

Because they can cover so many types of risk, contents policies vary considerably in what they cost. This is a field where a good insurance broker is invaluable. Give them a list of the types of risk for which you would like to be covered, then ask them to suggest any others which might be useful. Decide a final list, and ask them to find companies which will give a good price on those risks.

★ Insuring in a high risk area can cost 4 times as much as in a low risk one. But companies don't totally agree on what *are* high and low risk areas. Look for a company that doesn't rate the risk in your area too highly.

Exclusion Clauses
There are always exclusion clauses for such things as fair wear and tear, revolution, war, and anything may cease to be covered if you take it out of the house. (So cameras and jewellery should usually be covered by an all-risks clause within the policy.) What's more, some policies have a clause whereby cover ceases if you leave the house empty for over 30 days, which could be disastrous if you go on long trips or might be away in hospital.

Types of Policy
You can choose between several different types of policy.

With **indemnity** cover you don't get the full replacement cost. Instead you get the value of the item, bearing in mind the loss of value because of its age and wear. (Depreciation is not applied to objects which don't depreciate or which rise in value - such as antiques.) This is a relatively inexpensive type of policy.

With **replacement as new** cover you get the full cost of replacement. This is the most expensive type of cover but it is also the best. A slightly cheaper version is to get limited new-for-old cover in which you only get full replacement if the object is under a certain age (often 2 years old).

If a policy covers you for **accidental damage** you will be covered even if it is your fault.

You can't always choose which to have, as some objects are only insured on an indemnity basis. But some companies offer mixed policies which allow you to insure some things on one basis, some on another. Also different policies set different age limits for 'as new' replacement. This is something to compare before buying insurance.

How Much to Insure For
There's no short cut to working out insurance. You have to list the contents in every room, including things of value which are out of sight, and tot up the value. You *must* insure everything, you can't decide that the sofa is too old to be worth bothering about. Some policies won't allow items of value to exceed a certain percentage of the policy - on the assumption that people don't *just* have valuable things to insure - so if the balance looks wrong some must have been left out. Items like jewellery and antiques will need a special valuation. If some items

are on an indemnity basis (see left) ask what depreciation rules the company has and value them accordingly.

In making the valuation remember the rules about being underinsured may apply (page 506). For this reason it is much safer to have an index-linked policy.

> WARNING: Each time you buy something new of value you should tell the insurance company in writing and ask them to check that your cover is sufficient or you could be underinsured. Most policies will have a clause that you have to give details of individual items above a certain value.

★ In some policies items insured on an all-risks basis are not index linked. Check this and adjust their insurance each year if the index linking doesn't apply.

Life Insurance
In the dim and distant past, life insurance was simply a matter of a group of people getting together, saving some cash and the money in the kitty was paid to the family of whoever died that year. It was hardly a fair system: sometimes families had to share, at other times they won the equivalent of the jackpot and got three years' worth of savings. To get round these problems, in the middle of the eighteenth century a mathematician called James Dodson set about devising plans that were linked to how long people were expected to live. And so today's life insurance industry was born.

Life insurance salesmen are known for being the sharpest in the business. Don't tangle with one unless you have researched the matter quietly first and done a bit of reading. A broker may get the bulk of your first year's payment as commission for setting up these deals but since the Financial Services Act 1986 brokers have an obligation to give the client the *best* advice - not simply to recommend whichever company gives them the best commission. They must reveal the commission they will be getting on any insurance which could be an investment. So ask. However, they still have a vested interest in selling you *some* life insurance. The big question is - do you need it? If nobody would suffer financially if you died the answer is 'no'.

Don't let the terms life insurance and life assurance confuse you. Life assurance is the technical name for life insurance, that's all. As I don't like jargon I won't be using it.

Life insurance is very simple. You pay money every year and the company pays out if you die (or sometimes if you retire). It's a rather morbid gamble. The figures are geared to your personal life expectation. If you die young the company loses and you (in a sense) win. If you live long and pay long they win, you lose. But, as I write, no tax is saved on insurance premiums.

You can also take out life insurance on other people but, in case you were planning the perfect murder, there are limits to those whose life you may insure. You can't go round buying life insurance against the possibility of strangers dropping dead. You have to have an 'insurable interest', which is some legal or financial relationship which would justify you benefiting from the person's death. So it covers marriage partners, children and employees.

There are basically three types of life insurance:

Term Insurance

With term insurance you pay money to the insurance company *for a stated time* and if you die during that time your dependants get a cash sum tax free. You can choose how much will be paid at your death and how long you wish to pay the instalments. When you stop paying, the insurance stops, and if you have carelessly failed to die you get nothing for your money.

If you were a man aged 29 and wanted to buy a 20 year policy which would pay out £25,000 on your death, it would cost around £4 a month at current prices, but a woman would pay slightly less, as women live longer than men.

Level term gives a set sum which is fixed when you take out the policy. You can also buy a level policy which, if the holder dies, gives a fixed tax free income for a set period of time instead of a lump sum. **Increasing term** means that if you drop dead in year 5 your family gets more than if you die in year 4. The steps are usually pre-set and the money could be a lump sum or an income for a set period.

Whole Life

If you have whole life policy you keep on paying life insurance until you die. Then your dependents get either a lump sum or regular payments. The figures for these are set when you take out the policy and don't change. However, the policy can be bought 'with profits' or 'without profits' (see below). It will also have a surrender value if you want to cash it in, though doing that in the early days could mean you get back less than you pay in, as the broker's commission and setting-up costs come out of your early payments. This type of policy costs several times as much as a term insurance, but it does guarantee something for your money.

Endowment Policies

The system is that you pay premiums (monthly, quarterly, or annually) until a certain date, upon which you get a lump sum which was set at the start of the policy. If you die before the date your family gets all the money which would have been paid on that date. Within this there are two variations. A with-profits policy still guarantees a bonus, on top of the set sum, if the company has invested your premiums well (but if it has done badly you don't get less than the set sum). In a without-profits policy only the agreed sum is paid. This last is usually a bad buy. Your money would have done more for you elsewhere.

Unit-linked Insurance

This is a curious creature: an insurance policy mated with an investment fund. The money you pay is split, so part goes into buying units in an investment fund and the rest goes to pay for term insurance. However, a very small figure is usually set for the sum guaranteed by the insurance, and its value depends largely on the - unpredictable - value of the units at the end of the term. The payment can either be a lump sum or regular premiums.

What Happens if You Can't Pay

If you want, or need, to stop paying a life premium the policy will have a surrender value. But, as in war, there's not much joy in surrendering. Unless it has run more than half its time you are likely to make a loss - and that's on top of the value your money has lost with inflation.

A better option could be to ask the company to convert the policy to a 'paid up' basis. This means that it is frozen until it matures (ie until it would normally have paid out), they then pay less than they would have done on a fully paid policy but more than its surrender value would have been. There may also be the option of paying premiums again if your finances improve.

Travel Insurance

The key points of travel insurance depend entirely upon the value of what you're taking and the country you're going to and activities you intend to pursue while you are abroad. It is safer to buy through a broker and discuss your exact needs than to get a quick insurance from a bank or travel agent. And don't assume that any automatic cover provided by your credit card will be sufficient, often it will only cover certain aspects of travel insurance. Bear in mind that you are unlikely to be covered for active sports or hazardous activities so you need to take out special insurance. Cover for emergency fly-back is essential unless the medical facilities where you're going are excellent.

★ Check travel policies carefully. Some only cover you for loss from the time you leave home until you land on British soil. So if your valuables are stolen just after landing in Britain you can't claim.

School Fees Insurance

School fees have shot up much faster than inflation over the past few years and sending a child to a fee-paying school can now cost more than buying a house. The easiest way to pay school fees is to take out an insurance plan, when the child is very young indeed, which will pay out a certain sum each year over a set period of years, after a set date. How much is paid out is entirely a matter of the type of policy and what is put in. So work out how much the fees are likely to cost by the time the money will be needed - allow for at least 10 per cent increase a year on current costs. The **Independent Schools Information Service** (ISIS) 56 Buckingham Gate, London SW1E 6AG Tel: 01 630 8793 can give you the names of companies offering such policies.

Emergency Help

If you don't take out insurance early you can make last-minute arrangements. Banks have schemes for

Financial facts change daily, check the latest figures before making a decision.

borrowing for school fees on terms which allow the money to be repaid over a long period. But you must also take out insurance which guarantees that the bank can't lose its money if you die.

If you already have life insurance you may be able to get a loan from the insurance company, against this policy, without it affecting your life policy, provided the loan is paid back.

Schools have scholarships of all kinds and some also have trust funds for special cases. And sometimes you can get state help for private schooling (page 293).

> Choose an educational insurance scheme which will allow you to use the money for something else if circumstances change. Eighteen years is a long time and a government might ban private education before then.

More information
As always, the **Office of Fair Trading** has good leaflets.

The Association of British Insurers (ABI), Aldermary House, 10-15 Queen Street, London EC4N 1TT Tel: 01 248 4477 has a range of leaflets on different aspects of insurance.

British Insurance Brokers' Association, BIBA House, 14 Bevis Marks, London EC3A 7NT Tel: 01 623 9043

School Fees Insurance Agency Ltd, 10 Queen Street, Maidenhead, Berks SL6 1JA Tel: 0628 34291

Mortgages
With the present state of the market and tax relief, buying a home with a mortgage is the best investment you are ever likely to make. Whether the price boom will go on for ever is anyone's guess. But if it doesn't, at least you have something useful to show for your money. So it is hard to lose. But in budgeting for your down payment remember you will pay stamp duty to the government on the price of the property - in 1988 1% of its cost over £30,000.

How a Mortgage Works
Mortgages are very simple. If you can't, or don't want to, pay the full price of a home, you put down some of the money and ask the mortgage company to pay the rest to whoever is selling the property. When you buy a home with a mortgage you own it jointly with the mortgage company. You then pay them the money you owe on a monthly basis, plus interest on the loan. This means that if you don't keep up the payments the mortgage company has a right to sell your home and take back its share of the money plus the interest you owe. So there is a real danger in spending so much furnishing or doing up your home that you can't meet the mortgage payments if you fall ill or lose your job.

The main sources of mortgages are building societies and banks. You may get priority if you have saved with them so, as some companies give better terms than others, spread your savings so you stand a good chance of getting several offers. However, you don't *have* to save with a company to get a mortgage from it and,

when a company offers you a mortgage don't be so grateful you accept instantly. Take time to think, and talk to other companies. Remember the company giving you the mortgage isn't doing you any favours: you are putting money in its pockets. Whenever a financial institution lets you have money - you pay, they gain.

★ Some companies offer employees the best terms of all. But do check what would happen if you wanted to leave the job before the mortgage was paid off.

How Much You Can Borrow
The percentage you can borrow on a mortgage varies. Most companies will lend you 80 per cent of the value of a home, a few lend 100 per cent, and you should be able to find anything in between. It depends on your circumstances and on how eager companies are to lend.

The actual amount will depend on your income, and two incomes can be counted instead of one. You needn't be a couple, you could be friends of the same sex. As I write you can get tax relief on £30,000 of the loan per *home* - not per person. There are complicated Inland Revenue rules on whether they divide the tax relief between you (if you are both earning) or set it all against one income. Check with the Revenue - and possibly with an accountant too - before making an arrangement or you could lose out.

The formulas for how much you can borrow vary but 3 x the main borrower's yearly salary before tax is usual. On a shared mortgage you can add on 1 x the second income. The repayment time varies with the company and what you want. It's usually 5 to 25 years and generally the longer the time the more the total payment.

In deciding how much you can afford, don't forget that you also agree to pay interest - *at whatever rate the lender chooses*. This rate varies as the minimum lending rate goes up or down. So you must be prepared to pay a higher rate than the one in force when you borrow. However, some companies sell mortgages at fixed rates. These are a gamble. If interest rates drop you lose, if they rise you win. Look hard at the political scene before choosing.

Those who would find it hard to pay full interest may be able to find an equity scheme by which less interest is paid but the mortgage company takes part of the profits when the property is sold. Some building societies are offering special equity schemes for those in poorly paid jobs - such as nursing.

> If you have problems paying a mortgage you can renegotiate the loan and pay smaller sums over a longer time. It is much better to ask for this than to fall behind on your payments.

Types of Mortgage

Endowment Mortgages
Mortgage brokers may try to push this type. No wonder: they get commissions on the premiums you pay to the insurance company.

Financial facts change daily, check the latest figures before making a decision.

With an endowment mortgage you take out a life insurance policy which will pay out the value of the mortgage exactly when the mortgage must be repaid. Meanwhile you pay monthly premiums to the life insurance company and only pay interest to the mortgage company. Endowment policies are explained on page 508 and the fact that a mortgage is linked in doesn't alter the rules. You can use a with-profits policy or one without profits.

A **low-cost endowment** has cheaper premiums. This is a with-profits policy. But you insure for less than the full mortgage, gambling that the extra profits will pay the difference. If they don't, you have to find the balance out of your pocket.

Pros	Cons
You know your family will have a roof over their heads if you die.	You have to keep paying premiums even if you sell the house, pay the loan off and go abroad, or accept the surrender value.
You can transfer the endowment to a new home if you sell the first one, but see the cons.	When you want to sell one house and buy another you can't clear the first mortgage and start again as you can with a repayment mortgage.
When mortgage interest rates are under 10 per cent this system is a better buy than when they are over that.	If interest rates on the mortgage go up you can't renegotiate the mortgage to cover a longer period.
The system has advantages for high-rate tax payers as it keeps the tax relief at a higher level for longer than a repayment mortgage.	If you fall on hard times the DHSS may help with the interest on the mortgage but *not* with the premiums on the policy, whereas it may help with all of a repayment mortgage.

A key point is that the insurance premium is calculated on your age and fitness. The younger and fitter you are the less you pay. Once the premiums are set they stay the same until the end of the policy. The only exception is a low-start, low endowment mortgage in which you pay less in the early years of the premium than you do later on. This is geared to the young with low salaries but higher expectations - but the higher payments could be tougher to pay if a wife stops earning and children have to be paid for too. Don't rush into an endowment mortgage without looking at the other possibilities.

Repayment Mortgage

A repayment mortgage is a straightforward loan given for a set period of time. You then repay it month by month with interest. Your payments in the early years are mostly interest but, as the debt slowly drops, less of what you pay is mopped up by interest and a larger and larger proportion of the debt is paid off.

Repayments on a first (main) home qualify for tax relief (up to a certain value) and nowadays a system called MIRAS is used. This stands for Mortgage Interest Relief at Source. What happens is that if you owe £150

a month to the mortgage company and should get tax relief of £50, you pay only £100 to the mortgage company and the Inland Revenue pays the difference. (Those are not real figures incidentally but real figures are untidy.) MIRAS only gives relief at the basic rate, higher-rate tax payers have to get the difference back from the Inland Revenue.

This type of mortgage can be safeguarded with a mortgage protection insurance which will pay off the mortgage if you die. But it only pays out the amount needed to pay it off at that time. No extras, no bonuses. If you die the day you have taken out the policy it pays the whole lot, but if you die in the last year of the mortgage it pays out a few hundred. And if you don't die until the mortgage is paid it pays nothing. Provided you aren't a smoker, this is a cheap way of making sure a family isn't left homeless, and it can be taken out jointly if two people are paying towards the home. But premiums are higher for smokers.

By paying slightly more you can also be covered if you are unable to pay the mortgage during periods of illness or when out of work. Rates for these policies vary, so do the terms: some will only cover interest up to a certain level, while others have no ceiling. With some you can't increase your cover without a new health check, with others you can. And some trades unions will offer members cover of this sort at competitive rates.

Insurance companies you might look at include Equitable Life, Permanent, Cornhill, General Accident, GRE, Scottish Widows, NPI, Western Australian, Pinnacle, Royal Life and CIS. An insurance broker or the Association of British Insurers (page 509) will give you the addresses.

Pension Mortgage

This is very like an endowment mortgage except that the lump sum used to pay off the loan on the house is the one paid by a pension scheme. This is especially appealing if you pay a high rate of tax, as you get tax relief on both the interest to the mortgage company and on the pension plan. However, there are snags.
- It is harder to move house.
- The loan period has to run until you retire.
- If any government decided to tax the lump sum paid as part of a pension you could be in trouble.

This means that a pension mortgage is best suited to somone of 40 +, with a highish income and a nest egg to bridge the gap if tax rules change.

Financial facts change daily, check the latest figures before making a decision.

There is no guarantee that any pension plan will be able to pay out a sum large enough to pay off the mortgage. It may be *expected* to but if there is a slump the value of a pension normally slumps too.

Where to Find a Mortgage

There's no shortage of places to get a mortgage - banks, building societies, and mortgage lenders will all provide them. Some banks and building societies even run a scheme by which they guarantee to give you a mortgage, on a suitable property, if you save a set amount with them over a certain time (often 2 years). The offers aren't all the same when you start reading the small print. You don't need a mortgage broker to help you: you are usually better off going straight to the banks and building societies and talking to the managers.

Homeloan Scheme

Under the government backed Homeloan scheme a first-time buyer who registers for the scheme and saves a certain sum with a building society, over 2 years, will get a small interest free loan and a tax free bonus when buying a home costing less than a set amount. Building societies have the registration forms. If you haven't got a home and could save I suggest you sign on for this scheme immediately. If you don't want to buy you've lost nothing and if you do decide to buy you have gained interest free money. It may not be a lot but it usually covers the stamp duty.

Shared Ownership

Some local councils run shared ownership schemes in which you buy part of a home from a housing association, on a mortgage, and the council or a housing association buys the other part. You then rent the other part from them and, when you have the money, you can then buy more and more of the property - at the market price when you pay. For information contact the **Housing Corporation**, 149 Tottenham Court Road, London W1P 0BN Tel: 01 387 9466.

The trade association for the building society movement is the **Building Societies Association** (3 Savile Row, London W1X 1AF Tel: 01 437 0655), which produces a useful range of free booklets, a video, on the steps to buying a home, which is in some public libraries. The **Royal Institution of Chartered Surveyors** (page 214) also has leaflets.

Pensions

There is no getting round it: pensions have about as much charm as a fly and carry a nasty reminder of impending old age, the way a fly reminds of death and decay. But, as with any pest, the less you do about pensions the worse the situation becomes. If you take one out at 30 you could get several times as much pension for your money as you will get if you start at 40 - so it pays to take action fast. Particularly as a pension is usually the biggest investment anyone makes

in their life - even bigger than buying a home.

Until recently, the most notable feature of the pension system was its lack of choice. Now the rules have changed. There are more choices and more decisions to make.

State Pensions

Though the officials don't see it like that, the state pension scheme is, in a sense, in two tiers: the basic pension and SERPS.

Basic State Pension

So all embracing is the welfare state that it's easy to suppose one will get state benefits automatically, regardless of what one has paid, just as we get the Health Service. This isn't so. To get a state pension you must contribute to it. Everyone who reaches 16 is sent a National Insurance Number Card which should be kept safely as the number has to be given to any employer, or to the tax office if you are self employed. It may also be needed when claiming benefits. The most important benefit which has to be contributed to is the state pension. The full basic pension is the same for everyone, but National Insurance Contributions (NIC) are in 4 classes.

Class 1 is a flat rate paid by everyone who is employed.
Class 2 is a different flat rate paid by the self employed.
Class 3 is yet another flat rate paid by those who choose to keep up payments even when they aren't working.
Class 4 is an earnings related payment only for the self employed.

Anyone who is employed and earns over a set sum (£41 a week from May 1988) must pay NIC, and their employer must also contribute. And Class 2 must be paid by the self-employed who earn more than a set amount per year (£2,250 from May 1988).

In return for a lifetime of contributions you get a basic state pension which can be drawn, as a right, by any woman over 60 or man over 65 provided:
- they paid full NI contributions for 90 per cent of their working life
- they don't earn more than a set limit while drawing the pension.

'Working life' means about 16-59 for a woman and 16-64 for a man. Those whose payments and credits don't add up to 90 per cent still get some pension but on a sliding scale according to how much they have paid in. If you have paid NIC for half your official 'working life' you get half the basic pension. If you have paid it for three-quarters of it you get three-quarters of the basic pension. But if you have paid NIC for less than a quarter of your 'working life' you get nothing.

However, there are a host of special rules (see below). So *always apply for a pension* - even if you think you haven't contributed enough. The officials will soon say if you aren't entitled to it. And do remember there are special payments for those in special situations - widowed, with children, very old, and so on. So read the DHSS leaflets.

Special Rules to Note

- Years spent in full-time education between 16 and 18, are taken off the length of your 'working life' so you need only pay NIC for 90 per cent of a shorter period to get a full pension. That also applies to times of illness and unemployment when NIC could not be paid.

- The same goes for years women spend at home looking after children under 19 or the elderly or sick (called Home Responsibilities Protection - HRP). And from April 1988 it applied to SERPS (right) too. HRP also applies to the self employed who paid full contributions before stopping work. Either way HRP is limited to 20 years.

- On divorce a woman may apply for her husband's contribution record to be transferred to her card. This can be backdated 10 years. So if a woman didn't work before marriage and has now decided she wants to clock up the benefit of HRP this move could give it to her.

- It is possible to backdate contributions for up to 6 years by paying the voluntary rate to cover unpaid years. Years as a student, when over 18, are counted as part of your working life even though no contributions are paid. Ex-students may find it worth their while making backdated payments to cover these years.

- Girls should be sure to pay at least one year's employed NIC. This establishes their right to home responsibilities protection if they then marry fast and stay at home with their children.

- A married woman who hasn't paid enough contributions can get up to 60 per cent of a single person's pension on the basis of those her husband paid, but she has to wait until *he* reaches retirement age.

Graduated Pensions

The graduated pension was the grand-dad of SERPS. It is based on the level of your earnings in the years from 1961 to 1975. However, with rising prices its value has fallen dramatically.

The Self Employed

The self employed can only obtain the basic pension from the state, their additional earnings related payments don't count towards any extra pension. But for a long while they have been able to take out a Section 226A (non-state) pension for which contributions were and are tax free.

Earnings and Pensions

Governments tend to alter the amount a pensioner may earn. So pensioners should check the current figure before working. But you can choose to keep working and not draw a pension until up to 5 years later, then draw a slightly higher one. During those 5 years you don't pay your National Insurance but your employer does. But when a woman is 65 or a man 70 the pension is paid even if they carry on working - though it may be reduced in line with their earnings.

SERPS - Additional State Pension

SERPS sounds like a rather nasty disease but it stands for the State Earnings Related Pension Scheme. It was introduced in 1978 and is not for the self-employed. Under the scheme you make an extra state contribution - scaled to your earnings. (You have no choice as to how much this will be. If you pay SERPS you will pay exactly the same sum as everyone else with the same income.) Then, on retirement, you draw an extra pension linked to your earnings. The more SERPS you paid the higher your pension.

Until the 1986 Social Security Act you couldn't choose whether you paid this extra or not. Your employers decided for you. Now everyone can decide for themselves. The government set 1 July 1988 as the date from which anyone paying SERPS could decide to leave the scheme, and there is no closing date for leaving. But you *must* either buy a personal plan instead or go into a occupational pension plan run by your company. You can't just opt out of pensions altogether and decide you'll jump off the nearest bridge at 60 or 65.

In or Out of SERPS?

The big question is - will you be better off leaving SERPS ('contracting out') or staying in? The answer is, it's a gamble with risks both ways. Governments can cut pensions as well as raise them. And, with more and more people living into ripe old age, there will be increasing pressure to do just that (though the growing power of the geriatric vote might prevent any government going too far).

A personal pension plan spares you that risk. But nobody should imagine that a pension plan is necessarily a rock solid investment. Money can only be paid out if the fund managers have been able to make your money grow in the years before. That depends on the world economy as well as on their skill, and the crash of 1987 proved the fragility of the world's financial markets. When pension plans *guarantee* returns they tend to guarantee very small sums - often smaller than you would get with SERPS or a good company plan.

To encourage people to move out of SERPS the government will pay into the personal pension plan of anyone who leaves SERPS a tax-free sum equal to 2 per cent of their salary. (This is a government 'special offer' only running for 5 years from mid-1988.) The money someone has paid into SERPS up to that date will be held in the fund and go towards a larger pension when they retire.

★ To find out how much SERPS pension you've built up so far, and what it is likely to be if you don't opt out, use leaflet NP23 from a DHSS office. You can also ask your local DHSS office to give you a pension forecast on the basis of your contributions so far. Then you can see what you need to do to improve your final pension.

> The decision on SERPS is linked to whether or not you are well covered by a company pension plan. So read on.

Financial facts change daily, check the latest figures before making a decision.

Reasons for Staying in SERPS

You know, more or less, what you will get.

You are middle aged and won't have time to build up a good personal pension. So SERPS offers more.

You don't want the risk of perhaps buying the wrong plan.

Your employer won't pay into your personal pension plan so you would lose out by leaving SERPS.

The charges may be high for taking out a personal plan (some money will certainly go in commission).

You don't like your pension depending on a fund manager and the economic climate.

You are a woman and so have less time to build up a personal plan before retirement.

Ill health or disability may stop you working. SERPS ignores such gaps but with a personal plan you *must* keep up the contributions.

SERPS is indexed linked (at present).

Reasons for Leaving SERPS

You want to get the incentive payment the government will make into the personal plan, of those who opt out of SERPS - until 1993.

You believe you can buy a better pension scheme for the same money.

Your employer will definitely pay into your personal plan as much as into SERPS.

You get tax relief on your contributions. You don't on SERPS.

You can choose your own retirement age (within limits).

You can borrow money against a pension plan.

You can switch between being employed and self employed without it affecting your pension.

If you want to transfer it into a company scheme it should be easy after 1 July 1988.

More information

Your Rights for Pensioners, Age Concern (page 313).

DHSS Leaflets Unit, P.O. Box 21, Stanmore, Middx HA7 1AY Tel: 01 952 2311 - has free leaflets on all aspects of pensions (so does your local DHSS office). Say which aspect of pensions you want to read about or they may not send the leaflet you need. There is also a freephone information line on 0800 66655.

Occupational Pension Plans

Under the old scheme a company could decide to 'contract out' of SERPS provided it could give its staff an occupational pension scheme which met certain criteria.

Most employee contributions are below the maximum tax-free contribution of 15 per cent of earnings. Until June 1988 anyone wanting to contribute up to that maximum had to do so through Additional Voluntary Contributions (AVCs) to the occupational scheme. After June the law allowed the AVCs to be made to a free-standing personal pension plan instead.

Until the 1986 Social Security Act if your company had a pension scheme you had to join it willy-nilly, whether it was in addition to SERPS or instead of it. Now you can choose to pull out of the company pension plan, just as you can pull out of SERPS, and go into a personal pension plan instead. Whether this is a good idea will depend on your situation.

Pros to Company Schemes

There are two main kinds of company policy.
1 The **final pay** type (sometimes called 'Defined Benefits'), under which the size of your pension is linked to your earnings. This is usually via a formula which takes account of both your final pay and the number of years you have been contributing. A good scheme would provide 1/60th of your final pay for each year you paid contributions. So forty years of contributions would give you 40/60ths (i.e., two-thirds) of your final pay.
2 In the **money purchase** type (sometimes called 'Defined Contributions') instead of being paid a sum set by a formula, the money paid in is invested and when you retire the money which has built up is used to pay you a lump sum and a pension. This method tends to be favoured by small companies.

Either kind may be 'contributory' (i.e. both you and your employer contribute to it) or 'non-contributory' (i.e., only your employer pays in). Both types of contribution are tax free, so this is a cost-effective way of saving, and occupational schemes are index linked by the state just like SERPS.

By law a company *must* contribute something towards an employee's pension, over and above paying its whack towards the basic state pension. But it only has to pay into *one* extra scheme. So, under the new system, the company can either pay towards SERPS, or towards a company plan, or towards an employee's personal pension plan. As an employee you can choose to belong to any or all of these schemes, but if you belong to more than one all the contributions for the extra schemes come only out of your own pocket. Employers may also be prepared to contribute more towards one kind of scheme than another. So before you consider moving from a scheme you need to know what their attitude would be.

If a company goes into liquidation your pension should be safe. A company pension fund is normally administered as a trust and is not linked to the finances of the company. Ask the liquidators for the name and address of the trustee.

The Big Con of Company Schemes

The big snag to company policies is what happens when you change jobs. Until now there has been a Dickensian system where only lifelong loyalty to a single company guaranteed a decent pension. The new system is meant to change that. But some of the old rules may still affect certain sections of your pension.

From 1975:

If you worked for a company for under 5 years, contributions (but not those of your employer) to its pension scheme were refunded, with some deductions, on leaving. If you left after more than 5 years your money was stuck but you had a right to benefit from the scheme. However, the pension might be frozen at the value it had when you left the job.

From 1 January 1986 to 6 April 1988

You only had to pay into a company scheme for 2 years to get a right to benefit from it (and to lose your right to have your money simply refunded on leaving), but the pension due on those payments could not be frozen in value but had to increase in line with the pensions of those ·longer service.

Since 6 April 1988:

The 2 year rule still applies *but* now you must be given the option to transfer the full value of the pension into another pension scheme. This could be the scheme of your new company or a personal pension scheme of some kind. But the new company has no obligation to let you transfer money from your old company's scheme into its scheme. And even if it lets this happen there may be problems over how your old scheme is valued.

★ If you plan to change jobs negotiate your pension with the new employer before you accept the job. And, if you want to transfer the value of your current company pension into the new company's scheme, make sure they agree the figures as part of the deal, don't rely on general assurances.
★ If you are in a company scheme the personnel office of any company has a legal duty to keep you fully informed and tell you how your money is being invested - so ask. And if you aren't happy with the answers talk to the union representative.

Company Pensions Information Centre (CPIC), 7 Old Park Lane, London W1Y 3LJ Tel: 01 493 4757, offers a free information service giving the general facts about company pensions, and the rules and regulations surrounding them. But it does *not* give advice (s.a.e. for its free leaflets).
The Occupational Pensions Advisory Service, Room 327, Aviation House, 129 Kingsway, London WC2B 6NN Tel: 01 379 7311, has voluntary advisers around Britain.
The Association of British Insurers (page 509) has good leaflets on pensions.

Personal Pensions

From July 1988 the law allowed employees to choose to set up a personal pension scheme instead of belonging to a company scheme. Now that the government is encouraging everyone to buy personal pensions there has been an explosion in pension schemes and it may be some while before the dust settles. You can also be sure that the financial press will be full of articles appraising the various schemes. So watch the columns for the latest briefings.

The big problem isn't going to be finding personal pensions it's going to be avoiding them. Every possible financial institution is getting in on the act - not just the big companies, which have always offered pensions, but banks, building societies and unit trusts. The hard part will be getting unbiased advice. If you have an accountant or know a good accountant who is up on pensions he or she could be the best bet. But there is

nowhere you can go to get good free advice and information on all the possibilities.

The Society of Pension Consultants and the Association of Consulting Actuaries both have lists of firms whose staff offer unbiased pensions advice for a fee (the associations themselves do *not* offer advice). Until now such companies have tended to advise companies rather than individuals, so the fee schemes are still being worked out. But in time some of them should be able to offer some reasonably priced computerized advice systems.

Types of Personal Pension Plan

In choosing a personal pension plan don't forget that you can join more than one plan and even switch from one plan to another within a company. In fact it may be safest to have more than one plan.

In comparing the benefits of saving for your old age via a pension plan or by putting your money into some other investment, a key point is that your savings aren't tax free, but the money you pay into a pension plan is. So, in effect, the government pays about 30 per cent of any pension plan for you, which can't be bad. (Though there are, of course, limits to how much you can put into a pension tax free.)

A *deposit administration* plan is one similar to a deposit account. The amount you pay in stays safe (though it will lose value with inflation) and the pension you get depends on the interest rates when you retire. This seldom brings in very much, but it does guarantee a set minimum.

A *non profits* policy is one which guarantees to give you a set pension no matter what happens. This sounds ideal but, as it gives the company no leeway for adjusting to the economic situation, the sum is likely to be set very low.

In *unit-linked pension* plans your contributions are used to buy units in investment funds. The funds are invested in all kinds of things from shares to local authority loans. Your pension depends on the value of the fund at the time, and this is linked to the stock market. When the market is high you do well: when it falls you can do badly.

In *with profits* plans the policy usually guarantees a small pension and/or lump sum topped up by extra money from the profits the company has (with luck) made on the money. You should do better from this than from a non-profits policy.

An *annuity* is often thought of as a pension: it isn't, it's a kind of insurance policy. You pay a lump sum to a company, which then guarantees to give you an income until you die. Some annuities are fixed, some are index linked. A man usually gets a higher income than a woman of the same age paying the same money - as men die sooner. It is one way of getting an income out of a lump sum paid out by a pension plan, or from the sale of a house which is too big for someone elderly. The lump sum belongs to the company.

Points on Buying a Pension

The quality of your pension - and therefore of your life

in retirement - will depend on how good the pension plan is and on who is running it. Nobody should rush into buying a pension until they have looked at all the options and taken good advice. Never buy in a hurry, or buy the first you are offered.

- Compare several plans very carefully and *look at the track record of the company* (see the magazines listed below).
- Remember the years leading up to the crash of 1987 were a rising market: a company had to be pretty bad not to make profits during them. So don't be too impressed by growth during that time, unless it was greater than that achieved by other companies.
- If a company gives you a projection of the pension you will get, remember it is only a guess and no guarantee at all. You could get much less unless they are talking about a guaranteed sum.
- Ask how much any plan will cost you in commissions and other charges, especially in the first few years.
- In looking at the sums you will get on retirement allow for inflation. Ask if they can tell you what it will be worth in today's terms allowing for 5 or 10 per cent inflation.

One of the key attractions of personal pension plans is that they will have tax relief at source, and quite large sums will be able to benefit from this. Up to the age of 50 you will be able to put 17·5 per cent of your total salary into a personal pension plan tax free, and the percentage rises as you get older, to a top level of 27·5 per cent. The tax relief will use the same system as MIRAS (page 510). And, when the pension is paid, there will be further tax benefits (page 526).

The rules for calculating the permitted contributions for the self employed are complicated and you should consult an accountant if you need to know.

Association of Consulting Actuaries, Rolls House, 7 Rolls Buildings, Fetter Lane, London EC4A 1NH Tel: 01 831 7130

The National Federation of Retirement Pensions Associations, Melling House, 14 St Peters Street, Blackburn BB2 2HD Tel: 0254 52606 is a pensioners pressure group and information source.

Society of Pension Consultants, Ludgate House, Ludgate Circus, London EC4A 2AB Tel: 01 353 1688

Disclosure of Information to Pension Members, Sue Ward, The Industrial Society, clarifies the new rules about pension schemes, for employers and employees

Money Marketing magazine

Money Management magazine

Planned Savings magazine

Rosemary Burr (ed), *Make Your Pension Work,* Rosters

Age Concern, *Your Taxes and Savings in Retirement*

Savings

Sarah Bernhardt was right when she said, 'Money isn't everything, but it's so good for the nerves.'

Almost everyone's ideal is to win, save up, or inherit enough money to have a nice lump sum behind them: a nest egg for old age, a protection against a rainy day, or simply as a nerve soother. To lack it is the emotional equivalent of living without an overcoat. The slightest draught of misfortune strikes doubly chill. This means that it is enormously important to put any savings or windfalls into the right hands.

Money ought to be working for you every minute of its life. If you have more money in a current account which doesn't pay interest than is needed to avoid bank charges, you are throwing money away. It ought to be earning you interest in a deposit account at least. Money that isn't earning is like a factory sitting idle.

If you would be wealthy, think of saving as well as getting. The Indies have not made Spain rich, because her out-goes are greater than her in-comes.
Enquire Within, 1856

Savings v. Investments

Broadly speaking, there are two ways to place spare money:

1 Put it into a scheme which guarantees to let you have precisely the sum you put in - when you need it - and meanwhile provides interest at a set rate. This is a way of saving.

The snag here is that although you can take out the money you put in you may still lose because of inflation. If the rate of inflation is higher than the interest you are paid - or you don't have the interest added to the investment - the money you take out will have less buying power than it had when you put it in. So even if the figures are the same you have lost money.

Of course, if interest rates are higher than the rate of inflation, and you have the interest added to the investment, your capital is safe *and* making money.

2 You can invest the money. You gamble that it will grow but it could shrink instead and you may or may not get interest on the way.

Somehow investment has a glamorous air and saving is a bit down-market. (Although one of the smartest investments for a millionaire is in National Savings.) Don't let that glamour fool you into the common delusion that if money is invested some excellent alchemy takes place and it always comes out larger than it was before. This simply isn't true. Every time you read the word investment put 'risk' in its place and you will get a feel for the true situation. However, there is nothing wrong with risk if you can afford it. And - as in anything - there are degrees of risk. So the essence of placing money is to try to find the least risk with the most chance of either large growth or large interest.

Decisions Before You Place Your Money

Before you decide where to put your money, you need to think very clearly about what you want from it. This is a short checklist of points to consider - not in order of priority.

1 How much money do you want to place? (There may be a lower limit on how much you can place in a particular way.)

2 How long will you be able to leave the money without needing to use any of it? (Some investments have set lives.)

3 If you might want to get at some of the money how much notice might you be able to give?

4 Do you want to be *sure* you get out at least as much as you put in, or would you be prepared to risk losing it in the hope that it would get bigger?

5 Do you want to build up any goodwill for future borrowing by placing the money with an organization from which you may later want to borrow (e.g. you might need a mortgage at some time)?

6 Do you want any income from the investment or are you prepared just to have capital growth or plough any interest back in?

7 What is your tax position? Are you paying enough tax to benefit from a lower rate of interest which is tax free?

Your answers to these questions should help you to decide which of the following savings options should have your money.

Spreading the Load

The general rule is that if you have only a little spare money you should tuck it away as safely as you can, so at least the lump sum will be there, but this can be risky if inflation is high.

A second rule is that as soon as you have enough money to divide into sensible portions you should spread it between several forms of saving and investment with varied advantages and degrees of risk. Then what you lose on the swings you gain on the roundabouts.

Some of the Savings Options and what They Offer

Investment	Maximum	Minimum	Interest	Tax	Charges	Time	Notice	Comments
Building society or bank account paying interest	None	1p to many thousands, according to the account	Varies with the lending rate, the type of account and the company	Paid at basic rate by the account, *not refundable*	Usually nil	Any but you may need to give a few days' notice of withdrawal	The higher the interest the greater the penalty for sudden withdrawals	You can get at your money easily. A good place to keep funds for an emergency. *Not good for those who don't pay tax.* Check out the different types of account before placing your money.
Money market	None	Normally £10,000 but for money invested overnight £25,000–£50,000	Usually better than the best bank interest, but varies	Interest is paid gross	None	Subject to negotiation, often blocks of 7 or 31 days	The same as the time	Banks put it on the money markets for clients. A short-term move to make money work between other investments.
National Savings Ordinary Account	£10,000	£1	Rarely changes but not high	First £70 interest tax free, all paid gross	Nil	Up to a week	Up to £100 on demand, the rest within about a week.	Tax-free money is always good. Also useful for high earners and those who are not taxable as none is deducted.
National Savings Investment Account (3)	£100,000	£5	Varies each year	Taxable but paid gross	Nil	1 month	1 month	Much better interest than a National Savings ordinary account. The difference could cancel out the tax advantage of the ordinary account not paying high tax.
National Savings Yearly Plan (2)	£200 a month	£20 a month	Guaranteed for 5 years	Totally free of income and capital gains tax	Nil	1-5 years	14 working days	Tax free and safe but your money is tied up for a year; otherwise you lose interest.

Financial facts change daily, check the latest figures before making a decision.

Investment	Maximum	Minimum	Interest	Tax	Charges	Time	Notice	Comments
National Savings Certificates - Fixed Interest (2)	£1,000 (since the 33rd Issue)	£25	Fixed and paid when you cash in the certificates	Totally free of income and capital gains tax	Nil	Ideally 5 years	8 working days	You can take out the money any time, but the interest rate goes up for each year you leave it in, peaking in the 5th year. After that it drops to a flat rate just below the peak.
National Savings Certificates - Index Linked (2)	£5,000	£25	Interest at least equal to rate of inflation, bonuses on cashing in.	Totally free of income and capital gains tax	Nil	5 years (or some interest is lost)	8 working days	Most attractive when inflation is high.
National Savings Monthly Income Bonds (1)	£100,000	£2,000	Variable but one of the highest paid by National Savings	Interest paid gross but taxable	Nil	1 year (or some interest is lost)	3 months or you lose 3 months' interest	Interest is paid monthly - useful for those needing a regular income from savings. But withdrawals only in multiples of £1,000.
National Savings Deposit Bond (3)	£100,000	£100	Variable but usually very good	Interest paid gross but taxable	Nil	1 year minimum (or some interest is lost)	3 months	Gives a good interest rate if you can tie up a large sum for a longish time.
Premium Bonds	£10,000	£10	Nil	Any winnings are totally tax free	Nil	Any	8 working days	When inflation is high you lose heavily as the money loses value. But at least ERNIE is a gamble where you get your stake back.

National Savings

Most of the National Savings schemes can be bought over the counter of any post office but they can always be bought by post too.

You can also buy or sell those marked **1** by writing to The Controller, Bonds and Stock Office, Malton, Blackpool, Lancs FY3 9YP.

For those marked **2** contact Savings Certificate Office, Millburn Gate House, Durham, DH99 1NS.

For those marked **3** write to Deposit Bond Office, National Savings, Boydstone Road, Coveglen, Glasgow G58 1SB.

On all matters related to premium bonds write to the Bonds and Stock Office, Government Building, Lytham St Annes, Lancs FY0 1YN.

For information on National Savings Tel: 01 605 9461 (09.00 to 16.00). For information on National Savings interest rates there is a 24-hour recorded message on 01 605 9483/4 (south); 0253 723714 (north); 041 632 2766 (Scotland).

You can order a copy of *Investing in National Savings* by writing to the Professional Advisers' Liaison Officer, Charles House, 375 Kensington High Street, London W14 8SD.

Leaflets are in all post offices and information is also on Prestel ★50042; Ceefax page 223 and Oracle page 563.

Making the Most of Your Building Society

- Shop around. Rates on deposits change frequently. Keep an eye on the money pages of the national press.
- Don't expect the society which gives you the best deal on a deposit account to be the same one which gives you the best offer when it comes to a loan.
- Some societies sell travellers' cheques free of commission - saving you the 1 per cent charge.
- Several societies are linking up with travel companies to provide their savers with discounts - this may be worth considering.
- Many building societies are joining large national networks of cash dispensers - check whether your society is a member of such an organization and make sure you get a booklet giving you the relevant addresses.

Alternative Investments

Alternative investments include art, antiques, stamps, coins - and indeed anything which someone tries to sell you on the basis it will rise in price. The only way to make money on these is to be very knowledgeable. As a general rule don't think of them as investments. Buy what you like and pay the amount of money you consider it is worth to you: any future rise in price is a bonus and if the price falls you have at least enjoyed

Financial facts change daily, check the latest figures before making a decision.

it. Remember you will not be earning any income from such an investment, so unless it increases in value by a percentage greater than the rate of interest you will be losing money on it every year.

If you are offered a 'special' or 'limited' edition, check how many of the products have actually been made. Some of the objects and pictures offered in newspapers as 'investments' aren't even a decent gamble: you would be lucky to sell them for what you paid, let alone make money on them.

The Rising Cost of Living

In planning for the future it's useful - and frightening - to see how the value of money has changed in the past. If you had £100 in 1914 you would need the following sums to have the same buying power in the years which followed.

	£££		£££
1918	203·60	1960	446·85
1920	249·54	1962	477·48
1922	183·78	1964	502·70
1924	175·68	1966	546·85
1926	172·07	1968	587·39
1928	166·67	1970	658·56
1930	158·56	1972	772·07
1932	144·14	1974	977·48
1933	140·54	1976	1,415·32
1934	141·44	1978	1,775·67
1936	147·74	1979	2,013·51
1938	156·76	1980	2,375·68
no figures for 7 years		1981	2,657·66
1946	264·86	1982	2,886·49
1948	304·50	1983	3,018·92
1950	320·72	1984	3,169·37
1952	371·17	1985	3,362·16
1954	383·78	1986	3,476·58
1956	414·41	1987	3,620·00
1958	439·64		

I am indebted to the Central Statistical Office for these figures.

Several personal finance magazines concentrate on helping you plan your investments - although it is worth remembering the magazine is usually written some two to three months before it is published, so always check the rates, etc. are up to date.
Investors Chronicle, Greystoke Place, off Fetter Lane, London EC4A 1ND Tel: 01 405 6969
Money Magazine, Thames House, 18 Park Street, London SE1 9ER Tel: 01 378 7131
What Investment, Boundary House, 91-3 Charterhouse Street, London EC1M 6HR Tel: 01 250 0646
Money Observer, 120-6 Lavender Avenue, Mitcham, Surrey CR4 3HP Tel: 01 646 1031
Rosemary Burr, *Guide to Personal Equity Plans 1988*, Rosters
The Guardian Money Guide
Investors Chronicle Beginner's Guide to the Stockmarket, Penguin
Danny O'Shea, *Investing for Beginners*, Financial Times
Christine Stopp, *More Shares for Your Money*, sponsored by the Association of Investment Trust Companies, Rosters

Stocks, Shares and Relations

Investing in the stock market is a gamble. But it's like pontoon: skill counts and if you have it you can win handsomely. However, the unskilled are more likely to

lose, and even the cleverest can come unstuck. It is, however, infinitely more fascinating than any other form of gambling and if you have a few thousand *which you don't mind losing*, and enough time to follow the market, you can have a lot of fun.

The fascination lies in using your knowledge and your wits to decide which way a particular share will move. A company may have great profits today, and all the pundits may say its price is low for its potential. But does that necessarily make it a good buy? To decide, you need to know about its future prospects and about the competition. For example, is its 'go getting' managing director about to move elsewhere? Has a major competitor just brought out a product which could clean up? And so on.

You also have to be aware of national and international political events which may affect it, and the overall mood of the stock market. We all saw the crash of 1987 wipe pounds off the value of shares which had done nothing to deserve it. For example, ICI was £16½ (i.e. £16·50) at its peak and dropped to £9·37. Even when events are less dramatic, international affairs can still be a factor. A company may benefit from a drop in the price of oil, or suffer if there's a political coup in the country from which it gets its raw materials.

But, even if you don't have any money to invest, following the market can be a spectator sport as good as watching horse racing. If you find that investing in shares directly is not for you, but you want to put some of your money where there's a bit of excitement, you can opt for a PEP (page 523) or unit trusts or even investment trusts instead. You will still be investing in the market, but by proxy. But be wary of those who offer to teach you to invest in the stock market, and make it easy. It is always dangerous ground for the small investors and in the 1987 crash it was the small investors who made the wrong decisions most often.

A Toe in the Market

The only way to discover whether you have the time, energy and skill to play the stock market is to try it. But you can do this without risking a penny. Read the financial press and pick a handful of shares which you think are good buys. Write them down (then you can't cheat) plus their price and the number of shares you would buy if you were genuinely investing. Then follow those shares, noting their movement on paper, for at least six months, 'selling' them when you think it wise and reinvesting the money. But when you 'sell' a share still follow it to see whether you sold at the right time.

At the end of six months check your 'profit', or 'loss' - remember that each time you 'buy' or 'sell' you have to deduct the stockbroker's fees, plus VAT, plus stamp duty (see page 519).

If you did well you might be able to do well with some real investments, but don't forget almost anyone can make money in a rising market but only the very well informed can do so in a falling one. So before you decide that you are a financial genius or dunce compare the rise or fall of your shares with the overall performance of the market. For that is the only real measure of a

Financial facts change daily, check the latest figures before making a decision.

share's success. Then compare what you would have made had you put the same money into a building society, bank or National Savings. Don't forget to allow for the tax you would or would not pay according to how the money made its gains. It's the sum *after* tax which is the fair comparison.

Reading Share Prices
Share prices are very easy to read once you know the jargon. But though the jargon is the same everywhere, there is no god-given law as to how newspapers divide shares up. So don't worry if the *Financial Times* has a share in one place and the *Wall Street Journal* has it in another, nor if one is missing altogether. Companies pay to have their share prices put in the papers and hundreds of companies just don't bother. The Stock Exchange has a complete list which any broker or bank will have. Or the *Stock Exchange Official Year Book*, which should be in a good library, gives all listed companies.

The format for share price tables varies from paper to paper. Most try to divide companies into groups based on what they do, so if you know a company is a store or makes textiles, look under that heading. If you can't find it, try the miscellaneous column. This is a typical entry:

High	Low	Stock	Price	+ or –	Div Net	C'vr	Y'ld Gr's	P/E
70	27	Bigfoot Supershoes 5p	70	+4	1·5	2·7	3·1	14·6

The first two columns show you the highest and lowest prices at which that particular share has changed hands in the past year. Next you have the name followed by the nominal (or par) value of the share - 5p - which is no longer relevant, so forget it. Then comes the average price at which Bigfoot Supershoes shares changed hands the previous day - but buyers paid slightly more and sellers got slightly less. The + or - shows the amount the price rose or fell during that day's trading, compared with its price the previous day. It rose 4p, but when a share price stays the same this column is left blank.

After that come three bits of background information on the share. First the dividends: the 'Div Net' of 1·5 tells you the company paid out total dividends of 1·5p per share (after tax) in its last financial year. If the 1·5 had been preceded by a sign like a dagger pointing downwards it would have meant that the dividend rose that year. The C'vr tells you about the firm's ability to pay that dividend: the 2·7 tells you the profits were large enough to cover the dividend more than two and a half times. The 'Y'ld Gr's is the gross yield, which is the rate of interest you'd get on your investment if you bought at today's price. That was found by dividing the price by the dividend before tax was deducted. In this case it is 3·1 per cent.

Finally, P/E stands for Price to Earnings Ratio. The figure of 14·6 tells you that the present share price is more than 14 times as big as the net profits per share last year. A P/E can be high just because the whole stockmarket is booming, so you need to see whether it is high or low compared to other shares in its sector. If it's higher than average there has to be some reason why investors are interested in this share out of all proportion to its profits to date. And that is something which any would-be investor should look into.

How to Buy Shares
Nobody can go direct to a company or the Stock Exchange and buy shares, unless they are new issues. For all other shares you must use a stockbroker or a financial organization which will instruct a stockbroker for you. You can either pick your own stockbroker or approach one through a bank, solicitor or accountant. Going direct to a stockbroker may be the best course as only one person will be getting a commission and you can ask a stockbroker to advise you. The Stock Exchange, (London EC2N 1HP Tel: 01 588 2355) will supply a list of stockbrokers who are prepared to handle small investments, and it also has leaflets on the business of investing in shares, and runs an investors' club with a newsletter for small investors. There can be real dangers in buying shares across the counter of a bank, without anyone to warn you if they are a bad buy. And the cost may be more, or less, depending whether or not it has its own broking arm.

> You don't have to buy all forms of investment through a stockbroker: unit trusts can be bought direct, gilts can be bought through the post office, and even ordinary shares have new issues which allow you to buy without a broker.

The Cost of Buying and Selling Shares
Before you buy consider how much will have to be paid in fees, and then work out how much the share would need to rise before you made any money after these have been paid. Since the Financial Services Act 1986 brokers have ceased to charge a uniform rate. So it really pays to choose a broker carefully. Phone any firms you like the sound of, ask them if they handle your sort of business, and check their rates carefully. Then get them to send their prospectus and their latest newsletter giving investment advice.

When you buy shares brokers normally charge a percentage of the sum you are investing. They can charge what they like but 1·65 per cent wouldn't be unusual. And you will pay charges on selling as well as on buying. On small sums they often charge a flat rate, either way, so when buying £1,000 worth of shares the charges might look like this:

Fee to stockbroker, for example,	£15.00
VAT on broker's fee (only levied if he bought via another firm)	£2.25
Contract levy (flat rate on share deals of £1,000+)	£0.80
Stamp duty on £1,000 at ½ per cent	£5.00
Total	£23.05

Financial facts change daily, check the latest figures before making a decision.

How does the cost of the actual share affect the calculation? As you see, it's the *overall* sum you spend which decides the charges, but does the actual price of the share matter? In strictly mathematical terms the answer is no but, given the way the market operates, it is easier for a share to move up and down by 3 pence a day than by 33p. That's why penny shares have proved so popular.

£1,000 invested in 200 shares at £5.00 each
To cover share costs need a profit of £23.05
This is a rise per share of $\dfrac{£23.05}{200}$

= 12p per share (2·4 per cent)

£1,000 invested in 2,000 shares at 50p each
To cover share costs need a profit of £23.05
This is a rise per share of $\dfrac{£23.05}{2,000}$

= 1.2p per share (2·4 per cent). But you would need almost twice that rise simply to break even on the cost of both buying *and* selling because the same broker's charges apply.

What Happens if You Buy Shares

Buying shares involves remarkably little paperwork. When you buy shares you don't need to put your instructions in writing, you can simply telephone your broker. Millions of pounds worth of shares are bought and sold on verbal contracts each day - and what you say is binding, you cannot change your mind.

When a broker receives your telephoned instructions he sends you a contract note which tells you the account day. This is the day by which the money for the shares, plus any charges, *must* be with the broker's firm. The date is always 10 days after the end of the accounting period in which you bought the shares. Stockbroking uses fortnightly accounting periods, so if you bought at the start of one you would have 3½ weeks in which to pay, and if you bought at the end of one you would only have 9 days.

Some weeks later you will receive a share certificate from the company itself. This shows you are on the company's register. Keep the share certificate safely, it is the only proof that you own those shares. Even better, take a photocopy and get your bank or solicitor to hold it for you (unless they will charge for this).

When you sell, you will receive a contract note and also be asked to sign a form saying that you are selling. Your broker will send you this and you should fill it in and return it to him with your share certificate. Shortly after that, your name will be taken off the company's register of shareholders and the new buyer will be put on the list. You will receive no more information or dividends from the company once your name is taken off the register.

Dividends on Shares

Shareholders receive a dividend certificate - this pays you a certain amount per share and will be in two parts. Tear the certificate in two, keep the part headed 'tax voucher' as this proves the company has paid the basic rate tax for you. The other half should be paid into an account just as if it were a cheque.

In addition to dividends some shares offer perks. A hotel group may offer its shareholders discounts on rooms, a ferry company discounts on fares. It *isn't* usually worth buying a share for the perks but they're an amusing sideline.

Portfolios

If a lump sum has to be invested to create long-term income, you can hand the whole thing over to a broker to manage, provided it is large enough to be worth the stockbroker's time. Usually that means at least £25,000 and the bottom limit may often be a lot more. In those circumstances you give a stockbroker authority to buy and sell without asking you first, this is called a discretionary portfolio. As stockbrokers charge for moving money in and out of shares there can be a certain incentive for them to buy and sell more often than is strictly necessary. By no means all brokers do this, but it can happen. So some people prefer to have the portfolio managed on the basis that they will be consulted about transactions - even though this prevents a broker reacting rapidly to market conditions.

If a smaller sum needs to be invested to bring in an income, for example if you are a widow, approaching a bank with whom you have a long-standing relationship may be a good idea. Their investment departments are familiar with situations of that sort, and can advise across a wider range of types of investments. They may also take more trouble for a valued client than would a stockbroker you had only just met.

Whoever you use, you don't have to take the first investment plan which is offered. The experts usually give free advice hoping they will reap the percentage profit when you place your money with them. So make this system work for you by getting free advice from several sources. Only place your money when you have compared the lot and decided who is offering you the best service.

Terms Used in Stocks and Shares

Assets and Liabilities

A company's assets include everything it owns which is saleable. The fixed assets include not only obvious items like buildings, equipment and cars, but also valuable trade names, and even goodwill. Current assets is the term applied to the money it has in the bank, and any money due to it from goods or services already supplied, plus its stocks of raw materials. Liabilities are the exact opposite and cover outstanding debts.

Bears and Bulls

The difference between bulls and bears may be obvious to everyone else. But it was only when I fixed it in my head that bulls charge forward and toss prices upwards, whereas bears shamble away, that I was able to remember that, in stockmarket terms, bulls are buyers

Financial facts change daily, check the latest figures before making a decision.

(charging in to get the shares they want) and bears are sellers (backing away from shares they feel are not worth holding). Bulls are optimistic and bears are pessimistic. So when the market is said to be 'bullish' it means people feel prospects are good and share prices are rising overall. A bear market is the reverse.

Blue Chip

The term blue chip is said to come from the colour of the highest chip in poker (a useful reminder that even blue chip shares are a gamble). It is applied to shares in the companies valued at more than £500 million : ICI, Sainsbury, the major banks and so on. But is big also beautiful? Not necessarily so. Blue chip shares command hefty prices, but they are not always fast moving. So if you need to sell in the short term you may not cover the broker's fees, even if the price has risen. Nor is it easy to spot when a rise is coming. These are the shares into which the big institutions put their money. They are better informed and faster on the draw than the private investor. So when good news is in the wind they get in, and thereby push the price up, before you know what is happening. Nor are blue chips always safe. They are not likely to halve overnight but if you buy them at a high point in the market they could well drop considerably when the market falls.

Gilts and Gilt Edged Securities

When the government wants to raise money without increasing taxes it sells stocks on the stockmarket. The certificates registering the stock holders used to have gold edges so they came to be known as gilt edged securities, gilts for short. Each stock has a face value of £100, and a set interest rate. It also has a redemption date on which the government will pay £100 to the stock holder. Each stock gets its name from these facts. So if the Treasury offers stock at 3 per cent interest for redemption in 1999 it will be called '3 per cent Treasury Stock 1999'. Most stocks pay interest twice a year and you can check the exact date in the Monday issue of the *Financial Times*.

You are stuck with the interest rate, but £100 is unlikely to be what you pay for them, and you can get your money back before the redemption date. Interest is paid twice a year on the £100 face value of the stocks, but if you paid *less* than £100 the percentage value of the interest is higher than it seems.

New gilts are occasionally auctioned but are usually advertised for sale in the press on a tender basis (see 'New Issues' right) with a minimum price considerably below £100 a stock. The Bank of England sets a 'striking price' (i.e. the price people must pay) according to what offers it received. It is set so those who offered the striking price or more get the stock they applied for. Then, once listed, its price changes as it is bought and sold on the stockmarket like ordinary shares. But its popularity will depend on the interest it pays and how close it is to the redemption date. Unless the stock has changed hands in the 'ex-dividend' period, just before the dividend is due, the interest for the *whole* six months will go to whoever is holding the stock when it is paid.

There is also a period when stocks can be sold with or without that chunk of dividend - called 'cum' or 'ex' dividend.

You can buy gilts either through stockbrokers and banks or at the post office. The post office doesn't handle all the gilts issued, but the Bonds and Stock Office at Blackpool (page 517) will send you a list of those you can buy this way. Buying £1,000 worth of stock through the post office will cost about £4, through a broker it will cost over £15.

If you buy stocks from a stockbroker or direct from the Bank of England, which issues them, tax at the standard rate is deducted from the interest before it is paid to you. But if you buy through the National Savings Stock Register, interest is paid *without* deduction of tax - though you'll still have to pay it later if you are eligible. And, wherever you buy them gilts are free from capital gains tax provided you keep them for one year. Though if you make a loss on them you can't set that loss against other capital gains.

Gilts provide a secure investment, plus some growth and/or a regular income without risking your capital if you don't mind having your money tied up for quite a while. There are also index-linked gilts - new ones are issued, commission free, by the Bank of England. On these you get back the nominal value increased to keep pace with inflation.

Local Authority Loans

A local authority loan is rather like a gilt, but a local authority is raising money instead of the government. You lend money to the authority - it doesn't have to be your own - and they pay you fixed interest on it and return your lump sum at the end of the time. The loan periods can be as short as a week or much longer. You can find out which authorities are offering which terms by contacting **Sterling Brokers Ltd**, Colechurch House, 1 London Bridge Walk, London SE1 2SS Tel: 01 407 2767. In theory a local authority should be a safe investment, but today you never know.

New Issues

For the average investor the most important point about new issues is the opportunity they offer for stagging (page 522). Shares can come on the market in three ways: offers for sale, placings and introductions. But stagging only really applies to the first of these.

An offer for sale can be done in two ways. In a fixed offer the shares are offered at a fixed price, and you apply for however many shares you want at that price. Normally you get the shares you ask for. But if the applications exceed the number of shares for sale, then the issuing house usually limits the number of shares which any one person can buy. In an 'offer for tender' a minimum price is set and those who want to buy the shares have to bid for them by offering figures above

Financial facts change daily, check the latest figures before making a decision.

it. Then when the bids are in a 'striking price' is decided and bids equal to, or above, are accepted and those below it rejected. In either case there is a short time lag between the closing date for applications and the first day on which these shares are traded in the stockmarket. During this time successful applicants are sent letters of acceptance and unsuccessful ones have their cheques returned.

Offers for sale have to be well publicized. The prospectus, giving the company details, plus a form on which to apply for the shares, must - for a full listing - appear in two national newspapers (one is usually the *Financial Times*). Though the rules for a launch on the USM (see page 523) don't insist on this.

New Issues and Stagging
Stagging is buying a new issue and selling it within the first few days of it being traded on the stockmarket. The great advantage of stagging is that you pay no brokers' fees on the purchase and no stamp duty. So it is far easier to make a profit even if you invest a fairly small sum. And, of course, your money is only tied up for a very brief time. However, it is also possible to make a loss. Feeling can go against certain shares for no obvious reason. So the wise stag waits until very near the closing date before applying and only applies if all the signs are good. Shares are not usually allocated on a first come first served basis, so there is no need to fear that you will lose your chance.

Penny Shares
Penny shares sound appealing. The name seems to imply that all you need to make money on the stockmarket is a few pennies. This isn't the case. A penny share is a share priced on the stockmarket at under 20p (some purists say 10p). And they are bought and sold in just the same way as more expensive shares. But, despite the guides which urge you to believe that nothing is easier than making money on penny shares, there is a big difference between a share not costing a lot and it being good value. Essentially there are four kinds of penny shares: those of weak companies which don't deserve more recognition, potential shells, weak companies about to undergo a shake up (which therefore have potential), and stable concerns which just have an abnormally large share issue.

Since you pay the standard percentage commission on the buying and selling it still isn't practical to invest small sums. Before you buy penny shares you should work out how much the share will have to rise, in percentage terms, to cover the cost of investing. And, as penny shares can take a long time to rise, you should include in your calculation the interest your money could have earned had it been invested elsewhere.

Placing and Introductions
Placings and introductions are much quieter affairs than new issues. A share price is agreed, and buyers then found within the confines of the financial world. But placings can be very good buys, so it is worth discussing them with your stockbroker.

Rights Issues
When a company, which is already traded on the stockmarket, wants to raise more money it can do so by offering new shares for sale in a rights issue. To make them attractive these are usually offered at less than the current price of the company's other shares. The practice gets its name from the fact that existing shareholders have first rights to buy these bargains which they can then keep or sell at a profit.

Securities
This covers stocks and shares of all kinds.

Shells
A shell is a company which hard times have reduced to little more than a shell, despite its listing on the stockmarket. Having a stockmarket listing, it may attract a thriving company which lacks this. For, like a hermit crab finding a home, the thriving company can back its operation into the readymade listing of the shell and so gain access to the advantages of the stockmarket for raising capital. So someone with shares in that shell will suddenly find they have a stake in a very going concern. Shells are the secret behind many of the big rises in the value of penny shares.

Stocks
The word stock has two meanings, according to whether it is in the singular or the plural. In the plural it is used for securities which pay a fixed rate of interest, such as Government stocks or gilts. But stock in the singular is used to refer to a deal in shares with flexible rates of interest. So you could say, 'I sold my ICI stock today', meaning you had sold your shares in ICI. The Stock Exchange, of course, deals in both stocks and shares.

Various Alternatives to Shares
Buying shares through a stockbroker is by no means the only way to invest in the stockmarket. If you don't want to go to the time and trouble of choosing your own shares there are several products you can consider where the experts make the decisions. But even the experts can get it wrong. And choosing an investment company with a good track record is no guarantee it will keep on performing well.

Unit Trusts
Unit trusts get their name for two reasons: first, there is a trustee who is independent and who makes sure the fund managers do their job correctly and don't run off with your cash and, secondly, because you buy units in the trust itself, rather than shares. The trust buys shares jointly on behalf of all who buy units. So investing in a unit trust gives you a spread of investment. This provides some protection but not much: unit trusts fall in value when the stockmarket falls, and if the investment manager is poor, he can lose you money even in a rising market.

The trusts fall into two broad categories: those for income and those for growth. They also vary in the type of shares they specialize in. Some invest in British shares

Financial facts change daily, check the latest figures before making a decision.

in general, others specialize in a particular section or country, for example, small companies or Japan.

You can buy unit trusts yourself, direct from the firm, and it makes more sense than paying a bank or broker. The trusts are listed in the *Financial Times* with their phone numbers. Just ring and ask whether you can buy, and what the price would be and how you go about it. It will be very simple. Each company sets its own minimum investment. As you pay a set service charge per unit there is no advantage in sticking to large parcels of units. So if you have £1,000 to invest it would be best to spread it between several different unit trusts. Some also have savings plans where you pay in a small sum each month.

If you check the price of your units in the newspaper you will see two prices quoted: the offer price at which you can buy units and the bid price at which you can sell them. The offer price includes the initial charge which could be around 5 per cent. There is also an annual charge which is deducted from the trust's income *before it is paid out to unit holders.* This varies from trust to trust and may be anything from ¾ per cent to 1¾ per cent.

The interest you get on the units is paid after tax has been taken off at the basic rate. You *can't* claim this back if you don't pay tax, and if you make a profit on selling the shares you will pay capital gains tax.

Unit trusts are a good way of dabbling in the stockmarket with small sums and, as many specialize in foreign shares, they are an easy way of investing in overseas stock markets, but they aren't good for a quick return as the charges are quite high. There are also huge differences between the performances of different unit trust companies, so you need to pick your companies carefully.

Unit Trust Association, Park House, 16 Finsbury Circus, London EC2M 7JP Tel: 01 638 3071 has a leaflet on unit trusts. Send a sae.
Unit Trust Management,Money Management and *Planned Savings* are magazines covering unit trust performances.

Investment Trusts
Investment trusts do exactly the same job as unit trusts except that they are set up as a company, not a trust. The larger investment trusts are quoted on the Stock Exchange and you can buy shares in them in the same way as ICI and Marks & Spencer, (e.g. through a stockbroker or bank) and the charges for buying investment trusts are exactly the same as for buying shares (see page 519). The trust makes no annual charge but a small management fee of around ½ per cent is usually deducted.

Dividends from investment trusts are paid after basic tax has been taken off, but you can reclaim it if you should not have paid it. You also pay capital gains tax on any money you make by selling them.

Investment trust is a very reassuring name, and suggests that money put into it would be very safe. Don't be fooled. These aren't trusts and your money isn't safe. In fact they are only for those who can afford

to take a risk in the hope of a good return in the long term. The return can be very good, but the trust may rise and fall dramatically and if you sell through need, not choice, it is easy to lose.

Association of Investment Trust Companies, (Park House, 6th Floor, 16 Finsbury Circus, London EC2M 7JJ Tel: 01 588 5347) will supply a list of stockbrokers who will deal in small quantities of investment trusts.
The *Daily Telegraph* and the *Financial Times* give the figures for investment trusts on the fourth Saturday in each month.

Personal Equity Plans (PEP)
Personal Equity Plans are a government ploy to get small investors to buy shares. The carrot is that you can invest up to £3,000 each year and *provided the money stays in for a full year* any capital gains you make are tax free and so are all the dividends. This tax incentive isn't worth much on a single year, but if you treat PEPs as a long-term investment you could end up with a large sum tax free.

To reap these advantages the money *must* go into a managed plan approved by the Inland Revenue - you cannot simply put it into shares in the usual way. In most plans the plan managers make the investment decisions, as in a unit trust, however a few schemes do give you a degree of choice over the shares. PEPs have only been going since 1986 but there are over 100 plans to choose from. They are run by banks, unit trust companies, building societies and stockbrokers and the charges vary from plan to plan. Some include an initial charge, an annual charge and a dealing charge whenever they invest your money. Check the small print with *great care,* and remember, any investment in shares can lose money. It is essential to regard share package deals as long-term investments.

When you buy any type of packaged investment it is more expensive than investing by yourself. That's because you are paying both for the administration, marketing and distribution of the product and the investment skills of the fund manager. However, PEPs do offer small investors a good spread of shareholdings with the attraction of tax-free profits - provided a profit is made.

Money Management magazine has details of how funds compare in performance.

Unlisted Securities Market (USM)
The USM is where up and coming companies can first raise money by selling shares. To be quoted on the USM they only need to have traded for 3 years. This lack of track record makes USM companies a gamble. If you pick one that is on its way up you will buy its shares cheaply and perhaps be in a position to make a killing when it is launched on the main stockmarket. But some companies have an hour of glory and fade with the dawn. Don't invest unless you can afford to lose the money. The shares are bought through stockbrokers just like any others, and the tax rules are the same.

Reviews of USM shares are published in the *Financial Times* on Saturdays and in *The Times* on Mondays.

Financial facts change daily, check the latest figures before making a decision.

Securities and Investment Board, 3/4 Royal Exchange Buildings, London EC3V 3NL Tel: 01 283 2474 - has an entertaining booklet called 'Self Defence for Investors' which is useful reading.
Buying, Selling and Owning Shares Action Kit, Consumers' Association

RENDERING UNTO CAESAR

Everyone is liable to tax from the cradle to the grave - and slightly beyond it. As the Chancellor of the Exchequer decides not only the rates of tax but what they will be levied on - and changes at least some of these in the budget each year it isn't possible to give any tax guidance figures here. AND READERS SHOULD BEAR IN MIND THAT ALL THE FACTS IN THIS SECTION COULD CHANGE AT ANY TIME.

One thing which is unlikely to change, however, is that everyone has a duty to tell the taxman about any income or profit. Don't wait for the tax office to contact you. You can't claim ignorance of the law. It is no excuse for non-payment and interest is now charged on payments which are not made when they should be.

You need to declare *all* sources of income, not just those which you believe to be taxable. If you have any extra income at all on top of a wage or salary you must ask the local tax office (under Inland Revenue in the phone book) for a tax return form to fill in. The tax year runs from 6 April one year to 5 April the next. So get a form when 5 April is past.

The Inland Revenue will help with straightforward factual questions - but they can't give advice on tax planning. If you are self-employed or a higher rate taxpayer it will probably be worthwhile to consult an accountant. Anyone can set up as an accountant, even if totally unqualified, so do check you are dealing with someone from a reputable professional body. The Institute of Chartered Accountants in England and Wales or the Institute of Chartered Accountants of Scotland (see page 527) will send you a list of local accountants, but often the best course if possible is to choose someone recommended by a friend or business acquaintance.

However, in the budget of March 1988 the system was greatly simplified to give only two rates of taxation - a basic rate of 25 per cent, and a higher rate of 40 per cent on income over a set limit (£19,300 in that budget).

Capital Gains Tax (CGT)

Capital Gains Tax is a tax on the profits made on the sale of most assets, such as shares, unit trusts, antiques, stamps or a second home. But you can set losses against gains. And among the gains you can make *without* paying CGT are profits made on the following:

- your main home - provided it has not been used as a workplace (the rules on this are complicated - check with your accountant)
- private cars
- pools or betting winnings
- an asset with a limited life (e.g. a horse)

- gilts sold after July 1986
- cash from an insurance policy
- goods sold below a certain price each (£3,000 in April 1988)
- winnings from gambling
- cash from a personal equity plan
- cash from shares in a Business Expansion scheme which have been held for 5 years

Gains exceeding the exempt total (£5,000 in April 1988) are added *on top* of earned income, and taxed at the same rates.

Income Tax

There are two income tax systems for earned income running side by side. Both levy the same tax on the same amounts but the payments are made at different times.

Pay As You Earn (PAYE) is the system by which an employer takes tax out of a wage or salary before it is paid to an employee. So the employer acts as tax collector for the Inland Revenue.

Schedule D is the system used for the self employed. As there's often no telling how much someone self employed will earn in a year, the year's earnings are simply totted up at the end of each year and the sums sent to the Inland Revenue which then sends in a tax bill. There are slightly complicated rules on how late someone may be in completing their accounts and interest is now charged to those who don't get a move on. There are also rules which allow tax to be spread over several years - which is especially useful when starting a new business. So the self-employed need a good accountant to guide them.

Unearned Income is taxed at the same rate as earned income.

Taxable	Tax Free
perks and benefits if you earn over £8,500	pensions to those with gallantry awards
rent paid to you	compensation for loss of a job up to £25,000
interest on accounts	
pensions	interest on National Savings certificates
profits from any business	interest on SAYE schemes
tips and Christmas boxes	the first £70 earned in a National Savings account
interest on shares	
maintenance payments under a court order	the lump sum paid out by a pension scheme up to a set limit

You have to declare all income from these sources, but in many cases tax will have been taken out before the money was paid to you. But not all income is taxable.

Taxable unearned income is set on top of earned income and taxed accordingly. And until April 1990 a married woman's unearned income is added to her

Financial facts change daily, check the latest figures before making a decision.

husband's income, for tax, even if she has chosen separate taxation. When it comes to social security payments, the DHSS gives out with its right hand while the Inland Revenue sometimes takes it back with the left. The position here should be double checked as it changes occasionally.

Taxing Benefits

Taxable	Tax Free
Maternity Allowance	Child Benefit
Retirement Pension	Attendance Allowance
Widow's Pension	Mobility Allowance
Unemployment Benefit	Family Credit
Income Support to strikers	Sickness Benefit
and unemployed	Income Support if not on
Statutory Sick Pay	strike or unemployed
Industrial Benefit	Christmas bonus to state
Invalid Care Allowance	pensioner
	War Pensions
	Invalidity Benefit

Allowances Against Tax

Before anyone pays tax a certain amount of income is allowed to be tax free. The size of this tax free allowance varies with their situation. There is a set sum for a single person; a married person's allowance; an additional personal allowance for single parents, and allowances for each child in the family, plus an age allowance for those over 65 (a married couple can claim it the moment *either* is 65) which increases at 80. There are also other allowances for special situations such as having a dependent relative, for employing someone to look after you, for blindness and so on. All these allowances are usually changed at each budget. Your tax office will give you the latest rates.

Claiming Tax Rebates

If, for any reason, you have paid more tax than you should have done you simply write to the tax office and ask for a copy of the Notice of Assessment. This shows how your tax was calculated. If you find it doesn't agree with your figures you simply write asking for a refund and explaining why. You can claim up to 6 years after the error. You may also find that earnings or interest may have been paid to you after deduction of tax when you are not earning enough to be taxable. The Inland Revenue has numerous forms on which you apply for refunds in these circumstances but you can just as well apply with a letter. The only exception to this is a rebate on a covenant, which needs an R185 and R40.

★ Anyone doing temporary work should get a completed Form P45 from each employer they leave. This shows how much tax they have paid and enables them to get a rebate.

Marriage and Taxation

From 6th April 1990 a husband and wife will be assessed and taxed totally separately. Until then the Inland Revenue regards married couples as a single tax unit, who is responsible for filling in the tax form and paying the

tax. Married women can get *some* independence by opting for separate assessment. This does not affect your total tax bill but it means women can keep their financial affairs under their own control. To apply:
1 get a copy of form 11S from your tax office.
2 one of you must then complete and sign the form.
3 return the form between 6 January and 6 July for the tax year starting that April, i.e. if you want to be separately assessed in tax year 1989-90 then you must return it by 6 July 1989.

Normally when the taxman works out how much a couple should pay in income tax he adds their earnings together and deducts their allowances. Tax is then due on this sum. Suppose, for example, a couple have no unearned income and the husband earns £50,000 and the wife £15,000, and income tax starts at 25% and then rises to 40% on sums above £19,300 after allowances. The couple have no children so they are only entitled to a tax free allowance of £6,700.

Total income £65,000
Minus allowances of £6,700
Taxable income £58,300
Tax on first £19,300 at 25% = £4,825
Tax on next £39,000 at 40% - £15,600
Total tax bill - £20,425

Although the Inland Revenue regards a married couple as a unit the couple can ask for separate taxation. This *does* alter the tax bill, but only unearned income is taxed separately (page 524). One tax return, signed by the husband is used. For this:
1 get a copy of form 14 from your tax office
2 complete it and *both* sign it
3 return the form no later than 5 April following the tax year for which you want to be taxed separately - so for tax year 1989-90 this would be no later than 5 April 1991.

Each person can claim their own single person's allowance against their income, so separate taxation means less of their total income is taxed at the higher levels, and they save a considerable sum in tax.

Husband	Wife
Income £50,000	Income £15,000
Allowance £2,605	Allowance £2,605
Taxable income £47,395	Taxable income £12,395
Tax on first £19,300 at 25% -	Tax at 25% - £3,099
£4,825	
Tax on next £28,095 at 40% -	
£11,238	
Total tax - £16,063	

Couple's tax bill = £19,162
Saving of £20,425 - £19,162 = £1,263

★ Incidentally, a man no longer gets a whole year's married allowance regardless of when he marries. He now gets fractions according to how much of the financial year he was married for.
★ If parents give money to a child who is unmarried and under 18 and the child invests it, any income from the investment is counted as the parents' income.

Financial facts change daily, check the latest figures before making a decision.

Tax on Pensions

The income from a pension of any kind is taxed as earned income. But there are generous rules regarding the lump sum which can be paid out. In 1987-8 the tax-free lump sum could be up to a quarter of the total value of all someone's pension scheme put together.

Tax and First Jobs

If you are taking a job for the first time you can avoid paying tax you are not due to pay by immediately filling in a P15 form at the tax office. This will ensure you start paying tax at a lower rate until you have worked for long enough to need to pay full tax.

Tax and Divorce

The budget of 15 March 1988 made considerable changes to the taxation of maintenance for ex-partners and children, after which affect both the payers and receivers. However, the rules vary according to whether the payments were set before or after the budget. So check carefully with your tax office and accountant. On legal separation or divorce the wife goes back to single status for tax purposes.

- Some, legally binding, maintenance payments gain tax relief for the payer.
- If income is paid to a child it is either entitled to have the single person's tax relief set against it or may be totally untaxed.
- 'Small' maintenance payments are paid in full (small was under £48 per week in 1987-8). Until April 1989 larger ones have tax taken off before they are paid and the wife has to claim a rebate if she is entitled to one. After that *all* payments to ex-spouses and children will be gross (with no tax taken off).

Understanding Payslips

Whether you are paid weekly or monthly, by cash, cheque or direct into your bank account, if you are employed you will get a payslip. This will show you how much you earned and, equally important, what has been deducted by way of National Insurance and perhaps an occupational pension scheme.

Starting from the top left-hand corner in the example you will find the National Insurance number and name. Moving along, you come to the tax code - that's the shorthand instruction to the employer telling him how much income tax should be deducted from the pay.

Every employer acts as the unpaid tax collector for the government. *It is very important to make sure your tax code is correct as otherwise the wrong amount of tax may be deducted.*

Anyone with a knowledge of the tax code, for example, would be able to tell that Mr Smith is not married. That's because 'L' stands for someone receiving the single person's allowance or a wife's earned income allowance - and we did say 'Mr'. If you want to know all the codes they are in leaflet IR34, from your tax office but some of the other code letters are: H for married man's allowance, P for a pensioner who is single, V for being retired and married, F taxed at a higher rate.

On the slip there are details of the payment. In this case it's by cheque, which is common · for small businesses but large organizations often make payments directly to your bank or building society account.

There's also the date and the tax period. The tax year runs from 6 April to 5 April in the following year. So December is month nine of the tax year.

The first section is the taxable pay - sometimes called gross pay. This is the total earnings including bonuses before any deductions have been made.

Then come those nasty subtractions: income tax and National Insurance. You can check that you are paying the right amount of National Insurance - this will be affected both by the amount you earn and by any pension scheme your company runs. If it runs a scheme which replaces the government's earnings related scheme then there is a slight reduction in National Insurance contributions. Near the bottom there are the employer's contributions to Mr Smith's National Insurance. Finally, the crucial bottom line - the take-home pay, or net earnings.

Ways to Save Tax

Some of the legitimate ways to cut your tax bill include the following, but it's wise to take professional advice on which ones best suit your situation: some have disadvantages too.

- Buy your home with a mortgage - you can gain tax relief on the interest paid.
- Contribute to a pension plan which gets maximum tax relief on contributions.
- If you are a high-rate taxpayer invest in National Savings - which are tax free.
- Take the maximum permitted lump sum from any pension plan when it pays out.
- Make gifts to reduce your tax bill on death.
- Couples who both earn well should opt for separate taxation.
- Claim all the allowances you may be entitled to.
- If your work takes you abroad make sure you check the rules for reducing tax and abide by them.
- Make sure there is no mention of pay in lieu of notice in the terms of your employment. Payments written in are taxable, unwritten ones are tax free up to a certain level.
- Invest in a young company, under the Business Expansion Scheme (page 524).
- Give to charity through a 'Give as You Earn Scheme'.

MR SMITH				ABC LTD			
NI No: EF 123456C	Tax Code: 242L	Pay By CHEQUE		Date: 31.12.87		Tax Period: M9	
DESCRIPTION		UNITS DUE	RATE		AMOUNT	THIS YEAR	
1. BASIC PAY			1042.00		1042.00	9087.00	
3. PENSION CONTRIBUTION			− 25.00		− 25.00	−225.00	
5 BONUS			250.00		25.00	250.00	
			TOTAL TAXABLE PAY >>>		1267.00	9112.00	
INCOME TAX − PAYE					−287.55	−1968.30	
EMPLOYEE'S NI RATE A					−114.03	−821.61	
(EMPLOYER'S NI RATE A	132.40	TO DATE 953.98)					
			TOTAL NET PAY >>>		865.42	6322.09	

Inheritance Tax

Inheritance Tax is, in essence, the tax on whatever someone leaves when they die. It takes the place of Death Duties, Estate Duties and Capital Transfer Tax - all of which have been abolished - and covers the value of everything you own when you die.

You don't have to be very rich to pay it. As I write it is paid if the total sum left is over £110,000 and the rate for Inheritance Tax is 40 per cent.

The only way to avoid this tax is to give away part of what you own while you are alive. There is now no limit to how much you may give away each year. But for the gift to avoid inheritance tax you must live for 7 years after giving it. Though if you don't live that long the gift will only be taxed at its value when it was given, not when you die.

A vital point is that to count as a gift you may not continue to benefit from it. So you can't 'give' your home to your children and go on living there.

Within those rules there are special exceptions. If you die in under 7 years of making any of the following gifts they will still not be taxable.

- You can give away up to £3,000 a year (1988-9).
- A husband and wife can give each other unlimited amounts and the 7-year rule will not apply.
- Gifts of up to £250 are not counted.
- Wedding gifts up to £5,000 are not counted.
- Certain charitable and political donations are not counted.
- Gifts to the nation.

Rates and Local Taxes

Rates are a tax levied by local authorities to provide part of the money for local services, such as sewers and education. The authority raises money by deciding a 'rateable value' for each property based on its size, facilities and position. Each year it then levies a certain rate in the pound. So if the rate in the pound was 50p, a house with a rateable value of £400 would pay £400 x 50p which is £200 a year.

Once it is fixed the rateable value of a house stays unchanged for ever, unless it has additions or alterations, or unless you appeal for a reduction because some circumstance has changed. So the council adjusts its income by altering the rate in the pound. There are huge differences between the rate in the pound charged by different councils and the rates are one thing to ask about when buying a house.

Rates bills come in April. There are usually schemes whereby payment can be made in stages through the year instead of having to pay a large lump sum. But you will usually be paying a few pounds more for this privilege.

★ Rates are not paid on a house which is empty for 3 months, but a council may choose to charge rates on an empty property after that.

Poll Tax

The poll tax is a totally new system of local taxes for which Scotland will be the guinea pig in 1989. It is due to be visited upon England and Wales later but, as I write, it is still largely under wraps. All we do know is that it will be a system based on 'one man one tax', instead of the present method where 20 people could be in a house and pay the same rates as someone living alone.

Water Rates

Water Rates use the rateable value in the same way, but the rate in the pound is much smaller. An extra charge is made if you have an outside tap.

VAT

VAT is tax which uses every business and service as tax collectors - including the self employed. Anyone can register for VAT if they can show that they are trading. And if someone has earned or had a taxable turnover (*not* profits) of £7,500 in the previous quarter or £22,100 in the previous year, they *must* register for VAT. They must also do so if the coming year's figures will reach that sum.

The principle is simple. Someone who is registered for VAT adds VAT to every bill they charge to anyone else (unless the item is zero rated). The VAT so gathered then has to be paid to Her Majesty's Customs and Excise each quarter. But before it is paid, the individual who has collected it may deduct the value of all the VAT he or she has paid on goods and services needed for his or her business. The book keeping is a chore but it isn't hard and anyone who is within the band where there is a choice of registering or not would probably find the savings in VAT make registration worthwhile.

More information

Your local tax office should have the Inland Revenue leaflets on taxation, which are written for the public and reasonably easy to understand. They include leaflets for those with special problems, such as widows.

Institute of Chartered Accountants of England and Wales, Chartered Accountants Hall, PO Box 433, Moorgate Place, London EC2P 2BJ Tel: 01 628 7060

Institute of Chartered Accountants of Scotland, 27 Queen Street, Edinburgh EH2 1LA Tel: 031 225 5676

Financial facts change daily, check the latest figures before making a decision.

In Sickness

A-Z of Ailments • Alternative Medicine • Basic Medical Facts •
Dental Health • First Aid • Genital and Sexual Infections •
Handicaps and Disabilities • Social and Antisocial Drugs

In Sickness covers medical problems of every type. The first section is an A to Z of common illnesses and ailments. Then there are sections on medical terminology, on basic procedures like temperature and pulse taking, on the problems of drugs and sexually transmitted diseases, on handicaps, on infectious diseases and immunization, and on first aid. Both the information within each section and the sections themselves are arranged alphabetically - except on rare occasions when logic dictates otherwise.

The information is intended to help you to recognize when medical attention is needed, to provide basic home remedies for minor problems and to answer some of the questions which one can easily forget to ask a doctor. It also suggests other sources of information, help and support which may be valuable to the sufferer or to his or her family.

Some conditions seem to respond better to alternative treatments than to conventional ones, and many GPs now recommend alternative therapies for certain conditions. So the major branches of alternative medicine are explained.

Moreover, modern medicine is increasingly finding that health, like charity, begins at home and is placing new emphasis on prevention and on the need for patients to take an active part in their own recovery. So, both here and in the following section on health I have tried to provide the facts which could help people to prevent illness and to have more control over it when it does strike.

> The information given here should never be used as a substitute for seeing a doctor. Before using any remedy in this book *always* discuss it with your doctor. Only a doctor can say what is safe for a particular person.

A TO Z OF AILMENTS

Aches
What all aches have in common is that basic home remedies often ease the pain. Hot baths and hot water bottles help, whether the ache is from a period pain, overworked muscles or some medical conditions (though inflamed areas need cooling - see Sprains). Research also shows that firm rubbing can block the sensation of pain, because the nerves concerned can only carry one message at a time - so if the rubbing keeps them busy the pain can't get through. Some hospitals now use electric massagers in pain control, but the power of the human hand should never be underestimated.

Acne and Other Spots
To squeeze or not to squeeze, that is the question. Ask any two doctors and they'll give two different answers - and they'll both be right. If you squeeze any spot with dirty hands you spread the infection. And if you squeeze a spot which isn't ready to burst, you will push the pus deeper into the skin, increasing the problem. So *no* squeezing in either of those situations.

But blackheads should always be removed while still small, and you can safely remove small spots, with heads ready to burst, provided you gently press them out straight after a bath, when heat has opened the pores, using *perfectly clean hands and nails* and a soft tissue. Swab with witch-hazel (from a chemist) afterwards in order to tighten and disinfect the stretched pores.

In acne there seem to be three combined causes. The male hormone, androgen (which both sexes make), stimulates the skin to produce more oils, the duct to the skin surface becomes blocked, forming blackheads and whiteheads, and - for reasons nobody understands - bacteria build up underneath and form very nasty spots which can cause permanent scars. See a doctor; modern treatment can be very effective.

If necessary, ask to see a skin specialist, and basic care can make a difference.
- Wash the skin *very* well each day using a rough washing sponge or washing grains which rub off the dead surface layers of skin so the oils can seep out. Pat dry, preferably using kitchen roll - wiping and towels spread the bacteria.
- Eat a healthy diet - don't heap on the fats and sweets.
- Give up smoking.
- Use an anti-spot cream the moment a spot begins to appear.
- Keep the hair clean, so hair oil doesn't produce a spotty forehead.

Allergy

Good horsemen have known for centuries that oats put a zip in sluggish horses, but make others develop skin problems and get silly. Yet the extent to which diet can affect human health is only beginning to be realized. The body can react badly to any substance it meets - in the air, in food, in drink or even in clothing. Almost any persistent health problem might be due to an allergy. Common culprits include wheat, beef, milk products, caffeine, detergents, pets, feathers and certain garden plants and food additives.

Essentially, an allergy is the body's immune system over-reacting, and tests and avoidance can show which substances make it do this. If you think you have an allergy, and your GP isn't helpful, ask one of the organizations below where you can get expert help. Poor tests, badly interpreted, could just confuse the issue, and the government has warned about risks from desensitizing injections. In this field there are some unethical practitioners and inadequate testing laboratories.

Those allergic to medical treatments, such as penicillin, should carry a warning card or medic-alert bracelet (see page 569) saying so.

Action Against Allergy, 43 The Downs, London SW20 8HS Tel: 01 947 5082 - lists sources of products combating or avoiding potential allergens. RC, M£L, S, CS, O, F&F, L, B, F, EI, G, A, HD, large sae.

The Coeliac Society, P.O.Box 220, High Wycombe, Bucks HP11 2HY - has inf on allergy to gluten, B, L, V, F.

Hyperactive Children's Support Group, Maryfield House, Yapton Road, Barnham, West Sussex PO22 0BJ - M£L, CS, F&F, L, B, G, HD, diet sheets, sae.

National Society for Research into Allergy, PO Box 45, Hinckley, Leicester LE10 1JY - will direct to ethical practitioners in this field and away from dubious ones, sae. RC, M£L, S, CS, O, F&F, M, L, B, G, HD.

Dr H. Morrow Brown, *The Allergy and Asthma Reference Book*, Harper & Row

Amelia Nathan Hill, *Against the Unsuspected Enemy*, from Action Against Allergy

Mary Steel, *Understanding Allergies*, Consumers' Association

Alzheimer's Disease (Pre-senile Dementia)

This is a progressive disease, which can strike any adult, but affects 1 in 4 of the very old. It causes memory loss, and there may also be restlessness, loss of balance, irritability, over-reaction to stress and difficulty with basics like eating and dressing.

Nobody knows what causes it, but it can't be caught and there are physical changes in the brain, including marked loss of brain cells and unusual deposits of aluminium. There is no cure, but treatment may help and a sufferer should be registered as disabled, for entitlement to special benefits. Even so, sufferers are a great burden to their families and the future needs to be planned for: get advice at an early stage.

There is a growing body of evidence linking Alzheimer's Disease to aluminium. It is too soon to say what role it plays, at present it looks as if the cause could be exposure to high levels of aluminium *plus* an inability to stop the metal entering the brain - which may be inherited.

Cooking acid foods in aluminium pans, particularly with water containing fluoride, can dissolve the metal into the food, giving levels of aluminium up to 3,000 times those allowed in drinking water. Although there is no proof that this could cause Alzheimer's Disease it may be safest to avoid cooking in aluminium until there is proof that it *doesn't*.

Alzheimer's Disease Society, 158-160 Balham High Road, London SW12 9BN Tel: 01 675 6557 - RC, M£L optional, F&F, M, L, B, G, T, sitting service, Ad, sae.

Anaemia

If you have anaemia your red blood cells are inefficient, or in short supply. So too little oxygen reaches the body tissues and you easily become tired and breathless, and may have a very rapid heartbeat. But you can be anaemic and still have rosy-red cheeks. The paleness only shows in hidden places, like inside the eyelids.

Any slow insidious bleeding, for example from heavy periods, stomach ulcers or haemorrhoids, can cause anaemia. So can the extra demands of pregnancy and childbirth. But the most common cause is a poor diet. Lack of vitamin C makes it hard to absorb iron in the diet which is essential for making red blood cells. Lack of vitamin B12 and folic acid - found in liver and green vegetables - can also cause anaemia. But as there are other causes, those who think they are anaemic should see a doctor.

Anorexia and Bulimia

In anorexia it seems as if initial avoidance of food disrupts the body's mechanisms, setting up a vicious circle which causes loss of appetite and distorted thinking. Anorexics believe themselves to be fat, even when skeletal, and will lie outrageously about their food intake.

Starvation leads to loss of monthly periods, depression, severe constipation, dizziness and swelling of the face, stomach and ankles. Treatments vary. The main approaches are enforced eating and/or counselling or therapy. But recently people have also been successfully treated by adding zinc to the diet. This seems to restore the appetite and allow eating to begin again. This work is still experimental but there are good biochemical reasons for expecting zinc to help.

The professor of organic chemistry who has pioneered this treatment says the dose should be based on a zinc taste test which shows the severity of the zinc deficiency. He also claims that, though 15 mg of zinc per day can safely be taken anyway, very much larger doses may be needed in many cases. This treatment should be discussed with a GP.

again. This work is still experimental but there are good biochemical reasons for expecting zinc to help.

Bulimics may be a normal weight and seem happy but are caught in a compulsive cycle of bingeing and then purging or vomiting. This gradually disrupts the body's balance of mineral salts - which are vital for it to function normally - and there may be exhaustion, apathy and even coma and death. Bulimics often feel deeply ashamed and, whatever their outward appearance, may be exceedingly unhappy and depressed. Out-patient treatment, and joining a voluntary support group can help considerably. Meanwhile, bulimics should clean their teeth well after vomiting, as stomach acid rots the teeth. Zinc, as in anorexia, has been used successfully.

Anorexia Aid, The Priory Centre, 11 Priory Road, High Wycombe, Bucks HP13 6SL Tel: 0494 21431 - RC, M£L optional, S, F&F (bulimia too), M, G, L, B, Ad, sae.

Anorexic Family Aid, 44 Magdelene Street, Norwich, Norfolk NR3 1JE Tel: 0603 621414 National information centre (covering bulimia too). RC, M£L, S, CS, O, F&F, doctors, nurses, M, L, B, Rg, sae.

Bulimics Anonymous, 5 Chillingford House, Blackshaw Road, London SW1Y 0BQ Tel: 01 767 7029 is a small, but growing, organization in which bulimics meet anonymously for support and cure, as in Alcoholics Anonymous.

Society for Advancement and Research into Anorexia, Stanthorpe, New Pound, Wisborough Green, Billingshurst, West Sussex RH14 0EJ Tel: 0403 700210

Professor D. Bryce Smith and Liz Hodgkinson, *The Zinc Solution,* Century Arrow

Maureen Dunbar, *Catherine,* Penguin - a mother's story of her child's anorexia.

Appendicitis

The symptoms of appendicitis vary and are less precise in very young children than in older ones. They don't always have a stomach pain, but may have a high temperature, vomit and be irritable and off their food. Older children and adults are likely to vomit, have a stomach pain which starts around the tummy button, tenderness in this area if gently pressed, pain on coughing and a temperature of 37°-38°C (98·4°-100·4°F). In all ages there may also be a chest infection. ALWAYS CONTACT A DOCTOR IF YOU SUSPECT APPENDICITIS. Young children who get it need *swift* medical attention - an appendix can burst in eight hours, and that is dangerous.

Arthritis and Rheumatism

These terms have distinctly different meanings. Rheumatism is the pain caused by some 150 different rheumatic disorders in muscles, bones or joints, and affecting some 20 million people in Britain each year. Arthritis involves damage or disease in the joints. The most common forms are rheumatoid arthritis and osteoarthritis.

Rheumatoid arthritis is damage to the joint lining, which makes the smaller joints stiff and swollen. It mainly afflicts women and tends to start in their 30s and 40s. Osteoarthritis is the breakdown of the surface of the joints; it usually starts at about the age of 50, and particularly affects overworked joints - especially in the overweight.

The causes of these conditions are mysterious. Some, such as ankylosing spondylitis, rheumatoid arthritis, gout and osteoarthritis, seem to run in families. Fortunately, some forms clear up in a few years, others can be controlled with drugs, and reconstructive surgery can give mobility which once would have been impossible. Modern treatment tries to keep the sufferer mobile, and the joints should go gently through their full range of movement at least twice a day. This may be easiest when water is supporting the limb.

Some people undoubtedly find alternative medicine, such as acupuncture, chiropractic treatment or changes in diet, helps considerably. Others get relief from Balsona Ointment or Bengues Balsam, both of which contain oil of wintergreen, which is chemically a close relative of aspirin. This is also a field rich in folk remedies, such as copper bracelets, and my mother swears by a teaspoonful of honey and a teaspoonful of cider vinegar in hot water taken daily.

The Arthritis and Rheumatism Council, 41 Eagle Street, London WC1R 4AR Tel: 01 405 8572 - RC, S, CS, O, F&F, M, L, B, EI, sae

Arthritis Care, 6 Grosvenor Crescent, London SW1X 7ER Tel: 01 235 0902 - RC, M£L, S, CS, O, F&F, M, L, B, EI, G, A, H, C, Inf, welfare, groups for all ages, especially for the under 35s.

National Ankylosing Spondylitis Society, 6 Grosvenor Crescent, London SW1X 7ER Tel: 01 235 9585 helps sufferers cope with their condition - RC, M£L, M, G, A, Ad, V, TR.

Asthma

About 1 child in 10 gets asthma and, although more than half the children grow out of it, there are some 2 million asthmatics in Britain. The causes include allergies and viral infections, but asthma, hay fever and eczema tend to run in the same families, so there is probably a hereditary factor. Attacks may be triggered by exercise, suddenly breathing cold air, smoke, pollen, laughing or getting upset.

When we breathe in, the muscles round the tubes leading to the lungs normally tighten. During an asthma attack the tightening is exaggerated, so it feels like breathing in through a straw, causing coughing, wheezing, and distress. This happens very fast, and then the walls of the airpipe gradually become sore and swollen, and clogged with phlegm. Attacks often fade out untreated, but they need careful handling as they can be fatal. When someone has an attack:

1 Make sure they have taken their medicine and/or used their inhaler.

2 Stay calm and help them to stay calm and, if possible, avoid rapid breathing (gently distracting a child with a story may help).

3 Encourage them to sit with their arms resting on something slightly higher than their shoulders - this lifts the rib cage and makes breathing seem easier.

4 *Get medical help without delay if:*

a the condition isn't improving in 15 minutes
b breathing is exhausting them
c they cannot stand up or speak more than a few
  words
d they look blue
e the pulse is more than 120 a minute.

Modern inhalers and drugs can control asthma very well. And if children take their medicines regularly, as prescribed, attacks can be prevented and they can live perfectly normal lives. But keep spare medication handy, and take sensible precautions like clearing the bedroom of dust and fluff and keeping smokers at bay.

Asthma Research Council, 300 Upper Street, London N1 2XX Tel: 01 226 2260 - RC, M£L, S, F&F, M, very helpful L, B, G, A, sae.

Athlete's Foot and Ringworm

Athlete's foot is a fungal infection which makes the skin between the toes white, soggy, and uncomfortable. It can be caught wherever others go barefoot, and is worth curing fast, as it can spread to the upper thighs where it is most uncomfortable. Dry the area carefully after washing and use one of the powders sold for treating it. Wear cotton socks rather than man-made fibres and shake the powder into them before putting them on. Keep this up for several weeks after the symptoms disappear to kill the last traces of infection, or the infection will return.

Ringworm is a fungus in the same family, but it starts as an itchy red rash anywhere on the body, and gradually becomes ring-shaped with a paler centre and a scaly surface. It can be caught from people and animals (dogs, cats, cattle) and needs medical treatment to stop it from spreading.

Back Pain

Back pain has many possible causes, but it isn't normal - at any age - and the earlier it is treated, the faster and more permanent the cure. If left to itself it may go away, only to recur, more severely, months or years later. Pain is often attributed to pulled muscles. But it is extremely hard to pull a back muscle and a more likely cause is a small displacement in the spine itself. Having been totally immobilized by back pain, and totally cured, I confess to a prejudice. One effective treatment, in many cases, seems to me to be offered by fully qualified chiropractors who use gentle manipulation to correct the offending bones. This is now recommended by some GPs. However, by no means all back pain would be treated by chiropractors. A number of back conditions do need conventional medical treatment.

To avoid back pain lift heavy objects carefully, bending the knees, keeping the back upright and lifting from the legs. And don't risk your back by trying to lift something too heavy for you without suitable help.

Back Pain Association, 31-33 Park Road, Teddington, Middx TW11 0AB Tel: 01 977 5474 - Ad, Inf, RC, M£M, S, CS, O, F&F, M, L, B, EI, G, A, exercise classes, sae.

Bed Sores

Bed sores happen when someone, bedridden or chair-bound, stays too long in one position. Pressure then cuts off the blood supply to a patch of flesh, which dies, forming an open sore. Prevention is much better than cure. Any reddening of the skin should be taken as a warning and the position changed. Putting a sheepskin pad under any pressure point helps (good pharmacists sell these) and there are now ripple beds and cushions which vary the pressure by circulating water under the patient (organizations for the disabled have the details).

Birth Marks

Mongolian blue spots are small blueish patches found on the lower backs of black and Asian babies, but they usually fade as the child gets older.

A port wine stain (capillary naevus) is a dark-red patch with a raised edge. It doesn't change, but some NHS hospitals now treat these with a laser. They vary in how well they respond and there may sometimes be scars, but many people prefer pale scars to a dark stain, and cosmetic camouflage can hide either (see In Health).

Salmon patches (sometimes called stork-marks) are pinky-red marks on a baby's forehead and eyelids and at the nape of the neck. They go in a few months.

A strawberry mark starts as a small red dot on the face which grows during the early months and becomes a raised red lump. It usually starts to fade in the second year and vanishes by the time the child is 5 or 6.

Bites, Scratches and Stings

Bites and **scratches** from animals should be washed thoroughly and treated with a mild antiseptic. Deep bites also need an anti-tetanus injection, unless the victim is properly immunized (see page 551).

Insect bites from ants, gnats and so on do no great harm. The best antidote is bicarbonate of soda in a little water. Moist soap is also soothing and so is fresh urine. (Not perhaps a nice idea, but at least you always have it with you.)

The best treatment for **nettle stings** is the age-old one of rubbing them with dock leaves, which usually grow nearby, but sage or mint will do instead.

Wasp stings are painful but seldom do much harm. To minimize the pain bathe them with vinegar. **Bees** leave their sting in the skin, so pull it out with tweezers, then bathe the sting with water and bicarbonate of soda. Remember: 'Vinegar for Vasps; Bicarb for Bees.' An ice cube on either sting will soothe it.

There is a rare condition, called anaphylactic shock, in which someone can react violently to a sting and become extremely ill, needing immediate medical attention. Take someone to hospital RAPIDLY if they show any of the following signs:
● swelling *away* from the site of the sting
● blueness of the skin and/or lips
● difficulty in breathing
● a rash or flushed face
● a rapid pulse
● collapse.

Boils

A boil is a bacterial infection in one of the pores. The area swells and fills with pus until it bursts. Keep a boil covered when near to bursting and hurry it along by applying a hot poultice. The best poultice is from a chemist, and based on magnesium, which draws out the fluid. Failing that, bread mashed with very hot water, squeezed out and placed between gauze which is then bandaged on can help - provided it isn't so hot that it burns. If a boil is very painful a doctor may relieve the pain by opening it.

Brittle Bones (Osteogenesis Imperfecta and Osteoporosis)

There are two very different conditions which cause brittle bones.

Osteogenesis starts before birth and is sometimes inherited. In severe cases the bones are so fragile they fracture in the womb; in mild cases children may have several dozen fractures during childhood but live a normal life. Sadly, many are unable to walk, and repeated and inexplicable breaks have sometimes led to parents of such children wrongly being accused of ill treatment. It is incurable.

Osteoporosis has been called 'the silent epidemic': it will affect 1 woman in 4, and 1 man in 40 - and the figures are rising. Bones are living structures which constantly shed cells and replace them with new ones. In osteoporosis too little is replaced in later life. So, as people get older, the bones become small and fracture easily, and the bones in the spine weaken and crush painfully. Today, more British women die of complications following hip fractures than of cancer of the cervix, breast and uterus combined.

The cause of osteoporosis is still under research, but some of the risk factors are known. It is essential to have enough exercise and enough calcium in childhood and puberty to build strong bones. This regime must be continued. And in later life women need extra calcium, because hormone changes make its absorption less efficient (as does smoking, alcoholism and drug taking). Hormone replacement therapy may help here. People also need enough exercise, because without it the body doesn't renew bone so efficiently. However, black people seem to be very much better at making bones than white people, so osteoporosis isn't their problem.

The Brittle Bone Society, Unit 4, Block 20, Carlunie Road, Dunsinane Industrial Estate, Dundee DD2 3QT Tel: 0382 817771 - RC, M£L, L, Ad, sae.

The National Osteoporosis Society, P.O.Box 10, Barton Meade House, Radstock, Bath BA3 3YB Tel: 0761 32472 - RC, M£L, M, L, Ad, sae.

Bronchitis and Emphysema

Bronchitis attacks the air passages in the lungs. In acute bronchitis the sufferer has an irritating, dry and painful cough, and tightness in the chest, a temperature of 38°-39·5°C (100°-103°F), and may later cough up thick yellow, green, or blood-flecked phlegm. A healthy person will get over this in a few weeks without treatment, but chronic bronchitis is a long-standing problem causing breathlessness and a persistent cough. The more cigarettes a person smokes, the more likely they are to get this - and it can kill. Acute attacks can be treated with antibiotics, and those prone to it should talk to their doctor about having a flu vaccination, as colds and flu may trigger it.

Emphysema is when the lung tissue itself is damaged and becomes bad at transferring oxygen to the blood. It is linked to bronchitis and far more common in smokers. The lung damage of emphysema cannot be repaired, but those who stop smoking prevent greater damage, and if they stop before they get breathless, chronic bronchitis can be prevented. They should avoid cold, smoky or foggy air, get down to a normal weight and use hot drinks to help them bring up phlegm.

Cancer

Cancer is a fault in the mechanism which controls the development of body cells. So they multiply unchecked, forming a large growth in many cases (like an outsized internal wart) which gradually blocks the working of that part of the body. There are about 200 different types of cancer, and almost as many causes. But there have been dramatic improvements in treatment. Leukaemia in children can be cured in 50 to 75 per cent of cases, and cancers of the kidney, testicles and placenta are usually curable.

Recent developments in biochemistry have allowed cancer treatments to be more precise. At the same time, even in the bastions of conventional medicine, there has been a growing feeling that cancer may be related to the body failing to suppress it, and that this - in turn - may be linked to the mind as well as the body. This approach is partly due to the success of organizations, like the Bristol Programme, which encourage the patient to resist and fight cancer through changes in lifestyle, diet and attitudes as well as through more conventional medical means. Even those receiving conventional therapies could find it useful to read the two books on these methods details of which are given on page 534. They are written by former cancer patients and could help with the sense of isolation and distress which cancer inevitably brings. They also cover measures which may lessen the chances of cancer developing.

Bowel Cancer

Cancer of the bowel is less likely in those who eat plenty of fresh fruit and vegetables and fibre, and avoid excessive amounts of meat, fat and beer. The first symptoms may be alternating constipation and diarrhoea, blood in the stools and perhaps stomach pains. These can all have other causes but a doctor should be told. It may be treated by radiation, medicines or an operation to remove part of the bowel. If the cut ends of the bowel can't be joined, an opening is made in the stomach wall to replace the anus. This is a colostomy, and a disposable bag is attached to the opening to collect the stools. Afterwards the patient can live a normal life.

Breast Cancer

Breast cancer is the most common form of cancer in women, and the earlier it is caught the less drastic treatment need be. So every woman should be regularly checked by a doctor or check herself. Self-checking is taught at many local clinics. Checking the breasts at the same time each month, a few days after a period, is a first step to catching trouble early. See In Health.

- Does every part of the breast and nipple look normal - for you?
- Does every part of the breast and nipple feel normal - for you?
- Is the skin free from puckering?
- Is the skin surface its normal colour with no swelling, dimpling or puckering?
- Are the nipples free from any bleeding or weeping?

Any lump or abnormality should be seen by a doctor AT ONCE. Most lumps are *not* cancer, so your mind may well be put at rest. But if it is cancer, catching it early minimizes the treatment. Sometimes the lump can be checked by extracting a little fluid with a syringe; but sometimes a piece of tissue must be taken under general anaesthetic. In this case a woman may be asked to sign a form consenting to an immediate removal of the cancer if it is found. She does not have to consent, and should ask her doctor about the other options.

Breast Cancer Treatments

There is now a trend towards removing no more of the breast than is absolutely necessary, and treatment with radiation, chemicals or hormones may be used instead of or as well as an operation. There are three kinds of operation:

1 A lumpectomy is the removal of a small lump of breast containing the tumour and may change the breast very little.
2 A segmentectomy removes a larger section of breast, but shows relatively little on large breasts.
3 A mastectomy removes all the breast tissue, including the nipple, leaving the chest flat, and there is usually a curved scar towards the armpit. After the operation it will be tender and have pins and needles occasionally, and the arm and shoulder may be stiff.

Prostheses (falsies) are made to match every size and shape of breast, so people can swim and sunbathe without anyone spotting the difference. They are available on the NHS, and so are replacements - but some people prefer those sold privately.

Mastectomy isn't the end of everything: it's the beginning of life without cancer. Even so, it is hard to come to terms with losing part of one's body, especially when it is linked to one's identity as a woman, and it is better to talk about the sense of loss than keep smiling bravely. The Mastectomy Association (see page 534) can supply that need. And plastic surgery can often remake the missing breast if you wish.

Cervical Cancer

This cancer of the neck of the womb is probably caused by a virus transmitted during sexual intercourse. If so, the more a man sleeps around, the greater chance he has of passing it from one woman to another, and the more a woman sleeps around the greater her chance of meeting a carrier.

Regular tests are very important because cancer doesn't blossom overnight. Cells go through a stage when they are neither totally normal nor fully cancerous, and there are no symptoms. If a smear test finds them at this time they can be easily cured.

The smear test is nothing to worry about. A doctor slips a small wooden spatula into the vagina and brushes a few skin cells on to it. This only takes a moment or two and doesn't hurt.

One of the leading professional bodies in this field recommends that women have a cervical smear test every 3 years, from the first intercourse until they reach the age of 45, then every 5 years after that. But, ideally, a woman over 35 should have an annual check for diabetes, breast and other female cancers, with a smear test thrown in.

If tests show the cells are abnormal they can usually be burnt off *painlessly* with a laser, leaving tissue which quickly heals and is totally cured.

In 1 women in 10 the abnormal area extends deeper into the cervix and a cone biopsy, which removes a section of the cervix, is needed. This is also done in more minor cases if a hospital has no laser. As it sometimes makes miscarriages more likely it is always worth checking whether the laser method can be used - and asking to have it at another hospital if necessary.

If cancer is established in the cervix it may be treated with radiation, medication or surgery. Surgery usually involves the removal of the womb (a hysterectomy). This is a major operation needing up to 2 weeks in hospital and 3 months of taking things easy. Sexual intercourse has to be avoided for at least 6 weeks after, and if the ovaries have been removed the patient may experience the symptoms of the change of life. Sex may also feel different, but the loss of the womb doesn't prevent orgasm and after this operation is over a very full recovery is possible.

Lung Cancer

Of the 158,000 people in Britain who die of cancer each year 1 in 4 has lung cancer - and 9 out of 10 of those are smokers. The earliest symptom of lung cancer is often a cough. Smokers may think this is simply a harmless smoker's cough. There may also be an ache in the chest either on coughing, or taking a deep breath or all the time. If examination reveals lung cancer it may be treated by radiation, with chemicals or by removing all or part of a lung. This still leaves enough to breathe with if the cancer is not too advanced but, by the time lung cancer is diagnosed, cancer may have invaded other parts of the body.

Skin Cancer

There are three different types of skin cancer. One

(melanoma) can spread to other parts of the body if it isn't treated. And the cases of melanoma are doubling every 10 years. Eight out of 10 skin cancers are caused by too much sunlight. People with naturally blond or red hair are most at risk, but all white people should seriously limit their sunbathing and use a high protection sunscreen. The typical symptoms are a new lump or sore which refuses to go away after several weeks, or a change in the size or colour of a lump or sore which has been there for some while. Tell a doctor about these or about patches of skin of a different colour.

Most moles are harmless, but some can be cancerous. Consult a doctor if one changes shape or colour or bleeds. In 90 per cent of cases skin cancer can be cured by surgery, radiation or medicines.

Association for New Approaches to Cancer, Addington Park, Maidstone, Kent ME19 5BL Tel: 0732 848336 is the umbrella for local groups giving advice on diet, healing and the holistic approach. M£M, G, A, L, V, TR, B, Ad.

British Association of Cancer United Patients (BACUP), 121/123 Charterhouse Street, London EC1M 6AA Tel: 01 608 1661 9.30am-5pm (7pm Tuesday and Thursday) - RC, M£M, Inf line, excellent free L.

Cancer After-care and Rehabilitation Society, Lodge Cottage, Church Lane, Timsbury, Bath, Somerset BA3 1LF Tel: 0761 70731

CancerLink, 46 Pentonville Road, London N1 9HF Tel: 01 833 2451 - RC, S, CS, O, F&F,G, L, Inf, and emotional support for those with cancer and those who care for/about them. Self-help groups throughout the UK, sae.

The Colostomy Welfare Group, 38-39 Eccleston Square (2nd Floor), London SW1V 1PB. Tel: 01 828 5175

Hospice Information Service, St Christopher's Hospice, Lawrie Park Road, Sydenham SE26 6DZ Tel: 01 778 9252 - has information on hospices throughout Britain.

Hysterectomy Support Groups, 11 Henryson Road, Brockley, London SE4 1HL Tel: 01 690 5987 - M£L, S, M, G.

The Leukaemia Care Society, P.O.Box 82, Exeter, Devon EX2 5DP Tel: 0392 218514 - RC, S, F&F, M, Res, Inf, support, grants, H.

Marie Curie Memorial Foundation, 28 Belgrave Square, London SW1X 8QG Tel: 01 235 3325 - RC, Res, nursing homes, home nursing, research, financial help.

Mastectomy Association, 26 Harrison Street, Kings Cross, London WC1H 8JG Tel: 01 837 0908 - RC, S, EI, L, T. Concerned with *all* breast cancer treatment - not just mastectomy. Information and support throughout and mastectomy aids.

National Association of Laryngectomy Clubs, 4th Floor, 39 Eccleston Square, London SW1V 1PB Tel: 01 834 2857 - umbrella for local clubs throughout Britain. L, Ad, EI, Inf, B.

National Society for Cancer Relief, Anchor House, 15-19 Britten Street, London SW3 3TZ Tel: 01 351 7811 - RC, nursing homes for the seriously ill, grants and nurses for those at home.

Tenovus Cancer Information Centre, 11 Whitchurch Road, Cardiff CF4 3JN Tel: 0222 619846 - offers S, B, L, V, F, telephone counselling.

Women's National Cancer Control Campaign (WNCCC), 1 South Audley Street, London W1Y 5DQ Tel: 01 499 7532 offers Inf and screeening. RC, M£L, L, B, V, sae
Penny Brohn, *The Bristol Programme*, Century
Rachael Clyne, *Living with Cancer* Thorsons
Harriet Copperman, *Dying at Home* John Wiley & Sons
Shirley Harrison, *New Approaches to Cancer*, Century
Understanding Cancer of the Breast, from BACUP

Chilblains

When I was writing *Supertips to Make Life Easy*, a woman in Cambridgeshire wrote and told me that chilblains could be cured by bathing them with your own urine. When my daughter and I developed chilblains, we tried it. We both found it stops the itching almost instantly and that regular applications cure chilblains completely. But use it fresh. This is not the dirty remedy as it may sound: if we can go around unbothered by a whole bagful of urine *inside* us a few drops outside are no great matter. Alternatively, go to your GP for medication.

Cold Sores

Cold sores are caused by a virus in the same family as the one causing genital herpes. So it is very important not to do anything which might transfer the infection to your own or someone else's genitals, and direct contact with the cold sore should be avoided. A sore starts as itching and tingling, then blisters form, which crust in a couple of days. It normally clears up in 10 days without treatment, but it may recur and a child can feel ill and miserable and need to drink through a straw because opening the mouth wider hurts. Some people find covering the cold sore completely with lip balm or vaseline speeds healing. But don't stick a finger which has touched the sore back in the pot. Cold sores may also lead to impetigo (page 541).

Constipation

In the first edition of *Enquire Within*, the author wrote,

> In the spring time of the year the judicious use of aperient medicines is much commended ... for children nothing is better than brimstone and treacle.

He went on to recipes of ever-increasing power.

Some people still think the bowels should move regularly at the same time each day. So they sit straining until they do. This shouldn't happen. The time to go to the lavatory is when nature urges, and the modern definition of constipation isn't failing to go every day: it is having hard stools which are difficult to pass - even if they are passed daily. On a balanced diet, with plenty of roughage and enough fluid, stools should be soft enough to pass quickly and comfortably. The body may produce several a day, or none for a day or so. The pause is no disaster, the body isn't a machine.

The main treatment for constipation is therefore a change of diet. But a temporary way to add roughage is by taking 1 to 2 dessertspoonfuls of bran (the plain kind sold by Boots, not Allbran) in yoghurt, cereal or stewed fruit. But there is some evidence that raw bran like this may make it harder for the body to take up calcium. So this should not be a regular practice.

Laxatives should only be taken occasionally, and be the mildest which work. Taking them too often can make the bowels lazy and increase the problem. Children can also get very constipated and may need such temporary help, though the important point is to find out why they are constipated.

Corns and Callouses

Corns and callouses are best prevented. So whenever a layer of hard skin forms rub it well with a pumice stone at each bath. This can prevent a corn developing. Banishing established ones may need a chiropodist, but try treating them carefully with a good corn-removing solution and corn plasters. Alternatively, bread soaked in vinegar and applied to a corn at night under a plaster will soften it. Meanwhile, take the pressure off the area with a circular corn pad, and stop wearing the shoes which are causing the corns.

Colds and Coughs

The classic runny nose, sore throat, sneezing and feeling of being below par can be accompanied by a temperature of 37·5°-38°C (99°-100°F) and these symptoms usually last 4 to 10 days. Opinions are divided as to whether colds should be ignored or taken to bed for a day or so. Doctors tend to favour the former, but some psychotherapists say mild infections like this can be the body's way of telling you to let up, and that failing to take the hint can lead to more serious illness. As we meet germs every day and only get ill sometimes this seems eminently logical.

There is no magic cure. The medicines which claim to stop the symptoms only do so for a short period, then they come right back. Decongestant drops have the same effect if used for more than 5-6 days (3-4 for a baby). But home remedies can do a lot. To make breathing easier put a few drops of oil of eucalyptus in a pudding bowl, pour on very hot water and sit with your head over this, with a towel forming a tent over the top so that you breathe in the vapour. Do this three times a day. For children, place the bowl in a washbasin, then if it spills it won't scald them. Rubbing some Vick on the chest will produce a vapour which will make breathing easier at night. So will a few drops of oil of eucalyptus on the pillow case. If babies have trouble feeding, gently clean out their nostrils with a cotton bud before meals. They also sleep more easily on their sides, though older children may prefer to be propped up.

Coughing

Coughing is a device for keeping catarrh off the chest and there is really no need to spend money on cough mixtures - many of which do very little. It is just as good to give plenty of hot drinks, adding a little glycerine (from a chemist) or honey to soothe the throat. Or put a teaspoon of the spice turmeric in a saucepan with a cup of milk, and bring to the boil. Sweeten this with sugar or honey to taste and drink it three times a day. This is an Indian remedy and cures coughs better than any other I know. Turmeric has a soft, almost scented, flavour (though when old it can taste bitter), but the brilliant yellow stains badly, so watch where you put it. The full effects won't be felt for three days, but the cough may improve before that, and it is just as good for bronchitis. In both cases it attacks the catarrh which causes the cough - though it only works on chest catarrh, and doesn't clear the head. Use steam inhalations as described for colds, as well.

Contact the doctor about the cough so if:
- the cough lasts more than 10 days
- coughing produces yellow or green catarrh
- there is pain in the chest or shortness of breath
- coughing produces any blood
- the cough might be whooping-cough.

Flying with a thick cold can damage the ears as the air cannot get through the inner tubes to balance the pressure. Some ear specialists say people with heavy colds shouldn't fly, but if you *have* to do so ask your doctor for something to dry up the catarrh during the journey.

Cramp

Cramp is a painful and uncontrollable tightening of a group of muscles when lactic acid builds up in a muscle faster than the body can carry it away. This may be because an awkward position cuts off the blood supply, or because exercise makes the body produce more lactic acid than usual, or when there are extra demands on the blood supply, as in pregnancy. It is nothing to worry about. But don't swim for at least an hour after a heavy meal, especially if the water is cold: digesting food occupies the blood supply so it can't handle the lactic acid produced by swimming. This makes cramp a serious risk and people have drowned because of it.

A 'stitch' (rib muscle cramp) will go if you bend several times and try to kiss your knee; cramp in the foot will go if you turn your toes up, and so on. Massaging it afterwards will stimulate the blood supply and make the cramp less likely to return, and pregnant women who can't reach crampy insteps should roll their foot hard over a bottle. Some sports coaches advise drinking bicarbonate of soda in water before an event to counteract the acid. Those bothered by cramps could talk to their doctor about this.

Croup

Croup sounds like barking and is caused by a virus making the breathing tubes swell. It tends to happen at night to children under 4 years old. If they panic it aggravates the problem, so *be calm and reassuring*. Steam is the fastest way to relieve it. Just take the child into the bathroom and tell it you are going to make the cough better. Sit on the edge of the bath, holding the child upright on your knees, put the plug in and run the hot tap so the room fills with steam. (DO NOT put the child in the bath.) If there is no bath water boil up

In most cases, croup fades with the steam. But, if the child has such difficulty in breathing that the lower ribs are sucked in at each breath and the skin looks blue, call an ambulance IMMEDIATELY.

a kettle with the lid off and sit as near as is safe. Let the steam ease the coughing and then give the child a warm drink in little sips, *saying* that the drink will help. Once the croup is over a vaporizer lamp in the bedroom, until the infection goes, may stop a recurrence.

Cuts and Grazes

Most cuts and grazes are nothing to worry about, and they don't need the treatment usually meted out to them. Nor should children see that adults are worried. Be reassuring, wash any dirt out under lukewarm running water, and gently remove stubborn grit with a clean handkerchief or cotton wool. Failing clean water, the victim should suck a graze and spit out any grit. If there is a lot of bleeding raise the cut above the head. Research shows it is best *not* to use strong antiseptics. They kill the body's defences against infection. It is far better to use a gentle, painless antiseptic like Savlon cream or witch-hazel. And if neither is obtainable, either honey or sugar will help to keep down infection, but don't use these where ants might be attracted.

Grazes tend to heal best when left uncovered - unless they are in a place which gets dirty. Cuts may need a bandage or sticking plaster. Whether one needs stitches or not will depend on its length, depth and position - a cut on the face may need stitches when one of similar size on a knee wouldn't, but if in doubt consult a doctor.

Try not to get young children used to sticking plaster on the slightest hurt. Once it becomes an essential part of making cuts better they may cry blue murder when it isn't available. One wise mother I know taught her child that a kiss and/or a nice drink of cold water were the big healers - and there are few places where you can't get either.

> There is often confusion between antiseptics and disinfectants. Disinfectants do kill germs, but they should NEVER be used on the human body, as some could cause chemical burns. Use them on the loo, not on you.

Cystitis

Cystitis is an infection of the bladder which causes an urgent and frequent desire to 'pee'. Urinating causes a burning sensation, and the urine may be flecked with blood. There may also be a fever and a pain low in the abdomen. It's mainly a female problem, because the bacteria which cause it invade from outside the body and women have a far shorter urinary tube for it to travel up. The bacteria can come from the anus. So women should make a habit of wiping from front to back, and if they indulge in anal intercourse the man should wash well before making love in any other way.

Most attacks can be cured with medical treatment. But at the first sign of any symptoms the following steps may stop an attack developing:

1   Drink ½ pint of water (285 ml) containing 1 teaspoon bicarbonate of soda (those with kidney or heart trouble should consult their doctor first).

2   After that, drink ½ pint of a bland, non-acid, non-irritant liquid every half hour - milk, weak tea, water, herb tea, etc., but *not* fruit juice or coffee. And repeat the bicarbonate of soda every 3 hours.
3   Take a mild pain killer if you need it.
4   Sit or lie down if you possibly can.

As the attack passes, ease up on the drinking but stay off acid drinks and make sure you drink 4 to 5 pints of bland liquid a day for the next week or two. Don't use sprays or douches in that area, they will aggravate the problem, and follow the suggestions on page 565 for hygiene.

There are two other causes of cystitis symptoms. One is bruising of the tube leading to a woman's bladder, caused by rough lovemaking, or intercourse before a woman is excited enough to produce lubrication (often called 'honeymoon cystitis'). In these cases, let the bruising die down and then re-start lovemaking more considerately. Also a small proportion of cystitis sufferers have nothing clinically wrong and cystitis may be a sign of anxiety or some deeper emotional or sexual problem. It will go only when they sort this out.

Diabetes (Diabetes Mellitus, or Sugar Diabetes)

Diabetes is a breakdown in the mechanism by which the hormone insulin adjusts the level of sugar in the blood. So the amount of sugar in the blood, after meals, is far too high, too much sugar reaches the kidneys and they have to produce extra urine to handle it. The early symptoms are excessive thirst and excessive urine, coupled with loss of energy, loss of weight and possibly boils or thrush.

There are two forms. Insulin dependent diabetes starts in the young and thin and maturity onset diabetes mainly in the middle-aged, elderly, and overweight. There is no cure for either, but they can be controlled, and anyone with diabetic symptoms should see a doctor immediately. Proper control is important because diabetes can damage the walls of the blood vessels from the heart.

Control is by diet, plus possibly tablets or insulin injections. Treatment is less effective in the overweight, and the ideal diet is one which keeps the carbohydrate supply fairly steady. Once diabetes is under control diabetics need to eat regularly. This is especially important before driving because if the glucose balance suffers it causes faintness, sweating, headache, sickness, double vision, bad temper and - if not treated - unconsciousness. At the first signs of any of these symptoms a diabetic should take a sugary drink or glucose tablets.

Diabetics need to have regular eye checks and take care of their feet as they are prone to foot and eye trouble. They should carry a card saying they are on insulin, and declare diabetes on a driving application form and tell their car insurance company - but there should be no added premium.

The British Diabetic Association, 10 Queen Anne Street, London W1M 0BD Tel: 01323 1531 - RC, S, CS, F&F, M, very good L, B, V, E, G, A, T, C, recipes, sae.

The Stillbirth and Neonatal Death Society has a leaflet on how diabetics can prevent problems in pregnancy (see In Health).

Diarrhoea

Diarrhoea is defined as loose watery stools several times a day, and is often attributed to a change in diet or climate. Doctors now dismiss this theory. Some foods, such as chillies, figs and prunes, can act like dynamite but, those apart, diarrhoea is caused by bacteria.

Many of the diarrhoea medicines sold across the counter are no longer approved of by doctors. The modern method is to give the bacteria nothing to feed on. So drink *plenty* of water, and *eat nothing*. The quantity of water is important as a lot of fluid is lost and there is a danger of dehydration, particularly in young children in a hot climate. The World Health Organization (WHO) recommends giving the following solution to help prevent this. In 1 litre of water (2 pt) put 1 flat (*not* rounded) teaspoonful of salt, and 5 to 8 teaspoonfuls of sugar or glucose, and give this little and very often. It is important not to give too much salt as young children can be harmed by it. A similar mixture is available in chemists and is called the mixture for Oral Rehydration Therapy (ORT).

If a baby has diarrhoea see a doctor the same day and meanwhile give plenty of ORT mixture in cool boiled water. Children over a year should only be given the WHO mixture in boiled water and must be taken to a doctor if it hasn't cleared up in 36 hours - or sooner if really unwell. Any child with pinkish stools should also see a doctor.

If you can't stick to just water, plain boiled rice dressed with lemon juice is the least harmful food. An old home remedy, which was given to my grandmother by a doctor, is to starve and drink fluids as above but drink port too. It works well, and Mexican tequila also seems effective. If diarrhoea lasts see a doctor.

National Association for Colitis and Crohn's Disease, 98a London Road, St Albans, Herts AL1 1NX - general information on inflammatory bowel diseases only. RC, S, O, F&F, M, L, G, A, sae.

Ear Problems

The eardrum forms a barrier between the ear's outer tube and its inner workings, and problems can be roughly divided into those outside the eardrum and those behind it.

Otitis Media

The most common cause of earache in children is acute otitis media, in which an infection builds up behind the eardrum making it tight and painful. A child often has a cold at the time, and the pain tends to be worse at night because it is harder for the build-up to drain away when lying down. Sitting the child up for a while, to let the ear drain, and giving him or her paracetamol and a decongestant should help considerably. Placing a warm pad on the ear may also be soothing, but a doctor should be seen as soon as possible.

Glue Ear

Repeated infections can lead to a condition called 'glue ear' in which thick fluid collects behind the eardrum and gradually causes deafness - 20 per cent of children have this at some time. It may cure itself but, if not, it can be cured by a minor operation which drains it away. Any child who has had earache more than once should be watched for signs of deafness, because it is remarkably hard to recognize its gradual onset. Children who become partially deaf, (as my son did), may simply seem disobedient or may follow an instruction but get it oddly wrong (for example, 'take the cat outside' could be heard as 'take the cat upstairs'), they may do poorly at school or have temper tantrums. Hearing tests done in school aren't always sensitive enough to detect this sort of hearing loss. So, if a child has any sign of a hearing problem it should see a specialist immediately. Deafness in the early years at school is a handicap that takes a long time to overcome.

Minor Ear Problems

Loss of hearing can also be caused, at any age, by wax building up in the outer ear and a doctor can syringe this out. A boil in the tube of the outer ear is rather more painful and may need antibiotics. Young children may also get pain when they have something stuck in their ear. Unless it is very easy to remove, it may be best to let a doctor do it, rather than risk pushing it farther down.

Deafness as an Adult

Adults often deny their growing deafness until they have lost a great deal of hearing. By then they may have lost the habit of listening, and of selecting the words they want to listen to from the host of background noises. It is then far harder to adjust to a hearing aid than it might have been when only a little deaf. Both children and adults should see a doctor *as soon as* there is a possibility of deafness. The sooner action is taken to cure or relieve it the better.

Tinnitus

Tinnitus is a condition in which strange, often ringing, sounds are heard. Sufferers sometimes think they are going mad, because the rest of the world can't hear the sounds. It is not a sign of madness; it is an ear problem which has a variety of causes, including excessive use of aspirin. It is not usually curable, but it may go and masking the noise can give relief. Ask the Royal National Institute for the Deaf (page 568) about this.

Eczema

Eczema produces rough, itchy, red patches which may weep, especially where the skin is soft, such as the backs of the knees or wrists. But it can affect any part of the body. It may come and go for no obvious reason, but it can't be caught and most often starts in infancy. It seems as if about half of those who have eczema may have an allergy, and cows' milk and eggs are common culprits. Often relatives have eczema, hay fever, asthma or dry skin. So, when these conditions run in the family, some doctors recommend breast feeding for babies, and careful attention to diet. It may also be worth avoiding food additives. More drastic dietary changes should only be made on a doctor's advice, and creams may be prescribed which help considerably. Keep the skin soft by avoiding soap and using emulsifying ointment for washing instead (any chemist will order it). Apply basic moisturizing creams afterwards - different creams suit different skins.

Ninety per cent of cases improve during childhood, but eczema can also be an allergic reaction in adulthood, or be linked with varicose veins. Use pure soap for washing clothes, rinse garments very well and go for cotton which is often less irritating than wool or man-made fibres. Keep the nails short and clean, and scratch as little as possible (children may need mittens attached to the sleeves of their nightwear). *Most importantly*, sufferers could become seriously infected by contact with cold sores or impetigo, and must be kept away from anyone who has them. Very severe cases may qualify for financial help from the DHSS.

National Eczema Society, Tavistock House North, Tavistock Square, London WC1H 9SR Tel: 01 388 4097 - RC, F£L (but general enquiries welcome with large sae) S, CS, O, F&F, M, L, B, G, T, inexpensive Inf pack.

Epilepsy

Epilepsy affects about one person in a hundred and has a variety of causes, but most epileptics are intellectually normal and lead perfectly normal lives, and some children grow out of it completely. However, anyone diagnosed as epileptic must tell the DVLC and they may not drive for 2 years after the last fit. Fits can last from seconds to hours, and occur several times a day or only once in many months. What causes them varies greatly, but flickering light is a common trigger.

In a major fit (grand mal, tonic-clonic, or convulsion) there is usually no warning. Victims become unconscious and the muscles stiffen then relax, there are jerky movements, saliva may appear round the mouth, (blood-flecked if the tongue has been bitten) and they may wet themselves. Minor fits (petit-mal or absence) may be so slight that there is just a moment or two of blankness and clouded consciousness. Anyone who has fits of either type should see a doctor.

Epilepsy First Aid
- Get the sufferer away from hazards - sharp objects, fires etc.
- Put something soft under the head.
- Let the fit run its course without restraining movement.
- As soon as possible remove false teeth, check the airway is clear and place the victim in the recovery position (page 564).
- DO NOT put anything between the teeth - it could be bitten off and choke them - and don't put your fingers in their mouth.
- DO NOT give anything to drink until they wake FULLY.
- Gently loosen tight clothing round the neck.

- Only call a doctor if one fit follows another without a return to consciousness.
- Reassure them as consciousness returns.

British Epilepsy Association, Anstey House, 40 Hanover Square, Leeds LS3 1BE Tel: 0532 439393 - RC, S, CS, F&F, L, B, T, sae

National Society for Epilepsy, Chalfont Centre for Epilepsy, Chalfont St Peter, Gerrards Cross, Bucks SL9 ORJ Tel: 024 07 3991 - RC, S, CS, O, F&F, L, B, V, Cl, T, C, sae.

Medic-alert Foundation, 11 Clifton Terrace, London 6N4 3JP Tel: 01 263 8596 - provides warning bracelets engraved with the name of the sufferer's medical condition (e.g. 'epileptic' or 'diabetic'), plus a 24-hour emergency number which has access to computerized details on their problem and the dosage of any regular medication. (See also page 569.)

Eye Problems

Grit and Eyelashes
If a piece of grit, or an eyelash, gets into an eye, fold a clean handkerchief into a point, and use this gently to wipe the particle away. To see where it is, pull the lower eyelid away with the eyes up, or pull the upper lid up with the eyes down. If nothing can be seen try leaning under a cold tap and running cold water over the eye. But DON'T use an eyebath; it could wash the particle farther back, and don't try to remove a speck which is embedded in the dark area of the eye. See a doctor as the cornea can be scratched. See First Aid (page 560) for chemicals in the eye.

Eyesight
Sunlight is a major danger to the eyes: the delicate inner workings of the eye age in proportion to the amount of light which hits them. So the more eyes are exposed to bright light the faster they age, and the younger the failing vision and cataracts of 'old age' develop. Eye specialists recommend using fully protective sunglasses but most fashion glasses are *not* protective enough. Look for really dark glasses in shades of brown, orange or yellowy green. The time to have an eye check - whether you have glasses or not - is when you notice a change.

Fainting
Fainting isn't something to worry about. It happens when, momentarily, too little blood reaches the brain, so the person loses consciousness, and looks pale. It is most common in adolescence, but can be caused by fear (the classic 'strong' man fainting at the sight of an injection), shock, standing immobile for too long (guards on parade), extreme fatigue and standing up suddenly when hot. When someone faints leave them lying down, and raise their feet higher than their head. Let them come round in their own time and stay lying down until fully recovered. There is no need to give smelling salts or any other treatment.

Glandular Fever (Infectious Mononucleosis)
This virus infection is caught from saliva - which is why it is called 'the kissing disease'. Predictably, it is most common between the ages of 15 and 25, though you

can get it at any age. It causes a temperature for several days, then a sore throat and infected tonsils, and the glands down the neck below the angle of the jaw may become swollen and tender. There may also be a fine red rash - particularly if the sore throat is treated with certain antibiotics. It is always worth seeing a doctor about these symptoms and checking that it *is* glandular fever. Some other medical problems have very similar symptoms, and it often takes a blood test to tell which is which.

The treatment is complete rest, gargling with a soluble pain killer when the throat is very painful, and eating soothing foods. A young child usually recovers in 2 to 4 weeks, but someone older can take far longer and they may feel weak, depressed and very easily tired for some months afterwards. It may also recur, though usually quite mildly.

Hay Fever (Allergic Rhinitis)

Hay fever is an allergic reaction which causes watering eyes and a streaming nose. The allergy is usually to pollen but the same symptoms are produced by allergy to substances like dust, pets and feathers. It is best to keep away from the substance which causes the reaction, but see a doctor; there are now safe and effective remedies for hay fever.

Headaches

Headaches aren't a problem; they are a symptom of a problem. The most common causes of headaches are tension, eye strain, back trouble or the start of an illness. Or it could just be a need for love and attention. If a child gets a headache try curing it with a long drink of cool water and a soothing head massage rather than with pain killers. Giving pain killers too readily can teach a child that the solution to every problem is found in a tablet. Logically it isn't a very big step from this to thinking that the answer to the pains of adolescence lies in drugs. That doesn't mean pain killers should never be given, but it is better if they are not a *first* resort, and better for children to learn that love and cherishing are also healers. Nor need this be limited to children.

When a headache is combined with other signs of illness any sufferer should be watched carefully and a doctor contacted if necessary. A doctor should also be seen if headaches occur regularly - but it could be worth having an eye check first.

Migraine

Migraine is described as the worst headache imaginable, often accompanied by nausea and distorted vision. Recent research shows it has physical, not psychological causes. Pain killers are less effective than usual, as the gut functions poorly during a migraine. Attacks can be triggered by various factors, including alcohol, chocolate, cheese and coffee, or hunger or lack of sleep. Oral contraceptives, high blood pressure, menstruation, bright lights, loud noises, and television are others. Some find taking feverfew - a herb which grows anywhere - helps. The British Migraine Association has information on this and other measures. Help can also be got from the clinic of the Migraine Trust.

At the *first signs* of the migraine sufferers should:
1   Take 3 aspirin *or* 2 paracetamol (unless they have other medications).
2   Eat something to speed the absorption of the medicine.
3   Lie down in a dark room and try to sleep.

British Migraine Association, 1778a High Road, Byfleet, Surrey KT14 7ED Tel: 0932 352468 - RC, M£L, B, L, Inf, sae.

City of London Migraine Clinic, 22 Charterhouse Square, London EC1M 6DX Tel: 01 251 3322 (9 am-5 pm) is a specialist clinic (Dr) treating people from all over Britain. Plus emergency help, without referral, for anyone struck by a migraine while in London. RC.

The Migraine Trust, 45 Great Ormond Street, London WC1 3HD Tel: 01 278 2676 - RC, S, CS, F&F, Dr (to visit clinic), M, L, B, G, A, sae.

Heart Disease

Heart disease covers a whole range of disorders, from inborn defects to those which develop later in life. Modern surgery can now work miracles but nonetheless, there is a limit to what medicine can do, and heart disease is Britain's biggest single killer. The heart has to beat 60 to 90 times a minute (3 million beats a month), which is quite enough to ask of it without putting it under stress. Yet many of those who die of heart disease have dug their graves with their own fingertips. Smokers under fifty are 10 times as likely to die of a heart attack as non-smokers of their age. Those who are overweight and eat the wrong diet also carry a greater risk. Spoilsport though it may seem, those who want to live to enjoy the other pleasures of life should stop smoking and keep their weight down.

Angina (Angina Pectoris)

This is a painful cramp in the heart muscle brought on when the heart can't get enough oxygen from the blood. It happens after exercise, strong emotion, large meals or cold. It sometimes feels like severe indigestion, and occasionally it spreads to the left shoulder and arm, or the throat and neck. It shows that the heart is under stress and that an artery to the heart is narrowed either by a fatty lining or by a spasm.

There are several drugs which bring relief within about 5 minutes. If these fail surgery may sort out the problem. So someone with angina can usually live a perfectly normal life, but drivers must tell the DVLC in Swansea and their insurance company - or their insurance will not be valid. They need to learn to relax, and avoid overworking and excessive physical or emotional stress - though sex is allowed. They should also give up smoking, keep their weight down and eat a healthy diet.

Heart Attack (Coronary Thrombosis)

In a heart attack the blood supply to part of the heart is stopped. This can be because the artery has furred up, or because a clot of blood has blocked it, or when the wall of the artery splits. It causes severe pain in the centre of the chest, possibly spreading to the arms and

	Men			Women		
			naked weight (stones and lb)			
Height (ft and in)	Average	Acceptable weight range	Overweight	Average	Acceptable weight range	Overweight
4 10				7 4	6 8 - 8 7	10 3
4 11				7 6	6 10 - 8 10	10 6
5 0				7 9	6 12 - 8 13	10 10
5 1				7 12	7 1 - 9 2	11 0
5 2	8 11	8 0 - 10 1	12 1	8 1	7 4 - 9 5	11 3
5 3	9 1	8 3 - 10 4	12 5	8 4	7 7 - 9 8	11 7
5 4	9 4	8 6 - 10 8	12 10	8 8	7 10 - 9 12	11 12
5 5	9 7	8 9 - 10 12	13 0	8 11	7 13 - 10 2	12 2
5 6	9 10	8 12 - 11 2	13 5	9 2	8 2 - 10 6	12 7
5 7	10 0	9 2 - 11 7	13 11	9 6	8 6 - 10 10	12 12
5 8	10 5	9 6 - 11 12	14 3	9 10	8 10 - 11 0	13 3
5 9	10 9	9 10 - 12 2	14 8	10 0	9 0 - 11 4	13 8
5 10	10 13	10 0 - 12 6	14 13	10 4	9 4 - 11 9	14 0
5 11	11 4	10 4 - 12 11	15 5	10 8	9 8 - 12 0	14 6
6 0	11 8	10 8 - 13 2	15 11	10 12	9 12 - 12 5	14 12
6 1	11 12	10 12 - 13 7	16 3			
6 2	12 3	11 2 - 13 12	16 9			
6 3	12 8	11 6 - 14 3	17 1			
6 4	12 13	11 10 - 14 8	17 7			

The table is based on the Metropolitan Life Insurance Tables and reproduced with the permission of the Royal College of Physicians.

neck, and perhaps lasting several hours. This leaves the patient unwell and exhausted, and part of the heart muscle may die (myocardial infarction).

The greatest risk of a repeat attack is in the days afterwards. If there is no recurrence within several years the risk of another is no greater than for anyone else. The current medical thinking is that after a heart attack people should live normally but *give up smoking* get down to a better weight, eat sensibly and take gentle exercise. This includes sex after the first 6 weeks, provided it isn't too strenuous and doesn't provoke chest pain. The rules on driving are as for angina (p. 539).

The British Heart Foundation, 102 Gloucester Place, London W1H 4DH Tel: 01 935 0185 has excellent fact sheets on many heart conditions, the risk factors and their treatment. RC, S, CS, F&F, L, B, sae.
Coronary Prevention Group, 60 Great Ormond Street, London WC1N 3HR Tel: 01 833 3687 - has inexpensive booklets on heart disease prevention.

Heat Stroke and Sunstroke
Heat stroke and sunstroke are the same thing. The problem is that too much heat and sun upset the salt and water balance of the body. So the sufferer feels dizzy, feverish and sometimes sick, and may cease to sweat. The treatment is bed in a cool place, regular drinks of *very slightly* salted water, and sponging with tepid water. On rare occasions there may be high fever and even delirium. This needs IMMEDIATE medical attention in hospital.

Hepatitis
Hepatitis A is still a fairly common infection in Britain and is extremely common overseas. Hepatitis B is uncommon in Britain but quite common overseas.

Hepatitis A (often called infectious hepatitis) is caused by a virus which is most easily transmitted by the 'oral-fecal route'. For example, a carrier fails to wash after using the lavatory (the virus is in both faeces and urine), then handles food and you eat the food. Shellfish collected near a sewage outlet can also carry it, and so may primitive water supplies. Some 3 to 5 weeks after infection the victim has a fever, nausea, stomach ache and then jaundice - though in children it is often very mild and only 1 child in 10 who develops it gets the symptom of jaundice. The illness lasts at least 2 weeks and can go on for months, and sufferers are infectious from about 2 weeks before the symptoms start, until a few days after their onset. It is rarely fatal, but adults can be very ill for weeks and alcohol must be avoided for the next 6 months.

Hepatitis B (often called serum hepatitis) is not the fatal disease it is sometimes made out to be, though people can die of it. It is carried in the body fluids, especially in blood and semen, and must enter some break in the skin. It is caught in much the same ways as AIDS (see page 565), but it is far more infectious. The incubation period is 3 to 5 months and the victim usually feels below par and off food, and develops jaundice. The illness lasts about 6 weeks, but half of those who get it never have jaundice and many have no symptoms at all. Victims are infectious from several weeks before the first symptoms until several weeks after, and alcohol must be avoided for 6 months. A few people recover but remain infectious for up to 20 years; others are carriers who have never had any symptoms. Occasionally it causes liver damage.

Hernia (Rupture)
A hernia occurs when the wall surrounding one of the cavities of the body weakens at a particular point and allows an organ inside it to bulge through. Very young children can get hernias around the tummy button, but these usually right themselves within the first year.

By far the most common hernias are those in the groin, in which part of the bowel pushes through a weakness in the abdominal wall and bulges just under the skin. This is often provoked by a sudden strain on the area, such as when lifting a heavy weight, or even coughing violently. Normally it falls back when lying down, and is only mildly uncomfortable. The basic treatment is usually a support (truss) to push it back and hold it into position.

The only danger from a hernia is if the lump comes up and cannot be pushed back, and a doctor should be told immediately if this happens. In women the most common hernia is a hiatus hernia in which the abdomen presses up through a tear in the floor of the chest, and this is a fairly common cause of heartburn in pregnancy. But the same type of hernia can occur in men, particularly if they are overweight. In women it usually rights itself after pregnancy; in men the remedy is usually to diet. But any troublesome hernia may need an operation.

Hiccoughs
What infallibly cures hiccoughs is drinking a teaspoon of neat vinegar.

High Blood Pressure (Hypertension)
High blood pressure affects about 1 person in 5, and having high blood pressure increases the risk of heart disease, strokes and kidney disease. Someone who has high blood pressure at the age of forty is 30 times as likely to have a stroke as someone of that age with normal blood pressure. And the risk is increased if they smoke. Yet this problem usually has no symptoms and often goes unnoticed. Once detected, it can be treated with drugs and/or changes in diet and the risks reduced. The British Heart Foundation (page 540) has a leaflet answering queries about blood pressure and its treatment. But the best treatment is prevention:
- keep your weight down
- reduce the amount of saturated fat in your diet
- cut down on the salt in your diet
- some doctors also recommend eating more potassium - found in fruit like bananas - though this is controversial
- stop smoking
- take regular exercise

Impetigo
Impetigo is a bacterial skin infection which spreads very easily, so sufferers must avoid touching others, and their towels, flannels and bedding must be kept completely separate. It starts as rather large blisters which dry into golden-yellow scabs. Doctors usually prescribe an antibiotic cream which clears these up quickly.

Indigestion
Drinking milk, to neutralize the acid, will usually relieve the discomfort of indigestion. But the early signs of heart trouble can sometimes feel very similar. If the symptoms persist see a doctor.

Heartburn
This is a burning feeling high in the stomach, just under the centre of the ribs, often with a little regurgitation. Half a teaspoon of bicarbonate of soda in a glass of water usually helps.

Wind and Gripe
An effective remedy is to drink a glass or two of port. Don't ask me why it works, but it does. Obviously this isn't good for babies. For them the best solution is a remedy which has been used in Poland for centuries - fennel water. Just steep a teaspoon of fennel seeds in a mug of boiling water until the water is cool enough for the baby to drink. Strain the seeds out and sweeten it to taste. It works because fennel, like all this family of plants, contains a substance which stimulates the intestines and makes them get rid of the wind. It can work far better than gripe water.

Influenza (Flu)
The typical symptoms are achiness, a temperature and generally feeling below par. The cure is bed rest and reasonable doses of TLC (tender loving care). Flu will fade away in a few days. You can be immunized against it, but unfortunately the jabs need renewing each year.

Ingrowing Toe Nails
Ingrowing toe nails are better prevented than cured. If you are having problems, cut toe nails straight across, and don't wear shoes which are too small. Once one has developed it should be treated by a chiropodist.

Insomnia (Sleeplessness)

Time drags at night and even waking for short periods can seem like hours. So you may start worrying that you will be too tired next day, tense up and stay awake even longer. Sleeplessness is annoying but it is *not* something to worry about. There are no rules for how much sleep the body needs, and if it gets too little one day it usually makes up for it another. The only time when it becomes a real problem is when pain, deep depression or anxiety interfere with the body's natural ability to do this. Then sleeping pills taken for a few days (*not* weeks) may break the cycle of sleeplessness, tension and more sleeplessness. But never to *try* to go to sleep (the effort keeps you awake), instead use tricks to make it happen:

- Try to recognize the point when your body is ready to sleep, and go to bed then - however early it is.
- Do something which really relaxes you just before bed.
- Listen to the radio very quietly, close to you, in the dark (on headphones if you aren't alone in bed), abandoning all attempt to go to sleep and just relaxing. Ideally the radio should be the kind which turns itself off after an hour, then you won't be woken by the next loud music.

If you wake and can't sleep:

- Get out of bed and potter for a short while, letting yourself get a *little* bit cold. Meanwhile, make sure the bed is warm and cosy (switch on electric blankets, add hot water bottles). When you return to bed the warmth often brings a surge of relaxation and sleep with it.
- Read a book and enjoy the excuse to do so. If you read until morning you have still relaxed, but if your eyes feel sleepy stop instantly and turn off the light.
- Drink some hot milk laced with whisky. (Most effective for those who are not regular drinkers.)
- If worry and distress are going relentlessly round and round in your head, get up and *do* something. It doesn't matter whether you scrub the floor or garden at first light. Anything is better than lying there tense, worried and full of envy at the world of sleepers. The more active and satisfying the task, the more it will unwind the tension. If you feel tired later on don't feel guilty about lying down and sleeping. You worked when the rest of the world slept.

Jaundice

Jaundice isn't a disease; it is a sign of illness which involves yellowing of the eyes and face, and sometimes the whole body. The urine may also be dark and the stools pale. This shows that excess bile, from the liver, is entering the bloodstream. In a newborn baby the most common cause is an immature liver, and the baby usually grows out of it in 3 weeks, although babies can also have neonatal hepatitis, which takes longer to get over. In adults the most usual cause is infectious hepatitis (see page 540), but whatever the cause, it needs medical attention.

Kidney Disease

The kidneys are miniature purification plants which remove liquid waste products from the blood and get rid of them as urine. When the kidneys fail the waste is left in the blood and the sufferer essentially dies of internal pollution. This causes frequent urination - perhaps with blood in it (full kidney failure will have no urine output at all), pain at the waist level at the back, sometimes pain in the groin, and possibly a temperature and shakiness. It can affect any age, and the failure can be associated with high blood pressure or various infections. If a kidney fails the only treatments are dialysis, for 12 hours a day three times a week, on a machine, or a kidney transplant.

Anyone wondering about carrying a kidney donor card could talk to the following organization.

The British Kidney Patient Association, Bordon, Hants GU35 9JZ Tel: 042 03 2021/2 - RC, M£L, S, O, F&F, CS, L, H, T, Ad, Inf.
Stewart Cameron, *Kidney Disease: the Facts*, Oxford University Press
Elizabeth D. Ward, *Timbo - A Struggle for Survival*, Sidgwick & Jackson

Meningitis

Meningitis is an inflammation of the membranes covering the brain, caused by either bacteria or viruses and different types of bacteria cause meningitis in different age groups. (Encephalitis, which is a separate viral disease, looks initially like meningitis.) All of them are probably caught by general contact, but there is no set incubation period, and the infection can be carried by someone with no symptoms. Anyone who develops it will have some of the following symptoms:

- general unwellness and irritability
- severe headache (often with vomiting)
- dislike of light
- temperature of 38·5°C (101°F) or more
- a rash of red spots
- confusion (not recognizing parents perhaps)
- a stiff neck - less common in young children (not to be confused with the stiff neck which goes with tonsillitis).

Some of these symptoms also occur with other illnesses, so they don't always mean someone has meningitis, but a doctor should be told *immediately* because, if it is meningitis, *swift treatment can be vital.* The sufferer will usually be admitted to hospital for tests, and may need 10 to 14 days there. Even those who are severely ill with meningitis can recover totally, but there can be brain damage, ranging from mild problems to serious disabilities.

Mental Illnesses and Problems

Mental illness broadly divides into neurosis and psychosis. Someone with neurosis is in touch with the real world and behaves like anyone else, but there may be some aspect of their life in which they are off key. For example, they may have a phobia, and be terrified of something which doesn't frighten others, or be deeply depressed. Whereas someone with psychosis loses touch with reality, either all the time or in patches. Psychotics may believe they are someone they aren't, or hear voices, or believe that people are getting at them. Psychosis is so varied it is impossible to cover all its symptoms and cures. But, if a relative you suspect is mentally ill refuses to see a doctor, or gets no real help from a GP, you may ask the GP to arrange for a home visit by a psychiatrist. Those who are severely depressed or have other mental problems they cannot handle may ask a GP to refer them to a psychotherapist, but the NHS facilities are limited and overstretched.

Depression

Nobody should be ashamed of being depressed. It is either a natural aspect of grief, or an illness which is treatable. It is normal to be depressed after a divorce or the death of a loved one. But, in today's rushing society, people may feel they should recover from depression faster than is really natural. Recovery from mourning should be expected to be a matter of many months, not weeks, and nobody should be afraid to let this depression run its natural course. In fact, trying to rush the pace or brighten up with anti-depressants is seldom the best route to a full recovery.

When there is no obvious cause for depression doctors often call it endogenous (meaning in-built). Most psychotherapists would say that such depression stems from buried grief and pain in the past. For example, someone sexually molested or battered in childhood may become depressed as an adult, or someone who did not allow themselves to mourn a death may become depressed many years later.

Real depression cannot be simply snapped out of, as people often suppose. It usually passes with time - but the time can seem endless. Activities giving companionship and a new interest can help. But for the sufferer to talk, again and again, about the causes of the depression helps most. People with depression need to be listened to and encouraged to find their own solutions, not made to feel yet more inadequate by good advice. This may need professional counselling as well as the support of family and friends.

Other types of depression can be caused by changes in the brain's chemistry. There is now evidence, for example, that manic-depression runs in families, and the inherited fault is likely to be chemical. Also, as light can affect the balance of important chemicals which regulate our moods, some people have winter depression, caused by the lack of light. The treatment is extra artificial light - the amount needed to cheer up some people is phenomenal but others respond to even a slight increase.

Tranquillizers, such as Valium and Librium, are widely prescribed by doctors to help people deal with anxiety and depression. Some people find that they help considerably, but those who take them should realize that they also tend to reduce mental alertness and make people less skilful at driving, rather as alcohol does, and they can cause both physical and mental dependence. They need to be used with care because, in addition to

those dangers, large doses can be fatal, especially if combined with alcohol.

Unfortunately, recent research suggests that withdrawal problems can occur even from medically prescribed doses. The withdrawal symptoms vary, but they include nausea, insomnia, irritability and anxiety, panic attacks, shaking, loss of confidence and even agoraphobia (fear of going out of doors). These can make people feel that the solution lies in more tranquillizers, and the cycle is reinforced. It isn't easy to face up to the world without a familiar crutch - even if the crutch has become a handicap - but those who do it *do* return to normality and to a better life. However, this is still an area of medicine which is not fully understood; some doctors believe that tranquillizers are not addictive - but those who have experienced the ill effects of tranquillizers would say they are wrong. The best way to give up seems to be to come off tranquillizers little by little, with the help of a support group. The organizations below can help and advise.

British Association for Counselling, 37A Sheep Street, Rugby, Warwicks CV21 3BX Tel: 0788 78328/9 - has information on counselling services throughout Britain, both by individual therapists and through varied organizations. Some have low fees for those unable to pay more.

Depressives Associated, P.O.Box 5, Castle Town, Portland, Dorset DT5 1BQ offers support, contact, Inf for sufferers and relatives.

Samaritans, 17 Uxbridge Road, Slough SL1 1SN Tel: 0753 32713/4 is a free confidential service listening to the problems of those in despair. Branches throughout the UK listed in the telephone book, or write or call. Excellent book list, sae appreciated.

Tranx (National Tranquillizers Advice Centre), 17 Peel Road, Harrow, Middx HA3 7QX Tel: 01 427 2065/2827 - RC, M£L, S, F&F, G, L, Adv, A.

See also **Dawn** (page 570) and the book *Agoraphobia* (page 544) by a former tranquillizer 'victim'.

Phobias and Anxieties

A phobia is an overwhelming fear of something which doesn't normally cause fear - or fear on that scale. Agoraphobia is fear of open spaces; claustrophobia is fear of being in small spaces. But people can be phobic about anything. Unlike general 'free-floating' fear or anxiety, a phobia is triggered only by one particular thing, and tends to produce blind panic - with all the physical symptoms that go with it. Most phobias can be successfully treated, and GPs may refer patients to a specialist clinic, but people can also help themselves.

When people get very anxious it can cause a tightening of the throat which makes it hard to swallow. Often this increases their anxiety because they think it is a sign of some serious illness. A visit to the doctor, and something to relax the throat, may solve that part of the problem.

Action on Phobias, 8/9 The Avenue, Eastbourne, East Sussex BN21 3YA Tel: 0323 504755 - RC, L, TR, Inf, sae essential.

The National Association for Mental Health (Mind), 22 Harley Street, London W1N 2ED Tel: 01 637 0741 - RC, M£L, S, F&F, M, G, Rg, A, Ad, Inf, L, B, Res, carers.

National Schizophrenia Fellowship, 78 Victoria Road, Surbiton, Surrey KT6 4NS Tel: 01 390 3651 - M£H, M, G, L, B, Ad, Inf.

The Phobics Society, 4 Cheltenham Road, Chorlton-cum-Hardy, Manchester M21 1QN Tel: 061 881 1937 - RC, M£L, S, F&F, L, G, Inf, Ad, pressure group.

Dorothy Rowe, *Beyond Fear*, Fontana

Ruth Hurst Vose, *Agoraphobia*, Faber & Faber - by a former sufferer.

Myalgic Encephalomyelitis (ME) (Post-viral Fatigue Syndrome)

This disease has only recently been recognized, and is still not fully accepted, although definite biochemical differences have been found in some diagnosed as having it. It seems as if the body fails to make the normal immune response to a virus infection so the sufferer is left with long-term after effects. The major symptom is extreme fatigue. Sufferers are exhausted by simple everyday jobs and find mental activity equally tiring. They feel continually unwell and 'fluey', and there may be pain in the muscles, swelling, soreness, loss of memory, and speech and eyesight problems. There is no cure for ME. Some people recover slowly but completely; others recover but have relapses, and in a few, it becomes chronic.

It looks as if ME is more likely to attack those who refuse to rest up during a viral illness. So ME is a good argument for bed rest, even if it *is* only flu.

Myalgic Encephalomyelitis Association (ME), P.O.Box 8, Stanford-le-Hope, Essex SS17 8EX Tel: 0375 642466 - RC, M£M, F&F, M, group support, Inf, Ad.

Nappy Rash

The most common form of nappy rash is caused by bacteria changing the urine into ammonia, which burns the skin. So change the nappies often, wash the area clean each time, pat dry and apply a cream - such as zinc and castor oil ointment - which acts as a barrier to the urine. Thrush has very similar rash and needs special treatment. Any persistent rash should be medically checked. Rinse towelling nappies very well to avoid a build-up of detergent which can irritate any rash. Ideally, babies should spend as much time as possible during the day nappy-free. An old towel placed under them solves the problem.

Nosebleeds

The most effective way to stop a nose bleed is simply to pinch the nostrils very tightly together for about 20 minutes. But don't pinch a nose which is bleeding because of injury - it needs medical attention.

NSU - see Genital and Sexual Infections, page 564

Piles (Haemorrhoids)

These are varicose veins of the rectum which case itching, pain and even bleeding. The causes include constipation and straining on the lavatory, overweight and pregnancy and perhaps an inherited tendency. Treatment and more roughage in the diet can help.

Plastic Surgery

Plastic surgery for disfigurement of any kind can be obtained on the NHS. But not if the problem is too minor, or for cosmetic surgery. However, there are serious risks in having cosmetic surgery in some of the clinics which advertise in the press, as their doctors may lack the necessary qualifications or skills. The AMI helpline (see page 547) or the Medical Advisory Service can give the names of reputable London plastic and cosmetic surgeons.

To keep bruising to a minimum during plastic surgery, give up spirits and smoking for a month before hand. One top plastic surgeon advises his patients to take a 1 gram vitamin C tablet three times a day for a week before the opertation. (Vitamin C can be useful with any operation which causes bruising.)

Pneumonia and Pleurisy

Pneumonia is an inflammation of the lungs. It can strike any age from tiny babies to the very old, and there are several different types. One of the most common is acute bronchial pneumonia, which has much the same symptoms as bronchitis. Children get a cold and cough, but with a higher temperature. An adult will have a severe cough and high fever, and there may also be pain in the chest. It can usually be controlled with antibiotics, but it may be complicated by pleurisy, in which the membranes encasing the lungs become swollen. This makes breathing very sore, but it usually clears up with the pneumonia. Medical treatment is essential.

Psoriasis

Psoriasis is an unpleasant skin problem which causes reddish patches covered with dry flaky white skin -- which may or may not itch. It can start in childhood, but usually appears after the age of 14. It isn't infectious but, like eczema, it tends to run in families, comes and goes, varies in the area it covers, and increases with illness or emotional upset. Doctors can ease it with various ointments but there is no complete cure, and this is one of the few problems for which dermatologists recommended sunlight.

The Psoriasis Association, 7 Milton Street, Northampton NN2 7JG Tel: 0604 711129 - RC, M£L, M, L, Ad, Inf.

Sinus Trouble

The sinuses are spaces at the back of the nose. In acute sinusitis the tissue lining the sinuses becomes swollen, and full of catarrh, which presses painfully on the swollen tissue. The pain can reach across the forehead and along the cheeks and upper jaw. Use the steam and oil of eucalyptus treatment given on page 535 to ease it. Those who like herbal remedies can drink an infusion of a teaspoon of fresh or dried marjoram in boiling water 2 to 3 times a day while the sinusitis lasts and occasionally from then on. Any cold tea which remains can be sniffed up the nostrils. This is an old Austrian remedy which some sufferers find helpful but it works slowly. Severe sinus trouble needs medical attention.

Shingles

Shingles is a disease which strikes those who have had chicken pox in the past. It is most common in the elderly and the distinctive feature is that it only affects one side of the body. Usually an area becomes painful, then reddens and forms blisters which crust into scabs. Unfortunately, the pain may continue even after the skin has healed, and this is a disease which should always be seen by a doctor. These nasty symptoms are caused by the reawakened chicken pox virus, which has lain dormant in the body. Contact with chicken pox can cause this; the elderly should avoid those who have it.

Sore Throats and Loss of Voice

Most sore throats are caused by virus infections, they can't be cured with antibiotics. Most right themselves in 4 to 5 days, but see a doctor if a throat is getting worse after 2 days, or if there is earache, or the temperature rises above 39·5°C (103°F). Soothe with hot, sweet drinks with a teaspoon of glycerine.

If you have to talk the voice can be improved by gargling with neat whisky or with soluble aspirin in water. But don't give aspirin to young children.

Tonsillitis

Children's tonsils are often plump and look swollen, even when perfectly well: this isn't tonsillitis. Tonsillitis starts as a sore throat, with pain on swallowing and you may be able to see the reddened tonsils with white spots on them. There may also be swollen glands at the side of the neck, and a child will be decidedly unwell with a high temperature. Children usually recover in less than a week, but you should still tell the doctor. Nowadays doctors seldom remove the tonsils unless a child has suffered repeated attacks of tonsillitis.

Don't try to make a child with a very sore throat or infected tonsils eat if it doesn't want to. Just give plenty of soothing and nourishing liquid, and see whether hot or iced drinks are more comfortable.

Splinters, Thorns and Spines

Splinters can often be pulled out with tweezers. Most thorns will ease out with a hot bath and a slight squeeze. If that fails sterilize a fine needle in a flame until it glows red, let it cool and then gently use the tip to pick open the skin over the splinter until it can be pulled out with tweezers. Bathe the area with witch-hazel afterwards. Sea urchin spines won't easily come out that way. Instead, cover them with a piece of paw paw or pineapple for a few hours. Both fruits contain enzymes which cause the skin to open up and allow the thorn to be squeezed or pulled out. Failing that, mix castor oil, as hot as the skin can stand, with flour and apply this under a bandage for 12 hours. The thorn should then come out easily.

Sprains

A joint can be sprained if it's suddenly forced in an unnatural direction, causing bruising and swelling. Put a cold compress on the swelling and immobilize it. An ideal compress is a pack of frozen peas. (Place a cloth between the pack and the skin). Sprains shouldn't be tightly bandaged, but the less any sprain is used the faster it heals. One old-fashioned way to remind yourself of this is a loose bandage of stiff brown paper (hence the nursery rhyme about Jack going to bed 'in vinegar and brown paper'.) Sprains also seem to respond to sunshine. A bad sprain should be seen by a doctor.

Stammering

Nobody knows what causes stammering, but there are a number of speech therapy techniques which reduce it. Speech therapy should be available on the NHS, but not all authorities provide it. Meanwhile, some stammerers find that they can sing without hesitation, even if they can't speak. Worth remembering if the police ask for your licence number and you can't say it.

The College of Speech Therapists (6 Lechmere Road, London NW2 5BU Tel: 01 459 8521) can provide names of therapists in any area.

The Association for Stammerers (Finsbury Health Centre, Pine Street, London EC1R 0JH Tel: 01 278 2323) may also be able to advise on how to find help.

Stress

Probably the most important factor is how people feel about themselves. Those who feel they have failed in some important aspect of their life or who lack, or lose, the circle of warm, caring relationships which family and friends normally provide, or lose a cultural or ethnic identity which they value, feel bad about themselves and are more prone to illness - especially stress diseases.

Happily, reducing stress is easier than you might think. An American insurance company found that if a wife simply kisses her husband goodbye each morning she increases his life expectancy. Patients given a little time and attention by their doctors get well faster than those who just get the medicine. And those who have pets to stroke are less likely to get ill. The message is that being more affectionate to those around you, and joining a club if you are lonely, could do you as much good as a lot of jogging (not that exercise isn't good too). But if you do feel awful let it *out*. A good cry, by either sex, does more good than a drink or tranquillizers. Grief and tension, like bad food, are better out than in. And if you can get someone to hug you while you cry, do so. Human touch is one of the world's biggest healers and all too seldom used.

Stroke

Strokes are caused when the blood vessels of the brain get blocked or break open, damaging or destroying part of the brain. They range from a fleeting inability to speak, and a tingling sensation on one side of the body, to loss of consciousness followed by paralysis on one side. The effects depend on where the brain is damaged. Some people are left with restricted movement and speech but others recover completely, even from a major stroke, because, although damaged brain cells can't be replaced, other sections of the brain can learn to do their job. This only happens if the victim puts in a lot of work. The serious shortage of speech therapists means the family may need to do much of the speech work. (See below, also opposite).

Strokes are three times as likely in those who smoke 20 cigarettes or more a day. The risk is also greater in diabetics and those who have high blood pressure. The contraceptive pill also slightly increases the risk of strokes in young women, especially if there is arterial disease in the family.

Action for Dysphasic Adults (ADA), Northcote House, 37a Royal Street, London SE11 7LL Tel: 01 261 9572 - Ad and guidance on how to help adults who have speech problems following a stroke or head injury. RC, S, F&F, M, excellent leaflets, free help, M£L sae.

The Chest, Heart and Stroke Association, Tavistock House North, Tavistock Square, London WC1H 9JE Tel: 01 387 3012 - referral to stroke clubs, Ad rehabilitation schemes, RC, S, O, F&F, M, L, B, V, F, E, G, Res, sae.

Stye
A stye is an infected pore on the rim of the eye. It doesn't last long or do any harm, so the best course may be to let it cure itself. But bathing it with diluted witch-hazel can be soothing and doctors can prescribe ointments to clear up faster. A traditional cure - unlikely though it sounds - is to rub the stye several times a day with a gold ring.

Sunburn and Suntan
I once heard a woman invite a friend to 'come out and sunbathe'. 'You mean, come out and *age,*' her friend replied. And she was right. Tests have shown skin exposed to the sun gets old faster than uncovered skin.

Sunburn also increases the risk of skin cancer. So sunbathing should be limited and gradual. The nearer you are to the equator, the fiercer the burning rays - even if the heat is no greater. The rays are strongest between 11 am and 2 pm, regardless of temperature. So suit the protection factor of sunscreens to the time of day and place, not the heat - factor 6 is the recommended *minimum* for any white skin. On areas which stick out use a total sun block most of the time. Young children are especially vulnerable and they can even be burnt while swimming, so they should wear an old shirt in the water and a sun block on their face.

Cool sunburn down with a long cool shower, or by covering the area with a towel wrung out in cold water. Then soothe it, and put back some of the oils and moisture the skin has lost with an after-sun lotion. If you have none you can use rosewater mixed with glycerine or even milk, cream or yoghurt.

Testicles Problems
It is *very* important that a boy's testicles are properly in place from babyhood. Sometimes they remain higher up in the body. If this happens he may grow up infertile. So, in the early months, feel both sides, in the bath with a warm hand - when cold, they may rise out of the scrotum. They should feel like two very small eggs inside the bag of skin. If either can't be felt, see a doctor. The earlier this is corrected, the better.

Sometimes the testicles can twist out of place and a boy may get a sudden severe pain low down in the abdomen, and pain in the testicle itself. See a doctor FAST. This is called torsion and it can cut off the blood supply to the testicle and damage it permanently.

Travel Sickness
Research in America has shown that ginger is just as effective as most travel sickness pills, and it has the advantage of not making you sleepy. Eat crystallized ginger, or drink powdered ginger in hot water, sweetened to taste. The Chinese have for centuries drunk ginger tea after meals as a digestive, while in the Caribbean it has been used against morning sickness. So it could be worth trying it for either of these.

The build-up of static electricity in a car may be a factor in car sickness. Spraying the car thoroughly inside with an anti-static spray may therefore help. If queasiness starts, spit out the extra saliva that starts to gather in your mouth, and look ahead exactly as you would when driving.

Ulcers

Peptic Ulcers
These are thought to be due to stress and smoking. They usually cause stomach pains (often in the middle of the night), which may be relieved by drinking milk or taking anti-acids. Anyone who gets pain high in the centre of the stomach, just below the ribs - when hungry or full - possibly with burping or acid regurgitation should see a doctor, especially if the pain goes through to the back. Treatment is now very good and operations are needed far less often. This is one condition in which ancient and modern remedies can work hand in hand. It seems liquorice is still used alongside today's wonder drugs.

Mouth Ulcers
Occasional small mouth ulcers go in a few days without treatment. More severe, or repeated, ulcers should be seen by a doctor, as they can be a sign of illness.

Varicose Veins
Varicose veins are due to a weakness in the walls of surface veins. They start by showing too clearly through the skin, and gradually become twisted, lumpy and achy. As the action of the leg muscles helps push the blood round, the worst thing for varicose veins is standing still. Anyone prone to them should try to keep moving. It also helps to wear support stockings (on prescription) and raise the legs above the head whenever possible. If caught early enough, varicose veins can be treated with injections; they can also be operated on.

Vomiting
Occasional vomiting is seldom anything to worry about. It can be caused by eating too much, by a virus infection or by drink. Some children also tend to vomit whenever they are unwell or even nervous. If anyone feels queasy encourage him to bend over, relax and let it come up. If they feel awful but can't vomit they should put their

fingers in their throat and tickle their uvula (the little pink piece which hangs down above the throat). This usually does the trick and they feel a lot better, but if children are frightened stand behind them and support them gently and calmly. Rinse the mouth to remove the taste, avoid food that day and just drink liquid.

Consult a doctor if there is a stomach pain as well, a child has a temperature of over 38°C (100.4°F) or the vomiting lasts more than 24 hours.(See also pages 562 to 564).

Warts and Verrucas

Warts and verrucas (plantar warts) are both caused by a virus and often go away in time. Some anti-wart preparations may speed up the process and GPs can have them treated at a skin clinic. Doctors aren't agreed about whether covering a verruca stops the infection spreading. But it can't make it worse, so why not do it.

This is a great area for folk remedies. I even know of one skin specialist who 'bought' a patient's warts for sixpence - and they went. It certainly does no harm to try traditional remedies, but don't put plant juice on warts - some of the traditional anti-wart plants can cause skin cancer. For genital warts, see page 566.

Worms

Roundworms are not a common problem in Britain, but they can be picked up from the soil. The adults live in the gut, but the larvae move to the lungs, so they can cause problems in the lungs and in the stomach. They are a good reason to wash hands before eating.

Threadworms are very common, especially in school children. Itching of the anus (back passage opening) is the first symptom, and a check with a hand mirror may show tiny worms like white cotton threads. They may also be seen in the stools. The female worm lays eggs at the outside of the anus during the night. The worms tickle, so the sufferer scratches and eggs get under the fingernails - then go into the mouth when food or the mouth is touched - and are small enough to be breathed in. So some doctors treat the whole family together. Chemists sell effective treatments, but first get advice from a doctor.

Tapeworms can be caught from undercooked pork because the larval tapeworm lives in the pig's flesh. In humans it lives in the gut and takes nourishment from its host. Segments of tapeworm, like grains of rice, can sometimes be seen in stools. This problem is far more common in less developed countries.

Worms from Dogs and Cats

Toxocara canis (and *cati*) is a worm carried by dogs (and occasionally cats), which excrete the eggs. Small children who then crawl on soiled grass may pick up the eggs and transfer them to their mouth on eating. In a human the eggs develop into cysts which invade any part of the body - including the eyes and brain. Cases are fortunately rare, but infected children have been blinded and the cysts can be fatal. So it is better not to let children crawl about where dogs are exercised.

Other Useful Organizations Offering Help

AMI Health Care Ltd has a free help line staffed by nurses who provide basic medical advice or give you the address of any service in the private sector. Just dial 100 and ask for Freefone AMI Harley Street 9 am - 5.30 pm, or write to the **Harley Street Medical Advisory Service**, 46 Wimpole Street, London W1M 7DG.

Association for All Speech Impaired Children, 347 Central Markets, London EC1A 9NH Tel: 01 607 8851/2 helps parents to obtain speech therapy for children with any kind of speech problem. M£L, G, A, Inf, B, pressure group.

Association of Parents of Vaccine Damaged People, 2 Church Street, Shipston-on-Stour, Warwicks CV36 4AP Tel: 0608 61595 - Ad and Inf on compensation when children are damaged by immunization, sae.

The British Medical Association, BMA House, Tavistock Square, London WC1H 9JP Tel: 01 387 4499 — working party reports may be bought by the public.

The British Red Cross Society, 9 Grosvenor Crescent, London SW1X 7EJ Tel: 01 235 5454 offers first aid courses, nursing courses for those nursing someone at home, clubs, holidays and escorts on transport for handicapped and elderly, loan of nursing equipment, and cosmetic camouflage. Free international tracing service for lost relatives. L, sae.

College of Health, 14 Buckingham Street, London WC2N 6DS Tel: 01 839 1222 - has written information on aspects of health and illness, similar to Health Line, below. They also speak for the consumer in the NHS.

Health Education Authority, 78 New Oxford Street, London WC1A 1AH Tel: 01 631 0930 covers health care education, publishes good leaflets on many health topics.

Health Line, P.O.Box 499, London E2 9PU Tel: 01 980 626 is a Freefone help line on which you are connected to recorded information on whatever medical topic you wish to hear about. They also have an advice service on particular problems staffed by counsellors not medical staff.

Intractable Pain Society, Association of Anaesthetists of Great Britain and Northern Ireland, 9 Bedford Square, London WC1B 3RA Tel: 01 631 1650 is mainly for the medical profession but those with incurable pain can seek help and advice from this society. L. It is within the NHS.

Medical Advisory Service, 10 Barley Mow Passage, London W4 4PH Tel: 01 994 9874 (manned by nurses 24 hours a day) Advice on how to obtain all types of medical services, both NHS and private, and how to get in touch with organizations which help with specific problems. RC.

National Association for the Welfare of Children in Hospital (NAWCH), Argyle House, 29-31 Euston Road, London NW1 2SD Tel: 01 833 2041 has campaigned for parents to be able to be with children in hospital and for the emotional needs of children to be considered. M£L, M, G, L, B, Ad, Inf.

Patients' Association, Room 33, 18 Charing Cross Road, London WC2H 0HR Tel: 01 240 0671 - advises patients on their rights and campaigns on their behalf. RC, M£3, S, F&F, L, B, HD, sae.

St Andrew's Ambulance Association, 48 Milton Street, Glasgow G4 0HR Tel:041 332 4031 offers training courses in first aid and home nursing in Scotland.

St John Ambulance Association, 1 Grosvenor Crescent, London SW1X 7EF Tel: 01 235 5231 runs classes in first aid all over Britain. Plus other varied services.

The Scottish Health Education Group, Woodburn House, Canaan Lane, Edinburgh EH10 4SG Tel: 031 447 8044 has useful free leaflets on keeping healthy and also on coping with many health problems - obtainable from local Health Boards. *Well Woman - A Guide to Women's Health* is especially good.

Wider Horizons, Westbrook, Back Lane, Malvern, Worcs WR14 2HJ aims to widen the horizons of the physically disabled. Ad, RC, M£3, S, O, F&F, M, HD, sae.

Wireless for the Bedridden, 81b Corbets Tey Road, Upminster, Essex RM14 2AJ Tel: 040 22 50051 provides radio and TV sets for needy house-bound invalids and the aged throughout the UK.

Professor David Hull ed., *The Macmillan Guide to Child Health*
Peter Parish, *Medicines - a Guide for Everybody*, Penguin
Dr Andrew Stanway, *Prevention is Better...* Century

ALTERNATIVE MEDICINE

Alternative medicine covers all the approaches to healing which are not included in conventional medicine. In Britain more than 5 million people a year now use these therapies - and 1 in 10 are referred by their GP. But the training of practitioners who offer alternative therapy ranges from rigorous four-year full-time courses, similar to those of a conventional medical school, to brief postal courses and many have no qualifications at all. So anyone who uses any alternative therapy should take a hard look at the practitioner's qualifications: in the wrong hands even alternative therapies can be dangerous, yet referral by a doctor is not usually needed.

The most popular therapies are covered below, but anyone needing information on others, such as radionics, can get the details from the **Institute for Complementary Medicine**, (21 Portland Place, London W1N 3AF Tel: 01 636 9543). It keeps a register of qualified practitioners in all fields, and is establishing standards for training. Its information service will help you to find the branch of complementary medicine most suited to your problem and suggest suitable practitioners in your area.

Acupuncture

Acupuncture is an ancient Chinese treatment by which fine needles are inserted into the skin to influence the body's 'vital energy'. Practitioners believe this energy flows round the body along invisible channels and that when people are ill the energy is out of balance. So the aim of the needles is to correct the imbalance by stimulating or calming the flow at precisely the right points along the meridians. Treatments take about half an hour and are not painful like an injection.

Acupuncturists treat all kinds of conditions, ranging from headaches to addiction and strokes. They believe that, whatever the problem, putting the body into harmony can only do good. In France and Germany it is available under national health schemes. In Britain this is rarely so, but some health insurance schemes may cover it. But harm could be done by using it incorrectly; there are also risks from poorly sterilized needles - including AIDS and hepatitis. So it is unwise to go to anyone who is not fully qualified.

The British Acupuncture Association and Register, 34 Alderney Street, London SW1V 4EU Tel: 01 834 1012/3353 keeps a register of fully qualified practitioners.
Ruth Lever, *Acupuncture for Everyone*, Penguin

Chiropractic Treatment

Chiropractic treatment is more specific than many types of alternative medicine. It treats back and other pain arising from mechanical problems in spine and joints.

Nerves carrying messages to and from all parts of the body have to pass through the spinal column to join the spinal cord on their way to the brain. Chiropractors say that the normal alignment of the joints of the spine need only be fractionally altered to put pressure on vital nerves and cause not only back pain, but also pains such as headaches or sciatica which are not felt in the spine itself. Often pressure squeezes one of the discs between the vertebrae so it bulges (the mis-named 'slipped disc') and presses on a nerve, causing pain and immobility.

A fall, jolt or awkward movement can result in these problems, and so can the physical stresses of certain jobs. And, since nerves are extremely sensitive, very slight misalignments - which non-chiropractors may not detect on an X-ray - can cause pain. If a problem isn't treated muscles adapt, so a back problem may appear to go away when it has only been masked. This is why stress and tension will often trigger back pain, and also why it may come and go.

Treatment involves a careful diagnosis, often using X-rays. If a problem is found, precise manipulation is done with the hands to restore the back to normal. This doesn't hurt. I speak from experience - when I was crippled by back pain chiropractic treatment painlessly cured it in days. But a long-term problem will be harder to put right and a longer course of treatment may be needed. So it is always best to seek treatment soon.

There is often confusion between chiropractors and osteopaths. Both manipulate the spine, but chiropractors are more likely to use X-rays during the initial diagnosis: which could detect certain conditions which should not be manipulated. Chiropractors are also less likely to work on the soft tissue, and their manipulative technique is usually more precise. In Britain chiropractic treatment cannot be obtained under the NHS or on health insurance as it can in America, Canada, Switzerland and Denmark. A chiropractor should be a member of the British Chiropractic Association and have done a full-time four-year training at a recognized college with strict entry requirements.

British Chiropractic Association, Premier House, Greycoat Place, London SW1P 1SB Tel: 01 272 8866
Anthea Courtenay, *Chiropractic for Everyone*, Penguin

Herbalism

Herbalists believe they can cure a wide range of conditions with plant substances alone. But they like to look beyond the immediate symptoms, to the body's total state. Each person is seen as unique and their aim is to restore 'balance and health' by helping the body to heal itself. They take an equally holistic view of plant remedies. Nature, they believe, has balanced medically active chemicals so that using a whole plant avoids side effects, whereas isolating a particular chemical is far more hazardous. Most medical chemists would not agree with that. But the skill of the herbalist is in knowing which plants are beneficial and which harmful.

Herbalism isn't available on the NHS, although some GPs are also herbalists.

National Institute of Medical Herbalists, 41 Hatherley Road, Winchester, Hants SO22 6RR Tel: 0962 68776 - large sae for lists of qualified practitioners.

Homeopathy

The idea behind homeopathy is that giving a patient minute doses of natural remedies will stimulate the body's own defence and healing mechanisms. Choosing the right remedy involves both diagnosing the condition, and the general physical condition and personality. So two patients with the same disease may be given different remedies. Most remedies are made from pure animal, plant or mineral sources, which are then successively diluted - until many doctors would claim that too little of the active ingredient remains to be of any use. However, homeopathy enjoys Royal patronage and it seems to work well for certain conditions, particularly colds.

There are five homeopathic hospitals in Britain, with both out-patient and in-patient facilities and homeopathy has always been recognized by the NHS. Ask the Association below for the name of a properly qualified practitioner.

The British Homeopathic Association, 27a Devonshire Street, London W1N 1RJ Tel: 01 935 2163

Naturopathic Medicine

Naturopaths see illness as something affecting the body, mind and spirit of the whole person. They believe the body possesses the power to heal itself, and that disease is the outward sign that the body is fighting against some block which prevents it from functioning as it should. So the aim of naturopathic treatment is also to find out why the patient became ill and try to prevent future illness. This involves educating the patient to take responsibility for his or her own health through correct diet, rest, exercise and hygiene, as well as using specific therapies to remove the block to good health. Diet, fasting, relaxation techniques, chiropractic and osteopathic treatment, exercises, homeopathy, electrotherapy, herbalism and hydrotherapy may all play a part in this. So practitioners qualified in other fields, such as osteopaths, may also practise naturopathy (address under Osteopathy, below).

Osteopathy

Much of what I have written about chiropractic above applies to osteopaths. In both cases, a fully qualified practitioner will have done a four-year training which includes a considerable amount of basic medicine as well as specialist training. But the founder of osteopathy believed that the cures brought about by spinal manipulation were due to improved circulation of the blood, whereas chiropractors relate their treatment to the nervous system. Osteopaths also make broader claims for their treatment than chiropractors and usually believe it helps conditions which have no obvious link with the spine. This may be because they more often work on the soft tissues than do chiropractors.

Unfortunately, some osteopaths are fully trained, some are self-taught physiotherapists or masseurs and others are totally unqualified. Only members of a professional association should be consulted.

After a fall or whiplash injury it could be wisest to consult a practitioner who uses X-rays; then there is no risk of a fracture going undiagnosed.

British Naturopathic and Osteopathic Association, c/o W.V. Copeland Esq FCA, Slaters, 5 Guildford Road, Broadbridge Heath, Horsham, W. Sussex RH12 3JT Tel: 0403 65087 - £1 and a large sae obtains a list of members; there is also an out-patients clinic there.

Psychotherapy and Analysis

What distinguishes psychotherapy from other help for mental problems is that the treatment is purely talking. The patient may be depressed, afraid or have swings of emotion which seem to have no foundation. Psycho-analysis is a type of psychotherapy. It is usually longer and involves more frequent sessions than other forms of psychotherapy.

The patient sees the psychotherapist at regular intervals and talks about thoughts, feelings and memories. The aim is to allow the patient to understand the unconscious, as well as conscious, aspects of his or her feelings and behaviour, bring out what is happening inside them and realize how the roots of their behaviour have been formed. The therapist guides and questions, but does not tell the patient what to do. So it is a process of exploration, rather than advice. It is fundamental to psychotherapy that behaving in a new way will only work if the need for the old ways of behaving has gone.

The self-exploration may mean reliving memories which are distressing. So it can be important for the patient and psychotherapist or analyst to start with some rapport. See more than one for an initial consultation and choose whoever suits you.

Most sessions last 50 minutes, 1-5 times a week. Nobody can predict how long analysis will need to last. For some people it is 2 to 3 years, for others much longer.

One essential is that the analyst is properly trained and qualified but those who are well qualified don't normally advertise. So regard advertisements with suspicion. The following professional organizations will refer people to those who are properly qualified.

The Institute of Psycho-Analysis, 63 New Cavendish Street, London W1M 7RD Tel: 01 580 4952/3/4 has a good guide to psychoanalysis in Britain.

Society of Analytical Psychology, 1 Daleham Gardens, London NW3 5BY Tel: 01 435 7696

British Association of Psychotherapists, 121 Hendon Lane, London N3 3PR Tel: 01 346 1747

Lindsay Knight, *Talking to a Stranger - A Consumer's Guide to Therapy,* Fontana

Spiritual Healing

Spiritual healing is not limited to any one religion or denomination, and those with no religious faith can still be healed - provided they are determined to get well. The healer may touch the patient, or practise absent healing, for the basic principle is that divine energy is channelled to the patient by the healer. The healer asks for the patient to be healed in whatever way is best for him or her. So the result could be a cure, but it might equally be giving someone the tranquillity to handle their condition. Of course, that isn't healing in the medical sense, but the test is not whether doctors rate it as healing, but whether patients do. And some certainly do.

Members of the National Federation of Spiritual Healers work to a code of conduct which insists that diagnosis must be done by a doctor and that the healer must not countermand instructions or prescriptions given by a doctor. Nor may they ask patients to undress, or prescribe medicines. So healers should be told what medical treatment patients are having, and the doctor should be told about the spiritual healing, but it is not available on the NHS.

National Federation of Spiritual Healers, Old Manor Farm Studio, Church Street, Sunbury-on-Thames, Middx TW16 6RG Tel: 0932 783164

Transcendental Meditation

This is not a system of alternative medicine as such, and those who teach meditation don't claim to be healers. I include it because there is now medical evidence that regular meditation reduces the mental and physical symptoms of stress. The GPs' magazine *The Practitioner* in 1987 said studies showed 'a consistent reduction in blood pressure' after meditation and 'meditation may be a promising clinical intervention technique for stress-related disorders ranging from fear of enclosed spaces . . . to generalised anxiety, anxiety neurosis, back pain . . . rehabilitation after myocardial infarct and bronchial asthma.' The article added that there have been reports of 'a number of cases of regression of cancer after intensive meditation in the absence of any orthodox treatment which could have accounted for the regression'. Remarkably high praise from a doctor and courses training doctors in meditation are now provided by the British Postgraduate Medical Federation.

There are numerous meditation techniques but one of the most widely available is transcendental meditation (TM). It is a useful technique for anyone who wishes to iron out the emotional creases which modern living puts into most of us. I have far more energy when I meditate than when I don't. Although TM has a certain amount of philosophy and semi-psychology (which you can take or leave), it does not have religious overtones, so you can practise it whatever your belief, or unbelief.

Transcendental Meditation, Roydon Hall, Seven Mile Lane, East Peckham, Tonbridge, Kent TN12 5NH Tel: 0622 813243/812121

BASIC MEDICAL FACTS

Blood Pressure

There is no hard and fast figure which represents a 'normal' blood pressure, nor do doctors entirely agree on what is ideal. But somewhere between 110/70 and 125/80 is average for an adult — though some people with naturally low blood pressure may be closer to 100/60.

Blood doesn't circulate in an even stream, but in a series of spurts. So the pressure peaks in the blood vessels just after a heart beat and then ebbs until the next one. The two blood pressure figures represent the pressure when the force is at its peak and at its lowest. The stronger the arteries, the more they resist the force of the blood, and the lower the blood pressure. As you get older, and the elasticity arteries weaken, the figures tend to rise, but the lower figure should be under 90 until you are in your sixties.

Infectious Diseases

All the following diseases have one thing in common: the older you are when you have them, the worse they are likely to be. If you think someone has any of these illnesses phone a doctor and explain the symptoms, and which illness he or she has been in contact with - the doctor will probably prefer an infectious patient to stay away from the surgery.

	Chicken pox (varicella)	German measles (rubella)	Measles
Incubation period	14-16 days	14-21 days	10-14 days
Cause	Virus	Virus	Virus
Symptoms	Separate red spots which each form a blister, then a crust, and itch severely. Moderately high temperature peaking about day 2 and lasting several days more.	A mild illness lasting about 10 days. Lowish temperature tends to peak on 6th day. There is a fine rash on about the 5th day. Adults may be far more ill and have severe joint pains.	Begins like a bad cold, and cough. After 3-4 days a slightly itchy red rash starts behind the ears, and spreads. Fever usually peaks on 4th day, and is often high. The eyes and mouth may be sore, light may tire eyes.
Infectious period	Starts the day before the rash appears, and lasts until all the scabs have totally dried up.	Starts several days before the illness begins, ends a week after the spots appear.	Infectious from several days before the rash, until 5 days later, or when the child stops being ill - whichever is later.

	Chicken pox (varicella)	German measles (rubella)	Measles
Treatment	Keep spots dry in early stages (e.g. no bath). Soothe with calamine lotion. Do not scratch off scabs or scars will be left. Antihistamine will ease the itching.	Usually so mild it may not even need bed rest. But stay indoors.	Consult a doctor and give complete bed rest in a darkened room. This is not an illness to take lightly.
Special features	See Shingles, page 545.	Keep away from women who might be pregnant. In the first 3 months of pregnancy this illness may cause abortion, or a deaf, blind or heart-diseased baby.	There can be complications such as ear, eye and heart problems. Tell the doctor if there are signs of these. Signs of deafness should be watched for afterwards.

	Mumps	Scarlet Fever	Whooping Cough (pertussis)
Incubation period	16-21 days	2-4 days	7-10 days
Cause	Virus	Bacterium	Bacterium
Symptoms	Starts with a moderate temperature. After 1-3 days glands below the ear and along the jaw swell painfully, on one side or both. A very sore throat and earache are common. If males get swollen balls tell the doctor immediately.	Sore throat, headache, moderately high temperature. Fine red rash starts in 12 hours and spreads.	Feel ill and cough and catarrh for 1-2 weeks. Then cough becomes severe, with a whooping noise between coughs and usually vomiting. This lasts 4-6 weeks, and takes a long time to go.
Infectious period	Starts several days before the symptoms. Ends when the swellings are down to normal.	Starts several days before the first symptoms. Ends when fully recovered.	Highly infectious from the first symptoms, until 3 weeks after the start of coughing.
Treatment	There is no specific treatment, but the swellings should go in 7-10 days.	Bed rest while fever lasts. Calamine lotion may soothe the rash.	A doctor may use antibiotics to relieve the whoop, but the main treatment is rest and soothing drinks.
Special features	Tell a doctor IMMEDIATELY if there is a headache, dislike of light or a stiff neck. Males who have this after puberty, and have swelling in both balls, may become permanently sterile. Those with mumps should keep away from men who have not had it. Occasionally deafness afterwards; watch out for this.		

Immunization for Britain

No vaccine *guarantees* against an illness, but the following vaccines can give better than 90 per cent protection. The ages at which the injections should be given are regularly changed by the authorities, and there is now a new vaccine combining mumps, measles and German measles. So the table is only a rough guideline. Discuss the possibilities with a GP or Health Visitor shortly after a baby's birth.

Age	Disease	Method and Comments
Early days	Tuberculosis (BCG)	For babies born to high-risk families.
3 months	Diphtheria	Usually given in 3 doses with tetanus and whooping cough, second dose 6-8 weeks after the first, third dose 4-6 months after that. Mild feverish reaction is not unusual. **Booster** usually given before starting school.
3 months	Tetanus	Basic course is 3 doses, timed as for diphtheria. A **booster** at age 5 and at 15-19 years. Also after an injury which could be infected - though not within 5 years of a previous booster. Any puncture wound, or one in contact with soil has a risk of tetanus.

Age	Disease	Method and Comments
3 months	Whooping cough	Basic course is 3 doses, timed as for diphtheria. Mild feverish reaction usual shortly afterwards and the arm may be sore and red. Extreme reactions are exceedingly rare. **Boosters** are not needed.
3 months	Poliomyelitis	Basic course is 3 doses, as for diphtheria. **Booster** at age 5 and at 15-19. Adults may need extra **boosters** if travelling to high-risk areas.
1-2 years	Measles	Some children have a mild fever and/or a rash 7-12 days later. Serious side effects are rare.
10-14 years	German measles (Rubella)	For females only. One dose is enough. There may be a reaction 1-3 weeks later, with fever, sore throat and rash. Pregnancy *must* be avoided for 3 months after this injection.
10-14 years	BCG (tuberculosis)	One dose is normally enough. A reaction in 2-6 weeks on the site of the injection is normal. A light dressing can be used until the scab forms, but shutting out air may cause a large scar. Severe local reactions are possible.
Adults	Anthrax	Four spaced doses, plus annual **boosters** can be given to those who may encounter infected animal products during their work. Side effects are mild and rare.

Medicines

Analgesics

Government warnings have been issued against giving aspirin to children under the age of 12, except on medical advice. There is a rare, and possibly fatal, condition which aspirin can occasionally cause in young children. So children should be given paracetamol instead. Aspirin, paracetamol or neurofen are all suitable for adults. But - at any age - the soluble or specially coated versions of analgesics are safest: the ordinary tablets can stick to the lining of the stomach, and cause bleeding. Anyone who has to take analgesics regularly should see a doctor.

Antibiotics

Antibiotics are used to treat ailments caused by bacteria, but not those caused by viruses as viruses are not killed by them.

Doctors prescribe the amount of antibiotic needed for a course of treatment. Even if the illness seems to clear up before the medicine is finished it is important to keep on taking it. If you don't finish the treatment the remaining bacteria, which were the toughest to kill, may live on. This is how antibiotic-resistant bacteria are created.

Taking Medicines

Whenever any medicine is prescribed here are some questions which the patient ought to ask the doctor (as appropriate).

- Can I drink alcohol while taking them?
- May they make me sleepy?
- Is it safe to drive or operate machinery while taking them?
- Will they have any effect on the contraceptive pill? (Some stop it working.)
- Are there any side effects I should know about?
- Are there any over the counter medicines I shouldn't take at the same time?

Check precisely when any medicine should be taken. Some drugs need to be taken on an empty stomach (i.e. an hour before or after food), some must have food immediately before and after them, and others need to be taken straight after a meal. Some medicines won't work properly if you don't get this right. If you forget a dose don't just take a double dose next time: this could be dangerous - if the medicine is for a serious complaint ask a doctor or pharmacist what to do having missed a dose.

Temperature Taking

It is best to take a child's temperature in the armpit until he or she is about the age of 5. After that, a sensible, normal child can usually have it taken under the tongue, provided it knows the thermometer is fragile - though it's best for an adult to be there. For an accurate reading shake the thermometer to below normal by holding it firmly and giving several quick flicks of the hand, with a loose wrist. Keep the thermometer in place for 2 to 3 minutes, with the mouth closed, or the arm firmly against the body, so it has time to register fully.

It would be nice if I could tell you that below a certain temperature you didn't have to worry, and above it you had to ring the doctor. But temperatures aren't like that. Any fever shows someone has an infection, but the height of the fever *doesn't* show the seriousness of the infection because:
- some illnesses provoke higher temperatures, without being more serious
- some people get higher fevers than others without being any more ill
- young children run higher temperatures than older children or adults who are equally ill
- temperatures are often higher in the evening than in the morning
- the elderly can be quite ill yet have little or no temperature.

By the law of nuisance small children fall ill at

weekends, or near midnight, just when it is impossible to ring the surgery. In deciding if a child or adult is ill enough for you to telephone a doctor look at all the other indications of illness too. A very young baby may be really ill yet have no fever at all; equally, children can sometimes run quite high temperatures yet seem to be only a little poorly. In these cases the other symptoms would tell you not to go by the thermometer, and research has shown that mothers in particular are rather good at judging illness in their own children.

If a young baby is listless and off its food contact a doctor, even if there are no other signs of illness. This is not the same as a fretful child who is off its food and is clearly teething.

°C	°F	
40·6 –	– 105	Temperatures seldom go much above this.
40·0 –	– 104	A high temperature.
39·4 –	– 103	
38·9 –	– 102	
38·3 –	– 101	
37·8 –	– 100	
37·2 –	– 99	
37·0 –	– 98·4	The average temperature taken under the
36·1 –	– 97	tongue but some people register a
35·6 –	– 96	degree lower.
35·0 –	– 95	Below this temperature the patient has hypothermia.

Treating a Temperature
The traditional way of treating someone with a temperature was to put them to bed and keep them warm. However, some children under the age of 5 get convulsions when they have a fever. (This is more likely to happen if the temperature rises very rapidly and if fits run in the family.) So the latest nursing procedure is to bring the temperature down by giving paracetamol, *not* wrapping the child up or putting it to bed (unless it wants to be there) but sponging it cool with *tepid* water, leaving the water on the skin. I am assured that this won't give a child pneumonia. So this is probably the best course to follow with a young child, unless a doctor has advised otherwise.

However, some doctors believe that, like most of the body's reactions, a fever is a survival mechanism which helps to fight infection. They say, therefore, that although cool sponging may be soothing for adults and older children a fever should not be brought down with paracetamol unless it is uncomfortably high (40°C, 104°F).

Whether an adult or older child should go to bed or not is a matter of how they feel. If they want to be tucked up and warm let them. The body tends to know what it needs. Equally, if they feel more comfortable

and cool out of bed they should come to no harm.

If a child does have a fit it will become unconscious and may go stiff and jerk strangely. Fits usually end in a few minutes, but stay with the child until it does to make sure it doesn't hurt itself, then ring your doctor.

The surface temperature, measured under the armpit, is about 0·6°C (1°F) lower than the temperature measured under the tongue or (as on the Continent) up the bottom.

If you find conventional thermometers hard to read there is now an 'Easy Read' thermometer which really is easy to read.

★ Most adults have a pulse rate of about 60 to 80 beats a minute, but top athletes have considerably lower rates.

Travel Care

Medical Agreements with Other Countries
Britain has agreements with a number of countries which allow British passport holders to use their health services. The DHSS form SA30 lists the countries covered, the free treatment you may be entitled to and how to obtain it or get costs refunded. (Form SA35 shows what immunizations you may need. Both forms are in travel agents and DHSS offices.)

Within the EEC you can only use this concession if you have form E111, which you apply for on form SA30. If you leave in a rush you can, in theory, post the application for the E111 and ask them to send it to your overseas address - but they aren't geared for that.

If you don't have an E111 and find you need treatment, you can ask the health insurance authorities in that country to write to the DHSS Overseas Branch (as below) and obtain the form for you.

★ These forms don't cover anyone moving to live in another EEC country, and they should apply to the DHSS Overseas Branch, Newcastle-on-Tyne, NE98 1YX for details of their rights to EEC benefits.
★ Form E111 used to last for two years, it now lasts for ever - or until you have to give it to officials in another country to get treatment. If that happens you just get a new E111 before your next trip.
★ Take form SA30 with you when you go to a non-EEC country. Often you pay first then get a refund, the form tells you how to get it. Some countries need you to produce a passport; others want to see a driving licence or medical card to show you are *resident* in Britain. So take the necessary papers.

What You Get under these Agreements
In the EEC you are entitled to the same treatment as a national of the country. So in France we should get any free treatment a Frenchman would get and so on. It may be considerably less than you would get in Britain and the services usually cover sudden illness and accident; chronic illness may not.

In many other countries only certain medical needs are covered. For example, injuries from car accidents are not covered in some countries. On top of that, health scheme treatment may not be to the standard you are used to - and the cost of private treatment in some countries can be bankrupting. So it is never wise to assume that you don't need medical insurance.

If you do need treatment while away *tell* the medical staff that you wish to have it under their health scheme and have your passport with you.

Immunizations

Travel in other developed countries usually has health risks similar to here and, apart from checking the water, special precautions are seldom needed. But hot climates may foster diseases which are not found in Britain, and unhygienic conditions and food preparation increase the risks. There is also a big difference between the health hazards of staying in good accommodation, and of travelling rough. The immunizations which are advisable vary not only with the country but also with the circumstances of your visit. In addition, some countries may insist on evidence of certain vaccinations before you cross their borders. Three months before travelling abroad check whether any immunizations are needed.

The following table covers the most usual immunizations but get the latest information on what is needed where (see page 556).

Immunizations Which May be Needed When Travelling

	Cholera	Hepatitis A	Hepatitis B	Malaria	Polio
Immunization	2 injections not less than 1 wk apart	Injection of immunoglobulin	2 injections of vaccine 1 mth apart, booster in mth 6	None. Take preventative tablets from 1 wk before *until 6 wks after leaving malaria area.*	Unimmunized adults need 3 doses each 4 wks apart, and those immunized may need a booster
Timing	2+ wks before departure	Just before trip	1 mth before travel	Order tablets 2 wks before travel	4 months (if 1st time), only days if booster
Reaction	Tenderness where injected, fever, headache	Nil	Soreness where injected	Nil	Very rare cases develop polio
Protection	50-60%	Lessens the severity of the illness	Very variable	90%	95+%
Duration of protection	6 mths	3 mths	Perhaps 5 yrs	Only while tablets are taken	10 yrs
Other precautions	Avoid food or water which might be dirty. Low risk in reasonable tourist accommodation.	As typhoid	Avoid contact with blood, semen or saliva of potential carriers	Anti-mosquito spray on skin, knock down spray in rooms, covering clothes, mosquito nets	Nil
Incubation	Rapid	3-5 wks	60 days - 9 mths or symptomless	12-30+ days	3-21 days
Symptoms	Sudden watery diarrhoea, vomiting, collapse, rarely fatal	Fever, nausea, stomach ache, jaundice	Loss of appetite, slight stomach pain, nausea, possibly fever and jaundice. Rarely fatal.	Fever and sweating, then chills and shivering. In one form coma and possibly fatal shock.	Headache, stiff neck and back, fever, stomach upset.
Treatment	No food, *plenty* of clean liquid with 1 flat tsp salt and 5-8 tsp sugar per litre (or ORT preparation, see page 537, from a chemist)	Drink no alcohol		Drink no alcohol	
Notes	Some countries need evidence of immunization 6 days - 6 mths before crossing their border. Not recommended for children under 1 year.	In children it may be mild with no jaundice	A new and costly vaccine. Usually only given to those at high risk, such as health care workers.	Malaria in pregnancy is a danger to both mother and child. And some key drugs used in prevention cannot be taken when pregnant or given to the very young.	Not usually given in early months of pregnancy

	Rabies	Smallpox	Tetanus	Typhoid	Yellow Fever
Immunization	2 doses 4 wks apart, booster 12 mths, and as needed thereafter	In 1980 the WHO declared the world free of smallpox. Immunization is no longer given.	Normally given in childhood. Boosters every 10 years.	1-2 injections 4-6 wks apart	1 injection
Timing	5 wks before trip		Not critical	5-7 wks before departure	At least 10 days before departure, for certificate to be valid
Reactions	Soreness where injected, headache, muscle ache, vomiting, possible within 48 hrs		Rarely headache, lethargy	Soreness at injection, nausea, headache - worst in those over 35, and on repeat immuniz-ations - lasts 36 hours	Possibly slight headache and low fever 5-10 days later
Protection	Some doctors say it prevents rabies, others that it enables a faster response to preventative treatment if bitten. Recommend it.		95+%	70-90%	Almost 100%
Duration of protection	3 months		Around 10 years	1-3 years, boosters after that	10 years
Other precautions	Avoid bites, scratches or licks from *any* animals. If these occur wash the wound *fast and thoroughly* with antiseptic. Get IMMEDIATE medical treatment. DO NOT wait for symptoms.		Avoid getting wounds, and wash them well, use antiseptic	Avoid food, milk or water which could be contaminated with sewage or by flies	Against mosquitoes, as for malaria
Incubation	2-8 weeks normal, can be 9 days - 2 years		4-21 days	Usually 1-3 weeks	1-5 days
Symptoms	The wound feels odd, fever, headache, followed by either paralysis and coma, or hallucinations and wild behaviour. Usually fatal unless treated *before* symptoms occur.		Violent contractions of the muscles	Vomiting and diarrhoea, possibly fever	Sudden fever, vomiting, prostration, jaundice, can be fatal
Treatment	**Get medical attention at once**		**Get medical attention at once**	**Get medical attention at once**	
Notes	A relatively new immunization well worthwhile when visiting high-risk areas		Caught from the soil. Any skin puncture outdoors a risk. Keep immu-nization up to date in the UK and overseas.		Only available at special centres. Children under 9 months not immunized. Some countries require proof of immunization.

Some immunizations can only be given at special centres and even these may not carry all the vaccines. Check that a doctor or clinic has what you need before going.

Where to Get Advice
Any GP can give immunizations and prescribe anti-malaria tablets. But GPs get their information from government recommendations, which are likely to be out of date. In malaria there is a growing problem of drug resistance. So drugs which worked last year may not be safe this year. So it can be well worth getting up-to-the-minute information from the London School of Hygiene and Tropical Medicine. There is a recorded malaria information line on 01 636 8636.

The London School of Hygiene and Tropical Medicine also validates information for a highly efficient service called MASTA, in which you fill in a form giving all your medical details, where you are going and the conditions. They then tell you the health precautions you should take. Charges vary according to the level of information you want. You can simply get basic information on advisable immunizations and anti-malarial tablets, or have a general briefing on health precautions, or get a thorough run-down on all the health hazards in any area, how to prevent them, recognize the symptoms and treat them. This last could be invaluable to anyone travelling rough or doing VSO. Up to three other members of the family are covered at no extra charge.

Apply to MASTA 2 to 3 months ahead; then there is time to get immunizations and they can give you the latest facts on local epidemics and drug-resistant malaria. Regular travellers can have a subscription service. MASTA also sells items like small sterile medical kits for countries where unsterilized needles carry the risk of hepatitis and AIDS. The forms are available from the pharmacist in any branch of Boots, or by post from: **MASTA**, Keppel Street, London WC1 7HT or phone 01 631 4408.

Some travellers, needing blood transfusions or injections while overseas, have caught AIDS. It is not always easy to know whether blood is or is not adequately checked for AIDS but can be prepared for the worst.

- Know your blood group and agree mutual blood transfusion with a fellow traveller, of the same blood group, who seems unlikely to have AIDS.
- Take a kit of sterile medical needles (from MASTA, above) to countries where they might not be sterilized.
- Ask your doctor to prescribe Haemocell (a blood substitute, which can be used instead of a blood transfusion) to take with you, and take enough to last while you are flown to the nearest good medical centre. It comes in small packs, needs no special storage conditions, and will last the duration of an average trip.

British Airways Medical Centre, 75 Regent Street, London W1 Tel: 01 439 9584 Weekdays 08.30 - 16.30 - appointments preferred - gives immunizations and Ad on health precautions.

PPP Immunization Clinic 99 New Cavendish Street, London W1M 7FQ Tel: 01 637 8941 - open to anyone, without appointment, from 9.30 - 16.30 Monday to Friday (rabies is on Wednesday mornings only) and PPP subscribers get a reduction. A computer link keeps its information totally up to date, and they do some unusual immunizations, such as yellow fever.

Thomas Cook Ltd 45 Berkeley Street, London W1A 1EB Tel: 01 408 4157 - offers a walk-in service (08.30 - 17.30 weekdays, 9-12 am Saturdays) giving immunizations and advice on malaria.

General Precautions
It's easy to be unduly alarmed about hygiene and the risk of illness in strange countries. But being ill abroad can really spoil a trip. So judge which of the following precautions are needed and err slightly on the side of caution, but without seeing germs in every corner.
- Wear covering clothing - malaria is not the only disease carried by biting insects.
- Wear covering shoes - against ticks, bugs, hookworms, scorpions, etc.
- Do not enter fresh water (except swimming pools) - some exceedingly nasty conditions (e.g. bilharzia or liver fluke) can enter through the skin.
- Cover all wounds with plaster - some flies lay eggs in human cuts.
- Take a torch to countries which may have nasties underfoot, or wild animals in the bushes.
- Don't use scent or wear bright clothes in tropical countries which have stinging insects - they like both.
- Ask about possible hazards. Don't be embarrassed about seeming ignorant. Things aren't always the way common sense suggested - for example, some tiny African scorpions are far more poisonous than some large ones.

Serious Illness or Death
If you need to come home lying down, the airline has no obligation to transport you in that position unless you pay for the extra seat space. Such costs should be covered by holiday insurance. If you die while abroad you return as freight, in which case the airline may refund to your estate the difference between freight and passenger charges either as an obligation or as a favour depending on the type of return ticket.

More information
Dr Richard Dawood, *Travellers' Health*, OUP (paperback)

DENTAL HEALTH

Children's First Teeth
A child's first teeth are already in the jaw bone at birth. The first tooth cuts through at about 6 months - some sooner, some later. The other 19 will appear before the child is three.

Children often become fretful and flushed. Rubbing the bump where the tooth is coming through with a clean finger usually helps a lot. Teething rings also help, especially those filled with liquid, which can be

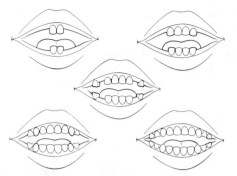

The Order in which Teeth usually Appear

refrigerated to soothe with coldness. But don't put all problems down to teething. It should never make the child ill. And *don't* comfort the child between meals with a sweetened drink - not even if it has 'health drink' written on the bottle. Any sweetness in a bottle just encourages the bacteria which are waiting to eat into the baby's lovely new teeth. The same goes for sweetened comforters.

Children's Second Teeth
The second teeth usually start coming through when the child is 5 to 7 years old and they keep on coming until adulthood.

Cleaning the Teeth
The time to start brushing is when the first tooth comes through. The sooner you start, the sooner the baby gets used to it. Use a soft, very small toothbrush with the child on your lap and its head cradled in your arm. Brush up and down rather than across the teeth, and do the inside surface as well as the outside. Until it is old enough to spit do without toothpaste, but use fluoride toothpaste when you can, and clean the teeth twice a day from then on - especially last thing at night. Once the teeth have been cleaned the child should not have food, drinks (apart from water) or liquid medicine, as they will all give the tooth decay bacteria a new feast to work on during the night.

Until the age of 8 or so children aren't thorough enough to do their teeth alone. When they do take over the job, occasionally use a disclosing tablet (most chemists sell them) which will (briefly) stain any badly cleaned patches a lurid colour and show a child which bits they haven't cleaned. Children usually find it fascinating and it is much easier than just nagging.

★ If you are ever out of toothpaste, salt makes a very good substitute.

Decay
Teeth decay when bacteria which live in a thin coating of plaque on the teeth have a chance to feed on sugar and change it into acid. The acid then dissolves the teeth. Each time we eat or drink something sweet the bacteria create acid for about one hour afterwards. So a child who eats about one sweet every hour bathes his or her teeth in acid for a whole day, and children's teeth are especially vulnerable.

Dental Checks
The first dental check is needed at about 2 to 2½ years old. However much you hate dental treatment yourself, don't let the child know. Say the dentist is going to count the child's new teeth - and tell the dentist, in front of the child. Then the dentist can take your cue.

How often dental checks are needed varies with the person, and dentists themselves are not totally agreed. But a child or teenager usually needs a check-up every 6 months, and an adult once a year.

Gum Disease - Gingivitis and Periodontis (Pyorrhoea)
Most adults have gum disease to some degree, and more teeth are lost because of it than from any other condition. The cause is a sticky film of bacteria forming on the teeth. This attacks the junction between teeth and gums. The rim of the gums then loosens, making access easier for the bacteria, and providing a pocket for food debris. Finally the bacteria attack the bone holding the teeth in place.

> Warning signs: a coating you can see or feel on the teeth; red or swollen gums; bleeding from the gums on brushing them; pain or soreness; a certain type of bad breath.

Prevent it by very thorough brushing, at least once a day, and by cleaning between the teeth with dental floss and/or special soft wood sticks such as 'Interdens', plus regular dental checks and descaling. For plaque which is left on the teeth hardens into calculus (tartar) which is hard to remove. Pregnancy and certain illnesses lower resistance to gum trouble, so more frequent checks are necessary, but I am assured that it is not infectious. So the kissing doesn't have to stop.

Orthodontics
Teeth can be crooked or badly placed for a lot of reasons. Orthodontics is the work of persuading the teeth to move into better positions. It used to be thought that orthodontic work couldn't be done in adulthood, but in America women in their thirties are to be seen in braces - and with beautifully straight teeth afterwards. But it is quicker and easier when done in childhood: talk to a dentist about it is as soon as you see the teeth aren't looking good.

This treatment is available on the NHS provided the dentist feels it is clinically necessary, and there is no hard and fast definition of what 'clinically necessary' means.

★ To deal with bleeding after a tooth extraction rinse the mouth with a solution of a dessertspoonful of salt in a tumbler of warm water. This cleans the socket and removes the taste of blood without interfering with the natural healing.
★ If the jaw aches after an extraction wrap an ice cube in a handkerchief and press it to the cheek. The cold both numbs the pain and reduces any bruising.

If a child's tooth is knocked out act fast - you may be able to save it. Rinse any dirt off it in lukewarm water swiftly and pop it in the pocket of your cheek (or get the owner to do that if she or he is old enough not to swallow it). It has to be kept moist and at mouth temperature and teeth don't mind alien saliva. Get the tooth and its owner to a dentist in 1 to 2 hours. If the root isn't fully adult it should be possible to put it back.

British Dental Association, 64 Wimpole Street, London W1M 8AL Tel: 01 935 0875 - will provide a list of dentists in your area, and answer queries, but it does *not* deal with complaints.

British Dental Health Foundation, 88 Gurnards Avenue, Fishermead, Milton Keynes, Bucks MK19 6AE - has leaflets, sae needed.

FIRST AID

First aid seems like the kind of thing which would be commonsensical and stay very much the same. In fact, even common sense isn't static and first aid is constantly changing and improving in the light of new developments. What follows is the very latest thinking in the field - so don't be surprised if it isn't what you've learnt. Experience has shown that some old techniques were none too safe.

In an Accident

In a serious accident which could have damaged the spine or internal organs NEVER MOVE THE PATIENT unless it is vital to get him or her out of greater danger. *Moving someone with a spinal injury can cause life-long paralysis.*

Never give injured people food or drink - especially not alcohol - as it may make it difficult for doctors to give an anaesthetic.

The order in which to act:
1 Prevent any further danger - e.g. turn off the electricity in electrocutions (page 561).
2 If the patient isn't breathing give artificial respiration (right).
3 If there is no pulse (pulse taking, page 561) give heart massage (page 562).
4 Treat any bleeding, starting with the worst (opposite).
5 If they are unconscious make sure the airway is clear and place in the recovery position (page 564).

Meanwhile, if possible, get someone else to dial 999 for help, and ask for Ambulance. When alone, take action needed to save life, as above, then call an ambulance.

Artificial Respiration

WORK QUICKLY. Tilt the head back and a gasp of air may go in. If not, feel whether the tongue has fallen back and blocked the throat - if so pull it forward. Then use one of the following methods to get breathing started.

Method 1 - Mouth-to-mouth Resuscitation
1 Put the patient on his back.

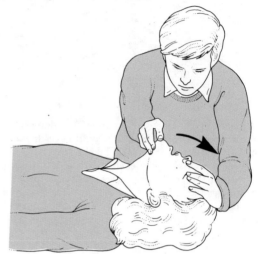

2 Tilt the head well back so the chin sticks up.
3 Open his mouth. Take a deep breath yourself.

4 Hold his nose shut and place your mouth firmly over his.
5 Blow out steadily (not too much for a young child or baby)
6 Raise your head; breathe in - looking to see that the chest is now falling.

Repeat once, ensuring the chest is fully inflated, quite quickly, then check that the pulse can be felt.

If it CAN - continue steps 1 to 6 at normal breathing speed until he is breathing or help comes.
If it CAN'T - give heart massage (page 562).

Chemists sell a tube which allows you to give mouth-to-mouth resuscitation without placing your mouth on the other person's. If you don't have one and really can't stomach mouth-to-mouth, use the Holger Nielson method on the right.

Method 2 - Holger Nielson method (less effective than 1)

1 Put the victim on his front.
2 Place his arms with elbows bent and head resting on hands.
3 Kneel above the head.

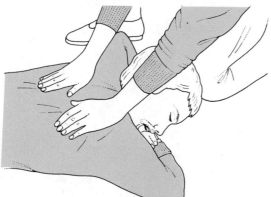

4 Press firmly down on the back, breathing out yourself (for timing).

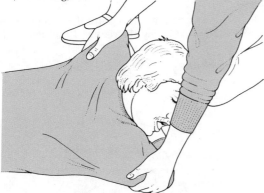

5 Take hold of each of the victim's elbows and raise them, lifting the chest slightly (breathing in yourself).

Repeat 4 and 5 three times, then check the pulse (see page 561). If it can be felt continue. If it can't give heart massage (see page 562).

If necessary, treat for unconsciousness (page 564).

Bleeding

If there is severe bleeding ACT FAST. Clean hands are best, but dirty hands are less harmful than no action at all. Arterial blood is bright red and its loss must be stopped RAPIDLY. Since AIDS, first aid instructors recommend putting a clean cloth, such as a handkerchief or scarf between the blood and your hand.

> When something (knife, pen, etc.) is stabbed deeply into the flesh DO NOT REMOVE IT. Removal could cause fatal bleeding.

- If bleeding is on an unbroken limb raise it above the heart - blood moves more slowly uphill.

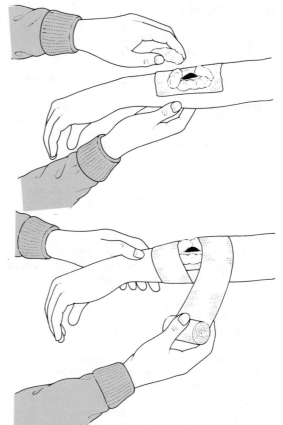

- If the blood is from a place which can safely be pressed, pressure will help stop the flow. Press cuts together or, on a larger injury, apply a pad of dressing and press.
- First aid experts no longer recommend applying a tourniquet to shut off the blood vessels. Bandages intended to stop blood flowing out through the injury can very easily block off the blood vessels carrying vital blood *back* to the heart, and this is *more* dangerous than the blood loss through the wound.
- Don't remove bandages to see how an injury is doing, this will slow down the good work. If blood oozes through, place a second pad on top.

• After treating bleeding *always* wash your hands well - the victim could carry a blood-borne disease.

Burns - Chemical

1 Rinse the area immediately, and *very* thoroughly, under running water. A few chemicals are activated by water. Try to check the container rapidly to make sure the chemical is not one of these. If it is, an alternative treatment may be given.
2 Remove any clothing containing the chemical.
3 Rinse again and get medical help.
4 If the chemical is in an eye rinse it IMMEDIATELY, AND VERY WELL, under a running tap (see box above). DO NOT use an eye bath; it washes the chemical back into the eye.

Burns - from Fire

1 Smother the flames on burning clothes with any thick material - towel, blanket, jacket - pressing it close enough to keep air from the flames. (Don't worry about bits of fabric stuck to the skin.)
2 Put the injury immediately under cold, running water or plunge it into a container of cold water, or - failing those - place a pad soaked in cold water over the burnt area. Leave the injury under cold water for at least 10 minutes. (It may hurt more but it *is* doing good.) Containers and pad will warm up, so keep adding fresh cold water.

> Plunging the whole body into a cold bath could increase the shock. Only plunge the burnt area.

As the body holds heat for a long time, so the cold water treatment helps even if it is not applied until 20 to 30 minutes after the accident.
3 Get medical attention if:
  a the burn is on a child and larger than a 50p piece;
  b the skin is charred or white;
  c burns are deep or cover much skin.

Be prepared to treat for shock (page 564) and give any burnt person frequent sips of tepid sweet water - this is doubly important with children.
4 Remove anything tight, if this can be done without further injury - rings, watches, shoes etc. - as the burnt area will swell. Don't try to remove any fabric which may have stuck to the burns, leave that to the professionals.
5 DO NOT apply lotions, creams, butter OR ANYTHING ELSE to the burns. Despite the folklore *none* of them helps and some may make medical treatment far more difficult and painful. Just cover the burn *lightly* with a *very clean* cloth such as a clean handkerchief, table napkin or pillow case - not a paper tissue or cotton wool as these will stick to the burn.

Chest Injuries

If an injury makes a hole in the chest there is a danger of air getting in and compressing a lung. Cover the wound IMMEDIATELY with a pad under your hand and bandage it as soon as possible to make it as airtight as you can.

Choking

Coughing is designed to remove whatever is blocking the throat. If coughing fails:
1 Try to have the victim's head down or hang a child downwards over your knee. Give 4 firm slaps between the shoulder blades. *Time the slaps to their coughs;* slapping as they breathe in could make them inhale the object. This could be dangerous.
2 If this fails, a small object like a fish bone may be dislodged by eating bread.

If the choking is serious and could endanger life use the following treatment - but do not use it for mild choking as it can cause internal injuries:
1 Get behind the person.

2 Place your fist thumb-side against the lower chest of the victim *just* below the centre of the ribs.

3 Cup your other hand over this and give a sharp pull inwards. Repeat several times.

4 Forcing the breath out suddenly like this should force the object into the mouth. Remove it quickly, before it can be breathed in again. If unconsciousness occurs give artificial respiration (page 558).

Drowning

If the body can be *briefly* held head down to drain any water, do so. Then apply artificial respiration - (page 558).

> Children can recover completely from surprisingly long periods under cold water. Keep trying to get them breathing, even if it seems unlikely that they will recover.

Electrocution - Domestic Current

1 If possible switch off the current.
2 If you can't turn off the current DON'T touch the victim directly, or with anything which could conduct electricity (e.g. metal). Using something made of wood (e.g. broom or chair), push the source of the electricity away from the person or vice versa. Rubber is another good protection against electricity, so wearing rubber gloves or pushing your arms down wellington boots is a safeguard.
3 Once separated from the electricity give whichever of the following is needed in this order:
artificial respiration (page 558)
heart massage (page 562)
burns treatment (page 560)

Then get medical attention - there can be a sudden collapse hours later.

Electrocution - High Voltage

> DO NOT try to rescue someone electrocuted by a high voltage such as a pylon or some factory supplies. It can reach out and 'grab' you if you get too close. Stay two normal room widths (18 m) away.

Fractures, Broken Bones and Dislocations

The signs of a break or fracture or dislocation are any of the following:
- the area looks out of shape
- there is swelling
- loss of normal movement below the point of the injury
- considerable pain.

> Whenever treatment under an anaesthetic may be needed DO NOT give *any* food or drink: it could delay the treatment.

Dress any open wound with as little disturbance as possible, and keep the patient warm. If the injury is to the skull or body DO NOT move the injured person (unless to save them from greater danger); get an ambulance to them. Keep them warm while it comes. DO NOT REMOVE ANY HARD HAT IF THERE IS RISK OF A HEAD INJURY.

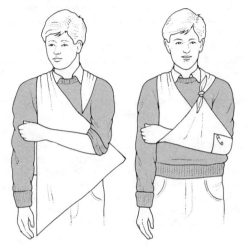

If the injury is to arm or collarbone use a triangular bandage or scarf, or a buttoned-up coat to support the limb. If necessary, take stress off the bone by supporting it with a splint - a whole newspaper rolled tightly is effective. If bending the arm is painful bandage it to the body in any position which relieves the pain.

Splint a broken leg to immobilize it completely, using anything to hand that is wider and longer than the limb you need to immobilize - a plank is ideal. Tie this to the leg firmly but not too tightly, avoiding ties at the

site of the injury. Unless it is clearly a very minor injury call an ambulance. Failing that, bandage the two legs together, so one bone supports the other and take the victim to hospital.

Frostbite

Frostbite must warm *slowly, without rubbing*. Remove anything tight or wet. Cover the frostbite with something warm and dry, or warm it with the body - tuck fingers under an armpit.

Heart Failure

Taking a Pulse

If you suspect heart failure take the pulse. To do this rest your fingers (not your thumb) lightly on the underside of the victim's wrist just below the base of his or her thumb. You should feel a slight beat in the

area between the bone and the tendon. *Don't press too hard* or you will block off the beat - practise on yourself. If there is no pulse ACT FAST.
1 Put the patient on his or her back.
2 Place the heel of one hand on the lower half of the breastbone (it runs down the centre of the chest).
3 Put the heel of the other hand on top with the fingers pointing in the *same* direction. Interlock the fingers. (This stops the lower fingers digging down into the chest.)
4 Repeatedly press down VERY HARD and FAST. Count 1 and - 2 and - 3 and - as you do it. Repeat 15 times, then give 2 breaths (page 558).

Once the heart is beating, check the breathing and treat that if necessary (see page 558).

> Forget the television series in which people doing heart massage press gently. It isn't easy to massage a heart through bone, and it is not unusual for correct heart massage to break a rib. Which is why you should never do it unless it really is necessary - but better a broken rib than dead.

Hypothermia
Hypothermia is a state of such great cold that it stops the body functioning. In conditions of extreme cold, such as icy water, anyone of any age can get it. But in normal life babies are at special risk because they have a large surface area from which to lose heat in relation to their total volume. The elderly are also vulnerable because in old age awareness of temperature changes becomes less acute - as eyesight does - and so they may not realize they are getting too cold. The symptoms are:
● the body is very cold
● adults look white, but a baby may be pink
● the pulse and breathing are feeble
● the victim is dozy, or unconscious.

Call medical help fast. While it comes:
1 remove any wet clothing
2 wrap the patient lightly in warm dry blankets or substitutes. DO NOT apply heat such as hot water bottles or electric blankets (if appropriate, cuddle them to share your body heat).
3 warm the room
4 DO NOT give alcohol; give warm - *not hot* - drinks if the victim is conscious.

Poisoning
There are a lot of false and dangerous ideas about poisoning. Forget what you have heard or seen on television. The action first aid experts recommend is this:
1 Watch the victim all the time; the conscious may become unconscious, the unconscious stop breathing.
2 Wipe the mouth area well, in case they have taken a chemical which burns. Then, if the patient isn't breathing, use artificial respiration (page 558).
3 If the patient is breathing but unconscious, place in

the recovery position (see page 564) - then ring for an ambulance. Keep them warm.
4 If conscious, find out what has been taken then ring for an ambulance and tell them what the poison was.
5 If the poison is a corrosive substance such as an acid or strong alkaline, DO NOT MAKE THE VICTIM SICK - *these are more dangerous coming up than in the stomach.* Instead give drinks of milk, or water to dilute the poison and soothe. Examples include:

petrol   bleach
white spirit   cleaning fluids
polishes   turpentine or turps substitute

6 Do not try to get rid of the poison by making the victim sick - unless a doctor advises it. Even poisons which could be brought up with relative safety do not act instantly, and will not be totally vomited by any first aid method. So give drinks of milk or water to dilute the poison and get proper medical attention FAST. One of Britain's top poisons units also recommends two products which use harmless activated charcoal to absorb the poison. Either can safely be taken, even by small children, and will help to stop the poison entering the bloodstream, so they are well worth keeping in any medicine cabinet. They are Carbomix and Medicol, and are obtainable from good chemists.

> Neither mustard nor salt should be given to make someone sick. Salt is particularly dangerous as high doses of salt are themselves poisonous - especially to children. *Children have died because parents gave them salt and water, though the poison they took would not have killed them.*

7 When the ambulance comes, give the attendants all the details of what has been taken, including whatever bottle or container held the poison, plus a sample of vomit.

The numbers of the major poison information centres are as follows:

Belfast 0232 240503   These numbers are for
Birmingham 021 554 3801   doctors: DO NOT
Cardiff 0222 709901   phone them unless you
Dublin 0001 379966   have a serious
Edinburgh 031 229 2477   emergency and cannot
Leeds 0532 430715   get local medical advice.
London 01 635 9191   A NEEDLESS CALL
Newcastle 091 232 1525   COULD BLOCK THE
                             LINE WHEN IT IS
                             URGENTLY NEEDED.

Poisonous Plants
The following plants, which are often found in the wild, in gardens or as house plants are poisonous. If you think someone has eaten one of them, see left. Just how ill someone would be after eating one of these plants would vary with the amount which was eaten and the age of

the eater. Young children are more easily poisoned than adults. How the poisons are presented is another factor. Some plants have poisonous juices which you encounter by just breaking a leaf or stem; others may have their most severe poison locked up inside a seed whose hard casing would take some determined chewing. The risk of poisoning also varies according to whether the plant looks inviting and tastes good. A child is far more likely to eat an attractive berry - especially if it looks like a familiar fruit - than leaves, and anything which tastes dreadful will not be eaten for very long - and many of them do taste vile.

If you have any of the following plants in your home or garden there is no need to get unduly alarmed. Just make sure that no one eats them or, in some cases, gets the juice on the skin. But children should be taught, from very young, that they do not pick or eat *anything* they find growing unless they have checked with you. This is particularly important if they ever see adults picking food from a garden, allotment or hedgerow: to a toddler blackberries and deadly nightshade are very similar. I emphasize 'anything' because many children like nothing better than to do the forbidden. So, if you point out the very poisonous plants in a garden, and tell them not to eat them, those will be the first ones they sample. But if you have children who are not able to learn to be cautious it may be necessary to remove poisonous plants from the garden. Be careful how you do it: don't load branches into a car and drive to the local dump. In the enclosed space of a car the fumes given off by the broken leaves could land you in hospital.

When making a barbecue in the wild, be sure that you recognize the wood you take for the fire or for skewering food. Even troops on survival training have been poisoned by carelessly skewering sausages on innocent looking, but highly poisonous shrubs.

Reactions to Poisonous Plants

★ ★ ★ extremely poisonous and possibly fatal
  ★ ★ very poisonous but rarely fatal
    ★ extremely unpleasant symptoms but not fatal

Assume *all* parts are poisonous unless otherwise stated.

Plant	Symptoms
Black Bryony (*Tamus communis*) ★ ★	vomiting, diarrhoea, also sap blisters skin
Castor Oil Plant (*Ricinus communis*) ★ ★ ★	vomiting, sweating, rapid pulse, weakness and collapse
Cherry Laurel (*Prunus laurocerasus*) ★ ★	headache, vomiting, dizziness, low blood pressure, dilated pupils, unconsciousness
Cowbane/Water Hemlock (*Cicuta virosa*) ★ ★ ★	dizziness, vomiting, unconsciousness, violent convulsions, coma
Cuckoo Pint (*Arum maculatum*) ★ ★	sore throat, diarrhoea, irregular pulse, coma
Deadly Nightshade (*Atropa belladonna*) ★ ★	vomiting, diarrhoea, convulsions, coma
Death Cap Mushroom (*Amanita phalloides*) ★ ★ ★	start after 6 to 24 hours, pain, vomiting, intense thirst, weak pulse
Foxglove (*Digitailis purpurea*) ★	nausea, weakness, rapid pulse, seeing yellow haloes round objects
Hemlock (*Conium maculatum*) ★ ★ ★	dilated pupils, lowered temperature, difficulty in moving, fluctuating pulse, rapid breathing, stupor
Henbane (*Hyoscyamus niger*) ★	nausea, dizziness, difficulty breathing, confusion, rapid pulse
Holly (*Ilex aquifolium*) ★	stomach pain, vomiting, diarrhoea
Laburnum (*Laburnum anagyroides*) ★ ★	stomach pain, vomiting, drowsiness, fever, rapid pulse, coma
Lily of the Valley (*Convallaria majalis*) ★ ★ ★	stomach pain, vomiting, cold clammy skin, delirium, coma, possibly death
Monkshood (*Aconitum napellus*) ★ ★ ★	burning mouth and throat, stomach pain, vomiting, intense thirst, headache, coldness, paralysis, convulsions, delirium, coma
Leopard Lily, Dumb Cane (*Dieffenbachia*) ★	extreme swelling of lips and tongue, pain
Oleander (*Nerium oleander*) ★ ★ ★	stomach pain, vomiting, diarrhoea, rapid pulse, dizziness, coma
Pokeweed (*Phytolacca americana*) ★	stomach pain, vomiting, diarrhoea, dizziness, exhaustion
Privet (*Ligustrum vulgare*) ★ ★	stomach pain, vomiting, diarrhoea
Rhubarb leaves (*Rheum rhaponticum*) ★	stomach cramps, vomiting, weakness, reduced blood clotting, liver and kidney damage
Thorn Apple (*Datura stramonium*) ★ ★	dry mouth, nausea, dilated pupils, loss of co-ordination, drowsiness, delirium, coma
White Bryony (*Bryonia dioica*) ★	diarrhoea, copius urine, also skin irritation
Woody Nightshade (*Solanum dulcamara*) ★ ★	vomiting, stomach pain, distressed breathing, flush, exhaustion
Yew Tree (*Taxus baccata*) ★ ★ ★ not the red flesh of the berry	vomiting, stomach pain, fever, drowsiness, stiffness, often death

The following plants are also poisonous:

Lupins	Daffodil bulbs
Buttercups	Hyacinth bulbs
Potato - leaves and	Poinsettia
stem, and green	Members of the spurge
sprouting tubers	(euphorbia) family
Broom	Meadow saffron
Marsh Marigold	(*Colchicum autumnale*)
Water Iris - Yellow Flag	Snowberries
Bluebells (Wild	Ivy
Hyacinth)	Rhododendron
Christmas Roses	Dog's Mercury
(Hellebores)	Ragwort
Wood Anemone	Daphne mezerium
Mistletoe	Buckthorn

All fungi should be regarded as poisonous unless you are experienced in telling which is which.

Poisonous Plants of Britain and Their Effects on Animals and Man, HMSO ref book 161

Shock
In shock the heart slows down and the victim becomes cold, pale, drowsy and possibly unconscious. It can be fatal, and needs medical attention. To avoid it:
1 Keep the patient warmly covered - DO NOT give hot water bottles. If it is safe to do so (page 558) get warmth under as well as over them.
2 Loosen any clothing which might hinder breathing.
3 If the injuries allow it (page 559) raise the feet higher than the head.
4 DO NOT give food or drink - it could cause vomiting.
5 Be reassuring and calm - even when seemingly unconscious they may be able to hear what you say.

The reason why hot water bottles must not be used is that they draw blood to the surface, away from other organs which need it.

Snakebite
Forget the stories about cutting open snakebites, sucking them and applying tourniquets. With the British adder the biggest danger is shock. Reassure the bitten person that adder bites are NOT fatal, and keep them calm. Move the bitten limb as little as possible (the more it is moved the more the poison will spread). Wash the bite or wipe it clean. Put a pad over it and bandage it

Always avoid contact with snakes in the wild, but don't assume all snakes are out to get you. Most avoid encounters with man and retreat at the vibration of footfalls, and some even shyly hide their head in their coils if surprised. However, this is not true of all of them. The black mamba, for example, has a reputation for aggression, and can rear and strike at a distance of up to two-thirds of its total length.

firmly. Immobilize the limb as if it was broken and get the person to hospital. Give paracetamol or aspirin to relieve the pain.

For most foreign snakes the treatment is the same - but get the victim to medical treatment FAST. The venoms of some tropical snakes work very rapidly, and try to get a good description of the snake as treatment varies with the type. With bites from certain highly poisonous types overseas there may be a need to apply a tourniquet. Before travelling in wild areas check the best first aid for those you may encounter.

Unconsciousness
If someone is unconscious and you *know* there is no injury put them in the recovery position; this prevents the tongue falling back into their throat and allows blood, saliva or vomit to flow out without choking them. It is most easily done by two people, with the victim on their back.
1 Remove anything from front pockets which might be hard to lie on.
2 Turn the head towards you.
3 Place one arm so it is folded across the chest.
4 Place the arm nearest to you by the victim's side.
5 Lift the leg on the side of the bent arm, cross it over the other one and bend the knee.
6 As the leg goes over roll the hips and shoulders with it - turning the casualty *towards* you.
7 Adjust to the position illustrated.

St John Ambulance Association (see page 547) and the British Red Cross Society (see page 547) each run courses in first aid all over the country. Your nearest course can be found from the local branch in the phone book, or failing that contact head office. **St Andrew's Ambulance Association** (see page 547) runs training courses in first aid in Scotland.
The First Aid Manual, Dorling Kindersley - the first aid bible produced jointly by the Red Cross and St John Ambulance - use the latest edition, it is regularly revised.

GENITAL AND SEXUAL INFECTIONS

General Facts
Anyone who thinks he or she may have a sexually transmitted (venereal) disease should stop all sexual activities and go to the 'Special Clinic' of a hospital for

tests - there is no need to see a GP first. The clinics are listed under Venereal Disease in the telephone book.

Sex being a private matter, there is (AIDS apart) remarkably little data on which sexual practices are most likely to transmit infection. So it is safest to assume that vaginal, anal and oral sex can all do so, though which is the most hazardous will vary with the nature and site of the disease.

It's no good thinking that you can tell the sort of person who would have VD. The patients in VD clinics look no different from those in an eye clinic. So the best protection is abstinence, the next best is a condom and a diaphragm is better than nothing. However, an IUD can actually increase the risk of infection. And how long any infection takes to show varies enormously.

You can - in theory - catch some sexual infections from lavatory seats. But the chances of two people both adopting the same (rather odd) position needed to bring the relevant bit of their anatomy in contact with the seat, *and* doing so in quick succession before the germs die in the cold, are *extremely* remote.

Hygiene

Women are especially vulnerable to minor infections because their genitals provide an ideal home for bacteria: warm and free from draughts, with plenty of body fluids to feed on - what more could a creature need? Our grandmothers knew better. Until the early years of this century women's knickers were open between the legs. Cooling the area prevents a lot of minor problems. Whenever possible, wear stockings or crutchless tights, with loose cotton pants - or no pants at all - and avoid tight-fitting trousers. That may sound impractical, unfashionable or indecent. But try wearing stockings, no pants and a fullish skirt round the house - you'll be surprised by how good it feels. And, when air-dried, moistness is not the problem you might think.

In its natural state the vagina's acidity is a good defence against bacteria. Excessive washing, or washing inside the vagina, removes this natural protection and makes infection more likely. This is counter-productive, as bacteria are far smellier than body fluids. A daily bath, plus an external wash after making love, if you wish, are quite enough. Vaginal sprays, deodorants and talcs and douches are totally unnecessary and even harmful - they *lower* the body's defences, and may also cause allergic reactions. Scented bath products should be used sparingly or not at all - too much can irritate the delicate tissue between the legs and create, or prolong, problems.

Men should wash the sexual organs regularly, including under the foreskin of the penis. But it is an old wives' tale that washing and urinating after intercourse prevent infection - they don't.

Acquired Immune Deficiency Syndrome (AIDS)

The AIDS virus (HIV) destroys the body's ability to fight off other diseases. As it is usually impossible to pinpoint the date of infection, there are no hard facts on how long AIDS takes to develop. Some people may get a glandular-fever-type illness within the first year, but many may have no symptoms for several years. Once symptoms develop, 3 out of 4 die within 3 years of diagnosis, but nobody knows how long the virus can be carried without symptoms, and a symptomless carrier is as infectious as any other AIDS victim. For tests you need only contact your nearest hospital.

The virus is carried in the body fluids - especially blood and semen - but it usually enters the body when a break in the skin lets it into the bloodstream. It *can't* be breathed in, or enter through the pores. So AIDS cannot be caught by sitting near someone, working with them, or even by normal social touching, or from lavatory seats. And the virus is easily killed by heat or household bleach. You can catch it from:

Sex - all forms of penetration carry some risk, but anal intercourse is the greatest danger because the lining of the anus and rectum (back passage) is most easily broken.

Needles - unsterilized needles used for drug abuse, ear piercing, tattooing, acupuncture or medical injections (a problem in less developed countries).

Shaving - sharing razors with an AIDS carrier could transmit the disease from his cut to yours.

Toothbrushes - there is a slight risk that sharing these could spread AIDS, as gums often bleed; and there is a greater risk of hepatitis B.

Overseas blood transfusions - in Britain the blood is checked and the government says there is only 1 chance in 1,000,000 of getting AIDS this way. But travellers who need a transfusion in less developed countries run a serious risk.

Spilt blood - if infected blood enters a cut or scratch it could cause AIDS so, when in doubt, wear rubber gloves and throw away what you use to clear it up, and if you have to do first aid put a pad, such as a folded handkerchief, between yourself and any bleeding.

The high-risk groups for AIDS are homosexuals, drug addicts, prostitutes, those who may have caught it in Africa and severe haemophiliacs (who may, in the early days of AIDS, have been given contaminated blood products before they were treated to kill the virus - as they are now). In Europe and the United States male AIDS victims vastly outnumber females, whereas in Africa the numbers are fairly equal. This difference isn't fully understood but, clearly, anyone can get it, and the more sexual partners you have, the greater the risk of sleeping with a carrier. The symptoms are numerous and varied, but they include:
- swollen glands, for example in the neck or armpits
- great fatigue for no special reason
- a persistent temperature and night sweats
- persistent diarrhoea
- shortness of breath and a dry cough which won't go
- pinky-purple blotches on the skin like a bruise or blood blister
- loss of more than 10 per cent of body weight.

The Haemophilia Society, 123 Westminster Bridge Road, London SE1 7HR Tel:01 928 2020

Healthline - recorded telephone information on AIDS: 01 981 2717, 01 980 7222, 0345 581151 (to call from outside London at local call rates)

Terrence Higgins Trust, BM/AIDS, London WC1N 3XX Tel:01 242 1010 - Vistel 01 405 2463 (3 pm-10 pm). RC, Inf, support, referral, befriending for AIDS victims.

Chlamydia (Chlamydia Trachomatis)

This is becoming very common and needs immediate treatment, as it can block the fallopian tubes and make a woman sterile. It can also be transmitted to the unborn child, causing serious eye infections and sometimes blindness. Women's symptoms vary, and include pain deep in the lower abdomen, pain on intercourse or on urinating. A man may have a slight discharge and mild inflammation of the penis, and/or discomfort on urinating. But, in both sexes, there may be no symptoms at all. It can be cured, and anyone who has slept around or whose partner has should consider tests to check they don't have it - especially if they intend to become pregnant. Sexual partners need to be treated.

Foreign Bodies

Occasionally something gets lodged in the vagina and allows bacteria to build up round it causing a smelly discharge. Even a small tuft left from a tampon can do this. Check this if there is a curious vaginal odour. Once the object is out the problem should end. If it doesn't, or you can't get it out, see a doctor. However odd it is the doctor won't be surprised. One doctor I know had removed statuettes of Napoleon from three different people in one week.

Genital Warts

A sexually transmitted virus causes warts in the genital area up to 9 months after infection. They start as hard whiteheads but can grow to large, uncomfortable, warty masses. Unfortunately, women who have had them may have a higher risk of cervical cancer - but this may depend on the type of wart virus. So anyone who develops them should stop intercourse and get treatment to avoid passing on the risk. After having them, women need a cervical smear each year.

Gonorrhoea

Gonorrhoea is the most common venereal disease, and probably the most widespread treatable infection in the world. A report in 1971 found it was the most common communicable disease in America after the common cold - and increasing. But it is more easily passed from a man to a woman than vice versa. The symptoms often start 2 to 10 days after infection. Men normally have a profuse yellow discharge from the penis, and a burning sensation on urinating - the French *chaudepisse* describes it well. If the anus is infected there may also be irritation and a discharge. Women may have discomfort on urinating, vaginal discharge, pain in the abdomen, occasionally aching joints and a fever. But many women, and some men, have *no* symptoms at all. It is infectious from the moment it is caught, not just when symptoms show. And in women the bacteria may be hard to trace, so most clinics do 2 tests on any woman

who is a gonorrhoea contact.

It is easily cured, but needs rapid treatment, and every sexual contact must be seen too. Untreated, it can damage the reproductive organs of both sexes, and produce other major complications. Babies who contact the infection during birth can develop eye problems, and may occasionally go blind. Unfortunately, some overseas forms are becoming resistant to penicillin and need other antibiotics.

Hepatitis - see page 540

Herpes

Herpes is a growing problem. There are two viruses involved: HSV_1 and HSV_2. HSV_1 usually causes cold sores, and HSV_2 usually causes genital herpes - but each *can* cause either. See page 534.

Herpes starts up to 10 days after infection. The genitals tingle, ache and itch, and develop red spots which turn into small blisters, then into ulcers. These clear up in 3 to 10 days, though it may take 3 weeks in a woman having a first attack. The glands in the groin may swell and it can be painful to urinate. Sufferers can feel ill, shivery, nauseous and have a headache. They should take pain killers, and see a doctor. The symptoms go in a few weeks and some people never get it again, but others have it in cycles. An attack can be brought on by exposing the genitals to the sun - so nude sunbathing is out.

As first aid, apply ice cubes in a plastic bag at the first warning signs, and try to relax - this could stop the attack: ice during an attack reduces the pain. Herpes sufferers are most infectious during an attack (from first tingling to total healing), and should avoid sex, but even between attacks small quantities of the virus may be passed on. Some people are also symptomless carriers. So between attacks, or if someone could be a carrier, it is safer if the man uses a sheath, and an infected woman uses a cap and spermicide. A baby passing through the infected area, during birth, can become infected and suffer potentially fatal brain damage, so a Caesarian birth is needed.

The Herpes Association, 41 North Road, London N7 9DP Tel. 01 609 9061 - M£L, S(and partners), M, G, B, L, A, 24-hr helpline.

NSU and Friends

NSU (non-specific urethritis) is the best known of a group of puzzling problems all referred to by initials. They include NGU (non-gonococcal urethritis), PGU (post-gonococcal urethritis) and NSGI (non-specific genital infections). The symptoms may suggest a sexually transmitted disease - genital discharge, discomfort on urinating and perhaps a pain low in the stomach - but basic tests may fail to reveal a cause. This can be either because the culture methods aren't good enough, or because there is nothing there to form a culture. Nobody knows for sure and British and American experts disagree, but this is a developing field and many cases once regarded as unidentifiable are now attributed to chlamydia (opposite), or TV (below). The rest may not respond to treatment, but most clear up in time. However, the lack of any high-flown name doesn't mean such infections should be treated lightly - some women may be sterile afterwards. So men with suspicious symptoms should *not* have sex.

Syphilis

This bogeyman of sexual diseases is now relatively rare in most highly developed countries, where it is largely a problem of gays. But it is far more common in Africa, the East and even in some of the less sophisticated parts of Europe. It should be treated rapidly, before serious damage is done. In pregnancy syphilis causes miscarriage, stillbirth or a handicapped child. Like the AIDS virus, this bacterium enters the body through a break in the skin. The first symptoms, 1 to 12 weeks after infection, are a sore at the point of infection - penis, vulva, vagina, anus, mouth - plus swollen lymph glands. However, the sore may be inside the anus or vagina where it can't be seen.

The sore heals after 3 to 10 weeks, and the disease enters its second stage. The symptoms now include dark-red skin rashes, swollen glands, ulcers in moist areas of the body and flue-like aches and pains. These go after several weeks or months. The third stage, which is very rare in the West, may come many years later. It can cause appalling sores on the body, severe heart disease, paralysis and insanity.

When syphilis is latent, or in the first or second stage, it can usually be cured. But not all syphilis sufferers know they have it, as the initial sore may be hidden and the secondary symptoms can go unrecognized. Those who have syphilis are infectious all the time, not just when the symptoms show, but their infectiousness gradually diminishes after the second stage.

Thrush (Candida Albicans)

This is an extremely common female problem, but rarely occurs in men - and then only causes a slight soreness. You don't need to have sex to develop it. The culprit is an organism, similar to yeast, which lives in the bowels. It often develops after a course of antibiotics, which have killed the body's natural defences, and when the vagina loses its acidity after the menopause. Thrush has no serious consequences, but it causes a thick creamy-yellow discharge which dries to a powder, and the genitals feel very itchy and sore. It is easily treated by a GP and home remedies also work well. Cleanse the area with olive oil rather than water to soothe the itching. Then put a little plain (not fruit) yoghurt into the vagina with the finger tips or with the end of a tampon (removing the tampon after), and spread more yoghurt on the outside. Do this regularly and follow the rules in 'Hygiene' (page 565). If you get a prescription do complete the full course of medicine, or these organisms may become resistant to the treatment and very hard to get rid of.

Trichomonas Vaginalis (TV)

This is a very common vaginal infection (probably affecting 1 woman in 5 at some time) caused by a protozoon (an organism considerably larger than a bacterium or virus). In women it causes a thin, greenish, frothy, very smelly discharge and genital itching and soreness, which may even cover the inner thighs and buttock cleft. In men the symptoms, if any, are as for chlamydia (opposite). It is easily treated and both partners must see a doctor.

David Barlow, *Sexually Transmitted Diseases: the Facts*, OUP

HANDICAPS AND DISABILITIES

The range of handicaps and disabilities is so wide, and their problems so individual, that it's impossible to do justice to them here. The best sources of information and help are the charities concerned, and some of the major ones are given below (see also page 547). There are more and more excellent aids and electronic devices for the handicapped and disabled, and it is well worth joining an appropriate organization to keep in touch with developments. A *Directory for Disabled People* by Ann Darnborough and Derek Kinrade is published by RADAR (see page 568) and the special programmes on Radio 4 are good sources of information.

Blindness and Partial Sight

Royal National Institute for the Blind (RNIB), 224 Great Portland Street, London W1N 6AA Tel: 01 388 1266 - Britain's largest organization for the blind, deaf-blind and partially sighted. RC, S, CS, O, F&F, M (braille), L, B (braille and Moon), Lib, E, EI, G, Rg, A, C, HD, TR (talking books), special accommodation, educational advice and units, holidays, rehabilitation courses, braille music, wireless provision, numerous benefits and concessions, sae.

Sense (National Deaf-blind and Rubella Association), 311 Gray's Inn Road, London WC1X ?T Tel:01 278 1000 - RC, M&L-Vol, S, CS, F&F, M, G, V, Ad, Inf, L, B, holiday programme, education service, further education establishments, some long-stay accommodation, grants.

Deafness

Specialists say that when talking to the very deaf one should use familiar words, and talk normally, but not too fast, facing both them and the light. Don't cover your mouth or smoke or eat. And treat them normally - they have ear trouble not brain trouble.

The British Association of the Hard of Hearing, 7/11 Armstrong Road, London W3 7JL Tel: 01 743 1110/1353 - offers help and information for those who gradually go deaf. RC, F&L, S, CS, M, very good L, B, E, G, A, T, C, sae.

British Deaf Association, 38 Victoria Place, Carlisle, Cumbria, CA1 1HU Tel: 0228 48844 Vistel: 0228 28719 is for those born deaf. RC, S, CS, O, F&F, M, L, B, V, E, G, A, T, C, HD, sae.

National Association for Deafened People, c/o 45 Broadway West, York YO1 4JN - caters only for people who become very deaf prematurely, not those born deaf. RC, M£L, S, F&F, M, L, B, E, A, C, sae.

National Deaf Children's Society, 45 Hereford Road, London W2 5AH Tel: 01 229 9272 - RC, CS, F&F, M, G, Inf on all aspects of child deafness.

Royal National Institute for the Deaf (RNID), 105 Gower Street, London WC1E 6AH Tel: 01 387 8033 - Excellent help and information source for all kinds of hearing disorders, including tinnitus. RC, S, F&F, L, B, E, EI, Lib, communication courses, residential care, large sae.

Talking Books for the Handicapped, 12 Lent Street, London SE1 1QH Tel: 01 407 9417 - postal listening service.

There are many other organizations, drama groups, sports associations, and so on. See the *Directory of Organizations for the Deaf and Hard of Hearing* published by Charities Aid Foundation (48 Pembury Road, Tonbridge TN9 2JD) or the similar list from RNID. See also page 537.

Mental Handicap

Down's Syndrome Association, 12-13 Clapham Common Southside, London SW4 7AA Tel: 01 720 0008 - RC, M£H-Vol, F&F, G, Rg, M, Ad, Inf, L, B, V, Ed, education adviser, resource centre.

National Autistic Society, 276 Willesden Lane, London NW2 5RB Tel: 01 451 3844 - runs schools and centres for the autistic and offers life-long care, and also does research. RC, M£L, F&F, M, G, B, L, Ad, Inf, parent-to-parent contacts.

Royal Society for Mentally Handicapped Children and Adults (MENCAP), 123 Golden Lane, London EC1 0RT Tel: 01 253 9433 - RC, M£Vol, S, CS, O, F&F, Dr, M, L, B, V, E, G, A, T, C, HD, sae.

General

Association for Research into Restricted Growth, 61 Lady Walk, Maple Cross, Rickmansworth WD3 2YZ Tel: 0923 7707591 — RC, S, M, G, L, Inf on specialists in this field and sources of clothing.

Association for Spina Bifida and Hydrocephalus, 22 Upper Woburn Place, London WC1H 0EP Tel: 01 388 1382 - RC, S, CS, F&F, M, G, B, L, C, HC, Ad, support, welfare grants.

The Association of Care Attendant Schemes Ltd, 10 Regent Place, Rugby, Warwicks CV21 2PN Tel: 0788 73653 - runs a scheme whereby care attendants will stand in, to give carers a break. This is a free service and will include the elderly if they have any illness.

Association of Disabled Professionals (General Secretary), The Stables, 73 Pound Road, Banstead, Surrey SM7 2HU Tel: 0737 352366 - fosters employment of disabled people in the professions. RC, M£L-M, S, F&F, Ad, Inf, pressure group, sae.

British Limbless Ex-service Men's Association, Frankland Moore House, 185/187 High Road, Chadwell Heath, Essex RM6 6NA Tel: 01 590 1124 - welfare for members and their widows, residential and convalescent homes, events to rehabilitate amputees, advises and assists on pensions and allowances. Also for ex-service women, will advise non-service amputees. RC, M£ optional, S, O, F&F, M, L, B, E, Rg, Res, A, C, HD, sae.

British Polio Fellowship, Bell Close, West End Road, Ruislip, Middx HA4 6LP Tel: 0895 675515 - RC, M£L, S, CS, F&F, M, O, G, Ad, Inf, EI, Res, grants, holiday homes.

Carematch, 286 Camden Road, London N7 0BJ Tel: 01 609 9966 - is computerized matching of young physically handicapped with suitable residential care. Free service, but they cannot inspect the homes, only say what is available. RC.

Contact a Family, 16 Strutton Ground, London SW1P 2HP Tel: 01 222 2695 - M£L, F&F, M, Ad, Inf, links parents of children with special needs.

Dial (National Association of Disablement Information and Advice Lines), 117 High Street, Clay Cross, Chesterfield, Derbyshire S45 9DZ Tel: 0246 250055 - gives free advice by phone, letter or visit on most aspects of disability.

Disability Alliance, 25 Denmark Street, London WC2 8NJ Tel: 01 240 0806 - RC, L, B, information on social security entitlements, pressure group. Publishes the *Disability Rights Handbook* annually.

Disabled Living Centres Council, c/o **Traids,** 76 Clarendon Park Road, Leics LE2 3AD Tel: 0533 700747/8 - has details of centres all over the UK where aids for the sick and disabled can be seen.

Disabled Living Foundation, 380/384 Harrow Road, London W9 2HU Tel: 01 289 6111 - covers almost every aspect of coping with most handicaps and disabilities, and the problems of old age. RC, S, CS, O, F&F, L, B, E, EI, Rg, HD, list of centres throughout UK where aids can be tried out.

In Touch, 10 Norman Road, Sale, Cheshire M33 3DF Tel: 061 962 4441 - supports and links parents whose children have similar mental handicaps or rare disorders. RC, M£L.

Invalid Children's Aid, Allen Graham House, 198 City Road, London EC1V 2PH Tel: 01 608 2462 - gives professional support and advice, school, centres, for chronic physical and mental disorders of all kinds. RC, M£M, CS, F&F, G, E, B, Res, sae.

The Leonard Cheshire Foundation, Leonard Cheshire House, 26-29 Maunsel Street, London SW1P 2QN Tel: 01 828 1822 - offers residential care, all over the UK. Mainly to physically disabled younger adults, also to mentally handicapped adults and children, and discharged psychiatric patients. Local groups run family support services.

The Multiple Sclerosis Society, 25 Effie Road, London SW6 1EE Tel: 01 736 6267 - RC, M£L, S, F&F, M, L, B, Ad, support, research.

Muscular Dystrophy Group of GB and NI, Nattrass House, 35 Macaulay Road, London SW4 0QP Tel: 01 720 8055 - RC, S, CS, F&F, G, L, B, Rg, Ad, Inf, EI, some grants, M - free on request, research, advises on genetic counselling.

Parkinson's Disease Society, 36 Portland Place, London W1N 3DG Tel: 01 255 24321 - RC, M£Vol, S, F&F, M, G, B, L, supports research, sae.

Royal Association for Disability and Rehabilitation (Radar), 25 Mortimer Street, London W1N 8AB Tel: 01 637 5400 - has over 400 affiliated organizations offer wide range of services and activities. Vast range of publications on all aspects of living as a disabled or handicapped person, correspondence courses, RC, C, E, L, A, sae welcomed.

Scottish Council on Disability, Princes House, 5 Shandwick Place, Edinburgh EH2 4RG Tel: 031 229 8632 - the voluntary body linking all Scotland's voluntary organizations for those with disabilities. Free enquiry service on equipment, facilities, access, clothing and employment.

Spinal Injuries Association, 76 St James' Lane, London N10 3DF Tel: 01 444 2121 - RC, M£L, S, CS, F&F, M, L, B, EI, G, A, T, Inf, link service HD, confidential welfare service, care attendant agency, holiday facilities, sae.

The Spastics Society, 12 Park Crescent, London W1N 4EQ Tel: 01 636 5020 - RC, S, CS, F&F, M, L, B, V, E, T, Th, Ed, F, G, Rg, A, C, HD, assessment, therapy, counselling, sports and leisure activities.

Technology Information Service, NDCS Technology Information Centre, 4 Church Road, Edgbaston, Birmingham B15 3TD Tel: 021 454 5151.

A Medic-Alert bracelet can carry details of the wearer's medical condition (see page 538).

SOCIAL AND ANTI-SOCIAL DRUGS

Some people may be surprised, or even affronted, to see smoking, drinking and gambling set alongside heroin and cocaine in a section on drugs. The grouping is scientific rather than critical. The *Collins English Dictionary* defines a drug as 'a chemical substance taken for the pleasant effect it produces' - which fits all of them, except gambling, very nicely. Gambling joins them because its thrill makes some people just as high as some drugs - which is not surprising, since extreme excitement makes the body produce chemicals very similar. All drugs share the ability to dominate those who enjoy them, to a point where they may be very hard to give up. Nor is there any neat line here between 'drugs' such as heroin and cocaine and more respectable substances like alcohol and tobacco. The heavy drinker who gives up alcohol may not suffer the withdrawal symptoms which are attendant on giving up heroin, but it can certainly be much harder than giving up a soft drug like marijuana. Finally, all drugs share the fact that even the mildest can make the user sacrifice friends and family to the need for them.

Those who feel this last statement isn't true of smoking should consider that every year families all over Britain suffer the grief of losing fathers, mothers, sons, daughters and grandparents prematurely, from diseases directly caused by smoking. What greater sacrifice is there?

Everyone however has the right to choose how to live their own life. This chapter is simply a route map to help people see the road they are on, and to provide signposts to where those who would prefer to go in a different direction can get help.

Alcohol

Alcohol is so much the socially accepted drug of the Western world that it is hard to think of it as a drug - let alone a harmful one. But it is. More young people die as the result of alcohol than from all the illegal drugs put together, and overall, in Britain and the United States, it is the third most common killer. By the year 2000 the World Health Organization predicts that alcohol may be the *biggest* killer in the industrial world, causing more deaths than cancer or heart disease.

It is not just alcoholics who are at risk. Vulnerability varies, and the young, the elderly and women are all rather more easily harmed by it than the average man. That doesn't mean men can drink without ill effect: 1 man in 5 admitted to hospital has an alcohol-related problem. It causes liver damage, high blood pressure, stomach problems, depression, damage to unborn children and personality changes. Yet alcohol consumption is rising.

Amounts of Alcohol

People generally think of spirits as strong, and beer as relatively weak. But we drink small measures of whisky and big glasses of beer, so the amount of alcohol consumed hardly differs. In alcohol content 1 glass of wine = 1 vermouth = 1 small sherry = 1 single whisky = ½ pint ordinary strength beer or lager.

The Health Education Authority (see page 547) uses units of alcohol to measure safe levels for drinking.

Units a Week

Men	Women	Level	Advice
up to 21	up to 14	low	Try never to exceed this.
22-35	15-21	moderate	Your chances of accidents and health damage increase.
35+	21+	high	Danger zone; cut down now, or you risk liver damage.

One unit =

single measure of spirits

small sherry

glass of wine

two-thirds can of ordinary beer

one-half pint of ordinary beer

one-half can of export beer

two-fifths pint of export beer

one-third can of strong ale or lager

one-quarter pint of strong ale or lager

one-third pint of ordinary cider

one-quarter pint of strong cider

one-quarter can of extra-strength beer or lager

one-fifth pint of extra strength beer or lager

Drinking and Driving
The official facts are these:
- Driving ability can be affected by even 1 to 2 units of alcohol in the bloodstream.
- It takes one hour for each unit of alcohol to wear off.
- 10+ units during an evening could make you unfit to drive the next morning.
- Tests with racing drivers have shown that drink made them far *more confident* of their ability to drive an obstacle course - but far *less good* at driving it. See also Law and Driving, page 456.

Drink alters the way the brain works and affects judgement, self-control, reaction time, memory and personality. When driving or operating machinery the most dangerous of these changes is in reaction time and judgement. Where relationships are concerned, the change to the personality is the killer. Most drinkers are their worst selves in their cups. But, as alcohol affects the memory, they may never know just how badly they have behaved. So they feel angry that others in the family aren't being as loving as they expect, and take refuge in more drink. This cycle breaks marriages and alienates children.

Those who become dependent on alcohol don't do so overnight: in some people it takes 5 years, but in most it takes 10 to 15 years. During that time most of them think they are just normal drinkers 'like everyone else'.

Women have less water in their bodies than men. So there is less to dilute the alcohol, and they are more easily harmed by it. A woman who drinks 8 units of alcohol a day is 36 times more likely to get liver disease than a man drinking the same amount. With the trend of women drinking more the number of women dying of liver disease has risen steadily. It is now 6 times more common than it was 20 years ago.

It is best not to drink when pregnant. Drink can get through to an unborn baby and harm it, and there is very new evidence which suggests that too much alcohol at the time when a baby is conceived may possibly cause abnormalities in the child.

There are NHS treatment centres, and increasing numbers of private clinics, which help people with alcohol problems. A GP can refer people to either. The organizations listed below have the latest information.

Warning Signs
Experts say these are some of the signs that alcohol may be getting a hold on someone:
- a need to have alcohol always available
- looking forward to drink as something they need to pep them up
- drinking playing an important part in their life
- having to increase the intake of alcohol to 'feel good'
- irritability if anyone else discusses their drinking
- feeling sick, irritable, having the shakes, sweating regularly in the morning or the middle of the night.

Al-anon Family Groups, 61 Great Dover Street, London SE1 4YF Tel:01 403 0888 (10 am - 4pm) - 890 self-help groups for relatives of problem drinkers. The Al-teen section helps teenagers who have an alcoholic relative. RC, F&F, L, B, G, sae.

Alcoholics Anonymous, P.O. Box 514, 11 Redcliffe Gardens, London SW10 9BQ Tel: 01 352 3001 - telephone counselling and over 2,000 self-help groups for those with alcohol problems. Local groups listed in phone directories. RC, S, CS, M, L, B, G.

Alcohol Concern, 305 Gray's Inn Road, London WC1 8QF Tel: 01 833 3471 - RC, P, F&F, L, B, sae. Referral to local centres.

Dawn, 39-41 North Road, Islington, London N7 9DP Tel: 01 700 4653 - L, Inf, for women with alcohol, tranquillizer and drug problems, sae.

Drinkwatchers, 200 Seagrave Road, London SW6 1RQ Tel: 01 381 3157 - Advice and groups to help heavy drinkers keep within sensible limits. L, G. **Accept,** at the same address but on 01 381 3155, caters for those who want to give up completely.

Galsworthy Lodge, Priory Lane, Roehampton, London SW15 5JJ Tel:01 876 6371/8261 - a private unit operating the Minnesota Programme for day or in-patients. GP, S, F&F.

Turning Point, 12 Long Lane, London EC1A 9HA Tel: 01 606 3947/9 - RC, S, F&F, G, Rg, C, residential rehabilitation projects, post-treatment for both alcohol and drugs, Inf and Ad, telephone 'druglines', industrial advisory service re employees with these problems, sae.

Ian Robertson and Nick Heather, *Let's Drink to Your Health,* the British Psychological Society - on how to cut down on drinking.

A Great and Growing Evil: the medical consequences of alcohol abuse, the Royal College of Physicians, Tavistock.

Gambling
The compulsion to gamble can be as strong as the compulsion to take drugs, is accompanied by the same delusions of being in control of the problem and is just as destructive. Wins just stimulate the urge to win more; losses - however serious - produce an urge to win them back. Normal, reasonable behaviour is steam-rollered by the compulsion and, thanks to fruit machines, even children as young as 8 years old are becoming hooked on gambling. The following organization helps gamblers overcome the urge to gamble.

Gamblers Anonymous, 17-24 Blantyre Street, Cheyne Walk, London SW10 Tel: 01 352 3060 - is like Alcoholics Anonymous (see above).

Gam-anon helps anyone related to a gambler, and is at the above address.

Smoking
Smoking is addictive - as most smokers who have tried to give up realize. But perhaps the greatest proof of its addictive power is that people continue to smoke despite the overwhelming evidence of the harm it does. The two harmful elements are tar, which condenses out of the smoke on to the lungs, and the poisonous gas carbon monoxide. Filter tips yield less tar but *more* carbon monoxide than other cigarettes. Research has *failed* to show that smoking low tar cigarettes is always much safer than other brands.

Effects on Those who Smoke
In its 6 years the Second World War killed only *half* as many British people as have been killed by smoking in the last 6 years. Of the 40,000 who die each year from lung cancer, 9 out of 10 are smokers. The younger

someone starts smoking, the more likely he or she is to get lung cancer. That is only the tip of the iceberg: consider the following facts.

- Smokers are twice as likely to get cancer of the bladder as non-smokers.
- Nine out of 10 who die from chronic bronchitis and emphysema are smokers.
- A smoker is 2 to 3 times more likely to have a heart attack than a non-smoker.
- Smoking while taking the contraceptive pill more than doubles the risk of a stroke or heart attack, compared to non-smoking pill takers.
- Smoking may cause abnormalities in sperm which lead to infertility.
- Smokers get the menopause 2 to 3 years earlier than non-smokers.
- Smokers are impotent more often than non-smokers.
- Smoking also increases the risk of cancer of the mouth, larynx and windpipe. It may also be linked with cancer in the pancreas, kidney and cervix.
- Of every 1,000 young British smokers on 20 cigarettes a day:
  1 will be murdered
  6 will die in road accidents
  250 will die from smoking.

Effects on Non-Smokers
Those who breathe the smoke from the cigarettes of others are smoking passively.
- Sizeable amounts of nicotine and tar (two harmful elements in cigarettes) are found in the blood and urine of non-smokers who have been with smokers in a poorly ventilated area.
- Those who work for years in a smoky atmosphere suffer measurable lung damage.
- Non-smoking women may have an increased risk of lung cancer if their husbands smoke, or if they work among smokers.

Unborn babies and children are also harmed by their parents' smoking. In all cases the more the adults smoke, the greater the likely harm to the child.
- A baby is more likely to be miscarried if its mother smokes.
- On average the babies of smokers are lighter and more likely to be stillborn or to die in the first week.
- Children whose mothers smoked 10 or more cigarettes a day throughout pregnancy do less well at school.
- Children whose mothers smoked 10 or more cigarettes a day throughout pregnancy are more likely to develop cancer.
- Children under one year old are twice as likely to have serious chest complaints if both parents smoke.

Giving up Smoking
The key to success is really wanting to give up. But the following methods can help:
- Make the first day without a cigarette a special day.
- Change your routine to cut out the events you associate with smoking.

- Find something else to do with your hands and/or mouth: sip water, chew gum, knit, carve wood - anything. If it's eating, make a bag of peeled carrots or washed celery each morning - not sweets.
- You may get no side effects, but if you do get irritable or depressed, start coughing or get stomach upsets be aware these *will* pass in several weeks - and they prove how much harm the cigarettes were doing you.
- Save up the money you would have spent on cigarettes for something you would really enjoy - or save your cigarette money for your favourite charity and see how quickly it mounts up.
- Learn relaxation or meditation techniques and use them when the craving starts.
- If you smoke a cigarette, don't feel defeated; give up again from then on.
- Remember over 9 million people have beaten the habit, and you are as good as any of them; so you can do it.

Health Education Offices and Community Health Councils, listed in the phone book, have information on clinics and self-help groups for those who wish to give up.

ASH (Action on Smoking and Health), 5-11 Mortimer Street, London WIN 7RH Tel:01 637 9843 - has Inf on smoking and the rights of non-smokers, Ad on giving up, referral to sources of help, sae and/or donation.

Soft Drugs and Hard Drugs
Each drug has its own particular effects, and people differ in their reactions. Generally, the lighter the body weight, the greater the effects. Also the more psychologically fragile someone is, the greater the risk of being pushed over the brink, even if others taking the same drug are affected very little.

Despite this, drug reactions do have some common characteristics. When 'high', users normally feel they are at their best - more relaxed, wittier, happier and more able to cope with those around them. To the observer the reverse is usually true: even relatively sociable drugs seem to put a distance between the users and non-users. Their reactions seem off-key and, being caught up in the distorted events of their own mind, they become unresponsive to other people's moods and needs. Anyone who has been teetotal at a drinks party has experienced a version of this phenomenon.

Teenagers and Drugs
One of the problems for parents and teachers is that most of the symptoms of drug taking mimic the behaviour of normal adolescence. Any parent whose child has reached its twenties without it ever being moody, irritable, depressed, over-confident, ill-washed, selfish, sleepless, insensitive to others, constipated, over-energetic, apathetic, late, off his or her food or obsessed with music, is either a very unobservant parent or has a very unusual child. Yet these can be the symptoms of drug taking.

Adults need to think very carefully before accusing a child of taking drugs. If the real problem is just adolescence, an accusation may produce the reaction of 'I may as well be hung for a sheep as a lamb' and push them into drug taking. So watch out for confirmation first - unusual tablets, capsules or powders, cigarette papers (if the child doesn't usually roll his or her own) or even needles or syringes or skin and hair looking lifeless. Meanwhile, try to find out if anything else is causing the symptoms - a child who is worried about something, or unwell, will also be moody, irritable and apathetic. This can also be the time to read up or talk to organizations which deal with drug problems and learn more about what you can do if drugs *are* being taken (opposite).

Unfortunately, there is no easy way to get an adolescent to admit to anything - let alone something illegal. But the adult who can *ask* a child calmly and caringly about the possibility that he or she may be taking drugs is more likely to learn the truth than someone who accuses. This means planning the moment carefully and not letting yourself be pushed into suddenly reacting to the child's behaviour. If drugs *have* been taken, try to find out how much, which ones, and why. Then discuss the future. Things need to be kept in proportion. A child regularly taking heroin has a serious problem, but a child experimenting with pot may be going through a passing stage - albeit an illegal one.

Such discussion isn't easy. Adolescents don't like talking about their lives. Equally a child's drug taking often makes adults feel rejected and furious. But it may be easier to handle if we take stock of our own drug taking first. Most of us take drugs of some kind, to keep others company or to make life more bearable or more enjoyable - the very reasons why adolescents take them. Our drugs are pain killers, sleeping tablets, tranquillizers, drink or cigarettes. Even if the first three are on doctor's orders, we all know that drink does us little good and that cigarettes are killers.

So shouting at adolescents for following the example which the adult world has set them is likely to be unproductive - however much we may feel like it. If *we* don't use our 'drug taking' as a route to understanding how they feel the risk is that *they* will use it to make us look foolish. They know that, as killers go, pot doesn't begin to compete with cigarettes. But they probably underestimate the risks of other drugs and the danger of one illegal drug leading to another, if those around them are taking them.

Common Hazards
People sometimes talk about drugs as if the slightest brush with them inevitably leads to addiction and death. This is simply not the case. But drugs do have risks attached to them which those who experiment with them tend to underestimate and the hazards involved *cannot* be judged by whether or not the law classes them as type A drugs. Some type B drugs are just as dangerous as those which are classified as type A.

First, the effects can be unpredictable, because the strength naturally varies from batch to batch, and sellers add impurities to increase their profits. Even if the strength doesn't vary, individual differences in people

still mean that there is no totally 'safe' dose. So there is *always* a risk of an experience getting out of control and causing distress, or possibly overdose. And even in the 'right' dose drug effects may not always be pleasant. People take drugs to make them feel better but, in reality, drugs strengthen the mood you are in. So if someone is feeling worried, depressed or aggressive, these feelings increase.

Most drugs reduce physical control and concentration and slow down reaction times, even though the user may feel alert and totally in control. So it can be dangerous to drive, use machinery or even cross a road. The emotions are affected in a similar way, and regular use can distort the user's view of the world to a point where it harms emotional development and the ability to function normally and have normal relationships. Drugs can also affect basic body functions. Amphetamines, for example, reduce the normal renewal of calcium in the bones, which could later lead to osteoporosis (see page 532), and both amphetamines and heroin play hell with the menstrual cycle and may stop it completely. In this situation girls should realize that they can still get pregnant and should not stop using contraceptives. In pregnancy there is also a risk of harming the baby, who may receive the drug through the mother's bloodstream. Drug users tend to have premature, underweight babies, and babies can experience withdrawal symptoms after birth.

Since the body adapts to drugs, this means the user needs more and more to get a buzz. In drugs that create dependence the body or the mind learns to 'need' that drug, and without it the user feels very ill. The cost can be disastrous for his or her lifestyle. Moreover, when combinations of drugs are used to get the desired effect it creates complex and unpredictable chemical interactions in the body, which are extremely dangerous and can be fatal. There are added risks from injecting drugs: it is more addictive and there is a greater danger of overdose, and sharing used needles causes infections such as abscesses, gangrene, hepatitis B and AIDS.

Coming Off Drugs
Relatives and friends may find it helpful to bear in mind that addiction is an escape from reality. So users may not know the truth, let alone tell it, and promises are often not remembered, let alone kept. The key to coming off drugs is the desire to do so. When someone really wants to give up, even the most addictive drug can be defeated, with help.

The first stop is the family doctor, but not all family doctors are experienced in this field, so it may be better to go to a specialist out-patient clinic. In-patient treatment is also available in some areas. Meanwhile it is safest to come off the drug gradually, and this will lessen the unpleasant symptoms of withdrawal. One useful trick is the slimmer's ploy of 'allowing' yourself the drug, but each time you feel like taking it, you tell yourself you will have some, but not until a little later. In that way you cut down the total amount taken in the day.

Once off drugs former users need other satisfactions

in their lives to help them stay off and to give them a new focus and source of relationships.

ADFAM (Aid for Addicts and their Families). 99-101 Old Brompton Road, London SW7 3LE Tel: 01 581 4163 - RC, M£L, S, F&F, L, G, A.

Families Anonymous, 5-7 Parsons Green, London SW6 4VL Tel: 01 731 8060 - helps family and friends of drug abusers. RC, F&F, L, B, G, sae.

Narcotics Anonymous, P.O. Box 417, c/o 47 Milman Street, London SW10 Tel: 01 351 6794 - Lists of self-help groups for ex-addicts.

Release Tel: 01 603 8654 - Ad on legal problems.

SCODA (Standing Conference on Drug Abuse) 1-4 Hatton Place, London EC1N 8ND Tel: 01 430 2341/2 - RC, CS, F&F, L, B, large sae for a list of your local clinics and services.

Turning Point and Dawn (see under Alcohol, page 570). The booklet 'Emergency Aid in Schools' covers first aid for drink and drugs, from St John Ambulance Association, Edwina Mountbatten House, 63 York Street, London W1H 1PS.

Pamphlets on giving up, and on helping drug takers can be obtained from ISDD (at SCODA address) or from Department DM, DHSS Leaflets Unit, P.O. Box 21, Stanmore, Middx HA7 1AY, and local Health Education Units.

Recognizing Drugs and their Effects

Amphetamines (Speed)

Amphetamines and other stimulants - sometimes described as the poor man's coke - are available in several forms. In the 1950s and 1960s they were often prescribed for depression, but are rarely used now. They are relatively cheap and easy to get and much used by teenagers, especially at weekends. The most common is amphetamine sulphate, a white or brown powder, which is sniffed or injected, small white tablets and capsules are also available. They speed up the body, raise the heart and breathing rate and widen the pupils. People become confident, energetic, bouncy, giggly and wakeful, and lose their appetite. The effects last 3 to 4 hours and it can take the body several days to recover.

As the body's energy runs down, the 'up' feelings can change to irritability, restlessness and extreme hunger, followed by depression and exhaustion. Tolerance can develop, and heavy use may cause heart problems, delirium, panic, hallucinations and feelings of persecution which can develop into a psychosis from which it may take several days to recover. With most teenagers speed is just a phase, but some youngsters take it compulsively and even inject it - which is particularly dangerous.

Cannabis (Marijuana, Pot, Dope, Hash, Grass, Gear, Ganja, Black)

Cannabis comes in two forms. One is a hard, dark-brown resin. The other looks rather like tobacco but is greener, sometimes seedy and less well chopped. It is smoked either in a pipe or in a cigarette paper, sometimes mixed with tobacco, but it is also brewed or put in food. The smoke smells distinctly herbal, and the strength is very variable, though resin is usually stronger than grass. The effects last from 1 hour to several, depending on the strength.

Cannabis distorts the sense of time and produces an exaggerated awareness of the world around. Some users become talkative and giggly, others withdraw. But not all its effects are pleasant: those who are feeling low, or are unused to it, can experience panic and distress. There are no obvious effects the next day, and almost no danger of overdose or physical dependence. But smoking it can aggravate both chest complaints and existing mental problems, and excessive use causes lethargy and loss of drive.

Cocaine (Coke)

Cocaine is a fine white powder which is a powerful stimulant. It is usually sniffed (snorted) off paper through a tube, but it can be injected (sometimes mixed with heroin) or tucked into the inner lip. Occasionally it is smoked (freebasing), which produces a sudden rush similar to injecting. Its effects are like those of amphetamines, but the much greater feeling of well-being, and loss of sensitivity to pain or fatigue, make it far more likely to lead to dependence. As the effects peak after 15 to 30 minutes, the dose may have to be repeated every 20 minutes to maintain the effect. Large doses, or too many repeats, can make people extremely agitated, anxious and paranoid, and may cause hallucinations. With frequent, heavy use the effects become increasingly unpleasant. Initial euphoria is replaced by restlessness, extreme excitability, nausea, insomnia and weight loss, then later by paranoia. But giving up cocaine usually cures these reactions and there are no physical withdrawal symptoms.

Regular use destroys the membranes inside the nose (and in time the division between the nostrils). So, even when they aren't high, regular users may sniff frequently. In rare cases excessive doses can kill through heart failure.

Crack

Crack is cocaine which has been refined and concentrated, then mixed with bicarbonate of soda to form a hard cake. But, contrary to popular belief, the refining doesn't free it from impurities. It is sold as tiny rocks which are vaporized into smoke with a match. It engenders the same euphoria as cocaine, but gives an instant 'rush' as high concentrations reach the brain within 10 seconds. Its other attraction is that inhaling smoke seems more 'normal' than sniffing powder or injecting, so those who might reject other forms of drug taking find crack acceptable. However, it is rapidly addictive both physically and psychologically and the ill effects are both unpleasant and dangerous. Regular use makes it increasingly hard to get a 'high', while its biochemical effects on the brain cause chronic depression, withdrawal and paranoid reactions. It can also cause high blood pressure, strokes and fatal brain seizures or heart failure.

Heroin (Smack, Skag)

Heroin is a fine white or brown speckled powder made from the milk of the opium poppy. The fumes are usually inhaled after heating it on silver foil ('chasing the dragon'), but it can also be sniffed, injected, and occasionally smoked. Using it for the first time may cause nausea and vomiting, but habitual users feel more alert. Like all opiates, it depresses the activity of the nervous system, so the blood vessels dilate (making the user feel warm and drowsy); reflexes like coughing are suppressed and the user begins to feel detached and content, free from pain, desire or stress. A heroin user may seem drunk and dopey to an onlooker. Gradually larger and larger doses are needed to produce these effects, and long-term users cease to feel good and need it even to feel normal.

Regular use produces both physical and psychological dependence, and withdrawal symptoms are similar to flu - aches, shaking, sweating, shivering, sneezing, yawning and muscular spasms. These start 8 to 24 hours after the last dose and usually last 5 to 10 days. In the short term it leads to constipation and loss of concentration, sex drive and appetite. And there is always a risk of infection if it is being injected.

Hypnosedatives (Downers, Blues)

These are prescribed drugs used to calm people down or to make them sleep - such as Tuinal, Seconal and Nembutal. But they are among the most dangerous drugs to misuse, and are the most dangerous of all if injected. Most are sold as coloured capsules. They damp down the nervous system in the same way as alcohol. Small doses make people just feel relaxed, but larger doses slur the speech and make them clumsy and prone to extreme emotional reactions and mental confusion. The effects last 3 to 6 hours, depending on the dose.

Heavy users are vulnerable to bronchitis and pneumonia, and large doses may cause unconsciousness and death. There is a constant risk of overdose, as the difference between a 'pleasurable' and a fatal dose is very small. Even a few barbiturate pills can be fatal and the dangers are increased if they are combined with alcohol. They cause both physical and psychological dependence, and the withdrawal symptoms include irritability, faintness, nausea, twitching, delirium and sometimes convulsions. There may be lasting brain damage. Sudden withdrawal can be fatal, so coming off must be medically supervised.

LSD (Acid)

Lysergic acid diethylamide is a very potent synthetic chemical which causes hallucinations. It is sold through drops on blotting paper, stamps or lumps of sugar - which are all sucked - and also as tiny coloured tablets. The trip starts within 30 to 60 minutes, peaks in 2 to 6 hours and fades in about 12 hours. The hallucinations range from the ecstatic and mystical to the very unpleasant. They may be accompanied by panic, disorientation and depression. While high, the user may seem either over-excited or deeply withdrawn, and may need reassurance on the way down. There is no physical dependence, prolonged psychological reactions are rare and deaths from LSD overdose are unknown. But heavy use can create acute confusion and ideas of persecution, and on occasions the hallucinations have proved fatal.

Magic Mushrooms (Psilocybin)

These mushrooms grow wild in Britain and elsewhere and are also sold dried on the black market. Eaten in large quantities they produce much the same effects as LSD, but, unlike LSD, there may be euphoria and often nausea, vomiting and stomach pains. The effects start within 30 minutes, peak after 3 hours, and last 4 to 9 hours. They can cause bad trips, for which reassurance and support may be needed, but there are no withdrawal symptoms, and there is no physical dependence. A major risk lies in confusing these mushrooms with poisonous ones. Curiously, it is illegal to cook or dry them for eating, but not illegal to eat them raw - though the effects are no different.

Other Opioids (Dikes, 118s)

A range of red, white or parti-coloured tablets, capsules and ampoules which are used clinically but sold on the black market. They have effects, and risks, similar to heroin.

Solvents

The solvents used in glues, paints, lighter fuel, hair spray and so on produce effects similar to alcohol, and some children increase the effects by sniffing them inside a paper bag. Users behave as if they are drunk, and an overdose can cause unconsciousness, vomiting and, occasionally, sudden death from heart failure or suffocation. Repeated sniffing produces a hangover, pallor, fatigue, loss of concentration and depression, and there are often spots round the mouth and red rings round the eyes. Glue can be addictive but physical dependence on solvents is rare. Heavy long-term (10 years) misuse, however, can permanently damage the brain, and there is a *very* great danger in getting high on the propellants in aerosols by spraying them into the mouth: they can freeze the throat, causing instant suffocation and death. Since 1985 it has been illegal to supply solvents to those under the age of 18 if misuse is suspected.

In Health

The Baby-Making Business • Contraception • Pregnancy •
Infertility • Sexual and Marital Problems • Menopause - Change
of Life • A Healthy Diet • Looking After the Face and Body

THE BABY MAKING BUSINESS

Puberty

Nobody really knows why the changes start, but puberty usually begins two years later in boys than in girls and no two people develop in exactly the same way. It is certainly tough to be the only flat-chested girl in the class, or to have friends shaving when you haven't a vestige of a hair. But nobody need worry if his or her timing is different from other people's or if things happen in a different order; that is perfectly normal.

The first changes are unseen alterations in the balance of hormones - the chemicals which make the body changes take place. After that, people often have sudden spurts of growth, and most girls start to round out over the hips, become slimmer at the waist and lose that pot-bellied little girl look. The hair on the head sometimes gets darker, and becomes curlier, or straighter. It may also become greasier as the hormones produce more oil - which is why spots are one of the hazards of the teens.

Girls' nipples get bigger and darker and the breasts begin to grow - often in fits and starts. They vary greatly in size, shape and even the position on the chest, and often one is slightly larger than the other. In both sexes, body smells alter and become stronger, and body hair starts sprouting on the fleshy mound over the pubic bone, between the legs and later under the arms, also on the chests of some boys. With these changes come new feelings and experiences. A girl's nipples become sensitive and sexual feelings may come when she touches them. This is perfectly natural.

There are also big changes in the genitals. The boy's penis begins to grow and his balls (scrotum) get bigger and drop lower. On girls the tightly-closed fleshy pads (the labia majora - literally big lips) between a girl's legs open out to reveal the tiny, but very sensitive, bump of the clitoris at the front where these 'lips' meet. Then further back are revealed the labia minora (little lips) and the entrance to the vagina, mid-way between the anus (back passage) and the urethra (urine opening). Stories make so much of the existence of a hymen, which has to be broken on first making love, that girls who look at this area in a mirror may be surprised to find that the hymen is only a small ring of tissue at the entrance to the vagina. It can be so

thin that it is almost transparent or up to 2 mm thick. It is often broken by girls and women inserting tampons.

Advertisements give the impression that to keep the genital area clean women need to use all kinds of douches, sprays and deodorants. This is totally untrue and just a ploy to sell products. Nature has arranged things so that the fluid of the vagina contains exactly the right balance of chemicals to keep it healthy. To wash inside or spray the area with deodorants just upsets the balance of nature and invites trouble.

Periods - a loss of blood from the vagina - usually start in girls about two years after the first signs of puberty. This is usually around the age of 12, but it can be anytime between the ages of 10 and 17. They are often erratic at first but they gradually settle down to about once a month (see page 576). A boy finds his voice may alter suddenly from his high-pitched boyish one to a deeper, more adult, tone. Disconcertingly, this comes and goes from day to day. And while his voice is breaking he also has what doctors call 'nocturnal emissions' - which means that he spurts a creamy liquid (seminal fluid) from his penis while asleep. The body is just practising for when he will make love.

Unfortunately, the hormones which cause these physical changes also have a strong effect on moods. Formerly reasonable pleasant children often become withdrawn, depressed, irritable, noisy, defiant and arrogant. Worst of all, they tend to think it is the rest of the world which is getting it wrong. Hormones are a kind of mind-changing drug, which the body produces, and adolescents should know this (and realize that adding other drugs will just confuse the issue). It isn't always easy for an adolescent to handle the moods which hormones produce, and putting up with them can be pretty hard on everyone else, but, unfortunately, growing older is the only cure. So both sides just have to keep reminding themselves that it *will* pass. They may be surprised to find how well they get on once the hormones stop moaning.

Masturbation

From early childhood most children enjoy touching the area between their legs. But even those who don't may find that in adolescence it becomes tender and itchy, so when they touch it they discover a rather pleasant sensation results. With a lot of touching and stroking the sensation may suddenly reach a climax and then fade (a boy also releases a spurt of liquid). The climax is an orgasm and the activity which leads to it is masturbation.

Because the genitals are so closely linked to the tubes for excreting and urinating some people think the genitals themselves are dirty and bad, and not to be touched. And all sorts of stories have been told about how people who touch themselves do damage and become ill. This is total nonsense.

Far from being immoral, touching and getting pleasure this way is very good preparation for both giving and receiving sexual pleasure from the opposite sex - which is an important part of a happy marriage. So nobody should be ashamed or worried about it. It can be far more than that. Masturbation is the dry ski slope of sex, where a boy can practise creating and controlling his own excitement, and a girl can learn what arouses and what checks arousal, so that when the time comes both can make love with more sensitivity. For it is very hard to understand other people's sexual needs unless you understand your own. Sexuality - like driving - takes practice and learner drivers are best without passengers.

Menstruation (Periods)

It's a pity menstruation has acquired bad names, like 'the curse', for it is not the problem such names suggests. What happens is that a complex chain of instructions from the hormones tells the ovaries to release an egg each month. While it travels slowly down the fallopian tubes the womb prepares a good home for a potential baby, thickening its lining and gaining more blood vessels. If the egg isn't fertilized within 14 days of its release the body realizes it has prepared the womb to no purpose. So the hormone levels change, making the new womb lining peel away and dissolve, releasing blood as a period. During the next 14 days or so the body ripens another egg ready for the whole cycle to start again. The hormones which control the cycle also affect the way in which water is stored in the body. So, in the early stages of a period, women often put on weight and feel bloated and swollen, and the breasts may be larger and rather tender.

The ripening time isn't always exactly 14 days so, although most periods come every 28 days, the cycle is seldom totally regular. Equally, some people have small periods lasting only 3 days, others heavy ones lasting 7 days. Even in the same person they may vary considerably from period to period. We aren't machines. Our body reacts to every aspect of our lives - feelings, diet, exercise, work, even our companions. (Nuns often menstruate in unison.) When deeply upset, for example, periods may suddenly stop for a while, or become very heavy. In fact, doctors are only just realizing just how much emotions affect a woman's rhythm, and how often female problems occur when something else - like their marriage - is going wrong.

False Ideas about Periods

Over the centuries the fact that periods come and go so mysteriously and uncontrollably, with bleeding but no wound, has led to all kinds of superstitions. Superstitions die hard, and odd ideas about periods persist, though it is high time they were abandoned.

Myths about Periods

False	True
Periods are dirty.	A healthy person's blood is one of the cleanest fluids - if it wasn't there would be no blood donor scheme.
Periods are smelly.	Fresh blood has almost no smell but bacteria love to live on it. The bacteria produce the smell. Normal washing and frequent changing banish it.
You shouldn't have a bath during a period.	You certainly should. It is failing to have a bath which makes periods smelly.
It is dangerous or unwise to wash your hair during a period.	Nonsense. Washing the hair has no link to periods at all, good or bad.
You can't do active sports or swim during a period.	You can do what you normally do. Tampons make swimming no problem - but don't swim where there are sharks, they are drawn to the blood. (No joke - women have died this way.)
During a period women should not cook or they will contaminate food.	An idea based on ancient ignorance and folklore. No harm comes to anyone if women cook during a period.
Sexual intercourse should be avoided during a period.	There is no health reason for avoiding sex. Some couples do; some don't. It's a personal choice. But, as the cervix is less tightly closed sexually transmitted infections are more easily caught (see also Diaphragm, page 581).
Tampons (internal sanitary towels) can only be used by non-virgins.	Anyone can use them and they are by far the neatest form of towel.
Tampons are dangerous as they can get lost in your insides.	No chance. The vagina is a short tube like the finger of a rubber glove, with no exit at the far end. The cervix which comes into it is far too small for a tampon to enter (see illustration, page 582).

Period Pains

A period is not an illness; it is just part of the body's functioning, like the heart beating or the lungs breathing, and for many women it is just as easy and unnoticeable. Unfortunately for others it isn't. There isn't one neat cause of period pains, there are different causes in different people. In young girls the hormones may be poorly balanced (the body is still learning its new role) and cause crampy pains in the womb, and there may also be nausea, diarrhoea and a headache. The mind also plays a part. A girl who is afraid of growing up or upset (perhaps at the beginning of term or before exams) is far more likely to have a painful period. It can also be a matter of temperament. Some people of both sexes tend to express their anxieties through pain of some kind. The pain is real, but the cause is emotional, and such women are more prone to get period pains.

Period pains can also possibly be caused by very small problems in the spine, and I have found that chiropractic treatment cures them totally (see page 548), but it may not do this for everyone. Equally, a friend of mine suffered so badly with pain that, in her twenties, she booked to have a hysterectomy (removal of the womb) despite the fact that she wanted children. Luckily, before the operation, she was told about vitamin B6, took it and the pain was cured. But this is a treatment to discuss with a doctor as it could be harmful if not used correctly. And, as B6 reduces the body's magnesium, it is a good idea to eat magnesium-rich foods, such as nuts, cereals and seafood, while taking it.

With most period pains you need only take it easy (if you can), put a hot water bottle where it comforts, and take a pain killer if necessary. But if pain occurs regularly see a doctor. There are various disorders of the womb which can make periods heavy and uncomfortable, so it is worth having a check-up. Claire Rayner's book *Woman* (Hamlyn) has a useful section on these.

Pre-Menstrual Tension (PMT) and Pre-Menstrual Syndrome (PMS)

Most women are not at their best in the week before a period, and many feel tense, irritable, depressed, bloated, forgetful, 'headachey' or generally low. Objective tests show women drive less well and perform less well in exams at this time. The reasons for this are still a mystery.

As the hormone changes make the body retain more fluid it may be that the fluid which cushions the brain increases, causing enough pressure to alter the emotions. Some specialists find it helps to prescribe a drug which lowers the fluid levels in the body. Others recommend vitamin B6 (see Period Pains, above). Research at St Thomas' Hospital suggests oil of evening primrose, which contains gamma linolenic acid, is effective - if costly. You can get it in health food stores. Some people need only take 250 mg a day; others need as much as 500 mg three times a day. If you try it, start low and only work up if necessary. Another possible treatment is hormone therapy, but this is still controversial.

Diet is also a factor. Salt makes the body retain fluid. A low salt diet helps, as does avoiding caffeine in tea or coffee, for caffeine greatly increases tension. A diet with less junk food, less sugar and less alcohol, but more raw foods and more fibre can also help. If you have dandelions include some leaves in salads, for dandelion makes the body hold less water.

National Association for Pre-Menstrual Syndrome, 2nd Floor, 25 Market Street, Guildford, Surrey GU1 4LB Tel: 0483 572715 Helplines: 0483 572806 (day) 095 92 4371 (night) - RC, M£L, support G, Ad, largely geared to the use of progesterone.

Pre-Menstrual Tension Advisory Service, P.O.Box 268, Hove, East Sussex BN3 1RW Tel: 0273 771366.

Breast Self-examinations

Every woman should check her breasts regularly for lumps, at the same time each month — a few days after her period (see page 533). These illustrations show how it is done. Self-checking is also often taught at local clinics.

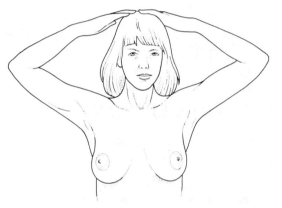

Stand before a mirror with your hands above your head and look at your breasts closely for puckering or any other changes.

Lie down with a towel under you and hunch your left shoulder up. Feel carefully for any lumps or other unusual signs at the top of your breast.

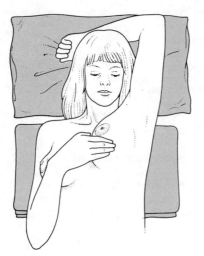

Raise your arm above your head and continue to feel around the breast, checking every part. Use your fingers rather than your palm.

Continue to check the area right into your armpit. Then repeat these stages for the other breast.

CONTRACEPTION

Contraception is a subject with almost as many myths as facts. And the myths are dangerous.

Myth	Truth
You can't get pregnant the first time you make love.	You can - and many do.
You can't get pregnant standing up.	Standing up makes no difference. Sperm can swim uphill.
You can't get pregnant with clothes on.	Yes you can. Clothes are no protection.
You can't get pregnant making love during a period.	Occasionally you can, sperm can live 5 days in the vagina.
You can't get pregnant if the penis never enters the vagina.	You can. If semen spills on to the area outside the vagina the sperm can find their way into it and up to the womb.
You can't get pregnant if the man withdraws before orgasm.	You can, very easily. Some semen often leaks well before orgasm.
You can't get pregnant if you are breast feeding.	You may be less likely to get pregnant if you are breast feeding *very* frequently. But, while breast feeding, a woman can release eggs before her periods return.
You can't get pregnant if you don't have an orgasm.	You certainly can. The world population would be a lot smaller if orgasm was needed.

Those are only some of the myths. There's another mythology about other, more effective, types of contraception. So the main ones are listed opposite. It is hard to be precise on effectiveness rates as they can vary with the sexual frequency and carefulness of the user. So all of them should be taken as approximate.

Sterilization - Male (vasectomy) *(3 failures in 1,000 men)*
The tubes carrying the sperm from the testicles to the seminal fluid (the liquid released when a man 'comes') are cut. This takes 10 to 15 minutes under local anaesthetic but, as some sperm are already part of the way down the tube, sterility isn't immediate. Other forms of contraception are needed for the next 20 or so ejaculations, until tests show the semen is sperm-free. A man's masculinity and sex drive are unaffected and, as sperm are only a tiny fraction of a man's seminal fluid, nobody notices any change.
Disadvantages: Normally, the tubes cannot be rejoined to restore fertility, though in rare cases this may be possible. It should only be used if a man is *sure* he will never want (more) children. However, it is sometimes possible to store semen before the operation.

VASECTOMY

Sterilization - Female *(Less than 1 failure in 100)*
The fallopian tubes, which pass the egg down to the womb, are cut or closed, under general anaesthetic, during a 24-hour stay in hospital. Occasionally they heal together on their own, but cutting is usually more certain than clipping. Another contraceptive is needed until after the first period following the operation.
Disadvantages: Usually there are no side effects. But it is normally impossible to restore fertility (though this can depend on how the tubes were closed). So it is only for those who will NEVER want more children in future.

STERILISATION

Injected Contraceptives *(97-98% effective)*
An injection of hormones which stop the woman producing an egg lasts 8 to 12 weeks according to which type is being used. It is only available from doctors and - though it sounds the ideal option - the possible ill effects should be thoroughly discussed first.

Disadvantages: Some women have fewer periods and no problems, but others may get heavy bleeding or irregular spotting, back pain or depression. It may take up to a year to regain normal fertility after the injections are stopped. There is also a question mark regarding the risk related to cancer of the cervix. More research is going on. Meanwhile it could be wise to opt for other methods - if you can use them.

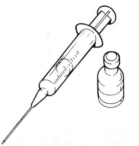

INJECTABLE CONTRACEPTION

The Combined Pill (99% effective)
This combines two hormones - oestrogen and progesterone - which stop the woman releasing an egg. One type of pill is taken daily for 21 or 22 days. Then there is a 6 to 7 day break for monthly bleeding, during which you are still protected because of the pills you have already taken. The other type is taken for 28 days and bleeding usually happens while still taking the pill. Some don't work for the first couple of weeks, so another contraceptive is needed then. It is also important to take some contraceptive pills in the correct order. Being on 'the pill' is convenient and may reduce the risk of some pelvic infections and of rheumatoid arthritis, and can also relieve pre-menstrual tension.
Disadvantages: This method is not suitable for lifelong use. Contact lens wearers may have problems. Some women may have nausea, headaches, tiredness, sore breasts, depression or increased weight. There is also a small risk of blood clots which can block a blood vessel and cause a stroke or heart attack. The women at greatest risk are those over the age of 35, the overweight, smokers and diabetics. Also at risk are those with high blood pressure, strokes or heart disease in the family.

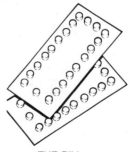

THE PILL

Both Pills

They may not work if you vomit or have diarrhoea - either can make you lose the pill before the hormones have time to work. Other medicines and drugs can interfere in the same way. So always check this possibility before taking any medication. It may be wisest *not* to take the pill when bedridden or with a leg in plaster, so discuss this with the doctor. It is essential to see a doctor every 6 months or if you have any unusual symptoms.

The Mini Pill *(97-98% effective)*

This 28-day pill uses only progesterone and may be less likely to produce problems with blood clotting or high blood pressure. But it *must* be taken at the same time each day - ideally in the early evening.
Disadvantages: there is a high risk of pregnancy if even one pill is missed. If you forget it for 12 hours or more, keep taking it but use another contraceptive for the rest of that month. It doesn't protect you for the first 14 days of taking it. It is less effective than the combined pill and offers less protection against ectopic pregnancy (pregnancy somewhere other than the womb). There may also be an increased risk of ovarian cyst - though this is not yet proved.

Intra-Uterine Device (IUD; IUCD or coil) *(96-99% effective)*

IUDs are a range of devices which are inserted by a doctor sliding them up the birth canal, when tightly folded. Then they open out in the womb and react with its lining so that an egg can't attach itself. For some women an IUD is the ideal contraceptive - trouble free and unobtrusive. Most are plastic or plastic and copper. Those with copper stay in place for 2 to 5 years; the plastic alone stay longer. They should normally be removed by a doctor. IUDs are best for those with children - especially if they intend to have no more.
Disadvantages: More effective with older women than with young ones. Some women get a pain and heavier periods; there can also be bleeding for a while after fitting. It is possible (though rare) to become pregnant with a coil in place. If a period is 14 days late see a doctor AT ONCE: there is an increased risk of ectopic pregnancy (other than in the womb) - which can be dangerous. Also pelvic infection, which can cause infertility, is more likely with an IUD, especially if a woman has several partners. Anyone who has pain after intercourse, abdominal pain or a vaginal discharge

should see a doctor immediately, especially if there is a fever. Anyone who has *ever* had a sexual infection of any kind should tell the doctor before an IUD is fitted.

Condom (sheath, rubber, French letter, Johnny *(85-98% effective)*

This is a thin rubber tube, like a long balloon, which is rolled over the length of the erect penis, so that the sperm are caught within it. It must be put on before the penis even touches the area round the vagina (most men trickle long before they 'come' and the sperm released that way can travel into the womb from outside the vagina). The big advantage is that condoms can be obtained from any chemist and it protects against sexually transmitted diseases.
Disadvantages: It can slip off; some men find it makes the penis less sensitive; sheaths have to be bought whereas most other contraceptives are on the health service. Also, some women find the interruption of the man putting one on may hinder orgasm. This is less likely to happen if she can put the sheath on him while he continues to excite her.

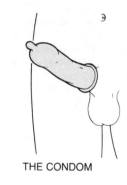

THE CONDOM

Diaphragm or Cap plus Spermicide *(85-97% effective)*

A circular device of arched rubber with a flexible reinforced rim. It is pushed high up in the vagina well before sex, blocking off the entrance to the womb, and stays in place for at least 6 hours afterwards. It must be coated with sperm-killing cream, and more cream should be squeezed into the vagina before making love again. Vaginas vary in size, so a doctor must choose the size, and this should be checked every 6 months, after weight gains or losses of 3 kg (7 lb) or more, and after childbirth. There are no side effects. It is not noticeable during lovemaking. Also it may be a

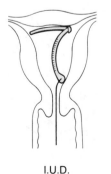

I.U.D.

protection against cancer of the cervix, and you can have sex during a period without leaking.

Disadvantages: The risk of forgetting to have it with you when you need it, and the spermicide tastes somewhat unpleasant. Also the effectiveness varies with the user. Careful users find it very effective; careless ones less so.

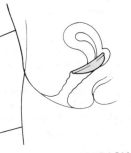

THE CAP OR DIAPHRAGM

Sponge *(unpredictable effectiveness)*
A man-made sponge, containing sperm-killing chemicals, which can be put high in the vagina up to 24 hours before intercourse. One size fits everyone and it can simply be bought at a chemist. It can stay in place throughout a love-making session - no matter how often intercourse occurs, but must remain in place for 6 hours afterwards and be thrown away on removal.

Disadvantages: Some authorities claim 75 to 91 per cent effectiveness, but one gynaecologist gave sponges to 7 women and all 7 became pregnant. It cannot be used during a period, and some women are allergic to the spermicide.

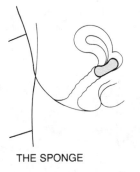

THE SPONGE

'Natural' Methods (safe period, rhythm method)
(variable effectiveness)
The old joke '"What do you call people who use the rhythm method?" Answer: "Parents!"' isn't entirely

true. But effectiveness rates for 'natural' methods are tricky. A leaflet by the Family Planning Association says, 'However careful you are, unplanned pregnancy occurs more often with this method than with any other method of contraception.' However, it also says the sympto-thermal method, correctly used, can be 85 to 93 per cent effective. This method uses a woman's daily temperature, and a number of other physical signs, such as day-to-day changes in her vaginal mucus, to decide when the egg is released. The advantages are that there is no interference with the body's chemistry and no side effects. However, women do not have textbook body changes. So these methods must be carefully taught and systematically used.

Disadvantages: Natural methods take care, and considerable self-control. For, since sperm can live in the vagina for up to 5 days, intercourse has to be avoided for more than half of every month. Also, irregular periods, disruptions through travel or illness, or the use of pain killers which lower body temperature can all reduce the accuracy. And, the so-called rhythm methods, which simply rely on avoiding intercourse at the mid-point between two periods, will have nothing like the success rate of the sympto-thermal method.

THE NATURAL METHOD

If You Forget - the 'Morning After' Method
If someone has had intercourse without using a contraceptive, pregnancy can usually be prevented if she acts *fast*. The first method is two doses of a special pill prescribed by a doctor. This treatment *must* start as soon after as possible, and at the latest within 72 hours of intercourse. This is usually effective but makes some women vomit and is not suitable for everyone. It is a one-off method and *not* a regular means of contraception.

The other method is the fitting of an IUD, which stops the egg attaching to the womb. Again it should be done as soon as possible, but up to 5 days after intercourse. Once there, it can remain as a permanent method of contraception. But IUDs don't suit everyone (see IUDs, opposite).

Contraceptive Advice and Help

Contraceptive advice and contraceptives are available free on the NHS to British residents (though GPs can't prescribe condoms). This applies to both sexes, whether single or married, and to everyone over the age of 16. It is available from NHS clinics all over the country, and from private clinics. You can go to your own GP - or, if you prefer, you may ask to see a different GP. Clinics are listed under 'Family Planning' in the phone book, A chemist, social worker, health visitor or midwife should have the address, or contact one of the following organizations.

Brook Advisory Centres, 153a East Street, London SE1 2SD Tel: 01 708 1234/1390 - centres in 7 major cities for those under 25. Cervical smears, pregnancy test if period 14 days overdue, free birth control, abortion advice, counselling on sexual and emotional problems. RC, optional M£M, L, B, V, tapes, E, HD, sae appreciated.

The Catholic Marriage Advisory Council, Clitherow House, IBI, The Mews, Blythe Road, London W14 0NW Tel: 01 371 1341 - will instruct in the use of 'natural' methods, and has branches.

Family Planning Association Information Service (FPA), 27-35 Mortimer Street, London W1N 7RJ Tel: 01 636 7866 - has free information on contraception, fertility, menstrual and menopausal problems. RC, optional M£L, P, L, B, V, E, Rg, Cl, HD, sae. Local branches under 'Family Planning' in the telephone book.

Health Education Authority, 78 New Oxford Street, London WC1A 1AH - information leaflets on contraception and pregnancy.

PREGNANCY

Preparing for Pregnancy

Responsible mothers often change their lifestyle once they know they are pregnant - giving up smoking and drinking, and taking more care of their diet. But, if you think about it, it's odd to make this change several weeks *after* the baby has been conceived, but to allow the embryo to bear the brunt of these things during the early weeks when it is, in some ways, at its most vulnerable. Logically, the time to change one's lifestyle is well before conception.

Any woman who might become pregnant, even by chance, should be tested for immunity to German measles - parental memories can be faulty. Those who aren't immune should be immunized *at least* 3 months before they intend to become pregnant. German measles in pregnancy can lead to severe mental and physical handicaps in the child. As some venereal diseases may be symptomless (see page 565), a VD check is also advisable.

Radical as it may sound, there is also a strong argument for *both* partners improving their diet and giving up alcohol and smoking (see page 569), and checking for hazards in the work place of both. A man is making sperm all the time, and smoking, drinking, drugs and environmental pollution can all damage the sperm and increase the chance of miscarriage or abnormality.

Farmers only mate a cow with a bull which is in prime health - so isn't it slightly odd that we often take less forethought for our children than a farmer would take for a calf? This is also a good time to research the best hospital for the birth (see page 584).

Foresight (The Association for Preconceptual Care), The Old Vicarage, Church Lane, Witley, Godalming, Surrey GU8 5PN Tel: 042 879 4500 - RC, M£L, S, F&F, L, EI, G, Inf on diet and forethought for pregnancy, sae.

The Maternity Alliance, 15 Britannia Street, London WC1X 9JP Tel: 01 837 1265 - RC, M£M, S, F&F, M, leaflets on preconceptual care, and maternity rights, sae.

Fertilization to Birth

Fertilization

The facts about human conception are quite extraordinary. Whatever lubricious magazines suggest, the average man ejaculates less than a teaspoonful of semen, but it carries some 400 million sperm, each about a five-hundredth of an inch long. Once in the vagina the race is on for the fastest, strongest sperm to get to the egg and fertilize it. Speed is vital for, after about fifteen minutes, the semen thins and the sperm can be killed by the natural acids of the vagina. Only 10 per cent make it to the welcoming, alkaline environment of the womb.

Sperm must travel about 9 inches, up the cervix and along to the other end of the fallopian tubes. Tadpole-like,

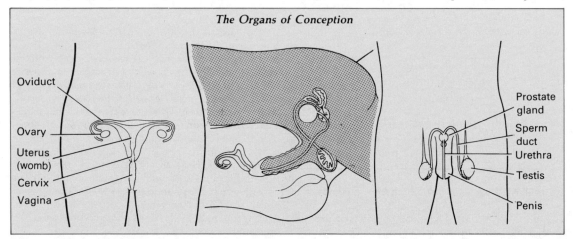

The Organs of Conception

Oviduct
Ovary
Uterus (womb)
Cervix
Vagina

Prostate gland
Sperm duct
Urethra
Testis
Penis

they swim with their tails, helped by minute hairs and small contractions inside the womb. It's survival of the fittest and only a small proportion of them manage this 45-minute Himalayan climb. Those that do, live on the sweet juices in the fallopian tubes for up to 72 hours while they wait for the egg - if it isn't already there.

On meeting the egg - which is vastly larger than them - they crowd round it, producing between them a substance which breaks down its outer layer and allows just one sperm to enter; the rest then fall away and die. If 2 separate eggs have been released they will each be fertilized and produce non-identical twins.

Deciding the Child's Sex
Conception itself doesn't happen until the fertilized egg is implanted. But, long before this, the 23 chromosomes of the sperm, which carry the genetic characteristics from father to child, link with the mother's 23 chromosomes in the egg to make one complete human cell. In some sperm the 23rd chromosome is a Y, in others it is an X. If a X-type sperm enters the egg it makes a girl; if an Y-type wins it's a boy. The complete 46-chromosome cell starts growing almost immediately, dividing and sub-dividing, making 2 cells, then 4, then 8, doubling in size at each division.

Implantation
It takes about a week for the fertilized egg to travel down to the womb. By the time it attaches itself and joins its own minute blood vessels to the mother's massive blood supply it has 64 cells. She is now pregnant, and her body is already releasing a pregnancy hormone - which tests can detect - but she hasn't yet missed a period. There are some 266 days to go before the birth - but to calculate when a baby is due count 280 days from the first day of the last period.

Ectopic Pregnancy
Occasionally cells implant on the way down the fallopian tube. Very rarely they even go the wrong way, and move out of the top of the fallopian tube and implant outside the reproductive system altogether. These are ectopic pregnancies, and are usually ended because they can cause serious complications. Some of the fallopian tube may have to be removed but the ovary is usually left, and a woman can have other perfectly normal pregnancies with eggs from the other tube.

The Vital Early Weeks
Between implantation and week 13 the cell will multiply and change to create almost all the human organs. These early weeks are crucial to the development of the baby. While the limbs and senses are forming they can be damaged if the mother takes certain drugs, or has infections like German measles, or even runs a high temperature. The range of infections which can disrupt a pregnancy is probably quite wide, so mothers need to keep away from anyone unwell, and any infection needs prompt treatment. But medicines of any kind should only be taken when really necessary and on doctor's orders.

Weeks 5 to 6
The baby floats in liquid inside a transparent bag (the amniotic sac) which cushions it until birth. It grows from 2 mm long to 6 mm long and the limbs begin to form. Gradually the chest and stomach cavities and the head and brain are formed, and the spine and nervous system develop.

Weeks 7 to 8
By the end of the 7th week the limb bulges have become arms and legs, with the first signs of fingers and toes. The heart begins to work, and the liver, kidney and lungs have developed - but don't yet work. The head grows rapidly, developing eyes, holes for nostrils, ears and a jaw. The body gains shoulders, the limbs develop joints, and genitals can be seen. But the baby is only as long as a finger joint (22 mm).

Weeks 9 to 10
The foetus looks more like a baby. Eyelids now cover the eyes, the nose and mouth develop fast, and the feet and hands have fingers and toes - though still webbed. The umbilical cord becomes complete and the placenta - the liver-like pad attaching the umbilical cord to the lining of the womb - is developing fast. The baby is definitely moving. It is as long as two joints of its mother's finger (4·5 cm) and weighs less than a Christmas walnut.

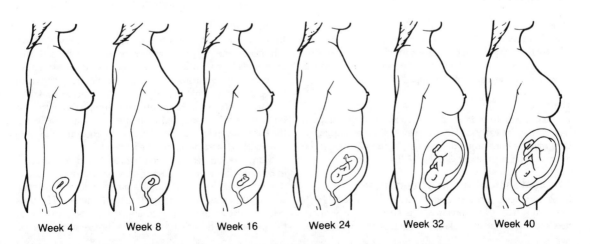

Week 4   Week 8   Week 16   Week 24   Week 32   Week 40

Weeks 11 to 12

Though only as long as a finger (5 to 6 cm) and weighing no more than a fat prune (10 g), all the main organs have formed and most are starting to work. The face is clearly human, the genitals are growing fast, and the details of the body are almost complete. From now on the foetus is far less vulnerable to outside factors which could damage it.

Weeks 13 to 14

At 13 weeks the mother is three months pregnant and the main risk of miscarriage is over. The womb has enlarged and can just be felt as a soft bulge above the pubic bone. The baby is about 7·5 cm long and has developed a neck. Its head can move, and some mothers may begin to feel movements - though many can't. By the 14th week the baby is fully formed. Now it must grow.

Week 16

Like the apes from which we descended, the baby begins to grow a layer of downy hair all over the body (lanugo) - plus eyebrows, eyelashes and head hair. It is now about 15 cm (6 in) long, and weighs about 135 g (almost 5 oz).

Week 20

It begins to move quite vigorously, and almost every mother can feel it. So can fathers if they put a hand on the still small bulge. This was once thought to be the time when life was 'breathed' into the baby and it got its soul.

Week 24

The organs are mature enough for the baby sometimes to survive briefly outside the womb if aborted or miscarried.

Week 28

From this week the baby is said to be viable - able to live without the mother.

Week 32

The baby is totally formed and can open its eyes. Its skin is covered with a greasy substance, called vernix, which protects the newly perfected skin against the water it lies in. But it is still only about 40 cm (16 in) long and weighs about 1·5 kg (3½ lb). It is getting ready to be born. By now half the babies lie head down.

Week 36

It is about 46 cm (18 in) long. If born at this stage it has a better than 90 per cent chance of surviving. Now the baby usually moves lower in the pelvis. People say the head has 'engaged' or the baby has 'dropped'.

Week 40

In theory, time to be born, but in practice perfectly normal babies may be early or late, as they will be as adults, so they may be born any time between 38 and 42 weeks. The average weight is about 3·2 kg (7 lb).

Medical Attention in Pregnancy

Pregnancy tests, on a sample of urine, by GPs or NHS clinics are free. Once pregnancy is confirmed a woman needs to have regular check-ups to see that all is going well, and paid time off work must usually be allowed for these. Check-ups are usually monthly until the 32nd week, then fortnightly until 36 weeks, and weekly after that. There are several options on how this is done.

1 If the baby is to be delivered at home, or in a nursing home, the GP who will deliver it may do all the check-ups himself, perhaps with the help of a midwife.
2 If a baby is to be born in hospital the GP usually refers the mother to the nearest one and she goes there for her check-ups.
3 Sometimes a GP does the ante-natal care in the early months and the hospital handles the later months and the birth.
4 Some areas have ante-natal clinics which may save a long journey to a hospital.
5 Those having their baby privately will see a GP or consultant - whichever will be delivering the baby.

Choosing a Hospital

If a woman would prefer a different hospital from the one her GP suggests she may ask to be referred there. If her GP doesn't agree she may still book into the hospital she wants - but she needs to book in early or it may be too full to take her. So it pays to research the local hospitals *before* getting pregnant and find out their policies on childbirth so you can book the instant you need to. *Choosing a hospital which does things the way you want is important.* Once under the care of a hospital you only have limited rights to insist on what you want and, in practice, demanding anything once in labour is almost impossible. Here are ten points you may want to check:

1   What is the policy on inducing labour?
2   What positions do women give birth in?
3   What types of anaesthetic are available?
4   Is the father allowed to be present *all* the time?
5   Do they always shave and give enemas?
6   What is the policy on episiotomies?
7   Do babies stay with their mothers?
8   Are babies put to the breast straight after birth?
9   What is the policy on breast feeding?
10   May mothers breast feed on demand?

More information

Sheila Kitzinger, *The New Good Birth Guide*, Penguin - useful reading before signing on with a hospital.

Home Births

In certain circumstances a home birth is risky, but Holland, which has one of the highest proportions of home births in the developed world, also has some of the lowest figures for babies dying during or soon after childbirth. The truth is that in Britain what makes home birth statistics look bad is that planned home births are often lumped in with data on women who concealed their pregnancy and delivered the baby themselves and/or those with problems who were caught short and never reached hospital.

Many doctors feel that first babies should be delivered in hospital. But if you had no trouble with your first labour there is probably no reason why you should not have the second, third and possibly fourth baby at home. (The risks begin to rise at the fifth birth and it may be wiser to go to hospital.) The advantages of a home birth can be considerable. It is much easier to relax and this alone makes labour easier, you can get to know your baby without the pressures of hospital routines or the risk that some nurse will foil your attempts to breast feed or leave the child crying when you want it comforted, and there is no risk of the baby picking up a hospital infection. There is also less disruption for your other children.

Some GPs do home deliveries, and so do some private gynaecologists, in which case they may have a midwife who works with them. But in law it isn't essential to have a doctor for a birth, a midwife is considered sufficient. If you need a midwife your local health authority has a statutory duty to provide one. So write to the Director of Midwifery Services in your health authority and ask to be provided with one. The alternatives are to obtain a private midwife through an agency (see page 547) or the association below.

Independent Midwives Association, 65 Mount Nod Road, London SW16 2LP - a small association of private midwives who offer a start-to-finish service for those wanting home births.

Body Changes and Problems in Pregnancy

Soon after conception a hormone is released which causes periods to stop. This is just the first of many changes which hormones cause during the 9 months. The hormone gives the body more elasticity. The skin on the breasts and stomach stretches more easily, and the gristly cartilage which links various bones in the body softens a little, so the pelvis can open slightly for the baby. The womb also stretches and grows new tissue. Quite early on the nipples darken and swell, and the breasts develop as they grow new tissue to make milk.

Unfortunately, not all body changes are beneficial. The softer tissues are less efficient and constipation, piles and varicose veins can result (see Diet, page 586). Some people also develop moles or freckles or darker patches of skin where it is exposed to the light, especially strong sunshine, and frequently in a line from tummy button to pubis. On the other hand, some people find their skin is better than ever, and positively glow. The hair may gradually alter - sometimes being glossier, sometimes greasier - and it can even change colour quite considerably. Mood swings are also common and emotions become so changeable that even a well-balanced woman can find herself suddenly tearful. She may also become victim to excessive worries about the baby. This is perfectly normal and isn't a sign that something is wrong with it.

Backache

When you consider how, during pregnancy, an extra couple of stone are carried amidships, with most of the weight dragging on the small of the back, it isn't surprising that many women get backache. Even a perfect back can ache, but if a woman has any specific back problems it's wise to get them sorted out before she becomes pregnant (see page 531).

The best relief for normal aching in pregnancy is to stand as little as possible, and, when you have to stand, avoid letting the weight simply hang. You can't pull your stomach in, but you can tuck in your bottom. Supporting the weight with a pregnancy girdle can also help - even if you wouldn't

be seen dead in one at any other time. Try to take plenty of rest and to lie down for at least half an hour each day.

Giddiness

As the mother breathes for both herself and the baby heavy demands are put on the oxygen-carrying red cells in her blood and she may feel faint or giddy and become anaemic. Doctors often prescribe folic acid to correct this. Neither the faintness nor the folic acid are bad for the baby.

Morning Sickness

Nobody should *expect* to feel sick during pregnancy. Pregnancy isn't an illness and you don't *have* to feel ill. In fact, 50 per cent of women never feel sick at all. However, the other 50 per cent do. As this is mainly in the early months of pregnancy, when the biggest changes are happening in the body, there may often be biochemical reasons for this. Each woman has her own pattern; some feel awful in the morning, some at night, often it only lasts a few months but in some it lasts throughout pregnancy. Avoid things which make it worse - some people, for example, find the smell of coffee disastrous. Get enough rest: everything is harder to bear when tired. This is easier said than done, but one of the things a woman needs to learn in pregnancy is to be a little gentle with herself.

Miscarriage

There is no need for a pregnant woman to be so afraid of a miscarriage that she wraps herself in cotton wool. She should steer a middle course between behaving as if ill and fragile and carrying on so much as usual as to be downright daft. Normal exercise is fine. But this is not the time for moving furniture, falling off horses or exerting any sudden strains on the body, especially at times when a period would normally be due - for this is when miscarriages most often occur. And smokers have more miscarriages than non-smokers.

If any bleeding occurs in pregnancy it could be the start of a miscarriage and the doctor should be phoned immediately. About 1 pregnancy in 7 miscarries. The causes vary: the mother's body rejecting the 'foreign body', the placenta not establishing its role properly, an inefficient cervix, problems with the uterus or severe illness or shock. But it can also be the body rejecting an imperfect foetal cell which would have made a handicapped baby.

For most women a miscarriage is the loss not of a foetus but a baby, and their grief needs all the understanding of those around them. It is all too easy to blame oneself, and feel as humiliated as a man who is impotent, for having failed in a basic female function. Understandable as these feelings are, there is no need for them, and another pregnancy will usually be fine. But it is hard to feel confident of this at the time.

More information

Miscarriage Association, 18 Stoneybrook Close, West Bretton, Wakefield, West Yorkshire WF4 4TP Tel: 092 485 515 - RC M£L, S, F&F, L, support groups, B, information on prevention.

Anne Oakley, Helen Roberts and Dr Anne McPherson, *Miscarriage*, Fontana

Hank Pizer and Christine O'Brian Palinski, *Coping with Miscarriage*, Norman & Hobhouse

Sex in Pregnancy

Neither intercourse nor orgasm normally causes miscarriages, and pregnancy needn't interrupt people's sex lives - though the positions may have to change as the bulge grows. But if a woman is prone to miscarry a doctor may advise her to avoid sex for the first 3 months and when periods would have been due. This is mainly to avoid the guilt a couple may feel if they have sex and then lose the baby. For even if making love didn't cause the miscarriage they will probably think it did.

Toxaemia (Pre-eclampsia)

Toxaemia is quite common towards the end of pregnancy. It is a condition in which the body stores more fluid than usual (e.g. in puffy ankles), blood pressure rises and protein is found in the urine. It is more likely to happen if the mother is especially tired or tense, and a high salt diet may possibly contribute to it. Bed rest in hospital is the usual treatment, but doctors may recommend inducing the birth early. This is because toxaemia reduces the blood supply to the placenta, on which the baby depends, and it can have serious consequences for both mother and child. Whether induction is needed or not will depend on the severity of the toxaemia, but mothers who don't want to be induced can always ask whether it is really necessary.

Diet in Pregnancy

There's a good word in the computer business - GIGO. It stands for garbage in garbage out. That is, what you get out is only as good as what you put in. The pregnant woman is feeding both her body and her child's. This doesn't mean she has to go along with the old wives' tale of needing to eat enough for two. But it does mean it is doubly important to have a good diet.

Unfortunately, researching the effects of women's diets on their babies is a long and complicated business. So there is a lack of hard data on how much a baby is affected. But some people are convinced that hyperactivity, and even major personality disorders, may be caused by the effects of certain substances - especially additives - taken by the mother during pregnancy. Whether that is so or not it would certainly be very odd if the ill effects of a bad diet on adults did not apply even more strongly to the far more vulnerable foetus. This means prospective mothers should try to avoid:

junk foods	tinned foods
dehydrated foods	instant packet foods
caffeine	man-made drinks

The foods to eat instead are:

fresh fruit	fresh vegetables
fresh meat	fresh fish
rice	dried beans
milk	nuts
cereals	pasta
milk products	eggs
frozen foods without	
dubious additives	

It's also a good precaution to adopt a high fibre, low sugar diet so as not to encourage piles by constipation, and for her to get enough calcium (see page 609). If there is risk of lead or high levels of chemicals in the tap water a pregnant woman should also avoid drinking it if she can - there is evidence that lead taken during pregnancy does get through to the baby, and lead is bad for the brain. The alternatives are bottled water or, failing that, using a water filter jug, such as the Crystal which removes a proportion of such metals.

And, of course, avoid alcohol and don't take drugs - not even ones from the chemist, unless a doctor says you need them. Both can get through to the baby and no baby needs alcohol or medicines. You should also talk to your doctor before taking extra vitamins and iron.

Two other changes can be useful. For centuries the Chinese have given up salt during pregnancy, because salt makes the body retain more fluid. As retaining unwanted fluid is one of the problems and hazards of pregnancy this makes a great deal of sense. It is easier than you might think. Another ancient practice is drinking raspberry leaf tea. If taken regularly, it seems to work on the womb and make labour easier. It is never possible to prove that such a thing works, as one can't re-run the labour without it for comparison. But some otherwise conventional doctors believe in it and, after three remarkably short labours, I personally swear by it. Many health food shops sell raspberry leaves and you just infuse a spoonful in boiling water and drink a cup or two each day, like ordinary milkless tea. But, like all unusual substances, it should not be taken in the first 4 months.

Tests during Pregnancy

Women may now be offered a number of tests during pregnancy to check that the baby is normal. Screening with ultrasound is fairly routine for everyone. But other tests are usually only offered to certain women. This is because there are three possible reasons for having them.

1   Women who are in a general 'at risk' category may be routinely screened. For example, screening for Down's syndrome in the babies of those over the age of 38 (35 in some areas), since the risk of having a Down's child increases with age. But, even at the age of 45, the risk of having a Down's baby is still only about 1 in 50.

2   Women who have a special risk of having an abnormal child will be tested to check the baby doesn't have a particular abnormality

3   A positive result in one test may be followed by other tests to double check it.

So don't expect *all* the tests below to be offered to everyone.

Detecting Abnormalities

At one time tests in pregnancy could only detect a narrow range of abnormalities. Now, they can pick up many more - though they will only find the abnormalities they look for, and the looking is selective. So having negative result does not *guarantee* a normal baby - though it makes it extremely likely.

Only a handful of tests are used, but this is now a sophisticated area of medicine and the samples obtained from the mother can be subjected to numerous different screening procedures.

How Soon the Results Come

With a test such as ultrasound scanning the results are there at once, but some analyses take time. So a mother may have to wait several weeks for certain tests following amniocentesis. Waiting weeks for the results is very hard on the parents, but some procedures simply cannot be hurried[?] and the delay does not mean that something dreadful has been discovered. A late result could be either negative or positive - just like any other.

Types of Test

Name	When Taken	How	Purpose	Advantages	Drawbacks
AFP Blood Test	16 to 18 weeks	A little blood is taken from the mother, as in any blood test.	To indicate whether the baby could have spina bifida or any other defect of the spinal cord.	It sounds a warning, through a test which is simple to apply and gives quite quick results.	It looks for raised levels of a particular substance, but these levels can also be raised by twins, or if the pregnancy is farther on than the mother calculated. So a positive result must be checked by amniocentesis.
Amnio-centesis	16 to 18 weeks	While 'looking' into the womb with a scanner, doctors choose a place where the baby isn't lying and insert a needle through the wall of the abdomen into the uterus, at that point, and draw off a little of the fluid in which the baby floats.	To detect a wide range of abnormalities including Down's syndrome, spina bifida and certain blood disorders.	Women who could not bear to have an abnormal child can abort it if they choose. It also reveals the sex of the child - if the couple want to know.	The sample of fluid from any one woman is only tested for a narrow range of defects. So, although a negative result usually means that the baby is fine, it does not *guarantee* a normal baby: the baby could have a defect for which the fluid was not tested. A very small proportion of positive results are incorrect. In about 1 woman in 100 to 200 the test causes a miscarriage.
Chorionic villus sampling (CVS)	8 to 10 weeks	Particles of the placenta are taken through a tiny tube inserted up the vagina and cervix.	It can detect many defects including Down's syndrome, and various inherited blood diseases found by amniocentesis.	The test can be done early in pregnancy and doctors have results quite quickly. So if an abortion is needed it can be done early in pregnancy when it is safer and less hard for the woman.	This is a new test and information on how often it causes miscarriage, and whether there are any other disadvantages for mother or baby, are still being collected.
Ultrasound	Usually routinely at 16 to 20 weeks. Occasionally more often.	Sound waves are sent into the womb which bounce off whatever they encounter and produce pictures on a screen. The strength of these waves can be adjusted to give more detail if an abnormality is suspected.	To check the development of the baby and get an accurate date for its birth. It also shows whether there are problems like the placenta lying across the cervix (which could complicate labour) and detects abnormalities in the baby, such as heart defects or other structural defects.	If it detects a defect there may be no need for amniocentesis. It also reveals twins (or more) and many mothers rather enjoy 'seeing' their baby.	The results can be inaccurate. Close to 16 weeks it is very good at telling the baby's age, but less good at picking up defects. Close to 20 weeks it is good for picking up defects but less good for dating. Around 18 weeks may be the ideal time. There is no evidence to suggest that ultrasound has any ill effect on the baby. But long-term ill effects cannot be entirely ruled out however unlikely.

Types of Test

Name	When Taken	How	Purpose	Advantages	Drawbacks
Doppler ultrasound	During pregnancy or during labour.	High intensity sound waves are sent into the womb through the mother's abdomen.	To monitor the baby's heart and make sure it is alive and well.	Heart defects are detected early, giving an opportunity for abortion or babies with weak hearts may stand a better chance as if an emergency operation may be needed at birth the hospital can be ready.	Nobody knows how upsetting the sound may be for the baby. The mother has to lie on her back, which may be uncomfortable and is not the best position for blood flow to the baby during labour.
Foetal blood sampling	From 18 weeks to the end of pregnancy.	Uses the same procedure as amniocentesis, except that a small sample of blood is taken from the umbilical cord, which links the baby to the placenta.	To test for some chromosomal abnormalities and blood and metabolic disorders after scanning has suggested they may be present.	It can be used to detect some of the same abnormalities as amniocentesis, but the results come back much faster. This saves waiting and may make abortion possible at a stage when it is easier for the mother.	There is a slightly greater risk of miscarriage than with amniocentesis, but this test is being used more and more and in the most practised centres the difference in risk is not very great.

Choosing to Have a Test

These are tests a woman *can* have; not tests she *must* have. Some doctors don't so much offer tests as tell the woman they want her to have them - or even that she will be having them. It's understandable that a busy doctor should word things this way, but this is not what is meant to happen and, as one leading doctor in the field put it, 'is to be deplored'.

Any test should be explained and the mother asked if she would like to have it. If not, she should ask for an explanation. If the doctor's explanation isn't enough the couple can ask to discuss the test with someone else. Most hospitals which do these tests have access to a genetic counsellor to help parents in this way. Once they understand the pros and cons of a test, it is up to them to decide whether or not they want it.

These tests should not be dismissed lightly, but a woman has a legal right to refuse to have any of them at any stage, and if the tests show that a baby is abnormal she and the father are free to decide whether they will or will not have it aborted. Equally, if a woman is not offered a test she wishes to have, she should ask the doctor whether she can have it, and discuss the pros and cons.

Preparing for Tests

Even with a routine test like ultrasound, which is looking for other things besides abnormality, there is always a risk of discovering the baby is not normal. Some doctors believe couples should think about and discuss this, before any test is even offered, and decide whether they would want an abortion if something was wrong. Some may prefer to have no tests and go through pregnancy not knowing; others may want to know if a child is handicapped so they can prepare for it, and may want these techniques used to give

it the best possible chance. Either way, it is better for all if the doctors know the parents' views from the start.

More information

Sheila Kitzinger, *Freedom and Choice in Childbirth*, Viking

Abortion

If pregnancy is risking the life of a mother, or tests show that a baby is severely abnormal, doctors may recommend an abortion. Equally, a woman who does not wish to continue a pregnancy can ask her GP to refer her for an abortion, or she can go to one of the organizations given below. Either way, an abortion should be done as early as possible.

The methods used vary according to how far pregnancy is advanced and this is always measured from the first day of the last period. (See also Law, page 467).

1   Up to 12 or 13 weeks it is possible to insert a thin tube into the womb and remove the foetus by suction.
2   Up to 18 or 19 weeks abortion can be by a process called D and E (Dilatation and Evacuation) which is essentially the same as a D and C (see page 589).
3   After 18 weeks drugs are given which cause premature labour. This is like labour at full-term, except that it produces a baby too young to live.

The number of weeks at which each of these can be done is only approximate, as each organization or hospital sets its own limits. In theory, abortions could be performed up to 28 weeks, which is the age at which a foetus is deemed to be viable (able to live once born). But there is a voluntary agreement with the Health Department that abortions will not be performed after 24 weeks - and in practice often 20 weeks.

Emotions

The moral issues which surround the ending of pregnancy are beyond the scope of this book, but there are also emotional factors.

Abortion is often seen as an easy option. For some women it may be. But for many it is a deeply distressing experience from which they may take months to recover. Even those who have no desire for a child, or who become pregnant through rape, may suffer deeply. And for anyone who wants to be a mother (even if not by that man), ending a pregnancy, even in its earliest stages, runs clean against her deepest needs as a woman. Those who accept an abortion, after discovering that a wanted child is abnormal, have the added burden of going through a labour which can only end in the loss of a wanted child. This loss can then be made more bitter by the fact that a late abortion causes the mother's breasts to fill with milk for the dead child.

This means there is maybe a deep sense of bereavement and intense grief, often coupled with feelings of guilt. Even the knowledge that the child was severely handicapped and might scarcely have survived birth, or have suffered terribly, may not blunt these emotions. And the woman can find them doubly hard to bear because the hormones which affect her moods have been disturbed by ending the pregnancy. This means that those who have lost a child through an abortion need not only good medical attention, but also loving support and comfort from everyone around them for some time afterwards, and a chance to talk about their feelings. For a grieving mother, or father, to bottle them up is to ask for depression later.

Devastating as an abortion may be, many people feel that some pregnancies have no 'good' solution. Women who put out for adoption a baby whom they cannot care for, or cannot love because it is the result of rape, may suffer just as deeply as they would have done from an abortion.

Risks

When a full D and C is needed there is the risk of physical complications which can occur in any operation. There is also a slight risk that a complication could lead to infertility. Anyone considering an abortion should realize that to have one without proper medical supervision can lead to complications which make it impossible to have children later. Backstreet and DIY abortions are very dangerous.

British Pregnancy Advisory Service, Austy Manor, Wootton Wawen, Solihull, W Midlands B95 6BX Tel: 056 42 3225 - offers pregnancy tests after 14 days late, abortion, contraception, morning-after birth control, infertility checks, artificial insemination by donor (AID), and by husband (AIH), sterilization, sperm storage, sexual counselling in some branches, all on fee-paying basis. RC, branches in major cities.

Life, 118-120 Warwick Street, Leamington Spa, Warwicks CV32 IQY Tel: 0926 21587 - is a pressure group opposed to *all* ending of pregnancy, even the post-coital pill. They try to help women avoid abortion by advising on accommodation, welfare, adoption and other matters.

Lifeline, 14 Beech Road, Reigate, Surrey RH2 9LR Tel: 073 72 21428 says it is neither pro nor anti abortion. Its branches, in major cities, offer free pregnancy testing, plus counselling and practical information where necessary. It also counsels on miscarriage, stillbirth and menopausal problems.

National Abortion Campaign, Wesley Hosue, 4 Wild Court, London WC2B 5AU Tel: 01 405 4801 - is a pressure group to retain abortion rights.

Pregnancy Advisory Service, 11-13 Charlotte Street, London WIP IHD Tel: 01 637 8962 - offers pregnancy testing, abortion advice, post-abortion counselling, birth control, artificial insemination by donor (AID), cervical smear tests, all on a fee-paying basis.

Society for the Protection of Unborn Children (SPUC), 7 Tufton Street, London SWIP 3QN Tel: 01 222 5845 - campaigns vigorously against abortion.

Preparing for Labour

Giving birth to another human being is one of the biggest things anyone can do in their lives. Because it is so important conflicting schools of thought have grown up about it. At one end of the spectrum, some doctors distrust nature and use every high-tech device at their disposal to organize, monitor and anaesthetize the birth. At the other, some natural childbirth fanatics insist that childbirth is a natural and deeply emotional event which *must* have no intervention and no pain killers if the mother is to experience the full joys of childbirth.

In their enthusiasm for the naturalness of birth, authors of books on natural childbirth invariably seem to depict women giving birth stark naked. You may like to know that it is by no means essential. It is for you to choose.

Many expectant mothers are either determined to have their baby naturally at all costs, or pooh-pooh preparation for childbirth and swear they will just have an epidural and leave it to the doctors.

Either way, the mother could be in for a shock. Epidurals don't always work, nor can anyone guarantee that the labour won't be too fast to set one up. Equally, although a totally natural and unaided labour can offer a great deal, nobody can promise that everything will go smoothly, or that the sensations of a particular labour won't be too tough to handle. So, to go into labour with a rigid view of how it will be is to invite disappointment in what should be the least disappointing event of your life.

I am all in favour of natural childbirth, but the most important thing about labour is not that you do it one way or another way, but that you give birth to a healthy baby. Going into labour is a journey into unknown territory: like walking alone down a dark street in an area you don't know. If you walk down it relaxed and confident that you can cope, not expecting mugging but knowing you can fight back if anyone tries it, you are far less likely to be a victim. But if a mugger does attack, you would be crazy to feel you were failing if you shouted for aid or accepted help. The same is true of labour. You shouldn't *expect* problems or intolerable pain, and should go into it confident that you know enough to cope with the sensations which will assault you, but if you are unlucky enough to have problems there is no failure in accepting help. Even if you need a general anaesthetic you won't miss the most satisfying moment. That moment is when you first see the baby, and hold in your arms the miraculously independent and whole human being whom you and your partner have created.

That, of course, means that every mother should go to ante-natal classes and learn techniques for coping without anaesthetics - even if she intends to be drugged up to the eyebrows. Understanding what is happening and learning good techniques for coping with the quite overwhelming sensations it produces can make labour a far easier experience and greatly reduce the pain, and will see some women through to the end without anaesthetics, even if the rest move on to anaesthetics when they feel it is right. Many hospitals run good classes but if you prefer private classes the National Childbirth Trust (see below) runs them: book *the instant* you are pregnant.

Fathers Attending Births

Fathers may be expected to attend the birth and they can be an immense help and support to their partners. There are very few times when a modern husband can take on the role of his wife's defender and champion, but this is one of them. A woman is at her most defenceless when in labour and it is easy for her needs to get steamrollered under hospital procedures or be misunderstood because the staff on duty have changed. The father can see this doesn't happen, and should be able to provide far better comfort and support than a stranger - however well qualified and caring. He can also be of practical help - the benefits of back rubbing, and similar help, in labour can be immense. However, fathers may be best able to handle the situation if they have attended some classes first.

The Association for Improvements in Maternity Services (AIMS), c/o Elizabeth Key, Goose Green Barn, Much Hoole, Preston PR4 4TD Tel: 0772 615840 - campaigns for better treatment of women in labour. M£L, M, L, Inf.

Association of Radical Midwives, 62 Greetby Hill, Ormskirk, Lancashire L39 2DT Tel: 0695 72776 - is committed to a more caring attitude to midwifery, less intervention, more choice for mothers, and more concern for what birth means to the parents. L, sae.

National Childbirth Trust, 9 Queensborough Terrace, London W2 3TB Tel: 01 221 3833 - runs ante-natal classes all over Britain, preparing for childbirth without fear, weekly for 8-10 weeks (book early). Free breast feeding advice, post-natal support via other mothers. RC, M£L, M, L, B, E, G, A, sae.

Twin and Multiple Births Association (TAMBA), Pooh Corner, 54 Broad Lane, Hampton, Middx TW12 3BG supports and advises those with twins - or more - including such matters as adoption or the death of a twin. M£L, M, G, A, Ad, L, B.

Dr Peter Huntingford, *Birthrights*, BBC
Sally Inch, *Birthrights*, Hutchinson
Sheila Kitzinger, *The Experience of Childbirth*, Penguin
The National Childbirth Trust, *Pregnancy and Parenthood*, OUP
Michel Odent, *Birth Reborn*, Fontana

Labour

In theory, labour occurs 280 days after the first day of the last period. But most babies are early or late. In the last twenty years there has been a dramatic increase in the number of labours which are started artificially. This can be best for both mother and child, but it isn't always. There are 'inducing doctors' just as there used to be 'hanging judges', and induced labours can be harder to cope with than those nature produces. The best way to avoid an unnecessary induction is to avoid such a doctor - so ask.

For all the wizardry of modern medicine doctors still don't know what makes labour start naturally. Labours don't all start the same way, even in the same woman. But one of three things always happens and the other two follow during the first stage:

1 a 'show' (a slightly blood-stained discharge) from the vagina;
2 the bag of waters cushioning the baby bursts and liquid floods out;
3 contractions begin.

Eating in Labour

Having tantalizingly gone into labour with my first child just as I was serving Christmas dinner, I remember vividly the old-fashioned rule that you couldn't eat a morsel once labour started. This was because eating before a general anaesthetic is dangerous. But very few women need a general anaesthetic and if they do it is seldom in the early stages of labour. So the new thinking is that a woman can eat what she feels like - in moderation - *in the early stages*.

First Stage Contractions

In films a woman who goes into labour immediately starts groaning and grimacing and promptly gives birth. This is artistic licence. The start isn't usually as painful nor the result so swift - nor is it always as long and awful as some 'old wives' like to make out. The truth is that labours vary hugely, and no two are alike - even in the same woman. What's more, some people are naturally good at handling stress and discomfort and take it in their stride, while others fall apart under it. So two identical labours would feel quite different to women at opposite ends of that spectrum.

The contractions of the first stage open the cervix (neck of the womb) and pull it out of the way, much as you'd prepare a sock to put your foot in. The contractions usually start weakly with big gaps between and gradually get closer and stronger, and some women even get practice contractions occasionally long before the start of labour itself. Contractions are just what their name suggests - muscles tightening. Try clenching your fist *as hard as you possibly can* for 30 seconds, and imagine that sensation inside your stomach - that's roughly the feel of it.

What Contractions Feel Like

The average labour is 10 hours, but it can be considerably shorter or longer. But that doesn't mean hours of agony. Early contractions are usually no more painful than clenching your fist, and they last under a minute and only come every 20 minutes or so. They gradually increase in length and strength and come more and more frequently. Some women would not define the sensation as pain, and for some they feel more like a massive orgasm (some of the same muscles contract in orgasm) than like normal pain. That's not as much fun as it sounds. Imagine having an overwhelming orgasm every two minutes for an hour or two and you get some idea of how exhausting labour can be. Any muscle which is worked hard in a way it isn't used to can ache enormously (backache is a common feature of the first stage too) and the worst part is you can't stop and rest from this abdominal marathon. Not surprisingly there comes a time when one tends to get irritable.

However, some women do have very severe pain. The chances of this are greatly increased in those who are untrained and frightened and therefore tense up against the contractions, setting up an internal war between opposing sets of muscles, but this isn't always the reason. You can have a painful labour even when previous labours have been easy.

In the early stages there is no need to sit down (unless you want to) - let alone lie down. But use each contraction to practise whatever exercises you have learnt for controlling it. You may feel like walking about, but doing it aimlessly creates tension. The early hours can drag, so do something constructive - clean the house, do some gardening, or cook and freeze food for later. When you feel like sitting have something really absorbing to do - a book you long to read, or a tape of some favourite music (plus Walkman, so you can take it to hospital), or a video film you can watch at home. But don't do as I did and leave your packing for hospital until you need to leave - by then bending may be impossible.

Help and When to Seek It
A woman often reaches a stage when it feels 'right' to go into hospital and she should act on this feeling. Failing that, medical authorities say any of the following indicate that it is time to go in:
- loss of fresh blood (not the same as the 'show' - see page 590)

- the waters breaking
- contractions coming every 10-15 minutes
- the contractions getting much longer and stronger.

Hospital Procedures
I spent the whole of my first pregnancy in a blue funk about the trivia of childbirth - the enema and shaving. In fact, neither are essential and many hospitals have now abandoned both practices. In those that like to give an enema the doctor may agree to you being given a suppository to insert yourself, if you ask well before labour. If your hospital hasn't abandoned shaving you can ask if they can keep it to a minimum.

Pain Killers
You are entitled to refuse pain killers during labour or to ask for the type you would prefer - though a doctor may have good reasons for not giving it. It is best to discuss the options with the doctor during an ante-natal check-up and not wait until labour, when you may be too busy to talk. It is also worth talking to other mothers about the effect pain killers had on them, and their babies. Whatever you opt for, do remember that no pain killer is 100 per cent certain to work, not even an epidural. The major options are these:

Anaesthetic	Possible Disadvantages
Entonox often called gas and air is given through a face mask. It makes you feel slightly woozy and dulls the edge of the pain	No known ill effects for mother or baby, but those who find breathing exercises helpful may lose their timing and feel out of control.
Pethidine is injected. Some women find it kills the pain and they float; others find the pain is there but seems farther away.	If given too late in the first stage the woman may have trouble pushing and the baby may be 'floppy', have difficulty breathing and be slow to suck. This can make breast feeding harder.
Epidural injections are given into the back near the spinal cord and most of the sensation in the lower part of the body is blocked. There should be no pain at all and a well-managed epidural will allow the mother to feel the baby emerging. But the effects of epidurals can vary.	Some women have a severe headache and bladder problems for a short while after. The labour may be longer and the baby is more likely to be delivered by Caesarian section or forceps. In *very* rare cases, it has permanently paralysed the mother.
Transcutaneous electrical nerve stimulation is a new system by which small pads are attached to the back which receive tiny electrical pulses from a battery-operated box the mother can carry about. The pulses stimulate the body's own pain-killing chemicals and also interfere with the passage of pain signals to the brain.	The big advantage is that there are no side effects for the mother or baby. In one trial 60 per cent of women found it helpful and felt it did reduce the pain. But opinions are divided on its effectiveness and it cannot be used when heart monitoring is needed.

Positions for Labour
Some hospitals allow a mother to adopt almost any position she wants, others insist on a certain position. Some methods of monitoring the progress of labour make movement almost impossible. In most cases, the doctor decides the position, not the mother - though you can always try persuasion - if you are up to it.

The Second Stage
Once the cervix is open the second stage starts, and lasts

20 minutes to an hour, with contractions about every 2 minutes. A quick vomit may be the start. Then an overwhelming desire to push downwards comes in waves. Women always used to go through this stage on their backs, but more and more doctors now allow women to do what feels right for them - whether standing, sitting or lying, though some anaesthetics make this impossible.

The baby is pushed down until the head presses on the mouth of the vagina. The skin should stretch, but it can tear, so some doctors or nurses then make a small cut (an

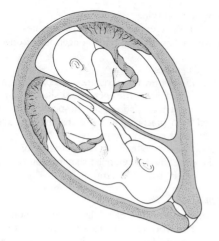

Twins in the Womb.
This picture illustrates the position of twins in the womb.

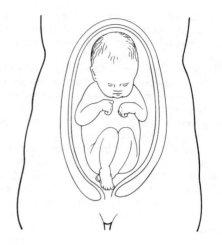

A 'Breech Baby'. This baby is the wrong way up for a normal birth and a doctor will try to manipulate it into the correct position.

episiotomy) instead. There is now medical evidence that this is not the advantage it was once thought to be. However, some hospitals still do it routinely rather than risk a tear - as tears are seen as bad practice. So discuss it with your doctor before labour. If you don't want one tell *all* the medical staff, then they will only do it if it can't be avoided. In either case, ask (at the time) for the stitches to be left with long tails, then they won't prick as you sit on them, (a tip some doctors tend to overlook).

Problems

If labour is not going smoothly doctors may, at any stage, decide it is safest to intervene. This may simply be helping the baby out in the normal way, or it may mean having a Caesarian section - in which a small cut is made above the pubic hair and the baby taken out - under local or general anaesthetic. Some women feel they have failed if they need such help. This is totally untrue. Some babies just don't adapt to the normal exit and that is no fault of the mother or the baby.

The Third Stage

The afterbirth - the placenta (and remaining umbilical cord) - has to be expelled. The womb contracts to push it out and to reduce the bleeding where it separates from its wall (though some bleeding usually lasts for 6 weeks). Ideally the baby should be put to the breast as soon as it is breathing easily. It will instinctively suck and nature is so well organized that the sucking stimulates a hormone which makes the womb contract. This helps the afterbirth to be expelled. Usually these contractions can hardly be felt, but in the early weeks of breast feeding they can occasionally be so strong that a mild pain killer is needed.

Problems at Birth and After

Premature Babies

A premature baby may have to be put straight into an incubator to give it the conditions it needs to survive. This can be very hard for the parents who are longing to hold it, but a good hospital will try to give them as much contact as the child's condition allows. Parents who use every chance to be with their baby will grow closer to it even if they can't hold it. But it can be frightening to have the responsibility for taking home a baby who has been frail, so support and advice from the organization below can be very useful.

Nippers (National Information for Parents of Prematures), c/o Sam Segal Perinatal Unit, St Mary's Hospital, Praed Street, London W2 INY gives help with the physical and emotion problems of a premature baby, practical information on clothes, equipment etc. M£L, M, L, B.
Glover and Hodson, *You and Your Premature Baby*, Sheldon Press

Stillbirth and Neonatal Death

Sadly some pregnancies result in a child who dies at birth or soon after. Legally a stillbirth is a baby born lifeless after 28 weeks of pregnancy. Doctors also use different terms according to when a child dies. A neonatal death is when a child dies within one month of birth, perinatal death is when a child dies just before labour, during labour or within 7 days of birth.

The grief and sense of loss which the parents experience are, unfortunately, not always understood. But the depth of grief can be frightening. If the child had some handicap there may be the added burden of guilt (however unnecessary) and the confusion of relief that it will not suffer or burden the rest of the family. These feelings can be hard to handle and nobody who loses a child should allow people to jolly them into putting a brave face on it, or feel ashamed if it takes a long time to get over the loss. Grief is just as natural as pregnancy, and those who let themselves mourn will recover more completely.

Many now feel that if parents see and say good-bye to the dead child, and have a chance to give it a name and a burial in a place they choose, the grieving is easier to handle in the end. Although hospitals may offer to 'dispose of' the child, parents have a right to ask for other arrangements.

Stillbirth and Neonatal Death Society (SANDS), 28 Portland Place, London WIN 3DE Tel: 01 436 5881 has support groups for the bereaved, plus experienced befrienders, information on new preventive measures. RC, Opt, M£L, S, F&F, M, L, B, Lib, G, sae.

Cot Deaths
Cot deaths are now called SIDS (Sudden Infant Death Syndrome) and are when a seemingly healthy baby, during its first year, is suddenly found dead when it was thought to be sleeping. Nobody quite knows why this happens, but several factors have been found which put a baby at risk. They are - low birth weight, having a mother who is under the age of 20, or who smoked in pregnancy or took drugs. However, babies who are breast fed for the first six months are *less* likely to die in this way.

Unfortunately, as the death has no known cause the coroner must be notified and in some areas the police will talk to the parents. This is routine procedure and does not mean the parents are being accused of anything, though it may be very upsetting.

The Foundation for the Study of Infant Deaths, 15 Belgrave Square, London SWIX 8PS Tel: 01 235 1721 - offers support and advice by letter, telephone and by individual befriending.

Post-natal Depression
Most mothers get depressed and tearful a few days after the birth - the baby blues - but feel better in a few days. But for a few it lasts longer and is far more severe, and there may be anxiety and panic as well as dislike of sex. During pregnancy huge changes take place in the levels of key hormones - an upheaval equivalent to going through adolescence in 9 months flat - and the body has to swing back to its normal hormone levels after the birth. Research shows that the brief baby blues - like adolescent dumps - are caused by these hormonal changes. Why long-term depression sometimes follows childbirth is less clear, but some doctors feel certain hormones *stay* out of balance and successfully use hormones to correct this, although others disagree and prefer to use anti-depressant drugs.

Association for Post-Natal Illness, 7 Gowan Avenue, Fulham, London SW6 has a nationwide network of volunteer supporters, who have been through it themselves. RC, membership free, S, F&F, L, B, G, sae.
See also **Meet-a-Mum** (page 329), **National Childbirth Trust** (page 590), and **Allergy** (page 529).
Katherine Dalton, *Depression After Childbirth* - a very readable book though not every doctor agrees with her conclusions.

Restoring your Figure
Post-natal exercises are the very last thing one feels like doing in the weeks after a baby is born, but they are worthwhile. Most important of all are those for the pelvic floor as this can be weakened by childbirth. Among other things, this can lead to an annoying condition called stress incontinence - a formal name for the fact that you can't help peeing slightly if you cough, lift a heavy weight or

do anything else which puts pressure on that area.

It is important to do the right exercises in the right way both during and after pregnancy or they could do more harm than good. A few hospitals have physiotherapists specializing in obstetrics and gynaecology, and you should ask your doctor about this.

Association of Chartered Physiotherapists in Obstetrics and Gynaecology, c/o The Chartered Society of Physiotherapists, 14 Bedford Row, London WC1 4ED Tel: 01 242 1941 this organization will put you in touch with those who supply leaflets on physiotherapy exercises for use after various conditions, including childbirth.
Barbara Whiteford and Margie Polden, *Post-Natal Exercises*, Century - written by gynaecological physiotherapists.

INFERTILITY

Anyone who has followed the exploits of Henry VIII knows that for centuries women took the blame for infertility. It was thought self-evident that a man who managed erection, penetration and orgasm was fertile. But potency and fertility are different and in fact men and women suffer equally from both infertility and low fertility, with sperm defects or problems being the biggest single cause in men.

Infertility is usually defined as failure to conceive within 12 months and it affects about one couple in six. Sometimes the causes are simple - excess weight, too much drink, tobacco or marijuana, or even the man wearing tight pants. Other causes may include the following.
- Incomplete intercourse or using the wrong opening (not as rare as you might think).
- The woman washing immediately after intercourse. This lowers the chances of conception (but it is not a contraceptive).
- Infertility after coming off the contraceptive pill. It can take a while to regain full fertility.
- Illness and anaemia.
- Infection of the cervix.
- Too little moisture in the woman for the sperm to travel (this may be treatable with hormones).
- Blockage of the fallopian tubes so the egg can't reach the womb. (Scars left by the venereal infections (see page 564) are unfortunately an increasingly common cause of this.)
- The woman's body reacting to the sperm as if they were germs and making a chemical which kills them. This is not easy to treat but it can be done.
- Recent research suggests that women who are too thin find it harder to conceive.
- A hormone imbalance causing the woman to release immature eggs or no eggs at all - surprisingly the periods can be normal while the eggs are not. In the past, boosting the hormones to cure this led to women having six babies, but now the risk of a multiple birth is far less.
- A woman's subconscious feelings may affect whether she conceives or not - which is why it is not unusual for pregnancy to follow an adoption.

Infertility in Men

The man plays some part in infertility in about half the cases. Sometimes he is the infertile partner; sometimes his low fertility combines with his wife's problems to make conception harder. The causes of male infertility include illnesses - such as mumps in the testicles during or after puberty, injury to the testicles, a block in the ducts carrying the sperm or a low sperm count. Some causes of male infertility can be treated; some cannot. But when a husband is seriously infertile some couples find a very happy solution in AID (see below).

Secondary Infertility

Secondary infertility is the term used when a couple have managed to have one child, but don't seem able to conceive another. Surprisingly, this is the case for as many as half the couples troubled by infertility. The tests and remedies are the same as for a totally infertile couple.

Increasing your Chances

When the problem is due to a low sperm count the chances of pregnancy may be increased by making love at just the right time. The Catholic Marriage Advisory Council (see page 582) (predictably) excels in this field.

More information
PAS - see page 589
Joseph Belina and Josleen Wilson, eds and rev. by Robert Newill, *The Fertility Handbook*, Penguin

Artificial Insemination by Donor (AID)

AID can be used when a fertile woman has an infertile husband, or one who carries a hereditary disease which he should not transmit. For AID a nurse or doctor inserts into the entrance to the womb semen from a donor who has been checked for good mental and physical health. Once pregnancy is achieved it proceeds as normal, though sometimes it takes several inseminations to achieve pregnancy.

AID is a solution which takes a bit of thinking about. But in Britain over 2,500 babies are conceived this way each year, and the AID parents I have talked to have had great joy from their babies. (See also Law, page 467). AID is available in a number of NHS hospitals, and is also offered by PAS and BPAS (see page 589) together with infertility counselling.

Artificial Insemination by Husband (AIH)

A man who is about to have a vasectomy or some medical treatment, which could damage his sperm, such as those for cancer, can have some of his semen frozen and stored (at some storage cost) against the day when he wants a child. In due course his wife can then be artificially inseminated with his sperm (as in AID) - this is called AIH. Unfortunately, this isn't always plain sailing. Semen is test frozen before storing and a small proportion of men are found to have semen which just won't stand up to freezing. And even if the semen stores well, some women who have no trouble conceiving through intercourse just don't conceive by artificial insemination. Finally, though sperm certainly keep for years, their exact life is a little speculative as the technique of freezing hasn't been around all that long. Both PAS and BPAS can advise on AIH (see page 589).

In Vitro Fertilization

Nowadays there is also increasing use of techniques for fertilizing a woman's egg outside her body - usually with her husband's sperm - and then putting the fertilized egg into the womb to begin an otherwise normal pregnancy. This is the method for the so-called test tube babies.

National Association for the Childless, Birmingham Settlement, 318 Sumner Lane, Birmingham B19 3RL Tel: 021 359 4887 - covers all aspects of childlessness including adoption, fostering and a list of clinics for AID, AIH and other methods of conception. RC, M£M (optional), S, M, L, B, self-help support G, A, Ad, Inf, sae.

Women's Reproductive Rights Information Centre, 52-54 Featherstone Street, London EC1Y 8RT Tel: 01 251 6332 - RC, M£L(optional), M, L, B, Ad & Inf related to infertility and clinics treating it, self-insemination and pelvic inflammatory disease. Also on aspects of abortion.

SEXUAL AND MARITAL PROBLEMS

At one time all sexual problems were thought to be psychological, but there is now evidence that some sexual difficulties may be linked to the body's chemistry. When this is so, the problem can sometimes be cured by purely physical treatment, but unfortunately the tests which are needed to establish such physical problems are not widely available.

When the problem is psychological the prospect is also very good. Sex therapy is one of the most successful areas of therapy, and it's possible for a therapist to bring about real change remarkably quickly, and make a great deal of difference to those involved. This is not an area in which therapy can only be obtained from psychoanalysts and psychiatrists. They have a role in some psycho-sexual problems, but there are excellent sex therapists among those with other backgrounds.

Sources of Help

For marital problems the main source of help and advice is Relate (National Marriage Guidance Council), and there is also a Catholic Marriage Advisory Council. These not only have counsellors who deal with general marital problems, but also people specially trained in psycho-sexual counselling, and you can ask to see either. You can find the local branches of either organization in the telephone book - usually under 'Marriage' or 'Catholic' - or through the head office address opposite. The Jewish Marriage Guidance Council is purely for general marital and family problems.

In many parts of Britain it is hard to find a sex therapist other than those involved in marriage guidance, but GPs and Family Planning Clinics may be able to refer you to someone in your area. Alternatively, you can write to the Association of Sexual and Marital

Therapists, which can refer you either to individuals who offer therapy or to clinics, and the clinics are often on the NHS. The British Association of Psychotherapists (see page 549) or the Institute of Psychosexual Medicine also have the names of sex therapists. Both associations cover trained sex therapists drawn from a number of disciplines - psychology, psychiatry, marriage guidance and so on - whereas the Institute is the professional body for medical doctors trained to help sexual problems, some of whom may offer help on the NHS.

Association of Sexual and Marital Therapists, P.O. Box 62, Sheffield S10 3TL

Catholic Marriage Advisory Council, - see page 582

Institute of Psychosexual Medicine, 11 Chandos St, London W11 9DE

Jewish Marriage Council, 23 Ravenshurst Avenue, London NW4 4EL Tel: 01 203 6311

Relate (National Marriage Guidance Council), Herbert Gray College, Little Church Street, Rugby CV21 3AP Tel: 0788 73241

Handicapped Sex

The sexual difficulties of the handicapped and disabled are the special province of SPOD (see below), which provides advice and information by phone or letter. Sometimes it can also put people in touch with professional counsellors, in their area, if they wish for face-to-face counselling. This is basically a free service for both the disabled and their partners, but those who want longer-term individual counselling may be able to obtain it through SPOD on a fee-paying basis. The leaflets and books available through MENCAP (see page 568) may also be useful.

SPOD (Sexual and Personal Relationships for the Disabled), 286 Camden Road, London N7 0BJ Tel: 01 607 8851 - L, B.

Homosexuality

There are numerous 'Gay Switchboards' which offer information and advice to homosexuals, of either sex. They are listed in the telephone book under 'Gay', 'Homosexual' or 'Lesbian'. Londoners, or those unable to find their local number, can contact the London switchboard given below, which is a national information source.

It is run entirely by homosexuals and keeps a nationwide list of switchboards, clubs, support groups, medical centres and other organizations related to homosexuality. There is a similar line purely for lesbians, but its hours are far more limited.

Lesbian Line, BM Box 1514, London WC1N 3XX Tel: 01 251 6911

London Lesbian and Gay Switchboard, BM Switchboard, London WC1N 3XX Tel: 01 837 7324/5/6 (24 hrs 7 days a week)

Sigma, BM Sigma, London WC1N 3XX Tel: 01 340 3924 (for referral to the support line) for heterosexual partners of homosexuals.

The help line for transvestites and transsexuals is on 01 729 1466 and is only manned for limited periods. An answering machine gives the hours of operation.

MENOPAUSE - CHANGE OF LIFE

Strictly speaking, the term 'menopause' means 'end of periods' and refers only to the point when periods stop; the term 'climacteric' means the time before and after periods stop. However, most lay people use menopause for the surrounding time, during which related changes take place. Periods usually stop at about the age of 49 - but 46 in smokers. But the change isn't always sudden, and the age isn't certain. Women vary widely in the symptoms they experience in the time around the menopause. Some have symptoms for as long as 5 years before their periods stop, or up to 5 years after. Others have symptoms for only months both before and after, and some have no problems at all.

What happens is that the ovaries cease to function properly and so the oestrogen level falls. This in turn effects an interaction with the pituitary gland, and it is these changes in body chemicals which cause the unpleasant symptoms. Because the ovaries play a key part in these changes, women whose ovaries are removed for any reason also experience a change of life which, being more sudden, can also be more severe.

Periods can become erratic, or suddenly heavy. There may also be hot flushes, when blood suddenly surges to the skin surface giving a fierce burning sensation, like all-over blushing, which the woman fears everyone can see (though if she goes to a mirror she will realize it hardly shows). With the flush may come sweating, nausea and all the symptoms of panic. The panic is only caused by hormones interacting and giving the body a sudden shot of adrenalin - the hormone which makes us act fast in emergencies. But it may also make her breathe too fast and bring on other symptoms, such as giddiness, pins and needles and cramps.

The symptoms go fastest if she relaxes and reminds herself that it is just the body playing tricks. It often helps to stand still, relax and take steady, slow and fairly deep breaths - thinking about the breathing - then, when calm, to run cold water over the pulse point in the wrists.

★ If she can't control her breathing an old, and effective, trick is to breathe into a paper bag until the symptoms go.

Physical Changes During the Menopause

As the hormone levels change the skin loses its bounce and elasticity - so, alas, lines become more obvious. The female hormone levels are no longer high and may not be enough to counteract the male hormones which all women have, so hair may appear on the chin and upper lip, muscle tone is reduced and the vagina produces less lubricant during sex (KY jelly isn't the only solution - see overleaf). The vagina also becomes less acid, and so more vulnerable to genital infections (see page 564). So, although the more sex a woman has at this time the better her hormone balance will be, promiscuity carries greater risks. At the same time, hormone changes make the body less efficient at taking up calcium (see page 609) and more is needed in the diet.

Mental Changes near the Menopause

A symptom which is often overlooked is difficulty in remembering things: usually little things, like appointments or what shopping is needed. Infuriating, but not the start of madness or senility. It ends when the menopause ends - and if it affects someone seriously, it can be treated.

There can also be swings of emotion rather like you get in adolescence, with depression and tearfulness striking out of the blue. The fact that the menopause often arrives just when children have left home and a marriage is rather tired may not make it any easier.

Help with the Hormones

There are creams containing oestrogen which can be used both to lubricate the vagina and slow down its ageing. As a proportion of the oestrogen in these creams is also absorbed into the body as a whole, they can't be used if someone has a condition which would be badly affected by it. There is also Hormone Replacement Therapy (HRT), in which the woman's hormones are boosted to the levels they were at when she was younger. This has been much vaunted as the answer to menopausal problems. Some doctors rate it highly, and many women find it an enormous help. But there are certain medical conditions which may make it unwise, and it has not been used for long enough for all its possible risks and side effects to be known. Even so, it may be helpful during a bad patch, and allow those whose menopause results from an operation to be eased into it more gradually. On the plus side there is some evidence that it protects against coronary thrombosis and osteoporosis (see page 532).

There are now a number of clinics specializing in the problems which are linked to the menopause, and if your doctor isn't getting to grips with your problems you can ask to be referred to one.

Self-help in the Menopause

Some women feel randier than ever during the menopause and, barring promiscuity, they should make good use of it. Sex is nature's way of keeping the hormones in balance. Some American research suggests that women who have sex fairly frequently maintain their female hormone levels for longer, and have fewer menopausal problems. Yoga exercises, which not only keep the muscles in trim but also stimulate the glandular system of the body, are another way to soften the blows of time.

A good diet, and learning to relax (see Transcendental Meditation, (page 550), also helps. It is also vital to have some real source of interest and satisfaction. The woman who has nothing to absorb her except her own symptoms is sure to notice every one of them.

More information

Dr Caroline M. Shreeve, *Overcoming the Menopause Naturally*, Century Arrow

Male Menopause

Although this term is bandied about, men can't have a menopause because there are no periods to stop. However, some men in their late 40s, 50s and 60s do have other symptoms very similar to those women experience. They have night sweats, lose muscle power and go off sex, and some even have a measurably low level of male hormones. But this only happens to a small percentage of men and the cause is not known.

Men usually retain their fertility all their lives and the sperm remain perfectly normal. But the ability to get, or maintain, an erection often lessens with age, as the body tissues lose their general elasticity and the blood flow becomes less efficient.

A HEALTHY DIET

Diet for Babies and Children

Breast Feeding

Some books say women should make up their minds in good time about whether they want to breast feed or not. I disagree. If someone is sure they want to breast feed that's fine. But to decide against it before you have the baby is a pity. How one feels about breast feeding is part of how one feels about oneself and one's own body. Few people emerge from giving birth feeling quite the same as they did before. So, whatever your reluctance, it may be wise not to make up your mind too firmly about not breast feeding until you have the baby in your arms. And, as putting a baby to the breast the instant it is born is the best way to get the placenta to detach, even those who are opposed to breast feeding may experience a baby suckling and discover it is very different from what they expected.

Those who do want to breast feed should tell the hospital beforehand but be prepared for the fact that everyone around them may not make it as easy as it should be. In the hospital there may be nurses who do unhelpful things like giving the baby bottle feeds when it should have been brought to the breast, or give strict advice which ends up making feeding harder than it need be. There is no expert quite so dogmatic as one who has only book learning.

There are, however, some excellent nurses who offer every support to the breast feeding mother. Some of them work as breast feeding counsellors. It may help to talk to one before going into hospital, so you have the confidence to handle any problems. The **National Childbirth Trust** (page 590) or **La Leche League** (page 599) may be able to put you in touch with one.

★ Research has shown that, in Western countries, the more educated a woman is, the more likely she is to breast feed.

Advantages for the Baby

● Breast milk is perfectly balanced to give a baby *exactly* what it needs to grow. Powdered milk formula is only close to what it needs.
● Breast milk is easier to digest than formula.
● There is less risk of the baby developing an allergy.
● Breast feeding gives a baby antibodies which protect it from infection, like flu, measles and polio,

especially in the early weeks.
- Breast feeding is cleaner - it carries no risk of infection from a poorly sterilized bottle. (Babies don't develop the stomach acids to kill germs in food until they are several months old.)

Establishing Breast Feeding
The size of a woman's breasts, or her nipples, are no guide to her ability to breast feed. So nobody should decide they won't be able to. Try to start the baby at the breast within the first 48 hours as that is when the baby establishes its sucking habits most easily. If it can't be put to the breast it can still learn later, but it will be harder.

A baby should be given *no bottles at all* in the early days of breast feeding so as to stimulate the breast milk to come in. Tell nurses in hospital that you don't want your baby to be given any bottles and that you want it brought to you each time it seems hungry. Otherwise they may give it a bottle to let you rest.

Colostrum
The first sign that the breasts are preparing to make milk may be a thick yellow substance called colostrum which sometimes leaks from the breasts in the last weeks of pregnancy. It is all the breasts produce for the first day or so. Colostrum contains everything that a baby most needs in the first days of life, especially antibodies which protect it from infection. If a baby is put to the breast whenever it wants it, it won't need any other feeds, and its regular sucking is exactly what is needed to help the body to produce milk. Only let it suck for a couple of minutes at a time in the first few days, so the nipples get used to it. A newborn baby may want to feed every couple of hours in the first week or two.

Even a mother who doesn't want to breast feed might consider letting her baby have the colostrum for the first few days, to give it those protective antibodies.

The First Milk
Almost every mother worries that she won't be able to produce enough milk. The great thing to remember is that *the body creates milk to meet the demands of the baby.* The more a baby demands the more the body makes. So the more often a baby is put to the breast in the early days, the sooner the breast milk will start flowing. During this time the mother should simply try to relax as much as possible and just enjoy and get to know her baby.

The milk starts to come in 2 to 4 days after the birth. At first it is mixed with colostrum and looks rich and creamy, later it becomes thin and watery. No one need ever worry that their milk is too thin and not good enough for the baby. This is one thing the body *always* gets right. Human milk is naturally watery looking, but it is very nourishing. Even if a mother is starving, nature will deprive the mother's body rather than let breast milk go short of what the baby needs. And, like colostrum, human milk contains antibodies which protect a baby against infections such as whooping cough, diarrhoea and flu.

Helping the Milk Come In
The first thing to do is to stop worrying that it won't. It's as natural for it to come as it was for the baby to grow once you'd conceived it - and there wasn't any trouble with *that*. The basics are very simple.
- Let the baby suck as often as it wants.
- Get as much rest as you can - including an afternoon rest if you can make time.
- Have a good diet pages 604 to 613).
- Have at least six pints of liquid a day - and put a glass of something beside you when you start the feed.
- When feeding practise any relaxation you learnt before childbirth and think of milk flowing.
- Don't go on the pill as it can reduce the amount of milk you make, and some of the hormones get into the milk.
- Start with the right breast at one feed and the left at the next, and so on.
- If there is milk left in the breast after the baby has finished express it into a sterilized jug in the early days and keep it in a sterilized bottle in case your own supply runs short later in the day. (If it hasn't been used by the evening freeze it in a sterilized container in case you are ever called away suddenly and a feed is needed.)
- If a baby refuses the breast it is probably because it can't breathe. Check if its nose is bunged up.

Demand Feeding
Since the breasts make milk in response to the baby's sucking it obviously helps the milk supply if babies are fed whenever they ask for food. But some people are afraid that letting the baby have food whenever it asks for it will make it spoilt and difficult.

Over the past fifty years opinions have see-sawed over whether babies should be fed to a timetable or when they cry. The logical solution seems to be to look at nature. Every animal which is suckled feeds whenever it wants and the fields of Britain are not littered with spoilt foals and fox cubs, nor are jungles filled with spoilt gorillas. With a small stomach and inexperienced digestion a baby, like all young animals, needs to be fed little and often. This is not the baby being naughty or demanding, nor are you spoiling it. There comes a time when children *do* get demanding but it is not for months. So, feed it as soon as it cries. Or, better still, feed it if it looks restless, *before* it cries. That teaches it that it doesn't need to cry to get attention (a good lesson for later). Babies do not need to cry to expand their lungs, as some believe. And if anyone says you are spoiling the baby you can point out that women fed on demand for centuries without the slightest evidence that it produced nations of spoilt children.

A newborn baby will usually need at least 6 feeds a day but in one survey a quarter of the babies wanted 8 feeds or more. As the weeks go by the feeds will gradually space themselves out. Nature has so well arranged it that, by then, the breasts will produce what milk is needed with far less frequent stimulation.

Babies are very variable in how many feeds they need.

Don't expect your baby to conform to any baby book or do what any other baby does. It has its own pattern which is right for it. However, at about 6 weeks old many babies are ready to give up the feed they have at around 2 a.m. If the baby is gaining weight well and is not small for its age, you could try offering it a bottle of warm boiled water at this time instead. Some babies get bored with waking up for boiled water. If your baby doesn't get bored or starts waking earlier in the morning go back to feeding it - it needs it.

Timing
The main thing a mother needs to know about timing breast feeds is - *don't*.

If nature had designed all breasts to give milk at the same rate and all babies to take it at the same speed she would have made all breasts look alike and all babies have the same faces. Differences in speed are as natural as differences in looks. And any woman who has breast fed several children, as I have, will be able to tell you that each child has its own speed, even on the same pair of breasts.

Simply put the baby to one breast for a few minutes, then switch it to the other when you reckon it is about half-way through (you will soon get to know how long the baby likes to suck). It can always go back to the first breast again if it wants to.

When it ceases to suck hard, it will normally have had the nourishment it needs. You don't have to take it off the breast just because it has finished eating. A baby enjoys just being at the breast and feeling it in its mouth, and, as it gets older, will start patting and pushing it. This is perfectly legitimate play: the breast is a child's first toy, its mother's skin its first real encounter with the textures of the world. It is learning through her body.

This means that the end of any feed is a good time to talk to a baby and get to know it.

Nipple Care
- Avoid washing the nipples with soap (and you don't need to wash before and after a feed).
- Some nipples get sore and can develop problems if sucked too long. If yours begin to get uncomfortable shorten the sucking time.
- Keep them as dry as possible - in the air if you can.

Engorgement
In the early days, the breasts can become so full of milk that they become hard and hot and painful. This is called engorgement.

If you feel the breasts getting very full, feed the baby *before* it becomes too painful. If this is impossible, squeeze out some breast milk by hand by pressing the breast rhythmically with a finger and thumb just behind the edge of the nipple. It helps the milk to come out if you imagine it flowing as you do this. Let enough flow to relieve the pressure but don't go on too long or you will just stimulate production. Then soothe the breasts with ice packs. Bags of frozen peas are ideal, but ice cubes in plastic bags are thriftier.

Pain when Feeding
Some women find breast feeding is perfectly easy and comfortable from the start. Others find it uncomfortable to start with but it becomes comfortable with time. Try varying the way you hold the baby, so it doesn't always chomp on the same bit of the nipple - lying down, or with its feet going back under your arm are good variations.

If it has been comfortable and becomes painful you should get a doctor, health visitor or breast feeding adviser to see what is going wrong. The breastfeeding book mentioned on page 599 has a careful analysis of possible causes and what to do about them. There are many reasons why it could hurt. If the cause is a lump in the breast and you feel as if you have flu see a doctor as soon as you can. You may have a blocked duct, mastitis, or an abscess which need prompt treatment.

Supplementary Feeds
It is always good to have a bottle and some formula in the home, just in case an emergency makes it impossible to feed a baby. As babies often dislike switching to a bottle teat it is a good idea to get a baby used to a little milk from a bottle from time to time - using expressed breast milk or formula - from early on. (But not before breast feeding is well established.) A bottle can also be used to supplement a feed if a baby is hungry and the breast milk has clearly finished. But, until the milk is well established, this should only be done *after* a feed, not instead of one.

Weight Gain
Breast feeding mothers often worry about whether their baby is getting enough to eat. The best guide is its weight. If it is gaining weight fairly steadily it is getting enough, however short or few its feeds.

Babies don't usually gain weight in the first week, but once feeding is established they gain fairly steadily, though the amount varies slightly according to their birth weight. On average a baby gains:

up to 2 months - 4-5 oz (110-140 g) a week
2-6 months 2-3 oz (55-85 g) a week.
By 6 months a baby will normally have doubled its birth weight.
By 12 months it will usually be 3 times its birth weight.

But don't expect a baby to meet these figures to the dot, week in week out. Some variation is normal.

It used to be thought that a fat baby was the ideal baby. But it has been found that those who are overweight as babies are more likely to be fat adults (with all the ills that flesh is heir to). Nowadays, they are chubby, not rolling in fat. The two big causes of babies being overweight, which you should guard against, are mixing more formula with the water than the manufacturers recommend, or giving sweet foods. Both are bad for the baby for other reasons beside fatness and are best avoided.

It's a good idea to have the baby weighed each week at a clinic. As babies aren't all born the same weight there isn't a right weight for a baby at a certain age. What matters is steady growth and weight gain (see page 598). If a baby is not gaining enough weight you should talk to a doctor.

Weaning

There are no rules about when to stop breast feeding. Most babies would like to go on nursing until well over 6 months old, and may even like it for far longer. Some women enjoy feeding until a child is long past its first birthday. Others want to stop well before 3 months are up.

But if a mother suddenly stops feeding, her breasts will become engorged and painful and the baby will be suddenly disappointed. Instead, let a baby have half a feed on a bottle (the first half - when it's eager), then half on the breast. Start doing this with just one feed, then with two and so on. Once this is established, cut out the breast entirely for one feed, then for another and so on. Exactly the same principle applies to weaning from bottle to cup.

Whether a baby *can* be shifted from breast to bottle or from bottle to cup or solid food is not the only issue. The breast or bottle are a major part of its pleasure in life. It is not just a matter of getting nourishment, it is the sensation of the whole business that it enjoys. Think how important our meals are and how deprived we would feel if someone decreed that, in future, we were to get our balanced diet through tablets taken with water three times a day. The day wouldn't be the same at all, would it? Yet we have all kinds of other pleasures to enliven our day which a baby doesn't have. To a baby the experience of the breast or bottle must be much more important than the experience of eating is to us, and it is unfair suddenly to take it away.

If a baby slowly switches from breast to bottle it can usually get a lot of satisfaction from the bottle, even if it prefers the breast. But it will get nothing like the pleasure if it is switched to a cup. So the fact that it can drink from one at about 6 months should *not* be the signal for depriving it of all the delicious sensations of sucking.

Often a child will want an evening feed by breast or bottle well after its first birthday and there is nothing wrong with that. You may also find that if it is unwell or especially tired a chance to suck may be a great comfort. This is totally natural. Don't worry if your child still enjoys a bottle long after other children have given up. It doesn't mean it's backward; it just means you are tolerant.

More information

La Leche League, BM 3424, London, WC1N 3XX Tel: 01 242 1278 - free help to women who want to breast feed. M£L (if you wish), M, L, B, G, Tel.Ad, visits.

The National Childbirth Trust offers advice and support (see page 590).

Norma Jane Bumgarner, *Mothering Your Nursing Toddler*, (only from La Leche, above - for those who wish to prolong feeding)

Maire Messenger, *Breast Feeding*, Century

Drs Penny and Andrew Stanway, *Breast is Best*, Pan

Bottle Feeding

A newborn baby's digestion is tailor-made to use breast milk. Cows' milk is very different in its richness and in the minerals it contains, so a tiny baby simply can't digest it. So the DHSS experts on child nutrition now say cows' milk shouldn't be given for the first year. If it isn't being breast fed a baby should be given a powdered milk formula made from cows' milk which has been treated to make it as close to human milk as possible. Only use those which say 'modified' on the container. Best of all look for those saying 'humanized' as these are the very closest to human milk. Unfortunately, they are also the most expensive.

From 6 to 12 months a baby can be put onto a formula made for the older baby. But these richer formulas should *never* be given to babies under 6 months old as they will strain their kidneys.

★ Mothers who think their babies are allergic to milk should consult their doctor. Babies should not be switched to a non-milk formula without a doctor's approval.

★ Most teats have rather small holes which make a bottle harder work than a breast. Enlarge the hole *carefully* with the tip of a darning needle heated to red hot in a flame. The hole should be large enough to allow a steady series of drops. But have a spare teat or two to hand in case you get it wrong. If the stream is too rapid the baby can choke - so be careful.

Keeping Bottles Clean

Until a baby is 6 months old bottles and teats must be sterilized. They should be rinsed after use and washed in clean soapy water, with a brush kept just for this, to remove *all* trace of milk. They should then be kept in a sterilizing solution when not in use, so should any spoon or jug used for mixing the formula. Whoever makes up the feed should wash their hands well, then remove the bottle and the teat from the liquid, fill it *without* rinsing them, and place the teat on the bottle without touching the part the baby will suck.

The sterilizing solution should be one specially made for babies' bottles and should be changed daily. But don't expect it to make a bottle safe to use if it is badly washed. The fats in milk can prevent the chemicals in the sterilizing solution from working at all.

★ If you run out of sterilizing fluid just boil the bottle and teat for at least 25 minutes in a pan of water.

Making Up a Bottle

Put the recommended amount of formula in the jug or bottle. Pour on the correct amount of boiling water (or use water which has boiled and cooled if the instructions say cool or cold water must be used). Put the lid on the bottle with the teat pointing inwards, and shake the bottle until it mixes. Put it in the refrigerator or a bowl of cold water to cool. Or stir the jug until the formula is mixed, pour it into several bottles, cap, and put them into the refrigerator.

★ Standing bottles in a plastic box in the refrigerator will stop them being knocked over.

> When a baby is on formula it should *only* be mixed to the strength recommended on the container: more is *not* better, it is harmful.

> Bottled water can contain mineral salts which would strain a baby's kidneys. However, it may be a good idea to use water which has been through a purifying jug (see page 586) that will remove some of the chemicals and metals, but it will still need to be boiled.

Giving Bottle Feeds

Babies tend to prefer slightly warm milk, but it does them no harm to have it at room temperature. However, germs breed very happily in milk, so made up bottles shouldn't be left sitting in the warm for longer than an hour. Equally what hasn't been taken at the end of a feed should be thrown away.

> WARNING: A microwave may seem the ideal way to warm a bottle but it may not be the same temperature right through. If you want to use a microwave always shake the bottle before testing it for temperature.

Before giving a bottle to a baby shake a few drops onto the inside of your wrist to check it's not too hot. It should be *just* warm. Undo the cap a half turn, so air can get in as the milk flows out, or the milk won't flow. Hold the baby in a half-sitting position and have the bottle tilting down towards the baby's mouth, not level.

★ If the baby doesn't open its mouth stroke the cheek nearest you with the end of the teat and it will open and root for it.

● Younger children can feel very left out with their mother sitting feeding a baby again and again. For some feeds try letting them feed the baby. They can sit on your lap and have a cuddle, while they cuddle and feed the baby. The safest place for this is a big bed - so no harm comes if the baby isn't held too securely.
● A young baby should never be left alone with a feeding bottle - it could choke and suffocate.

Burping and Posseting

Babies vary in how prone they are to wind. Just hold it upright against your shoulder, and gently rub its back (don't pat it firmly or it may vomit). Even with gentle handling, a baby may 'posset' (i.e. bring up part of its feed). This is nothing to worry about; lots of babies do it, and you can easily spot the difference between vomiting and posseting.

When to Feed and How Much to Give

Some people try to make feeding very regimented, giving feeds at regular intervals and giving the same amount at each feed, or taking the same time on each feed. This is just to make a rod for your own back. It also seems to assume that a baby is either a machine or very, very stupid - which is a poor basis for your relationship with it. We all feel more hungry on some days than others, and more hungry at certain times of the day. Babies are just as varied. When a baby seems hungry offer it a bottle straight away (see page 597). Just let it drink for as long as it seems to want to. If it hasn't had enough it will either ask for another meal sooner, or drink more next time. You may want to guarantee it won't yell for food when you are out. The fact is you can't, and you can waste a great deal of time trying to force food down it. It is much better to take a bottle with you in case it does cry.

At first, babies need a lot of small feeds — usually under 3 to 4 ounces a feed in the first 6 weeks. From then on most babies begin to find their own routine, taking less and less interest in certain feeds as they have rather more at each of the others. They usually take about an extra ounce per feed per month. So let the baby guide you.

However, if you know it's nearly time for it to get hungry and you want to get a feed out of the way, offer it a bottle. If it will drink, fine. If it won't there's no way you can make it, so don't try.

> If a doctor prescribes a vitamin D supplement for a child *it must only have the recommended dose*. A little is good. Too much can do harm.

Introducing a Mixed Diet

Amazingly, some mothers give babies solid food in the first weeks of life. This is not a good idea. When babies are very young their bodies have not yet developed the enzymes needed to get the goodness out of anything except milk. Nor are their kidneys able to get rid of extra salt in the way more mature kidneys can. Giving solid foods to a very young baby, when its body isn't ready, could harm it.

Babies vary slightly as to when they are ready to start mixed feeding, but the timing recommended by a DHSS report is as follows.
● Most babies can begin a mixed diet at between 4 to 6 months old.
● Some babies are ready to start at 3½ or even 3 months old.
● All should start a mixed diet before 8 months old.

Ordinary foods are added while the baby is still on baby milk, and it is recommended that:
● sugar should not be added to a baby's solid food or bottle
● salt should *not* be added to a baby's food as its kidneys cannot cope with it

- extra vitamins should be given from 1 month onwards and up to 2 years old, or preferably 5. (Clinics supply these.)

Drinks Other than Milk

What the recommendations boil down to is that *unsweetened water is the best drink you can give your child between meals.* They don't need vitamin C drinks; it is better for them to get that vitamin in drops without the sugar. Up to 6 months water should be boiled. Bottled water may have too many minerals so it may be an idea to use a filter jug to remove some of the chemicals, boiling the water afterwards.

Approaching Mixed Feeding

Solid food gives a baby two new experiences: a totally new flavour (which must be most surprising) and a food which needs a new tongue action before it can be swallowed and doesn't trickle conveniently towards its throat. At first keep one of these new experiences to a minimum by making the purée very runny by stirring in mixed formula, boiled water or breast milk.

Most mothers start with a baby cereal. Baby rice is now thought to be best because it looks as if some babies become allergic to gluten (which is in flour, bread, and most cereals) if given it too early, and rice has no gluten. For this reason bread and biscuits should not be given until the baby is 6 months old.

There is no evidence that cereal is the best food to start with, but it may be the one most like plain milk, and therefore least likely to be rejected. But don't think a baby is rejecting food just because a lot comes out. It can't get the tongue action right at first, so a lot *always* comes out. Just scrape it off its cheeks and pop it in again. Once it gets used to the feel of spoon food it will make it very clear when it rejects something. If it dislikes a food miss it out for a while. Babies tend to know the foods which don't agree with them.

Home-Made Food v Bought Baby Foods

There are no rules which say home-made food is better than baby food or vice versa. It depends which foods you buy and how you cook.

When a mother gives her baby food she is also giving her love. It can be hard not to feel hurt when a baby spits the food out and turns it head away from the proffered spoon. You can remind yourself that the food is being rejected not you. Try not to make meals a battleground as this can pave the way to food fads later.

Making Baby Food

- Choose the freshest fruit and vegetables — they have more vitamins.
- Cut them up small so they cook quickly — long heat destroys vitamins.
- Cook them with as little water as possible then goodness isn't lost in the water.

- Stop cooking them *the moment* they are soft enough to purée.
- Use any cooking water to thin the purée.

If you cook enough for the whole family you will all benefit from the extra goodness of cooking this way.

★ Keep baby food in a refrigerator once made or opened, transferring tinned food into some other container. Don't feed the baby directly from the container. It is safest to throw away what isn't eaten after 24 hours.

★ For thrift, sterilize an ice cube tray, and when you make or open baby food put enough for one meal in each ice cube section. Pop the tray in a new plastic bag and freeze it. Then less is wasted.

Tips for Starting Mixed Feeding

- Only introduce one new food a day. Then, if it disagrees with your baby, you will know.
- Make the food into a smooth purée: check for lumps: they can choke a young baby.
- Give puréed food on a teaspoon, *never* in a bottle.
- At 6 months you don't need to sterilize the cup and spoon you use, but you should wash your hands before preparing the food.
- Start with ½ to 1 teaspoon — but don't try to put it all in at once. Give it *before* the breast or bottle feed.
- Food which is puréed looks much less than food in lumps. Don't worry if a baby seems to eat very little. The figures overleaf are only guidelines. If your baby wants less (or more) that's fine.
- Don't try to force a baby to eat more than it wants. Babies may be young but they aren't stupid: they don't starve themselves. They know how much food they need better than you do.
- Once a baby is eating one food try to give two different foods a day at different feeds.
- Build up gradually until by 1 year the baby is eating almost normal meals, at your mealtimes, plus a bottle or breast if it wishes at other times, or drinks of water.

You may be thinking that the human body needs salt and wondering what will happen to the baby if you don't add any. It does need salt but salt occurs naturally in almost all foods.

★ Many baby rusks contain sugar. Check their packets and choose one which has no sugar or as little as possible. And don't give babies sweet biscuits.

What to Give When

Both the baby and its digestion need to get used to new foods in easy stages. If it starts mixed food a little late don't suddenly put it on to the food for that age. And do read the tips above before using the chart overleaf.

Age	What You Can Give When
6 weeks	baby rice (see page 601)
4 months	Steamed, boiled or microwaved fresh carrots, cauliflower, green beans, potatoes. Mashed bananas, stewed dessert fruit such as pears, apples (see page 601). Give ½ – 1 teaspoon before a breast or bottle feed at one or two of its meals, each day.
5-6 months	Include egg yolk, plus a wider range of vegetables and fruit, meat broth. Also rusks when wanted. A baby can have a total of about 3-4 teaspoons of food a day divided between 3 meals. Give breast or bottle afterwards and for other feeds.
6-7 months	Include puréed meat of all types (try to give some liver), beans and lentils, white of egg, fish – with *all* bones removed, cottage cheese, grated cheese in other food, yoghurt, porridge. Simply build up the variety and give milk by breast, bottle or cup afterwards and for other meals.

If the baby is already used to purées, its food can be a little coarser from now on. If not, keep to purée a little longer.

Age	What You Can Give When
9-12 months	Most ordinary food, if not too fatty. Not sweetened drinks or other sweet foods.
1 year	From now on a baby can eat small amounts of ordinary family meals. Salt and extra sugar should still be avoided as much as possible. (It could benefit the whole family to cut down on these - see page 603.) Food should be cut into tiny pieces and the baby can begin to feed itself.

Not to be given under 1 year	Foods to watch carefully as some children react to them
Bovril or Marmite (too salty)	Eggs – especially the white
Smoked meat or fish (too salty)	Cheese
	Pork

Not to be given under 1 year	Foods to watch carefully as some children react to them
Bovril or Marmite (too salty)	Eggs – especially the white
Smoked meat or fish (too salty)	Cheese
Salted meat or fish (too salty)	Pork
Shellfish	Tomatoes
Coffee or tea (children don't need stimulants)	Strawberries
Alcohol	Citrus fruit
Dried fruit (too sweet and a child may choke)	Peanuts
Nuts (often salty and a child may choke)	Shellfish
Chunky peanut butter (a child may choke)	
Oily fish	
Sugary foods	
Fizzy drinks	
Fruit with seeds	
Sweets or chocolates	
Unripe or acid fruit, such as rhubarb (possible indigestion or diarrhoea)	

WARNING: In the past few years there have been cases of young children, in normal well-off families, being admitted to hospital because they were under-fed. Believing that a low fat diet was healthy their mothers to put them on to skimmed or semi-skimmed milk and only gave them small amounts of other fats. *The low fat diet was never meant for young children.*

Children under 5 *must not* be put on the very low fat diet adopted by some adults. In the first year a child grows faster than at any other time outside the womb. To grow they need far more calories for their size than adults do.

Half the calories in human milk come from fat. So babies are 'programmed' to grow on a relatively high fat diet. The fat they most need is found in milk. Like a cake, fat is made with several different ingredients which can't be seen. Those in milk are ones the body uses to build cells and which are important for other aspects of growth. A child should have 1 pint (500 ml) of ordinary pasteurized milk a day - or its equivalent in cheese or yoghurt.

Feeding Itself

You don't need to buy special bent spoons and forks for a baby to learn to feed itself, an ordinary teaspoon is fine. A baby will tell you when it wants to try this by holding your hand or grabbing the spoon. If it wants to feed itself let it. Attempts to be independent are worth encouraging, so praise it. Don't worry that quite a lot will go anywhere *but* in its mouth. When it flags you can always offer it some more. If a baby doesn't try to feed itself by about 8 months let it have the food in front of it with a spoon in for a minute or two while you are 'busy' in the same room. Or, if it's old enough, it may prefer to eat finger foods like bananas or bread.

A baby is learning all the time. The *feel* of puréed food is a totally new experience and it will want to discover the sploshiness of food by sploshing. This is not naughty. It is good - the baby is using its intelligence to learn what the world is like. However, in doing so it may look perfectly revolting and make a dreadful mess. So I strongly recommend feeding a baby in a low chair which sits on the floor, rather than a high chair from which it can spread the food in a wider arc and be a most off-putting sight at meal-times.

Some people will feel this deprives the child of a role in family meals. Maybe. But a baby won't think it's bad being below the table (particularly if it has never known any different) and there are other times when it can be part of the scene. Babies can dominate meal times too much, when adults and other children need attention too. (And there's no risk of the baby toppling out if left alone for a moment - but see below.) There also comes a time for a toddler to give up being so messy, but it will often continue just to get attention. Below the table it has no such incentive, and joining adults and any older children at table is a great reward for civilized behaviour - when it can manage it. It also means that once elevated to table status, a badly behaved child can be put back in the 'baby chair' on the floor - where it can't show off with bad behaviour - which it won't like at all.

A table full of people can be a marvellous audience and few toddlers can resist playing havoc at a meal sooner or later, and some try it regularly. If you have a suitable remedy, like this, it is very useful.

> A baby or toddler should never be left alone while actually eating: it can choke.

Diet in Childhood
Starting a child on solid food is much more than a matter of just giving it nourishment. The food a child eats when very young sets the pattern for its eating later in life. The types of flavours it learns to enjoy will probably be the ones it returns to for comfort even as an adult. When most of us were babies giving sugary foods was a sign of love, and it can be difficult to abandon that idea. But developing a sweet tooth can mean no teeth at all: most people need dentures in old age, and a horrifying proportion have them by the age of 18. Sugar also plays no small part in the fact that of half those over 50 are overweight - and few of them thank their mothers for it. So, if we really want to do our children a favour, we should tell ourselves that sugar may taste lovely but it isn't loving.

Not buying sweets, cakes, biscuits, canned and bottled drinks, and packets of snack food frees a lot of the family budget to buy food that *is* good for you and tastes a lot better, which means that treats can take the form of out of season fruit or a better cut of meat or fish - so teaching your child to turn to good food when it wants comfort in later life. The British Dietetic Association's report says the following.
- Once solids have been introduced, and the child is on a mixed diet, milk, lean meat, poultry, fish, eggs, cheese, fruits, vegetables, and cereals - preferably of the wholegrain type - should form the major dietary sources of nutriments and energy.
- Sugary foods should continue to be limited.
- Fried foods and high fat foods such as chips, pastry, fatty meat products and crisps should be limited or reserved only as occasional foods rather than for everyday. (The right fat is good, but not all fat is the right fat.)
- If children want to eat between meals they should be given milk, fruit, or bread: not sweets or fatty foods.

Fibre and Young Children
There has been very little research on the right amount of fibre for a young child. What is known is that they need a balanced diet in order to get the full range of vitamins and minerals. For that they need to eat several different fruits and vegetables at some time in a week, and a whole grain cereal or wholemeal bread. Once they can cope with it leave the skins on most fruit and vegetables: it saves you work and it does them good. That way they will get enough fibre anyway.

Food Fads
The great thing to remember is *never* to worry or fuss if a child refuses food. Otherwise it will learn to use food refusal to get attention.

If a child, of any age, dislikes a *new* food don't try to persuade it to eat it. Stop offering it that food at that meal, and *without fuss* offer something else - even if it is only milk. Don't offer the disliked food again for days, weeks, months or years - according to the age of the child. Children's palates change, what they loathe at a year they may love at 2.

If a child just goes off a familiar food let it. We do. But don't try to make something *nicer* to cajole it into eating. If you could turn down cod and get smoked salmon wouldn't you think you were onto a good thing? If it refuses something in a main course it can always fill itself up on everything else, and if it has had enough main course, doing without pudding will do no harm. Do this so that it's not *you* making the child go without food as a punishment but simply the child choosing not to eat, so it doesn't.

The lesson a child needs to learn is that it has a right to choose what it eats, and you are not going to try to push it about, by anger or persuasion. But it also needs to learn that it can't push you into cooking special things to pander to its likes and dislikes. This applies whether it is a toddler or considerably older.

Sometimes, children restrict their diets to quite bizarre combinations: one child I knew would only eat fish fingers and chocolate. If this happens the chances are that the child is enjoying your reaction. Behave as if you totally take its behaviour for granted and have *no* desire for it to change. This is much easier said than done. The following may help the situation.

- Let it have the food it wants, without comment, and don't even offer anything else.
- Talk to your doctor *without* your child, so he can reassure you that the lack of variety for a time won't harm it.
- Get the doctor to prescribe, or recommend, some vitamin and mineral tablets you can give the child so you *know* it is not going short of those. (Give similar suitable tablets to the whole family - then the child won't feel you are worried about it.)
- Don't let it overhear you saying you are worried or upset by its behaviour.
- If the child is old enough (even a 3-year-old can get something out of a cupboard), let it get as much of its own meal as it is able to. You can be busy making the other family food and just ask it to help you by doing its own. *Praise* the way it does it, and ask for its help next time. If it can manage (even badly), gradually shift the responsibility for its food away from you and onto the child. If the battle was really a power struggle you are putting the power to make what it wants into its own hands - and transferring your attention away. It also makes it easier for the child to sneak new foods into its diet without the loss of face involved in asking for them.

* Milk is such convenient nourishment that it's a nuisance if young children go off it. If they liked it before and aren't allergic to it try simply adding safe food colouring. Sometimes they are just bored with white milk and green milk through a straw will be bolted down.

Unhealthy Food
There is a stage when children seem to crave the very foods which are least nourishing. You offer them gourmet cooking and they complain that they aren't having Bloggins Bursting Burgers. If they learnt to like good food when younger this is a phase. Let it ride. It will do no harm if some meals in a week would make a dietician weep.

Vegetarians and Vegans
In general, vegetarians need to be careful that their children eat enough high protein food (pulses and so on). Other vegetables and cereals are filling and a small child can become full on them without taking enough calories for normal growth. They should discuss their child's need with their doctor.

A Good Diet for Life

People are not identical, nor are their needs. What follows is based on dietary reports by the medical profession, but it is not meant to be a substitute for discussing diet changes with your doctor, and following his or her recommendations. Major changes in diet should only be made with medical approval.

The Body's Needs
The body needs energy, fibre, certain fats, about 10 vitamins and 20 minerals. If you eat when hungry you will get enough energy, so the question is how to get enough vitamins, minerals and fibre.

Having found out roughly how much we need of each I decided to construct the perfect diet. So I sat down with the latest scientific analyses and, after hours of arduous calculation, I had it. I'd hoped for a revelation. There was none. The list was precisely what my grandmother had always told me to eat - a little meat and fish, some dairy products and cereals, some vegetable oils and plenty of varied fresh fruit and vegetables. The good old balanced diet. The only modern touch was that added sugar and salt simply didn't appear because they contain nothing the body needs which it won't get from other sources.

The message for a healthy diet is: eat everything which is natural, eat it in varied ways so it tastes delicious - both raw and cooked if appropriate - and eat everything in moderation. The rest of this section is simply an explanation of why that is true. However, you are unlikely to get a balanced diet through eating a wide range of processed and manufactured foods. As I write I have ringing in my ears the words of one of the most noted authors on the subject of diet who, on hearing that I was writing about it, told me firmly, 'Don't tell them about nutrition; tell them about good food.'

Some people say a good diet is too expensive. It needn't be if you buy what is in season and keep to the cheaper cuts of meat and fish. In processed food you are always paying for the labour as well as the food: with fresh food you aren't. The real problem with a healthy diet isn't the cost, it's the rethinking.

Why Variety is Important
We tend to think of each food as adding to our total diet rather like pieces in a jigsaw puzzle. It isn't quite like that. Foods interact to make it easier (or occasionally harder) for the body to use the goodness in them. Some substances can't be used at all unless those from other foods are there. So, the more varied your diet, the better the chances of foods helping each other, and the maximum amount of goodness getting into the blood.

Variety is also good because vitamins and minerals are often absorbed better from one source than from another. So, for example, iron from meat is very well absorbed, but less than 5 per cent of the iron you eat in vegetables will get in your blood.

About Digestion
Before food can do us good it has to work its way through a series of extraction chambers.

1   Down the gullet from mouth to stomach is a 3-second chute.

2 Stomach juices containing an enzyme and hydrochloric acid then get to work on it.

3 How long food stays in the stomach varies with the emotional state of the eater and the type of food. Rice goes through fastest, fats and pasta go slowly: 2 to 4 hours is average.

4 Next it travels through the small intestine being bombarded with body chemicals to get the goodness out of it.

5 The goodness is absorbed through the walls of the intestine into the bloodstream, while the the debris is shunted to the bowel.

The journey takes 1 to 7 days depending on what was eaten. A high fibre diet passes through fastest.

> The 1856 *Enquire Within* recommended 'feeding' those who were ill with a nourishing enema of beef tea - which just shows how little the digestion was understood in those days. What a waste of good broth.

Indigestion

Indigestion happens when food isn't digested so it ferments, causing gas and discomfort. This can happen because of the nature of the food, or the nature of the eater. I believe there is also a wind-producing bacterium. But this is a personal theory which is totally unproved.

Calories

Officially Britain has gone metric and works in kilojoules not calories. 1 Calorie (also called a kilocalorie) = 4·2 kilojoules. A calorie is a measurement of the amount of energy food will provide.

Calories Needed

The number of calories someone needs varies with the amount of energy they use and with their age, size, and sex.

Age	Girls	Boys	Age	Men	Women
1 yr	1100	1200	18 to 34 not active	2500	2000
2 yrs	1300	1400	18 to 34 fairly active	2900	2100
3-4 yrs	1500	1560	18 to 34 active	3350	2500
5-6 yrs	1680	1740	35 to 64 not active	2400	2000
7-8 yrs	1900	1980	35 to 64 fairly active	2750	2100
9-11 yrs	2050	2280	35 to 64 active	3350	2500
12-14 yrs	2150	2640	55 to 75 not active	2400	1900
15-17 yrs	2150	2880	75+ not active	2150	1680
			Pregnancy		2400
			Breast feeding		2750

What Foods Are Made Of

Carbohydrates

These are sugars and starches. Both provide energy, but any surplus is changed into body fat. We get starch from potatoes, rice, cereals, pulses (peas, dried beans) bread, biscuits, cakes, pasta.

Sugars include - glucose, fructose, lactose, sucrose and maltose. Any of those on a label is sugar by another name - so are corn syrup, and corn syrup solids. Sorbitol and mannitol are related to sugar but are absorbed more slowly, which makes them suitable for diabetics. But saccharine, aspartame and acesulfame K are not even related.

Sugar provides no vitamins or minerals. Even brown sugar, which is less refined, has only a trace of minerals. So, it isn't much better for you. Treacle and golden syrup contain iron and calcium, but not a lot.

Sugar encourages the bacteria which rot teeth and you get used to it and gradually add more and more - so building your calorie load (and probably your waistline too). It has been claimed that it increases the risk of appendicitis, heart disease and bowel cancer, but this is not certain.

The average person eats about 46 kg (100 lb) of sugar a year - about 110 g (4½ oz) a day. NACNE (National Advisory Committee on Nutrition Education) recommended halving this to about 20 kg (44 lb) a year. A BMA report recommends that sugar intake should be cut from 18 kg (40 lb), to 11 kg (24 lb) per person a year. That's about 4 teaspoonfuls a day. Easy if you eat fresh food, and give up sugar in tea and coffee, but very hard if you eat processed foods. Many processed foods are sugar-loaded. Even savoury foods such as tinned soup, ketchup, pickles, salad dressings and even peanut butter.

Fats and Oils

An old Dutch saying is:

> *Eat butter first, and eat it last*
> *And live till a hundred years are past.*

and, according to Paracelsus, the Greeks used to present newly weds with a 'pot of butter, which they esteem the foundation of their lives'. Today's newly weds might think it a less happy omen. But few foods are surrounded by more confusion and misinformation than fats and oils.

Since word got around that saturated fat could cause

heart trouble the media story which has emerged is that butter and animal fats are saturated fats and therefore bad, while margarine and vegetable oils are unsaturated fats which are good. The truth is rather different and a recent survey showed that in trying to buy what is good for them many people are getting it wrong.

The animal versus vegetable distinction is not valid. Duck fat, for example has much *less* saturated fat than many brands of margarine, while coconut oil has *twice* as much saturated fat as butter. What's more, there aren't two types of fat, there are three: saturated, mono-unsaturated and polyunsaturated. All fats and oils contain all three types; it's the proportions which matter.

How Saturated Is Your Food?

Fats and Oils	Satur %	Mono %	Poly %	Vit E mg per 100g
almond oil	5		95	
beef fat	41	47	4	
butter	68	23	4	
chicken fat	30	45	20	
coconut oil	89	8	2	1·6
corn oil (maize)	13	25	58	73·2
duck fat	29	57	13	
herring oil	22	56	20	
lamb fat	52	41	5	
lard	44	44	9	
mackerel	20	49	20	
margarine - hard	39	47	10	
margarine - soft	30	41	26	
margarine - 'polyunsaturated'	17	27	52	
olive oil	14	73	12	5·1
palm oil	45	45	9	78·5
peanut oil	15	53	30	37·0
pork fat	35	42	15	
rapeseed oil	4	24	25	57·6
salmon oil	27	42	26	
sardine oil	20	57	20	
sesame oil	14	40	43	
safflower	9	13	74	80·0
soya	14	24	60	95·8
sunflower	12	33	58	54·6
tuna oil	19	41	38	
turkey fat	36	27	34	
walnut oil	8	15	75	

No two tables agree exactly. On margarine and animal fats I have used figures given by the Ministry of Agriculture, Fisheries and Food.

One study showed that out of 27 brands of margarine a quarter of them had more saturated fat than beef and half had more saturated fat than pork. It pays to read the labels.

> What are saturated fats? Essentially, it's a case of hydrogen strikes again - not the hydrogen bomb but the hydrogen bond. Fats are made of atoms bonded together. And the difference between saturated, mono-unsaturated and polyunsaturated fats lies in the number of hydrogen atoms which are bonded to the carbon atoms of the fat. The more hydrogen atoms are bonded in, the greater the hydrogen saturation is said to be. Hence saturated fats. The difference between mono-unsaturated and polyunsaturated is simply in the number of bonds which are used to hold the atoms together. Polyunsaturates are more firmly bonded.

Fat Intake Recommendations

The big dietary issue is, how much fat should we eat? In Britain the average person eats about 40 per cent of their daily calories as fat.

The government *Manual of Nutrition* suggests only taking 35 per cent of calories as fat. While the report by COMA (the Department of Health's Committee on Medical Aspects of Health) suggested no more than 33 per cent and NACNE recommended cutting it to no more than 30 per cent of total calories, (10 per cent saturated fats, 20 per cent unsaturated fats).

The Case Against Fat

There is no doubt at all that fat is a high calorie food which makes it very easy to put on weight. And being overweight makes people more prone to a whole range of diseases. So there is a strong case for keeping the intake of fat moderate. And *all* fats are high in calories, whether saturated or unsaturated.

The argument against *saturated* fat concerns cholesterol. The body gets cholesterol in two ways: it takes it in through food, and it makes it in the liver. It looks as if saturated fat increases blood cholesterol levels, while eating polyunsaturated fats lowers it (monounsaturated fats have no effect either way).

Those who recommend lowering our fat intake believe that raised levels of cholesterol cause heart disease, and that reducing the nation's fat intake would reduce the toll taken by it. This is, however, not the open-and-shut case many people believe. In fact, there is a serious division in the ranks of both doctors and dieticians. Some eminent members of these professions question whether the evidence against saturated fat justifies the recommended cut-backs.

If the case is not proven, the question is - how can we hedge our bets until the scientists get it sorted out?

The answer is surely to avoid going to extremes. If you eat a lot of saturated fat (see page 606) you may want to cut back, and/or substitute polyunsaturated fat for some of it (see page 606). If you eat almost no saturated fat you might consider increasing it slightly - in some studies in which saturated fats were sharply cut deaths from heart disease went down, but those from cancer went up. Paracelsus said, 'The dose makes the poison', and there can be a risk in taking anything in excess - even good advice. But if you start manipulating the fats in your diet you may like to consider the following.

- There is some evidence to suggest fish oils may protect against heart attacks.
- There is beginning to be evidence that vitamin E may help to protect against heart attacks. There is most vitamin E in whole grains, in certain cooking oils (see page 613) and in eggs.
- The seed oils contain 'essential fatty acids', which the body must have is to work properly.
- Some experts say butter may be better for you than margarine. To make a consistent product, most margerines are filtered, bleached and deodorized, then emulsified, coloured and flavoured with an alarming variety of chemicals, then hydrogenated to make them become solid. So eating margarine is just adding yet more chemicals to the chemical load you are already carrying. They say that those who want to cut down on saturated fat should simply use less butter, and if necessary use unsaturated oil for more of their cooking.

> Young children should not be put on a low fat diet (see page 602).

Fatty Delights
Food is for pleasure as well as nutrition and the individual virtues of the various fats and oils deserve more consideration than they get. They are not tasteless mediums for cooking in, as water is, each has its own special flavour which suits some dishes but not others. A simple carrot salad sprinkled with sesame oil can be excellent, anointed with corn oil it can be very unappealing; potatoes roasted in duck or beef fat are delicious, cooked in lard they are more ordinary. Equally, each has different keeping qualities and smoking points, and different properties as a cooking medium. If we are going to be eating less of them, there is a case for getting the most enjoyment out of what we do eat.

Fibre
Fibre is a carbohydrate which the body cannot break down and use, and until about 1969 most experts said fibre was useless. Then a doctor discovered that cancer of the bowel, and several other diseases, were almost unknown in parts of Africa where a high fibre diet was eaten. Research soon began to confirm that fibre could help prevent, or relieve, a whole range of conditions.

Fibre is whatever is toughest in a plant, often its skin but sometimes part of its flesh too. That is why high fibre food produces big soft stools which are easy to pass, but it does a great deal more than just prevent or cure constipation.

- By keeping the bowels moving high fibre stops one kind of bad breath.
- Increasing the amount of fibre *from pectins* - in apples and other fruit - lowers the levels of cholesterol in the blood.
- Increased fibre is recommended for diabetics.
- Those with healed duodenal ulcers may be less likely to have more if they eat a high-fibre diet.
- It has been suggested that speeding the passage of waste products through the colon lowers the chances of any harmful substances damaging, or being absorbed through, its walls.
- Fibre helps to prevent piles.
- Eating enough fibre may prevent diverticular disease. It also relieves it.

However:
- If you suddenly increase your fibre intake you may get wind and very loose stools until your body gets used to it; so a gradual change is better.
- Fibre reduces the absorption of certain minerals, such as calcium, iron and zinc. So the intake of these should be increased.
- As fibre holds water those who switch to a high-fibre diet should drink more liquid.

How Much Fibre is Good
The average Britisher eats about 20 g a day. The recommended level is at least 30 g and Passmore and Eastwood (in their diet textbook, *Human Nutrition and Dietetics,*) say up to 50 g a day will do no harm. But they add: 'Enthusiasts who pour large quantities of bran on their food gain no benefit from the excess and expose themselves unnecessarily to hazards, known and perhaps unknown.'

The British Medical Association report, *Diet, Nutrition and Health,* says, 'Dietary fibre should be derived from [natural] foods and *not* [my italics] from either dietary fibre preparations or from foods to which fibres are specifically added.' It adds that fibre intake should be increased by eating more whole grain products.

Bran can reduce the body's ability to use other nutrients, especially when raw. But if you eat whole wheat which contains both bran and calcium the fact that bran lowers the percentage of calcium your body takes in should be balanced by the extra calcium the grain gives you.

★ A high fibre diet saves time: scrub potatoes don't peel them; don't peel cucumber; eat fresh fruit rather than puddings; and eat them with their skins on.

Fibre Content of Food
The list overleaf shows milligrammes of fibre per 100 grammes.

Food	Fibre g per 100g
Dried apricots	24
Haricot beans	7
Dried figs	19
Spinach	6
Puffed wheat	15
Sweetcorn	5
Weetabix	13
Celeriac	5
Shredded wheat	12
Butter beans	5
Frozen peas	12
Broad beans	4
Wholemeal pasta	10
Broccoli tops	4
Blackcurrants - raw	8
Leeks	4
Muesli (typical)	7
Lentils	4
Raspberries	7
Blackberries	7
Oatmeal	7
Baked beans	7
Brown rice	varies
Wholemeal bread	varies

	Sodium	Chloride	Fibre per 100 g
All bran	1670 mg	2440 mg	26.7 g
Cornflakes	1160 mg	1780 mg	11 g
Puffed wheat	4 mg	50 mg	15 g
Shredded wheat	8 mg	53 mg	12 g

(Figures from McCance and Widdowson's *The Composition of Foods,* HMSO)

Protein

Protein is found in milk, eggs, meat, fish, cereals and pulses. The quality (i.e. usefulness) of any protein depends on its ability to supply the body with essential amino acids. As the various amino acids complement one another, and different proteins have these acids in different amounts, the best diet is one which combines several types of protein in a single day, or even a single meal, especially as the body has no way of storing them from day to day.

Just how these amino acids are used at different stages in the human life is still under research. But it is known that certain ones are needed for children to grow; that is why milk is an important food for young children (page 596).

Minerals

We seem to need about 20 different minerals: some we take in quantity; some have only a tiny trace in the diet (called trace elements). Only some of their roles and interactions are understood, but most are only needed in very small amounts and too much can be poisonous.

> Some high bran cereals and cornflakes contain very large amounts of sodium and chloride (essentially salt). Compare the levels in these four cereals.

The Role of Minerals

Mineral	Role	Major Sources
Calcium (Ca)		see pages 609-610
Iron (Fe)	Making red blood cells which carry oxygen. Lack causes anaemia.	Meat especially liver, eggs, apricots, pulses, wholemeal bread, spinach. Absorbed well from meat, poorly from vegetables.
Magnesium (Mg)	Vital for all body cells, and the work of enzymes which create energy from food. Present in bones.	Most foods, especially wholemeal bread, cheese, fish, vegetables, milk.
Phosphorous (P)	Strengthens bones and teeth. Allows energy in food and vitamin B to be used.	Plentiful in most foods. Deficiency unknown.
Potassium (K)	Used in body cells. Vital for muscles (heart). Interacts with sodium.	Most natural foods.
Sodium (Na)	Keeps the body's water balance. Needed by muscles and nerves.	Most foods, especially eggs, celery, milk, meat, fish.

Trace Elements

Chromium (Cr)	Probably enables the body to use glucose.	Black pepper, liver, wholemeal bread.
Cobalt (Co)	Needed for creating blood and maintaining nerve cells.	Only used as part of vitamin B12 - page 612.

Mineral	Role	Major Sources
Copper (Cu)	Enables body to use iron, needed for some enzymes to work.	Liver, shellfish, meat, bread
Fluorine (F)	Strengthens teeth and bones.	Tea, fish bones, water with fluoride.
Iodine (I)	Vital for the thyroid gland.	Sea food, milk, meat, eggs.
Manganese (Mn)	Used in making bone and cartilage.	Tea, nuts, spices, whole grains.
Selenium (Se)	Needed by an enzyme in the blood.	Fish, meat, cereals.
Molybdenum (Mo)	May strengthen teeth and excess may cause gout.	Plants.
Zinc (Zn)	Wound healing, activity of many enzymes, DNA repair possibly appetite.	Oysters, cheese, milk, beef, chicken, eggs, grains.

Calcium in the Diet

The importance of calcium in the diet has only been recognized fairly recently. It is used in the functioning of muscles, nerves and certain hormones and enzymes but most of all in bones. There are 4 possible stages to its use.

1 From birth to the age of 20 builds strong bones and teeth.
2 In adults it maintains the constant renewal of the bones.
3 When pregnant or breast feeding a woman needs calcium for two; if she eats too little the baby takes it from her bones.
4 From middle age onwards it is still needed to replace the bone structure, but the body is less efficient at absorbing it - especially in women.

Lack of calcium makes the bones slowly weaken, becoming more likely to break and much harder to mend. It can also make bones crumble - causing the painfully stooped backs of old age.

The body excretes large amounts of calcium daily and a healthy diet must put back more than is lost. It is also important that it is absorbed (see below).

> People are now taking less calcium than they used to, possibly because of low fat diets. Those who cut down on fat should not give up milk, which is the richest and most usable form of calcium (see page 43). And, they should make sure they get enough vitamin D, and enough protein; both are needed for the calcium to be used by the body (see above).

Opinions vary as to just how much calcium we need. The levels recommended by the DHSS are among the lowest in the world, and some British experts feel they are far too low. In America they recommend about double the DHSS level. Lack of calcium causes osteoporosis (see page 532).

Recommended Calcium Intake

	DHSS	Other UK experts
children under 9	600 mg	600-850 mg
adolescents 9-14	700 mg	1100 mg
adolescents 15-17	600 mg	1100 mg
adult of 18+	500 mg	800 mg
pregnancy and breast feeding	1200 mg	1000-1500 mg
women over 40	500 mg	1000-1500 mg

Even the best figures cannot be exact. As with all the essential food elements, the amount which is taken up by the body is affected by whether the rest of the diet helps or hinders its absorption.

Factors Which Affect Calcium Absorption

Without vitamin D in the diet calcium cannot be absorbed properly. During middle age hormone changes in women make calcium absorption inefficient. So from then onwards women need to take more in order to put the same amount into the bones. The factors which help calcium absorption are vitamin D in sunlight, oily fish, eggs, liver, butter/margarine, yeast, unskimmed milk. Also, daily exercise of any kind and lactose in milk. The factors which hinder calcium absorption are smoking, alcohol, inactivity, uncooked bran, laxatives, coffee, lack of protein, some medication, hormone changes in middle-aged women.

Sources of Calcium
milk (see page 43)

yoghurt	5 oz	270 mg
cottage cheese	4 oz	60 mg
hard cheeses (like cheddar)	1 oz	220 mg
sardines (with bones)	2 oz	220 mg

broccoli and other greens	4 oz	30-76 mg
beans (baked, butter etc)	4 oz	45 mg
peanuts, almonds, brazils	2 oz	34 mg
apricots, dates, figs	(roughly) 2 oz	52 mg

N.B. 1 oz = 28.35 grammes

★ It is sometimes claimed that too little calcium can cause period pains. Keeping calcium levels up could carry a bonus for those troubled by them.

Sodium and Chloride

Salt is sodium chloride, a combination of sodium and chlorine. Many doctors (though not all) think that people should limit their salt intake, and that too much salt can lead to high blood pressure. There is less agreement on what represents a suitable amount for an adult. A major committee in the United States opted for 3 g a day. A British Medical Association report recommends that we bring our average intake down from 12 g a day to 9 g.

The most compelling argument is surely that man did not evolve with a salt pot in his hands. So it would be logical to assume that the human body is geared to run well on naturally occurring salt rather than needing additions to food. Evidence suggests that some people are more vulnerable to excess salt than others - but no one can tell who is and who isn't.

In cutting down on salt the major step is to stop eating processed foods. Stick to fresh meat, fish and vegetables, fruit and frozen foods. High salt levels are not limited to food which you would expect to find salt in, such as crisps and bacon (see page 608). Watch out for salt, sodium or chloride on the label.

> It may also be useful to keep up your potassium intake. Salt and potassium have a double act which controls the way the body uses water and it looks as if potassium may be able to counteract the effect of sodium.

Vitamins

I think ascorbic acid [vitamin C] is fundamental; it is involved in the simplest processes of which life is built.
Szent Gyorgyi, Nobel Prize winning researcher 1978

The more research is done on the substance, the more intriguing it appears. Thus there is a nagging suspicion that there is a very important use for the vitamin and we are just not smart enough to see it.
A.L.Tappel on vitamin E 1973 - and the mystery still exists

Vitamins are one of the great discoveries of this century but we are only beginning to understand what they do, and huge research projects are in progress to discover their roles in a whole range of diseases - especially cancer.

Very often their role is to enable some kind of food stuff to be converted into a form which the body can use. So the lack of certain vitamins can make the goodness in other foods unusable.

The big divide is between vitamins which dissolve in fat and those which dissolve in water.

Fat Soluble	Water Soluble
Vitamin A	Vitamin C
Vitamin D	Vitamin B family
Vitamin E	
Vitamin K	These are destroyed by: long-cooking, alkali (*don't* put bicarb in cooking water),
These are not easily destroyed but, as most can be stored in the body, there is risk of overdosing.	long storage, leaving food standing in water (e.g. peeled potatoes) too long.

As we don't totally understand what vitamins do, the recommended levels are very hazy. I have used British figures, unless only those from the USA were available. Every country sets recommended intakes, but no two countries agree on every one. For example, Sweden and West Germany both recommend twice as much vitamin C as the British authorities suggest.

★ A survey in 1985 showed that 90 per cent of people have diets low in key vitamins and of iron.
★ To eat more salads made of really varied vegetables, and dress them with a little oil high in vitamin E would be a major step forward in any diet.

More information

The British Nutrition Foundation, 15 Belgrave Square, London SW1X 8PS Tel: 01 235 4904 publishes a series of inexpensive leaflets on various aspects of diet. The foundation is funded by the food industry, but its sponsors have competing interests.

The London Food Commission, 80 Old Street, London EC1V 9AR Tel: 01 253 9513 is a watchdog on consumer interests and an information source. Hard-hitting reports on issues like irradiation and diet for the under 5s.

The National Eczema Society (see page 538) produces a diet guide for those with eczema.

Scottish Health Education Group, Health Education Centre, Woodburn House, Canaan Lane, Edinburgh EH10 A5G Tel: 031 447 8044

The Vegan Society, 33-35 George Street, Oxford OX1 2AY M£M, M, B, L.

The Vegetarian Society, Parkdale, Dunham Road, Altrincham, Cheshire WA14 4QG

Geoffrey Cannon and Caroline Walker, *The Food Scandal*, Century

'Manual of Nutrition', HMSO (page 615)

See also Health Education Authority leaflets (page 582).

The Role of Vitamins and Adult Daily Requirements

Babies often need less and adolescents more of many vitamins. But all children need the vitamins which fresh food provides. The higher figures in the chart below usually apply to the young and/or active, especially males. The requirements of babies and children vary greatly with age and health so always check with your doctor before giving extra vitamins to your children.

During breast feeding the vitamins a woman eats provide the baby with its vitamins too. So it is particularly important to have the whole range of vitamins. More vitamins are needed when breast feeding than at any other time.

The old need more fibre to prevent constipation, and more vitamin D if they don't spend so much time in the sun.

The following chart gives the recommended daily amounts of vitamins for adults in either milligrams or micrograms. A microgram is one-thousandth of a milligram.

Vitamin	Normal Daily Need	Need When Pregnant	Need When Breast Feeding	Uses	Sources	Lost Through
Vitamin A Retinol (micrograms)	750	750	1200	Night vision, healthy skin, hair and mucus membranes. Can prevent cancer in animals — may do so in man. Excess can be poisonous.	Fish oils, liver, kidney, dairy products, eggs, orange fruit and vegetables and dark-green vegetables. An average diet gives plenty.	High temperatures, light, air, copper or iron.
Vitamin B1 Thiamin (milligrams)	0·8 - 1·3	1	1·1	Vital to the enzyme system and in breaking down carbohydrate into energy. Shortage may cause fatigue, irritability and anxiety. Excess excreted.	Many foods, especially grains, pork, peas, rice, potatoes, nuts, wheatgerm.	Heat, alkaline, leached in thawing. Absorption reduced by alcohol.
Vitamin B2 Riboflavin (milligrams)	1·3 - 1·6	1·6	1·8	Growth. Maintenance of various tissues. Lack gives tired 'gritty' eyes.	Liver, kidney, dairy products, eggs, meat. Milk easily loses it in sunlight on a doorstep. Those on the pill need more, so do smokers and drinkers.	Light — 50% lost in two hours of sunlight.
Vitamin B Niacin Nicotinic Acid (milligrams)	15-18	18	21	Releases energy from food. Linked to lung enzymes. Lack causes severe skin conditions.	In many foods, especially liver, kidney, meat, whole grains, pulses, brewers yeast, peanuts. Some forms in cereals need alkalis to become usable by the body e.g. bicarbonate.	

Vitamin	Normal Daily Need	Need When Pregnant	Need When Breast Feeding	Uses	Sources	Lost Through
Vitamin B Folic Acid Folate Folacin (micrograms)	300-400	300-400	300-400	Assists cell division. Shortage causes anaemia. Surplus stored in liver.	In many foods especially liver, broccoli, spinach, cabbage, runner beans, oranges, wholemeal bread, nuts, bananas.	Much lost in water and in long cooking.
Vitamin B6 Pyridoxine (milligrams)	2-2·2	2·6	2·6	Metabolism of amino acids from protein. Helps make red blood cells. Doses over 10 mg can be harmful.	In many foods especially meat, fish, eggs, grains and some vegetables.	Oral contraceptives reduce its uptake, so more may be needed.
Vitamin B12 (micrograms)	3	3	3	Cell division, especially in bone marrow. Lack causes anaemia. Maintains myelin coating in nervous system. Excess is stored in the liver.	Only occurs in meat, fish, eggs and dairy produce. Liver best source. None in vegetables.	Dissolves in water.
Vitamin C Asorbic Acid (milligrams)	30	60	60	Present in all body tissues. Aids healing of skin and bone, may be needed for iron absorption. Vital for connective tissue. Stress and cold increase the need for it. Unknown role in adrenal gland and other functions not yet understood.	Almost entirely in fruit and vegetables especially black-currants, green peppers, sprouts, broccoli, mangoes, cauliflower. Deficiency not uncommon in Britain.	Very easily lost by storage, heat, cooking in water.
Vitamin D Cholecalciferol (micrograms)	sunlight	10	10	Vital for bones to grow and for calcium to be used to make them strong. Too little leads to bone softening and rickets. Too much is poisonous.	Fish liver oils, herrings, salmon, liver, made by the skin in sunlight. Dark skins need more sunlight for this than pale skins.	

Vitamin	Normal Daily Need	Need When Pregnant	Need When Breast Feeding	Uses	Sources	Lost Through
Vitamin E (milligrams)	8-10	8-10	8-10	Animals short of E show disorders in every system of the body. Role in man uncertain but probably key. May lessen risk on heart disease. Seems to lower blood cholesterol.	Vegetable oils especially wheat germ and sunflower, grains, eggs.	
Vitamin K (micrograms)	40	40	40	Makes blood clot. Too much can cause anaemia.	In most vegetables especially spinach, cabbage, cauliflower and our body can make it.	Antibiotics reduce Vitamin K production.
Pantothenic Acid (milligrams)	3-10	3-10	3-10	Releases energy from fat. Stops rats going grey but no evidence it does this in people.	Most foods, especially grains and pulses.	
Biotin (micrograms)	300	300	300	Lack causes fatigue, depression, nausea, loss of appetite and the skin becomes dry. Positive role not certain except for using fat.	Liver, kidney, eggs.	

Slimming

Extra weight puts a strain on the heart, and makes you far more prone to a whole range of diseases. However, medical opinion is against sudden crash diets. The more faddy and extreme the diet, the greater the risk that you will deprive yourself of vital nutrients without which your body will not be able to process even those you are getting, and such imbalances can make you seriously ill. If you do decide to keep your expansion within limits, talk to your doctor first.

Incentives to Dieting

To diet successfully the whole of your mind has to be doing it, if you need to convince one half of your mind that the other half is talking sense, here are some ways to do it.

1   Work out how much heavier you are than you ought

to be, then fill a rucksack, or suitcase, with that amount of weight and carry it everywhere you go for a whole day.

2   Stand in front of a full-length mirror and take off your clothes little by little. At each stage look at yourself from the front, the back and the side in a good light.

3   Try on some garments from the time when you were your right weight.

4   Next, find yourself some incentive to keep at it. For example, buy a coveted garment one size too small.

Dieting Methods

Whatever anyone says, you can't change the way the body works.

The easiest way is to think of it as a steam engine. Instead of shovelling coal into our steam engine we shovel in food. The body burns up the food to produce the power it needs to keep going, just as the steam engine burns coal. This is why food values are measured in calories - a calorie being a unit of energy.

Unfortunately, if it is given more fuel than it needs for the work in hand it stores it as fat, ready to be used on some other day when there is less fuel than the work demands. A great system in the days when primitive man never knew when the next elk would pass by; but a bore with a supermarket round the corner.

The good news is that eating less fuel than we need will force the body to draw the energy it needs from our fund of fat, and we will just as surely lose weight.

Whatever wrapping is put round them, these facts are central to the success of every diet ever invented.

The Calories You Need

Health experts recommend the following calorie levels for slimming.

Man: to lose 1 lb a week eat only 2,300 calories a day
to lose 2 lb a week eat only 1,700 calories a day
Woman: to lose 1 lb a week eat only 1,500 calories a day
to lose 2 lb a week eat only 1,000 calories a day

That weight loss of 1 to 2 lb a week may not sound dramatic, but if you diet gradually you change your eating habits and the weight is more likely to *stay* off.

The Snags of the High Fat Diet

Because calories are what count you can diet on *anything* - beer, cream cakes, doughnuts, baked beans, chocolate, cheese, coconuts, cabbages - or even, if you're a cannibal, kings. But there are snags to dieting on high calorie foods. First, you may lack vital vitamins and minerals needed for health (so you may look and feel lack-lustre). Second, the higher the calories of any food, the *less* you must eat to keep below your fuel needs. So it takes a great deal of self-control. For example: to take in 1,000 calories you could eat just:

4½ oz (125 g) cream cheese *or*
2½ buttered crumpets *or*
5½ oz (160 g) milk and nut chocolate *or*
8 rich biscuits *or*
2 lb (1 kg) smoked haddock *or*
12 cucumbers *or* 14 oranges
16 apples *or* 16 lettuces

On half that amount of fish in a day, plus lettuce and cucumber salad, you would be amply full, but on 2½ crumpets you'd be decidedly peckish.

Calories in Food
All are calories per 100 g (4 oz)

Food	Cal	Food	Cal	Food	Cal
Bacon, grilled	393	Beetroot, boiled	44	Peaches, canned in syrup	87
Beef, average cooked	225	Brussels sprouts, boiled	18	Pears	41
Chicken with skin, roast	213	Cabbage, raw	22	Pineapple, canned in juice	46
Chicken (no skin), roast	148	Cabbage, boiled	15	Plums	32
Duck with skin, roast	339	Carrots, boiled	23	Prunes, dried	161
Duck meat only, roast	189	Cauliflower, boiled	9	Raspberries	25
Fish - white, baked	77	Celery	8	Rhubarb, cooked with sugar	45
Fish - white, fried	235	Courgettes, raw	29	Strawberries	26
Fish - herrings	251	Cucumber	10	Sultanas	250
Fish - trout	135	Leeks	24	Almonds	565
Ham	166	Lentils, cooked	99	Coconut, desiccated	604
Kidney - pigs', fried	202	Lettuce	12	Peanuts	570
Lamb, roast	266	Mushrooms, raw	13	Biscuits - chocolate	524
Liver - lambs', fried	237	Onions	23	Digestive	471
Pâté, average	347	Parsnips	56	Bread - white	230
Pork chop	332	Peas, frozen, boiled	72	Bread - wholemeal	215
Sausages - beef, cooked	267	Peppers, green	14	Cake - rich fruit	322
Sausages - pork, cooked	317	Potatoes, boiled	76	Cake - chocolate with butter icing	500
Tongue	293	Potatoes, chips	234	Jam tarts	368
Turkey with skin, roast	189	Potatoes, roast	150	Porridge	374
		Spinach, boiled	30	Rice (approx)	350
Brie	300	Sweetcorn, canned	85	Spaghetti (approx)	330
Cheddar cheese	406	Sweet potato	91	Chocolate - milk	529
Cottage cheese	96	Tomatoes, raw	14	Cocoa powder	312
Cream - double	447	Turnips, steamed	14	Coffee - instant powder	100
Cream - single	195	Watercress	14	Coffee - ground infused	3
Eggs, boiled	147			Curry powder	325
Eggs, fried	232	Apples	46	Drinking chocolate	366
Yoghurt - low fat natural	65	Apricots, dried	182	Honey	288
Yoghurt - low fat fruit	89	Bananas	76	Jam	262
Custard	118	Blackcurrants	28	Ketchup	98
Butter	740	Cherries	47	Peanut butter	623
Lard	892	Dates, dried	248	Pickles - sweet	134
Margarine, average	730	Figs, dried	213	Sugar - white	394
Oil for cooking, average	899	Grapes	63	Tea	0
Aubergine	14	Grapefruit	22	Beer	37
Avocado pear	223	Mango	59	Spirits	222
Runner beans, boiled	19	Melon	23	Wine - typical white	89
		Oranges	35	Cider - typical	43
		Peaches	37		

The figures below left were taken both from the Ministry of Agriculture Fisheries and Food **Manual of Nutrition** and from the 4th revised edition of McCance and Widdowson's **The Composition of Foods** (HMSO).

Your Greatest Guide to Calories, *Slimming* Magazine - on manufactured food.

The No-Diet Diet
If you normally eat a very well-balanced diet then the best way to lose weight is probably to eat slightly less of everything, and little by little the weight should come off. Try to get up from every meal feeling slightly hungry.

However, it may be easiest to diet by changing your eating pattern entirely and only eating low calorie foods, so you can create feasts and still lose those pounds.

The Diet That's a Feast
If you look at the calorie list on page 614 you'll see you can eat a vast amount of vegetables before you begin to approach your calorie limit. They don't have to be raw, but the best feast of all is raw vegetables because they take time to eat and bulk out the stomach, leaving you feeling nice and full for some time afterwards. So try a salad diet. The salads I'm talking about are delicious concoctions of every vegetable imaginable. Avoid the higher calorie salad items like avocados and tomatoes.

For dressing use freshly ground black pepper, a sprinkling of Maldon sea salt and some lemon juice or plain low fat yoghurt.

The Whole Meal
After your salad have a smallish portion of grilled or roasted meat or fish, or any plain protein that the rest of the household is having, provided it isn't fried or fatty. If you feel like something sweet afterwards make it a piece of raw fruit with no extra sugar.

For the rest of the day allocate yourself 2 slices of wholemeal bread, and half a pint of skimmed milk. Have no sugar, and avoid alcohol, squashes, mixers and fresh fruit juice - all packed with calories.

> Even with half a pint of milk a day you may run low in calcium. Ask your doctor whether you should take calcium tablets.

★ If you are a nibbler choose some vegetables you like eating raw - such as celery or carrots and prepare a bag of them in the morning.

Keeping Up the Burn
Only keep to a strict diet for three days. Then have two days of eating normal meals in smaller quantities than usual, so you neither lose nor gain. (This means keeping off sweet snacks and drinks.) Then go back on the diet for three days more - and so on. Research has shown that when the body is short of food for any length of time it changes into a different 'gear' and learns to make far better use of what it is given. So, if you diet hard

without a break, it actually makes it harder to lose weight.

Weighing Yourself
It's hard to lose weight unless you have scales to show you the pounds you are shedding. I find by far the most effective are the new electronic ones which allow no self-deception in unambiguous dulcet tones, 'Your weight is 19 stone 3 pounds' - or whatever it happens to be. Weigh yourself at the same time of day each time and wear exactly the same clothes, if you can't be naked.

★ Take a long hot or cold calorie-free drink.
★ Chart your drop in weight day by day, but don't expect it to drop evenly *every* day. It is normal to have slight ups and plateaus, as well as downs.
★ Never have serving dishes on the table while eating.
★ Carry that loaded suitcase mentioned on page 613 whenever you feel yourself weakening.
★ *Most important of all:* if you break your diet don't feel a failure and give up totally. A slip is a slip, accept that you are human and get on with dieting from that point on.
★ Never eat while standing up.
★ Only let yourself eat in one room of the house.

LOOKING AFTER THE FACE AND BODY

Skin and body care are often looked upon as mere fripperies. Some people certainly get through life perfectly well without ever introducing their skin to anything more cosmetic than a bar of soap. That, however, does not suit everyone and it has been discovered that looking good contributes far more to someone's sense of well-being than has been appreciated. This means that when people feel that they look good they are more likely to look after their health and even to recover more quickly from illness. So beauty and relaxation are, in their own ways, important factors in health.

The Body
Beauty care starts at the toes, not at the neck. After all, it's the people we really care about who see the whole of us. Even if we aren't all shaped like Marilyn Monroe or Robert Redford the surface can at least be good to touch.

Rough Dry Skin
Few people have skin as smooth as a baby's, but there are plenty of cures for the roughness which adults are heirs to.

A long-term solution to dryness is to rub liquid paraffin (the laxative from a chemist, not the kind used for fires) all over the body before getting into a bath. Let your skin absorb the oil in the heat of the bath for a while before washing in the usual way. Do this at each bath when the skin is dry, or several times a week when it isn't. It can produce velvety results, especially if you combine it with the bumpy skin prevention below. But to clean the bath you will need the method on page 154.

> *Don't* oil the soles of the feet or use oil before showering - you could slip.

Bumpy Skin
I'm not talking here about the under-the-skin bumps of cellulite but about the goose-pimple bumps *on* the skin. To prevent them, wash with a loofah at each bath. But, if you already have bumps, set to work with soap and a pumice stone. They won't vanish in one go, but a week or two should cure them. After the bath smoothe on skin lotion.

Scars
Rubbing vitamin E cream on potential scars has long been said to be a cure. Doctors now say that it's the rubbing - and not the vitamin - which stimulates the skin to heal better. It is a technique well worth using if a scar might form.

Stretch Marks
Stretch marks can occur anywhere that the skin is stretched by excess weight, and cannot be removed. The most annoying are those across the stomach as a result of pregnancy. As they are partly caused by hormone changes people dispute whether they can be prevented. I think that it's certainly worth a try. Avoid excessive weight gain, cut out salt to keep down the fluid gain, and start preventive measures on the skin. Stretch marks occur more easily on dry skin, so give any area which is liable to be stretched a daily massage with a rich hand or body lotion such as one based on cocoa butter. To this add a little wheatgerm oil, as the vitamin E it contains seems to help skin to renew itself.

Broken Veins
When fine spiders' webs of broken veins appear on the legs, as part of the early stages of varicose veins, they can be removed by injections - though NHS doctors are unlikely to bother with this cosmetic treatment.

A small spider of blood vessels on the face is called a naevus and it can usually be removed permanently.

Face Facts
It may sound a curious thing to say, but the most important thing about making-up is getting to know your face. You may think you know what you look like, but very few of us really do.

A face is like a river, always the same and yet always changing: our health, our moods, our diet and the amount of sleep we get are reflected in it, as surely as clouds in water. So we each have many faces, not one.

A shade of lipstick or eyeshadow which looks wonderful on Monday can be a disaster on Tuesday after a late night. To look her best every woman needs to take a few moments to *look honestly* at her face as it is *that day.*

The other factors in looking good are diet, exercise and skin care. Unless we get all four right we are painting make-up on to a badly prepared canvas and

it will show. But if you decide to eat better, sleep more and revise your beauty routines don't expect your face to be like new the next morning. Skin is remade from the bottom layers upwards, to replace what flakes off the top. It will take *at least* three weeks before those layers reach the surface and show even the first sign of improvement.

Sleep and Diet
It is only during sleep that our body can give its undivided attention to feeding and remaking the cells of our skin. Of course, it will make new skin cells whatever happens, but somehow they don't seem to look as good.

How much sleep is enough varies from person to person. You can only let your body guide you, but if you've become used to very little, yet feel tired, you will need to re-educate it little by little.

Diet is also important. The body will chug along on almost any food. But it needs a whole complex of vitamins and minerals to work at its best. Nobody should expect to stay looking good on a poor diet any more than they would expect to get the best out of a Rolls Royce if they ran it on 2-star petrol.

Smoking and alcohol both affect the amount of vitamins which are available for skin renewal. By tightening the fine blood vessels smoking also reduces the amount of oxygen which reaches the surface of the body, so making it function less well. As a result smokers have sallower, spottier skins than non-smokers and develop lines measurably sooner. Alcohol gives skin a coarser, slacker texture and can produce the venous and swollen nose of the heavy drinker on either sex.

Cleansing
Make-up is best removed with a cream cleanser - which will remove both dirt and make-up. Whether it's basic cold cream or the most expensive cleanser, it will do the same job. Apply it with upward strokes (gravity pulls the face down quite enough without us helping it) and massage it into the make-up. Then remove it with clean cotton wool and repeat. It's amazing how much comes off the second time.

★ If you want to feel extra fresh you can now splash your face with warm water. Those with a high colour should avoid using very cold or very hot water on the face; either will increase the problem. So will temperature extremes in sauna and steam baths, or skin tonics with alcohol in them.

If You Have to Wash
If soap upsets your skin you can use a soap-free washing cream. The big cosmetic companies make expensive ones but you can wash just as well with emulsifying ointment which is a fraction of the price. Dermatologists recommend it for people who can't take soap - such as those with eczema - so the pharmaceutical counter of most chemists will produce it if you ask. It's a thick cream which you apply to a wet face, lather up like soap and rinse off. It leaves the face feeling perfectly clean but with none of the dryness of soap.

Open Pores

For an oily skin, with no tendency to broken veins, put boiling water in a bowl in a wash basin, and lean over it with a towel over your head so all the steam is trapped under it. When the face is thoroughly hot and the pores are open any blackheads can be very gently pressed out *with well scrubbed fingers*. Then wipe a slice of lemon all over the open pores and leave it to dry. Finally rinse the face with tepid water.

Face Packs

Face packs can be as varied as cakes - and contain many of the same ingredients. A pack by any good cosmetic company will do the job, and the ones which peel off afterwards are appealing, but you can easily cleanse and tighten the skin by applying simple home-made mixtures provided you remember the rule that anything which disagrees with you as a food is likely to disagree with your skin too, and that food put on you should be as fresh as food put *in* you.

For cleansing and tightening use a mixture of plain yoghurt and Fullers Earth (from a chemist) - the earth absorbs the grease while the yoghurt nourishes and tightens. One famous French beauty of the last century swore by a mixture of strawberries and cream - without the sugar, of course. This does have a tendency to slide off the face unless you keep very still, but the astringency of strawberries certainly tightens the skin and refreshes it.

Whatever the pack, rinse it off with very cool water and pat dry.

★ If you go swimming both salt and chlorine are equally bad for the skin. Rinse them off with cool water and cleanse, tone and moisturize the skin as soon as possible afterwards.

Exfoliation

Exfoliation is a smart word for removing the top layers of skin. You can buy washing grains which are just rough enough to rub off rather more of the surface than washing would remove. These can be excellent for skin. But most are not for fine dry skin.

There are also more drastic forms of exfoliation which go as far as peeling the upper layer of skin off with chemicals. It is said that this allows new young skin to grow. Anyone who is considering such harsh treatment would do well to discuss it with more than one beauty therapist.

Toning

You might think that the best toning lotion you could get would be a gleaming bottle from a big cosmetic company. Not so. Many branded ones contain alcohol which is positively bad for sensitive skins, especially black skins, very fair Celtic skins and those with a high colour. But you can tone with cosmetic rosewater from a pharmacy counter. Use the rosewater neat or mix it with witch hazel (which is a mild odourless antiseptic extracted from a shrub). For a normal skin try one spoonful of witch hazel to three of rosewater. The witch hazel is especially good for greasy skins and those with

a tendency to spottiness, so for that type of skin increase the proportion of witch hazel - but don't expect it to scotch full-blown acne.

For dry skins add a little glycerine (also from a pharmacy), as glycerine has the ability to hold moisture in the skin. Suit the proportions to your skin.

Nourishing

Just how much skin can or cannot be fed is debatable, but it is certainly worth applying an oil or cream at night - at worst it will protect it from the drying effect of the atmosphere. To feed your skin you don't need to confront your nearest and dearest with a face like a lard bag. A rich moisturiser which sinks invisibly into the skin is all you need or, better still, use a vitamin A or vitamin E cream or oil. Both vitamins are said to help the skin restore itself. Do include your neck; it too is exposed to the elements. The old saying is, 'A woman is as old as her hands and her neck', and in these face-lifting times it was never truer.

Moisturizer

The face, neck and hands are the only parts of our bodies we expose to the elements day in day out. And if they can take the water out of clothes on a washing line they must be doing just the same to the skin. Of course, some people who never use moisturizer reach old age none the worse for the lack of it - but no one can know how their skin will weather, until it's too late. So if you don't want to end up looking like a Cox's Orange Pippin apple after long storage you should wear moisturizer on your face and neck every day, whether or not you use other make-up.

The effectiveness of different moisturizers *may* be related to the price, but if any cream could be scientifically proved to be much more effective than all the rest the fact would be advertised in bold letters on its packing and splashed across the women's press: that hasn't happened. So buy whatever suits you.

Moisturizer and Sun Block

There is now ample scientific evidence that sun is bad for skin. It creates what are called 'free radicals' - skin saboteurs which damage it internally, speeding up the skin's ageing and reducing its bounce and elasticity. In fact, strong sunlight hitting the skin is equivalent to a classroom of schoolchildren jumping on a sprung mattress. Worse still, it affects the cell's biochemistry and causes skin cancer. Even among the British, who get little strong sun apart from summer holidays, the incidence of skin cancer is rising dramatically in the generations who have sunbathed. (See page 533.) In summer sunshine your moisturizer should contain a total sun block.

Concealer

One make-up artist who teaches the general public says concealer is the most under-used make-up of all. It's a very dense form of foundation which you apply to small areas where something needs to be blotted out. It works equally well on spots, blemishes and on shadows under the eyes, and lightens the effect of long lines bracketing the sides of a mouth. Choose one slightly lighter than your skin, and towards beige rather than pink. Apply it with a fine brush, working it to nothing at the edges. Properly blended in it should be invisible. It can be used with or without foundation - and more men use concealers than you might think. (For covering major marks see Cosmetic camouflage, page 620.)

★ Be very careful how you apply it if you have bags under your eyes. If you put it *on* the bags it will highlight them and make them look bigger. It must only go on the shadow *under* the bag.

Foundation
If nature didn't give you a perfect complexion having the correct foundation correctly applied is *the* most important part of make-up. If it isn't right you won't look good whatever else you do.

Choosing Foundation
Whatever the publicity machines of the big cosmetic companies imply, foundation should be the same colour as your skin: keep changing it to suit fashion and you risk looking like a doll with its neck a different colour. That doesn't mean there is only one shade which is right; hardly any make-up is *exactly* the colour of skin. So there will be several similar shades which look like your skin when you apply them - and some may be more flattering than others. You may even find that to get a good match you need to mix two together. They usually mix best if they are the same type - both liquid or both block - but they don't need to be the same brand.

When looking for the right shade the golden rule is not to be fooled by the lights in the shop where you buy it.

Only buy what looks good in *daylight*, and buy one that is no heavier than is necessary. A good foundation looks and feels light but gives as much coverage as you personally need. And there *are* foundations which block out even the reddest veins yet look natural - they just take a bit of finding.

★ If you can't face shopping for foundation with no make-up on get several of the little plastic cylinders which camera film comes in (photographic counters usually have empties) and ask the sales girls to put a test dab of the foundations you like in each so you can take it home to try. But do label them as the dabs go in or you'll be none the wiser.

Applying Foundation
No professional make-up artist would dream of applying foundation with anything except a moist sponge - and it really does give much the best finish. Wet the sponge and then squeeze it *very* hard in a tissue to remove all the excess water. Apply the foundation with it, working from the middle of the face outwards. If you have a good skin you can even use it simply to cover small blemishes or excess rosiness; it doesn't have to be wall to wall - provided nobody can spot where it ends. Don't forget the neck. Foundation needs to shade to nothing under the jaw line.

★ To take a little foundation down the upper part of the neck without it showing and to blend it away to nothing, mix a little with your moisturizer as you apply it.

Powder
Fashions for powder come and go. Its great advantage is that it helps foundation to stay on. So, if powder isn't out of fashion use it. Unless you have very dark skin, choose a colourless translucent powder. (For films, television or photography beware of those with a sparkle - they can make you look as if you are sweating.) Take some on a clean puff, knock the surplus off on your hand and then apply it all over, pressing it lightly into the foundation - but not dragging at it. Then brush off every loose particle with a big soft brush.

★ Some make-up artists say older women with fine lines under the eyes should avoid powdering this area at all; others say the big secret is to brush every extra atom out of the creases - it may depend on the powder. So, if time has added a tracery, try both ways and see what suits you.

Blusher
Blusher tends to be over-used or not used at all. The point about blusher is that red creates optical illusions. When I learnt theatrical make-up, from a splendid old pro, he showed us how colouring something red makes it seem more prominent than it would be if it were flesh colour. (This is one reason why the Chinese, who have none of the rosiness of Europeans, seem to have flatter faces.) So by putting a redder tone on the cheekbones, we make the bone structure seem stronger and more prominent. This adds essential definition to a face, but needs a light hand or it creates a clownish look.

Blusher should never be a feature *of* the face, it should only bring out the features *in* the face. So choose a blusher only a few shades darker than your skin tone. Take some up on a large brush - use the sort that looks like an artist's brush but with a very big head. Brush most of it off on the back of your hand, and smile. Then apply it to the outer part of the bulge, working it very lightly in a pear shape, along the cheekbone, to *slightly* wider than the eyes.

★ If you put too much on blot it and powder over to kill the colour.
★ If you aren't wearing foundation, powder the area before applying blusher or it will cling too brightly on any oily patches.

Eyes
Most people regard eye shadow as eye colouring, look for a 'pretty colour' and apply it. There is more to it than that. In fact, there are two totally different aspects to using eye make-up - eye shaping and eye colouring. And the first is the most important.

Eye Shaping
Most eyes are a fairly similar shape and size. Where they differ greatly is in the shape of the sockets. So the object of eye shaping is to use light and shadow to sculpt the area around the eyes, improving the shape and

concealing any faults. To do this you don't need dramatic colours; in fact, it is much easier to work with milk chocolate tones, or browny-grey ones, and these suit almost any eye colour. Use a fairly fine brush, rather than the applicators the cosmetic houses supply.

Big eyes are almost always beautiful, and the illusion of size can be created by having enough space between the brows and the lashes. To make this area seem larger apply a highlighter to the bone just under the outer half of the eyebrows. Or apply a light eye make-up base over the whole lid and up to the eyebrows - a good base does double duty by helping the eyeshadow to stay on and prevent it creasing.

Once you have created the space you can begin to shape the eye with light and shadow. There are no fixed rules for how to do this, but with most eyes the aim is to make them look bigger and wider than they really are. So avoid shading heavily near the nose or you will make them seem closer together. Try to imagine your ideal eye and how the shadow would fall on it, and try painting those shadows on your lids. Then imagine where the highlights would come and paint those on. Finally blend the edges of the light and shadow together so nobody would know where either began or ended. Few people's eyes are symmetrical so don't try to apply the shading in exactly the same way on both eyes. Instead, look at them from a slight distance and shade them to *look* the same.

★ If you find it hard try reversing the process. Imagine you are trying to make yourself up for a stage part in which you have to look old, or tired, or ugly. Then make-up for that part. You will discover what you *mustn't* do and from there it is far easier to see what should be done.

Once you have the eyes shaped you can decide whether or not to use a colour. If you do, don't apply one colour all over or you will kill the effect you have just created. Instead use touches of several colours, which blend well, to recreate the basic shading.

The tones should be chosen to go with your skin shade, and with the lipstick you plan to wear. Olive tone skins look great with lipsticks which lean towards coppery tones, and with brown, golden or sludgy green eye-shadow. Pinker toned skins look better with pinker toned lipsticks, and eye-shadows in greys, silver, light gold and certain blues (though blue is much harder to wear than grey). Seductive as glittery shadows may be, flat colours are far easier for most people to wear.

If you are lucky enough to have a mid-toned skin you may be able to lean either way - wearing blues and greens, greys and browns with equal success. But most people have a smaller range of shades which really show them off at their best.

The young can use spectacular colours with great effect - if they apply them well - but, unfortunately, spectacular colours get harder to wear with every year. Basically a face is a very small place, and it doesn't look its best when it's too ornamented. We may not think of lines as ornamental but each one adds a new 'busy-ness' to the face, until there comes a point where quite enough is happening in it without bright colours as well.

★ If you want a slightly dramatic look at times when eyeliner is out of style try using a *very* fine brush to put minute dots of liquid liner right in the base of the eyelashes. The dots should be invisible, but the eyes should have an extra something.

Eyebrows

The face has two frames - the hair and the eyebrows. The hair frames the whole face but it is the eyebrows which frame its most important feature - the eyes. If the eyebrows aren't right the picture just isn't set off properly. It is currently fashionable to leave the eyebrows looking unplucked and have them brushed away from the eyes but slightly shaggy. Fine, if it suits you - and thin highly plucked brows now look ridiculous - but most eyes have less space between them and the brows than is ideal. So a *little* judicious plucking *under* the brows at the outer half opens up the eyes and makes them seem much larger. Eyebrows can be shaggy but still have a defined shape, and hairs growing down the lid do nothing for anyone.

The best way of darkening the eyebrows isn't to use an eyebrow pencil because, being hard, it forces you to draw on the skin. A far more natural effect is achieved by brushing a little block mascara onto the hairs of the eyebrows, or by using a soft eyeshadow to colour them - an eyeshadow pencil is ideal. Avoid black, unless you are genuinely raven-haired; a soft brown gives as much definition and looks more natural. Finally comb the hairs away from the eyes, and - if you don't want a shaggy look - smoothe the comb along the upper edge.

Mascara

Mascara should be the last item of make-up you apply. There are basically two kinds - one kind smudges when wet, the other smudges on oil. (There is also a third kind, which manufacturers don't admit to, which smudges whatever you do.) When using the oil-smudge type avoid taking mosturizer and foundation close up to the eyes. To apply mascara neatly just pull your chin in and hold the mirror high while doing the under lashes. Then tilt your head back and hold the mirror down for the upper ones. Brush it on in the direction the lashes grow - a sideways movement will make them clump together and, as Raymond Chandler put it, look 'like miniature iron railings'. For a thicker effect without iron railings apply mascara lightly to both sides of the upper lashes. If any do clump together comb them apart with a tiny eyelash comb before the mascara dries.

Tired or Sore Eyes

Two easily made eye-packs are slices of cucumber or cold tea bags (old used ones which have been in the refrigerator). However, I'm told tea may not suit some skins - and if it doesn't suit yours don't use it. Whatever you use, lie down and relax (see page 624). If your eyes are tired the rest of you probably is too.

Lips

It's easy to envy the model girls their lovely mouths. The truth is most of them don't have them. They simply redraw the lines to achieve perfection, and anyone can do the same. Vast changes in outline look silly on the young and only create the look of an ageing vamp on an older woman: but you don't need vast changes. It's amazing how much difference can be made by drawing the lips *slightly* fuller or narrower or curvier than nature intended. Experiment in private; it's a skill which takes practice but it's well worth practising.

★ Keep soft lip and eye liners in the refrigerator for a while before sharpening them, then they will break less easily.

If you use foundation take it right over the lips, so you have a blank canvas to start on. Hold the mirror so you can see your entire face and imagine your ideal mouth. Then see how close you can get to it without it being obvious. It needs to be a combination of the mouth you have, the mouth which would best suit your other features and the mouth which is in fashion - for mouth shapes do change. Start with a lip pencil and only fill in with lipstick when the outline is right.

★ To check whether the upper lip line is even on both sides pull your chin in and hold the mirror above the mouth. To check the bottom lip line do the reverse - stick your chin out and hold the mirror low.

To be unobtrusive the lip pencil can match the lipstick. But if very pale lipsticks are in vogue, using a slightly darker liner can prevent that vague amorphous look which pale lipstick gives. If you want a more dramatic mouth a darker liner can be used with a medium-toned lipstick. Equally, by night or for photographs, I have seen a paler liner or even a *minute* line lighter than the foundation used to give the illusion of a strong lip angle. But be careful with this or it can look decidedly odd. Whatever the shade, blot the pencil before applying the lipstick.

★ To prevent lipstick creeping into any, otherwise invisible, lines in the upper lip: outline the lips with lip pencil, blot with tissue. Powder over the line. Brush off the excess powder, and apply the lipstick keeping just *inside* the lip line. This works better than most special products designed to stop lipstick creeping - and it costs nothing.

The Shades of Lipstick

Different shades of lipstick can make an enormous difference to the look of a mouth. Nothing makes a small mouth look smaller and meaner than a really dark lipstick, whereas the same mouth with a lighter tone can look a perfectly normal size. In the same way big mouths can look like cushions when painted pale pink.

There is also the matter of age. The very young and beautiful can get away with almost any shade - but the rest of the population needs to be wary of extremes. Very pale tones can look too baby-doll after a certain age and dark tones are hard and ageing. This doesn't mean the over-25s have to ignore fashionable colours. When deeper tones are in fashion they can be softened by applying a light shade first, then the dark one, and finishing with a glosser. Then the darkness has some life to it. When very pale tones are 'in' you can do the reverse and put a mid-tone underneath.

★ When buying lipstick try the shades out on the pads of your fingers. They are pinker than the back of your hand and you will get a better idea of how it will look on your lips.
★ There's never any need to be stuck with a lipstick shade. With a lip brush you can mix several together. You can even put the stubs in a plastic container in a low microwave and melt them to make a totally new colour.
★ If you find the acid in your skin turns lipstick bluer than it should be, you can minimise this effect by putting foundation base over the lips before the lipstick.

Any scent can react with sunlight to cause ugly dark patches on the skin. So it should not be applied before sunbathing nor should scented skin lotions be used before going in the sun.

More information

Joan Price's Face Place, 33 Cadogan Street, London SW3 2PP Tel: 01 589 9062 - sells almost every brand of make-up and there are dressing tables at which you can sit down and try them out before you buy. The assistants are trained beauty therapists and will help and advise.

The Make-up Centre, 26 Bute Street, London SW7 3EX Tel: 01 584 2188 - run by a make-up artist with 20 years' experience in films and making up the faces of the famous. She will make someone up and the shop also sells make-up ranges which are normally reserved for professional make-up artists.

Colour Counselling

A friend of mine rang me one day to say her life had been revolutionized: she had been to a colour counsellor and discovered what colours of make-up and clothes really suited her. She has been looking twice as attractive since. The international organization which offers colour counselling is **Colour Me Beautiful**, 56 Abbey Business Centre, Ingate Place, London SW8 3NS Tel: 01 627 5211. There are representatives all over the UK, but - and it's a *big* but - they pay to be trained by the organization and then essentially have a franchise to operate the scheme. This means that there is no guarantee that all the operatives have a real flair for the job.

Cosmetic Camouflage

To cover up a heavy mark on the skin takes make-up with more density than the usual foundation. But there are several ranges on the market designed to do just that. So almost any skin blemish, anywhere on the body, can be camouflaged with the right technique. As many of these cosmetics are waterproof, you can even swim with confidence.

If you want to find a beauty therapist trained in this kind of work the association given on page 623 will put you in touch with one. In addition, the British Red Cross have a cosmetic camouflage service. Their representative will visit patients in need of this while they are in hospital and show them how to use make-up to cover marks and disfigurements - as it is possible to disguise marks without leaving the skin looking made up, the service is available to both sexes, and to children.

Patients are only given this help after referral by a doctor, but anyone who needs it may ask his or her doctor to refer them.

Most of the companies which make these special cosmetics will supply samples, for a small fee, so you can try them out at home. Some of the major manufacturers and distributors of cosmetic camouflage are given below and some products can be obtained on a NHS prescription or through a hospital pharmacy. A word of warning though. To achieve perfect camouflage you need to blend several shades together to produce one which exactly matches your skin, and then apply it with considerable skill so as to minimize any problems in the texture of the disfigured area. This is a skill which anyone can acquire, but very few people will have it the first time they try to apply the make-up. To get good results you may need either a lot of practice or a lesson from an expert - or both. You may need to experiment to find a brand which suits you.

Boots (most branches) - Covering Cream
Charles H. Fox, 22 Tavistock Street, London WC2E 7PY Tel: 01 240 3111 (Dermacolour)
Flori Roberts, 158 Notting Hill Gate, London W11 Tel: 01 229 4224 has camouflage products especially suited to dark and black skins.
Stiefel Laboratories (UK) Ltd, Holtspur Lane, Wooburn Green, High Wycombe, Bucks HP10 0AU Tel: 062 85 24966 (Covermark)
Joyce Allsworth, *Skin Camouflage*, Stanley Thornes

Feet and Legs

Most feet are like a pair of ancient retainers working away below stairs with never a thank-you. They benefit from being given a good scrub to stimulate the circulation. After scrubbing, rub down every bit of dry skin with a pumice stone, or it may crack painfully on the heels or turn into nasty corns on the toe joints. If the skin is hard and dry rub some glycerine on at night.

Chiropodists say people shouldn't treat corns at home with bottled chemicals in case they let the acid damage normal skin around the corn. Instead they advise using a pumice stone to remove the first signs of a corn forming or to rub it down if it has already formed. This isn't a job which can be done in one session. Do, meanwhile, apply a corn ring to remove the pressure when in shoes. You can also try the old-fashioned remedy of soaking some bread in vinegar and putting this on the corn under a plaster. It isn't so strong it will damage the skin, but it will make the surface of the corn a lot easier to rub off.

Tired Feet

The most basic treatment for tired feet is to remove not only your shoes but your socks, stockings or tights as well. Feet weren't designed for footwear and they benefit from going barefoot for part of the day.

If the feet are tired soak them for 5 to 20 minutes in a basin of warm water containing a handful of salt. Wiggle your toes as you sit, to undo the cramping effect of shoes. Next, lie on your back and put your feet up the wall. Having your feet above your head will rest all the veins in your feet and legs which have been under pressure from walking, standing and tight footwear.

Hands

The counsel of perfection is to put handcream by each basin and apply it every time you wash them. Failing that, at least try to spare them the worst assaults by household products. There is no substitute for rubber gloves. Most of the products used for such jobs are made to strip off grease - and they are even more effective on the delicate natural oils in the skin.

★ When about to do a job which will push dirt up under the nails scratch them into vaseline or lanolin so the grease gets well under the nails and prevents the dirt embedding.

Rough Hands

When the skin is roughed up by jobs like decorating and gardening handcreams don't smooth it. Much better is an old-fashioned remedy given to me by a man who was forever tinkering with cars. Pour into a cupped hand a teaspoonful or so of cooking oil. Add a teaspoonful of granulated sugar. Then rub the mixture *very* thoroughly all over the hands for about 2 minutes. Then rinse the mixture off and dry. It works because the sugar acts as very gentle sandpaper rubbing off all the little rough corners of skin, while the oil softens the skin and lets the sugar slide enough to do its job painlessly.

At night apply a few drops of neat glycerine or a mixture of glycerine and rosewater to keep the hands (or body skin) soft. If they are very chapped, apply lanolin cream as well and put on cotton gloves to stop the lanolin getting everywhere. (A few people are allergic to it, so if you get any reaction stop using it.)

Smelly or Stained Hands

By tradition, finger bowls always contain a slice of lemon. This is because lemon removes smells from the skin. So if you are doing a smelly job it's useful to keep an odd wedge of lemon to rub over the skin afterwards. Failing that you can rub them with vinegar, salt or dry mustard. Each removes a slightly different spectrum of smells. Whatever the smell, don't wash your hands in hot water: the smell penetrates the skin more deeply.

Lemon is almost as good for stains on the hands as it is for curing smells. It needs to be rubbed on and left to act as a bleach. For nicotine stains the only solution is hydrogen peroxide. Chemists sell it in different strengths. Ask the chemist to advise you on how much you should dilute the one he sells, to make it safe for your hands.

Nails

Manicurists sometimes take clippers to the cuticles. This is not a good idea. The cuticles are there to protect the nail bed. In time it can also produce a thickened edge to the skin around the nail which is most unattractive.

If the cuticles really grow too far over the nails try a tip recommended by The Body Shop: soak the finger tips for 30 minutes in a mixture made from 2 tablespoons of egg yolk, 2 tablespoons of pineapple juice and ½ teaspoon of cider vinegar. Then gently push the cuticles back with an orange stick.

Scissors may fracture the nail layers as they cut through them, so it is better to shorten them with an emery board. It should be rubbed from the sides towards the middle - not used like a saw, because sawing to and fro overheats the nail and makes it more likely to break later. So does a metal file. But even the most careful filing won't prevent some nails from breaking because nails reflect our general state of health. If they keep breaking the cause is likely to be an unbalanced diet or some kind of strain.

If you improve your diet and reduce the strain don't expect strong nails in a trice. They take about 6 months to renew themselves.

★ Toe nails should be cut straight across; angling them down at the corners risks very painful ingrowing toe nails.
★ Nails stained with vegetable juices can be bleached with lemon juice, but the best way to whiten nicotine-stained nails is to scrub them with smoker's toothpaste regularly.

Hair

Hair is one of those curious substances which, like ivory, is both dead and delicate. In more than one detective story the murderer is caught because he shows traces of arsenic in his hair - having fiendishly built up an immunity to it and then administered it to both himself and his victim. These revelations appear in the hair because it is fed by the blood supply and everything we eat and drink is reflected in it. So the first step to beautiful hair is a good diet.

To look its best it also needs to be treated gently. Mild shampoos are better than harsh ones, gentle brushes better than scrapers, and most hair looks better with conditioner. Apply the conditioner to the ends of the hair, not to the roots; it's the hair which has been exposed to the elements for longest which most needs its soothing touch.

Bleaching
The idea that gentlemen prefer blondes has an ancient history: it is said that the prostitutes of ancient Rome were required either to dye their hair yellow or to wear a blond wig. The bleaches they used were probably horrific, but hair can be made fairer quite gently. To lighten fair hair gradually without the harshness of bleach, infuse camomile flowers (as for camomile tea) and pour the mixture over the hair as a last rinse.

Alternatively, pour dilute lemon juice all over your hair before going in the sun, or draw strands of hair through a wedge of lemon to get a streaked effect. Using lemon and sun is not good for the hair. But then neither is bleach - and lemon is the milder of the two.

Be very careful about trying to bleach hair suddenly with strong peroxide. If hair has any undertone of red - and a lot of brown hair does - peroxide can turn it pure carrot. If this happens don't assume you can just blot it out by dyeing over it. Get professional advice: some dyes turn it green.

★ If you have already made the mistake of using strong peroxide on your hair - which can be most unpleasant for the skin - neutralize it with a strong solution of bicarbonate of soda and water.

> *DYEING THE HAIR - It may be stated once for all that this practice is decidedly injurious. It may fail altogether in producing the desired result; it is never unattended by a certain amount of unpleasant circumstances, and frequently with evil results.*
> Enquire Within 1856

★ An infusion of sage leaves used as a final rinse will reduce the greyness of hair which is just beginning to go grey.

Conditioners
One reason why conditioner improves the look of hair is that it restores its acid/alkali balance. But, if you don't want to use bought conditioner, a touch of vinegar in the last rinse helps to remove the alkalinity of the soap and makes the hair shine. You can also infuse a few sprigs of fresh rosemary in boiling water and when it has cooled pour it over the hair. This also leaves the hair shiny and manageable, and smelling perfectly delicious. If you don't have rosemary but have nettles in reach, use them instead. You won't smell as sweet but there is the bonus that nettles help prevent dandruff.

Dandruff
Dandruff is a condition in which dry flakes of skin fall from the hair in excessive amounts. It's nothing new, though the cures of the past could well have been fatal. One seventeenth-century recipe for preventing it includes among its ingredients old wine dregs, cyanide and vitriol. It probably has more than one cause and is linked to both a bacterial infection and to stress, possibly also to a lack of vitamin B.

The first step, if you think you have dandruff, is to rub the scalp regularly with witch hazel and to switch to a mild medicated shampoo. This should deal with the infection. At the same time improve your diet and get more vitamin B.

However, not all dry flaking skin is dandruff, so if you think you have dandruff but it doesn't respond to a medicated shampoo quite quickly you should see a trichologist. There are some conditions which look like dandruff which need expert treatment and could lead to hair loss if they aren't treated properly.

★ To cure dandruff: age. The over-60s don't get it.

Dry Hair
Sun, salt, chlorine, heated rollers, hair dryers, bleaching and perming can all individually - let alone combined - wreak havoc with the condition of the hair. To have healthy hair keep all of them to a minimum. If you must use heated rollers put a layer of tissue between the roller and the hair to lessen the damage.

It was a West Indian mother of a pupil of mine who taught me that if hair does become dry and tired one of the best treatments is coconut oil. It is remarkably effective. Rub it well into the hair, wrap a hot towel round it and leave it for several hours (or smother the pillow in towels and go to sleep on it). Then shampoo the hair as usual. The hair will look shiny and restored and not at all oily. If you find yourself with dry hair on a Mediterranean holiday use olive oil in the same way.

For dull dry hair, when you haven't time to oil it, beat up an egg and massage it well in. Leave it a few minutes, then rinse off with almost cold water - unless you want scrambled hair. This can also be used instead of conventional washing if you run out of shampoo.

Hair Loss
Hair loss can be caused by illness, pregnancy, sudden weight loss, certain types of medical treatment (such as some cancer therapies and certain drugs), the menopause and an hereditary tendency to baldness.

Baldness may not simply be an hereditary tendency. It looks as if the male hormone androgen is bad for hair growth. This hormone is produced in greater quantities when either sex is under stress. So those who push themselves will increase their chances of hair loss. It is interesting that hair loss among women in highly competitive jobs is an increasing problem.

There is also a condition called *alopecia areta* in which bald patches appear randomly on the scalp. The precise causes of alopecia are unknown but in most cases the hair starts to regrow 1 to 2 years later.

Hairdressing Council, 12 David House, 45 High Street, South Norwood, London SE25 6HJ Tel: 01 771 6205 - the state registry for qualified hairdressers who have completed a set training and taken exams, but membership is voluntary. The council has a disciplinary committee to which you can complain. But, it can't, alas, get you compensation. So if you have a major problem go to you local Trading Standards Officer or to a Citizens Advice Bureau.
Institute of Trichologists, 228 Stockwell Road, Brixton, London SW9 9SU Tel: 01 733 2056 Trichologists are trained to deal with every kind of hair problem. To find your nearest trichologist send a sae.

Unwanted Hair
Unwanted hair is one of the most unmentionable of beauty topics. As a result most women who have hair in the 'wrong' places feel they are uniquely blighted. But anyone in the beauty business will tell you it is one of the most common problems of all. Hair can grow absolutely anywhere it shouldn't be, so no misgrowth is uniquely embarrassing.

Plucking
For small areas, such as the eyebrows, or a slight excess on the bikini line, plucking is probably easiest Numb the area with an ice cube, or by stretching the skin very tightly, before you pluck. But DON'T pluck hair out of a mole (see opposite).

Shaving or Waxing
Larger areas, such as the legs, can be waxed or shaved. Some experts say that shaving doesn't increase the hair growth. Many women disagree. Experience suggests it is coarser and thicker after shaving, whereas after waxing it seems to regrow a little less each time. But be warned: both professional and DIY hot waxing carry a risk of burning if it isn't done carefully, and this is one of the most common causes of claims against beauty therapists.

Depilatories
Cream depilatories are usually effective but they may not suit some skins. Also they should only be used in the areas of the body recommended by the manufacturers.

Electrolysis
Electrolysis can permanently remove areas of unwanted hair from almost any part of the anatomy. It involves passing an electric current into the area of the hair root, to kill the root. Using a fairly strong current will kill most strongly growing hair at one session. But it can produce soreness and scabs. On the delicate skin of the face there is a special risk that if these scabs are knocked off they will leave a scar. The alternative is to have a far weaker current, which may take several treatments to remove the more stubborn hairs, but is far less likely to cause scabs. The right current is a matter of judgement so it is important to have it done by someone who is both qualified and experienced. And if you get any bad reaction at all, have no more done. UNDER NO CIRCUMSTANCES risk trying to do it yourself (see below).

Unwanted Hair in Moles
Moles with hair in present a special problem. They should not be plucked and can only be treated with electrolysis if you have a doctor's approval. This is because certain kinds of moles can be the beginning of cancer, and interfering with such moles could spread cancerous cells to the rest of the body. However, most moles are perfectly healthy and a doctor can tell whether a mole is healthy or cancerous. If your doctor gives the all-clear for electrolysis, there is a chance that it will not only remove the hair but cause the mole to vanish too.

More information
British Association of Beauty Therapy and Cosmetology, Suite 5, Wolseley House, Oriel Road, Cheltenham, Glos GL50 1TH Tel: 0242 570284 - will tell you where to find beauty therapists qualified in electrolysis, cosmetic camouflage and general beauty therapy.
Institute of Electrologists, 18 Stokes End, Haddenham, Bucks HP17 8DX Tel: 0844 290721 - will put you in touch with someone qualified in electrolysis in your area.
The Body Shop Book, Macdonald
Christina Probert, *Vogue Book of Beauty and Health*, Octopus

Relaxation
If you need to relax in preparation for something which makes you tense, such as making a speech, use the trick actors have used for generations. Close your eyes, drop your shoulders and breathe slowly and deeply for a few

minutes. Make it very slow and calm, and concentrate all your attention on your breathing. You will soon be far calmer than you were.

It works because the body and mind work as one. Slow breathing and calmness go together. When you feel calm you automatically breathe more slowly. But equally, when you behave in a calm way, and breathe slowly, it tricks the body and tells it the crisis is over, so it can stop producing all the chemicals it jets into the bloodstream in an emergency. It's those fight or flight chemicals which hype us up to a point of tension which may be too much for the situation.

You don't have to be doing anything special to try this technique. You can use it to unwind before going to sleep or on the journey home at the end of a hard day, but, like anything else, it takes practice.

Eye Relaxation
This is a good way to rest a little if your eyes are sore and tired. Put your elbows on a table in front of you, with your hands up at eye level. Rest your closed eyes on the heels of your hands, with the rest of the hands supporting your forehead. Then think black and 'see' the black getting blacker and blacker. Stay like this for as long as you feel like it. Your eyes will feel odd when they first come back to the light, but they should be refreshed.

Bath Relaxation
Those who believe in aromatherapy claim that if you use the right aromatherapy oil it will make you relax. Certain herbs and smells do seem to have a relaxing effect, and herbs have been used in baths for centuries. If you have no special oils but do have a herb garden try throwing a sprig or two of rosemary in the water as the bath is running.

Finally, for really in-depth relaxation, there is meditation - see page 550.

Animals

Bees to Tortoises, Terrapins and Turtles

Pet choosing, like marriage, is all too often done by falling in love. What it really needs is some good, old-fashioned matchmaking, in which each side carefully examines the other to see if it will meet its needs. Having an animal is a matter of give and take, on both sides, and nobody should go into the partnership without very clear ideas of what will be demanded and what will - and won't - be given in return.

In this chapter I have tried to give the basic information on the pleasures, pitfalls and needs of each of the popular domestic animals. Books and specialist societies are listed, wherever possible, to help you take your enquiries a stage further; other major animal organizations are given at the end of the chapter. Between them they provide a wealth of excellent leaflets - mostly free - which are well worth reading. You may fall in love with an animal, but there is no divorce - and a marriage of inconvenience can last a long time.

Basic Medical Facts
If first aid has to be given to any creature follow the basic rules given in In Sickness for people. The biggest problem with animals is shock, so it is most important to keep them warm, and calm. Also a *very* small blood loss can be a large proportion of a small animal's blood, so treat bleeding *rapidly*. If you lack antiseptics a mild solution of salt and water is a good cleanser.

Giving Tablets
If you have a dog which likes chocolates, as many do, the easy way to give it tablets is to push the tablet into the middle of a soft centre and pop it into its mouth.

Cats won't be fooled that way, and usually detect a tablet in any other food. If so, the only method is to tilt its head up, open its mouth and drop the tablet well in, then hold its mouth shut, with the chin pointing upwards, until it swallows. This is hard to do with a resistant and angry cat unless you adopt the right position. The easy way is to sit it on your lap with its back towards you, and its back legs gently but firmly between your thighs; you can then hold the front paws with one hand and use the other hand to give the tablet. Most animals will easily accept such handling if you do it confidently and without dithering.

Black's Veterinary Dictionary, A C Black
Geoffrey P. West (ed.), *First Aid for Pets*, A C Black
Francis Hunter MRCVS, *Before the Vet Calls*, Thorsons Ltd: a book of homeopathic first-aid for pets.

Bees
It is possible to keep bees in any quiet garden, including a suburban one - provided the neighbours don't object - and there is even an Inner London Beekeepers Association. But the best honey flows come when bees have access to heather, clover, beans, raspberries, sycamore or lime trees. The Scottish Beekeepers Association has a booklet (see overleaf) which lists trees, shrubs and plants providing abundant pollen or nectar for bees - which could be planted by anyone who cares about these fascinating creatures. But keeping bees is not something to be undertaken lightly, as the hive requires skilled and systematic attention. I strongly recommend anyone considering this hobby to read *Teach Yourself Beekeeping* (see overleaf). Join an adult education class on beekeeping and/or a local beekeeping association. It can also be useful to talk to people at the National Honey Show, which the British Beekeepers Association (see overleaf) organizes each October at the Porchester Hall, in London.

Buying Bees
Bees from a member of a local association are adapted to the weather in your area. But there is a risk that an amateur could sell ill-tempered or diseased bees. So ask for a written undertaking that they are disease-free. Alternatively, buy from one of the dealers advertising in beekeeping magazines. There are really two kinds of worker bee: summer bees and winter bees. Summer bees only live about 6 weeks, whereas those born in August and September live right through to the following spring.

The hive needs a site which is sheltered and faces south, with no overhanging trees or dampness. Avoid placing it within the magnetic fields of high tension electricity cables as bees become aggressive.

Some hives may yield no honey at all, others as much as 200 lb, but the average is 30 to 40 lb. To obtain this you need to supply the hive with about 50 lb of sugar as winter feed. So honey is not the bargain it might seem.

Be careful what you wear near bees. Bees are angered by red, dark-blue or black clothing and may also be upset by woollen garments if they become entangled in them. Nylon also seems to irritate them - perhaps because of the static electricity.

British Beekeepers Association, National Agricultural Centre, Stoneleigh, Kenilworth, Warwickshire CV8 2LZ Tel: 0203 552404 - Rg, G, A, L, B, HC, Ad, tours.

Scottish Beekeepers Association, Craigi, 9 Glenhome Avenue, Dyce, Aberdeen AB2 0FF Tel: 0224 722598 (evenings) - M£5, M, L, B, F, G, A, Ins, sae. Special facilities.

'Starting with Bees', leaflet 283, free from Ministry of Agriculture, Fisheries and Food, Lion House, Willowburn Trading Estate, Alnwick, Northumberland NE66 2FF Tel: 0665 60288.

An Introduction to Bees and Beekeeping, Scottish Beekeepers Association.

Frank Vernon, *Teach Yourself Beekeeping,* Hodder & Stoughton.

Birds

Birds may seem like trouble-free pets, undemanding and contained. This isn't necessarily the case. All birds are gregarious and it is cruel to keep them singly unless you are prepared to spend all day with them yourself. Parrots, in particular, need constant attention throughout the day, and resort to feather plucking when bored. Some also need a new branch to gnaw daily, and many indulge in raucous screeching, loud enough to disturb the neighbours. Some can also become very attached to one person and may live as long as a human and all birds litter the floor with seeds and feathers. So the general rule is: the smaller the bird, the smaller the problems.

Many are bred in Britain, but some of the exotic birds are captured in the wild and transported in horrific conditions. To buy any which have suffered this fate is to encourage cruelty to animals. So check a bird's origins before buying.

It is safest to buy from a specialist shop or breeder. The signs which indicate a healthy bird are: preening, standing on one leg, alertness, bright eyes, a clean vent unstained with droppings and a plump breast. Hollows felt beside the breast bone could be due to illness. If you want a bird to talk buy it young. A budgerigar should be 6 to 9 weeks old, and at this age should have no white ring round the eye; the dark lines or flecks in the feathers should come down to above the bill, and the dark spots on the throat shouldn't be well defined.

Cages

If a bird is deprived of flying its muscles waste away and it is unlikely to be happy. As birds fly horizontally, having enough width and length is far more important than the height. The *minimum* sizes of cage *per bird* are as follows and you should try to give them more.

Bird Type	Height		Width		Length	
Budgies, canaries, finches	30	×	30	×	60 cm	(1×1×2 ft)
Cockatiel, love birds	60	×	60	×	90 cm	(2×2×3 ft)
Small parrots	60	×	90	×	90 cm	(2×3×3 ft)
Large parrots	60	×	90	×	120 cm	(2×3×4 ft)
Macaws	60	×	120	×	120 cm	(2×4×4 ft)

See the table opposite for bird lengths.

Wall cages which are large enough are advertised in some of the specialist bird magazines. It's important to avoid anything which might injure the birds, such as wrongly spaced bars which could catch a bird's head. Parrots need 16-gauge wire (not the standard 19-gauge) on tougher supports, well encased in wire on the inside. Perches, preferably of chemical-free washed branches, should be of varied diameters (within the bird's grasp) so it doesn't get sores from always gripping with the same part of its feet. Small birds like finches need pot plants to perch on too. The cage must be put out of direct sunlight - or birds overheat - and away from draughts.

Softbills, like macaws, are messy and need their cages cleaned daily; others every 2 days. Line the floor with newspaper which can quickly be removed. The cage needs to be thoroughly scrubbed and disinfected every 2 weeks.

Care

They are creatures of routine and so they are happiest when feeding and cleaning follow a predictable pattern. They need 9 to 12 hours' sleep, according to the season. Erratic hours and staying up late can make them tetchy and neurotic. They also need the sunlight; use a special bulb which compensates for this.

Birds need a daily 'bath' - some like to nestle in damp plants; others like to splash in a shallow dish, and the larger parrots often like to be sprayed with a plant sprayer - or even to shower with their owner.

It is also good for birds to be allowed to fly freely in the house. But, before releasing them, vet the room for hazards - they don't know they mustn't go near the vacuum cleaner or into cooking pots or down lavatories, and may bang into windows unless the curtains are closed.

Entertainment

Birds are naturally active and like to have things to play with and sound is also important to them. Birds left alone will often be happiest with the radio quietly on. But even with plenty to do a caged bird may get bored, distressed or sexually frustrated. The result is usually feather plucking, but occasionally they will take to compulsive eating or chronic egg laying. Sometimes a mate is the solution, but even so some birds can't stand captivity.

Feeding
All birds need water constantly and like to feed morning and evening, as they would in the wild. Dr Axelson's book (see overleaf) gives the food needs for each species. The basics are these. Good quality bird seed mixtures are sold for parrots, canaries and budgerigars. Those of in-between sizes, such as parakeets, can be given some budgerigar food and some parrot food. Birds (especially parrots) also need fresh food each day - fruit or green vegetables cut in pieces can be left in the cage. But be sure to wash them well - birds are not as tolerant of chemicals as we are. Mung beans, soaked and sprouting (but mould-free) can also be given to larger birds, and chickweed is good if there are no chemical sprays on it. A cuttlefish bone hung in the cage provides the calcium they need, and a vitamin supplement must be given on some fruit to avoid vitamin D deficiency. They also need grit occasionally, or the food cannot be digested in the gizzard: the larger the bird, the larger the grit.

Softbills, like mynah birds, are fruit and insect eaters and need the proprietory food designed for them, supplemented by fruit such as peeled apple in half-inch chunks or seedless grapes. Insects can be provided for softbills by obtaining mealworms or by putting in their cage sprays of garden plants carrying aphids - provided no chemicals have been used.

Health
A major threat to birds is dirty air. They may get breathing problems if kept near smokers, drying paint or aerosols of any kind, and also from kitchen smells such as burning fat or the fumes from non-stick pans.

Some birds carry almost invisible mites. Using a proprietary spray immediately after purchase should get rid of the problem.

It is normal for birds to moult, dropping old and damaged feathers and replacing them with new ones. Some do it once a year, some twice a year and it can take several months, during which they may constantly preen the new feathers and stop singing. This is perfectly normal, but they are more vulnerable to chilling and illness at this time and will benefit from quiet and a good diet.

The signs of a sick bird are abnormal droppings, loss of appetite, listlessness, soiled or matted feather around the nostrils or difficulty in breathing. Some experts say all birds should be taken to a vet 3 to 4 times a year for a health check and a nail (and possibly beak) trim - nails have blood vessels in so they need careful cutting. When carrying the bird outside, cover the cage with a blanket and pre-warm the car in cold weather.

Birds which are newly imported, or have been in contact with imported birds, may develop a disease called Parrot Fever (chlamydiosis, psittacosis or ornithosis). This is not common but it can be transferred to humans and is occasionally (if rarely) fatal. It is,

therefore, wise to avoid putting one's mouth close to a bird, and to wash after handling and cage cleaning.

Talking
Among the birds available in Britain canaries win as singers, and the Roller is the best variety. They sing best if there are two male birds *each in a separate cage.* To stand a good chance of teaching a bird, like a budgerigar, to talk, you need a young bird on its own. A budgerigar bought at 6 weeks old should start after 5 to 6 weeks. Some find that if the bird is put in an empty cage, and this is covered with a cloth while the bird is talked to for just 10 minutes a day, it will talk far sooner. Start with one word or short phrase. Once that is mastered gradually introduce new words and phrases, including perhaps your address or phone number, in case the bird ever escapes. Don't put a mirror in its cage until it has learned to talk or it will just twitter to its alter ego.

Whatever bird you have, don't shout at it or let it hear you shouting. Birds will copy anything and if you shout so will they. If this advice comes too late Dr Axelson gives a cure for shrieking in his book (see overleaf). In the list below the best talkers are star-rated - *** being the best talkers. Of course, it varies from individual to individual: some birds are brighter than others.

Bird	Talking Ability	Life Span in Years	Length
Budgerigars	***	6-8 (but sometimes to 20 years)	20 cm (8 in)
Cockatiel	*	10-14 (but sometimes to 30 years)	31 cm (12 in)
Cockatoos	*	25-45 (but sometimes to 100 years)	31-67 cm (12-27 in)
Love birds	*	10-14 years	14 cm (5 in)
Macaws	*	up to 60 years	30-100 cm (12-40 in)
Mynah birds*	***	up to 25 years	30-45 cm (12-18 in)
Parrakeets	*	10-15 years	13-36 cm (5-15 in)
Parrots	**	20-70 according to type	25-52 cm (10-21 in)

*(Greater Hill variety only)

A newly acquired bird can be as bewildered as a small child in a new school. So give it time to settle into a new home in peace. Let it get used to you gradually; and talk to it quietly as you offer it its regular food. Do this so it has to come to you to get it. Once it eats happily from your hand you can begin to stroke or scratch it gently on the head and chest, keeping every movement slow so the bird is never startled. Most birds will try to bite in the early days, or with strangers, and the largest ones can remove a nasty chunk of flesh or part of a finger, so don't allow small children near large birds. Never hold out one finger for a new bird of any size to hop on to - it's a nice beakful. Instead hold out your hand, palm down, with the fingers together, while talking gently and catching its attention with a movement of the other hand - and if necessary wear thick protective gloves at first. If it does bite, *never* hit it or it will become scared and redouble its attack next time. Just put it in its cage immediately and leave the training for that day. When it is tame you can begin to teach it to talk.

The Aviculture Society, Warren Hill, Hulford's Lane, Hartley Wintney, Hants RG27 8AG - M£M, M, A, advice, use of library at the Linnean Society, open to non-bird owners, sae.

British Waterfowl Association, 6 Caldicott Close, Over, Winsford, Cheshire CW7 1LW Tel: 0606 594150 - M£L, M, Rg reps, some A, advisory panel, buyers' guide, open days, annual show.

The Budgerigar Society, 49-53 Hazelwood Road, Northampton NN1 1LG Tel: 0604 24549 - M£L, M, G, Rg, L, B, shows, sae.

The National Council for Aviculture, 87 Winn Road, Lee, London SE12 9EY Tel: 01 857 4208 - M£L, G, Ad, the linking body for a mass of societies covering individual species.

The Parrot Society, 19a De Pary's Avenue, Bedford MK40 2TX Tel: 0234 58922 - M£L, includes junior members 8-16, M, L, will recommend vets for birds.

David Alderton, *Looking After Cage Birds,* Ward Lock
Jim Allcock, *A Pet Bird of Your Own,* Sheldon Press
Dr R. Dean Axelson, *Caring for Your Pet Bird,* Blandford

Pigeons

Racing pigeons are a subject on their own. A good starting point is the book *Racing Pigeons* by D.V.Belding (published by Saiga, 1 Royal Parade, Hindhead, Surrey GU26 6TD). The same publisher also has books on ornamental wildfowl, and on domesticated ducks and geese.

Royal Pigeon Racing Association, The Reddings, Cheltenham, Glos GL51 6RN Tel: 0452 713529 - keeps the records of 18 million racing pigeons, supplies rings, supervises racing, age 8-10+ upwards, free booklet for children. M£L, G.

Cats

We probably owe today's felines to the ancient Egyptians, who 3,000 years ago domesticated them to keep down the rats and mice in their grain stores. It is even said that the word 'puss' derives from Basht (pronounced Pasht), the Egyptian cat goddess. But it was the Romans who introduced cats to Britain, and much prized they were. By the ninth century a mouser was valued at two pennies - a sum which, given 1,000 years of inflation, makes today's pedigree pussies a bargain.

Buying

Before falling in love with some adorable kitten take stock of what it will be like as an adult cat. Long-haired cats need daily grooming if their coats are not to mat into painful hair balls. Siamese are decidedly noisy, and Burmese have a penchant for climbing - curtains included. So a plain moggy may be a better bet for most households. And before taking on a cat remember that it could live for at least 14 years.

To find a young cat ask your local vet for a good source, go to a show and find a breeder whose animals you like, or write to a cat society for information on

breeders offering a particular kind. As with all animals, look at the parents to see what the offspring will be like. A kitten can leave its mother when over 8 weeks old, but get a diet sheet from the breeder so it can eat what it is used to, at first.

If cats are neutered there is nothing to choose between males and females in affection, but it is a great joy, and education, for children to experience one litter of kittens, *provided they can be found good homes.*

Food

Cats need a varied diet of cooked or raw meat and fish to stay healthy, with quite a lot of fat or fish oil to provide enough vitamins A, D and E. Most cats prefer food at room temperature and usually eat about 200 g (7 oz) of meat or fish a day, in two meals. Kittens and cats which are growing, pregnant or feeding babies need larger and more frequent meals. All cats need clean water.

Offer kittens a little cow's milk as soon as they are 2 to 3 weeks old, and begin to add a little minced meat and cereal soon after. So by 8 weeks they are weaned and on four meals a day. Give them a very varied diet so they won't be faddy.

Branded cat foods usually provide a balanced diet, but dog foods (which cats often enjoy) have too much vegetable and cereal to be used regularly. Most cats also like about a quarter of a pint of milk a day - though some do better on milk and water. Non-milk drinkers need a calcium supplement until they stop growing. If a cat is fed on dry food it is essential that it drinks plenty of liquid or it may develop bladder problems.

Grooming

Long-haired cats need daily grooming, with a good quality metal comb, to stop the hair matting. First sprinkle on grooming powder or unscented baby powder, leave it for 10 minutes to absorb any grease, then comb it out systematically.

Health

The three most dangerous infections are rabies (outside the UK), feline enteritis and cat 'flu'. The last two are easily picked up by any cat allowed out, and enteritis is usually fatal. So kittens should be vaccinated against both, at about 3 months old, and given regular boosters as your vet recommends. If boosters have been missed make sure a cat has one before moving to a new area or going into a cattery, and also if there is an epidemic. Good catteries won't accept cats without a certificate of recent vaccination.

House Training

A kitten quickly learns to be clean. Start with a shallow box of cat litter close to its box, and if it seems about to 'go' pop it on it. If you have a garden, start taking the kitten outside first thing in the morning and at intervals during the day. If it performs out there praise it warmly. But if it makes a mess indoors don't punish it - it won't understand. Just clean it up and eradicate the smell - cats home in on any place where they smell previous use. So, ideally, keep kittens away from carpeted areas until they are trained. But the easiest way to clean up solids is with a flat scraper like a wallpaper stripper.

Housing

The ideal home for a cat is a cardboard box lined with scrunched-up newspapers and an old jumper. It keeps out the draughts and can be burnt if the cat gets fleas, but cats are nocturnal and, if it is safe for them to be out at night, they enjoy it.

Mating

The breeding season for a queen (female) can be all year, peaking in spring and autumn. She will become increasingly restless and start crying. If kept in she may even try to jump from a high window, go off her food and spray urine in the house. She will only mate when fully on heat. Cat societies can often recommend suitable mates, but unmated moggies will quickly find their own.

A cat pregnancy takes about 65 days. Some get morning sickness and vomit occasionally. Make sure she has extra food and enough calcium. Some can get all they need from milk, but those which can't digest it need a calcium supplement.

In week 7 she may start looking for a warm dark place to give birth. Provide one or she may well use your cupboard. Get a cardboard box large enough for her to stretch out fully and line the base well with newspapers. Then place the box on a sheet of plastic and more newspapers somewhere warm and quiet. When about to give birth she may refuse food and perhaps vomit. Have a litter tray near the birth box in case she needs it.

Many like to be alone during labour; others need their owner. Sometimes the first thing out is an empty sac - this is quite normal - and the kittens may emerge head or tail first, each encased in a thin sac. The mother should lick the sac off. Having bitten through the umbilical cord she usually eats the membrane, cord and placenta. These are rich in hormones and are thought to encourage her milk.

Human intervention shouldn't be needed. But if a cat strains for a long time, with the kitten half in half out, you may need to take hold - with a piece of towelling - and gently help on the next contraction. If the cat fails to lick the membrane from a kitten you can wipe it clear, and stroke the kitten into breathing. Do this near the mother's head so she can finish the job and eat the placenta - there is no rush to cut the cord. But if things go seriously wrong and the cat is in distress call a vet.

To check the sex of a kitten press gently near the genital area - on males a penis will emerge, but not when they are very young.

Moving with a Cat

Cats often get more attached to places than to people, and need time to get adjusted to a new home. You need to keep them indoors for a few days and give them time to learn that the new home is now the source of food and comfort, or they could stray.

Neutering

Male kittens are sexually mature at 6 to 8 months and will start looking for a mate. They will mark out their territory, by spraying their strong-smelling urine all round your home. It is one of the hardest smells to eradicate, so get a tom neutered at 5 to 6 months old.

Female kittens don't start 'calling' for toms until about 10 months old, but some breeds can be precocious and call long before it would be safe for them to have kittens. Cat contraceptives are advisable, as a frustrated female can make herself ill and become infertile by calling for a longed-for tom. Vets usually neuter a cat at 6 months old, but it can be done after she has had kittens. As a general anaesthetic is used, the cat must not eat for 12 hours before.

Parasites

Worm treatment should come from a vet and, as fleas can infect a cat with worms, the cat should be treated for these at the same time. Vets can now provide tablets which make the fleas die when they bite the cat. This is a very convenient way of treating fleas or you can use an aerosol from your vet. The easiest way to apply it is to spray it on to cotton wool and wipe this over the animal as if you were stroking it. Burn the bedding at the same time and spray the rooms with a long-acting insecticide from a vet.

Opinions vary on the effectiveness of flea collars and there is a danger that tree-climbing cats will catch them on a branch and hang themselves.

When You Go Away

The best place for a cat is at home, and pet sitters are provided by some agencies or the **Feline Advisory Bureau (FAB)** (1 Church Close, Orcheston, Nr Salisbury, Wilts SP3 4RP Tel: 0980 620251) runs a Boarding Cattery Approval Scheme and will send a list of approved catteries. Inspect any cattery before booking. Even approved ones may have changed hands since the last inspection. Catteries should provide food, warmth, shelter, genuine care and thoroughly clean conditions. Outdoor catteries are healthier than indoor ones, and cats from different households should be housed separately to prevent infection. If a cattery is inadequate report it to the local Environmental Health Officer *and* to FAB if they approved it.

Cat Protection League, 17 Kings Road, Horsham, West Sussex RH13 5PP Tel: 0403 65566 - RC, cat welfare, with cat shelters and a placing system finding good homes for cats.

The Governing Council of the Cat Fancy, 4-6 Penel Orlieu, Bridgewater, Somerset TA6 3PG Tel: 0278 427575 - Inf on local clubs and shows, L.

James Allcock, *A Pet Cat of Your Own*, Sheldon Press
Bradley Viner, *The Cat Care Manual*, Stanley Paul

Dogs

At first sight there seems to be a dog to fit every family. This isn't quite the case. Dogs are demanding: even tiny ones need careful training and regular exercise. 'Going walkies' may be enchanting on long summer evenings, but it is less delightful in driving snow. If you aren't prepared to feed and exercise it daily, for about 14 years, regardless of the inconvenience, don't buy a dog. The welcome companion to a woman at home looking after toddlers can be a bind when she wants to return to work. But if you do decide to buy a dog here are some points to consider:

- Size isn't a good indication of how much exercise a dog will need - some small breeds, such as terriers, are very active.
- Long-haired dogs need daily grooming - have you time?
- Large dogs cost a great deal more to feed.
- All breeds need careful training and some can be dangerous if they lack discipline.
- Are you likely to be good at dog-training? If not, buy one you can manhandle when fully grown.
- Some breeds have in-bred health problems - especially very small and very large dogs.
- Dogs which need clipping run up bills with their hairdressers.
- What other animals are in the house? I include small children here. In guard dogs and hunting dogs, like Dobermanns and German Shepherds, the fighting instinct is not far below the surface. Others have a slower fuse with toddlers.

It's true that having a dog to pet will help keep down your blood pressure, reduce your risk of heart attack and make you recover from illness more swiftly. But the strain of a large dog in the average house or flat can practically *give* you high blood pressure. It is also very bad for the dog to be captive in too small a space. So the *Sunday Times* asked experts on dogs to name their top six for town living. They were:

1 Cavalier King Charles Spaniel
2 Dachshund
3 Chihuahua
4 Yorkshire Terrier
5 Pekinese
6 Miniature or Toy Poodle

Buying a Dog

Many of the qualities of a dog depend on the character and health it inherited. So one sure way to get a good dog is to buy a puppy from a friend who has a bitch of good health and character, which had an equally reliable mate.

Another good, if expensive, source is a pedigree dog from a specialist breeder. The Kennel Club or Dog Breeders Associates (see below) will send you a list of breeders for any breed.

Taking pity on an animal from a market stall, pet shop or dogs' home is the least reliable way to get a good animal. Though many lovable creatures end up in such places, it is often a route to disappointment. These animals may carry infections and, in some cases, unkind

treatment may have made them nervous or aggressive. But some dogs' homes, such as Battersea, do have good dogs which have been rejected by callous owners.

The ideal age is 8 to 10 weeks, and the animal should seem in perfect health - bright eyes, moist nose, clean ears and no parasites or raw patches - and be alert, inquisitive and friendly to everyone, neither barking without provocation nor backing away. An independent animal which neither cowers nor advances may have a lot of character, but will not be so easy to train. Don't buy a dog which doesn't seem to like you - dogs tend to stick to their prejudices.

- Make your purchase conditional upon it being examined and given a clean bill of health by a vet. This is normal practice and nobody should be insulted. If the seller won't agree go elsewhere.
- When you pay you should be given: its pedigree, if it has one, its registration certificate, a diet sheet telling you what it eats, and how often to feed it, information on whether, and when, it was treated for worms, the dates and type of any preventive injections. If you don't get the papers, they shouldn't get the cheque.

The journey home will be frightening for the puppy, so prepare the car against puddles, and at home have ready a cosy box or basket, lined with something warm like an old pullover. Place the puppy in it immediately, so it has somewhere to belong; then let it explore from there. But don't let children maul or over-excite it. It may well howl the first night. Treat it as you'd like to be treated if you were frightened - a cuddle, a warm hot-water-bottle (it's used to the warmth of other dogs), and a cheering tit-bit when it's quiet. But don't let it do things you won't want it to do later (like sleep in your bed). Training starts the moment it enters your home.

Exercise
Dogs need daily exercise (a marathon at weekends won't make up for 5 days cooped up), but don't take a puppy where other dogs have been until at least 2 weeks after it has been inoculated. A good play in a garden, where it can stop when tired, is better than a walk. Large dogs in particular, have soft bones and should not be walked too soon. Once a dog is grown, suit the exercise to its size and energy. Short-legged, or snub-nosed, dogs shouldn't be given long walks on hot days. And all dogs should be on a lead when there is livestock or game about.

Feeding
Good breeders provide a diet sheet for a puppy. Stick to it for 2 weeks. But get the puppy used to all kinds of flavours and gradually switch it from minced meat to chunks.

Puppies need food little and often and each meal should be the amount the puppy will eat in 10 to 15 minutes.

2 to 4 months	*Breakfast:* minced or tinned meat + dry dog meal *Lunch:* cereal and cow's milk *Tea:* cereal and cow's milk *Supper:* as breakfast, and time it for an hour before bedtime to encourage the puppy to open its bowels on its bedtime walk.
3 to 7 months	Cut out the 'teatime'.
7 to 12 months	Cut down to two meals a day by dropping the mid-day feed, but it can still have milk and cereal as part of another meal.
12 to 18 months	Drop the milk and feed it once a day.

On average a young dog needs about ½ oz meat for every pound of its body weight, while a full-grown dog needs only about ⅓ oz. Beef can be raw, other meat cooked. Dogs also need cereal in the form of biscuits or meal, or toasted wholemeal bread, plus some cooked vegetable matter. Small bones, especially poultry, are dangerous, but raw marrow bones are excellent - unless the dog is so big it can even splinter these. A diet of fresh food usually needs added vitamins, but most branded dog foods have vitamins already added - check this on the tin. There should always be clean water out for a dog - cow's milk can cause diarrhoea in adult dogs.

Dogs should be fed from their own bowls and not from plates used by humans, and their bowls should be washed up separately. There is a small and avoidable risk of catching worms or disease from dogs.

Health and Grooming
Regular brushing with a suitable dog brush, or combing with a smooth, toothed, metal comb, is better for a dog than frequent bathing. Any washing must be with a dog shampoo which won't irritate the skin.

Inoculations against a number of infections are usually given at 10 to 12 weeks, but the timing depends on weaning. So check earlier with a vet. Make sure a booster is given before a dog goes into kennels or moves to a new area.

A healthy dog is alert and active, with bright eyes and a glossy coat (if its type permits), and its temperature (taken up its bottom, not under its tongue) is 101° to 102°F (38·5°C). Illness needs swift attention from a vet. Some diseases are fatal, even with modern drugs; others, like distemper, are highly infectious, and some can be given to humans.

There is more to dog **first aid** than can be covered here, but it is really very like human first aid (see In Sickness) except that an animal in pain may bite. If necessary, prevent this by tying something round its nose. The British Veterinary Association (page 640) has a free leaflet on first aid for dogs and cats.

Most dogs get **fleas** or **lice** at some time and they are easily recognized. The treatment for both is tablets, flea powder or aerosol. Treatments must be every 4 to 7 days for at least a month to be effective, burning the bedding at each treatment.

Mites are too small to see but may cause mange or ear infections, and one type can be given to humans - take a dog to the vet even for mild skin problems. All dogs and cats in a house should be treated at the same time, as mites get passed around.

Roundworms are usually in puppies from birth and stools free of worms are *not* a proof that the dog is worm-free. Worm the puppy at 2, 4, 6, 8, 12 and 16 weeks old, then every 3 months, especially if there are young children in the house.

Tapeworms can be caught from fleas which carry the eggs. Segments of tapeworm may show, like grains of rice, in the stools or near the dog's anus. A vet will prescribe and it usually takes several treatments to kill them.

Ticks look like rather faded baked beans. They must *never* be just pulled off or the head will remain in and cause infection. First make them let go by painting them (but not the dog) with surgical spirit, meths or paraffin. Cover the dog with flea powder to kill any unattached ticks.

Holidays
A Herald Holiday Handbook, called *Pets Welcome*, lists establishments which welcome pets. It also gives boarding kennels and catteries, and these are also listed in the Yellow Pages. But some pet sitter rates compare favourably with boarding two animals. If you have to board pets do inspect the place before you book, and

book well in advance. The best places get booked up and the worst you wouldn't put a louse in.

House Training
A young puppy has a very limited ability to control itself and can't go through the night without wetting. Let it sleep where an accident won't be a disaster. Make a habit of putting it outside whenever it wakes up, after any great excitement, and after food, and praise and pet it lavishly if it performs - even accidentally - in the right place.

If it looks about to go take the puppy straight outside (stay with it so you can praise its achievement). Say 'no' firmly if you catch it doing it indoors - and growl for good measure. It will learn in a few weeks. But it is pointless to get angry or smack a young puppy or rub its nose in it after the accident has occurred: it hasn't got the brain to link the mess or puddle with the making of it. That method won't teach it to be clean, but it will teach it to distrust you.

Pregnancy
Bitches can only conceive when 'on heat' (in season). This usually happens twice a year and lasts about 3 weeks. Special sprays may make a bitch less seductive, and there are now pills which remove the bitch's appeal to males. But if you want puppies, mate her when the discharge becomes clear. During mating dogs are anatomically locked; forcibly separating them can harm both animals, and the act itself can take 5 to 60 minutes.

There are no pregnancy tests for dogs, but a vet can often tell at 4 weeks and pregnancy lasts about 63 days. The mother needs milk and some jelly from boiled-up bones, plus extra food in the last few weeks, and a vet should check her.

Make a birth-bed with a warm blanket, and get her used to it well before the birth - you don't want her to choose your bed. When the puppies are due, line it with newspaper and let her get on with it. Puppies may come every half hour or with a gap of an hour or so. If she fails to lick the membrane from a puppy's head you may need to break it and rub its chest to get it breathing. Break the umbilical cord with your nails - it bleeds less than a smooth cut - about 2 inches from the puppy, but don't tug or you could cause a hernia.

Bitches seldom need assistance. So only call a vet if:
- the puppies are overdue by 2 days
- she has strained for 2 hours without producing a puppy (first or other)
- a puppy is stuck half in, half out, and a gentle pull hasn't helped
- she is very excitable
- something else seems abnormal.

Spaying and Castration
Most male dogs are routinely castrated to prevent straying and fighting. Some people favour doing it at 6 months. Other breeders and trainers say that doing it at a year old allows the dog to develop its adult character in a way which it may not if its hormone balance is altered before this. A castrated dog is usually less aggressive and more obedient and affectionate.

If puppies aren't wanted many vets recommend spaying bitches to avoid unwanted pregnancies, or 'female problems' in old age. The surgical risk is slight - but it does exist. Vets differ in the age they do the operation, but some claim that if a bitch is spayed after her first season she is less likely to have incontinence problems. If they are not spayed, dogs stay fertile all their lives.

Training
Training a dog is easy. The hard part is training yourself. You can't vary from day to day; you always have to follow the rules and be entirely consistent.

Dogs are pack animals. Your family becomes its pack and it will feel safe and happy if it knows its place in the pack - as a bottom dog who obeys. Dogs are most devoted where they are most obedient - a devoted undisciplined dog is a contradiction in terms.
1 Use *exactly* the same command words *every* time (not 'sit' one day and 'sit down' the next).
2 Always say the word *first*, then help the dog to obey it (eg. press its bottom down); then the word will gradually trigger the action.
3 Teach the formal commands - heel, sit, stay, come, lie - one at a time, only introducing a new one when another is well learnt. By 8 to 9 months it should come when called, walk well on a lead and stop what it is doing on the word 'no'.
4 At first let it know you are *delighted* if it even begins to get it right. Keep repeating the *same* words of praise (e.g. 'good dog') and *follow* them with petting. Then the dog associates 'good dog' with the reward of your pleasure, and the words themselves slowly become a reward. Gradually become more demanding until you only reward immediate obedience.
5 Punish bad behaviour *instantly* (see punishments below): the dog must learn to associate bad behaviour with something bad *immediately* happening to it, and say 'no' as you punish. Then 'no' becomes linked to the idea of punishment. But don't use any other words which might muddle it - 'bad dog' and 'good dog' sound too alike. And don't use its name when punishing. If you want it to come when called it mustn't link its name with punishment.
6 Remember dogs don't discriminate. If you love your Alsatian jumping up and licking your face when you get home, and reward it for doing so, don't expect the dog to work out that smartly-dressed women, frail old ladies and tiny children will not welcome the same treatment.

Once you are clear about the rules you want it to obey you *must* win *every* time. Dogs don't respect pack leaders who don't. Nor do they respect those who fly off the handle. If 'no' doesn't work, stop the dog doing what it shouldn't by using only as much force as is necessary. Your advantage is psychological not physical. As punishment, don't hit it with a newspaper; do as dogs would - growl at it, hold it by the scruff of the neck and shake it hard (the hardness being adjusted to the size and strength of the dog) or glare into its eyes or, if necessary, tap it firmly on the nose with two fingers (using an open hand to hit a dog makes the start of a pat look like the start of a slap and confuses the animal). If it's on a slip lead jerk it - just enough for the size of dog. Banishment is another punishment.

> Dogs can die if they are left in a car in the sun with too little air. The windows must be left open a crack so cool air can come in, and while the car is still they need some water.

Dog Breeders Associates, 1 Abbey Road, Bourne End, Bucks SL8 5NZ Tel: 062 85 20943

The Kennel Club, 1-5 Clarges Street, London W1Y 8AB Tel: 01 493 6651

National Dog Owners Association, 39-41 North Road, Islington, London N7 9DP Tel: 01 609 2757 - M£1M4 (OAPs less) - L, Ad, Inf, A, Ins.

Scottish Kennel Club, 6b Forres Street, Edinburgh EH3 6BJ Tel: 031 226 6808 - M£L0, Ad and Inf.

James Allcock MRCVS, *A Pet Dog of Your Own,* Sheldon Press

John Holmes, *The Family Dog: its choice and training,* Century Hutchinson

Joan Palmer, *Training Your Dog,* Salamander

Trevor Turner B.Vet Med, MRCVS, *How to Feed Your Dog,* Century Hutchinson

Robert C. White MRCVS, *The Care of the Family Puppy,* Century Hutchinson

Manual of Canine Behaviour, British Small Animals Veterinary Association

Frogs, Toads and Relatives

Frogs and toads have different images: frogs are seen as attractive, smooth, moist-skinned creatures and toads as ugly, lumpy, dry-skinned ones. Although true in Britain, worldwide the distinction fails to stand up. So, many scientists refer to both as frogs, and so shall I.

Frogs lead a double life: first in water, then on land. As ponds have been infilled and ditches ploughed out, they have increasingly lost the water they need for breeding. The Great Crested Newt and the Natterjack Toad are already rare enough to be protected, and there are moves to have them all protected. Anyone planning to collect frogs' spawn or frogs should first take advice on whether there are enough frogs in that particular area for it not to matter, and on which types are protected. Most counties have a Naturalists' Trust or a Natural History Society which can be found through the public library and will be only too glad to advise you; or you can read up the restrictions in the Wildlife and Countryside Act. If in doubt don't take any spawn.

If you take a little spawn it deserves careful treatment. Put it in rainwater or pondwater, not chlorinated tap water. As the tadpoles hatch from the eggs, they need algae to eat, so add plants or objects which have algae on. Christopher Mattison's book *The Care of Reptiles and Amphibians* recommends lightly-boiled lettuce or

flaked fish food. But be careful not to overfeed tadpoles; rotting food fouls the water and kills them. As they grow, their appetites increase and they need more protein - or they will eat each other to get it. Finally, as the legs sprout, their appetite reduces but they need something on to which they can climb to get air; they must also have a diet which includes small flies and white worms (from tropical fish dealers). If well fed they may be sexually mature in 6 weeks and ready to be released into the wild, or a garden pond, to start the extraordinary cycle all over again.

Michael J. Tyler, *Frogs,* William Collins Pty, Sydney (from libraries only)

Gerbils and Jirds

One of the little-known secrets of the pet world is that most gerbils aren't really gerbils at all: they are jirds. Gerbil is a blanket term used to refer to about a hundred different species. These include true gerbils, jirds, fat-tailed rats and other small rodents related to voles and lemmings. They are all about half-way in size between a mouse and a rat, with long tails. True gerbils, or *Tatera*, have a long-nosed ratty look, whereas jirds have shorter noses. In either case, they make excellent pets, clean, disease-free and tame - though they are not ideal for very young children.

It is the clawed jird, *Meriones unguiculatus* (sometimes called the Mongolian gerbil), which is most often found as a pet, but the slightly larger Libyan Jird and the Indian Gerbil are also sold. To find which you have, check its feet: jirds have furry soles, gerbils don't; and Libyan Jirds have white claws, while Clawed Jirds have black claws. They are happiest in pairs and, if you don't want to breed, two males or two females will live together provided they are from the same litter and have grown up together. For breeding, the pairs need to be of the same species.

When tame, they will run into an outstretched hand; otherwise pick them up by the tail *close to the body* - but never farther down or the skin may pull off. But they shouldn't be over-handled and, as they are very active, they must be held over something so there can be no long fall.

Provided they are kept in clean conditions, don't eat too much fruit or vegetable matter and have a good diet, they should have few problems and may live to 5 years old.

Breeding

Start matchmaking when the couple are under 4 months old, so they mature together and are less likely to fight.

If mates introduced as adults start fighting they should be separated at once and reintroduced another time, but once mated they mate for life. A litter of 4 to 8 is usually born 22 to 25 days after mating, and a female can have several litters a year. The male can remain in the nest, but the female may abandon or destroy the young if she is disturbed by people. The babies open their eyes after 3 weeks or so and wean themselves naturally at 4 weeks. As the mother can mate immediately after giving birth the young may then need to be removed to make room for the new arrivals. At about 4 months the males may need to be separated to prevent fighting. This tendency to produce numerous litters can give you an awful lot of babies to find homes for each year.

Feeding
A good hamster mix from a pet shop feeds them well, or you can make your own mix from peanuts, flaked maize, wheat, sunflower seeds and spray millet. To either you need to add pieces of apple, carrot and green vegetables to give them vitamins and moisture. They also like the occasional treat of meat or a live meal-worm or two, and there must always be a drinking bottle filled with water.

Housing
As these creatures live in desert areas they like to burrow out of the sun. So, though they can be kept in a cage, it may be more interesting to use an aquarium, at least 51 cm (20 in) x 46 cm (18 in), with the top covered with wire. You can then construct a little cave out of stone and clean dry sand and watch them underground. If they are in a cage give them a deep layer of sand, and plenty of unprinted shredded paper or hay in which to burrow and nest. They also like a few twigs to climb and to gnaw, as their front teeth grow extremely fast. The ideal temperature for them is above 5°C (40°F) and below 20°C (70°F); damp and draughts are harmful. As their droppings are dry and odourless, cages need only be cleaned out once in three weeks.

National Mongolian Gerbil Society, c/o Miss Debbie Allan, 23 Exeter Drive, 212 Partick West, Glasgow G11 7UY. Tel: 041 334 3874 - M£L, M, G, shows, sae.
David Alderton, *A Pet Keeper's Guide to Hamsters and Gerbils*, Salamander
Chris Henwood, *Love Your Gerbil*, Foulsham

Guinea Pigs
Though descended from the wild cavies of South America, guinea pigs have been kept as pets for hundreds of years, and vary greatly in size, colour, and coat length. There are three main sorts: the kind with short smooth hair, those with long straight hair - such as the Peruvian - and the Abyssinians with short hair in rosettes. Their needs vary slightly, so ask about them before you buy. Whatever the kind, choose a lively young animal with no scars or wounds.

Guinea pigs need to feel secure. So handle them calmly, using two hands until they are used to you, or their wriggling may lead to a fatal fall.

Breeding
It is quite easy to get cross-bred guinea pigs to breed, but pure breds are harder. Females can be mated at 6 months old and pregnancy lasts 9 to 11 weeks. A mother may have 2 to 3 litters a year, and is able to mate again on the day she has just given birth. So if you don't want a production line keep males and females apart. Babies are born furry and adorable and can be weaned at 3 weeks on to the same food as adults. What's more, males are so oversexed that they may start mating their mother if you don't remove them.

Feeding
Guinea pigs *must have* plenty of vitamin C every day. They need fresh green vegetables, like lettuce, cabbage or dandelions, hay, root vegetables, such as carrot or raw beetroot, and a handful of guinea pig mix. They also need constant fresh water in a heavy dish or drinking bottle. They aren't usually inclined to overeat, so let them guide you on quantities unless they begin to get fat.

Health
Healthy guinea pigs can live for 7 years, but 3 years is average. They tend to fight, and scratches may turn into abscesses, so it is worth cleaning them with a mild antiseptic such as you'd use on a human cut. Mites and lice sometimes trouble them and need to be treated with an insect powder recommended by a vet. It is also important not to let them become very fat or they may die suddenly, especially if they are pregnant. Penicillin is also fatal to them - but not all vets realize this.

Housing
They can use an outdoor cage during the summer, if it is out of sun and wind, has stilts against the wet and a waterproof roof. But some need to be indoors in winter, so check the hardiness of any guinea pig before you buy it. A single animal needs a hutch about 60 cm (2 ft) long, by 45 cm (18 in) wide and high, with about a third partitioned off for sleeping and 18 mm (¾ in) wire mesh across the front. A family group of three females and one male needs a hutch twice as long. Put paper on the floor and cover this with 2½ cm (1 in) of wood shavings, then add hay for bedding. The bedding should be changed daily if there is no separate sleeping quarter, or weekly if there is. (Don't use sawdust: it gives them breathing trouble.) In summer guinea pigs enjoy having a wire run on a lawn, provided they are well protected from larger animals and the lawn has not been treated with chemicals.

The National Cavy Club, 9 Parkdale Road, Sheldon, Birmingham B26 3UT Tel: 021 742 3772 - M£L, A, G, B, shows.
Isabel Day, *Guinea Pigs*, Hamlyn Pet Guides

Hamsters

Hamsters were domesticated in this century, and make excellent pets provided you buy the Golden Hamster - which is not always golden. Their only disadvantages are that each one needs a separate cage and they tend to sleep by day and rush about at night. Choose a lively animal, in good condition, with no scars or scratches, and 8 to 10 weeks old. Either sex makes a good pet, but you can tell which is which by looking at their hind quarters: males have an elongated rump, whereas females have a rounder one. Females also have two rows of teats from about 8 days old.

Handle hamsters very carefully. In the early days, before they are tame, hamsters may need to be picked up gently by the loose skin at the back of the neck. But as soon as possible get them used to cupped hands. Handle them while sitting on the floor - if they fall more than 23 cm (9 in) they may be killed.

Breeding

Before breeding hamsters, think whether you have the space. You need separate cages to keep old from young and male from female or they will fight. They can breed at only 6 to 8 weeks old, but the female (doe) should be 3 to 4 months old before she is mated. She is most likely to be broody in the summer and will be in season every 4 to 5 days, but mating needs to be watched carefully as you may have to separate them if they fight. They should also be separated straight afterwards. A litter of 4 to 7 naked young will be born 15 to 18 days later. Their eyes open and they start eating dry oatmeal after about 5 days and chopped greenstuff after 10 days. However, they should not be handled at all for over 2 weeks. Segregate them at 4 to 5 weeks to stop them from fighting - even siblings scrap.

Food and Drink

Hamsters need to be fed once a day - ideally in the evening - and will thrive on pellet seed preparations made for rats or mice. But they will eat almost anything, and some people claim they do well on a firm, crumbly, chopped-up mixture of left-over meat, fish, eggs, vegetables and biscuits. But they also need mixed grains and fresh green and root vegetables. Avoid oats in the husk, as the pointed tips can pierce a hamster's cheek pouches. If they are fed at the same time each day they become tamer, but only give them enough food for one day or they will store it, and it will become mouldy and unhealthy. They like water from a bottle hanging in the cage and can have milk occasionally.

Health

Hamsters get fewer fleas and lice than other rodents and should not get ill if properly fed and housed. They live 3 to 4 years. Treat any problems as for guinea pigs or gerbils.

Housing

As the rule for hamsters is only one hamster per cage, they are not as easy to house as some other rodents. They need a strong house which will resist their large teeth. Many hamster pens are too small, for they like to climb and move about a lot, especially at night. Each one needs a separate cage at least 60 cm (2 ft) by 30 cm (1 ft) and 30 cm (1 ft) high, though there is no need for a separate sleeping section. The cage can be in plastic, metal or wood, but metal tends to be cold and if wood is used it must be strong hardwood at least 2 cm (⅝ in) thick, painted inside with non-poisonous hard gloss paint, and protected on tempting edges with metal strips. A thick floor covering of wood shavings and a supply of fresh meadow hay or shredded white paper (from pet shops) for bedding is all a hamster then needs. Don't use sawdust, newspaper, feathers, cotton wool or artificial fibre bedding as they can cause health problems.

Keep them at an even temperature of 18° to 21°C (65° to 70°F), away from draughts and direct sunlight. For when the temperature falls below 5°C (40°F) they may go into a coma, and seem dead. If this happens revive them in a warm place and offer warm sweet milk.

They are remarkably clean creatures, and will learn to leave their droppings in one place if you put a flat container there and give them the idea by putting some of the soiled litter on it when you clean the cage. Clean the whole cage out once or twice a week, but remove wet patches daily.

The National Hamster Council, c/o Chris Henwood, 179 Pavilion Road, Worthing, W Sussex BN14 7EP Tel: 0903 35008 - M£L, M, G, handbook, Ad, shows.
Chris Henwood, *Love Your Hamster*, Foulsham Press

Horses

Owning a horse is a major undertaking, needing more than an ability to ride. Only someone who will be totally committed should take a horse on. Care and exercise can take at least 3 hours a day - *every* day. It is one thing to help a friend muck out a stable on a summer's day, and quite another to do the job, twice a day, week in week out - especially with the temperature below freezing, and everyone else in the warm. They also cost more to keep than any other animal.

Horses also require more detailed information than I have space for. Anyone wanting to buy a horse should first talk to other owners, read books on the subject and gain practical experience in horse care - it could just change their mind. There are also courses in stable management which are well worth taking before a horse is purchased. And someone with spare land who simply wants to own a horse may get a great deal out of giving a retired horse a good home.

The following can give you all the information on horses that you need.

Association of British Riding Schools, Old Brewery, Brewery, Penzance, Cornwall TR18 2SL Tel: 0736 69440

Bransby Home of Rest for Horses, Bransby, Saxilby, Lincoln LN1 2H Tel: 0427 788464 - cares for old and sick horses, donkeys and mules.

The British Horse Society (and the Pony Club), British Equestrian Centre, Stoneleigh, Kenilworth, Warwick CV8 2LR Tel: 0203 52241 - covers both riding and carriage driving through numerous affiliated clubs and branches. Pony clubs for under 21s. Riding schools are inspected and given the BHS 'seal of approval'. M£L-M, M, L, F, V, A, Inf, B, E, EI, HD - see below, sae preferred.

British Equine Veterinary Association, Hartham Park, Corsham, Wilts SN13 0QB Tel: 0249 715723.

British Show Jumping Association, British Equestrian Centre, Stoneleigh, Kenilworth, Warwicks CV8 2LR Tel: 0203 55251 - M£L-H, M, A, Ins.

The Donkey Breed Society, Manor Cottage, South Thoresby, Alford, Lincs LN13 0AS Tel: 05216 320.

Equine Management Consultancy Service, c/o Gillian McCarthy, 20 Victoria Road, Bulwark, Chepstow, Gwent NP6 5QN Tel: 0291 71023 - advises on all aspects of horse management, especially feeding. Sells tapes which calculate a horse's weight from its girth.

Horses and Ponies Protection Association, Greenbank Farm, Fence, Nr Burnley, Lancs BB12 9QJ Tel: 0282 65909 - M£L, G, loans horses, ponies and donkeys, sae.

The National Pony Society, Brook House, 25 High Street, Alton, Hants GU34 1AW Tel: 0420 88333 - for pony breeders.

Riding for the Disabled Association, National Agricultural Centre, Stoneleigh, Kenilworth, Warwicks CV8 2LY Tel: 0203 56107

Brian Giles, *Safety with Horses*, Stanley Paul (paperback)
Susan McBane, *Your First Horse*, Stanley Paul
Gillian McCarthy, *Horse Feeding*, David & Charles
C. Vogel B Vet Med MRCVS, *Horse Ailments and Health Care*, Ward

Lizards

Buying
Lizards are increasingly popular as pets, and should live for about 5 years. But far too many die young because of improper care, and some are too delicate to be kept in captivity at all. Their needs are very varied. So do check on their special needs before you buy. Some won't drink from a dish, but only sip water sprinkled on plants in their environment - which gives you the role of rain-maker. Worst of all - some eat lizards of other species if they are kept together. This range of needs makes it hard to generalize about their care, but there are certain needs they all have in common.

Feeding
Most lizards adore eating spiders, as well as many insects and a wide range of other foods. They like bran-fed mealworms (which are often fed to them), but these contain too few vitamins and minerals and too little calcium unless they have been on a special diet. Varied

fruit, vegetables and insects should be offered, plus multi-vitamins and powdered cuttlefish bone and, of course, water. The larger lizards, in particular, benefit from the extra vitamins and minerals in tinned cat or dog food. They may also accept a small whole mouse. But not all their likes are so distasteful - it seems iguanas have a penchant for rose petals.

Housing
The right temperature is vital, for it dictates the rest of their behaviour and in the wrong temperature they cannot thrive. Most lizards thrive at 25° to 30°C (77° to 84°F) and need a lamp to bask under and a cooler place to retire to.

Being active creatures they easily entangle themselves in wire mesh and become injured, so a glass aquarium (correctly called a terrarium), with enough room for them to run around, is the best home. As most lizards are wall climbers, it needs a firmly attached perforated lid too. Cover the bottom with newspaper or cardboard, for ease of cleaning, and then give them a good layer of earth or sand. Other details should be adjusted according to the species. Study, and try to mimic, their natural habitat; tree climbers should have twigs to climb and those which bury themselves in the sand should have sand. Like any creature, they must be kept clean if they are to stay healthy.

Joan Palmer, *Reptiles and Amphibians*, Blandford - covers the special needs of each type of lizard.
Robert G. Sprackford, *All About Lizards*, THF Publications
R. H. Wynne, *Lizards in Captivity*, THF Publications

Mice and Rats

Mice and rats are often considered dirty creatures. Wild ones are disease-carriers, but a cleanly-kept caged mouse or rat is no dirtier than a rabbit or a hamster, though they do have a strong smell, especially if you fail to clean them out regularly or give them the wrong diet.

If you intend to exhibit get advice from the relevant society (see below) on which type to choose. The best rat or mouse to buy is one which looks alert and lively and whose coat is in good condition. If you want a happy mouse, get it a friend of the same sex. When choosing a rat pick a female - they're less smelly than males - but avoid the wild Brown Rat: it may carry disease.

To find the sex of rodents you need to compare several. The anal-genital distance is greater in a male than in a female. But don't press around hoping to extrude a penis and confirm your diagnosis - as you could on a rabbit or kitten: it won't work.

Breeding
Rats reach maturity at 2 months, mice at 6 to 7 weeks. Rats can produce 6 litters a year, but it's best to delay the first pregnancy by separating the sexes, and separate them again during pregnancy. This lasts 17 to 22 days in mice, and 20 to 22 days in rats, and the mother may produce from 6 to 16 young. The baby mice can be taken from their mother at 3 weeks, rats at 4 weeks.

Feeding

Ready-mixed rat and mouse food gives a balanced diet, or you can make your own mixture of oats and other cereals. These animals also need green foods such as lettuce, chickweed and rose hips and haws, fruit according to the season, biscuits and bread in a little milk and table scraps. Give the food at night and remove any that isn't eaten by the morning. But avoid cheese, it makes them smelly; and provide a constant supply of water.

You can buy water bottles which hang upsidedown on the cage or fix a piece of very narrow metal tubing, in a small cork, in the neck of a medicine bottle and hang this up.

Handling

Mice need gentle handling. Don't grab them; lift them by grasping the tail near the base, and then place them on your hand. Rats are too heavy for this; so grasp them round the middle, with your thumb and first finger beneath their chin. Handle both creatures calmly, even tame ones may bite if you startle them.

Health

Mice don't need grooming, but children enjoy polishing their coats by stroking them gently with a piece of silk - a trick which is just as good for smooth-haired dogs. Treat fleas with a powder recommended by a vet. Sores can be cured by adding arrowroot to the diet and applying a skin ointment from your vet. A healthy rat may live 3 years, a mouse slightly less.

Housing

Rats are very active and need a cage 75 x 50 x 45 cm (30 x 20 x 18 in). But two mice are happy in a standard mouse cage 46 x 25 cm (18 x 10 in) and both creatures need play wheels and things they can climb. Metal or strong plastic are the best materials for rat cages as these can't be gnawed through and don't absorb the smell of urine. Mice are best in a wooden cage, as plastic cages attract condensation, which is bad for them. Mice also need to be indoors, away from damp and draughts, but cover any cage ventilation holes with wire mesh - believe it or not, a mouse can squeeze through a hole only a third of an inch across. Both creatures need plenty of sawdust or wood shavings in their cages to mop up the urine, and the cage must be completely cleaned 1 to 3 times a week, and scrubbed out every month.

The National Mouse Club, c/o 85 Forest Road, Cuddington, Northwich, Cheshire CW8 2ED Tel: 0606 882908.
The National Fancy Rat Society, 18 Browns Lane, Uckfield, East Sussex TN22 1RY Tel: 0825 4537

Rabbits

Rabbits which get used to being petted when young make good pets and seem to enjoy company. I knew some that loved to watch the television, and sat so close the family had to watch it between their ears. The more a rabbit is handled when young, the more friendly it will be. Lift it carefully, and *never* by the ears. There

are several different types of rabbit, each kind having its own advantages and disadvantages. Ask about these before you buy. For example, Rex get very large and may weigh 3 to 4 kg (6-8 lb), English Lop have excessively long ears which are easily damaged by children, and Angora need careful daily grooming.

Feeding

Water must always be available, and an upside down bottle with a metal tube to drink from is ideal. Rabbits will eat as much green food as you care to give them, plus any root vegetables except raw potatoes. But to keep a rabbit happy include a handful of hay in the morning (or have a hay rack in the hutch) and pellets of meal - oats, wheat, barley or sunflower seeds - in the afternoon. They also appreciate cooked potato peelings or wholemeal (not white) bread toasted or mashed with milk.

Food should be stored away from the hutch, and leftovers cleared up so as not to attract rats or mice. Rabbits must *not* be overfed: folds of fat may become raw and attract flies whose maggots will then eat into the animal. This also happens if their rump is unclean.

Health

One of the advantages of rabbits as pets is that they seldom get ill, but they do have an odd habit of eating their night droppings. This is perfectly normal. If rabbits get parasites *don't* use an insect powder based on DDT, get a safer one from your vet. If there is ear canker it also needs veterinary treatment.

Housing

The hutch must be about 1 m (1 yd) long and 60 cm (2 ft) wide for one rabbit, or half as big again for two, with a sloping waterproof roof. The wire front should be ½-inch mesh - if it's larger they can put a foot through and cut it on the wire. About a third of it needs to be enclosed for a sleeping compartment and the whole hutch must be safe from foxes, and even dogs and cats. Cover the floor with sawdust and bed the sleeping compartment with hay, changing it whenever it is soiled. Whenever possible rabbits should be allowed out for a run - preferably on grass. They are not solitary animals, so if you can't keep 2 give them the company of people or other pets. If keeping several choose females, as bucks may fight.

Pregnancy

Does can become pregnant 10 times a year and produce 4 to 8 young in a litter. Keeping the sexes apart is the only birth control. To mate them deliberately take the doe to the buck, not vice versa or there will be territory squabbles. Pregnancy averages 31 days and the doe needs to be alone and to have extra food and materials she can use for a 'nest'. She also needs considerably more food while feeding her young.

The British Rabbit Council, Purefoy House, 7 Kirkgate, Newark, Notts NG24 1AD Tel: 0636 76042 - M£M, G, A, shows.
David Robinson, *Encyclopaedia of Pet Rabbits*, THF Publications
Care for Your Rabbit, the RSPCA offical guide, Collins

Snakes

Snakes are in some ways perfect pets: silent, clean, deliciously silky to touch, and requiring food very infrequently. But one must face certain facts before buying this ancient symbol of wisdom. First, most snakes feed almost entirely on other live animals. In captivity they may be persuaded to eat dead food, but it can't be counted on. Even then, you may need to kill the food yourself and give it to the snake while it is still warm and - preferably - kicking. Second, they are expensive to care for properly and need special attention. Finally, most snakes manage to escape from their cages - so if you'd mind one underfoot think again. You also need to consider your responsibility under the Dangerous Wild Animals Act.

Obviously, no sane amateur is going to buy a poisonous or semi-poisonous snake. But even those snakes which lack venom in the fangs have venom in their saliva - not strong venom, but it can produce ill effects in certain people. This means that even the least poisonous snake needs careful handling and that you should only buy from a responsible and knowledgeable pet dealer who can advise you about this. The London Zoo suggests looking in *Exchange and Mart* for a snake dealer who also deals in equipment and books.

Feeding
Snakes must always have fresh water available, as they may refuse to drink stale water, and they must not be overfed as this shortens their life and affects their fertility. Don't handle them for several hours after they have eaten and, if you have several, separate them for feeding.

How often they must eat varies with the type and their individual preference, and the details can be found in the books listed below. Once a week is average for a medium-sized snake, like a Garter Snake, but some can go much longer. Favourite foods vary with the species, but baby hamsters, mice, guinea pigs and rats are usually popular, though some prefer fish. It is kindest to kill the creature yourself, but if you can't bear to do this, stay and watch the snake kill and eat its

dinner. If it doesn't go for the creature quickly the snake may be the one that gets bitten. When live animals can't be obtained snakes will usually eat raw fish, especially if you wiggle it to make it look alive. When about to change their skin it is natural for most snakes to refuse food and for their eyes to look milky, but they are very hungry afterwards.

Health
To know whether a snake is well you need to observe its feeding and excreting patterns. If these are abnormal, or it vomits, something is wrong. But don't worry if a snake doesn't seem to sleep: it just sleeps with its eyes open.

Housing
Snakes need cages to suit their size. The minimum is a rectangular cage about 50 cm (20 in) by 50 cm (20 in) by 100 cm (39 in). This can be a wooden cage or a lidded terrarium, and the bottom can be lined with wood shavings, or shredded newspaper, but earth may carry parasites. Try to mimic the snakes' natural habitat and include somewhere they can hide if they wish, as they tend to like privacy. The housing should be heated to about 24°-28°C (75°-80°F) for temperate species or 26°-30°C (77°-86°F) for tropical ones, with only a slight drop at night. If the temperatures are too low a snake will eat, but the digestive enzymes won't work and the food will remain undigested and make it ill.

Scrupulous cleanliness is essential if snakes are to stay healthy. Remove large droppings as soon as possible and clean the cage thoroughly with Milton disinfectant every 2 to 3 weeks. Snakes have an excellent sense of smell, although curiously they smell with their tongue. To avoid being bitten when cleaning out the snake's house wear rubber gloves and put something strong-smelling - such as alcoholic spirits - on the gloves. The snake will then avoid your hand.

Klaus Griehl, *Snakes, Giant Snakes, and Non-Venomous Snakes in the Terrarium*, Barron Educational Series, New York
Christopher Mattison, *The Care of Reptiles* and *Amphibians in Captivity*, Blandford
Joan Palmer, *Reptiles and Amphibians*, Blandford.
Mervin F. Roberts, *Snakes*, TFH Publications Ltd - mainly on constricting snakes.

Tortoises, Terrapins and Turtles
Toothless and gentle, these creatures are living fossils, far older than the dinosaurs, and almost unchanged in 100 million years. In the wild many live as long as a man, and longer, but it is rare to find any British family with a tortoise which has survived more than a few years. So to keep a tortoise in the average family is, essentially, to kill it, and their popularity as pets has helped to make European tortoises an endangered species. The Wildlife and Countryside Act of 1981 made it illegal to import these. Some are now bred and sold in Britain, but many are imported from America, and may need far warmer conditions than can easily be provided. Terrapins may carry salmonella bacteria,

which cause food poisoning, and transfer them to humans. So neither could really be called an ideal pet.

A fall could fatally break their shell, so they must be handled with great care. The shell must never be painted or pierced as it is a living part of the creature. If necessary, a label can be attached with a *small* dab of superglue.

Feeding Tortoises

Tortoises are often put in a garden and left to fend for themselves. Although European tortoises may munch your greenery this is *not* all they need, and some are unlikely to survive such treatment. They usually eat about 1 to 1½ cups of varied meat and vegetables a day, with more vegetables than meat - and they may enjoy cat or dog food. Try them on green vegetables (well washed because of chemical sprays), carrots, sweetcorn, bananas and non-poisonous weeds - dandelions are a great favourite. Leave them to munch slowly, but throw fruit away before it becomes overripe or they will get stomach upsets. To stay healthy they also need direct sunlight and extra calcium and phosphorous in their food.

Feeding tortoises early in the morning makes them less prone to stray, and if you always choose the same place and time they will learn to arrive there on the dot. If you call them, or make some other noise each time before you feed them, they will even learn to come when called. When kept indoors give them 3 meals a day to mimic their natural browsing. Put the food on a clean piece of ground - they are not designed for eating off dishes. Water should always be available, and they love to paddle in hot weather, so a shallow dish sunk in the ground doubles for drinking and bathing, but only give them a little water or they drown.

Health - Tortoise

Most tortoise problems need a vet, but if they get a cold keep them at 18 to 21°C (67°F) until they get better, and treat ticks as for ticks on dogs (page 631). Cuts should be cleaned, smeared with Savlon and covered with a plaster or flies may lay eggs in them.

Hibernation of Tortoises

When the temperature drops in autumn and a tortoise slows down and eats less, it is ready for hibernation. Put it in a box at least a foot cubed, with plenty of shredded paper, dry leaves or litter, but not woodwool as this could cut it. Then fix wire over the top and put the box in a garage or garden shed - provided there are no rats of mice - until the spring. Check it weekly, if it wakes too soon, keep it indoors until the weather is warm. On waking, its eyes may be sticky and need bathing with 1 teaspoon of boracic acid (from a chemist) in 5 teaspoons of water. It may also need lots of water and some vitamins, such as Abidec, to stimulate its appetite, and if it seems slow to get going put it in *shallow* lukewarm water and splash the water over it. However, some American tortoises do not hibernate.

Housing Tortoises

A tortoise can wander in the garden, if there are no poisonous plants around, or be given a large run - though it may well burrow out of either. It also needs a waterproof wooden house with space to move about in. This must be made with a doorway allowing for growth. The underside needs battens to keep it off the ground, and the ramp up to the door should have some anti-slip device, like strips of wood attached in a V. David Robinson's book (see overleaf) has detailed instructions. A litter of shredded newspaper inside is better than straw, which can cut a tortoise, or hay, which grows fungus when damp. The house must be cleaned out regularly. At night, or when the temperature is below 15°C (60°F), they should be brought indoors and put in a pen well-lined against droppings.

Sex

To tell the sex of a tortoise look at the undershell. In a female it curves slightly outwards; in a male it curves inwards. Males also have longer tails. Mating and breeding are well covered in David Alderton's book (see overleaf).

Feeding Turtles and Terrapins

Terrapins like ¾ of meat to ¼ of vegetable or fruit. Finely chopped fresh fish or meat (without fat, and not liver or heart), tinned tuna fish or sardines, earthworms, mosquito larvae, mashed berries or tiny pieces of tomato are all suitable. Sprinkle a little cod liver oil, for vitamins, and ground cuttlefish bone on all the food or their shells will weaken from lack of calcium. Feeding them in a separate bowl avoids polluting the aquarium and cuts down the cleaning, though a lettuce leaf can be floated on the water for browsing. A bunch of aquarium plants is also a good idea.

They will only eat if the temperature is right. If cold they withdraw into their shells and refuse to eat or, having eaten, are unable to digest their food and become ill. Feed young ones daily, when the temperature has been right for some hours. Those 13 cm (5 in) or over only need food 3 to 4 times a week; and only offer what they can eat in 15 minutes. Include a few drops of Vionate vitamin supplement each week: lack of vitamin A can lead to a fatal infection.

Health - Turtles and Terrapins

Terrapins can suffer from colds, pneumonia, eye infections and fungus infections. The fungus shows as a halo in the water round the terrapin, and immersing in a solution of 1 teaspoon of salt to each cup of water for 15 minutes a day may cure it. Other conditions are best seen by a vet as terrapins are delicate creatures.

Housing Turtles and Terrapins

These need an aquarium giving slightly more than a cubic foot per creature. Put 2·5 to 5 cm (1 to 2 in) of coarse aquarium gravel in the bottom, and a water depth twice the creature's length from head to tail. Keep it at 23° to 29°C (75° to 85°F) with a heating element. As basking is their delight, they need a flat stone, under a lamp, to climb out on to. Like all reptiles, turtles cannot adjust their body temperature. So they depend totally on the environment and must have a temperature of 29° to 34°C (85° to 92°F) by day. You can buy ready-made aquarium lids complete with a light fitting, and an ultraviolet bulb should be used to give them 8 hours of 'sunlight', but switch it off at night.

Sudden temperature changes harm them. Get the water temperature right, then float the plastic bag you bought them in on the water for 30 minutes, so it takes on the same temperature. Then release them in the tank. A dirty aquarium causes sick terrapins, so the tank must be cleaned every 2 days, unless it has a filter. With a filter it need only be cleaned 3 times monthly. But never empty the water by first sucking it up a tube - there is a risk of salmonella poisoning.

The Association for the Study of Reptilia and Amphibia (ASRA), Cotswold Wild Life Park, Burford, Oxon OX8 4JW Tel: 099 382 3006 - M£L, M, G, A, Lib.

British Chelonia Group, c/o Mrs Pat Murray, 105 Burnham Lane, Slough, Berks SL1 6LA Tel: 06286 62721 - Ad and Inf.

British Herpetological Society, c/o The Zoological Society of London, Regents Park, London NW1 4RY Tel: 01 452 9578
David Alderton, *Tortoises and Terrapins*, Saiga (paperback)
C. Mattison, *The Care of Reptiles and Amphibians in Captivity*, Blandford Press
David Robinson, *Tortoises, Turtles and Terrapins*, Bartholomew (paperback)

Animals for Smallholdings

The Agricultural Development and Advisory Service (ADAS) is the best source of information if you want to keep creatures like goats, pigs, poultry or even a cow. The regional ADAS offices are listed in the phone book under Ministry of Agriculture but, although the leaflets are free, they now charge for personal advice. They urge people not to take on livestock too lightly. Inexperienced neighbours may happily feed a cat while you take a holiday, but leaving them with chickens may not be so successful. If you can't track down your local ADAS office, the London number is 01 216 7342.

British Goat Society, Moreton House, The Square, Moretonhampstead, Devon TQ13 8NF Tel: 0647 40781 - M£M, M, yearbook, herdbook, affiliated societies.
David Mackenzie, *Goat Husbandry*, Faber

Animal Organizations

Many of the animal organizations have no fixed address, but rove as the secretaries succeed each other. If you can't trace such an organization, the RSPCA or BVA (see below) may have the latest address. The Charities Aid Foundation publishes a *Directory of Organizations for the Protection and Welfare of Animals* which may be in your public library - but, as with this book, things may have changed while it was being printed.

Amateur Entomologists Society, 355 Hounslow Road, Hanworth, Feltham, Middx Tel: 01 755 0325 - for those with a passion for insects.

Blue Cross Victoria Hospital, 1 Hugh Street, London SW1 Tel: 01 834 4224 - provides free veterinary care for the animals of those who can't afford a vet. By appointment only, with evidence of inability to pay. Branches also in Hammersmith and Wandsworth. RC.

British Small Animal Veterinary Association, 5 St George's Terrace, Cheltenham, Glos GL50 3PT Tel: 0242 584354

British Veterinary Association (BVA), 7 Mansfield Street, London W1M 0AT Tel: 01 636 6541 - book series on pet care.

National Association of Private Animal Keepers, c/o D. H. Keeling, 13 Pound Place, Shalford, Guildford, Surrey GU4 8HH Tel: 0483 37547 - for family pet keepers and professionals.

Pedigree Petfoods Education Centre, Waltham-on-the-Wolds, Melton Mowbray, Leics LE14 4RS Tel: 06642 410000 - inf and free leaflet service.

People's Dispensary for Sick Animals, PDSA House, South Street, Dorking, Surrey RH4 2LB Tel: 0306 888291 - 57 centres give free treatment to sick pets and wildlife, and neuter male cats, when their owners are unable to pay fees. Vets displaying a PDSA Auxiliary Service sticker also do this. 24-hour emergency service. Take proof that you are receiving state benefits or rebates. Busy Bees Club for children with pets. M£M, M, G, L.

The Pet Health Council, 4 Bedford Square, London WC1B 3RA Tel: 01 255 1100 - leaflets on pet health.

Royal Society for the Prevention of Cruelty to Animals, The Causeway, Horsham, West Sussex RH12 1HG Tel: 0403 64181 - animals clinics, and welfare centres. RC, M£free, M, L, G, F, V, B, charts, junior membership and magazine.

Small Mammals Genetic Circle, 179 Pavilion Road, Worthing, Sussex BN14 7EP Tel: 0903 35008 - Inf forum - especially on unusual creatures or breeding developments. M£L, M, L, Ad.

The Wild Life Hospital Trust, 1 Pemberton Close, Aylesbury, Bucks Tel: 0296 29860 - Ad and Inf - on caring for injured wildlife if your vet can't help - including a hedgehog helpline.

Organizations

Consumer Bodies • Government • The Law • The Media
and the Arts • The Medical Services • The Police • Religious
Faiths • Services • Travel and Transport • Work-Related
Organizations

CONSUMER BODIES

Citizens Advice Bureau (CAB)

Citizens Advice Bureaux are one of Britain's most useful institutions. Their role is to make sure that nobody fails to get their entitlements because they don't know their rights, or are unable to fight their own case. CABx offer a free, and confidential, service in which they explain social security entitlements, help people make complaints against public bodies of all kinds, show them how to cope with financial problems and assist with legal problems. How far they can go in helping with a problem depends very much on what it is. They will guide a desperate battered wife through the legal steps needed to get her legal protection, but they can't hold someone's hand right through a divorce.

You can phone up with a problem or visit them - with or without an appointment and when the team at a Citizens Advice Bureau don't know the answer, they can always tell you where else to go. They also carry the leaflets and explanatory pamphlets put out by government departments and quangos. CABx are funded by local authorities, and listed in the phone book under Citizens Advice Bureau.

National Association of Citizens Advice Bureaux, Myddelton House, 115/123 Pentonville Road, London N1 9LZ Tel: 01 833 2181

Federation of Independent Advice Centres

There are some 500 independent advice centres around the country which offer free advice on a wide range of problems, such as benefits, housing and discrimination. Unlike the CABx they are funded from a range of sources, and they often specialize in certain issues or sectors of the community, such as the disabled, single parents or some ethnic group. So they will take on in-depth work on particular cases, and some centres will even represent people in tribunals. Although you may find them in the 'Advice' section of some telephone directories, such as Thompsons, there is no general name under which you can look them up in an ordinary phone book. To find your nearest, ask your public library, or contact the address below.

Federation of Independent Advice Centres (FIAC), 13 Stockwell Road, London SW9 9AU Tel: 01 274 1839/1878

National Consumer Council (NCC)

The National Consumer Council is financed by government and its members are appointed by the Secretary of State for Trade and Industry, but otherwise it is entirely independent. It represents the interests of consumers in every area, from goods and services to the health service, public transport and amenities like gas and water. The Council does *not* help with individual complaints but reports to governments on faults in services and legislation, and lobbies them for improvements. This means that, although it will not deal with your particular problem, you can write and tell the Council if there are flaws in the system about which the NCC should lobby the authorities.

National Consumer Council, 20 Grosvenor Gardens, London SW1W 0DH Tel: 01 730 3469

The Money Advice Association is an independent organization at the same address. It has *no* role in relation to the public except to supply the name of your nearest Money Advice Centre which in certain circumstances will give advice on serious personal financial problems such as debt if you have been unable to find it through your local CAB.

Office of Fair Trading (OFT)

The Office of Fair Trading is a government organization looking after the interests of consumers. It approves the codes of practice of trade associations, alerts the Monopolies Commission to potential monopolies, and is the body to which Trading Standards Officers report. It also publishes excellent free leaflets on consumer rights - available from CABx *not* direct from the OFT.

If you think a company has broken any consumer law (see Law) ask the Trading Standards Officer, at your local council, to look into it: the OFT doesn't deal with individual complaints. However, the OFT does like to be alerted to the fact that a code of practice is not being properly applied. In that case, write to this address:

Office of Fair Trading, Field House, Bream Buildings, London EC4A 1PR Tel: 01 242 2858

GOVERNMENT

The European Economic Community (EEC, the Common Market)

There are 12 members of the EEC. The founding 6 - France, Germany, Italy, Belgium, Luxembourg and Holland - signed their agreement in 1957 and formally united in 1958. Britain, Norway, Denmark and Ireland then joined in 1973, followed by Greece in 1981, and Spain and Portugal in 1986. Forming a community of 320 million people, with special trading relationships with many African, Caribbean and Pacific countries, the EEC is the largest trade bloc in the world.

Council of Ministers

The Community is run by the Council of Ministers. It creates all major EEC legislation, and its laws are binding on EEC members. The major work is done by the specialist ministers from the various departments of state, such as the Minister for Agriculture. They stand up for the interests of their countries, and each country has a voting strength, on the Council, proportional to its size. Major issues demand a unanimous decision, but minor ones can be passed by a majority. The presidency of the Council passes to a different member state every 6 months, and the heads of the various governments also meet at 6-monthly intervals.

European Commission

The Commission has 17 members, appointed for a 4-year term by agreement between the member governments. Unlike the members of the Council, they are sworn to uphold the interests of the *whole* Community and ignore their national interests. The Commission's job is to see that the EEC rules are kept. It is also the policy planning body which makes proposals to the Council. The only way members can be removed from office is by a motion of censure, on the entire Commission, from the EEC Parliament.

European Parliament

The members of the European Parliament were voted in for the first time in 1979. There are 81 British members (MEPs), elected for 5 years, from candidates put forward by the political parties, most of whom are not already MPs at Westminster. The elections are held in each country, according to its own electoral system. So, in Britain, MEPs are elected on a majority vote from constituencies which embrace several Westminster ones.

Anyone can get the name and address of their MEP from their local library and may write to him or her direct.

In the European Parliament MEPs belong to party groups, according to their political complexion, regardless of national boundaries. They meet once a month and debate issues and sit on special committees in much the same way as they would in the House of Commons. Commission proposals are usually submitted to the European Parliament for an opinion before decisions are taken in the Council, though the Parliament and the Council have joint powers in deciding the ill-fated EEC budget.

Economic and Social Committee

This is a large committee made up of representatives of employers' organizations, trade unions and special interest groups. It has to be consulted on a wide range of EEC aims, but it operates purely in an advisory capacity. In theory, it can be lobbied via one of the groups represented on it - in reality, this is hard.

Financing the EEC

The EEC budget is a perpetual problem. Originally, the income was a fraction of each country's Gross Domestic Product (GDP), now it's a portion of VAT revenue, plus farming and import levies. This contribution is then used mainly to finance the various funds, the prime ones being those of the Common Agricultural Policy (CAP) and the Social Regional Development Fund. Income and expenditure have to balance but, thanks to the seemingly insatiable demands of CAP, this doesn't always happen, and extra payments from member states have had to be agreed.

How the EEC Affects Us

The major influence of the EEC is through common policies agreed by the members and incorporated into our legislation. These policies cover every area of economic life, including energy policy, food prices, industrial standards, steel policy, training and employment, transport and fishing. They also cover issues such as women's rights, pollution and aid to the Third World.

Our Rights in Relation to the EEC

Both houses of the British parliament have scrutiny committees which examine proposed EEC legislation, and British ministers are answerable to parliament for their actions in the EEC Council of Ministers. Anyone who wishes to lobby or protest at EEC proposed legislation can approach: (a) his or her MP, (b) the relevant minister, (c) a member of the European Parliament.

Commission of the European Community, 8 Storey's Gate, London SW1P 3AT Tel: 01 222 8122
European Parliament UK Office, 2 Queen Anne's Gate, London SW1H 9AA Tel: 01 222 0411 - purely provides general information.

Parliament

The two, unequal, sections of parliament - the House of Commons and the House of Lords - are officially headed by the Queen. She therefore opens each session in October or November and lays out the government's intended policy in the Queen's Speech - which is actually prepared by the Prime Minister's office.

House of Commons

At a general election 650 Members of Parliament are elected - one for each constituency. The party with the greatest number of MPs forms a government by its leader appointing a cabinet of about 22 senior ministers, plus 80 other ministers. The majority are from the Commons, but some can be from the Lords. The leader of the largest defeated party appoints an equivalent 'shadow cabinet'. Ministers and shadow ministers sit on the front seats on their sides of the House. All the other MPs are known as back-benchers.

The Public and Parliament

In theory, the role of an MP is to represent the views of his constituency in parliament, and every citizen has the right to contact his MP on any issue he feels strongly about. An MP can also take up a constituent's case with certain authorities outside parliament. The best way to reach an MP is by letter to the House of Commons, or by visiting one of the 'surgery' sessions which most MPs hold. But any constituent may simply turn up at the House of Commons, fill in a green card and give it to a doorkeeper who will find the MP, if he is in the House. The MP usually meets the constituent in the central lobby - hence the term 'to lobby'. There is also an unwritten rule that constituents must reach other MPs through their own MP, and not contact them directly.

Ministers are an exception to this rule: anyone may write to any minister, and may even ask to see him or her. Alternatively, they can ask their MP to deal with a ministry. An MP usually writes to the minister and can also raise the matter in the House at Question Time or in an Adjournment Debate.

The Structure of a Ministry

All ministries, except Agriculture, are headed by a Secretary of State, and under him come one or more Ministers of State, and one or more Parliamentary Under Secretaries of State. Each has special responsibility for an area of the ministry's field, and one of them usually sits in the Lords - though this is not essential.

Acts of Parliament

Changing things is the very life-blood of politicians and the main instrument of change is an Act of Parliament. An act starts life as a bill - a draft law - and it then has to come before both Houses of Parliament in a set sequence before it can be made law. It is during this sequence that members of the public, who have noticed flaws in the bill, can point them out to their MP and ask him or her to take them up. So it's useful to know the sequence. It is even possible for an MP to press for an amendment very late in the day, via a member of the Lords. Most bills start in the Commons and the pattern is as follows (when a bill starts in the Lords the process is exactly reversed).

At the **First Reading** the Commons is formally notified that a bill of a certain name is being introduced. There is no debate. The bill is then printed and available to the public through **Her Majesty's Stationery Office**, P.O. Box 276, London SW8 5DT, and telephone orders are through (orders): 01 622 3316 or enquiries 01 211 5656 (which has a queuing system on the line).

The **Second Reading,** at which the bill is explained and the minister cross-questioned, is usually several days later. If a majority of the House are then in favour of the bill it goes to the Committee Stage. But it may be voted out.

In the **Committee Stage** a small group of MPs go through it clause by clause, agreeing to cuts and improvements. They are usually selected because they know something about the subject of the bill and all parties are represented in about the same proportions as in parliament. The altered bill is then printed.

The bill then goes to the **Report Stage** and is presented to the Commons and debated by MPs, who have a chance to make further changes.

In the **Third Reading** the bill comes before the Commons. It has to be accepted or rejected as it is. If the Commons reject it, that is the end of it. If it is accepted it goes before the House of Lords.

In the Lords the bill goes through exactly the same stages as it did in the Commons, except that the Committee Stage is the whole of the Lords, not just a small group, and changes can be made in the Third Reading. If the Lords have made no changes the bill can go straight to the Queen for Royal Assent. But, if changes have been made, the bill must go before the Commons first. Once a bill receives Royal Assent it becomes an act, and is law, but it may not come into force straight away.

MP's Attendance at Parliament

MPs have considerable freedom, but each party uses a system of 'whips' to let MPs know whether they need to attend. A whip is a document giving the business of the day. If a section is underlined once they should try to attend. Two underlinings mean they should either attend or 'pair' with a member of the opposition who also agrees not to be there. A three-line whip, with three underlinings, is an emergency and every MP is expected to be there unless actually dying. This system is administered by the Chief Whip for each party.

House of Commons, London SW1A 0AA Tel: 01 219 4272 Information on the Commons, by letter or telephone *only*, from **the Public Information Office,** Norman Shaw Building (North), Victoria Embankment, London SW1A 2JF.

House of Lords

The House of Lords has about 1,178 members, consisting of hereditary peers, life peers created by the Queen, the 26 most senior archbishops and bishops, and a group of judges. Some, however, may never go there. Until 1958 there were no women in the Lords, but there are now more women there than in the Commons. The Lords divide along party lines, and the same whip system applies. But, with no constituents to offend, the Lords can afford to be more controversial. Some of the most progressive legislation of the last 20 years owes much to this chamber.

The House of Lords has five main activities:

1 It is the supreme court of appeal in legal cases. These appeals are only heard by a specially appointed group of law lords, not by the whole House, and about 70 cases are brought before them a year.

2 It is a forum for debates - which may or may not have any influence on the rest of parliament.

3 It can originate legislation - which is then passed through both Houses.

4 It considers and amends bills which have started in the House of Commons.

5 It questions the government on its activities.

It has a special role in relation to bills on issues which affect only one or two people. If you need a bill to be brought you first have to find a peer or peeress to sponsor it. Obviously, it is a good idea to lobby a peer or peeress who is already in sympathy with the topic. A run through Dod's *Parliamentary Companion* should help here, and any member of the House of Lords may be approached in writing by a member of the public.

Journals and Information Office, House of Lords, London SW1A 0PW Tel: 01 219 3107

Visiting Parliament

Parliament sits for about 37 weeks a year, taking holidays (known as recesses) for 4 weeks at Christmas, 1 week at Easter, 1 week at the Spring Bank Holiday, and a summer recess from early August to October. The House of Commons usually sits at 2.30 pm on Mondays, Tuesdays, Wednesdays and Thursdays, and at 9.30 am on Fridays. A normal sitting may last until after 10 pm. The House of Lords sits at 2.30 pm on Tuesdays, Wednesdays and Thursdays and 11 am on Fridays.

The best way to watch the Commons in session is to write to your MP, about 6 weeks in advance, asking if he or she can obtain a ticket for you (maximum two tickets) and giving a selection of dates. This lets you watch Question Time - which is often the liveliest part of the proceedings. If you simply queue outside St Stephen's entrance, you get in later. You queue in the same way to watch the Lords. The queues are shortest on Fridays, as the sitting ends at 3 pm.

Parliamentary Ombudsman

If you have suffered as the result of injustice by a department of central government, such as the Department of Social Security or the Inland Revenue, you can ask your MP to take your case to the Parliamentary Ombudsman. The Ombudsman investigates and, if an injustice is found, can instruct the department to make amends either by apologizing

or by making an appropriate payment. You may not take your case to the Ombudsman yourself, but you can get an information leaflet direct from his office.

Parliamentary Ombudsman, Church House, Great Smith Street, London SW1P 3BW Tel: 01 212 7676/6271

Political Pressure Groups

Campaign for Lead-Free Air (CLEAR) and **Campaign for Freedom of Information,** 3 Endsleigh Street, London WC1H 0DD Tel: 01 278 9686. The names say it all. RC M£M, M.

Campaign for Nuclear Disarmament (CND), 22-24 Underwood Street, London N1 7JG Tel: 01 250 4010. Campaigns for unilateral nuclear disarmament.

Council for Environmental Conservation (COENCO), 80 York Way, London N1 9AG Tel: 01 278 4736. A coalition of organizations concerned with environmental issues. Membership is not open to individuals, but individuals can alert the council to problems.

Families for Defence, 21 Cloudesley Street, London WC1A 2RA Tel: 01 831 0180, is a political pressure group against unilateral disarmament and for multilateral disarmament.

Greenpeace, 30-31 Islington Green, London N1 8XE Tel: 01 354 5100, is an organization campaigning against pollution of all kinds and in favour of conservation worldwide. M£M.

Political Parties

Political parties are hard to summarize and easy to misrepresent. What follows is taken entirely from information supplied by the parties themselves, and the quotes are their own words.

Communist Party

The Communist Party wants to see 'the end of the capitalist system', 'the means of production, distribution, and exchange' publicly owned, and a state-planned economy. It also wants to see a 'revolutionary transformation' to a society in which working people rule. It is funded by voluntary contributions and, unlike most parties, it is evangelical and lays obligations upon those who join.

Communist Party of Great Britain, 16 St John Street, London EC1M 4AL Tel: 01 251 4406

Conservative Party

The Conservative Party stands for 'personal freedom', 'free enterprise', 'the rule of law' and a strong defence policy. It also claims to be a party which cares for every sector of society regardless of class, colour or creed. There is no fixed membership subscription and, though industry does contribute to it, most of its funds come from subscriptions and from money raised by constituents.

The Conservative Party, Conservative Central Office, 32 Smith Square, London SW1P 3HH Tel: 01 222 9000

Green Party

The Green Party wishes to promote an economic system which does not exploit resources or people and emphasizes locally based work and finance - without multinationals or big banks - so that people's needs may be met without 'damaging each other or the planet'.

Green Party, 10 Station Parade, Balham High Road, London SW12 9AZ Tel: 01 673 0045

Labour Party

The main aims of the Labour Party stated in Clause 4 of the constitution are 'to secure for the workers ... common ownership of the means of production, distribution and exchange, and the best obtainable system of popular administration and control of each industry or service' and 'to co-operate with the General Council of the Trades Union Congress, or other kindred organizations, in joint political or other action...'

Only a small proportion of the party's funding comes from members, and in recent years between 78 per cent and 86 per cent of the party's total income has come from Trade Union Affiliation fees, and some candidates are directly funded by a union.

The Labour Party, 150 Walworth Road, London SE17 1JT Tel: 01 703 0833

Plaid Cymru

Plaid Cymru means 'Party of Wales' and it was founded in 1925 to work for self-government for Wales by peaceful means. It would like to see the restoration of the Welsh language, and Wales under an independent democratic socialist government, which would play a part in world affairs through the United Nations. Its policies are broadly socialist, decentralist and environmentalist. The funding is entirely from members of the party.

Plaid Cymru, 51 Cathedral Road, Cardiff CF1 9HD Tel: 0222 31944

Scottish National Party

This claims to be a moderate left-of-centre party. It stands for self-government for Scotland, and greater decision making within its local communities. Having gained independence, it would also like to renegotiate Scotland's conditions of entry into the EEC. It is dedicated to unilateral nuclear disarmament and the removal of all foreign bases from Scottish soil.

Scottish National Party, 6 North Charlotte Street, Edinburgh EH2 4JH Tel: 031 226 3661

Social Democratic and Labour Party

This is a socialist party, formed in 1970, which aims to produce peace in Northern Ireland, by democratic means, and works for 'Irish unity based on the consent of the majority'.

Social Democratic and Labour Party, 38 University Street, Belfast BT7 1FZ Tel: 0232 323428

Social Democratic and Liberal Parties

At the time of going to press the Liberal Party and the Social Democratic Party were only beginning their union and no decisions had been made on their combined structure and policies. Their individual policies are, therefore, given below. They share the fact that both are funded almost entirely from personal subscriptions and local fund raising.

The Liberal Party

The party stands for the devolution of power from the centre to local communities, greater worker participation in decision-making in the workplace, freedom of information and a written bill of rights. It is also commited to NATO, but in favour of arms control.

The Liberal Party, 1 Whitehall Place, London SW1A 2HE Tel: 01 925 0025
The Scottish Liberal Party, 4 Clifton Terrace, Edinburgh EH12 5DR Tel: 031337 2314
The Welsh Liberal Party, Dumfries Chambers, 91 St Mary's Street, Cardiff CF1 1DW Tel: 0222 382210

Social Democratic Party (SDP)

The SDP is committed to a mixed economy; to decentralization in both industry and government; and to fairer election procedures. It also believes in Britain playing a full part in the EEC, NATO, the UN and the Commonwealth.

Social Democratic Party (SDP), 4 Cowley Street, London SW1P 3NB Tel: 01 222 7999

Ulster Democratic Unionist Party

The stated objectives of this party, led by Ian Paisley, are to 'smash Sinn Fein', and 'annihilate the IRA'. It is fiercely Protestant, and wants to maintain Northern Ireland's position as part of the United Kingdom.

Ulster Democratic Unionist Party, 296 Albert Bridge Road, Belfast BT5 46X Tel: 0232 458597

Ulster Unionist Council

Originally formed in the struggle against 'Home Rule' as a coalition of Liberals and Conservatives, this party is dedicated to remaining British and *not* uniting with the Irish Republic. But it wants to see less direct rule from England.

Ulster Unionist Council, 3 Glengall Street, Belfast BT12 5AE Tel: 0232 324601

Non-Party Political Organizations

Electoral Reform Society, 6 Chancel Street, Blackfriars, London SE1 0UU Tel: 01 928 9407, is a pressure group favouring a single transferable vote.

The Green Alliance, 60 Chandos Place, London WC2N 4HE Tel: 01 836 0341, works to persuade each of the political parties to become aware of environmental issues by lobbying and information. Membership is by invitation only but the public can alert this organization to environmental issues which should be taken up with politicians.

The 300 Group, 9 Poland Street, London SW1V 3DG Tel: 01 734 3457, a cross-party group to help women to get into parliament. M&H, assists in building the necessary skills.

Government Departments

One seasoned campaigner claimed that the great advantage of the British system of government was that there was so much confusion and overlap that on any issue he could approach at least a dozen different departments. Here are the addresses of those departments; defining which does what to whom is more than there is space for - but we all know who pays. I wish you luck in approaching them.

Board of Inland Revenue, Somerset House, The Strand, London WC2R 1LB Tel: 01 438 6622

British Coal Board, Hobart House, 40 Grosvenor Place, London SW1X 7AE Tel: 01 235 2020

Countryside Commission, John Dower House, Crescent Place, Cheltenham, Glos GL50 3RA Tel: 0242 521381

Countryside Commission for Scotland, Battleby, Redgorton, Perth PH1 3EW Tel: 0738 27921

Crafts Council, 8 Waterloo Place, London SW1Y 4AT Tel: 01 930 4811

Department of Education and Science, Elizabeth House, 39 York Road, London SE1 7PH Tel: 01 934 9000

Department of Employment, Caxton House, Tothill Street, London SW1 9NF Tel: 01 213 5551/3000

Department of Energy, Thames House South, Millbank, London SW1P 4QJ Tel: 01 211 3000

Department of the Environment, 2 Marsham Street, London SW1P 3EB Tel: 01 212 3434

Department of Health and Social Security, Alexander Fleming House, London SE1 6BY Tel: 01 407 5522

Department for National Savings, Charles House, 375 Kensington High Street, London W14 8QH Tel: 01 605 9300

Department of Trade and Industry, 1/19 Victoria Street, London SW1H 0ET Tel: 01 215 7877

Department of Transport, 2 Marsham Street, London SW1P 3EB Tel: 01 212 3434

Forestry Commission, 231 Corstorphine Road, Edinburgh EH12 7AT Tel: 031 334 0303

Health and Safety Executive, St Hugh's House, Stanley Precinct, Bootle L20 3QY Tel: 051 951 4000

HM Customs and Excise, King's Beam House, Mark Lane, London EC3R 7HE Tel: 01 626 1515

HM Treasury, Treasury Chambers, Parliament Street, London SW1P 3AG Tel: 01 270 3000

Home Office, 50 Queen Anne's Gate, London SW1H 9AT Tel: 01 213 3000

Land Registry, 32 Lincoln's Inn Fields, London WC2A 3PH Tel: 01 405 3488

London Regional Transport, 55 Broadway, London SW1H 0BD Tel: 01 222 5600

Lord Chancellor's Department, Trevelyan House, 30 Great Peter Street, London SW1P 2BY Tel: 01 210 8500

Manpower Services Commission, Moorfoot, Sheffield S1 4PQ Tel: 0742 753275

Meteorological Office, London Road, Bracknell, Berks RG12 2SZ Tel: 0344 420242

Ministry of Agriculture, Fisheries and Food, 3-10 Whitehall Place, London SW1A 2HH Tel: 01 270 8080

Ministry of Defence, Main Building, Whitehall, London SW1A 2HB Tel: 01 218 9000

National Economic Development Office, 21-24 Millbank Tower, Millbank, London SW1P 4QX Tel: 01 211 3100/6198

National Radiological Protection Board, Chilton, Didcot, Oxon OX11 0RQ Tel: 0235 831600

Nature Conservancy Council, Northminster House, Peterborough PE1 1UA Tel: 0733 40345

Northern Ireland Office, Whitehall, London SW1A 2AZ Tel: 01 210 6470 *and* Stormont Castle, Belfast BT4 5T Tel: 0232 63011

Prime Minister's Office, 10 Downing Street, London SW1A 2AA Tel: 01 930 4433

Scottish Office, Dover House, Whitehall, London SW1A 2AU Tel: 01 270 3000 *and* New St Andrew's House, St James Centre, Edinburgh EH1 3TD Tel: 031 556 8400

United Kingdom Atomic Energy Authority, 11 Charles II Street, London SW1Y 4QP Tel: 01 930 5454

Welsh Office, Crown Buildings, Cathays Park, Cardiff CF1 3NQ Tel: 0222 825111

Local Government

The relationship between central and local government is essentially the same as between husband and wife in an old-fashioned marriage: central government says what should be done; local government does it. Central government handles the broad issues - defence, international affairs. Local government deals with those which affect our daily lives - health, education, welfare, sewage, parking, libraries, consumer protection. But, true to the marriage simile, it does so within constraints placed by the appropriate department of central government, which ultimately holds the purse strings. So, predictably, local government has second-class status.

Administration

A local authority is, in theory, the epitome of government by the people for the people. Its policy is decided by local councillors who are elected from those in the area. Their work on the council is virtually unpaid and is done in their free time from other jobs. Provided they stay within the law, local authorities can more or less run themselves as they wish. However, since the 60s local politics have become dominated by party politics and the decisions of councillors increasingly made along party lines.

Councillors oversee the authority, but the day-to-day work is done by full-time staff and supervised by local government officials.

Financing Local Government

Local authorities are among Britain's largest land owners, shareholders, and employers, and the budget of the Greater London Council *alone* was, in its day, larger than that of many nations. The income for all this has two main sources - rates and taxes. Of these, rates used to be the most important, but now more than half the money spent by local councils is from government grants, out of taxes, applying the Robin Hood principle of funding the poorer boroughs out of taxes paid by those in the richer ones.

The Structure and Role of Local Authorities

The structure of local authorities in Britain was totally changed in 1974. Apart from in the major cities, there is now a basic three-tier system, which varies slightly in Scotland. (Borough councils and district councils have the same powers and functions, except that a borough is headed by a mayor and a district by a chairman.)

London
Since the abolition of the Greater London Council (GLC) the London Residuary Body has been giving back to the 32 London boroughs the powers which once belonged to the GLC. Essentially they have the powers of county and borough councils combined. The City of London is not a London borough but a separate corporation, with similar powers.

Large Cities - England
City areas like Liverpool and Manchester are under city councils which have the powers of both county and borough councils. In many cases these councils link with other authorities, in the same region, to form joint authorities for administering services like fire and the police.

Scotland
- Regional Councils - broadly similar to county councils
- District Councils - much the same as those in England and Wales borough councils
- Community Councils - very similar to town or parish councils

Grievances, Complaints and Suggestions
Local libraries have lists of the local councillors, with their home addresses and phone numbers, which can be used if you want to discuss any local issue or make a complaint. How much a councillor can, or will, do is very variable but, at the very least, he or she should be able to help you pinpoint the level of local government you need to complain to.

Unfortunately, most authorities lack a good system of dealing with complaints. So it is often a case of suiting the method to the complaint. Start with the chief officer of the department in question. Failing that, try the chairman of the relevant committee or sub-committee. There is also the local ombudsman (see below) and if local authorities break the law they can be taken to court, but most problems aren't on that scale.

Another route is to complain to your MP, who probably has experience on a local council and can help you through the maze. Also, certain local authority schemes must be approved by a government minister before they are implemented, and can be halted by a minister if he objects. If your complaint falls into one of these categories complain to the appropriate minister either directly or via your MP. Such areas include planning, housing and education, the appointment of senior officials, such as chief constables, and the making of by-laws.

The Local Ombudsman
There are three local ombudsmen who cover the whole of England between them, and one each for Scotland and Wales. They offer a free service dealing with complaints in connection with the following public bodies:
- Local Authorities - except town or parish councils, which are not under any such supervision

- Joint Planning Boards
- Water Authorities
- Police Authorities - but not a complaint against a police officer
- Inner London Education Authority (others are automatically covered by the local authority)

Before approaching an ombudsman you must try to resolve the problem yourself. So, if you have a grievance against one of these organizations your first move must be to complain to them directly. If you are still not happy, ask a councillor to take up your complaint - the local library has a list of councillors. If this produces no result ask the councillor to send your written complaint to the local ombudsman. You cannot send it yourself unless the councillor refuses to act or drags his feet.

The local ombudsmen are concerned with *injustices* created by what these organizations do, or fail to do. You cannot take a complaint to them just because you don't like what has been done, and the ombudsmen can only deal with something which occurred after 1 April 1974. There are also a number of other situations they may not handle, so it is best to get their leaflet first. Once they have your complaint it will be investigated and you may be asked for more details. If they find the complaint justified they contact the organization concerned and encourage it to put things right. But, unfortunately, the ombudsman cannot insist it does so.

Voting for Local Councillors or Members of Parliament
To vote you must be over the age of 18, be a British subject (or a citizen of the Irish Republic) and have your name on the electoral register of your local council. You can check the draft list in a public library in early December and notify the Electoral Registration Officer of the council, before 16 December, if your name is not there. The people not allowed to vote are those in prison for more than a year, those detained in psychiatric institutions, or (in parliamentary elections) peers.

Proxy votes, in which you appoint someone to vote for you, are only allowed to those working outside Britain (e.g. servicemen).

Postal votes are allowed if you cannot go to the polling station for the following reasons:
- Illness or incapacity (a doctor or nurse must vouch for this)
- Work which prevents you (e.g. long-distance lorry drivers)·
- You have moved to a new area and are not yet on the electoral register there (this only applies in parliamentary elections)
- You are engaged in religious observance that day.

Enquiries about both proxy and postal votes should be made some weeks before the election. And neither type of vote is allowed for those who are away on holiday.

Those entitled to vote are sent a numbered polling card, shortly before the election, telling them which polling station to vote at. They simply take this with them and place an 'X' by the name of the candidate they prefer. Whichever candidate gets the most votes wins.

Association of County Councils, Eaton House, 66A Eaton Square, London SW1W 9BH Tel: 01 235 1200

Association of District Councils, 9 Buckingham Gate, London SW1E 6LE Tel: 01 828 7931

Association of Metropolitan Authorities, 35 Great Smith Street, London SW1P 3BJ Tel: 01 222 8100, represents the 32 London Boroughs and 36 local authorities of other big English cities, plus the Inner London Education Authority and the City of London. It presents a unified face in pay negotiations for professions - such as the teachers - which are paid by local authorities, or in fighting government attempts at centralization. Its committees are among the most powerful in the local authority scene.

Convention of Scottish Local Authorities, Rosebery House, 9 Haymarket Terrace, Edinburgh EH12 5XZ Tel: 031 346 1222

National Association of Local Councils, 108 Great Russell Street, London WC1B 3LD Tel: 01 637 1865, is the organization for parish, town and community councils.

The Commission for Local Administration in England, 21 Queen Anne's Gate, London SW1H 9BU Tel: 01 222 5622 (for the Ombudsmen for England)

Local Ombudsman (Scotland), Princes House, 5 Shandwick Place, Edinburgh EH2 4RG Tel: 031 229 4472

Local Ombudsman (Wales), Derwen House, Court Road, Bridgend, Mid-Glamorgan CF31 1BN Tel: 0656 61325

The Open Spaces Society, 25a Bell Street, Henley-on-Thames, Oxon RG9 2BA Tel: 0491 573535 campaigns for the protection of all open spaces, such as commons, greens and public paths. RC M£M.

Tony Byrne, *Local Government in Britain*, Pelican

The Municipal Yearbook (in public libraries) lists every authority and gives a breakdown of their responsibilities.

THE LAW

European Court of Human Rights

Britain signed the European Convention for the Protection of Human Rights and Fundamental Freedoms. So British citizens have a right to appeal to the European Court of Human Rights if they are the victims of a breach of the rights set out in that convention. However, they can only apply if they have already appealed through each stage in the British legal hierarchy which is open to them, and their appeal must be made within 6 months of the last appeal decision. Written evidence is submitted, and from this the court usually tries to arbitrate without the case going to a court hearing. But it can go to trial if necessary.

European Court of Justice

This is concerned with disputes over the application of EEC rules and regulations, so it is mainly used by companies.

The British Courts

The courts of England and Wales have different names from those of Scotland, but in both cases they are arranged in a strict hierarchy which has two effects. First, it means that cases of different degrees of seriousness are tried at different levels. Second, it means that if there is an appeal against the decisions made in one court the appeal is always heard in the next court up the tree. Within some of the levels there are also

divisions which specialize in certain types of case.

The hierarchy also varies slightly according to whether it is a criminal or a civil case. Acts of Parliament always say whether something is a criminal or a civil offence. For a criminal offence someone is almost always prosecuted by the state; whereas in a civil case one citizen sues another.

Civil Courts

The Courts of Session and the High Court of Justiciary are both facets of one Supreme Court, with the same judges acting in different capacities. Two key differences are that the criminal court travels to several main cities, while the civil court does not, and there is no appeal from the criminal court to the British House of Lords, whereas you can appeal a civil case.

The Scottish system also includes specialized courts such as the Land Court; the Lyon Court and tribunals similar to those in England and Wales.

Criminal Courts

In Scottish criminal cases there is no appeal to the House of Lords.

Small Claims - England and Wales

The 'small claims' procedure, operated by the County Courts, is designed to deal with claims for damages. These can be for trespass, negligence, breach of contract and so on: for example, against a company which took your money and failed to do the work, or a dry cleaner that ruined a garment.

If you are claiming less than a certain sum (£5,000 at the time of writing) you can do so in the County Court in England and Wales. If the sum is under £500 it normally comes within the small claims procedure which is usually heard by a registrar rather than by a judge. The aim is to make the process quick and easy, so people can claim without always using a solicitor. However, it is usually advisable to get some initial advice from one even if you conduct the case yourself from there on. Remember that for the smaller claims for damages (currently up to £500) each side must pay their own costs, win or lose, unless the case is especially complex. This means that you will pay for that advice, even if you win. Also if you are claiming slightly more than £500, and you are not certain to win, it may be worth reducing your claim to £500. Then you may not need to pay the other side's legal costs if you lose. If you need legal advice and are short of money use a law centre or the Green Form Scheme operated by solicitors (see Law).

If you want to make a claim it must be made to the court in the area where the offence occurred - for example, where you bought the goods. The procedure is as follows:

- You must give the court the key facts of your claim against the company or individual, in writing.
- You also have to complete a request form asking for the case to be heard.
- You then pay a plaint fee to the court, based on the sum you are claiming.

- The court then sends a summons to the other side.
- They may then decide to accept your claim and make you an offer.
- You then have 14 days in which to tell the court whether or not you accept the offer.
- But if the trader plans to fight your claim the court will arrange an informal 'preliminary consideration', which you have to attend, and tries to get the matter settled without the full court procedure.
- If the preliminary consideration fails the case goes to arbitration.

In the arbitration the case is heard by a registrar in private, not in a court, but you can take along a witness if you wish. The registrar decides who shall win the case, and although the winner can't claim solicitor's fees he or she can claim expenses (e.g. the court fee, the cost of photocopying evidence for the court, phone calls, fares etc), so keep track of everything you spend and have this account with you - with receipts where possible - when you go to this last hearing.

Northern Ireland

In Ireland the ceiling for the small claims scheme is lower than in England and Wales (currently £300). The procedure is much the same, but the names are different; here you make an 'application for arbitration'.

Scotland

In Scotland the Sheriff Courts cover claims of up to £1,000 under the 'summary cause procedure' and solicitors' costs may be charged against the loser. Sheriff Courts have a leaflet on the details of this procedure.

Chartered Institute of Arbitrators

The Chartered Institute of Arbitrators is a body which deals purely with disputes on civil matters, which those concerned decide to take to arbitration. An arbitration is a judgement by a lawyer without the usual formalities of a court. The purpose of arbitration is to settle disputes quickly and fairly without the cost of going to law in the usual way. So many arbitrations are on the basis of written evidence alone, and when there is a hearing it has fewer formalities than a normal court. The lawyer who arbitrates is someone with experience in cases of that sort and who is chosen by the Institute of Arbitrators.

The usual form is that each side pays a registration fee, plus a further fee nearer the hearing. Whoever loses can be ordered to pay the fees for the other side, but costs are limited to that. Knowing the limits to what a case could cost - even if you lose - is designed to make legal redress more available to the ordinary person. For this reason many trade associations have codes of conduct for their members which offer arbitration to members of the public who are dissatisfied with the treatment that a complaint has received and want to take things further. Each trade association which operates such a scheme has its own agreement with the Institute, and in many cases the trade association bears the bulk of the cost of the arbitration. Some codes of practice allow only written evidence to be submitted,

while others may allow a hearing or even an on-site inspection. In terms of speed, cheapness and ease, arbitration has much to offer, but anyone considering arbitration should be aware of the following facts:

- Arbitration is an alternative to going to a court, such as the Small Claims Court. The important difference is that the arbitrator's decision is *final* and both sides are bound by it; there is no appeal precedure - except in very rare circumstances. So you lose some of the rights of appeal which would exist if the case were heard in court.
- Even when the trade association subsidizes the cost of arbitration it could still run you into costs of three figures - though only just.
- Under most arbitration schemes all the evidence is in writing. You get no chance to put your case face to face. This saves the time and possible upset of going to court, but unless you are very good at putting your points in writing (or get good help with it) most companies have an advantage over you, as they probably do have someone who is experienced in putting their case.
- Because codes of conduct can draw up terms of reference which limit the evidence you can use, you may be prevented from putting strong points on your side.

A copy of the general rules used in arbitrations can be obtained from the institute: **Chartered Institute of Arbitrators**, 75 Cannon Street, London EC4N 5BH Tel: 01 236 8761

Jury Service

To sit on a jury you must be on the voting register and have lived in Britain or the Channel Isles or Isle of Man for 5 years. And you must not have been a barrister, advocate, solicitor, policeman (woman), clergyman, prison official or probation officer within the past 10 years. Nor may you have been sentenced to prison within the past 10 years - and those sentenced to 5 or more years in prison are disqualified for life, as are judges and JPs.

If someone who is ineligible or disqualified sits on a jury it is a serious offence punishable with a substantial fine. You can also be fined if you fail to go for jury service when summoned - and an employer who fails to release someone can be punished for contempt of court.

Payment for Service

Jurors are paid their travelling expenses, plus a laughably small sum for subsistence and loss of earnings.

Release from Jury Service

When called to a jury some professions such as midwives, MPs, vets, nurses, doctors, dentists and pharmacists can ask to be excused as of right. So can anyone who has served during the previous 2 years. You may also be excused for a 'good reason' such as exams, or a booked holiday. Whatever the reason, put it to the court as soon as you are called. If the officials do not excuse you, appeal to the judge. In an emergency, such as illness, a juror may be excused during the case and the trial may continue with fewer than 12 jurors.

Provided a person has lived in Britain for the necessary period, an inability to understand English does not bar him or her from jury service, as there is no test of language ability. But it does count as a valid reason for being excused from serving if someone requests it.

Hearing the Case
In Scotland there are 15 jurors for criminal cases. For civil cases in Scotland and all cases in the rest of Britain there are 12. In Scotland a majority verdict of 8 out of 15 is needed to convict someone.

Lawyers
In Scotland the legal system comes under the Lord Advocate; in the rest of Britain it is the Lord Chancellor. Both are government ministers, senior members of the bar and a member of the House of Commons or House of Lords.

In the British system solicitors are the vital bridge between the public and the major courts. For almost all High Court cases they recommend, and work with, a barrister (advocate in Scotland) and only he or she may take the case through the courts - unless someone wishes to defend themselves. But in county and magistrates' courts and in tribunals solicitors represent the client in court. At all levels, from the magistrates' courts to an appeal in the House of Lords, anyone may do without lawyers and defend themselves, though the intricacies of the legal system make this far harder to do than you might suppose.

Finding a Solicitor
In Scotland you can ring the Law Society or look for a solicitor in the Directory of Services which they publish annually and is in most public libraries. For the rest of Britain there is a Solicitor's Regional Directory in libraries, courts and town halls, or you can ask a Citizens Advice Bureau. The ways of finding solicitors who do Legal Aid work are listed on page 483. Whatever method you choose, it makes a big difference if you choose someone who specializes in whatever you want that person to do. A run-of-the-mill solicitor may take very much longer to convey a house than a firm which does it all the time, but charge no less, and in some cases using someone with experience in a particular field of law is essential to have any good chance of winning the case.

Fees
In Scotland many solicitors charge nothing for the first interview and they are allowed to advertise this fact. They are also unusual in accepting payment by most major credit cards. The Scottish Law Society also publishes recommendations on fees, but these fees are not set fees, just guidelines. There are no guidelines in the rest of Britain and solicitors can charge anything they like. As some cost well over £100 an hour, the Law Society advises that people should always ask what a solicitor charges. The easiest way is to ask a clerk or secretary before even booking the first appointment. But many solicitors are taking part in a Law Society scheme whereby they only charge a token sum (about £5) for a half-hour first interview. Having had an initial interview, a client should *always* ask a solicitor for an estimate of what it will cost if he or she goes ahead with the case. You can also ask the solicitor to let you know if, as the case progresses, it looks as if the cost will exceed the estimate. It is wise to put this request in writing and ask the solicitor to confirm that he or she will do this, making clear that if it costs too much you may have to withdraw.

Those who cannot afford a solicitor in the normal way can go to a Law Centre (see Law) or use Legal Aid (see Law).

Complaints
In Scotland complaints against a solicitor should be sent to the Law Society of Scotland. In the rest of Britain complaints against solicitors are dealt with by the Solicitors Complaints Bureau (Portland House, Stag Place, London SW1E 5BL) set up by the Law Society. They will look into complaints about delays in dealing with your case, failure to handle your money properly, dishonesty and other unprofessional conduct. If a solicitor has been negligent the situation is slightly different as you may be able to bring a case against him, and obtain compensation. So the Bureau will put you in touch with a solicitor who will give you a free 1-hour interview in which to discuss the case.

The Bureau has a free leaflet on the complaints procedure and Citizens Advice Bureaux will help with such a complaint. Under the 1985 Administration of Justice Act the Bureau was given the power to make a solicitor who has done shoddy work either redo it correctly without further charge, or refund money which he has already been paid, or pay for another solicitor to complete the case.

Supporting Organizations and Pressure Groups
Amnesty International, 5 Roberts Place, London EC1 0EJ Tel: 01 251 8371 - campaigns for the release of prisoners of conscience.

Council on Tribunals, 7th Floor, 22 Kingsway, London WC2B 6LE Tel: 01 936 7045 - is the advisory body to the government on tribunals and public enquiries. It will also look into individual complaints about the procedure of tribunals - but it is not an appeals body.

Court of Protection, Stewart House, 24 Kingsway, London WC2B 6JX Tel: 01 405 4300 - administers the estates of those mentally unable to do so.

Howard League for Penal Reform, 322 Kennington Park Road, London SE11 4PP Tel: 01 735 3317 - campaigns for reform of the system of sentences and maintains contacts with both offenders and the victims of crime. M£5-17, M, sae.

Immigration Appellate Authorities, Thanet House, 232 Strand, London WC2R 1DA Tel: 01 353 8060 - hears appeals on immigration decisions.

Industrial Tribunals are independent legal bodies set up to hear cases related to most aspects of employment. A senior barrister is chairman and there are two lay advisers who sit with him.

Judge Advocate General's Office, 22 Kingsway, London WC2B 6LE Tel: 01 430 5335 is the department which provides Judge Advocates for courts-martial.

Judicial Committee of the Privy Council is the final court of appeal from the courts in the British dominions and colonies, such as Australia, New Zealand, Malaysia and Jamaica.

Lands Tribunal, 48-49 Chancery Lane, London WC2A 1JR Tel: 01 936 7200 - decides issues relating to the cost of land, compensation for compulsory purchase, and rating appeals.

Law Centres Federation, Duchess House, 18-19 Warren Street, London W1P 5DB Tel: 01 387 8570 is the head office for some 50 law centres around Britain which offer free legal advice to those who need it. They are staffed by both lawyers and experienced non-lawyers and specialize in the areas of personal law such as housing, welfare rights, juvenile crime, employment - and do not cover things like divorce, conveyancing or commercial work. The amount of help a centre gives varies from one-off advice to representation in court. The Federation or your local library can tell you of your nearest Law Centre. Most operate on a walk-in basis, but those who are unable to get to a centre, for example because of illness, can ask for a visit. The Federation also sells a range of publications.

Law Commission, Conquest House, 37-38 John Street, Theobalds Road, London WC1N 2BQ Tel: 01 242 0861 - reviews law reform in England and Wales.

The Law Society (113 Chancery Lane, London WC2A 1PL Tel: 01 242 1222) sets the professional standards solicitors must keep to and administers a compensation fund for those who suffer loss through defaulting solicitors. There is a similar fund in Scotland. Unlike the Law Society in London, the **Law Society of Scotland** (The Law Society's Hall, 26 Drumsheugh Gardens, Edinburgh EH3 7YR Tel: 031 226 7411) will deal with public enquiries. It cannot give legal advice but it will answer questions of fact and direct people to where they can find help. It also publishes clear readable guides as to what to do in many common situations, such as when someone dies, or when buying a house.

Lay Observer, Royal Courts of Justice, The Strand, London WC2A 2LL Tel: 01 936 6000/6695 - investigates complaints made by members of the public about how the Law Society has handled complaints against solicitors.

Legal Action Group, 242 Pentonville Road, London N1 9UN Tel: 01 833 2931/2/3 - RC, works to improve legal services, laymen representing themselves might find their books useful. Does not give legal advice but publishes a directory of legal advice and law centres throughout the UK.

The Lord Chancellor's Department, Trevelyan House, 30 Great Peter Street, London SW1P 2BB Tel: 01 210 8500 - administers most of the legal system of England and Wales, bar certain tribunals which come under other government departments.

National Council for Civil Liberties, 21 Tabard Street, London SE1 4LA Tel: 01 403 3888 - lobbies government and advises individuals on issues of civil liberty. Useful leaflets and books on a wide range of legal matters from maternity rights to nuclear power. M&M, L, B, sae.

The Northern Ireland Court Service, 5/18 19-21 Floors, Windsor House, 9-15 Bedford Street, Belfast BT2 7LT Tel: 0232 228594 - covers both the courts in Northern Ireland and the legal aid scheme.

The Office of the Social Security Commissioners, Harp House, 83 Farringdon Street, London EC4A 4DH Tel: 01 353 5145 - hears appeals against entitlement to benefits after they have failed in an appeal to the Social Security Appeals Tribunal or the Medical Appeals Tribunal. Appeals forms available direct.

Official Solicitor to the Supreme Court, Penderel House, 287 High Holborn, London WC1V 7HP Tel: 01 936 6000 officially acts as guardian for children or those needing guardianship, and also monitors the cases of those admitted to prison for contempt of court.

Pension Appeals Tribunal, 48-49 Chancery Lane, London WC2A 1JR Tel: 01 936 7034 - hears appeals against DHSS decisions relating to war pensions, the disabled, or widows and children.

Public Trustee Office, Stewart House, 24 Kingsway, London WC2B 6JX Tel: 01 405 4300 - this body can be appointed to act as trustee, in a will, and administers estates and funds.

Special Commissioners for Income Tax, Turnstile House, 98 High Holborn, London WC1V 6LQ Tel: 01 438 6622 - hears appeals against tax assessments, usually after referral from the revenue, but an individual may ask for a hearing.

VAT Tribunals, 15-17 Great Marlborough Street, London W1V 2AP Tel: 01 437 6337

THE MEDIA AND THE ARTS

Advertising

Two sets of rules govern what appears in advertisements. First, they are controlled by a whole range of laws - for example, they may not break the Race Relations Act, infringe copyright or libel someone. Second, there is the British Code of Advertising Practice (BCAP) which establishes the rules to which every advertisement must keep. This is a self-regulatory code agreed among all those involved, and applies to every kind of printed advertisement - in newspapers, magazines, on posters, on documents put through your door - and to those in the cinema, and on video.

The code is regularly reviewed and amended, in line with public feeling, and copies of it are available in libraries and Citizens Advice Bureaux. Basically, in addition to being legal, an advertisement must be:
- decent (i.e. it must respect accepted UK standards of propriety)
- honest (i.e. it must present facts clearly and not exploit consumers' lack of knowledge or experience)
- truthful (in all respects it must be accurate, unambiguous, not exaggerate or omit relevant facts)
- safe (i.e. it should not show or advocate dangerous behaviour)
- harmless to children (i.e. must contain nothing which could harm them physically, mentally or morally, or exploit their credulity or loyalty)
- fair (i.e. not make unfair comparisons with competitors, or denigrate them, or exploit the goodwill of a trademark).

There is also a British Code of Sales Promotion and Practice (BCSPP) which covers promotional lotteries, competitions, and so on. Both codes are administered by the **Advertising Standards Authority (ASA),** Brook House, 2-16 Torrington Place, London WC1E 7HN Tel: 01 580 5555, which is funded by the industry, but independent of it. It handles all complaints about breaches, except those on radio and television - which are dealt with by the IBA (see page 653).

Complaints

Complaints to the ASA should be made in writing; if possible, send a copy of the advertisement or exact details of where and when it appeared. If the secretariat feel a breach of the codes has been committed - the advertiser is asked to withdraw, or amend, the advertisement, and undertake not to repeat the breach. If this fails the branches of the media carrying the advertisement are asked to block it - which they do. Details of complaints, both upheld and rejected, are given in an ASA bulletin. Reading it you'll find even well-known companies make totally false claims.

The ASA has a useful leaflet on the do's and don'ts of complaining. It emphasizes that they deal only with the *content* of advertisements and promotions. If you object to anything else it isn't their problem - so don't write to them because you think drink shouldn't be advertised, or because an advertised washing machine develops a fault.

The Arts

The arts, like almost every other area of British life, have a surfeit of administrative bodies. At the top there is the **Arts Council** 105 Piccadilly, London W1V 0AU Tel: 01 629 9495 through which government money is channelled to Scottish and Welsh Arts Councils, and to 12 Regional Arts Associations. Money is also channelled into the associations by local councils, the British Film Institute, the Crafts Council and industry.

Most arts organizations supported by these bodies are registered charities and anyone starting an arts project should investigate the benefits of this through the **Charities Commission** (Registration of Charities Department, St Alban's House, 60 Haymarket, London SW1Y 4QX Tel: 01 210 4405). In addition to support for arts groups, all these organizations may award grants and bursaries to individuals - but applications usually have deadlines.

British Broadcasting Corporation (BBC)

The BBC is established under Royal Charter, licensed by the Home Secretary and funded by licence fees paid by the public, and must present audited accounts to parliament. The powers of the BBC are vested in 12 governors, mainly from outside broadcasting, appointed by the Queen in Council, on the recommendation of the Prime Minister. But the powers are exercised by a permanent staff headed by the Director General. In Scotland, Wales and Northern Ireland responsibility for the policy and content of BBC programmes is shared with their National Broadcasting Councils, each headed by a BBC governor and staffed by BBC appointees. A series of advisory councils also cover different subjects and areas.

Ceefax from the BBC

Ceefax, Room 7013, BBC Television Centre, Wood Lane, London W12 7RJ Tel: 01 743 8000 is a 600-page .

news and on-screen information and entertainment service, obtainable on any television with a teletext decoder, and offers up-to-the-minute news, and financial, travel and consumer information. It also gives subtitles to an inceasing number of TV programmes (for those with hearing problems) and has a Telesoftware service giving computer programs and information for users of the BBC Microcomputer.

Complaints About Subject Matter

If you want to complain about anything you don't like on the BBC ring Television Centre, Broadcasting House, or Bush House, as appropriate. A duty officer will note your complaint, and a daily log of complaints is passed on to the Board of Management and heads of department. If you want a reply you must write to the Head of Programme Correspondence at Broadcasting House (see opposite), who handles all written comments, whether praise, complaint or suggestion, for both radio and television. From there your comment may, or may not, be referred to the programme makers.

Frequencies

The frequencies on which different services are transmitted vary with the transmitter which relays them. BBC Engineering publishes booklets listing all domestic radio and TV transmitters and advising on reception. They can be obtained from **BBC Engineering Information,** Broadcasting House, London W1A 1AA Tel: 01 972 5040. There is also a government booklet 'How to Improve TV and Radio Reception', obtainable from a post office, covering both BBC and independent stations. Devotees of the World Service, who want to know transmission times, can subscribe to London Calling from P.O. Box 76, Bush House, Strand, London WC2B 4PH Tel: 01 240 3456.

> There is a new radio data system by which an inaudible digital signal is now transmitted with broadcasts. This signal can be read by specially equipped radios and allows them to home in on a particular channel and display data about the programme being transmitted, so by-passing normal tuning in.

Publications

BBC books, journals, language courses and computer software are available from booksellers, but also from BBC bookshops at Broadcasting House, Television Centre and Bush House. Mail order books and computer software can be obtained - post extra - from **BBC Books,** P.O. Box 234, London SE1 3TH Tel: 01 580 4468.

Radio Weather Forecasts

The usual weekday times for general forecasts are: on Radio 4 Long Wave 06.00, 06.55, 07.55, 08.57, 12.55, 17.55, 22.29, 00.10 (VHF: 05.55); for shipping forecasts they are: 05.55, 13.55, 17.50, 00.33.

Warnings of dangerous conditions - fog, icy roads,

etc - are broadcast rapidly on Radios 1 and 2 and as soon as possible on Radios 3 and 4. When necessary, there are fog alerts on Radio 2 after every news summary on the hour.

SOS Messages
Free messages seeking relatives of anyone *dangerously ill* are transmitted, after medical confirmation of the emergency. The broadcast is made once only, either before the 07.00 or 18.00 news. Requests to Broadcasting House in London, Glasgow, Cardiff or Belfast.

Tickets for BBC Programmes
Anyone may ask for free tickets for any BBC show which has an audience. Apply in writing 6 weeks before the date, giving the type of show you want and the ages of any children in the party. But be warned - many shows are recorded months before transmission, so your favourite may not be available. Send a sae to **Radio Ticket Unit**, BBC, London W1A 4WW Tel: 01 580 4468 or **TV Ticket Unit**, BBC, London W12 7SB Tel: 01 743 8000.

Writing for the BBC
You may find it helpful to read the BBC publication 'Writing for the BBC'. Typed scripts (with a sae) should be sent to the Script Editor of the appropriate section - Radio Light Entertainment, Television Drama, or whatever. But scripts do get lost, so keep a copy yourself.

BBC Radio, Broadcasting House, Portland Place, London W1A 1AA Tel: 01 580 4468

BBC Television, Television Centre, Wood Lane, London W12 7RJ Tel: 01 743 8000

BBC World Service, Bush House, London WC2B 4PH Tel: 01 240 3456

Broadcasting Complaints Commission
The **Broadcasting Complaints Commission** (Grosvenor House, 35-37 Grosvenor Gardens, London SW1W 0BS Tel: 01 630 1966) was set up under the 1981 Broadcasting Act to handle complaints from those who felt any broadcast had infringed their privacy, or treated them unfairly. It covers all sound, television and cable programmes, including advertisements and teletext transmissions and also programmes broadcast by the BBC's External Services. All it lacks is teeth.

Having assessed your complaint, they send copies of their adjudication to both you and the company concerned, and the company may be instructed to publish the finding in the *Radio Times* or *TV Times*. The Commission has no other sanctions and cannot insist on either an apology or compensation.

Alternatively, if you feel you have been unfairly treated by programmes you have appeared in, or been approached by, complain to the editor of the programme, or to the head of the company concerned. But, before you complain about money, remember that the basic rule is that if a programme wants to use you and you want a fee, you must make this clear from the moment they contact you. The reporter, or researcher, in question usually has no authority to agree fees and will have to put your request to an editor. In some cases a fee will be impossible; in others it could be substantial. And if you don't want to appear make this equally clear.

Broadcasting Support Services (BSS)
BSS (252 Western Avenue, London W3 6XJ Tel: 01 992 5522) is the back-up service which works for both BBC and the independent companies, operating helplines after broadcasts and supplying follow-up literature through their P.O Box 7 and 4000 address. They keep fact sheets for some while after any broadcast, so it is always worth asking for the sheet you forgot to write in for.

Independent Broadcasting Authority (IBA)
The **Independent Broadcasting Authority (IBA)**, 70 Brompton Road, London SW3 1EY Tel: 01 584 7011, is controlled by the Broadcasting Act 1981 and is the governing body for independent television and independent local radio - but not for cable. It is funded entirely through receiving a share of the advertising revenue from the companies under it. It:
- selects and appoints programme companies (e.g. Central, Thames)
- supervises programme planning
- controls advertising
- transmits programmes.

Complaints about programmes on independent channels can be sent to anyone involved, from the IBA (see below), down to those who made the programme.

Independent Television Companies
Anglia Television, Anglia House, Norwich NR1 3JG Tel: 0603 615151

Border Television, Television Centre, Carlisle CA1 3NT Tel: 0228 25101

Central Television, Central House, Broad Street, Birmingham B1 2JP Tel: 021 643 9898

Channel 4, 60 Charlotte Street, London W1P 2AX Tel: 01 631 4444

Channel Television, Television Centre, Rouge Bouillon, St Helier, Jersey, Channel Isles Tel: 0534 73999

Grampian Television, Queen's Cross, Aberdeen AB9 2XJ Tel: 0224 646464

Granada Television, Granada TV Centre, Manchester M60 9EA Tel: 061 832 7211

HTV Wales, Television Centre, Culverhouse Cross, Cardiff CF5 6XJ Tel: 0222 590590

HTV West, Television Centre, Bath Road, Bristol BS4 3HG Tel: 0272 778366

ITN (Independent Television News Ltd), ITN House, 48 Wells Street, London W1P 4DE Tel: 01 637 2424

London Weekend Television (LWT), South Bank Television Centre, London SE1 9LT Tel: 01 261 3434

Scottish Television, Cowcaddens, Glasgow G2 3PR Tel: 041 332 9999

Thames Television, Thames Television House, 306-316 Euston Road, London NW1 3BB Tel: 01 387 9494

TSW (Television South West), Derry's Cross, Plymouth PL1 2SP Tel: 0752 663322

TV-AM, Breakfast Television Centre, Hawley Crescent, London NW1 8EF Tel: 01 267 4300

TVS (Television South), Television Centre, Northam, Southampton SO9 5HZ Tel: 0703 634211

Tyne Tees Television, Television Centre, City Road, Newcastle upon Tyne NE1 2AL Tel: 091 261 0181

Ulster Television, Havelock House, Ormeau Road, Belfast BT7 1EB Tel: 0232 328 122

Yorkshire Television, The Television Centre, Leeds LS3 1JS Tel: 0532 438283

Television and Radio Advertising

Advertising is limited by law to an average of 6 minutes an hour on TV, and 9 minutes an hour on radio (i.e. some ad breaks may be less, some more, provided the total keeps within the limit). The content of advertisements is controlled by the 1981 Broadcasting Act and by various consumer acts. The IBA has a duty to ensure that advertisements meet the standards laid down. So all advertising scripts must be approved before transmission, and those unsuitable for children may not be transmitted before 9 pm.

Complaints about advertisements should be sent to the IBA (previous page), and if the codes have been breached the advertisement will be withdrawn. The IBA is ultimately responsible to parliament for everything transmitted on independent television. So if complaining to the IBA doesn't get results, the next step is your MP.

Local Radio

As stations tend to come and go it isn't practical to list them, but the BBC and IBA will supply a list of their respective local stations. Some, such as Capital Radio, PO Box 958, London NW1 3DR Tel: 01 388 1288, offer a wide range of local services.

National Viewer's and Listener's Association

The **National Viewer's and Listener's Association** (Ardleigh, Colchester, Essex CO7 7RH Tel: 0206 230123) is the pressure group started by Mrs Mary Whitehouse. If you object to what you see or hear on TV or radio you can write to her. You don't have to be a member to complain. The organization is avowedly Christian and anti-humanist (M£L).

The Press Council

If you have been wronged by something printed in a newspaper, magazine or periodical, you should complain to the editor. You may also complain in writing to the director of the **Press Council,** 1 Salisbury Square, London EC4Y 8AE Tel: 01 353 1248, sending a copy of the offending article and of any correspondence between yourself and the paper. The Council will investigate and if they find that an offence has been committed, they can insist that the publication publishes the details of the judgement against them, in a position of reasonable prominence.

If a publication has broken the law the alternative is to take it to court - though this is prohibitively expensive. However, if you take the matter to the Press Council you can be asked to agree not to go to law if the editor accepts the Council's investigation. A leaflet giving all the details on making complaints is available from the Council.

THE MEDICAL SERVICES

The Health Service

The **Department of Health and Social Security** is under the Secretary of State for Social Services.

Below that there are 14 **Regional Health Authorities** which allocate money to the District Health Authorities under them.

The **District Health Authorities** are responsible for the hospitals and other medical services in their area.

Each District Health Authority usually has a **Community Health Council** (CHC) with members from both the local authority and voluntary organizations to bridge the gap between the public and the health service. Anyone may attend their meetings and, if you are having problems with the local health service, they are there to give advice and help with complaints. In Northern Ireland the equivalents are District Committees.

Family Practitioner Committees (FPCs) are independent bodies which may not cover the same area as the District Health Authority. NHS general practitioners, dentists, pharmacists and opticians are all under contract direct to their FPC.

Joint Consultative Committees are the link between the District Health Authority and the local authorities in the same areas, and voluntary authorities are also included. Sub-groups within these committees cover particular problems such as the mentally ill.

The Scottish health service is under the **Scottish Home and Health Department,** which comes under the Secretary of State for Scotland.

Scotland is divided into **Health Boards** which administer all levels of health care and have links to both local authorities and local Health Councils.

The Family Practitioner Committees are called **General Practitioner Committees.**

Finding your Local Health Authorities

The naming of the various levels of the health authority might have been designed to make it hard to find them. They are listed in the telephone book under the name of the region, district and so on, which is fine if you know the name. Most of us don't because, confusingly, health service boundaries aren't usually the same as those of the local authorities. The best source of this information is the local public library, or your GP's receptionist.

Using the Health Service

The health service has a mass of detailed rules and regulations. Those who want to know the full details of any aspect of it will find the book *A Patient's Guide to the National Health Service* (Which? and the Patients Association) invaluable.

Dentistry

The best way to choose a dentist is to ask around, and find someone who is known to be good at the sort of dentistry you want - whether it's treating children or making dentures. Failing that, you can find one in the same way as a GP (see right) but using the Dental List. However, you don't sign on with a dentist as you do with a GP, and if you are not happy with any treatment you can go to another dentist for a second opinion.

Strictly speaking, each time you start a new course of treatment, you must make it clear to a dentist that you want to be treated on the NHS. If he or she agrees to treat you on the NHS you may be asked to sign a form and give your NHS number; the dentist is then obliged to give you a course of treatment on the NHS to make you 'dentally fit'. After that the 'contract' ceases and next time you should go through the whole routine again. Make sure you get the dentist's agreement *before* you sit in the chair.

Dentists' Charges
Dentistry on the NHS is not free; you are simply charged a special scale of fees. Dentists can ask for payment before a course of treatment starts, and may also charge for an appointment a patient misses without notice.

Before certain work is done a dentist must get permission from the **Dental Estimates Board (DEB)**. If permission is refused the dentist may appeal, to the FPC, against the DEB decision within 4 weeks.

Free dental treatment is given in certain circumstances, but you must ask the dentist before he starts treatment.

Emergency Dentistry
If an NHS dentist sees you as an emergency out of hours there is no extra charge. But even if your dentist does NHS work, a stand-in on an emergency rota may not - so check. Some areas have an emergency service set up by the health authority - the local hospital or police may know the number. In London, **Capital Radio Helpline** is another source.

Eye Treatment

Finding an Optician
You don't need to be referred by a GP to have your eyes checked, nor do you have to sign on with anyone. Post offices, libraries and Yellow Pages all have lists of ophthalmic opticians and you can use whoever you wish.

Who Does What
The terms used in this field of medicine have been changing, so any of the following may be involved in eye treatment.

- A **dispensing optician** makes up spectacles.
- An **ophthalmic medical practitioner** is a doctor who treats eye diseases, tests eyesight and prescribes lenses.
- An **ophthalmic optician** tests eyesight, looks for eye diseases and prescribes lenses.
- An **ophthalmologist** (once called an oculist) is a senior doctor specializing in eye diseases and may also be an eye surgeon. You have to be referred to an ophthalmologist.
- An **orthoptist** treats children's eye problems, such as squints, and works under an ophthalmologist.

General Practitioners

Changing Your GP
If you are moving, just tell your GP you are leaving and find one in the new area. Changing because you are dissatisfied is harder. First find someone you might prefer and arrange to see him or her. In these circumstances the doctor usually regards it as a one-way interview to decide if he or she will accept you, not vice versa - so try to be sure this is the right doctor. Doctors distrust patients who have fallen out with their colleagues, but one fairly acceptable reason for changing is that you want a doctor of the opposite sex to your present one.

If a new doctor will take you on, you either ask your present GP to complete a section of your medical card and then take it to your new GP or you write to the Family Practitioner Committee saying you want to change from GP A to GP B and enclosing your medical card. By the last method you may register with the new GP 14 days later - and *must* register within the month, or the whole procedure has to start again.

Finding a GP
The best way to find a GP is through neighbours who can give you the low-down on the doctors in the area. Failing that, your local library, main post office or CAB should have a Medical List giving the doctors in your Family Practitioner Committee's area. Having found some reasonably close to your home, which you can reach by the transport available, you can check their sex, qualifications and various other details in the Medical Directory in the reference library - letters after their names are explained in the abbreviations section of this book.

Before arranging to register with any doctor it is worth ringing his receptionist to ask about any points which matter to you, for example:
- Is it a group practice? In these, doctors usually stand in for each other when away, so you are always seen by someone you know, whereas in a solo practice the stand-ins may constantly change.
- What are the surgery hours? (Saturday and evening surgeries are becoming less common.)
- Is there an appointments system?
- Does the doctor deliver babies - if you want a home delivery?
- Does the doctor deal with contraception?
- Does the practice hold any preventive clinics e.g. 'Well Woman'?

Registering with a GP
Having chosen a doctor, ask to see him or her and explain why. But, *don't* take your medical card, or the receptionist may take it from you on arrival. If you don't like the doctor it is embarrassing to have to ask for it back, but if you do like him or her you can always post it. Fill in part A of the card before sending it to the doctor, who then registers you formally, via the Family Practitioner Committee (FPC). If your doctor ceases to practise, you are automatically registered with his or her successor. If you don't want this you must tell the FPC within 14 days. The committee will also supply a new medical card if your

old one is lost.

A doctor can refuse to accept a patient or remove a patient from his or her list, and need give no reason. But if you can't persuade a doctor to accept you, you should tell the FPC, which will allocate one.

Prescriptions

Most people have to pay for their prescriptions, but there are many exceptions to this such as pensioners, those under 16, pregnant women, those who have had a baby in the last 12 months (even if it was stillborn), also those on low incomes and with certain medical conditions. Form P11 from the Post Office gives the details.

Hearing Problems

Hearing Aids

If you need a hearing aid your family doctor will refer you to a consultant. The NHS loans hearing aids, free of charge, to those who need them and also supplies batteries and accessories and sees to their servicing. The range of NHS aid has been extended and now meets most needs.

If you have a problem the **Royal National Institute for the Deaf (RNID)** (see In Sickness) will test aids without charge and gives free advice on all aspects of deafness both by post and to personal callers. You can also make an appointment to see their range of aids. The RNID also has information on devices which make it easier to hear the telephone, listen to the television and so on, and these can be provided on the NHS if the local authority social services decide you need them.

You don't need any referral to buy a hearing aid privately. But, despite the glowing advertisements, they vary greatly in price and performance. *It is never wise to buy one without trying it first or getting medical advice* - you could be wasting a lot of money.

Patients' Rights

Children under 16 can be treated in an emergency, without their parents' consent, if the parents cannot be reached or refuse consent to treatment which would save the child's life. Otherwise consent must be obtained from the parent or from the child if it is able to understand. However, a girl under 16 may obtain contraceptive advice provided the doctor is sure she understands what is involved, and has tried to persuade her to tell her parents.

Confidentiality is a difficult issue. In theory, the information on a patient's medical record can only be passed on if the patient agrees. In practice, doctors pass it on to other health care professionals when they believe it is in the patient's best interests. However, since AIDS, they are less likely to release information to organizations like insurance companies or to prospective employers unless the patient specifically agrees.

Patients must **consent to treatment,** but consent can be either implied or expressed. If you go to a chest X-ray unit you imply that you agree to a chest X-ray. But if you are about to have an operation you must express consent by signing a form agreeing to it. The consent form names the operation and then has some general words that mean the doctor is free to do whatever else seems to be necessary

to relieve the condition. Most people are happy to accept this wording. But if an operation might reveal a condition - such as breast cancer - which could be treated by surgery *or* by medication it isn't so easy. The doctor might choose surgery - since you are already on the table - but *you* might prefer medication. The answer is to tell the doctor how you feel *before* signing the form, and agree with him a change of wording which will leave the surgeon free to act in a sudden emergency but not to do anything you don't want.

Since the doctor you agree this with won't necessarily do the operation, it is important to get this in writing not just agree it in words. Some doctors and nurses may not like this, but it can be done, and there is no reason why anyone should sign away their rights over their own body. Nor do good doctors want them to. Private patients can insist on having a particular doctor to operate and they should cross out any wording which allows a change of doctors, except in an emergency.

Patients may *leave* a hospital whenever they want - unless they are held for certain mental illnesses or have a notifiable disease like cholera. But if you leave before the doctors advise it, you will be asked to sign a form saying you are no longer the hospital's responsibility. You don't have to sign it to leave, and it is best not to sign it if you have a serious complaint against the hospital.

Official **medical records** belong to the Secretary of State for Social Services. Amazingly, patients have no legal right to see their own medical records, let alone change anything on them. This is one of the big problems in bringing cases for medical negligence.

If doctors want you to accept treatment which is part of **medical research** they are usually obliged to explain the treatment and get your permission. If no effective treatment exists for your condition, an experimental one may be your best chance. But ask questions and think very carefully before agreeing. You are free to say no and ask for other treatment.

Whether you are seeing a GP or a consultant in a hospital, you have a right to privacy and can ask for **medical students** not to be present and refuse to be examined by them. If a doctor (or would-be doctor) examines or treats a patient without his or her consent it is assault and civil proceedings can be brought.

A **husband** has *no* absolute right to be with his wife during labour or childbirth; it is at the consultant's discretion. So it is very important to find out the policy on this before registering with a hospital. However, if any member of staff *physically* ejected a husband it might be assault. So, in practice, politely standing firm could work, as it can if a hospital refuses to let you be with a young child. However, the situation needs careful judgement. It is one thing to stand firm against hospital staff who are throwing their weight around, but it is quite another to get in the way of responsible staff carrying out vital procedures.

Organs can only be removed after death if the donor gave written consent, or gave verbal consent in front of at least two witnesses. Also, whoever is 'lawfully in possession of the body' can authorize the organs' removal if, after reasonable enquiries, there is no reason to think the donor would have objected, or that the surviving relatives would object. If someone dies in hospital the hospital is 'lawfully in possession of the body' until the relatives claim it. In practice, the relatives are almost always asked, but it is easier for everyone if those who want to give organs carry a donor card, and if those who wish *not* to give them also carry a card saying so.

If you feel a relative is **mentally ill** and the GP is failing to recognize this, you may ask for him or her to be seen by a consultant - if necessary in the patient's own home. And the GP should arrange this.

Services Which Can Be Used
All the following services may be contacted through your GP, or via your Community Health Council.
- **Chiropody** is provided mainly for the elderly, handicapped or disabled, pregnant women and school children. Some chiropodists will come to the home. Check the qualifications of chiropodists before having treatment; the letters MChS or FChS are safeguards.
- **Day centres** will care for, and feed, special groups during the day. For example, the mentally handicapped or elderly.
- **District nurses** give nursing care in the home and can provide certain aids and equipment, such as incontinence pads.
- **Health visitors** can call at the home and advise on baby care or the care of the sick or old. They also have information on equipment you may be able to get on the NHS.
- **Home adaptations** for someone handicapped or disabled may be partly paid for by the NHS, or provided by local authority social services.
- **Laundry services** are sometimes available for those in special need.
- **Meals on wheels** will provide a hot mid-day meal to the home.
- **Speech therapy** should be available both for children with speech problems, and for adult problems like stammering or speech difficulty after a stroke.
- **Transport** to and from hospital can be provided for those not able to use public transport or where suitable transport is not available.

Complaining
You are entitled to complain if:
- a service is not provided which should be provided
- if the standard of any service is not good enough.

There are time limits for many complaints (see below), but these may be extended if you were clearly unable to complain at the proper time.

The health service is a complex organization and it is important to address your complaint to the right person. Try to start with the person concerned - there may just be a misunderstanding. If that fails try that person's immediate superior. If that too fails, start writing to those above them. The basic procedures for each section of the health service are given below; your **Community Health Council (CHC)** (address from the telephone book or public library) and local CAB are there to advise you. The DHSS

leaflet 'Comments, Suggestions and Complaints About Your Stay in Hospital' also has practical advice.

The Sour Fruits of Success
If your complaint is upheld, the person concerned may be penalized - but you don't get any compensation. All you can get is a refund of any money you spent (e.g. on incorrect dentures) and of any expenses the complaint has cost you. *But you only get these if you ask the Family Practitioner Committee at the time.* DHSS leaflets give full details - the DHSS office or CHC should have them.

Dentists
If treatment is unsatisfactory, and complaining to the dentist fails, contact the Family Practitioner Committee (see page 654) within 6 months of treatment or 8 weeks after becoming aware of the problem - whichever is soonest. Complaints about improper conduct should go to the **General Dental Council** (37 Wimpole Street, London W1M 8DQ Tel: 01 486 2171).

GPs
Complain about general services in writing to the Family Practitioner Committee (see page 654) within 8 weeks (6 weeks in Scotland). If the complaint is about unethical conduct complain to the **General Medical Council** (44 Hallam Street, London W1N 6AE Tel: 01 580 7642).

Hospitals
The best time to complain is usually when the trouble occurs, and the best people to complain to are the staff involved. If you aren't getting the information you need about your illness, or the treatment, you should tell the staff. Medical staff tend to use technical jargon without realizing it and genuinely believe they have given a proper explanation. But if you say you haven't understood they will usually explain more clearly.

If you have left the hospital write to the Hospital Administrator or, to the District General Manager (ask the hospital for the address). Patients, or their relatives, have a year in which to make a complaint. If your complaint is about hospital organization, complain to a senior member of staff and, failing that, to the District General Manager. Your CHC will advise on these procedures. See also the Health Service Commissioner (overleaf).

Local Authority Health Services
The right person to complain to will vary according to which department organizes the service. Talk to your CHC and, if the medical routes fail to get results, complain to your local councillor, and/or MP.

Mental Illness
Most complaints in connection with the mentally ill are made as for any other complaint against a hospital or medical staff, and relatives are allowed to complain on a patient's behalf. If these complaints fail they can be taken to the **Mental Health Act Commission** (Hepburn House, Marsham Street, London SW1P 4HW Tel: 01 211 8061). And **Mind** (see In Sickness) will advise on making complaints about the care of the mentally ill or handicapped.

Opticians

If an ophthalmic optician fails to give proper service complain to your Family Practitioner Committee. If a dispensing optician is unsatisfactory complain to the **Association of British Dispensing Opticians** (22 Nottingham Place, London W1M 4AT Tel: 01 935 7411). The right way to complain about improper conduct varies greatly with the qualifications, so consult the *Which?* book (see page 654).

Other Disciplines

The methods of complaining about chiropodists, district nurses and others slightly outside the mainstream of the system are in the *Which?* book (see page 654), but there is not space for them here.

Health Service Commissioner

If other remedies fail write to the **Health Service Commissioner** (Church House, Great Smith Street, London SW1P 3BW Tel: 01 212 7676) - Scotland and Wales have their own Commissioners (addresses from the above office). The Commissioner can investigate complaints regarding Regional Health Authorities, District Health Authorities, Family Practitioner Committees, Boards of Governors and those areas of the Health Service under them. You should write giving details of the person you are complaining about, the name of the health authority concerned, and an account of the problem and of the action you have so far taken, plus copies of any relevant letters. However, the Commissioner may not investigate complaints which involve clinical judgement - for example, whether a particular treatment was appropriate.

When Legal Action is Needed

If complaints are upheld certain penalties may be imposed on whoever was at fault, but the patient gets no compensation or damages. For these you must take the matter to a court within 3 years, and the usual case is for negligence. Medical cases are complicated and expensive, so it is essential to get good advice before starting and *only* to use a solicitor who has handled medical negligence cases before. Your CHC or Citizens Advice Bureau will help and so will the Patients Association (see In Sickness) and the organizations listed below. They may also be able to put you in touch with others who have had similar problems. This type of case is eligible for the Legal Aid and for the Green Form Scheme.

Vaccine damage is a special case. There is an established procedure for compensating for damage caused by a routine childhood vaccination. Forms are available from the **Vaccine Damage Payment Unit** at the Department of Health and Social Security (Room 112G, North Fylde Central Offices, Norcross, Blackpool FY5 3YZ Tel: 0253 856123).

Action for Victims of Medical Accident, 24 Southwark Street, London SE1 1TY Tel: 01 403 4744. This is an organization which gives preliminary advice to those who have suffered as the result of a medical accident. This includes such things as misdiagnosis, failure to treat and incorrect treatment. Its lawyers will not take a case for you but, they *will* advise on whether there is a case to be taken, and can put you in touch with lawyers experienced in this field. Send a brief outline of the problem when you write, sae

appreciated. RC.

Medical Victims Association, 137 Morriston Road, Elgin IV30 2NB Tel: 0343 41339 (for those in Scotland)

Private Medicine

The chief advantage of private medicine, over the NHS, is that with private treatment you can see a doctor of your choosing - instead of a succession of doctors, as one often gets on the NHS - and arrange the timing to suit you and your work. Doctors working in the NHS will have had their qualifications checked by the authorities. With private medicine, however, it is up to you to check that doctors are what they say they are. Surprisingly, it is legal for anyone to call himself or herself a doctor - if doctors are qualified they will be in the *Medical Register*, in your public library.

It is perfectly possible to straddle both systems. For example, a NHS doctor may be happy to deliver a baby in a private hospital or a nursing home. Equally, if you are with a NHS GP you can get a second opinion from a private doctor, or go for private health checks and screening, or have alternative medicine without it affecting your NHS status at all. You don't even have to tell your GP you are doing this - though, if another medical doctor treats you, he or she will normally notify your GP, even if you feel it is none of your GP's business.

Complaining

One disadvantage of private treatment is that you are in a much weaker position if you need to complain as there is no hierarchy to complain to. However, you do have the sanction of refusing to pay the bill (at the risk of prosecution) and private doctors do rely on their patients recommending them to others. Apart from that, you can complain to the General Medical Council (see previous page) about improper conduct or go to the courts for compensation. See also Health Insurance, in Money.

THE POLICE

The police have no central organization. Broadly speaking, they come under the Home Office, but there are 43 totally independent forces. Their boundaries roughly correspond to those of local government, and they are funded both by local and central government. The Metropolitan Police come directly under the Home Secretary, but each of the others has its own Police Authority made up of magistrates and councillors from that region.

Each force is headed by a Chief Constable and both he and his senior officers are appointed by the Police Authority, with the approval of the Home Secretary.

Most police forces do a great deal more than catching criminals, and it is worth asking your local station about extra services they offer. There is usually a crime prevention officer who will give free advice on the choice of locks and burglar prevention devices, and many forces run courses in self-defence, or cycling or road safety classes for children. Your nearest station is in the phone book under 'Police'.

EMERGENCY - always dial 999 and ask for police.
Be ready to tell them the exact address they need to come to. Dialling 999 gets a faster response than dialling the local police station, even if you know its number.

Complaints

If the complaint is about the behaviour of a particular officer make a note of the number on his or her shoulder tab, at the time, and give it in your complaint.

Any complaint can be sent, in writing, to the police station in question. If the incident was away from your home area, and you don't know which police station that would be, ask telephone directory enquiries. But, unless it is something quite trivial, it may be better to send it to the **Police Complaints Authority (PCA)** (10 Great George Street, London SW1P 3AE Tel: 01 213 5392), which is a totally independent body staffed by people who are not in the police, and never have been. It is, however, purely concerned with disciplinary action. It cannot make sure that you receive compensation.

If a complaint is about the police causing death or serious physical harm the Authority will deal with it directly. If it is not, they will forward the complaint to the police authority concerned. Police forces have departments for dealing with complaints, and officers from it are likely to visit you to discuss the complaint. If necessary, an investigating officer may even be appointed. After investigations a report is filed and (if you complained through the PCA) a copy of this will go to the authority to see if they are happy about the action which has been taken. It is then up to them to accept the report or take matters further if they feel it necessary. In rare cases, the matter may go to the Director of Public Prosecutions.

If you are wrongfully arrested, or injured by the police, or have your property damaged and want compensation, either you or your insurance company must make a claim, in writing, to the police force in question. For the other two, you yourself make the claim. These claims can be made to the station in question, but on major matters it makes sense to address them to the Chief Constable. It is then up to the force in question to assess liability and either to agree to meet your claim or negotiate a compromise sum with you, or refuse to do anything at all. There seems to be no appeals procedure, but you can ask them to review their offer, try bringing pressure to bear through a letter to the Chief Constable personally, or by contacting local councillors who are members of the Police Authority. Your local library should be able to tell you who they are. You may also be able to get advice and support from local law centres and CABx. You could even go further and contact the Home Secretary, through your MP, but there seems to be no central body which will act as final arbiter between the police and a member of the public who is seeking compensation.

You can, however, seek compensation in the courts for wrongful arrest and wrongful imprisonment, and if a policeman is found guilty of criminal assault you can be compensated by the Criminal Injuries Compensation Board.

RELIGIOUS FAITHS

The brief summaries here are not intended as a full introduction to these faiths but simply as a starting point towards understanding.

The Baha'i Faith

This faith started in 1863 when an Iranian, later called Baha'u'llah (Glory of God), announced he was the prophet of the unification of all religions. Since then it has become one of the most widespread, but least known, faiths and has a growing British following. The central belief is the oneness of all mankind, and of all religions. For Baha'is believe that the prophets of all religions have, each in turn, taught the basic truths about the one God, and added social laws suited to their period and country. They also believe that each successive prophet improves man's understanding of God. So Baha'is acknowledge the teaching of Moses, Zoroaster, Krishna, Buddha, Christ and Mohammad and see Baha'u'llah's teaching as an extension and refinement of their teachings. Equally, they expect other prophets to come in the future and extend his teaching.

Baha'is dedicate their lives to peacefully breaking down the prejudices and intolerance regarding race, class, country, sex or creed which divide man from man.

Baha'i Centre, 27 Rutland Gate, London SW7 1PD Tel: 01 584 2566
Mary Perkins and Philip Hainsworth, *The Baha'i Faith*, Ward Lock

Buddhism

The Buddha was a nobleman born on the border of India and Nepal in the sixth century BC. Through meditation he achieved a new vision of the world, and set about teaching others to achieve this too. This ideal is a state of transcendent spiritual insight and awareness, coupled with intense love and compassion towards all living things, and inexhaustible mental and spiritual energy. The Buddha (the Enlightened One) emphasized that although a monk might find it easier to reach this state it was open to anyone.

Most Buddhists are vegetarian, but not all. Tibetan Buddhists, for example, found vegetables hard to grow and vegetarianism there is restricted to the deeply devout. Equally, though most Buddhists are teetotal, there are exceptions. In the same way, Buddhist festivals, though usually set by the moon, vary from country to country.

The London Buddhist Centre, 51 Roman Road, Bethnal Green, London E2 0HU Tel: 01 981 1225
The Buddhist Society, 58 Eccleston Square, London SW1 Tel: 01 834 5888

Christianity

Christianity was started by a Jew, Jesus of Nazareth, as a movement within Judaism. His followers believed him to be the chosen one, 'Christ', which God promised to Abraham. It became a separate movement when the

Jews failed to accept him, and after his death the apostle Peter led the small group of believers. Being based on Judaism, Christianity retained the teachings of Moses and other Jewish scriptures but the Christian bible added the teachings of Jesus, as they were written down by his followers after his death, to form the New Testament or Gospel.

The key beliefs of Christianity were laid down in AD 481 when the bishops of the Christian world assembled and produced the Universal Councils. But by AD 325 the Nicene Creed had been established and it is still used, not only by churches in Britain but also by Churches of the East, such as the Greek Orthodox.

Nicene Creed (from the Alternative Service Book 1980)

> We believe in one God, the Father Almighty, maker of heaven and earth, of all that is seen and unseen.
> We believe in one Lord, Jesus Christ, the only Son of God, eternally begotten by the Father, God from God, Light from Light, true God from true God, begotten, not made, of one being with the Father. Through him all things were made. For us men and our salvation he came down from heaven; by the power of the Holy Spirit he became incarnate of the Virgin Mary, and was made man. For our sake he was crucified under Pontius Pilate; he suffered death and was buried.

> On the third day he rose again in accordance with the scriptures; he ascended into heaven and is seated on the right hand of the Father. He will come again in his glory to judge the living and the dead, and his kingdom will have no end.

> We believe in the Holy Spirit, the Lord and giver of life, who proceeds from the Father and the Son. With the Father and the Son he is worshipped and glorified. He has spoken through the Prophets.

> We believe in the holy catholic and apostolic Church. We acknowledge baptism for the forgiveness of sins. We look for the resurrection of the dead and the life in the world to come.

Although the creed may represent the beliefs which lie at the core of Christianity, each denomination tends to emphasize different elements in those beliefs, and some would add elaborations not found there. The book *Reflections - how the churches view their life and mission* (published by the British Council of Churches, 2 Eaton Gate, London SW1W 9BL) has sections written by each of the Christian denominations in Britain and is eye-opening, if only in the saddening obscurantism of some of the statements.

Anglicanism - Church of England
This is the official Church of England which separated from the Church of Rome in the sixteenth century at the instigation of Henry VIII. This separation formalized a growing feeling in England that the absolute authority of the Pope was not acceptable.

The Church of England sees itself as a reformed part of Christ's universal Church, founded by St Peter. The key points of belief are the Trinity - of God, his son Jesus and the Holy Ghost, eternal life after death, and God's forgiveness of human sins through belief in Jesus

Christ and through repentance. So it differs from other Christian Churches mainly in matters of organization For example, it rejects the authority of the Pope in moral and doctrinal matters, but has a more structured hierarchy and form of worship than many Non-conformist Churches

Admission to the Church is through baptism, which commits the individual to Christ. But each priest accepts a 'caring responsibility' for everyone in his parish whether baptized or not and this is most often expressed through marriages and funerals.

The Church of England General Synod, Church House, Great Smith Street, London SW1P 3NZ Tel: 01 222 9011

Baptists
There are various types of Baptist Church in Britain. Some are extremely strict and basically Calvinist. The main Baptist body is the Baptist Union. It has beliefs and practices very similar to the Congregationalists (see below), except that the Baptists returned to the New Testament baptism of total immersion in water to symbolize death and resurrection into a new life as a believer. As they hold that all believers are taken to God in the after-life, the emphasis is on hope.

The Baptist Union, Baptist Church House, 4 Southampton Row, London WC1B 4AB Tel: 01 405 9803

Roman Catholicism
Roman Catholicism sees itself as the Church of Christ on earth, with the Pope being in direct succession to St Peter and acting as God's spokesman on earth. At every stage the Church is the vital mediator of God's will, love and forgiveness. In contrast with Churches like the Congregationalists, which place the emphasis on the individual, the Catholic Church places the emphasis on the Church itself and the priests have an important role as channels for God's forgiveness. The Church is 'the sacrament of God's salvation', the 'sign and instrument of the coming Kingdom of God'. It does, however, recognize 'sanctification and truth in other Christian communities which have a real degree of ecclesiality and are rightly called churches' - a statement which shows that the Roman Church also judges other Churches by their priestly hierarchy, not simply by their beliefs.

The Catholic Enquiry Centre, 120 West Heath Road, London NW3 7TY Tel: 01 455 9871 or call at any presbytery or convent.

Christian Scientists
Christian Science was started by Mary Baker Eddy in 1879 to 'reinstate primitive Christianity and its lost element of healing'. The church takes the 'inspired Word of the Bible' as its 'guide to eternal Life' and regards the crucifixion and resurrection of Jesus Christ as the central events of history. A key belief is that God made man in his image - spiritual, good and eternal. Therefore mortal man is a false manifestation which must be outgrown through 'spiritual regeneration'. Christian

Scientists believe in healing illness, fear, grief and sin through prayer, rather than through conventional treatment.

Christian Science Committee on Publication, 108 Palace Gardens Terrace, London W8 4RT Tel:01 221 5650
Mary Baker Eddy, *Science and Health with Key to the Scriptures*

Congregational Churches
This Church started as a splinter group from the Church of England when, in 1662, some 2,000 clergymen decided to throw off the constraints of a Church governed by the state and form independent congregations. Two centuries later these independent churches formed a Congregational Union which sees itself as the most free of the Free Churches.

The Congregationalists base their worship on Jesus's saying that 'whenever two or three are gathered together' in his name God would be with them. So the Congregationalists have no hierarchy. The minister is ordained, but is part of that congregation, not a superior with a hot-line to God and services are informal and bible-based with no prayer book or formalized liturgy.

Congregational Federation, Congregational Centre, 4 Castle Gate, Nottingham NG1 7AS Tel: 0602 413801

Methodist Church of Great Britain
Methodism was started by John Wesley, an Anglican minister, in the early eighteenth century, as a revivalist movement trying to take Christianity closer to its beginnings, when it carried a message of personal redemption. The name started as a taunt at the earnest group of Oxford students who joined Wesley in this.

Wesley's four key points, which are still fundamental to Methodism, all centre on salvation - that men can be saved from their sins, that they know they can be saved, that they can be saved utterly, and that this is achieved 'by grace through faith in the personal saving grace of Jesus Christ'.

The Methodist Church, 1 Central Buildings, Westminster, London SW1H 9NH Tel: 01 222 8010

Quakers - Religious Society of Friends
The movement was started in Britain by George Fox in the mid-seventeenth century. Fox rejected the Church's emphasis on formalized services and argued for the importance of spiritual awareness in each human being. To the Church this was blasphemy. But he soon attracted followers who were equally dissatisfied with the straitjacket they felt the Church then imposed.

Fox and his 'Friends' claimed that religious insight came from human experience, and an overwhelming awareness of the closeness of God and of the spirit of Christ within. They rejected the need for the Church and its priests, as interpreters of the bible and mediators between them and God. For them religion involved following Christ's teachings in daily life, rather than obedience to dogma. Quaker beliefs are still essentially the same.

Quaker Home Service, Friends House, Euston Road, London NW1 2BJ Tel: 01 387 3601

Salvation Army
The Salvation Army was founded by William Booth in 1865 following the main tenets of the Christian Church.

They hold that the 'first parents' of man fell from innocence and that as a result 'all men have become sinners, totally depraved, and as such are justly exposed to the wrath of God.' Therefore repentance is necessary for salvation, and continued salvation depends on 'continued obedient faith in Christ'. They also believe in the immortality of the soul and the resurrection of the body. But prospects for the after-life are bleak for those who have not been saved - a general judgement at the end of the world in which the wicked will be endlessly punished and the 'righteous' eternally happy.

The Salvation Army Information Service, 101 Queen Victoria Street, London EC4P 4EP Tel: 01 236 5222 (sae welcome).

Unitarians
The origins of Unitarianism lie in radical thinkers like Erasmus, who in the sixteenth century questioned whether the Trinity - the idea of God as three persons, Father, Son and Holy Spirit - had any basis in scripture. At that time such questioning was blasphemy, and in Britain, this belief was illegal until 1813.

Today, their central belief is a 'reverence for life' combined with a search for individual truth. Most Unitarians follow the teaching of Jesus Christ without seeing him as the unique incarnation of God, and regard the reliance on him for salvation as being contrary to the need for individual moral responsibility. For, fundamental to Unitarianism is the belief that no *one* prophet, book or religious tradition possesses the whole and absolute truth, and that value can be found in all of them.

General Assembly of Unitarian and Free Churches, Essex Hall, 1-6 Essex Street, London WC2R 3HY Tel: 01 240 2384
Rosemary and Jeremy Goring, *The Unitarians*, Religious, Moral and Educational Press

Hinduism
It is almost incorrect to talk about Hinduism as a religion. Hinduism is a way of life. Its origins are unknown, but some priests believe this philosophy grew up in India over 10,000 years ago. Hindus believe that there is one God, who may have different aspects. They also believe the soul travels through many incarnations and that the aim of life is to get rid of the bad qualities - like violence, selfishness and love of material things - in order to travel up the ladder of incarnation and eventually attain union with God. This state of blissful union is called Nirvana, but the journey upwards is not inevitable. Bad deeds can lead to a Karma (destiny) of reincarnation at a lower level of being, such as an animal or a tree.

This belief in reincarnation means that all living creatures are thought to possess a soul, and even trees and rivers have something of the divine.

Hinduism developed differently in different regions. The oldest branch is Shaivism, from the south of India. In the north there grew up Vaishnavism, in which Vishnu is the supreme deity, but for the educated Hindu, Shiva and Vishnu are not opposing gods, but the same God seen from different angles.

At one time Hindus were vegetarian, but a great many of them now eat meat - but not beef. However, they must not eat meat for 24 hours before entering a temple, and must bathe after eating it. So, as Friday is the important day for attending the temple it is usually a vegetarian day, even for the non-devout. No dead creature may ever enter the grounds around a temple. Any woman should respect the rule that she may not enter a temple while menstruating.

The Highgate Murugan Temple, 200a Archway Road, London N6 5BA Tel: 01 348 9835 (Shaivism)
Geeta Bhaan Mandir, 107-115 Heathfield Road, Birmingham B19 1HL Tel: 021 554 4120/021 523 7797 (Vaishnavism)

Humanism

Since religion is about belief humanism is, in a sense, a religion. Its keynote is a belief in the power of mankind to work for a better life for everyone, and in man's absolute obligation to do so - if we are to have a society which is worth living in. Humanists believe there is a moral imperative which does not come from 'God', but from an acceptance of man's responsibility for the world around him. A responsibility which, logically, devolves upon him, as the most intelligent creature on the planet. To a humanist, the power for good is fundamentally the power of each individual. So each person is responsible for fulfilling his or her potential, both individually and to the world around them.

The British Humanist Association, 13 Prince of Wales Terrace, London W8 5PG Tel: 01 937 2341

Islam

Muslims believe the Koran was revealed to Mohammad, in Mecca, by an archangel in about AD 610, and he dictated it to his companions. Unlike most other religions, Islam insists that its founder was a man, who was a mouthpiece for the one God, not semi-divine. The Koran speaks of the mercy of God, his absolute power, of the resurrection of the dead and judgement, and of the bliss of paradise for the good and the pains of hell for the wicked. It also lays down a framework of earthly law. In all its teaching the keynote of Islam is submission: submission to Allah (God).

The prophets listed in the Koran include Moses and Jesus Christ. However, Islam is thought to correct and purify the errors which have developed in both Judaism and Christianity. This means that both are seen as early stages in the route to the one God which is perfected in Islam.

The big division in the faith is between Shiite and Suni Muslims. This dates back to a dispute over who should succeed Mohammed. The Shiites believed that Mohammad's cousin, Ali, had to succeed him, whereas the Suni said that it was up to the community to choose the next leader and successfully selected Abu Backr, and from this seed complex philosophical differences developed.

Islamic Cultural Centre, 146 Park Road, London NW8 7RG Tel: 01 724 3363
Suzanne Haneef, *What Everyone Should Know About Islam,* Kazi Publications

Judaism: The Jewish Faith

The Talmud, the chief book of Jewish religious teaching and history, tells of a heathen who asked Hillel to teach him the whole of the Torah in the time he could stand on one leg. The sage replied : 'That which is hateful unto thee do not do unto thy neighbour. This is the whole of the Torah. The rest is commentary.' I am sure he was right - but there's a lot of 'commentary'. Strictly, the word 'Torah' is used for the five books of Moses but it is often used for the body of religious teaching, and 'Judaism' for the whole body of Jewish values - spiritual and secular.

The foundations of Judaism date back to Moses to whom the 'word of God' was 'revealed'. Central to the faith, as it developed, was that there was one God who demanded holiness, righteousness and justice from all mankind, and that this God was a loving and compassionate God who wanted men to both love and respect him. The other key beliefs were that a Messiah would come, that the dead would be resurrected, and that it was forbidden to make any 'graven image', or any manner of likeness.

The Board of Deputies of British Jews, Woburn House, Upper Woburn Place, London WC1H 0EP Tel: 01 387 4044

Herman Wouk, *This is My God,* Fontana
R. C. Zaehner ed., *The Concise Encyclopaedia of Living Faiths,* Open University - takes an in-depth, philosophical look at most religions.

SERVICES

Gas

British Gas

British Gas is a public company administered by a board and executive, and has responsibility for supplying gas, and ensuring its safety. It is divided into 12 regions headed by regional chairmen. However, prices are set nationally and the only variation between regions is a fractional difference in standing charges. There are also 2 parallel bodies set up by government - The Gas Consumers' Council and the Office of Gas Supply.

The Office of Gas Supply is headed by a Director General of Gas Supply, appointed by the Minister for Energy, and has ultimate responsibility for approving the gas prices proposed by the Board of British Gas, and for authorizing new gas suppliers.

Complaints

If you have a complaint about gas write first to your local gas board - the address is on your gas bill or under 'Gas' in the telephone book. If that fails to get results you can contact the Gas Consumers' Council (right).

> The 24-hour emergency service is under 'Gas' in your telephone book - for use if you think there is a gas leak.

Paying

- The cheapest way to pay for gas is to pay a quarterly bill based on the meter reading, and use cash or a cheque to pay.
- You can also buy stamps towards your gas bill, but that means you are putting money into stamps which could be earning you interest in an account in a bank, building society or post office - so you lose money.
- You can also use budget payments in which the gas board estimates how much the year's bill will be and you make twelve equal payments through the year, the difference in either direction being adjusted in the last bill.
- Gas slot meters mean you only use the gas you pay for. But the coins in the meter are your responsibility. If they are stolen you have to replace them.

Anyone finding it hard to pay their bill should talk to the gas board immediately. The boards try to arrange payment systems which will make it easier for people in trouble, or advise them on how to get the social services to help with heating bills. Special consideration is given to old people who cannot pay during the winter months, and there are 'pay as you go' schemes for those who find budgeting hard.

Paying Landlords for Gas

When tenants have a gas meter, or use gas paid for on a landlord's bill, the landlord may make a profit on the cost of the gas. However, landlords may not charge more than a resale price, for gas, set by the Office of Gas Supply. Your local gas showroom or Consumers' Council can give you a leaflet with the permitted charges. As coins and gas units don't always match a refund may be payable when the meter is emptied.

Modern meters show how many cubic feet you get for each coin they take. If a meter doesn't do this ask the landlord to have it changed for a modern one.

Safety

If you smell gas or see a brown stain appearing on or around a gas appliance call the gas company immediately and say you think there is a leak. They make no charge for the first 30 minutes spent making a supply safe. The old and handicapped who live alone may have free safety checks to their appliances once a year.

Servicing

To function safely and efficiently gas appliances such as boilers need regular servicing. Gas boards offer service contracts and they are worth taking up, as it removes the possibility of simply forgetting to have a service done. If you don't use the gas board make sure that any work is done by a member of CORGI (see A Roof Over Your Head). The emergency call-out service if there is a leak is available to anyone - even if the customer has no contract with the board.

Special Needs

There are adaptors to help people use gas appliances safely despite handicaps or old age; these can include controls marked in braille. Some charities linked to particular handicaps also have information on specific aids or you can ask your local gas authority for a visit from the British Gas Home Service Advisor.

The blind and partially sighted can arrange for meter readers to have a special password, so there is no risk of them admitting someone who is not a genuine meter reader.

Gas bills will be lower if there is proper insulation. In some areas there are neighbourhood insulation groups which insulate the homes of those who are not able to do it for themselves. **Monergy Saver** (Freepost Newcastle on Tyne NE1 1BR Tel: 0800 234 800 - a Freefone call) can tell you if there is a group in your area. Even if you can get it done yourself you may be able to get a grant to pay for it. Ask at your town hall about home insulation schemes - but to get a grant you must ask *first*. The grant will not pay for anything you get before the grant is awarded.

The head office is **British Gas**, Rivermill House, 152 Grosvenor Road, London SW1V 3JL Tel: 01 821 1444, but consumer queries should be addressed to the regional offices.

Gas Consumers' Council

The Gas Consumers' Council, Abford House, 15 Wilton Road, London SW1V 1LT Tel: 01 931 0977 was set up by parliament to help consumers with problems and complaints, regarding both the gas industry and gas-related companies. The council is totally independent and champions the cause of consumers both with the industry and with government. It will also give free expert advice, to any gas user, at any time. However, it only takes up complaints after your own complaints have failed, and though it can suggest and advise, it cannot force British Gas to take action.

Gas Otherwise

In addition to piped gas there are a large number of private companies supplying bottled gas to those not on the gas system. The largest of these is **Calor Gas Ltd**, Appleton Park, Riding Court Road, Datchet, Slough SL3 9JG Tel: 0753 40000. Its customer service division has an information pack on cooking and heating by bottled gas and on appliances which are suited to it.

Electricity

The electricity industry comes under the Secretary of State for Energy, who has no executive control but can influence its policies. The Electricity Council is the industry's co-ordinating body on finance, tariffs and industrial relations for England and Wales - and the last resort of the aggrieved consumer.

Electricity is produced by the Central Electricity Generating Board (CEGB) and supplied to the 12 Area Electricity Boards in England and Wales. These Area Boards then supply it to consumers, run local services and showrooms and act independently on prices and policy.

In Scotland and Ireland things are arranged differently. The South of Scotland Electricity Board, the North of Scotland Hydro-Electricity Board and the Northern Ireland Electricity Service both generate and distribute electricity in their areas.

The interests of the consumer are represented by two types of statutory body: nationally there is the Electricity Consumers' Council, and within each Area Electricity Board region there is an Electricity Consultative Council. The latter is the main source of information and advice if you need it.

Paying for Electricity

Electricity is charged at two rates; a day rate, and a much lower Economy 7 tariff between about midnight and 8 am GMT (but check your board for the exact times in your area). You only get the benefit of the lower rate if you have an Economy 7 meter which measures night use separately. These meters are installed free, but the standing charge is increased. It may be worth getting one if you run appliances overnight.

Electricity bills are normally sent out every quarter. But many boards have flexible payment schemes, or there are electricity stamps or slot meters - though a slot meter greatly raises your standing charge. Anyone who has difficulty in paying should tell his board immediately and explain all the household circumstances. They may be especially understanding where people are old, infirm or very young.

If the meter reader can't get in you will receive an estimated bill. *Beware:* if several estimates result in you underpaying you could have a whopping bill when the meter is read. So, it's best to use the card provided to read it yourself.

Which Bit Do You Own?

All the wiring which supplies your electricity, up to and including the meter, belongs to the Electricity Board and it is its responsibility. Everything in your home, beyond the meter, is yours. But if you let your trees, for example, interfere with the cables you could be liable.

Complaints

As with all complaints there is a sequence of moves.
1 First complain to your local Electricity Board.
2 If that fails, you can take any complaint on the distribution of electricity to your Area Electricity Consultative Council. They take the case up with the Board if they think action is needed.
3 In rare cases, if you think there is 'a defect in the Electricity Board's general plans and arrangements' - as opposed to goods or services - you can write to the Electricity Consumers' Council.
4 If steps (2) or (3) fail the Electricity Council is your last resort. The procedure is complex and could end in a hearing. What you need to do is spelt out in a leaflet called 'Statutory Representations to the Electricity Council' from the Electricity Consumers' Council (see below).

More information

Electricity Boards are listed under 'Electricity' in the telephone books and there should be special numbers for emergencies out of office hours.

The address of the **Electricity Consultative Council** for your area is in your telephone book and on your bills.

Electricity Consumers' Council, Brook House, 2/16 Torrington Place, London WC1E 7LL Tel: 01 636 5703, has leaflets on budgeting but is *not* really a body for individual consumers, despite its name.

Electricity Council, 30 Millbank, London SW1P 4RD Tel: 01 834 2333, has information for consumers.

Postal Services

The Post Office is a financially self-supporting, nationalized industry, directly responsible to the Department of Trade and Industry. Internally it is divided into several interdependent businesses run like subsidiary companies. This means that although the letter service, parcel post and Post Office Savings can all be used through a single post office, they are each run separately and have different area managers.

The following information comes from a tome called *The Post Office Guide* which anyone can buy from their main Post Office for about £1. Not the most entertaining book for the money but probably the biggest. It is worth consulting if you want to know the full details of any service.

Basic Weight Limits

● You pay extra on 1st and 2nd class letters weighing over 60 g.
● 1st class letters have no maximum weight.
● 2nd class letters may not exceed 750 g.
● On letters and postcards to the EEC you pay extra for over 20 g.
● On other airmail letters and postcards you pay extra for over 10 g.
● The basic rate for surface mail to all overseas countries is for up to 20 g.
● Packets up to 2 kg can be sent at letter rate if they are not more than 60 cm (2 ft) long at any point. Printed matter has special rules.
● Parcels can weigh up to 20 kg, for most countries, and can be up to 1.5 m (5 feet) long.
● An international datapost service is available.

Proof of Posting

You can obtain a form giving proof of posting, for any

letter or parcel, *free of charge* from main post offices and some sub-post offices.

Dangerous Items

Nobody will be too frustrated by the fact that the Post Office specifically bans the sending of mustard gas through the post. However, some of the banned items, such as aerosols and paints, might not seem dangerous at first sight, so the Post Office list should be consulted before sending anything unusual.

Recorded Delivery

Anyone can send a letter by recorded delivery, but only from a post office. However, all you get for the extra cost is a certificate of posting and an assurance that the Post Office will get a signature when they deliver it. You *don't* get any more compensation than an ordinary letter, and *no* compensation will be paid if you send money or jewellery this way.

Registered Letters

Any 1st class letter can be registered, at a post office, for an extra fee. The fee covers compensation: the more you might wish to claim, the higher the fee. Check how much compensation you would get - it may be much less than you would expect but, for *another* fee, the Post Office will arrange insurance if you wish. Any item to be registered must be sealed with sticky tape or glue, not just tied up, and any adhesive tape should have the sender's signature or initials across it. *Compensation will only be paid on money if it is sent in a registered envelope bought from the Post Office.*

> The Post Office delivers registered letters to the address, *not* to the individual the letter is addressed to.

Datapost

Datapost is a courier service for urgent mail and goods. The weight limit is 27.5 kg and only hazardous and high-value items (gems, precious metals) are disallowed. The charge includes insurance against direct loss of the item and losses resulting from that. The service is either same day or overnight. For more information ask the operator for Freefone Datapost and check value of the insurance cover.

Royal Mail Special Delivery

Special delivery ensures that if an item is received by a certain time it will be delivered the next day to any destination except the Channel Isles and the Isle of Man. The charge is 1st class plus a supplement. The Channel Isles and Isle of Man are covered by an Express Delivery service.

Parcels

Fragile articles must be packed so as to protect them adequately and labelled *Fragile with care* or *Do not bend* as appropriate, and *The Post Office Guide* has detailed

advice on how to pack different types of objects. There is also a leaflet on sending food by post. Items of value can be sent by compensation fee parcel post, for which you pay an additional fee for insurance.

★ The Post Office will deliver printed unaddressed material to every household in a given postal area (e.g. a local business publicizing its opening).

★ A wide range of items may be sent to the blind free of charge provided they are within a limited size, wrapped according to set rules and carry the words 'Articles for the Blind' on the outside.

Complaining

In theory, if the Post Office is to blame for something being lost or damaged in the *inland* post you are entitled to compensation - provided the object was properly packed, marked, and so forth. But you must have proof that it was posted, and compensation on anything sent by ordinary post is decidedly limited. Moreover, this does not cover money, in *any* form, or jewellery. For these there is only compensation if they are sent by registered post or by compensation fee parcel post (see page above).

The first step is to contact your local Head Postmaster - the address is available from your local office. If it is a question of something failing to arrive, give the full details of the date and time of posting and where it was going to. If there has been a serious delay, let him have the wrapper, if you can. But if you have received something in a bad condition and will be claiming compensation keep the wrapper and the article, and complete and send in form P58 from the Post Office as soon as possible. If you have suffered loss the Post Office is able to give you compensation.

If that fails, write to the Regional Director of the Post Office - your local CAB or Trading Standards Department can give you the address - or to POUNC (see below), and ask them to take it up.

If you are still dissatisfied (or wish to bypass the step above) you can take your claim for compensation to the Small Claims Court (page 648) or to the Chartered Institute of Arbitrators (page 649). You pay a small fee to apply to the Institute, but this is refunded if the decision is in your favour. However, the Post Office has limited legal liability for postal orders and items lost in overseas post, so you won't always get compensation for these even if the decision goes against the Post Office.

Post Office Headquarters, 33 Grosvenor Place, London W1X 1PX Tel: 01 235 8000

Post Office Users National Council (POUNC)

POUNC is a statutory body, set up under the Post Office Act 1969, but independent of the Post Office, with additional councils for Scotland, Wales and Northern Ireland (addresses from POUNC). The Post Office has an obligation to consult them about policy changes. So write to these organizations if you dislike proposed changes in Post Office policy or charges. POUNC will also take up a personal complaint (see above) only after you have failed to get satisfaction from the District Customer Services Unit. There are also some 160 local Post Office Users' Advisory Committees which may be able to help with complaints of a local nature.

However, POUNC does not handle services such as the Girobank, Intelpost, or philatelic services - nor, oddly, datapost or special delivery. Nor, of course, anything related to the telephone.

Post Office Users National Council (POUNC), Waterloo Bridge House, Waterloo Road, London SE1 8UA Tel: 01 928 9458

Telephone

British Telecom is a public company licensed for 25 years by the Secretary of State for Trade and Industry to run a telecommunications system. The licence contains certain limitations to guard the interests of the consumer and BT has no monopoly of such services. In Hull there is an independent telephone service, which links to the BT network. There is also **Mercury**, P.O. Box 49, Birmingham B1 1TE Tel: 0800 424194, which operates a limited network, covering a number of major cities. People living within the scope of its network can have a Mercury line which allows them to call anyone on its own or the BT system (major users have their own fibre optic link into the building; ordinary subscribers have a BT line which links to the Mercury network). As I write, Mercury calls cost less than those of BT.

British Telecom

Since British Telecom became a public company its organization has fallen outside the government domain. But its activities are burgeoning. A huge array of services are on offer and, being a high-tech industry, the facilities are expanding constantly. If you think the telephone is just for talking on, you could be missing out.

Charges

Only BT is legally allowed to install telephone lines to a building, and it makes graduated charges according to whether a line is being installed for a first time user, or for an established user (even at another address), or for transferring a line to a new address. There is then a quarterly rental charge for using that line.

Once you have the initial socket, which allows you to plug in the telephone as you would a fire, you may install as many other sockets as you wish, but there is an exorbitant installation charge if BT installs the extension sockets. DIY kits for installing these are available from BT or from telephone shops and it is easy to do yourself - but see below.

The charge for each call varies with the length and distance of the call, and the time of day. It is far cheaper to call at off-peak times. There may also be special cheap rates over holiday periods, such as Christmas. The rates for calls of different distances, whether within Britain or overseas, fall into graded price groups labelled a, b, c and so on. Overseas peak times and cheap rates vary with the country. The rates and things are in your code

book. Charges made via the operator, either direct or using the reversed charge system, cost considerably more than those directly dialled. Charges are made in units, with so much time per unit; if you go even fractionally into the time for a second unit you are charged for two units. There is no charge for ringing directory enquiries.

Elderly and handicapped people can apply to be listed under a 'Protected Service Scheme' by which they name someone who can be told if a bill reminder is unpaid. This means that BT will delay cutting off the phone so that person can deal with the bill, and someone sick will not return from hospital to find their phone has been cut off.

Complaints

If you feel the bill is larger than it should be for the amount you have used the phone you should not pay the bill but should ask to have it checked. Unfortunately, the company has no legal obligation to check your line within any set time, or under conditions comparable to those for the period of the bill - which can make a nonsense of the whole procedure.

For any problem the first person to complain to is the local telephone manager. You can dial 100 and ask to be connected without charge, but on any major complaint - especially if money is involved - it is wise to confirm your conversation in writing afterwards. If complaining to him does not get you satisfaction, contact the Telephone Advisory Committee for your area - a CAB should have the address - or one of the 4 national advisory committees.

There are 4 independent advisory committees to the telephone industry - one for each section of Great Britain. They handle complaints relating to any aspect of the telephone industry, not just BT. They should be listed in the telephone book under '**Office of Tele-communications**' or '**OFTEL**'. Failing that, the office for England is **English Advisory Committee** (Atlantic House, Holborn Viaduct, London EC1N 2HQ Tel: 01 822 1600) and it will have your committee's address. If that too fails contact OFTEL, which is the prime body with responsibility for seeing that consumers get fair treatment, at the same address as the **English Advisory Committee** but on Tel: 01 353 4020. OFTEL also publishes information leaflets for consumers on using services and equipment.

Decoder

BT now sells a book which lists telephone codes in numerical order, so you can find out where someone lives before making the call - but it isn't cheap.

Equipment and Extensions

Although you can install as many sockets as you like there is a limit to the number of phones which can be run from a domestic line. On each phone you should find REN followed by a number. REN stands for ringer equivalent number. Domestic lines are only able to handle a total of 4 RENs, between all the phones in the house. So if you have 3 phones all at 1.5 RENs, since

$1.5 + 1.5 + 1.5 = 4.5$ you may not be able to install a fourth phone, as if you exceed 4 RENs some phones may not ring out properly. But BT errs on the cautious side about REN values and in practice you can sometimes run more phones than the RENs would indicate.

Your telephone equipment does not need to be made by BT but it does need to be approved by it. Approved equipment carries a label with a green circle. Non-approved equipment, carrying a red triangle, may be sold in Britain but it is a criminal offence to *use* it here, as it can damage the telephone system. However, small wiring accessories may be used which carry neither sticker.

There is now a far wider range of telephone equipment than there used to be. Telephones are far more sophisticated, you can rent table-top coin-operated machines, and you can buy monitors which will print out the exact cost of each call - very useful with telephone-addicted teenagers. The phone cost monitors vary greatly in ease of use; avoid those which need the dialling codes programmed into them.

Facilities for the Handicapped
There are numerous devices, services and modifications to help those who find a normal telephone hard to use, or need a special emergency service. Details are in a booklet from any BT District Sales Office - dial 100 and ask for Freefone Telecom Sales. There are also demonstration centres all over Britain. Or contact **BT Action For Disabled Customers**, Room B4036, BT Centre, 81 Newgate Street, London EC1A 7AJ Tel: 0345 581456 (local price charged all over the UK).

Maritime Radio
There is a BT international radiophone network designed for use on boats, with a special distress channel monitored by maritime rescue services. More information from **Maritime Radio**, BT International, First Floor, 43 Bartholomew Close, London EC1A 7HP Tel: 01 583 9416.

Payment from Coin Boxes
In addition to payment by coins or phone cards, a growing number of boxes will accept calls which you charge either to your credit card or to your own telephone account. There are also BT credit cards which can be used in phone boxes. Unfortunately, they charge a quarterly rent for the card, then charge extra for calls made with them.

Phoning Home from Abroad
BT has instituted a system which allows a special code to be dialled from coin boxes in certain countries which will connect you straight to any British number you want.

Another system connects you straight to a British operator (no more struggling with Japanese ones) when you want to make a transfer charge call. BT has a leaflet giving the details; to get it call the operator and ask for Freefone BT1.

Prestel
Prestel is a system which allows you to use your telephone to dial into a vast information system providing facts on travel, finance and a host of other subjects. The information then comes up either on the screen of a specially modified television or computer. You pay a quarterly subscription and calls are charged by time during the day, but not usually after 6 pm.

Repairs and Maintenance
Any fault which is reported to the engineers (dial 151) should be repaired within 2 working days of it being reported to them. If they fail to do so ask for the rental charges to be adjusted to allow for loss of use.

Telemessages
Telegrams may be dead but you can still send a costly telemessage through the operator. It is delivered by post the next working day.

Telephone Information
You can find a growing range of information by telephone: recipes, horoscopes, racing results, financial news and so on. Most services are advertised in the press. But the trade association is the **Association of Telephone Information and Entertainment Providers** (48 Grafton Way, London W1P 5LB Tel: 01 387 2838) and it can tell you what is available.

These Callstream services have numbers starting 0898, 0055, 0066, 0077, and the more expensive ones are charged at the 'm' rate - as for calls to Northern Ireland and with the same cheap times. BT has a code of practice for Callstream services which you can obtain by telephoning 0345 345005, and if you feel the code is being broken write to **The Secretary, ICSTIS**, (Third Floor, 2-12 Gresham Street), P.O.Box 488, London EC2V 7AG.

Telephone - Business Services
Links between computers and telephones have been around for a long time, but their sophistication is relatively new. Telecom has a range of business facilities including access to a series of databases with information of use to businesses and business travellers. There are also other BT routes by which you can link into telexes using a computer, or obtain telex messages through a BT office.

Cellnet mobile telephones are available through dealers. Calls are charged at a special 'm' rate which is considerably higher than a normal call.

Solid Fuel

Approved Coal Merchant Scheme
The **Approved Coal Merchants Scheme** Victoria House, Southampton Row WC1B 4DH Tel: 01 405 1601, is designed to regulate coal merchants and make sure they give the public a reliable service. It is backed by both British Coal and the Coal Merchants' Federation. Approved coal merchants are meant to abide by a set

of rules which, for example, say he or she must:

- offer good quality fuel,
- have it properly described,
- write on the delivery ticket which coal he has supplied
- give the name and weight on any pre-packed fuel,
- employ staff with a basic knowledge of solid fuel.

The scheme has regional officers who visit and approve a would-be coal merchant, and make spot checks after membership. In practice, anyone not a member of this scheme must find it hard to have a job being a coal merchant at all, as the NCB will only supply to 'Approved Merchants' and foreign coal may not compete on price.

If you are dissatisfied complain to the coal merchant. If that fails contact the regional official of this scheme, either directly or via the head office.

British Coal
Being a nationalized industry, **British Coal**, Hobart House, Grosvenor Place, London SW1X 7AE Tel: 01 235 2020 is directly responsible to the Department of Energy. British Coal is purely concerned with the mining of coal and its only links with the public are through the Solid Fuel Advisory Service.

Domestic Coal Consumers' Council
Domestic Coal Consumers' Council, Freepost, London EC1B 1DT Tel: 01 638 8914/8929, is Britain's oldest consumer council. It is involved in setting coal prices and is a source of information and advice. It will also take up complaints about coal merchants and put them to the Approved Coal Merchants Scheme, but it has no 'teeth' of its own. It advises customers who suspect short weight when coal is delivered to contact their local Trading Standards Officer immediately so he can see what was delivered, or ask him to be present at the next delivery.

Solid Fuel Advisory Service (SFAS)
Solid Fuel Advisory Service (SFAS), address as British Coal (above), has the job of promoting coal (and similar solid fuel, including smokeless fuel - but not wood) to the general public. It does this through regional offices, through links with over 350 showrooms, and through leaflets and information on how to use solid fuel. It also runs a free advisory service, its advisors will visit you and suggest which appliances would suit both your home and your needs. It also has technical experts who will come and advise you on how to clear up problems with existing fires, and will recommend heating contractors to do the work. Predictably, all this is funded jointly by the Coal Merchants' Federation of Great Britain and British Coal.

Solid Smokeless Fuels Federation
Solid Smokeless Fuels Federation, Devonshire House, Church Street, Sutton-in-Ashfield, Notts NG17 1AE Tel: 0623 550411, is a far smaller and more specialized organisation than SFAS. It is sponsored by those who produce and distribute smokeless fuels and tries to promote their use. It will give advice on smokeless fuels or provide literature on them.

> It is illegal to burn non-smokeless fuel in a smokeless zone.

See also **WARM**, in A Roof Over Your Head.

Water
This is an industry which is due to be privatized. What follows is the structure before privatization. If you need advice and information on post-privatization changes your Citizens Advice Bureau should help, or contact the National Consumer Council (page 641).

Water supplies in England and Wales are dealt with by 10 totally independent bodies, which are responsible directly to the Secretary of State for the Environment. In some areas they have small private companies under them which act as agents for the authority, both supplying the water and billing the customers. In Northern Ireland water is handled directly by the Department for the Environment and in Scotland water comes under the 12 regional councils. In England and Wales your authority will be found under 'Water' in the telephone book, but in Scotland it may be under the local authority and on all bills plus emergency numbers should be listed in each case.

Water authorities handle not only the supply of fresh water and the disposal of sewage, but also river management, pollution control, flood prevention, land drainage, sea defences, conservation, fishing and the use of water for sports and recreations. All this is paid for out of charges made to water users.

Charges
The price of water is arrived at between each board and the Department of the Environment, so charges vary from area to area. On average a family pays about 25p a day and this is based on the rateable value of its home, with an additional charge for outside use. However, anyone can ask for a water meter, costing about £100. Then the charges will be made on the amount of water used. This may be cheapest if you use very little water and live in a property of high rateable value.

Complaints
Complaints have to go to different places according to where you live.
- In England and Wales to the Regional Water Authority
- In Scotland to the Water Services department of your Regional Council
- In Northern Ireland to the local Divisional Office of the Department for the Environment.

Every authority has several Consumer Consultative Committees covering different divisions within its area to take up complaints. The water authority, or your local library, will give you the address. However, since they are appointed by the authority, they are not always as forceful as they might be. Your Citizens Advice Bureau may be able to advise you. Unfortunately, the lack of any central consumer body makes it hard for a consumer to get satisfaction, but in Ireland there is a **Water Appeals Commission** (Carlton House, 1 Shaftesbury Square, Belfast BT2 7LB Tel: 0232 244710).

Regulations
Water by-laws vary from area to area and may cover details such as the size of cistern you can have or the design of your water system. If you have done alterations to plumbing in a house in one area and then move it is not safe to assume that the same rules will apply. However, one rule is general: any water leaks on your property are your problem; any leaks on public property are the Water Board's job.

Water Authorities Association, 1 Queen Anne's Gate, London SW1H 9BT Tel: 01 222 8111, is basically a trade association little related to consumers.

TRAVEL AND TRANSPORT

Air Transport

Air Transport Operators Association (ATOA)
The Air Transport Operators Association, Clembro House, Weydown Road, Haslemere, Surrey GU27 2QE Tel: 0428 4804 is the association which looks after the interests of air taxi operators and commuter airlines. It has no formal arbitration scheme, but it does have a code of practice and would investigate complaints against members. If you need to get from A to B in a hurry - and have mislaid your private jet - this organization can give you the names of companies from which to hire one.

Air Ambulances
ATOA members include several air ambulance services. Most operate only when the sick person has insurance with fly-back cover, but the following organizations will handle cases which lack insurance, provided someone will meet the bill. Some conditions would be made far worse by the pressure changes of a flight and any organization is unlikely to agree to a flight until their medical team has all the facts. Often they can arrange for someone to be brought back by scheduled flight and provide doctors and nurses in attendance. Compare prices and try to suit the plane (and with it the cost) to the degree of urgency. Their 24-hour, 7 days a week, numbers are:

St John's Ambulance Tel: 01 730 0318 (only from abroad to Britain)
International SOS Assistance Tel: 01 876 2929/392 1666 from anywhere to anywhere, even China. Also referral to doctors in overseas countries.
Europ Assistance Tel: 01 680 1234

Planes in a Hurry
If you need an air taxi in a hurry, one of ATOA's members

operates a round-the-clock, 7 days a week, worldwide air charter service. Before you ring work out how you could guarantee to pay a substantial sum: the size most people would only pay in a serious emergency. The Gatwick based company is: **Air London - The Aircharter Centre** Tel: 0293 549555.

Air Transport Users Committee
Air Transport Users Committee, (129 Kingsway, London WC2B 6NN Tel: 01 242 3882) is a committee of unpaid members representing the general public, with a supporting secretariat. Its job is to look after the interests of consumers, and it covers every aspect of civil aviation, monitoring and advising on changes, and taking up complaints (see CAA, below). They supply various consumer leaflets.

Civil Aviation Authority (CAA)
The Civil Aviation Authority, 45-59 Kingsway, London WC2B 6TE Tel: 01 379 7311, is the body which advises the government on aviation issues, monitors all aspects of air safety and regulates the aviation industry. This means that it runs air traffic control services, licenses airlines and air travel organizers, approves air fares, sets the standards for testing both private and commercial pilots and issues pilots' licences. In addition, it owns and runs 8 aerodromes in the Scottish Highlands and Islands through its subsidiary, Highlands and Islands Airports Ltd.

Complaints and Problems
The CAA's main link with the general public is when things go wrong. One of its objectives under the Civil Aviation Act 1982 is to 'further the reasonable interests of the users of air transport services'. So, complaints about the flight aspects of package tours, which have not been dealt with satisfactorily by the company concerned, can be sent to the CAA. However, those related to a British airline, but not part of a package tour should go first to the Air Transport Users Committee, which was set up by the CAA to represent consumers. Either organization may be able to get redress, and possibly compensation. If that fails it may be possible to get compensation in the courts.

The CAA also issues the Air Transport Organizer's Licence (ATOL) to tour operators. Companies may only offer travel based on charter flights if they have this licence. Before obtaining it companies are vetted financially, but that is no guarantee against later problems. If an ATOL holder ceases to trade the CAA will bring home stranded holiday makers or make refunds to those who have bought tickets but lost their flight. This applies if the flight was a charter flight, or if the booking was on space *chartered* on a scheduled flight. It does not apply to seats booked, in the ordinary way, on a scheduled airline. Moreover, the fund only refunds basic costs; it is not able to compensate people for inconvenience or loss of holiday. To claim ask the CAA for a claim form.

International Air Transport Association (IATA)
International Air Transport Association (IATA), Greener House, 66-68 Haymarket, London SW1Y 4RF Tel: 01 839 2490, (London office) is purely a trade association for airlines, and operates from a head office in Montreal. It

does, however, claim to check the financial status of travel agents selling full-price air tickets.

Buses outside London

Since the 1985 Transport Act the bus system has been revolutionized - whether for good or ill only the users can decide. Under it, anyone may run buses on virtually any route, provided the buses meet the safety standards set by the Ministry of Transport. If they can show they meet these standards they just register with the Traffic Commissioners for the region 6 weeks before they start the service (6 weeks' notice must also be given before discontinuing any service). As buses only choose to run profitable routes, councils fill in the gaps with subsidized bus services which are operated by private companies under contract.

Most companies have discount fares such as local travel cards and Explorer tickets.

The Local Traffic Commissioner (listed under 'Traffic' in the telephone book) is the person who should know what companies are operating where.

Complaints

Any complaint about buses should go to the company concerned. By law the company's name and address must be written on the side of its buses - usually near the door. If complaining fails, and the company is operating under licence to the council, you can complain to your local councillor. Bus companies are also vulnerable to bad publicity. So if one behaves really badly talk to the local media - or threaten to do so.

If it breaks its terms of registration - which the public have a right to see either at the office of the Traffic Commissioner or at the County Council - you can report it to the Local Traffic Commissioner. If a company breaks the safety regulations you can also report it to the Ministry of Transport.

Unfortunately, there is no statutory body representing the needs and complaints of bus users, so if such complaints fail there is little you can do except go to court - if the case is suitable. However, CABx will advise you, at any stage, and you may be able to get help from the pressure groups listed below.

Lost Property

Bus regulations oblige bus operators to check buses for lost property and notify the owner if an item with a name and address is found. They must also hold lost property for 12 months after finding it and keep a record of it. However, they may charge for returning your belongings, and throw away perishable goods after 48 hours.

Bus and Coach Council

The Bus and Coach Council, 52 Lincoln's Inn Fields, London WC2A 3L2 Tel: 01 831 7546, is a trade association which sets standards within the industry and has a code of conduct for driving standards. It has a voluntary bonding scheme for members who offer coach tours, and if a member of the public has a grievance against a bonded company it will refer the complaint

to arbitration - at the expense of those concerned. However, it has no powers over its members, no conciliation service and its only real role in relation to the public is to put people in touch with companies offering particular services.

National Federation of Bus Users

National Federation of Bus Users, 6 Holmhurst Lane, St Leonards-on-Sea, East Sussex TN37 7LW Tel: 0424 752424, is open to both individuals and local user groups, and represents their interests to local and national government. It covers all bus services except those in London and will take up complaints and advise on rights in law. M£L, M, L.

London's Transport

London Regional Transport (LRT)

Travel on the Circle line, between Paddington and Farringdon, and you go back to the origins of London's public transport: in 1863 those very tunnels carried not only London's first underground train, but the world's. But the roots of today's transport go farther back - to the stage coaches of the eighteenth century and to London's first horse bus in the 1820s, later superceded by trams, which were, ironically, started by a Mr Train.

Today London's transport system comes under **London Regional Transport (LRT),** 55 Broadway, London SW1H 0BD Tel: 01 222 5600, operates to guidelines and financial objectives set by the Secretary of State and, although funded by fares, it is underpinned by a government subsidy. It has two main companies - London Buses Ltd, which runs the main London bus services, and London Underground Ltd - with additional subsidiaries for bus engineering, consultancy and the Docklands railway. Most of London's bus services are run directly by London Buses Ltd, although private companies operate some routes, under contract to LRT, for a fixed fee. Under their contracts they must charge standard fares (which are passed on to LRT) and accept LRT passes and travel cards.

Travellers usually deal with the bus division or the underground division. But, as LRT approves fare structures and budgets for both, protests and suggestions on these can be sent direct to LRT.

You can take a bicycle on the underground system, but not on all lines and not at peak times - so you need to check.

Dogs, other than guide dogs, are accepted on buses only with the approval of the conductor or driver.

Complaints

The first complaint should go to the company concerned. The addresses of London Buses Ltd and London Underground Ltd are the same as for LRT. The addresses of other companies should be on the side of the buses. If you don't get satisfaction through the company concerned complain to the **London Regional Passenger's Committee** (see opposite).

Fares

On undergrounds fares are charged according to the zone, and on ordinary single and return tickets you cannot break your journey and keep your ticket, but ask about the following possibilities.

- Bus passes - giving unlimited travel in all London buses for a day, a week, a month or a year, within set zones.
- Cheap day returns - issued after 09.30 on weekdays, and anytime during weekends and public holidays.
- London Connection Through Tickets - take you from a London underground station to a British Rail destination outside London.
- Travelcards - giving unlimited travel on both buses and undergrounds within a given zone. Valid for 1 day or longer but day tickets only operate after 09.30; long-term cards are valid anytime.
- Capitalcards - Travelcards which also cover British Rail.
- The Visitor Travelcard - which can *only* be bought outside London - giving reduced fares on buses and undergrounds and on the entry to a number of London's sights.

> You need a photocard before you can buy or use a Bus Pass or Travelcard (except Day or a Visitor's). Take a passport-sized photo to the ticket office to get one.

- Travel- and Capitalcards valid for 2 or more zones can be used on Green Line Coaches in London. Ring 01 668 7261 for details.
- Those with BR Senior Citizens' or Disabled Rail Cards can travel at a child's fare at the times given for cheap day returns.
- Refunds can be obtained on Travelcards and Capitalcards if you are sick and off work.

Information

You can get free maps and information of all kinds from information centres at major stations and at Heathrow, and from the Travel Information Service at LRT headquarters. 01 222 1234 is a 24-hour personal enquiry service and 01 222 1200 a recorded message of the latest information on buses and undergrounds.

Lost Property

LRT *never return* lost property. If it has a name and address on it, a card is simply sent saying property has been found. To get it back you *must* claim it within 3 months. After that it is sold.

If you have lost something on a train or bus go to the manager of the first station you come to, or to the bus garage, and ask if it can be traced *immediately*. They will usually try to trace it for you, and if it is urgent - such as a live animal - they will go to considerable lengths to help. If your property can't be found ask for a lost property enquiry form at a station or bus depot.

Once your belongings are in the system they cannot be extracted quickly. No enquiries about lost property are handled on the phone, but a recorded message on 01 486 2496 will tell you the procedure. It involves *writing* to the Lost Property Manager (200 Baker Street, London NW1 5RZ) or calling at that address between 09.30 and 14.00 on Mondays to Fridays.

All lost property is sold by auction through Greasby's Ltd (211 Longley Road, London SW17 Tel: 01-672 1100). A great place to go if you want a job lot of a dozen umbrellas - but little is sold singly.

London Regional Passenger's Committee (LRPC)

The London Regional Passenger's Committee, Golden Cross House, 8 Duncannon Street, London WC2N 4JF Tel: 01 839 1898, is the odd one out among the passenger's committees under the CTCC (see over), since it represents passengers on *buses* as well as on underground trains, the Docklands Light Railway and British Rail within its area. Its remit extends beyond London proper and covers an irregular circle around Aylesbury, Hitchin and Bishops Stortford, Gravesend, East Grinstead, Horsham and Windsor.

The committee looks at suggestions and complaints related to any of those services and makes recommendations to both the organizations themselves and to government. It also pursues transport issues with local government, and will back individuals in their complaints if it feels they are justified. However, it will only take up your cause if you have tried yourself, and failed.

Railways

As a nationalized industry British Rail is directly responsible to the Secretary of State for Transport, who sets standards and financial targets. The major business decisions are then made by five Business Directors - one for freight, one for parcels, and three covering the different sectors of the passenger network, some of which have state subsidies. The day-to-day running of all services, whether passenger or freight, is under 6 Regional General Managers, and their Area Managers.

Code of Practice

Under the 1985 BR Code of Practice:

- You can get a refund on an unused ticket if you submit it within 28 days to a ticket office, travel centre or appointed travel agent, and explain why it is unused. For refunds on season tickets, hand them in with 7 days unused (3 days for a weekly ticket). (Exceptions are made for the ill.) There is a service charge unless it was BR's fault that you didn't travel.
- There are no refunds on lost tickets, but BR may replace a lost season ticket.
- If you leave property in Left Luggage or park on railway premises you may be able to claim compensation if the railway breaks the terms of the implied contract.

Complaining

If you have a complaint about any aspect of a passenger

train service first complain to the Area Manager - the address and phone number are displayed in stations. If you want compensation (apart from a refund) don't forget to say so, and give all the details which justify it. A reply to a written complaint should come within 4 weeks - at most.

The Area Transport Users' Consultative Committees are nine committees set up by parliament to represent the interests of rail users throughout Britain. It is to them that you should complain if you are dissatisfied with the services or have a personal complaint which has fallen on deaf ears at BR. An area's committee should be in the telephone book under 'Transport', or ask your local CAB or the CTCC, below.

If all else fails, you can apply for arbitration by the Chartered Institute of Arbitrators (page 649), but this is not a free service, so do use the consultative committee first.

If BR disputes your claim it may be worth checking the rules it is governed by. These are the International Uniform Rules, and the Byelaws and Conditions of Carriage. The latter can be seen at booking offices; the former can be bought from HMSO or seen in the office of the Claims Manager at Marylebone Station - or your library might get a copy.

> BR officials may say that you should take the complaint up their hierarchy before going to your users' committee. In fact, the choice is yours: the committees welcome complaints from those whom Area Managers have failed to satisfy.

The Central Transport Consultative Committee is the organization, set up by the transport acts, to represent rail passengers - despite its name, it has no link with buses. Although government sponsored, it operates independently and is the co-ordinating body for the 8 Area Transport Users' Consultative Committees and the London Regional Passengers' Committee (and through the committee for Scotland also covers certain Scottish ferry services). The CTCC is formed by the chairmen of these area committees plus a number of outside members. The CTCC:

- monitors the policy and performance of BR's passenger services
- makes recommendations to British Rail and to government
- takes note of complaints and comments from rail users.

However, parliament imposed certain limitations on it. It may not deal with individual fares or reductions in services. It *can*, however, deal with closures and the fare structure. So if you object to your local line being closed or feel the fare structure needs a rethink, this is the body to protest to: **Central Transport Consultative Committee**, First Floor, Golden Cross House, Duncannon Street, London WC2N 4JF Tel: 01 839 7338

British Railways Board, Euston House, 24 Eversholt Street, P.O. Box 100, London NW1 1DZ Tel: 01 928 5151

Fares
The discounts and price variations on British Rail need a tome in themselves. Bear in mind that discounts can be had through:

- a senior citizen's railcard
- a young person's railcard
- disabled person's railcard, which includes all disabilities
- family railcards
- travelling at off-peak times
- season tickets.

> **Warning:** If you don't buy a ticket and have to pay on the train it is likely to cost more. If you travel in any part of a first class carriage - even standing in the corridor - you are liable to pay the difference between a Standard Class ticket and a First Class one. And if travelling on a season ticket you pay the *full* First Class fare - not just the difference.

Luggage and Other Items
There is a limit to how much luggage you may take on a train without paying extra. (It cost my daughter more to take her books to university by train than it would have done to hire a car.) The free allowance is 70 kg (154 lb) First Class, 50 kg (110 lb) Standard Class. After that you pay about £2 per 5 kg (10 lb) overweight.

Luggage can be sent to and from many stations in advance. It is charged by weight, with a set minimum fee, and takes 48 hours. Do remove or cross out all labels for other destinations, or BR may not accept responsibility if it is lost.

Dogs pay half the Standard Class fare, but pets are only allowed in the passenger compartments if they don't annoy other passengers, and are never allowed in sleepers or dining cars (guide dogs travel free and are usually an exception). If muzzled or in suitable containers pets can travel in the guard's van.

For motor cycles and other two-wheeled vehicles with motors you pay a full Standard Class fare - and they are not allowed on certain trains, so it's best to check first.

Passengers' bicycles travel free in the guard's van, except on certain trains - check before travelling.

Phoning for Information
Frequent British Rail users will increase their life expectancy by buying a timetable (there is also an international timetable). They come out each year in May and October. If, however, you are reduced to hanging on for one of those overburdened lines, remember they have a stacking system and take calls in order - so hold on or you lose your place in the queue. *There is no special number to ring in emergencies.*

Red Star
The Red Star parcels service offers two options: the parcel can be collected from you and delivered, or go station to station. On station to station, it goes on the next train; with door to door it takes 24 hours. Both are charged by weight, and neither is cheap. If there's no rush it is cheaper to disguise your parcel as luggage and use the advance luggage service (opposite).

Reservations
Seats can be reserved on most Intercity trains and on others indicated in the timetable. You can do this through travel agents or at major stations up to 3 months before. There is a small fee for reservations, but up to 4 seats can be reserved for the price of 1.

Shipping

Passenger Shipping Association (PSA)
The Passenger Shipping Association is the trade association of companies running shipping lines. If you have a complaint about a shipping line first take it up with the shipping line itself. If the issue is major and you want compensation *make sure that you put your case as well as possible and give all the evidence clearly.* If you get no satisfaction from the company and it has to go to arbitration this first letter will be your evidence to the court of arbitration and it may be impossible to add further arguments later. If necessary, get a CAB or Law Centre to help you with this first letter, and keep copies of all correspondence.

If that fails, it may fall within the PSA conciliation and arbitration service. However, this service is only available if:

- You booked on the shipping line as part of an inclusive holiday with a ferry line, or it was a cruise or a fly/cruise holiday.
- You live in Britain and booked the holiday here.

You can use the PSA conciliation service by simply asking the shipping line to forward the written claim to the conciliator at the PSA. The conciliator is an independent solicitor who will consider the written evidence and advise on whether the company should compensate you (his or her fee will be paid by the shipping line). Neither side has to accept the advice.

If you still can't agree you can either take the matter to court (if appropriate) or ask the company to let you have a form to apply for arbitration with the Chartered Institute of Arbitrators (see page 649). The arbitrator then considers the written evidence (excluding the conciliator's decision - unless both sides agree to it being revealed) and says what should happen. This may include ordering one side to pay the other's arbitration fee. Both sides are legally bound by this decision.

Passenger Shipping Association, 93 Newman Street, London W1P 3LE Tel: 01 491 7693

Transport Pressure Groups
Campaign to Improve London's Transport, Tress House, 3 Stamford Street, London SE1 9NT Tel: 01 928 9179
Cyclists' Touring Club (see Free Time) acts as a pressure group for cyclists.
Friends of The Earth (see Free Time) has a transport section.
The Railway Development Society, 48 The Park, Great Bookham, Surrey KT23 3LS Tel: 0372 52863 is for the development of railways and improvement of services. Its members are both individuals and local users' groups. M£M, M, Rg, A.
Transport 2000, Walkden House, 10 Melton Street, London NW1 2EJ Tel: 01 388 8386 is a federation of those who would like to see public transport improved, more use of rail and water for bulk carriage, and better facilities created for pedestrians, cyclists and public transport users. M£M, M, G, L, B.

Travel

The Association of British Travel Agents (ABTA)
The Association of British Travel Agents (ABTA), 55-57 Newman Street, London W1P 4AH Tel: 01 637 2444, represents 90 per cent of the travel agents and tour operators in Britain. It tries to maintain standards within the industry and the code of conduct for its members has been agreed with the Office of Fair Trading. ABTA travel agents only sell holidays by ABTA tour operators, and the holidays provided by those tour operators are only sold through ABTA agents. So you won't find yourself partly covered by the code of conduct and partly not. The only possible confusion could be if your complaint was to do with the flight and the ABTA operator was an ATOL holder, as many are. In this case, contact ABTA first, and let ABTA and the CAA sort it out. You can never get compensation from *both* ABTA and the CAA; it is one or the other.

Rules Under the Code of Conduct
- Brochures
Brochures should be clear, comprehensive and accurate.

> Brochures are often optimistic, even fanciful, but for a brochure to describe any aspect of a holiday in terms which are seriously untrue is illegal. Compensation may be obtainable in the Small Claims Court.

- Flights
A Companies may pass increased fuel costs on to the customer in a surcharge - and there is no time limit - but *only* if they can prove that it is necessary.
B Someone is entitled to compensation if a flight is delayed, or its time altered for a period with takes away a *substantial fraction* of the holiday. (So, a 12-hour delay would be considered a substantial fraction of long weekend, but it might not be considered grounds for compensation on a fortnight's break.)

The Code does *not* say that if flights are delayed passengers should be given meal vouchers, nor that they must be given a hotel room if a flight is delayed overnight. It is up to the airline. Nor does the Code govern what happens if a flight booked by an ABTA agent is overbooked.

● Hotels

A Companies may not add a surcharge on hotel costs, because of exchange rate changes, less than 30 days before departure.

B If a hotel overbooks and notifies the tour operator, the operator must offer its clients the choice of equivalent accommodation or a full refund before departure. There is no compensation for loss of holiday.

C If a hotel overbooks and it isn't realized until the client gets there then the operator must provide equivalent accommodation or compensation.

D If the tour operator overbooks it must pay compensation.

Company Failures

ABTA runs a bonding scheme which ensures that if one of its members goes out of business customers won't lose their money. If an ABTA company goes bust after you have paid your deposit or paid for your holiday in full and the holiday is no longer available ABTA will refund your money, but it will not give you compensation for loss of holiday. In some cases ABTA may offer an alternative holiday.

If the company liquidates while you are on the holiday ABTA will make sure you still have somewhere to stay and will arrange your return flight, at no extra cost.

The only major gap in the system concerns compensation relating to a flight or a boat journey without any holiday attached to it. These tickets fall into a grey area. They are not covered by the PSA scheme or by ATOL and the chances of compensation from ABTA would depend on the circumstances.

Complaints

The first place to take your complaint is the local representative of the company concerned. If you are on holiday try to get the representative to put things right then and there. If that fails you may have a fight on your hands - so gather evidence.

● If it was something you can photograph (like peeling paint in a 'de luxe' hotel or a factory blocking a 'sea view') photograph it.
● If other holiday makers are just as dissatisfied, or will witness to your problem, get their home addresses.
● Get the names of any members of staff who failed to put things right when you complained.
● Keep all proof of what you paid for the trip/holiday.

● Keep all bills for any extra expenses incurred because of the problem. For your own sake, be reasonable. If your 3-star hotel is overbooked and you have to find accommodation for yourself get 3-star accommodation. If you go to a 5-star hotel instead, *you* will be meeting the bill - unless you can *prove* that every 3- and 4-star hotel in the area was totally full.

Once home write to the customer complaints department at the tour operator's head office, giving details of what went wrong and saying what you would like them to do about it. *Keep a copy of your letter and of every piece of evidence you send them* and get the post office to give you proof of posting (free) when you send the letter. If necessary, also complain to the travel agent who booked you.

If you fail to get satisfaction *write* to ABTA with the facts and evidence. ABTA operates a free conciliation service *for those who have already complained without success.* If ABTA feels your complaint is justified, it will try to persuade the company to treat you better. It cannot, however, enforce this. If persuasion fails ABTA can give you information on low cost arbitration by the Chartered Institute of Arbitrators (see page 649). The arbitration is based entirely on written evidence, so anyone who is not confident about writing should get help from a CAB.

ABTA will *only* act if it gets your complaint within 9 months of your return from the holiday.
ABTA only deals with complaints against ABTA members.
ABTA will not deal with complaints involving serious sickness or injury. For these you need legal advice. Go to a CAB or Law Centre if you have no solicitor.

Association of Independent Tour Operators
The Association of Independent Tour Operators is a trade association for small tour operators. It does not have a code of practice or any scheme for dealing with complaints, but operators are bonded, so if one goes out of business the association should be able to refund your money.

The Association of Independent Tour Operators, The Knoll House, Pursers Lane, Peaslake, Surrey GU5 9SJ Tel: 0306 730476

WORK-RELATED ORGANIZATIONS

Advisory Conciliation and Arbitration Service (ACAS)

ACAS is an independent organization set up to improve industrial relations. These services are equally available to trade unions, employers and individual employees.

If you complained to an industrial tribunal about an infringement of your rights - say, unfair dismissal or unequal pay - the complaint would be passed to ACAS and one of its conciliation officers would try to sort the problem out before it reached the tribunal. The conciliation officer does not take sides, he simply helps the two sides to agree to a settlement which they choose themselves. The service is free, and anything said to a conciliation officer is strictly confidential. Equally, if either side wishes to refuse conciliation and simply goes to the tribunal it has a right to do so. There are ACAS offices in many major cities and you can approach them with queries about problems, such as employment rights, and redundancy, either in person or on the phone.

Advisory Conciliation and Arbitration Service, 11-12 St James's Square, London SW1Y 4LA Tel: 01 210 3000. Regional offices are listed in the phone book under 'Advisory'.

Central Arbitration Committee (CAC)

The CAC acts as arbitrator in trade disputes using a committee of three arbitrators: one from management, one from the unions and one independent member with expertise in this field. When conciliation fails at ACAS those in dispute may have a choice of using ACAS arbitration or being referred to the CAC, unless arbitration solely by the CAC is written into a collective agreement. This organization also arbitrates when a union wishes an employer to disclose information which it considers relevant to collective bargaining. If the employer refuses, the matter can be taken directly to the CAC without going via ACAS.

Central Arbitration Committee, 15-17 Ormond Yard, Duke of York Street, London SW1Y 6JT Tel: 01 210 3737/8

Certification Office

The full title of this organization is the Certification Office for Trade Unions and Employers' Associations, and it is really the office of the Certification Officer. His (or her) job is to approve the way trade unions and employers' associations conduct certain aspects of their operations and see that they abide by certain rules. He approves union mergers, and the ballot rules of trade unions in relation to political funds. He also runs the ballot refund scheme for postal ballots and holds the audited accounts for all unions and employers' associations - and allows the public to inspect them.

By law, if a trade union member feels the rules on the political funds have been broken, or that there has been a breach of the rules on the election of someone to the executive of a union, he should contact the Certification Officer who will investigate, however his powers are limited. So, if the election rules are broken the trade union member may also ask for an injunction in the High Court.

Certification Office, 15-17 Ormond Yard, Duke of York Street, London SW1Y 6JT Tel: 01 210 3733/4

Low Pay Unit

This independent body exists to help the low paid, through its regional offices. It will advise any individual who has a problem over pay, without charge, and put him or her in touch with other organizations which can help. It also campaigns for a minimum equal wage and sells a range of leaflets.

Low Pay Unit, 9 Upper Berkeley Street, London W1H 8BY Tel: 01 262 7278

Confederation of British Industry (CBI)

The CBI is an independent organization representing British business. Its members include large businesses, small companies and trade and commercial organizations. Its policy is set by by its ruling council and chairman, but a range of standing committees and regional councils, plus a Small Firms Council, bring their views to bear on decisions. It claims to speak for every sector of industry, and, has close links with both the EEC and Westminster. It also provides a specialist advice and information service, in a number of business fields, for its member companies.

Confederation of British Industry (CBI), 103 New Oxford Street, London WC1A 1DU Tel: 01 379 7400

Industrial Society

The Industrial Society is a campaigning charity which tries to foster greater employee involvement, better leadership at all levels of industry, better communication within industry, and more productive industrial relations. Its members are employers, in companies of all sizes, and many of the major unions. It tries to achieve these ends by links with schools, by conferences, by a large number of courses all over Britain, and by offering a wide range of services. These include an extensive business library, a telephone advice service on any aspect of employing people, management advice and help on drafting documents, and a monthly newsletter covering changes in legislation which affect businesses. There is also a 'Small Company Information and Personnel Service' which will advise on personnel and organizational problems and help those running small business to build management skills. All those services are for members only.

In addition, its Enterprise and Head Start scheme helps young people, who are not members, start up in business. It also has information on other agencies which will help in starting a business. Its publications list covers a wide range of work-related topics, from how to find a job, through business knowledge and skills, to successful retirement.

Industrial Society, Peter Runge House, 3 Carlton House Terrace, London SW1Y 5DG Tel: 01 839 4300

Institute of Directors

The institute is both a club and a pressure group for company directors, senior executives, sole proprietors and certain other business professionals. It aims to improve the industrial and economic climate in which business operates and to provide an effective voice to represent the interests of its members. It also tries to bring the experience of business to bear on the conduct of public affairs and to help its members to 'improve their competence as business leaders'. It has an information and advice service for members, and a research facility based on a business library with direct links to business databases and news services. In addition, it runs a series of events aimed at bringing business people together, including a major annual convention, and offers short courses in business skills which are open to non-members.

Institute of Directors, 116 Pall Mall, London SW1Y 5ED Tel: 01 839 1233

Small Businesses Bureau

Although this is a pressure group linked to the Conservative Party, it is also a useful association for those involved in small businesses - you don't have to be a Conservative to join. It offers an advice and information service, runs Europe's largest conference for small businesses, and incorporates 'Women into Business', which advises and assists women who want to make a career in business or run their own company. It also provides information to young people who want to set up on their own.

The Small Business Bureau, 32 Smith Square, London SW1P 3HH Tel: 01 222 0330 M£H, M, L, B, G, A.

Trade Unions and the Trades Union Congress (TUC)

There is no blanket description which fits all trade unions. To 'protect the interests of their members at work' is the most general aim, but each has created its own set of rules. Provided unions do not break the Employment Act 1984 and register with a government Certification Officer, they can do as they like.

The most usual hierarchy is this: a workplace group is headed by a shop steward (though possibly under another name). The shop steward then represents his or her group of workers in a district committee. This committee, in turn, sends delegates to a regional body, from which the national representatives are then chosen. In some unions ordinary members, or their local representatives, play a more direct part in policy making at a national level. National policy decisions are usually made at an annual national conference and implemented by an executive committee.

Unions are free to levy any subscription they wish. Part of this may be put into a political fund, and used to support any political group the union leaders favour - usually the Labour Party. However, not all unions have such a fund and, by law, members must be given the chance to opt *out* if they wish, and no pressure may be brought on them to pay the levy.

The shop steward or area representative will help employees with any problems related to pay and conditions. A union representative can also act on behalf of a member in an industrial tribunal. However, if your union representative fails to act properly on your behalf, or you are being unfairly treated by the union itself, you can approach the General Secretary of the union with your complaint - the TUC can supply the head office address.

Most trade unions are affiliated to the TUC, but they don't have to be. The TUC is governed by a General Council of 48 union representatives, and is the official voice of the unions to the government. It also arbitrates in disputes between unions, but only in very rare cases can the TUC act on behalf of an aggrieved individual.

Trades Union Congress, 23-28 Great Russell Street, WC1B 3LS Tel: 01 636 4030 - has a range of publications.

Wages Inspectorate

This is the body appointed to see that employers keep the law on wages and hours. It consists of officers from the Department of Employment who investigate complaints made by employees. They have power to enter business premises and have access to records and personnel, and they can bring a case against an employer in the Crown Court. In their turn they are answerable to the Secretary of State for Employment and the Parliamentary Commissioner (Ombudsman).

If you want to check that *you* are getting your due get the leaflets on your occupation, and on the Wages Act 1986, from the Wages Inspectorate. The rules are set by wages councils, representing both employers and workers. However, the 1986 Act largely pulled the teeth of these councils. They usually set a basic working week and give maximum charges for food and accommodation, when the job involves them. But one minimum hourly rate must often cover a whole industry and waiters get the same as kitchen staff - even though the tips are one-sided. Under this legislation, there are *no* minimums for anyone under the age of 21. The addresses of Divisional Offices of the Inspectorate can be found at Jobcentres, Law Centres and Citizens' Advice Bureaux, and all complaints are treated as completely confidential.

Wages Inspectorate, Gatliff House, 93 Ebury Bridge Road, London SW1W 8RE Tel: 01 730 9161 X 294/266

Books on Britain's Organizations
Central Office of Information, *Britain: an Official Handbook,* HMSO - covers most public bodies.
Consumer Congress Directory, **National Consumer Council** (paperback) - embraces most organizations which bridge the gap between public and bureaucracy.

Facts and Figures

Abbreviations • Alphabets • Astrology • Calendar Dates • Clothing Sizes • Collective Nouns • Frequencies • Gems • Historical Figures • Inventions and Discoveries • Names • Roman Numerals • Sports Winners • Temperatures • Useful Maths • Weather • Weights and Measures

This section of the book may look like a rag-bag of assorted information. It is, quite deliberately, just that. Its aim is to answer the diverse, ill-assorted questions of fact which are raised in every household — whether the issue is how to decipher Roman numerals, signal SOS in Morse, or do long division.

ABBREVIATIONS

The vexed question, when it comes to abbreviations, is when to put full stops. At one time they were always put after an abbreviation in which the first part of a word or the first and last letters were used, as in illus. (illustration), Dr. (doctor) or Rd. (road). Full stops were also put between letters used to stand for the first letters of words - as in M.P. Then came the trend for pronouncing abbreviations like ASLEF as if they were words, so the full stops were gradually omitted. Now there is no one rule as to what is correct, but the modern trend is, increasingly, to leave full stops out unless this creates confusion. But even within any one dictionary there are contradictory uses, so it is really a matter for your own discretion.

@ at , as in 'at a certain price'

A1 or A-1 First class (Lloyd's Register of ships); first rate

AA Automobile Association; Athletic Association; Alcoholics Anonymous

AAA Amateur Athletic Association (referred to as 'the three As')

AAM air-to-air missile

A&M Ancient and Modern (hymn book); Agricultural & Mechanical

A&R concerning artists and repertoire (in the recording industry)

ABA Amateur Boxing Association; American Booksellers Association

ABC Australian Broadcasting Commission; American Broadcasting Company

ABM antiballistic missile

ABO the system for classifying blood; there are four types (A, B, AB and O)

AC alternating current; Air Corps; athletic club; before Christ (Latin: *ante Christum*)

ac used in prescriptions to mean 'before meals' (Latin: *ante cibum*)

a/c account; air conditioning (also A/C)

ACAS Advisory Conciliation and Arbitration Service

AC/DC bisexual (slang) - from the two types of electric current

ACE Advisory Centre for Education

ACGI Association of the City and Guilds Institutes

ACTU Australian Council of Trade Unions

ACW aircraftwoman

AD in the year of our Lord (Latin: *anno Domini*)

ad active duty

Ad hoc for this special purpose

Ad lib as much as you please (Latin: *ad libitum*)

ADP automatic data processing

AEA Atomic Energy Authority

AEC Atomic Energy Commission

AEU Amalgamated Engineering Union

AFA Amateur Fencing Association; Amateur Football Association

AFAM Ancient Free and Accepted Masons

AFB Air Force Base

AFC Association Football Club; automatic frequency control; automatic flight control

AGC automatic gain control

AGR advanced gas-cooled reactor

AH in the year of the Mohammedan calendar (Latin: *anno Hegirae*)

AHM Association of Head Mistresses

AI artificial insemination

AIA Association of the Institute of Actuaries

AICC All India Congress Committee - the national assembly of the Indian National Congress

AID Army Intelligence Department; artificial insemination by donor; acute infectious disease; Agency for International Development

AIDS   Acquired Immune Deficiency Syndrome

AIF   Australian Imperial Force

AIH   artificial insemination by husband

AIR   All India Radio

ALU   arithmetical and logical unit - computer jargon

AM   Alpes Maritime; in the year of the world (Latin: *anno mundi*); Ave Maria; associate member

am   before noon (Latin: *ante meridiem*)

AMA   American Medical Association

anon   anonymous

ANU   Australian National University

ANZAC   Australian and New Zealand Army Corps

ANZUS   Australia, New Zealand and United States - defence alliance

A/O or a/o   for the account of - used in accounting

AOB or aob   any other business - as in timetable for a committee

AOD   Ancient Order of Druids

AOH   Ancient Order of Hibernians

APR   annual percentage rate

APS   American Protestant Society; American Peace Society; Aborigine Protection Society

APT   advanced passenger train

AQ   achievement quotient

AR   Autonomous Region

ASA   Amateur Swimming Association

ASE   Amalgamated Society of Engineers

ASEAN   Association of South East Asian Nations

ASGB   Aeronautical Society of Great Britain

ASIO   Australian Security Intelligence Organization

ASLEF   Associated Society of Locomotive Engineers and Firemen

ASM   air-to-surface missile

ASSR   Autonomous Soviet Socialist Republic

AST   Atlantic Standard Time

ASTMS   Association of Scientific, Technical and Managerial Staffs

AT or at   automatic transmission

ATC   air traffic control; Air Training Corps

ATV   Associated Television

AU or au   angstrom unit; astronomical unit

AUEW   Amalgamated Union of Engineering Workers

AWOL or awol   Absent without leave (Forces)

BA   British Academy; British Association (for the Advancement of Science)

BAA   British Airports Authority

BALPA   British Airline Pilots Association

BAR   British Auction Records

BBA   British Beekeepers Association

BBC   British Broadcasting Corporation

BC   before Christ

BCG   Bacillus Calmette-Guérin (anti-tuberculosis vaccine)

BCh/BChir   Bachelor of Surgery - a fully qualified surgeon

B/D   bank draft; bills discounted - commercial

BDA   British Dental Association

be or B/E   bill of exchange

BEF   British Expeditionary Force

B/L, b/l, Bs/l   bill of lading

BM   Bachelor of Medicine

BMA   British Medical Association

BMJ   *British Medical Journal*

BO   body odour; box office

B/O   brought over - used in book keeping; buyer's option

BOA   British Olympic Association; British Optical Association

BOAR   British Army of the Rhine

BoT   Board of Trade

BP   British Pharmacopoeia

bp   boiling point (also bpt); below proof - re alcohol

B/P or bp   bills payable

BPC   British Pharmaceutical Codex

bpi   bits per inch - used of computer tape

BR   British Rail

B/R or br   bills receivable

BRCS   British Red Cross Society

BRS   British Road Services

BS   precedes catalogue number of the British Standards Institution

bs   balance sheet; bill of sale

BSI   British Standards Institution

BSS   British Standards Specification

BST   British Summer Time

BThU   British Thermal Unit

BTU   Board of Trade Unit

bu   bushel

B/W   black and white - in photography

BWR   boiling water reactor

BYO   an unlicensed restaurant where you bring your own wine (Australian)

C   Centigrade; Celsius; coulomb (electricity); Conservative

c   about (Latin: *circa*)

©   copyright

CA   Chartered Accountant; chief accountant; Central America; consular agent; Consumers' Association

C/A   current account; credit account; capital account

CAA   Civil Aviation Authority

CAB   Citizens' Advice Bureau; Civil Aeronautical Board (US)

CAF   cost and freight

CAP   Common Agricultural Policy - of the EEC

c&b   caught and bowled - cricket

C&G   City and Guilds

C&W   country and western

CARE   Cooperative for American Relief Everywhere - charity federation

CARICOM   Caribbean Community and Common Market - trade alliance

CARIFTA   Caribbean Free Trade Area

CAT   College of Advanced Technology

CB   Citizens' Band - radio frequency

CB   County Borough

cb   centre of buoyancy - in boats etc.

CBC   Canadian Broadcasting Corporation

CBD, cbd   cash before delivery; central business district

CBI   Confederation of British Industry

CBS   Columbia Broadcasting System

CC   County Council/Councillor; County Court; Circuit Court; Chamber of Commerce cc carbon copy; cubic centimetres; chapter

CD Civil Defence; Corps Diplomatique - visiting diplomat

cd cash discount

c/d carried down - in accounting

CD Acts Contagious Diseases Acts

CE Common Entrance - exam; civil engineer; chief engineer

CEGB Central Electricity Generating Board

CENTO Central Treaty Organization - for military and economic co-operation between Iran, Pakistan and Turkey

CERN Conseil Européen pour la Recherche Nucléaire - European centre for research into particle physics, based in Geneva

CET Central European Time - 1 hour ahead of GMT

c/f carried forward - book-keeping

CFE College of Further Education

CG Coast Guard; Coldstream Guards

cg centre of gravity; centigram

ch chain; chapter; chief; church

CI Channel Islands

CIA Central Intelligence Agency (US intelligence and espionage)

CID Criminal Investigation Department

CIF or cif cost, insurance and freight - included in quoted price

CM or cm Court Martial

cm centimetre

cml commercial

CMS Church Missionary Society

CMUA Commercial Motor Users Association

C/N, c/n or cn credit note

CNAA Council for National Academic Awards - degree awarding body

CND Campaign for Nuclear Disarmament

CNR Canadian National Railways

CNS central nervous system - brain and spinal cord

CO conscientious objector

Co county; company; the others

c/o care of

COD cash on delivery

C of C Chamber of Commerce

C of E Church of England (sometimes also CE)

C of S Church of Scotland

COI Central Office of Information

COM computer output on microfilm

com committee; commercial; comedy

COMECON Council of Mutual Economic Assistance - Eastern bloc alliance

Cons Consul; Conservative; constitution

cont continued; containing; contents; continent

CORE Congress of Racial Equality (US)

COSPAR Committee on Space Research

CP Command Post; Canadian Press; Communist Party; Common Prayer; Court of Probate

cp compare

cpd compound

CPR Canadian Pacific Railways

cps cycles per second

CPSU Communist Party of the Soviet Union

CPU central processing unit - computer technology

cr credit; creditor

cres crescendo

CRP Central Reserve Police

CS Chemical Society; Civil Service; Court of Session; Christian Science; Capital Stock

CSB chemical stimulation of the brain

CSC Civil Service Commission

CSE Certificate of Secondary Education

CSIRO Commonwealth Scientific and Industrial Research Organization (Australian)

ct cent; certificate; court

CTC Cyclists' Touring Club

CTO cancelled to order - in stamp collecting

CTV Canadian Television Network Ltd

CU Cambridge University

CUP Cambridge University Press

CUSO Canadian University Services Overseas - voluntary work

CWS Co-operative Wholesale Society

cwt hundredweight

D Democratic; Deus (God); Department

d date; penny; diameter; daughter; dose; dollar; drachma

D/A or da deposit account; documents for acceptance

DC direct current; District Court; District of Columbia

dc direct current

D and C dilatation and curettage - dilation of cervix and cleaning out of the uterus

DCH Diploma in Child Health

DCL Distillers Company Ltd

DCLI Duke of Cornwall's Light Infantry

DDT Dichlor-diphynl-trichlorethane — insecticide

DDS Dewey Decimal System - used in classification of library books

deb debenture

deg degree

del delegate

DES Department of Education and Science

DEW line distant early warning line - Arctic sensors of air attack

DF, D/F Direction Finding (or Finder)

DG thanks be to God (Latin: Deo gratias); Dragoon Guards

dg decigram

DH, D/H, DHC drop head coupé - car with removable roof

DHSS Department of Health and Social Security

di or dia diameter

dig digest - i.e. book summary

dim diminuendo

Dip, dip diploma

div divide; dividend; division; divorce(d)

DIY, diy do-it-yourself

DJ, dj dinner jacket; disc jockey

dkg decagram

dkl decalitre

dkm decametre

D/L demand loan

dl decilitre

DLI Durham Light Infantry

DLO Diploma in Laryngology and Otology (ear, nose and throat)

DLO Dead Letter Office

DLP Democratic Labor Party (Australia)

dlr dealer

DM Deutsche Mark - German currency

dm decimetre

DMA direct memory access - computer term

DMS Diplomatic Management Studies

DMZ demilitarized zone

DNB *Dictionary of National Biography*

DNS Department for National Savings

D/O, do delivery order

DOA dead on arrival

DOD Department of Defense (US)

DOE Department of the Environment

DP Displaced Person

DPH Diploma in Public Health

DPW Department of Public Works

DR dead reckoning

Dr Doctor

dr dram; debit; drachma; debtor

DS *dal segno* - in music, meaning repeat from the mark

DST daylight saving time

DTI Department of Trade and Industry

DTs delirium tremens - delirium caused by alcohol damage to brain

D/W dock warrant

dwt pennyweight

dwt deadweight tonnage

dz dozen

E East; energy; electro-motive force

e engineering

ea each

EACSO East African Common Services Organization

E&OE, e&oe errors and omissions excepted

EAROM electrically alterable read only memory - in computers

ECG electrocardiogram

ECOWAS Economic Community of West African States

ECGD Export Credits Guarantee Department - a government department providing facilities for UK exporters

ECSC European Coal and Steel Community

ECT electroconvulsive therapy - electrical stimulation of brain

EDC European Defence Community

EDP electronic data processing

EEC European Economic Community

EEG electroencephalogram; electro-encephalograph

EFTA European Free Trade Association

Eg Egyptian

eg for example (Latin: *exempli gratia*)

ELDO European Launcher Development Organization

EMU, emu electromagnetic unit

ENE east-northeast

ENT ear, nose and throat

EP extended-play gramophone record

Ep epistle

ep in passing conversation (French: *en passant*)

EPA educational priority area

EPNS Electroplated Nickel Silver

eq equal; equation; equivalent

ERNIE electronic random number indicating equipment

ESN educationally subnormal - of below average intelligence

ESP extrasensory perception

ESRO European Space Research Organization

EST electric-shock treatment; Eastern Standard Time (US)

est established; estate; estimated; estuary

ETA estimated time of arrival

et al and others (Latin: *et alii*)

etc and so forth, and the others (Latin: *et cetera*)

ETD estimated time of departure

et seq and the following (Latin: *et sequens*)

ETU Electrical Trades Union

EURATOM European Atomic Energy Community - treaty by EEC members

EV English Version (of Bible)

ex div without dividend

ex int without interest

F Fahrenheit; fellow; force; France

f forte - loudly in music

FA Football Association; Field Artillery; Fanny Adams

FAO Food and Agriculture Organization

FBI Federal Bureau of Investigation

FC Football Club

FCO Foreign and Commonwealth Office

ff fortissimo - music; folio, following pages or lines

FHC fixed-head coupé - coupé in which roof is not removable

FI fuel injection - of car

FIFA Fédération Internationale de Football Association

Fl Flanders; Flemish

FM frequency modulation - radio receiving high frequency

FO Foreign Office

FOB, fob Free on board - i.e. free delivery to freight vehicle

FP, fp freezing point; fully paid

FPA Family Planning Association

fps feet per second; frames per second - photographic

frt freight

fs foot-second

fwd forward; front-wheel drive; four-wheel drive

G, g guilder; gauge; guinea

GA General Assembly

GATT General Agreement on Tariffs and Trade

GB Great Britain

GBH grievous bodily harm - legal

GCM, gcm greatest common measure

Gdns gardens

GDP gross domestic product - a country's flow of goods and services during a year

GDR German Democratic Republic

gds goods

GG Girl Guides

GHQ General Headquarters

GLC Greater London Council

GMC General Medical Council

GMT Greenwich Mean Time

GNP gross national product - GDP plus overseas real earnings

GO general order

GP graduated pension; Gallup poll

GPI general paralysis of the insane

GPO general post office
GQ general quarters
gr wt gross weight
GS General Staff
gtd guaranteed
GTC, gtc goods till cancelled - on orders

HAC Honourable Artillery Company
Hb haemoglobin
HC House of Commons; Holy Communion
HCF, hcf highest common factor
hdbk hardback
HE high explosive
HEW Department of Health, Education and Welfare (US)
HF, hf high frequency
HG Home Guard
HGV heavy goods vehicle
HJ here lies (Latin: *hic jacet*)
HL House of Lords
HM headmaster; headmistress
HMS Her Majesty's Service; Her Majesty's Ship
HMSO Her Majesty's Stationery Office - publisher of government papers
HNC Higher National Certificate
HND Higher National Diploma
HO Home Office; head office
HP, hp horse-power; hire purchase; high pressure; Houses of Parliament
HQ headquarters
HR House of Representatives (US)
HT high tension
HV, hv high voltage
HW, hw high water
HWM high water mark
hyp hypothesis; hypotenuse

IAEA International Atomic Energy Authority
IAS indicated air speed
IATA International Air Transport Association
IBA Independent Broadcasting Authority
ICA Institute of Contemporary Arts
ICAO International Civil Aviation Organization
ICBM intercontinental ballistic missile
ICE Institution of Civil Engineers

ICFTU International Congress of Free Trade Unions
IChemE Institution of Chemical Engineers
ICJ International Courts of Justice
ID identification
ie that is (Latin: *id est*)
IEE Institution of Electrical Engineers
IFC International Finance Corporation
IGY International Geophysical Year
ILEA Inner London Education Authority
ILO International Labour Organization
ILS instrument landing system
IMechE Institution of Mechanical Engineers
IMF International Monetary Fund
IMinE Institution of Mining Engineers
IMunE Institution of Municipal Engineers
IND in the name of the Lord (Latin: *in nomine Dei*)
IUD intrauterine device - contraceptive in the womb
IPA International Phonetic Alphabet
IQ intelligence quotient
IR Inland Revenue
IRA Irish Republican Army
IRO Inland Revenue Office; International Refuge Organization
ISBN International Standard Book Number
ita, ITA Initial Teaching Alphabet
ITV Independent Television

JA joint account - in bank
JCR junior common room

KANU Kenya African National Union
KB King's Bench
KD, kd knock down - as in furniture which is sold in kits
KE kinetic energy
kg kilogram
KGB Soviet secret police
KKK Ku Klux Klan - secret anti-black organization in US
KO knock out

LA Legislative Assembly; Library Association

LAMDA London Academy of Music and Dramatic Art
LC letter of credit
LCM, lcm lowest common multiple
LD lethal dose
LDCs less developed countries
LEA Local Education Authority
LED light-emitting diode
LF low frequency
LH, lh left hand
lhd left-hand drive
LI Light Infantry

lit literary
LP long player
£sd term for UK currency before decimalization - pronounced as LSD
LSE London School of Economics
Ltd Limited Company
LV luncheon voucher
LW long wave, low water
LWM low water mark

M medium
M3 a fairly broad measure of the money supply which includes notes, coins, bank accounts and savings in the UK. M 1 and 2 are narrower, excluding coins, notes and certain savings
MA mental age; military academy
MCC Marylebone Cricket Club
met meteorological
MF medium frequency - radio
mfd manufactured
mg milligram
MHz megahertz
MI Military Intelligence
MI5 Military Intelligence section 5 - British counter intelligence
MIDAS Missile Defence Alarm System
MIRV multiple independently targeted re-entry vehicle - i.e. missile
MIT Massachusetts Institute of Technology
mkt market
MLD minimum lethal dose
MLF multilateral force - nuclear
MLR minimum lending rate
MO, mo mail order; money order
MOD Ministry of Defence
MOT Ministry of Transport

MP Metropolitan Police; Mounted Police; Military Police; Member of Parliament
mp melting point
mpg miles per gallon
mph miles per hour
MRA Moral Rearmament
MRC Medical Research Council
MS, ms manuscript (plural Mss or mss)
MSG monosodium glutamate - food additive used to enhance flavour
Mt mount, e.g. Mt Everest
MV megavolt
MVD Ministry of Internal Affairs - Soviet police
MW 1 megawatt, medium wave - radio frequency
MY motor yacht

N north; National; Navy
n born (Latin: *natus*); noun; noon; number
NAAFI Navy, Army and Air Force Institutes - organized canteens
NALGO National and Local Government Officers Association
NAS National Association of Schoolmasters
NASA National Aeronautics and Space Administration
NATO North Atlantic Treaty Organization - defence alliance
NATSOPA National Society of Operative Printers, Graphical and Media Personnel - trades union
NB, nb note well (Latin: *nota bene*)
nb no ball - cricket
NBC National Broadcasting Company (US)
NBG no bloody good
NCB National Coal Board
NCCL National Council for Civil Liberties
NE northeast
neg negative
NERC Natural Environment Research Council
NF National Front
NFS National Fire Service
NFU National Farmers Union
NFWI National Federation of Women's Institutes
NG National Guard (US)
NGA National Graphical Association

NHS National Health Service
NI National Insurance
NIRC National Industrial Relations Court
NKVD Soviet police and secret police, 1934-43
nl not permitted (Latin: *non licet*)
NLC National Liberal Club
NLF National Liberation Front
NLLST National Lending Library for Science and Technology
nm nautical mile
NNE north-northeast
NNW north-northwest
NPA Newspaper Publishers Association
NPL National Physical Laboratory
nr near
NSB National Savings Bank
NSF, N/S/F not sufficient funds - banking
NSPCC National Society for the Prevention of Cruelty to Children
NSU non-specific urethritis - mild venereal infection
NT National Trust
nt wt net weight - weight without the packaging
NUAAW National Union of Agricultural and Allied Workers
NUGMW National Union of General and Municipal Workers
NUJ National Union of Journalists
NUPE National Union of Public Employees
NUR National Union of Railwaymen
NUS National Union of Seamen, or Students
NUT National Union of Teachers
NW northwest
NZBC New Zealand Broadcasting Corporation

O ocean
O & M organization and methods - work study
OAP old-age pensioner
OAS Organization of American States; Organisation de l'Armée Secrète - European settlers opposed to Algerian independence

OAU Organization of African Unity
o/c overcharge
OCAM Organization of French-speaking African States
OCTU Officer Cadets Training Unit
OD on demand - banking; overdraft - banking
ODM Ministry of Overseas Development
OECD Organization of Economic Co-operation and Development
OED Oxford English Dictionary
OEEC Organization for European Economic Co-operation
OHMS On Her Majesty's Service
OK expression meaning all right, fine, I agree
OMS Organisation Mondiale de la Santé (French: World Health Organization)
ono or nearest offer - meaning offers of a lower price considered
OP, op out of print
OPEC Organization of Petroleum Exporting Countries
OR other ranks - military; operational research
OS outsize; Old School; Ordnance Survey
OST Office of Science and Technology
OTC Officer's Training Corps; over the counter - stock exchange
OU Open University; Oxford University
OUP Oxford University Press
ovno or very nearest offer - they won't accept a much lower price

P parking
p penny - since decimal coinage
PA personal assistant; press agent; Publishers Association; power of attorney; public-address system; personal appearance
pa each year (Latin: *per annum*)
PABX private automatic branch exchange - telephone system (also PB handling internal and external calls in a large firm)
P&L profit and loss

P&O Peninsular and Oriental - shipping company

p&p postage and packing - referring to the cost of these

Pat Off Patent Office

PAYE pay as you earn - system of tax deductions from earnings

PB Prayer Book; British Pharmacopoeia

pc post card; per cent; after meals - medicine (Latin: *post cibum*)

PD Police Department

pd paid

pdq pretty damn quick

PDSA People's Dispensary for Sick Animals

PE physical education; potential energy

PG paying guest; post graduate; parental guidance - film category

pg page

PGA Professional Golfers Association

PK psychokinesis

pkg package

pkt packet

pl place

PLA Port of London Authority

PLO Palestine Liberation Organization

PLP Parliamentary Labour Party

PLR Public Lending Right - authors' remuneration scheme

PM, pm after noon (Latin: *post meridiem*)

PN, P/N, pn promissory note

PNdB perceived noise decibel - sound measurement

PO Post Office; personnel officer

po postal order

POB Post Office Box

POE point of embarkation - military

pp pages; parcel post; past participle; privately printed; post paid

ppd prepaid; post paid

PPE philosophy, politics and economics - university course

PR Proportional Representation

pr pair; price; pronoun; to be inserted in the anus - medicine (Latin: *per rectum*)

PS postscript - note added after signature on a letter

PT physical training; physical therapy; pupil-teacher

pt pint; part; payment; point

PTA Parent-Teacher Association

PW policewoman

Q question; quarto

q quart; quarter; question

QARNC Queen Alexandra's Royal Army Nursing Corps

QB Queen's Bench - legal

QED which was shown or proved (Latin: *quod erat demonstrandum*)

ql as much as you please - prescriptions (Latin: *quantum libet*)

qm every morning - medicine (Latin: *quaque mane*)

QS quarter sessions

qv denotes a cross-reference (Latin: *quod vide*)

R royal

RAAF Royal Australian Air Force

RAC Royal Automobile Club

RADA Royal Academy of Dramatic Art

RAEC Royal Army Educational Corps

RAF Royal Air Force

RAFVR Royal Air Force Volunteer Reserve

RAM Royal Academy of Music

RAMC Royal Army Medical Corps

RAN Royal Australian Navy

R&B rhythm and blues

R&D research and development

R&R rest and recreation

RAOC Royal Army Ordnance Corps

RAS Royal Agricultural Society, or Astronomical Society

RATO rocket-assisted take-off

RAVC Royal Army Veterinary Corps

RC Roman Catholic; Red Cross

RCA Radio Corporation of America; Royal College of Art; Royal Canadian Academy

RCAF Royal Canadian Air Force

RCM Royal College of Music

RCMP Royal Canadian Mounted Police

RCN Royal College of Nursing; Royal Canadian Navy

RCO Royal College of Organists

RCP Royal College of Physicians

rcpt receipt

RCS Royal College of Surgeons; Royal Corps of Signals; Royal College of Science

RDC Rural District Council

RE Royal Engineers

REM rapid eye movements - in dreaming sleep

RFC Rugby Football Club

RGS Royal Geographical Society

Rgt regiment

RH, rh right hand

RHA Royal Horse Artillery

RI Royal Institution

RIBA Royal Institute of British Architects

RIC Royal Institute of Chemistry

RICS Royal Institute of Chartered Surveyors

RIP rest in peace - as on tombstones (Latin: *requiescat in pace*)

RM Royal Mail; Royal Marines

RMA Royal Military Academy (Sandhurst)

RNAS Royal Naval Air Service, or Air Station

RNLI Royal National Lifeboat Institution

RNVR Royal Naval Volunteer Reserve

RNZAF Royal New Zealand Air Force

RNZAN Royal New Zealand Navy

RoSPA Royal Society for the Prevention of Accidents

rpm revolutions per minute; resale price maintenance

RSA Royal Society of Arts; Republic of South Africa

RSGB Radio Society of Great Britain

RSJ rolled-steel joint - used to support building structures

RSL Royal Society of Literature

RSM Royal Society of Medicine

RSPB Royal Society for the Protection of Birds

RSPCA Royal Society for the Prevention of Cruelty to Animals

RSV revised standard version - of Bible

RSVP please reply (French: *répondez s'il vous plaît*)

RTR Royal Tank Regiment

RU Rugby Union

RV revised version - of Bible

S saint; Socialist; sea; senate; society; small
SA Salvation Army
SABC South African Broadcasting Corporation
SALT Strategic Arms Limitation Talks
SAM surface-to-air missile
SAYE save as you earn - deduction from earnings scheme
SCE Scottish Certificate of Education
SCR senior common room
SDP Social Democratic Party
SE southeast
SEATO South East Asian Treaty Organization
SERC Science and Engineering Research Council
sgd signed
SHAPE Supreme Headquarters Allied Powers Europe
SLADE Society of Lithographic Artists, Designers, Engravers and Process Workers - a trade union
SLR single lens reflex - type of camera
SNAKE EEC scheme for harmonizing fluctuations in EEC currencies
so seller's option; shipping order
SOP standard operating procedure
SPCK Society for the Promotion of Christian Knowledge
Sr Sister - religious
SRCN State Registered Children's Nurse
SRO standing room only; Statutory Rules and Orders
SS steamship; Schutzstaffel (protection detachment, i.e. originally Hitler's bodyguard)
SSW south-southwest
St street; saint; statute
sta station; stationary
suf suffix; sufficient

TA Territorial Army
TAVR Territorial and Army Volunteer Reserve
TGWU Transport and General Workers' Union
TM transcendental meditation
TPI Town Planning Institute
tr translated; trustee; treasurer
TT teetotal(ler); tuberculin tested

TTL through the lens - type of light metering on a camera

U category of film suited to all ages
UCCA Universities Central Council for Admissions
UDA Ulster Defence Association
UDC Urban District Council
UDR Ulster Defence Regiment
UGC University Grants Committee
UHF ultra high frequency
UN United Nations
UNCTAD United Nations Commission for Trade and Development
UNDRO United Nations Disaster Relief Organization
UNESCO United Nations Educational, Scientific and Cultural Organization
UNICEF United Nations Children's Fund
UNO United Nations Organization
UP United Press
USAF United States Air Force
USM unlisted securities market - for certain shares
USS United States Senate
USW ultrashort wave
UU Ulster Unionist
UV ultraviolet

V volt
VAD Voluntary Aid Detachment
V&A Victoria and Albert
var variety; various
VAT value-added tax
vb verb
VD venereal disease
VDU visual display unit - screen part of a computer
VLF, vlf very low frequency
VO very old - to imply brandy, port and similar are old
VSO very superior old - to imply brandy or port is twelve to seventeen years old; Voluntary Service Overseas
VSOP very superior old pale - shows brandy or port is twenty to twenty-five years old
VTOL vertical take-off and landing

W watt
WAAAF Women's Auxiliary Australian Air Force

WAAC Women's Army Auxiliary Corps
WAAF Women's Auxiliary Air Force
WASP white anglo-saxon protestant - slang for classy, white American
WC, wc water closet - lavatory; West Central - London postal district
WCC World Council of Churches
WEA Workers' Educational Association
WHO World Health Organization
WI Women's Institute
WL, wl water line
WLM women's liberation movement
WNP Welsh Nationalist Party
WNW west-northwest
WP weather permitting
WPB, wbp waste paper basket
WPC woman police constable
wpm words per minute
WRAAC Women's Royal Australian Army Corps
WRAAF Women's Royal Australian Air Force
WRAC Women's Royal Army Corps
WRAF Women's Royal Air Force
WRNS Women's Royal Naval Service
WRVS Women's Royal Voluntary Service
WSW west-southwest
wt weight
WVS Women's Voluntary Service

XL extra large

YHA Youth Hostels Association
YMCA Young Men's Christian Association
YMHA Young Men's Hebrew Association
yr year
YWCA Young Women's Christian Association

ZANU Zimbabwe African National Union
ZAPU Zimbabwe African People's Union
ZPG zero population growth

Ranks and Titles

If you need to know what the letters after someone's name stand for, or are generally curious, the following list covers those most commonly used. Among academic qualifications a bachelor is junior to a master, and a master junior to a doctor, and members of institutions are normally junior to fellows. Unfortunately, where titles are concerned it isn't possible to offer any neat rules, it's an immensely complex business with one order of knighthood being senior to another and different orders having different orders of seniority within them. On all matters of precedence, from university degrees or monastic orders to dukedoms, the bible – which is even used by the honours department of 10 Downing Street – is Debrett's *Correct Form*. If you can't get hold of a copy, the *Daily Telegraph* information service (ring 100 and ask for custom call, the *Daily Telegraph* Information Bureau – there is a fixed charge for every query of £2.85 + VAT which will be automatically added to your telephone bill) can will look up what you need to know. Other useful reference sources in this area are Debrett's *Peerage, Burke's Peerage, Who's Who,* and *Dod's Parliamentary Companion.*

AB Able Bodied Seaman

ACA Associate of the Institute of Chartered Accountants of England and Wales

ACP Associate of the College of Preceptors

ADC aide-de-camp

ADG Assistant-Director General

ADMS Assistant Director of Medical Services

AE & P Ambassador Extraordinary and Plenipotentiary

AFA Associate of the Faculty of Actuaries in Scotland

AFC Air Force Cross

AFM Air Force Medal

AGSM Associate of the Guildhall School of Music

AIA Associate of the Institute of Actuaries

AIC Associate of the Institute of Chemistry

AIG Adjutant Inspector General

AM Albert Medal, Master of Arts (US) (Latin: *Artium Magister*)

AMICE Associate Member of the Institution of Civil Engineers

AMIChemE Associate Member of the Institution of Chemical Engineers

AMIEE Associate Member of the Institution of Electrical Engineers

AMIME Associate Member of the Institution of Mining Engineers

AMIMechE Associate Member of the Institution of Mechanical Engineers

AMInstCE Associate Member of the Institution of Civil Engineers

AMInstGasE Associate Member of the Institution of Gas Engineers

APS Associate of the Pharmaceutical Society

ARA Associate of the Royal Academy

ARCM Associate of the Royal College of Music

ARCO Associate of the Royal College of Organists

ARCS Associate of the Royal College of Science

ARIBA Associate of the Royal Institute of British Architects

ARMCM Associate of the Royal Manchester College of Music

ARSA Associate of the Royal Scottish Academy; Associate of the Royal Society of Arts

ARSM Associate of the Royal School of Mines

ASAA Associate of the Society of Accountants and Auditors

ASAM Associate of the National Society of Art Masters

ATCL Associate of Trinity College London (Music)

AVM Air Vice Marshal

BA Bachelor of Arts

BAgric Bachelor of Agriculture

BArch Bachelor of Architecture

Bart Baronet

BCh Bachelor of Surgery

BChD Bachelor of Dental Surgery

BCL Bachelor of Civil Law; Bachelor of Canon Law

BCom Bachelor of Commerce

BD Bachelor of Divinity

BDS Bachelor of Dental Surgery

BE Bachelor of Education; Bachelor of Engineering

BEd Bachelor of Education

BEng Bachelor of Engineering

BHy Bachelor of Hygiene

BLit Bachelor of Literature

BLitt Bachelor of Letters

BM Bachelor of Medicine

BME Bachelor of Mining Engineering

BMet Bachelor of Metallurgy

BMus Bachelor of Music

BPharm Bachelor of Pharmacy

BPhil Bachelor of Philosophy

BS Bachelor of Surgery

BSc Bachelor of Science

BSSc or BSoc Sc Bachelor of Social Science

Bt Baronet

BTh Bachelor of Theology

CB Companion (of the Order) of the Bath

CBE Companion (of the Order) of the British Empire

CEng Chartered Engineer

CF Chaplain to the Forces

CG Consul General

CGM Conspicuous Gallantry Medal (Naval)

CGS Chief of General Staff

CH Companion of Honour

ChB Bachelor of Surgery (Latin: *Chirurgiae Baccalaureus*)

ChE Chemical Engineer

ChM Master of Surgery (Latin: *Chirurgiae Magister*)

CIGS Chief of Imperial General Staff

CMG Companion of the Order of St Michael and St George

CO Commanding Officer

Cons Consul

CPC Clerk of the Privy Council

Cpl Corporal

CPO Chief Petty Officer

CPS (Latin: *Custos Privati Sigilli*) Keeper of the Privy Seal

CR (Latin: *Custos Rotulorum*) Keeper of the Rolls

CS Clerk of Sessions; Clerk to the Signet; Common Sergeant; Keeper of the Seal; Chartered Surveyor

CSC Conspicuous Service Cross

CSE Certificate of Secondary Education

CSI Companion of the Order of the Star of India

CSO Chief Signals Officer; Chief Staff Officer

CVO Commander of the Royal Victorian Order

D Don (Spanish); Director

DA District Attorney (US)

DBE Dame Commander of the Order of the British Empire

DC Deputy Consul

DCB Dame Commander of the Order of the Bath

DCL Doctor of Civil Law

DCM Distinguished Conduct Medal

DCVO Dame Commander of the Royal Victorian Order

DD Doctor of Divinity

DDEng Doctor of Engineering

DDS or DDSc Doctor of Dental Surgery, or Science

DF Defender of the Faith

DFC Distinguished Flying Cross

DFM Distinguished Flying Medal

DG Director General

DHy Doctor of Hygiene

DIC Diploma of the Imperial College of Science and Technology

Dip or dip diploma

DipAD Diploma of Art and Design

DipEd Diploma in Education

DipN Diploma in Nursing (a senior qualification)

DLitt or DLit Doctor of Letters, or of Literature

DM Doctor of Medicine

DMD Doctor of Dental Medicine

DMus Doctor of Music

DO Doctor of Optometry; Doctor of Osteopathy

DObstRCOG Diploma in Obstetrics of the Royal College of Obstetricians and Gynaecologists

DPH Diploma of Public Health

DPhil or DPh Doctor of Philosophy

DPM Diploma in Psychological Medicine

Dr doctor

DSc Doctor of Science

DSC Distinguished Service Cross (Naval)

DSM Distinguished Service Medal (Naval)

DSO Companion of the Distinguished Service Order

DTh Doctor of Theology

DVM Doctor of Veterinary Medicine

E Earl

ER Elizabeth Regina - Queen Elizabeth

Exc Excellency

FAI Fellow of the Auctioneers' Institute

FBA Fellow of the British Academy

FCA Fellow of the Institute of Chartered Accountants

FCI Fellow of the Institute of Commerce

FCP Fellow of the College of Preceptors

FES Fellow of the Entomological, or Ethnological Society

FFA Fellow of the Faculty of Actuaries

FFPS Fellow of the Faculty of Physicians and Surgeons

FGS Fellow of the Geological Society

FIA Fellow of the Institute of Actuaries

FIC Fellow of the Institute of Chemistry

FIH Fellow of the Institute of Hygiene

FLA Fellow of the Library Association

FO Field Officer; Flying Officer

FoC Father of the Chapel - trade union official

FPS Fellow of the Philharmonic Society, or Philosophical Society

FPhysS Fellow of the Physical Society

FRCGP Fellow of the Royal College of General Practitioners

FRCO Fellow of the Royal College of Organists

FRCOG Fellow of the Royal College of Obstetricians and Gynaecologists

FRCP Fellow of the Royal College of Physicians

FRCPsych Fellow of the Royal College of Psychiatrists

FRCS Fellow of the Royal College of Surgeons

FRGS Fellow of the Royal Geographical Society

FRHistS Fellow of the Royal Historical Society

FRHortS Fellow of the Royal Horticultural Society

FRMetS Fellow of the Royal Meteorological Society

FRNSA Fellow of the Royal School of Naval Architecture

FRPS Fellow of the Royal Photographic Society

FRS Fellow of the Royal Society

FRSA Fellow of the Royal Society of Arts

FSA Fellow of the Society of Antiquaries

FSI Fellow of the Surveyors' Institution

FZS Fellow of the Zoological Society

GBE (Knight or Dame) Grand Cross of the British Empire

GC George Cross

GCB Knight Grand Cross of the Bath

GCIE Knight Grand Commander of the Indian Empire

GCMG Knight Grand Cross of St Michael and St George

GCSE General Certificate of Secondary Education

GCSI Knight Grand Commander of the Star of India

GCVO Knight Grand Cross of the Royal Victorian Order

GG Governor General

GI soldier in US army, esp. an enlisted man

GM George Medal

GOC General Officer Commanding

GOC-IN-C General Officer Commanding-in-Chief

GP General Practitioner

GS General Secretary

GSO General Staff Officer

HBM His (Her) Britannic Majesty

HE His Eminence; His (Her) Excellency

HG His Grace

HIH His (Her) Imperial Highness

HIM His (Her) Imperial Majesty

HMIS Her Majesty's Inspector of Schools

HRH His (Her) Royal Highness

HRSA Honorary Member of the Royal Scottish Academy

HS Home Secretary

HSH His (Her) Serene Highness

HSM His (Her) Serene Majesty

IGM International Grandmaster (chess)

ISO Imperial Service Order

IM International Master (chess)

JA Judge Advocate

JAG Judge Advocate General

JP Justice of the Peace

KB Knight Bachelor; Knight of the Bath

KBE Knight (Commander of the Order) of the British Empire

KC King's Counsel

KCB Knight Commander of the Bath

KCH Knight Commander (of the Order) of Hanover

KCIE Knight Commander (of the Order) of the Indian Empire

KCMG Knight Commander of St Michael and St George

KCSI Knight Commander of the Star of India

KCVO Knight Commander of the Royal Victorian Order

KG Knight of the Order of the Garter

KH Knight of the Order of Hanover

KSG Knight of St Gregory

KStJ Knight of the Order of St John

KT Knight of the Order of the Thistle

Kt, Knt Knight

LAC leading aircraftman

LACW leading aircraftwoman

LCJ Lord Chief Justice

LCP Licentiate of the College of Preceptors

L/Cpl Lance Corporal

LDiv Licentiate of Divinity

LDS Licentiate of Dental Surgery

LittD Doctor of Letters

LJ Lord Justice

LL Lord Lieutenant

LLA Lady Literate of Arts

LLB Bachelor of Law (Latin: *Legum Baccalaureus*)

LLD Doctor of Law (Latin: *Legum Doctor*)

LLI Lord Lieutenant of Ireland

LLM Master of Civil and Canon Law (Latin: *Legum Magister*)

LM Licentiate of Medicine; Licentiate of Midwifery

LMRCP Licentiate in Midwifery Royal College of Physicians

LMS Licentiate in Medicine and Surgery

LMSSA Licentiate in Medicine and Surgery Society of Apothecaries

LP Lord Provost

LPS Lord Privy Seal

LRAM Licentiate of the Royal Academy of Music

LRCP Licentiate of the Royal College of Physicians

LSA Licentiate of the Society of Apothecaries

Lt Lieutenant

LtCol Lieutenant Colonel

LtComdr Lieutenant Commander

LtGen Lieutenant General

LtGov Lieutenant Governor

M Monsieur (French); Majesty

MA Master of Arts

MB Bachelor of Medicine (Latin: *Medicinae Baccalaureus*)

MBA Master of Business Administration

MBCPE Member of the British College of Physical Education

MBE Member of the Order of the British Empire

MC Master of Chemistry; Military Cross; Master of Ceremonies; Member of Congress

MCh/MChir Master of Surgery (Latin: *Magister Chirurgiae*)

MChD Master of Dental Surgery

MComm Master of Commerce

MCP Member of the College of Preceptors

MD Doctor of Medicine (Latin: *Medicinae Doctor*); Managing Director

MDS Master of Dental Surgery

ME Marine Engineer; Mechanical Engineer; Mining Engineer; Most Excellent

MEng Master of Engineering

MFH Master of Foxhounds

Mgr Monsignor

MGTI Member of the Gymnastic Teachers' Institute

MHA Member of the House of Assembly (Australian)

MHK Member of the House of Keys (Isle of Man)

MHR Member of the House of Representatives (USA & Australia)

MHy Master of Hygiene

MIEE Member of the Institute of Electrical Engineers

MIJ Member of the Institute of Journalists

MIME, MIMinE Member of the Institute of Mining Engineers

MIMechE Member of the Institution of Mechanical Engineers

MIMM Member of the Institute of Mining and Metallurgy

MIMunE Member of the Institute of Municipal Engineers

MINA Member of the Institute of Naval Architects

MInstCE Member of the Institution of Civil Engineers

MInstGasE Member of the Institution of Gas Engineers

MISTM Member of the Incorporated Society of Trained Masseuses

ML Licentiate of Medicine; Licentiate of Midwifery

MLA Member of the Legislative Assembly; Member of the Library Association

MLC Member of the Legislative Council

Mlle Mademoiselle

MM Military Medal; Master Mason

MM Messrs (French version)

Mme Mmes Madame, Mesdames

MNAS Member of the National Academy of Sciences

MNSPE Member of the National Society of Physical Education

MO Medical Officer

MOH Medical Officer of Health

MP Member of Parliament

MPhil, MPh Master of Philosophy

MPS Member of the Pharmaceutical Society, or Physical, or Philological Society

MR Master of the Rolls

MRAS Member of the Royal Academy of Science, or Asiatic Society

MRCGP Member of the Royal College of General Practitioners

MRCOG   Member of the Royal College of Obstetricians and Gynaecologists

MRCP   Member of the Royal College of Physicians

MRCS   Member of the Royal College of Surgeons

MRCVS   Member of the Royal College of Veterinary Surgeons

MRI   Member of the Royal Institution

MRIA   Member of the Royal Irish Academy

MRSA   Member of the Royal Society of Arts

MRSL   Member of the Royal Society of Literature

Ms   title instead of Mrs or Miss

MS   Master of Science; Master of Surgery

MSA   Member of the Society of Apothecaries

MSc   Master of Science

MTech   Master of Technology

MtRev   Most Reverend

MusB, MusBac   Bachelor of Music (Latin: *Musicae Baccalaureus*)

MusD, MusDoc   Doctor of Music (Latin: *Musicae Doctor*)

MusM   Master of Music (Latin: *Musicae Magister*)

MVO   Member of the Royal Victorian Order

MVS   Master of Veterinary Surgery

MVSc   Master of Veterinary Science

NCO   Non-Commissioned Officer

NGO   Non-gazetted Officer

NP   Notary Public

OBE   Officer of the Order of the British Empire

OC   Officer Commanding

OL   Officer of the Order of Leopold

OM   Order of Merit

OND   Ordinary National Diploma - qualification in technical subjects

ORC   Order of the Red Cross

OS   Ordinary Seaman

OSA   Order of St Augustine

OSB   Order of St Benedict

OSD   Order of St Dominic

OSF   Order of St Francis

OSMA   Order of St Michael and All Angels

P   Prince; President; priest

PhB   Bachelor of Philosophy (Latin: *Philosophiae Baccalaureus*)

PC   Privy Councillor; Police Constable; Perpetual Curate

PhD   Doctor of Philosophy (Latin: *Philosophiae Doctor*)

PM   Prime Minister; Provost Marshal; Post Master; Paymaster

PMG   Postmaster General; Paymaster General; Provost Marshal General

PO   Petty Officer; Pilot Officer

PP   Past President; parish priest

PPE   Philosophy, Politics and Economics (a combined degree course)

PPS   Parliamentary Private Secretary

Pr   Prince

PRA   President of the Royal Academy

PRIBA   President of the Royal Institute of British Architects

PRS   President of the Royal Society

PRSA   President of the Royal Scottish Academy

PRSE   President of the Royal Society of Edinburgh

QC   Queen's Counsel

QM   Quartermaster

QMG   Quartermaster General

QMS   Quartermaster Sergeant

RA   Rear Admiral; Royal Academician

RD   Rural Dean

RE   Right Excellent

RGN   Registered General Nurse (now the main nursing qualification)

RH   Royal Highness

RHV   Registered Health Visitor

RM   Resident Magistrate; Registered Midwife

RP   Regius Professor

RSA   Royal Scottish Academician

RSM   Regimental Sergeant-Major

RtHon   Right Honourable

RtRev   Right Reverend

RW   Right Worshipful; Right Worthy

SAS   Fellow of the Society of Antiquaries (Latin: *Societatis Antiquariorum Socius*)

ScB   Bachelor of Science (Latin: *Scientiae Baccalaureus*)

ScD   Doctor of Science (Latin: *Scientiae Doctor*)

SEN   State Enrolled Nurse (the most basic qualification)

SG   Solicitor General

Sgt   Sergeant

SgtMaj, SM   Sergeant-Major

SL   Solicitor at Law

SMLonSoc   Fellow of the London Medical Society

SRN   State Registered Nurse

SSC   Solicitor Before the Supreme Court (Scotland)

SSD   Most Holy Lord (the Pope) (Latin: *Sanctissimus Dominus*)

ThB   Bachelor of Theology

ThD   Doctor of Theology

TRH   Their Royal Highnesses

UKA   Ulster King of Arms

V   Viscount; Venerable; Vice (in title)

VA   Vice-Admiral; Order of Victoria and Albert

VC   Victoria Cross; Vice Chancellor; Vice Consul; Vice Chairman; Vicar Apostolic

VD   Volunteer Officers' Decoration

VMD   Doctor of Veterinary Medicine (Latin: *Veterinariae Medicinae Doctor*)

VO   Victorian Order

Science Abbreviations

The Periodic Table

Dimitrii Ivanovich Mandeleev in 1869 discovered the periodic law which forms the basis of today's periodic table. But it was H.G.J. Moseley who, in 1913, realized the key to classifying the elements was not their mass but their atomic number - that is the number of positive charges in the nucleus. This set the pattern for the periodic table (opposite) in which the elements were arranged in order of their atomic number (1, 2, 3, 4 etc). For then certain properties keep recurring at regular intervals (or periods).

There is a dispute over the name of element 104 which is called either kurchatovium or rutherfordium - according to whether you belong to the Eastern bloc or the West.

Periodic Table of the Elements

Period	Group 1 Alkali metals	Group 2 Alkaline earth metals																Group 3	Group 4	Group 5	Group 6	Group 7 Halogens	Group 8 Inert gases
1	1 Hydrogen **H** 1.00794																						2 Helium **He** 4.00260
2	3 Lithium **Li** 6.941	4 Beryllium **Be** 9.01218																5 Boron **B** 10.81	6 Carbon **C** 12.011	7 Nitrogen **N** 14.0067	8 Oxygen **O** 15.9994	9 Fluorine **F** 18.99840	10 Neon **Ne** 20.179
3	11 Sodium **Na** 22.98977	12 Magnesium **Mg** 24.305																13 Aluminium **Al** 26.98154	14 Silicon **Si** 28.086	15 Phosphorus **P** 30.97376P	16 Sulphur **S** 32.06	17 Chlorine **Cl** 35.453	18 Argon **Ar** 39.948
4	19 Potassium **K** 39.098	20 Calcium **Ca** 40.08	21 Scandium **Sc** 44.9559	22 Titanium **Ti** 47.90	23 Vanadium **V** 50.9414	24 Chromium **Cr** 51.996	25 Manganese **Mn** 54.9380	26 Iron **Fe** 55.847	27 Cobalt **Co** 58.9332	28 Nickel **Ni** 58.70	29 Copper **Cu** 63.546	30 Zinc **Zn** 65.38						31 Gallium **Ga** 69.72	32 Germanium **Ge** 672.59	33 Arsenic **As** 74.9216	34 Selenium **Se** 78.96	35 Bromine **Br** 79.904	36 Krypton **Kr** 83.80
5	37 Rubidium **Rb** 85.4678	38 Strontium **Sr** 87.62	39 Yttrium **Y** 88.9059	40 Zirconium **Zr** 91.22	41 Niobium **Nb** 92.9064	42 Molybdenum **Mo** 95.94	43 Technetium **Tc** 97.9072	44 Ruthenium **Ru** 101.07	45 Rhodium **Rh** 102.9055	46 Palladium **Pd** 106.4	47 Silver **Ag** 107.868	48 Cadmium **Cd** 112.40						49 Indium **In** 114.82	50 Tin **Sn** 118.69	51 Antimony **Sb** 121.75	52 Tellurium **Te** 127.75	53 Iodine **I** 126.9045	54 Xenon **Xe** 131.30
6	55 Caesium **Cs** 132.9054	56 Barium **Ba** 137.34	57 Lanthanum **La** 138.9055	72 Hafnium **Hf** 178.49	73 Tantalum **Ta** 180.9479	74 Tungsten **W** 183.85	75 Rhenium **Re** 186.207	76 Osmium **Os** 190.2	77 Iridium **Ir** 192.22	78 Platinum **Pt** 195.09	79 Gold **Au** 196.9665	80 Mercury **Hg** 200.59						81 Thallium **Tl** 204.37	82 Lead **Pb** 207.2	83 Bismuth **Bi** 208.9804	84 Polonium **Po** 209.9871	85 Astatine **At** 209.9871	86 Radon **Rn** 222.0176
7	87 Francium **Fr** 223.0197	88 Radium **Ra** 226.0254	89 Actinium **Ac** 227.0278	104 Unniquadium **Unq** 216.109	105 Unnilpentium **Unp** 262.114	106 Unnilhexium **Unh** 263.120	107 Unnilseptium **Uns** 262																

Transition Elements Series

Element Key

1
Hydrogen
H
1.00794

atomic number
name
symbol
relative atomic mass

Lanthanide series

57 Lanthanum **La** 138.9055	58 Cerium **Ce** 140.12	59 Praseodymium **Pr** 140.9077	60 Neodymium **Nd** 144.24	61 Promethium **Pm** 144.9128	62 Samarium **Sm** 150.36	63 Europium **Eu** 151.96	64 Gadolinium **Gd** 157.25	65 Terbium **Tb** 158.9254	66 Dysprosium **Dy** 162.50	67 Holmium **Ho** 164.9304	68 Erbium **Er** 167.26	69 Thulium **Tm** 168.9342	70 Ytterbium **Yb** 173.04	71 Lutetium **Lu** 174.97

Actinide series

89 Actinium **Ac** 227.0278	90 Thorium **Th** 232.0381	91 Protactinium **Pa** 231.0359	92 Uranium **U** 238.029	93 Neptunium **Np** 237.0482	94 Plutonium **Pu** 244.0642	95 Americium **Am** 243.0614	96 Curium **Cm** 247.0703	97 Berkelium **Bk** 247.0703	98 Californium **Cf** 251.0786	99 Einsteinium **Es** 252.0828	100 Fermium **Fm** 257.0951	101 Mendelevium **Md** 258.0986	102 Nobelium **No** 259.1009	103 Lawrencium **Lr** 260.1054

ALPHABETS

The Deaf and Dumb Alphabet

These deaf and dumb hand signals are included not only for those who would like to talk to people with these handicaps but also because I have fond memories of using them to signal across classrooms as a child, and I feel these little pleasures should not be lost.

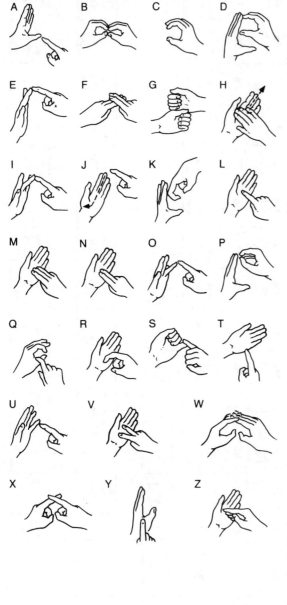

The Modern Greek Alphabet

Printed Form		Handwritten Form		Name of Letter
A	α	A	α	alfah
B	β	B	β	veetah
Γ	γ	Γ	γ	gamah
Δ	δ	Δ	δ	deltah
E	ε	E	ε	epseelon
Z	ζ	Z	ζ	zeetah
H	η	H	η	eetah
Θ	θ	Θ	θ	theetah
I	ι	I	ι	yeeotah
K	κ	K	κ	kahpah
Λ	λ	Λ	λ	lahmdhah
M	μ	M	μ	mee
N	ν	N	ν	nee
Ξ	ξ	Ξ	ξ	ksee
O	ο	O	ο	omeekron
Π	π	Π	π	pee
P	ρ	P	ρ	ro
Σ	σ ς	Σ	σ ς	seeghmah
T	τ	T	τ	tahf
Y	υ	Y	υ	eepseelon
Φ	φ	Φ	φ	fee
X	χ	X	χ	khee
Ψ	ψ	Ψ	ψ	psee
Ω	ω	Ω	ω	omehghah

Pronunciation

Vowels

α	a as in park
ε	e as in bell
η, ι, υ	ee as in feet
ο, ω	o as in spot

Consonants

β	v as in vain
γ	1) before α, ο, ω, ου and consonants like the 'ch' in the Scottish 'loch' but voiced
	2) before ε, αι, η, ι, υ, ει, οι, y as in yellow
δ	th as in the
ζ	z as in zebra
θ	th as in thought
κ	k as in king
λ	l as in like
μ	m as in many
N ν	n as in never
ξ	x as in fix
π	p as in paint
P ρ	r as in road
Σ σ, ζ	1) before β, γ, δ, ζ, μ, ν, ρ, z as in zebra
	2) elsewhere, s as in sea
τ	t as in ten
φ	f as in four
χ	ch as in Scottish loch
ψ	ps as in dropsy

Morse Code

Morse code is essential not only for boy scouts but for all whose Walter Mitty dreams include being imprisoned in a good cause and tapping out courageous dying messages to the cell next door. The code of signalling devised by Professor Samuel Morse is now universally used. The complete alphabet is as follows:

A	.—		N	—.
B	—...		O	———
C	—.—.		P	.——.
D	—..		Q	——.—
E	.		R	.—.
F	..—.		S	...
G	——.		T	—
H	....		U	..—
I	..		V	...—
J	.———		W	.——
K	—.—		X	—..—
L	.—..		Y	—.——
M	——		Z	——..

Figures are represented as follows:

International Code		Army Signalling Code	
1	.————	1	.—
2	..———	2	..—
3	...——	3	...——
4	....—	4	....—
5	.....	5	.
6	—....	6	—....
7	——...	7	——...
8	———..	8	—..
9	————.	9	—.
0	—————	0	—

.	......	;	—.—.—	?	..——..
,	.—.—.—	:	———...	!	——..——

The Russian Alphabet

Printed Form		Handwritten Form	Name of Letter	Pronunciation
А	а	*A a*	ah	a as in fatter
Б	б	*Б б*	beh	b as in boy
В	в	*B в*	veh	v as in victor
Г	г	*Г г*	geh	g as in get
Д	д	*D д*	deh	d as in dog
Е	е	*Е е*	yeh	ye as in yes
Ё	ё	*Ё ё*	yoh	yo as in yonder
Ж	ж	*Ж ж*	zheh (soft z)	s as zh in pleasure
З	з	*З з*	zheh	z as in zebra
И	и	*И и*	ee	ee as in feet
Й	й	*Й й*	ee krahtkoyeh	y as in toy
К	к	*К к*	kah	k as in kitchen
Л	л	*Л л*	ehl	l as in leaf
М	м	*М м*	ehm	m as in man
Н	н	*Н н*	ehn	n as in not
О	о	*О о*	o	o as in pot
П	п	*П п*	peh	p as in pot
Р	р	*Р р*	ehr	r as in rabbit but slightly rolled, as in a Scots r
С	с	*С с*	ehs	s as in sit
Т	т	*Т т*	teh	t as in top
У	у	*У у*	oo	oo as in tool
Ф	ф	*Ф ф*	ehf	f as in food
Х	х	*Х х*	khah	kh as in ch of loch
Ц	ц	*Ц ц*	tseh	ts as in seats
Ч	ч	*Ч ч*	chah	ch as in chocolate
Ш	ш	*Ш ш*	shah	sh as in shop
Щ	щ	*Щ щ*	shchah	shch as in posh chips
Ъ	ъ	*ъ*	tvyordiy znahk	ignore it - it is merely to show that the consonant before it stays hard, an effect too subtle for foreigners
Ы	ы	*ы*	yehree	similar to i as in sin but no English equivalent
Ь	ь	*ь*	myahkee znahk	this is a sign which softens the previous consonant by putting a slight y after it
Э	э	*Э э*	eh oborotnoyeh	e as in pen
Ю	ю	*Ю ю*	yoo	u as in universal
Я	я	*Я я*	yah	ya as in yard

ASTROLOGY

Chinese Astrology

According to the Chinese, every year belongs to an animal, and those who are born in that year have the animal's characteristics. Twelve animals occur in succession, and their qualities aren't always the ones the West would attribute to them, so don't worry if you find you're a pig.

Rat	1888	1900	1912	1924	1936	1948	1960	1972	1984
Buffalo/Ox	1889	1901	1913	1925	1937	1949	1961	1973	1985
Tiger	1890	1902	1914	1926	1938	1950	1962	1974	1986
Cat/Rabbit/Hare	1891	1903	1915	1927	1939	1951	1963	1975	1987
Dragon	1892	1904	1916	1928	1940	1952	1964	1976	1988
Snake	1893	1905	1917	1929	1941	1953	1965	1977	1989
Horse	1894	1906	1918	1930	1942	1954	1966	1978	1990
Goat/Sheep	1895	1907	1919	1931	1943	1955	1967	1979	1991
Monkey	1896	1908	1920	1932	1944	1956	1968	1980	1992
Rooster	1897	1909	1921	1933	1945	1957	1969	1981	1993
Dog	1898	1910	1922	1934	1946	1958	1970	1982	1994
Pig/Boar	1899	1911	1923	1935	1947	1959	1971	1983	1995

To know your Chinese animal sign find your date of birth and see what animal names that line. The snag is that the Chinese New Year begins at the first new moon after the sun enters Aquarius. It therefore falls on a different date each year - somewhere between 21 January and 19 February on our calendar. So those with birthdays at the beginning of the year take the sign of the year before. If you want to know the exact change-over date *Chinese Horoscopes* by Barry Fantoni (Sphere) has the answers, but they are too lengthy to give here.

Characteristics
Rat charming, quick-witted, loves company, spendthrift

Snake attractive, sexy and wise, but can be possessive and conceited

Buffalo/ox calm, dependable, self-contained, a leader, but stubborn and inclined to shift blame on to others

Horse sociable and likeable, sporty, practical and logical, but can be prejudiced and intolerant

Tiger thoughtful, strong, brave, dynamic and imaginative, but inclined to be rash and touchy

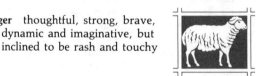

Goat/sheep harmony-loving, humorous, easy to get on with, but impressionable and easily lead

Cat/rabbit/hare methodical, cautious, comfort-loving, tactful and lucky, but also gossipy and moody

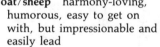

Monkey intelligent, fast-talking and good with figures, but insecure and sometimes superficial

Dragon eccentric, self-confident, dynamic, perfectionist, highly sexed and loyal, but proud and incapable of routine

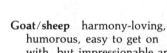

Rooster hard-working, great organizers, punctual, competitive, but either very thrifty or very wasteful

Dog honest, loyal, idealistic, but a fault-finder who needs to be led

 Pig well-mannered, industrious, domesticated, but obstinate, egocentric and bad at planning

Some Chinese marriage proverbs for these animals are:
- The sheep and rat are always at war.
- When the pig meets the monkey there are sure to be tears.
- The cock and snake are always at odds.
- When a dragon meets a rabbit good luck is shattered.
- The ox and tiger always quarrel.
- The cock and dog always end in tears.
- When a tiger meets a snake there is always battle.
- The horse fears the ox.
- The serpent with the hare gives supreme happiness.

But I wouldn't take them too seriously.

The Chinese calendar has a 60-year cycle in which your character and fate are thought to be influenced by the interaction of two cycles. These are the Ten Heavenly Stems and the Twelve Heavenly Branches, so the animals which represent the branches (see above) are only part of the picture. Those who want to delve into the complexity of the two cycles can read: Theodora Lau, *Chinese Horoscopes*, Arrow.

European Astrology

Astrology has scarcely changed since Ptolemy's time, when in about AD 140 he warned that if Saturn was not tempered by Venus it could make men licentious, libidinous, practisers of lewdness, careless, and impure in sexual intercourse; obscene, treacherous to women...

It's odd to think that we send rockets to the moon yet still refer to star charts which grew out of a belief in all-powerful planet gods, and that some tycoons still place as much trust in astrology as did the kings of the ancient world. However, though Shakespeare's Cassius

may have been right in saying, 'The fault, dear Brutus, is not in our stars, but in ourselves...' it is nonetheless amusing to see how our image of ourselves squares with our star sign.

Here is a quick distillation of what a number of astronomers attribute to different star signs. But to know what astrologers really say the stars hold for you you need a proper star chart for the instant of your birth. For the truth is that the traits of your star sign are as close to astrology as an egg is to a soufflé.

ARIES
the Ram

DATES: 21 March-20 April   RULING PLANET: Mars   ELEMENT: fire
Aries are pushy, energetic go-getters who take on a challenge, think quickly and get things done. Though courageous, enterprising and highly-sexed, they are less good at considering the options (or the needs of other people) and at paying attention to details.

TAURUS
the Bull

DATES: 21 April-20 May   RULING PLANET: Venus   ELEMENT: earth
Bulls are pleasure-lovers with a thrifty and methodical streak. They love beauty, food and luxury, but they like to hold on to what they have. So they are seldom extravagant. They are affectionate and sensual but may get stuck in a rut and become possessive, boring and self-centred.

GEMINI
the Twins

DATES: 21 May-21 June   RULING PLANET: Mercury   ELEMENT: air
Geminis are adaptable, responsive and good at communicating. They are naturally resourceful wheeler-dealers, with a restless energy. But at worst they are shallow, cunning, and two faced in business and love.

CANCER
the Crab

DATES: 22 June-22 July   RULING PLANET: Moon   ELEMENT: water
Crabs are loyal, patriotic, imaginative and sympathetic. They are also moody, untidy and prone to self-pity. They like to protect and be protected and are inclined to be introverted and are happiest when surrounded by their loved ones.

LEO
the Lion

DATES: 23 July-22 August   RULING PLANET: Sun   ELEMENT: fire
At their best Leos are natural leaders, with warm, energetic personalities which command respect. They tend to be generous, broad-minded, and good organizers, and also sincere and sensual lovers. But they can be too power-loving and become opinionated and domineering.

VIRGO
the Virgin

DATES: 23 August-22 September   RULING PLANET: Mercury   ELEMENT: earth
Virgos are reserved (as befits a virgin), analytical and often clever. They are also discerning, methodical and thorough, but taken too far this precision and reserve makes some virgos into up-tight, over-critical worriers.

LIBRA
the Scales

DATES: 23 September-22 October   RULING PLANET: Venus   ELEMENT: air
Librans can spend so much time weighing things in the balance that they never make up their minds. But they are also charming, kind and able to create harmony and compromise, though secretly perfectionist. As lovers, they caress the mind more than the body and may lack fire, and they can be untidy and unreliable.

SCORPIO
the Scorpion

DATES: 23 October-22 November   RULING PLANETS: Mars and Pluto
ELEMENT: water
Scorpios tend to hide their true selves away, rather as a scorpion hides. But they have strong personalities which are intuitive, analytical and passionate. These qualities can become warped and turn into jealousy, vindictiveness and secretiveness.

SAGITTARIUS
the Centaur with bow and arrow

DATES: 23 November-22 December   RULING PLANET: Jupiter   ELEMENT: fire
The symbol stands for a man's intelligence combined with animal power and speed. Sagittarians are meant to be ambitious, freedom-loving, optimistic and deep thinkers; good at sport and sincere in love - if you don't tie them down. But they can be careless, tactless and have a playboy streak.

CAPRICORN
the Goat

DATES: 23 December-20 January   RULING PLANET: Saturn   ELEMENT: earth
Capricorns are self-disciplined, resourceful and cautious. They are great planners and take life rather seriously, working their way carefully to where they want to get. However, they can be unaffectionate, over-reserved, pessimistic and conventional.

AQUARIUS
the Water-Carrier

DATES: 21 January-18 February   RULING PLANETS: Uranus and Saturn
ELEMENT: air
Aquarians are expressive, spontaneous, inventive and idealistic - even revolutionary. They are also artistic, friendly and unpredictable. The qualities may not add up to a faithful lover, but they are fun while it lasts. Some Aquarians go too far and become cranky and rebellious.

PISCES
the Fish

DATES: 19 February-20 March   RULING PLANETS: Neptune and Jupiter
ELEMENT: water
The least worldly of the twelve signs, Pisceans are very intuitive, emotional and creative. They are also highly compassionate, loving and sensitive to others, but they find it almost impossible to conform to any set patterns of living, and organization eludes them.

More information
Derek and Julia Parker, *The New Compleat Astrologer*, Mitchell Beazley
For those with an interest in palmistry: Lori Read, *How to Read Hands*; The Aquarian Press

CALENDAR DATES

The year is still based upon religious calendars, which are in turn dominated by the moon and sun as they were in ancient times.

Christmas apart, the major dates of the Christian calendar are set in relation to Easter; and Easter is the first Sunday after the full moon following the vernal equinox of the northern hemisphere (sometime between 22 March and 25 April). The vernal equinox is the time when the position of the sun in relation to the equator is such that day and night are of equal lengths. (The Book of Common Prayer also contains a table showing how to find Easter.)

The Jewish calendar has twelve lunar months of 29½ days long, so the dates of religious festivals shift each year in relation to the Western calendar. Since the festivals are also linked to the seasons, adjustments are made every few years to ensure that they stay within the right seasons, so there is no predicting when they will occur.

The Muslim calendar dates from Mohammed's journey to Medina and also operates to a totally different set of dates from the Western calendar. What is more, the major Muslim festival of Ramadan happens in the ninth month of the Muslim year but cannot start until someone in that country sees the new moon. It last 27 to 29 days and ends in great festivities.

Exact Hindu dates are set for each year by holy men, with reference to the moon, and the process is slightly obscure to the layman.

Epiphany	6 January
Candlemas	2 February
Septuagesima Sunday	Three Sundays before Ash Wednesday
Sexagesima Sunday	Two Sundays before Ash Wednesday
Quinquagesima Sunday	One Sunday before Ash Wednesday
St David's Day	1 March
Ash Wednesday	Wednesday before the 7th Sunday before Easter
Lent	Ash Wednesday to Easter Sunday
Quadragesima Sunday	First Sunday after Ash Wednesday
St Patrick's Day	17 March
Holi (Hindu Spring Festival)	March
Mothering Sunday	Third Sunday before Easter
Annunciation Day	25 March (but if this is Easter, then first free Monday after that)
April Fool's Day	1 April
Rama Navami (Ram's Birthday - Hindu)	April
Palm Sunday	Sunday before Easter
Holy Week	Sunday before Easter to Easter Sunday
Good Friday	Friday just before Easter
Easter	see introduction
St George's Day	23 April
Low Sunday	First Sunday after Easter
Rogation Sunday	Fifth Sunday after Easter
Pentecost/ Whitsunday	Seventh Sunday after Easter
Trinity Sunday	Ninth Sunday after Easter
Corpus Christi	Thursday after Trinity Sunday
Mayday Bank Holiday in Britain	First Monday in May
Liberation Day (Channel Isles)	9 May
Spring Bank Holiday in Britain	Last Monday in May
Ascension Day	Forty days after Easter on a Thursday
Father's Day	Third Sunday in June
St Peter and St Paul	29 June (RC)
Salvation Army Founder's Day	2 July
Martyrdom of Bab (Baha'i)	9 July
Obon (Japanese spirit festival)	13-15 July
St Swithin's Day	15 July
Assumption	15 August (RC)
August Bank Holiday in Britain	Last Monday in August
Festival of Hungry Ghosts (Chinese Buddhist)	18 September
Shubun No Hi (Japanese autumn equinox)	23 September
Michaelmas	29 September (C of E)
Navaratri/ Dassehra/Durga Puja (Hindu nine-day celebration of Ram's victory over the demons)	October
Birth of Bab (Baha'i festival)	20 October
All Saints' Day	1 November (C of E/RC)
All Souls	2 November (C of E/RC)
Birth of Baha'u'llah (Baha'i)	12 November
Remembrance Sunday	Second Sunday in November
Divali (Deepavali - Hindu festival of light)	November
Thanksgiving Day	Fourth Thursday in November
St Andrew's Day	30 November
Advent	From the fourth Sunday before Christmas until 24 December
Christmas Eve	24 December
Christmas Day	25 December
Boxing Day	26 December

The dates for when the clocks go forward and back, called British Summer Time, are set by arrangement with the EEC every four years.

The Queen's official birthday is the first, second or third Saturday in June and is set each year by Buckingham Palace and approved by the Queen.

Law Terms

Hilary	11 January - until the Wednesday before Easter Sunday
Easter	Second Tuesday after Easter Sunday until the Friday before the Spring Bank Holiday (last Monday in May)

| Trinity | Second Tuesday after the Spring Bank Holiday until 31 July |
| Michaelmas | 1 October to 21 December |

The Parliamentary terms are decided by the Leader of the House and the whips, according to parliamentary needs, at as little as two weeks' notice.

Cambridge University terms are set in relation to Easter. The system is so complex that even the vice-chancellor's department couldn't explain it. However, the actual dates for the next 10 years can be obtained from 0223 337733. The Oxford system is simpler - but would take a page to define; the University of Oxford offices will answer queries on future dates (Tel: 0865 270001). Other university terms vary with the university.

Whittaker's Almanac gives the exact dates of movable festivals to the year 2000.

More information

Shap Working Party on World Religions in Education (7 Alderbrook Road, Solihull, West Midlands B91 1NH) publishes an annual booklet listing the exact dates of the festivals of the major religions and what they signify.

CLOTHING SIZES

Clothing sizes are not as exact as you might suppose. It seems that different makers in each country use slightly different sizing and numbering. The following tables are therefore the most usual ones in the judgement of some of Britain's top clothing buyers.

Men's suits

UK/USA	32	34	36	38	40	42	44
Europe	42	44	46	48	50	52	54
Metric	81	86	91	97	102	107	112

Men's Shirt Collar

| UK/USA (in) | 14 | 14½ | 15 | 15½ | 16 | 16½ | 17 | 17½ |
| Europe (cm) | 36 | 37 | 38 | 39 | 40 | 41 | 42 | 43 |

Women's clothing

UK	10	12	14	16	18	20	22
USA	8	10	12	14	16	18	20
Europe	38	40	42	44	47	50	52

Hats

| UK | 5½ | 6 | 6½ | 7 | 7⅛ | 7¼ | 7⅜ | 7½ |
| Europe | 53 | 54 | 55 | 57 | 58 | 59 | 60 | 61 |

Shoes - Men's, Women's and Children's

Young children's shoe sizes are the same in America as in Britain. The following chart, for which I am indebted to Clarks Shoes, shows how the bands of measurements overlap in Europe, the UK and the USA.

Comparison of Shoe Sizes

Centimetres	Paris Points	English Sizes	US Women's Sizes	US Men's Sizes
11	16	1		
	17			
12	18	2		
13	19	3		
	20	4		
14	21			
		5		
15	22			
	23	6		
16	24	7		
17	25	8		
	26			
18	27	9		
19	28	10		
	29	11		
20	30			
		12		
21	31		15	5
	32	13		
22	33		25	15
		1		
23	34	2	35	25
	35	3	45	35
24	36		55	45
	37	4		
25	38	5	65	55
26	39	6	75	65
27	40	7	85	75
	41		95	85
28	42	8		
29	43	9	105	95
	44	10	115	105
30	45	11	125	115
31	46		135	125
	47	12		

Children's Clothing Sizes

Most manufacturers simply give an age for children's clothing sizes, but the following chart is an approximate guide to what measurements correspond to any age. Err on the large side. Other people's children are usually larger than you remember them, and your own will grow with purse-draining speed.

Children's Clothing Sizes

Age	Height (cm)	Chest (cm)	Waist (cm)
0–6 months	70	46	48
12 months	80	50	50
18 months	86	52	51
2 yrs	92	53	52
3 yrs	98	55	53
4 yrs	104	57	54
5 yrs	110	59	55
6 yrs	116	61	57
7 yrs	122	63	58
8 yrs	128	66	60
9 yrs	134	69	61
10 yrs	140	72	62
11 yrs	146	76	63
12 –13 yrs	154	78	64

COLLECTIVE NOUNS

I am indebted to the Game Conservancy for the following list of old and charming collective nouns for birds and animals:

A shrewdness of apes
A cete of badgers
A sloth of bears
A singular of boars
A tok of capercailzie
A covert of coots
A paddling of duck

A labour of moles
A watch of nightingales
A covey of partridge or grouse
A muster of peacocks
A flight of pigeons
A congregation of plovers

A gang of elk
A business of ferrets
A skulk of foxes
A gaggle of geese (at rest)
A skein of geese (in flight)
A charm of goldfinches
A trip of hares
A sege of herons
A band of jays
An exultation of larks
A leap of leopards
A pride of lions
A tidings of magpies
A sword of mallard

A bevy of quail
An unkindness of ravens
A building of rooks
A dopping of sheldrakes
A walk of snipe (at rest)
A wisp of snipe (in flight)
A murmuration of starlings
A pack of stoats or weasels
A herd of swans
A sounder of swine
A spring of teal
A company of widgeon
A trip of wildfowl
A fall of woodcock

FREQUENCIES

We tend to think of heat, light and radio waves as being entirely different from each other. This isn't quite true. Just as red, blue and yellow seem entirely different, but are all part of a spectrum of colour, so heat, light and radio waves are all part of an electromagnetic spectrum. They all consist of waves which travel at the speed of light. How they differ is in the length of those waves.

The greater the length of the waves (wavelength), the less frequently they occur in a given period - hence low frequency. Just as our ears can only hear part of the range of possible sounds, and therefore can't hear a dog whistle, so our eyes can only see a small central section of the electromagnetic spectrum. The fact that we can't see it all doesn't mean it isn't there. While dogs can hear both ordinary voices and a dog whistle, bees, for example, see many of the wavelengths we see and also ultraviolet which we can't see.

The Electromagnetic Spectrum

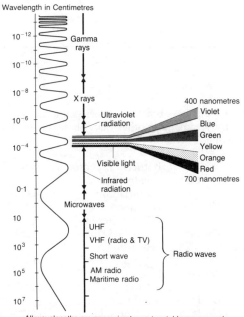

All wavelengths are approximate: no two tables agree and some 'functions' overlap

GEMS

Gems are classified by the form the crystals take - aquamarines, for example, are hexagonal - and by the way they refract light. In air light travels at 669,000,000 miles an hour, but in a diamond it slows down to 276,000,000 as the separate rays produce the brilliance in it.

Gems are measured in carats, a measurement which goes back to keration, derived from the Greek word for the carob beans which for centuries were used as weights. But gem carats are quite different from those used for gold. In gems a carat is 200 mg ($1/5$ g or $3 \cdot 086$ grains troy weight) so 5 carats are 1 gram. But, as even a 1 carat diamond is scarcely part of everyday trade, diamonds are usually referred to as pointers, so you may be offered a '10 pointer' or a '25 pointer'. A 10 pointer is one weighing $0 \cdot 10$ of a carat, and a 25 pointer weighs $0 \cdot 25$ of a carat.

Occasionally jewellers sell diamonds by carat *width*, as shown in the gauge below. So a stone which fits in the hole marked 3 could be referred to as '3 carats'. This is easily confused with weight, but a stone 3 carats wide may well be shallow and *weigh* much less than 3 carats. As the value of diamonds is by quality and *weight* — not width — make sure you ask what type of carat a jeweller is talking about and get the carat weight not just its width.

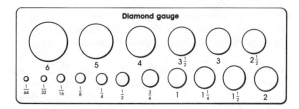

Pearls

Cultured pearls were first produced by the Japanese in the 1920s by inserting a bead made of mother of pearl into an oyster, which then coats it in pearl. X-rays can tell a natural pearl from a cultured one because they can detect the structure of mother of pearl on the inside. But, though natural pearls are usually more expensive than cultured pearls, they are both 'real' pearls because an oyster has formed both of them.

The twisted pearls sold as freshwater pearls, and sometimes called 'rice crispie pearls' are also real pearls but are made by mussels.

Pearls are usually sold by their diameter in millimetres - usually 3 mm to 9·5 mm - though larger pearls can be bought. Any size will vary in price according to its colour and lustre, with the pinker toned pearls costing most. When buying look at them in a good light and always try them against your skin. They look best against certain backgrounds and clever shopkeepers always show them against the colour which will flatter them.

★ To tell whether a pearl is real or simply a fake coated with a pearly substance rub it against the flat of your front tooth. If it feels smooth it's a fake, if it feels slightly rough it should be real. It's so well known in the trade that nobody turns a hair.

Hardness
In 1816 Friedrich Mohs developed a scale of hardness which is still used. The higher the numbers the harder the substance; anything can scratch a substance with a lower number - so the idea that only a diamond can cut glass is untrue.

Amber	2 - 2 ½	Quartz	7
Ivory (and finger nails)	2 ½	Topaz	8
Calcite	3	Sapphire	9
Window glass	5 ½	Diamond	10

Jewellers' Measures
1 metric carat = 200 milligrams
1 troy ounce = 155·52 metric carats

Troy ounces are not the same as standard ounces; a standard ounce is 28 g, but a troy ounce is 31 g. A standard gold bar weighs 400 troy ounces, though bars are sometimes made with 250 troy ounces.

Gemmological Association of Great Britain, St Dunstan's House, Carey Lane, London EC2V 8AB. Tel: *01-726 4374*

Birth Stones
At one time much was made of birthstones for the qualities which were associated with them. Today they seem almost forgotten and the list somehow has an Edwardian flavour.

Jan.	garnet	purply-red	constancy
Feb.	amethyst	purple	sincerity
Mar.	bloodstone	green with red flecks	courage
Apr.	diamond	glassy	innocence and lasting love
May	emerald	green	success and hope
June	pearl	pearly white	health and purity
July	ruby	red	love and contentment
Aug.	agate	pale green	married happiness
Sept.	sapphire	blue	wisdom
Oct.	opal	white with coloured flecks	hope
Nov.	topaz	yellow, brown	fidelity
Dec.	turquoise	greeny blue	harmony

HISTORICAL FIGURES

Famous Artists
Artists are often known by either their first name or their surname alone. In this list the names are given in their correct order but those which are seldom used are put in () brackets. Where an artist is known by something other than his real name the real name is given in [] brackets after.

Phidias	c.490-420 BC
Praxiteles	active 390 BC
Duccio (di Buoninsegna)	AD1255-1319
Giotto (di Bondone)	c.1266-1337
Donatello [Donato di Niccolo]	c.1386-1466
Fra Angelico [Giovanni da Fiesole]	1387-1455
Jan van Eyck	c.1390-1441
Uccello [Paolo di Dono]	c.1397-1475
Roger van der Weyden	1399-1464
Luca della Robbia	c.1400-1482
Masaccio	c.1401-1428
Fra Filippo Lippi	c.1406-1469
Piero della Francesca	c.1416-1492
Andrea Mantegna	c.1428-1506
Botticelli [Sandro Filipepi di Mariano]	c.1440-1510
Hieronymus Bosch [Jerome van Aeken]	c.1450-1516
Leonardo da Vinci	1452-1519
Hugo van der Goes	active 1467-1482
Matthias Grünewald	c.1470-1528
Albrecht Dürer	1471-1528

Michelangelo Buonarroti	1475-1564	(Jean-Honoré) Fragonard	1732-1806	Georges Pierre Seurat	1859-1891
Giorgione [Giorgio da Castelfranco]	c.1477-1510	(Francisco de) Goya	1746-1828	Gustav Klimt	1862-1918
		Jacques-Louis		Edvard Munch	1863-1944
Raphael [Raffaello Sanzio]	1483-1520	David	1748-1825	Henri (Marie Raymond) de	
		William Blake	1757-1827	Toulouse-Lautrec	1864-1901
Correggio [Antonio Allegri]	1489-1534	Joseph Mallord William Turner	1775-1851	Vassili Kandinsky	1866-1944
				Pierre Bonnard	1867-1947
		John Constable	1776-1837	Henri Matisse	1869-1954
Titian [Tiziano Vecelli]	c.1490-1576	(Jean-Auguste-Dominique) Ingres	1780-1867	Georges Rouault	1871-1958
				Piet Mondrian	1872-1944
Hans Holbein the Younger	1497-1543	(Jean Louis André)		Maurice de Vlaminck	1876-1958
Benvenuto Cellini	1500-1571	Théodore Géricault	1791-1824	(Constantin) Brancusi	1876-1957
Tintoretto [Jacopo Robusti]	1518-1594	(Jean-Baptiste Camille) Corot	1796-1857	Raoul Dufy	1877-1953
				Kasimir Malevich	1878-1935
Veronese [Paolo Caliari]	1528-1588	(Eugène) Delacroix	1798-1863	Paul Klee	1879-1940
				Sir Jacob Epstein	1880-1959
Pieter Bruegel the Elder	c.1530-1569	Samuel Palmer	1805-1881	André Derain	1880-1954
		Honoré Daumier	1808-1879	Fernand Léger	1881-1955
El Greco [Domenikos Theotokopoulos]	c.1540-1614	Jean François Millet	1814-1875	Pablo (Ruiz) Picasso	1881-1973
		Jean-Désiré Gustave Courbet	1819-1877	Edward Hopper	1882-1967
Pieter Bruegel the Younger	1564-1637			Georges Braque	1882-1963
				Maurice Utrillo	1883-1955
Caravaggio [Michelangelo da Maresi]	1573-1610	Gustave Moreau	1826-1898	Amedeo Modigliani	1884-1920
		William Holman Hunt	1827-1910	Max Beckmann	1884-1950
Peter Paul Rubens	1577-1640	Dante Gabriel Rossetti	1828-1882	Oskar Kokoschka	1886-1980
				Marc Chagall	1887-1985
Frans Hals	c.1580-1666			Marcel Duchamp	1887-1968
Nicolas Poussin	1594-1665	Sir John Everett Millais	1829-1896	Josef Albers	1888-1976
Gianlorenzo Bernini	1598-1680	Camille Jacob Pissarro	1830-1903	(Giorgio) de Chirico	1888-1978
				Egon Schiele	1890-1918
Anthony van Dyke	1599-1641	Edouard Manet	1832-1883	Man Ray	1890-1976
Diego Velazquez	1599-1660	(James Abbot McNeill) Whistler	1834-1903	Max Ernst	1891-1976
				Sir Stanley Spencer	1891-1959
Rembrandt [Harmensz van Rijn]	1606-1669	Hilaire Germain Edgar Degas	1834-1917	George Grosz	1893-1959
				Joan Miró	1893-1983
(Bartolomé Esteban) Murillo	1617-1682	Paul Cézanne	1839-1906	Henry Moore	1898-1986
		Auguste Rodin	1840-1926	Marino Marini	1901-1966
		Claude (Oscar) Monet	1840-1926	Mark Rothko	1903-1970
Pieter de Hooch	1629-1684			Barbara Hepworth	1903-1975
Jan Vermeer	1632-1675	Pierre Auguste Renoir	1841-1919	Salvador Dali	1904
Jean-Antoine Watteau	1684-1721			Rex Whistler	1905-1944
		Henri (Julian Felix) Rousseau (Le Douanier)	1844-1910	Francis Bacon	1909
Giovanni Battista Tiepolo	1696-1770			(Paul) Jackson Pollock	1912-1956
				[Adolf] Ad Reinhardt	1913-1967
William Hogarth	1697-1764	Paul (Eugène Henri) Gauguin	1848-1903	Joseph Beuys	1921-1987
Canaletto (Giovanni Antonio Canal)	1697-1768			[Andrew] Andy Warhol	1928-1987
		Vincent van Gogh	1853-1890	Frank Auerbach	1931
Joshua Reynolds	1723-1792			Frank Stella	1936
Thomas Gainsborough	1727-1788	John Singer Sargent	1856-1925	David Hockney	1937
				Anselm Kiefer	1945

Famous Composers

Guillaume de Machaut	1300-1377
Josquin des Prés	1440-1521
Thomas Tallis	1505-1585
Giovanni Pierluigi da Palestrina	1525-1594
William Byrd	1543-1623
John Dowland	1563-1626
Claudio Monteverdi	1567-1643
Jean Baptiste Lully	1632-1687
Arcangelo Corelli	1653-1713
Giuseppe Torelli	1658-1709
Henry Purcell	1659-1695
Alessandro Scarlatti	1660-1725
François Couperin	1668-1733
Antonio Lucio Vivaldi	1678-1741
Jean Philippe Rameau	1683-1764
Johann Sebastian Bach	1685-1750
Domenico Scarlatti	1685-1757
George Friedrich Handel	1685-1759
Carl Philipp Emanuel Bach	1714-1788
Christoph Willibald von Gluck	1714-1787
Franz Joseph Haydn	1732-1809
Wolfgang Amadeus Mozart	1756-1791
Luigi Cherubini	1760-1842
Ludwig van Beethoven	1770-1827
Carl Maria von Weber	1786-1826
Gioacchino Antonio Rossini	1792-1868
Franz Schubert	1797-1828
Gaetano Donizetti	1797-1848
Vincenzo Bellini	1801-1835
Hector Berlioz	1803-1869
Mikhail Glinka	1804-1857
Jacob Ludwig Felix Mendelssohn-Bartholdy	1809-1847
Frédéric François Chopin	1810-1849
Robert Schumann	1810-1856
Franz Liszt	1811-1886
Richard Wagner	1813-1883
Giuseppe Verdi	1813-1901
Charles Gounod	1818-1893
César Franck	1822-1890
Bedřich Smetana	1824-1884
Anton Bruckner	1824-1896
Johannes Brahms	1833-1897
Alexander Borodin	1834-1887
Camille Saint-Saëns	1835-1921
Georges Bizet	1838-1875
Modeste Petrovich Mussorgsky	1839-1881
Pyotr Ilyich Tchaikovsky	1840-1893
Antonin Dvořák	1841-1904
Arthur Sullivan	1842-1900
Edvard Hagerup Grieg	1843-1907
Nicolai Andreyevich Rimsky-Korsakov	1844-1908
Gabriel Fauré	1845-1924
Edward Elgar	1857-1934
Giacomo Puccini	1858-1924
Gustav Mahler	1860-1911
Claude Debussy	1862-1918
Richard Strauss	1864-1949
Carl Nielsen	1865-1931
Jean Sibelius	1865-1957
Ralph Vaughan Williams	1872-1958
Sergey Vasilyevich Rachmaninov	1873-1943
Arnold Schoenberg	1874-1951
Charles Ives	1874-1954
Maurice Ravel	1875-1937
Manuel de Falla	1876-1946
John Ireland	1879-1962
Béla Bartók	1881-1945
Zoltan Kódaly	1882-1967
Igor Stravinsky	1882-1971
Anton Weber	1883-1945
Arnold Bax	1883-1953
Alban Berg	1885-1935
Sergei Prokofiev	1891-1953
Arthur Honegger	1892-1955
Paul Hindemith	1895-1963
George Gershwin	1898-1937
Aaron Copland	1900
Sir William Walton	1902-1982
Sir Michael Tippett	1905
Dimitri Shostakovich	1906-1976
Olivier Messiaen	1908
Benjamin Britten	1913-1976
György Ligeti	1923
Pierre Boulez	1925
Hans Werner Henze	1926
Karlheinz Stockhausen	1928

Presidents of the United States of America

George Washington	Federal	1789
John Adams	Federal	1797
Thomas Jefferson	Republican	1801
James Madison	Republican	1809
James Monroe	Republican	1817
John Quincy Adams	Republican	1825
Andrew Jackson	Democrat	1829
Martin Van Buren	Democrat	1837
General William Henry Harrison	Whig	1841
John Tyler	Whig	1841
James Knox Polk	Democrat	1845
General Zachary Taylor (died in office)	Whig	1849
Millard Fillmore	Whig	1850
General Franklin Pierce	Democrat	1853
James Buchanan	Democrat	1857
Abraham Lincoln	Republican	1861
Abraham Lincoln (assassinated 14 April)	Republican	1865
Andrew Johnson	Republican	1865
General Ulysses Simpson Grant	Republican	1869
General Ulysses Simpson Grant	Republican	1873
Rutherford Birchard Hayes	Republican	1877
General James Abram Garfield (died in office)	Republican	1881
General Chester Alan Arthur	Republican	1881
Grover Cleveland	Democrat	1885
General Benjamin Harrison	Republican	1889
Grover Cleveland	Democrat	1893
William McKinley	Republican	1897
William McKinley (assassinated)	Republican	1901
Theodore Roosevelt	Republican	1901
William Howard Taft	Republican	1909
Dr Woodrow Wilson	Democrat	1913
Dr Woodrow Wilson	Democrat	1917
Warren Gamaliel Harding	Republican	1921
Calvin Coolidge	Republican	1923
Herbert Clark Hoover	Republican	1929
Franklin Delano Roosevelt	Democrat	1933
Franklin Delano Roosevelt	Democrat	1937
Franklin Delano Roosevelt	Democrat	1941
Franklin Delano Roosevelt	Democrat	1945
Harry Shippe Truman	Democrat	1945
Harry Shippe Truman	Democrat	1949

Dwight David
Eisenhower   *Republican* 1953
John Fitzgerald Kennedy
(assassinated)   *Democrat* 1961
Lyndon Baines Johnson
Democrat 1963

Lyndon Baines Johnson
Democrat 1965
Richard Milhous Nixon
Republican 1969
Richard Milhous Nixon
Republican 1972

Gerald Rudolf Ford
Republican 1974
James Earl Carter *Democrat* 1977
Ronald Wilson Reagan
Republican 1981
Ronald Wilson Reagan
Republican 1984

Prime Ministers of Britain

Sir Robert Walpole was the first person who could be termed Prime Minister in anything like the modern sense, and party affiliations were very loose until about 1782.

Sir Robert Walpole   *Whig* 1721
Earl of Wilmington   *Whig* 1742
Henry Pelham   *Whig* 1743
Duke of Newcastle   *Whig* 1754
Duke of Devonshire   *Whig* 1756
Duke of Newcastle   *Whig* 1757
Earl of Bute   *Tory* 1762
George
Grenville   *Independent* 1763
Marquis of
Rockingham   *Whig* 1765
Earl of Chatham
(William Pitt
the Elder)   *Tory* 1766
Duke of
Grafton   *Independent* 1767
Lord North   *Whig* 1770
Marquis of
Rockingham   *Whig* 1782
Earl of Shelburne   *Whig* 1782
Duke of Portland *Coalition* 1783
William Pitt
(the Younger)   *Tory* 1783
Henry Addington   *Tory* 1801
William Pitt
(the Younger)   *Tory* 1804
Lord Grenville   *Whig* 1806
Duke of Portland   *Tory* 1807
Spencer Perceval   *Tory* 1809
Earl of Liverpool   *Tory* 1812
George Canning   *Tory* 1827
Viscount Goderich   *Tory* 1827
Duke of Wellington   *Tory* 1828
Earl Grey   *Whig* 1830
Viscount Melbourne   *Whig* 1834
Sir Robert Peel   *Tory* 1834
Viscount Melbourne   *Whig* 1835
Sir Robert Peel   *Tory* 1841
Lord John Russell   *Whig* 1846
Earl of Derby   *Liberal* 1852
Earl of Aberdeen   *Tory* 1852
Viscount Palmerston *Liberal* 1855
Earl of Derby *Conservative* 1858
Viscount Palmerston *Liberal* 1859
Earl Russell   *Liberal* 1865
Earl of Derby *Conservative* 1866
Benjamin Disraeli
Conservative 1868

William Ewart Gladstone
Liberal 1868
Earl of Beaconsfield
(Benjamin Disraeli)
Conservative 1874
William Ewart Gladstone
Liberal 1880
Marquis of Salisbury
Conservative 1885
William Ewart Gladstone
Liberal 1886
Marquis of Salisbury
Conservative 1886
William Ewart Gladstone
Liberal 1892
Earl of Rosebery   *Liberal* 1894
Marquis of Salisbury
Conservative 1895
A.J.Balfour   *Conservative* 1902
Sir H. Campbell-Bannerman
Liberal 1905
H.H.Asquith   *Liberal* 1908
H.H.Asquith   *Coalition* 1915
David Lloyd
George   *Coalition* 1916
A. Bonar
Law   *Conservative* 1922
Stanley
Baldwin   *Conservative* 1923
Ramsey MacDonald *Labour* 1924
Stanley
Baldwin   *Conservative* 1924
Ramsey MacDonald *Labour* 1929
Ramsey MacDonald *Labour* 1931
Stanley
Baldwin   *Conservative* 1935
Neville
Chamberlain   *Coalition* 1937
Winston Churchill *Coalition* 1940
Winston Churchill
Conservative 1945
Clement Attlee   *Labour* 1945
Sir Winston Churchill
Conservative 1951
Sir Anthony Eden
Conservative 1955
Harold Macmillan
Conservative 1957

Sir Alec Douglas-Home
Conservative 1963
Harold Wilson   *Labour* 1964
Edward Heath *Conservative* 1970
Harold Wilson   *Labour* 1974
James Callaghan   *Labour* 1976
Margaret Thatcher
Conservative 1979
Margaret Thatcher
Conservative 1983
Margaret Thatcher
Conservative 1987

Famous Writers

Homer *probably*
born between   1050 and 850
Sappho *probably*
born   mid-7th C
Aesop   7th/6th C
Aeschylus   525-456
Sophocles   496-406
Herodotus   *c.*484-425
Euripides   480-406
Thucydides   *c.*460-*c.*400
Aristophanes   *c.*448-388
Plato   *c.*427-348
Marcus Tullius
Cicero   106-43
Virgil [Publius
Virgilius Maro]   70-19
Horace [Quintus
Horatius
Flaccus]   BC 65-8

(Gaius? Cornelius)
Tacitus   AD*c.*55-c.117
Dante Alighieri   1265-1321
Giovanni
Boccaccio   1313-1375
Geoffrey Chaucer   *c.*1342-1400
François Villon   1431-unknown
(Niccolo)
Machiavelli   1469-1527
Francçois
Rabelais   1494(?)-1553
(Miguel de)
Cervantes
(Saavedra)   1547-1616

Edmund Spenser	1552(?)-1599	(Wilhelm Carl)		Fyodor	
Francis Bacon	1561-1626	Grimm	1786-1859	Mikhailovich	
Christopher		(George Gordon)		Dostoevsky	1821-1881
Marlowe	1564-1593	Lord Byron	1788-1824	Dante Gabriel	
William		Percy Bysshe		Rossetti	1828-1882
Shakespeare	1564-1616	Shelley	1792-1822	Jules Verne	1828-1905
John Donne	1572-1631	John Keats	1795-1821	Henrik Ibsen	1828-1906
Ben Jonson	1572-1637	Heinrich Heine	1797-1856	Count Lev	
John Webster	1580(?)-1625(?)	Alexander		Nikolaevich	
Robert Herrick	1591-1674	Sergeyevich		Tolstoy	1828-1910
Pierre Corneille	1606-1684	Pushkin	1799-1837	Lewis Carroll	
John Milton	1608-1674	Honoré de Balzac	1799-1850	[Charles	
John Evelyn	1620-1706	Victor (-Marie)		Lutwidge	
Jean de La		Hugo	1802-1885	Dodgson]	1832-1898
Fontaine	1621-1695	Alexandre Dumas		Mark Twain	
Molière		(father)	1803-1870	[Samuel	
[Jean-Baptiste		Alexandre Dumas		Langhorne	
Poquelin]	1622-1673	(son)	1824-1895	Clemens]	1835-1910
John Bunyan	1628-1688	George Sand		Algernon Charles	
John Dryden	1631-1700	[Armandine		Swinburne	1837-1909
Samuel Pepys	1633-1703	Aurore Lucile		Émile Zola	1840-1902
Jean Racine	1639-1699	Dupin,		Thomas Hardy	1840-1928
Daniel Defoe	1660(?)-1731	Baronne		(Etienne)	
Jonathan Swift	1667-1745	Dudevant]	1804-1876	Stéphane	
William		Hans Christian		Mallarmé	1842-1898
Congreve	1670-1729	Andersen	1805-1875	Henry James	1843-1916
Sir Richard		John Stuart		Gerard Manley	
Steele	1672-1729	Mill	1806-1873	Hopkins	1844-1889
Alexander Pope	1688-1744	Henry		Paul Verlaine	1844-1896
Voltaire		(Wadsworth)		August	
[Francçois		Longfellow	1807-1882	Strindberg	1849-1912
Marie Arouet]	1694-1778	Edgar Allan Poe	1809-1849	Guy de	
Henry Fielding	1707-1754	Nikolai		Maupassant	1850-1893
Samuel Johnson	1709-1784	Vasilevich		Robert Louis	
Laurence Sterne	1713-1768	Gogol	1809-1852	(Balfour)	
Tobias (George)		Alfred Lord		Stevenson	1850-1894
Smollett	1721-1771	Tennyson	1809-1892	Oscar (Fingal	
Oliver Goldsmith	1730(?)-1774	Alfred de		O'Flahertie	
Edward Gibbon	1737-1794	Musset	1810-1857	Wills) Wilde	1854-1900
(Johann		William		George Bernard	
Wolfgang von)		Makepeace		Shaw	1856-1950
Goethe	1749-1832	Thackeray	1811-1863	Joseph Conrad	1857-1924
Richard Brinsley		Théophile		Sir Arthur Conan	
Sheridan	1751-1816	Gauthier	1811-1872	Doyle	1859-1930
William Blake	1757-1827	Charles Dickens	1812-1870	Anton	
Robert Burns	1759-1796	Robert Browning	1812-1889	(Pavlovich)	
(Johann Christoph		Anthony		Chekhov	1860-1904
Friedrich von)		Trollope	1815-1882	Rudyard Kipling	1865-1936
Schiller	1759-1805	Charlotte Brontë	1816-1855	W.B. (William	
William		Emily Brontë	1818-1848	Butler) Yeats	1865-1939
Wordsworth	1770-1850	Ivan Sergeyevich		H.G. (Herbert	
Sir Walter Scott	1771-1832	Turgenev	1818-1883	George) Wells	1866-1946
Samuel Taylor		George Eliot		John Galsworthy	1867-1933
Coleridge	1772-1833	[Mary Ann		Luigi Pirandello	1867-1936
Jane Austen	1775-1817	Cross née		Maxim Gorky	
William Hazlitt	1778-1830	Evans]	1819-1880	[Alexei	
Stendhal [Henri		Herman Melville	1819-1891	Maximovich	
Beyle]	1783-1842	Charles		Peshkov]	1868-1936
(Jacob Ludwig		Baudelaire	1821-1867	André Gide	1869-1951
Carl) Grimm	1785-1863	Gustave Flaubert	1821-1880	Marcel Proust	1871-1922

Sidonie-Gabrielle Colette	1873-1954	Rupert (Chawner) Brooke	1887-1915	George Orwell [Eric Blair]	1903-1950
G.K. (Gilbert Keith) Chesterton	1874-1936	Eugene (Gladstone) O'Neill	1888-1952	Evelyn (Arthur St John) Waugh	1903-1966
Robert Frost	1874-1963	T.S. (Thomas Stearns) Eliot	1888-1965	(Henry) Graham Greene	1904
(William) Somerset Maugham	1874-1965	(John Ronald Reuel) Tolkien	1892-1973	Jean-Paul Sartre	1905-1980
Thomas Mann	1875-1955	e.e. cummings	1894-1962	Arthur Koestler	1905-1983
Hermann Hesse	1877-1962	Aldous (Leonard) Huxley	1894-1963	Anthony Powell	1905
P.G. (Sir Pelham Grenville) Wodehouse	1881-1975	Robert (Ranke) Graves	1895-1985	Samuel (Barclay) Beckett	1906
James (Augustine Aloysius) Joyce	1882-1941	F. Scott Fitzgerald	1896-1940	W.H. (Wystan Hugh) Auden	1907-1973
Virginia Woolf	1882-1941	William Faulkner	1897-1962	Simone de Beauvoir	1908-1987
Franz Kafka	1883-1924	Bertolt Brecht	1898-1956	Anthony Burgess	1910-1987
D.H. (David Herbert) Lawrence	1885-1930	Ernest Hemingway	1898-1961	Mervyn Peake	1911-1968
Alain Fournier	1886-1914	Frederico García Lorca	1899-1936	Albert Camus	1913-1960
Siegfried Sassoon	1886-1967	John Steinbeck	1902-1968	Dylan Thomas	1914-1953
				Tennessee Williams	1914-1983
				(Alexander Isayevich) Solzhenitsyn	1918
				Günter Grass	1927

INVENTIONS AND DISCOVERIES

3300	the wheel	in Sumeria
250-226	basic laws of mechanics	Archimedes
200-176	concrete used for building	by the Romans
75-51	glass blowing invented	Levant
46 BC	Julian (modern) calendar began	on Caesar's orders
105 AD	paper invented	China
232	wheelbarrow thought to have been invented	China
250	algebraic notation began	Diophanus of Alexandria
450-74	metal stirrup first used	horsemen of Asian steppe
467	earliest known sighting of Halley's comet	China
525-49	silk worms smuggled into Europe	from China
550-74	decimal notation began	India
575-99	first porcelain produced	China
751	earliest known printed book - Buddhist Diamond Sutra	in Korea
1042	first recorded use of movable type in printing	China

1138	first use of Arabic numerals in the West	on Sicilian coins
1167	first distillation of alcohol	Salerno
1190	first evidence of use of the mariner's compass in West	in De Utensibus
1232	first use of rockets in warfare	China
1276	first European papermill	at Fabriano — 'Italy'
1280-84	spinning wheel appears in West	from China
1289	convex spectacles first used	Roger Bacon - England
1315-24	first clock escapement	Western Europe
1315-24	development of guns	Western Europe
1377	first specific quarantine period recognized	Ragusa - 'Italy'
1408	first windmill to pump water	Holland
1455	first book in the West	Johann Gutenberg
1462	first watch	Bartholomew Manfredi - 'Italy'
1477	first English printing press	William Caxton
1515-19	coffee came to Europe	from Arabia
1520-24	chocolate came to Europe	from Mexico

1581	pendulum's motion understood	Galileo	
1589	water closet invented	Sir John Harrington - England	
1590	the microscope was invented	Zacharias Janssen - Holland	
1621	slide rule invented	William Oughtred - England	
1628	circulation of blood discovered	William Harvey - England	
1644	barometer invented	Evangelista Torricelli - 'Italy'	
1661	first definition of chemical elements	Robert Boyle - England	
1665	experiments on gravitation	Sir Isaac Newton - England	
1666	the prism invented	Sir Isaac Newton - England	
1670	first minute hands on watches	unknown	
1679	first pressure cooker	Denis Papin - France	
1680	dodo became extinct		
1680	phosphorous matches invented	A.Hunckwitz	
1690	first steam-driven piston pump	Denis Papin - France	
1698	first steam pump engine	Thomas Savery	
1714	first mercury thermometer with temperature markings	Gabriel Fahrenheit - Germany	
1718	first machine gun invented	James Puckle - England	
1720	first inoculation against smallpox	Lady Mary Wortley Montagu - England	
1733	the flying shuttle invented for weaving	John Kay - England	
1742	Centigrade scale developed	Anders Celsius - Sweden	
1752	first lightning conductor	Benjamin Franklin - America	
1764	Spinning Jenny invented	James Hargreaves - England	
1769	first steam-driven car	Nicholas Cugnot - France	

1776	first commercial steam engine	Watt and Boulton - England	
1776	first submarine	David Bushnell	
1777	circular saw invented	Samuel Miller	
1779	first iron bridge	at Colnbrook-dale - England	
1780	first fountain pen	Scheller	
1782	first hot air balloon	Joseph Michel and Jacques Étienne Montgolfier - France	
1784	shells invented	Henry Shrapnel - England	
1785	seismograph invented	Salsano	
1785	parachute invented	Jean Pierre F.Blanchard	
1787	first iron ship	John Wilkinson - England	
1792	gas lighting	William Murdock - England	
1794	first telegraph used (Paris to Lille)		
1799	invention of bleach for cloth	Tennant and Mackintosh	
1800	first electric battery	Alesandro Volta	
1803	morphine discovered	Sertürner	
1808	typewriter invented	Pellegrine Tarri - 'Italy'	
1810	food canning started	Durand	
1812	local analgesia by freezing	Baron Larrey - France	
1816	stethoscope invented	Réné Laënnec - France	
1821	the electric motor devised	Michael Faraday - England	
1823	rubberized waterproof fabric	Charles MacIntosh - Scotland	
1825	first passenger railway	George Stephenson - England	
1826	the safety match	John Walker	
1829	photographic processing perfected	J. N. Niepce and Louis Daguerre - France	
1831	chloroform discovered	Guthrie and Jastus von Liebig	

1834	forerunner of the computer designed	Charles Babbage - England	
1835	Colt revolver patented	USA	
1836	first propeller-driven ship	John Ericson - Sweden	
1837	the Morse telegraph code	Samuel Morse - USA	
1839	bicycle invented	Kirkpatrick Macmillan - Scotland	
1845	patent for a pneumatic tyre	R. W. Thompson - England	
1846	solid rubber tyres for cars	Thomas Hancock	
1846	patent for a sewing machine	Elias Howe - USA	
1849	safety pin	Walter Hunt	
1850	first machine-chilled cold storage unit	James Harrison and Alexander Catlin Twining	
1851	first practical sewing machine	Isaac Singer - USA	
1854	first lift	Elisha Otis - USA	
1856	first aniline dye - mauve	William Perkin	
1858	first burglar alarm	Edwin T. Holmes - USA	
1859	first sleeping car for trains	George Pullman - USA	
1859	theory of evolution	Charles Darwin - England	
1862	plastics discovered	Alexander Parkes - England	
1866	theory of plant genetics	Gregor Johann Mendel - Czecho-slovakia	
1867	dynamite invented	Alfred Nobel - Sweden	
1869	DNA discovered	Friedrich Meischer - Switzer-land	
1873	barbed wire invented	Glidden - America	
1876	telephone invented	Alexander Graham Bell - Scotland	

1878	gramophone invented	Thomas Alva Edison - USA
1878	motorized tricycle	Karl Benz - Germany
1879	first electric light bulb	Thomas Alva Edison - USA
1879	first electric train	William Siemens - England
1885	first patent motorcycle	Gottlieb Daimler - Germany
1885	successful inoculation against rabies	Louis Pasteur - France
1886	first three-wheeler car patented	Karl Benz - Germany
1887	first four-wheeler car	Gottlieb Daimler - Germany
1888	first three-wheeler car ran	Karl Benz - Germany
1888	pneumatic bicycle tyres introduced	John Boyd Dunlop - Scotland
1891	first zip fastener	Whitcomb L. Judson
1895	safety razor	King C. Gillette - USA
1895	X-ray invented	W.K.Röntgen - Germany
1896	radioactivity from uranium discovered	Alexandre Becquerel - France
1898	discovery of radium	Marie and Pierre Curie - France
1900	first escalator	in America
1900	first loudspeaker	Horace Short - Britain
1903	Wright brothers' first flight	North Carolina, USA
1907	first electric washing machine	Hurley Machine Co - USA
1913	machine to measure radioactivity	Hans Geiger - Germany
1915	first tank used	Sir Ernest Swinton - Britain
1915	first fighter plane built	Hugo Junkers - Germany
1922	radar invented	Dr Albert H. Taylor and Leo C. Young

1924	first helicopter invented	Étienne Oehmichen - France
1926	first TV picture transmitted	John Logie Baird - Britain
1926	first 16-mm movie film made	Kodak - USA
1927	first electronic television	Philo Taylor Farnsworth
1928	penicillin discovered	Alexander Fleming - Britain
1931	the electric razor	Colonel Jacob Schick
1932	first nuclear disintegration	John Cockcroft and E. T. S. Walton - Britain
1933	discovery of polythene	ICI
1935	first parking meter	Carlton C. Magee - USA
1937	nylon created	Dr Wallace H. Carothers
1938	first practical ballpoint pen	Lajos Biró - Hungary
1939	first helicopter produced	Igor Sikorsky - USSR
1941	portable military bridge invented	Donald Coleman Bailey - Britain
1942	first atom split	Joliot-Curie Frédéric - France
1943	first electronic computer	Dr Alan M. Turing
1947	sound barrier first broken by an aeroplane	Major Charles Elwood Chuck Yeager - USA
1948	first long-playing record	Dr Peter Goldmark

1948	semiconductors introduced	
1948	first transistor	John Bardeen, W. Shockley and W. Brattain - USA
1952	first atomic powered submarine	USA
1953	discovery of the structure of DNA	James Dewey Watson and F. H. C. Crick - Britain
1955	the hovercraft invented	Sir Christopher Cockerell - Britain
1956	world's first large-scale nuclear power station	at Windscale - Britain
1957	launch of first space satellite	by USSR
1959	first craft to land on moon (unmanned)	USSR
1960	laser invented	Dr Charles H. Towne
1961	first man in space	Uri Gagarin - USSR
1966	first plastic heart used	USA
1969	first men on the moon	Neil Armstrong and Edwin (Buzz) Aldrin - USA
1969	first supersonic passenger plane flown - Concorde	Britain and France
1975	Rubik cube invented	Professor Ernö Rubik - Hungary
1982	first successful artificial heart transplant	USA

NAMES

The origins and meanings of many names are highly debatable. Often a name seems to have cropped up in different places at much the same point in history and it's anybody's guess who started it. The following list does not pretend to be scholarly, but simply provides a useful checklist if you are trying to name a child, and gives a rough guide to some of the possible origins and meanings. Alternative spellings, short forms and diminutives are given with the name from which they stem.

o/u stands for origin unknown
m/u stands for meaning unknown

Girls' Names

Abigail, *Hebrew*, father's delight

Ada, *German*, same as Edith, *q.v.*
Agatha, *Greek*, good
Agnes, *Greek*, chaste
Aileen, *Celtic* form of Helen, *q.v.*

Alexandra, *Greek*, helper of men
Alice, Alicia, *Old French*, m/u
Alison, pet name for Alice
Amabel, *Latin*, lovable
Amanda, *Latin*, fit to be loved

Amelia, *Old German*, m/u

Amy, *Latin*, a beloved

Andrea, modern from Andrew, — manly, brave

Angela, *Greek*, from angel - messenger

Angelina, *Greek*, lovely, angelic

Ann, Anne, Anna, Annette, *Hebrew*, gracious

Annabel, *Latin/French*, lovable

Antonia, Antoinette, from Anthony

Arabella, *Latin*, a fair altar

Aurelia, Aureola, *Latin*, like gold

Aurora, *Latin*, morning brightness

Barbara, *Greek*, foreign or strange

Beatrice, *Latin*, making happy

Belinda, *Latin*, useful

Bella, *Italian*, beautiful

Benedicta, *Latin*, blessed

Bernice, *Greek*, bringing victory

Blanche, *French*, fair, white

Bona, *Latin*, good

Brenda, *Norse*, from the male Brand

Bridget, *Irish*, shining bright, strength

Bryony, climbing plant

Camilla, *Latin*, attendant at a sacrifice

Candida, *Latin*, white

Cassandra, *Greek*, a reformer of men

Catherine, Catharine, Katherine, Katerina, Kate, *Greek*, o/u

Cecilia, Celia, Cecily, Cicely, *Latin*, m/u

Charlotte, Carlotta, Carla, Caroline,
Carol, *French*, from Charles, *q.v.*

Charmian, *Greek*, joy

Chloe, *Greek*, a green herb

Christabel, *Greek/Latin*, beautiful Christian

Christine, Christina, *Greek*, belonging to Christ

Clare, Clara, Clarice, Clarinda, Clarissa, *Latin*, clear or bright

Claudia, *Latin*, lame

Clementine, Clementina, *Latin*, gentle

Colette, *French*, from Nicole

Constance, *Latin*, constant

Cordelia, *Latin*, warm-hearted

Cornelia, *Latin*, m/u

Cressida, *Greek*, daughter of the golden one

Daisy, Victorian pet name for Margaret

Daphne, *Greek*, laurel

Davina, *Scottish*, from David, *q.v.*

Deborah, *Hebrew*, a bee

Delia, *Greek*, from Delos

Denise, from Denis

Diana, *Latin*, Jupiter's daughter

Dinah, *Hebrew*, judged

Dorcas, *Greek*, a gazelle

Dorothea, Dora, Dorothy, *Greek*, gift of God

Edith, *Saxon*, happiness, a rich gift

Edna, *Hebrew*, pleasure

Elaine, Eleanor, Elinor, from Helen

Elizabeth, Beth, Betty, Betsy, Bessie,
Elsie, Elspeth, *Hebrew*, oath of God

Emily, corrupted from Amelia

Emma, *German*, a nurse, industrious

Erica, from Eric

Esme, *French*, beloved

Esther, Heather, *Hebrew*, secrets

Ethel, *Saxon*, of noble birth

Eugenia, *Greek*, well-born

Eunice, *Greek*, fair victory

Eva or Eve, *Hebrew*, causing life

Evelyn, *Latin*, hazel

Fanny, diminutive of Frances, *q.v.*

Felicia, *Latin*, fortunate, happy

Felicity, *Latin*, happiness

Fenella, *Gaelic*, from white shoulders

Fiona, literary invention

Flora, *Latin*, flowers

Florence, *Latin*, blooming, flourishing

Frances, Francesca, Fanny, *German*, a Frank

Frederica, *Saxon*, abounding in peace

Gail, from Abigail

Gemma, *Italian*, a gem

Georgina, Georgia, Georgiana, from George, *q.v.*

Geraldine, *Saxon*, strong, spear power

Gertrude, *Old German*, from spear and strength

Gladys, *Welsh*, a fair maiden

Grace, *Latin*, grace

Hannah, *Hebrew*, gracious

Harriet, Henrietta, from Henry

Helen, Helena, Ellen, Ella, Nell, Nella, Nellie, Nelly, *Greek*, the bright one

Hilda, *Old English*, war and battle

Ida, *Saxon*, like a goddess, happy

Imogen, o/u

Iona/Ione, o/u

Irene, *Greek*, peaceful

Isabella, Ella, *Spanish*, fair Eliza

Jacqueline, Jacquetta, *French*, from Jacques

Jane, Jean, *Scots*, Jeanne, Joan, feminine of John, *q.v.*

Janet, Jeanette, little Jane

Jasmine, *Persian*, from the flower

Jemima, Gemima, *Hebrew*, dove

Jennifer, *Welsh*, from Guinevere, m/u

Jenny, pet name for Jane

Jessica, probably *Hebrew*, m/u

Joanna, Johanna, form of Joan, *q.v.*

Josephine, *French*, from Joseph

Joyce, *Latin*, sportive

Judith, *Hebrew*, praising

Julia, Juliana, feminine of Julius, *q.v.*

Juliet, *Italian* diminutive of Julia

June, from the month

Justina, *Latin*, just

Karen, *Danish* form of Katherine

Kirsten, Kirsty, *Scandinavian*, Christine

Laura, *Latin*, a laurel

Lavinia, *Latin*, of Latium

Leila, *Persian*, dark-haired as night

Leitia, *Latin*, joy or gladness

Leonie, *Greek*, lion

Leslie, Lesley, *Scottish*, m/u

Lilian, Lily, *Latin*, a lily

Linda, *German*, m/u

Lisa, Liza, Lizzie, from Elizabeth

Lois, *Greek*, better

Lorna, invented for Lorna Doone

Louise, Louisa, *French*, from Louis, *q.v.*

Lucretia, *Latin*, a chaste Roman lady, light

Lucy, Lucinda, Lucia, *Latin*, from Lucius

Lydia, *Greek*, native of Lydia

Mabel, *Latin*, lovely or lovable

Magdalen, Madeline, *Syriac*, magnificent

Maia, Maya, *Latin*, exalted

Marcella, *Latin*, m/u

Margaret, Madge, Maisie, Maggie, Greta, Minnie, *Greek*, a pearl

Marina, *Latin*, of the sea

Marjorie, Margery, *French*, from Marguerite

Marlene, devised for Marlene Dietrich

Martha, *Hebrew*, lady

Martina, from Martin

Mary, Maria, Marie, Marion, Marilyn, Molly, *Hebrew*, bitter

Matilda, *German*, a lady of honour

May, *Latin*, month of May, or dim. of Mary, *q.v.*

Melissa, *Greek*, a honey bee
Mildred, *Saxon*, speaking mild
Millicent, *Latin*, a sweet singer
Miranda, *Latin*, admirable
Miriam, *Hebrew*, exalted
Moira, Moyra, *Irish* for Mary
Myra, *Greek*, grieving
Nancy, a form of Anne
Naomi, *Hebrew*, bitterness, consolation
Natasha, *Russian* diminutive of Natalia
Netta, Nettie, forms of Henrietta
Nicola, *Greek*, feminine of Nicolas
Nina, *Russian* diminutive of Anne
Nora, *contraction of* Honora
Olive, Olivia, *Latin*, an olive
Ophelia, *Greek*, a serpent
Pamela, invented by Sir Philip Sidney
Patience, *Latin*, bearing patiently
Patricia, feminine of Patrick, *q.v.*
Pauline, Paula, Paulina, from Paul
Penelope, *Greek*, a weaver
Philippa, *Greek*, feminine of Philip
Phoebe, *Greek*, the light of life
Phyllis, *Greek*, a green bough
Polly, variation of Molly, dim. of Mary, *q.v.*
Priscilla, *Latin*, somewhat old
Prudence, *Latin*, discretion
Rachel, *Hebrew*, a lamb
Rebecca, *Hebrew*, a noose
Rhoda, *Greek*, a rose
Rita, short for Margaret, *q.v.*
Roberta, Robina, from Robert
Rosa, Rose, Rosie, *Latin*, a rose
Rosabella, *Italian*, a fair rose
Rosalie, Rosaline, *Latin*, little rose
Rosalind, *Latin*, beautiful as a rose
Rosamond, *Saxon*, rose of peace
Rosemary, o/u
Rona, Rhona, *Gaelic/Welsh*, m/u
Roxana, *Persian*, dawn of day
Ruth, *Hebrew*, friend
Sabina, *Latin*, sprung from the Sabines
Sally, form of Sarah, *q.v.*
Samantha, modern
Sandra, Sandy, from Alexandra
Sarah, *Hebrew*, a princess
Sasha, from Alexander (also for boys)
Selina, *Greek*, the moon
Serena, *Latin*, calm
Sharon, biblical place name
Sheila, *Irish* for Celia, *q.v.*
Sheena, Shena, *Gaelic* for Jane

Shirley, from the surname
Sibylla, *Greek*, a prophetess
Siobhan, *Irish* form of Joan
Sonia, Sonya, *Russian* diminutive of Sophia
Sophia, Sophie, *Greek*, wisdom
Stella, *Latin*, a star
Stephanie, *French*, from Stephen, *q.v.*
Susan, Susanna, *Hebrew*, a lily
Tabitha, *Syriac*, a roe
Tamsin, version of Thomasina
Tania, Tanya, *Russian* diminutive for Tatyana
Teresa, *Greek*, a gleaner
Theodora, Theodosia, *Greek*, given by God
Tracy, from Teresa
Una, *Irish*, one
Ursula, *Latin*, a she bear
Valerie, Valeria, *Latin*, m/u
Vanessa, invented by Swift
Venetia, possibly *Latin*, for Gwyneth
Vera, Vere, *Latin*, true
Verity, o/u
Veronica, *Latin*, true image
Victoria, *Latin*, all conquering
Viola, Violet, *Latin*, a violet
Virginia, *Latin*, chaste
Vivien, *Latin*, lively
Wendy, first used in *Peter Pan*
Winifred, *Saxon*, winning peace
Yvonne, Yvette, *French* diminutive
Zoe, *Greek*, lively

Boys' Names

Adam, *Hebrew*, red
Adrian, *Latin*, from Adria
Albert, *Saxon*, nobly bright
Alexander, Alastair, Alex, Sandy, *Greek*, defending men
Alfred, *Teutonic*, good counsellor
Algernon, *French*, bearded
Allan, Alan, Allen, *Celtic*, m/u
Ambrose, *Greek*, immortal
Andrew, *Greek*, manly
Angus, *Celtic*, excellent virtue
Antony, Anthony, Tony, *Latin*, m/u
Archibald, *German*, a bold observer
Arnold, *German*, strong as an eagle
Arthur, o/u
Barnaby, *Hebrew*, a prophet's son
Barry, *Irish*, spear
Bartholomew, *Hebrew*, the son of him who made the waters to rise
Basil, *Greek*, kingly

Ben, *Hebrew*, son
Benedict, *Latin*, blessed
Benjamin, *Hebrew*, the son of a right hand
Bennet, *Latin*, blessed
Bernard, *German*, bear's heart
Bertram, Bertrand, *German*, bright raven
Beverley, from beaver stream
Brendan, *Irish*, hill
Brian, Bryan, *Celtic*, strong
Bruce, place name
Byron, *Old English*, at the cowsheds
Caleb, *Hebrew*, a dog
Cary, *Old English* place name
Cecil, *Latin*, blind
Charles, *German*, manly
Christopher, *Greek*, bearing Christ
Clarence, *Latin*, illustrious
Clark, from the surname
Claude, *Latin*, lame
Clement, *Latin*, mild-tempered
Clifford, from a place name
Clive, from the surname
Colin, *French*, from Nicolas
Conrad, *German*, able counsel
Constantine, *Latin*, resolute
Craig, *Old Welsh*, crag
Crispin, *Latin*, having curled locks
Cuthbert, *Saxon*, known famously
Cyril, *Greek*, commanding
Damian, *Greek*, tamer
Dan, *Hebrew*, judgement
Daniel, *Hebrew*, God is judge
David, *Hebrew*, well-beloved
Dean, o/u
Denis, Dennis, *Greek*, from Dionysius belonging to the god of wine
Derek, Derrick, Deric, Dirk, *Old German*, ruler of the people
Desmond, *Old Irish*, south of Munster
Dominic, *Latin*, of the Lord
Donald, *Gaelic*, proud
Douglas, *Gaelic*, dark grey
Duncan, *Celtic*, brown chief
Dunstan, *Saxon*, most high
Edgar, *Saxon*, happy hour
Edmund, *Saxon*, happy peace
Edward, *Saxon*, happy keeper
Edwin, *Saxon*, happy conqueror
Egbert, *Saxon*, ever bright
Emmanuel, *Hebrew*, God with us
Enoch, *Hebrew*, dedicated
Eric, *Anglo-Saxon*, kingly
Ernest, *Old German*, vigour

Eugene, *Greek*, nobly descended

Evan, *Welsh*, young warrior

Fabian, *Latin*, bean grower

Felix, *Latin*, happy

Ferdinand, *Old German*, from 'journey' and 'risk'

Fergus, *Celtic*, manly

Francis, *Latin*, a Frenchman

Frederick, Fredric, *Old German*, from peace and ruler

Gabriel, *Hebrew*, the strength of God

Gareth, *Welsh*, high land

Gary, *French*, Gerard

Gavin, *Celtic*, hawk of battle

Geoffrey, Jeffrey, *Old German*, peace

George, *Greek*, a husbandman

Gerard, *Saxon*, spear power

Gideon, *Hebrew*, a destroyer

Gilbert, *Saxon*, bright as gold

Giles, *Greek*, a little goat

Glenn, *Celtic*, valley

Goddard, Godard, *Old German*, from God and hard

Godfrey, *Old German*, God's peace,

Gordon, *Scottish* surname

Graham, *Scottish* surname

Gregory, *Greek*, watchful

Griffith, Griffin, *Welsh*, m/u

Guy, *French*, a leader

Hamish, pseudo *Gaelic*, for James, q.v.

Harold, *Saxon*, a champion

Hector, *Greek*, a stout defender

Henry, *Old German*, house ruler

Herbert, *Old German*, from bright and army

Herman, *Saxon*, a valiant soldier

Horace, Horatio, *Latin*, m/u

Howard, recent, from the surname

Hubert, Hugh, Hugo, *German*, from heart and mind

Humphrey, *Old English* or *Old German*, m/u

Ian, *Celtic*, for John

Ingram, *Old German*, m/u

Isaac, *Hebrew*, laughter

Ivan, *Russian*, for John

Ivor, *Celtic*, Lord

Jack, pet name for John

Jacob, *Hebrew*, a supplanter

James, Jamie, Jacques, Jim, Jimmy, *Old French*, m/u

Jason, *Greek*, m/u

Jasper, Caspar, m/u

Jeremiah, Jeremy, Jerry, *Hebrew*, exalted of the Lord

Jerome, *Greek*, holy name

Jesse, *Hebrew*, wealth

Job, *Hebrew*, sorrowing, persecuted

Joel, *Hebrew*, acquiescing

John, *Hebrew*, the grace of the Lord

Jonathan, *Hebrew*, the gift of the Lord

Joscelin, Jocelyn, *Old German*, m/u

Joseph, *Hebrew*, addition

Joshua, *Hebrew*, a Saviour

Jude, *Hebrew*, confession

Julian, Julius, *Latin*, soft-haired

Justin, *Latin*, just

Keith, *Gaelic*, wood

Kenneth, *Gaelic*, leader of men

Kevin, *Irish*, comely birth

Kieran, *Old Irish*, black-haired

Kim, from Rudyard Kipling, used for either sex

Kirk, *Scottish* surname

Lambert, *Saxon*, a fair lamb

Laurence, Lawrence, *Latin*, from a town name, meaning crowned with laurels

Leonard, *Old German*, bold

Leopold, *Old German*, from people and bold

Leslie, *Scottish*

Lewis or Louis, *French*, famous warrior

Liam, *Irish* form of William

Lionel, *Latin*, a little lion

Llewellyn, *Celtic*, lightning

Lloyd, *Welsh*, grey

Lucius, *Latin*, shining

Luke, *Greek*, a wood or grove

Magnus, *Latin*, great

Malcolm, *Gaelic*, m/u

Manfred, *German*, great peace

Mark, *Latin*, a hammer

Marmaduke, *Saxon*, noble and powerful

Martin, *Latin*, martial

Matthew, *Hebrew*, a gift or present

Maurice, *Latin*, sprung of a Moor

Meredith, *Old Welsh*, lord

Michael, *Hebrew*, who is like God?

Miles, Myles, *Old German*, m/u

Morgan, *British*, a mariner

Nathaniel, Nathanael, Nathan, *Hebrew*, God has given

Nicholas, Nicolas, *Greek*, victorious over the people

Nigel, Neil, Neal, Neale, Niall, obscure - probably *Irish*

Noël, *Old French*, for Christmas-day babies

Norman, *French*, a North man

Oliver, *Latin*, an olive

Orlando, *Italian* form of Roland, q.v.

Orson, *Latin*, a bear

Oscar, *Old English*, from god and spear

Osmund, *Saxon*, house peace

Oswald, *Saxon*, ruler of a house

Owen, *Old Welsh*, well-born

Patrick, *Latin*, a nobleman

Paul, *Latin*, small, little

Paulinus, *Latin*, little Paul

Percival, *French*, a place in France

Percy, *English*, adaptation of pierce eye

Peregrine, *Latin*, stranger

Peter, Piers, *Greek*, rock

Philip, *Greek*, a lover of horses

Phineas, *Hebrew*, of bold countenance

Quentin, Quintin, *Latin*, from quinctus - fifth

Ralph, contracted from Randolph, or Randal, Ranulph, *Saxon*, house wolf

Raymond, *Old German*, from counsel and protection

Reginald, *Saxon*, ruler

Reuben, *Hebrew*, the son of vision

Rex, *Latin*, king

Richard, *Saxon*, powerful

Robert, Robin, Rupert, Bob, *Old German*, fame

Roderick, *German*, rich in fame

Rodney, Somerset place name

Roger, *Old German*, from fame and spear

Roland, Rowland, Rollo, *Old German*, from fame and land

Ronald, *Old German*

Rory, Roy, *Irish*, red

Rufus, *Latin*, reddish

Samuel, *Hebrew*, heard by God

Saul, *Hebrew*, desired

Sean, *Irish*, for John

Sebastian, *Latin*, man of Sebastia

Shamus, Seamus, *Irish* for James

Sidney, Sydney, from the surname

Silvester, *Latin*, born in the woods

Simeon, *Hebrew*, hearing

Simon, *Hebrew*, obedient

Solomon, *Hebrew*, peaceable

Stanley, from the place name

Stephen, *Greek*, a crown or garland

Stewart, Stuart, from the surname

Terence, *Latin*, m/u
Theobald, *Saxon*, bold over the people
Theodore, *Greek*, the gift of God
Thomas, Tom, *Hebrew*, twin
Timothy, *Greek*, a feãrer of God
Titus, m/u
Tobias, Toby, *Hebrew*, God is good

Tristram, *Celtic*, a herald
Valentine, *Latin*, powerful
Victor, *Latin*, conqueror
Vincent, *Latin*, conquering
Vivian, *Latin*, lively
Walter, *Old German*, from rule and folk
Warren, *Old German*, folk name
Wilfred, *Saxon*, bold and peaceful

William, Bill, Willy, *Old German*, from will and helmet
Winston, family name in the Churchill family

More information
Leslie Dunking, *The Guinness Book of Names*, Guinness Superlatives

ROMAN NUMERALS

Since Latin is a dead language publishers and film makers conveniently obscure their release dates by printing them in Roman numerals, thereby leaving those unversed in Latin totally mystified. To frustrate this ploy here is how you decipher them.

Roman numerals are written with seven capital letters of the alphabet:
$I = 1$ $V = 5$ $X = 10$ $L = 50$ $C = 100$
$D = 500$ $M = 1000$

For most numbers the symbols are written in order of size, with the largest first, so they add up to the number intended.

$2 = II$ i.e. $1 + 1$
$3 = III$ i.e. $1 + 1 + 1$
$6 = VI$ i.e. $5 + 1$
$7 = VII$ i.e. $5 + 1 + 1$
$8 = VIII$ i.e. $5 + 1 + 1 + 1$
$12 = XII$ i.e. $10 + 1 + 1$
$15 = XV$ i.e. $10 + 5$
$17 = XVII$ i.e. $10 + 5 + 1 + 1$
$20 = XX$ i.e. $10 + 10$
$35 = XXXV$ i.e. $10 + 10 + 10 + 5$
$60 = LX$ i.e. $50 + 10$
$75 = LXXV$ i.e. $50 + 10 + 10 + 5$
$200 = CC$ i.e. $100 + 100$
$600 = DC$ i.e. $500 + 100$
$735 = DCCXXXV$ i.e. $500 + 100 + 100 + 10 + 10 + 10 + 5$

Some numbers can't be made this way. So the other rule is, that if any letter has a smaller value than the one that follows it you subtract it from the one after it. So:

$4 = IV$ i.e. 1 taken away from 5
$9 = IX$ i.e. 1 taken away from 10
$19 = XIX$ i.e. $10 + (1$ taken away from 10)
$40 = XL$ i.e. 10 taken away from 50
$90 = XC$ i.e. 10 taken away from 100
$900 = CM$ i.e. 100 taken away from 1000

The year 1988 is written MCMLXXXVIII.

SPORTS WINNERS

American Football - Superbowl
This developed from soccer and rugby in the late nineteenth century, and the first programme was played in 1895, in Pennsylvania. Superbowl started in 1967.

1967	Green Bay *35* Kansas City *10*
1968	Green Bay *33* Oakland *14*
1969	New York *16* Baltimore *7*
1970	Kansas City *23* Minnesota *7*
1971	Baltimore *16* Dallas *13*
1972	Dallas *24* Miami *3*
1973	Miami *14* Washington *7*
1974	Miami *24* Minnesota *7*
1975	Pittsburgh *16* Minnesota *6*
1976	Pittsburgh *21* Dallas *17*
1977	Oakland *32* Minnesota *14*
1978	Dallas *27* Denver *10*
1979	Pittsburgh *35* Dallas *31*
1980	Pittsburgh *31* Los Angeles *19*
1981	Oakland *27* Philadelphia *10*
1982	San Francisco 49ers *26* Cincinnati Bengals *21*
1983	Washington Redskins *27* Miami Dolphins *17*
1984	Los Angeles Raiders *38* Washington Redskins *9*
1985	San Francisco 49ers *38* Miami Dolphins *16*
1986	Chicago Bears *46* New England Patriots *10*
1987	New York Giants *39* Denver Broncos *20*
1988	Washington Redskins *42* Denver Broncos *10*

Oxford and Cambridge Boat Race
This was first rowed between Hambledon Lock and Henley Bridge in 1829. It moved to the present course of 6·779 km (4 miles 374 yards) from Putney to Mortlake in 1845.

	Winner	*Min*		*Winner*	*Min*
1900	C	18.45	1911	O	18.29
1901	O	22.31	1912	O	22.05
1902	C	19.09	1913	O	20.53
1903	C	19.33	1914	C	20.23
1904	C	21.37	1920	C	21.11
1905	O	20.35	1921	C	19.45
1906	C	19.25	1922	C	19.27
1907	C	20.26	1923	O	20.54
1908	C	19.20	1924	C	18.41
1909	O	19.50	1925	C	21.50
1910	O	20.14	1926	C	19.29

	Winner	Min		Winner	Min		Winner	Min		Winner	Min
1927	C	20.14	1947	C	23.01	1961	C	19.22	1975	C	19.27
1928	C	20.25	1948	C	17.50	1962	C	19.46	1976	O	16.58
1929	C	19.24	1949	C	18.57	1963	O	20.47	1977	O	19.28
1930	C	19.09	1950	C	20.15	1964	C	19.18	1978	O	18.58
1931	C	19.26	1951	C	20.15	1965	O	18.07	1979	O	20.33
1932	C	19.11	1952	O	20.23	1966	O	19.12	1980	O	19.20
1933	C	20.57	1953	C	19.54	1967	O	18.52	1981	O	18.11
1934	C	18.03	1954	O	20.23	1968	C	18.22	1982	O	18.21
1935	C	19.48	1955	C	19.10	1969	C	18.04	1983	O	19.07
1936	C	21.06	1956	C	18.36	1970	C	20.22	1984	O	16.45
1937	O	22.39	1957	C	19.01	1971	C	17.58	1985	O	17.11
1938	O	20.30	1958	C	18.15	1972	C	18.36	1986	C	17.58
1939	C	19.03	1959	O	18.52	1973	C	19.21	1987	O	19.59
1946	O	19.54	1960	O	18.59	1974	O	17.35	1988	O	14.35

Cricket

The Ashes

1901/2	Aus.	1930	Aus.	1962/63	Aus.
1902	Aus.	1932/3	Eng.	1964	Aus.
1903/4	Eng.	1934	Aus.	1965/6	Aus.
1905	Eng.	1936/37	Aus.	1968	Aus.
1907/8	Aus.	1938	Aus.	1970/1	Eng.
1909	Aus.	1946/7	Aus.	1972	Eng.
1911/12	Eng.	1948	Aus.	1974/5	Aus.
1912	Eng.	1950/1	Aus.	1975	Aus.
1920/1	Aus.	1953	Eng.	1977	Eng.
1921	Aus.	1954/5	Eng.	1978/9	Eng.
1924/5	Aus.	1956	Eng.	19781	Eng.
1926	Eng.	1958/59	Aus.	1982/3	Aus.
1928/9	Eng.	1961	Aus.	1985	Eng.

County Championships

The championships, which are contested by 17 counties, date from 1864, but were made official in 1890.

1900 Yorks.	1949 Middx/Yorks.	1930 Lancs.
1901 Yorks.	1931 Yorks.	1963 Yorks.
1902 Yorks.	1932 Yorks.	1964 Worcs.
1903 Middx	1933 Yorks.	1965 Worcs.
1904 Lancs.	1934 Lancs.	1966 Yorks.
1905 Yorks.	1935 Yorks.	1967 Yorks.
1906 Kent	1936 Derbys.	1968 Yorks.
1907 Notts.	1937 Yorks.	1969 Glam.
1908 Yorks.	1938 Yorks.	1970 Kent
1909 Kent	1939 Yorks.	1971 Surrey
1910 Kent	1946 Yorks	1972 Warwicks.
1911 Warwicks.	1947 Middx	1973 Hants
1912 Yorks.	1948 Glam	1974 Worcs.
1913 Kent	1949 Middx/Yorks.	1975 Leics.
1914 Surrey	1950 Lancs./Surrey	1976 Middx
1919 Yorks.	1951 Warwicks.	1977 Kent/Middx
1920 Middx	1952 Surrey	1978 Kent
1921 Middx	1953 Surrey	1979 Essex
1922 Yorks.	1954 Surrey	1980 Middx.
1923 Yorks.	1955 Surrey	1981 Notts.
1924 Yorks.	1956 Surrey	1982 Middx
1925 Yorks.	1957 Surrey	1983 Essex
1926 Lancs.	1958 Surrey	1984 Essex
1927 Lancs.	1959 Yorks.	1985 Middx
1928 Lancs.	1960 Yorks	1986 Essex
1929 Notts.	1961 Hants	1987 Notts.

Golf - Open Championship

This is the world's oldest open golf championship, having first been held in October 1860, at the Prestwich Club in Ayrshire.

1900 John H. Taylor (GB)
1901 James Braid (GB)
1902 Alexander Herd (GB)
1903 Harry Vardon (GB)
1904 Jack White (GB)
1905 James Braid (GB)
1906 James Braid (GB)
1907 Arnaud Massy (GB)
1908 James Braid (GB)
1909 John H. Taylor (GB)
1910 James Braid (GB)
1911 Harry Vardon (GB)
1912 Edward (Ted) Ray (GB)
1913 John H. Taylor (GB)
1914 Harry Vardon (GB)
1920 George Duncan (GB)
1921 Jock Hutchinson (USA)
1922 Walter Hagen (USA)
1923 Arthur G. Havers (GB)
1924 Walter Hagen (USA)
1925 James M. Barnes (USA)
1926 Robert T. Jones Jr (USA)
1927 Robert T. Jones Jr (USA)

1928 Walter Hagen (USA)
1929 Walter Hagen (USA)
1930 Robert T. Jones Jr (USA)
1931 Tommy D. Armour (USA)
1932 Gene Sarazen (USA)
1933 Denny Shute (USA)
1934 Henry Cotton (GB)
1935 Alfred Perry (GB)
1936 Alfred Padgham (GB)
1937 Henry Cotton (GB)
1938 Reg White (GB)
1939 Richard Burton (GB)
1946 Sam Snead (USA)
1947 Fred Daly (GB)
1948 Henry Cotton (GB)
1949 Bobby Locke (SA)
1950 Bobby Locke (SA)
1951 Max Faulkner (GB)
1952 Bobby Locke (SA)
1953 Ben Hogan (USA)
1954 Peter Thomson (Aus)
1955 Peter Thomson (Aus)
1956 Peter Thomson (Aus)
1957 Bobby Locke (SA)
1958 Peter Thomson (Aus)
1959 Gary Player (SA)
1960 Kel Nagle (Aus)
1961 Arnold Palmer (USA)

1962 Arnold Palmer (USA)	1968 Gary Player (SA)
1963 Bob Charles (NZ)	1969 Tony Jacklin (GB)
1964 Tony Lema (USA)	1970 Jack Nicklaus (USA)
1965 Peter Thomson (Aus)	1971 Lee Trevino (USA)
1966 Jack Nicklaus (USA)	1972 Lee Trevino (USA)
1967 Roberto de Vincenzo (Arg)	1973 Tom Weiskopf (USA)
	1974 Gary Player (SA)
	1975 Tom Watson (USA)

1976 Johnny Miller (USA)	1983 Tom Watson (USA)
1977 Tom Watson (USA)	1984 Severiano Ballesteros (Sp)
1978 Jack Nicklaus (USA)	1985 Sandy Lyle (GB)
1979 Severiano Ballesteros (Sp)	1986 Greg Norman (Aus)
1980 Tom Watson (USA)	1987 Nick Faldo (GB)
1981 Bill Rogers (USA)	
1982 Tom Watson (USA)	

Football

FA Cup Winners

This competition started in 1872 but only found a permanent home at Wembley in 1923. There were replays of the Cup Final in 1901, 1902, 1910, 1911, 1912, 1970, 1981, 1982 and 1983.

1900 Bury 4 Southampton 0
1901 Spurs 3 Sheffield Utd 1
1902 Sheff Utd 2 Southampton 1
1903 Bury 6 Derby County 0
1904 Man City 1 Bolton Wanderers 0
1905 Aston Villa 2 Newcastle 0
1906 Everton 1 Newcastle 0
1907 Sheffield Wed 2 Everton 1
1908 Wolves 3 Newcastle 1
1909 Man Utd 1 Bristol City 0
1910 Newcastle Utd 2 Barnsley 0
1911 Bradford City 1 Newcastle 0
1912 Barnsley 1 WBA 0
1913 Aston Villa 1 Sunderland 0
1914 Burnley 1 Liverpool 0
1915 Sheff Utd 3 Chelsea 0
1920 Aston Villa 1 Huddersfield 0
1921 Spurs 1 Wolves 0
1922 Huddersfield 1 Preston 0
1923 Bolton Wanderers 2 West Ham 0
1924 Newcastle 2 Aston Villa 0
1925 Sheff Utd 1 Cardiff City 0
1926 Bolton Wanderers 1 Man City 0
1927 Cardiff City 1 Arsenal 0
1928 Blackburn Rovers 3 Huddersfield 1
1929 Bolton Wanderers 2 Portsmouth 0

1930 Arsenal 2 Huddersfield 0
1931 WBA 2 Birmingham 1
1932 Newcastle 2 Arsenal 1
1933 Everton 3 Man City 0
1934 Man City 2 Portsmouth 1
1935 Sheffield Wed 4 WBA 2
1936 Arsenal 1 Sheff Utd 0
1937 Sunderland 3 Preston 1
1938 Preston 1 Huddersfield 0
1939 Portsmouth 4 Wolves 1
1946 Derby County 4 Charlton 1
1947 Charlton 1 Burnley 0
1948 Man Utd 4 Blackpool 2
1949 Wolves 3 Leicester 1
1950 Arsenal 2 Liverpool 0
1951 Newcastle 2 Blackpool 0
1952 Newcastle 1 Arsenal 0
1953 Blackpool 4 Bolton Wanderers 3
1954 WBA 3 Preston 2
1955 Newcastle 3 Man City 1
1956 Man City 3 Birmingham 1
1957 Aston Villa 2 Man Utd 1
1958 Bolton Wanderers 2 Man Utd 0
1959 Nottingham Forest 2 Luton 1
1960 Wolves 3 Blackburn Rovers 0
1961 Spurs 2 Leicester 0

1962 Spurs 3 Burnley 1
1963 Man Utd 3 Leicester 1
1964 West Ham 3 Preston 2
1965 Liverpool 2 Leeds 1
1966 Everton 3 Sheffield Wed 2
1967 Spurs 2 Chelsea 1
1968 WBA 1 Everton 0
1969 Man City 1 Leicester 0
1970 Chelsea 2 Leeds 1
1971 Arsenal 2 Liverpool 1
1972 Leeds 1 Arsenal 0
1973 Sunderland 1 Leeds 0
1974 Liverpool 3 Newcastle 0
1975 West Ham 2 Fulham 0
1976 Southampton 1 Man Utd 0
1977 Man Utd 2 Liverpool 1
1978 Ipswich 1 Arsenal 0
1979 Arsenal 3 Man Utd 2
1980 West Ham 1 Arsenal 0
1981 Spurs 3 Man City 2
1982 Spurs 1 QPR 0
1983 Man Utd 4 Brighton 0
1984 Everton 2 Watford 0
1985 Man Utd 1 Everton 0
1986 Liverpool 3 Everton 1
1987 Coventry 3 Spurs 2

Football League

1900-01 Liverpool
1901-02 Sunderland
1902-03 Sheffield Wed
1903-04 Sheffield Wed
1904-05 Newcastle
1905-06 Liverpool
1906-07 Newcastle
1907-08 Man Utd
1908-09 Newcastle
1909-10 Aston Villa
1910-11 Man Utd
1911-12 Blackburn
1912-13 Sunderland
1913-14 Blackburn
1914-15 Everton
1919-20 WBA
1920-21 Burnley
1921-22 Liverpool
1922-23 Liverpool

1923-24 Huddersfield
1924-25 Huddersfield
1925-26 Huddersfield
1926-27 Newcastle
1927-28 Everton
1928-29 Sheffield Wed
1929-30 Sheffield Wed
1930-31 Arsenal
1931-32 Everton
1932-33 Arsenal
1933-34 Arsenal
1934-35 Arsenal
1935-36 Sunderland
1936-37 Man City
1937-38 Arsenal
1938-39 Everton
1946-47 Liverpool
1947-48 Arsenal
1948-49 Portsmouth
1949-50 Portsmouth

1950-51 Spurs
1951-52 Man Utd
1952-53 Arsenal
1953-54 Wolves
1954-55 Chelsea
1955-56 Man Utd
1956-57 Man Utd
1957-58 Wolves
1958-59 Wolves
1959-60 Burnley
1960-61 Spurs
1961-62 Ipswich
1962-63 Everton
1963-64 Liverpool
1964-65 Man Utd
1965-66 Liverpool
1966-67 Man Utd
1967-68 Man City
1968-69 Leeds

1969-70 Everton
1970-71 Arsenal
1971-72 Derby Co.
1972-73 Liverpool
1973-74 Leeds
1974-75 Derby Co.
1975-76 Liverpool
1976-77 Liverpool
1977-78 Nottm Forest
1978-79 Liverpool
1979-80 Liverpool
1980-81 Aston Villa
1981-82 Liverpool
1982-83 Liverpool
1983-84 Everton
1984-85 Liverpool
1985-86 Liverpool
1986-87 Everton
1987-88 Liverpool

European Cup Winners Cup

1961	A.C. Fiorentina 4 Glasgow Rangers 1
1962	Atletico Madrid 3 A.C. Fiorentina 0
1963	Tottenham Hotspur 5 Atletico Madrid 1
1964	Sporting Club, Lisbon 1 M.T.K. Budapest 0
1965	West Ham United 2 T.S.V. Munich 0
1966	Borussia Dortmund 2 Liverpool 1
1967	Bayern Munich 1 Glasgow Rangers 0
1968	A.C. Milan 2 S.V. Hamburg 0
1969	Slovan Bratislava 3 Barcelona 2
1970	Manchester City 2 Gornik Zabrze 1
1971	Chelsea 2 Real Madrid 1
1972	Glasgow Rangers 3 Moscow Dynamo 2
1973	A.C. Milan 1 Leeds United 0
1974	F.C. Magdeburg 2 A.C. Milan 0
1975	Dynamo Kiev 3 Ferencvaros 0
1976	Anderlecht 4 West Ham United 2
1977	S.V. Hamburg 2 Anderlecht 0
1978	Anderlecht 4 Austria Vienna 0
1979	Nottingham Forest 1 Malmo 0
1980	Nottingham Forest 1 Hamburg 0
1981	Liverpool 1 Real Madrid 0
1982	Aston Villa 1 Bayern Munich 0
1983	S.V. Hamburg 1 Juventus 0
1984	Liverpool 4 Roma 2 (on penalties)
1985	Juventus 1 Liverpool 0
1986	Steaua Bucharest 2 Barcelona 0 (on penalties)
1987	F.C. Porto 2 Bayern Munich 1

Horse Racing

The Derby

This has been run at Epsom, over 1½ miles, since 1780.

1900	Diamond Jubilee
1901	Volodyovski
1902	Ard Patrick
1903	Rock Sand
1904	St Amant
1905	Cicero
1906	Spearmint
1907	Orby
1908	Signorinetta
1909	Minoru
1910	Lemberg
1911	Sunstar
1912	Tagalie
1913	Aboyeur
1914	Dunbar II
1915	Pommern
1916	Fifinella
1917	Gay Crusader
1918	Gainsborough
1919	Grand Parade
1920	Spion Kop
1921	Humorist
1922	Captain Cuttle
1923	Papyrus
1924	Sausovino
1925	Manna
1926	Coronach
1927	Call Boy
1928	Felstead
1929	Trigo
1930	Blenheim
1931	Cameronian
1932	April the Fifth
1933	Hyperion
1934	Windsor Lad
1935	Bahram
1936	Mahmoud
1937	Mid-Day Sun
1938	Bois Roussel
1939	Blue Peter
1940	Pont l'Eveque
1941	Owen Tudor
1942	Watling Street
1943	Straight Deal
1944	Ocean Swell
1945	Dante
1946	Airborne
1947	Pearl Diver
1948	My Love
1949	Nimbus
1950	Galcador
1951	Arctic Prince
1952	Tulyar
1953	Pinza
1954	Never Say Die
1955	Phil Drake
1956	Lavandin
1957	Crepello
1958	Hard Ridden
1959	Parthia
1960	St Paddy
1961	Psidium
1962	Larkspur
1963	Relko
1964	Santa Claus
1965	Sea Bird II
1966	Charlottown
1967	Royal Palace
1968	Sir Ivor
1969	Blakeney
1970	Nijinsky
1971	Mill Reef
1972	Roberto
1973	Morston
1974	Snow Knight
1975	Grundy
1976	Empery
1977	The Minstrel
1978	Shirley Heights
1979	Troy
1980	Henbit
1981	Shergar
1982	Golden Fleece
1983	Teenoso
1984	Secreto
1985	Slip Anchor
1986	Shahrastani
1987	Reference Point

The Grand National

A steeplechase of 4 miles 856 yards held at Aintree, Liverpool.

1900	Ambush II
1901	Grudon
1902	Shannon Lass
1903	Drumcree
1904	Moifaa
1905	Kirkland
1906	Ascetic's Silver
1907	Eremon
1908	Rubio
1909	Lutteur III
1910	Jenkinstown
1911	Glenside
1912	Jerry M
1913	Covertcoat
1914	Sunloch
1915	Ally Sloper
1919	Poethlyn
1920	Troytown
1921	Shaun Spadah
1922	Music Hall
1923	Sergeant Murphy
1924	Master Robert
1925	Double Chance
1926	Jack Horner
1927	Sprig
1928	Tipperary Tim
1929	Gregalach
1930	Shaun Goilin
1931	Grakle
1932	Forbra
1933	Kellsboro' Jack
1934	Golden Miller
1935	Reynoldstown
1936	Reynoldstown
1937	Royal Mail
1938	Battleship
1939	Workman
1940	Bogskar
1946	Lovely Cottage
1947	Caughoo
1948	Sheila's Cottage
1949	Russian Hero
1950	Freebooter
1951	Nickel Coin
1952	Teal
1953	Early Mist
1954	Royal Tan
1955	Quare Times
1956	E.S.B.
1957	Sundew
1958	Mr What
1959	Oxo
1960	Merryman II
1961	Nicolaus Silver
1962	Kilmore
1963	Ayala

1964 Team Spirit
1965 Jay Trump
1966 Anglo
1967 Foinavon
1968 Red Alligator
1969 Highland Wedding
1970 Gay Trip
1971 Specify
1972 Well To Do
1973 Red Rum
1974 Red Rum
1975 L'Escargot
1976 Rag Trade

1977 Red Rum
1978 Lucius
1979 Rubstic
1980 Ben Nevis
1981 Aldaniti
1982 Gritta
1983 Corbiere
1984 Hallo Dandy
1985 Last Suspect
1986 West Tip
1987 Maori Venture
1988 Rhyme 'n Reason

Motor Racing

World Drivers' Championship
The championship is made up of certain Formula One Grand Prix races and started in 1950.

1950 Giuseppe Farina *(It)*
1951 Juan Manuel Fangio *(Arg)*
1952 Alberto Ascari *(It)*
1953 Alberto Ascari *(It)*
1954 Juan Manuel Fangio *(Arg)*
1955 Juan Manuel Fangio *(Arg)*
1956 Juan Manuel Fangio *(Arg)*
1957 Juan Manuel Fangio *(Arg)*
1958 Mike Hawthorn *(GB)*
1959 Jack Brabham *(Aus)*
1960 Jack Brabham *(Aus)*
1961 Phil Hill *(USA)*
1962 Graham Hill *(GB)*
1963 Jim Clark *(GB)*
1964 John Surtees *(GB)*
1965 Jim Clark *(GB)*
1966 Jack Brabham *(Aus)*
1967 Denny Hulme *(NZ)*
1968 Graham Hill *(GB)*

1969 Jackie Stewart *(GB)*
1970 Jochen Rindt *(Ger)*
1971 Jackie Stewart *(GB)*
1972 Emerson Fittipaldi *(Bra)*
1973 Jackie Stewart *(GB)*
1974 Emerson Fittipaldi *(Bra)*
1975 Niki Lauda *(Austria)*
1976 James Hunt *(GB)*
1977 Niki Lauda *(Austria)*
1978 Mario Andretti *(USA)*
1979 Jodi Scheckter *(USA)*
1980 Alan Jones *(Aus)*
1981 Nelson Piquet *(Bra)*
1982 Keke Rosberg *(Fin)*
1983 Nelson Piquet *(Bra)*
1984 Niki Lauda *(Austria)*
1985 Alain Prost *(Fr)*
1986 Alain Prost *(Fr)*
1987 Nelson Piquet *(Bra)*

Wimbledon Tennis Championships

Men's Singles
1900 Reggie Doherty *(GB)*
1901 Arthur Gore *(GB)*
1902 Laurie Doherty *(GB)*
1903 Laurie Doherty *(GB)*
1904 Laurie Doherty *(GB)*
1905 Laurie Doherty *(GB)*
1906 Laurie Doherty *(GB)*
1907 Norman Brookes *(Aus)*
1908 Arthur Gore *(GB)*
1909 Arthur Gore *(GB)*
1910 Tony Wilding *(NZ)*
1911 Tony Wilding *(NZ)*
1912 Tony Wilding *(NZ)*
1913 Tony Wilding *(NZ)*
1914 Norman Brookes *(Aus)*
1919 Gerald Patterson *(Aus)*
1920 Bill Tilden *(USA)*
1921 Bill Tilden *(USA)*
1922 Gerald Patterson *(Aus)*
1923 William Johnston *(USA)*
1924 Jean Borotra *(Fr)*
1925 René Lacoste *(Fr)*
1926 Jean Borotra *(Fr)*
1927 Henri Cochet *(Fr)*
1928 René Lacoste *(Fr)*
1929 Henri Cochet *(Fr)*

1930 Bill Tilden *(USA)*
1931 Sidney Wood *(USA)*
1932 Ellsworth Vines *(USA)*
1933 Jack Crawford *(Aus)*
1934 Fred Perry *(GB)*
1935 Fred Perry *(GB)*
1936 Fred Perry *(GB)*
1937 Donald Budge *(USA)*
1938 Donald Budge *(USA)*
1939 Bobby Riggs *(USA)*
1946 Yvon Petra *(Fr)*
1947 Jack Kramer *(USA)*
1948 Bob Falkenburg *(USA)*
1949 Ted Schroeder *(USA)*
1950 Budge Patty *(USA)*
1951 Dick Savitt *(USA)*
1952 Frank Sedgeman *(Aus)*
1953 Vic Seixas *(USA)*
1954 Jaroslav Drobny *(Cze)*
1955 Tony Trabert *(USA)*
1956 Lew Hoad *(Aus)*
1957 Lew Hoad *(Aus)*
1958 Ashley Cooper *(Aus)*
1959 Alex Olmedo *(Peru)*
1960 Neale Fraser *(Aus)*
1961 Rod Laver *(Aus)*

1962 Rod Laver *(Aus)*
1963 Chuck McKinley *(USA)*
1964 Roy Emerson *(Aus)*
1965 Roy Emerson *(Aus)*
1966 Manuel Santana *(Sp)*
1967 John Newcombe *(Aus)*
1968 Rod Laver *(Aus)*
1969 Rod Laver *(Aus)*
1970 John Newcombe *(Aus)*
1971 John Newcombe *(Aus)*
1972 Stan Smith *(USA)*
1973 Jan Kodes *(Cze)*
1974 Jimmy Connors *(USA)*
1975 Arthur Ashe *(USA)*
1976 Bjorn Borg *(Swe)*
1977 Bjorn Borg *(Swe)*
1978 Bjorn Borg *(Swe)*
1979 Bjorn Borg *(Swe)*
1980 Bjorn Borg *(Swe)*
1981 John McEnroe *(USA)*
1982 Jimmy Connors *(USA)*
1983 John McEnroe *(USA)*
1984 John McEnroe *(USA)*
1985 Boris Becker *(W. Ger)*
1986 Boris Becker *(W. Ger)*
1987 Pat Cash *(Aus)*

Women's Singles

1900 Blanche Hillyard (GB)	1930 Helen Wills Moody (USA)	1962 Karen Susman (USA)
1901 Charlotte Sterry (née Cooper) (GB)	1931 Cilly Aussem (Ger)	1963 Margaret Smith (Aus)
1902 Muriel Robb (GB)	1932 Helen Wills Moody (USA)	1964 Maria Bueno (Bra)
1903 Dorothea Douglass (GB)	1933 Helen Wills Moody (USA)	1965 Margaret Smith (Aus)
1904 Dorothea Douglass (GB)	1934 Dorothy Round (GB)	1966 Billie Jean King (USA)
1905 May Sutton (USA)	1935 Helen Wills Moody (USA)	1967 Billie Jean King (USA)
1906 Dorothea Douglass (GB)	1936 Helen Jacobs (USA)	1968 Billie Jean King (USA)
1907 May Sutton (USA)	1937 Dorothy Round (GB)	1969 Ann Jones (GB)
1908 Charlotte Sterry (GB)	1938 Helen Wills Moody (USA)	1970 Margaret Court (Aus)
1909 Dora Boothby (GB)	1939 Alice Marble (USA)	1971 Evonne Goolagong (Aus)
1910 Dorothea Lambert Chambers (GB)	1946 Pauline Betz (USA)	1972 Billie Jean King (USA)
1911 Dorothea Lambert Chambers (GB)	1947 Margaret Osborne (USA)	1973 Billie Jean King (USA)
1912 Ethel Larcombe (GB)	1948 Louise Brough (USA)	1974 Christine Evert (USA)
1913 Dorothea Lambert Chambers (GB)	1949 Louise Brough (USA)	1975 Billie Jean King (USA)
1914 Dorothea Lambert Chambers (GB)	1950 Louise Brough (USA)	1976 Christine Evert (USA)
1919 Suzanne Lenglen (Fr)	1951 Doris Hart (USA)	1977 Virginia Wade (GB)
1920 Suzanne Lenglen (Fr)	1952 Maureen Connolly (USA)	1978 Martina Navratilova (USA)
1921 Suzanne Lenglen (Fr)	1953 Maureen Connolly (USA)	1979 Martina Navratilova (USA)
1922 Suzanne Lenglen (Fr)	1954 Maureen Connolly (USA)	1980 Evonne Cawley (Aus)
1923 Suzanne Lenglen (Fr)	1955 Louise Brough (USA)	1981 Christine Evert-Lloyd (USA)
1924 Kathleen McKane (GB)	1956 Shirley Fry (USA)	1982 Martina Navratilova (USA)
1925 Suzanne Lenglen (Fr)	1957 Althea Gibson (USA)	1983 Martina Navratilova (USA)
1926 Kathleen Godfree (GB)	1958 Althea Gibson (USA)	1984 Martina Navratilova (USA)
1927 Helen Wills (USA)	1959 Maria Bueno (Bra)	1985 Martina Navratilova (USA)
1928 Helen Wills (USA)	1960 Maria Bueno (Bra)	1986 Martina Navratilova (USA)
1929 Helen Wills (USA)	1961 Angela Mortimer (GB)	1987 Martina Navratilova (USA)

TEMPERATURES

°C	°F		°C	°F		°C	°F	
100°	212°	boiling point of water	40°	104°		20°	68°	warm weather
95°	203°		39°	102°		15°	59°	
90°	194°		38°	100°		10°	50°	
85°	185°		37°	98·4°	normal body temperature	5°	41°	
80°	176°		36°	96·8°		0°	32°	freezing point of water
75°	167°		35°	95°		- 5°	23°	
70°	158°		34°	93·2°		-10°	14°	
65°	149°		33°	91·4°		-15°	5°	
60°	140°		32°	89·6°		-20°	-4°	
55°	131°		31°	87·8°		-25°	-13°	
50°	122°		30°	86°		-30°	-22°	
45°	113°		25°	77°				

On average the air temperature falls 0·6°C for every 100 metres above sea level - hence the snow line on mountains.

Converting Temperatures

To convert Centigrade to Fahrenheit: multiply the temperature by 9, and divide that answer by 5, then add 32.

To convert Fahrenheit to Centigrade you do the reverse, in the reverse order. So you first *subtract* 32 from the temperature, then multiply the result by 5, and divide that answer by 9.

Or - if you prefer formulae:

$$C \text{ to } F = \frac{(temp \times 9)}{5} + 32$$

$$F \text{ to } C = \frac{5(temp - 32)}{9}$$

If you forget which version produces which result remember 32 F = 0 C. So you can test one version of the formula on one of these figures and see if it comes out right.

Centigrade temperatures are the same as Celsius and Kelvin. In some parts of Europe where the term Celsius is used, Centigrade is a measurement of angle - worth bearing in mind with doctors overseas, if you don't want them to mistake your inclination.

USEFUL MATHS

It's a pity mathematics is often seen as an unconquerable mountain. It shouldn't be. It *can* be rarified and hard, but few people climb Everest and in its early stages mathematics is just a useful game in which the rules never change: 2 and 2 always make 4. In an uncertain world that is really rather reassuring, and some of the patterns numbers form have a decided charm. Before you dismiss the idea as crazy take a look at this:

1×1	=	1
11×11	=	121
111×111	=	12321
1111×1111	=	1234321
11111×11111	=	123454321
111111×111111	=	12345654321
1111111×1111111	=	1234567654321
11111111×11111111	=	123456787654321

Mathematics is full of curious patterns and though that palindrome may not be useful I hope it will convince you that numbers can have their own unexpected charm.

Nobody should feel insulted by the simplicity of what follows, as much of it is written to make it easier for parents, and other adults, to help children, or for children to read up alone. But I hope that if anyone, who is teaching a child, turns to these pages for the rules of maths, they will also turn to the section on teaching children (page 284). It is not so much *what* you teach a child that matters, but how you teach it. The right facts given in the wrong way will run from the mind, as easily as rain runs off stone.

Getting to Grips with 10
The basis of our mathematical system is that figures have *two* meanings. The first comes from the *quantity* they stand for: 5 means five apples, cars, people or whatever. The second meaning comes from their *position* in relation to other numbers. We arrange numbers in columns. One column tells us about single figures (units), the next about tens, the next about hundreds, the next about thousands and so on. So the 5 in 50 means 5 lots of ten because it is in the column devoted to tens, in 500 it tells us how many hundreds there are. Those columns increase in value as they move to the left, with each column being ten times as large as the previous one.

Obvious perhaps, but it can be overlooked that the rule also holds good in reverse. Moving from left to right on the chart above right, each column is made by dividing the previous one by 10. Divide 10 by 10 and you get 1, divide 1 by 10 and you get one-tenth, and so on through the whole range of decimal fractions.

Notice that whole numbers are separated from fractions by a dot (point) in the line. This always stays still as a fence dividing one field from another and the numbers move across it as you multiply or divide them (although people talk about moving the point when what they mean is that they move the figures).

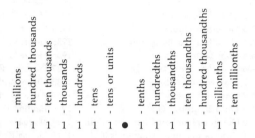

1 1 1 1 1 1 1 ● 1 1 1 1 1 1 1

(columns, left to right: millions · hundred thousands · ten thousands · thousands · hundreds · tens · tens or units · tenths · hundredths · thousandths · ten thousandths · hundred thousandths · millionths · ten millionths)

Addition
The tens rule applies to every move in basic maths. So when you add

  7
+3

10 you have written it to show you have one ten and no spare units.

Subtraction
Subtraction is the most commonly misunderstood process in basic maths, and the first one children get muddled by. One of the most muddling methods is that in which you borrow and pay back. It gets the right answer, but doesn't relate to the real situation. So, if you are helping children, it is best not to use that method, as it can make it harder for them to understand what numbers are really about. A better method to use is borrowing without paying back. Children can grasp it very quickly if you make it concrete with some objects.

Before a child can even begin to do sums with borrowing, he or she must be totally confident about what numbers mean. So, if there's any doubt about this, spend time letting the child set up groups of tens and groups of ones using small objects like beans or Lego. So 52 is five groups of ten and two ones. (The term 'units' can be muddling and it is clearer to talk about '2 ones'.) Once a child sets them up correctly every time, try taking away simple numbers, say 25−12, or 34−21. Once simple subtraction with beans or Lego is going well you can move on to borrowing.

If the sum is: 23−15 or 23
                 −15

set up two heaps of Lego each with 10 pieces in, and establish that 2 in the tens column means *two lots of* 10. (This idea of numbers in the tens column standing for groups of ten is the really important thing for a child to grasp, so still use that phrase all the time.) Then set up a heap of 3 pieces to the right, to represent the 3 ones.

Young children like owning things. So make the 23 pieces theirs, and say you are coming to take away 15 of the pieces for yourself. Show them that you can't take 5 when there are only 3 there. So you have to use one of the tens. Do this by moving a group of 10 to sit above the 3.

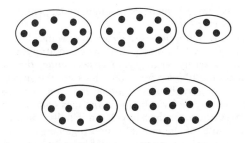

Take 5 from the 13 - using the Lego - and let the child count up how many it has left from the 13. Explain that taking away 15 means taking away one lot of 10 as well as one lot of 5 and take the heap of 10 away. So the child can see it has 8 left.

Repeat this, with you owning the heaps and the child taking 15 away. Once sums like this have been mastered with just beans or Lego it is time to do it on paper too.

Try this process, from the top, with different combinations of numbers, using bricks each time. Even better, use tiny sweets and let the child eat them if it gets the sum right. Bad for the teeth but good for the memory, and the teeth can always be cleaned afterwards. The same principle can be applied to borrowing from the hundreds column, but here you point out to the child that borrowing one lot of 100 is the same as borrowing ten lots of ten (easy to demonstrate with beans if you have enough of them).

Fractions

Basic fractions are those in which the two numbers are put one above the other with a line separating them. So ½ and ¼ are basic fractions.

The top number is called the   numerator
the bottom one is called the   denominator.

The denominator tells you how many pieces you *need* to make one whole. The numerator tells you how many pieces *there actually are.*

So, if you cut a cake into 4 pieces each piece is one ¼. The 4 tells you that 4 pieces make a whole cake. The 1 is one bit of those 4.

Fractions in which the top number is smaller than the bottom are called proper fractions. So

$$\frac{5}{6}, \frac{7}{10}, \frac{9}{35} \text{ and } \frac{125}{150}$$

are proper fractions.

Fractions in which the top number is larger than the bottom one are called improper fractions. So

$$\frac{15}{6}, \frac{32}{10}, \frac{48}{35}, \frac{165}{150} \text{ and } \frac{100}{90}$$ are improper fractions.

Improper fractions can also be written as a whole number and fraction combined. For example,

$$\frac{15}{6} = 2\frac{1}{6} \text{ and } \frac{100}{90} = 1\frac{10}{90}$$

The names don't matter but the rules of handling the fractions do. They are very simple.

Adding and Subtracting Fractions

To add two fractions you have to make the denominators (bottom numbers) the same. You do that by multiplying the top and bottom of each fraction by the bottom number of the other.

$$\frac{1}{2} + \frac{7}{9} \text{ can be converted to } \frac{1\times9}{2\times9} + \frac{7\times2}{9\times2} = \frac{9}{18} + \frac{14}{18}$$

This is the same as $\frac{9+14}{18} = \frac{23}{18}$

Subtraction is just the same except that in the final stage you take away.

Multiplying Fractions

This is really easy. You just multiply the two top numbers together and the bottom two together.
So $\frac{1}{2} \times \frac{7}{9} = \frac{1\times7}{2\times9} = \frac{7}{18}$

Dividing Fractions

To divide one fraction by another you simply do a rather neat trick and turn the second fraction upside down. Then proceed as for multiplying. (Don't worry about *why* it works - it takes a bit of explaining - but it does.)

$$\text{So } \frac{1}{2} \div \frac{7}{9} = \frac{1}{2} \times \frac{9}{7} = \frac{1\times9}{2\times7} = \frac{9}{14}$$

Multiplication

The easiest multiplication of all is by 10. Suppose you need to multiply 137 by 10. You know that each column to the left is ten times larger, so all you need to do is move each figure one column to the left to get the answer. So 137×10 becomes 1370 (you put a 0 in the gap to keep the columns right).

Multiplying by 100 is really multiplying by 10, and then by 10 again, so the figures move two places to the left and you fill in the gap between the last figure and the point with 0s. So 137 x 100 becomes 13700 (you fill in the gaps with two 0s).

Or if you need to multiply a number by, say, 70 you can multiply by 7 and then by 10. So 70 x 55 is most easily calculated as:

```
  55
 ×7
```

385 multiplied by 10 = 3850

You can use the same system for 700 x 55 except that you'd multiply by 100 at the end, and therefore add two 00s to the answer, making it 38500. The method works for multiplying by 20, 40, 80 or 300 or any other number ending in a zero. So 4·25×100 becomes 425·0 which is written as just 425 because points are only used if there are figures to their right.

Obviously, to multiply by 1000 you move the figures *three* places to the left. (Notice that the number of columns the figure moves is always the same as the number of zeros in the figure you are multiplying it by).

Since division is the opposite of multiplication to *divide* by 1000 you do the opposite. So you move the figures three places to the *right*.

So   137 divided by   10 becomes 13·7;

and   137 divided by   100 becomes 1·37;

and   137 divided by 1000 becomes   ·137.

The decimal point has been put in to show which column each figure belongs in. There is an invisible point after every whole number but it is only shown if there are figures to the right of it.

A table of answers for multiplication by other numbers is given below. For long multiplication without a calculator you just need to apply the table, keeping the columns right. Always write a long sum down so the tens come under the tens and the hundreds under the hundreds and so on.

So 3472×37 is written as

$$\begin{array}{r} 3472 \\ \times\ 37 \\ \hline 24304 \\ 10416\ \\ \hline 128464 \end{array}$$

First multiply each of the top numbers by 7, starting at the right. When any figure is more than 9 you write down the unit and carry the tens into the answer in the next column. Whichever column it happens in you always carry ten.

Having multiplied 3472 by 7 you now multiply 3472 by 3. The vital point is that when multiplying you always start by writing your answer *under the figure you are multiplying by*. So, in this sum, the answer or multiplying by the 7 starts under the 7 and the answer for multiplying by a figure in the tens column (the 3 here) starts under the tens column. Finally you add the two results of the multiplication together.

The same holds good for multiplying by hundreds or thousands. So a longer multiplication looks like this.

$$\begin{array}{r} 1987472 \\ \times\quad 2145 \\ \hline 9937360 \\ 7949888\ \\ 1987472\ \ \\ 3974944\ \ \ \\ \hline 4263127440 \end{array}$$

So 145·87 + 43·12 is

$$\begin{array}{r} 145\cdot87 \\ +\ 43\cdot12 \\ \hline 189\cdot99 \end{array}$$

And 189·43 — 37·01 is

$$\begin{array}{r} 189\cdot43 \\ -\ 37\cdot01 \\ \hline 152\cdot42 \end{array}$$

Multiplication and Division Table

For those who have forgotten their tables and their calculator:

		Col	Col	Col	Col	Col	Col	Col	Col	Col	Col	Col	Col	Col	Col
		2	3	4	5	6	7	8	9	10	11	12	13	14	15
Row	2	4	6	8	10	12	14	16	18	20	22	24	26	28	30
Row	3	6	9	12	15	18	21	24	27	30	33	36	39	42	45
Row	4	8	12	16	20	24	28	32	36	40	44	48	52	56	60
Row	5	10	15	20	25	30	35	40	45	50	55	60	65	70	75
Row	6	12	18	24	30	36	42	48	54	60	66	72	78	84	90
Row	7	14	21	28	35	42	49	56	63	70	77	84	91	98	105
Row	8	16	24	32	40	48	56	64	72	80	88	96	104	112	120
Row	9	18	27	36	45	54	63	72	81	90	99	108	117	126	135
Row	10	20	30	40	50	60	70	80	90	100	110	120	130	140	150
Row	11	22	33	44	55	66	77	88	99	110	121	132	143	154	165
Row	12	24	36	48	60	72	84	96	108	120	132	144	156	168	180
Row	13	26	39	52	65	78	91	104	117	130	143	156	169	182	195
Row	14	28	42	56	70	84	98	112	126	140	154	168	182	196	210
Row	15	30	45	60	75	90	105	120	135	150	165	180	195	210	225

To find the answer when two numbers are multiplied together go down the column headed by one of them until you come to the row belonging to the other. So 13×11 is 143.

To divide one number by another go down the column for the smaller number until you find the row for the other number. The answer will be where the column and row meet. So 98 divided by 7 = 14.

If you can't find the exact number in the table take the next number smaller than it and take it away from the number you are looking for. So 100 divided by 7 = 14 remainder 2

Decimals

Adding and Subtracting Decimals

To add or subtract decimals you just put the points under one another and treat the numbers just like any others (see page 716), applying just the same rules.

Multiplying Decimals

The basic multiplication is the same as for other long - or short - multiplication (see page 717), and while you do the multiplication you ignore the points.

So $12 \cdot 25 \times 1 \cdot 7$ can be written as

$$
\begin{array}{r}
1225 \\
\times\ \ 17 \\
\hline
8575 \\
1225 \\
\hline
20825
\end{array}
$$

You then look at the original numbers which you multiplied together, and see how many figures were after the decimal point *altogether*. In this case there were two ($\cdot 25$) in one case, and one ($\cdot 7$) in another. So altogether there were 3 numbers after the decimal. This tells you that you must place the decimal point in your answer 3 figures in, counting from the right.

So 20825 becomes $20 \cdot 825$

Dividing Decimals

To divide decimals you have to convert the one you are dividing by into a whole number. This is easily done by just multiplying it by 10, or 100 or by whatever is needed (see page 717). So if the sum is $8147 \cdot 25 \div 2 \cdot 7$ you first multiply $2 \cdot 7$ by 10 to make it 27.

To keep the two parts of the sum in balance you *must* then multiply the other number by 10 too.

So $8147 \cdot 25 \times 10 = 81472 \cdot 5$

Then you can divide $81472 \cdot 5$ by 27 using the ordinary rules of long division. (See right.)

Decimal Places

The farther to the right you go with decimals, the smaller the fraction they represent. Unless you are calculating something of infinite fineness, it isn't worth bothering with these tiny amounts. So, for most purposes, you only need answers to one or two decimal places. This simply means you only write down that number of figures to the right of the point. But always check the figure to the right of them. If it is 5 or larger you increase the figure to its left by 1, if it is under 5 you do nothing. This is called rounding up. So $564 \cdot 13596$ to two decimal places may seem to be $564 \cdot 13$ *but* as the 3 is followed by 5 the correct answer is $564 \cdot 14$.

Similarly, in both decimals and non-decimals an answer may be needed to a certain number of 'significant figures'. Obviously, a number is more significant (important) the bigger it is. So the farther to the left a number is, the more significant it is. This means that in picking out significant figures you start from the left.

Suppose you are asked for $4828 \cdot 04$ to four significant figures. You'd take the four left-hand figures and drop the rest = 4828. Easy.

But suppose you were asked for $4828 \cdot 04$ to three significant figures? The answer is *not* 482. What you actually do is replace any non-significant numbers to the left of the point (in this case an 8) with 0s. And if the left-most of the numbers you drop is 5 or greater you increase its significant neighbour by 1. In this example the left-most figure is 8. So $4828 \cdot 04$ to three significant figures is 4830. But $4828 \cdot 04$ to two significant figures would be 4800 as the 2 which was dropped was smaller than 5.

Long Division

Long division without a calculator is tedious, but not hard. This is one case where there is no choice but to just do the steps without thinking too hard about the mathematical realities.

Suppose you need to divide 15965 by 52.

$$
\begin{array}{r}
3 \\
52 \overline{)\ 15965} \\
-156 \\
\hline
3
\end{array}
$$

$$
\begin{array}{r}
30 \\
52 \overline{)\ 15965} \\
-156\!\downarrow\!\downarrow \\
\hline
365
\end{array}
$$

$$
\begin{array}{r}
307 \\
52 \overline{)\ 15965} \\
156\!\downarrow\!\downarrow \\
365 \\
-364 \\
\hline
1
\end{array}
$$

$$
\begin{array}{r}
307 \cdot 01 \\
52 \overline{)\ 15965 \cdot 000} \\
156\!\downarrow\!\downarrow \\
365\ \downarrow\downarrow \\
-364\ \ \ \downarrow \\
\hline
1\ 00 \\
-52 \\
\hline
480
\end{array}
$$

Working from the left, find the first number that 52 can be divided into. It won't go into 1, or into 15 but it will go into 159. Work out how many times it will go, on a bit of scrap paper.   i.e.
$$
\begin{array}{r}
52 \\
\times 3 \\
\hline
156
\end{array}
$$

Put a 3 above the 9 of 159, and write 156 under the 159 and subtract it.

That leaves 3.

Now bring down the 6 from the upper line. 52 can't go into 36, so put a 0 in the top line and bring down the 5. 52 will go into 365; a quick calculation shows it goes 7 times.
$$
\begin{array}{r}
52 \\
\times 7 \\
\hline
364
\end{array}
$$

Put 7 in the top row and put 364 under 365 and take it away.

For most purposes the answer 307 remainder 1 will do. But if you need to be fanatically accurate just put a point after the figures and keep on dividing bringing down a zero each time. etc. etc.

Binary

The tens system isn't the only one possible, it's just the one mankind found convenient (having ten fingers). Computers, having switches instead of fingers, don't find it convenient. So their creators chose to work in the binary system - so-called because instead of each column being ten times as big as the one to its right it is just *twice* as big.

thirty twos	sixteens	eights	fours	twos	units
1	1	1	1	1	1

So instead of 11 standing for 1 lot of ten and 1 unit, it means 1 lot of 2 and one unit - in other words 3. And 111, stands for one 4, one 2 and one 1 - that's 7 to you and me. You add or subtract just as with tens, but using the values of the columns given above.

Percentages

Discounts

The situation in which percentages are most often encountered is when discounts are offered. To calculate a percentage discount on a price divide the price by 100, and multiply the answer by the percentage discount being offered. So a 12 per cent discount on a bed costing £499 goes like this: $499 \div 100 = 4 \cdot 99$

$$4 \cdot 99 \times 12 = 59 \cdot 88$$

So the 12% discount is worth £59.88. Take that away from the original price of £499 and you find the bed is reduced to £439.12.

Percentages as Part of a Price

This is how to find a percentage element of a price - for example, the VAT element.

1 Add 100 to the percentage VAT (or whatever other percentage you need to calculate). Say 15 (VAT) + 100 = 115.
2 Divide the price by this figure.
3 Multiply the result by the original VAT (or other) percentage.

So, with VAT at 15%, the calculations to find the VAT element on a car costing £10,500 would be:

$$15 + 100 = 115$$
$$£10,500 \div 115 = £91.304347$$

The last four figures (4347) are fractions of a penny and may not seem worth writing down, but don't get rid of them, they make a difference to the final answer.

$$£91.304347 \times 15 = £1369.5652$$

So the VAT is £1,369.57 (to the nearest penny).

The price is $£10,500 - £1,369.50 = £9,130.43$ without VAT.

Percentages Added to a Price

This is how you do the calculation to increase a price by a given percentage.

1 Divide the price by 100: this gives you 1 per cent of it. (See page 716 for the quick way to divide by 100).
2 Multiply that answer by the percentage.
3 Add the result to the original price.

To increase £110.67 by 23% the calculation is this:

$$£110.67 \div 100 = £1.1067, \text{ which is 1\%}$$
$$£1.1067 \times 23 = £25.45$$

So the price +23% is $£110.67 + £25.45 = £136.12$.

Converting Fractions to Percentages

Fractions are converted into percentages by multiplying them by 100.

As a fraction always means that you divide the upper figure by the lower one to get an answer in simple figures, 100 can be written as $\underline{100}$. So to convert 3/5 to a percentage:

$$\frac{3}{5} \times \frac{100}{1} = \frac{3 \times 100}{5 \times 1} = \frac{300}{5} \qquad 300 \div 5 = 60\%$$

The same rule applies with decimal fractions.
So $0 \cdot 35$ becomes $(0 \cdot 35 \times 100)\% = 35\%$.

Converting Percentages into Fractions

Percentages are converted into fractions by dividing them by 100.

So $12\% = \dfrac{12}{100}$ $20\% = \dfrac{20}{100}$ $75\% = \dfrac{75}{100}$ and so on.

To make large fractions more manageable divide both the top and bottom by any number which goes exactly into *both*. So $\dfrac{12}{100}$ can be divided by 4

$$\frac{12 \div 4}{100 \div 4} = \frac{3}{25}$$

> In any calculations in which a percentage is one of the figures it *must* be converted into a fraction in this way. You *can't* just drop the % sign, as you might drop a £ sign, and tack it on at the end of the calculation. Doing that would give the wrong answer.

Positive and Negative Numbers

Positive and negative numbers are extremely simple to understand if you use a method my daughter learnt from a brilliant maths mistress at her school who had that rare knack of making the obscure perfectly obvious. The system is called heaps and holes. Think of a positive number as a heap. So +7 is a heap 7 cm (or 7 in) high.

Now think of a minus number as a hole the same size. So −3 is a hole 3 cm (or 3 in) deep.

Therefore, if the sum was −3 + 7 you could use a heap of 7 cm high to fill in a hole of −3 cm deep and you'd be left with 4 cm above the ground so 4 is the answer.

But if the sum was 3 − 7 you would put the 3 cm into a hole 7 cm deep and still leave 4 cm unfilled. So the answer would be −4.

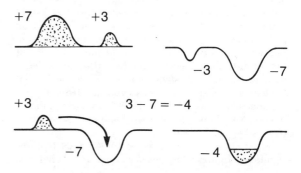

In the same way, the tricky concept of $(-2)+(-2)$ is bound to be two holes each 2 cm (or whatever) deep – which is the same as one hole 4 cm deep. So the answer is -4.

The other thing to remember is that the $+$ or $-$ always belongs to the number which follows it. So provided you keep each sign firmly attached to the number it belongs to you can switch the order of the numbers to make it easier to do the sum. It is often easier, for example, to gather up all the plus numbers then deal with all the negative ones.

Powers

Powers are shown as a small figure at the top right-hand corner of another figure, or a bracket. They indicate the number of times the number they are attached to must be multiplied by itself. 2^2 is called 2 squared.

It means there are two lots of 2 which must be multiplied together.

So $2^2 = 2 \times 2$ which is 4, and $3^2 = 3 \times 3$ which is 6. And $5^3 = 5 \times 5 \times 5$ making 125 $7^3 = 7 \times 7 \times 7$ which is 343 And $10^{10} = 10 \times 10 \times 10 \times 10 \times 10 \times 10 \times 10 \times 10 \times 10 \times 10$, so $10^{10} = 10,000,000,000$.

There are books of tables which give you the answers for calculations of this sort. But you can just as easily do the maths on your calculator provided you keep track of how many times you have multiplied.

There is also a short cut which can be useful: 2^6 is the same as $2^2 \times 2^4$ i.e. 2^6 is $2 \times 2 \times 2 \times 2 \times 2 \times 2 = 64$ but 2^2 is $2 \times 2 = 4$ while 2^4 is $2 \times 2 \times 2 \times 2 = 16$ And $4 \times 16 = 64$

Notice that if powers *add* together to make the power you want to calculate the answer by *multiplying* their products together.

Rules of Geometry

180°	a half circle	
360°	a circle	
less than 90°	an acute angle	
90°	a right angle (square corner)	90°
greater than 90°	an obtuse angle	
180°	a semi-circle	180°
greater than 180°	a reflex angle	

The angles inside a triangle total 180°.

The angles inside any figure with 4 sides total 360°.

The circumference of a circle (measurement right round) is worked out by the formula $2(\pi)r$. r = radius − the measurement from the centre of a circle to its edge.

$\pi = 3 \cdot 142$ or $\dfrac{22}{7}$ (approximately).

The area of a circle is $\pi \times r^2$.

Signs and Symbols

In maths signs and symbols often show not only what you have to do but the direction in which you have to do it. We all know $6-3$ means you take the 3 from the 6, and not the 6 from the 3. The other rules of direction are just as simple, but it is important to get them right.

$+$ add
$-$ subtract (ie $6-3$ means take 3 from 6)
$\times$ multiply
a . on the line, not raised as in decimals, also means multiply
$4(5+2)$ is the same as $4 \times (5+2)$ and means the numbers inside the brackets are multiplied by 4, but the calculation inside the bracket must be done first.

÷ divide; $\dfrac{6+8}{7}$ means the 6 and 8 are added then divided by 7.

> means 'is greater than'. So an elephant > a mouse, and 56 > 3.

< means 'is less than'. So an elephant < a castle, and 15 < 60.

≥ means greater than or equal to. So one dog ≥ another dog.

∞ means infinity

≈ means approximately

: means 'is to'

∴ therefore symbol — means therefore

∵ because symbol — means because

√ square root symbol means square root. The square root of a number is the one which multiplied by itself makes that number.

So 2 is the square root of 4 (i.e. $2 \times 2 = 4$) and 10 is the square root of 100 (i.e. $10 \times 10 = 100$)

( ) { } [ ] - brackets like these indicate that the calculations inside them need to be done before any numbers outside the brackets are brought into the action. If there are brackets within brackets start inside the innermost pair.

WEATHER

Beaufort Scale of Wind Force

Force	Wind Type	mph	kph	knots	Effect on Land and Sea
0	none	0-1	0-2	0-1	Smoke rises vertically. Sea like a mirror
1	faint breeze	1-3	2-5	1-3	Smoke drifts but wind vane stationary. Sea slightly rippled
2	light breeze	4-7	6-12	4-6	Wind felt on face, leaves rustle,vanes move. Sea has wavelets
3	gentle breeze	8-12	13-20	7-10	Wind extends light flag, twigs move. A few white horses on sea
4	moderate breeze	13-18	21-29	11-16	Raises dust and loose paper, small branches move. Small waves, more white horses
5	fresh breeze	19-24	30-39	17-21	Small, leafy trees sway. Moderate waves, some spray
6	strong breeze	25-31	40-50	22-27	Large branches move. Telegraph wires whistle. Umbrellas a problem. Large waves with foam crests, extensive spray
7	moderate gale	32-38	51-62	28-33	Whole trees in motion. Hard to walk against the wind. Sea heaps up and foam blows with the wind
8	fresh gale	39-46	63-74	34-40	Twigs break off trees. Walking difficult. Moderately high waves of greater length, streaks of blown foam
9	strong gale	47-54	75-87	41-47	Slight structural damage. Chimney pots and slates blown off. High waves, blown foam begins to limit visibility
10	whole gale	55-63	88-102	48-56	Trees uprooted and major structural damage. Very high waves and sea white with foam. Worse visibility
11	storm	64-75	103-120	57-65	Widespread damage. Rare in Europe. Exceptionally high waves, can mask medium-sized ships from view. Bad visibility from blown foam
12	hurricane	75+	120+	65+	Very great damage - typical of revolving storms in the tropics. Air filled with foam, sea totally white, very bad visibility

Shipping Forecast Areas

For those who go to sea and those who, like me, are bemused by the shipping forecast.

There is a new station to the south of FINISTERRE called TRAFALGAR

WEIGHTS AND MEASURES

Capacity

UK Imperial

8 fluid drachms	=	1 fluid oz
5 fluid ounces	=	1 gill
4 gills	=	1 pint
2 pints	=	1 quart
4 quarts	=	1 gallon
2 gallons	=	1 peck (only used for dry goods)
4 pecks	=	1 bushel (only used for dry goods)
8 bushels	=	1 quarter (only used for dry goods)
31½ gallons	=	1 barrel
2 barrels	=	1 hogshead
36 gallons	=	1 bulk barrel

American pints and gallons are not the same size as British ones. (See page 107 for measurement in US cups.)

Metric

10 millilitres	=	1 centilitre
100 centilitres	=	1 litre
1,000 millilitres	=	1 litre
100 litres	=	1 hectolitre
1,000 litres	=	1 kilolitre

Conversion Factors

1 fluid ounce = 28·4 millilitres
1/4 pint = 142 millilitres
1 pint (UK) = 568 millilitres
1 quart = 1·136 litres
1 gallon = 4·546 litres
1 litre = 2·1134 pints US
1 litre = 1·7598 pints UK

Circular and Angular Measures

60 seconds (")	=	1 minute
60 minutes (')	=	1 degree
30 degrees (°)	=	1 sign
45 degrees (°)	=	1 octant
60 degrees (°)	=	1 sextant
90 degrees (°)	=	1 quadrant
4 quadrants	=	1 circle
12 signs	=	1 circle

Conversion Factors

Multiply number of	by	to obtain equivalent number of
inches	25·4	millimetres
	2·54	centimetres
feet	30·48	centimetres
	0·3048	metres
yards	0·9144	metres
miles (land: 5,280 ft)	1·609344	kilometres
miles (UK sea: 6,080ft)	1·853184	kilometres
miles (international nautical)	1·852	kilometres
sq inches (in²)	645·16	sq millimetres (mm²)
	6·4516	sq centimetres (cm²)
sq feet (ft²)	929·0304	sq centimetres
	0·092903	sq metres (m²)
sq yards (yd²)	0·.836127	sq metres
	4,046·86	sq metres
acres	0·404686	hectares (ha)
	0·004047	sq kilometres (km²)
sq miles	2·58999	sq kilometres
cu. inches (in³)	16·387064	cu centimetres (cm³)
UK pints	34·6774	cu inches
UK pints	0·5783	litres
UK gallons	4·54609	litres
US gallons	3·785	litres
cu feet (ft³)	28·317	litres
cu feet	0·028317	cu metres (m³)
UK gallons	1·20095	US gallons
US gallons	0·832674	UK gallons
ounces, avoirdupois (oz)	28·3495	grams
ounces, troy (oz tr)	31·1035	grams
ounces, avoirdupois	0·9115	ounces, troy
pounds avoirdupois (lb)	453·59237	grams
	0·45359	kilograms
short tons (2,000 lb)	0·892857	long tons
	0·907185	tonnes
long tons (2,240 lb)	1·12	short tons
	1·01605	tonnes

Multiply number of	by	to obtain equivalent number of
millimetres	0·03937	inches
centimetres	0·3937	inches
centimetres	0·03281	feet
metres	39·3701	inches
metres	3·2808	feet
metres	1·0936	yards
metres	0·54681	fathoms
kilometres	0·62137	miles (land)
kilometres	0·53961	miles (UK sea)
kilometres	0·53996	miles, (international nautical)
sq millimetres	0·00155	sq inches
sq centimetres	0·1550	sq inches
sq. metres	10·7639	sq feet
sq. metres	1·19599	sq yards
hectares	2·47105	acres
sq kilometres	247·105	acres
	0·3861	sq miles
cu centimetres	0·06102	cu inches
litres	61·024	cu inches
litres	0·0353	cu feet
litres	2·1134	US pints
litres	1·7598	UK pints
litres	0·2642	US gallons
litres	0·21997	UK gallons
hectolitres	26·417	US gallons
hectolitres	21·997	UK gallons
hectolitres	2·838	UK bushels
hectolitres	2·750	UK bushels
cu metres	35·3147	cu feet
cu metres	1·30795	cu yards
cu metres	264·172	US gallons
cu metres	219·969	UK gallons
cu metres	6·11026	UK bulk barrels
grammes	0·03527	ounces, avoirdupois
grammes	0·03215	ounces, troy
kilogrammes	2·20462	pounds, avoirdupois
metres quintals (q)	220·462	pounds, avoirdupois
tonnes	2,204·62	pounds, avoirdupois
tonnes	1·10231	short tons
tonnes	0·984207	long tons

Approximate Conversions

Miles to kilometres: multiply by 8, then divide by 5
Kilometres to miles: multiply by 5, then divide by 8
Square metres into square yards: add one fifth
Acres to hectares: multiply by 2 and divide by 5
Hectares to acres: multiply by 5 and divide by 2

Distance

Imperial

12 inches	=	1 foot
3 feet	=	1 yard
5½ yards	=	1 rod, pole or perch
4 rods (66 ft)	=	1 chain
10 chains	=	1 furlong
5,280 feet	=	1 mile
1,760 yards	=	1 mile
8 furlongs	=	1 mile

Metric

10 angstroms	=	1 nanometre
1,000 nanometres	=	1 micrometre
1,000 micrometres	=	1 millimetre
10 millimetres	=	1 centimetre
100 centimetres	=	1 metre
100 metres	=	1 hectometre
1,000 metres	=	1 kilometre
10 hectometres	=	1 kilometre

Approximate Equivalent Distances

1 inch	=	2·5 cm
1 foot	=	30 cm
1 yard	=	91 cm
1 mile	=	1,609 m
1 centimetre	=	0·4 in
1 metre	=	3 yd 3 in
1 kilometre	=	1,093 yd
1 kilometre	=	almost ¾ mile

Nautical Distance

6 feet = 1 fathom
100 fathoms = 1 cable length
6,080 feet = 1 nautical mile
1 international nautical mile = 1,852 metres

Old British Currency

Until February 1971 British currency was pounds, shillings and pence which were abbreviated to £ s d, from the Roman coins Libra, solidus and denarius.

4 farthings	=	penny (1d)
2 half pennies (½d)	=	1 penny
12 pennies (12d)	=	1 shilling (1s)
4 threepenny pieces (3d)	=	1 shilling
2 sixpences (6d)	=	1 shilling
2 shillings (2s)	=	1 florin
2 shillings and sixpence (2/6)	=	1 half crown
5 shillings (5s)	=	1 crown
10 shillings (10s)	=	1 half-sovereign
20 shillings (20s)	=	1 pound (£1)
1 pound (£1)	=	1 sovereign
1 pound 1 shilling (£1 1s)	=	1 guinea

Paper Measures

Writing and Drawing Paper
24 sheets	=	1 quire
480 sheets	=	1 ream
20 quires	=	1 ream

Printing Paper
516 sheets	=	1 ream
2 reams	=	1 bundle
5 bundles	=	1 bale

Weights

Imperial
437½ grains (gr)	=	1 ounce
16 drams (dr)	=	1 ounce
16 ounces (oz)	=	1 pound
14 pounds (lb)	=	1 stone
28 pounds	=	1 quarter
8 stone	=	1 hundredweight
4 quarters	=	1 hundredweight
2,240 pounds	=	1 ton
20 hundred-weights	=	1 ton

Metric
1,000,000 microgrammes	=	1 gramme
1,000 milligrammes	=	1 gramme
1,000 grammes	=	1 kilogramme
100 kilogrammes	=	1 quintal
1,000 kilogrammes	=	1 tonne

Approximate Equivalent Measures
1 ounce	=	28 grammes
1 pound	=	454 grammes
1 stone	=	6.3 kilogrammes
1 cwt	=	50.8 kilogrammes
100 grammes	=	3½ ounces
200 grammes	=	7 ounces
1 kilogramme	=	2 pounds 3 ounces
1 tonne	=	just under 1 ton

Conversion Factors
1 ounce	=	28.35 grammes
1 pound	=	0·4536 kilogrammes
1 gramme	=	0·035 ounces
1 kilogramme	=	2·204 pounds

> Under the Weights and Measures Act 1963 the rod, pole or perch, quarter (capacity), bushel, and peck are no longer legal measures. The old apothecaries' measures with their quaint drachms, scruples and grains have also passed into history.

BIBLIOGRAPHY

Many of the books which form part of the bibliography are recommended in the relevant chapters. The rest are as follows.

David Alderton, *Looking After Cage Birds*, Ward Lock, 1982

John Arlott (ed.), *Oxford Companion to Sports and Games*, Oxford University Press, 1975

Peter Arnold (ed.), *The Complete Book of Indoor Games*, Hamlyn, 1981

Denis Arnold (ed.), *The New Oxford Companion to Music*, Oxford University Press, 1983

British Dietetic Association, *Children's Diets and Change*, 1987

British Medical Association, *Diet, Nutrition and Health*, 1986

Stefan T. Buczacki and Keith Harris, *Collins Guide to Pests, Diseases and Disorders of Garden Plants*, Collins, 1986

Stefan T. Buczacki, *Gardeners' Questions Answered*, Collins, 1985

James R. Busvine, *Insects and Hygiene*, Chapman & Hall, 1983

Pamela Carmichael, *The She Book of Cats*, Ebury Press, 1983

Collins English Dictionary, Collins, 1973

The Concise Oxford Dictionary, Oxford University Press, 1982

Robert Dearling (ed.), *Guinness Book of Musical Facts and Figures*, Guinness, 1976

Department of Health and Social Security, *Present Day Practice in Infant Feeding*, HMSO, 1983

Diagram Group, *Official World Encyclopedia of Sport and Games*, Paddington Press, 1979

Margaret Dibben, *The Guardian Money Guide*, Collins Willow, 1986

Directory of British Associations, C.B.D. Research, 1986

Alexandre Dumas, *Dumas on Food*, trans by Alan and Jane Davidson, Michael Joseph, 1979

John and Peter Filbey, *The Astrologer's Companion*, Aquarian Handbooks, 1986

Maureen Foster, *Preserved Flowers*, Pelham, 1973

H.W. Fowler, *Dictionary of Modern English Usage*, Oxford University Press, 1965

Frohne & Pfander, *Colour Atlas of Poisonous Plants*, Wolfe Medical, 1984

A.R. Gennaro (ed.), *Blakiston's Gould Medical Dictionary*, McGraw, 1979

Brian Giles, *Safety with Horses*, Stanley Paul, 1985

Glanz, *Mosby's Medical and Nursing Dictionary*, Mosby, 1985

William R. Gondin and Edward W. Mammen, *The Art of Speaking Made Simple*, W.H. Allen, 1975

Conal Gregory, *Caterer's Guide to Drinks*, Northwood, 1979

James M. Haig, *The Householder's Guide to Plumbing*, Stanley Paul, 1984

Maurice Hanssen, *E for Additives*, Thorsons, 1986

Arthur G.L. Hellyer, *The Amateur Gardener*, Collingridge, 1972

Norman Hickin, *Pest Animals in Buildings*, George Godwin, 1985

Betty C. Hobbs and Diane Roberts, *Food Poisoning and Food Hygiene* (5th edition), Edward Arnold, 1987

Ingrid Holford (ed.), *Guinness Book of Weather Facts and Feats*, Guinness, 1977

James Holgate and David Coulter, *Speak with Confidence*, Stanley Paul, 1974

Angela Hollest and Penelope Gaine, *Parties for Older Children*, Piatkus Books, 1986

Derek Hull and Derek I. Johnston, *Essential Paediatrics*, Churchill Livingstone, 1980

Investors Chronicle, Financial Times Business Publishing Ltd, London

Hugh Johnson, *World Atlas of Wine*, Mitchell Beazley, 1977

Felicity Lawrence, *Additives: Your Complete Survival Guide*, Century, 1986

Margaret Leach, *Freezer Facts*, Forbes Publications Ltd, 1975

Jeff Mayo, *Teach Yourself Astrology*, Hodder & Stoughton, 1981

Susan McBane, *Keeping Horses*, Collins, 1986

Susan McBane, *Your First Horse*, Stanley Paul, 1985

R.A McCance and E.M. Widdowson, *The Composition of Foods*, HMSO, 1978

Diane McCrea, *Opening the Floodgates*, London Food Commission, 1987

The Macdonald Guide to French Wines, Macdonald, 1988

Norris D. McWhirter (ed.), *Guinness Book of Answers*, Guinness, 1978

A.G. Mears, *The Right Way to Speak in Public*, Elliott Right Way Books, 1987

Mims Magazine, Medical Publications Ltd, London

Ministry of Agriculture, Fisheries & Food, *Manual of Nutrition*, HMSO, 1985

Ministry of Agriculture, Fisheries & Food, *Poisonous Plants in Britain and Their Effects on Animals and Man*, HMSO, 1984

National Consumer Council, *Consumers and Credit*, 1980

The New England Journal of Medicine, Massachussetts Medical Society, Boston, Mass.

Maureen O'Connor, *A Parent's Guide to Education*, Fontana, 1986

Derek and Julia Parker, *A History of Astrology*, André Deutsch, 1983

David Parlett, *Penguin Book of Card Games*, Penguin, 1979

R. Passmore and R.A. Eastwood, *Human Nutrition and Dietetics*, Churchill Livingstone, 1986

The Practitioner, Morgan-Grampian Ltd, London

David Robinson, *Tortoises Including Turtles and Terrapins*, Bartholemew, 1976

David Rubenstein and David Wayne, *Lecture Notes on Clinical Medicine*, Blackwell, 1976

W.E. Shewell-Cooper, *Soil: Humus and Health*, David & Charles, 1975

Felicity Taylor, *How to Invest Successfully*, Kogan Page, 1983

W.A.R. Thomson, *Black's Medical Dictionary*, Black, 1984

Alan Titchmarsh, *Down to Earth Gardening*, Ward Lock, 1984

Alan Titchmarsh, *How to be a Supergardener*, Ward Lock, 1988

United Kingdom Bartenders' Guild, *International Guide to Drinks*, Century Hutchinson, 1987

Update: The Journal of the Post Graduate Practice, Siebert Publications Ltd, Guildford

Frank Vernon, *Teach Yourself Beekeeping*, Hodder & Stoughton, 1986

Caroline Walker and Geoffrey Cannon, *The Food Scandal*, Arrow, 1986

Derek Walters, *Chinese Astrology*, Aquarian Handbooks, 1987

The Which? Guide to Your Rights, Consumers' Association, 1981

Michael Wright and Sally Walters (ed.), *The Book of the Cat*, Pan, 1980

INDEX

Numbers in **bold** are main entries;
italic are illustrations/diagrams